A TRADITION OF EXCELLENCE

CANADA'S AIRSHOW TEAM HERITAGE

A TRADITION
OF EXCELLENCE

CANADA'S AIRSHOW TEAM HERITAGE

Daniel V. Dempsey

Canadian Cataloguing in Publication Data

Dempsey, Daniel Vance 1952 –
  A tradition of excellence

Includes bibliographical references and index.
ISBN 0-9687817-0-5

1. Air shows—Canada—History. 2. Air shows—Canada—Pictorial works.
3. Canadian Armed Forces—Aviation. 4. Stunt flying—Canada—History.
5. Stunt flying—Canada—Pictorial works. I. Title.

UG632.3.C3D45 2002   797.5'4'0971   C2001-911157-6

Consulting Editor: Vic Johnson, Ottawa

Design: James W Jones, Aerographics Creative Services, Ottawa

Photo reproduction and retouching: Ed Drader, Drader AV Consultants, Winnipeg; James W. Jones, Aerographics Creative Services, Ottawa; John Groot, Wizard's Eye Digital Foto, Victoria; Kelly Oltean, Edmonton

Graphics: James W. Jones, Ottawa ; Jason D. Dempsey, Victoria

Proofreading: Vic Johnson, Ottawa; Ruth Dempsey, Victoria

Cover Illustration: Robert Dallabona, Montreal

Printed and bound in Canada by Friesens Corporation, Altona, Manitoba, Canada

Published by
High Flight Enterprises Ltd.
Daniel V. Dempsey, Publisher
1174 Sloan Terrace
Victoria, British Columbia V8Y 3C4
Canada

Front end paper: Top – The 1963 RCAF Golden Hawks photographed at their home base in Trenton, Ontario. Inset, W/C Frank Hatton and S/L Lloyd Hubbard, the last commanding officer and team leader respectively. (RCAF photos via Bill Briggs)

Left to Right – A note is handed to airshow chairman Dennis Yorath by the AOC North West Air Command, Air Vice-Marshal K.M. Guthrie, to officially open the second annual Calgary Air Show in 1947. Guthrie is dangling from the cockpit door of the RCAF's first helicopter, S-61 serial 9601. (RCAF Photo courtesy Canada's Aviation Hall of Fame). The 1964 Red Knight, F/L Bill Slaughter, climbs aboard his T-33 (DND PL 99029). The Golden Centennaires thrilled Canadians during Canada's Centennial year in 1967. (Canadair 92500). The Snowbirds saluted the 25th anniversary of the Canadian flag with their Maple Leaf Burst in 1990 (Ron Miller).

Title Page: The most famous photograph ever taken of the RCAF Golden Hawks. (DND PCN 164, Cpl George Hardy)

Copyright page: The author leads the 20th anniversary edition of the Snowbirds over the top of a Big Diamond loop on April 5th, 1990. The location is Vancouver Island, British Columbia, just south of 19 Wing Comox where the team traditionally completes its spring training. (Rafe Tomsett)

Dedication page: S/L Fern Villeneuve, the first leader of the Golden Hawks, leads his diamond formation through a loop in September 1959 during what was expected to be the team's last ever photo flight. Strong public demand led to the re-establishment of the team on March 1st, 1960. (DND PCN 1067, Cpl George Hardy)

Contents Page: The beautiful symmetry of the Snowbirds Double Diamond silhouette is evident in this dynamic shot captured by Bill Johnson, the Snowbirds first official photographer. (Bill Johnson)

Introduction Page: Brian Willer photo taken for *Maclean's* magazine, December 1990. (Brian Willer)

Back end paper: Left page, top to bottom – the Golden Hawks display the symmetry of a perfectly executed flat turn (RCAF Photo via Bill Briggs); the Goldilocks demonstrate their famous "crazy" formation in their Harvard trainers (DND PCN 4553); the Golden Centennaires presented a contrast in aviation history – from the sleek Tutor jet trainer of 1964 to the Avro 504K of 1924. (DND CAT 67-008-9)

Right page, top to bottom – The Snowbirds trademark Big Diamond formation following a nine-plane takeoff at Comox, British Columbia; the Snowbirds await their turn to start engines at Abbotsford 1973. (Bill Johnson)

Dedication

*To all those who have
known the magic
of aerobatic flight ...
and the families
who supported them.*

Contents

Foreword

"Now look straight ahead for the nine twinkling lights as the Team Lead calls for the Snowbirds to check in." With these words, the ensuing pull-up of the "trademark" nine-plane formation and the stirring sounds of Steven Vitali's musical tribute *In Flight*, another Snowbird show begins.

For the next 30 minutes, audiences ranging in size from a few hundred in Canada's Far North, to several hundred thousand at other major showsites across Canada and the United States, will be treated to a display of aerial skill and professionalism by Canada's world famous air demonstration team. The show is, in every sense of the word, a virtual aerial ballet, choreographed with an unmatched precision in time and space.

Members of today's Snowbird team shoulder a significant responsibility – one which is subliminal, and thus unspoken, but which is very real. For the Snowbirds, that responsibility is threefold. First, it is to execute the team's primary mission; specifically to demonstrate the professionalism of each member of the Canadian Forces. Second, it is one of "stewardship;" that is, to maintain the very high reputation established by those aircrew and groundcrew members who have preceded them in the team's proud history. Finally, it is to preserve the "tradition of excellence" established by such eminent predecessors as the Siskins, Blue Devils, Golden Hawks and Golden Centennaires – a proud legacy created during eight decades of aerial demonstration by Canadian teams. Even today, these teams still evoke powerful memories for those fortunate enough to have seen them fly – each an integral part of Canada's proud aviation heritage.

Through his book, Dan Dempsey makes an invaluable contribution to the preservation of this "tradition of excellence." Only someone who has "been there" and who has established such credibility within the airshow team community, both past and present, could have elicited so many rich first-hand accounts of their experiences from members of that unique fraternity. Coupled with outstanding collections of photos and artwork, his book provides a truly superb chronicle of the distinguished history and proud legacy of Canada's aerial demonstration teams.

This wonderful book must and will serve as a constant and vivid reminder, to both the people of Canada and to our country's civilian and military decision makers, that the Snowbirds are the visible and very popular custodians of our airshow heritage. By discharging their role with such singular excellence during their 32-year history, and by touching millions of lives in such a positive way, they have become, in every sense of the word, a national treasure – a treasure which simply must be preserved for future generations of Canadians to experience.

Fred Sutherland

Fred Sutherland CMM, CD
Lieutenant General (Ret'd)
Honorary Colonel
431 (AD) Squadron

Introduction

It has been over 80 years since Canadians witnessed a formation display for the first time at the Canadian National Exhibition in Toronto. In the decades that followed, dozens of different teams emerged to represent Canada at airshows spanning two continents – North America and Europe. There are few words which can adequately describe the excitement of an airshow. Seasoned airshow fans from years gone by might still remember some of the nation's earliest teams that flew Harvards, Mustangs or Vampires. T-33s, Sabres, Voodoos and Starfighters thrilled audiences for decades with their speed and precision. But for the last three decades, the team that has secured a place in the hearts and minds of Canadians is the Snowbirds. No matter which era one wishes to consider, Canadian pilots have established an enduring legacy in the airshow business, captivating audiences of all ages with their unique talents and flare for the spectacular.

My own fascination with flying and airshows began at an early age. This had much to do with the fact that the earliest days of my childhood were spent in Ottawa, not far from RCAF Stn Rockcliffe and the National Aviation Museum. I can still remember, quite vividly, the very first time I was in an airplane, an RCAF North Star which was then considered a mammoth machine. That was back in 1956 and at four years of age I got my first glimpse of a cockpit, on the knee of a navigator!

One of my earliest recollections of jets came on a sunny morning two years later when my father was filling up his old '48 Chevy at the station gas pumps. The sound was barely audible at first but suddenly grew louder and I looked up just in time to see the sky full of jets in a giant formation spelling out R C A F. "T-Birds" my Dad called them, practicing for the big airshow coming up that weekend. As he was to be on duty during the show, I saw my first airshow at Rockcliffe at the ripe old age of six years, thanks to my mother. The date was June 6th, 1959 and what a show it was. It seemed the sky was full of airplanes for hours … and probably was. The show was a salute to the 35th anniversary of the RCAF and 50th anniversary of powered flight in Canada – celebrated on National Air Force Day. As we sat on the hillside overlooking the runway, two of the aerial acts mesmerized me. One was a bright red T-33 known as the Red Knight. The other was a team of six golden jets which glinted beautifully in the sunlit sky as they raced around at incredible speed. They were the Golden Hawks flying the famous F-86 Sabre. The love affair was on …

Moving to RCAF Stn Lincoln Park, Calgary, in 1961 brought me into contact with more renowned aircraft – older ones this time – surplus F-51 Mustangs and B-25 Mitchell bombers – awaiting disposal from the RCAF inventory. And every year there was another wonderful airshow featuring the Red Knight, Golden Hawks and just about every aircraft type in the RCAF inventory. What a thrill it was to get all of the Hawks' autographs in 1963 when they returned to Lincoln Park by

helicopter after landing back at McCall Field. Earlier that morning I had been picked up by one of the support officers while walking alone from our home in the Married Quarters to the airfield – his Golden Hawks nametag standing out like a beacon to my 10-year-old eyes. Just the day before my father had taken me to McCall Field to watch the Red Knight and Hawks practice. We had parked on a side road that got us very close to the taxiway – close enough that the gleaming Hawks passed right in front of us. A friendly wave from the pilot of the seventh Sabre was a great thrill, an experience still indelibly etched in my mind. Now, just a few days later, here I was staring up at S/L Lloyd Hubbard, the Hawks' leader, as he and the rest of the team signed the special autograph cards designed with kids like me in mind.

With these youthful encounters, the dream of flying in the air force became an all-consuming passion. From the fantasies conjured up from our makeshift cockpit under a childhood friend's dilapidated porch in Calgary – where our imaginations ran wild with daring aerial feats – to somehow sneaking on board a B-25 Mitchell bomber with another friend a few years later at Edmonton's Industrial Airport to "check it out" – to all those magnificent airshows – I did everything I could to work towards that singular goal. I went for my first "real" airplane ride in 1964, crammed into the back seat of a crop-duster in Milestone, Saskatchewan with my younger brother. Our pilot was Marvin Omoth, a family cousin and one of those salt-of-the-earth prairie farmers who did it all. That first lesson in barnstorming left us wide-eyed, but smiling. What a proud moment it was then to have all of those childhood fantasies come to pass 11 years later when my father pinned on my air force wings at CFB Moose Jaw on June 29th, 1975. The venue couldn't have been more perfect – the Saskatchewan Air Show.

Twenty-seven years have passed since that monumental day, including four magnificent years spent flying with the Snowbirds, the successors to my childhood heroes. It was at the third Aerobatic Pilots Reunion held in conjunction with the Snowbirds 25th anniversary in October 1995 that I finally decided it was time to fulfill a long-held ambition to record the history of Canada's airshow teams. Within these pages are the names of hundreds of military personnel who have served their country with distinction. But for every name recorded there are many more whose contribution to this story will unfortunately go unrecognized. This book is a reflection of their dedication as well, and I hope that as they leaf through these pages they too will derive great pride and satisfaction in knowing they were part of it all.

In the seven years since I started my quest, the passing years have claimed some of the great aviators and technicians who helped create the wonderful aerial legacy represented in this book. One of my greatest regrets is that they were unable to see the finished product before they left us – people like Ralph Hawtrey of the Siskins, "Irish" Ireland, one of the original "Kerosene Kids" and member of the CFS Vampire Team, Lou Hill of the first post-war Harvard team and founder of the Silver Stars, Jim Giles of the Golden Hawks, Jake Miller, Rob McGimpsey and George Greff of the Golden Centennaires and Gus Youngson of the Deadeye Zips. Sadly, young Michael VandenBos of the Snowbirds was also lost during this period, never having had a chance to reflect back on the career he relished so much.

I've always held the greatest respect for historians and the years spent researching this book have given me a new appreciation for the challenges of their profession – scholars like John Griffin, George Fuller, Fred Hotson, and Hugh Halliday. Their work has all contributed to the completion of this book in one way or another. But the greatest influence of all has come from author Larry Milberry whose dedication to Canada's aviation history as witnessed by his prolific collection of aviation titles never ceases to amaze me. He has been a constant source of inspiration. So, to Larry and the others, I offer a most sincere thank you.

Taking on a project of this magnitude, which literally doubled in size from that first envisioned, has necessitated the cooperation of hundreds of people. I am indebted to all of those acknowledged on the following pages but would in particular like to single out the dozens of former team members who contributed their personal recollections, memorabilia or photographs in helping record this history. I shall also be eternally grateful to the professional photographers and artists who contributed their work to the cause, entire collections in some cases. Special thanks to James Jones, Dave O'Malley and Vic Johnson for their expertise and incredible patience, to Ed Drader and Peter Mossman for their phenomenal dedication and sense of humour, to

Bill Johnson for his ever-present inspiration and friendship, to John Miller, John McQuarrie and Earl Schmidt for their wise counsel and to Janet Lacroix for having put up with endless requests for photographic information.

My most heartfelt appreciation must naturally be reserved for my family – to my children Stephanie and Jason for their encouragement while having endured considerable inconvenience and especially to my wife Ruth for her extraordinary patience and contribution to the project over seven long years. Her expertise and attention to detail are visible on every page of this book – which she has read more times than she will ever care to remember. She is certainly equally deserving of any accolades the recording of this history may bring.

One starts to run out of superlatives in attempting to adequately articulate how important all of the teams described in this book have been to Canada – simple words don't seem to be enough. As I sat at my well-worn laptop pondering my final thoughts prior to going to press, I received a congratulatory letter from Tom Reid saluting the completion of my "labour of love." Tom is one of those countless thousands of Canadian servicemen who worked tirelessly behind the scenes to help ensure that Canada's airshow team heritage continued, in his case with the formation of the Snowbirds over three decades ago. As commandant of 2 CFFTS in 1971, he played an integral role in helping select the first team pilots, all of whom were working for him as instructors in Moose Jaw. In reflecting on the personnel who contributed to this unique Canadian story he wrote:

"This will undoubtedly be a hallmark in the historical recordings of special Canadians – serving their country, applying unique skills and being national ambassadors. They were all such. But more, they were part of the fabric, woven together, that exemplified the capability, spirit, togetherness and dedication of the members of Canada's Air Forces – regardless of the official title of the time."

I couldn't have said it better myself. So thank you Tom, and thank you to the hundreds of others who accompanied me on this wonderful odyssey. This is their story … and their legacy.

Dan Dempsey
October 2002

Acknowledgements

Dave Adamson, George Adamson, Fred Aldworth, Stu Allen, Brent Anderson, Dave Anderson, William J. Anderson, Vicki Andrew, Ralph Annis, Art Armstrong, Skip Armstrong, Roger Ayotte, Bob Ayres, Reg/Sandy Bach, John Bagshaw, Robert Bailey, Stu Baines, Bob Baird, Grant Baker, Adrian Balch, Bob Banks, Jean Pierre Baraton, Curt F. Barlow, Adrian Barry, Vic Bartlett, David L. Bashow, Bob Bauer, Russ Baxter, Gord Beaman, Barb Beardsall, Spike Bell, Jim Belliveau, Al Benell, Geoff Bennett, Richard Bennett, Russ Bennett, David (Badger) Berger-North, Don Bergie, Earl Berlie, Ron Berlie, Carole Berthelette, Carl Bertrand, Dennis Beselt, Ken Beselt, Jerry Billing, Doug Bing, Pat Bing, Jake Birks, Bill Bland, Dave Bligh, Bill Bliss, Laura Bonikowski, Bill Books, Dick Bos, Yves Bossé, Don Bosworth, Paul Boucher, Bob Bouchard, James A. Boutilier, Russ Bowdery, Bob Bowles, Jim Bowman, Robert Bradford, John Bradley, Mike Bradley, Cajo Brando, Julie Brazeau, Harold Breadner, Peter J. Brennan, Doug Brenton, Tony Brett, William (Bill) Briggs, Don Brodeur, Rick Brosseau, Al Brown, Bob Brown, Doug Brown, Gord Brown, Ken Brown, Jim Bruce, Greg Bruneau, Ross Buckland, Doyle Buehler, Jim Burant, Dave Burroughs, Syd Burrows, Lowell Butters, Kerri Button, Tom Byrne, Palmiro Campagna, B.R. Campbell, Bert Campbell, Brenda Campbell, Eddie Campbell, Gray Campbell, Mrs. Gray Campbell, L.C. Campbell, Al Camplin, Greg Carlow, Anne Marie Caron, Chuck Caron, Ken Carr, W.K. Carr, Lance Carroll, Bill Carswell, Bill Carter, Doug Carter, Ron Carter, Bob Caskie, Ken Castle, Clive Caton, Peter Caws, Will Chabun, Roger Champagne, Harry Chapin, Ross Chapman, Steve Charbonneau, J.G. Charlebois, Vic Charlebois, Joe Chermisnok, Nick Chester, Terry Chester, Tom Chester, Walt Chipchase, Jim Christie, Robert Christie, Garth Cinnamon, Joel Clarkston, Ted Climenhaga, Andrew Cline, Dale Cline, Linda Cobon, John J. Cockburn, Chuck Coffen, Ron Coleman, Kay Collacutt, Bill Collier, Don Connolly, Al Cooper, John Corrigan, Roger Cossette, Garry Cotter, Bill Cottrell, Rick Cottrell, Keith Coulter, Bill Cowan, Stu Cox, Sam Cramb, Geoff Craven, Alicia Crawford, Ray Crone, Kelly Cross, Ray Cryderman, John Cudahy, Dave Curran, Doug Cushman, Robert Dallabona, Barney Danson, Doug Dargent, John David, Jerry Davidson, Paul Deacon, Jack Deakin, Reg Décoste, Dave Deere, Louis DeGagne, A.V. Dempsey, Jason Dempsey, Rick Dempsey, Jack Des Brisay, Peter DeSmedt, Henry Devison, A.M. DeQuetteville, Hank Dielwart, Garth Dingman, Rod Dingwell, Andy Dobson, Len Dodd, Mike Dolan, Elmer Dow, B.K. Doyle, Bert Doyle, Michael F. Doyle, Ed/Alice Drader, Tim Dubé, Cy Dunbar, Barney Dunlevy, Pat Dunn, Richard Dunn, Christine Dunphy, Ray Dunsdon, Guy Dutil, W.H. "Bill" Eckley, Tony Edmundson, Gordon Edwards, J.F. (Stocky) Edwards, Scott Eichel, Brehn Eichel, Jerry Elias, Art Elliott, Rod Ellis, John England, Dale Erhart, Doug Erlandson, Rod Ermen, Jodi Ann Eskritt, Lucie Ethier, Don Evans, John Evans, Guy Fabi, R.H. Falls, Hani Farag, Chuck Fast, Eric (Speedy) Fast, Mike Fehr, Bob Fenn, Doug Fenton, Ian Ferguson, Ray Ferguson, Robert Finlayson, Sam Firth, George Fitzgerald, Len Fitzsimmons, Gary Flath, William Floyd, Billie Flynn, Bob Flynn, Andy Fok, Drew Folds, Garth Foley, Monique Fortin, Jeff Foss, David Foster, Marg Fowler, Alec Fox, Rick Franks, W.C. (Bill) Fraser, Jack Frazer, Carrie Friend, Frank Friesen, George Fulford, Don Fynn, Dick Gaff, Claude Gagnon, Jean Gaudry, Denis Gauthier, Rick Gibbons, Tom Gigliotti, Frank Gilland, William Gilson, Richard Girouard, William Gladders, Clair Gleddie, Chester/Judy Glendenning, Chris Glover, Shirley Gobeil-Gravelle, Ray Goeres, Tom Gosling, Jim Graham, Bob Granley, Bud/Carol Granley, Jim Grant, Chris Grasswick, Herb Graves, Jim Grecco, Steve Green, George M. Greenough, Scott Greenough, Jim Gregory, John Griffin, A.T. Griffis, Ron Guidinger, Jean Guilbault, Tony Gunther-Smith, Dale Hackett, Steve Hale, Terry Hallett, Hugh Halliday, Craig Halliwell, Bob Hallowell, Mario Hamel, Ken Hamilton, Laurie Hamilton, George Hammond, Gord Hannam, Milt Harradence, Chris Harris, Chuck Harris, Steve Harris, Mrs. Grant Harrison, Gord Hatch, Frank Hatton, Al Hauff, George Hawey, Laurie Hawn, Ian Hawtrey, Ralph C. Hawtrey, Paul Hayes, Mike Head, Glenn Heaton, Russ Heinl, Paul T. Hellyer, Steve Hemenway, Tom Henry, Hayden Henwood, Ryan Hildebrand, Bob Hill, Lou Hill, Robin Hill, Steve Hill, Tom Hinton, Mark Holmes, Roman Holowatyj, Fred Holtslag, Gary Hook, Dale Horley, Fred Hotson, Joe Houlden, Norm Hoye, Warren Hruska, Bill Huckstep, Peter Hulbert, A. Chester Hull, Terry Humphries, Larry H. Hunt, Terry Hunt, Jim Hunter, Bob Hurst, Yogi Huyghebaert, Tom Ianella, Bob Imre, Bruce D. Inring, E.G. (Irish) Ireland, Leonard Jenks, Bill/Nancy Johnson, Keith Johnson, Rolly Johnson, Vic Johnson, Curt Johnston, Bob Jones, James W. Jones, Matt Joost, Jim Jotham, Ken Jubenvill, William Jupp, Charles Kadin, Vince Kavic, Chuck Keating, Sean Keating, Mark Keller, Harry Kelly, Gordon Kemp, Jim Kendall, Gwen Kerr, Lyle Kettles, Dave Kingstone, D.N. Kinsman, George Kirbyson, John Kitchen, T.K. Klassen, Marion Knight, Mike Kobierski, Rhinehart Koehn, Dave Koski, Les Koski, Ben Kooter, Simon Kooter, Jordy Krastel, Dave Krayden, Raimo Kujala, Al Kucinskas, Janet Lacroix, Ron LaGrange, John Lahey, Don Laidler, John Laidler, Bob Lake, Romeo Lalonde, John Lameck, William E. Lamon, Roger Lamothe, George Landry, Dud Larsen, Robert Larocque, Colin Latta, Don Laubman, Anthu Lauzon, Baz Lawlor, Brooke Lawrence, Bud Lawrence, Chuck Lawrence, Brenda Lea Austin, T.J. Leblanc, Carolle Leboeuf, Bill Lee, Don Leonard, Ian Leslie, K.C. Lett, Terry Leversedge, Omer Levesque, Gary Liddiard, Dick Lidstone, Ken Lin, Clark Little, Jerry Lloyd, Larry Lott, Ron Lowry, Gene Lukan, Connie Lupton, William Lupton, Terry Lyons, Jim Lyzun, Joe MacBrien, Joanne MacDonald, Rod MacDonald, Haggis Mackay, Wayne MacLellan, Mal Macnair, Bob MacWilliam, Charles Maier, R.K. (Dick) Malott, Paul D. Manson, Paul Marsden, Doug Marshall, Rick Martin, Michael Marynowski, Art Maskell, Eric Matheson, Denis Matte, Mike Matthews, George Mayer, George McAffer, Peter McCague, Evelyn McClelland, John McClenaghan, Jim McCombe, Earl McCurdy, Alf McDonald, Keith McDonald, Pat McGale, Ed McGillivray, Rob McGimpsey, Joe McGoldrick, Jay McGowan, John McGowan, Richard McIntosh, Bob McIntyre, Ev McKay, Peter McKeage, Ed McKeogh, Dan McLaren, Doug McLennan, Gary McMahon, Carl McNally, Gord McNulty, John McQuarrie, Al Mehlhaff, George Meldrum, Bob Merrick, Bob Middlemiss, Larry Milberry, Sam Millar, Vance Millar, Fred Millard, George Miller, Glen Miller, John Miller, Ron Miller, Carl Mills, Debbie Millward, Rob Mitchell, Paul Molnar, Cindy Molyneaux, Dan Montschak, Pieter Montyn, Yvette Moore, Bob Morgan, Pierre Morissette, Dan Morley, Carol Morrisette, Dan Morrison, Gordon Morrison, Larry Mosser, Peter Mossman, Roy Mould, Harry Mueller, Rollie Muloin, Bill Munro, Doug Munro, Mark Munzel, Mike Murphy, Jim Murray, Tom Murray, Eddy Myers, Mike Nash, Murray Neilson, Grant Nichols, W.H. (Bill) Nichols, Gerry Nicks, Walter Niemy, Steve Nierlich, Paul Noack, Mick Nordeen, Ken Nott, Neale Nowosad, David O'Blenis,,

David O'Malley, Tim O'Rourke, Tom O'Sullivan, Kelly Oltean, Marvin Omoth, Jack Orr, Mary Oswald, Marc Ouellet, Bob Painchaud, W.G. Paisley, Joe Parente, Brodie Partington, Val Pattee, Gerry W. Patterson, Ross Patterson, Holmes Patton, Herb Paul, Steve Peach, Don Pearsons, Bing Peart, Wally Peel, Wally Peirson, Jon Pellow, Pete Pellow, Jacquie Perrin, Phil Perry, William Perry, Serge Peters, Carl Peterson, Bill Petro, Leo Pettipas, Jack Phillips, Pat Phillips, William S. Phillips, Maeve Philp, James Pickett, Pietsch Family, Walt Pirie, Ron Platt, Claude Poirier, John Politis, Todd Pomerleau, Sid Popham, Les Price, Kevin Psutka, George Quigley, Rick Radell, Manfred Radius, Dean Rainkie, Wayne Ralph, Jason Ransom, Jack Rathwell, Carol Reid, Tom Reid, J.H. (Jack) Reilly, J.P. (Jack) Reilly, Jim Reith, Dave Reyenga, Mike Reyno, Gary Richards, John Richkun, Roy Riley, Jack Ritch, Al Robb, Keith Robbins, Peter Robertson, Don Robinson, Pierre Rochefort, Andrew Rodger, Tony Roeding, Hugh Rose, John Rose, Mike Ross, John Roulston, Manny Roussey, Dave Rozdeba, Fred Rudy, Ron Russell, John Rutherford, Rusty Rutherford, B.J. Ryan, Patrice Ryan, Tom Sabean, Pierre Saucier, Bob Saunders, Ernie Saunders, Brad Schmidt, Earl Schmidt, Don Schmidtt, Gary Schwindt, Cpl Scott, Russ Scott, Walt Scott, Ian Searle, John Searle, Paul Seguna, René Serrao, Norm Shaw, Norm Shrive, Scott Shrubsole, Darryl Shyiak, Hank Siemens, K.O. Simonson, Rae Simpson, Tom Sinclair, Don Sinel, Joseph Singerman, Mike Skubicky, Bill Slaughter, Wally Sloan, Bob Small, Kent Smerdon, Bob Smith, Eric Smith, G.N. Smith, Grant Smith, Kevin Smith, Fiona Smith-Hale, Manny Soberal, Eric Sommerfeld, Rein Sommerfeld, Rodger Sorsdahl, Stu Soward, Wilf Speck, Jim Speiser, Mike Spooner, John Spronk, Robert St. Pierre, Chuck Steacy, Bob Stephan, Al Stephenson, Bill Sterne, J.W. (Bill) Stewart, W.C. (Bill) Stewart, George Stewart, Ray Stone, Wally Stone, Mel Storrier, Gerry Stowe, Terry Strocel, Tim Strocel, Ian Struthers, Doug Stuart, John Stuart, Wayne Stuart, R. Sturgess, F.R. Sutherland, Michael Swanson, Rod Sword, Gord Symmuck, Nev Symonds, Cliff Symons, Gerry Takach, William (Turbo) Tarling, Dave Tate, Marty Tate, Brodie Templeton, Chris Terry, Yves Tessier, Jacques Thibaudeau, Claude Thibault, Rich/Jay Thistle, Dave Thom, Rick Thompson, Wayne Thompson, Frank Thorne, Eric Thurston, Ben Toenders, Katsu Tokunaga, Rafe Tomsett, George Topple, Jonathan Totti, Bob Tracy, Guy Trudeau, Chris Tuck, Bob Turner, Paul Tuttle, Ed Ukrainetz, Bill Upton, John Ursulak, Mike Valenti, Ray H. Valentiate, Henry Van Keulen, L.G. (Rocky) Van Vliet, John Veevers, Jerry Vernon, Jean Veronneau, André Viens, Chops Viger, Fern Villeneuve, Steven Vitali, Bryan Volstad, Bob Wade, Dave Walker, Jay Walker, Myrna Wallis, Dick Walton, Marcus Walton, Duke Warren, Mel Warren, Bruce Warwick, Paul Washington, Jack Waters, Bob Webber, Jeff Welch, Lee Wenz, Bill Werny, Pat Whitby, Randall Whitcomb, Bud White, Grant Whitson, Dan Whittle, Bart Wickham, David Wightman, Cathy Wiley, Steve Will, Fred Williams, Frank Willis, Dave Wilson, Leah Wilson, Rob Wilson, Peter Wiwcharuck, Mike Woodfield, Cynthia Woods, Bob Worbets, Bill Worthy, Graham Wragg, Harv Wregget, Brian Wright, Al Young, Glen Younghusband, Grant Youngson, Gus Youngson, Gord Zans, Pete Zinkan, Rick Zyvitski.

Organizations

Abbotsford International Airshow
Aerographics Creative Services Inc.
Air Force Association of Canada
Airforce Magazine
All Weather Fighter Association
Atlantic Aviation Museum
Aviation World
BGM Imaging
Canada Aviation Museum
Canadair Ltd.
Canadian Aerophilatelic Society
Canadian Aviation Artists Association
Canadian Aviation Hall of Fame
Canadian Fighter Pilots Association
Canadian Forces – Chief of the Air Staff,

1 Canadian Air Division, 1 CAD Heritage and History, 1 CAD Wings, Squadrons and Units (3 Wing Bagotville, 4 Wing Cold Lake, 15 Wing Moose Jaw, 17 Wing Winnipeg, 19 Wing Comox, 410, 414, 416, 417, 419, 424, 425, 431, 433, 434, 435, 439, 441, 442, 443 Sqns, 2 CFFTS, 3 CFFTS, Aerospace Engineering and Test Establishment), Air Force Public Affairs, Army Public Affairs, Navy Public Affairs, Canadian Forces Joint Imagery Centre, Canadian Forces Skyhawks, Canadian Forces Snowbirds (431 Air Demonstration Squadron)
Canadian International Air Show
Canadian Starfighter Association
Canadian War Museum
Canadian Warplane Heritage
Canadian National Exhibition Archives
Cold Lake Courier
Department of National Defence – Director of History, Director Intellectual Property
Friesens Corporation
Glenbow Museum
International Council of Air Shows
Macleans Magazine
Moose Jaw Times Herald
National Archives of Canada
National Library of Canada
Nova Scotia International Air Show
Ottawa Sun
Portage la Prairie Daily Graphic
Regina Leader Post
RCAF Memorial Museum
Saskatchewan Air Show
Shearwater Aviation Museum
SPAADS (Sabre Pilots Association of the Air Division Squadrons)
Specialty Jets Unlimited
The Boeing Company
Toronto Globe and Mail
Toronto Star
Vancouver Province
Vanwell Publishing
Veritas - RMC Club of Canada
Victoria Times Colonist
Windsor Star
WINGS Magazine
World Airshow News

The author wishes to acknowledge the special assistance provided by the following corporations and organizations:

The New Adventure

Thousands of Canadians young and old alike thronged to new airfields across the country to witness the aerial phenomena known as the airshow during the "Roaring Twenties" and "Dirty Thirties." This was the scene at Edmonton, Alberta's Blatchford Field where the city hosted its first major airshow in September 1930 to coincide with the arrival of the Ford Reliability Air Tour, a precursor of things to come during the great Trans-Canada Air Pageant of 1931. The Canadian pageant created scenes similar to this at 26 cities from coast-to-coast as 500,000 spectators took in the exhibition flying. (Provincial Archives of Alberta BL.87/2)

For Canadians, the new adventure in human achievement began in the middle of winter on February 23rd, 1909 over a frozen, windswept bay at Baddeck, Nova Scotia. Although only a handful of aviation pioneers and curious onlookers were in attendance to watch the event, the occasion marked the advent of powered flight in the Dominion of Canada. A young 22-year-old Canadian by the name of John Alexander Douglas McCurdy was sitting at the controls of a strange looking, double-winged flying machine powered by a propeller-driven, 35 horsepower Curtiss engine as it began to move slowly over the ice under its own power, gradually picking up speed. Four young men on ice skates chased along but were losing ground when the "heavier-than-air" flying machine dubbed the Silver Dart lifted gently into the air to an altitude of about 30 feet, the first to do so anywhere in the British Empire. McCurdy stayed aloft for just over half a mile (800 metres) before easing himself down onto the ice again, allowing the machine to skate along to a stop. Within a few minutes the euphoric group of fellow colleagues from the Aerial Experiment Association had caught up again and greeted McCurdy as he climbed out of the ungainly looking, 800 pound biplane with the tricycle landing gear. Months of determined work and endless experiments had paid off – history had been made in Canada.

J.A.D. McCurdy's first flight in Canada came just over five years after Orville and Wilbur Wright had fulfilled their dream of powered flight and, by so doing, changed the world forever. By defying gravity at Kittyhawk, North Carolina on December 17th, 1903 with that first 12 second flight of their motorized glider (the Wright Flyer), the two brothers set in motion a revolution in technology to rival Thomas Edison's invention of the light bulb. The revolution would ultimately captivate some of the world's brightest inventors and engineers as they sought more efficient ways to escape the boundaries of earth and emulate the birds. It was a bold new frontier that within a generation would see man propelled to speeds of twice the speed of sound, a notion that not even science fiction could have imagined at the turn of the 20th century. With the new technology would eventually come two new industries that would consume hundreds of thousands of citizens in industrialized nations around the world – one industry fulfilling the quest of highly skilled engineers and workers to design and build bigger and better flying machines for transportation, exploration and eventually military applications; the other a direct result of the first – a fascination of flight that, in capturing the imagination of ordinary people everywhere, would see early air exhibitions ultimately mush-

room into one of the world's largest and most popular spectator events – the Airshow.

Canada's Earliest Aerial Feats

The earliest aerial events recorded in what is now Canada predate the birth of the nation in 1867 by over three decades. It was the *British Whig* newspaper of Kingston, Upper Canada that reported what is believed to have been the first successful deployment of an unmanned hot air balloon over the city on May 18th, 1835 by one F.E. Butterfield, a travelling comedian. Before long, the novelty could be witnessed at summer fairs and exhibitions stretching from Upper Canada to the Maritimes as entrepreneurs used every trick in the book to lure fairgoers to their wondrous, "never-before-seen" scientific experiments. Even Queen Victoria's coronation was celebrated by the release of a bal-

Mr. L.A. Lauriat, Professor of Chemistry and Aerostatic Exhibitions, respectfully announces that he will Monday next, make a grand ascension in his splendid balloon, the "Star of the East," within the Barrack Square – being the first in the Province. Should the weather prove to be unfavorable, the ascension will take place the next fair day.

An advertisement for Canada's first manned flight, as reported by the *New Brunswick Courier* in August 1840.

The flight of the Silver Dart (inset right) was the first powered flight of an "aerodrome" in the British Empire, taking place near Baddeck, Nova Scotia on 23 Feb 09 in the hands of a young Canadian engineer and aviation pioneer, J.A.D. McCurdy. The excitement of that historical moment was reenacted 50 years to the day later in 1959 when W/C Paul Hartman of the RCAF flew a replica of the Silver Dart (below) at the same location. (National Archives of Canada PA-061741, DND Photo)

loon in Halifax on June 28th, 1838 to entertain her loyal subjects. A scant two years later, the Maritimes also recorded the first manned ascent in Canada of a hot air balloon over Saint John, New Brunswick. The honour went not to a Canadian however, but to aeronaut Louis Anselm Lauriat from Boston, Massachusetts. His 2,500 square foot balloon named "Star of the East" was an attraction not to be missed and rose majestically over the city on August 10th, 1840 to a reported altitude of over 7,000 feet, eventually landing some 21 miles away.

As if to underscore the slow evolution of man's quest for flight, it would be another 16 years before the first successful voyage of a balloon constructed in Canada was to take place. Built and put on public exhibition in Montreal, Canada East on September 4th, 1856, French aeronaut Eugène Godard made a short voyage four days later with three passengers aboard his balloon – appropriately named "Canada." As Canadians slowly became acclimatized to seeing members of the upper class ascending above the masses in a hot air balloon, it was only a matter of time until someone decided to introduce a new gimmick to gain publicity. This took the form of aerial acrobatics performed on a trapeze suspended below an ascending hot air balloon. The venue for this "first" in Canada was the Toronto Cricket Ground in May 1875, self-proclaimed Professor Justin Buislay providing the drama below his balloon, "Meteor." By that summer, balloons had become a popular attraction at circuses, P.T. Barnum even constructing his own balloon to transport friends and associates around southern Ontario and New York State. All that remained now to further the cause of entertainment was for someone to *jump* out of a balloon and drift to the ground

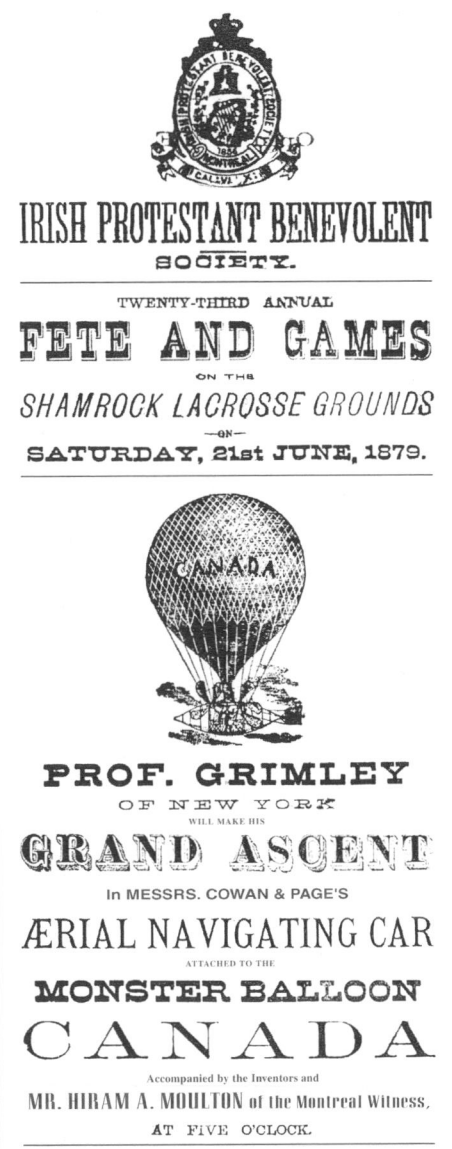

IRISH PROTESTANT BENEVOLENT
SOCIETY.

TWENTY-THIRD ANNUAL

FÊTE AND GAMES

ON THE

SHAMROCK LACROSSE GROUNDS

—ON—

SATURDAY, 21st JUNE, 1879.

PROF. GRIMLEY
OF NEW YORK
WILL MAKE HIS

GRAND ASCENT

In MESSRS. COWAN & PAGE'S

ÆRIAL NAVIGATING CAR

ATTACHED TO THE

MONSTER BALLOON

CANADA

Accompanied by the Inventors and

MR. HIRAM A. MOULTON of the Montreal Witness,

AT FIVE O'CLOCK.

CAPTIVE ASCENTS will be made during the day.

All persons desirous of getting a charming view of the City and Country
ought to embrace this rare opportunity.

One Dollar Each Person will be charged

THE BAND of the SIXTH FUSILIERS

WILL BE IN ATTENDANCE.

via parachute. This occurred for the first time in Canada on September 4th, 1888 at the Great Eastern Exhibition in Sherbrooke, Quebec when Canadian-born Edward Hogan

The first manned balloon flight in Canada took place in 1856. Over the next five decades, clever advertising made such flights the highlight of fairs and exhibitions across the nation, witness this example in 1879 when Professor Grimley of New York was the second aeronaut to name his hot air balloon "Canada." Equipped with side propellers and a directional rudder, he flew it from Shamrock Lacrosse Grounds in Montreal to St. Jude, Hyacinthe County, Quebec with a reporter on board to record the event. (CAHS Collection)

of Jackson, Michigan became the first to accomplish the daring feat. But for every successful flight there were dozens of failures, some catastrophic. Hogan's fame was fleeting as he became the first casualty of his new daredevil parachute act when he miscalculated the winds and drowned after being blown out to sea off Long Island, New York several months later. And Canada recorded its first aerial casualty on September 26th, 1888 when a young volunteer by the name of Tom Wensley was inadvertently carried aloft by a hot air balloon while dangling from one of its mooring lines at the Ottawa Exhibition. As reported by the *Ottawa Free Press* the next day, the aeronaut, Professor C.W. Williams, was unable to assist the young man who lost his grip and promptly fell to his death to the horror of 15,000 spectators.

From Dirigibles to Gliders

By 1906 a new novelty reached Canada as more Americans ventured north to show off the latest in "lighter-than-air" craft – the dirigible. Unlike the simple balloons that preceded them, dirigibles were eventually powered by an engine-driven propeller and became steerable through the use of a boat-like rudder. The first such flights took place in Montreal between July 13th and 16th as Montrealers descended on Dominion Park to witness the spectacle. It was also in Montreal that the first "heavier-than-air" glider was successfully tested a year later in August

Exhibitions in Canada began to include dirigibles or airships in 1906 which became a feature attraction, as evidenced by this rare envelope. The largest airship ever to fly in Canada was the mammoth R-100 which arrived at St. Hubert from Cardington, England on 1 Aug 30. Its custom-built mooring mast, constructed by Canadian Vickers of Montreal, towered 60 metres into the air. Over one million Canadians flocked to Montreal, Ottawa, Toronto and Niagara Falls to see the R-100 during its two week visit. It departed St. Hubert for the return trans-Atlantic trip on 13 Aug, never to return again; the grand Imperial Airship Scheme was cancelled following the catastrophic loss of her sister ship in France. (courtesy Dick McIntosh, RCAF Photo via Fred Hotson)

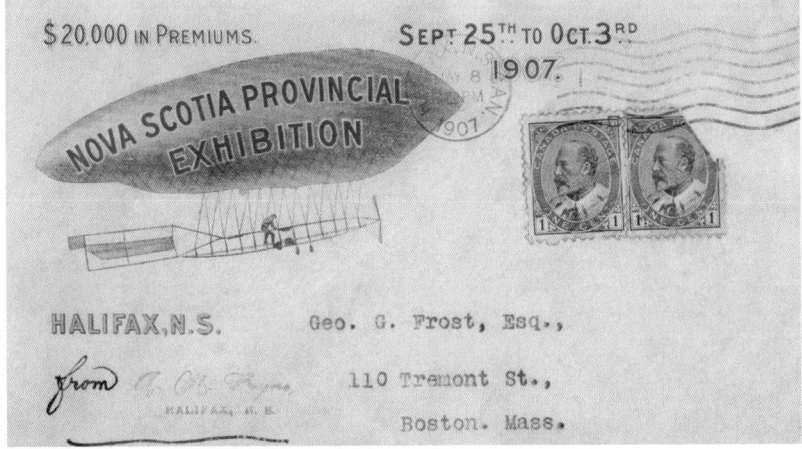

Two amazing photographs from 1907 depict teenager L.J. Lesh gliding in his "Montreal No. 2" glider near the city, the first person to do so in Canada. He subsequently was also the first person in Canada to add ailerons to his glider, giving him the ability to turn. He used one of two power sources to get airborne – a horse or a powerboat on the St. Lawrence River. (CAHS Collection)

1907. Amazingly, the flight was conducted by a 15 year-old American-born teenager by the name of Lawrence Jerome Lesh in a glider of his own design, the "Montreal No. 1." Lesh relied on a horse to tow him into the air on his first flights of short duration, truly a sight to behold. Then, in a moment of brilliance, he decided to try a motorboat on the St. Lawrence River as a tow vehicle. The experiment worked and his most successful test saw him stay aloft for a phenomenal 24 minutes in which he covered over six miles, making him the talk of the town! Only a month later, after demolishing his first glider in a crash, the young man became the first aviator in North America (and only the fifth in the world) to fit ailerons to a flying apparatus, his "Montreal No. 2" glider. Lesh later also became the first innovator to take a photograph from a glider, doing so over Montreal and thus making him Canada's first aerial photographer.

Alexander Graham Bell

While many Canadians are familiar with the legend of the Silver Dart, few realize that the driving force behind the building of the machine and the advent of powered flight in Canada was none other than the inventor of the telephone, Alexander Graham Bell. Born and raised in Edinburgh, Scotland on March 3rd, 1847, Bell emigrated to Canada with his parents in 1870, settling in Brantford, Ontario. It was in this city that he and his father initially worked together as speech therapists for the deaf. However, lured by a greater calling south of the border, Bell moved to the United States in 1871 where he began his experiments in the electronic transmission of voice signals that led to the invention of the telephone on March 10th, 1876 and the subsequent founding of the Bell Telephone Company. While telephone patents had made him a rich man by the time he was 35, Bell fell in love with Canada during visits every summer. He was fascinated by the country's unspoiled beauty and in 1890 bought land near Baddeck, Nova Scotia where he would later build himself a summer home which he named "*Beinn Bhreagh*" (Beautiful Mountain in Gaelic). Perched on a headland overlooking Baddeck Bay in the heart of Cape Breton Island, some 44 kilometres west of Sydney, it became Bell's favourite place on earth. Of the area the millionaire inventor later wrote, "I have travelled around the globe. I have seen the Canadian Rockies, the Andes and the Highlands of Scotland. But for simple beauty, Capt Breton outrivals them all."

The Aerial Experiment Association & The Silver Dart

Alexander Graham Bell's scientific mind and fascination with the accomplishments of the Wright Brothers prompted him to begin his own experiments on the principles of flight at *Beinn Bhreagh* in the summer of 1907. To assist his research, he secured the services of two young engineering graduates from the University of Toronto, J.A.D. McCurdy and Frederick W. "Casey" Baldwin. Encouraged by experiments with kites towed by power boats, the trio formalized their relationship by founding the Aerial Experiment Association (AEA) in Halifax, Nova Scotia on October 1st, 1907 with the express purpose of building a flying machine capable of carrying a man into flight. To help them achieve their goal, two Americans equally enthusiastic about the prospect of manned flight, engine-maker Glenn H. Curtiss from Hammondsport, New York and Lt Thomas W. Selfridge from the U.S. Army, were invited to join the team. With Bell and his wife using their wealth to finance the group, the team forged ahead with their flying experiments.

As the leaves began to fall in the autumn of 1907, Bell moved his research team to the shops of Glenn Curtiss' successful engine business in Hammondsport. It was from this location that several gasoline-powered biplanes (which they called aerodromes) were designed over the winter months of 1907-1908. The first design ready to test was dubbed the "Red Wing" and was powered by

The five founding members of the Aerial Experiment Association. L to R – F.W. "Casey" Baldwin, Lt T.E. Selfridge, Glenn H. Curtiss, Dr. Alexander Graham Bell and J.A.D. McCurdy. Pictured with them (far right) in this May 1908 photo from Hammondsport, New York is Augustus Post, secretary of the Aero Club of America. Casey Baldwin had two months earlier become the first aviation pioneer in North America to give a public demonstration of flight. (Bell Family Photo/CAHS Collection)

The Canadian militia was not convinced of the practical applications of flight when Casey Baldwin and J.A.D. McCurdy demonstrated their "Baddeck No. 1" biplane at Camp Petawawa, Ontario in August 1909. The Baddeck 1 was the first all-Canadian aircraft built by the duo's "Canadian Aerodrome Company." (National Archives of Canada C-020260)

John Alexander Douglas McCurdy seen in Toronto in 1911, two years after he had made his first historic flight. (CAHS Collection)

a 40 hp engine. The aircraft made history by being the first airplane to fly a public demonstration in North America on its inaugural flight on March 12th, 1908. Ironically, it was not flown by one of the Americans, but rather by Casey Baldwin, thus immortalizing his name in the annals of Canadian aviation.

Baldwin also flew the first test flight of the association's next aircraft, the "White Wing," two months later. McCurdy followed suit a few days later to mixed reviews – he crashed the aircraft but lived to fulfill his destiny. The team's next "aerodrome" was called the "June Bug" which became the first aircraft to fly a full kilometre under test conditions on July 4th, 1908. Finally, the team's last machine – McCurdy's "Silver Dart" – took to the skies over Hammondsport on December 6th, 1908 with the designer at the controls. Following this successful flight, the aircraft made of steel tubing, bamboo, friction tape, wire and wood covered with rubberized silk balloon-cloth was partially dismantled and shipped to Canada. There it was reassembled, tested and made its historic flight on February 23rd, 1909.

Their mission accomplished, the AEA was disbanded at the end of March. However, at the encouragement of Bell, his two Canadian protégés remained a team, founding the nation's first aviation firm at Baddeck – the Canadian Aerodrome Company – in April 1909. Eager to market their new-found fame, McCurdy and Baldwin made what might be considered Canada's first aerial demonstrations in a powered aircraft on August 2nd, 1909 – a series of demonstrations of the Silver Dart for the benefit of the militia at Camp Petawawa, Ontario. With 46 successful flights of the Silver Dart under their belts, including one which had covered a distance of 32 km, the two aviators were very confident they could impress the military.

Unfortunately, pushing their luck a little too far, the Silver Dart crashed and was destroyed beyond repair on its fourth flight of the day when a gust of wind flipped it over. This left the military audience highly sceptical of any potential use of flying machines in the foreseeable future.

Undaunted by this temporary setback, McCurdy and Baldwin went to work finalizing preparations for the inaugural test flight of the first Canadian-built aeroplane, the Baddeck No. 1. Powered by a 42 hp Kirkham engine, McCurdy got airborne at Petawawa on August 12th and less than two weeks later flew a sister aircraft, the Baddeck No. 2, back at their home base on Cape Breton Island.

Early Aerial Milestones in Canada

18 May 1835	F.E. Butterfield launches the first reported unmanned hot air balloon in Kingston, Upper Canada.
10 August 1840	American Louis Anselm Lauriat makes the first aerial voyage in Canada in a hot air balloon in Saint John, New Brunswick.
8 September 1856	French aeronaut Eugène Godard makes the first successful voyage of a balloon constructed in Canada and carries the first aerial passengers at Montreal, Canada East.
24 May 1875	Professor Justin Buislay performs the first aerial stunts on a trapeze suspended beneath an ascending hot air balloon in Toronto.
4-6 September 1888	American Edward D. Hogan makes the first parachute descents from a hot air balloon at Sherbrooke, Quebec.
13 July 1906	American Charles Keeney Hamilton makes the first engine-powered, directed flight of a dirigible in Montreal, Quebec.
16-18 August 1907	American-born teenager Lawrence Jerome Lesh makes the first successful glider flight in Montreal, Quebec – towed by a horse.
1 October 1907	The Aerial Experiment Association is inaugurated in Halifax, Nova Scotia by Alexander Graham Bell.
12 March 1908	Canadian Casey Baldwin makes the first public demonstration of an aircraft in North America at Hammondsport, Connecticut.
23 February 1909	Canadian J.A.D. McCurdy makes the first powered "aerodrome" flight in the British Empire at Baddeck, Nova Scotia in the Silver Dart.
2 August 1909	J.A.D. McCurdy conducts Canada's first aerial demonstration in the Silver Dart for the benefit of the militia at Camp Petawawa, Ontario.
2 September 1909	American Charles Foster Willard makes the first "contracted" public exhibition of an aeroplane at Scarborough Beach Amusement Park near Toronto. His aircraft, a Curtiss pusher biplane named the "Golden Flyer," ended up in Lake Ontario after a 300 yard flight.

(Data via Canadian Aviation Historical Society)

Many western Canadians saw their first aeroplanes courtesy of the Curtiss Exhibition Team which performed in a number of cities from 1910 to 1913. At left, C.K. Hamilton draws a crowd at Minrou Park near Vancouver in Mar 1910 as he prepares to take off in a Curtiss Pusher. At right, a later version built by the famous American designer is being demonstrated by Hugh Robinson at Edmonton, Alberta in Apr 1911. (CAHS Collection)

A Fascination With Flight

Notwithstanding their initial disappointment with the militia, McCurdy and Baldwin had spurred the imagination of Canadians right across the country. This led to the founding of more organizations devoted to the concept of flight. On March 31st, 1909, the Aero Club of Canada was formed in Winnipeg, Manitoba "to assist and promote practical aeronautics by encouraging Canadian inventors." This was followed by the formation of the Aeronautical Society of Canada in Toronto on September 2nd, the very same day that patrons at the Scarborough Beach amusement park witnessed an amazing sight – a Curtiss pusher biplane flown by Charles F. Willard flying along the beach for some 300 yards before it splashed into Lake Ontario. Known as the "Golden Flyer," this was the first contracted public exhibition of an aeroplane in Canada. Dozens more would soon follow.

Still, for the balance of 1909, it was dirigible flights that continued to dominate public fairs and exhibitions across the country. The West Coast saw its first demonstrations of a Strobel dirigible in Victoria on September 22nd at the annual Fair and Horse Show followed by the Provincial Exhibition at Queen's Park, New Westminster in mid-October. While these were exciting, the best was yet to come only five months later.

Canada's First Aviation Meets

The year 1910 was a pivotal period in the growth of aviation in Canada. With further refinements, McCurdy and Baldwin managed to convince a member of the militia, Maj G.S. Maunsell, to go flying with McCurdy on March 10th at Baddeck. Having cheated death once, Maunsell agreed to a second flight the same day. Still, the militia

remained unconvinced about the benefits of manned flight. Nevertheless, Canadians right across the nation were eager to see this new flying phenomena. Many saw their first aerial demonstrations of manned flight courtesy of two American demonstration teams that toured the country between 1910 and 1913. Not surprisingly, their founders were the legendary Wright Brothers and Glenn Curtiss. The Curtiss team made its first appearance in Canada on March 25th, 1910 with several flights at Minrou Park race track (near Vancouver) flown by C.K. Hamilton in a Curtiss pusher biplane. Hamilton became the first aviator to fly over a Canadian city, New Westminster, the very next day. Curious about how fast a flying machine could really go, Hamilton's last demonstration at Minrou Park was a race – against a horse! It is not clear who won …

Anxious to make their own mark in Canada, the Wright Brothers Exhibition Team made its debut at Lakeside (Point Claire), Quebec on June 25th, 1910 with their Wright Flyer, edging out J.A.D. McCurdy for the privilege of being the first to do so in that province. McCurdy had crashed just the day before attempting a flight in the Canadian Aerodrome Company's Baddeck No. 2 biplane and was to have a frustrating week trying to get airborne. The venue was the

scene of Canada's first aviation meet sponsored by the Automobile & Aero Club of Canada. It lasted 11 days during which time spectators were treated to daily flights by several members of the Wright team, the first Canadian flight of a Bleriot XI monoplane (le Scarabée) flown by Count Jacques de Lesseps of France, dirigible flights and balloon ascensions complete with parachute jumps. The successes and failures of the meet were dutifully reported every day by the Montreal Herald.

Not to be outdone, the Ontario Motor League ran the first aviation meet in Ontario history just three days after the Quebec affair had ended, with many of the same performers in attendance, led by the Wright team. Based at Trethewey Farm at Weston (then just outside Toronto), large crowds once again gathered to witness the spectacle of manned flight for nine straight days. On July 13th, Count de Lesseps gave Torontonians a taste of what they were missing by flying right over the heart of the city in his Bleriot XI. Meanwhile, it was the Curtiss pusher biplane that was all the rage in western Canada, being the first to demonstrate powered flight at the Winnipeg Industrial Exhibition in the summer of 1910. The City of Edmonton followed in April 1911, Saskatoon and Fort Erie in June, Calgary and Lethbridge in July,

The Montreal Aviation Meet of June/July 1910 held at Lakeside, Quebec was a first for Canada and lasted 11 days, drawing aviators from Canada, the United States and France. Depicted here are two aircraft demonstrated by Count Jacques de Lesseps of France, both Bleriot XI monoplanes. (P.A. Reid/CAHS Collection)

Canadian-born Harold Blakeley (above) conducted numerous flying demonstrations in Manitoba and Saskatchewan during the summer of 1913 flying a Curtiss pusher. That same year young American Cecil Peoli became the first aviator to fly in New Brunswick and Prince Edward Island in his Baldwin "Red Devil" biplane. (CAHS Collection)

Regina in August. It was in Fort Erie on June 21st, 1911 that J.A.D. McCurdy became the first Canadian to conduct a professional flying exhibition in Canada, having incorporated the McCurdy Aeroplane Company only the day before for the express purpose of manufacturing and displaying aeroplanes.

By the end of 1911, hundreds of thousands of Canadians from coast-to-coast had seen an aeroplane fly for the first time. Crashes were commonplace however, and it was on August 15th that the first Canadian was killed during an aviation meet in Chicago, Illinois. Toronto-born St. Croix Johnstone had taken his flying training at the Bleriot School of Flying in Hendon, England, earning Royal Aero Club Certificate No. 41 on December 31st, 1910. This made him the second licensed pilot in Canada, J.A.D. McCurdy having become the first just two months earlier. Johnstone had subsequently repatriated with his new-found knowledge and joined the International Aviators Exhibition Team in July flying a Bleriot-type Moisant monoplane. He had proudly flown the aircraft over Windsor, Ontario on July 3rd – just six weeks before he lost his life in the same aircraft.

The trend of exhibition flights continued through 1912 with many eager new faces taking to the skies in Canada. One was William McIntosh Stark of Vancouver. He took his flying training at the Curtiss Flying School in San Diego, graduating with his "certificate" on March 22nd. Less than a month later he flew his Curtiss pusher biplane at Minrou Park near Vancouver for the first time. With this heady experience under his belt, he gave three flying exhibitions on April 20th before making history a few days later by taking up the first female passenger to fly in Canada – his wife. He later became the first to conduct a demonstration in Victoria and was also a big hit at the Dominion Day ceremonies in Armstrong, British Columbia. Meanwhile, the Curtiss Exhibition team had returned to Ontario in June and made its way into the Maritime Provinces for the first time. A young American aviator by the name of Cecil Peoli made the record books by being the first aviator to fly in New Brunswick (Saint John – September 2nd) and Prince Edward Island (Charlottetown – September 25th). His demonstrations were flown in a Baldwin "Red Devil" biplane, patented and built by none other than Casey Baldwin. It was from this same aircraft that Peoli took the first photographs from an aircraft in Canada the day following his historic flight in Charlottetown. He would also be the first aviator to circle the Parliament Buildings in Ottawa one year later while performing at the Central Canada Exhibition.

In 1913 another Canadian-born aviator made a name for himself in Brandon, Manitoba at the Dominion Livestock Show and Fair in July. Harold Wilton Blakeley not only flew more than 20 flights during his engagement at the fair, he made history by making the first night aeroplane flight in Canada on July 23rd. With only small electric lights on the aircraft's leading edges, an electric headlight and a landing area outlined by fires, this particular feat seemed downright foolhardy. Yet, he got away with it and continued to impress prairie spectators as he crossed back and forth between Manitoba and Saskatchewan for the balance of the summer giving demonstrations in his Curtiss pusher at numerous fairs. For pure entertainment value however, the humorous act of the year had to go to young Cecil Peoli when he arrived at Fletcher's Field in Montreal on December 13th – dressed as Santa Claus – courtesy of Goodwin's department store who reaped the benefits of the publicity.

The Loop-the-Loop

For all of the antics demonstrated by various Canadian and American aviators in the first four years of powered flight in Canada, there was really nothing to compare to the day American Lincoln Beachey showed up for a flying exhibition at Maisonneuve Park in Montreal, Quebec. It was June 27th, 1914. Beachey was no stranger to aerial demonstrations in Canada, having first flown his dirigible at Sherbrooke, Quebec in September 1907. Four years later he had been a member of the Curtiss Exhibition Team when the group performed in Fort

Legendary aerobatic pioneer Lincoln Beachey of the United States flew both lighter-than-air and heavier-than-air machines in Canada. He was the first to demonstrate a loop-the-loop in his Curtiss pusher, flying the radical manoeuvre in Montreal on 27 Jun 14. Below, he is shown taking off to perform the daring deed in his standard flying attire, a business suit. Up until his untimely death in 1915, he was revered as the foremost aerobatic pilot in North America where millions had watched him perform. (CAHS Collection via Larry Milberry, A.H. Sandwell)

Erie, Ontario in June 1911. His most famous and daring stunt had come just after the Fort Erie show when he flew through the Niagara Gorge, dangerously low over Niagara Falls and then dove under the steel arch bridge which spanned the Niagara River at the time. The tremendous downdrafts associated with the disturbed airflow over the falls had nearly cost him his life. Yet, it apparently did nothing to dampen his enthusiasm for flight or penchant for the spectacular.

Now, three years and innumerable demonstrations later, Beachey was once again dressed in his business suit, sitting out in the open on his Gnome-powered special Curtiss-type pusher biplane, this time in front of a Montreal audience. After a routine takeoff he turned and lined up along the edge of the spectator area as he eased his nose down to gain speed. Then, only a few feet off the ground, he pulled back on his steering column to cause the aircraft to climb rapidly. Seeing the aircraft suddenly climbing straight up would have stunned even the most experienced aviation buffs in the crowd – but watching Beachey *keep pulling* until the aircraft was upside-down was beyond belief. Then, just as suddenly, he was heading straight down at the ground again – a

madman about to meet his maker! A collective sigh of relief swept the crowd as Beachey suddenly recovered to level flight and flew away. Few knew how to describe the incredible manoeuvre they had just witnessed. But Lincoln Beachey did – he had just completed a "loop-the-loop" for the first time in Canada. And he repeated the exhibition the next day to convince the sceptics that the stunt was no fluke.

Lincoln Beachey went on to establish a reputation as the greatest aerobatic pilot of his day. He demonstrated his incredible manoeuvre again at the Winnipeg Industrial Exhibition over a seven day period commencing on July 11th, doing the stunt twice on all but one day. This was just another stop on a 126 city tour in 1914 that saw average audiences peak 100,000 at almost every performance. In one 30-week period, 17 million Americans watched his performance … and the superlatives flowed. "The Genius of Aviation," "The Divine Flyer," "Master Birdman," "The Eighth Wonder of the World" and "The Man Who Owns the Sky" were all accolades used to describe Beachey. When it came to flying, he knew no fear. Nor, however, was he as foolhardy as he appeared. Rather, Beachey calculated each

manoeuvre carefully in practice before trying any stunt in front of a crowd. After mastering the loop-the-loop, he was the first to develop a spin recovery and the first to dive an aircraft vertically from high altitude until maximum velocity was reached. Of his flying, Orville Wright reflected, *"I have watched him closely with my glasses and have never seen him make an error or falter. An aeroplane in the hands of Lincoln Beachey is poetry. His mastery is a thing of beauty to watch. He is the most wonderful flyer of all."* This was high praise indeed from the first man in the world to fly a powered aircraft.

Lincoln Beachey's revolutionary flying and superman status made it all the more difficult for aviation fans in the United States to accept his death when tragedy struck in March 1915 at the Panama Pacific International Exposition. Flying in front of a hometown crowd in San Francisco, 28-year-old Beachey became an early victim of aircraft structural failure due to high G forces when he pulled the wings off of his new aircraft while pulling out of a high-speed dive from 3,500 feet, plunging into the harbour just inside the Golden Gate bridge. His funeral was the largest in San Francisco history.

While war raged on in Europe between 1914 and 1918, citizens back at home continued to be entertained by aviation exhibitions. American aviatrix Ruth Law created a stir in Toronto when she raced Gaston Chevrolet at the Exhibition grounds on June 29th, 1918. Although well ahead initially, she lost the race in the corners due to her larger turning radius. This dynamic work by Jim Bruce of Montreal, Quebec has been displayed in the Glenn Curtiss Museum in Hammondsport, New York and won first prize in 1997 at the annual *Artflight* competition sponsored by the Canada Aviation Museum. The painting is now part of the museum's permanent collection. (courtesy Jim Bruce)

CANADIAN NATIONAL EXHIBITION 1919 SPECIAL EVENTS

FORMAL OPENING BY PRINCE OF WALES – Monday, August 25th

GENERAL CURRIE'S VISIT – Saturday, August 30th

GRENADIER GUARDS' BAND – Full two weeks of Exhibition. Afternoon concerts, main band stand, west of Manufacturers' Building.
Evening, Victory Spectacle, Huntsville's famous Band – three days in second week. There will also be daily concerts on both band stands, by a number of veterans' military and other bands from Toronto and other Ontario points.

WAR MEMORIALS PICTURES – The present art sensation of the world will be exhibited for the full term of the Exhibition in the Fine Arts Gallery. The Canadian section will be found in the Applied Arts Building where the International Photographic Salon is also located.

WAR TROPHIES – Mammoth display of relics of the Great War, owned by the Dominion Government in the Educational Building, north side of the grounds, opposite Fine Arts Gallery.

AEROPLANE FLIGHTS – Under supervision of Cols. Bishop and Barker, aeroplane exhibitions will be given daily in captured German and other enemy aircraft. There will also be a number of enemy and other machines exhibited on the grounds. An aerial contest from Toronto to New York and return will also be a feature of the first week of the Exhibition.

A colourful programme cover at the Canadian National Exhibition in 1919 celebrated Canada's contribution to victory in "The Great War" which ended on Armistice Day, November 11th, 1918 (the 11th hour of the 11th day of the 11th month), now commonly referred to as "Remembrance Day." The Special Events calendar at the 41st annual CNE included a strong military presence. (courtesy the CNE Archives)

Canadian Flyers in World War I

The death of the United States' most prolific aerobatic pilot did not go unnoticed north of the 49th parallel but America's northern neighbours had far bigger concerns at the time – Canada was at war – and had been for seven months! Great Britain's declaration of war on Germany on August 4th, 1914 automatically committed her "self govern ing colonies" like Canada to the war in Europe. Notwithstanding the militia's early trepidations about manned flight, Col Sam Hughes, Minister of Militia and Defence, authorized the formation of the Canadian Aviation Corps (CAC) on September 16th, a fledgling air force for Canada. It proved to be a dismal failure. Allocated only two officers and a single mechanic to service a well-used, demonstration model Burgess-Dunn pusher floatplane purchased for $5,000, the CAC set sail for Great Britain with the Canadian Expeditionary Force. The aircraft was lashed to the deck of a troop transport, the S.S. *Athenia*, and bobbed its way across the Atlantic, being damaged in the process. It never flew again. The rapid demise of the CAC resulted in the Royal Flying Corps (RFC) and Royal Naval Air Service

(RNAS) in Great Britain offering the only opportunities for Canadian servicemen wishing to fly. To obtain the necessary qualifications, civilian flying schools such as the Curtiss School of Aviation established at Toronto Island and Long Branch began to flourish. However, as the war raged on, civilian schools could not keep up with the demand which led to the formation of RFC training wings in Ontario at Camp Borden, North Toronto and Deseronto. It was at Camp Borden that the first RFC flying training took place commencing on April 2nd, 1917. It would remain the nation's largest flying station until the RCAF opened a new air station at Trenton in 1931.

By the time the armistice was signed on November 11th, 1918, some 22,811 Canadians had served in the British air services, 1,563 losing their lives in "the war to end all wars." Countering this sobering statistic was the fact that 10 of the 27 leading aerial "aces" among the allies were Canadians. Names like Bishop, Collishaw, MacLaren and Barker became famous in Canada. World War I had created a new brand of aviator with his own special mystique – the fighter pilot.

Canada's First Formation Display

The exhilaration of victory over the despised Germans was not something that would soon pass after four years of bloody war. In fact, it would last for many months in Canada as more of the nation's war heroes returned home, thousands with shattered bodies. Two fighter pilots that received much acclaim were Majors Billy Bishop and William Barker. Both had gained fame in the Royal Flying Corps/Royal Air Force as multiple "aces" and both had been promoted to the rank of lieutenant colonel within the new Canadian Air Force before they came home. They shared a love of flight, had eagle eyes and had won a chest full of decorations, including the Victoria Cross – the British Empire's highest award for gallantry. Although they never crossed paths during the war, they would go into business together afterwards, forming Bishop-Barker Aeroplanes Limited as pioneers of commercial flight. Although it was Billy Bishop who won the greatest acclaim for his reported 72 victories overseas, it was William Barker who gained the distinction of leading the first public display of formation flying in Canada in the summer of 1919.

Following the allied victory in World War I, numerous "war trophy" machines were claimed by the victors, including this Fokker D.VII, one of Germany's most famous combatants. Showing off one of the aircraft in early 1919 at Upper Heyford, Oxfordshire, England is Maj A.E. McKeever, commanding officer of No. 1 Sqn, Canadian Air Force which was formed in May 1918. Note the addition of the No 1 Sqn maple leaf insignia in contrast to the Iron Cross. (National Archives of Canada PA-6011)

William Barker had grown up a farm boy in Dauphin and Russell, Manitoba, the eldest of 10 children. It had been a pretty routine existence for a young boy growing up on the Canadian prairies, routine that is until he saw American Eugene Ely of San Francisco put on a flying display at the Winnipeg Industrial Exhibition on July 15th, 1910. It was the first time a powered flying machine had ever appeared in Manitoba, and watching Ely swoop low to the ground and then climb suddenly while rolling his machine from one side to the other captivated young Barker – this looked like great fun. He made sure his father took him back to the big city again the following year where he watched Frank T. Coffyn perform in his Wright Model B biplane. The flashy aviator even had a 20 lap race with a motorcycle ... and won, to the delight of the Winnipeg faithful who cheered the young man as a hero. These eye-witness accounts changed Barker's life forever, giving him a focus and passion for flight that would eventually drive him to his destiny. Watching the master himself, Lincoln Beachey, do his loop-the-loops in July 1914 only reinforced the 19-year-old's desire. However, getting the opportunity to learn how to fly didn't come easily and was expensive. Thus, Barker had to do it the hard way – by joining the army first.

In November, 1914, just three months after war had broken out in Europe, Will Barker joined the 1st Regiment, Canadian Mounted

Rifles with long-time friend Duncan Leigh. Before his 21st birthday, Trooper Barker was at war in Flanders, Belgium as a machine gunner. To his relief, after five moribund months in the trenches, Barker's application to transfer to the Royal Flying Corps was approved in February, 1916. Initially employed as a lieutenant observer, when he finally did get the opportunity to become a pilot, Barker excelled at flying training and by war's end had become one of the deadliest shots in the world. His celebrated one-sided dogfight in his Sopwith Snipe against at least 15 German fighters on October 27th, 1918 (embellished to as many as 60 fighters by some exuberant reporters) was considered one of the greatest single dogfights of World War I and made him a legend, one of the great popular heroes of the day.

Barker's passion for flight did not end with the war. His new focus became aerobatic flying and air racing. It was on August 23rd, 1919 that Barker led three RAF compatriots flying "war trophy" German Fokker D.VIIs in a display of formation and solo aerobatics for the patrons attending the opening day of the 41st annual Canadian National Exhibition. The use of these particular aircraft came about due to the initiative of LCol

The Canadian National Exhibition is home to one of Canada's largest and most famous airshows. The nation's first formation display took place over the Toronto waterfront in August 1919 during "Victory Year" celebrations. Widespread advertising ensured hundreds of thousands of spectators bore witness to the historic event. (courtesy CNE Archives)

Arthur Doughty, the Dominion archivist. In May of 1919, he had arranged for a collection of "war trophies" to be shipped from England to Toronto. Among them were a number of Fokker D.VII scout planes which were highly regarded as a fighter pilot's airplane – fast, manoeuvrable and stable, making the aircraft an ideal gun platform. Upon docking in Toronto, the aircraft were unloaded and sent to Leaside airfield. Having tried out the aircraft, Barker received permission to "borrow" six Fokkers, four of which would be used at the upcoming CNE to give a display of the prowess of RAF pilots that had fought over the skies of Europe. A description of the show was reported in detail by *The Globe*, Toronto's leading newspaper of the day in their Monday edition on August 25th, 1919:

"STUNT" FLYING THRILLS CROWD

Spectators at Exhibition Gasp at Feats of Daring Airmen

FAMOUS AVIATORS THERE

Thousands See Pilots Manoeuvre Machines as in War Days

Headlines of the in-depth report on the air display put on by LCol William Barker's Fokker team as reported in *The Globe*, Toronto, Monday, August 25, 1919

"Exhibition visitors Saturday evening saw about the best series of "stunt" (sic) the Fair patrons have ever witnessed. For over forty minutes four of the crack Canadian airmen flew above the heads of the people on the grounds and twenty minutes of this time was spent in trick flying. Spiral dives, loop-the-loop, side slips and the Immellmann turn, invented by the famous German "ace," featured the performance. Below on the ground crowds stood gazing upward while the birdmen flew. Gasps and cries of "Oh!" and "Ah!" came when one of the quartet performed some spectacular feat.

Col Barker, V.C., D.S.O., D.F.C., Capt James, M.C., Capt Dallin, M.C., and Capt Pearson,

Two of Canada's leading aces of World War I, Billy Bishop and William Barker, went into business together after repatriating to Canada as heroes. They are pictured here at Leaside airfield in Toronto with one of their "borrowed" Fokker D.VII Scouts. (DND RE68-5450)

M.C., were the four aviators who performed. In Col Barker Toronto people had the opportunity to watch in flight one of the foremost aviators of the world war. His feats, notably that in which he encountered and fought 60 Hun planes, need not be recounted.

In Squadron Formation

Commencing, the four flew in squadron formation with Col Barker in the lead. In this formation, which is the battle formation, the leader and two planes form a flying wedge, while another remains in the rear as a rear guard. Flying well up the four airmen turned and wheeled, changing formation. They flew far out over the lake, and then turned and came over the grounds. After this Col Barker and Capt James led off with trick-flying in pairs. For ten minutes they side-slipped, performed the Immellmann turn, which was invented to turn the tables when an enemy plane "had got on his tail," i.e. secured a position directly behind whereby the plane in front is helpless ...

Spectators Breathless

During a good many of the "stunts" the spectators were breathless. They thought the airman was plunging down

The other three continued squadron flying for some time. On one occasion two of the machines approached each other. People below gasped with apprehension, thinking that a smash-up was coming. But just before they came together one smartly dived under the other.

Streamers on Plane

While Col Barker's plane had streamers to distinguish the famous Canadian "ace," a good many of the people were not able to identify the plane. The streamers were scarcely distinguishable except when the airman came low.

In the "stunt" flying all four airmen appeared to perform equally well. To the many returned men the squadron brought back memories of watching British fighting planes, the roar of their propellers mellowed by the height, flying steadily in formation over the German lines, while the "Archie" shells, like pieces of white popcorn floating in the air, burst around them.

Crowds See It All

Although the airplane is now nearly as common as was the motor car a few years ago, watching the airmen never seems to lose its charm. There were many who stood for the entire course of the flights gazing up at the

Canada's most decorated fighter ace, LCol William Barker VC, DSO, MC, ADC made history by leading the first formation demonstration in Canada at the CNE on 23 Aug 19. He is shown at Armour Heights, Ontario preparing for a flight. (DND RE69-1418, RE75-306 courtesy Dr. Steve Harris)

to destruction ... Capt Dallin and Capt Pearson then took up the stunt flying and went through the whole bag of tricks. The aviators flew quite low and the crowds were able to get a good view of the machines. After the "stunt" flying was finished, one of the machines, evidently having engine trouble, flew off to the landing ground.

planes as they wheeled and turned. Even around the bandstand the crowd listening to the music found that they could watch and listen at the same time, and necks were craned to follow the airmen in their flight. A novelty no longer, the airplane, particularly when flown by such famous pilots, is still a strong attraction."

Of the aerial exploits by Barker's team, the 1919 annual report of the Canadian National Exhibition was equally complimentary. *"During the Exhibition daily flights were given by Col Barker and associates who demonstrated some of the reasons why Canadians gained the reputation of being among the most daring and successful flyers at the front. Their exhibitions were at all times most interesting, bordering indeed on the sensational and thousands waited daily for their flights over the grounds and lake."*

Barker did not confine his flying during the CNE to the daily airshow however. He also made headlines by participating in the "Great Toronto-New York Air Race" of 1919, the first post-war international air race. The round trip race, which could be started from either location, covered 1,150 miles. Barker's chosen aircraft for the race was also the Fokker D.VII. Although he didn't win the race, he did make headlines for his tenacity in just completing it. With his left arm all but immobilized as a result of wounds suffered during his famous dogfight, he froze the arm during an 80 minute flight from Albany to Roosevelt Field, New York on August 24th while battling sleet and freezing rain in his open cockpit. Ignoring this minor nuisance, he was back in the air just under two hours later for the return trip to Toronto. Such was the bravado of the day – and Barker was not alone in displaying it.

It was unfortunately that same bravado that would later get both Barker and Bishop in trouble. The duo continued to perform at the CNE in 1920 and 1921 until they were finally fired "for performing stunts at a dangerously low altitude over the crowds, with aircraft painted conspicuously with the Bishop-Barker name." In his outstanding biography, *Barker VC* (Doubleday 1997), Canadian author Wayne Ralph offers an explanation as to why both Barker's personality and flying habits began to take on an aura of recklessness:

"Receiving the Victoria Cross had thrust Barker into a public role, and a social milieu, that he was not well equipped to handle. Fame or wealth conferred impunity from social consequences and, despite Prohibition, alcohol was still the drug of choice. Will began to drink. He drank far more than he had during the war, firstly to be social and then, later, to numb the pain. The gradual onset of painful arthritis in his arm and legs was a constant reminder to him of his last battle.

The stunts performed by Barker and Bishop at the CNE, as well as by other flyers after the Great War (and also the Second World War), were sometimes the result of post-traumatic stress disorder (PTSD), but often were just a craving for a peak experience. Risk taking, what might be labelled the 'flying low' syndrome, was the war pilot's way to recapture the intense rush felt only in combat … What was surprising about Barker was not that he occasionally behaved recklessly, or was socially inept, but that he retained the regard of his peers and most of the public in spite of it. He was the hero of heroes to his own generation, the man that even the most egotistical of scouts aces could admire and praise unreservedly."

Wayne Ralph

The much decorated William Barker left the RCAF in 1926 and was appointed vice president and general manager of Fairchild Aircraft's new factory in Montreal. On March 12th, 1930 he was flying an impromptu demonstration of a new Fairchild KR-21 biplane for the RCAF at Rockcliffe when, not sufficiently aware of the aircraft's aerodynamic performance, he stalled it at the apex of a steep pull-up. The two-seater flipped on its back, the nose pitched down and the KR-21 hit the frozen surface of the Ottawa River. Barker was killed instantly. He was only 35.

The Barnstormers

While Bishop and Barker were gaining fame (and later notoriety) for their antics at the CNE, they were but two of scores of young men who returned from the Great War eager to make a living in aviation. Two more veterans that became famous in Western Canada (especially Alberta) were Captains Wilfrid "Wop" May and Fred McCall. They too were "aces" several times over and had been decorated for their victories over France. And they too formed their own aviation companies, May Airplanes Limited and McCall Aero Company Limited in Edmonton and Calgary respectively. When the two became partners, one of their business ventures included "barnstorming" the prairie fairs' circuit together over the next three years. McCall survived an amazing crash at the Calgary Exhibition on July 5th, 1919 when his Curtiss JN-4D-2 (serial number 34214) suffered an engine failure shortly after takeoff from the infield of the exhibition racetrack during a joyride flight. With insufficient altitude to make it back to the racetrack, McCall was faced with the

unpleasant predicament of having to crash land in the crowded midway. He skilfully planted the stricken aircraft in the only place not packed with fairgoers, the top of the twirling merry-go-round named the Carousell (sic). He and his two young passengers (Ronald and Herbert Richardson – the fair manager's children!), along with everyone on the ride, walked away shaken but unscathed. Of the startling incident the *Herald* reported the next day, *"It was a wonderful exhibition of daring aviation, quick thinking and pluck."* Ultimately, the names of Wop May and Fred McCall became synonymous with the commercial success of aviation in Edmonton and Calgary respectively and both played important roles in the British Commonwealth Air Training Plan during World War II.

The week long Calgary Exhibition of 1919 highlighted the aerial proficiency of two home-grown World War I barnstormers, Capt Fred McCall and Capt Wilfrid "Wop" May. (NA-1473-17)

By comparison, decorated flyers like Bishop, Barker, May and McCall had a relatively easy time establishing flying businesses after the war as opposed to many of their peers. With so many young men having learned how to fly during the war, the cessation of hostilities meant that the vast majority found themselves without jobs when they returned home. Yet, in flying they had found that same adventure that created an adrenalin rush unlike anything they had ever experienced. Thus, they too yearned to keep that feeling of high adventure and euphoria alive. It was from these emotional ties to aviation that the post-war era of barnstorming boomed throughout the Roaring Twenties. Surplus military aircraft made redundant after the war were plentiful and acquired by hundreds of wartime-trained

pilots on both sides of the border. For many, their livelihood then became a gypsy's life of barnstorming from airfield to airfield throughout every region of the county. Stunt flying and air racing were their favourite activity, not only because they were fun, but because they offered the most glamour. Spectators were mesmerized by these free-wheeling displays which in turn made the prospect of taking these curious bystanders for their first aeroplane rides all that more likely – for a fee of course. The increasing frequency of flying exhibitions also led to direct advertising as commercial enterprises saw an opportunity to exploit the popularity of flying. Before long, all manner of advertisements were appearing on the fuselage and wings of performing aircraft. And aerial photography would soon become a booming business.

As the decade wore on a new generation of flyers started to take to the skies as well, the sons of veterans of the Great War. One of these was Z.L. "Lewie" Leigh whose family had emigrated to Canada from England in 1909, the same year that J.A.D. McCurdy had made his famous flight. The elder Leigh had subsequently fought overseas in France as a member of the 39th Battery, Canadian Field Artillery. His father's pride in Queen and country led the younger Leigh to join the militia in Lethbridge, Alberta where the family had settled, but by 1929 Lewie had seen enough of aeroplanes to know that it was time for a career change. Taking flying lessons at Southern Alberta Airlines in a de Havilland Gipsy Moth, he spent much of his solo time practicing loops, rolls and spins – all trademark manoeuvres of barnstormers. Once he had attained the prerequisite minimum of 50 hours of solo time, Leigh passed a series of exams and attained his commercial licence which entitled him to carry passengers. So began his early part-time barnstorming career – enticing prairie citizens with his aerobatics and then taking them for joyrides in a Moth or Curtiss Robin monoplane powered by a 180 hp engine.

When in 1930 some of the novelty of "routine" barnstorming began to wear thin, Leigh teamed up with long-time friend Ernie Boffa in Medicine Hat, Alberta for some truly bizarre stunts using Boffa's appropriately named "Waco 9" biplane. They started off with a variation of the daredevil antics popularized by aerial gymnasts known as "wing walkers." One stunt had Botha climb out onto Leigh's wing and then dive off to the spectators' horror, only to be "saved" by a

specially designed parachute pulled out of a bag tied to one of the wing struts. In his entertaining memoirs, *And I Shall Fly* (CANAV Books 1985), Leigh explains what transpired following the success of this death-defying act:

"Then Ernie and I decided to *really* create a stir. Our idea, concocted appropriately in a beer parlour, was for our Waco to fly over a crowd towing a daredevil hanging by his teeth to a rope that dangled from the undercarriage. At least, that was the way the spectators would see it, and that was how we advertised our plan. Actually we were cheating a little. The rope, 12 feet long, was tied to the undercarriage. About every foot along it

It was on the last day of the 1919 Calgary Exhibition that McCall experienced an engine failure on his JN-4D-2 that resulted in this incredible "controlled crash." (Glenbow Archives, Calgary, Canada NA 1451-27)

was a large knot and at the end of the rope there was a steel snap hooked to his harness. Ernie was to climb out of the front cockpit onto the wing while I flew low over the crowd. From there he was to reach the undercarriage and climb down the rope, then hang onto that last knot with his hands near his mouth, thus simulating the 'hanging by his teeth.' I would circle the crowd, after which he would climb the rope again and return to the cockpit.

For this stunt Ernie was not to wear a parachute. We posted some friends in the middle of the field with the understanding that if anything went wrong they were to wave to me, for once Ernie climbed off the wing he

would be out of my sight. The problem was that though they could signal that something was amiss they could not describe exactly *what* was wrong. In our beer parlour schemes we never considered this point.

A substantial crowd had gathered on and around the Medicine Hat airfield when we took off. I climbed to 300 feet and then flew over the onlookers, keeping the aircraft in a wide circling turn. Ernie crawled out onto the wing, then grimly let himself down over the leading edge, heading for the undercarriage. His body created wind resistance, so I opened the throttle more. The underpowered Waco was fighting to maintain altitude. I waited for a minute or two, giving Ernie time to ease himself down the rope, then

began my circuits over the crowd. As I completed the routine I glanced towards the centre of the airfield. There were our friends, waving frantically. Something was wrong – but what?

Exhilaration turned to sobriety. I decided to do one more pass over the crowd and see what happened. The waving became more frenzied. I guessed, rightly, that for some reason Ernie could not climb back up the rope and that he was still dangling there. My job was to try to get the airplane down without killing him. For a start I selected a smooth, grassy part of the field, far away from the crowd, the flatter the better, Then, too, I figured I should keep the tail up as

long as possible, lest the iron tail-skid shoe bash him. At that time three-point landings were normal; of necessity this must be a wheel landing.

Down I touched, then rolled. I could visualize Ernie being dragged along behind at 40 miles an hour, then 30. How was he? As I came to a halt I sat there frozen with fear. 'I must have killed him!' I thought. From under the plane crawled a figure in white flying overalls, dirty, somewhat bloodied about the knees, elbows and nose. Our eyes met, and without a word, as sober as judges, we shook hands. At that moment our friends arrived, Lin among them (Lin Bowker was Leigh's future wife). She looked from Ernie to me and back again, then uttered the most appropriate words for the occasion: 'Come to my house and have a drink. You both need it.'

I learned afterwards that Ernie had been unable to climb back again because of the slipstream, aggravated by the extra power I had applied to maintain altitude. Snapped to the rope, he could not fall, but he was whipped around in the slipstream. As I settled down he was pumping his legs like crazy bounding along in giant 30-foot strides behind the Waco. In the crowd there was pandemonium; more than one woman fainted.

Subsequently I received a ticking off from Inspector Ingram of the Civil Aviation Division, Department of National Defence. I promised never to try a similar stunt again."

Z. Lewis Leigh

By the spring of 1931, Leigh had pretty much purged barnstorming from his system, helped along when he survived a close brush with death when he overstressed a Command-Aire biplane while doing a loop with two "hefty" passengers aboard. In completing the loop, he had managed to break the welds on all of the front centre section struts, pulling them away from the fuselage! He then nervously watched his upper wings sway back and forth as he came in for landing; he never did aerobatics with heavyweights aboard again … Faced with a failing business as The Great Depression gripped the prairies, Lewis Leigh joined the RCAF in December 1931 and went on to a distinguished career that helped earn him a place in the Canadian Aviation Hall of Fame.

The Birth of the RCAF

Some 14 months after the end of the First World War, the government of Canada under Prime Minister Sir Robert Borden authorized the formation of the first home-based Canadian Air Force (CAF) on February 18th, 1920 (Order-in-Council 395). Its Latin motto was "*Sic Itur Ad Astra*" (This is the Way to the Stars). An organization by the same name had been formed in England on September 19th, 1918, initially under the command of LCol W.A. Bishop. However, comprised of a single wing and two squadrons (No. 1 and No. 2), all had been disbanded in England by February 5th, 1920.

Granted Royal approval by King George V, the Canadian Air Force was officially redesignated the Royal Canadian Air Force on 1 Apr 24.

The new CAF was a non-permanent organization designed to provide 28-day refresher training on a biennial basis to former officers and airmen that had served with the RAF. The provisional establishment for the new air force was set at 1,340 officers and 3,905 airmen at the end of June 1920, although only a fraction of that number saw active service. By the time the training was suspended at the end of 1922, only 550 officers and 1,271 airmen had completed the course at Camp Borden, Ontario. Clearly, a more permanent arrangement was required.

The first step towards a permanent air force for Canada had already been taken in June 1922 when the Civil Operations Branch and Canadian Air Force were consolidated into a single military organization. Simultaneously, the formation of a Department of National Defence (DND) was approved to take effect on January 1st, 1923. The new DND became responsible for the former Department of Militia and Defence, Department of Naval Service and the Air Board that had originally

been formed on June 6th, 1919. From an air force perspective, the significance of these changes was that the CAF became a permanent entity responsible for all flying operations and the control of civil aviation across Canada.

Of historical interest, King George V granted Royal approval to use the prefix "Royal" in front of Canadian Air Force on February 15th, 1923 with the designation first appearing in Air Force Orders on March 13th. However, the prefix was not officially approved by the Canadian government for over a year, until April 1st, 1924 which was subsequently considered the birth date of the Royal Canadian Air Force. With a permanent force established at only 68 officers and 307 airmen, it was a humble beginning for an air force that would eventually grow in wartime to over 215,000 personnel by December 1943.

Flying operations in the early days of the RCAF mirrored those of the CAF in that they were distinctly unmilitary in nature, much to the chagrin of combat veterans like Will Barker. He wanted to see Canada develop a more robust air force with some teeth, along the lines of the RAF. Yet, the varied tasks that the RCAF was assigned initially were vitally important to the development of the nation. These "civil" tasks included exploration, surveying, mapping and aerial photography, fishery and forest fire patrols and transportation of everything from fire fighters to snowshoes. Aircraft in use at the time were the remnants of an Imperial Gift of some 114 surplus aircraft that Great Britain had donated to Canada in 1919. Of these, 62 Avro 504s and a dozen each de Havilland D.H. 4s and D.H. 9s plus some Curtiss HS-2L flying boats acquired from the US Navy had proven most useful in accomplishing these tasks. However, as a fighter force, the RCAF was anything but.

All of this began to change on January 5th, 1926 when two all-metal Armstrong-Whitworth Siskin fighters (J7758 and J7759) arrived at Camp Borden for winter trials at the request of the RCAF. Subsequent testing in High River, Alberta that summer and into the next winter convinced the RCAF that the Siskin was an aircraft they could use as a training platform to eventually develop a fighter force. By the summer of 1929 a total of 10 Siskins (including two duals) had been purchased from the Air Ministry in Great Britain and were assigned to Training Squadron B Flight at Camp Borden.

The Siskins – The RCAF's First Demonstration Team

The summer of 1929 marked the 10th anniversary of the first successful non-stop trans-Atlantic crossing of an aeroplane (a twin-engine Vickers Vimy) which was accomplished by two British Empire aviation pioneers, John Alcock and Arthur Whitten Brown. On June 15th, 1919 they had been the first intrepid aviators to successfully meet the challenge laid down by Lord Northcliffe of the London *Daily Mail* to make the flight, taking 16 hours and 12 minutes to fly the 1,800 mile journey between St. John's, Newfoundland and Clifden, Ireland. Although their triumphant flight ended in a bog, they were rewarded handsomely with a £10,000 prize, their own statue in London and a knighthood from King George V to go with it!

To mark the occasion, the government of Prime Minister William Lyon Mackenzie King had been urged to acknowledge the achievement in an appropriate fashion by a Toronto citizen, Mr. Benjamin F. Wilson. When the request reached the Director of the RCAF, W/C L.S. Breadner, he suggested an exhibition flight at Borden be formed using two Siskins, one (Siskin No. 20) inscribed with "Captain Sir Arthur Whitten Brown" under either side of the cockpit, the other (Siskin No. 59) with "Captain Sir John

Alcock D.S.C." The dedication of the two aircraft took place on July 19th, 1929 with Brigadier A.H. Hill, District Commanding Officer, District No. 2, officiating.

The camp commandant at Borden at the time was W/C G.M. Croil who was destined to become the RCAF's first Chief of the Air Staff in December 1938. He had a very experienced instructional staff which included S/L C.M. McEwen (chief flying instructor and an original member of the CAF's No. 1 Fighter Sqn in England) and three flight commanders. Of these, F/L G.R. Howsam was a Canadian veteran of the Great War and the other two were post-war RAF instructors seconded to the RCAF to assist with flying training – F/Ls D.A. Harding and F.V. Beamish. Croil wanted two of his young Canadian charges to show off the commemorative aircraft and selected two who had shown much promise with their flying abilities. Pilot officer Edwin A. "Mac" McGowan was placed in charge of the exhibition flight with Ernest A. "Ernie" McNab as his partner. They later became the nucleus of the RCAF's first formation demonstration team.

McGowan's logbook reveals that he had commenced flying training at Camp Borden on July 3rd, 1926 with a familiarization flight that lasted all of five minutes. It is not clear whether he or his flying instructor had seen

enough in that short time span! Nevertheless, two days later he commenced his formal flying training with a 25 minute flight and on August 19th he slipped into the wild blue on his first solo flight – that magic and unforgettable day when a young aviator gets the thumbs up from his instructor and goes flying with no one but himself to talk to. McGowan was undoubtedly thrilled with his "exhibition flight" assignment in July 1929, in spite of the fact he had never flown the Siskin. He had however done plenty of flying in the Avro 504N, including formation aerobatics. McGowan took Siskin number 20 up for a test flight on August 5th and over the next week flew eight more practice sorties. Unfortunately, an incident during his third trip of the day on August 13th kept him on the ground for the team's first big weekend of shows. P/O McNab therefore got all of the glory with solo shows at several southern Ontario locales, including Hamilton, St. Catharines and Oshawa.

From Ottawa to Cleveland to Toronto – the Summer of 1929

As time drew near for Eastern Canada's two major exhibitions of the year, the Central Canada Exhibition in Ottawa and Canadian National Exhibition in Toronto, the RCAF received invitations to participate in both. F/L Victor Beamish, who had been instruct-

Camp Borden, Ontario was the initial home of the Siskin Exhibition Flight. The team typically took off and landed in a loose three-plane formation as depicted in this fine study by Graham Wragg of Gibson's Landing, British Columbia. The background for this painting is Rockcliffe Air Station in Ottawa circa 1932. (courtesy Graham Wragg)

Members of the RCAF's first aerobatic team, the Siskins, pose for a casual photo at Rockcliffe on 26 Aug 29 in front of one of their team aircraft bearing the Alcock-Brown dedication. L to R – P/O Ernest A. McNab, F/L F. Victor Beamish (RAF) and P/O Edwin A. McGowan. Above is the detailed inscription on Siskin 59. (RCAF Photos via Shirley Gobeil-Gravelle)

ing on the Siskin at RAF Cranwell immediately prior to his posting to Canada, had impressed everyone at Camp Borden with his aerobatic expertise within days of his arrival in April 1929. To that end, W/C George Croil had invited him to put on a solo display for the opening of the new airport at Kingston, Ontario on June 4th. With the success of that show and others that McNab and McGowan had flown in the region, Croil then tasked Beamish to work up a three-ship "non-aerobatic" formation display for the exhibition in Ottawa on August 22nd and 23rd. It was a basic formation routine worked up over five practices and the team set out for Rockcliffe (Ottawa) on the morning of August 22nd via a refuelling stop at Deseronto. They flew their first official formation show that afternoon to a large and appreciative crowd followed by two more the next day. As Beamish was scheduled to go on leave during the period of the CNE, leadership of the new team was passed to F/L Dave Harding who would lead the same wingmen to Toronto.

In spite of the best laid plans, an unforeseen development towards the end of August pressed Beamish back into service to accommodate a late request for an RCAF demonstration at the ninth edition of the highly regarded U.S. National Air Races to be held at Cleveland, Ohio for the first time. This show would later come to be regarded as the start of the "golden age" of air racing. In view of the fact that the US Air Corps, US Navy demonstration team (the High Hats) and now world-famous Charles Lindbergh would be in attendance, the show offered an exceptional public relations opportunity for the RCAF to enhance its reputation. Presented the details, Beamish felt an aerobatic demonstration was in order. He therefore decided that, with only two days to practice, it would be prudent to put on a show with his fellow flight com-

manders, Howsam and Harding, rather than push his new protégés beyond their experience level.

If it was publicity the RCAF was looking for in Cleveland, they certainly got it on August 29th, 1929. As special guests of the races along with a Canadian Band and Drill Team, the Siskins were invited to close the show following a mock dogfight by six US Air Corps Curtiss Hawks and the three-plane Navy Demonstration Team. Beamish wasted no time in getting the crowd's attention. Commencing with a formation takeoff, the team climbed to several hundred feet and then proceeded to totally ignore any so-called showline. Breaking from an echelon formation, they dove straight at the crowd, terrorizing the grandstand area with mock strafing runs scant feet above the spectators' heads. Then, working at flag pole height, they did loops, rolls and "double-bunts," keeping some 45,000 race fans riveted for a

F/L David A. Harding, an RAF flying instructor, led the RCAF Siskins during their first appearances at the CNE in 1929, introducing a three-plane formation spin to their repertoire. Behind him is the 425 hp rotary engine of the Siskin IIIA. (DND PL 117106)

full 30 minutes before finally joining up in a "V" formation for one last pass across the field. It was in the eyes of some witnesses the most skillful and daring flying ever seen, even if race officials were distressed at the visitors' disregard for the rules. The thunderous roar the three aviators received when they taxied up to the speaker's stand moments after landing left no doubt that they had won the day. Two newspaper accounts the next morning in Cleveland said it all, *"Royal Aces Burn Up Sky in Most Daring of Stunts"* and *"Canadians Rocket over Heads of Crowd to Outdo Lindbergh and High Hats In Mad Loops."*

Following the Cleveland escapade, F/L Dave Harding led McGowan and McNab through a somewhat tamer, but nevertheless impressive formation demonstration at the CNE in Toronto. One manoeuvre stood out from all the others – a three-plane formation spin. On looking back at the 1929 CNE many years later, Ernie McNab explained how the manoeuvre came to be introduced into the Siskin show:

"Two days before the CNE Dave decided that as the U.S. Air Corps were bringing up a full squadron of Curtiss Hawks we had to do something spectacular so he added to our few manoeuvres, *spinning in formation*!! We had one practice at Camp Borden consisting of No. 1 and 2 wingmen moving out two spans from the leader; the three aircraft then picked a point on the horizon, put the aircraft in a right hand spin coming out on the picked point on the third turn. It worked! During the years I spent on flight formation flying I never heard of any unit in the U.S. or U.K. even contemplating incorporating this manoeuvre in their program, but they didn't have a Dave Harding and two dumb wingmen … If I knew then what I knew after with more experience, I'd have walked right back to Borden!

The infamous Siskin show over the grandstand of the Cleveland Air Races in 1929 was led by F/L Victor Beamish. This depiction by artist Don Connolly won first prize at the *Artflight* exhibition at the Canada Aviation Museum in 1999. (courtesy Don Connolly)

The 1930 Siskin team was officially designated the "Siskin Exhibition Flight" and flew from their home base at Camp Borden, Ontario. Four pilots were assigned to the team, three flying in each show. L to R – F/L F. Victor Beamish (RAF), F/O Ernest A. McNab, F/O Ralph C. Hawtrey, F/O Fowler M. Gobeil. (DND PL117434 to 117437)

Gaining Official Status

In the spring of 1930 a regular aerobatic flight was formed at Borden under the command of F/L Victor Beamish … The other pilots were P/Os Ralph Hawtrey, Fowler Gobeil and myself with F/O R.C. Minnes to fly the transport aircraft. F/L Beamish was a perfectionist and expected his pilots to be the same, resulting in a summer of rigid training. Three hours a day and more of formation aerobatics can be very trying on all concerned. He also was a fanatic on the subject of body conditioning, for example, in playing golf, after every shot one picked up his bag and ran. It was not a fun summer.

The aerobatic flight put on shows at the larger centres – Montreal, Ottawa, the CNE and others in the lower St. Lawrence and lakes area. It was a satisfactory summer, in that all exhibitions went well, and all aircraft remained whole. One incident that happened in training had its exciting moments. The adjutant of the training wing wanted to experience flight aerobatics, so Vic took up a dual with the adj as passenger. Everything went well until during an over-the-vertical left steep turn, Hawtrey on the left slipped ahead a bit and his prop chewed off the dual's left aileron. From my position on the high side I immediately kicked away but not before noting the greenish pallor of our visitor. Beamish did a remarkable job in righting his aircraft from the vertical to an even keel, and landed safely. We had no further requests for passengers!"

E.A. McNab

Another of the newcomers in 1930 was P/O Fowler Gobeil, a 1929 graduate of the Royal Military College in Kingston, Ontario who completed his wings training in October of that year. Within eight months he had been assigned to the Siskin Exhibition Flight. Some 43 years after joining the team he was asked to reflect back on his glory days during the Canadian Aviation Historical Society Annual Convention in 1973. His humorous anecdotes kept his audience well entertained and are reproduced here in part courtesy of his daughter, Shirley Gobeil-Gravelle. Gobeil left no doubt as to his first impressions on arriving at Camp Borden for the first time … or the effect that Victor Beamish had on his flying career:

"In June of 1927, while still a cadet at RMC, I reported to Camp Borden as a goggle-eyed pilot officer (provisional) for the 5th RCAF flying training course. Those were the glory days! WW I pilots carried on the RCAF Reserve Air Force list came up to Borden for refresher training. To say that they were gods to us is to put it mildly. When I first saw one of these gods, dressed to kill in long boots, whipcord riding breeches, a beautiful 'maternity jacket,' complete with medal ribbons – well, I just damned near to keeled over in a dead faint! THAT was really living … I see from my logbook that I accumulated 11 hours 40 minutes dual and 30 minutes solo in my first year. Aircraft types were the rotary Clerget-powered Avro 504K (castor-oil lubed which gave off the most delightful odour of dead fish!), the Lynx-powered Avro 504N and the Avro Viper. These were all open-cockpit jobs with a long fish pole sticking out in front to keep from nosing over …

For the first three months of 1930, we were still on 504s, FC-2s and Moths. At the end of March 1930, the 504s were finally withdrawn and replaced by the de Havilland Moth. Now, glory be, in April 1930 I was posted to 'A' Flight, No. 3 Sqn RCAF, the first service squadron in the RCAF – on Siskin fighters! I wish I could describe to you in adequate terms what this meant to an early RCAF pilot – a kid really – to make our first fighter squadron! It was the realization of every pilot's dream …

All our Siskins were new from Armstrong Siddeley in England, and they all smelled swell. You know, like a brand new car, or a brand new pigeon! We officer pilots washed them, polished them, and dusted them, with love! They had an open cockpit – nothing of this sissy, closed-in jazz of today. You sat out in your glory and got sunburned, soaked with rain, or frozen to death, depending on the weather conditions.

They had a 14-cylinder radial engine of some 300 HP – again none of this pansy, cowled-in, rocker-arm-covered nonsense. Everything was right out where the pilot could see it working – push rods pumping up and down, rocker arms pivoting in plain sight, oil blowing back over the windscreen and the pilot! A real threshing-machine of a motor, but by God, it never stopped. In many hundreds of hours on Siskins, I never had a forced landing due to engine failure. In those days, the Siskin was a lot of aeroplane for a kid pilot with some 100 hours of flying experience to be horsing around in, but when that huge wooden prop up front started spinning – we LOVED it!

Francis Victor Beamish (was) a man who had a very great deal to do with teaching the RCAF responsible flying. He was a wild Irishman in the RAF – a Cranwell grad, international rugger type, possessed of one outstanding attribute of *complete and utter*

impatience with incompetence. We all admired him all to hell, and were scared to death of him. He was a dedicated officer.

Francis Victor introduced me to Siskin flying in April 1930 – an experience I'll NEVER forget, so help me! He was nothing if not direct. His opening gambit was, with a fishy stare: 'I presume you can fly, Gobeil?' To say that this threw me a little – me, with my nice new wings that I still marvelled at – is putting it mildly. I remember coming up with a remarkably intelligent reply, along the lines of: 'Oh YES, Sir – I … I think I can.' Francis Victor, wearing an expression of complete scepticism, said only: 'Well, that's nice to know. Get in the back seat of '63' (our dual trainer Siskin) and for God's sake try not to kill me.'

In those early days we wore back chutes in the Siskin trainer; somebody, somehow, had forgotten to put a cushion on the seat. When I finally crawled on board and collapsed into the seat, with trembling limbs and shaking hands from pure excitement, I found that I was so low in the seat that I couldn't see out of the damn aeroplane. However, that was a small point. I was finally in a Siskin, so I dutifully connected up my Gosport, strapped myself in to the limit of my belts, only to discover to my horror that my belts, even done up to the maximum, let me wander about the cockpit like the feet in a farmer's galoshes.

By this time, Francis Victor had started up, run up, and waved 'Chocks away.' We started to move out for takeoff. We lined up. As far as I was concerned, we could have been lined up, down or sideways! I faintly heard Francis Victor 'Gosport' me: 'Ready, Gobeil?' Knowing his famous reputation for impatience, and being thoroughly terrified of him anyway, I thought quite simply: 'Christ, here goes nothing!' I croaked: 'Yes, sir,' and away we went into the wild blue yonder. (I'll never forget the kick in the back that seat gave me!)

Well, we got up to about 3,000 feet, straight and level. Faintly via Gosport I heard Francis Victor: 'Aerobatic experience, Gobeil?' I quavered back: 'Oh yes, sir!' (I was at my scintillating best that day – conversation-wise.)

My aerobatic experience to that time encompassed the vast ability to loop, spin and do the tremendous 'falling leaf' in a 504. Turn an aircraft upside down? Not on your jolly likely! Faintly, faintly, I heard: 'On the con-

trols – lightly now – we'll loop first.' Nose down – speed up – nose up – up – over and away! What a piece of cake, I thought. What's all this jazz about high speed fighters? After all, it's quite impossible to fall out of an aircraft in a normal loop, even if you can't see over the cockpit coaming.

Then came terror, pure and undiluted. From some other planet, a disembodied voice whispered to me: 'We roll – hands and feet on LIGHTLY!' Something completely beyond my comprehension happened to the aircraft, and I completely fell out of it to be brought up short by my belts. I was head and shoulders out – up above the windshield, feet off the rudder hanging by the toe straps, with a fingertip death grip on the control handle spade grip, mouth open gasping for breath. And then I ingested the most fascinating collection of debris from the inside of the aircraft – dust clouds, dirt, small rock particles, chewing gum labels, etc. We hung there for an interminable period of time, and that imperishable Air Force ballad flashed through my mind. It goes something like this:

'Come all you people who have heard,
Join the Navy and see the world,
For contemplation I leave this text,
Join the Air Force and see the next!'

Well, we rolled level, the seat of my pants hit the seat and the aeroplane with a thump that damn near snapped my head off, and I returned to this life. I heard Francis Victor coo ever so sweetly: 'My, did you EVER experience such a filthy aeroplane? We MUST speak to the boys about THIS when we land.' (He did and if I remember correctly the riggers ran around the aerodrome long enough to pick up two promotions from LAC to Sergeant!)

The next delightful flow of conversation from front to rear and back went something along these lines:

'Get that roll, Gobeil?'
'Oh yes, sir.' (Right up to par.)
'You try one.'
'Oh yes, sir.' (Here goes nothing.)

I put myself completely in the hands of God, Francis Victor and Armstrong Siddeley and pushed and pulled blindly. Same script – same scenario – same results! Terse summation by Francis Victor: 'Gobeil, that was positively the worst manoeuvre I have ever been forced to endure in any aeroplane. You are nothing but a butcher! We're going back.' 'Oh yes, sir.' (Just let me out of here and I'll be a good boy for the rest of my life Lord!)

To digress for a moment, Francis Victor was a grand man, a real leader – capable, thorough and actually really patient. After a couple more check rides, he turned me loose in a solo Siskin and, thanks to his training, I went on to roll up the top Siskin time in the next few years.

Once on the Siskins, we spent a very happy six months flying our pet. Francis Victor taught us formation and precision flying in his own inimitable fashion – rigid control and position holding were his watchwords. However, despite his careful training, things did not always go as they should. I recall one day (in a three-plane training flight, flying in the left wing position) watching the upper man in a left-hand turn slide slowly but inexorably down the hill into Francis Victor's plane, his prop neatly chopping pieces out of Victor's right aileron. With our open cockpits, the noise was quite audible, and terrific!

F/O Fowler Gobeil proudly poses in front of his beloved Siskin 23 (prop spinning!) with his crewman, LAC Stanyard in the summer of 1930. At right, the architect of the RCAF's first formation team, F/L Victor Beamish, RAF in front of Siskin 59. (RCAF Photos via Shirley Gobeil-Gravelle)

Sitting about three feet off Victor's left wing, all I wanted to do was to get the hell out of it, but I was too damned scared to break off. Not on account of a potential disaster, but because Francis Victor had impressed on us the cardinal sin of EVER breaking formation without the leader's signal. Sitting there in the choice grandstand seat, I watched in utter fascination as the unflappable Francis Victor gently waved his finger at the other pilot who was using his right aileron for a light snack. With his hand leisurely motioning at the end of a limp wrist, Francis Victor gently eased his boy away. Then he looked my way to see if I was still with him. I was, and he gave me the old 'thumbs up' signal. Believe me, I was proud of that! After we landed, all he said was a mild: 'My, chaps, we mustn't have any more of that. Let's go over it again.' And that was that.

At this time, I might say that if the Siskin had one fault, it was a rather weak undercarriage. We had a number of crash landings at Borden from this; no paved runways in those days, only grass and sand holes. In May of 1930, I joined the Siskin 'left-handed club' by folding up an undercarriage when I hit a pothole on landing.

During the summer, I was allotted my very own fighter – Siskin IIIA No. 23 – which I flew for the next two years and one month, until she was written off in a mid-air collision at Trenton … What a life that was! Young, single, in good shape, crazy about flying – one of the first RCAF fighter boys, with a fighter all my own (except for the Government's share!) and unlimited popsies! Ho, boy – to go back, if only for half an hour!

In August 1930, led by Francis Victor, we put on our first three RCAF exhibition flights over the Central Canada Exhibition in Ottawa where we were enthusiastically received. We landed and refuelled at the old WW I Deseronto field to and from Camp Borden. This year, we also flew exhibitions over the CNE using the old Weston airport on Bathurst Street, now a fully built-up area. After the CNE, we flew exhibitions for the Montreal Light Aeroplane Club at St. Hubert, we showed at Kitchener and again at the Ottawa Flying Club Field Day (on October 5th). After the Ottawa Show, we turned over our aircraft for overhaul and modification and the Siskin Flight closed down for the year …"

F.M. Gobeil

By the end of the 1930 season the Siskins had brought great fame to the RCAF in Central Canada, some 154 hours having been flown in support of exhibitions. Many new flying clubs had started to spring up all over the country along with new airfields to support the growth of commercial aviation. Having the Siskins appear at "official openings" added much prestige and a carnival atmosphere to these events while affording the RCAF welcome press coverage. It was good PR and was recognized as such by the senior officers running the air force. It also helped drive home the notion that the RCAF was capable of con-

As Canadians became more and more enamoured with "stunting" introduced by the barnstormers, airshow audiences grew from hundreds to thousands. Although the Siskins would not make a western tour until 1931, the City of Moose Jaw, Saskatchewan hosted its first highly successful airshow in Jul 1930. (via Tom Reid)

ducting far more than just "civil" flying operations. Nevertheless, the season was still quite short with just 13 shows completed over an eight week period.

It was not long after the team returned to Camp Borden in October that the snow began to fall. It was as if to signal not only the end of the season but also the end of Victor Beamish's days at Borden. As a just reward for the outstanding leadership and flying instruction he had brought to the RCAF, he was posted on October 21st to Vancouver to command the RCAF's major seaplane training base at Jericho Beach. It was only a five month "plum posting" to close out his two year secondment to the

RCAF. After a final farewell visit to Borden and Ottawa, Beamish bade farewell to Canada and set sail from Saint John, New Brunswick for Liverpool on March 20th, 1931. Sadly, his story did not have a happy ending. After winning a fierce personal battle with tuberculosis, surviving an incredible 126 fighter sorties in a Hawker Hurricane during the Battle of Britain and rising to the rank of group captain with three medals for gallantry, Beamish was later shot down by a *Luftwaffe* FW-190 while leading his Spitfire wing from Kenley on March 28th, 1942. Having plunged into the English Channel, no trace of him or his Spitfire (FV-B) was ever found …

Practice Makes Perfect

The third young pilot of the trio to have served under Victor Beamish on the Siskin Exhibition Flight in 1930 was P/O Ralph Hawtrey. Like McNab and Gobeil, he had great respect for Beamish and learned much from him. Hawtrey's logbook is replete with formation and aerobatic sorties. From April 22nd to 25th he flew four training trips with Beamish in Siskin 63 at Camp Borden and then did *nothing but* formation and aerobatics for the next three-and-one-half months, chalking up 98 sorties leading up to the Camp Borden Sports Day Exhibition on August 8th which he flew in Siskin 23. This was a clear reflection of Victor Beamish's insistence on perfection. Following that initial show, it was more of the same until the team flew its last show over the Ottawa Flying Club on October 5th.

All three of the young pilots would rejoin the team the next spring for their greatest adventure of all – the famous Trans-Canada Air Pageant of 1931. Command of the team was passed to a new leader from the RCAF, F/L Henry W. "Sam" Hewson, a veteran World War I flyer who was awarded the rank of temporary squadron leader for the tour, and a new flight commander, F/L William I. "Bull" Riddell. Proving that fond memories do last a lifetime, Ralph Hawtrey, as the last surviving pilot of the Siskins, recorded his memories for the express purpose of this book in May 1996. Remarkably, he was 90 years of age at the time and wrote from a veterans' home in Manotick, Ontario. Aside from the addition of sub-titles, dates and clarifying notes, his unedited letter is reproduced below for the first time:

The flight of the Siskins was immortalized decades ago when famed Canadian aviation artist Robert Bradford completed this unique perspective of the team as they crested the top of a formation loop. (courtesy Robert Bradford/Canada Aviation Museum)

"The Siskin Formation Aerobatic Flight was formed at Camp Borden in 1930 under F/L Beamish, an RAF officer seconded to the RCAF. The squadron was composed of five Siskins, a Trimotor Ford and a Fairchild. The Ford carried the groundcrew and the Fairchild spare parts. We were trained to fly the Siskin in a dual seat aircraft. At first just circuits and bumps as we called it, later aerobatics.

The Armstrong Whitworth Siskin

The Siskin was an extension of the First World War fighter aircraft. It was not equipped for night flying and had no radio. There was no tail wheel, but rather a skid which we called a spade on account of its shape. It was somewhat underpowered, but fully aerobatic for that period (although I never saw the aircraft do a bunt), it gained height in a loop, and the control stick had to be moved forward in order to complete a proper loop. The aircraft spun readily and

came out of the spin readily. No two aircraft flew in the same way – each had its own characteristics. This was somewhat disconcerting.

The undercarriage wheels had no brakes and were somewhat weak. Landings had to be made carefully. In those days a three-point landing was always made; a wheels only landing was a rumble, just not done. In most Siskins, the seat was made for a seat pack parachute. The front seat in the dual aircraft was constructed for a back pack. The engine was started by swinging the prop. Three or four airmen formed a line, hand-in-hand, to do this.

The Armstrong Whitworth Siskin IIIA was the RCAF's first fighter-type aircraft. Powered by the Armstrong Siddeley Jaguar IV 14-cylinder, two row radial engine, the aircraft had a top speed of 156 mph (251 km/hr) at sea level. It had a wingspan of 33 ft 2 in (10.1 m) and length of 25 ft 4 in (7.72 m). (RCAF Photo via R.C. Hawtrey)

The Siskin had a relatively weak landing gear considering the unprepared fields it operated from. Many pilots of the day suffered the embarrassment of gear collapse on takeoff or landing. (DND RE 15852 via Larry Milberry)

We did not have any back parachutes, so the pupil flew without a chute! This was not too bad when doing circuits and bumps, but I will never forget the first aerobatics. I thought that my seat belt was tight but when we did a slow roll I hung out of the cockpit so far that my feet came off the rudder bar, and I could only just touch the control stick. After that when fastening the belt I crouched down in the seat to make sure that the belts were too tight. They never were TOO tight.

In a formation takeoff with F/L Beamish leading in the dual machine my aircraft (Siskin 61) hit a bump, became airborne then came down going slightly sideways. The undercarriage collapsed and I hit the front rim of the cockpit with my nose. I spent three days in the hospital. I have what is called a 'Siskin nose.'

We did a few aerobatic shows in 1930 during the summer, but the main operation was in 1931, in the Trans-Canada Air Pageant. We transferred to St. Hubert, Quebec because this aerodrome was only occupied by the flying club, which was not very active. We lived in tents on the airfield. The pilots of the Trans-Canada Air Pageant were: Flying Siskins – S/L Hewson, F/O Riddell, F/O McNab, F/O Gobeil and myself, F/O Hawtrey. Flying the support aircraft – F/L Boret, Flt Sgt (forgotten his name).

(Historical note: Of interest, Hawtrey flew a 20 minute check ride with F/L Riddell at Camp Borden on May 5th, 1931 and the team deployed to St. Hubert via Kingston the next day to commence their workups. The workups for the 1931 season under S/L Hewson consisted of 78 dedicated sorties. However, with the three wingmen all now being very experienced, they were permitted to take team technicians flying with them from time to time to demonstrate to them both the joys of flight … and the importance of the technician's job! Hawtrey's logbook reveals he took Corporals Ramshaw, Cantley and Watts, Leading Aircraftman Gould and Aircraftmen Turner, Winden, Bensou and Partridge for practice flights.)

The 1931 Siskins' Show

Our formation aerobatic procedure was – take off in open formation, steep turns around the airfield, formation loops (as many as three continuing), line-ahead formation with turns and half rolls-off-the-top, dive bombing on a selected place on the airfield. We approached the target in very open formation; the leader went down first, then the starboard aircraft, and last mine. We did three dives. Once or twice I blacked out at the bottom, but only for a fraction of a second. After this we did individual aerobatics over our part of the airfield.

In order to carry the extra fuel needed for our journey the incidence of the lower wings was increased by four degrees. At the bottom of a dive on a converging bombing target I hit a bump. While climbing to regain position for the next dive I saw that the leading edge of the lower wing on the port side had collapsed against the main spar. The fabric of the wing had ripped fore and aft, (thank goodness), in a number of places. I did a very gentle right wheel only landing and the aircraft dropped the left wing only at the last minute. Needless to say the leading edge of all the Siskins was strengthened. At that time I felt a bit of shock. The metal parts had been painted a dark grey on the Siskin aircraft. We were told to remove the paint with paint remover. What a job! So we spent much time sitting on the grass until the job was finished.

Cross Country Adventures

On June 30th, 1931 we left St. Hubert and started the journey with the Trans-Canada Air Pageant. Because there were no facilities to land planes north of Lake Superior area, we flew through the USA to Winnipeg. On the takeoff in the mid-western airfields, the smell of roasting grasshoppers was not nice. Over the prairie provinces, it was noticed that the dust had piled against the fences like snow in winter.

In Regina we stayed in a hotel downtown. That night there was a thunderstorm. In the morning it was mud, mud and more mud; streaks down the buildings and on the roads. The airfield was a sea of mud. It was decided that one Siskin should attempt a takeoff. I was selected. I took off ok with a lot of mud flying around. I flew to Moose Jaw were I did a few aerobatics before landing. When the rest of the squadron arrived I was told that the mud had cracked my propeller. I asked how they knew. They said 'by the sound.'

During our ab initio training we were told, when on cross country, always fly from one possible forced landing field to another and do not use the smoke from a moving train engine as the wind direction. When we crossed the Rocky Mountains to Vancouver I was of course on the lookout for possible landing fields. There were some in the valleys. On one mountain I noticed a sheet of very blue ice – no snow.

At Vancouver we did some flying in civilian aircraft and RCAF seaplanes. It was a very happy time. When returning over the mountains some of the forest was on fire. All I could see was mountain tops. No possible landing fields at all; just smoke. I was glad to get to Lethbridge.

On the flight from Calgary to Edmonton it was very dark, and was raining. At Edmonton they had the floodlight shining across the field. Since the Trimotor Ford was the only aircraft with lights, I followed it around the airfield. I managed to land alright and in conversation with my fellow pilots found that they had followed the Trimotor also. I hadn't seen them!

On the way from Fargo to St. Paul I fell asleep for a second. It seemed that someone was rocking my bed. When I woke up I was still in my right place in the open formation.

From Madison to South Bend I heard a thump. When I looked around my aircraft I saw that the port flying wire was lying on the lower wing with a large piece of metal on the end. It seemed to me that my controls were becoming stiff. There were many possible landing fields in view. I decided that I had better go down. So I picked a good field near a farm house. I landed okay. The American National Guard made a new fitting and placed the flying wire in position. The farmer and his family were very good to me. I took off and joined the squadron in South Bend.

On the flight from Rimouski east at 2,000 ft altitude my engine started to fail. It was banging with smoke coming out. I looked around for a possible landing field, and all that I saw were lakes, rocks and bush. I felt my hair press against my helmet. But then I noticed some green fields some way south. I left the squadron and headed for the green. I arrived over a field, it looked just right at a low altitude, then I saw that the field was full of boulders. I was at low altitude and had to land, so I picked an adjacent field which was not into wind, and rather small. Before I hit the soft fence I decided to ground loop, but the ground was fairly soft and the tail skid tended to keep the aircraft straight. I had just

started to turn when the port lower wing hit the snake fence alongside a country road. The aircraft stopped in a ditch by the side of the road. The rest of the squadron flew over and I waved to show that I was not hurt.

Two young men came down and escorted me to their farm house a short distance away. I suppose that I looked very dejected. They offered me a beer, which I readily accepted. They went down to their basement and returned with two bottles and a large jug, which they took outside. I wondered why we were going outside, so I had a look. They opened the first bottle, and the contents headed for the roof of the house! They then opened the second bottle and I had some of that. Rather fizzy …

Next day the airmen arrived with a low loader. They took the wings off and loaded the aircraft onto the loader platform and left. I rejoined the squadron at Moncton and flew

in formation as usual. The Air Pageant ended in Montreal and we all went on leave.

The next year (1932) we did a few shows. I did not fly in formation since I rejoined the flight at the last minute. I did the single aerobatics at the show."

R.C. Hawtrey

G/C Hawtrey passed away in Ottawa on July 14th, 2001 – just 11 days short of his 96th birthday. He remained proud of his air force heritage right up to his final days, including a healthy respect for the military protocol that had been ingrained as a young officer. In discussing Hawtrey's military service with members of the Canadian media, Hawtrey's son Ian revealed with a smile: "As far as he was concerned, a non-commissioned officer didn't talk to a high ranking officer without being spoken to first … except the nurses, he loved the nurses."

The scene at Blatchford Field in Edmonton (now the municipal airport in the heart of the city) on 28 Jul 31 during the Trans-Canada Air Pageant. At top, the aircraft in the foreground are members of the local flying club waiting their turn to perform. Below, the pageant aircraft lined up and ready to go. The civilian aircraft are in the front row led by the Saro Cloud amphibian (CF-ARB). Behind them is the RCAF contingent – the Ford Trimotor (WZ), Fairchild 183 and five Siskins (serial numbers 23, 59, 22, 210 and 60), four of which performed in the show. (Provincial Archives of Alberta BL. 87/7, BL. 87/6)

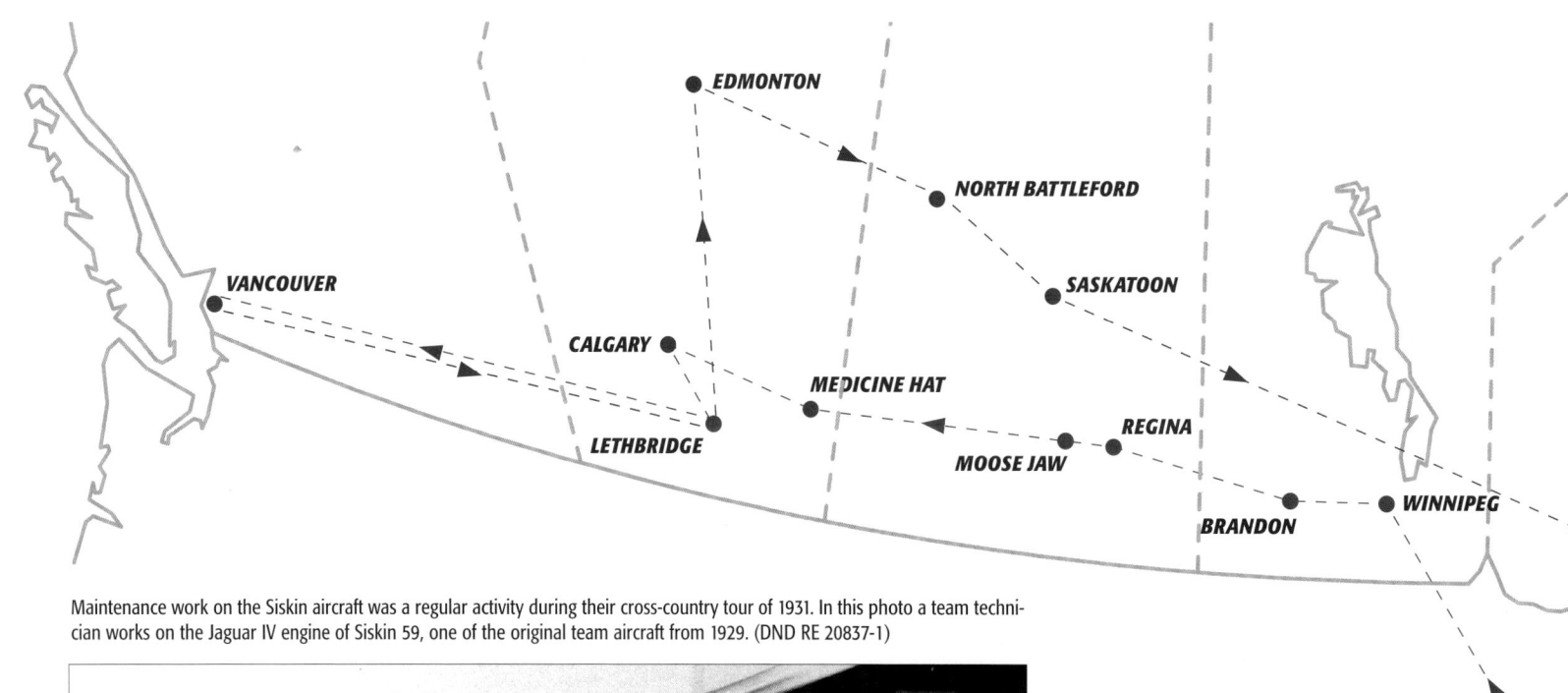

EDMONTON

NORTH BATTLEFORD

SASKATOON

VANCOUVER

CALGARY

MEDICINE HAT

REGINA

LETHBRIDGE

MOOSE JAW

BRANDON

WINNIPEG

MINNEAPOLI

Maintenance work on the Siskin aircraft was a regular activity during their cross-country tour of 1931. In this photo a team technician works on the Jaguar IV engine of Siskin 59, one of the original team aircraft from 1929. (DND RE 20837-1)

The Siskins were the feature attraction of the 1931 Trans-Canada Air Pageant. The RCAF team comprised 16 personnel. L to R – LAC Partridge, Sgt Riggs, LAC Wilcox, Flt Sgt Elliott, Sgt Laidlaw,
F/O McNab, F/L Boret, S/L Hewson (team leader), F/L Riddell, F/O Gobeil, F/O Hawtrey, WO2 Hems, LAC Gould, Cpl Ramshaw, Cpl Cantlay, Sgt Roberts. (DND RE11148)

TRANS-CANADA AIR PAGEANT
1 July - 12 September 1931

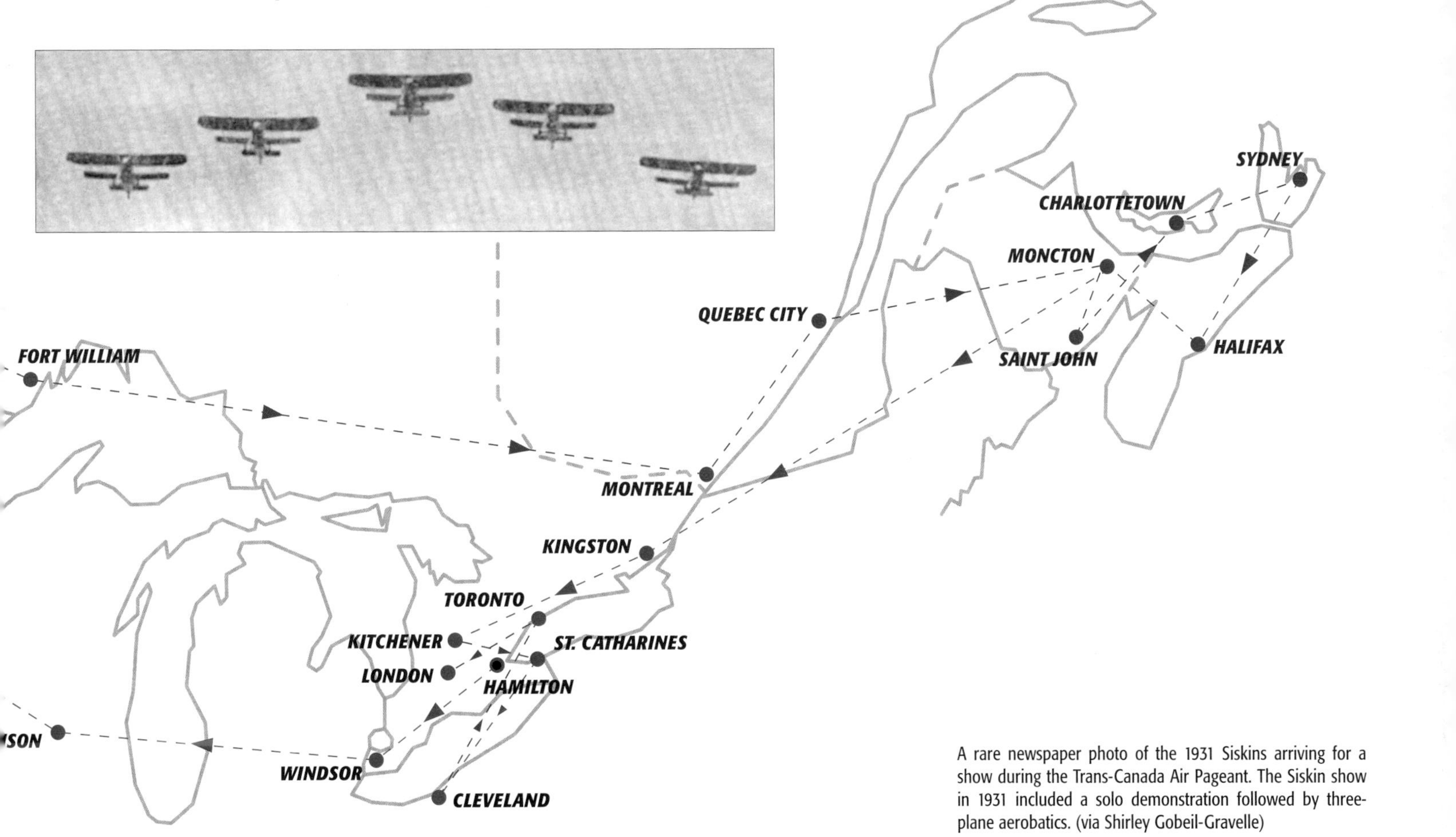

FORT WILLIAM

QUEBEC CITY

SYDNEY

CHARLOTTETOWN

MONCTON

SAINT JOHN

HALIFAX

MONTREAL

KINGSTON

TORONTO

KITCHENER

ST. CATHARINES

LONDON

HAMILTON

...SON

WINDSOR

CLEVELAND

A rare newspaper photo of the 1931 Siskins arriving for a show during the Trans-Canada Air Pageant. The Siskin show in 1931 included a solo demonstration followed by three-plane aerobatics. (via Shirley Gobeil-Gravelle)

The Trans-Canada Air Pageant

Much has been written about the Trans-Canada Air Pageant of 1931 and for good reason – it was an overwhelming success. By demonstrating the sheer thrill of aviation to thousands of spectators, the combined civilian and military team achieved its stated aim of promoting and stimulating public interest in all branches of aviation in Canada. Between July 1st and September 12th, some 500,000 Canadians took in the aerial spectacle as it stormed 26 Canadian cities stretching between Sydney, Nova Scotia and Vancouver, British Columbia. Ultimately, the tour demonstrated the potential for a robust airshow industry in Canada, although this would not be realized until after the end of World War II and the stifling depression that preceded it.

The idea for an all-Canadian air pageant had its genesis in an air racing exhibition south of the border that had been started years earlier by Edsel B. Ford, the only son of the Ford Motor Company magnate. Known as the Ford Reliability Air Tour, it had been traversing the breadth of the central United States since 1925 when it conducted its first trial tour with 15 aircraft. As more and more American aviation companies became interested in providing their latest aircraft as a means of advertising, the tour grew in both scope and prestige. Since each race started and ended in Detroit, in 1929 the tour included four stops in Eastern Canada for the first time – at Windsor, Toronto, Ottawa and Montreal. Then, in 1930 the race made a major foray into Western Canada to the delight of prairie residents of Manitoba, Saskatchewan and Alberta who badly needed a distraction from successive crop failures caused by drought. Assisted by the fledgling Canadian Flying Clubs Association (CFCA), whose local members also got a chance to perform during the show, extensive planning and advertising for the race/airshow resulted

in thousands of spectators turning up at every venue to welcome the visitors. Led by Capt Frank Hawks, the "speed demon of the skies" in his TravelAire "Mystery Ship," the 1930 extravaganza included 28 aircraft (18 racers and 10 support aircraft) and was advertised as the greatest air race in the history of aviation. The race took in 32 cities as far north as Edmonton and as far south as Enid, Oklahoma.

From Concept to Reality

One of the tour stops in 1930 was Moose Jaw, Saskatchewan, a city that had already staged a major "air meet" of western flying clubs earlier that summer on July 5th. It was the architect of that highly successful meet, George M. Ross, who was subsequently inspired to organize the Trans-Canada Air Pageant after he witnessed the popularity of the Ford tour. Recruited to the position of executive-secretary of the CFCA in Ottawa later that year, Ross began his campaign for support at the end of January 1931. Delegates to the annual convention were unanimous in their support for the initiative and Ross received an enthusiastic response when he requested support from the RCAF. The popularity of the Siskins the previous summer in Ottawa, Toronto and Montreal made them a natural choice to partake in this much grander scheme, in which they would naturally become the top attraction.

The inclusion of the RCAF's official aerobatic team highlighted a major difference between the Ford tour and the Air Pageant. The Canadian affair was not a race but rather an airshow – a celebration of the technological advances that aviation had brought the country while highlighting the skills of Canadian aviators. It also became a model of cooperation between the civilian and military participants in the show and local flying clubs across the country that would benefit from the exposure the exhibition would bring.

Tour leader for the overall pageant was T.M. "Pat" Reid who was affectionately nicknamed "Moses" as he led the cavalcade of 16 aircraft from coast-to-coast. Also playing a key role was Marshall Foss, the pageant's publicity and show manager who doubled as airshow announcer. Each show commenced with a "rat race" around the host city by all participating aircraft to advertise the commencement of the show. As soon as everyone was back onto the ground, F/L "Bull" Riddell of the Siskins kicked off the formal part of each show with a dramatic 20 minute solo aerobatic routine in his Siskin fighter that immediately captured the crowd's attention. With his shockingly low loops and stunt combination that included a spin, falling leaf, rolls, dives and an inverted pass, Riddell established a reputation as one of the finest aerobatic pilots in the world.

Following Riddell's display, the civilians took to the air in turn to demonstrate their prowess. Their show featured a variety of interesting acts – from the wild antics of Bernard Martin in his Fairchild KR 21 biplane and tiny Aeronca, to a low-level parachute jump by George Bennett, to the truly bizarre autogiro – a thrashing marvel of a machine flown by Godfrey W. Dean that made tremendous noise and could almost takeoff and land vertically. Local flying clubs were also afforded the opportunity to strut their stuff and promote their membership just before the grand finale – the breathtaking display of formation aerobatics by S/L Hewson and his Siskin team.

As the Air Pageant weaved its away across Canada, it was preceded by an avalanche of publicity as the popularity of the show gained momentum. Having survived a disastrous opening day on July 1st in Hamilton, Ontario when a TravelAire crashed taking the lives of its five occupants, the show never looked back. By the time it reached Vancouver as the feature attraction of the

Of the civilian aircraft that participated in the great Trans-Canada Air Pageant, the Pitcairn autogiro (CF-ARO) flown by Godfrey Dean was by far the most unique. In September 1931, Dean got up enough gumption to loop the aircraft. Getting a photograph taken alongside the intrepid aviator was popular with airshow spectators. (CAHS Collection, M. Mumford via G. Greenough)

One of the highlights of the Trans-Canada Air Pageant included the opening of Vancouver's new Sea Island Airport. Team members were given a royal welcome to the city where over 100,000 spectators watched them perform two shows. One of the gala dinners associated with the pageant yielded this rare set of autographs. Thirty-three years later, four of the original Siskins met the successors of their bravado at the first aerobatic pilots' reunion in Moose Jaw. Pictured here are, L to R – Ernie McNab, Chuck Keating (Fireballs), "Mac" McGowan, Syd Burrows (Fireballs) and Ralph Hawtrey. Missing from the photo is Fowler Gobeil. (via Shirley Gobeil-Gravelle, Syd Burrows)

official opening of the new Sea Island Airport (officially the Vancouver Civic Airport and Seaplane Harbour), the people of British Columbia were primed. It is estimated that between July 22nd and July 25th when the pageant was in town, over 100,000 spectators flocked to the new airport. These impressive numbers were not unique, similar statistics being recorded later in both Montreal and Toronto.

Although not on the itinerary for all of the pageant aircraft, several did join the Siskins for a short detour to the United States to accommodate a return engagement at Cleveland's National Air Races on September 4th and 5th, 1931 where they were welcomed in grand style, at least on the first day. Over the two day affair, the Siskins once again dazzled the air race patrons (if not the officials) with some very low flying, finishing their third consecutive loop below the height of the start/finish pylon according to McNab's memoirs. This even led one enthusiastic newspaper to publish a plethora of accolades which included this rather humorous description of the individual pilots: S/L Hewson – "a mild looking man with a black moustache, a ruddy face and a calm manner;" F/L Riddell (the solo pilot) – "Never saw a squarer jaw. Comes out of a loop two feet from the ground;" F/O McNab – "Ruddy face, clear-eyed, about five feet six inches tall, soft spoken, one of Canada's aces;" F/O Hawtrey – "Slim, young, clear-eyed, one of the stars, though he can't be much over 20;" and finally F/O Gobeil – "Another slim kid." To elicit such detailed commentary in the American press, the RCAF's aerobatic team had obviously left its mark.

Flying back into Canada to rejoin the rest of the team, the last performances of the summer were conducted at Toronto on September 7th (Aviation Day at the CNE), followed by London on September 12th where they completed their final show in front of a glowing Minister of National Defence, D.M. Sutherland. As the team dispersed for the last time the next morning following their 11,000 mile tour, the unanimous sentiment across the country was that the Trans-Canada Air Pageant had indeed presented "the finest exhibition of flying ever seen in Canada."

Surviving the Cuts

Coming on the heels of such a fine showing just the summer before, the RCAF was ill prepared for the budgetary cutbacks that began to take their toll on the service the next year. In 1930-31 the budget appropriation for all air operations in the country had been just under $7.5 million; for 1931-32 it had been reduced to $5.3 million. Then came the "Big Cut" of 1932-33, a staggering 67 percent reduction in the air services appropriation that saw the budget slashed to just under $1.6 million. Personnel strength in the RCAF was reduced to 694 officers and men from 906 only two years before and an additional 110 civilians lost their jobs. Recession was strangling the country. Yet, in spite of the massive cuts, the importance of the Siskin Exhibition Flight as a public relations tool saved it from the axe as the RCAF clung to the hope that in better days the country would see a renewal that would allow the service to expand and obtain modern aircraft. That in turn would necessitate the recruiting of more young men and women to join the service. The Trans-Canada Air Pageant had certainly generated the interest – there was just no way of taking advantage of it in the immediate future.

With this philosophy in mind, F/L Hewson, having reassumed that rank on June 1st due to the cutbacks, was given the go ahead to form another team for 1932 but with a significantly reduced schedule. In 1931, the Siskins had flown a total of 1,376 hours traversing Canada in support of aerial exhibitions; for 1932, only 200 hours would be expended. Fowler Gobeil's logbook, now an artifact in the Canadian War Museum, reveals that in

F/L Henry W. Hewson, team leader of the Siskins during the Trans-Canada Air Pageant, was enlisted in the Royal Flying Corps as an air mechanic during a recruiting drive in Toronto in May 1917. He was subsequently commissioned as an officer during the Great War and became one of the first pilots of the Canadian Air Force (shown here) and Royal Canadian Air Force. (via Rocky Van Vliet)

preparation for a new season he took Siskin 23 out of storage at St. Hubert on June 20th, flew it on a 15 minute test flight and then ferried it to its new home in Trenton, Ontario, the RCAF's newest station. A similar sojourn three days later with Siskin 63, the dual seater, was interrupted by engine problems which necessitated an unscheduled landing near Ottawa. He completed the trip to Trenton on June 25th following repairs and practices got underway in earnest.

The Loss of a Leader

F/L Hewson wasted no time in getting his new team into the swing of things with an aggressive training program that included two newcomers, F/O Larry Wray and F/O Doug

Edwards. While Siskin shows had previously comprised a formation of three aircraft flying formation aerobatics with a separate solo demonstration, Hewson wanted all five aircraft to commence the show in formation before splitting up to move into a newly choreographed routine. By July 25th, Hewson had his charges looping in a five-plane formation, doing so on two separate sorties that morning. The very next day, a Tuesday, calamity struck, as Fowler Gobeil's memoirs reveal:

"We became more adventurous in our formation flying – in practice we added five-plane Vs, close-up rolls in line astern, tight converging bombing, synchronized aerobatics in pairs, and the now famous 'Prince of Wales Feathers' used by show teams from most air forces.

We began to feel that we were pretty hot, when disaster struck. On 26 July 1932, it was decided to try three consecutive loops in a five-plane half-V (an echelon 'squirrel cage' loop). I was flying the No. 3 position on the right. We completed the first two loops normally when I lost sight of the plane on my left. I sensed trouble immediately and pulled up straight ahead to clear the formation. At that moment the leader's plane hit me from below. It was a thoroughly unpleasant experience. I could hear and see the two props thrashing one another and the screech of the engines as they broke off. The solid thud of the impact left no doubt that dear old '23' had come to the end of her days. It was time to get out of it! I had never done a parachute jump before, but I pulled the pin on my safety harness and pushed up as we had been told to do. I waited for the harness to break clear and leave me free to depart – nothing went according to the book! The more I tried to get out, the more the harness held me in.

It's odd how one reacts in such an emergency. I spoke to myself quite severely: 'Gobeil, you clot,' I said. 'You'll never get out this way. Take it easy – relax.' I sat back in the seat, picked each belt off the stud separately, one by one, deliberately … and I was free!

We had started our first loop at about 1,200 feet. By the time I got free, '23' was in a tight right-hand spin. I began to think of the ground. Believe me, it took some hard clawing to get out of the cockpit, but I had plenty of incentive with the ground about 600 feet away. I remember taking about two steps

along the top of the upper wing and worrying that my feet would go through the fabric and that I'd be trapped. I could have spared myself that worry. Old '23' just threw me off her wing into space. I yanked that ripcord so hard that it splashed in Lake Ontario halfway to Rochester, the chute popped and there I was – the first RCAF emergency chute jump. I looked down and saw '23' spin in and blow up, and thanked the good Lord that I wasn't in her.

A 24-foot emergency chute lets you down pretty fast; you have an unsavoury rate of descent. There was quite a breeze blowing, I hit the ground like a side of beef – drifting backward – and that was that."

F.M. Gobeil

F/L Hewson flying Siskin 61 wasn't so lucky. His aircraft was chopped in half by Gobeil's propeller as he pulled into him from below. With no radios, he probably had no idea that Gobeil had even pulled out of the formation until he heard and felt the sickening crunch. Either incapacitated or trapped, Hewson plummeted to the ground in his aircraft as station vehicles raced to his assistance. He succumbed to his critical injuries in a Belleville hospital 32 hours later. The demise of such a distinguished aviator was a sobering loss for the RCAF and "Fighter Flight," as the Siskin Flight had been renamed after moving to Trenton.

Notwithstanding their tragic loss, the team was authorized to continue with F/O Gobeil

A page from F/O Gobeil's logbook reveals the various aircraft types flown by members of the Siskins in the formative years of the RCAF. (via Shirley Gobeil-Gravelle)

BASE	COURSE		REMARKS
	Summary Service Flying June 20th, 1927 – November 20th, 1932		
Aircraft Type	Solo	Dual	Passenger
Avro 504N	98·15	30·50	3·35
Moth	L6700 98·55 WN 55	·FF10 18·15 W1H	· 7·15
C.Courier w	4·45 w	·55	· ·20
Vedette	32·35	6·25	3·00
B.Rambler x	26·45		
Av. Tutor	·40		
H.Tomtit	1·00		
T. Moth	2·10		
Av. Trainer	·30		
Avian x	26·45		·20
Hawk Moth	·40		
F.C. 31	4·15		3·55
F.C. 71			10·10
Belanca			·45
Ford Tri			3·20
Fleet	197·55	12·20	1·45
Atlas	12·40	·25	8·25
Siskin x	414·35	3·55	
Total	919·25	73·05	43·25

being appointed the new team leader and F/O Hawtrey rejoining the team as a solo aerobatic pilot. Gobeil was back in the air on August 8th in his newly assigned Siskin (No. 210) leading a three-plane formation comprised of himself, Edwards and Wray. Hawtrey's logbook reveals he began to work up his solo routine the same day. The next 12 days were spent re-working the show under Gobeil's leadership in preparation for the main event of the season, the Central Canada Exhibition in Ottawa. It had been two years since the team had flown at the CCE, having been otherwise engaged on tour with the Trans-Canada Air Pageant in the Maritimes the previous year. Thus, there was great anticipation by exhibition officials as local newspapers advertised the team's return: *Siskins to Roar Over Exhibition – Crack Pilots of RCAF Again on Bill at Lansdowne Park.*

For six straight days from August 22nd through 27th the Siskins did not disappoint those eagerly waiting their return. With a repertoire that included formation loops, double loops and half rolls plus a bevy of solo manoeuvres such as spiral dives, Immellmanns and the like, all concluded with the ever-popular Prince of Wales Feathers, press releases once again featured splashy headlines to describe their performance: *Daring Display Siskin Bombers – Three Skilled Pilots Thrill Crowds at Central Canada Exhibition.*

Following their return home, the Siskins flew one last series of shows for the local residents of nearby Belleville to help them celebrate their annual fair, climaxing on September 2nd, 1932. In comparison to the previous year, the season was all too short, especially considering that winter was late in arriving and the Siskins were not put into storage until January 1933. Nevertheless, the team had at least ended the season on a high note and they continued to practice together in Trenton right into late fall.

There is a footnote to the airshow activity of 1932. It is popular legend that the Siskins flew some of their airshows with their three aircraft tied together. In fact, it only happened once, in practice, on November 18th, 1932 as noted in Gobeil's logbook: "*Formation with aircraft fastened together with light string. OK.*" This is a clear indication that the team was expecting to fly again in 1933 and no doubt planned to introduce the stunt under the right conditions.

The RCAF's newest air station at Trenton, Ontario became the home of the Siskins in 1932, as depicted here in another fine work by Don Connolly. Three-plane practices early in the season soon gave way to five-plane loops. On 26 Jul 32, a mid-air collision took the life of the team leader, F/L Henry Hewson. (courtesy Don Connolly)

F/O Fowler Gobeil took command of the Siskin Exhibition Flight for the balance of the 1932 season, leading the team to the Central Canada Exhibition in Ottawa. (RCAF Photo via *Airforce* Magazine).

Clipped Wings

As it transpired, 1932 marked the end of the Siskin Exhibition Flight as a formal demonstration unit. With their numbers having been reduced to only nine aircraft as a result of the previous year's crash, they were brought out of storage again in the spring of 1933. Including five additional "Army Cooperation" Atlas fighters, the RCAF's so-called fighter force consisted of only 14 obsolete aircraft. Flying training had all but ceased as there was little money for flying training and not much more for operational missions. The RCAF's desire to move towards a more operational military force was definitely on hold. In some cases, aircraft sat idle for months and many pilots were transferred to the "reserve of officers" pending better times. Dozens of other young men wanting to join the RCAF had to put their aspirations on hold; those who couldn't wait applied to the RAF. Thus, with the limited funding available, there was simply no way the Siskin team could continue under such crippling conditions. As it transpired, only five solo exhibitions were given in the entire year in addition to a good will tour to Manitoba to break the monotony. For his part, F/O Gobeil only flew the Siskin a few more times that spring and summer. Fittingly, his very last flight was a solo demonstration in Siskin 210 at Trenton during an open house on August 26th, 1933.

A Glimmer of Hope

The year 1934 brought a glimmer of hope for the resurgence of airshows in Canada, thanks in large part to a visit by the Royal Air Force's No. 1 Sqn Aerobatic Team flying five Hawker Fury biplanes. Based in Tangmere under the command of W/C G.C. Pirie, the unit arrived in Montreal on June 18th aboard two ships. During their month-long visit the team helped Toronto celebrate its centennial from June 30th to July 6th and then gave demonstrations in London, Kitchener, Hamilton, St. Catharines and Camp Borden. The biggest show of all however, was reserved for RCAF Stn Ottawa (Rockcliffe), just east of the nation's capital on the Ottawa River, on July 14th, 1934. Piggy backing on the better fortunes of the RAF, the RCAF pulled out all the stops to help stage the display.

Kicking off the hour-long show, F/L Elmer Fullerton from Camp Borden put on a skilful demonstration of aerobatics in a Fleet Fawn I from the training school. It was then four Atlas Is from the RCAF Army Cooperation Flight in Trenton led by F/L A. Lewis that displayed formation flying and a unique technique of using hooks to pick up messages from army troops on the ground. One of the young pilots in the formation was F/O Hugh Campbell, a future Chief of the Air Staff who would play a pivotal role in the

formation of one of the RCAF's most famous aerobatic teams 25 years later.

Making a comeback of sorts, Fighter Flight from Trenton put up a four-plane Siskin show (Siskins 210, 21, 20 and 60) led by a member of the 1932 team, F/O D.M. Edwards. Although one of the aircraft had to land due to mechanical difficulties, the other three continued the performance, ending their nostalgic show with a Prince of Wales Feathers. But on this day, it was the much more modern RAF Furies that captured centre stage with a highly polished performance that included a three-plane formation roll, another step in the advancement of formation aerobatics. The RAF team subsequently visited Quebec City to perform a show prior to setting sail for home again from Montreal on July 27th.

Notwithstanding these sparse flashbacks to previous glory, the Siskin Flight fell on hard times in 1935 with only three serviceable aircraft. With no hope of obtaining newer aircraft, the Siskin fleet of five aircraft was put into an overhaul program in an attempt to keep them airworthy for a few more years. Exhibition flights were conducted on a limited basis and recruiting was sparse, with more Canadians able to join the RAF (a total of 37) than the RCAF for flying training. And it wasn't until October 1937 that the aircraft finally had two .303 Vickers

machine guns mounted to enable some real gunnery training.

A change in organization saw the Siskin Flight redesignated No. 1 Sqn in 1937 with an impending move to Calgary, Alberta the following summer. The last Siskin demonstration out of RCAF Stn Trenton was flown in Ottawa on August 20th, 1938 to commemorate the opening of the new Uplands Airport. Nine days later the squadron commanding officer, S/L Elmer Fullerton, led the five remaining Siskins westward to their final home where they commenced operations on September 16th. The tired old aircraft soldiered for a few more months until S/L Fullerton finally led a party of 20 other ranks to Vancouver on February 16th, 1939 to uncrate and assemble the first of her replacements – the state-of-the-art Hawker Hurricane. Having delivered the first aircraft to Calgary on June 1st, Fullerton gave one of the earliest demonstrations of the RCAF's newest acquisition on July 29th to a most interested spectator, Air Marshal W.A. "Billy" Bishop. The fine new machine would make its debut at the CNE the next month, just days before Europe was plunged into war again with Germany's invasion of Poland on September 1st. Before long, hundreds of Hurricanes would be built in Canada as the nation rose to the challenge and became totally engrossed in the war effort to support England and her allies in their fight for survival.

Elmer Fullerton went on to command the RCAF stations at Summerside, Prince Edward Island, then Centralia, Ontario, retiring shortly after the war with the rank of group captain. An aficionado of the bagpipes, Fullerton was credited with conceiving, designing and incorporating the distinctive RCAF Tartan in 1942, a tartan still proudly worn by air force pipes and drums bands.

As for the original RCAF members of the Siskin Exhibition Flight, all would continue with distinguished service careers. S/L Fowler Gobeil would gain fame in May 1940 by being the first RCAF pilot to engage the enemy over France as commanding officer of No. 242 Sqn, RAF, flying the Hawker Hurricane. Just two days later, on May 25th, he had his first kill on a Messerschmitt Bf 110 over Belgium. Meanwhile, his old teammate, S/L Ernie McNab, also made history three months later by achieving the first RCAF victory in the Battle of Britain when he shot down a Dornier Do 215 while temporarily seconded to the RAF's No. 111 Sqn. Both Gobeil and McNab earned the Distinguished Flying Cross for their combat actions. Ralph Hawtrey's career took a different path as he was attending university in London when hostilities broke out. Upon graduation, he returned to Canada to play an important role in the development of the British Commonwealth Air Training Plan, eventually being promoted to the rank of group captain.

Through Adversity to the Stars

The 30 years that elapsed between J.A.D. McCurdy's first flight in the Silver Dart and the commencement of World War II saw a quantum leap in the evolution of manned flight worldwide thanks to a dedicated group of aviation pioneers. Attracted by the earliest barnstormers and airshow pilots, thousands of young Canadians eventually took to the skies, eager to shed their earth-bound ties for the pure magic of flight. Many eventually joined the RCAF, their perseverance in mastering the art of flight embodied in the RCAF Motto, *Per Ardua Ad Astra*, (Through Adversity to the Stars).

Sadly, hundreds of these keen young men would lose their lives in World War II, includ-

ing a young American-born native son, Pilot Officer John Gillespie Magee, Jr. who joined the RCAF to fly and fight for the cause of freedom. A member of 412 (F) Sqn flying Spitfires, he lost his life during a training flight from an airfield near Scopwick, Lincolnshire, England on December 11th, 1941. He was only 19. Not long before his fateful accident, he had penned a letter to his parents which included a poem on the back. Of the poem he noted, "I am enclosing a verse I wrote the other day. It started at 30,000 feet, and was finished soon after I landed."

For the millions of spectators that would come to marvel at airshows in the post-war era and ponder the inner feelings of the pilots flying them, some of those feelings might best be personified by Magee's famous poem:

High Flight

Oh, I have slipped the surly bonds of earth
And danced the skies on
* laughter-silvered wings;*
Sunward I've climbed,
* and joined the tumbling mirth*
Of sun-split clouds –
* and done a hundred things*
You have not dreamed of –
* wheeled and soared and swung*
High in the sunlit silence, Hov'ring there,
I've chased the shouting wind along,
* and flung*
My eager craft through
* footless halls of air.*
Up, up the long, delirious, burning blue
I've topped the windswept heights
* with easy grace*
Where never lark, or even eagle flew.
And, while with silent,
* lifting mind I've trod*
The high untrespassed sanctity of space,
Put out my hand,
* and touched the face of God.*

Foreign visitors in 1934 helped keep interest in aviation high as Canada struggled to recover from the lean years brought on by the Great Depression. At left, a Royal Air Force aerobatic team comprising Hawker Fury Is which toured Ontario and Quebec. At right, a squadron of US Army Air Corps Martin B-10 bombers on their way to Alaska drew a crowd in Edmonton during a refueling stop. (DND HC-6985, Provincial Archives of Alberta BL. 168/1 via Larry Milberry)

The Easy Aces of RCAF Stn Centralia, home of No. 1 Flying Training School, epitomized the free-wheeling spirit of post-war air-show teams in Canada. Led by veteran instructor F/O Bob Ayres, his teammates were Ernie Saunders (right wing), Ray Embury (left wing) and Frank Pickles (box). The stunt shown here happened only once, F/O Gord Plyley providing the drama. However, in a scene reminiscent of the Siskins, the Easy Aces flew their last aerobatic show on 20 Oct 52 with lead, two and three tied together wing tip to wing tip with rope. They landed in vic formation with the rope still intact. (via Bob Ayres).

Post-War Exhibitions

Canada emerged from the Second World War with an enormous air force, the 4th largest among the allies, and a solid reputation to match. From its humble beginnings in 1924, the RCAF had grown in wartime to a peak strength of 215,200 men and women in December 1943, at which time 77 squadrons were in active service. A total of 48 RCAF squadrons saw service overseas during the war along with some 94,000 personnel, many of whom were seconded to the Royal Air Force. From the Battle of Britain to the Battle of the Atlantic to the D-Day invasion, Canadian aircrews did their part in the allied war effort. Back at home, 37 "home war establishment" squadrons conducted coastal defence, shipping protection and other duties as Canadian factories churned out hundreds of aircraft – from Hurricanes to Mosquitos to the mighty Lancaster bomber. Canada was also the birthplace of the British Commonwealth Air Training Plan which saw dozens of airfields spring up all over the country. RCAF instructors helped train a total of 131,553 aircrew, of which 72,835 were Canadians.

The hard-earned victory of WW II took a heavy toll on the RCAF and her sister services. Some 17,000 RCAF personnel lost their lives in the war, a grim reminder that freedom was not easily won. When victory was finally declared, a mixture of relief and elation swept over the allied forces, tempered only by the numbing grief of so many comrades lost. The end of the conflict led to the first post-war "airshows" of a sort – in part as a tribute to their fallen comrades, and in another as a final show of contempt for their crushed enemy, the allies staged large-scale victory flypasts in the immediate days following Germany's surrender. In some cases, they would go on for a month or more all over Europe.

One massive show of force involved the four Spitfire wings of 83 Group, namely 122, 124, 126 and 127 Wings. Both 122 and 124 were RAF Wings, although the "wing commander flying" of the latter was a Canadian at war's end, W/C George Keefer. The other two wings were dedicated RCAF Wings, 126 led by W/C Geoff Northcott and 127 by W/C J.F. "Stocky" Edwards at the end of the war. It was Stocky Edwards who was bestowed the honour of leading the group in their victory flypasts – he was all of 23 years old! In his 400 sorties during the war in the P-40 Kittyhawk and Spitfire, he became one of Canada's leading aces with 16½ confirmed air-to-air kills (15 plus three shared-destroyed), eight probables and a host of ground kills.

Edwards led the first flypast of 127, 126 and 122 Wings on May 12th, 1945 over Bremerhaven, only four days after Germany's surrender. Then on May 15th it was over a demoralized "Hun airfield" and the surrounding countryside. The next areas to see their sky filled with victorious Spitfires were Kiel and Lubeck, Germany followed by Copenhagen, Denmark. The latter on June 12th was the largest of them all as Edwards led all four wings in the victory parade, some 144 aircraft in total. For 127 Wing, their final salute to fallen comrades was on August 3rd and fittingly took place over their final staging area of the war, a grass strip near Schneverdingen, Germany (50 km southwest of Hamburg) annotated as "B124." Exactly one week later 127 re-deployed to Dunsfold, England to prepare for their final journey – it was their turn to go home … Of those last sorties in the Spitfire, and the final dissipation of adrenaline, Stocky Edwards reminisced a few years ago, "That was a sad day when we flew back to England. You knew

W/C J.F. "Stocky" Edwards, DFC and Bar, DFM alongside his trusty Spitfire at "B154" near Schneverdingen, Germany in May 1945. He led as many as four wings of Spitfires in large-scale victory flypasts in the days following VE Day in Europe. (via J.F. Edwards)

everybody was happy the war was over, but we were also sad because we knew we'd never fly the Spitfire again. They just took those beautiful Spitfires and put them in the junkyard. You know, when you're talking amongst a bunch of fighter pilots, there were different types of airplanes, and some were pretty good. But there was nothing like the Spitfire … nothing. In fact, you couldn't have asked for anything better …"

Within weeks of the unconditional surrender of Germany, RCAF squadrons in Europe began to disband. The process accelerated with the end of the war in the Pacific, the Japanese officially surrendering on September 2nd, 1945. Canada rapidly downsized to a peacetime air force with tens of thousands of personnel taking their release from the RCAF in an attempt to restore some sense of normalcy to their lives.

With thousands of Canadian civilians also having been involved in the war effort at home, especially in the manufacture of aircraft, there continued to be a fascination with aeroplanes. If there had been a positive side to the war, it was the rapid technological progress which had resulted from the endless quest to build better and better fighters and bombers. Millions around the world hoped that these advances could now be directed to more peaceful ends.

de Havilland Aircraft of Canada Ltd

In spite of the rapid downsizing of Canada's three military services and the resultant loss of military contracts, aviation manufacturers were eager to take advantage of the profound advances in aviation technology. One was de Havilland Aircraft of Canada Limited. Incorporated in Canada on March 5th, 1928 as a branch of its English parent, the company was determined to build on the success of its original founder, Maj Geoffrey de Havilland, who had turned to commercial ventures following the end of WWI. His vision had created the legendary Moth with its many variants and the Tiger Moth trainer. The scourge of Nazi Germany had changed all of that, leading to the production of legendary aircraft such as the Mosquito, many of which were built in Canada. Meanwhile, towards the end of the war, the company was secretly working on an aircraft that would take advantage of the most revolutionary advance of them all, jet propulsion. It would yield the Vampire which was destined to become Canada's first operational jet fighter. And with peace restored, de Havilland went on to produce some of Canada's most versatile and successful aircraft – the Chipmunk, Beaver, Otter, Caribou, Buffalo and later the Dash series of STOL (short takeoff and landing) aircraft.

The Toronto International Air Show 1946

It was also de Havilland that provided the venue for Canada's first precedent setting "international" airshow spectacle in the post-war era, the event taking place at the de Havilland Airport from August 30th to September 7th, 1946. Sponsored by the National Aeronautical Association of Canada in cooperation with the City of Toronto and Canada's three military services, the Toronto International Air Show eventually developed into the world-famous Canadian International Air Show.

The 1946 show was officially opened by the Minister of National Defence, the Honourable Colin Gibson, and featured both ground and air displays. Two hangars provided by the Toronto Flying Club were jammed full of exhibits, one catering to civilian exhibitors and the other to the RCAF, RCA Airborne Division and the RCN. The US Army Air Force was also a welcome participant in the show, providing a C-54 transport, P-51 Mustang, Black Widow night fighter and P-47 Thunderbolt for static display. The highlight of their involvement however, at least for the first few days, was the P-80 Shooting Star – America's first jet fighter. Its over exuberant demo pilot bent the aircraft during one of his early demonstrations, actually rippling the whole fuselage. As Bill Munro recalls, the aircraft left Toronto for the return trip to Dayton on a flatbed truck and was likely written off!

In addition to their extensive ground exhibits which featured everything from aircraft to radar to jet propulsion, Canada's services staged a mock invasion which featured army veterans jumping from three RCAF C-47 Dakotas after the "landing area" had been sanitized by five Seafires of the Royal Canadian Navy.

Royal Canadian Naval Air Arm

The General Badge of the Royal Canadian Navy

From Seafires to Sea Furies
1946-1953

Up until the end of WWII, the responsibility for all maritime coastal patrol had been handled by the RCAF. This changed with the cessation of hostilities when the Canadian government authorized the formation of the Royal Canadian Naval Air Arm in December 1945. It was a modest start with only four squadrons being formed, the crews coming from the RCAF and those RCN Voluntary Reserve airmen who had served with the Fleet Air Arm of the Royal Navy during the war. Indeed, Canada's first naval aircraft were obtained from the Royal Navy in June 1946 and included Supermarine Seafires and Fairey Fireflies. They sailed to Canada aboard the first of three aircraft carriers (HMCSs *Warrior*, *Magnificent* and *Bonaventure*) that Canada would purchase over the next 12 years. Their shore-based home would be RCAF Stn Dartmouth, Nova Scotia which was transferred to the navy and renamed HMCS Shearwater on December 1st, 1948.

803 Sqn Seafire Team

The four Seafire Mk XVs which appeared at the international show in Toronto in 1946 were among 35 taken on strength in what became the first of three generations of single-seat fighters to serve with the RCN. The Seafires were from the RCN's first fighter squadron, 803 Sqn, a member of the 18th Carrier Air Group. The squadron also had the distinction of forming Canada's first post-war demonstration team. One of the team members was a young naval aviator by the name of Robert Falls who would go on to a distinguished career in the RCN and Canadian Forces, eventually becoming a full admiral and Chief of the Defence Staff. He provides a brief overview of the Seafire team, some 56 years later:

The Seafire Mk XV, Canada's first naval fighter, operated off the deck of the nation's first aircraft carrier, HMCS *Warrior*. This shot of SR 545 was taken at de Havilland Airport on 30 Aug 46, the first day of the Toronto International Air Show. (Jack McNulty via Leo Pettipas)

Man and machine. Lt Bill Munro joined the Seafire team off of leave and impressed Toronto crowds for eight consecutive days with a fully aerobatic solo show in the Seafire XV. (via Bill Munro)

few years which of course became part of the Canadian National Exhibition. My log shows that we flew from Dartmouth to Toronto via Moncton, Presque Isle (Maine), Quebec, Montreal and Trenton on August 12th (no drop tanks). We flew in the show daily from August 30th to September 7th doing various formations, some simple formation aeros and simulated ground attack. Bill Munro did solo aerobatics, usually after our formation display. We were then invited to stop in at Ottawa on the way home to shake the hand of the Chief of Naval Staff! I have a copy of Naval Message 161946Z/ 9/46 from Naval Service Headquarters (NSHQ) to Warrior, Naval Air Station Dartmouth, which reads *'Unclassified. The flying of the Seafire formation at Toronto was of a high standard and the conduct of all personnel was a credit to the service. The fact that the Seafires were maintained at 100 percent serviceability throughout the week of the display is particularly creditable.'* Subsequent teams of Seafires participated in this event in Toronto, but three years later both Clunk Watson and Chuck Elton were killed near Toronto while practicing for the show."

Robert Falls

"In 1946 I was a member of a team of four Seafires led by Lieutenant Commander Cliff (Clunk) Watson, CO of 803 Sqn, who took part in the de Havilland Air Show at what is now Downsview Airport. The others were Hal Fearon and Monk Geary. Bill Munro, who was on leave in the area, joined us just for the heck of it as did some of the squadron groundcrew. This was the first major post-war airshow in Canada, and evolved into the Canadian International Air Show within a

Canada's first post-war naval demonstration team en route to Toronto on 12 Aug 46. Note the 803 Sqn crest below the cockpit. L to R – Lt Neville "Monk" Geary, Lt Hal Fearon, Lt Bob Falls, LCdr Clifford Watson. Missing from this photo is Lt Bill Munro who joined the team in Toronto while on leave. (via Robert Falls)

The Seafires of 803 Sqn wind up in preparation for one of their displays. They were supported by a mixture of their own groundcrew (in uniform) and technicians from de Havilland Aircraft (in white coveralls). (via Jim Lyzun)

A Lesson Learned

The Toronto show paved the way for several world-class annual shows in Canada that would come into their own over the next three decades. Over 100,000 spectators had crammed de Havilland airfield over the eight day event, with 78,000 paying their way in to see the show. Approximately $250,000 in aircraft sales were credited to the event, but with the success came some embarrassment. The sponsors had neither anticipated nor were prepared for the huge crowds.

The day before the show opened, the *Toronto Telegram* had produced headlines designed to capture the imagination – "*Show Opening Packs Program With Speed, Skill And Wallop*." The advertising went on to praise Canadians for their sacrifice during the Second World War and invited them to come and witness firsthand some of the aircraft that had helped win the day. Each of the eight days of the show was given a theme, from Exhibitor's Day to Youth Day to Women's Day to Flying Club's Day and so on. The advertising worked well – too well! The early success of the show created a crisis on Labour Day, September 2nd. Headlines in the *Telegram* the next day reported "*50,000 Jam Air Show, Strip Planes Of Gadgets, Bayonet Guard Called In*." The paper went on to report that "*Long before the show opened the invasion started and soon cars were lined up for miles around the airport.... The crowds were so dense that few could observe what was going on for the solid wall of humanity ...*" With totally insufficient food and facilities at the tiny airport, things eventually got out of hand. Following their show, several of the Seafires were vandalized by souvenir hunters. Police reinforcements from North York had to be airlifted into the airport due to the worst traffic jam in Toronto history.

By the time the last bars of *God Save the King* had played on September 7th, the organizers were acutely aware of Canadian interest in airshows – and had a whole new outlook on the importance of logistic planning ...

LCdr "Clunk" Watson in "Z" leads his charges over the field in finger-left formation. On his right wing is Lt "Monk" Geary, on his immediate left is Lt Hal Fearon and on the outside is Lt Bob Falls. (via Jim Lyzun)

Back in service! One of 10 Seafire Mk XVs pulled out of storage to fulfill the RCN's commitment to the 1949 CNE. This shot was taken at Dartmouth on 27 Jul 48 as pilots and technicians prepared for the official stand-up of the "Seafire Exhibition Flight" on 1 Aug. This aircraft is having its batteries charged. (National Archives of Canada PA 135896)

One of the Seafires is prepared for a test flight on 28 Jul 49. (National Archives of Canada PA 141118)

Seafire Exhibition Flight – Watson's Flying Circus

Only one other RCN Seafire team flew in Canada and it was formed on very short notice for the 1949 CNE. The navy had originally intended to send a Sea Fury team to Toronto for the annual exhibition but the entire fleet was grounded due to engine problems upon arrival at the Canadian Joint Air Training Centre in Rivers, Manitoba in June. When it became apparent that repairs were going to take some time, naval headquarters decided to reactivate the Seafire for the 1949 show.

A message from headquarters to the Flag Officer Atlantic in mid-July 1949 got the ball rolling. A reply message on July 26th reported the selection of team pilots from 803 Sqn, including the appointment of Acting LCdr C.G. "Clunk" Watson as commander of the operation. Responsibility for the selection of a groundcrew team from 19 Carrier Air Group was given to a Royal Navy engineer on exchange at Shearwater, Lt Brian Dawbarn. The unit would form on August 1st and would be officially known as the Seafire Exhibition Flight. However, in a tribute to its leader, the team became more commonly known as "Watson's Flying Circus."

Although having had a three year hiatus from his first shows in Toronto in 1946, that previous experience was invaluable in allowing Clunk Watson to move quickly to establish his team. It would comprise 10 demo pilots (of which at least eight would fly in each show), a commentator and a 39 man ground

Clunk Watson briefs his team prior to departure for Toronto on 21 Aug 49. (RCN DNS 1787 via Bill Munro)

The Royal Canadian Navy's "Seafire Exhibition Flight" 1949. L to R, Front Row – Lts Anton Schellinck, Mike Wasteneys, Al Bice, Jack Hartle, Ed Myers. Back Row – Lt Pat Whitby, LCdr Bill Munro, Lt Brian Dawbarn (RN), LCdr Clifford Watson, Lt Charles Elton, Lt Joe MacBrien. Missing is commentator, Lt Harry Swiggum. Watson and Elton were killed in a mid-air collision while practicing a formation roll on 23 Aug 49. (RCN DNS 1786 via Pat Whitby)

support team. They had precious little time, their first show being scheduled for August 26th. Lt Pat Whitby was Watson's right-hand man when practices got underway and explains how the show was developed:

"From its inception in late July '49 to our first show at the CNE, our aircrew had to re-familiarize on the Seafire XV (having been flying Sea Furies for the previous year) and work up an aerobatic routine. The ground support staff had to reactivate the Seafires that had been in mothballs for a like period of time, a formidable task in itself. The Seafire XV was a navalized version of the Spitfire XII – both had the Griffon engine. To permit carrier operations the Seafire was given folding wings and a strengthened fuselage for catapult launching and arrested landings. It was a delightful aircraft to fly but not a good deck landing machine – too frail with its narrow undercarriage, etc. It was good for aerobatics, but not so for lateral formation aerobatics due to very pronounced torque which occurred with throttle changes.

When we formed up I was 'senior pilot,' naval air terminology for 2 i/c or executive officer. We had been together for about a week when one of the pilots decided that this airshow stuff was not for him, so he left and was replaced by Acting LCdr Bill Munro. Although senior in rank, Bill generously deferred to me and I continued as senior pilot.

After some discussion, the unit was divided into two flights for administrative purposes, each consisting of five pilots. Red Flight comprised Clunk with Lts Joe MacBrien, Chuck Elton, Al Bice and 'Doc' Schellinck. Black Flight consisted of LCmdr Bill Munro, Lts Mike Wasteneys, Eddy Myers, Jack Hartle and myself. Our commentator was Lt Harry Swiggum.

Following trial flights, it was decided that MacBrien and Elton would fly in a three-plane vic with Clunk after breaking off 'Smokey' Bice from the formation who was our designated solo. I would lead a two-plane element and Bill Munro would lead a four-plane to demonstrate the variety of formations normally used – finger-four, diamond, echelons and line-astern. We eventually put together a 20 minute show with the various elements rotating in front of the crowd. Watson did the range of aeros possible in vic formation – loops, rolls, lazy 8s – my element did much the same in line-astern and Bice did Cuban-eights, vertical rolls and eight-point rolls."

Pat Whitby

Mid-Air Tragedy

One young naval aviator who got his first taste of organized airshow formation flying under the tutelage of Pat Whitby was Eddy Myers. He flew his first re-familiarization flight on the Seafire Mk XV on August 1st,

1949 after a year of flying the Sea Fury with 883 Sqn of 19 Carrier Air Group. He describes the events leading up to a tragedy which shook the team before the Toronto shows got underway:

"We had just over one month to work up an airshow including close formation flying and low-level aerobatic routines with aircraft that most of us had not flown for over a year. Fortunately, the Scafire was a pilot's aircraft that one felt part of in very short order. From August 1st to August 21st when we deployed from HMCS Shearwater to Malton Airport in Toronto, we got approximately 15 hours practicing 'formation aeros' for the CNE. The flight to Toronto took just under four hours with stopovers at Bangor, Maine and Dorval, Quebec. While the en route formation was loose and relaxed, we tightened up our exhibition formation during arrivals at and departures from airports and large populated areas.

At Bangor, our Seafires were given a heretofore unheard of priority for takeoff over the resident USAF jets because of the risk of our Griffin engines overheating if takeoffs were delayed due to prolonged taxiing and idling. The American pilots were astounded at the small size of the Seafire, given its reputation during WWII.

After arriving at Malton on August 21st and settling in, it was during our first rehearsal

The Seafire Exhibition Flight ground support crew were transported to Toronto courtesy an RCAF North Star. L to R, Front Row – Bough, O'Neil, Williams K., Williamson, Adams, Baily, Turnbull, Fletcher, Weston, Clermont, Dewell, Nunnerly, Gurling, Carey, McColm. Centre Row – Hoare, Langlois, Clarke, Bent, Trott, Payne, Coughlin, Thomas, Williams J., Becker, Wade, Hill, Taylor, Spratt, Hall, Volkes, Smith. Back Row – Knowles, James, Turner, Chalifour, Bisset, Pelley. (RCN photo via Eddy Myers)

Able Seamen David Adams and Len Bough chock a Seafire XV following a team performance at the CNE. (via Leo Pettipas)

over the airfield on the 23rd that a mid-air collision occurred killing the CO and Chuck Elton. This of course had a serious effect on the morale of the flight – from a high of anticipation of performing at the CNE to a low of burying two of your flying mates. Acting LCdr W.D. "Chiefy" Munro assumed command of the flight and as a well-liked and respected pilot reorganized the flying display and led us through the remainder of the rehearsals and airshows. We relocated to Downsview Airport from Malton for the last week of the show to facilitate operations in a less congested air space."

Eddy Myers

The accident which took the lives of Clunk Watson and Chuck Elton, who were good friends, took place mid-way through a practice over Malton Airport just as the team was beginning an integrated practice with eight aircraft. Watson's vic had already done several practice manoeuvres back-to-back, including their show opener – three loops in a row in vic formation. Their second manoeuvre was a low and tight vic roll to starboard, a difficult manoeuvre but one which the trio had performed many times. Halfway through the roll, just past the inverted position, something happened and Elton's aircraft collided with his lead. Joe MacBrien on the left wing was just able to avoid the collision by pulling hard out of the formation. Within seconds both Watson and Elton had plummeted to the earth. Fortunately, no one else on the ground was hurt. The RCN Board of Inquiry was "unable to determine the exact cause of the collision."

Given the tragedy and the widespread press coverage it received, the fact that the remaining team members were able to regroup and still perform their first show at the CNE three days later speaks highly of their dedication and courage of conviction. This dedication was very much appreciated by the thousands of airshow fans who showed up at the CNE each day to watch them perform alongside many aircraft from the RCAF and American military. The revamped seven-plane show led by Acting LCdr Bill Munro went smoothly, the final performance taking place on September 10th. As Pat Whitby recently

reflected, "We changed the show only slightly, foregoing the three-plane vic routine since we felt we could not get another three ready in time. We reduced the time to 15 minutes as well. I don't recall any concern about safety – we were all quite confident." Their nostalgic performances in the Seafire completed, the team flew home to HMCS Shearwater and disbanded. Bill Munro's logbook reveals that he flew a total of just over 20 hours during the operation, including the 14 shows the team flew in Toronto. The Seafires would never fly again, their place at the CNE being taken by the Sea Fury.

The Hawker Sea Fury

The Sea Fury era in Canada effectively began with the arrival of Canada's second aircraft carrier, HMCS *Magnificent*, which sailed into Halifax harbour on June 1st, 1948. Aboard were 27 FB 11 Sea Furies along with the pilots and groundcrew of 803 Sqn who had sailed to RNAS Eglinton in Northern Ireland the previous August to train on the navy's latest fighter-bomber.

As naval historian Leo Pettipas has documented, the Sea Fury marked a significant improvement over the Seafire Mk XV:

"As a fighter-bomber, the Sea Fury was vastly superior to the Seafire – the latter could carry 500 pounds of bombs compared with

A classic formation shot of Hawker Sea Fury FB 11s belonging to 803 Sqn. They demonstrated formation flying and weapons deliveries at the CNE in 1952 and 1953. (via Leo Pettipas)

Two views of Sea Fury BG-C (TG 120), denoting it as the aircraft assigned to the Commander 19 Carrier Air Group, LCdr Jim Hunter. He put on the first formal display of the aircraft for dignitaries at RCAF Stn Rockcliffe on 24 Jun 48. (National Archives of Canada PA 168860 and 168862)

1948. The first major encounter with airshow fans in Canada came less than two months after the aircraft's arrival when the RCN staged a major naval air display at Dartmouth (soon to be renamed HMCS Shearwater) on July 21st. Stars of the show were a Royal Navy team which had been designated 806 Sqn RN and given the mandate of carrying out an airshow tour of North America. They were uniquely equipped with two Sea Fury FB 11s, two Sea Hornet F.20s and a single Sea Vampire F.20, all of which had accompanied 803 Sqn on its maiden voyage to Canada aboard *Magnificent*. Not only did the team put on an impressive display of formation and solo aerobatics, but one of the Sea Fury pilots managed to overspeed his engine during a series of vertical rolls resulting in an engine failure and dead-stick landing in front of the crowd. This one-day show was attended by 15,000 spectators and was the predecessor to the now famous Shearwater International Airshow which is held annually over two days each September.

CNE fairgoers also got their first look at the Sea Fury in 1948 when 803 Sqn dispatched three aircraft to Toronto in August to participate in the annual show. Their participation was somewhat unusual as two of the fighters flown by Lts Al Bice and Jack Sloan joined the 806 Sqn (RN) team during the airshow. The entire contingent was hosted by A.V. Roe Canada and flew out of their facility at Malton

the Fury's 2,000. Unlike the Canadians' Seafires, fitment with rocket projectiles was standard on the Sea Fury. And although the Seafire was armed with six wing guns compared with the Fury's four, the Seafire carried only two cannons whereas all of the Sea Fury's guns were cannons. The Seafire was powered by an in-line, liquid-cooled engine of 1,850 horsepower, whereas the Sea Fury's 'Bristol Centaurus 18' was an air-cooled radial capable of delivering 2,550 horsepower … This gave the Fury a maximum speed of 460 mph at 18,000 feet and 415 mph at 30,000 feet."

Leo Pettipas

Two RCN stalwarts which appeared at the 1951 CNE, Grumman Avenger BD-A and Hawker Sea Fury BC-F. Note the non-standard "NAVY" painted on the side of the aircraft. (via Jim Lyzun)

Those who have seen the Sea Fury perform at airshows or air races over the years will know first-hand what an incredible sight the aircraft can be on a high-speed, low-level pass. The first RCN pilot to put on a display in the new aircraft was LCdr Jim Hunter, Commander 19 Carrier Air Group, who put on a show for the navy brass and other dignitaries at RCAF Stn Rockcliffe on June 24th,

Airport. The third Canadian Sea Fury joined an RCN Firefly on static display. Jack Sloan was later promoted to lieutenant commander and became the first Canadian to fly the Banshee while on exchange with the U.S. Navy.

The 1949 CNE featured 803 Sqn's Seafire Exhibition Flight, the entire fleet of Sea Furies being grounded by engine problems at the time. The extent of navy participation at the 1950 and 1951 CNE shows is unknown, but it is highly likely that a limited number of Sea Furies, Fireflies and perhaps Avengers participated one or both years. It was also during the spring of 1951 that the RCN introduced several changes to the numbering system of their squadrons and aircraft. In order to comply with the Commonwealth numbering scheme, 803 Sqn was redesignated 870 Sqn, the fighter component of the 31st Support Air Group (formerly designated the 19th Support Air Group). The squadron's total complement comprised nine Sea Furies and they were paired with the anti-submarine warfare Avengers of 880 Sqn.

31st Support Air Group CNE Team 1952-1953

Although the RCN never authorized the formation of another official aerobatic team fol-

lowing the Seafire tragedy of 1949 at Malton, considerable participation did take place at each of the 1952 and 1953 shows by 870 Sqn (Sea Furies) and 880 Sqn (Avengers).

The 1952 team was commanded by the CO of 31 SAG, LCdr J.B. "Pop" Fotheringham. A total of nine Sea Furies were deployed to Malton by 870 Sqn, led by their CO, Lt Doug Peacocke. In addition to Fotheringham and Peacocke, other Sea Fury pilots included Lts Mike Wasteneys, Al Shimmin, Bob Falls, "Whitey" McNichol, Dave Tate, Ken Nicholson and "Doc" Schellinck. Dave Tate was a young lieutenant at the time who would ultimately go on to play an important role in the establishment of squadron status for the Snowbirds in 1978 while base commander at CFB Moose Jaw. He reflects back 50 years to those heady days at the CNE as a young naval fighter pilot:

"We did 13 shows at the CNE between August 18th and September 6th. These were primarily weapons displays on the waterfront with five-inch rockets (cement heads) and 20mm cannon. We also did several formation passes. I flew most of my trips in Sea Fury 106, but had four in 113 and a couple in 102 as well. During the same time frame, we

TG 128 sports the RCN's new livery at Malton Airport on 3 Sep 52. This aircraft was flown by both Bob Falls and Dave Tate during the two week CNE exhibition. (via Leo Pettipas)

NAVY 113

In September 1953, four Sea Furies and an Avenger continued to the West Coast following the CNE to "show the flag". Note the flashy spinner on the VF 870 Sea Fury. (via Leo Pettipas)

also did a couple of shows at Hamilton for a regatta. I particularly remember a lot of low passes and a lot of formation …"

Dave Tate

It goes without saying that the ground attack simulation part of the show was a lot of fun and a real crowd pleaser. Although the names of the 1952 Avenger pilots have been lost with the passage of time, their contribution has not. The September 1952 issue of HMCS Shearwater's newspaper, the *Crowsnest*, reported that *"The daily (CNE) naval air demonstration was brief but spectacular. It consisted of Sea Furies and Avengers carrying out rocket attacks on a dummy submarine in Lake Ontario some 600 yards off the breakwater. Record crowds of spectators thronged the waterfront each evening to witness the submarine attacks, and invariably they saw the target demolished in swift order."*

In November of 1952 yet another change was made to RCN squadron designators when it was decided to add letter prefixes in front of

squadron numbers to make them compatible with the US Navy. This was done in order to facilitate joint exercises with the larger American fleet which were commonplace. Thus, 870 Sqn became VF 870 and so on.

The 1953 CNE team was led by the new commanding officer of 31 SAG, LCdr Don Knox, an Avenger pilot. They did preliminary airshows at Lakehead from August 10th to 12th prior to heading to Toronto where they also did daily demonstrations in front of the CNE grandstand from August 27th to September 11th. The Sea Furies blasted away with their 20 mm cannons and the Avengers fired three-inch rockets followed up by their half-inch machine guns at the wooden submarine target. VF 870 Sea Fury pilots included their new CO, LCdr "Pappy" Macleod, Lts Stu Soward, Jeff Harvie, Vern Cunningham and S/Lts Jake Birks and Marty Brayman. In addition to Don Knox, the Avenger attackers included the CO of VS 880, LCdr Ted Davis with Lts Doug Fisher and George Noble. Stu Soward also joined them for a couple of sorties since he was also

checked out on the Avenger at the time.

Following the CNE, the team put on one last show at London on September 14th at which time the bulk of the aircraft headed home to Shearwater. Four Sea Furies and an Avenger continued on to the West Coast to pay a short visit to the Pacific Fleet. While there is no record of any airshow activity per se, there is little doubt that this group made their presence well known to western Canadians during this sojourn.

The fall of 1953 marked the end of major Sea Fury and Avenger activity at airshows in Canada, certainly on the scale of that seen at the CNE. At the end of March 1954, VF 870 disbanded until being stood up again with the Banshee fighter. The air group system was also abolished later in June. The last remaining operational squadron on the Sea Fury was VF 871 which continued until August 31st, 1956 when it too converted to the Banshee. It was that same summer that Canada's naval aviators made their grand return to the CNE in their newly acquired jet fighters.

The Inauguration of Air Force Day

It was in 1947 that the RCAF officially got back into the airshow business after the rapid downsizing following World War II. With thousands of veterans having retired or been released, Canada's air force soon needed an infusion of young blood to complement the substantial experience which had remained in the RCAF. The popularity of pre-war airshows and exhibitions had left no doubt that this was the best forum for attracting young recruits to the military. While the print and visual media were important, there was nothing that could compare to the firsthand experience of getting up close to air force aircraft on the ground and then watching them perform at close quarters in the air.

It was to this end that the Chief of the Air Staff, Air Marshal Robert Leckie, authorized planning for an annual "Air Force Day" which would be celebrated across the country at all of the major RCAF stations. Aircraft stationed in the local area would be featured in static and flying displays and station personnel would be available to host the citizens of the surrounding area. However, the biggest show would be held in the nation's capital at RCAF Stn Rockcliffe. The inaugural show took place on June 14th, 1947 under rainy skies which resulted in a number of flying displays being cancelled. Nevertheless, as the show developed in the

ensuing years, it would become a showcase for the RCAF with virtually every aircraft in the inventory being featured, often in large formations. The first post-war aircrew trainees, 21 cadets in total, began indoctrination training at No. 1 Manning Depot in Toronto in November, 1947. Hundreds would follow in their footsteps …

The introduction of Air Force Day was A/M Leckie's lasting legacy to Canada's airshow heritage. Soon after the inaugural show, he retired as Chief of the Air Staff and handed the reins to an equally strong proponent of the concept of public relations, A/M W.A. Curtis.

National Air Force Day at RCAF Stn Rockcliffe in Ottawa became the showcase for the air force starting in 1947. Rituals such as this were common every year as thousands of Canadians flocked to the station to see their air force in action. NAFD 6 Jun 64. (DND PL 144500)

RCAF Piston Teams 1947-1953

The F-51 Mustang IV

One of the first RCAF aircraft involved in post-war exhibitions was the legendary North American P-51D Mustang, also referred to as the Mk IV in British nomenclature. With a distinguished combat record in the war (9,081 enemy aircraft destroyed), the Mustang fulfilled an important role in Canada's air defence system as the RCAF entered the jet age. The first of 130 Mustangs taken on strength arrived in Canada from Homestead Army Air Force Base in the United States in late May 1947. Two regular force and six auxiliary squadrons were eventually equipped with the fighter and it was not until 1961 that the last of the RCAF's Mustangs were struck off strength. The RCAF generally adopted the use of the designation F-51 to denote "fighter" rather than the designation "P" which stood for "pursuit." However, research has revealed that both designations could be found on either side of the Canada-U.S. border.

With a maximum speed of 395 mph at 5,000 ft and a service ceiling over 41,000 feet, the Mustang was an impressive performer and an immediate hit with airshow crowds in Canada. Even today, dozens are still flying around the world, their appearance at airshows or air races always a thrilling sight.

A/M Robert Leckie, CB, DSO, DSC, DFC
Chief of the Air Staff 1 Jan 44 – 31 Aug 47

417 (FR) Sqn Mustang Team

The first squadron to be equipped with the Mustang was 417 "City of Windsor" Sqn which was re-formed in Rivers, Manitoba on June 1st, 1947 as a fighter reconnaissance squadron. Its initial complement included four aircraft with seven pilots, an engineering officer and 31 airmen.

The history of 417 is unique in that it was the only RCAF fighter squadron to serve in the Mediterranean theatre during the Second World War. Flying Spitfires and Hurricanes with the famed Desert Air Force, squadron pilots fought in support of the Eighth Army from Tunisia to northern Italy. Some of the seasoned veterans who re-formed the squadron and participated in airshows were equally famous, as Chuck Keating recalls:

The line up of 417 Sqn Mustang IVs in Trenton for the CNE airshow in September 1947. (DND PL 135285)

"I was a very junior sprog in 1947 when I had the chance to re-enter the RCAF after getting my wings in May 1944 at No. 4 Service Flying Training School Saskatoon, a short tour at No. 7 Bombing and Gunnery School at Paulson, Manitoba and a year at the University of British Columbia. Completely out of the blue I had this posting to 417 Sqn at Rivers! I had always wanted to be a fighter pilot but since the war was over there didn't seem to be a chance of that happening. When I got the posting I didn't even know the air force was thinking about raising fighter squadrons again. When someone told me that 417 was a fighter squadron (with MUSTANGS yet!!), I just about flipped. When I got to Rivers I was in further shock to find I would be flying with legendary types like S/L Jack Mitchener, DFC and Bar, with 17 destroyed, F/L Bob Kent, a Desert Rat, F/O Ray Oldfin, a Typhoon train buster and W/C Stan 'Marble Eyes' Turner of 242 Sqn Battle of Britain and Douglas Bader fame. Some said 'who do you think you are taking up a spot that should be for more worthy types?' I had to agree. I had a grand total of 350 hours, fresh out of flying Mk I Ansons at some obscure bombing and gunnery school in Canada.

The 417 (FR) Sqn Mustang team for the 1947 CNE. L to R, Front Row – F/L Ed Geddes, S/L Jack Mitchener, F/O Ray Oldfin. Back Row – F/L Bruce "Duke" Warren, F/L Tony Stephens, F/L Bob Kent. Missing is F/O Chuck Keating, no doubt at the Trenton Officers' Mess making preparations … (DND PL 135287)

When we were young seems to be the theme of this PR photo taken in Trenton. F/L Tony Stephens barely suppresses a smile as he runs up his mighty Packard-built Rolls-Royce Merlin engine (1490 hp) for the cameraman. Those are some of his teammates sharing a laugh behind him with some of the station nursing sisters. (DND PL 135288)

However, I checked out in the 'Mousetrap' and after five hours was hustled off to Trenton to take part in airshows at the Canadian National Exhibition from August 17th to September 7th. Being the junior pilot that I was, my logbook shows only two brief trips for the show. My job was to have the drinks ready in the Trenton mess after each day's sorties at the CNE. Sloe gin was the drink of choice. Maybe it helped to preserve me … I doubled my time on the Mustang by flying one back to Rivers, logging 5:00 hours with a refuel at Kapuskasing, Ontario.

Three weeks later we were off to the Calgary Air Show – a six-plane formation, 2 hrs 30 mins each way, and we did one 30 minute show. A who's who in the formation: W/C Stan Turner – many gongs – Battle of Britain; F/L Tony Stephens – Mustang wartime photo recce squadron; F/L Stan Knight – Mustang wartime photo recce squadron; S/L Bev Christmas – many gongs – Battle of Britain; F/L Ed Geddes – DFC; and finally, F/O Chuck Keating – that's me – the only survivor today!

During the next year-and-a-half we did a lot of airshows in conjunction with local air cadet squadrons in many small towns in Manitoba and Saskatchewan. Usually it was several towns on one sortie. As an example, on March 8th, 1948 we did Neepawa, Strathclair (Manitoba), Yorkton, Estevan, Wilcox (Saskatchewan) and Melita (Manitoba) – a

three-plane for 2 hrs 50 mins! On one trip to Estevan we did a full stop for a short static display. There was no local air traffic control – in fact, it was an abandoned airfield. On takeoff as a three-plane we were tails-up ready for lift off when we were confronted by a farmer driving a team of horses with a full load of hay across the runway. We just managed to hop over top of them. I'm sure the farmer had more than hay on his load going home!

A couple of long-range airshows were sort of interesting. In 1948 new runways were being laid at Rivers so they moved the squadron to Winnipeg for the summer. On June 19th we flew to Saskatoon (1 hr 40 mins), refuelled, did an airshow and then returned to Winnipeg (1 hr 55 mins). On September 4th I was sent as a solo from Winnipeg to Calgary to do a show (3 hrs 10 mins) where I refuelled, did a 45 minute aerobatic airshow and returned the next day (2 hrs 45 mins)."

Chuck Keating

With re-formed squadrons having so few pilots, airshows often became an entire squadron affair. That certainly had been the case when 417 deployed to Trenton with six aircraft for the CNE, groundcrew in tow. It was the start of a busy fall in 1947 – between October 18th and November 22nd, the squadron put on shows at no less than 18 locations ranging from Fort William, Ontario

to as far west as Edmonton, Alberta. The trend continued in 1948 as airshows gained popularity in North America.

The North American Harvard

Another performer to gain fame on the airshow scene in the 1940s was the venerable Harvard on which thousands of Canadian and allied pilots learned to fly across Canada during its lifespan of 25 years. The RCAF had taken delivery of the first of 15 Mk I Harvards on July 19th, 1939. With the outbreak of the Second World War and the rapid build-up of forces that ensued, the RCAF soon ordered another 90 from the North American Aviation Company in the United States. More significantly, Noorduyn Company of Canada received a government contract to build the Mk II in Canada, supplying the RCAF with almost 2,000 airframes by the end of the war.

Although many of the Harvard IIs were put into storage at the end of the war due to the phase-out of the BCATP, the highly reliable and rugged trainer continued as the RCAF's basic trainer until 1964. The location for post-war pilot training, minimal as it was immediately following the war, became No. 1 Flying Training School at RCAF Stn Centralia. It was from this location that the first "semi-official" RCAF aerobatic team in the post-war era was born, piloted by veteran instructors F/Ls Lou Hill and Ray Greene:

The first post-war Harvard aerobatic team was formed in Centralia in the fall of 1948. Leading the formation in Mk IIB 3034 (GG-Q) is F/L Lou Hill with his partner F/L Ray Greene neatly tucked to his side in 3337 (DB-O). (via Lou Hill)

A fine portrait of the Centralia Harvard Aerobatic Team circa 1949 by Canadian artist Robert Durnan. (via Lou Hill)

Centralia Harvard Aerobatic Team

"In the fall of 1948 at No. 1 Flying Training School, Centralia, F/L Ray Greene and I were authorized to establish a two-plane formation aerobatic team using stock Harvard Mk IIB trainers. Practice sessions were carried out into the spring of 1949. The team performed at many Armed Forces Day celebrations and civilian airshows throughout southwestern Ontario and was disbanded in July of 1950 when F/L Greene was posted to the USAF Test Pilot School. I later received an exchange posting with the USAF Training Command in September.

Our program comprised a coordinated start, taxi and formation takeoff. We usually proceeded to a designated holding point to await the time to commence our show. This also allowed time to climb to 3,000 feet to perform our first manoeuvre which was a coordinated spin. Led by F/L Greene at this point, flying with wing tip clearance, a spin was initiated on lead's command. Each aircraft would then spin about its own axis for two-and-a-half turns at which time recovery was initiated. This required another half-turn with the two aircraft coming out in their pre-spin formation position. Recovery was completed by 800 to 1,000 feet allowing the dive to be carried out to near ground level. At that time no specified minimum altitudes were dictated for shows – other than don't hit the ground or anyone else! After this opening act there followed a series of loops, rolls and formation changes led by myself. The formation would then separate to perform synchronized head-on loops and rolls followed by a rapid rejoin. The final manoeuvre, with Ray Greene leading, would be a series of three formation snap-rolls. Similar to the spin, each aircraft would rotate about its own horizontal axis but maintain the formation integrity on recovery. We would then position for a formation landing. Initially, our performance was designed to finish with a formation landing off a loop, but we found the loop had to be performed too far back from the viewing area in order to decrease to landing speed, so it was deleted. All manoeuvres were planned to be within the confines of the airfield so that the aircraft would be in sight of the spectators at all times.

Our aircraft carried no special markings other than the black cowl designated to "B" Flight as they were used daily for pilot training. We were authorized to perform our own

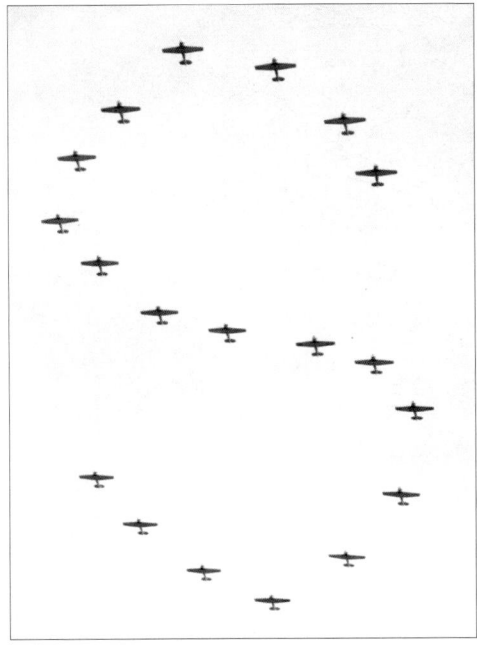

While serving as a staff instructor at CFS Trenton in September 1949, F/O Bob Ayres participated in this impressive flypast of 19 Harvards led by F/L Ed Gray to welcome A/V/M Slemon as the new AOC Training Command. Two years later at Centralia, Ayres designed an ungainly but extremely effective smoke system with which he became one of the great "smoke writers" of the day. (via Bob Ayres)

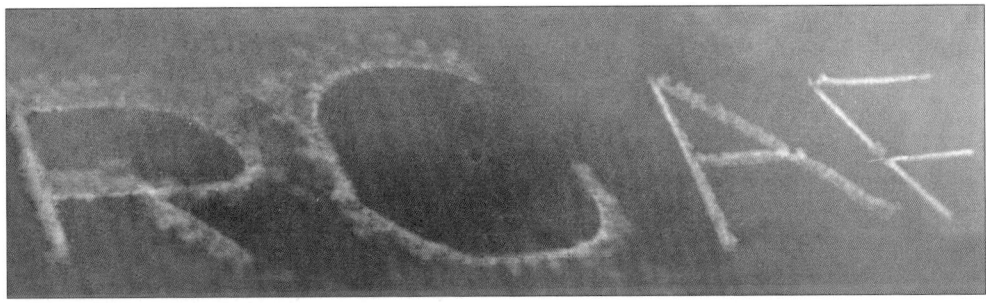

aircraft daily inspections and refueling when operating away from home base. The same aircraft, Harvards 3034 and 3337, were always used so that we were familiar with their flying characteristics."

Lou Hill

As Lou Hill and Ray Greene were setting the stage for future teams in Centralia, another veteran RCAF instructor was testing the waters for an aerobatic team at Central Flying School, RCAF Stn Trenton, Ontario. F/O Bob Ayres would go on to a distinguished 30 year flying career in the RCAF and Canadian Forces, ultimately becoming the first Canadian to fly 2,000 hours in the CF-104 Starfighter and the first to zoom the aircraft to over 100,000 feet. He reflects back on how he first got involved with airshows in a clear demonstration of the importance of perseverance:

"Having served as a wartime pilot instructor in the RCAF, I was discharged in September 1945. I immediately resumed a flying career in civil aviation as a flying instructor and bush pilot in northern Ontario, Quebec and Manitoba. For the next four-and-a-half years, I flew commercially. I re-enlisted in the RCAF as a so-called 'retread' pilot in April

1949. My first posting was to a flying instructors' course at Central Flying School. On completion, I remained on staff at CFS, instructing on all types of aircraft from Harvards to Expeditors, Vampires, Mitchells, Lancasters, Chipmunks and the Norseman, holding an A1 category on all types. Being on staff at CFS also gave me the opportunity to participate in flying activities such as seaplane flying, cross-country flights to distant destinations across Canada and weekend airshows in Ontario. Those were the good old days … as long as you were back to work on Monday morning.

In May 1949, I initiated and led a two-plane Harvard formation aerobatic team with F/O Ken Marlatt. He was later killed while doing solo low-level aerobatics over Sturgeon Lake near Peterborough, Ontario. That September I was posted to No. 1 FTS in Centralia as a flight commander to instruct NATO, French and other allied flight cadets. In March of 1951 I tried to form another two-plane Harvard formation aerobatic team, this time with F/O Tex Weatherly as my number two but this venture only lasted about a month.

Undaunted, I again attempted to work up a Harvard team in May and June with a USAF exchange instructor, Capt Marc Tinsley. We became pretty proficient, only to have Marc

The addition of billowy smoke to airshow routines highlighted the beauty of aerobatic flight, as clearly evidenced in this photo as Bob Ayres zooms skyward in his specially modified RCAF Harvard. (via Bob Ayres)

get posted back to the USA. It was also in May 1951 that I designed a smoke generator for the Harvard exhaust. It was subsequently used as the lead aircraft during formation aerobatic demonstrations as well as doing some sky writing with smoke.

Following Marc's departure, I attempted to keep the team alive by trying out several other instructor pilots. F/O Chris Frost ended up working out best and we performed at a few airshows together. On July 1st, 1951 (Dominion Day), we did a two-plane formation aerobatic show at each of Exeter, Elora and Goderich, Ontario. We did little more than practice after that.

The Easy Aces

It was finally the following spring, April 1952, when I received authorization to form a Harvard formation aerobatic team with three flying instructors that I found to be the most enthusiastic and capable of all the pilots with whom I had previously flown formation aerobatics. We had the full support of the station commander (G/C Bean), chief operations officer (W/C Bruce Miller) and chief flying instructor (S/L Freddie MacDonell). Ultimately, we also received the approval of the AOC of Training Command Headquarters, A/V/M Roy Slemon.

The Easy Aces. L to R – F/Os Ray Embury (left wing), Frank Pickles (box), Bob Ayres (leader) and Ernie Saunders (right wing). (RCAF photo via Ernie Saunders)

My No. 2 was F/O Ernie Saunders, No. 3 F/O Ray Embury and No. 4 F/O Frank Pickles. Many hours of formation aerobatic practice culminated in a very polished demonstration team with the "Easy Aces" representing the RCAF, No. 1 FTS Centralia. While flying with the aerobatic team, all of the pilots carried a full slate of students under pilot training, including Italian, French, Dutch, Norwegian, Belgian and Canadian flight cadets.

The Easy Aces had a busy summer in 1952. On June 14th, Air Force Day, the team flew

'EASY ACES' STEAL THE SHOW

A name is born. The station newspaper in Centralia as the headlines appeared on 20 Jun 52.

four airshows in one day at London, Aylmer, Clinton and Centralia. Chatham, Ontario followed on June 29th at an airshow sponsored by the RCAF Association's 411 Wing. On July 1st we flew shows at Exeter and Kitchener. Of course, our biggest show of the year was our appearance in Toronto for the National Air Show on September 20th. Then, on October 18th, we did an airshow at the Royal Military College of Canada in Kingston, Ontario.

Although we continued to fly together until December 1952, our last public show was on October 20th in Centralia. By the end of the year I was posted to the F-86 Sabre OTU at Chatham, New Brunswick and the team was disbanded. Postings followed shortly thereafter for Ernie Saunders to F-86 Sabres

and Frank Pickles and Ray Embury to CF-100s."

George R. "Bob" Ayres

It is unusual for an airshow team to get "instant" recognition on the strength of a one day performance, but this certainly seems to have been the case with Bob Ayres' team. The four shows they performed on AFD 1952 were enthusiastically reported by all of the community newspapers. The London *Free Press* had this to say about the show, "*The largest number of aircraft ever to be massed for an airshow in this district put on a sizzling demonstration of hot flying Saturday afternoon....Although all types of aircraft, from perky T-33 jet trainers to docile, dowager Dakota transports (performed), it was the time-honoured Harvard trainers which sent gasps of excitement coursing through the crowds at London City Airport.*" This was a reflection of just how polished the team's routine had become after six weeks of practice. Their show finale at Centralia on this day had been a "high-speed" line-astern pass which culminated with Bob Ayres pulling his smoking Harvard up into a loop, lowering the landing gear over the top and then landing in front of the crowd, with the remaining team members spacing themselves neatly behind him. The performance led to an enthusiastic report by the station newspaper, the *Centralia Coronet*, the following week which not only praised the team, but gave them a name. Since all four team members came from "E" Flight at 1 FTS, and the letter "E" was referred to in the old phonetic alphabet as "Easy," the exuberant station reporter entitled his report "*Easy Aces Steal The Show.*" It was strictly an unofficial name, but one that stuck and is now part of air force history.

The Easy Aces left their mark over southern Ontario in 1952 and drew widespread praise for their efforts. (via Bob Ayres)

"Bumps" between aircraft were fortunately rare, but did create a close call on one occasion.

IN REPLY PLEASE QUOTE
No. 000-2 (AOC)

Department of National Defence

Royal Canadian Air Force

Training Command Headquarters

CANADA

Trenton Ont 21 Oct 52

STATION HEADQUARTERS
CO
OCT 23 1952
23-5
R.C.A.F. CENTRALIA, ONT.
3760

Commanding Officer
RCAF Station
Centralia Ontario

Appreciation of Services

1   The Air Officer Commanding Air Defence Command has informed me of the valuable assistance rendered by units of Training Command in the presentation of the RCAF portion of the National Air Show held in Toronto on 20 Sep 52. His letter states in part,

> "The high rate of serviceability and the excellent flying discipline displayed by the aircrew -- is a credit to Training Command, and the RCAF as a whole. I would be grateful if you could compliment all those in your Command who participated."

2   Please add my personal congratulations for a task well done and pass the above information to those personnel under your command who contributed to this successful display.

(C R Slemon) A/V/M
AOC   TC

① OC FIS.
Des. plan on
x/Reg/c
x/c.

③ F/O Ayres
Toronto, plan
J.v. macdonell

RCAF G32
1000M—1-50 (6149)

Although timing was a critical component while flying the Harvard inverted, it became a regular feature of the Easy Aces routine. (via Bob Ayres)

As a formation performer, the Harvard was a handful and it took some deft handling by team members to maintain position, particularly during rolls when the outside aircraft would need all of the power the old Pratt and Whitney Wasp would deliver. This situation was compounded when different versions of the Harvard were used, from the Mk II to the Mk IV, each having different performance and stall characteristics. The leading was of course critical as the Harvard was not known for its high-speed performance! Loops were entered at 155 knots with 2,000 RPM and 28 inches of manifold pressure. As they staggered over the top, the pilots had to lean out the mixture if rough running developed, all the time jockeying to maintain position. Thus, what was meant to look easy from the ground, was anything but … Another manoeuvre that took some experimentation at altitude was inverted flying since the Harvard did not have an inverted flying system. Ayres found that by turning the fuel pump off just prior to rolling inverted, he could trap some fuel in the lines thereby preventing air cavitation. This gave him 30 to 40 seconds of inverted time.

As the Easy Aces continued to practice and perform throughout the summer of 1952, their proficiency and confidence continued to grow. For their last public appearance on October 20th, they decided to perform a stunt not seen since the barnstorming days of the Siskins. The wingtips of lead, No. 2 and No. 3 were tied together via their tie-down rings and they took off in vic formation. Joined by No. 4, they went through their repertoire of formation loops and rolls, landing again with the rope still intact.

Although this was the swan song for the Easy Aces, Bob Ayres continued to perform solo

demonstrations. Following graduation from Farnborough as a test pilot, he checked out on a wide variety of aircraft from helicopters to supersonic fighters. Between 1957 and 1959 at the Air Armament Evaluation Detachment in Cold Lake, he demonstrated the RAF Javelin Mk IV, F-86 Sabre and Argus at several Air Force Days prior to being seconded to the USAF in May 1960 to check out on the new F-104A Starfighter, the first RCAF pilot to fly the aircraft operationally.

As for the Harvard, it continued to be in high demand for demonstrations but it wasn't only the flying schools who got in on the act. The Air Armament School in Trenton also provided Harvards and Mustangs to satisfy air display requests in the early '50s. F/L Bud Lawrence remembers leading four Harvards over the Bay of Quinte in a "fire-power" demonstration in Sep '52 during

which they bombed local reserve units with small bags of flour – much to their surprise! Centralia did form one more aerobatic team for the 1953 airshow season, this one led by an RAF exchange instructor at 1 FTS, F/L John Towler. The rest of the team were all young Canadian instructors and included F/L Doug Bing (right wing), F/O Stu Allen (left wing) and F/O Al Mehlhaff (box). Al Mehlhaff remembers John Towler as an expert leader who had the team's complete confidence in his ability to lead them through their aerobatic routine, even in marginal weather conditions such as those encountered during their last show of the season, the National Air Show on September 19th, 1953. It would be nine years before the largest and most famous Harvard team of them all was born near the end of the aircraft's remarkable run in the RCAF. That team gained fame as the "Goldilocks"…

The 1 FTS Harvard Aerobatic Team performed at the Canadian National Exhibition and National Air Show in 1953. L to R – F/O Stu Allen, F/L Doug Bing, F/L John Towler (RAF), F/L Al Mehlhaff. Allen and Bing later both lost their lives in unrelated T-33 accidents. Downsview Airport, 9 Sep 53. (DND PL 65370)

416 (F) Sqn Mustang Team

This photo was taken to celebrate 416 Sqn's record breaking non-stop formation flight from Vancouver to Ottawa on 29 May 51, some 2,300 miles. It also happens to include the six team members who participated in AFD 1951 at Rockcliffe. L to R, Back Row – F/O Carl Longmuir, F/O Chuck Steacy, S/L Don Laubman (OC), F/O Bill Peterson, F/O Ken Lewis. Front Row – F/O Ray Howey, F/O Harold Wilson, F/O Roy Bamford. (DND CM72-459-11 via Gerry Patterson)

The second regular force squadron to be equipped with the Mustang was 416 (F) Sqn which was re-formed on January 15th, 1951 at RCAF Stn Uplands. The first flight of the Mustang IV was appropriately made by the new squadron commanding officer, S/L Don Laubman, who was fresh off a tour flying the Vampire with 410 (F) Sqn, the first operational squadron in the RCAF to be so equipped.

With Laubman's previous experience as leader of the Blue Devils, it was not long before he turned his boys loose for some challenging formation practice. By June, much of the squadron's allotment of flying hours was being used to practice for the upcoming Air Force Day show at Rockcliffe, the fifth annual show. S/L Laubman authorized the formation of a four-plane demonstration team which was supplemented by a solo performance and an additional two-plane which did a rocket firing demo – impressive stuff in front of a civilian audi-

ence! Squadron members who participated at Rockcliffe included F/O Roy Bamford (leader) with F/Os Bill Peterson, Ken Lewis and Ray Howey as wingmen and F/Os Chuck Steacy and Harold Wilson doing the rocket firing. Steacy would conclude the show by demonstrating the maximum performance characteristics of the Mustang in an aerobatic show.

A total of 8,000 cars and 39,000 spectators converged on Rockcliffe for the 1951 show and they were not disappointed. The *Ottawa Journal* had given the Mustangs from 416 Sqn high billing as "Train Busters" for their rocket firing display – it would take place at the edge of the airfield against a mock locomotive and cars built for the sole purpose of being blown to smithereens. How successful Steacy and Wilson were in actually hitting the target was not mentioned the day following the show, but as Gerry Patterson, another part-time airshow performer recalls, hitting a pinpoint target with the practice

warheads of the day was questionable at best. The five-inch diameter rockets had dummy warheads made of concrete with blunt heads, so the ballistics were anything but predictable. As they could only be fired in salvo (six to eight rockets per wing), they "went in all directions." Notwithstanding, the crowd loved the show as the commentator played up the "attack" and Chuck Steacy won praise for his skillful aerobatics in the Mustang, especially his "upside-down flying."

By the middle of September 1951, 416 received its first jet aircraft, a T-33 Silver Star. It would be used to convert squadron pilots to jet aircraft in preparation for the fighter that everyone was clamouring to get their hands on, the F-86 Sabre. Thus, 416's era of demonstrating the F-51 Mustang was a short one. However, exciting days lay in the future for one lucky squadron pilot who would fly with 2 Wing's Sabre team in Europe in 1955, the Sky Lancers.

Two views of 416 Sqn Mustang IVs that thrilled spectators at the National Air Force Day at Rockcliffe in 1951. Their show included a formation demonstration, rocket firing against a ground target and a solo aerobatic routine. (DND PL 53281 via CAHS Chronology, Halford/Milberry Collection)

F/O Roy Bamford leads his 416 Sqn Mustang team across RCAF Stn Rockcliffe during National Air Force Day on 9 Jun 51. Three classic World War II aircraft on static display included the PBY Canso, Lancaster and B-17 Flying Fortress. A total of 39,000 spectators took in the show, arriving in 8,000 cars. (National Archives of Canada PA-067415)

These were the good 'ol days when you could leave your civilian life aside for a few hours and jump into the cockpit of an RCAF Auxiliary Mustang for a little fun. This beauty from 424 "City of Hamilton" Sqn operated out of Mount Hope Airport, now the home of the Canadian Warplane Heritage Museum. (Harry Tate via Larry Milberry). Inset are the pilots of the 424 Sqn Mustang team that performed in 1951. L to R - F/O Fred Alport, S/L Norm Shrive, F/O Ray Sherk. (RCAF Photo XP 1039 via Norm Shrive)

420 & 424 (F) Sqns Auxiliary Mustang Teams

Although use of the Mustang IV by the two regular force squadrons equipped with them was relatively short-lived, the aircraft would fly for many years with the RCAF Auxiliary. Within the RCAFA, at least two squadrons were to mount part-time display teams, 420 "City of London" and 424 "City of Hamilton" Sqns. The 420 team flew out of Crumlin Field in London and was led by S/L George Lee in 1951. He gave way to F/L D.G. Gray in 1952 who led a four-plane team with wingmen F/Ls Jack Baxter and Ivor Williams, F/O Murray Quinney flying the box. As the London *Free Press* reported following the annual AFD show in 1952, the 420 team *"demonstrated types of formation flying used in aerial operations and showed how formations of fighters would attack an invading bomber wave. Stooging along in Harvards to simulate slower bomber formations were F/Os Don Ingram, M.L. Lalonde, Jack Greenwood and Charles Duncan."* To complement the formation and tactical show staged by his pilots, the CO of 420 Sqn, W/C A.D. Haylett, did a solo aerobatic show in the Mustang.

The 424 team also flew in 1951 out of Mount Hope Airport in Hamilton under the leadership of S/L Norm Shrive. For the 1951 CNE, 420 and 424 combined forces, each providing a three-plane vic for each of the 14 evenings of the show. Their show was a simple one – like many in that era, it was highlighted by a fire-power demonstration. As Norm Shrive vividly recalls, the Mustangs opened their show with a

low pass from the west in two vic formations, one behind the other. As they approached stage centre, they pulled up over the crowd and changed to line-astern. They then repositioned for their live firing passes, coming in from behind the crowd, directly over the bandshell. They then let loose – first with rockets followed by the six .50 calibre machine guns carried on the Mustang. Shrive also recalls that rockets would occasionally ricochet off the water, much to the delight of the crowd, and shell casings were known to hit the top of the bandshell if there was a strong wind from the south!

With so many aircraft participating in the show each evening, TOTs (time-on-target) were hard – just be there, no excuses accepted! The coordinator of the Mustang show was a hard-nosed perfectionist by the name of W/C William Lupton, affectionately known as "Willy the Whip." It seems that Norm Shrive was a whop-

ping four seconds early on his 6:15 p.m. TOT on one of the first evenings of the show. Lupton's debriefing was to the point: "You do that again and you're off the lead!" Although this was Shrive's most humorous recollection from the 1951 CNE, it was by no means his most memorable. The Mustang on occasion had difficulty with its carburetor diaphragm which in turn had a nasty habit of causing the engine to fail. This highly undesirable situation is precisely what happened to Shrive one evening after firing his rocket salvo. A roar as his rockets headed for their floating target was followed by deathly silence as his four-blade prop sputtered to a halt. Fortunately, the engine revved to life again just as Shrive was preparing to ditch in Lake Ontario and he managed to get the aircraft back onto terra firma in short order. Lucky for him, as swimming during the show was strictly forbidden – and "Willy" would *not* have been impressed!

Two impressive views of the 420 "City of London" Sqn Mustang team at work during an airshow in 1951. S/L George Lee led the team. (via John Bradley)

For the 1951 CNE, 420 and 424 Sqns combined forces to put on an exciting formation and firepower demonstration. Members of the team were L to R, Front Row – F/O J. Malone, F/O Fred Allport. Back Row – F/L W. Fox, S/L George Lee, S/L Norm Shrive, F/O Ray Sherk. (RCAF HN-424-14-A via Norm Shrive)

Static displays are today a vital part of airshows. In 1952 the CNE went out of its way to put this beauty belonging to the Winter Experimental Establishment in Edmonton on display outside the grandstand at Exhibition Place. The Mustang would eventually be replaced by the F-86 Sabre, but its legend lives on forever. (courtesy CNE Archives)

Canada Enters the Jet Age

The most revolutionary development to come out of the Second World War – one which would change aviation forever – was the introduction of jet propulsion. Germany had won the race to deploy the first operational jet fighter in mid-1944, but the Messerschmitt Me.262 was soon countered by the British when they flew the production model of the Gloster Meteor F.1 very shortly thereafter. However, the concept of the jet engine had been theorized years before. The first British engineer to do so was Frank Whittle who eventually got the attention of the War Ministry once he had built an engine that actually developed thrust without blowing up. Whittle had joined forces with Gloster Aircraft to build an experimental jet aircraft and it was on February 7th, 1941 that the Ministry signed a contract for 12 (later

reduced to eight) twin-engined "Gloster-Whittle aeroplanes" which eventually became known as the Meteor. All of this was being done in absolute secrecy of course and very few people knew anything about the program, let alone understood what it was all about.

The Canadian connection to this story was purely accidental but is an important, if little known, chapter of our aviation heritage. As it transpired, the first RAF Sqn earmarked to receive six of the prototype fighters was 616 Sqn which at the time was flying combat missions on the Spitfire VII out of West Malling. Two of the squadron pilots were Canadians, F/Ls Bill McKenzie and Jack Ritch. In April 1944 they and their squadron mates were advised that 616 Sqn had been chosen to convert onto a new aircraft, one with two engines. No one had any idea what it was but something was in the wind with respect to a new fighter aircraft using new technology. Jack Ritch recalls hearing the terms "*jet, mach and speed of sound*" for the first time, and then the term *Meteor*. "What the hell is that?" he had asked a fellow squadron pilot. "I don't know," was all his compatriot could reply.

Soon enough, 616 pilots were introduced to their new machine under special security at RAF Farnborough. The sight of it drew blank stares of disbelief – it had no props! "Good God, what the hell is that?" was Bill McKenzie's first reaction. He would be the first fighter pilot to fly the Meteor F.1, a Canadian to boot ... Once the entire

Canada's first jet pilots, shown here at RCAF Stn St. Hubert shortly after the arrival of Meteor EE311 in September 1945. L to R – S/L Shan Baudoux, F/L Bill McKenzie, F/L Jack Ritch. Both McKenzie and Ritch flew combat missions against the V1 "Buzz-bombs" towards the end of WW II. Jack Ritch became the RCAF's resident aerobatic expert on the machine. (DND RE 2949-2)

Thousands of Canadians turned out to witness history in the making as the first jet aircraft to fly in Canadian skies was shown off in 1945. (via Jack Ritch)

squadron had been checked out, they were transferred down to Manston and started their operational combat sorties – chasing buzz-bombs!

Following the end of the war, after some confusion, both McKenzie and Ritch found themselves posted back to Canada to the Test and Development Establishment at RCAF Stn Rockcliffe in Ottawa. They were to demonstrate a Meteor F.3 which had been donated to the RCAF by the RAF for evaluation. They were joined by their new boss, S/L Shan Baudoux, a former Coastal Command pilot who had just completed the test-pilot course at Boscombe Down.

The First Jet Shows in Canada

F/L Jack Ritch flew his first trip in the Meteor at Farnborough on June 10th, 1944. The comment entered alongside the 40 minute trip recorded in his logbook was "Jet Propelled Job – Nice." It was on September 18th, 1945 that he flew the first jet aerobatic show in Canada in Meteor EE311. His audience was a group of air attachés invited to Rockcliffe for the special showing. By now, Ritch was totally comfortable with low-level aerobatics in the aircraft and he put on a fine show on a miserable day – cloudy with rain. He used the cloud to advantage however, recalling that for his finale he pulled up into the cloud in a looping manoeuvre, disappeared and then reappeared from behind the old photo unit at the far end of the runway going as fast as the

aircraft would go. The Russians were particularly impressed ... and crawled all over the aircraft after it had landed.

What followed was a tour by the aircraft in Central Canada as the principal attraction behind a Victory Bond drive which raised millions of dollars. Between McKenzie, Ritch and Baudoux, demonstrations were held in Ottawa, Montreal, Quebec City, Toronto, Hamilton, London and Windsor between the 23rd of October and 7th of November. This incidentally included an infamous low pass down Danforth Avenue in Toronto by Jack Ritch in a special salute to ... his mother! Thousands of Canadians witnessed history in the making as the jet attained speeds of over 500 mph during its demonstrations, making front page news in every city. The aircraft was then crated and shipped by rail to the Winter Experimental Establishment (WEE) in Edmonton, Alberta.

Winter trials were flown in Edmonton on a wide variety of aircraft, including both the Meteor and Vampire. Over the next several years sporadic airshows were flown to slowly show off jet aircraft to Western Canadians. The first of these naturally took place in Edmonton itself on May 5th, 1946 where eager spectators were permitted to get right up to

YEAR 1945		AIRCRAFT		PILOT, OR 1ST PILOT	2ND PILOT, PUPIL OR PASSENGER	DUTY (INCLUDING RESULTS AND REMARKS)
ONTH	DATE	Type	No.			
—	—	—	—	—	—	— Totals Brought Forward
		TEST & DEVELOPMENT EST.		RCAF ROCKCLIFFE OTTAWA ONT.		
Aug.	23	HARVARD	867	SELF	F/L McKENZIE	LOCAL
"	23	HUDSON	630	S/L BAUDOUX	SELF	ST. HUBERT TO RCK R.R.
"	27	"	630	S/L BAUDOUX	"	ST. HUBERT TO RCK R.R.
"	27	"	630	S/L BAUDOUX	"	RCK - ST HUBERT R.R
"	28	"	630	S/L BAUDOUX	"	RCK - ST HUBERT R.R.
				SUMMARY FOR AUG. 1945	A/c TYPES	
				UNT: T&D. EST.	HARVARD	
		—S/L		DATE: SEPT. 1, 1945	HUDSON	
		O.C. FLYING T.&D. EST.		SIGNATURE: Ritch F/L		
SEPT.	4	ANSON	12177	S/L BAUDOUX	SELF	RCK TO ST. HUBERTS R.R.
"	4	"	12172	S/L BAUDOUX	"	ST. HUBERTS - RCK R.R.
"	5	"	12002	SELF		TO UPLANDS + RETURN
"	7	HUDSON	456	F/O MILLIKEN	SELF	TO MONCTON R.R
"	8	"	456	"	SELF	TO RCK R.R.
"	10	"	456	S/L BAUDOUX	"	RCK TO ST. HUBERTS R.R.
"	11	"	456	"	"	ST. HUBERTS TO RCK R.R.
"	11	ANSON	12172	"	"	RCK TO RSH R.R.
"	12	"	12172	SELF		RSH TO RCK R.R.
"	13	METEOR	EE311	SELF		LOCAL
"	18	"	EE311	"		LOCAL DEMONSTRATION AIR ATTACHÉS

GRAND TOTAL [Cols. (1) to (10)]   747 Hrs 25 Mins.   TOTALS CARRIED FORWARD

Jack Ritch's logbook, showing the first airshow in Canada in the post-war era on 18 Sep 45. Although this performance was a special one for air attachés, the general public would get their chance to see the new jet a month later.

Calgary Annual Air Show

CALGARY - ALBERTA

Office:
BOARD OF TRADE ROOMS
Renfrew Bldg.

October 6th 1947.

Flt. Lt. J. Ritch,
Northwest Air Command,
R.C.A.F.,
Edmonton, Alberta.

Dear Flight Lieutenant Ritch:

It is very difficult for me to thank you enough for the marvellous performance you put on at our Air Show on September 27th in the Vampire.

It was the highlight of the Show and is still being talked about by the citizens of Calgary, and your cooperation is very greatly appreciated.

Yours very truly,

D. K. Yorath,
Chairman.

DKY:EFJ

The biggest challenge for any air display chairman is lining up aircraft to perform at their show. The City of Calgary received a major boost to their event when North-West Air Command of the RCAF approved the appearance of F/L Jack Ritch in the Vampire on 27 Sep 47.

the Meteor to examine it. Calgarians had to wait another 16 months to see their first jet, Jack Ritch put on a thrilling demonstration in Vampire 372 at their annual airshow on September 27th, 1947. By this time the RCAF had selected the Vampire over the Meteor as its first operational fighter, based largely on the recommendations of Shan Baudoux and his staff. It would be July of 1948 before Canadians on the West Coast would get their first look at the Vampire, doing so on the final day of the Abbotsford "International" Airshow east of Vancouver. The show was opened on July 1st by Air Vice Marshal K.M. Guthrie, AOC of North-West Air Command, with over 15,000 spectators taking in the three day event. No one could have imagined that from those early roots would slowly evolve one of the world's premier airshows.

The de Havilland Vampire

Once the RCAF had made the decision to go with the Vampire instead of the Meteor as its first operational jet fighter, it took time to set up a delivery schedule with de Havilland. Nevertheless, Canada was still at the leading edge of allied countries to attain jet fighters and many Canadians would be surprised to learn that the first flight of a Vampire Mk 3 designated for the RCAF (17014) was flown at Downsview by test pilot Russ Bannock on January 7th, 1948. Twelve days later the first Vampires were handed over to the RCAF for instructional use at Central Flying School in Trenton.

The de Havilland Vampire Mk 3, Canada's first operational jet fighter, made many airshow appearances in Canada and the United States between 1947 and 1956. (via Jack Phillips)

Vampire Mk 3 17014, the first jet flown by Irish Ireland and Stocky Edwards at Central Flying School in Trenton in 1948. (DND PL 38751 via Jack Phillips)

The Vampire Flight at CFS was initially manned by a staff of two young fighter pilots who had plenty of combat experience. F/L "Stocky" Edwards was in charge with F/L "Irish" Ireland his right-hand man. Together they became known as "the Kerosene Kids," in reference to the new type of fuel used in the jets. Ireland was the first to get up in 17014, flying a 30 minute trip on February 4th. The next day was Edwards' turn and he did two short but highly enjoyable trips in the machine. In comparison to everyone else that would follow, they were now experts on jet fighters!

With the brief indoctrination to jet aircraft that Canadians had received courtesy the Meteor two years earlier, it was only a matter of weeks before requests for airshows started to reach CFS. However, there were more important matters to attend to first, such as exploring the operational envelope of the aircraft, at high and low altitudes, and mastering the Vampire's handling characteristics. This was essential if the jet instructors were to impart any meaningful knowledge to their students, the first of whom were destined to form Canada's first operational jet fighter squadron. Those steps taken however, Stocky Edwards did his first of many Vampire demonstrations on March 15th near Trenton in conjunction with an army co-op program. Irish Ireland relates how his demonstration days got started:

"As the first jet-propelled aircraft in Canadian service (aside from Experimental, Ferry and Acceptance Units), the Vampire was much in demand for flying and static displays by both military and civilian organizations. Initially the flying displays consisted of single aircraft executing high and low speed flypasts, maximum rate turns, loops and rolls – all very impressive with the new sound and somewhat higher speeds of the jet aircraft. The demonstrations progressed into

three and four-plane formations – the first three-plane display recorded in my logbook (in Vamp 17013) was for the opening of the 'World's Trade Fair' in Toronto on May 29th, 1948 with Governor General Viscount Alexander in attendance. That was a straightforward flypast and was followed by another of the same three aircraft on the same day for the 'Ontario County Flying Club' at Oshawa.

Let not the wrong impression be given that these displays were a flagrant waste of flying hours. Most, if not all, of the simple flypasts were formation training flights for the numerous experienced pilots who were being 'converted' to jet aircraft operation. Scheduling of the flight and timing by the

leader to appear at the right location at the appropriate time were critical features of the training flight.

Our first 'international' flying and static display was given at the 'Detroit International Airshow' held at Romulus Airport on June 26th and 27th, 1948. The aircraft and support crews were based at Selfridge Field, Michigan and the entire affair was a great success."

Irish Ireland

One young officer who played a different, but vital role in the introduction of the Vampire to the RCAF was the engineering officer charged with the responsibility of supervising the groundcrew technicians on the new fighter. Norm Hoye relates the good fortune which saw him become an important link in the success of Canada's first post-war aerial demonstration on American soil:

"My introduction to the Vampire jet fighter was at the de Havilland factory in England where I was sent on a jet engine course in 1946. The RCAF had decided to start replacing wartime piston aircraft with a jet and ordered some Vampires. I was still in

Engineering Officer F/L Norm Hoye steals a little thunder from his boss as he shows off the bells and whistles of the Vampire to a young lady in Detroit. Ever the gentleman, S/L Barry Barrett lends a, er, helping hand. (via Irish Ireland)

A typical PR shot of the post-war RCAF as demo pilots Jack Phillips, Stocky Edwards, Barry Barrett (RAF) and Irish Ireland examine a site layout in preparation for the CNE. While the formation team did 12 displays at the 1948 CNE in Toronto, Stocky Edwards was flying the Canadian flag down south in solo performances at the Cleveland Air Races. All four pilots earned the Distinguished Flying Cross in WW II. Trenton, Aug 48. (RCAF Photo via Irish Ireland)

craft. It was small and light so it could stay in close to the spectators. We had some very experienced wartime fighter pilots on the team, Stocky Edwards and Irish Ireland in particular. I travelled with them for shows away from base. In June 1948, a memorable trip was to Selfridge Field near Detroit from where we staged a show over Romulus Airport in conjunction with a USAF team. They were flying Shooting Stars, the single-seat fighter version of the later T-33 trainer. A bigger and heavier aircraft with essentially the same engine, the 'Stars' were no match for the agile little Vampires and the skill of our pilots. Stocky led a three-plane formation through various formation passes while Irish did a solo act interspersed between the formation manoeuvres. They stole the show."

Norm Hoye

CFS Aerobatic Team

With the Detroit spectacle behind them, in addition to an earlier show for the Joint Defence Staff on June 10th (filmed by *Associated Screen News*) and popular appearances of the CFS Vampires at Air Force Day in Aylmer, Camp Borden and Hamilton on June 12th, CFS suddenly found themselves the focus of a lot of attention. Stocky Edwards would continue to do many solo aerobatic displays in the Vampire, most notably a three day stint at the Cleveland Air Races from September 4th to 6th, but for Irish Ireland a new development was about to take place:

Yorkshire on the last base remaining from Canada's No. 6 Bomber Group, so I got the course. It was a fortunate break which led to many interesting assignments as the jet programs grew over the years.

After returning home from England later that year on one of the earliest trans-Atlantic flights (in a converted Liberator bomber), I was attached to Western Air Command HQ on 4th Avenue in Edmonton – but not for long. During the winter of 1946/47 the RAF had a Vampire at Namao (just north of Edmonton) on winter trials so I was sent there to get some experience on maintaining the Vampire and monitoring the winter trials. There were some problems, mostly with hydraulic seals in very cold weather, but the engine was quite happy in the cold and produced more power. Learning both jet aircraft operations and winter trial procedures made it an interesting winter. Both would stand me in good stead later.

When the trials finished, I had a short sojourn at London, Ontario and then was sent to Trenton in March 1948, about the time of the arrival of the first Vampires in the RCAF. My job was to maintain the aircraft and train the airmen who would be going to 410 Sqn which was to be the first operational jet squadron. There were no dual trainers so the pilots were trained on Harvard and

Mustang propeller aircraft, then soloed the Vampires after ground school and a cockpit check. The excellent visibility from the forward cockpit, the tricycle undercarriage and the simplicity of the controls made it an easy aircraft to fly. I do not recall anyone having a problem on their first solo.

In addition to training, CFS was given the task of setting up the first jet airshow team. The Vampire was a very good airshow air-

The Central Flying School Aerobatic Team originals, F/L Jack Phillips, S/L Barry Barrett (RAF) and F/L Irish Ireland, seen flying down the CNE waterfront in Sep 1948. (via Jack Phillips/Irish Ireland)

"An increasing number of requests for the appearance of jet aircraft on every occasion from unit Air Force Days to local county fairs soon dictated more than a 'catch-as-catch-can' type of operation. Accordingly, A/V/M E.E. Middleton, AOC Central Air Command, directed W/C F.R. (Freddie) Sharp, Officer Commanding CFS, to form an officially recognized jet aircraft display team. The appointed leader was S/L Barry Barrett (an RAF exchange officer), with right wing F/L Jack Phillips, left wing myself and part-time slot pilot F/L Les Banner. Solo aerobatics were shared by Banner and myself.

As well as carrying on with our regular instructional duties, we proceeded to develop a three-plane aerobatic routine. Training began on August 20th and, having survived the first three-plane formation slow roll in line-astern, proceeded quickly. We did our first show in Trenton five days later and then it was off to the CNE for 12 daily displays. On Sunday, September 12th we performed at the third annual Windsor Flying Club Air Show followed by an American show at Niagara Falls, New York on the following Saturday. It was the next day that F/L Banner became the only casualty of the display season when he inexplicably crashed during the return cross-country flight from Niagara Falls.

By October of 1948 the display season was running down and the pilots associated with the initial Vampire conversion were dispersed to other flying duties, many to the newly-formed Air Defence Group in St. Hubert which would take up the responsibility for aerobatic teams in Canada for a number of years."

Irish Ireland (with Jack Phillips)

It was indeed unfortunate that Les Banner lost his life on his return trip to Trenton, unable to reap the rewards for his contribution to the success of the team. Each of the remaining members received letters of appreciation from the AOC of Central Air Command on behalf of the RCAF. The positive public relations they had achieved on both sides of the border paved the way for the creation of the RCAF's most famous Vampire team the following year at RCAF Stn St. Hubert, Quebec.

A happy group of demo pilots. Jack Phillips, Barry Barrett, Irish Ireland and Les Banner prior to their show at Niagara Falls, New York. Tragically, Banner was lost on 19 Sep 48 when his Vampire hit a hill during his cross-country flight home. (via Irish Ireland)

The Windsor Daily Star

PHONE 4-1111   WINDSOR, ONTARIO, CANADA, MONDAY, SEPTEMBER 13, 1948

Huge Throng Jams Windsor Airport Area for Flying Show

The scene at Windsor, Ontario on 12 Sep 48. Canadians have long been fascinated with airshows – 12,000 spectators turned up for Windsor's third annual show over 50 years ago. (Courtesy *Windsor Star* via Jack Phillips)

A typical box formation flown by the CFS Vampire team in 1948. Led by S/L Barry Barrett of the RAF, Jack Phillips flew right wing, Irish Ireland left wing and Les Banner the box. (via Graham Wragg)

410 (F) Sqn Aerobatic Team - The Blue Devils

The first operational jet fighter squadron in RCAF history was 410 (F) Sqn which was re-formed on December 1st, 1948 coincident with the formation of Air Defence Group in St. Hubert. The Cougars were about to enter an exciting new era following their distin-

guished record of achievements with the Mosquito during WW II. The first squadron commander in the post-war era was S/L R.A. (Bob) Kipp. His squadron was tasked to train in jet interceptor operations, to develop tactics using the new jet and to set the standard for other squadrons that would follow. By the summer of 1949, aerial duels were daily events as fighter pilot pride pushed the Vampire to the edge of its operational envelope.

Formation flying has always been a necessary skill in fighter operations and 410 pilots, all of whom were veterans of WW II, easily adapted to the responsive Vampire. With the widespread interest that the advent of the jet had created in Canada, it was to be expected that public appearances by the RCAF's most advanced aircraft would continue to be in high demand. It was in the spring of 1949 that F/L Don Laubman stepped to the forefront and created the enduring legacy known as the Blue Devils. Laubman had impressive credentials with 15 aerial kills to his credit as a WW II fighter pilot. So too did his initial cadre of teammates – Joe Schultz with nine enemy aircraft and Omer Levesque with the distinction

S/L R.A. Kipp, DFC. OC 410 (F) Sqn, 1 Dec 48 – 25 Jul 49 (DND PL 48031 via Omer Levesque)

of being the first allied pilot to shoot down the dreaded Fw.190 Focke-Wulf. Laubman's first candidate for a formation trial was a young 25-year-old flying officer by the name of Mike Doyle. He had only joined the RCAF in 1942 but still saw action with 411 Sqn scoring two kills in air-to-air combat. He explains how the 410 team got started:

The original 410 (F) Sqn Blue Devils pose for a publicity shot at RCAF Stn St. Hubert on 14 Jul 49. L to R – F/L Joe Schultz (solo/slot), F/L Don Laubman (team leader), F/O Mike Doyle (left wing) and F/L Omer Levesque (right wing). S/L Bob Kipp, the squadron officer commanding, is in the cockpit. (DND PL 48038)

A famous shot of the original three-ship. By the time the 1949 Canadian National Exhibition had rolled around, the Blue Devils had expanded their show to six Vampires, a formation of four plus two solos. (RCAF Photo)

"The de Havilland Vampire aerobatic team, known as The Blue Devils, was born on May 4th, 1949 when F/L D.C. Laubman, a flight commander on 410 (F) Sqn based at St. Hubert, invited (ordered?) me to 'have a go' at some formation aerobatics. Soon, on May 12th, another Vampire, flown by F/L Omer Levesque, was added to the duo and the initial element of 410's aerobatic team became a fact of life.

This threesome practiced often throughout May and the early part of June. To add some activity to our repertoire while the formation was away from the airfield preparing for our next run, we added a solo Vampire flown by F/L Joe Schultz. He performed solo aerobatics during the formation's temporary, but sometimes prolonged, absences and joined up as No. 4 in the box for our finale which was to be a loop.

Our first airshow performance was held at RCAF Stn Rockcliffe on Air Force Day,

F/O Mike Doyle sports the flying gear of the day in this typical "hero" shot. Flying suits were nothing more than white coveralls with wings and rank insignia sewn on. (RCAF photo via Mike Doyle)

June 11th, 1949. The team was a great hit as few of the spectators had seen formation aerobatics flown in jet aircraft at low level before. It was not too long after this display that G/C W.R. MacBrien, Commander of Air Defence Group, authorized our OC, S/L Bob Kipp, to form and develop an aerobatic team that could perform at airshows in Canada and the USA. Thus, the Blue Devils became the first organized and officially sanctioned Air Defence Group aerobatic team in the post-WW II period. Shortly after this, a second solo Vampire, flown by F/L Bill Tew was added to the team – he would coordinate his simultaneous solo aerobatics with Joe Schultz. Also added in time for the CNE was a permanent No. 4 flying box in the person of F/O Bill Bliss who rounded out the symmetry of the team previously added by Joe Schultz during the final pass. Bill also added a new dimension to the team's social life!

Chicago Daily Tribune
THE WORLD'S GREATEST NEWSPAPER

72 PAGES
★★★ SPORTS
FINAL

AN AMERICAN PAPER FOR AMERICANS

VOL. CVIII—NO. 158   [REG. U.S. PAT. OFFICE, COPYRIGHT 1949 BY THE CHICAGO TRIBUNE]   MONDAY, JULY 4, 1949   FOUR CENTS – PAY NO MORE

AIR SHOW DRAWS 145,000

The Blue Devils hit the big time with their first show in the United States. By the end of the second day, 300,000 Americans had watched the pride of the RCAF perform. (via Mike Doyle)

International Exposure

Local airshows at Trenton and Drummondville, Quebec were flown and then at the end of June our newly formed aerobatic unit flew off to Chicago to perform at the National Air Fair on July 3rd and 4th. This event was held at O'Hare International Airport and was one of the major airshows in the United States at that time. According to the *Chicago Daily Tribune,* which wrote up the previous opening day extensively, 145,000 people attended the show on the first day. There were all kinds of US Air Force aircraft present, from the B-36 strategic bomber to the F-86A fighter. There was Betty Skelton, female world aerobatic champion, and her wonderful little Beechcraft biplane in which she executed all kinds of manoeuvres, including an outside loop. Also present were the Acrojets flying F-80 Shooting Stars, except for the man in the box who flew a T-33 because of its longer nose. The Blue Devils

Invitations to participate in major American shows such as the 1949 National Air Races in Cleveland were a measure of the high esteem in which Canadian teams were held by their neighbours to the south. (via Omer Levesque)

weren't worried because we figured we were the stars of the show! In the event, however, it was the Acrojets with their precision flying, all within the boundaries of O'Hare and always within easy sight of the 145,000 spectators, who stole the show. They were good – after talking to them over a few (?) drinks in a downtown Chicago hotel and learning their tricks of the trade, we resolved to become as good as they were. And we did!

Our next show was at RCAF Stn Rockcliffe on July 22nd. Following our return to St. Hubert, S/L Bob Kipp, who had accompanied us to Chicago flying the spare aircraft, decided that he would participate in a solo capacity on the team replacing F/L Bill Tew. Unfortunately, during a team practice over the airfield at St. Hubert on July 25th in preparation for the Michigan Air Fair, he was killed when his aircraft crashed during an inverted opposing pass with Joe Schultz. Nevertheless, we participated in the

As the RCAF prepared to expand to fulfill new responsibilities, National Air Force Day offered a prime opportunity to attract the youth of the nation to service careers. Media advertisements such as this were common across the country. (via Omer Levesque)

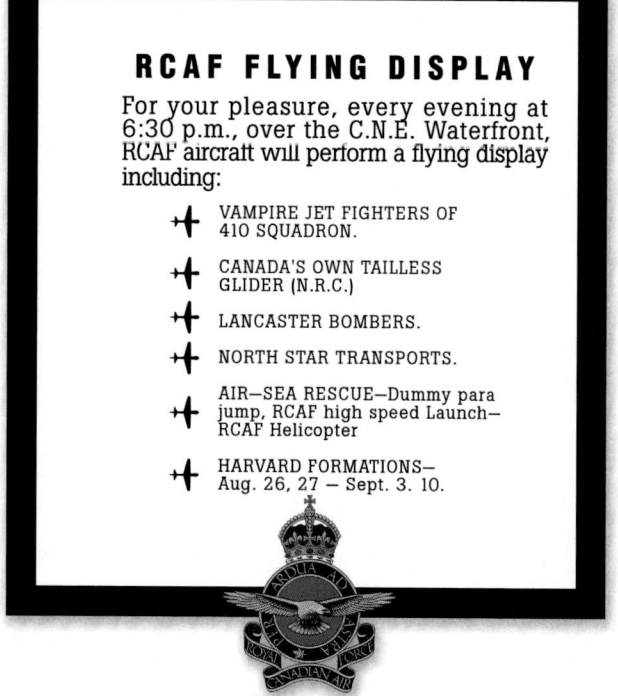

The Blue Devils were the feature attraction of the CNE Air Show in 1949. (via CNE Archives)

The final version of the 1949 Blue Devils featured a full-time slot man and additional solo. L to R – Omer Levesque, Bill Bliss, Joe Schultz, Mike Doyle, Don Laubman, Bill Tew. (RCAF Photo)

Michigan Air Fair at Willow Run Airport, Detroit on August 6th and 7th – Bill Tew resuming his former role as partner to Joe Schultz in performing solo aerobatics.

The next airshows we flew that first year were 11 successive shows at the Canadian National Exhibition starting on August 25th plus a two-day show at the National Air Races in Cleveland, Ohio on September 3rd and 4th. We were given the honour of closing the show on the first day and opening it on the next. We flew the Windsor Air Show

the following weekend prior to our finale for the year at the dedication of the British Commonwealth Air Training Plan Memorial Gates at RCAF Stn Trenton on September 30th, 1949. This latter ceremony was attended by various figures who played a prominent part in establishing and running the British, Australian, New Zealand, Canadian and other Commonwealth nations' aircrew training in Canada during World War II. This was a significant event in RCAF history. In all, we had flown 26 shows in our first season.

Air Defence Group Aerobatic Team

In 1950, now officially known as the Air Defence Group Aerobatic Team, we opened our season by flying to Chicago, Illinois for the Chicago Fair on June 1st. As well that year, we flew numerous airshows in Canada, including Air Force Day on June 10th and again the CNE. As F/L Bill Tew had left 410 Sqn for other duties and F/L Joe Schultz was posted to the RAF Central Fighter Establishment at West Raynham as RCAF

Reality check! For those fortunate to serve on an aerobatic team, fame is fleeting. From a high of having your name announced to tens of thousands of spectators during a season follows the low of a frozen cockpit in the middle of winter. About to embark on *Exercise Sweetbriar* in Feb 1950 are F/L Omer Levesque, F/L Mac Graham and F/O Bill Bliss, still smiling following their summer of adventure. (RCAF Photo via Omer Levesque)

ANNOUNCER:

This afternoon the crack exhibition aerobatic team of the R.C.A.F.'s first post-war fighter squadron, 410 Squadron, based at St. Hubert, will give a display of formation and single plane aerobatics similar to that which caught the fancy of audiences at the Canadian National Exhibition the Cleveland Air Races and other American and Canadian centres where it performed this summer. Pilots of the Vampire jet aircraft are F/L W. R. Tew, D.F.C.; F/L D. C. Laubman, D.F.C. and bar; F/L R. D. Schultz, D.F.C. and bar; F/L J. A. O. Levesque, and F/O M. F. Doyle. All these men are experienced wartime fighter pilots and all are graduates of the British Commonwealth Air Training Plan. One of the squadron pilots, F/O M. G. Graham, D.F.C., is at present in the Control Tower; he is in direct contact with the pilots of the aerobatic team, and will give you a running commentary of the manoeuvres.

FLYING DEMONSTRATION BY 410 FIGHTER SQUADRON

Liaison Officer, F/O Fred Evans of 421 Sqn undertook the solo role. On one occasion he also extracurricularly entertained the rest of the team by his antics on a fire escape on the outside of a downtown Chicago hotel! Also joining the team from 421 were F/Os Larry Spurr who flew right wing (replacing F/L Omer Levesque who was posted on exchange to the USAF to fly the F-86A Sabre) and Bill Paisley who became our spare.

It was in Boston immediately prior to the CNE that we had one of our more humorous incidents take place. By now we had become recognized, for all intents and purposes, as the RCAF's official aerobatic team. As such, we were invited to take part in the airshow associated with the annual USAF Association convention which had also extended an invitation to the CAS, A/M Wilf Curtis, and the chairman of the Canadian Joint Staff in Washington, A/V/M Hugh Campbell, among others. The airshow was to take place at Logan Field and Don Laubman was briefed by organizers that he was to conduct his show over an inlet or river about a mile away from the spectators. This was an absurd restriction which was placed on our team for no apparent reason – at that distance, hardly anyone would see us! Canadian pride was at stake.

After takeoff, Don managed to 'get lost,' miraculously ending up very close to the thousands of spectators who had turned out for the show. We completed our normal show to great applause from the Americans. That evening at the gala banquet, we were milling around in the presence of our American hosts when A/M Curtis approached our group. He placed himself squarely shoulder to shoulder with Don Laubman, and after exchanging pleasantries, quietly proceeded to publicly chastise him for having flown too close to the crowd. What no one else could see however, was that with his right arm which was hidden from view, he was patting Don on the back as he scolded him …

Following the Boston affair, we proceeded directly to the CNE for the annual airshow from September 1st to 9th. These were to be the last appearances for the Blue Devils and

A/M W.A. Curtis, CB, CBE, DSC, ED
Chief of the Air Staff 1 Sep 47 - 31 Jan 53.

we disbanded on September 11th to prepare for the F-86 Sabre and our impending move to Europe as part of the new No. 1 Canadian Air Division.

As it turned out, 1951 was a most interesting year. The squadron re-equipped with F-86 Sabre aircraft and Don Laubman was promoted to squadron leader. He was posted to RCAF Stn Uplands where he was appointed OC of 416 (F) Sqn which was forming at that base on Mustang fighters prior to getting their Sabres. No thought was given to the now extinct Blue Devils until one morning early in August when someone way up the command ladder realized that a commitment had been made to field an aerobatic team at the forthcoming Michigan Air Fair at Detroit on August 17th, 18th and 19th.

As a result, the Blue Devils were hastily reformed on August 8th with Don Laubman being sent to St. Hubert on temporary duty. I temporarily relinquished my duties as a flight commander on 410 (now in the process of converting to Sabres), Bill Bliss was

recalled from staff duties at Air Defence Command HQ and F/O Jerry Billing was thrust into the right wing position in the formation replacing Larry Spurr who was now in Korea flying with the USAF. As well, F/L Dean Kelly was drummed into service as the solo performer, replacing Fred Evans. Needless to say, six intensive formation aerobatic practice sessions were flown to re-acquaint the pilots with the Vampire and with the demands of formation aerobatics. The new and hurriedly assembled team then flew off to Detroit where we performed for three successive days, once again upholding the honour and prestige of the RCAF. This was the final airshow flown by the Blue Devils.

Altogether over a period of three years, the Blue Devils performed in 45 airshows in Canada and the United States. The initial assembly of the team was done on 410 (F) Sqn strictly as a squadron matter and it was not until after our first performance on Air Force Day at RCAF Stn Rockcliffe that any official recognition was forthcoming. Subsequently, of course, the Blue Devils became the Air Defence Group Aerobatic Team, although support from that higher headquarters was mostly moral with the pilots of the team having, for example, to paint the distinguishing insignia of our team on our aircraft ourselves. We did a pretty good job!

The Air Defence Group Aerobatic Team, better known as the Blue Devils, continued to bring fame to the RCAF with its performances at home and abroad. Shown here at the USAF Association banquet in Boston in August 1950 is the Canadian airshow contingent that performed earlier in the day. L to R – F/O Larry Spurr, F/L Don Laubman, F/O Bill Bliss, F/O Mike Doyle, S/L F.H. Darragh, Bill Waterton (Avro CF-100 test pilot), F/O Bill Paisley, F/L Bruce Warren (RCAF test pilot) and F/O Fred Evans. With the exception of Darragh, those in uniform are the Blue Devils. The Canadian delegation was led by the Chief of the Air Staff, A/M Wilf Curtis. (*Roundel* Magazine)

Ground support for the Blue Devils Aerobatic Team was provided throughout our existence by the groundcrews of 410 (F) Sqn, with WO2 Charlebois being in charge all three years."

Michael F. Doyle,
with Don Laubman and Joe Schultz

The final disbandment of the Blue Devils in August 1951 was not the end of an era, but the beginning of a new exciting one. Jet aircraft teams would slowly take prominence in Canada as the piston-engined teams gradually took their honoured place in history. And Canadians would continue to throng to airshows from coast-to-coast to watch the transition unfold …

As much as Canadians were fascinated by the speed and noise of the nation's first jet fighters, they were equally intrigued by the young men who flew the nimble machines. At the 1950 Canadian National Exhibition, legendary Canadian journalist Gordon Sinclair caught up with some of the Blue Devils for an interview. On the left is team leader F/L Don Laubman; on the right are F/Os Bill Paisley, Bill Bliss and Fred Evans. (via Bill Paisley)

The Blue Devils are remembered in this magnificent portrait by Geoff Bennett of Bridgewater, Nova Scotia. The team helped pave the way for one of the most exciting decades in Canadian airshow history. (courtesy Geoff Bennett)

The Sky Lancers Aerobatic Team of the RCAF's No. 1 Air Division Europe was formed at 2 Wing Grostenquin, France in March 1955.
A total of seven Canadian F-86 Sabre teams were formed in England, France and West Germany between 1952 and 1956. (DND PC 1043)

Jet Teams of the Fabulous Fifties

The popularity of the Blue Devils in their little Vampire fighters from 1949 until their final appearance in 1951 paved the way for one of the most exciting decades in Canada's airshow team development. The jet age quickly gripped Canadians from coast-to-coast – no one was immune to the thrill of watching a high-speed aircraft flash across an airfield in a matter of seconds, suddenly zooming skywards towards the heavens. Watching man and machine then do it upside down, or with a series of aileron rolls thrown in, only added to the mystique of the aircraft and the lucky souls flying them. The 1950s were unprecedented years of peacetime expansion for the Royal Canadian Air Force and, to a lesser extent, the air arm of the Royal Canadian Navy. The Cold War was on, and with it came a booming aviation industry in the heartland of Canada. The expansion also led to a preponderance of airshow teams. Collectively, they would generate great fame for Canada's military services, both at home and abroad.

The RCAF kicked off the new decade with its annual Air Force Day on 10 Jun 50 which was celebrated across the country. Advertisements such as these were seen nationwide as the air force prepared to accept three new high performance jet aircraft into its inventory. (via Syd Burrows)

In the early part of the decade, the propeller driven day fighters of the RCAF and RCN, the Mustang and Sea Fury respectively, continued to make popular appearances at airshows in Canada. So too did the venerable Harvard trainer, the "yellow peril" becoming one of the greatest trainers in the history of manned flight. Although each of these aircraft would become legends in their own right, it was really the jet aircraft that caught the imagination of airshow audiences around the world.

The RCAF received its Queen's Colours from Governor General Viscount Alexander on June 5th, 1950 in a moving ceremony on Parliament Hill, just five days in advance of the annual Air Force Day. Once again the annual salute to the air force was a resounding success nation-wide as thousands of

The pilots of the 1950 Air Defence Group Aerobatic Team, popularly known as The Blue Devils, kicked off a fabulous decade of airshow flying in Canada. L to R - F/O Fred Evans, F/O Bill Bliss, F/O Larry Spurr, F/L Don Laubman, F/O Mike Doyle, F/L Bill Tew. Inset is the youngest pilot to join the team in 1950, F/O Bill Paisley. (RCAF Photos via Bill Paisley)

Canadians flocked to RCAF stations to see the latest in aerial wizardry. With the Blue Devils now operating into their second season, they were the feature attraction of the big show in the nation's capital held at RCAF Stn Rockcliffe. However, since they couldn't be everywhere, many other pilots had the opportunity to put on shows in front of appreciative audiences – the Vampire was in high demand. One pair who did many shows together in the Vamp in 1949 and 1950 were F/L Hal Knight and F/O Jerry Billing. Both would perform numerous solo shows as well, including the CNE, Knight in the Vampire (and later T-33), Billing gaining fame as the longest flying Spitfire demo pilot in the world. Also remaining on the airshow scene in the first part of the decade was Irish Ireland who performed in the Vampire at RCAF Stn Chatham on Air Force Day 1950, 10,000 Miramichi residents taking in the show. Of his performance, *The Moncton Daily Times* wrote "*Individual show honours for the afternoon went to S/L 'Irish'*

A proud groundcrew team pose in front of the Blue Devils' spare Vampire at Chicago's O'Hare Airport on 1 Jun 50. They added an RCAF crest to their standard issue coveralls and painted "Air Defence Group Aerobatic Team RCAF" on the nosewheel door of each aircraft. (via Doug Hudson)

Ireland, commanding officer of the jet Operational Training Unit at the base … With conventional rolls, loops and chandelles, he produced an eight-point hesitation roll … inverted runs and vertical rolls following a high speed dive."

Notwithstanding the early popularity of the Vampire, three new jet aircraft defined airshow development during the 1950s in

The Vampire was in high demand for airshows in the early part of the 1950s. Shown flying 17021 in CFS livery is F/L Hal Knight who performed many demonstrations across central Canada, including a solo aerobatic demonstration every day at the 1951 CNE in Toronto. (RCAF photo via Marian Knight)

Canada. They were the F-86 Sabre, T-33 Silver Star and CF-100 Canuck. All of them would feature prominently in air displays across Canada over the next 10 years.

Canadair Ltd

The name Canadair became synonymous with the success of the RCAF in the 1950s as it became a full-fledged partner in the expansion of the air force. Incorporated on October 3rd, 1944, Canadair took over the Canadian Vickers plant at Cartierville Airport in Montreal on November 11th of the same year and has never looked back. By the beginning of the 1950s, the company had earned a fine reputation for technological expertise which led to the procurement of many key government projects. Thus, as plans unfolded for the expansion of the air force, so too did Canadair grow to meet the demand. Indeed, from 1947 until the early 1960s, fully 80 percent of Canadair's production effort was devoted to the Canadian military. From an employee work force of approximately 3,500 at the beginning of the decade, the Canadair payroll mushroomed to over 13,000 by April of 1953.

The Canadair F-86 Sabre

The introduction of the F-86 Sabre to the RCAF inventory in the early 1950s is one of the great success stories in Canadian air force history. Built by Canadair under licence from North American Aviation of California, the rugged and highly manoeuvrable day fighter became a classic and all-time favourite among many of Canada's fighter pilots. It was put to the ultimate test early in its development, thanks to the Korean War in which it dominated the Soviet built MiG-15. Within a few short years, the Sabre became the mainstay of air defence in

Europe for over a decade under the auspices of the North Atlantic Treaty Organization (NATO), of which Canada was an original signatory on April 4th, 1949.

The first Canadair-built Sabre prototype (19101) took to the air on August 9th, 1950 in the capable hands of Canadair test pilot, Al Lilly. Designated the CL-13 Sabre Mk 1 by Canadair, it was powered by a General Electric J47-GE-13 turbojet producing 5,200 lbs static thrust. It was the only Canadair Sabre built to F-86A standards; rapid design improvements by North American allowed Canadair to launch its production model of the F-86E, the CL-13 Mk 2, only two months later. It was the Mk 2 that would see widespread service in the RCAF's newly formed Air Division in Europe as part of Canada's NATO contribution to the defence of the continent. Canadair would ultimately build 350 Sabre 2s with their "all flying tailplane" before further improvements yielded later versions.

For most Canadians, initial exposure to the F-86 was in the form of news releases dealing with the Korean War which had broken out on June 25th, 1950 when the North Korean army invaded South Korea. Canada

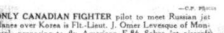

SABRE JET FIGHTERS are being battle-tested in Korea by American F-86 Sabre aircraft

THE F-86 JET plane is shown skimming tree top at Malton airport, near Toronto.

ONLY CANADIAN FIGHTER pilot to meet Russian jet planes over Korea is Flt.-Lieut. J. Omer Levesque of Montreal, preparing to fly American F-86 Sabre jet aircraft

CANADA FIGHTER PILOT TELLS HOW HE CHASED RUSSIANS AT 55 BELOW

OF THE SOVIET MIG-15, shown in flight. Levesque says: "They're fast alright, but as soon as you get near enough to shoot they hightail it over the border again." He could see the planes, which hit 658 miles an hour, take off and land in Manchuria.

Below – The Canadair Sabre assembly line in building P2 at the Montreal plant. In total, the company produced 1,815 Sabre variants from the prototype Mk 1 to the final production model, the Mk 6. At its peak, the plant was turning out 50 Sabres per month. (courtesy Canadair Ltd.)

was one of 17 nations to ultimately commit combat troops against the North in conjunction with United Nations Security Council military sanctions. Although no RCAF fighter aircraft were committed to the fray, 22 RCAF pilots saw combat as "exchange pilots" with the USAF who had rapidly deployed the F-86A to the region. The first Canadian involved was former "Blue Devil" Omer Levesque of Mont-Joli, Quebec, a fact not lost on the press. Levesque had already been earmarked as the first RCAF pilot that would fly the Sabre on exchange with the USAF – he was in the process of checking out on the F-86A at Langley AFB in Virginia when hostilities broke out. On December 15th, 1950, he found himself flying his first of 71 jet combat missions in Korea, this one out of Kimpo Air Base in Seoul. This novelty led to a half page spread in the *Toronto Daily Star* on January 5th, 1951 when Levesque was invited to comment on "how he chased Russians at 55 below," a reference to his MiG adversaries and the decidedly frosty conditions in which the aerial battles were taking place. The paper took pride in the fact that Levesque had been a performer at the local CNE Air Show, the inference being that his previous experience as an airshow pilot had honed his flying skills to a fine edge. F/L Levesque lived up to the fame garnered in the article, becoming the first Commonwealth pilot to get a jet kill against a MiG-15 in a dogfight on March 31st, 1951. He led the way for the small group of RCAF pilots who eventually accounted for nine confirmed MiG-15 kills, two probables and 10 damaged – a fine accounting by any standards.

413 (F) Sqn Sabre Team

Notwithstanding the early success demonstrated by the Sabre in Korea, the purchase of the new fighter by the Canadian government

was not without controversy due to its substantial cost in comparison to the Vampire fighter it would replace. There was no question within the RCAF that the F-86 was the best fighter in the world, but the sceptics and Canadian taxpayers needed to be convinced. It therefore wasn't long before demands to see this new "swept wing" jet led to an eastern Canada tour by 413 (F) Sqn which had been re-formed at Bagotville in August 1951. The squadron was initially equipped with Vampires and had been earmarked as an all-weather squadron to be re-equipped with the CF-100. However, when production delays with the all-weather interceptor ensued, the squadron's role was changed to that of a day fighter unit and squadron pilots found themselves in the cockpits of shiny new Sabres starting in December. Under the command of S/L Doug Lindsay, with two veteran flight commanders in the personas of F/Ls Phil Brodeur and Ken Lett, the squadron was tasked to organize and conduct *Operation*

Apple Tree to show off the new fighter starting in the spring of 1952. Ken Lett picks up the story:

"During the May to September period of 1952, 413 Sqn was highly involved in showing the Sabre to the voters of eastern Canada. We joked about being used to justify the Honourable Brook Claxton's decision to equip the RCAF with modern fighters.

During the month of May we flew 18 'show the flag' displays with 12 brand new Canadair Sabre Mk 2 aircraft. The list of locations where we performed was impressive: Summerside, Halifax, Truro, Amherst, Moncton, St. Hubert, Shawinigan, Three Rivers, Toronto, Oshawa, Peterborough, Hamilton, Orillia, Barrie, Camp Borden, Stratford, London, St. Thomas, Gravenhurst, North Bay, Sudbury, Huntsville and Midland. The air force stations got a fly-by plus a sonic boom and a generous 'beat up.' The cities and towns got a 12 plane fly-by in three diamonds of four aircraft each. We treated the Halifax and Shearwater area to a little 'extra' because of the naval environment. As a squadron, we had limited experience – all pilots were fresh out of the Sabre OTU except for Bill Paisley and Mark Sauder. However, our routine was simple – low and fast with lots of noise!

Shortly thereafter, in the late spring of '52, our O/C Doug Lindsay was posted to Korea on exchange with the USAF and Phil left the squadron to become chief administration officer (CAdO) in Bagotville. This left me as acting squadron commander with Mark and Bill as flight commanders. Early in August

The 413 Sqn team which introduced the Sabre to thousands of Canadians in 1952, seen here during a visit to A.V. Roe Canada Limited. L to R, Front Row – Ken Branch, Tom Mulrooney, Ken Lett, Mark Sauder, Art Maskell, Al Wilson. Centre Row – Bob Moncrief, Ernie Glover, Bill Paisley, Doug Lindsay (OC), Bill Pettit (SSupO), Phil Brodeur, Len Fine, Brian Burns, Barney Barnett. At back – Dan Kaye, Don Schneider. (*Avro Canada News*, via Ken Lett)

Seen in uniform at Canadian General Electric with some of their unidentified groundcrew are members of the CNE team. Front row to back, L to R – Doug Williams (engineering officer), Ken Lett, Mark Sauder, Bill Pettit (supply officer), Ken Branch (in civvies), Bill Paisley, Jud Killoran, Arnie Cavett, Jack Nichol, Harry Hrishenko, Don Schneider and Gene Nixon. (via Ken Lett)

we were tasked to develop a show for the CNE which we would perform for 19 consecutive days in addition to two shows for the National Air Show at the waterfront in mid-September. We decided to organize a more structured routine.

We flew a 12-plane plus a spare and one T-33 for solo aeros. It was flown by F/O Harry Hrischenko who performed flawlessly every day. The 12-plane flew along the waterfront east to west followed by Harry who did his thing while the Sabres executed a large 270 degree turn to fly straight at the grandstand. We then pulled up into a sort of 'Prince of Wales,' the two outer sections peeling off at about 30 degrees and the centre section continuing over the top with the wingmen separating at about 80 degrees. Mark Sauder's section on the left side flew two fairly steep 360 degree turns at low speed in front of the stands while Paisley's section lined up for strafing runs. They used an overhead break 'weapons range style' and fired all six guns at a float in the harbour very close to the spectators. Imagine turning in for a live firing pass with the nose of the aeroplane pointing at the spectators in today's world!

The grand finale was an unorganized line-astern pass across the viewing area – low, fast and noisy. The whole thing was a fun routine that an inexperienced fighter pilot could handle."

Ken Lett

The squadron's appearance at the CNE and National Air Show in September 1952 wound up the unit's involvement with Sabre airshows in Canada. They would soon be off to Europe. However, the exercise had been a highly successful PR endeavour. For the younger pilots on the squadron, it had been a license to pick up some valuable flying experience while getting their egos stroked at the same time – at the CNE each was introduced in turn by name and hometown as they sped individually down the showline on their last pass. This was also a thrill for the many family members in attendance, jet fighter pilots still being a rare breed in Canada at the time.

The Birth of the T-33 Silver Star

As the F-86 Sabre was gaining fame in an international forum, another highly successful jet design was coming into its own in the United States, this one by Lockheed Corporation. Lockheed was the first aviation company in the United States to design and build a jet fighter, the P-80 Shooting Star. While the fighter version of the aircraft turned out to be relatively short-lived due to the evolution of the swept wing, an adaptation of the aircraft did lead directly to the development of the most successful jet trainer in history, the T-33 Silver Star. Design of the trainer variant had actually begun in 1947 when the P-80 was stretched by some 41 inches to allow for a second ejection seat. The prototype trainer, initially known as the P-80C, took to the air on its first test flight on March 22nd, 1948 powered by an Allison J33-35 turbojet engine developing 4,600 lbs of static thrust.

One of the most versatile aircraft ever to serve with the RCAF, RCN and Canadian Forces, a long line of T-33 Silver Stars is seen in final production at Canadair circa 1954. Of the 656 T-Birds built at Plant 2, a total of 26 were still in active service with Canada's air force in the year 2001. Final phase-out of the aircraft took place in March 2002, resulting in the disbandment of 414 and 434 Combat Support Sqns based in Comox, British Columbia and Greenwood, Nova Scotia respectively. (Canadair Photo)

Training Command's jet contribution to the 1953 CNE Air Show comprised eight T-33 Silver Star advanced jet trainers, seen here at RCAF Stn Trenton. The CFS instructors that flew them are shown below, L to R – F/L D. Payne, F/L A. Lehman, F/L R. Leather, S/L L. Hill (leader), Maj M. Felts (USAF), F/L G. Frostad, F/L R. Scott. Missing is F/L J. Seaman. (RCAF Photo via Lou Hill)

With Canada's decision to enter the NATO alliance and support it with an entire air division overseas came the need for a jet trainer that would be at once forgiving for the *ab initio* jet pilot, yet powerful enough to serve as an introductory platform for fighter conversion later. The T-33A fit the bill perfectly. In 1951 the RCAF borrowed 20 of the tip-tanked Lockheed trainers from the USAF for a trial. Liking what they saw, they received 10 more as negotiations got underway for a major procurement program. Once again, the government turned to Canadair as the prime contractor and an agreement was reached with Lockheed in September 1951 which would allow Canadair to build the T-33 under license for the RCAF. However, the Canadian version of the jet trainer would be powered by the Nene 10 turbojet engine designed by Rolls Royce in the UK and rated at 5,200 lbs static thrust. It too would be built under license in Canada by Orenda Engines Limited in Malton, a subsidiary of A.V. Roe Canada Limited.

The first Canadair built T-33 was delivered to the RCAF on January 3rd, 1953. The entire program turned out to be a wonderful arrangement for all four parties as Canadair eventually supplied the RCAF with 656 of the Nene-powered trainers. The "T-Bird" ultimately developed into the most versatile aircraft in Canadian air force history, seeing service as a basic and advanced jet trainer, instrument trainer, weapons trainer, utility aircraft and electronic warfare platform during its lifespan. Its most visible role in the eyes of the average Canadian however, was that of an aerobatic performer. The aesthetically pleasing and unique lines of the aircraft were seen by millions of spectators at airshows for almost five decades.

Training Command Aerobatic Team - The Silver Stars

By the summer of 1953 the T-33 had become an instant hit with the instructional core of the RCAF. Due to its speed and manoeuvrability, there was no comparison to the lumbering Harvard trainer. Although converting to a jet aircraft for the first time was somewhat daunting for many young pilots, they would become comfortable with the increased speed soon enough and most would ultimately look back on their T-Bird days with great fondness.

The T-33's first foray into the airshow business was directed by Training Command to show off the new trainer to the Canadian taxpayer – the venue was to be the largest airshow of its kind in North America, the CNE in Toronto. W/C Cam Mussells was the OC of Central Flying School in Trenton at the time and was very active in promoting the concept of a demonstration team to represent Training Command. After careful consideration, he chose one of his most experienced instructors to form and command the team. S/L Lou Hill had been one of the first postwar RCAF pilots to be posted to an exchange tour with the USAF's Training Command where he had picked up valuable experience on the T-6 Texan, T-33 Silver Star and F-80 Shooting Star. Upon his return to Canada and a posting to CFS, he was immediately put in charge of Harvard basic training. With the introduction of the T-33 to the RCAF inventory, he was given the added responsibility of

The Silver Stars aerobatic team first performed at the National Air Show in Toronto on 19 Sep 53. Here they are photographed in practice from an RCAF B-25 Mitchell bomber near Trenton in 1954. (RCAF Photo via Lou Hill)

developing the jet curriculum as officer in charge of the newly formed Jet Training and Visiting Flight. He explains how an initial eight-plane non-aerobatic team eventually got clearance to do formation aerobatics:

"In August of 1953, CFS was tasked to provide a formation demonstration team to perform at the CNE at Toronto. For 18 consecutive evenings at 6 p.m., eight T-33 Silver Star aircraft rose from the runway at Trenton en route to the waterfront at the CNE. The aircraft were scheduled to be on stage at precisely 1818 hours (6:18 p.m.) and off stage at 1830 hours. For the 12 minute program, a demonstration of various formation patterns took place. On the final run, with two aircraft of the second section formed on each side of the box position of the lead flight, the lead flight would pull up into a vertical climb and perform an upward bomb burst. The second section would fly straight ahead and rejoin into a box formation. The two flights would then rejoin for the return flight to Trenton.

My right wing was F/L Russ Scott, left wing F/L Jack Seaman and in the box position was Major Mick Felts, a USAF exchange officer. The second flight was led by F/L Doc Payne, with F/Ls R. Leather, A. Lehman and G. Frostad completing the formation.

It was while performing at the CNE that CFS was requested to provide an aerobatic team to perform at the National Air Show at the Toronto waterfront scheduled for Saturday, September 19th, 1953. Although we had only two weeks to work up a program, a four-plane aerobatic team was established, led again by myself with F/L Scott, F/L Seaman and Maj Felts. The program included loops and rolls with formation changes during their execution and concluded with the upward bomb burst. The fact that a formation aerobatic routine was accomplished with such a short work up time was a tribute to the professional ability of the other three members of my team. A second

formation, again led by F/L Payne with his previous wingmen, flew various formations between our aerobatic manoeuvres.

On the day of the national show, low cloud and rain prevented us from completing our full program. Maj Felts complained that he was having difficulty seeing me due to the heavy rain on his windscreen as he flew the box position. We were also entering cloud during looping manoeuvres. I therefore directed the formation to discontinue and we returned to Malton from where we were operating for the

show. It was during this show that S/L Ray Greene, my partner from the Centralia Harvard team, unfortunately lost his life while performing solo aerobatics in an F-86 Sabre.

With the completion of the 1953 display season, the formation did not start to practice again until the spring of 1954. It was decided that only a four-plane formation would be utilized for future displays. Maj Felts had completed his exchange tour and the number four position was filled by F/L Alex Bowman. Since the aircraft we were flying were Silver Stars, this name was adopted for the team for the 1954 season.

A more challenging and variable flight program was implemented. A typical show would commence with each of us strapping in and starting together on my signal. We lowered our canopies half way and pulled forward together to taxi in trail to the takeoff position. We took off in a finger-four formation with number four moving into the box position as soon as possible after clearing ground. Our opening pass was a double loop with four moving to finger-four position at the top of the second loop. Tight dumbbell turns were executed between manoeuvres so that we remained in sight of the spectators as much as possible. This was the most difficult part of our routine due to the rapid climbing and descending rolling G to maintain position.

Our second manoeuvre of the show was a barrel roll carried out in finger-four formation changing to box formation during the roll. This was followed by completing two leaves of a clover leaf which placed the formation back parallel with the spectators. On return with the formation in line abreast, a loop was carried out with the formation returning to the box formation at the top of the loop. Forming echelon right on turn around, the formation went into a

A classic shot of the Silver Stars in diamond formation. Led by S/L Lou Hill, right wing was flown by F/L Russ Scott, left wing by F/L Jack Seaman and box by F/L Alex Bowman. (RCAF Photo via Lou Hill)

The Silver Stars swoop low over the Princess Gate at the Canadian National Exhibition in Toronto in this recent work by Charles B. Kadin of Toronto. (courtesy Charles Kadin)

barrel roll to the right changing to the box formation in the roll.

The final manoeuvre was in the box formation with a vertical pull-up and bomb burst after which all aircraft would individually complete the back side of a loop and criss-cross from four different directions at high speed. A crossing position would be designated at briefing and if at an airfield, the runway parallel to the spectators was used. Lead and four would use opposite sides of the runway while two and three would approach at right angles to the runway. Each pilot would be responsible for clearing the aircraft to his left as well as the oncoming aircraft. The two aircraft parallel to the runway would be at the same height but below the two aircraft approaching from right angles. In those days, there was no limitation on flying towards the spectators and the height limitation was 100 feet. After completing the criss-cross the lead would pull up vertically and recover to level flight, two and three performed tight climbing turns into lead while number four completed a roll-off-the-top of a loop. This

allowed a rapid rejoin in box formation. If the length of runway permitted, we would land in finger-four formation or perform a one second overhead break to land in close stream on shorter runways. Taxi back to the ramp and shut down was again completed in formation.

In 1954, the Silver Stars formation performed at many armed forces displays as well as civilian airshows in southern Ontario. Our spare aircraft was flown by F/L Payne who also acted as servicing coordinator. If ground personnel did not accompany the formation, the aircraft inspections and refueling operation would be handled by the pilots.

The highlight of the season was when the team became part of *Operation Prairie Pacific* under the command of W/C Cal Lee. This was a cavalcade of jet aircraft which toured the Western Provinces partaking in airshows at the major cities of each province. In addition, on days not scheduled for a show the team would fly at 500 feet over the local countryside zigzagging from community to

community to display the current jet aircraft used for the operational and training roles of the RCAF. Due to the tandem seats in our T-33 aircraft, we also flew many media, VIP and photo flights during this exercise. After *Operation Prairie Pacific* completed its final performance on September 11th at the CNE, all participating aircraft returned to their respective bases.

Not to be overlooked is the tremendous contribution that the ground personnel made to the success of the Silver Stars Aerobatic Team. Under the leadership of Sgt G. Munro, they worked countless hours, often extending into the darkness, to clear up the unservice-abilities and servicing the aircraft. The long, noisy and fatiguing flights in the C-119 Flying Boxcar across the countryside, ability to improvise with a minimum of facilities and personal dedication to their profession with little recognition, speaks highly of the participating NCOs and airmen.

With the winding down of the 1954 airshow season, the Silver Stars' personnel resumed

their regular duties with CFS. In the spring of 1955, we resumed practices. Shows were flown at London, Windsor, Centralia and Trenton. Our final displays were again at the CNE in September 1955. These comprised six formation demonstrations with no aerobatics involved as I was on temporary duty at the time. The team leadership was temporarily passed to F/L Russ Scott. The team was disbanded when I was posted to No. 1 Air Division in Europe to fly the F-86 in the spring of 1956, followed shortly thereafter by F/Ls Scott, Seaman and Payne. F/L Bowman was posted as well to the Empire Test Pilot School in England.

During the late '40s and '50s there was only limited support from higher levels for air displays, thus the performance of these air displays was not to interfere with regular Central Flying School commitments of personnel or aircraft. Therefore, practice by pilots was carried out on a voluntary basis, usually on evenings and weekends. Our aircraft had no special markings other than a red and white stripe on the upper part of the fin and rudder. We had no special flight dress, wearing only the issued flying and G suits and the ground personnel wore issue coveralls or working dress. Ground transport consisted of a bus and driver on call. Except at Toronto and Vancouver, accommodation was in barracks. Although funds were tight and amenities few, the spirit was high and everyone put their heart and pride into being able to represent that "branch of service" they represented, the RCAF.

One of the more humorous incidents that I recall from my airshow days occurred in Vancouver. As I was walking back to the crew room after completion of our team demonstration, I was handed a pamphlet by an elderly lady. On reading the pamphlet, the headline in bold print stated, 'Are You Prepared to Meet Your Maker?'"

Lou Hill

All told, the logbooks of Lou Hill and Russ Scott record 68 airshows by the Silver Stars during the summers of 1953 to 1955. These shows were performed with grace and style, and for the first time team members were able to share the pride of their profession with the Canadian public from inside their aircraft as eager media scrambled for a ride. This added an important new dimension to the public relations aspect of airshow teams and did much to increase their popularity.

A.V. Roe Canada Limited

While Canadair was busy setting up tooling for the F-86 and later T-33 assembly lines, another major player in the rapidly expanding Canadian aviation industry had made significant inroads in the design of a brand new "all-weather" interceptor for the RCAF. A.V. Roe Canada Limited had been formed in 1945 when the Hawker Siddeley Group of Great Britain had purchased the Crown-owned assets of Victory Aircraft. From these humble beginnings the company grew in size and stature, representing the largest single

investment of British industry in Canada. By 1954, following the delivery of the initial batch of 70 CF-100 interceptors, the company had grown from a workforce of 300 to 16,000. In 1954, the directors of the company led by Chairman Sir Roy Dobson and President and General Manager Crawford Gordon decided to form two new subsidiary companies, Avro Canada Limited and Orenda Engines Limited while purchasing a third, Canadian Steel Improvement Limited. With another new fighter design in the works that would come to be designated the CF-105 Avro Arrow, the future looked exceptionally bright for the A.V. Roe Canada group.

The Avro CF-100 Canuck

The twin-engine CF-100 was the first jet aircraft to be completely designed and built in Canada. Dubbed the "Canuck," it was pro-

duced to RCAF specifications as a long range all-weather interceptor to counter the Soviet bomber threat of the 1950s and early '60s. Nine RCAF squadrons were eventually equipped with the two seat interceptor and it provided the mainstay of Canadian air defence until the early '60s when the RCAF obtained the supersonic F-101B Voodoo from the USAF. Four CF-100 squadrons also eventually found themselves in Europe with Canada's Air Division to complement the RCAF's unparalleled day fighter, the F-86 Sabre, thereby giving each of Canada's fighter wings an all-weather air defence capability.

The Mk 1 prototype of the CF-100 took off on its maiden flight at Malton, Ontario on January 19th, 1950 in the hands of test pilot Bill Waterton. It was powered by two Rolls-Royce Avon engines. This was followed by the Mk 2 in June 1951 with the first Orenda 1 power plants. A skilled team of engineers worked steadily to iron out the inevitable (and many) wrinkles in the new jet but it was not until April 1953 that the first production aircraft went into service with the RCAF, the Mk 3 powered by the Orenda 8. The Mk 4A variant boasted a weapons package which consisted of 52 spin-stabilized 2.75 inch unguided rockets mounted in each wingtip pod combined with the eight 50-calibre machine guns of earlier models, now enhanced with a "gun-laying" radar. It was the Mk 4B in a new camouflaged paint scheme powered by Orenda 11 engines that was deployed across the Atlantic with four squadrons under the code name "Nimble Bat" beginning in 1956. The last version of the CF-100, the Mk 5, also went into squadron service in 1956. Avro Canada built a total of 692 CF-100 interceptors before production was completed in December 1958. Of these, 53 were delivered to the Belgian Air Force.

The Avro CF-100, the only indigenous interceptor to ever go into service with the RCAF, was built in the Malton plant near Toronto. Shown here on 23 Jul 53 is a Mk 3 of No. 3 AW (F) OTU from RCAF Stn North Bay bearing the unit's "JF" designator and "witch" emblem. (DND AAE2830 via Tony Gunter-Smith)

445 AW(F) Sqn Formation Team

The RCAF's first formation demonstration of the CF-100 was conducted by crews from the first operational squadron to be equipped with the new interceptor, 445 "Wolverine" Sqn. Shown here is part of the 445 team and their groundcrew. The aircrew are, L to R – P/O Vic Bartlett, F/O Bill Begy, F/L Doug Turner, F/L Mike Kobierski, F/O Jim Brown, F/O John Kitchen, F/L Jack Baxter, F/L Lloyd Chambers, F/O Bob Kirkpatrick, S/L Tom Futer (team leader). Missing are the crews of F/L Phil Etienne / F/O Russ Baxter and F/L Pat McGale / F/L Mel Bolton. The team also performed at the 1953 CNE and the National Air Show in Toronto on 19 Sep 53. (*Avro Canada News* via Vic Bartlett)

The honour of forming the first formation team on the CF-100 went to the first operational squadron to be equipped with the long range interceptor, 445 AW(F) Sqn being re-formed on April 1st, 1953 under the command of W/C George Nickerson. Nickerson selected S/L Tom Futer to form the team and he put together a five-plane team which performed at a special show for the Canadian press on August 20th, 1953. On September 1st, the squadron moved to its new home at RCAF Stn Uplands in Ottawa. It was from their new digs that the squadron then sent five CF-100s to perform at the 1953 Canadian National Exhibition in Toronto, along with three from 423 Sqn in St. Hubert. They performed simple flypasts in vics of three aircraft each interspersed with solo aerobatics by F/L Mike Kobierski of 445 Sqn.

CF-100 Aerobatics

Initial demonstrations of Canada's new interceptor were made by Avro test pilots. The first to do so was Bill Waterton who had been seconded from Gloster in the UK to be program test pilot due to his extensive experience. With Avro eager to market the CF-100 to other allied air forces, Waterton would wring out the aircraft, pushing it to the edge of its operational envelope. In 1950 he flew demos at Ottawa, Montreal, Washington and Boston as well as the CNE. One of the Boston shows was rather infamous when he lost an engine on takeoff – rather than doing his normal maximum rate of climb (as described by the commentator), he had his hands full just keeping the aircraft safely climbing at all. If nothing else however, it

was a powerful demonstration of the advantage of having two engines!

Another famous Avro pilot to demo the Canuck was Jan Zurakowski (later of Avro Arrow fame). He performed at the National Air Show in Toronto in each of 1952 through 1954 and then took his CF-100 act to Farnborough in September 1955. While there, he reportedly stole the show with a magnificent display according to *The Aeroplane* magazine.

The first RCAF unit to be equipped with the CF-100, No. 3 AW(F) OTU based in North Bay, finally took acceptance of its first CF-100 (18108) on July 22nd, 1952. It was delivered by S/L Paul Hartman, an RCAF graduate of the Empire Test Pilot School. Unfortunately, the aircraft was nine months

behind schedule and both Avro and the government were taking a beating in the press.

Also arriving in July was former Blue Devil solo Joe Schultz, now a squadron leader and appointed chief flying instructor at the OTU. He had picked up a wealth of jet experience while on exchange with the Central Fighter Establishment in the UK and with his previous operational jet experience with 410 Sqn (not to mention his exploits as a Mosquito night fighter pilot in WW II) was a prime candidate for the job. He was the first pilot of the unit to make an appearance at the CNE Air Show, doing so on September 20th, 1952 with only three hours on type. His spectacular high-speed pass at 500 kts followed by a rapid pull-up into the vertical was most impressive, a bit too impressive for the unit groundcrew as the aircraft came back somewhat overstressed.

Following in the footsteps of legendary Avro test pilot Jan Zurakowski, F/O Tony Gunter-Smith was one of only a handful of RCAF pilots authorized to do low-level aerobatic demonstrations in the CF-100, shown here in 18130. (via Tony Gunter-Smith)

It would be almost a year before the OTU endeavoured to do too much more in the way of demonstration flying, the principal task at hand being to get initial crews for the operational squadrons checked out. That accomplished however, the young instructor given the responsibility of working up an aerobatic routine in the late summer of 1953 was F/O Tony Gunter-Smith, 29, a former member of the RAF.

Gunter-Smith had enjoyed a rather unique career in the RAF when, as an experienced instructor, he was seconded to the Ministry of Supply late in 1948. This gave him the opportunity to check out on a wide variety of aircraft, from the Mosquito and Lancaster to all of the new jet aircraft. He took his release from the RAF in January 1952 and immediately emigrated to Canada with his family, joining the RCAF the same month. He had been exposed to the dynamic flying of Jan Zurakowski at Farnborough in 1951 and in particular to an incredible manoeuvre which he later flew himself. It became known as the "Zurabatic Cartwheel" which was eventually banned in the RAF. He describes both the manoeuvre and the show he ultimately perfected in the CF-100:

———————

"All aerobatics are combinations and variations of loops, rolls, stalls, high/low speed passes, etc. At Farnborough I had seen Zurakowski perform this entirely new, never before seen, aerobatic manoeuvre dubbed the "cartwheel." He did it in a Meteor 4 I believe – I was lucky and did it in a Meteor 8. The cartwheel began with a low-level pass along the runway, pulling up at the end into the vertical (and it had to be absolutely true vertical) both engines at 100 percent. As the speed dropped off to 60 knots, the throttle on the left engine was slapped shut and full left rudder applied. The right engine, still at 100 percent, rotated the aircraft to the left through 360 degrees, still in the vertical plane. It was imperative to shut the right throttle as the nose came up through 270 degrees and the momentum carried the nose through the last 90 degrees of rotation. It was equally important to slam on full right rudder as the nose passed 360 to 450 degrees. If it was done correctly, rudders could be centralized at 540 degrees (i.e. straight down vertically), the aircraft eased out of the dive and power applied to round out and pass down the runway on a reciprocal heading. The height at which the cartwheel was executed was between approximately 2,500 and 3,000

feet. If you did not get true vertical, or forgot to shut off the right engine at the right moment, or failed to use the rudders correctly, you were in big trouble. Hence, the eventual ban on the manoeuvre. The Meteor engines were separated sufficiently away from the fuselage to provide the required torque. The CF-100, on the other hand, had the engines too close inboard to allow a cartwheel.

Since I had flown many public displays in the RAF on Tempests, Vampires, Meteors and the Canberra, displaying the CF-100 was a natural follow-on so my boss at the OTU, W/C Ed Crew, asked me to work up a show. I initially displayed the Mk 3, then later at Cold Lake the Mk 4. Although I test flew the Mk 5 at A.V. Roe, I never flew it in displays. Later, when at CEPE Cold Lake, I gave public displays in the Sabre and again as a CEPE test pilot in Scotland (under the control of 1 Air Division) I was authorized to give public displays in the CF-100, Sabre and T-33.

I always flew solo in my displays, with one exception. I was called down from North Bay to Air Defence Command HQ in St. Hubert on February 16th, 1954 to give a display for a visiting USAF senior officer, General Twyning. My navigator, F/O Dave Brown, elected to occupy the rear seat for my show. The problem was that my routine included my "speciality" (if it can be called that), a ground-level, 360 degree turn inside the airfield perimeter flown at 300 knots with a constant 6.5 to 7 G throughout. I never wore a G-suit and was able to withstand a continuous 7 G for the full turn without blacking out – but not so for most in the rear seat. Dave Brown was the only volunteer I ever had! My routine varied somewhat from show to show but generally included loops, a Cuban-eight, inverted pass, slow roll, eight-point roll and, occasionally, a vertical eight in the CF-100. But the show always included the 360 degree 7 G turn – apparently the sound and wind effects were quite impressive to the spectators. Sometimes this was followed by an inverted turn onto base leg, lowering the undercarriage inverted, and then a very slow pass in front of the crowd prior to landing."

Tony Gunter-Smith

———————

Gunter-Smith's first official show on the "Canuck" was performed on August 20th, 1953 in CF-100 18163, his favourite aircraft for display flying. This was a special show at

RCAF Stn North Bay for the Canadian media (some 50 in total) designed to alleviate concerns about the state of Canada's new interceptor – several of the aircraft had crashed since the maiden flight of the prototype and the aircraft had experienced a myriad of problems. The show was therefore a vitally important occasion played up heavily by both the RCAF and Avro Canada who had unwavering faith in the aircraft.

The show began with a formation display by pilots of 445 AW(F) Sqn. Led by S/L Tom Futer, they did a series of formation passes across the field. Then it was Gunter-Smith's turn. By all accounts from the press in attendance – from North Bay to Toronto and Ottawa thru to Montreal – he put on a daz-

Pilot Tosses CF-100 Around Sky Like Toy in Thrilling Air Show

F/O Tony Gunter-Smith, 29, of 3 AW(F) OTU North Bay dazzled the press with a fully aerobatic display, including a roll after takeoff, on 20 Aug 53. (via Tony Gunter-Smith)

zling display. The *North Bay Daily Nugget* enthusiastically extolled how Gunter-Smith had "*tossed the CF-100 around the sky like a toy … Roaring down the runway, he rolled the aircraft when he was barely off the ground. Then he took it upstairs climbing at a 90 degree angle. Operating a few hundred feet above the ground, he twisted, turned and looped the plane while veteran airmen stood by in awe. They confessed they had not seen some of the stunts performed before in a CF-100.*" By the end of the show, the naysayers had been quieted (at least temporarily) as it was impossible to criticize the performance they had just seen. After three

long years of development, testing and troubleshooting of the indigenous interceptor, it was a relieved group of RCAF personnel that left the station that day.

Tony Gunter-Smith would be called upon to show off the CF-100 twice more in 1953 and would do half a dozen shows in 1954 out of North Bay in between his instructional duties, most notably the National Air Show on June 12th. He would repeat his performances several times after No. 3 AW(F) OTU moved to Cold Lake in 1955. Many other RCAF pilots would fly the CF-100 in displays across Canada, primarily in formation flypasts, including some incredibly large ones. However, relatively few pilots were authorized to do low-level aerobatic demonstrations. Another who was granted special dispensation was F/O Al Hesjedahl of 423 AW(F) Sqn based in St. Hubert. His opportunity came in the summer of 1954 when a special RCAF unit was created …

Operation Prairie Pacific

It was touted as the largest peacetime aerial exhibition of its kind in history and was an important catalyst in building a future for the airshow industry in Canada. *Operation Prairie Pacific* was conceived by Air Force Headquarters in 1954 and placed under the command of W/C Cal Lee of RCAF Stn Trenton. He was joined by S/L Roy Wood, command public relations officer at Training Command who helped coordinate much of the PR side of the operation. Its threefold mission included: stimulating interest in air force careers for young Canadians; acquainting the people of Western Canada with the RCAF's expanding roles and new jet aircraft; and finally, testing the coordination and mobility of over 100 RCAF personnel and equipment from Training, Air Defence and Transport Commands.

W/C C.C. Lee commanded Operation Prairie Pacific in 1954. (DND PL 87203)

The composite squadron officially comprised 19 aircraft, including five T-33s, five F-86 Sabres, five CF-100s, three C-119 Flying Boxcars and an amphibious Canso. The concept was to put on a 50 minute air display at selected centres across Western

More Than 50,000 Hear Jet Shatter Barrier

First jet-dive through the sound barrier ever made on the West Coast was heard by more then 50,000 people at Sea Island Sunday as the RCAF put on the biggest and best airshow in its history.

Even the frustration of the worst traffic jam in B.C.'s history didn't detract from the thrills as the people packing the perimeter of the airport heard a 21-year-old fighter pilot hurtle his F-86 jet straight down from 42,000 feet.

Veteran Air Force officers called the the show "fantastic."

The $15,000,000 worth of Sabres, CF-100 Canucks and

T-33 Silver Stars — 18 planes in all — went through an aerobatic routine as graceful and well timed as aerial ballet.

Formation aerobatics with wing tips less than 30 inches apart at more than 500 mph — that a single conventional airplane could never do, kept the crowd breathless for almost an hour and a half.

Post show PR in Vancouver by F/O Al McIlraith. (via Fred Rudy)

Canada over a four week period in an operation that would ultimately put a total of 80,000 miles on the team aircraft. It was a formidable undertaking and was successful beyond anyone's expectations.

In effect, the team comprised three teams that were brought together for the first time on July 22nd, 1954 at US Navy Station Argentia, Nfld, where they spent three days waiting out the weather for a show. This was a prelude to Prairie Pacific but the show had to be cancelled when the weather failed to clear. On the 13th of August, they regrouped at Stevenson Field in Winnipeg. Two of the teams, the Silver Stars Aerobatic Team from CFS in Trenton and 431 (F) Sqn Aerobatic Team from Bagotville had already performed shows earlier in the year while the third, the CF-100 team from 423 AW(F) Sqn in St. Hubert, was formed specifically for Prairie Pacific.

The show opened with a Sabre flown by F/O Al McIlraith coming in high overhead the spectators in a steep dive in which he broke the sound barrier, dropping a sonic boom on the awed crowd. With the whole "sound barrier" phenomena still being a novelty to most Canadians, this made the young 21-year-old very popular with audiences across the country and the press alike. As the spectators reacted to the boom, the Silver Stars swept on stage to begin their show. They were followed by the 431 Sqn team and then 423 Sqn who wrapped up the show.

Training Command Aerobatic Team The Silver Stars

The Silver Stars were Training Command's contribution to Prairie Pacific and were again led by S/L Lou Hill. They performed a fully aerobatic routine with four T-33s, the RCAF's new advanced jet trainer. Since the principal role of the mission was public relations, the T-33 added an important dimension as the team crossed Western Canada in that it was the only team aircraft that could give "press rides" at the time.

The concept of the press ride was initiated to further enhance the relationship between the air force and the general public it served. Heretofore, team members from the various teams had always been readily available to conduct interviews with the press and would continue to do so. However, the offer to take a member of the press flying in one of Canada's new jet aircraft immediately caught the imagination of thousands of average Canadians as they wondered how a lowly civilian could possibly withstand the speed and G forces they would surely experience! The fact of the matter is many fared well, but some did not – airsickness being the most common problem. The claustrophobic feel-

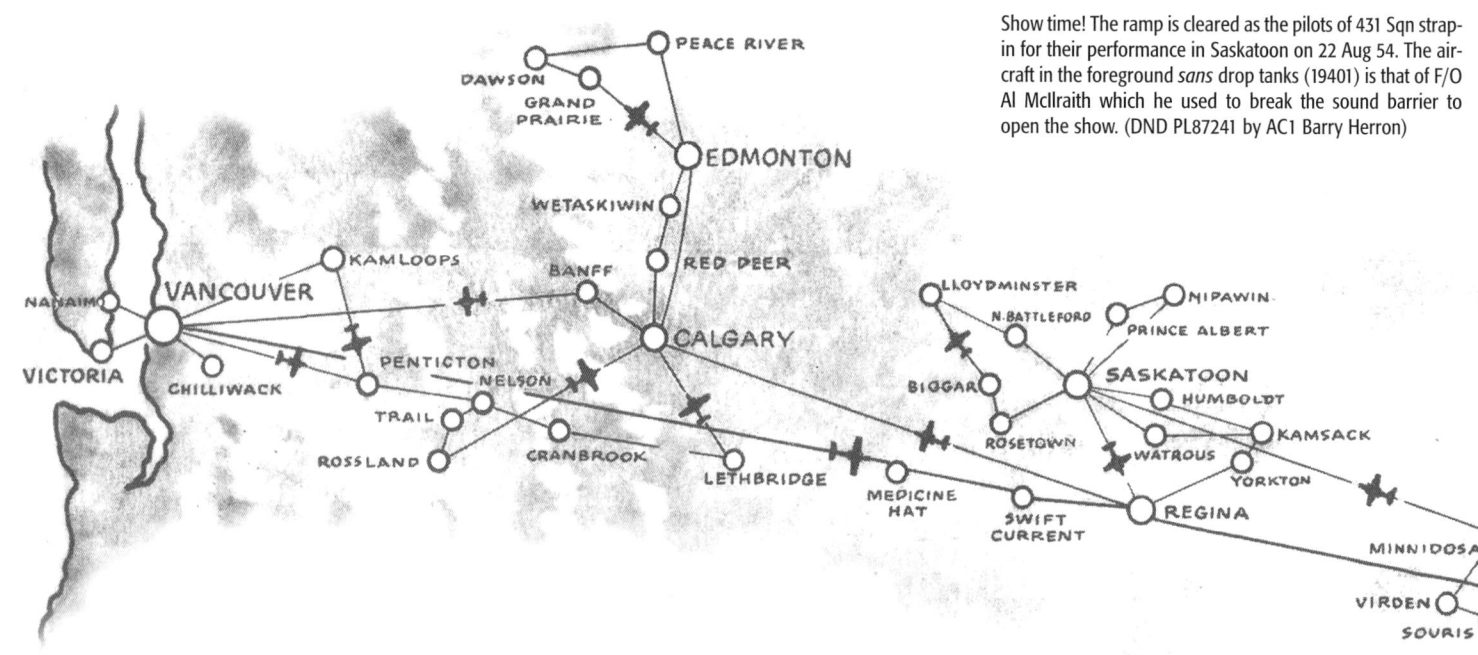

Show time! The ramp is cleared as the pilots of 431 Sqn strap-in for their performance in Saskatoon on 22 Aug 54. The aircraft in the foreground *sans* drop tanks (19401) is that of F/O Al McIlraith which he used to break the sound barrier to open the show. (DND PL87241 by AC1 Barry Herron)

S/L Pat Bing leads his CF-100 team across the field in Saskatoon for the benefit of 30,000 spectators, the biggest crowd in the city's history. (DND PL 87239 by AC1 Barry Herron)

Three C-119 Flying Boxcars provided essential airlift support for Prairie Pacific and were put on static display at each of the main showsites. RCAF photographer AC1 Barry Herron set up this PR shot of some of the crews. Pictured are, L to R kneeling – F/L C.N. Agar, F/Os R.H. Theissen, A. Pickering. Standing are LACs J. Watson, J.M. Brown, N.S. Justice, F/O A. Edwards, F/O J.L. Nelson, LAC M. La Plante. (DND PL 87252 by AC1 Barry Herron)

OPERATION PRAIRIE PACIFIC
1954

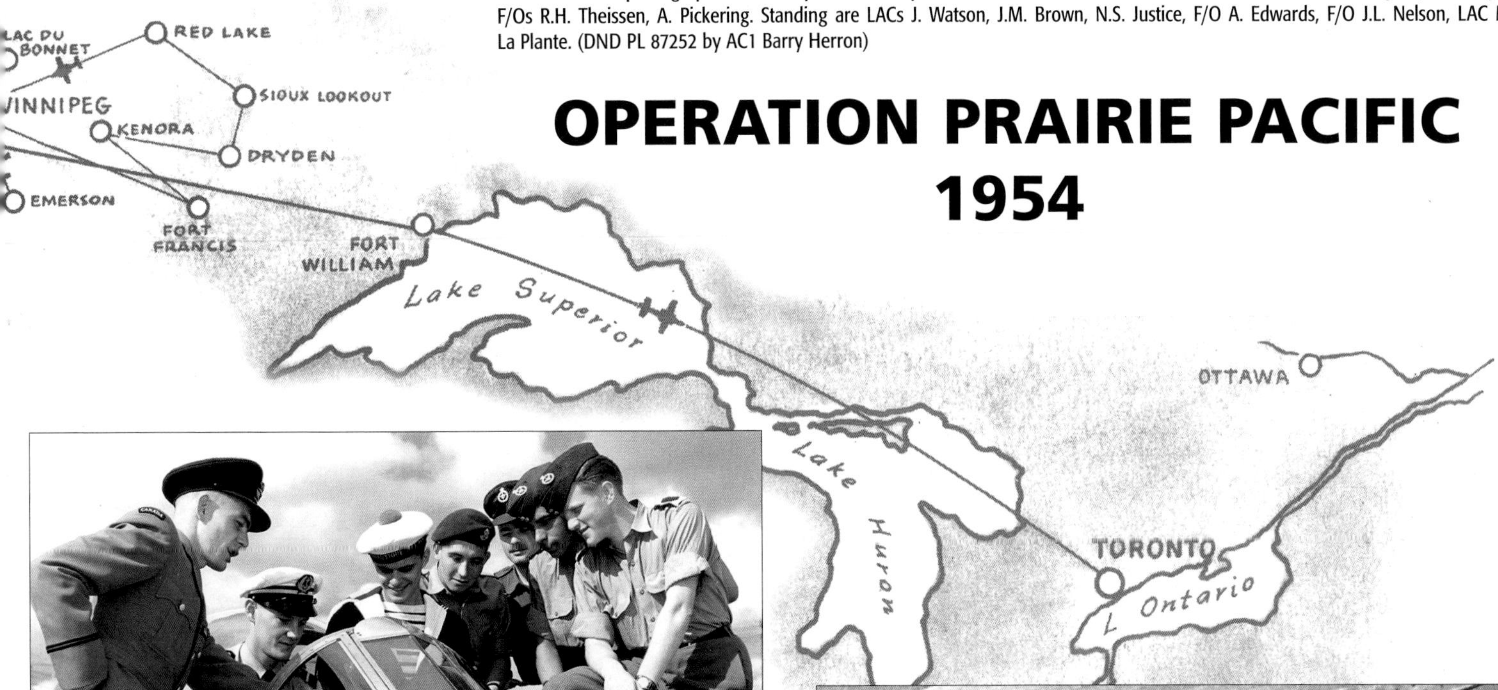

F/O Rod MacDonald of 431 Sqn gives a briefing on the Canadair Sabre 2 to a group of NATO students on course at the RCAF Air Navigation School in Winnipeg on 15 Aug 54. (DND PL 87253 by AC1 Barry Herron)

One of Vancouver's roving radio newsmen was taken up by S/L Lou Hill, leader of the Silver Star jet aerobatic team. Throughout the tour, the RCAF let Canada's newsmen and radio commentators do the talking—calling the shots as they saw them. Verdict? "Terrific." (*Jet age* by AC1 Barry Herron)

S/L Lou Hill of Central Flying School, leader of the Silver Stars. (RCAF photo via Lou Hill)

The Silver Stars fly their diamond formation over the Canadian prairies as depicted by John Rutherford of Kamloops, B.C. (via Lou Hill)

ing of being strapped into a parachute, stuffed into a tiny compartment and then having an oxygen mask seemingly glued to one's face has always been the major obstacle for the novice passenger – and that was before you even started to taxi! Then of course there was always the reassuring smile and last words from the crewman who had helped strapped the "volunteer" into the ejection seat, "Good luck, keep this bag handy and, whatever you do, don't touch those yellow handles!" Some of the press rides also produced unique problems, as team right winger F/L Russ Scott recalls: "The one I remember was in Vancouver when a young lady showed up for a flight dressed in a skirt! Lou assigned her to Jack Seaman to be fitted with a parachute since Jack was a low key,

casual type who could cope with that kind of pressure …"

The team groundcrew were led by Sgt G. Munro and played a pivotal role throughout the tour, as they always have on demonstration teams. Russ Scott characterizes their performance:

"The groundcrews were most impressive. They were volunteers, they worked hard and after normal duty hours in most cases, and they did not receive nearly the recognition

they deserved. They were dedicated to keeping those T-Birds in the air and looking good, and as a result the pilots were seldom without their chosen aircraft. They did not have team badges, special clothing or any other items to identify them as team members, so the *esprit de corps* was maintained by the individual's desire to be a part of something special, recognized or not. I no longer remember the names of the individual technicians, but I will not forget their contribution."

Russ Scott

F/L Russ Scott briefs reporter Ted Greenslade prior to a press flight in Vancouver on 29 Aug 54. (DND PL 87261 by AC1 Barry Herron)

The 1954 Silver Stars Aerobatic Team in Trenton just prior to departing for Prairie Pacific. Pilots L to R are F/L D. Payne, F/L R. Scott, S/L L. Hill, F/L J. Seaman and F/L A. Bowman. The NCO in charge of the ground personnel, Sgt G. Munro, is in the middle row, third from left. (RCAF photo via Lou Hill)

431 (F) Sqn Aerobatic Team

The second team to make up Prairie Pacific was an F-86 Sabre 2 aerobatic team from 431(F) Sqn, the first Sabre team to be authorized formation aerobatics in Canada. The team was made up of veteran Sabre pilots who had all served in the Air Division in Europe and was led by F/O Fern Villeneuve. His original wingmen were F/O George Fulford (right wing), F/O Fred Rudy (left wing) and F/O Art Maskell (slot). The oppor-

tunity to form the team early in 1954 transpired due to a unique set of circumstances, as Art Maskell recalls:

"431 Sqn was re-formed early in 1954 because A.V. Roe wasn't producing CF-100s quickly enough to form new squadrons. The CF-100 Sqn in Bagotville at the time was 440 AW(F) Sqn and since they were designated to go to Europe in the near future, it was decided to form an interim Sabre outfit to fill in until another CF-100 Sqn was ready. As a result, six of us who had reasonably high Sabre time were sent from the Air Div to 'Bagtown' while the squadron OC, two experienced flight commanders and remaining line pilots were all freshly graduated Sabre OTU pilots from Chatham.

We started flying in early February and it didn't take long for Fern Villeneuve to canvass us to see who wanted to form an aerobatic team. As a result, we started practicing formation aeros on March 22nd and did a few local airshows when requested plus a major airshow at the National Air Show in Toronto on June 12th."

Art Maskell

Fern Villeneuve was the obvious choice as leader of the team, having led the 441 Sqn aerobatic team in North Luffenham, England in the latter part of 1953. Since all of the teams of the day were considered secondary duties, it was not unusual for team members to swap in and out. It was up to the team leader to ensure that whatever repertoire had been designed remained safe. The only way to do so was through careful briefings and practice. When George Fulford left the team to go on a T-33 instrument course in late April, he was replaced on the right wing by F/O Rod MacDonald and another practice regimen had to begin. Art Maskell's logbook reveals the team did 10 successive daily practices leading up to the National Air Show on June 12th, and nothing else …

"100,000 JAM WATERFRONT" was the headline the day following the National Air Show in Toronto, reaffirming that city's standing as one of the premier locations for an aerial display in Canada. The show had been inaugurated in 1952 as a showcase for both the civilian and military aviation industries in Canada and had grown in popularity each year. The 1954 edition included an opening flypast of 16 RCAF jet aircraft and performances by a CF-100 formation from North Bay, Vampires from the local auxiliary

F/O Fern Villeneuve, formation leader and soloist of the 431 Sqn Aerobatic Team, prepares to mount his Sabre 2 for a solo performance at the Windsor Centennial Air Show in Jul 54.

The originals. The first 431 Sqn team to perform an official show did so at the National Air Show in Toronto on 12 Jun 54. Kneeling is leader Fern Villeneuve; behind are Rod MacDonald (right wing), Art Maskell (box) and Fred Rudy (left wing). (via Art Maskell)

squadrons, the Silver Stars Aerobatic Team and another sterling solo display by Zurakowski in the CF-100. Various flypasts also took place, including the Avro Jetliner, USAF F-86Ds, Scorpion interceptor and new B-47 strategic bomber. However, according to the *Toronto Telegram*, the highlight of the afternoon was the formation aerobatic display by 431 Sqn – "*A brilliant display of close pattern flying was given the record crowd of more than 100,000 by RCAF Sabre jets from Bagotville, Que. The jets reached a speed of 570 mph over the CNE waterfront.*" Obviously, the hard work by the team had paid off.

Canada Magnificent-Doolittle

The good…and the not so good. Two headlines – one which praised the RCAF for a superb display at the National Air Show and another a few days later which scolded it for low flying jets. The latter was unintentional and resulted when 431 Sqn took off from Downsview under a VFR clearance and was forced to stay at low altitude due to a lower than expected cloud ceiling over the city. (via Fred Rudy)

**JETS BUZZ CITY
HUNDREDS DUCK**

George Fulford rejoined the 431 team for Prairie Pacific, replacing Maskell who went on leave to get married. MacDonald and Rudy remained on their respective wings. Of his experience flying with the team, George Fulford has many fond memories that have lasted a lifetime: "That it was memorable and lots of fun goes without saying, and even now I will assert that Fern was the finest jet jockey I ever flew with. He could out fly me and anyone else in the sky, yet his personality was gentle and unassuming."

The Sabre portion of the Prairie Pacific show was similar in nature to the show performed by the Silver Stars, with one significant difference. At the conclusion of the four-ship formation aerobatics, Fern Villeneuve dropped off his wingmen and then went into a high performance solo aerobatic routine designed to demonstrate the superb handling characteristics of the Canadair Sabre. Weather permitting, his repertoire included a spin and an amazing eight consecutive vertical rolls straight up. No sooner was he off stage than in came the CF-100 team.

431 Sqn's Aerobatic Team for Prairie Pacific. Kneeling L to R – F/Os Fern Villeneuve (team leader), Rod MacDonald and Fred Rudy. Standing are F/Os George Fulford, J. Landreville and Al McIlraith. Landreville ferried in a spare aircraft and McIlraith opened the show with a sonic boom. (DND PL 87263, AC1 Barry Herron)

The groundcrews of Prairie Pacific played an indispensable role in the success of the operation. Three members of the team were LAC J.D. Sauve of 423 Sqn and Cpls A. Olynyk and O.W. Conn of 431 Sqn. (DND PL 87249, AC1 Barry Herron)

423 AW(F) Sqn Demonstration Team

The 423 Sqn Demonstration Team of Prairie Pacific. L to R, Front Row – the pilots, F/O Jack Des Brisay, F/L Don McNichol, S/L Pat Bing, F/O Al Hesjedahl, F/L Stu Woolley. Behind are their navs, F/Os Bill Cole, Larry Parakin, Peter Hawkes, "Shorty" McFarland and Ron Pratt. Missing are the crew of F/Os Ray Komar and Alex Martin who flew the first half of the tour. (DND 87264)

When the Chief of the Air Staff at AFHQ in Ottawa approved the concept of Prairie Pacific, there was no question that a team of CF-100s would be included. Like the Canadair Sabre and T-33, the CF-100 also carried the "Made in Canada" label, but with a difference – it had the distinction of being the only one of the three which had been totally designed in Canada as well. It was also the only all-weather interceptor in the RCAF inventory. With aviation design and manufacturing in Canada booming, this was a fact Avro Aircraft and her sister company, Orenda Engines, were eager to advertise. Orenda was building engines for all three aircraft in what was the beginning of a very long relationship with the RCAF and later Canadian Forces.

Air Defence Command tasked 423 Sqn, which had been re-formed on July 1st, 1953 at St. Hubert, to represent the CF-100 contingent in Prairie Pacific. Command of the team was handed to S/L Pat Bing. He explains how 423 Sqn first got involved in displaying Canada's new interceptor:

The team leader of 423 Sqn's CF-100 team, S/L Pat Bing, DFC. On the left and right respectively are F/Os Al Hesjedahl (solo) and Ray Komar (slot pilot). (DND PL87260)

"As we were the second CF-100 squadron to be formed with what was essentially a development aircraft only in operational service since April 1st, 1953, we were called on to show it off on many occasions. The first "formal" one was at the CNE in 1953 where we flew three aircraft in company with a similar flight from 445 Sqn in various changing formations. We flew every evening for 15 straight days (August 28th through September 11th) over the waterfront in front of the CNE grandstand. We flew out of Malton (now Pearson International) from the A.V. Roe plant where they provided us with a small shed which acted as a crew/operations room – pretty primitive conditions really. I led the formation with F/L Don McNichol and F/L Stu Woolley as wingmen. On September 19th we did the same show at the National Air Show.

The next summer we were tasked to form a team for Prairie Pacific which was designed to show the people of Western Canada the jet aircraft their air force was now using; there were no jets based west of North Bay at the

time. This operation ran from August 13th through to September 11th, 1954. The 423 Sqn crews comprised S/L Pat Bing / F/O Peter Hawkes (lead), F/L Don McNichol / F/O Larry Parakin (right wing), F/L Stu Woolley / F/O Ron Pratt (left wing), F/O Ray Komar / F/O Alex Martin (box), F/O Al Hesjedahl / F/O 'Shorty' McFarland (solo) and F/O Jack Des Brisay / F/O Bill Cole who flew the box for the second half of the tour.

We did flypasts all over the western provinces and airshows at major locations. Our show consisted of a four-plane display of various formations and at several of the shows F/O Al Hesjedahl did a solo aerobatic display of loops and rolls to close the show. Throughout the operation, we were supported by our own groundcrew under the supervision of engineering officer F/O Curt Barlow. They flew from showsite to showsite in one of three C-119 Flying Boxcars accompanied by tools and essential spares. At the end of Prairie Pacific, we flew at the CNE in Toronto on September 11th before returning to our base at St. Hubert. The tour had kept us on the road for an entire month and our groundcrew successfully kept us airborne throughout."

Pat Bing

Spectators by the Thousands

Although they had done a practice show the previous day for hundreds of air cadets, the Prairie Pacific tour formally got underway in Winnipeg on Sunday, August 15th when the RCAF opened Stevenson Field to the general public at 2 p.m. for a static display of the team's aircraft. At 3 p.m. the jets took to the air to wow the crowd, estimated to exceed 25,000. Although the full aerial displays were reserved for the major population centres in Western Canada, carefully plotted (and advertised) cross-country routings allowed dozens of communities to see the jets up close as they thundered over main streets in formation. For example, in a two-day period following the Winnipeg show, the Manitoba towns of Neepawa, Minnedosa, Brandon, Souris, Clear Lake, Dauphin, Carman, Morden, Winkler, Morris, Steinbach, Emerson, Teulon, Pine Falls, Lac du Bonnet, Chatfield, Winnipeg Beach, Grand Beach, Victoria Beach, Selkirk and Beausejour were all treated to flypasts by the 15 aircraft team. This was typical of what happened in every province along the way

and by the end of the tour some 79 prairie and western Ontario communities had seen the team. Wherever they appeared, thousands of citizens were waiting to see them. On occasion, pilots from one of the teams received approval to be dropped off at their hometown following the formation flypasts to do a little extra for the hometown crowd, as was the case on August 19th when F/O Fred Rudy thrilled the residents of Langenburg, Sask, he being *"well known in these parts."*

As the team moved west, shows were held in Saskatoon, Regina, Lethbridge, Calgary, Vancouver and Victoria. Unfortunately, weather played havoc with the tight schedule, resulting in cancellations of scheduled

In Toronto for one more performance at the CNE Air Show at the end of their 28 day tour, a clearly exhausted 423 Sqn groundcrew team join their aircrew for one last photo at A.V. Roe Canada's Malton plant. The groundcrew in front of the CF-100 Mk 3B are: L to R, Back Row – LAC Lindbloom, LAC Fontaine, Sgt Cleland, LAC Roberts, LAC Langerak (hand on aircraft), FS McNally (NCO i/c 423 Sqn Det). Middle Row - LAC Roussey, LAC Chadwick, LAC Demers, LAC Barret, LAC Wood, LAW de Sansoucy, F/O Barlow (423 Sqn Engineering Officer), LAW Koehn, Cpl Goulet, LAC Sauve, LAC Warwick. (via Pat Bing/Curt Barlow).

displays in Moose Jaw and Edmonton and severely restricting the show in Calgary. The show created the largest traffic jams in the history of Saskatoon and Vancouver and attendance records were broken at every location. The press had a field day – newspaper headlines included: "Large Crowd Watches Jet Display" (*Winnipeg Tribune*), "Thousands See and Hear Daring Jet Aerial Show" (*Saskatoon Star Phoenix*), "Thousands Watch Jets Despite Traffic Tangle" (Calgary *Herald*), "100,000 See

Sound Barrier Crashed" (*Vancouver Sun*) and "Traffic Record Broken – Cars Jam Airport" (Vancouver *Province*). The traffic jam in Vancouver was atrocious, as reported by the *Province*: *"The worst traffic jam in city history tied up an estimated 100,000 people in the Richmond-Sea Island area Sunday. Half of them packed the airport to watch an RCAF jet show; the other half never did get there. After the show, it took five hours for traffic to return to normal on narrow roads leaving the airport."*

On the return trip east from Vancouver, a show was held at Port Arthur/Fort William (Lakehead) on September 5th. By this time the RCAF had already tasked all three teams to perform at the CNE in Toronto on September 11th. This was the 10th and final show for the Prairie Pacific entourage, some 200,000 spectators taking in the CNE show. The following day the teams headed back to their respective bases, 431 to be disbanded again in October. *Operation Prairie Pacific* had been a highly successful endeavour, exceeding everyone's expectations and once again demonstrating to Canadians that the RCAF was operating at the leading edge of technology. Almost half a million Canadians had taken in the show.

The Lancers – No. 1 Fighter OTU Chatham

The disbandment of 431 Sqn in October 1954 left the Sabre community in Canada without an aerobatic team. With the overwhelming success of Prairie Pacific, this simply would not do. The seeds had been planted and with No. 1 (F) OTU at RCAF Stn Chatham being the repository of experience in the country, the air force had to look no further to find a leader amongst the instructional staff. F/L Garth Cinnamon, with experience on both the 410 and 1 Wing aerobatic teams, happily found himself tasked to form a new team in March 1955. Sadly, it would turn out to be the shortest-lived team in Canada's air force history, as he explains:

"I left 410 Sqn in October 1954 and arrived at the Sabre OTU early in December '54. Around Christmas time the chief flying instructor, S/L Eric Smith, told me that AFHQ was considering the idea of having an aerobatic team tour Canada in the summer of 1955. He indicated that he planned on leading the team and wondered if I was interested in being on it. Nothing more was said about it until March when he told me there was to be a team and he offered me the opportunity to form and lead it. Once I accepted, I was sent over to the Air Div in Europe to select four more team members. The Air Div pilots had to be selected from the single guys who were being transferred back to Canada that summer.

I spent the last two weeks of April 1955 at 4 Wing Baden selecting from a group of seven or eight pilots who were interested in being on the team. The selection of the pilots was difficult enough, but it was compounded by a lack of support from "the brass" at 4 Wing and Air Div HQ – the usual problem of lack of aircraft and hours. We were to have six aircraft for the tryouts. One of the six was in periodic inspection the whole time. One other only had six hours left to inspection. No replacement! Another had a "minor" entry in the blue sheets 'ailerons tend to snag during rolls.' Needless to say, not too happy a camp! With time running out, I made my selections by the end of April after 20 sorties and headed back to Chatham with Jack Frazer, Norm Garriock, Danny Campbell and Doug Evjen.

The Chatham Lancers official PR photos taken on 18 May 55. The team was cancelled two days later. Top to bottom – F/L Garth Cinnamon, F/O Norm Garriock, F/O Jack Frazer, F/O Dan Campbell. (RCAF Photos)

There seemed to be disagreement at AFHQ in Ottawa at the time about the need for an RCAF display team in Canada. The one person very much in favour of having a team was the Chief of the Air Staff himself, A/M C. Roy Slemon. The fact that he left on a four week tour of India, South Asia and Australia about the same time I went over to Air Div to select pilots may have reflected in the treatment we received while at 4 Wing. As for support at RCAF Stn Chatham, it was nothing but the best. The station CO was G/C McKenna, the OC of the OTU, W/C Bill Smith and the CFI, S/L Eric Smith. We were given our pick of Sabre aircraft and were assigned an engineering officer and ground-crew team to travel with us. The national tour was to begin in mid-to-late June and go through to the end of August.

By mid-May 1955 we were finally getting everything organized and had just started to work up a four-plane aerobatic program when we had a mid-air and Doug Evjen was killed on only our second practice. The mid-air didn't happen during a manoeuvre however, but in the circuit downwind following the practice. The accident occurred on Friday, May 13th at the end of our second training flight of the day at Chatham. We had been cleared into the circuit for a low pitch from 200 feet AGL, at two second intervals to downwind at 1,500 feet. Ground and tower observers reported this went smoothly and the four aircraft rolled out nicely spaced about a 1,000 feet apart downwind. At this time, the tower told us we were number two to a T-33 on base. I looked and looked, quite a few seconds, and finally spotted the T-bird two to three miles out on base leg. I told the tower we would all be on the ground before he turned final, reached for the undercarriage and started to turn base when the collision occurred. For some unexplained reason, Doug, who was flying number 2, overtook me and collided with me from below. The tip of his vertical stab hit the belly of my aircraft putting him into a violent pitch-up. The rudder and part of his vertical stab ended up stuck over the leading edge of my left wing.

His aircraft went into a flat spin but he never made any attempt to eject. The only explanation that I could see for these actions was that he was unconscious during all this, possibly due to hyperventilating or having had a problem with his oxygen. I was able to control my aircraft down to 210 or 220 knots, so managed to get away with a fairly high-speed landing. The T-33 in the transport type

Two rare photos of Sabre 23286, the only Sabre 5 ever painted in Lancer colours. (via Eric Smith and Larry Milberry)

circuit turned out to be the first T-33 solo of a 426 Sqn North Star driver who wanted a jet check-out on his record.

We resumed practices the following Monday but on Friday, the 20th, we suddenly received a message cancelling the team. In the week following our accident, a Harvard aerobatic team also had a fatal accident during practice. The net result – AFHQ cancelled all aerobatic teams in Canada – the detractors had won the day. The team name was to have been 'The Lancers.'"

Garth Cinnamon

At the time of the team's sudden disbandment, they had just received their first Sabre 5 in new team colours, featuring a unique diamond paint scheme on its nose, wings and tail. Unfortunately, none of the team members ever got a chance to fly Sabre 23286. It was kept in its colours at the OTU for several weeks, perhaps in the hope that the higher echelons would change their minds. The only public appearance the aircraft ever made was in the hands of S/L Eric Smith when he led a massive RCAF flypast to open the Canadian International Air Show in Toronto on June 4th, 1955. Ironically, like the team, Sabre 23286 also suffered an early demise, being written off in an 'A' Category accident (total write-off) in Chatham on October 27th of that year.

Notwithstanding this setback, the desire to field a national jet aerobatic team in Canada became deeply ingrained in the minds of many RCAF personnel, not the least of which were the Sabre pilots in Chatham. Success of several squadron and wing teams in Europe had filtered back to the OTU – this would be way more fun than instructing! When the unit was invited/ordered to participate in a flypast at the CNE Air Show on September 9th, 1955, someone came up with the brilliant idea to paint the aircraft red, as if to send a not so subtle message to the Canadian public and brass alike. So off they went to Trenton on September 6th with eight bright red Sabre 5s, Eric Smith leading one section and Garth Cinnamon the other. Someone laughingly referred to them as the "Red Eyed Vultures." Trenton and the Toronto waterfront were a blaze of red as they practiced the mass flypast on each of the 6th, 7th and 8th with the "official" flypast taking place on the 9th. But their quest for a new Sabre team would go unheeded for another three years – for now, most of the fun would remain with the boys in the Air Div.

The No. 1 (F) OTU instructor's version of 'painting the town red' for their appearance at the CNE Air Show on 9 Sep 55, seen en route to Trenton and on the ramp after arrival. (John Ursulak, via Larry Milberry)

Flying the Flag in Europe – The Air Division Teams

The decision to commit an entire air division comprising four wings and 12 squadrons of brand new Sabre 2s to Western Europe in support of NATO was the largest peacetime overseas basing of fighter aircraft in Canadian history. The first Sabre squadron to deploy was 410 Sqn which had been the first RCAF Sqn to take possession of the new fighter on May 19th, 1951. Their Sabres, along with those earmarked for 441 Sqn (35 in total), were initially ferried from Dorval to Norfolk, Virginia. At Norfolk, the US Navy lent a hand by loading the aircraft onto HMCS *Magnificent* at which time she sailed for the UK, arriving at Glasgow, Scotland on November 13th. From there it was a short hop to North Luffenham – the home of No. 1 Fighter Wing for the first three years. On February 13th, 1952, 441 Sqn pilots and groundcrew set sail from Saint John, New Brunswick aboard the *Empress of France* to catch up with their aircraft. Much to the delight of the pilots of 439 Sqn, which had been re-formed at RCAF Stn Uplands on September 1st, 1951, the squadron got the nod to be the first to fly their aircraft to Europe. They departed Uplands on May 30th, 1952 on "Leapfrog 1" and arrived at North Luff on the 14th of June, thus rounding out 1 Wing.

By the time the last three Canadian squadrons arrived at 4 Wing on September 4th, 1953 via "Leapfrog 4," the Air Division comprised 12 squadrons, as illustrated by Ray Cryderman:

The first public appearance by Canadian Sabres in England took place on 12 Jul 52 courtesy 410 Cougar Sqn. L to R – F/O Garth Cinnamon, S/L Duke Warren, F/Os Bob Gibson, Len Bentham, Francis Sylvester. (DND PL 62323)

1 Wing North Luffenham and Marville

441 "Silver Fox" Squadron

410 "Cougar" Squadron

439 "Sabre Tooth Tiger" Squadron

2 Wing Grostenquin

421 "Red Indian" Squadron

416 "Lynx" Squadron

430 "Silver Falcon" Squadron

3 Wing Zweibrücken

427 "Lion" Squadron

413 "Tusker" Squadron

434 "Bluenose" Squadron

4 Wing Baden-Soellingen

422 "Tomahawk" Squadron

414 "Black Knight" Squadron

444 "Cobra" Squadron

The arrival of 410 Sqn in England with their Sabre 2s was big news as it marked the first time in history that a Commonwealth squadron had more modern equipment than the Royal Air Force. With the USAF having already deployed the F-86A in Europe, the RAF was feeling decidedly behind the power curve. They badly wanted into the Sabre program – when North American Aircraft could not oblige the Air Ministry's request, they turned to Canadair who came to the rescue. The RAF finally joined the "swept wing" club in January 1953, eventually taking delivery of 430 Canadair Sabres, primarily Mk 4s.

Meanwhile, 410 pilots were merrily adapting to their new environment in North Luff – engaging in air-to-air GCI (ground control intercept) exercises and air-to-ground gunnery practice on a routine basis. For the locals, it was impossible to miss the clean lines of the Sabre or the beautiful contrails the Canadian gaggles were weaving over the English countryside whenever the weather permitted. Being keen aviation enthusiasts, it was only natural that British citizens wanted to get a closer look at the new aircraft. One of their first opportunities to do so was at the National Air Races held at Newcastle on July 12th, 1952. Led by their new OC, S/L Duke Warren (an ex-Spitfire pilot), the Cougars were happy to oblige a request to put on a display for the air race fans, doing so with five Sabres. Warren's wingmen were

F/Os Garth Cinnamon, Bob Gibson, Len Bentham and Francis Sylvester. By all accounts, they put on a dazzling display, demonstrating "a new high in aerial wizardry" according to the 410 Sqn History Book. News of the Cougar participation made it all the way back to Canadian newspapers, complete with photographs.

Originals From All Over Ontario

Windsor Jet Plane Pilot Figures in British Display

News of the 410 Sqn appearance at the National Air Races in England made it back to Canada, this photo appearing in the *Windsor Daily Star* on 2 Aug 52. (via Garth Cinnamon)

At the end of July, Duke Warren led the squadron to Soosterburg, Holland to participate in a major airshow at Ypenburg Airport (The Hague) on August 2nd and 3rd. Over 100,000 spectators took in the three-and-a-half hour non-stop show. One of many fascinations with the Sabre was its ability to break the sound barrier, dropping a sonic boom that could be heard for miles. The mere thought of an aircraft going that fast stirred the imagination and naturally, the Dutch airshow organizers were eager to have the Canadians show off this capability. Holland is of course a beautiful land of windmills, canals, fields-upon-fields of flowers and … greenhouses … lots of them! Duke Warren was careful to warn the airshow organizers that sonic booms would break glass in the area. "Do you really want the booms?" They did – and they got them – along with a lot of broken glass. There were no repercussions, however, the locals being suitably impressed. Press accounts the next day praised the Canadian presence – "*One of the highlights of the demonstrations was the formation of twelve Canadian Sabres, creating waves of sensation among the crowd by sweeping again and again across the field at the rate of more than 1,000 km an hour.*" (*Haarlems Dagblad*, Haarlem); "*The exhibition of the twelve Canadians, in three teams of four, over Ypenburg was bewildering.*" (*De Maasbode*, Rotterdam); "*The Sabres punctured the barrier with an almost deafening bang.*" (*Dagbl.voor N.Limberg*, Venlo)

410 (F) Sqn Aerobatic Team

The appearances at Newcastle and Ypenburg planted the seed for the RCAF's first foreign-based aerobatic team. The squadron had participated in a number of public flypasts, including those commemorating the Battle of Dieppe in August and the Battle of Britain in September. It was following a similar multi-national flypast over Fontainbleau, France that the subject of a dedicated team came up. F/L Grant Nichols was the senior member of 410 Sqn present at the time and explains:

"Whilst debriefing at a local *café* in Reims over a couple of jugs of champagne, F/O Garth Cinnamon suggested that 410 should form an aerobatic team before some other squadron thought if it. By this time I was a flight lieutenant and a flight commander, so that made me the leader! On the next flight after returning to base, Garth and I tried some formation loops and rolls – no problem. A few flights later, F/O Len 'Speed' Bentham went up with us; we put him in the box and he liked it. We then tried two or three others in the left wing position until F/O Al Robb asked to go along – he fit in the No. 3 slot like an old glove.

All of this was done on the sly and took some time since we did our practice aeros at the tail end of our regular flights. It wasn't always possible to get the prospective team members up together. I think we had only flown one or two flights with the four of us together when I approached the squadron OC, S/L Duke Warren, and suggested it would be a splendid idea to have a 410 Sqn aerobatic team! When he agreed, I then allowed that, in fact, we could have one right then and there as we had done a couple of practices. He said 'show me' and then flew his Sabre in trail to watch the four of us put on a short practice routine. Happy with what he saw, he subsequently went to the station CO and got permission for us to do a 'show'

The 410 Sqn Aerobatic Team. L to R – F/O Len Bentham (slot), S/L Duke Warren (OC 410 Sqn), F/L Grant Nichols (leader), F/O Al Robb (left wing), F/O Garth Cinnamon (right wing). (*Flight* via Al Robb)

for a visiting dignitary, Field Marshal Alexander. That took place on November 14th, 1952 and was our first chance to use the airfield and go on 'public' display.

Our concept was to stay close to the display area at all times by doing high climbing and diving dumbbell turns, constantly changing speed, altitude and direction. I timed the completion of the dumbbells to be in front of the focal point and then proceeded into the next aerobatic manoeuvre without a break. We changed formations during the dumbbells. In due course the four of us got very comfortable flying together. 'Speed' took great pride in the fact that his tight flying in the box resulted in the top of his tail being blackened by my exhaust. A black nose painted on my Sabre was the only non-standard marking – other than that there were no official team markings. There weren't any altitude restrictions to begin with, so we used about 100 feet. Of course, a big problem in England was the weather and the routine had to be modified as necessary from time to time. We did four-plane formation takeoffs but a normal fighter break and stream landing. In those days the break constituted a power off, hard 360 degree turn, rolling out just before touchdown. It was a point of pride to pull 'streamers' on the break.

I was posted to Korea in January 1953 and returned to the squadron in early June. At that point S/L Warren was sent to Korea and I took over 410 Sqn for six months. We started up the team again and put on a few more shows at RAF bases. The only official 'media' comment I am aware of was a favourable one in *Flight* magazine. We were doing an 'official' day at a Royal Navy flying base in southern Wales and the weather was quite poor with low overcast cloud and rain. The other performing teams contented themselves with straight flypasts in different formations, as did we – except I decided to show the flag a bit. We did a slow roll in box formation which got everyone's attention and received favourable comment in the magazine. One of our last shows was for Air Force Day at North Luff in 1953. By this time, both 441 Sqn and 439 Sqn had aerobatic teams which performed as well. Later that year, 410 was chosen to perform for the Chief of the Air Staff at the official opening of 2 Wing in Grostenquin, France. We got airborne out of Luffenham but were recalled when the weather deteriorated over Grostenquin, culminating in a hangar roof blowing off.

Grant Nichols leads his charges through a roll for *Flight* magazine's John Yoxall, crammed in the back seat of an RAF Gloster Meteor 7. (via Al Robb)

Because we had relatively little practice, 'we' meaning all of these first Sabre teams, we had some interesting moments. We were practicing between cloud layers one day and just as I started up in a barrel roll, an Oxford appeared in front of us. We cleared him nicely in the inverted position and never heard anything later. I often wonder if he ever saw us, and if he did, if he rechecked his instruments! Our bomb burst manoeuvre was always interesting. We would pull up into the vertical in box formation at which point Speed would roll 180 degrees, Garth and Al 90 degrees, and we would all loop through, coming back across the field from four different directions. The idea was to adjust the speed so all four aircraft crossed centre stage simultaneously as low as possible, with each

man watching out for the man on his right. With a runway as a guide it wasn't too bad with lead and No. 4 each flying down the right edge of the runway, but it was a bit exciting at times …"

Grant Nichols

Within three weeks of their first show in mid-November 1952, *Flight* magazine of the UK sought and received permission to fly with the 410 Sqn team. Two flights were made on the 4th and 7th of December with the resultant photo spread on the team being released on December 26th. As Al Robb recalls, the flights were not routine: "The two seat Meteor 7 with the cameraman could not stay with us at our normal aerobatic manoeuvring speeds. The rolls were okay, but to accomplish a loop we had to formate on him at a lower speed. The top of the loop produced a good picture despite the fact we were almost stalled – 'Speed' ran out of power in the slot which caused him to fall back from his normal position." Nevertheless, this exposure by a very highly respected aviation magazine did much to heighten the awareness of the Canadian presence in Europe and underscored the valuable role an aerobatic team could play in fostering good will among its allies and their citizens. This was clearly evidenced by the huge

crowd of over 35,000 spectators that turned up for the "At Home" Air Force Day at North Luffenham on September 19th, 1953. It was a busy day for the 410 team – after doing a full show at Luffenham, they landed, refuelled and then took off again to do abbreviated performances at three RAF stations, all on the same flight!

The fun and challenge of doing airshows in the Sabre was by no means limited to a dedicated "team" of pilots, and most squadron pilots got the opportunity to do their thing "solo" at various venues around England and on the continent. Low-level aerobatics required a high degree of skill, knowledge and discipline (not to mention a healthy dose of self-preservation), but were a natural extension of low-level flying and air-to-air combat which all squadron pilots were required to do. Fighter aircraft of all descriptions were always in high demand around Battle of Britain Sunday each September. In 1953 for example, 410 had three pilots do low-level aerobatic displays that day: F/L Gibson at North Luffenham, F/O Potter at Thorny Island and F/O Knox-Leet at Weston Zoyland. Pilots who weren't involved in doing aerobatics of some description on these days were usually wrapped up in some kind of formation fly-past with the rest of the wing.

King of the Solos – F/L Dean Kelly

In terms of solo aerobatics, one Sabre pilot deserves special mention. F/L Dean Kelly of 441 Sqn fame is widely regarded by his peers as having probably been the greatest solo aerobatic pilot ever to fly in the Sabre era. A veteran of WW II on the Spitfire and Hurricane, he flew solo for the Blue Devils on the Vampire in the summer of 1951 prior to being posted to 441 Sqn as a flight commander. But it was his airshows in the Sabre that created his legendary status. He put on his first "public" show over North Luffenham for a small group of visitors in terrible weather on March 18th, 1952, less than three weeks after the squadron had commenced flying in theatre. His next audience was somewhat larger – 100,000 at an airshow at Yeadon, Yorks on June 2nd!

F/L Dean Kelly of 441 (F) Sqn, regarded by many as one of the finest demo pilots ever to fly in the RCAF. (DND PL 62278)

There are probably not too many superlatives in the English language that haven't been used to describe Kelly's shows, but here is a fairly representative commentary by someone who watched him perform many times, Grant Nichols of 410 Sqn: "Dean put on the most hair-raising solos I've ever seen. One famous photo in the English *Flight* magazine shows Dean recovering from a slow-speed loop started below the height of the control tower. He recovered at the same height – below the tower with big 'streamers' coming off each wingtip. This was not a mistake on his part – this and other similar manoeuvres were all done deliberately and expertly." Others who flew with Kelly marvelled at his

A "before and after" through the lens of John Yoxall's camera. On the bottom, the 410 diamond sets up for a loop; approaching the top the Meteor 7 hangs in on the wing to capture a superb shot, but the relatively slow speed has caused the slotman to stretch out of the photo. (via Al Robb)

Dean Kelly runs in for a manoeuvre during a practice at North Luffenham. In the foreground, his commanding officer's Sabre 2 is being readied for a gunnery mission. (RCAF photo via Larry Milberry)

abnormally high tolerance for sustained G and the fact that he could fly the aircraft safely outside the airspeed design envelope. This he did with regularity during his show, on one manoeuvre going from a slow pass into the first half of a loop and then gently doing a roll-off-the-top below the advertised stall speed of the Sabre.

As any demonstration pilot will readily admit, the toughest audience to perform for is another group of aviators, especially fighter pilots and test pilots. Why? Simply because these aviators aren't easily impressed by routine aerobatic manoeuvres flown at standard altitudes – they know what is difficult and what is not. One of Kelly's most critical audiences was undoubtedly that at RAF West Raynham on July 1st, 1952 when a large number of pilots put on demonstrations. Their aircraft included the DH 110, Avro 707B, Supermarine Swift, Supermarine 508, Hawker 1067 as well as production aircraft such as the Seafire, Venom, Attacker, Vampire, Meteor, F-84 Thunderstreak, B-45, B-29 Superfortress and Vickers Valiant jet bomber. There was even a "live" ejection from a Meteor. But it was Dean Kelly that stole the show with his ultra low-level Sabre demo, causing one seasoned British test pilot to remark, "I've never seen an aircraft flown so close to the bone." Not bad publicity for the RCAF!

441 (F) Sqn Aerobatic Team

With squadron *esprit de corps* and rivalry being major players in the fighter community, it was no surprise that 441 Sqn pilots aspired to form their own formation team shortly after 410 Sqn got their team up and running. The "Silver Fox" squadron had been re-formed on March 1st, 1951 at RCAF Stn St. Hubert and their airshow involvement began before they arrived in England. The squadron's diary reveals that 441 selected ex-Blue Devil, F/O Larry Spurr, to lead a three-ship Vampire formation aerobatic display with wingmen

Simmons and Weeks over Quebec City on June 3rd, 1951, where they received a very warm welcome. The OC of the squadron, S/L A.R. "Andy" MacKenzie, also got involved when he took part in an early Sabre airshow with F/Os Simmons and Atherton at Trenton on October 12th – this one to salute the Royal Visit of Princess Elizabeth and the Duke of Edinburgh.

Once in England, Battle of Britain Sunday became the focus of a huge squadron effort – on September 20th, 1952 no less than 10 squadron pilots put on Sabre displays at 10 different RAF bases. Gar Brine did the honours for the hometown crowd at North

The original members of the 441 (F) Sqn Aerobatic Team. L to R – F/Os Jean Gaudry (slot), Ralph Annis (left wing), Fern Villeneuve (right wing) and Gar Brine (leader). (RCAF Photo)

A magnificent shot of the 441 team passing through the vertical of a loop. On leader Villeneuve's left wing is F/O Bob Haverstock, on his right is F/O Norm Ronaasen and in the box is F/O Jean Gaudry. The chase T-33 was flown by former team member Ralph Annis, later selected to join Villeneuve on the RCAF Golden Hawks. (RCAF Photo via Ralph Annis)

Luffenham. Little wonder then, that when F/Os Gar Brine, Fern Villeneuve, Ralph Annis and Jean Gaudry approached their boss in late 1952 with a request to do some formation aerobatics, he readily approved. With blessing in hand, they began some limited practicing, initially in two-plane elements. Fern Villeneuve's logbook records his first formation aerobatic sortie on December 5th, the next one not occurring until the 11th. However, this was a beginning. The winter doldrums put the usual damper on flying in England but by mid-April the team was back together and raring to go. Practices became more commonplace and gradually the four developed a safe and appealing four-plane show. Their first opportunity to strut their stuff came on a most auspicious occasion – the visit of His Royal Highness the Duke of Edinburgh to 1 Wing on May 21st, 1953. This was a major event for the entire station and nothing was overlooked in preparing for the Royal Visit. The Duke was treated to a wing flypast of 12 Sabres, a *"breathtaking display of solo aerobatics"* by F/L Dean Kelly followed by *"a beautiful display of precision flying in the form of formation aerobatics"* by the 441 team according to the station's local newspaper. *The Tailpipe* summed up the visit in this way: *"A great honour has been bestowed on Number 1 Fighter Wing in this, its first opportunity to be host to a mem-*

show at the National Air Races at Southend-on-Sea, their last demonstration with Gar Brine as leader. Having given a glowing report on the solo aerobatics of F/O Bob Gibson of 410 Sqn, *Flight* magazine added this tribute to the 441 team: *"The four other Sabres of 441 Sqn gave as graceful and effortless a formation display as could a corps de ballet. Their slow, slow rolls, the speed with which they were back for the next manoeuvre and finally, their bomb shell breakaway – and high-speed criss-cross – were all outstanding examples of master demonstration flying."*

At the end of the summer Brine was transferred back to the OTU in Chatham and Ralph Annis proceeded to Zweibrücken to instruct at the Air Div Instrument Training Flight. Fern Villeneuve took over leadership of the team, recruiting Norm Ronaasen to fly right wing and Bob Haverstock to fly left; Jean Gaudry remained in the box. Villeneuve led the team through 13 practices starting on the 31st of August in preparation for what would turn out to be their last two shows – RAF Stn Horsham St. Faith on the occasion of their Battle of Britain Open House and the North Luffenham "At Home," both taking place on September 19th, 1953. Although this ended the season for the 441 Sqn team, they would fly a rare photo trip

439 (F) Sqn Aerobatic Team

The last group of intrepid aviators to arrive at North Luffenham were the Tigers of 439 Sqn. They did so in style, flying 21 Sabre 2s across the Atlantic for the first time. Thanks to Mother Nature, it wasn't the smoothest of operations, taking the squadron over two weeks by the time they finally landed at North Luffenham on Sunday, June 15th, 1952. In a classy gesture, 441 Sqn scrambled five Sabres to intercept the weary travellers and escort them in to North Luff on the last leg of their journey.

Like their predecessors, it took 439 several months to get comfortable in their new surroundings. Since 410 and 441 Sqns were by now both well ensconced in their NATO roles, the pressure was on 439 to catch up as quickly as possible. Although airshows were clearly of secondary importance at the time, it didn't take the squadron long to get into the public eye. World War II veteran, F/O Ken Cheesman, was given the honour of leading a four-ship of Tigers over Brighton on August 17th in a salute to the Canadian soldiers that had been billeted in the area prior to setting sail on the ill-fated Dieppe raid 10 years earlier. As for dedicated airshows however, the other two squadrons were eagerly lapping up all of the requests. Naturally, it wasn't fair for the other guys to be having all the fun – and getting all of the publicity – so it was finally F/L Harry Wenz who instigated the formation of a 439 team. F/O Laurie Hamilton was eager to participate and flew right wing with the team:

RCAF 1 Wing North Luffenham received a visit by HRH The Duke of Edinburgh on 21 May 53. Escorted by G/C Ed Hale and W/C Doug Lindsay, Prince Philip is about to be introduced to F/O Gar Brine, leader of the 441 Sqn aerobatic team. (via 441 Tac (F) Sqn)

ber of the Royal Family and in the hearts of everyone is the fond wish that we may be so privileged again in the not too distant future."

On June 4th, the team put on a display for the troops at 3 Wing in Zweibrücken. This was followed on the 20th by another major

on October 8th with Ralph Annis who flew over from Zweibrücken in a T-33. Fern Villeneuve would also do one more solo aerobatic display at RAF Wattisham on October 25th prior to being posted back to Canada. But this stint with 441 Sqn was not the end of his career in the airshow business, it was only the beginning …

Two views of 439 Sqn Sabre 2s and the tigers who flew them across the Atlantic on Leapfrog 1. L to R, Front row – Al Seitz, Ken Cheesman, Ken Jennett, H.F. Reischman, A. Everard, T.D. Wheeler, *Len Pappas*, Tom Wilson. Centre row – S. Hannah, *Laurie Hamilton*, Blake Smiley, *Harry Wenz*, Cal Bricker (OC), Bill Bliss, *Dick Wingate*, Charles Wilkinson. Back row – Ray Laroche, Ray Contly, Ray Bedard, Frank Fowler, Frank Raymond, Herb Ruecker, George Fitzgerald. Pilots who flew on the squadron aerobatic team are shown in italics. (George Fitzgerald, sqn photo DND PL 54293)

The 439 team was officially formed in August 1953 and remained in existence until May of 1954 when a composite wing demonstration team was formed. The 439 team consisted of F/L Harry Wenz (lead), F/O Laurie Hamilton (right wing), F/O Dick Wingate (left wing) and F/O Len Pappas (slot).

After a short but intensive workup, we performed at North Luffenham's Battle of Britain Open House on September 20th, 1953 and at a number of similar RAF and 'Royal Air Forces' Association events. In October 1953, both Dick Wingate and Len Pappas were transferred and F/O Mac Gillies and F/O Jeb Kerr took their places. The English winter of 1953-54 was one of the worst on record for snow, fog and freezing temperatures which severely restricted a great deal of our flying activities. Consequently, between December 1953 and March 1954, we did very little formation aerobatics except for a few flights to maintain our skills.

We performed on April 23rd, 1954 for the newly appointed Chief of Air Staff, Air Marshal C.R. Slemon. As it turned out, this was to be our final performance as in May of 1954, Harry Wenz and I were transferred back to Canada."

J. Laurie Hamilton

By early 1954, 1 Wing had been in operation for over two years and many of the "original" squadron pilots began to get posted to new assignments. This natural evolution necessitated a period of adjustment for all of the squadrons as new "sprogs" arrived fresh out of the OTU in Chatham, eager to take advantage of the superb flying (and *après* flying!) that a fighter tour in Europe had to offer. The loss of experience also began to have an effect on each of the three squadron aerobatic teams. Competition being what it was among the squadrons to be the best, in all facets of flying, led to the conclusion that the time was ripe for a new approach. This change of philosophy ushered in the era of the "Wing" aerobatic team.

The 439 Sqn Aerobatic Team in the winter of 1954. It gave way to the formation of a 1 Wing composite team in May '54. L to R – F/O Jeb Kerr (slot), F/O Mac Gillies (left wing), S/L Mars Belleau (OC 439 Sqn), F/L Harry Wenz (leader) and F/O Laurie Hamilton (right wing). (RCAF photo via Laurie Hamilton)

A photo from the 1 Wing newspaper, *The Tailpipe*, praising the performance of the 439 Tigers during their home base show for the Chief of the Air Staff on 23 Apr 54. (via 439 Combat Support Sqn)

1 (F) Wing Aerobatic Team

Dick Wingate had been cooling his heels as a simulator instructor on the station and was rewarded with an offer to become the leader of the 1 (F) Wing team. It probably didn't take more than a nanosecond to accept that offer! He was joined by F/Os Mac Gillies (439), Norm Ronaasen (441) and Jeb Kerr (439). Since all four already had experience with their respective squadron aerobatic teams, it didn't take them long to work up a fine show from the time they started practicing together on May 31st, 1954. Their first show was a two-day affair at the National Air Races at Badington aerodrome (near Coventry) on June 18th and 19th. They were accompanied by Dean Kelly and as usual the Canadians acquitted themselves very well, in spite of poor weather. Two additional shows were flown in June at St. Evans and North Luffenham. July and August were quiet months for the team and just as they were about to gear up again in September, disaster struck – Mac Gillies was killed in a car accident. This was a great loss for the team and left them in a bind.

A quick tally of wing personnel revealed that the only pilot left with any team experience under his belt was F/O Garth Cinnamon of 410 Sqn, who was preparing to depart on a posting to the OTU in Chatham. However, he readily agreed to help out the team and on September 13th four Sabres leapt into the sky again for the first of six practices over four days. On the 18th they performed two shows as scheduled at Horsham St. Faith and Castle Bromwich. This was Battle of Britain day and once again it was a maximum effort

for the entire wing – 441 Sqn alone put up 10 solo displays at 10 RAF stations, generating almost 18 hours of flying time. The last show for the 1 Wing team took place over home plate in North Luffenham on September 24th – a special performance for the new Minister of National Defence, the Honourable R.O. Campney. This performance marked the end of the airshow era for North Luffenham. Within a few months the entire wing would be packing up for a move to its new home in Marville, France, 439 being the last to leave on April 1st, 1955. The squadrons would also bid a fond farewell to the Sabre 2 which had made them masters of the sky in Europe. But a much improved Sabre was coming off the Canadair assembly line, a more powerful beast with a new Orenda engine – the Sabre 5.

3 (F) Wing Aerobatic Team – The Fireballs

It was in the spring of 1954 that 3 Wing got into the aerobatic team business to mirror the success of her sister wing in England. Comprised of 413, 427 and 434 Sqns, the wing had arrived en masse at their new home in Zweibrücken on April 7th, 1953 via "Leapfrog 3." It was almost a year to the day later when F/L Chuck Keating was appointed team leader of the new team. He looks back on those fun-filled days with a sense of humour that served him well throughout his air force career:

"The Fireball aerobatic team was formed at 3 (Fighter) Wing Zweibrücken, West Germany in April 1954. The OCs of the three squadrons selected two pilots each to try out for the team. The team was formed just as 3 Wing was converting to Sabre 5s, so the decision was made to hold back six Mk 2s for the team. There were several reasons for this, but the main reason seemed to be that the slotted leading edge wing was preferable from a manoeuvring and safety point of view at lower speeds during our performances. This idea probably stemmed from a desire to stay with something more familiar, rather than get into a new airplane whose performance we were unfamiliar with.

Our first training flight took place on April 9th. The next two weeks consisted of a lot of flying on my part with each member of the team. The first few trips were about an hour of close formation with the wingman flying various positions – left, right and line-astern. In this way we determined which position

109

The Fireballs became an overnight sensation at 1 Air Division, finding themselves featured on the cover of 3 Wing's *Flugplaz* magazine as well as the 1 Air Div magazine. The latter shows the team performing at Volkel, Holland on 3 Sep 54 as a section of 413 Sqn Sabres from Zweibrucken wait for clearance to start up. (via A. Chester Hull, Syd Burrows)

each man was best suited for. Following the tryouts, team positions were assigned as follows: from 434 Sqn – myself (leader) and F/O Syd Burrows (right wing); from 427 Sqn – F/O Jack Frazer (left wing) and F/O Bill Grip (spare); and from 413 Sqn – F/O Rick Mace (slot). F/O Nick Nixon ended up being transferred before the workups were completed. By April 23rd we were ready for our first four-plane sortie. Unfortunately, this commitment was only a secondary duty from Sqn Ops and Training, therefore time available for the team was very restricted. In fact, a lot of sorties were flown after normal hours throughout the summer. Only six four-plane formation sorties had been flown by April 27th when Syd and I departed for Rabat, Morocco for gunnery training. We were gone for a month.

On our return from Rabat, we were met at our aircraft with a message to refuel and get the team airborne over Air Div Headquarters in Metz for a review of our 'performance' for a possible show in Rennes, France on the anniversary of D-Day. No practice, just git there! We weren't exactly in prime shape after three legs and almost four hours in the air from Rabat. However, off we went …

The first roll over the HQ was wonderful. When I rolled out, there were no aircraft with me! Talk about rusty … About four

manoeuvres later we returned for a landing at Zweibrücken to await our blast from the AOC 1 Air Division, A/V/M Hugh Campbell. To our surprise, we got the green light to prepare for the 6th of June. This was the 27th of May! With regular squadron commitments, we managed only two practice sessions before the show. One of them was on the way there!

Our set routine of manoeuvres lasted for 12 minutes and consisted of an opening silhouette pass in a tight diamond, a loop, roll, cloverleaf of four loops, a change of formation (diamond to line-astern to diamond) followed by a vertical bomb shell. We found the best power setting to be 80 percent RPM, which I maintained throughout; all manoeuvres were entered at 360 knots. Takeoffs were always made in finger-four formation and landings in box.

On one of our occasional visits to the USAF base at Sembach, we befriended a pilot, Lt Russ Tanzy, who happened to fly an RF-80 photo recce aircraft with a side mounted camera. After much arm twisting and a few mint-juleps, we persuaded him to come along on one of our practice flights on July 12th and fly a wing position suitable for snapping close-ups of our super formation. The resulting pictures are now part of the team history. Tragically, Russ was

killed later that summer in a mid-air accident. We were grateful for his help and missed his visits.

Because of our part-time employment as an aerobatic team, there seemed to be little direction or interest from Air Div HQ to give us a standing in name, or a colour scheme. A name was originally tagged on us by F/O Fred Allport who did an amazing job composing a video of our show on his 8mm movie camera. (Unfortunately they were all from the ground so there were few good close-ups.) His title page dubbed us 'The Four Aces.' However, it didn't seem to catch on and over much discussion and a few beers one Friday night, F/O Bernie McComiskey yelled from the bar, 'Why don't you guys just paint your airplanes fire-engine red and call yourselves the FIREBALLS?' It stuck!

A large number of our shows were put on for visiting dignitaries from the Department of National Defence, AFHQ and other countries. These included A/V/M Frank Waite, Sir Basil Embry, the Hon George Drew, A/M Wilf Curtis and the Hon Ralph Campney. Besides these and the D-Day show, the team also performed shows at: the 86th Fighter Bomber Wing in Landstuhl, West Germany (July 10th); Vichy, France (Aug 22nd); Volkel, Holland (Sep 3rd); Nancy and Sedan, France; 2 Wing; 3 Wing; and 4 Wing (all on Sep 5th).

F/L Chuck Keating leads the 3 Wing team through a loop with Lt Russ Tanzy of the USAF flying formation while snapping away with the recce camera of his RF-80. (DND PL 81246 via Chuck Keating)

Letters of appreciation to the RCAF extolling the virtues of Canadian airshow displays in Europe clearly demonstrated the strong bond Canada had formed with her NATO partners. (*Flugplatz*, Sep 1954 via A. Chester Hull).

The Fireballs pulling up in line-astern during their show in Volkel, Holland on 3 Sep 54. Following Chuck Keating are Syd Burrows, Jack Frazer and Rick Mace. Bill Grip replaced Burrows on the right wing following the latter's "1 v 1" with a hawk 10 days later (the hawk lost). (DND PL 81361)

The French had an organization known as '*Le Meeting National de l'Air*,' whose job it was to organize airshows throughout France and North Africa in order to interest the populace in air power. It was this organization which had hosted our first show in Rennes. In all, the Fireballs performed in four French airshows, at Rennes, Vichy, Nancy and Sedan. These were great occasions. The towns were in a holiday mood and huge crowds converged on the aerodrome to witness the feats of the French, British, Canadian and American aircraft. The shows usually included aerobatic teams, parachutists, stunt fliers and occasionally high-speed demonstrations by the latest types of French fighter aircraft. In the evenings, a banquet and grand ball were usually held, to which all participants were invited, and which was attended by the mayors, air attachés of various countries and French military personnel. The dinner was abound with speeches and toasts and all the participants were presented with silver cups, cut glassware or medallions in memory of the occasion.

The largest show of the summer was at Vichy on August 22nd. We were based at Lyon, along with the USAF Skyblazers (flying F-86Fs), the French team with their Ouragans, the RAF Meteor team and a flight of RAF Canberras. Our busiest day, by far, was September 5th when we flew five shows in one day! The last show of the day at 4 Wing was at dusk. Our next scheduled show would also take place in Baden, this time for the Chief of the Air Staff.

The Fireballs accept the accolades of the president of the aero club of Sedan, France during a reception at 1 Air Div HQ in Metz on 5 Sep 54. L to R – Bill Grip, Rick Mace, Chuck Keating, Syd Burrows, Jack Frazer, Monsieur J. Ronnet, G/C L.H. Randall (1 Air Div HQ), Monsieur S. Ronnet. (DND PL 81650)

Two rare photographs. On top, the only group shot of the "red" Fireballs known to exist. (Jeannie Hallowell via Chuck Keating). Below, a close-up view of the infamous paint scheme on Jack Frazer's Sabre 2. (via Jack Frazer)

Disaster Strikes

Although our aerobatic performances were accident free, on September 13th Syd Burrows had a severe mid-air with a large bird while flying a Sabre 5. He was returning low-level to 4 Wing following a four-plane attack on Zweibrücken when the bird crashed through his canopy. It struck him in his left eye, from which he eventually lost his vision. Even with splintered canopy, blood and guts, and severe pain, Syd managed to bring his aircraft safely in. After many repairs, Syd was back on duty but without his aircrew category. Through his determination and help from several people, the 'brass' were eventually persuaded to let this one-eyed pilot back at the controls. He was also written up for and received the Air Force Cross for his efforts. Fortunately, we were able to use our spare pilot, F/O Bill Grip, to finish off our season. He performed admirably as our right winger in place of Syd.

Red is a Canadian Colour…Sir!

Although we had adopted the name Fireballs, up until then we had been flying our four Sabre 2s in standard squadron markings. Our request for a red paint scheme had fallen on deaf ears. There had been no reply from Air Div HQ – but at least they hadn't said NO! I therefore decided to approach our station commander, G/C A.C. Hull, personally with the request.

('Chuck Keating came to me one day and said that our team would like to have their aircraft painted in some distinctive colour. The USAF and French teams that were usually performing at the same events as us had been painted fancy colours, and we looked like 'country cousins' without a paint scheme. He suggested fire-engine red as a colour, as it would stand out against the blue sky and/or white clouds. I agreed.' – A.C. Hull)

So, with our intrepid squadron servicing NCO in charge, Flight Sergeant Phil Perry made all haste to paint the team red. At the time, we were temporarily based at 4 Wing while the Zweibrücken runways were under repair. We managed a few unofficial display practices over open country (now with Bill on the right wing) and then tucked the aircraft away in the trees at 4 Wing to await our performance for the CAS, Air Marshal Curtis.

On September 17th, the reviewing stand was full of brass as they awaited our performance – when we taxied and poked our red noses out of the trees, there was apparently a bit of apoplexy from the upper ranks. Unauthorized show of initiative and all that! (As Chester Hull recalls, 'In addition to the CAS, the AOC (A/V/M Campbell) and the SASO (G/C Pollard) were there. When the AOC noticed the colour of our team, he quietly turned to Pollard and asked, 'What do you think of the colour of the team?' Mike replied (I think facetiously), 'Makes them look like the Russian team.' With that response, the AOC said 'Tell them they have 24 hours to get it off!' As it was a lot harder to take off than it was to put on, and only 24 hours to do so, I had some pretty unhappy airmen.')

After the CAS's inspection there was of course the inevitable mess dinner. I had been given the word that the paint scheme was a goner since RED was a *communist* colour and might startle the locals. 'Not so,' said I, 'RED is Canadian – witness our fire engines, the Montreal Canadiens' hockey uniforms, the Liberal Party and the Red Ensign, well known in Europe through two world wars.' To no avail, the colour had to go, which it did before the next performance. The only picture ever taken of the red aircraft together was by nursing sister Jeannie Hallowell, a still photo of the aircraft parked in the 4 Wing dispersal area.

The Red Hat

Our station chief operations officer (COpsO), W/C Lyte Gervais, had supported our efforts to name the team and paint the aircraft – by looking the other way! At the mess dinner, the word was out that the coloured aircraft must go. Some of our friends at 4 Wing decided to honour the occasion with a presentation of a red hat. They painted some poor officer's flat hat brilliant red and presented it to W/C Gervais, unbaked! This trophy resided in the Officers' Mess bar at 3 Wing until it closed, a funny reminder of our one official performance in that colour. Its fate today is unknown.

We finished our tour for the summer at Baden with one last show for the Minister of National Defence, Ralph Campney on September 29th, 1954. This was our last flight as a team. But it was a marvellous summer. We met some grand people and shared in the various celebrations with many pilots of other nations. Our team had become one of the best known in Europe, and we were sorry to see it disbanded."

Chuck Keating

With the end of the 1954 airshow season in Europe, it was time to pass the torch to the next wing that would fly the flag on behalf of the RCAF. The honour now went to 2 Wing in Grostenquin, France. Sixty Sabres from the three squadrons comprising the wing (416 Uplands, 421 St. Hubert and 430 Sqn North Bay) arrived on the continent on October 11th, 1952, having completed the 3,600 mile journey in 13 days. Led by W/C 'Stocky' Edwards, they flew the standard leapfrog routing: Goose Bay, Bluie West 1 (southern tip of Greenland), Keflavik

(Iceland), Prestwick (Scotland), then on to Grostenquin. They encountered the usual bad weather, but that paled in comparison to the mess they arrived at in Grostenquin, a newly built base that was still a sea of mud in many areas. It took months to get everything finished and running smoothly, but the 2 Wing team persevered and overcame the initial adversity. By the time their turn came around to field an aerobatic team, there was a strong contingent of experienced pilots available to select from.

Also well ensconced in theatre by now was the latest generation of the Canadair Sabre, the Mk 5, easily identified by its five-inch high "wing fences" located at 70 percent of the span. Most importantly, it arrived in Europe with its much improved Orenda 10 power plant sporting 6,355 lbs static thrust – this would be the mount for Canada's next aerobatic team.

2 (F) Wing Aerobatic Team - The Sky Lancers

The 2 Wing team was selected in March 1955 and began practicing in April for what promised to be a very busy airshow season. Led by Acting S/L Tony Hannas of 421 Sqn, the balance of the team was made up of No. 2 - F/O B.R. Campbell (430 Sqn), No. 3 - F/O Len Eisler (421 Sqn), No. 4 - F/O Gerry Thériault (430 Sqn) and No. 5 - F/O Herb Graves (416 Sqn) who fulfilled the role of solo pilot. Once the team went on the road, a dedicated servicing team of approximately 10 technicians led Flight Sergeant Art Elliott accompanied them.

Solo aerobatics by Canadian pilots in the Air Div had become very common and, thanks to

The heraldic badges of the three F-86 Sabre squadrons that comprised 2 Fighter Wing during the Sabre era. Of the four Canadian fighter wings and 12 squadrons based in Europe, 2 Wing was the only one that was never assigned an official heraldic badge prior to its disbandment early in 1964.

An impromptu but rare photograph of the 2 (F) Wing Sky Lancers taken at 2 Wing Grostenquin, France in June 1955. L to R, Front Row – F/O Len Eisler, F/O Gerry Thériault, Acting S/L Tony Hannas (team leader), F/O B.R. Campbell, F/O Herb Graves. Back Row – LACs Anderson, Bowers, Bruce, Thibeault, Cpl McCabe, Flt Sgt Elliott (Crew Chief), Cpl Innis, LACs Paterson, Hollywood and Lunn. (via Art Elliott)

the likes of Dean Kelly, quite legendary. The addition of a solo pilot to the formation team was a new twist. Even the tightest formation in the world could not remain in front of the crowd at all times, so the addition of an integrated solo into the act guaranteed there was always something going on to hold spectator interest. It was a highly successful development which became standard for aerobatic teams in the future.

The RCAF's 2 Fighter Wing at Grostenquin, France as it existed on 2 Jul 53. It was to become the birth place of the Sky Lancers. (DND PL 80296 via Larry Milberry)

During an early team meeting, the pilots decided they wanted a name, finally coming up with "Sky Lancers." A modest addition to the now standard camouflage regalia of Canadian Sabres was also approved by 1 Air Div HQ in Metz. It consisted of a black and white "lance" painted on the side of the aircraft, from just forward to just aft of the canopy. Emblazoned above it was *Sky Lancers* and below *No. 1 Air Division RCAF Europe*. It was a simple but attractive scheme which served two important purposes. The most obvious was that it gave the team a distinct identity as the air division's aerobatic team and a sense of permanency previous wing teams had longed for. The 2 Wing Sky Lancers were also the first RCAF team to design and wear a distinctive patch on their flying suits.

The Sky Lancers put on a show for a special visitor to Zweibrücken on 13 May 55. L to R – S/L Tony Hannas, F/O B.R. Campbell, F/O Len Eisler, Hon Lester B. Pearson, F/O Gerry Thériault, F/O Herb Graves. (DND PL 82087)

The advent of a modest team badge and poster for PR purposes began with the 2 Wing Sky Lancers in 1955. (via Herb Graves)

SKY LANCERS

F/O "LEN" EISLER / F/O "GERRY" THERIAULT / F/L "TONY" HANNAS / F/O "BR" CAMPBELL / F/O "HERBIE" GRAVES

2 (F) WING
GROS TENQUIN FRANCE
1955

The second equally important factor was that the team was eventually supplied with dedicated aircraft which, aside from maintenance requirements, ensured that once the show season began the pilots could fly the same aircraft all the time. This is an important factor

The RAF, RCAF and USAF join forces for an historic aerobatic sortie. B.R. Campbell flew right wing, Len Eisler the left. (DND LR82-433-1 via Larry Milberry)

in the realm of precision formation aerobatics. Every aircraft handles slightly differently and individual idiosyncrasies soon become apparent with repeated practice of set manoeuvres such as loops and rolls. These differences manifest themselves in any number of ways – roll and/or pitch rate, trim effectiveness and engine acceleration to name a few. With four aircraft flying in extremely close proximity, consistency in performance of both man and machine are vital.

The human factor became all too evident when the team had a mishap during a particularly bumpy practice on July 13th, the most serious incident involving an Air Div team to that date. While flying in a tight line-astern formation, a bump caused a chain reaction that resulted in three aircraft damaged as noses came in contact with tails. The only aircraft left unscathed was that of the leader. B.R. Campbell relives the incident:

"I remember the July 13th formation practice mishap well. It was the day that my respect for the robust characteristics of the F-86 airframe was reinforced. Because there was moderate turbulence that day, Tony Hannas increased our minimum recovery altitude to about 2,000 feet. In any event, we were executing a loop in diamond formation with a change to line-astern over the top. On the recovery, with the line-astern formation in about a 35 to 45 degree dive, the number three aircraft accidentally hit the rear of my F-86 from below. The nose of my aircraft abruptly pitched downward heading for the trees. I pulled 8 to 10 G and recovered safely, immediately heading for Grostenquin at reduced power because of high exhaust temperature readings on my engine. Upon landing I was startled to find that the tailpipe opening was somewhat reduced and one side of the flying tail (elevator) was sheared off near the vertical stabilizer. Being able to pull 8 to 10 G with only one side of the flying tail provided ample proof that the Sabre was indeed a sturdy aircraft."

B.R. Campbell

It is indeed fortunate that Tony Hannas had taken the prevailing conditions into account that day and had elected to increase the safety margin of the team by conducting the practice well above show altitude. His airmanship likely saved the lives of both B.R. Campbell and Gerry Thériault who had been flying at the

This beautiful portrait of the Sky Lancer diamond over France was taken on 23 Aug 55 and featured on the cover of the January 1956 edition of *The Roundel* as a tribute to their highly successful season. (DND PL 82637 by LAC J. Scrimger, via Herb Graves)

back of the pack and had been forced to push down out of the formation. It was a valuable lesson learned for all.

At the time of the accident, the team had already performed publicly three times since starting a concentrated training regime on the 12th of April – at Chaumont on April 25th, 4 Wing Baden on May 6th for the Chief of the Air Staff, and 3 Wing Zweibrücken on May 13th for Minister of External Affairs Lester B. Pearson. Fortunately, they were able to continue their schedule on July 17th with a show at Auxerre, France. The team was a big hit at the show in Metz Frescaty on July 31st, home of 1 Air Div HQ, so much so that the USAF Acrojets (T-33 team) and RAF Hunter Aerobatic Team of 54 Sqn followed them back to Grostenquin for a party! It was undoubtedly during this social affair in the 2 Wing Officers' Mess that someone came up with the brilliant idea of doing a composite team flight for some publicity shots. The next day they made it happen. With B.R. Campbell and Len Eisler flying their normal wing positions, they were led by an RAF Hunter with the USAF slotman in the box – perhaps the only time in history three air forces have done loops and rolls together in the same diamond formation.

Although August was quiet for the team, they did several big shows in September. These included Volkel, Holland (September 2nd), Tours, France (September 11th), Düsseldorf, West Germany (September 18th) and Grostenquin, France (September 20th), winning praise for Canada at every location.

The Box Takeoff

While previous teams had landed in box formation following their shows, the Sky Lancers were the first to take off in box as well. This required some deft handling on the part of slotman Gerry Thériault who would start the takeoff roll with his nose just right of the lead's tail. As soon as safely airborne and climbing away, he would then slide down and across a few feet into his show position as the formation raised their gear in unison. It was an impressive sight for the spectators, especially if the runway paralleled the showline and it happened right in front of them.

With audiences reaching as high as 300,000 at some of the larger shows, the Sky Lancers soon became famous across Western Europe. They prided themselves in their very tight formation, most evident in their beautifully symmetrical diamond. Herb Graves, who

The Sky Lancers head downhill on the backside of a loop. (RCAF photo via Graham Wragg)

had almost 350 hours on the Sabre when he joined the team, would open the display with a sonic boom (weather permitting) just as the diamond formation arrived overhead for their opening pass. He would then reposition and come on stage to do solo loops and rolls, demonstrating the maximum capability of the Sabre 5, as the formation turned around for their next manoeuvre. The show finale was a bomb burst as in previous years, but this time with Herb Graves rocketing up the centre behind the four-ship as fast as he could go, climaxing with vertical rolls until he ran out of airspeed. This was a first for jet demonstration teams.

It was at Düsseldorf on Sunday, September 18th, when the team suffered another minor setback. There were few regulations with respect to airshows in those days, the principal one being don't hurt yourself, or anyone else! Unfortunately, while operating in very close proximity to the Sky Lancers parked on the ramp, German glider pilot Albert Falderbaum lost control of his sailplane during his aerobatic performance and promptly crashed, upside-down, into Thériault's Sabre 5. Fortunately, Falderbaum survived, but the Sabre would need repairs. Thériault therefore had to use Herb Graves' aircraft to keep the diamond intact, with a disappointed Graves watching from the ground. Someone else watching from the ground that day was a young Canadian airman from 2 Wing by the name of Bob Jones. He explains how the

An advertising poster for the Düsseldorf airshow. By the fall of 1955, airshows were drawing mega crowds in Europe, occasionally as high as 300,000. The translation reads "With the fastest and best jet flying squadrons in the world from the USA and Canada." (via Herb Graves)

Sky Lancers used tactical surprise to liven up the audience on what was otherwise a very cloudy and drizzly airshow day:

"I had been late getting back from leave and, as punishment, was flown to Düsseldorf in an Expeditor with three others to guard our

aircraft during the show. I watched the Sunday show in which the four-ship took off and flew a wide circuit. As the crowd watched a solo civilian performer exit the area, the four-ship came in low and fast from behind the crowd and scared the hell out of them! As I watched the crowd, they seemed to physically jump as the noise hit them. I don't know how low those F-86s were, but I would guess at less than 100 feet."

Bob Jones

With their final shows in Dortmund, Germany and Cambrai, France on the 2nd and 6th of October respectively, the 2 Wing version of the Sky Lancers disbanded – it was time to pass the public relations role to 4 Wing in Baden-Soellingen. Years later, team leader Tony Hannas reflected back on the glory days of the 2 Wing team:

"I'm sure all the members of the Sky Lancers would allow me to say that being part of a formation team was the highlight of our flying careers. The Sabre was a good sturdy beast and a pleasure to fly. Putting a show sequence together from scratch, refining the manoeuvres and then putting on shows in the competitive atmosphere of the European theatre was the ultimate in flying experience."

Tony Hannas

The end of a gratifying season. The formation pilots of the 2 Wing Sky Lancers stroll into the sunset and history on 12 Oct 55 at RCAF 2 Wing Grostenquin, France. L to R – F/O Gerry Thériault, S/L Tony Hannas, F/O Len Eisler and F/O B.R. Campbell. (DND PL 82891)

4 (F) Wing Aerobatic Team – Sky Lancers

By February of 1956, 4 Wing in Baden-Soellingen had been in operation in West Germany for just under two-and-one-half years. In terms of location, they had won the lottery! Nestled in the Rhine Valley between the Rhine River and the Schwarzwald, better known as the Black Forest, Baden was perfectly placed to take advantage of all the finer things in life – the Roman baths and casino in Baden-Baden, some of the finest food in Europe in quaint French villages only 20 minutes away and, for those slightly more adventurous, Switzerland beckoned from the south only 90 minutes down the autobahn. And THEN there was the flying … over some of the most scenic terrain in all of Europe. If there was a fighter pilot mecca, this was it! Ultimately, the wing would thrive for an incredible 40 years through four different fighter aircraft: the F-86 Sabre, CF-100 Canuck, CF-104 Starfighter and CF-18 Hornet. She would be the last European bastion for the Canadian fighter pilot.

"Leapfrog 4" had been the final big push to get the last three of the 12 RCAF squadrons into theatre and they had done so in record time, arriving on September 3rd, 1953. The young men flying at 4 Wing in 1956 were a highly motivated group. They loved their jobs and their aircraft and were as eager as any for their chance to show their stuff on the European airshow circuit. Once again, as in the previous two years, the team would be represented by pilots from each of the wing's squadrons, in this case 414, 422 and 444 Sqns.

The station sign that greeted RCAF personnel reporting for duty at 4 (F) Wing commencing in 1953. Thousands of military personnel passed through the gates over the 40 year lifetime of the base in support of Canada's NATO commitment during the Cold War. (Claude H. Gray via Paul Pomerleau)

The 4 Wing Sky Lancers Aerobatic Team captured in Baden on 22 Feb 56. L to R – F/Os Jake Adams (right wing), Dale McLarty (team leader), Les Price (solo), Fred Axtell (slot) and Ed Welters (left wing). (DND PC 1167)

AUF WACHT

TOTIS VIRIBUS

THIS ARM SHALL DO IT

STRIKE SWIFT STRIKE SURE

As the 1955 team had been officially recognized as the "No. 1 Air Division RCAF Europe Aerobatic Team," the decision was made to retain the name Sky Lancers and to continue to select new pilots annually on a rotational basis from the four wings. For 1957, aerobatic team tasking would go back to 1 Wing, now located in Marville.

The five young men chosen to fly the 4 Wing version of the Sky Lancers were F/Os Dale McLarty (414 Sqn) as leader, Jake Adams (444 Sqn) as right wing, Ed Welters (414 Sqn) as left wing, Fred Axtell (422 Sqn) as slot and Les 'Stretch' Price (444 Sqn) as solo/deputy leader. Since the team members had actually been selected in the fall of 1955, they were able to get a head start on their training for the next season. Les Price reviews the early days of the team and the circumstances behind the tragedy which ultimately befell them:

"Our first training flights occurred on November 14th, 1955 flying two-plane formations in looping and rolling manoeuvres. After a short indoctrination period, we switched to four-plane formation practicing basic diamond, line-astern, line-abreast and wedge formations. Formation manoeuvres included loops, rolls, 360 degree silhouette passes, chandelles and lazy eights. My solo routine was being worked up at the same time with manoeuvres between formation passes. My routine included close-in loops, rolls, a Cuban-eight, cloverleaf, low-level 360 degree max rate turn and a coordinated end of show bomb burst where I went straight up the middle behind the four-ship.

We had flown close to 50 missions together by the end of the year and were 'gelling' quite nicely as a cohesive unit. We flew another 23 missions as a team in January 1956, battling the usual Rhine Valley weather which was notorious for low cloud and fog during the

midwinter time frame. Thus, a lot of our flying was in marginal weather. The team placed limits of 3,500 foot ceiling and two miles visibility as mandatory for looping manoeuvres (the top third of the loop would be in cloud) and something slightly less for rolling manoeuvres.

February was a terrible month for weather and we flew only six or seven missions together that month. Our aircraft did not turn a wheel from February 13th until March 1st. Needless to say, we were chomping at the bit to get on with the job.

Finally, March 1st opened with a break in the weather. I was able to get in two solo practices and the formation team flew four missions in clear weather that day. Two of the missions were photo opportunities where official pictures were taken of the team by the Air Division's senior photographer, F/O Louis Le Compte, from a T-33 piloted by myself. We had just had our six Sabres painted and this was our first chance to show them off in their new paint scheme which had been designed by F/O Jerry Davidson of 414 Sqn. These aircraft had been carefully serviced over the past three months by a very talented and dedicated group of technicians assigned to the team as our groundcrew. Through their efforts, each of the team's Sabres had been carefully "tweaked" to suit the desires of its particular pilot depending on which position he flew.

Marginal weather again dogged the team on the morning of March 2nd and thus the formation team did not get a chance to take off on their first mission until approximately 1:45 p.m. that afternoon. The mission was to be a rather routine practice flight with nothing new involved. Regrettably, at approximately 2:20 p.m. the team crashed in close formation

while recovering from what was likely a looping manoeuvre.

Weather reports revealed a ragged ceiling close to 3,500 feet with one-and-a-half to two miles visibility in the area of the accident, which was just southwest of the airfield. The accident investigation board did a thorough investigation of all aspects of the team's operation to that time and the actual accident itself, but were unable to pinpoint exactly what went wrong that day. Needless to say, there was a lot of conjecture from the armchair experts.

Our team had had a good record up to the time of the accident with only one incident to report – which was my fault. I was flying the No. 3 position on a practice flight in mid-January when I stuck the pitot tube on my right wing through Dale's left aileron. Weather was marginal with heavy cumulus embedded in a ragged stratus layer of cloud. We entered cloud going straight up and at the top of the loop flew into the bottom of a heavy CU. It got very dark, very scary and very exciting all at once. Everybody was moving and the cloud was so dense that we kept loosing sight of each other. It was at this point that I hit Dale and left my pitot tube in his aileron. We finished our practice and returned to base without further incident, landing in formation.

The formation team genuinely enjoyed aerobatic flying and with over 70 practice missions behind them had become quite proficient at their routine. Dale was a particularly smooth and capable leader and we all had a lot of confidence in him. The members worked well together and like most teams spent a lot of their off-duty time together, forming fast friendships in the process.

An extremely rare shot of one of the Sky Lancers Mk 6 Sabres taken at 4 Wing Baden-Soellingen just days before four of the five team pilots lost their lives. Sabre 470 went on to serve with the Golden Hawks. (Claude H. Gray via Todd Pomerleau)

A silhouette of the Sky Lancer diamond in their new livery over Baden illustrates the precision of their formation. (via Les Price)

In Memoriam – the Sky Lancers proudly show off their new paint scheme on 1 Mar 56. Tragically, all four formation pilots were killed during a practice in poor weather the next day near Strasbourg, France. (DND PC 1229 by F/O Louis Le Compte)

It was indeed tragic that four fine young men of the calibre of Dale, Jake, Ed and Fred should lose their lives flying for the 4 (F) Wing Sky Lancers aerobatic team. They were all respected, admired and capable pilots and all had a great capacity for life. I can still remember clearly the easy confidence with which they went about their work and the fine sense of humour which was so much a way of life with them. Standing by their grave sites at the Canadian Cemetery at Choloy, France, I and many others felt a great personal loss as they were laid to rest."

Les Price

The loss of the Sky Lancers on March 2nd, 1956 shocked the entire Air Division and sent reverberations throughout the RCAF back in Canada. The accident was to result in dark days for the future of Canadian teams. The previous year, 1955, had not been a good one for fighter fatalities, with 17 Sabre pilots alone having lost their lives dur-

F/O Les Price chased his teammates twice in a I-33 on 1 Mar 56 with Louis Le Compte shooting from the back seat to get this fine study of the 4 Wing Sky Lancers (DND PL 83547)

ing training. This included F/O "Swede" Evjen who had been killed at the end of a training sortie with a new team in Chatham in May 1955, resulting in the cancellation of the team. With the hammer having fallen so quickly on that team in Canada, it is little wonder that the Minister of National Defence, the Honourable Ralph Campney, decreed within days that there would be no more RCAF fighter aerobatic teams in the foreseeable future. The entire concept of aerobatic displays had come into question and would undergo close scrutiny – while there was no doubt about their popularity, some began to question the negative effects such a tragedy had on the Canadian psyche. There was a fine line between public relations glory … and public relations disaster.

It would take the RCAF, and even more so the Canadian government, a few years to come to grips with the notion of "inherent risk" which some attached to demonstration flying. The fact is, under normal circumstances demonstration flying should never be risky – it requires the highest discipline of any form of flying and it is no place for an amateur. Underlying this debate in 1956 however, was a disturbing flight safety record during the mid '50s which had taken the lives of many young fighter pilots. Were these young men pushing the edge of the envelope too far during fighter training? In many cases the answer was yes. However, bravado was the culture of the day, when the old adages "you fight like you train" and "train to win" were taken literally on a day-to-day basis. The enemy threat was real and only a few minutes flying time away. The problem was, many young pilots did not

have the experience to recognize imminent danger, often not reacting until it was too late. In other cases, they attempted to force-land crippled aircraft instead of ejecting. This was not a unique problem for the RCAF, but indeed was one which all post-war allied air forces had to come to terms with. However, it was a problem which could not be ignored and didn't go away … nine more Sabre pilots lost their lives in accidents by the end of 1956.

In the case of the Sky Lancers, it was easy for the critics to point to the flight safety record of the day and make sweeping generalizations about the accident. But it was also unfair, especially in the absence of any conclusive proof of the cause. The four young men who died that day were not run-of-the-mill pilots, nor were they trying to prove anything – there was no one watching when they commenced what would be their last manoeuvre that cloudy afternoon. Les Price remembers them as mature professionals, not brash in any way. They had a calm measured approach to the team and took the responsibility very seriously. Their only goal

in flying that day was to get in some much needed practice in preparation for their first public appearance. They knew the weather was marginal and had talked about it over lunch together in the Officers' Mess in Baden only hours before. Like many before them, and hundreds after, they decided to launch to check out the weather to see if they could find a "hole" in which to work …

Ultimately, the debate over aerobatic demonstrations was resolved in part by those for whom they were designed – the citizens of Canada. Although the RCAF would not field any major teams for several years, tens of thousands of Canadians continued to flock to airshows across the country to watch military and civilian aircraft alike. None was larger than the CNE in Toronto, and in each of 1956, 1957 and 1958 airshow fans turned up in eager anticipation along the Lake Ontario waterfront. The RCAF continued to devote large numbers of aircraft to the show, including large formations and solo aerobatic performers, but no dedicated aerobatic team. Now it was the Royal Canadian Navy's turn to step into the limelight.

The best and worst of times. At left, a happy group of 4 Wing Sky Lancer pilots (L to R – Les Price, Ed Welters, Dale McLarty, Jake Adams and Fred Axtell) stride in from the flight line following an enjoyable practice. At top and bottom, a sad reminder of the team's ill-fated practice on 2 Mar 56 in which four of the five were killed. United States Air Force Europe F-86 Sabres paid tribute to their Canadian colleagues as the four were laid to rest in the Canadian cemetery in Choloy, France a few days later. (Top photo by Claude Gray, RCAF Photos via Les Price and Larry Milberry)

The RCN enters the Jet Age

The Royal Canadian Navy's foray into jet aviation did not get underway until the middle of the decade. VF 870 had bid a fond farewell to their fleet of Sea Furies late in March of 1954 in eager anticipation of taking delivery of used McDonnell F2H-3 Banshee fighters under a purchase agreement with the US Navy. Unfortunately, they were at the mercy of the USN and when delivery of their new F3H Demon was delayed, so too was the RCN's acquisition of the Banshee. It was therefore not until November 1st, 1955 that VF 870 was re-formed under the command of Lieutenant Commander Robert H. Falls.

Since the intervening months waiting for delivery had been used to train the aircrew and groundcrew in the United States, the first order of business was to take delivery of the "new" aircraft. The CO wasted no time in putting together a team of pilots and ground-crew to proceed to NAS Quonset Point, Rhode Island to take delivery of their Banshees which had been pre-positioned by various US Navy squadrons. The team departed Shearwater on November 20th courtesy an RCAF Flying Boxcar. What they found on arrival was depressing – a group of aircraft in decrepit condition, some barely airworthy; in effect, they were US Navy cast-offs. With a distinct lack of spares, it took a superhuman effort by engineering officer, Lt Gord Cummings, and his team to get the aircraft airborne again – and that was just for the short flight back home to Shearwater!

The first two Banshees to arrive in Shearwater, still in US Navy markings, swept in over the station on November 25th, 1955 in a high-speed pass led by Bob Falls with Lt Walter Sloan on his wing. Notwithstanding the initial disappointment, this was an exciting day for Canadian naval aviation and a throng of station personnel were there to meet them on landing. It would take several more weeks to get the remaining aircraft to Canada, the last two finally arriving on December 16th.

All told, VF 870 took delivery of 10 Banshees. With an extraordinary effort by squadron technicians, the jet aircraft were revitalized to combat condition. By the time a new attractive paint scheme was applied by Fairey Aviation, the gleaming Banshees looked like new. Morale was soon booming again in the squadron which, by RCAF standards, was small with only

10 pilots and 57 men on establishment. Of course, many a steely-eyed naval aviator would have argued that they only needed half the manpower and aircraft of an RCAF squadron to do a better job! It did not take long for the Banshees to be "welcomed" by the Sabres from the OTU in Chatham with intensive dog fighting often taking place over Shearwater and Chatham, and everywhere in between!

VF 870 Aerobatic Team

The arrival of a new fighter aircraft into any military force is always met by a certain amount of public curiosity, and so it was with the Banshee. The initial months of 1956 were spent in intensive training which soon ground to a near halt due to problems with speed-brake assemblies and landing gear doors, exacerbated by a lack of spares. Repairs were effected in due course and training continued. Meanwhile, with the RCN's previous involvement with the International Air Show in Toronto still remembered, they once again received an invitation to participate in the Canadian International Air Show which would take place for the first time in conjunction with the CNE. Organizers were particularly eager to ascertain whether the RCN would provide a "team" since the RCAF had cancelled their proposed Sabre team in May 1955 in the aftermath of their fatal accident. An added incentive was the scheduled appearance, for the first time, of the famed US Navy Blue Angels in their five Grumman F9F-8 Cougar fighters.

As luck would have it, Lt Gord Edwards had approached his boss early in June with a request to form a squadron aerobatic team. Approval was granted, with the understanding that LCdr Falls would ultimately lead the team. As Gord Edwards recalled some years ago, "That was okay by me of course, as long as I was still in it!" A four-plane aerobatic routine was developed and worked up over the next two months with Gord Edwards leading the team on their first public display on August 11th at the Maritime Air Show in Moncton, New Brunswick. One of his favourite manoeuvres was an inverted pass down the showline with wingmen Jake Birks and Frank Willis tucked in upside right. This must have impressed the Maritimers because after the show "the locals were very friendly" as Wally Sloan recalls.

The VF 870 Aerobatic Team of 1956. L to R – Frank Willis, Walter Sloan, Gord Edwards, Robert Falls (CO), Derek Prout, Frank Herrington (USN), John Searle and Jake Birks. (via Robert Falls)

The RCN was featured towards the end of the show with VF 870 taking the stage following the flypast of a Grumman CS2F Tracker submarine hunter. Their 20 minute show opened with Lt John Searle doing a low and slow pass just outside the breakwater, deploying a large target banner depicting "NAVY" which fluttered open as he approached stage centre. Simultaneously, Bob Falls came in with his five-ship of Banshees at high-speed, overtaking Searle and pulling up into the vertical to drop off the two solos who would take turns demonstrating the maximum performance characteristics of the Banshee as the remaining three-plane formation set up for their next manoeuvre. Lts Gord Edwards and Jake Birks remained Fall's wingmen with the solo manoeuvres being alternated by Lts Frank Herrington and Walter Sloan on September 7th and Lts Frank Willis and Derek Prout on the 8th.

Of their performance at the CIAS, Bob Falls reflects:

No airshow team can function without a dedicated groundcrew team. Shown here are the men who kept the RCN's eight Banshees in prime shape for the 1956 CIAS. L to R - PO1 Ross Steene, CPO2 Buck McCallum, AB Barry Whyte, PO2 Marvin May, AB Ivan Pilkington, AB Leonard Thompson, PO2 William Bruce, PO1 Milt Droeske, C2 George Blackwell, PO1 Robert Potter. (DND via Carl Mills)

As anticipated, Bob Falls took over command of the team for the balance of the 1956 season. He decided not to adopt a team name "in order to emphasize that 870 was an operational squadron first and foremost, and that anyone in the squadron could fly on the aerobatic team ... most of the guys did airshows at one time or another." Indeed, the team added a solo to their repertoire in the personage of Frank Herrington, the squadron's US Navy exchange pilot, which greatly enhanced the presentation. The team's next formal display was for the hometown crowd during Navy Day at Halifax/Dartmouth on

August 31st which naturally was enthusiastically received. Then it was on to Toronto for the big show with the Blue Angels.

It had been three years since the last appearance by naval aviators of the Royal Canadian Navy at the CIAS and they were determined to remind Canadians of their existence, at the same time stealing back some of the publicity the RCAF had enjoyed each year. Eight Banshees were deployed to Malton supported by a C-45 Expeditor. Six Banshees were flown in each of the two-day show.

"I think the show was well received and we all flew on to St. Louis to visit McDonnell Douglas feeling very proud of ourselves. Although we couldn't return the following year because we were getting ready to embark on the *Bonaventure*, others, including the Grey Ghosts, performed at the Canadian International Air Show in subsequent years."

Robert Falls

The VF 870 Aerobatic Team performed for the last time in 1956 on October 6th in Quebec City for "Navy Day" celebrations.

Lined up and ready to go, the VF 870 team parked alongside the US Navy Blue Angels at Malton for the 1956 Canadian International Air Show. (via Carl Mills)

They performed two shows that day, one in the morning and another in the afternoon, with Falls and Edwards taking turns leading. Much to the delight of the locals, the team even went so far as to tow Banshee 104 through the streets of the city to put it on static display at the Citadel. On their return to Ancienne Lorette Airport after their last show over the St. Lawrence (in front of the Citadel), the team did an impromptu beat up for the considerable crowd which had also gathered there. Solo Frank Herrington lived up to his reputation as "lowest of the low" by starting a small grass fire in the infield during some ultra low passes. The team had barely shut down their aircraft on the tarmac before they were mobbed by well wishers seeking their autographs.

In May of 1957 the squadron deployed to Rivers, Manitoba for live weapons firing at the range at Shilo, including strafing, high velocity rockets and delivery of 500-lb bombs. As the town of Brandon was celebrating its 75th anniversary on the 15th of May, VF 870 was invited to participate in an air display at the Brandon Airport. The Navy's willingness to participate added much to the show and was well received by the prairie folk from the surrounding area. As fate would have it, this would be the only airshow performed by 870 in 1957 – a fatal accident which took the life of Lt Derek Prout on May 30th revealed a structural defect in the wing locking mechanisms which grounded the fleet for several weeks in June. More maintenance problems dogged the squadron in July and August and by the time all of the problems were rectified all priorities were geared to preparing

The original Grey Ghosts in 1958. L to R – LCdr Wally Walton (CO/leader), Lt Walter Sloan (left wing), LCdr Alec Fox (right wing), Lt Ed Hallett (USN – slot). (via Alec Fox)

to set sail on HMCS *Bonaventure* in late September for much anticipated carrier qualifications. So while the navy presence was missed at the 1957 CNE in Toronto, Canadians had not seen the last of the Banshee at the show. A new team would soon be born.

The Grey Ghosts

By the end of 1957, VF 870 had completed its first deployment on *Bonaventure* and inevitable postings began to dwindle the pilot population on the squadron. One of the arrivals in February 1958 was a new

CO, LCdr Wally Walton. His first task on taking over the squadron was to address the winter doldrums of the remaining members who had not departed or were not on leave – by now down to a measly four pilots, including himself! Some years ago, he explained how he helped alleviate the problem:

"I had just arrived as the new CO and to get a bit of spirit and colour into the squadron, I decided to establish a more formal aerobatic display team. We didn't have an airshow season or any requests for displays, it just

The 1959 version of the Grey Ghosts comprised, L to R – Wally Walton, Walter Sloan, Alec Fox, Ed Hallett and Geoff Craven. Missing from this photo is Frank Willis who performed as a second solo during Shearwater shows. (RCN Photo via Walter Sloan/Alec Fox)

seemed to be a natural thing to do and besides this, it would be a showpiece for the Navy and would be well received.

I discussed the proposal with the Staff Flag Officer Atlantic (SFOA) and he gave me a verbal approval to form the 'unofficial' team. I was told to use my own judgement and discretion and he wished me good luck. As there were only four of us, we were all automatically included. I assumed that most of the manoeuvres would be done in diamond formation and I asked the others which position they would prefer to fly. Lt Ed Hallett, our US Navy exchange pilot, picked the slot and Lt Walter Sloan and LCdr Alec Fox (the squadron executive officer) picked left wing and right wing respectively. It wasn't long before the topic of a team name came up and Ed Hallett suggested the 'Grey Ghosts.' This was due to the two-tone grey of the aircraft and the fact that a Banshee (an Irish death spirit) was ghost-like. The name appealed to everyone and we were in business.

It was early in the year and there was no rush to get the team together, so I spent a good deal of time practicing by myself in the low flying area, getting myself in shape and developing a suitable routine. I did loop after loop and many rolls, checking the entry speeds and recovery altitudes until I was satisfied that they could be done easily and consistently. I then started again with another pilot in his assigned position. When he could do it all with me, I then added a third member and we practiced in threes. Finally,

I added the fourth member and we practiced as a team, attaining the perfection necessary to perform safely but spectacularly. Safety was paramount – we were very careful and flew with good safety margins.

As in the agreement that I had with SFOA, this wasn't part of our main job and was done in our spare time after the combat readiness tasks were completed. We squeezed time in here and there and after a few months the four of us were flying well together and had a 20 minute routine down pat. We were now ready for our first show. We added a solo position later to fill in the quiet minute or so while the main team was turning around. Lt Geoff Craven was our solo in 1958 and 1959.

The airshows were all by invitation and occasionally we did military exhibitions such as air demos for visiting VIPs on the carrier. On one trip, we had a combined mission in that we also had three-inch HVARs (high velocity aircraft rockets) aboard for a firing demonstration, so we could only do a rolling airshow with no loops. Unfortunately, on takeoff, 'Foxy' hit a seagull and lost an engine. He flew single engine back to Shearwater and we did a three-plane show for the carrier and her guests."

Wally Walton (via Carl Mills)

The addition of a solo to the Grey Ghosts was of course an important development and something the 1956 squadron team had done with great success. There is always a certain

stigma surrounding a solo aerobatic performer, the pilot whose job it is to wring out the aircraft, pull maximum G and make it all look easy. Geoff Craven worked hard to perfect his solo routine, but as he recalls, there were always those willing to help!

"That was great, do it again!"

"One or two perfectionists in the squadron complained on one occasion that my low level loops were not round enough, that they looked like arabesques rather than nice round 'Os.' The next time I practiced for a show at Shearwater, Wally Walton went up to the tower to coach me. With the circuit to myself and half the base watching, I came in from the south over the Eastern Passage golf course at 20 feet and around 400 knots. At the button of runway 34L, I eased back on the stick and I went into a huge, fat, round loop. At the top, upside down, Wally said to me, 'Now, hold it off a little,' so I eased the stick forward a bit before pulling it back in the downward half of the loop. 'WOW,' I thought, 'this is super!' Then, 'Holy *+%!! – I'd better start pulling some G on my way out of this, or I'm going to bore a big hole right in the middle of the runway!' Well, I reefed back on the stick like I've never reefed before or since, the runway numbers coming straight up at me, the Banjo's nose slowly pulling out along the centre line, then faster as I got lower. I almost grayed out, still not knowing if there

The Grey Ghosts diamond from the bottom showing the distinct lines of the Banshee. (DND EKS 701)

was enough room to make it – I finally did, but recovered at no more than 10 feet off the runway going like hell … Then Wally says 'That was great! Do it again!' I allowed as how I didn't have enough fuel left, vowing to myself I'd never fly a loop as round ever again. That was the only time in my solo career that I ever thought I just might not make it in a Banshee."

Geoff Craven

According to Alec Fox's logbook, the Grey Ghosts put on their first semi-official show on March 11th, 1958 at Shearwater during the visit of the Secretary General of NATO. They then had two months to refine their performance before doing their first public show at RCAF Stn Greenwood on May 17th to herald the arrival of the Canadair CL-28 Argus submarine hunter into operational service. This was an historic day for the RCAF and Canadair, and no doubt a proud day for the Grey Ghosts to be able to strut their stuff in front of the air force which didn't have a fighter demo team at the time. Several more local shows were put on in Shearwater over the summer, including "Navy Day" on August 6th.

On to the Canadian International Air Show

The biggest show of the year was the CIAS on September 5th when tens of thousands of spectators once again lined the Toronto waterfront to watch the annual spectacle. Although the RCAF dominated the show with the first 16 acts, the ending was all navy with the Grey Ghosts show preceding the Blue Angels second appearance in Toronto. The Angels were now sporting six new Grumman F11F-1 Tiger fighters in their show, with coloured smoke to boot. Not to be outdone, VF 870 planned to put eight Banshees into the air, the Grey Ghosts diamond plus an additional flight of four. Geoff Craven again recalls his experiences working up for the Toronto show:

"We were scheduled to perform in two flights of four aircraft each in Toronto. The first flight, the Grey Ghosts team led by Wally Walton, would go through a 15 minute precision aerobatic display. We new boys would form a second flight and would do two or three low-level formation passes, carrying all the weapons we could hang on our airplanes.

In our case, we practiced in June and July, performing the full routine at Shearwater. The Grey Ghosts practiced even harder than we did. They'd taxi out in formation, blast off, depart for the low flying area, and come back an hour later with their flight suits (and G-suits underneath) wringing wet with sweat. Their competition was the Blue Angels and the Thunderbirds, so they had to be perfect.

We flew eight aircraft to Downsview at the beginning of September and stayed at a 'less than exclusive' hotel off Jarvis Street. The best that could be said for it was that it had a very good buffet-style dining lounge. This wasn't much of an advantage, in that our opinion of food was that it took up space better used for liquid refreshments …

The day of our practice display on September 3rd dawned hot and sunny, and got progressively hotter and less sunnier as the Toronto smoke and haze of late summer intensified. We set out for Downsview, arriving there to find our groundcrew had loaded our four aircraft with a deadly-looking array of bombs, rockets, dummy Sidewinder missiles, tip tanks and an air-to-air banner canister.

We all briefed together, Alec Fox and Ed Hallett having already attended an airshow briefing earlier. By now the visibility on the ground was down to about a mile in haze and we knew it wouldn't be much better in the air. Undaunted, we all climbed into our birds together and put on a great show for our own groundcrew and those at Downsview with a formation start, taxi and takeoff.

As we taxied out it was boiling in the cockpit – the air conditioning making little perceptible improvement. I was carrying quite a lot more power than usual to keep my bird and its load of four 500-pound bombs rolling; the sensation was of taxiing through mud. Wally Walton led his flight out to the button, with my flight close behind. They rolled off down the runway in their neat finger-four formation and disappeared into the shimmering haze. I lined up my murderous-looking flight, held it on the brakes while we turned up 100 percent and said 'Go' over the radio. I released the brakes, and oh, so slowly, Banshee 126414 started to roll, my wingmen beside and behind me.

Downsview's runways are not long, and in addition to the heat there was no wind. We

had full fuel loads with the weapons onboard and when we got halfway down the runway, I thought we weren't going to make it. At the two-thirds point, I knew it was going to be very close so at the end I pulled the poor old birds up off the runway. We mushed along at 50 feet over Wilson Avenue for about a mile before we started to gain any airspeed. Those people south of Downsview got a real show that day – probably better than the spectators in the CNE grandstands later on.

We had to work hard to stay close behind Wally's flight in the bumpy holding pattern east of the fairgrounds. Eventually our time came and we roared in past the grandstands as low as we could inside the breakwater. Eight Banshees at low-level, first on a high-speed pass, then a slow-speed pass with gear and flaps down and power up at 90 percent, deafened the crowd. Wally's flight then separated from mine going into their precision aerobatic routine. While Wally and the others were rejoining after their 'palm tree,' I led my flight on two more tight passes by the grandstand, bellies toward the crowd so they'd see the weapons. We then exited to rejoin the Boss and his flight, heading back to Downsview via Whitby and Kleinburg in the smooth air above the haze.

Both flights switched to right echelons, broke and made stream landings, low on fuel now and relieved to be back. These kinds of flights were pretty demanding and not without pucker factor. On Friday, September 5th, we repeated the show, but the CO reduced our holding time so we in the weapons flight could take off with a reduced fuel load. Downsview dwellers did not get a repeat performance of the previous encounter."

Geoff Craven

Unfortunately, the scheduled show for Saturday, September 6th at the CIAS was a total washout and had to be cancelled due to terrible weather. This disappointed thousands of airshow fans who had been unable to attend the Friday show. It was equally disappointing for the participants and organizers who had spent a great deal of time and energy preparing for the show.

Only one more show was flown by the 1958 Grey Ghosts, this one at Brandon, Manitoba on October 25th in conjunction with their training deployment to the Canadian Joint Air Training Centre at Rivers. However, the team would get an early start in 1959.

"Just like Presley , eh?"

It was customary for the Banshee squadrons to head south on occasion to do intercept training with their US Navy counterparts. With great skill and cunning, these trips were usually scheduled in mid-Canadian winter to escape the incessant maritime rain, fog and occasional snow that would plague the operation. So it was that Wally Walton organized a six week deployment to Naval Air Station Boca Chica in Key West, Florida in January 1959. As it transpired, an airshow was to take place in Miami at the end of the month to commemorate the opening of the new international air terminal. Alec Fox recalls how the Canadians came to be invited to participate:

"We had performed at the CIAS in Toronto in 1958 with the US Navy Blue Angels and had spoken up on their behalf when the airshow chairman virtually gutted their show for safety reasons. They never forgot this.

When VF 870 arrived in Key West for annual night intercept training in January 1959, the Blue Angels were there, but going on the road. They were unable to fly in the upcoming Miami International Air Show to celebrate the opening of the new civil airline

terminal because their rules did not allow them to fly in the same show as the USAF Thunderbirds. They told the show committee that we were coming and might fly for them.

Soon a gentleman in a Cadillac convertible arrived in Key West and invited us. We sent messages to the Canadian Defence Liaison Staff in Washington and naval headquarters for permission to do some of our formation aeros. They wouldn't allow us to do much. We hesitated in accepting while waiting for answers, and then for fear of embarrassment due to our restrictions. The show people thought we were playing 'hard to get' and offered nationwide TV coverage; they would also bus our groundcrew 125 miles to Miami, provide complimentary cars for the CO and XO (me) and throw a cocktail party for us. All of this they did, although I did not verify the TV coverage.

The CO (Wally Walton) sent me in a Banshee to Miami and back on January 29th to make final arrangements. I got the show organizers to separate us from the Thunderbirds so we wouldn't show up too badly in contrast.

Friday we flew from Key West, did the show at Miami and landed back at Key West. Saturday we flew from Key West, did the show at Miami and then landed there. The

show was at Masters Field, as civil air traffic at Miami International could not be interrupted. The Thunderbirds did not land there in their F-100s but flew from a base in southern Florida.

We did what we were allowed, including low and slow, close by with lots of noise. We closed our show with low carrier circuits to touch and go landings with a madly waving unqualified batsman (Lt Fred Goodfellow) close to the crowd. He was blown about and sprayed with pebbles to the delight of the spectators. We landed, folded wings by radio on the way in and shut down almost amongst the people, with our groundcrew looking smart in gunshirts and bell bottoms. The crowd mobbed us for autographs and a Miami cop remarked to me as he eventually cleared our way to the complimentary car 'Just like Presley, eh?'

After the cocktail party we met a little guy at the bar who appeared to be drowning his sorrows alone. He was the Thunderbirds PR man. The *Miami News* had shown only a picture of our Banshees in formation captioned *'Royal Canadian Air Force Banshees Thrill Crowd at Airshow.'* We were given three paragraphs including *'Some 10,000 air enthusiasts ... saw the Royal Canadian Air Force steal yesterday's show with precision high-speed aerobatics. They flew four twin-*

Two Royal Canadian Navy icons from the past, the Grey Ghosts and HMCS *Bonaventure* circa 1959. (courtesy Paul Seguna)

engined Banshee jets only feet apart, whizzing over the sweltering crowd in a tight diamond formation …' The Thunderbirds put on a super show, with coloured smoke, but got only a four line mention for making noise when they cut in their afterburners!"

Alec Fox

While at Key West, the members of VF 870 had occasion to watch the Blue Angels practice for their upcoming 1959 season and were suitably impressed with their show, especially their two solos who apparently had no restrictions whatsoever placed on them. The Grey Ghosts therefore decided to add a second solo when an aircraft was available. Lt Frank Willis, who had flown with the 1956 team, had recently returned to the squadron following a three year instructional tour with VT 40 on T-33s and was recruited to join the Ghosts. By now, the RCAF had also formed a new six-plane team called the Golden Hawks, including opposing solos, so the pressure was on!

Unfortunately, the Grey Ghosts were still very much an "unofficial" team with relatively few resources so getting official blessing for anything dramatic was near impossible. Thus, when they did have occasion to put on a show using two solos, it was only in the Shearwater area. Nevertheless, they worked up a routine, as Geoff Craven explains:

"When performing at Shearwater, Frank and I sometimes did crossover aerobatics in the intervals between the formation passes. This was fun and relatively safe – although the crowd's perception from the ground was that the two solos were separated only by a hair's breadth during the crossovers, in profile we made sure we had plenty of room. At one Shearwater airshow, Frank and I started our takeoffs from opposite ends of the long runway and crossed in the middle, both of us having kept well to the right of the centre line. It wasn't smart, but the crowd loved it! We stopped short of landing at opposite ends, though."

Geoff Craven

The Ghosts get Smoke

The final touch that the Grey Ghosts added to their show was smoke, white at first and then coloured. Although the team did not have any dedicated groundcrew attached

LCdr Wally Walton gives the Canadian fleet a close look at his team circa 1959. On his right wing is Alec Fox, on the left is Walter Sloan and in the box is Ed Hallett of the US Navy. With the posting of the four original members of the team, the Grey Ghosts faded into history early in 1960. (RCN Photos via Shearwater Aviation Musuem)

specifically to them, the support offered Wally Walton and his team from the squadron aircraft engineering officer (AEO), Lt Peter Wiwcharuck, and his technicians was first class. Among the first of them to get involved with a smoke system for the Banshee in the spring of 1959 was aircraft tradesman Roy Valentiate:

"The AEO gave me an unofficial project to prototype a smoke rig that could be used in the forthcoming airshows. He already had a tank complete with pump that fit in the port side ammo bay and all I had to do was run the plumbing from there to the engine exhaust plus do the electrical hook up. No

authority, no paper, just a pat on the back and the usual comment that 'ATs' can do anything. It was beg, borrow and steal, and fortunately Red Atkins in the hydraulic shop was helpful in assisting with the piping. Alloy plumbing was fine but for the portion in the jet stream I had to use a piece of common steel water pipe. An oil spray of sorts was achieved by flattening the end. The initial trial was a total success.

The tank/pump assembly was placed on an engine stand with a flex hose connected to the aircraft. The pump was activated by a remote switch on an auxiliary power unit with the whole business parked on the 'A' Hangar flight line. Initial pump/nozzle tests

didn't quite satisfy the AEO. You can imagine the stares and comments while I was proceeding from hangar stores with a sledge hammer, the biggest ball-peen hammer available and a pipe wrench in my hands, as these were not common tools used on the Banshee. 'Calibration' entailed placing the sledge hammer under the steel pipe nozzle and pounding the orifice into a different shape with the hammer. The engine was started and brought up to a mid-power setting. The remote switch was made and a huge white cloud of smoke went rolling up tower hill. The AEO was elated. Congratulations all around – but no pay raise. A few minutes later the AEO was on the phone calming a highly annoyed 'commander air' whose tower was momentarily clouded in smoke!"

Roy Valentiate

Although the white smoke proved very successful, it wasn't long before the team wanted coloured smoke as well. Gord Synnuck was a young ordinary seaman in Shearwater at the time and remembers the prestige that the Grey Ghosts brought to the RCN. There was no question that coloured smoke would enhance the show, as the Blue Angels had demonstrated many times, but creating red and blue was easier said than done:

"That's where we ordinary seamen came in, the worst part of rigging for smoke. There was powdered dye that had to be mixed with an awful smelling sort of chemical, much like a toluene thinner or perhaps a ketone … We had to mix this concoction up and what a mess it was. Invariably, the dye mix would get into everything and it would not wash out very easily, if at all.

They gave us coveralls after the first couple of sessions of mixing but it still got into everything and we looked weird with red and blue splotches on our faces. This mixture was then blended in with the 10/10 oil and put into the special tanks in the ammo bay. The coloured smoke added to the air display – besides, the 'civvys' were suitably impressed! It was nice, but the poor 'oil rag' had a real job on his hands cleaning the aircraft. All in all it was great sport."

Bob Cansfield and Gord Synnuck

Following the short notice Miami shows, the Grey Ghosts fulfilled a modest schedule of half a dozen shows in the spring and summer of 1959. Operational priorities kept them close to home. The two main shows of the summer came on the 5th and 12th of August for the Dartmouth and Shearwater Naval Days respectively. Disappointingly, preparations for embarkation on HMCS *Bonaventure* scheduled for September 15th precluded them from paying a return visit to the CIAS in Toronto, the squadron being engrossed in day and night mirror controlled landing practice. Thrown in for good measure was an air defence exercise, *Operation Cueball*, which kept everyone on their toes. Notwithstanding, Wally Walton still got his troops airborne for the odd local practice and on September 12th led the Grey Ghosts in what would be their final show in Shearwater.

A Short Lived Legacy

With the start of a new year came renewed air defence priorities and the inevitable changing of the guard. The Grey Ghosts diamond flew together for the last time on February 1st, 1960. On the 14th, VF 870 bade a fond farewell to LCdr Wally Walton (soon to be promoted) who handed over command to LCdr K.S. Nicholson. Also leaving the squadron were Alec Fox and Ed Hallett, with Wally Sloan soon to follow. With the departure of these four stalwarts, the Grey Ghosts Aerobatic Team faded into history. Although the Banshee soldiered on with the Canadian navy until September 30th, 1962 with occasional flypasts and airshows, nothing that followed compared to the efforts of 1958 and 1959.

What is most remarkable about the legacy of the Grey Ghosts, is that they achieved so much with so little in the way of dedicated resources, a true testament to team spirit and *esprit de corps*. As Frank Willis recently summarized, "We were an informal and low key operation, but had a wonderful time doing it."

The Quest for a National Team

As the 1950s unfolded, the success and popularity of the part-time airshow teams in Canada began to foster a desire for something bigger and better – a permanent team all Canadians could identify with. The RCAF's Blue Devils at the start of the decade and the RCN's Grey Ghosts towards the end were certainly important catalysts in developing that desire. So too were the Silver Stars which were followed by many regional T-33 teams such as the ones led by F/L Gordon "Moe" Morrison from 1955 to 1957 at No. 1 Flying Instructor School in Trenton. They flew four-plane shows all over southern Ontario, from Windsor to Ottawa. F/L Max Preston took over the team in 1958 to continue the tradition, publicizing his team with some beautiful photographs. Meanwhile, out west the T-33 flying schools were doing the same. F/L Bob Hallowell put together a four-ship at 2 AFS in Portage la Prairie in 1957 accompanied by fellow instructors from "Argo" flight. They performed at Air Force Day and opened the Red River Exhibition in Winnipeg. Two years later he would gain fame as the RCAF's Red Knight, the same year that 3 AFS in Gimli would form the

The 1955 No. 1 FIS team from Trenton flew T-33 shows all over southern Ontario, demonstrating the skills of RCAF pilots to thousands in the heartland of Canada. L to R - F/Os Dunc McLeish, Ken Blackmore, Ross McGillivray and team leader F/L Gordon "Moe" Morrison. (RCAF photo via Moe Morrison)

Gimli Smokers. Like most of their predecessors, these teams were strictly part-time ventures flown by volunteers who loved to fly. Such teams provided an excellent opportunity for flying instructors to hone their skills while at the same time providing strong motivation for students on the station. However, their principal role was to promote positive public relations and they could be available on relatively short notice to participate in community activities such as fairs, parades and other special events. All of these teams invariably did an excellent job in representing the Canadian services.

No. 1 FIS Aerobatic Team captured during a practice loop on 2 Sep 58. Following team leader F/L Max Preston are Capt Ted Guy (USAF) on the right wing, F/O Doug Fraser on the left and F/O Bill Kelly in the box. Regional airshow teams such as this helped foster a desire for a full-time aerobatic team in Canada. The standard day-glo orange featured on F/L Max Preston's lead aircraft became the signature colour of a famous RCAF T-33 solo performer. He also began performing in 1958 – and was soon known as the Red Knight. (DND PCN 682, PCN 681)

The CIAS Leads the Way

Another vital factor in building support for a full-time team was simply the public response to annual "Air Force" and "Navy" days in addition to dozens of civilian airshows which had sprung up across the country. On the civilian side, no show was more prominent than the Canadian International Air Show in Toronto.

The first post-war show in 1946 at de Havilland Airport had provided some important lessons, underscoring the fact that Canadians loved to watch airplanes fly. The show in 1948 was switched to Malton where *"over 80,000 people stormed the airport"* according to the *Globe and Mail*. To cater for the growing crowds, the venue eventually switched to Exhibition Park at the CNE grounds. Known as the "National Air Show" between 1950 and 1954, the event was a single day affair sponsored by the City of Toronto on behalf of the Toronto Flying Club. It was held separately from the aerial exhibitions held during the CNE itself. The chairman of the show was Frank Young, a man with extraordinary vision who expanded the National Air Show into the Canadian International Air Show in 1955. The June 4th, 1955 show was the last one held in late spring with the 1956 CIAS becoming the feature attraction of the annual Canadian National Exhibition. The show is now held every Labour Day weekend.

Frank Young was chairman of the Toronto show for 18 years. In thanking the many contributors to his show in 1954, he summarized the importance of airshows to Canadians in a short dissertation which in many respects is as valid now as it was then:

"The Twentieth Century has witnessed, as no other period of infinite time, one of the greatest accomplishments of man – his ability to fly. His progress has been rapid and continues at supersonic pace in the field of design, distance and speed. The latest aircraft in the civil and military field in the air today is already in second place to the blueprint on the engineer's table for tomorrow's production.

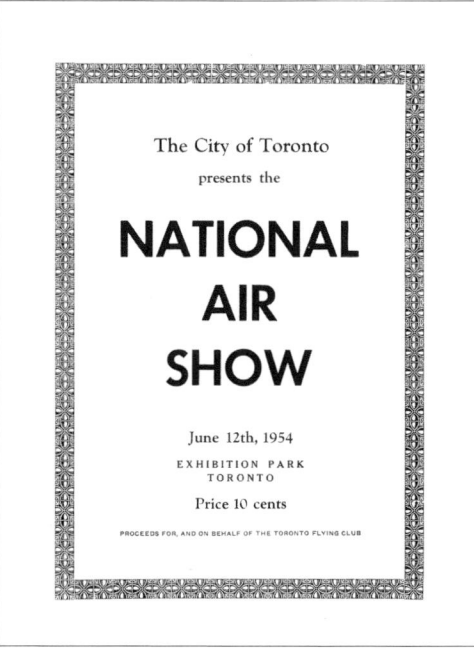

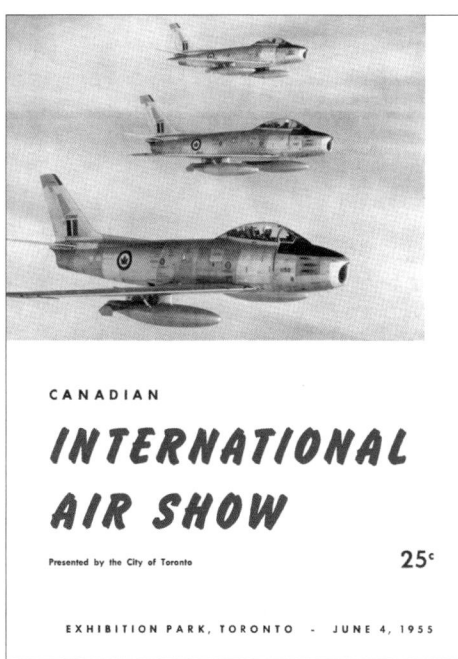

The City of Toronto hosted the first "National Air Show" in 1951 at Malton airport under the chairmanship of Frank Young. The venue changed to Exhibition Park in 1952 and in 1955 the show was formally renamed the "Canadian International Air Show." With the growing reputation of the show came increased sponsorship and more lavish programs, eventually featuring some of the most famous aircraft in the RCAF inventory. (via Peter Brennan)

The National Air Show mirrors man's accomplishments in the sea of space for all Canadians to see, both in the air and on the ground, whose country is the fourth ranking air power in the military field and whose commercial wings cast their shadows about the globe."

Frank Young

As the CIAS grew in stature it became a magnet for the aviation industry and the annual showcase for Canadian manufacturers. This stature was instrumental in attracting some of the world's best airshow acts. It was the appearance of two flashy American teams at the CIAS for the first time, the US Navy Blue Angels in 1956 and US Air Force

Thunderbirds in 1957, that undoubtedly contributed to the quest for a full-time Canadian team. Both teams were warmly received by the City of Toronto and their rapidly escalating worldwide fame was a real boon to Canada's international show. The Blues returned again in 1958, the two teams alternating appearances at the CIAS for the next 30 years.

One aircraft that was also eagerly anticipated at the CIAS in 1958 was the Avro Arrow. Although in the midst of a busy test schedule, plans were made to have one of the prototype aircraft make its public debut on the last day of the show, Saturday, September 6th. Although Arrow 25202 was standing by on the day, the show was cancelled due to

adverse weather. As an historical sidelight, that same Arrow did not fly again until September 14th when it achieved a speed of Mach 1.86 at 50,000 feet at the hands of Jan Zurakowski. Ironically, the Arrow never did perform publicly, the program being scrapped on February 20th, 1959.

Nevertheless, by the fall of 1958 the wheels were turning at Air Force Headquarters in Ottawa as a new aerobatic team was contemplated. An upcoming special anniversary in Canada would provide the perfect backdrop for a full-time team, one which would provide a fitting tribute to Canada's flourishing role in the world of aviation. The RCAF was about to form one of the finest teams the world would ever know …

$2·75

CFB TRENTON

RCAF
60TH ANNIVERSARY

© MICHAEL SWANSON

Although weather at the 1958 Canadian International Air Show and subsequent program cancellation prevented the Avro Arrow from ever making a public airshow appearance, the aircraft retains a mystical legacy among many Canadians. In 1984 it was remembered at CFB Trenton as Air Command celebrated the 60th anniversary of the RCAF. (*Ghost Flight RL206* courtesy Michael Swanson)

AIM HIGH...
GO AIRCREW

If you are between the ages of 17 and 24.... have at least junior matriculation... have the desire to fly... you can apply for Aircrew training in the RCAF.

To the qualified young man, the RCAF offers:

★ the Queen's Commission
★ the best flying instruction
★ the opportunity to develop executive and technical skills
★ excellent pay

New courses for Pilots and Observers are starting now. Visit your nearest RCAF Recruiting Unit or fill in the coupon below and mail to:

Director Personnel Manning,
RCAF Headquarters, Ottawa, Ontario

Please mail to me, without obligation, full particulars regarding training, pay and other benefits for Aircrew in the RCAF.

NAME ....

ADDRESS ....

CITY .... PROV. ....

EDUCATION (by grade and prov.)..................

.... AGE............
AF-58 4CAS

Royal Canadian Air Force

THESE ARE THE PEOPLE...

...the people of the Royal Canadian Air Force who serve Canada and her allies.
Their tasks are significant, varied and complex. Some fly supersonic jet interceptors, others transport men and supplies in multi-engine giants, or keep aircraft operational and keep watch on our skies. Their success as a team is reflected in the outstanding world-wide reputation of the RCAF.

Find out from your RCAF Career Counsellor about the exciting opportunities for young men and women.
AF-60-4M

ROYAL CANADIAN AIR FORCE

As the RCAF moved towards the establishment of a full-time aerobatic team, it continued to recruit personnel through advertisements in airshow programs across Canada. (CIAS Programs via Peter Brennan)

The Golden Anniversary of Flight in Canada. With the 50th anniversary of flight to be celebrated in 1959, Avro Aircraft, de Havilland and Canadair prepared for a major advertising campaign to celebrate the milestone. Airshows across Canada became the major focus for the celebration. (via Bill Briggs)

COMMEMORATING THE 50th ANNIVERSARY OF POWERED FLIGHT IN CANADA

FAIRCHILD 71
One of a long line of Canadian bush flying aircraft, built by Fairchild Aircraft at Longueuil, Quebec. Used by R.C.A.F. and commercial operators throughout 1930's.

SISKIN 111A
Single seat fighter, flown by R.C.A.F. during late 1920's and early 1930's. Built by Armstrong Whitworth and powered by Armstrong-Siddeley Jaguar 14 cylinder engine.

HARVARD TRAINER
Built by Canadian Car. This two-place trainer was used with outstanding success in the British Commonwealth Air Training Plan in the 1939 to 1945 War.

VICKERS VEDETTE
Three-place flying boat, designed by W. T. Reid of Canadian Vickers, Montreal. The first Canadian-designed aircraft to go into quantity production in 1924. Used by R.C.A.F. and civil operators —it was also exported. Powered by Armstrong-Siddeley Lynx. In limited use at the outbreak of war in 1939.

AVRO LANCASTER
Built by Victory Aircraft, Toronto. Was used by R.C.A.F. 6th Bomber Group in the 1939-1945 War. In post-war years used in Canada in the Arctic Explorations. The last active Operational Squadron, Number 407 Maritime Squadron, Comox, B.C., is retiring this wartime-built Aircraft in this Golden Anniversary Year.

MOSQUITO 35
This Fighter Bomber, built by deHavilland of Canada Ltd. Powered by Rolls-Royce Merlin Engines. Was used extensively in Second World War. Still being used for Air Survey in Canada.

deHAVILLAND OTTER
This Canadian designed freight carrier is one of the most successful aircraft ever to be built in this country. It is used in large numbers by R.C.A.F. and Commercial Operators and is being exported all over the world.

DH-9
Manufactured by deHavilland— powered by various engines such as the Beardmore, Liberty, etc. Served from 1916 until late 1920's in Canada.

1909 1959
Golden Anniversary of
FLIGHT IN CANADA

SABRE JET
Built by Canadair, Montreal, powered by Canadian designed and built Orenda engines. This jet fighter is used in Canada and overseas by No. 1 Air Division, R.C.A.F.

CF-100
Designed and built by Avro in Toronto. The CF-100 is employed in North American defense as its outstanding all-weather, long-range, fighter. Powered by two Orenda engines.

J N 4 CANUCK (JENNY)
Built by Canadian Aeroplanes Limited, Toronto. Was used as first war trainer and post-war barnstorming aircraft. The first airmail in Canada was carried in a Jenny by Captain Brian Peck, June 24th, 1918, from Montreal to Toronto. Curtiss OX-5 90 h.p. engine.

AVRO ARROW
The Avro Arrow Supersonic All Weather Interceptor, has given Canada the world lead in Aviation on Canada's Golden Anniversary of Powered Flight. Speed 1000 m.p.h. plus.

DOUGLAS DC-8
This aircraft will be delivered in December, 1959. Cruising speed—550 m.p.h. Number of passengers—127 Length—150 feet, 5 inches. Wing span—139 feet, 8 inches. Gross weight—287,500 lbs. Engines—Rolls Royce Conway 17,000 pound thrust per engine.

THE SILVER DART

In 1909 J. A. Douglas McCurdy completed the first powered flight in Canada, when, at Baddeck, Nova Scotia, the Alexander Graham Bell's Aerial Experiment Association culminated many years of trial when the "Silver Dart" took off from the frozen surface of Bras d'Or Lake under its own power. The "Silver Dart" with a wing spread of 49 feet used a V8 water cooled engine manufactured by Glenn Curtiss. This engine developed approximately 30 h.p. at 1,000 RPM's.

BRISTOL BRITANNIA
Now in service of CPA. Speed—400 m.p.h. at 23,000 feet under normal conditions. Maximum seating—130. Length—124 feet, 3 inches. Wing span—142 feet, 3.5 inches. Weight, less fuel and payload—95,000 lbs. Engines—Four Proteus 755 Turboprop engines of 4,120 EHP.

TODAY, CANADA IS ONE OF THE LEADERS IN THE AIRCRAFT INDUSTRY, EARNING WORLD-WIDE ACCLAIM FOR FORWARD THINKING. KEY MANUFACTURERS ARE: AVRO AIRCRAFT LIMITED, TORONTO • de HAVILLAND OF CANADA LIMITED, TORONTO • CANADAIR LIMITED, MONTREAL

It was in 1959 that the RCAF established its first full-time national aerobatic team since the Trans Canada Air Pageant of 1931. For those fortunate enough to have seen the Golden Hawks fly, simple mention of the name will bring back vivid memories of a fabulous team that thrilled Canadians from coast-to-coast for five airshow seasons. If the modern day Snowbirds owe their legacy to any one predecessor, then it is arguably the Golden Hawks, for it was this team that first earned Canada and the RCAF widespread international recognition for having a world-class aerobatic team. As Canadian aviation historian Larry Milberry has pointed out, "The Golden Hawks represented everything that was glorious about the RCAF."

S/L Fern Villeneuve leads the 1960 Golden Hawk diamond over Fox Island in Miramichi Bay, New Brunswick on 22 Jun 60, not far from their home base at RCAF Stn Chatham. (DND PCN 1137, Cpl Bill Noice)

The RCAF Golden Hawks

With the 50th anniversary of powered flight in Canada to be celebrated in 1959, coincident with the 35th anniversary of the RCAF itself, the seeds were planted in the fall of 1958 for a new aerobatic team. The Chief of the Air Staff, Air Marshal Hugh Campbell, had tasked his director of public relations (DPR) at Air Force Headquarters (AFHQ) in Ottawa to come up with a range of public relations activities to celebrate these special anniversaries. Wing Commander Bill Lee had served in the Air Division overseas at the same time as Campbell and had been specifically recruited to join Campbell at AFHQ. He knew his boss well. Among a variety of options, he presented A/M Campbell with the proposal to field a full-time national aer-

With J.A.D. McCurdy watching, G/C Paul Hartman relives history at the controls of a Silver Dart replica, complete with linen fabric and bamboo elevator and rudder supports. Baddeck, Nova Scotia, 23 Feb 59. (via CAHS Chronology)

Chief of the Air Staff, A/M Hugh Campbell, and J.A.D. McCurdy do the honours as former CAS, A/M W.A. Curtis, looks on. Royal Canadian Air Force Association Annual Dinner, Montreal 1959. (DND PL 114963 via Larry Milberry)

obatic team that would tour Canada coast-to-coast in 1959 in celebration of the two anniversaries.

Campbell immediately endorsed the plan and adopted it as his own. From his days as the Commander of 1 Air Division in Europe, he had witnessed firsthand what his fighter pilots could accomplish at airshows with both little practice and little in the way of dedicated support. Time and again they had demonstrated that they were as good as anyone in

the world, whether plying their trade on daily sorties in the skies of Europe or winning their share of tactical weapons meets with their NATO allies. The notion of an aerobatic team given a full-time mission with dedicated aircraft and crews – and a mandate to represent the entire RCAF – was inspiring. Placing the RCAF in the limelight through a team that would tour the entire country was the best way of promoting the air force to the people of Canada. It would also be a fitting tribute to an aviation industry that had grown dramatically across the nation over half a century, opening up virtually every region of the coun-

Part of the public relations team involved with the formation of the Golden Hawks in 1959. L to R, Bob Turner, Duke Palmer, Bill Lee (Director) and Terry Axell. (via Bill Lee)

try including the Canadian north. Canadian airmen had distinguished themselves in two world wars in Europe as well as the Korean conflict, and thousands of skilled labourers had found employment in the aviation industry over 50 years. Much had transpired since J.A.D. McCurdy had coaxed the Silver Dart into the skies of Baddeck, Nova Scotia on February 23rd, 1909.

Surprisingly, the Chief of the Air Staff's proposal to the RCAF Air Council for a new aerobatic team was not unanimously welcomed by all members of the council. Many questions were voiced and there was concern expressed about the negative publicity an unfortunate accident would create. Previous tragedies were well known to all. Nonetheless, A/M Campbell persevered and convinced both the council and Minister of National Defence George Pearkes of the rationale for his team. With that approval, he once again enlisted the support of his public relations experts, as without public support a new team had little chance of longevity.

The public relations team was an all ranks committee which, in addition to W/C Lee, included S/L Duke Palmer (deputy director), F/Ls Bob Turner, Ken Roberts, Mo Morrison and Terry Axell, Sgt Paul Larouche and Cpl Ray Stone. They were joined by S/L Russ Bowdery, Cpl Bob Tracy and photographer Cpl George Hardy from Training Command Headquarters (TCHQ) in Trenton. Lee and his staff worked tirelessly in developing a public relations strategy that would involve the new team in far more than airshows alone. With team membership would come responsibility for a host of social activities as well, from signing autographs following a show to visiting sick children to attending a

wide variety of public and private receptions. If the RCAF had learned anything about the airshow business since the Trans Canada Air Pageant of 1931, it was that Canadians held a fascination for not only airplanes and airshows, but for the pilots themselves who created the aerial artistry.

Formation of the Team

Responsibility for the as yet unnamed aerobatic team would in fact devolve to two RCAF Commands while remaining under the watchful eye of A/M Campbell. Since there was no question that the team would fly the RCAF's front line fighter, the F-86 Sabre, it would be formed and train in Chatham, New Brunswick, home of Air Defence Command's Sabre Operational Training Unit. This was where all budding Sabre fighter pilots learned their trade prior to embarking on an operational tour with 1 Air Division in Europe. However, the CAS directed that the team would form part of a larger unit to be known as the "RCAF Air Display Unit." Thus, the new team would tour Canada as part of a package which was to include a replica of the Silver Dart, the first airplane to fly in the British Empire. Overall responsibility for the Air Display Unit and planning of the 1959 tour was assigned to Training Command. Air Vice Marshal J. G. Bryans, Air Officer Commanding (AOC) of Training Command, was assigned responsibility for the unit. After due consideration of the importance of this new unit and the national exposure it would receive, he selected W/C J.F. "Jake" Easton as its commanding officer. The CO would be responsible for all administrative matters relating to the team, whereas responsibility for the development and flying of the show would devolve to a team leader of squadron leader rank.

Having settled the command and control aspects of the new team, the next task was to select a name. The name, like the original concept, was subject to some controversy. At the time these decisions were being made in 1958, S/L Russ Bowdery was the staff officer for public relations for Training Command and later would be selected as the first Golden Hawks' public relations officer. Over 40 years later, he recalls some humorous anecdotes from those hectic early days:

"The Hawks were tentatively called the "Golden Falcons" until someone told the powers-that-be that Studebaker had a car called the Silver Falcon. Rather than approach the car company, they decided on 'Hawks.' I'm sure that if the problem had been broached with some of us in the PR department, we would have solved the problem toute suite and had the Studebaker people providing cars for our 'Falcons' at every show location as part of the bargain … By the way, the eventual gold colour of the Hawks was a special mix chosen from four gold colours – over the objections of A/V/M Bryans who was rooting for Harvard yellow – 'to save money' he said. We managed to convince him that the chosen gold would look much better on the ground, and in the air for that matter. He and I had more than one encounter, which were interesting for him and sweaty for me!!"

Russ Bowdery

Selecting a Leader

The selection of a team leader for the newly-named Golden Hawks was a critical decision for the fledgling team. What was required was a veteran Sabre pilot, preferably with airshow experience, flying skills and leadership abilities that would allow the team to operate safely under often difficult circumstances. He would also have to lead his troops into the sensitive realm of public relations – foreign territory for most fighter pilots! After careful

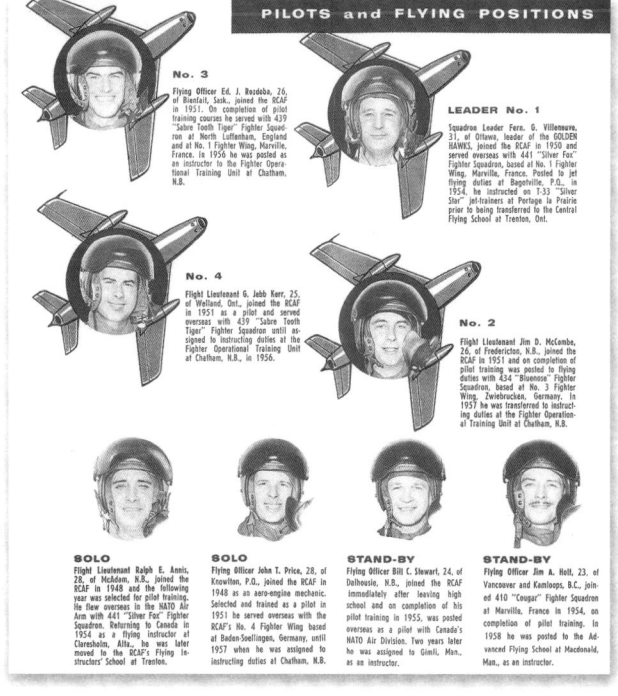

scrutiny of several suitable candidates, the young man chosen for the job was S/L F. G. "Fern" Villeneuve, a 31-year-old fighter pilot with almost 3,000 hours of jet experience. He had attracted the attention of A/M Campbell while leading Sabre "four-ships" through aerobatic routines with 441

W/C Jake Easton, the first Commanding Officer of the Golden Hawks Display Unit. (RCAF Photo)

Sqn in the Air Division in 1953 and the following summer with 431 Sqn's contribution to the "Prairie Pacific Team." His tour across Canada from Ottawa to Victoria that summer would provide valuable insight and practical experience to this new, much larger operation. He was the natural choice – and he had a penchant for perfection …

Fern Villeneuve led the Golden Hawks through the 1959 and 1960 seasons, helping foster the enduring legacy which all those who were members of the team still enjoy over 40 years later. He reflects back on those heady days …

"My appointment in January 1959 to select, train and lead a formation aerobatic team for the RCAF was, without a doubt, the highlight of my life as a pilot. A summary of my prior experience might just clarify, for those who wonder, why I was selected for this most challenging assignment.

My passion for flying was simultaneous with my realization that manned flight existed. My teens were the years of WWII and the British Commonwealth Air Training Plan. How many times did I bicycle to Uplands Airport and watch those Harvards take off and land? After the war many flying clubs and commercial flying schools came into being, and in 1946 I took flight training. I got a private pilot's certificate and then qualified for a commercial pilot's licence. My budget was a simple one during those years. Since I lived at home, all my meagre pay cheque was spent on transportation to and from the airport and on aircraft rental. In 1950 the RCAF was recruiting, and I joined at the earliest opportunity.

What has this civilian flying got to do with the Golden Hawks? Well, I credit those four hard years of very limited funds being responsible for my unending urge to make sure that every minute spent in the air be devoted to learning the capabilities of the aircraft and to perfect my craft. So it went during my pilot training and on my first squadron assignment flying the F-86 Sabre. I studied my aircraft, and I knew it well. I was with 441 Sqn based at North Luffenham, England in 1952. We were part of the first Canadian fighter wing in Europe, and flying the best fighter aircraft in the western inventory – the first operational aircraft not affected by the dreaded 'sound barrier.' Consequently, our wing received many visitors, and whoever was going flying was usually authorized to make a few passes and dramatic zoom climbs. So it happened one day as I was scheduled to fly that I was requested to show off the aircraft for a group of visitors. I requested authorization to perform some aerobatics. I was authorized, with the concise briefing that I was 'not to perform anything beyond my capability.' I put on a display that I was quite proud of, and subsequently one that was good enough to find myself assigned to give airshow demonstrations at other bases in England and on the continent. Mention of these in aviation magazines was most complimentary and gratifying.

A few pilots at 441 Sqn were interested in exploring formation aerobatics. Four of us got together, agreed on positions within the formation, and requested authorization, which was granted. So in early 1953, 441 Sqn had an aerobatic team. Gar Brine was the leader, I flew right wing, Ralph Annis left wing and Jean Gaudry the box. That summer Gar returned to Canada and Ralph was posted to the instrument flight at

Zweibrücken, West Germany. For the remainder of the year I assumed leadership of the team with Norm Ronaasen and Bob Haverstock flying wing. We did not get many chances to practice, but the experience was great, and we did get half a dozen official displays, including one at Luffenham on the occasion of a Royal Visit by HRH the Duke of Edinburgh.

Early in 1954, after two years in England, I was posted to 431 Sqn at Bagotville. This was an interim Sabre squadron awaiting production of the CF-100 all-weather fighter. The squadron was not to exist to the end of the year, and was replaced by a CF-100 squadron in October. 431 Sqn was small by most standards. The squadron officer commanding (OC) had just completed operational training at Chatham and the two flight commanders were former instructors at the OTU. Six pilots were returning from tours in Europe and six were right out of OTU training. The young pilots were a wild bunch, by-and-large, and we had a great time. The Air Division pilots knew of the 441 Sqn team, and of my participation. They

Two key supporters of the Hawks in the early days of the team, A/V/M J.G. Bryans, OC Training Command and G/C N.W. Timmerman, CO RCAF Station Chatham in 1959. (RCAF Photos)

badgered the OC to authorize us to form a team. I trained them, one at a time, to perform rolls and loops, and soon we had a team. My cohorts were George Fulford, Fred Rudy and Art Maskell. Rod MacDonald started flying with us at the end of April, substituting in for Fulford who went on a T-33 instrument course. We performed several shows, including the National Air Show in Toronto on June 12th, 1954. Then came a tasking for 431 to provide a Sabre flight to perform on the Prairie Pacific team, along with a team of T-33s and a formation of CF-100s. Art Maskell was to be married during the period of Prairie Pacific, so George Fulford rejoined the team to fly in the box. This was a great operation, allowing many Western Canadians to see jets for the first time. Flypasts were carried out over many west-

ern towns and cities. Airshows were performed at the following airports: Winnipeg, Saskatoon, Regina, Lethbridge, Calgary, Vancouver, Patricia Bay and the Pacific National Exhibition (PNE) in Vancouver. Returning east, an airshow was performed at Lakehead, now called Thunder Bay, and on September 11th at the Canadian International Air Show (CIAS) as part of the Canadian National Exhibition (CNE) in Toronto. At all of these airshows I led the Sabre team through four-plane loops and rolls, including formation changes during some of the manoeuvres. I then came in solo to perform manoeuvres that cannot be done with formations, such as rhubarb rolls, inverted flight, roll-off-the-top and a three turn spin from 4,500 feet. In October 1954, 431 Squadron was scattered to the wind and I was dispatched to Training Command in Trenton.

A Training Command tour could not be avoided, so I gave it all I had. Following Flying Instructor's School (FIS), I instructed on T-33s at Portage la Prairie and within two years had 1,000 hours of instructional duties and had risen from the provisional 'C' category instructor to an 'A1' rating. Early in 1957 I was transferred to Central Flying School (CFS) back in Trenton as an examining officer. During the last few weeks of 1958, there were rumours of forming an official aerobatic team. As I pondered how I could get in on such a team, I did not realize that I was already under consideration.

One day my flight commander came in and advised me that on the next day I was to report to the Air Operations Branch of TCHQ for an interview – reason unknown.

I reported as directed, and was introduced to W/C John Buzza from AFHQ. The wingco got right down to business and outlined the program for an aerobatic team … Yes, there was to be an official, full time, aerobatic team – for one year. It was to be called 'The Golden Hawks.' The aircraft were to be Sabre 5s – yes, 6s were desired, but there were none in Canada. The aircraft were to be

painted gold with a stylized hawk on the side. He showed me a blueprint of the design, which was exactly as the aircraft were eventually painted. The team was to form and train in Chatham, under Air Defence Command, and then would tour Canada as part of a larger organization known as the 'RCAF Air Display Unit.' The tour and the Air Display Unit were to be the responsibility of Training Command. Air Force Day, which had hitherto been on the same day at all RCAF stations across Canada, was being changed and each location would have its own Air Force Day so that the Hawks could be there to perform.

I interrupted the wing commander to let him know that I volunteered to fly on this team, and that I would gladly fly any position. He then advised me that his job was not to pick a team, that would be up to the team leader. His task was to interview prospective candidates for the lead appointment. The driving force behind this operation was the Chief of the Air Staff himself, A/M Campbell. The purpose was to do something special to celebrate the 50th anniversary of powered flight in Canada and the 35th birthday of the RCAF. The wing commander then asked me a direct question: 'Do you wish to volunteer to be considered for the leader's position on the Golden Hawks team?' I think that my positive reply must have been heard throughout the headquarters. This was December 1958.

There was so much to be done and time was so short, but the planning was outstanding; this was going to be an exhilarating program. I wanted … REALLY wanted … to be in!

Then in January 1959 the OC CFS came in one day and told me to get my best uniform on because I was to report to the AOC Training Command. He had nothing to offer and I proceeded to the headquarters wondering what the news was to be. When I entered the AOC's office it was the biggest I had ever seen. As the door closed behind me I saluted. A/V/M Bryans said, 'Come forward, young man.' As I approached his desk he stood up extended his hand and said, 'Congratulations, you have been selected to lead the Golden Hawks.' I was speechless! He went on, saying that he was glad to be the first to inform me. CFS would be directed that I had free rein to perform tasks associated with the formation of the team and in due time I would be transferred. My instructions would come from W/C Buzza at AFHQ.

Orders from W/C Buzza were issued by telephone. Sabre 5s were being readied out of storage at Mountain View, near Trenton, by a civilian contractor. I was to contact them and let them know that I was to test-fly the aircraft when they were ready. If an aircraft was serviceable and did not exhibit undesirable characteristics during the test flight, it was then to be landed at Trenton and delivered to

No. 6 Repair Depot (6 RD) for painting. If the aircraft was deemed undesirable for formation aerobatics, it was to be landed back at Mountain View and returned to storage. The first two aircraft were test flown, and found acceptable on February 2nd and 3rd, 1959.

On February 5th, I reported to Air Defence Command Headquarters (ADCHQ) at St. Hubert, as directed, for a briefing. I was to see the senior air staff officer (SASO). His greeting was not cordial. He made it clear that he was not in favour of the team and if it were not for the Chief of the Air Staff, the thing would not fly. He gave me a list of seven pilots on strength at the OTU in Chatham from which the team was to be picked. As I understood him, those were the remainder from all the Chatham volunteers after vetting by the personnel staff. The SASO then introduced me to one of his staff officers, a squadron leader from the Royal Air Force on exchange duty. That poor squadron leader had just been appointed as my taskmaster. I had to report to him weekly, informing him of what I had done, in what direction we were proceeding and obtain approval before working on any particular manoeuvre. I left immediately after the business-at-hand had been concluded knowing that if I had any friends or supporters in ADCHQ, I had not met them. I returned to Trenton and took a Sabre up for a flight, wringing out the poor machine to vent my disappointment.

A fine study of the Golden Hawk diamond near Chatham in May 1959. Glued to Fern Villeneuve are Ed Rozdeba (near side), Jim McCombe (far side) and Jeb Kerr in the box. (DND PL 64219)

The next day I proceeded to Chatham; the OC of CFS agreed that I should arrive there via Sabre, after all, it would make a more favourable impression. In Chatham I reported to the station CO, Group Captain Timmerman, 'Big T', as he was affectionately known. He was most affable; the station would provide us with aircraft until such time as our own were ready. The OTU flying would be arranged so that the airfield would be ours for a practice every day between 1630 and 1700 hours (4:30 and 5:00 p.m.). Offices and a briefing room were made available for the operation. Aircraft technicians were being transferred in; they would be integrated into the base maintenance organization and our engineering officer would be allowed to choose from all the available personnel to ensure that we had a very high level of expertise. He could not have been more helpful – what a relief!

I called on the OC of the Sabre OTU and then interviewed the pilots on the ADCHQ list, one-by-one, to establish their experience and aspirations as far as the team was concerned. This being Friday, the 6th of February, I advised them that I would return to Chatham the following week for flight trials. This I did on February 9th, and by the end of the 12th

had briefed and flown eight two-plane formation aerobatic flights and selected the team pilots. That part was not too difficult however, since there had already been some agreement between Jim McCombe, Ed Rozdeba and Jeb Kerr as to what position they wanted on the team. They were not competing with each other, and since no one else could compete with them on experience or ability, they were in!

The problem at this point was that none of the other available pilots had any experience at formation aerobatics or low-level aerobatics. I conferred with W/C Buzza, telling him I had a formation team, but needed pilots for the solo positions. In three months I had to have a display ready to go. There were many experienced pilots who wanted to do this, but they were not at Chatham. The program was too important not to avail ourselves of their expertise. 'You'll have to give me this on paper,' Buzza said, 'so that I can try to move things.' I put this in a message to Ottawa, then returned to Trenton.

F/O George MacDonald, team commentator in 1959 and 1960, provided a vital link between the men in the air and the viewing spectators on the ground. Live commentary was broadcast at every airshow and often on local radio stations as well. (RCAF Photo)

On Friday, February 13th, I test flew Sabre 23135. Also on that day, I was advised that the first aircraft I had delivered to 6 Repair Depot in Trenton (23042) had been painted in Golden Hawk colours. I flew it to Ottawa on the following Tuesday for the Chief of the Air Staff's approval. I was pleased to learn that the Chief did not approve the colour, which was closer to a brown than a gold. So it was back to the drawing board for the painters, and they eventually came up with a beautiful gold colour.

Between February 19th and 25th, I test flew six more aircraft from Mountain View to Trenton. During this period I had several contacts with W/C Buzza. Did I have any pilots to suggest for the team? I gave him several names. He later informed me that Air Defence Command steadfastly refused to make any more pilots available. Training Command would supply them.

The originals – the 1959 Golden Hawks began the team's first tour on 14 May 59. L to R - F/O Bill Stewart, F/O Jim Holt, F/O John Price, S/L Fern Villeneuve, F/L Ed Rozdeba, F/L Ralph Annis, F/L Jim McCombe, F/L Jeb Kerr (DND PCN 149)

The first official PR shots of the Hawks included this echelon break taken on 12 May 59 from the open door of an RCAF North Star transport. (DND PCN 183)

During this period I also sought information about what latitude and limitations I had with regard to the airshow program. Could I put up six aircraft in the show? The operation order called for seven Sabres on tour. Yes, I could fly as many as I wanted. The manoeuvres and composition of the show were up to me. Safety and good judgement were paramount. Minimum altitudes were: single aircraft passes 50 feet; formation fly-pasts 100 feet; single aircraft aerobatics 150 feet; and formation manoeuvres 200 feet.

Before the end of February, Training Command had posted in Ralph Annis and Sam Eisler, both of whom had previous aerobatic team experience in the Air Division. Bill Stewart and Jim Holt were also posted in as spare pilots and standby commentators as was George MacDonald who would be our designated commentator. I don't know how they found George, but his voice and personality were outstanding for the public address system.

Officially, the Golden Hawks team came into being on March 1st, 1959. The first task on Monday the 2nd was to assemble the pilots and outline the objectives, review the limitations and restrictions and formulate a plan for training. The pilots were eager to develop a show that would be second to none. I emphasized that, to be successful, our performance would have to be not only impressive to the professional airman, but also had to be interesting to the general public. Another key principle was that, once on stage, the Golden Hawks' performance had to ensure there was always something going on to hold the spectators' interest; the sequence of manoeuvres had to be from the ordinary to the spectacular so that there would not be an anticlimax during the performance. We stuck to these principles and they proved to be a good formula for a most spectacular presentation.

The solo pilots would practice independently from the formation in a suitable area about 15 to 20 miles from the station. The formation would do likewise in a different location, to develop their manoeuvres and improve their skills. Training would begin at altitude, at least 3,000 feet AGL, and as competence and confidence increased, altitudes would gradually be lowered. Once the team and the solos felt that their repertoire was adequately developed, we would carefully link them together to create the continuous performance and we would start prac-

The original Golden Hawk crest designed by F/L Ken Roberts of the RCAF's public relations team. This crest was used only in 1959, giving way to the more famous version to match Robert's stylized Hawk design on the aircraft. (via Phil Perry)

ticing over the airfield. And so it went. We carried out eight training sessions during that first week, with thorough briefings before each flight and a complete debriefing on landing.

The training routine was now three flights per day, weather permitting, and by the second week the third flight of the day was over the aerodrome. We were now operating comfortably at 1,000 feet above ground. The formation would practice over the field for about half an hour and then the solos would do the same. Then, on Thursday, March 12th, during our off-field training, Sam Eisler crashed. The Board of Inquiry was inconclusive. The aircraft was too badly destroyed to

Airshow programs across the nation celebrated the 50th Anniversary of Powered Flight in Canada and 35th Anniversary of the RCAF. (via Syd Burrows)

establish a malfunction. None of us, to this day, believe that it was the manoeuvre or that Sam was too low. The manoeuvre which preceded the accident was a coordinated loop. The two aircraft approach from opposite directions with lateral separation, each performs a loop so as to cross at the top, inverted, one above the other. Ralph Annis was the low man on this cross and his altitude was 5,500 feet, just right for a 1,000 foot AGL manoeuvre. There would have had to have been a major distraction to cause Sam to misjudge his pull-out – not likely – there had to have been some malfunction. The loss of Sam was a terrible blow to all. However, the three practice sessions over Chatham, where this manoeuvre had been witnessed several times by most of the station personnel, including 'Big T,' saved the day as far as our program was concerned. There was no condemnation of the manoeuvre or our program. F/O J.T. Price, a member of the OTU staff who had not previously volunteered, came forward and asked to replace Sam on the team.

Training resumed, still three flights a day if possible, as we had only two months before our first public display. F/O Ray Grandy had been appointed engineering officer for the team; he was a no-nonsense man. If he was not chewing on the end of a cigar, he was probably chewing somebody out, and not necessarily someone subordinate in rank or position. W/C Easton, the appointed CO of the RCAF Air Display Unit, and S/L Bowdery, the PRO, visited the team in Chatham. The tour program was being finalized.

In mid-April our team aircraft, in their beautiful gold colours, started arriving. After the technical formality of an acceptance check, these were put on the flight line. From then on we flew a mixture of unpainted OTU Sabres and our own 'gold plated' aircraft.

I never initiated any calls to report to ADCHQ, so periodically the squadron leader from the SASO's staff would call for a report update. I answered in general terms… the manoeuvres were loops and rolls and the show sequence had definitely not been finalized. I did not want to have to obtain the approval of the SASO and his staff for anything. They were too much against this team in the first place. After three or four of these communications, I received a call from the squadron leader who informed me that I had been too evasive and uncooperative. As a

The pride of the RCAF – the 1959 Golden Hawks during their first deployment to RCAF Stn Trenton, Ontario in May 1959. (DND PCN 1011)

consequence, the Chief of Staff of ADCHQ, Air Commodore Bradshaw, was personally going to fly to Chatham to inspect the team. I asked him if the station commander was aware of this. He stated that G/C Timmerman would be advised. A couple of days later the station commander and I met the air commodore on arrival. He accompanied me to our briefing room, where I introduced the team members, gave him a complete briefing on our operation, and asked him if he would like to attend our pre-flight briefing. He did, and so I briefed the team for a practice over the airfield. The practice went well and on landing the air commodore attended debriefing. Upon conclusion he addressed the team, stating that we had obviously done some hard work, and there would be more. He singled out a couple of manoeuvres, indicating that these needed refinement and polish. He concluded his remarks by wishing us a successful tour. The station commander and I saw A/C Bradshaw off as he departed, solo, in his T-33 for St. Hubert. A question was raised about the air commodore's remarks. I took the opportunity to point out to the team that this had been a momentous day… we now had ADCHQ's blessings, and would probably not hear from the SASO again. And we didn't!

Prior to our first public appearance, we were tasked to put on a display for Air Force Headquarters personnel at RCAF Stn Rockcliffe, in Ottawa. It was only fair that the AFHQ staff see the result of all the effort and to have a preview of what was to be presented to the country on behalf of the RCAF. The date chosen was May 12th, 1959. We deployed to Ottawa on the morning of the 11th. Air-to-air photos were required for PR

purposes, so two missions were flown, one on the afternoon of the 11th and the other one on the morning of the 12th. The photo ship was a North Star. Movie footage and stills were shot from the open side door. Some of the resultant photos appeared in publications across the country. The preview performance at Rockcliffe went well and, by all accounts, our sponsors were pleased.

On the Road in 1959

Following a quick turnaround at Uplands we returned to Chatham to prepare for deployment to Torbay, Newfoundland, for the first public display of the Golden Hawks on May 17th – 'Air Force Day Torbay'.

With this deployment the tour was underway; home base was now effectively RCAF Stn Trenton. Transport Command supported the tour with two C-119 aircraft. 'Flying Boxcars' they were called, and you knew why when you travelled in one. One carried the team's spares and equipment, the other a hand-picked team of some of the best aircraft technicians in the RCAF.

After Torbay we were in Trenton for two weeks doing shows at Camp Borden, Kingston and Trenton. Then on to Ottawa for an unofficial show for the personnel at Uplands, and 'Air Force Day Rockcliffe.' From there it was Val d'Or, St. Hubert, Bagotville, Sydney, Chatham, Halifax, Greenwood, Moncton,

The travelling maintenance crew for the Golden Hawks' trans-Canada tour in 1959. Back row – LACs Tardiff, Savoie, Levesque, Donaldson, Cpl White, Cpl Terrio, Sgt Mooney. Front row – LAC Lunn, LAC Hodgins, Cpl Gemmel, LAC Nickerson, Cpl Maahs, Cpl Latraverse and Cpl Cote. (via Bill Briggs)

The '59 Hawks ham it up with movie star and swimming champion Esther Williams prior to their first public show in Ottawa. The photo appeared in newspapers across the country. RCAF Stn Uplands, 4 Jun 59. (DND PCN 1002)

Fredericton, St. John and Summerside. En route west for the Calgary Stampede it was 'Air Force Day North Bay' and 'Air Force Day Falconbridge.' We flew for 'Air Force Day Calgary' on July 5th and over the Stampede grounds for the rest of the week. An airshow in Moose Jaw the same week, on to Vancouver for two performances on the weekend, to Namao (Edmonton) for a show at the station and then six more at the Edmonton Exhibition. 'Air Force Day Cold Lake' was followed by presentations at Saskatoon, Portage la Prairie, Gimli, Regina, Prince Albert, Lethbridge, Winnipeg and Lakehead.

The next day, August 10th, we proceeded back to Calgary via a refuelling stop at Portage la Prairie. Calgary weather on arrival was a few high-scattered clouds, visibility more than 15 miles, and a wind out of the north at about 20 mph. Calgary Airport at that time had a north/south runway of 6,000-7,000 feet, and an east/west runway of 4,000-5,000 feet. The north/south runway was closed for maintenance. At Calgary's elevation, with no headwind component, the east/west runway was not long enough for our normal diamond formation landing. I requested permission from the tower to perform a loop and fan break over the runway, for a stream downwind entry. This was approved. The loop, break and circuit were normal but when I was about three-quarters

down the runway I heard a call for an overshoot. The aircraft flew over my head as I turned off into the holding bay. The runway did not have a parallel taxiway. The overhead aircraft pulled up into a close downwind leg. I stopped, looked back at the runway, saw No. 2 turn off the runway and No. 3 about a thousand feet back. I completed a post-landing check, put away my charts and looked back expecting to see the fourth aircraft. I did not see one. The tower then called and cleared us for backtrack down the runway. I advised the tower that we would not backtrack until the last aircraft was down. Then someone said, 'He crashed.' Jeb Kerr's aircraft had collided with a light aircraft at 500 feet AGL, about halfway through base leg, and within a half mile of the runway. We were devastated! The next day we spent a long time discussing our course of action concerning the three shows scheduled over the next five days. We could not answer for Jeb, but we were all cut from the same cloth. What would each one of us decide if he was the unlucky one? We were unanimous … each of us would want the team to rally and press on.

Ralph Annis took over the box position. J.T. Price moved up to the lead solo position, and No. 5 in the card-five formation. Our two spare pilots, Jim Holt and Bill Stewart, were brought in to participate, taking turns flying

the opposing solo position. We were able to do two practice flights the morning of the 13th of August and put on a show in the afternoon. I remember the show was a special one for youngsters. They arrived by busloads from homes, institutions, and orphanages… many of them handicapped. The show itself was not as tight as we liked, and the altitudes were a bit higher as a safety margin. We were probably the only ones who realized this, but we were satisfied. We did three practice flights on the 14th, 'Air Force Day Penhold' and an airshow at Rocky Mountain House on the 15th.

On August 16th we proceeded to RCAF Stn Comox, B.C.; our next show was 'Air Force Day Comox,' scheduled for the 22nd. We took a day off. The pilots took a day off that is, while our poor, hard working technicians prepared the equipment for a rigorous four day program to sharpen the demonstration as much as possible. We did 10 practice airshows out of Comox, having found an ideal place to train – a large, abandoned airport on the other side of Vancouver Island, at Tofino. Ten times, over a four day period, we hopped the mountains, put on a full-scale rehearsal – there was never a soul to be seen – and then returned to Comox to debrief and refuel. 'Air Force Day Comox' on August 22nd was followed by an airshow at Victoria and four demonstrations at the PNE in Vancouver.

Throughout these performances our spare pilots, Holt and Stewart, alternated; the idea was to keep them in full practice in case of some other misfortune or illness. After the PNE we returned east. Then it was Toronto for the CIAS, the Quebec Provincial Exhibition, 'Air Force Day Centralia' and two performances at the Windsor Air Show on September 19th and 20th.

That was to be the end of the year, and the end of the Golden Hawks. We were overjoyed when advised that two requests for performances in the U.S. had been approved! The first request was for two appearances at the Eastern States Exposition in Springfield, Massachusetts. These were flown out of Westover AFB. The other was for the dedication of Kinross AFB – just southwest of Sault Ste Marie, Michigan – to the memory of Ivan C. Kincheloe, chosen as the first U.S. astronaut, but killed in an F-104 Starfighter accident before going into space. With that last public show on September 25th, our season ended.

Only a rickety fence prevented S/L Fern Villeneuve from being mobbed by the enthusiastic crowd at Rockcliffe following the National Air Force Day airshow on 6 Jun 59. Over 100 aircraft flew in the show. (via Bill Briggs)

On Saturday, September 26th, 1959 the Golden Hawks ceased to exist. On the tarmac at RCAF Stn Trenton the entire team was on parade – a stand down parade called by the Chief of the Air Staff. After his inspection as reviewing officer, the Chief addressed the unit. His comments were a tribute to the team. These included the following: 'I have heard nothing but the highest compliments for the superb performances of our flying team. In the space of a few months you have established yourselves as one of the outstanding aerobatic teams in the world – in my opinion, the best … the Hawks have given the 51,000 members of the RCAF an even greater pride in their Service!'

At a reception in the Officers' Mess the CAS talked quite candidly – there was no doubt this was his team. A/M Campbell was the driving force behind the Golden Hawks and he made it clear that he wanted this team to be a permanent unit of the RCAF. He needed the approval of the Air Council to keep the team, but within his authority he had ordered that the aircraft be put in ready storage and that all of the Golden Hawks' pilots, and as many of the technicians as possible, be posted to Chatham. He would obtain the necessary support and approval to reactivate the Golden Hawks for 1960. There had been outstanding support from the public and news media for the Hawks. They were a symbol of national pride. While aerobatic teams do not compete internationally, they are an indicator of a nation's capability in the specialized field of fighter operations. The Hawks again showed that Canada was second to no one in the operation of high performance fighter aircraft.

The Golden Hawks quickly gained an affinity with their American counterparts. Seen here during a photo shoot are two F-100 Super Sabres of the USAF Thunderbirds prior to both teams performing their last show at the Canadian International Air Show in Toronto on 12 Sep 59. (via John Lameck/Turbo Tarling)

As CO Jake Easton looks on, A/M H. Campbell and A/V/M J.G. Bryans congratulate the Golden Hawks during the team's stand down parade in Trenton on 26 Sep 59. The CAS subsequently succeeded in his quest to have the Golden Hawks revived in 1960 to continue to represent the RCAF. (DND PCN 1101)

During the 1959 season the RCAF estimated that some 2.5 million spectators saw the Hawks perform during their 65 shows at 42 locations. It was also estimated that the RCAF received more than $1 million worth of publicity through the team, more than its entire recruiting budget. WO2 Charles Raizenne admires the results at AFHQ in Ottawa, 7 Oct 59, in a promotional shot that was used to help re-form the team. (DND PL64547 via Mo Morrison)

The Hawks sparkle during a late afternoon loop at the end of the 1959 season. Cpl George Hardy captured the shot from a T-33 chase aircraft. (DND PCN 1067)

One of the Hawks gets up close and personal with the photographer in this classic Mk 5 Sabre shot. (RCAF Photo via Bill Briggs)

The 1960 Season

During the winter of 1959-60, I was an instructor with the OTU's Tactics Flight. As promised by A/M Campbell, on March 1st, 1960 the Golden Hawks were re-established, this time on a permanent basis under the AOC of Air Defence Command. From this welcome development came a requirement to implement a personnel rotation. The decision came from Ottawa; the three married pilots would be transferred off the team at the end of the season. The three single pilots would remain for a third year, thus maintaining continuity. I was to provide sufficient practice to one of the remaining pilots so that he could fill the lead position in 1961. Jim McCombe was selected and we flew a number of practices with Jim and I changing position.

W/C Jack Allan, Commanding Officer 1960-1962 (RCAF Photo)

In 1960, W/C Jack Allan became the commanding officer. Having a CO was a great help to the team and the team leader. W/C Easton had been unique in that he was not jet qualified and left all of the questions about flying and the show to me. He looked after all of the administrative and social requirements. He seemed to know all of the station com-

manders personally and after the first greeting would talk to them on a first name basis. I was impressed by his broad knowledge of protocol and service procedures. Although Jack Allan had been a Sabre squadron commander, he had no experience in the field of formation aerobatics or demonstration flying. He, like Jake Easton, was most supportive of our needs and took all of the administrative requirements from us.

For our second year of operation, McCombe and Rozdeba remained my wingmen and Bill Stewart flew the No. 4 position. Annis and Price continued the fine solo work they had done in 1959. F/L Dave Tinson

became our spare pilot. F/O George MacDonald continued as commentator and the PR duties were taken over by F/L L.G. 'Rocky' Van Vliet. Management of the aircraft maintenance and servicing program became the responsibility of F/L Dan McKinnon.

The number of performances and the schedule in 1960 were very similar to the previous year, with the exception of several very fine opportunities to perform in the U.S. in May and again in October. In May we were tasked to participate in the U.S. 'Armed Forces Week' program at Andrews AFB, near Washington, D.C. Saturday and Sunday, May 14th and 15th, were the show dates. This was a high calibre presentation of two and a

Fun in the sun - not quite. The boys keep their sense of humour as mother nature keeps them on the ground in Chatham in March 1960. (via Jim McCombe)

The 1960 Golden Hawks show off their new flight suits in a typical PR shot of the period. Joined by Miss M. Powell, Miss United Provinces of Canada, the Hawks are, L to R, Back row – F/L J.T. Price, S/L Fern Villeneuve, F/L Jim McCombe, F/L Ed Rozdeba. Front row – F/L Dave Tinson, F/L Rocky Van Vliet (PRO), F/O Bill Stewart and F/L Ralph Annis. Below, newcomer Dave Tinson quickly adapted to the team's public relations role. Meeting a pilot from the Golden Hawks was a great thrill for youngsters (and parents alike) across the nation. Many aviation careers were born of such an encounter. Inset is the cover of the team's 1960 brochure. (DND PCN 1168, 1194, via Bill Briggs)

THE GOLDEN
Hawks

The 1960 groundcrew team under the leadership of F/L Dan McKinnon pose proudly in front of one of the team's F-86 Mk 5 Sabres. The line crew are in white, the maintenance crew in standard RCAF uniform. (DND PCN 1185)

half hours duration which also included performances by the USAF Thunderbirds and the USN Blue Angels, plus a host of high performance operational aircraft. As is customary in such circumstances, the visiting team opens the airshow and it is closed by the home team. Therefore, we opened the show on both days and it was closed by the Blue Angels one day and the Thunderbirds the other. These were gala performances for us, with the largest audiences ever!

While we were at Andrews AFB there was a reception at the Canadian Embassy in Washington to which we were invited. It was a grand function and a very festive occasion. I was impressed by the pride and the exuberance of the ambassador and the members of the Canadian delegation. Everyone expressed their appreciation for our performance and, as was stated over and over again, Canada was as advanced in the field of aviation as anyone and our air force was indeed second to none. We were all very proud Canadians.

While at Andrews there was another event, one of a much lighter vein, but one that I also will never forget. After the Sunday airshow, I was walking on the flight line with Major Fitzgerald, the leader of the Thunderbirds, and two other pilots. All four of us were in blue flying suits and red jackets. We showed little originality in choosing our colours,

although ours were a different shade than the Americans'. Coming towards us, in the typical day-glo orange flying suit of the air defence crews was a USAF pilot. As we approached he stretched his arms out and said, 'Excuse me, gentlemen, I'm an F-102 pilot here on static display with my aircraft and I just have to say this …' He glanced over our epaulettes. My guess is that our rank stripes did not mean anything to him because he locked on to Major Fitzgerald's insignia. He put his hand out to the major and as he shook it vigorously, he said, 'That was a great show – you Canadians came down here and showed our boys how to do this formation stuff!' Fitzgerald replied, 'Thank you very much Captain, we appreciate your comments.' As we continued down the flight line, Fitz slapped me on the shoulder and said, 'See, that's what we think of you guys!' Major Fitzgerald was without doubt an outstanding officer and a gentleman.

Sometime during the summer we were pleased to learn that our 1960 season had been extended into October. AFHQ had accepted requests from Washington for us to do two shows, one at Vandenberg AFB, California, the other at the USAF Tactical Air Command firepower demonstration at a weapons range just north of Las Vegas, Nevada. We would be operating from Nellis AFB, the home of the Thunderbirds.

Since the firepower demonstration was some 30 to 40 miles from Nellis, we were asked if we would put on a performance over the base for the personnel who would not have the opportunity to attend the main event. We welcomed the opportunity to practice. Prior to this Nellis presentation, we were asked if we had objections to having our performance filmed. The Thunderbirds had a bomber hydraulic gun turret with three cameras, each with a different lens, that they used to film their practices for self-evaluations. They would make a complete film of our show for us. Some time later I saw that film and it had all of our performance in great detail – it was a fine account of the Golden Hawks. This was a great time for us; we opened the firepower demonstration with our full aerobatic display. We had a superb visit and enjoyed great camaraderie with Major Fitzgerald and his team. I was terribly grieved to hear, the following year, of the accident in which he lost his life.

1960 was a most outstanding and successful season. We did not have a serious accident and as we wrote our year-end reports we rejoiced in the knowledge that we might just have made Canadians more proud of themselves – we had shown others our very real interest and abilities in aviation."

Fern Villeneuve

Media Exposure

Russ Bowdery worked endlessly promoting the Hawks in their inaugural year and wrote several fine articles about the team both during and after his tenure. Acting as "advance man" as the team moved across the country, he seldom stayed around to receive the plaudits of appreciative audiences. Instead, he jumped into a Beech 18 Expeditor immediately after each show and lumbered off, often flying solo (or occasionally with George Hardy) to the next showsite to ensure all was in order for the team's arrival. His successor in 1960, Rocky Van Vliet, did the same, often with photographer LAC Rolly Johnson as his "co-pilot."

S/L Russ Bowdery, the public relations officer for the Golden Hawks in 1959, was a tireless worker in promoting the team. He later served on the CIAS Committee in Toronto for many years. (RCAF Photo via Phil Perry)

Throughout their operation, it was inevitable that the Golden Hawks would be compared to their more senior compatriots south of the border, the USN Blue Angels and the USAF Thunderbirds. It was also inevitable that a friendly rivalry, which already existed between the two American teams, would now encompass the Golden Hawks. Part of that rivalry was to get as much public exposure as possible, thereby winning the hearts and minds of the North American airshow fan.

"While in Saskatoon in the summer of '59, our Hawks saw an American magazine come out with a front cover featuring the Blue Angels over Niagara Falls. Fern Villeneuve accosted me and said, 'You see this? Why don't you get something like that for us Bowdery?' 'Over Niagara Falls?' I countered. 'Sure, over Niagara Falls' said Fern. 'Well Fern, you fly the Hawks over Niagara Falls and I'll get you on a front cover.' 'Great! And we'll do it upside down!'

What followed was a meeting with both the mayors of Niagara Falls, Ontario and Niagara Falls, New York. They were both enthusiastic and very supportive, each receiving a framed picture of the team. The Yankee mayor was most put out that he would not be able to witness the fly over as he had to be elsewhere on the day of the deed.

In order to get the shot, the Hawks' four-plane first flew over the Falls in a practice flight with Bill Stewart flying a chase T-33 with team photographer Cpl George Hardy riding in the back seat with a Speed Graphic 4x5 format camera. The Speed Graphic was a large cumbersome beast with 4x5 inch sheet film in holders which had to be slipped in and out of the back of the camera – but it sure took great pics. Using it in the back seat of a twirling T-33 was anything but easy. George did a terrific job. The first day was a dummy run followed by a black and white photo run. The next day Hardy shot in colour which resulted in the famous shot which graced the front cover of the *Star Weekly*, a weekend supplement to the *Toronto Star*. The *Star Weekly* was overjoyed to get an exclusive and *Federal Newsphotos* used a black and white shot to service their many outlets worldwide."

Russ Bowdery

Co-Solo Aerobatics

Flight Lieutenant Ralph Annis had already established quite a reputation for himself by the time he joined the Golden Hawks. One of the all-time great Sabre pilots, he was responsible for putting together a coordinated solo show which would set the standard for all future Canadian teams. In later years, he would play a pivotal role in ensuring the longevity of the Snowbirds while base commander of CFB Moose Jaw from 1973 to 1976. A passionate believer in the need for a national aerobatic team, he reflects back on some special memories from the formative years of co-solo aerobatics:

"Fern Villeneuve and I first flew on an aerobatic team together in England in 1953. Our 441 Sqn team was among the first Sabre teams and was set up by our squadron commander, Andy MacKenzie, who thought we should have one. Fern flew right wing and I flew on the left. The best and biggest airshows we did were the National Air Races at Southend-on-Sea and another for HRH The Duke of Edinburgh at North Luffenham. Therefore, Fern and I knew each other well long before the Golden Hawks were formed in 1959. We were great friends and flew together occasionally when we were on staff in Trenton in the summer of 1958. I was instructing on Harvards with FIS and he was instructing on T-33s with CFS. But quite often we would get together a couple of T-Birds and go out and do some formation aeros on the side. So when it came time to form the Golden Hawks, Fern invited me to join the team but he wanted current Sabre pilots for the formation. I was chosen to work up a co-solo routine as this was one of Fern's motivations, to have two solo pilots doing opposing aerobatics. I should add that it was also Fern's idea to do the bomb burst way back in 1953; I believe we were the first team ever to do that manoeuvre.

Once we got started, the practice sessions in Chatham were very long and involved. Early in the workups, I was experimenting with airspeeds for the low-level manoeuvres, especially the rolls. I was out over a cut in the forest one day and started a roll at 500 knots at low-level. I got inverted and realized it wasn't the right speed and I wasn't doing it correctly. I therefore hit the aileron as hard as I could and as soon as I got 90 degrees of

The 1960 Hawks strap in for a spring practice in Chatham using a mix of OTU aircraft and their own Sabre 5s. (Bill Briggs)

Cpl George Hardy's famous shot of the Hawks inverted over Niagara Falls on 29 Sep 59. F/O Bill Stewart put the T-33 chase aircraft in a perfect position to capture the shot. (DND PCN 1057, Cpl George Hardy)

Good morning!! Solo J.T. Price races past the tower in Chatham with his hair on fire during an "altimeter check." The pass was caught on motion picture camera and appears in the joint DND/National Film Board of Canada film released in 1971 as a tribute to the team. (DND Photo PMR 76-659)

bank I pulled as I was coming mighty close to the pine trees. Fortunately, I got the thing out but overstressed the aircraft to the tune of about 9 G! I'd felt I didn't have enough aileron authority so I tried rolling a few more times, at higher altitude. Although I was hitting the aileron stops, the rate of roll seemed fairly slow. I kept flying that same machine and one day I got behind Billy Stewart who was a spare at the time. So I said 'Bill, when I say roll, you do a maximum rate roll.' I did the same thing and as it turned out Billy was back out straight and level again while I still had about 90 degrees of roll to go. Having been unable to determine the problem, the groundcrew decided to put the gauges on the aircraft and found out that the ailerons were not giving a full rate of roll because the bell cranks had been installed backwards!! This was a lesson learned for all concerned.

The saddest part of our workups was when Sammy Eisler was killed only 12 days into the team's existence while working up our solo routine. As lead solo, I was doing all of the calls for turning in to the showline and starting the manoeuvres. Since we didn't have an airfield to work over, we were working up over a swamp southwest of the station. Sammy had replied to every transmission I made until that fateful loop. I saw him over the top of the loop and again on the backside cross so I called the turn to start the next manoeuvre. When he didn't answer, I turned and looked back to see the smoke rising out of the forest and realized that he had gone in. I don't know what happened, but there is a possibility something distracted him and he hit one of those so-called 'widowmakers,' those tall burned pine trees that stayed standing after the great Miramichi fire. They used to stick up 50 or 60 feet above the surrounding forest and were very

difficult to see. Regardless, it was a most unfortunate tragedy as Sammy had been doing a great job.

The accident led to J. T. Price joining the team as my opposing solo and John and I worked very, very hard to get everything rolling again. We continued to experiment with the co-loop which was quite difficult when we started. We tried starting the loop at different speeds and G combinations and eventually settled on 350 knots as the best speed to get around the loop with a reasonable cross over the top and again on the bottom. The only way we could get a good cross over the top was to pull up as tight as possible initially and then relax the G over the top, thus allowing a very close cross. We ended up with a good looking manoeuvre but did an awful lot of practicing before we came up with it. Meanwhile of course, Fern and the boys were working up their formation show.

Lead solo Ralph Annis corkscrews skyward over English Bay, Vancouver on 11 Jul 59 as his colleagues set up for the four-plane crossover. (DND PL 64504 via Larry Milberry)

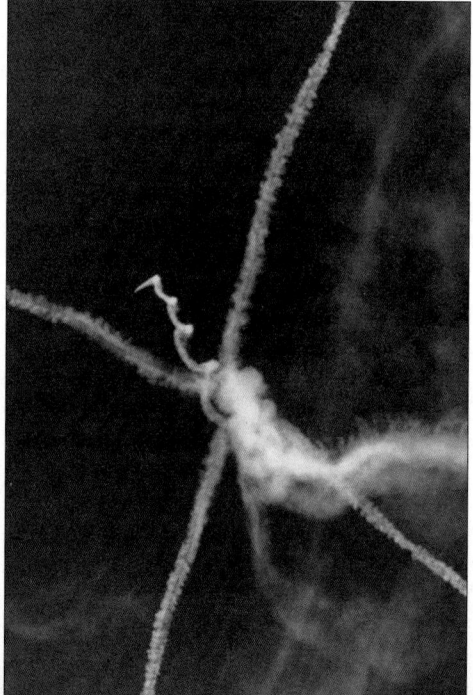

Virtually from the start we were flying three trips a day and it was mighty rough work. We never begged off, but every once in a while Fern would call us all together in a loose line astern and we'd go into a tail chase which was always relaxing. I remember Fern once pulled up with the six aircraft all in loose line astern and he kicked his Sabre into a spin. So everybody in the line astern formation kicked their aircraft into a spin. We spun around for awhile, then all recovered, jumped back into the tail chase and kept on going. It was an interesting sight, six Sabres spinning down pretty well at the same time, not in formation mind you, but we weren't very far apart either. So it was a lot of fun. We did relax quite a bit but we worked our butts off and came up with a pretty decent show.

During our workups in Chatham we used to fly the OTU aircraft until we got our own Sabres back from maintenance. I went up in a machine one day and John and I were practicing over the station doing high-speed passes and solo manoeuvres. Fuel was getting a little low, but not terribly so, when the engine quit on me. I pulled up and got it started again and we came in and landed. The groundcrew couldn't find anything wrong with the engine so the next day I took it up and it happened again. Following another extensive check by the maintainers, who still couldn't find any serious problems, they decided to send it up for an air test with test pilot Jerry Westfall. The thing flamed out on him when he was on the pitch for landing and he ejected. So that got rid of that problem for us! Jerry had a successful 'silk descent' so there was no real harm done.

Each Sabre had its own personality even though they all came off the same Canadair production line. Once you got used to your own machine, it was noticeably different to fly another aircraft. I know that I flew Ed Rozdeba's airplane two or three times and it was very heavy on the controls. As a solo, I wasn't terribly happy with it. I said 'Ed, how the heck do you fly that machine that heavy?' and he said 'Don't do anything about it. I like it that way!' He carried on with his heavy ailerons. John and I had some of the ballast in the front of our aircraft removed so they were quite light in the pitching plane, thus making it easier to pull G.

We didn't have much in the way of flying suits in our first year, just standard RCAF issue. We quite often looked like raga-

muffins. Most of the boys did wear a G suit, even though the formation didn't pull as much G as we solos did. It was good for fatigue. They wore their G suits on the inside of their flying suits and John and I, to be different, wore our G suits on the outside of our flying suits. The suits helped a great deal as we did pull a tremendous amount of G. It was almost continuous except when straight and level downwind or on the actual run-in. Once we started on the road with the show we worked our way across the country, getting better as we went. We didn't go into the States very much but we did do an airshow at Selfridge AFB. By this time, John and I were getting pretty good at this solo stuff and I guess maybe pretty cocky since our limits were 50 feet in those days, that is we were allowed to run in at 50 feet. However, we interpreted this as doing the manoeuvre at 50 feet. For the opposing rolls, we would start on the deck and then pull up a little for the roll, but not a whole heck of a lot. Now Selfridge had a nice flat runway and a nice flat run-in with no obstructions. It was one of those beautiful days with unlimited visibility, so John and I were really on the deck during our show. We came down thumping ourselves on the back believing this to be our best show ever. Then our commentator, George MacDonald, came over and said 'What the hell were you crazy fools doing up there?' We replied 'What do you mean? It was the best show we've ever flown!' He said, 'Well, you were so low no one could see you from the second row back!' This caused us to change our thinking a little and we were reminded that the air commodore had warned us months earlier to 'keep it up where people can see you.' At the time, being young brazen fighter pilots, we had dismissed him as a 'crazy old kook' who didn't know what he was talking about. However, having received this criticism from our own George, we decided 'hey, maybe the guy was right.' So we did pull our show up a little … well, at least so people could see us!

I can't say enough for our groundcrew – they were absolutely superior, really top notch people. The team was transiting into Saskatoon one morning when I had an engine bearing go on me. I ground my way into Saskatoon at reduced power and did a flameout approach, but the old engine kept grinding away until I was off the runway. The groundcrew went to work and two hours later they had the engine out even though it was still too hot to handle. In no time they had a new engine in my aircraft which I air tested and shortly after noon I was able to fly

Each of the seven pilots on the Hawks were assigned a crew chief and deputy crew chief. Shown here with supervisor Cpl Norm Gray are the 1960 Crew Chiefs, LACs Bill Briggs, Ed Harnum, Nick Nichols, Rod Embree, Mick Nordeen, T.T. Thompson and Dave Merriam. (via Bill Briggs)

our show in the same aircraft. That was just one example of the tremendous work our boys did on a regular basis.

It was after that show when we were moving on to do the Regina Exhibition that Bill Stewart pulled a little stunt. On transits, Billy had to wait until everyone was airborne to make sure that we didn't need his aircraft as a spare. Fern would take off with the four-ship first, followed by me and John. At any rate, we were well on our way to Regina when we all heard Billy call Saskatoon tower on the RT and ask for a low pass from east to west. Although we couldn't hear the tower, they obviously cleared him because a couple of minutes later he said 'Saskatoon tower, low pass west to east.' I called him and said 'Billy, get that airplane down here.' Anyway, Fern had landed in Regina with the formation and John and I had just touched down, when along came Billy. The next thing I heard was

'Regina tower, low pass north to south' and I said to myself, 'Oh the SOB.' We were rolling down the runway when he came right over our heads, just at tail height. Billy was feeling pretty rambunctious that morning …

Fern put up with an awful lot from us. We had a great time. Fern was married but he had no children. I was married with four kids. It must have been awfully difficult for my wife because I was on the road a lot and she had to raise those four young people. As the family had stayed behind in Trenton when I went to Chatham to join the team, they of course were eager to see the show when we came through Trenton. During the bomb burst I was the one that went straight up through the formation and did vertical rolls until I ran out of airspeed. I recall my young son, who was only six or seven at the time, asking his mother if I'd ever come back down again?

F/L Ed Rozdeba is invested into the Blood Indian Tribe in Calgary by Chief "Shot-Both-Sides," Chieftain of the Blood Confederacy, 7 Aug 59. At right, F/O Jim Holt spends a few minutes with some curious onlookers after the ceremony. (DND PCN 1034, 1041)

W/C W.I. "Bull" Riddell, a 1931-32 member of the RCAF's first aerobatic team (The Siskins), makes a presentation to the Hawks during Air Force Day Trenton on 28 May 60. (RCAF photo)

We worked hard during that first year. I remember the month of July '59 in particular, as we only had one day off the whole month. The rest of the time we were either doing airshows or transiting from one show site to another. There wasn't much money either. We weren't given an allowance to go anywhere except on station. This was difficult in more ways than one because everywhere we went was a big celebration – Air Force Day or Stampede or Exhibition. We were always on call to attend receptions but we also needed our rest. There were times it was difficult with big parties going on in the mess and we had to go home and go to bed because we had a pretty strenuous job ahead of us. Flying airshows back in those days was quite different as we often flew our shows right over the middle of cities. I can recall in Calgary when the Palliser Hotel was the tallest building around and my run-in to the Exhibition grounds was right beside it. You'd never get away with that today, but back then no one thought too much about it. We were always treated very well in Calgary

The Golden Hawks flew an extremely tight box formation as evidenced by this vertical shot taken following a practice on 21 Jun 60. (DND PL 64800 via Bill Briggs)

and were made honorary Calgarians by the mayor. We were also made honorary members of the Blood Indian tribe by their Chief and all given Indian names. My name was 'Warrior Brave One Spot' and the ceremony was very moving, one I will never forget.

It was back in Calgary a few weeks later that we regrettably lost Jeb Kerr. Since I had taken training in all of the formation positions, Fern decided to put me in the slot for the remainder of the 1959 season. John took over my job as lead solo and Billy Stewart was brought in as the second half of the co-solo show, occasionally spelled off by Jim Holt. It took me a couple of shows to get used to flying the slot. I recall that during an airshow at Rocky Mountain House we were doing our formation change from line astern to diamond over the top of a loop. On Fern's command, I put on all the power I had to try and catch up to the formation at the top of the loop. I then came thundering up on the formation, pulled off the power to kill the overtake and then hammered the power back again after getting in the box. I then had a compressor stall which was rather interesting at the top of the loop as we headed back down the other side. I got the stall cleared but dropped back two or three plane lengths and was very embarrassed that such a stupid thing should happen to me. It was a rough throttle handling of course and falling back out of position was a terrible blow to my pride. It didn't happen again.

When the 1959 season ended it was back to Trenton for a big closing down ceremony with planes, pilots and the groundcrew on parade. Everybody was given a hardy handshake and we thought that was the end of that. However, through the good offices of A/M Campbell we re-formed again in 1960 and were made a permanent organization, or

so we thought at the time. The 1960 season was a lot better. We got nice light blue flying suits and flying jackets. I went back to my familiar lead solo position and we had a fabulous season without incident. We were also allowed to stay in hotels/motels off station pretty much all the time since we had learned the hard way this was necessary to get any degree of rest and relaxation.

Throughout our tenure, we did far more than the strict 'air demonstrations' approved by AFHQ. For example, in Saskatoon one day we did a show for the Hospital for Crippled Children. They brought the little kids out on the runway and we put on a special show just for them. Afterwards, we joined the children on the tarmac and spent some time with them. We always had a wonderful time talking with young people, whether at shows, schools or hospital visits. We saw it as an important part of our job.

Flying with the Golden Hawks in 1959 and 1960 was the highlight of my career. We flew the finest fighter in the world and flew it to its maximum limits in all respects. It was a great, great two years. Years later, when Ken Lett and I went out to the Abbotsford Airshow in 1972, we spotted a Sabre with a Boeing paint scheme on it. I hadn't seen a Sabre for a long time so I wandered over to have a look at it and, lo and behold, it was my old airplane '096' that I had flown 242 missions in. Well I almost kissed it! I patted it on the nose and looked it all over; it was still in beautiful shape. Boeing had taken very good care of it. It was like meeting an old friend, one I hadn't seen for 12 years. It was a nostalgic reunion."

Ralph Annis

It wasn't all hard work! Fern Villeneuve and Ed Rozdeba enjoy the company of Margot Turney, Miss Calgary Stampede, during the annual extravaganza in July 1960. (RCAF photo via Bill Briggs)

The Golden Hawk Show

Jim McCombe had the good fortune of serving three years with the Golden Hawks, flying the right wing in 1959 and 1960 and as leader in 1961. In all he flew in some 200 shows and over 500 practice sessions. He describes the show manoeuvres and some special memories from the first three years of the Golden Hawks …

"The formation show we flew with the Mk 5 in 1959 and 1960 basically consisted of an opening plan view of the diamond formation, a loop, a roll, a double loop with a change to line astern on the first and back to diamond on the second, a reverse echelon roll, an echelon roll back to diamond, a card-five loop and roll (the lead solo pilot joined the formation for these latter two manoeuvres), a bomb burst through a circle of smoke laid by a solo, rejoining into a diamond formation, a loop and landing.

As a rule of thumb, loops were done into wind and rolls downwind. This creates the illusion of a rounder loop and flatter roll. Also, the manoeuvres were initiated in order to be centred mid-crowd as often as possible. This presented a difficult task at times, especially for the solos who had to centre their crosses on the crowd.

Looping manoeuvres were normally started at 350 kts on the Mark 5 Sabre and 330 kts on the Mark 6, which we flew from 1961 onwards. This speed was much lower than the 570 kt maximum airspeed allowed below 10,000 feet. These airspeeds were calculated to give adequate control around the loop while gaining as little altitude as possible. The loops were entered at 4.5 G which decreased to about half a G over the top. The reason for relaxing some G over the top was to keep the loop rounder; higher G over the top resulted in an L-shaped loop. Our loops were topped at about 5,500 feet on the Mk 5 and 4,500 feet on the Mk 6. Double loops were started about 20 kts faster since G forces would cause about that much decay in airspeed during the first loop.

Formation rolls were commenced at 350 kts after a 2.5 to 3 G entry pull-up. The rolls were topped at 1,500 feet AGL with the Mark 5 Sabre and 1,200 feet AGL with the Mark 6. The purpose of the relatively slow speed was to prevent 'dishing' and maintain aileron performance. 'Dishing' during a roll

The Golden Hawks diamond took off and landed in formation whenever runway and wind conditions permitted. (DND PL 131167)

is a phenomena created because the aircraft on the inside of the roll needs less bank than the leader because he is describing a smaller circle. Conversely, the aircraft on the outside needs more bank due to the larger circle. The faster the rate of roll, the more pronounced the dishing. To keep the wings flat, the inside aircraft would use inside rudder which, because of some cross-control, would flatten his wing angle to that of the leader's. Similarly, the outside wingman would also rudder into the lead to keep his wings level with lead's. We also attempted to keep as much 'barrel' out of the roll as possible in order to keep our heading change to 10 degrees or less and altitude gain to a minimum. This may be contrasted to the Snowbirds who, because of their larger formations, use a lot of barrel in their rolls with heading changes up to 45 degrees and more altitude gain.

The solo show was comprised of a coordinated head-on, high-speed pass (up to 540-550 kts) with a wing span separation, a co-loop, a head-on roll (both aircraft crossing exactly inverted), a Cuban-eight and a head-on four-point roll. At this point, the lead solo joined the formation in card-five with the second solo conducting an eight-point roll and a very tight 360 degree turn between the formation's passes. The second solo would then describe a circle for the bomb burst with the lead solo following the formation into the vertical where he would complete several vertical rolls. Meanwhile, the four formation pilots would set up for the 'crossover'. After the bomb burst, the four pilots would theoretically be heading away from each other at 90 degree angles at 5,500 feet AGL. Upon a signal from the leader, each aircraft would roll inverted and complete the back half of a

loop. They would then be heading back to the centre of the airfield attempting to cross over one another simultaneously. The leader would be the lowest with the other aircraft ensuring that they passed over their teammate on the right. It took some airspeed adjustments (due to wind) to get a good crossover, but often you could feel the 'bumps' from compression of the aircraft crossing above and below you. This was the end of the show except for the loop/landing sequence mentioned earlier.

Each aircraft was capable of carrying two colours of smoke out of a selection of red, blue and white. The pilots selected the different colours according to the manoeuvre being flown. The solution, which was pumped into the jet wash immediately behind the tailpipe, would be vaporized by the heat, thereby providing the coloured smoke. The boys on the smoke mixing/loading detail would spend the summer adorned in patriotic colours since the waxoline dye used was almost permanent. I have a flying suit which is still sporting bright red dye stains after 41 years and numerous cleanings.

Either carnea oil and the dye could be used for smoke or, alternatively, turbo oil and dye could be mixed with numerous additives to keep the dye from clotting. At first, we used carnea oil until some supply weenie observed that this oil had to be specially ordered whereas the turbo oil was already 'in the system.' We were therefore obliged to use the turbo oil and additives even though the cost was several times higher. Also, our poor smoke mixers would have to open several hundred one-quart oil cans per show versus pumping it straight out of 45 gallon drums. Some things never change!

Three classic views of the Canadair Mk 5 Sabre flown by the Golden Hawks in 1959 aand 1960. On the left, the 1959 team passes through the vertical during a loop. Above and below, the 1960 team shows off the diamond and line-astern formations. The Sabre 5 had a top speed of 696 mph (1,112 km/h) at sea level and a service ceiling of 50,700 ft. (DND PL 64566, PCN 1146, PCN 1135)

Fond Memories

Our first airshow season in 1959 had been a busy one with 65 shows completed at 42 locations, a lot of good times and some very sad times too. On May 14th, we had taken the show on the road for our public debut at RCAF Stn Torbay, Newfoundland (St. John's). The first demonstration was to be on the 15th, but St. John's weather being what it is, we were kept on the ground until the 17th. My introduction to 50 knot winds and WOXOF (fog) was on the 15th when I came out of the barracks heading for breakfast and met a Newfie outside the door. He said it all when he commented 'Beys oh beys, she's some tick.' The show was postponed until the weather cleared on the 17th of May.

Following the Torbay opening show, the team did several shows in Ontario and Quebec, several more in the Maritimes before heading west on the 4th of July for such events as the Calgary Stampede, the Edmonton Exhibition and the Pacific National Exhibition in Vancouver. Interspersed were various other airshows and 'Air Force Days' in the west. In those days, airshows were authorized over built-up areas and we did so at the foregoing exhibitions plus in several cities such as Saskatoon, Regina, Lethbridge, Victoria, etc. I recall threading our way along a Calgary street except that in order to centre the show in front of the grandstand, we had to fly directly over the livestock exposition barns. The animal owners were justly furious; however, the show directors cast their votes in favour of the airshow. Proper priorities!

After our last show at newly dedicated Kincheloe AFB in Michigan and our stand down parade in Trenton the next day, Fern and I ferried all of the aircraft the 15 miles from Trenton to Mountain View for storage. Although we were officially disbanded, pressure to re-form the team worked and one year to the day of our first ever practice (March 2nd), we started again! Our second season followed the first year pattern pretty well except for more shows in the United States, nine in total. Mid-summer found us at the Calgary Stampede again. At most exhibitions, the team was introduced to the public during the evening stage performance at the grandstand. At one of these, W/C Jack Allan was invited to have the individual pilots introduce themselves. Just as he stepped up to the microphone, Bill Stewart whispered loudly, 'Psst, Sir, your fly is open.'

Jack instinctively grabbed for his zipper, which was of course closed. However, it brought the house down. Shortly after, as the pilots were introducing themselves, one took the opportunity to announce his single status, his hotel room and telephone number. As soon as the ceremonies were over, he proceeded back to his room, via the liquor store, to wait for the calls to come in … none came!

The 1960 season progressed without incident and we left for Las Vegas on the 28th of September via Ottawa, Bunker Hill AFB (Indiana), McConnell AFB (Kansas) and Kirkland AFB (New Mexico), finally arriving at Nellis AFB just outside Las Vegas. My VHF went unserviceable, both transmitter and receiver, five minutes after departing Chatham so it was a quiet series of legs for me. The old 'coffee grinder' ADF provided some music for diversion. On arrival at Nellis, we took a day off, did two practices

The 1960 Golden Hawks ended their season in style at Nellis AFB in Las Vegas. This late afternoon shot was taken by crew chief, LAC Mick Nordeen. (Mick Nordeen)

and then an impromptu Nellis show. The next day we left for Oxnard AFB to do a show at Vandenburg AFB. We returned to Nellis via the same route with some low flying over Death Valley both ways. It is interesting flying 50 feet below sea level! Nellis AFB is of course the home of the USAF Thunderbirds and they were great hosts. Their PR folks were instrumental in getting North American Aircraft to put us up in the Riviera Hotel and Casino and they also picked up our meal tabs. This was fortunate for some of the boys who got wiped out at the gaming tables during the wee hours of the morning. Not having access to 'plastic money' in those days resulted in quite a few panic calls for bank drafts.

The next show was again at Nellis, this time at their formal Armed Forces Day show along with the Thunderbirds. After their show, we went to their lounge where I soon found out where the term 'blue room' may have originated. Upon entering the men's washroom, you quickly noticed its navy blue colour, pictures and mementoes of the U.S. Navy Blue Angel team as well as the Blue Angel logo on each toilet seat! Nothing like a little friendly rivalry …

The next day we did a show for a 'firepower demonstration' at Indian Springs AFB, which is a weapons range near Nellis. There are bleachers there for people to watch weapons deliveries and other flying demonstrations. Right beside the bleachers was the control tower which was built in a fire tower manner, i.e. a steel ladder up the inside with entry onto the floor of the tower via a reverse trap door arrangement. Now in the United States, FAA inspectors monitor ALL public airshows whether they are held on military reserves or not. They have the power to direct deletions of any part of a show that they don't like, and they get particularly upset if you point an aircraft directly at any spectators. Now, our show contained many FAA 'no-no's,' some of which had been toned down for previous shows.

So, to get back to Indian Springs and the trap door, the Thunderbirds wanted us to do our full 'no holds barred' show so, as part of their plan, they had one of their pilots located in the tower. Immediately before our show started, the Thunderbird driver convinced the FAA inspector that he should check some-

thing in the stands which he departed to do. As soon as he saw the first part of our show from ground level, the inspector quickly headed back to the tower to call off the show but, too late!!! All the boys in the tower were standing on the trap door and they stayed there until the show was completed.

The following day was our turn to watch the firepower demonstration and airshow as guests at Indian Springs. The commentator advised us that, due to technical problems, the supersonic pass by an F-105 Thunderchief (the Thud) would be done instead by an F-104 Starfighter. The F-104 had been requisitioned on short notice from Westover AFB in Massachusetts and, unfortunately, the pilot did not have time to get a site briefing prior to the show. Rumour has it this was the same pilot of the F-104 which had removed most of the windows of RCAF Stn Uplands and the Ottawa airport while doing a 'demo' in November of 1959, a few months after our government had ordered Starfighters for the

RCAF. His 'unintentional' supersonic pass had not been well received in Canadian government and military circles as it had caused $500,000 damage to the newly renovated terminal. True to form, he maintained his reputation at Indian Springs.

The base site for Indian Springs is about four miles south of the demonstration area; the idea was that the 104 would go supersonic after passing the base side. But the pilot, not knowing the site position, had his Starfighter wound up to about Mach 1.2 prior to passing the buildings. Once again, all windows were blown out, but even more spectacular was watching the four walls of the NCO Club open outward and the roof falling to the floor. We could see the aircraft approaching the stands because the shock waves were lifting the desert floor. He passed the bleachers about 200 feet in front and only 50 feet above. The shock waves literally raised everyone about a foot out of their seats. Spectacular!!

Nellis was our last show of 1960 and the team stood down on October 12th for vacations, etc. Because the team was now permanent, a crew replacement program had been set up which saw Fern Villeneuve, Ralph Annis, J.T. Price and Dave Tinson leave the team. Ed Rozdeba, Bill Stewart and myself stayed on to maintain continuity.

Selecting Mark 6 Sabres

On November 16th, 1960 the three of us proceeded to No.1 Air Division stations in France and Germany to select Mk 6 Sabres for the coming season. Of course, flying units which have to give up airplanes are not in the habit of offering up their best and, in reality, we had to select the best of a generally bad lot. Three aircraft were taken from each wing for a total of 12. They were transported to Trenton via C-130s, which were then new to the RCAF inventory. The trip to Europe was in reality a vacation in itself with visits to Marville and Grostenquin in France and Zweibrücken and

Artist Don Connolly captured the glory of the Golden Hawks in this limited edition work entitled *"In the Golden Age"* which became the most famous painting of the team ever completed. (courtesy of Don Connolly)

Baden-Soellingen in West Germany. We renewed friendships with former squadron mates and ex-students from Chatham and had the opportunity to visit more notable spots away from the military environment.

Once the aircraft reached Trenton they were carefully inspected, rebuilt and modified as necessary before being painted in Golden Hawk colours. The excellent work done by No. 6 Repair Depot in Trenton was crucial due to the demands placed on our demonstration aircraft. They were consistently flown to, and occasionally beyond, design limitations, yet were expected to maintain a high serviceability rate.

The 1961 Season

Pilot selection for the 1961 team started on December 14th and was completed by the end of the month. After tryouts, the following team was selected – B.R. Campbell on right wing, Lloyd Hubbard on left wing, Ed Rozdeba in the slot and myself as leader. Bill Stewart became lead solo, Alf McDonald as opposing solo and Jim McCann as spare. The practices for the new season started on January 5th and continued until our first show at St. Hubert, Quebec on April 27th. During the practices, Bill Stewart was obliged to bail out at low altitude due to an engine seizure but fortunately was not injured. A fatality did occur on February 22nd however, when Jim McCann somehow collided with the left wingman during a low-level echelon right turnaround causing him to lose most of his right wing. Jim was replaced by Jack Frazer who had flown with the 3 (F) Wing aerobatic team, the 'Fireballs.'

Our 1961 show changed somewhat with a new entrance manoeuvre. All six aircraft pulled up vertically in front of the crowd in

The 1961 Golden Hawks pose in front of one of the team's Mk 6 Sabres (23433). L to R – F/L Jack Frazer, F/L Ed Rozdeba, F/L B.R. Campbell, F/L Lloyd Hubbard, S/L Jim McCombe, F/O Bill Stewart, F/L Alf McDonald, F/O Bob Dobson. Not included are CO Jack Allan, PRO F/L Rocky Van Vliet and EO Phil Perry. (DND PCN 2028)

'wedge' formation, with the two solos breaking off 90 degrees at the vertical in order to go outbound and reposition for their coordinated high-speed pass. The formation team then conducted a roll-off-the-top and began entry for a loop. After this, the show remained pretty well the same until after the card-five roll when we continued that formation into what we called a 'flag' formation with the five aircraft pulling out into line abreast at the top of the loop, continuing into a second loop, then returning to card-five. While the aircraft were line abreast, red, white and blue smoke was used to give the impression of a flag fluttering from a pole. The solo routine was changed by the addition of a coordinated 360 degree turn (a picture of which made *Life Magazine*), a slow pass and a vertical eight by one of the solos. Even though extra manoeuvres were added, the show time remained the same because of the tighter turns possible in the Mk

6 Sabre. A tight show is a requirement to keep a crowd entertained; long gaps between manoeuvres will result in a diversion of attention and people wandering away.

Of special note in 1961 were two shows at Pensacola, Florida – the home of U.S. naval aviation. Again, the FAA inspectors became our nemesis which resulted in our not being able to participate in the Pensacola 'military family day' because, if the FAA were to see the show the day previous to the main show days, most of our show manoeuvres would have been cancelled. Instead, while the Thunderbirds and Blue Angels did their thing at the air station, we proceeded out over the Gulf of Mexico and did a practice over a U.S. Navy aircraft carrier. The boys on the ship appreciated it and we found out how difficult it is to centre a show over water with a moving target having an angled deck!

The 1961 groundcrew under the command of Engineering Officer F/O Phil Perry. RCAF Stn Chatham, New Brunswick is in the background. (DND PCN 2050)

The next day we were scheduled for two shows, one in the morning and one in the afternoon. The cloud base was about 2,500 to 3,000 feet which resulted in many formation and some solo manoeuvres entering cloud … no great problem in Canada. Even though we modified the first show, omitting some of the manoeuvres which would have had the FAA cancel the second show, they violated us every time we entered cloud. The FAA called a special meeting between shows and read the riot act to the Thunderbirds and ourselves. The inspectors wanted us to again modify our show, to which I took exception. I don't know how they could satisfy themselves that doing a new manoeuvre near a crowd would be safer than doing those which had been practiced hundreds of times. In any case, the leader of the Thunderbirds, 'Hoot' Gibson, pulled me aside, suggested that we tell the FAA we would meet their criteria, and then do our own thing. 'After all,' he said, 'who cares about FAA violations after you return to Canada?'

The skies cleared for the afternoon show and it was very hot and muggy. After we were cleared by the tower to commence our show, we changed to our designated UHF show frequency and did our full show, only returning to tower fre-

quency after the show had been completed. The FAA were furious; however, the show had delighted the public …

One aspect of this particular show was the formation double loop. Because of the hot temperature and associated power degradation, the No. 4 man, Ed Rozdeba, had trouble getting from line astern back into his slot position in the diamond. As I normally did, I would slack off the top of the loop and wait until I could see Ed's aircraft pulling into position in my rear view mirror. However, this day I waited and waited, losing altitude in an inverted position until I was forced to pull out to complete the loop. Ed made it into position. However, we all got a thrill because there was barely enough altitude for us to complete the loop … except for one thing. Pensacola is on a peninsula and the displacement of our second loop took us over the edge of the shoreline and the relatively cool water. As a consequence, we regained lots of lift so everything turned out well. The crowd of course loved it as they thought it was part of the show.

The new entrance manoeuvre for the 1961 Hawks, a six-ship wedge loop. The two solos, Bill Stewart and Alf McDonald, are just about to split off to set up for their first head-on pass. (via Bill Briggs)

The Hawks' visit to NAS Pensacola in June 1961 offered a rare opportunity for this unique photo. Blue Angel Commander Zeb Knott has his six-ship of Grumman F11F-1 Tigers tucked in behind slot man Ed Rozdeba of the Hawks. (via Bill Briggs)

That night there was to be a cocktail party in the Officers' Wardroom and the three aerobatic teams were expected to be there. However, through some oversight, neither the Hawks or Thunderbirds received invitations. We therefore gathered around the swimming pool instead with plenty of liquid refreshment at hand. The pool was surrounded by a tall hedge so that anyone who was interested in seeing who was there had to enter the pool area. Some members of the Blue Angels team, curious about our whereabouts, ventured into the pool area upon which they were all thrown into the pool, navy whites notwithstanding, along with their escorts! One by one, others would come out to find out where everyone had gone, until many of the team, leader included, had been immersed. So much for the cocktail party, more fun at the pool …

We returned home the next day and continued the Canadian itinerary without incident until July 2nd at North Bay when Alf McDonald (our opposing solo) had his engine flame out in the middle of the show. After a quick relight, the engine quit again about 20 seconds later so he was forced to deadstick the aircraft in. After prolonged and frustrating efforts to find the problem, the engine finally had to be replaced.

Another interesting show was at Chatham where unforecast high winds came up just before the start of the show. Wind speeds rapidly became 55 knots gusting to 70, with peak gusts of 80 knots! Crowd control fences, tents, chairs and everything else not battened down were blowing around. We got airborne and did a show, one of the bumpiest on record with the wind 60 degrees across the runway. A peculiar aspect of doing loops in such a high crosswind was keeping about a 30 degree crab into the wind in order not to get

Two impressive low passes. Top, Jim McCombe rolls out on Jack Frazer's Sabre 6 for RCAF photographer Rolly Johnson in Edmonton on 8 Jul 61. (DND PL 131129) Immediately above, Frazer has joined the team for the "crazy" formation back in Chatham in Sep 61. (DND PL 131156)

In spite of the cloudy weather, thousands showed up at RCAF Stn Rockcliffe to take in the annual Air Force Day on 24 Jun 61. (DND PCN 3 256)

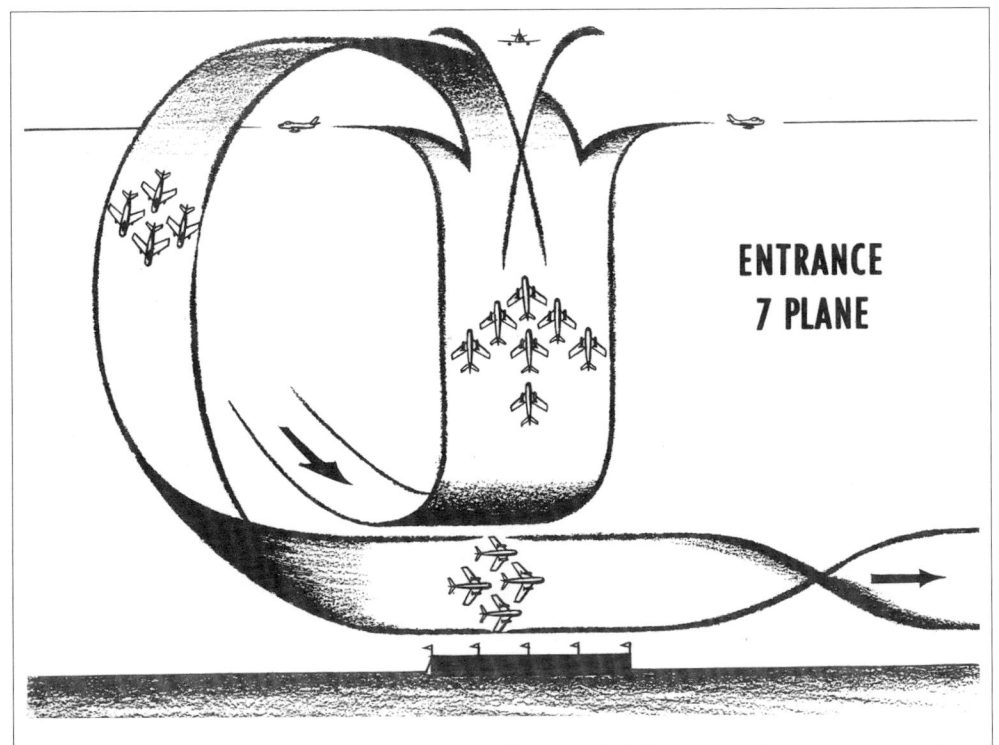

ENTRANCE 7 PLANE

By mid-1961 the Golden Hawks were regularly using seven Mk 6 Sabres for selected manoeuvres in their show, including the show opener. (via Phil Perry)

blown over the crowd. Of course we had to do a stream landing instead of our normal formation; at the slower approach speed we had almost 45 degrees crab on landing. Not so interesting was the fact that every aircraft's accelerometer was pegged off the clock, both positive and negative G. Thus, our ground-crew had to conduct 'overstress' inspections prior to our departure for St. John's.

The CNE in Toronto was always one of our more challenging showsites. One reason is that our shows were flown in the late afternoon when the sun was about 30 degrees above the western horizon, with industrial haze usually very heavy. By geographical necessity, the showline is east-west and therefore, when recovering from any manoeuvre heading west, you have the problem of defining the horizon which blends into the water through the haze. By choice, we did rolls to the east so that Toronto Island could be used for height reference. Looping into the western sun required one to use the shoreline to your right for height reference which was not an accurate method of recovery. Hence, it was never an easy routine.

Our 1961 season ended with our last show at Dow AFB in Bangor, Maine. This went well, culminating with the famous 'stolen horse buggy' incident (see Phil Perry's account). I wasn't one of the returning party as I had been called across A/V/M 'Iron Bill' MacBrien's carpet to explain the 47 violations submitted by the FAA over our Pensacola shows!

Fortunately, our Air Officer Commanding couldn't get very excited about the violations either, and I was let go with a 'tut tut.'

On return to Chatham, we did one week of photo flying and then Ed, Bill and I left the team, all to get married shortly thereafter and to lead a more civilized life. The airshow circuit is fine provided you don't mind being on the road all summer with your luggage and laundry sometimes two stops behind you.

So, three fine seasons, over 900 hours of aerobatic flying and over 200 airshows made up my Golden Hawk tour. A lot of hard work, some tragedy, much fun and excitement. It wasn't until 1962, the team's fourth season, that I saw my first ever Golden Hawk show from the ground. Up until then, I had participated in all of the Hawk practices and shows."

Jim McCombe

A Day in the Life

What was it like flying with the Golden Hawks day-to-day? It was seldom routine and days off were rare. However, the hospitality afforded the team at civilian showsites was often first-class. Veteran Sabre pilot Alf McDonald flew as a solo with the Hawks in 1961 and 1962. He gives us a flavour of what it was like being a member of the showcase of the RCAF. It starts with an 8 a.m. takeoff

from Vancouver on August 7th, 1961, on one of those days you just never forget:

"The seven golden Sabres rolled onto the taxiway at Vancouver's Municipal Airport as if tied together. Golden Leader received take-off clearance on informing the control tower that we would be airborne for 30 minutes under visual flight rules to Kelowna.

The jets were lined up for takeoff and stopped for a final test. Black smoke and noise spewed from their tailpipes as we tested their engines at maximum power. I checked out: engine pressures and temperatures – within limits; oxygen – functioning; fire-warning lights – out; and then watched the leader's cockpit for the brake release signal that would start six aircraft rolling simultaneously. We became airborne at 140 knots. Roz's crisp command 'wheels,' brought all wheels folding up into the fuselage at the same instant. The lead cleared us from Vancouver area control to our tactical radio frequency.

It was a beautiful day, sunny and crystal clear. The formation had swung out over the Straits of Georgia and turned towards the northeast. From two miles high, the strait was mirrored blue, flecked with the startling white of canvas. We left the indented rugged coastline behind and flew above the vast coastal range. Everywhere ahead were deep chasms and awe-inspiring mountains of green timber. Jack Frazer broke the reflective silence transmitting, 'The hills of home.' His voice carried great pride and humbleness for this beautiful part of our country.

Lake Okanagan, a long, slender finger of quiet blue water cradled in gentle mountains, appeared in the distance. We slipped quickly down its 80 mile length, (sort of a notice of arrival) turning at its northern end over the town of Vernon, and set course for the strip of cement outside of Kelowna.

At the airport we were officially met by Mayor Dick Parkinson, a tall, ramrod erect gentleman, the president of the Chamber of Commerce and Harold Long, a committee of one who volunteered to look after us during our stay. The lovely 'Lady of the Lake,' Miss Valerie Deacon, extended an invitation to join the regatta activities. Later that week I discovered that this charming person is selected every year from Kelowna and vicinity contestants by the mysterious, well-man-

The 1961 Golden Hawk postcard, now a rare collector's item. (via Alf McDonald)

nered water serpent Ogopogo who inhabits the lake. None of us had the good fortune to meet the monster but we all thought highly of his ability to choose.

The old Colonial Empire Hotel, our home for the next three days, was reminiscent of a past, Victorian era. It appeared out of place amongst its contemporaries yet it added much charm to the street. The same tone prevailed throughout its interior. The floors were richly carpeted. The walls were panelled in dark mahogany and of course there was no elevator. It was apparently considered a modern triviality not worthwhile.

The following day, Rocky Van Vliet, our public relations officer, received a call from a Mr. Capozzi, who had invited the entire team to visit his winery. Since most of us were amateur connoisseurs, the home of Calona Wines was invaded shortly after we came off duty that afternoon. Mr. Capozzi, a rotund personable man, conducted us on a tour through the maze of presses, massive vats and barrels. He assured us that maidens' feet were no longer used to press the juices from the grapes. Mechanized presses were found to be much more efficient; however, he added 'Something was lost between the antiquated and modern system.' The wines were excellent. A lot of the team members got to bed rather early that night.

The airshow started for us in front of the grandstand at 7 p.m. the following evening with the seven aircraft pulling up in front of the display area in the arrow formation. The formation explodes when the aircraft are vertical with the solos (5, 6 and 7) breaking away leaving the four-plane diamond. The diamond then continues in a shadow pass as Bill Stewart and myself climb away. Gold 5's timing to coordinate the solo manoeuvres between the formation display is critical to the success of the overall show.

His radio call, 'Go now, six' was the cue command to roll my Sabre inverted and pull through towards show centre. The ideal was to have the two aircraft pass centre stage at 200 feet in opposite directions, at 550 knots. The aircraft at these speeds with the moisture conditions at this time of the evening caused a vapour cloud to appear off the aircraft. The noise and speed of the jets with this added phenomenon was spectacular, we were told after the show by our golden voice, Bob Dobson.

The display was in fact a coordinated show of formation and solo flying that had aircraft in front of the spectators at all times. The finale was the bomb burst that got all seven aircraft together with the four-plane formation always hitting a bull's eye smoke ring put up by Gold 6 – then the four aircraft broke to the four points of the compass with the two other soloists climbing through the centre of it to disappear vertically rolling out of sight. The four aircraft reappeared at low-level to cross paths at high-speed. The trick was to be above the plane coming in on your right.

After the show we were informed by our groundcrew about errors (they were experts by this time), smoke problems, scuffed tires caused by improper braking technique and of course, our own complaints about the aircraft. These latter were usually very few and far between.

At the debriefing, Wingco Jack Allan would outline the next day's activities. These often included PR visits to children's hospitals or TV interviews, usually on the early morning shows.

We departed Kelowna the following day knowing that we had helped in a small way to make the Regatta a success."

Alf McDonald

Lead solo Bill Stewart (Gold 5) and opposing solo Alf McDonald (Gold 6) execute a perfect cross in the summer of '61. Note the Avro Lancasters on the ramp below. (Bill Briggs)

The 1962 Hawk pilots strut their stuff for the cameraman in a spring PR shot. L to R - Jack Frazer (slot), Norm Garrioch (left wing), Ed McKeogh (second solo), Lloyd Hubbard (leader), Alf McDonald (lead solo), BR Campbell (right wing) and George Miller (solo). (DND PCN 2076)

The 1962 Season

With the end of the 1961 season came the end of a three year tour with the Golden Hawks for Jim McCombe, Ed Rozdeba and Bill Stewart. Collectively they and their teammates had accomplished a great deal. The team was now well ensconced as an integral component of the RCAF. W/C Jack Allan would continue to command the team as it entered its fourth season; he selected Lloyd Hubbard as the new team lead who was promoted to the rank of "acting squadron leader."

Following another round of intense tryouts, F/Ls Norm Garriock (left wing), George Miller (solo) and Ed McKeogh (second solo) won spots on the team. F/L Jim Giles was selected as the new public relations officer. Seventy shows were scheduled at 60 locations across Canada and the United States where the team had also now garnered widespread recognition and admiration. In fact, the 1962 season opened with two shows at Andrews AFB in Washington on May 12th and 13th. As in previous seasons, it was a gruelling four-and-a-half month airshow season with the team almost constantly on the road. Cross-country transits and shows on the same day became the norm rather than an

The Golden Hawks were often featured on the cover of the RCAF's *The Roundel* magazine, seen here in the issue advertising their 1962 schedule. (via Bill Briggs)

THE *Roundel*

VOL. 14, NO. 4
MAY 1962

The men who kept them flying, F/L Ray Grandy (1959), F/L Dan McKinnon (1960), F/O Phil Perry (1961-62), F/L Carl Peterson (1963). These four engineering officers supervised some of the finest technicians the RCAF had to offer. (RCAF Photos)

exception. This made it exceptionally hard on the groundcrew who flew from showsite to showsite crammed in a C-119 Flying Boxcar with enough spare parts to keep the seven Sabres airworthy at all times. There was no such thing as regular hours for these unsung heroes – their day began long before the pilots arrived at the field for a show and would not end until well after the show had ended. For more complex snags, this often involved working late into the night.

The Groundcrew

Four officers carried the mantle of engineering officer over the Hawks' five airshow seasons: Ray Grandy (1959), Dan McKinnon (1960), Phil Perry (1961, 1962) and Carl Peterson (1963 to disbandment in February 1964). Each was ultimately responsible for the serviceability of the team's 10 Sabre aircraft and had under their command some of the RCAF's finest technicians. Phil Perry outlines how the groundcrew team worked and some of the finer technical details of supporting the team:

"After completing a tour at 3 Wing in 1956, I was posted back to Trenton where I was commissioned to the rank of flying officer in 1958. I had never lost my love for the Sabre, so a few years later in 1961 when Jim McCombe asked me to join the Golden Hawks as engineering officer, I quickly grabbed the opportunity. This was probably the highlight of my air force career. Just a wonderful bunch of highly skilled professional servicemen doing what they loved best. We had top priority when it came to support and equipment and were treated by everyone, service and civilian, in a first class manner. I had approximately 48 groundcrew on the team who carried out all of the main-

The refueling operation following a show in 1962. The open gun bay compartment reveals a portion of the specially designed smoke system. (Bill Briggs)

The Hawks' 1962 Snag Crew. L to R Standing – Sgt. Latraverse, Cpl Paiment, LAC Lariault, Cpl Young, Cpl Terrio, LAC Savage, Cpl Enman, unknown. Kneeling – L AC Grey, LAC Briggs, LAC Brenton, Cpl Lundahl, Cpl Nolin, Cpl Lacking, LAC West, LAC Donaldson. (via Bill Briggs)

RCAF photographer Bill Noice captured a contingent of Hawk groundcrew giving a newly painted Sabre 6 (23457) the once-over in Chatham on 15 Mar 62. The automatic leading edge slats and dual smoke lines on top of the fuselage are clearly visible. (DND PCN 2086)

tenance on the aircraft during the winter when the pilots were training. This was at Chatham until November 1962 when the team moved to Trenton.

When we were on tour from May to September, the team was broken down so that we had 20 techs on the road with us and 28 back at Chatham or in Gimli (when we were doing the western part of the tour). Prior to a tour we would preposition engines, rudders and canopies at different locations. While on the road we were quite self-sufficient. The different trades were responsible for their own pack-up boxes and did very well to prepare themselves for most unserviceabilities. We used various methods of resupply from our base group and normally if it could be squeezed into a Sabre or T-33, that was it! If necessary, we would leave the aircraft and have a spare flown out as a replacement. This was very unpopular with the pilots as they loved their own aircraft and hated flying the spare. Believe me, we would rectify the situation by getting a pilot's aircraft back as soon as possible and get him off my back. The same routine was necessary when an aircraft was due for an inspection.

My right-hand man was Flight Sergeant 'Tousie' Tousignant who supervised our elite group of NCOs and airmen. I cannot say

enough about the technicians. Being on the road for five months working out of pack-up boxes to maintain seven Sabres was not easy. However they did it and we never missed a show with less than the six aircraft, and very seldom without the seventh as a flying spare. It took a lot of work, long hours and above all, teamwork. It didn't matter what their trade was; they all pitched in to get the job done. At the same time our station maintenance crew backed us up with inspections and always had the aircraft ready to go when repaired.

Each aircraft had a crew chief who was responsible for its serviceability and appearance. This was a good system as it allowed a close liaison between the pilot and the groundcrew which was so important in this type of operation. It also set up a very competitive rivalry between the crew chiefs. Morale was always high, mainly because they were proud of belonging to the Hawks and the job they were doing. We had some characters that helped too, like LAC 'Newf' Faulkner who knew everyone wherever you went and could scrounge, beg or steal what-

Coloured smoke was an integral part of the Golden Hawks' show. (RCAF Photo via Terry Leversedge)

With a closing speed of some 700 mph, capturing a solo cross was a real feat. Here, solos George Miller and Alf McDonald commence their co-360 manoeuvre on 9 Jun 62 during National Air Force Day in Ottawa. (DND PL 139663)

ever was required. This took some explaining at times but we didn't have a lot of time when we had a show to do. On one occasion at Edmonton there were no trucks available to off-load our equipment when we arrived and we had a show to do not long after arrival. So I called Newf over and told him to get a stake truck. He was back pronto driving a stake truck. But not long after I had a raging warrant officer after my tail to find out who stole the truck out of the Motor Transport Section. Good Old Newf …

Technical Maintenance

There were not any major maintenance problems with either the Mk 5 or Mk 6 Sabre aircraft. The big difference between the aircraft was the added performance of the 6 over the 5, particularly in this type of flying. It is interesting to know how the Mk 6 aircraft were selected from the Air Division in Europe and ended up with the Hawks. During the break after the 1961 tour (November 1961), Lloyd Hubbard, Jack Frazer, B.R. Campbell and myself were sent over to the Air Division. We went to each of the three wings where I checked the aircraft over and the pilots flew those selected. We then proceeded to Scottish Aviation at Prestwick, Scotland and went through the aircraft in storage the same way. From this we selected 12 of the best aircraft for shipment to No. 6 Repair Depot in Trenton. We were not very popular but it indicates the support we had from headquarters in Ottawa.

The aircraft were dismantled and shipped to 6 RD by C-130 Hercules. We returned with the first Herc. In fact, I am probably the only 'ground pounder' who ever took off in the cockpit of a Sabre inside a Herc! These aircraft were subsequently overhauled, modified, painted and used on the 1962 tour.

Smoke System

The smoke generating system was designed by 6 RD at Trenton. The ammunition cans located in the lower forward fuselage directly below the cockpit were removed and two tanks (one on each side) were manufactured and installed in their place. Each tank held approximately 15 gallons of fluid. Two Dakota (DC-3) feathering pumps located above the tanks in the gun bay, one for each side, were used to pump the fluid to the transfer lines. These stainless steel lines (approximately half an inch inside diameter) ran from the pump back to the aft end of the fuselage. On the Mk 5 Sabre they were on the inside of the fuselage; on the Mk 6 they were on the outside. The reason for this was

Having just flown over the site of the World's Fair during "Canada Week," the Hawks overfly one of "Her Majesty's Canadian Ships" in Seattle Harbour in Sep 62. (DND PCN 7003)

to prevent overheating of the fluid and improved access for cleaning and other maintenance. Smoke nozzles were attached to the end of the lines and designed to give a suitable spray of fluid into the jet blast. The normal fluid we used for white smoke was ordinary 1010 engine oil (the same as that used in the engine of the aircraft). We also experimented with other fluids such as furnace oil, mixtures of engine oil and trichlorethylene (cleaning fluid).

For the blue and red coloured smoke, the fluid was a mixture of a blue or red waxoline dye (a very fine powder made in England which came to us in 2.5 gallon pails), 1010 oil and trichlorethylene fluid. The white smoke did not present any problem. However, the coloured was a different story; it presented our major maintenance problem in handling, maintenance and dependability. It was mixed in 45 gallon drums with a paddle away from any built-up area, normally out in the airfield away from the aircraft and hangars. The reason for this was the powder. Even with the utmost care when you opened a pail the light powder would spread, so you can imagine what it was like in a breeze. There were usually two mixers and you could always recognize them; they would sweat blue and red for days after. It was necessary to vary the consistency as the colour was affected by the humidity and temperature. If it wasn't right you would get pink and purple rather than red or blue and then the *!?#@! would pass down the line. If it was a hot day you left the mixing and filling of the aircraft until the last as it would thicken in the lines and then come out in spurts. On these days pilots would not check their colour systems before takeoff as extreme hot temperatures could bake the fluid in the lines. This was one of the big problems on the Mk 5s with the smoke lines inside the fuselage.

Immediately after a show the crews were required to clean out the smoke system. This was accomplished by pumping 1010 oil through the lines and then purging with air. Occasionally, an aircraft would develop a leak in the smoke system and if it was on the coloured side, what a mess! The poor crew chief would almost cry, in fact I think some did as they were very proud of their aircraft and worked hard to keep them perfect. If it was a bad coloured leak a repaint of the aircraft was required which we often did on the

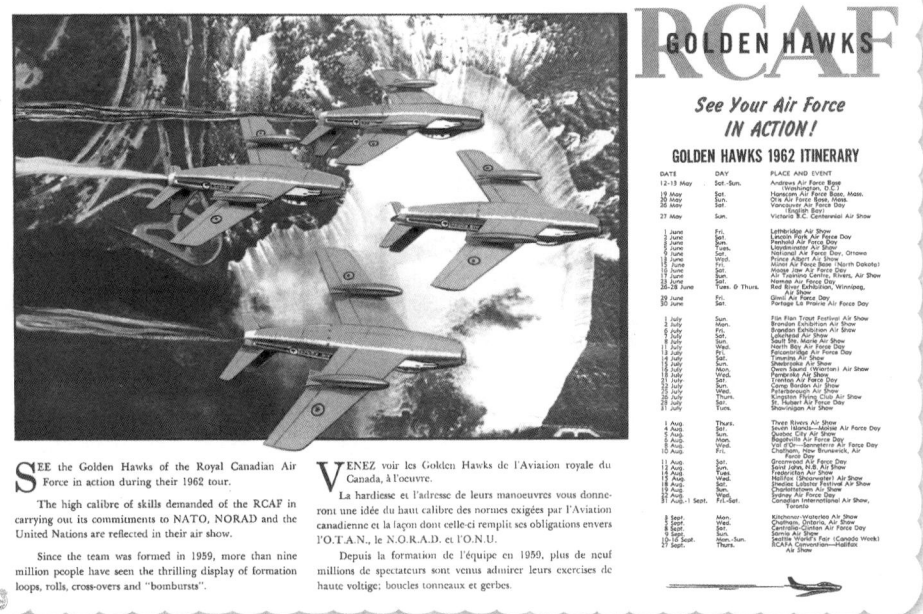

The RCAF took every opportunity to promote the Golden Hawks, including the use of distinctive table placemats each year to advertise the team's schedule. (via Bill Briggs)

road. Although the smoke colour was very temperamental to humidity and temperature, in most cases we got it right and it was a major part of the Hawks' display. Aside from coloured smoke problems, our maintenance crew became very adept at carrying out overstress checks, normally with little or no damage found. Our solo aircraft would often pull six positive G, particularly on the co-360 degree turns, so it didn't take much to get an overstress on the meter, particularly on a hot day with turbulence or by hitting the slipstream of each other or the formation team. This is why the solo aircraft were limited to one year; they were then used in the four-

plane formation or put into storage.

We occasionally had problems with rudders and canopies. If the slot pilot flew low in the box, then the rudder would take a beating, usually at the top hinge point. These were beefed up but we would still go through a lot of rudders on a tour. If the pilot flew higher in the box, then the heat from the lead aircraft would get his canopy occasionally. This would result in crazing of the canopy, requiring replacement. With the box man flying so close behind lead, his vertical stab would get very dirty. One of my first big mistakes with the Hawks was having the vertical stabilizer on Gold 4 repainted – Ed Rozdeba really got on my back. 'Blankety blank, Perry, do you realize how long and what it has taken me to get that tail dirty?' I think he went back to the flight line after we had painted it and blackened it with shoe polish! Aside from the smoke system and the beefed-up rudder hinges, there were few modifications to the Golden Hawk aircraft. In 1962, we did modify the bungees in the elevator control system which provided artificial feel to the hydraulic control system. The standard bungee required a heavy pull on the elevator which became very tiring on the pilots during a show, so we had lighter ones installed which relieved the strain. The only pilot I knew that the heavy bungee did not bother was B.R. Campbell, commonly known as 'The Arm' among the group. The 1962 season was also the only year we flew with blue numbers on the tails.

The smoke makers, LAC Doug Brenton (Smoky 2) and Cpl Ron Lundahl (Smoky 1) prepare the team's coloured smoke for another performance in the summer of '62. (RCAF Photo via Bill Briggs)

The Hawks' flashy T-Bird (21500) was painted in 1961. The first T-33 taken on strength by the RCAF in January 1953, it was normally flown by the CO, W/C Jack Allan, with Phil Perry in the back seat. By the end of 1962, the team's second T-Bird (21616) was also decked out in Hawks' colours. (Rae Simpson)

The T-33 Support Aircraft

When I joined the team, they were usually using a Beech 18 Expeditor for the CO, EO, PRO and commentator to get around the country. This was terrible as you can imagine as it was so darn slow we were always behind. Somehow we managed to exchange it for two T-33s, one of which (500) we had painted in the same scheme as our Sabres. This one was of course for the CO and EO, and 616 looked after the PRO and commentator. By the end of the '62 season, 616 was also painted in Hawk colours. During my tour with the team I put in over 300 hours flying in these aircraft. A lot of this was in the front seat, especially when lanky Jack Frazer and I were together. Jack liked the back as it had more room. For a ground pounder, I became very adept flying the aircraft. Of course, I had the best of instructors.

The gold-painted T-33 was a real crowd pleaser, so there were many low passes made on arrival and departure. It's a wonder we didn't put a smoke system on it. This aircraft made the front page of the Timmins, Ontario newspaper when the Hawks were to put on a show for the opening of their airport. On that day, as we often did, we preceded the team in so I could check the parking area, etc. At the end of our landing roll while completing a 180 degree turn to taxi back, the nose wheel collapsed right in the centre of the new runway. We were sure popular as we had to wait until our groundcrew arrived to get the aircraft back on three wheels and clear the runway. This took a couple of hours and blocked an Air Canada flight from departing. The front page picture of the aircraft showed the T-33 down on its nose with the headlines 'Golden Hawks arrive to open our new airport.'

The Pensacola Show

The year 1961 represented the 50th anniversary of the U.S. Navy and Pensacola was the home base of the Blue Angels. It was a big event as all three teams, the Blue Angels, Thunderbirds and the Golden Hawks were taking part. We were there for five days and the competition was keen throughout the practices and the actual big airshow.

Our chief smoke mixer was Cpl Ron Lundahl who was a great big armourer. He had volunteered for the job at the start of the tour just to be with the team. The heat at Pensacola was causing the smoke systems on the aircraft to plug, so we had to vary our formula to try and prevent this. Consequently, on our practices we would occasionally get pink instead of red, or purple instead of blue. Well, our CO, W/C Jack Allan, was on my back and I was on Tousi's back and poor Lundahl was ending up with it all.

The night before the big show there was a great party put on for all three teams which lasted to the early hours. I remember seeing Lundahl there sweating blue and red through his white shirt having a ball. I knew that we were on fairly early that next day which meant the mixers had to be at their job much earlier. I thought to myself, 'more pink and purple!' Anyway, the next morning bright and early I was on the flight line and it was already 90 degrees F. I went over to the field where they were mixing the smoke and there was poor old Lundy. He could hardly hold his head up and was he sick… right into the barrel! Well, we put on one of our finest airshows that day with the best smoke you could ask for. W/C Allan was elated and said 'Whatever your boys did Phil, tell them not to change it.' I related this to Lundy and his reply was 'To hell with you.'

Dow Air Force Base – The Stolen Surrey

Our last show in 1961 was at Dow Air Force Base in Bangor, Maine. Outside their officers' quarters they had three (almost antique) surreys mounted on cement pedestals with their wheels strapped down. They had been loaned to the club by the local farmers around the base. I don't know who got the bright idea, but we thought it would be a great skit to swipe one and take it back to Chatham, paint it gold and mount it outside our Hawk building. This took a lot of planning as Dow was a Strategic Air Command base with top security; to get that surrey to Chatham we had to get through the hangar line security where our C-119 Flying Boxcar support aircraft was parked.

About 2 a.m., a group of us dismounted the surrey, wheeled it away from the mess and loaded it into the stake truck that we had been allotted. It had a tarp over the back which concealed the surrey. We then backed the truck up against one of the supply buildings so that no one could see in the back. We were scheduled to depart early the next morning for Chatham so our crew got the truck and loaded our baggage all around the surrey so it was not visible. They then headed for the hangar line and our Boxcar. On the way they had to pass through the security gate where the guards actually checked the truck over and passed it through. While all this was going on all hell broke loose when the Yanks found the surrey missing. They knew we must have been the culprits and set about trying to locate it. After passing through the security gate we quickly loaded it into the front end of the Boxcar and surrounded it with our equipment. Before we were allowed to leave, an American security

The "borrowed buggy caper" – safe on home turf again, Jim McCombe and Phil Perry are all smiles as the ever present "Newf" Faulkner prepares to drag their new trophy away. (via Phil Perry)

detail actually came and looked the Boxcar over for the surrey before we were cleared to depart.

As far as we were concerned this was a tremendous skit and was sure to set up some inter-base rivalry. We off-loaded the surrey at Chatham and stored it in our hangar. That was on a Sunday afternoon. The next morning S/L Jim McCombe and I had to go down to Montreal – fortunately we were not around for the fireworks. The base commander at Dow called our station commander at Chatham and gave him an ear full. I guess we had created an international incident and that surrey had to be returned intact to Dow, like yesterday!

The next morning B.R. Campbell and Jack Frazer headed for Bangor, in a yellow pickup truck with the surrey in the back. They had a hell of a time explaining the reason for the mission at the border, but were finally allowed back into the USA. Their welcome at Dow was not warm, so they quickly off-loaded the thing and headed for home. Those Yanks just couldn't take a joke!"

Phil Perry

Of the dozens of technicians posted to a tour of duty with the Golden Hawks, only six served with the team for all five airshow seasons. Five of them were slated to stay on for 1964. Each technician was selected for demonstrated excellence in his respective trade and regardless of how long they served with the team, each came away with vivid memories of a tour like no other. Canadian air force technicians have always taken a

great deal of pride in the aircraft they have serviced, but the opportunity to do so in a public forum comes only once in a lifetime for most. One such individual was a young leading aircraftman by the name of Bill Briggs. An aero engine technician, he was working in the Gunnery and Maintenance Section of RCAF Stn Chatham in February 1959 when he was selected to join the Golden Hawks. He was there from start to finish and to this day, almost 40 years later, still cherishes the experience:

During my tenure with the Golden Hawks, I served as crew chief for Gold 1 (S/L Fern Villeneuve) in 1959 and 1960, Gold 6 (F/L Alf McDonald) in 1961 and Gold 2 (F/L Al Young) in 1963. I also spent one year on our snag crew in 1962.

When the team got underway, the 10 aluminum skinned Mk 5 Sabres selected for use were identified with a yellow painted square on each side of the aircraft. On receipt of the Sabres tested out of Mountain View and accepted by the team, 6 RD in Trenton inspected each aircraft, had the tail section beefed up, removed the bottom guns on both sides and installed the smoke system. Finally, the aircraft were painted in the team colours. As each was tried and tested, the aircraft made their appearance at Chatham one by one. It was a proud moment to witness that first sight of a 'golden bird' and to be part of it.

Six members of the groundcrew served all five seasons with the Golden Hawks. L to R – LAC Bill Briggs, Cpl Ken Terrio, Flt Sgt Guy Latraverse, LAC Ed Harnum, LAC John Elmose and LAC Graham Faulkner (kneeling). (via Bill Briggs)

A stunning shot of the diamond formation in an exceptionally low pass over the runway in Chatham during spring workups. (RCAF 34 38 via Al Brown)

Our safety systems techs painted the pilots' helmets gold and had small hawks emblazoned on either side of the helmets. The groundcrew had white coveralls (from stores on station) and obtained gold coloured baseball caps. A small Golden Hawks crest of the hawk was sewn on the baseball caps and an initial Golden Hawks crest was developed and sewn on the coveralls and flight suits.

All the equipment, spares, baggage and groundcrew were crammed into a C-119 Flying Boxcar supplied by Transport Command. This aircraft, built by Fairchild Aircraft, was rotated from Downsview for the eastern tour and Winnipeg for the western tour. We nick-named this aircraft the 'Fairchild Inn' due to hours, days and months we spent in it. We flew, ate and indeed slept on top of the spares, engines, canopies or baggage. Long flights and long

hours, but never did an aircraft miss a performance on the road. We changed engines on tarmacs, in open fields, in a barn – wherever needed. In addition to the C-119, spare parts were transported by T-33, Expeditor, H-51 helicopter and, on occasion, even a USAF C-124 Globemaster when we were in a tight spot.

From my perspective, the most influence on the groundcrew operation came from F/O Phil Perry. Through his drive and commitment we obtained decent uniforms of tailored blue coveralls with 'Golden Hawks' emblazoned in gold on our backs and a great team emblem at last sewn on the shoulders.

We had a lot of characters on the team such as LAC 'Newf' Faulkner, our metal tech. A jack of all trades, master of none type, he was a scrounger who could cajole the gold

fillings out of anyone's teeth and they'd thank him for it. Newf had a moped motorcycle and we had it painted gold with a hawk on either side of the gas tank. This went with us wherever we went and saved us many a day in obtaining that needed item.

Memorable moment – showtime at RCAF Stn Sea Island, British Columbia The pilots are ready to taxi out for the show. All the groundcrew are lined up on the edge of the tarmac with F/O Phil Perry in front of us. Now Perry had a habit of standing just so straight, then combing his hair in place. Must look pretty for the public you know! Well, on this day, Newf quietly took a position five feet behind Perry (who didn't realize he was there) and then parodied every move that Perry made. Needless to say, it was a riot to watch. Newf had to make coloured smoke for a week for

Solo George Miller in Hawk 6 dusts off the "Fairchild Inn" in a low pass down the ramp upon arrival at The Pas, Manitoba on 30 Jun 62. The team flew a show in Flin Flon the next day. (via Bill Briggs)

that but it was worth it. Newf was invaluable as a technician, a solid team member and vital to lifting one's spirits.

Camaraderie and pride amongst the ground-crew were always evident. The crew chiefs even bet each other on who could marshall his pilot to a perfect park after a show. For all the good times we enjoyed together, however, there were also incidents which were not so funny. During an airshow at Sea Island (Vancouver), F/O's Price's solo air-craft appeared to be changing colour every time he flew by, from gold to a faint reddish colour on the starboard side. Oops! The smoke cap was left off and the red dye poured out over the aircraft. On landing,

As a groundcrew team, we too had our own close call on a flight from Edmonton to Comox in 1959. We were all packed into the 'Fairchild Inn.' Since we had to climb over the Rockies in a storm, we were all on oxy-gen for a few hours. On descent into Comox, the aircraft captain announced that the oxygen cease light would be illuminated and we could remove our masks. No sooner had we taken our masks off than our pho-tographer, Cpl George Hardy, popped a cig-arette in his mouth and lit it. A bright blue flash careened down the centre of the air-craft and the fuselage seemed to expand a foot on both sides. Time stood still as we all held our breath in shock. After the bang subsided all eyes were on George, who was

or right. All seven got down safely. Needless to say, a few hours were spent get-ting them back to the line and cleaned up.

The occasions when we performed with our counterparts, the USAF Thunderbirds and the USN Blue Angels, were always wonder-fully special occasions. They even remarked that the Golden Hawks were something to try to top. There was nothing finer than all three teams getting together in a social atmosphere such as at Corpus Christi, Texas – on the beach with a few vans full of beer. Camaraderie went a long way. So many sto-ries, so many people, so many memories, but none more sobering than the loss of F/L Jeb Kerr in Calgary when he was killed in

Another fine portrait of the Golden Hawks diamond formation, one of a series on Canadian teams painted by artist Geoff Bennett. (courtesy of Geoff Bennett)

and for the next 24 hours, we all scrubbed that aircraft clean. It was a terrible mess.

It was also J.T. Price that gave all of us one of our scariest moments during an airshow. At Halifax, a seagull struck the top of his windshield during the solo high-speed pass over the waterfront. The canopy fragment-ed, Price's helmet visor shattered and due to the cuts inflicted on his face, he couldn't see. Ralph Annis came to the rescue, coached him back to the airport and talked him down to a safe landing. The aircraft looked like something from the Korean War, with holes all over it. Fortunately, Price recovered and the aircraft was fixed and returned to service.

as white as a ghost. Nobody said a word, we all just slowly started breathing again – close baby!

Then there was that stormy, lightning filled day in Thunder Bay the summer of '61 when we awaited the arrival of the team from North Bay. We all knew that this was going to be a dicey landing. One by one the golden Sabres made their approach. The runway was waterlogged and the rain poured down. S/L McCombe landed first and we lost sight of him in a huge spray ball of water as he veered off to the right side of the runway. Each successive aircraft landed, spraying water and hydroplaning down the runway, eventually veering off to the left

the collision with the light aircraft on approach to land. His loss really hit home for all of us.

As I reflect back on five years with the Golden Hawks, I would have to say that LAC Ed Harnum, one of our aero engine techs, was the all around top team player. This individual exemplified the real mean-ing of *esprit de corps*. Tireless, unselfish and keen to perform any task, he was loved and admired by all and will always remain that special person whenever we think of the team."

Bill Briggs

A Technician's Pride

LAC Bill Briggs was among the first group of technicians assigned to the RCAF Golden Hawks in the spring of 1959 and one of the last to leave the unit in February 1964. Over the team's five-year history, he took dozens of photos which comprise a unique collection ... rare treasures from four decades ago. MWO Briggs retired from the Canadian Forces in 1993 following a 37 year career servicing military aircraft. (courtesy Bill Briggs)

Ready for another stellar season, the 1963 version of the Hawks pose with their new boss in Trenton. L to R standing - F/L Bruce Lebans (commentator), F/L Norm Garriock (left wing), S/L Lloyd Hubbard (lead), W/C Frank Hatton (CO), F/L Dave Barker (solo). On the wing are - F/L C.B. Lang (slot), F/L Ed McKeogh (lead solo), F/L Al Young (right wing) and F/L Bill Grip (second solo). Missing is F/L Jim Giles (public relations officer). (DND PCN 7005)

W/C Frank Hatton, Commanding Officer 1963-1964. (RCAF Photo)

Into a Fifth Season

Following the end of the 1962 season it was Jack Allan's turn to move on. He had enjoyed a three year stint as commanding officer of the Golden Hawks and was replaced by W/C Frank Hatton. Lloyd Hubbard would stay on for a third year with the team, his second as team leader. Only Norm Garriock and Ed McKeogh remained with him which left four open slots for new pilots. In November of 1962, the Hawks also bade a fond farewell to Chatham to take up their new home in Trenton. The move of the team to Trenton was a great disappointment to the citizens of Chatham who had enjoyed bragging rights as home of the Golden Hawks. However, the logic at the time was to move the display team to a more central location; Trenton was an attractive choice as it was already home to 6 RD where major modifications to the team's aircraft took place. Thus, the Hawks became an Air Defence Command "lodger unit" on Air Transport Command's largest station.

By now, after four years of unprecedented publicity, the Golden Hawks were becoming a household name in Canada. It was difficult to escape their presence. They had performed at every major exhibition in Canada and had been featured in most of the nation's newspapers and magazines. They had earned their rightful place among the world's best aerobatic teams.

Naturally, with fame and glory seemingly at every turn, the Golden Hawks were not having any trouble attracting new candidates for team pilots or groundcrew to replace departing members. One such pilot who would ultimately make the team was F/L Al Young, a veteran of three flying tours prior to joining the Hawks:

"Following a tour at 2 Wing in Grostenquin, France on the Sabre and an instructional tour on the T-33 at Gimli, I served as an exchange instructor on USAF T-33s from 1960-62 at Reese AFB in Lubbock, Texas. The summer of 1962 saw me posted to the Sabre Transition Unit at Chatham as an instructor.

I decided to give the Hawks a shot and applied by memorandum for a place on the team. I recall being asked by my flight commander, Jack Craig, whether I had any air-show type experience. I could only come up with a very short season with the 'Gimli Smokers' in 1959 when Ken Lett, Tony Bosman, Ollie Fritsch and I had performed at a few shows in the T-33 doing a 'Prince of Wales feather' with smoke. I had of course done a couple of sloppy, unauthorized shows over my home town in Nova Scotia, as I suppose most young pilots with the opportunity had done, but these were not disclosed.

For reasons which I do not recall, I applied for the team without consulting my wife Geraldine, who was pregnant with our second child. When I was accepted for the trials at Trenton, I then had to break the news to her.

Lloyd Hubbard guides the diamond through the Rocky Mountains southeast of Lake Louise on 2 Aug 63. On his right is Al Young, on the left Norm Garriock and in the slot C.B. Lang. (DND PCN 7035)

I have the utmost admiration for the way she reacted during what was a difficult period for her. She had seen a good deal of the hazards of air force life since our marriage in 1957 and must have felt a good deal of trepidation at the prospect of my serving on the team. She quickly became a strong supporter and is now very proud of my Golden Hawk service.

During the period before the flying trials which took place at Trenton, while my log-book does not show an abundance of aerobatic practice flights, I certainly took every opportunity to practice using the Point Escuminac area east of Chatham. I recall being mindful of avoiding those grey fingers of burnt trees which stuck out of the post-fire new growth which had resulted in/caused the crash and death of F/L Sam Eisler in 1959 when he was practicing for the first year of the Golden Hawks.

Late in November 1962, those pilots who had volunteered and been selected for team tryouts proceeded to Trenton. These included myself, Dave Barker, C.B. Lang, Bill Grip and Dave Steeves. Dave Barker had been the 'Red Knight' in 1962, Bill Grip had flown with the 3 Wing 'Fireballs' in

1954 and Dave Steeves had been tentatively earmarked as a spare in the latter part of the 1962 season. Given the background of the prospective members, it looked like C.B. Lang and I would be in a contest for the fourth opening. Initial F-86 checkouts were given since only Dave Steeves and I were current on the Sabre, although C.B. Lang, Dave Barker and Bill Grip had all flown the F-86 in the Air Division. The flying trials, which began on November 26th, 1962, consisted of solo practice and two-plane formations. With hold-over pilots Hubbard, Garriock and McKeogh taking turns leading, Garriock and Hubbard evaluated the two-plane formation performance of the volunteers. Ed McKeogh conducted the solo evaluations. Manoeuvres were generally conducted above show altitudes and kept quite simple, although no height restrictions were formalized. I certainly remember practicing solo loops at Mountain View. We were all conscious of the oval form of a loop. On one occasion, in attempting to perform a more rounded loop, I let the aircraft float over the top and down the backside too long with the result that on the pullout I was so low that I was able to see individual blades of grass. I raise this point to illustrate

that the trials were not for the purpose of instructing but purely for testing the prospective team members. I do not actually recall being given any tips as to technique to apply when performing solo manoeuvres, or formation for that matter.

It must be mentioned that the prospective team members were not vying for a particular position on the team. One was being evaluated as a potential solo performer and as a formation member. Also, of course, we were being evaluated as to our personal compatibility with other members of the team. This is a sometimes unrecognized aspect of selection for aerobatic team membership, but is as critical to the success of a team as piloting skills. The team must get on well with each other. Personality clashes or petty disputes have no place in this kind of work. Confidence in each other's flying ability and personal compatibility are of paramount importance.

At the conclusion of the flight trials in mid-December 1962, we were individually called into the CO's office where W/C Frank Hatton and S/L Lloyd Hubbard debriefed us on our performance and on our

Another flashy work demonstrates why the Golden Hawks were such a popular subject for Canadian artists – at any angle. (courtesy of Geoff Bennett)

acceptance or rejection. Barker, Grip, Lang and I made it as second solo, third solo, slot and right wing respectively. Lloyd Hubbard and Norm Garriock retained their previous positions for 1963 thereby providing continuity in the diamond and Ed McKeogh moved up to lead solo.

New team members returned to their respective units to move their families to Trenton and to be ready for the training period which began the first of the new year.

Training for 1963

The 1963 team began training for the season on January 14th and continued into May. We were scheduled for 14 flights per week, three per day Monday through Thursday and two flights on Friday. Our sorties were approximately one hour in duration. Friday afternoon was a non-flying period to allow the groundcrew additional time for aircraft maintenance.

The flight schedule had the potential to yield something over 200 practice sorties but the winter weather prevented that number being flown. My log book shows 147 sorties of practice before the team's approval show for the AOC of Air Defence Command, A/V/M Max Hendrick, which we flew on May 3rd.

The solos and the formation practiced initially on a separate basis, the formation utilizing the abandoned BCATP field at Deseronto just east of Belleville and only five minutes flying time from Trenton, while the solos used the airfield at Mountain View just to the southeast of Trenton.

Lloyd Hubbard, whom I regarded as an outstanding flight leader and individual,

believed absolutely in making maximum use of flying time. The typical formation training sortie consisted of takeoff from Trenton, close formation to Deseronto and immediately into manoeuvres, loops and rolls along the main runway which was oriented east-west. Each manoeuvre was followed at the end of the runway by a 90-270 degree turn, 3 G pull-up and reposition for the next manoeuvre. The practice continued in this fashion for the

With canopy open, F/L Dave Barker staggers down the showline low and slow at RCAF Stn Lincoln Park in Calgary on 3 Aug 63. The author, 10 years old at the time, is watching from the fenceline. The budding aviator in the foreground was obviously undeterred by a simple snow fence! (Glenbow Archives Calgary, Canada NA-2864-2141(g)-11)

Two fine shots taken by aviation buff Jerry Vernon at Comox AFD, 17 Aug 63. Top – with F/L Bill Grip's aircraft in the foreground, seven Hawks are joined by another RCAF icon of the era, Training Command's Red Knight (F/L Bud Morin). Bottom – the Hawks' paint scheme in all its glory. The "GH" on the tail only appeared in 1963. (Jerry Vernon)

duration of the sorties except that at the halfway point, the lead would pull up and fly a downwind leg allowing us to loosen out and relax a minute or so. We were then called back into close formation for a 3 G turn into the airfield for the next manoeuvre. Return to Trenton was in close formation for a diamond formation landing sequence. This eventually consisted of a loop, pull-up to a landing pattern and a 'box' landing.

Three sorties of this kind (at least early on) were quite fatiguing and it was always a relief to get to the top of the loop where lead was constrained by a lower airspeed from pulling his customary 3 G. The formation pilots did not wear G suits. I have always thought that during the training period my right bicep became an inch larger in diameter than my throttle arm. As in previous years, we flew Mk 5 Sabres during the initial period of selection and training, switching in April to the Mk 6 which was then used through to the end of the show season.

As one would expect, training was begun with the simple manoeuvres of loop and roll. Early on these were carried out at a higher altitude but altitude was reduced as

experience was gained and more complicated manoeuvres were introduced. There was not, as I recall, a lot of individual technique passed from a team member to his successor. B.R. Campbell, whom I succeeded, had been posted away before I arrived and the team had moved to Trenton. The trials and training period were therefore a time of learning virtually by oneself. I had a wealth of formation flying experience from my tours on the F-86 and T-33, so was as well prepared as anyone. However, close formation under G and in aerobatic manoeuvres was not something which I had experienced. I was aware of course that in formation flight the primary means of maintaining position was by the use of throttle. Hitherto, I had always advocated an aircraft in formation should be trimmed so that one's workload was reduced to the minimum. During training to fly the close right wing position in the diamond, I adopted a trim position where left rudder trim cocked the nose slightly into lead and right aileron trim was used to drop the right wing very slightly. The result was a slight cross-control which helped to control any cocking tendency (i.e. to remain wings level with the lead) during a rolling manoeuvre.

The formation typically entered and recovered from a manoeuvre at 200-250 feet. Entry and recovery airspeed was usually 350 kts. From my logbook, the introduction of our more complex manoeuvres occurred as follows: card-five and reverse echelon rolls (Jan 24th), diamond to line astern loop (Feb 5th), bomb burst and crossover (Feb 7th), four-plane line abreast roll (Mar 5th). Our first integrated practice with the solos took place on sortie 92, the 25th of March. Finally, on April 24th, 1963, after 134 practices, we did our first seven-plane full smoke show.

The only new manoeuvre introduced in the formation in 1963 was the four-plane line abreast roll. The positions of the pilots in the manoeuvre were, left to right: left wing, lead, slot, right wing. The roll was always to the right and our first efforts were disappointing. I maintained a fore and aft position by staying where I could just see the inside of the left arch of C.B. Lang's windscreen. Vertically, I could just see the left cockpit rail of his aircraft over the right. Lateral separation was a matter of developing the correct 'whole aircraft' picture.

As the inside aircraft during the first half of the roll, I would come all the way to idle on the engine to avoid going forward of the abreast position. As the roll continued past the inverted position, I would fall back of the line abreast position because engine response to throttle movement was not fast enough to maintain position. One solution was to open the speed brakes and keep the power up to where engine acceleration was faster. This was deemed unsatisfactory as the use of speed brakes would be seen by the audience.

The solution finally decided upon was to perform a roll of higher vertical displacement than the card-five roll and for me as right wing pilot to firewall the engine when I saw the horizon coming up in the inverted position. I maintained my relative position on Gold 4 by a cross-control condition to prevent going forward of line abreast when engine acceleration was too great. Cross-control was reduced as the manoeuvre continued so as to maintain position. Vertical displacement of the line abreast roll was finally settled on at approximately 2,000 feet, as compared to 1,500 feet for the card-five roll and a mere 1,100 feet for the diamond roll. Incidentally, late in the practice season, Lloyd pulled off an 800 foot diamond roll; the roll rate was so fast that I for one was just barely in control of my aircraft.

The Show Routine - 1963

As with any other aerobatic team, we had not one show, but four. Weather and location of the performance determined the show content. The team always went through a standard start-up and takeoff routine, starting on lead's signal and taxiing in a seven-plane echelon formation (fuselage aligned to the drop tank of the aircraft ahead) with a crossover to the opposite echelon at turns in the taxiway. Oxygen was at 100 percent, canopy closed and a rise in EGT was experienced when directly line astern during a crossover because only slightly more than nose/tail clearance was maintained. Taxi in after landing was the same. Takeoff was in two sections with about a five second interval, the diamond leading and the solos following in a vic of three aircraft.

The full show began with a seven-plane pull-up head-on to the showline. When vertical the solos rolled to three cardinal points, the diamond continued over the top to perform a half-roll and pull around to do a diamond silhouette pass. Thereafter, the formation and solos alternated manoeuvres at show centre. As in previous years, the high show had a full complement of manoeuvres i.e. rolls, loops, formation changes and opposing solo manoeuvres. Apart from the entry manoeuvre, the solos and formation integrated when the lead solo joined the formation for the card-five roll and the third solo performed vertical rolls through the diamond bomb burst. The ensuing four-plane crossover saw four aircraft at 90 degrees to each other attempting to cross at the same instant with minimal vertical clearance. In practice, a perfect crossover was virtually impossible to accomplish. After the crossover, the formation pulled up and rejoined at 4,000 to 5,000 feet, although this was not part of the show.

When the full show was being performed at a departure or arrival airfield, the landing sequence was made part of the show. This consisted of the diamond formation performing a loop at the landing end of the runway followed by a pull-up to downwind, lowering gear and flaps, and doing a standard base turn and diamond formation landing as previously described. Meantime, the solos were positioning for a run-in from initial to perform a roll-around break and individual landings. Typically the roll-around break took place with the formation on late base or touch down. Our full remote show lasted

about 26 minutes while a full show at base had another six or seven minutes added for the landing sequence.

The medium or rolling show was performed when a cloud base below 2,500 feet existed. Manoeuvres were limited to those in a rolling plane, formation changes and flypasts. A flat show (1,500 feet) was performed when the weather would only permit formation changes and flypasts, although the solos were still able to do head-on rolling manoeuvres.

On the Road - 1963

The show season for the 1963 team lasted from May to late September. In all, 65 shows were scheduled and 66 shows were flown. Some originally scheduled shows were not flown because of weather but a compensating number were added.

Shows were performed in all 10 provinces, with an additional nine shows scheduled in the southern USA in September. Our most easterly show was St. John's, the most northerly was Cold Lake, westerly Comox and in the south, Corpus Christi.

The team on the road comprised seven F-86 Mk 6 aircraft, two T-33s and one Cosmopolitan support aircraft which had replaced the old Boxcar of previous years. The only exception to this standard deploy-

ment occurred during our last swing to the States when we were supported by a C-130 Hercules which carried our groundcrew and additional spares.

Once on the road, the team pilots flew the same aircraft except of course when that aircraft was returned to Trenton for major maintenance. I flew Mk 6 tail number 23410 about 53 percent of the time. While occasionally one flew one's own aircraft to Trenton for replacement, more typically S/L Fern Villeneuve (then staff officer flight safety at ADCHQ) delivered a replacement and flew the returning aircraft to Trenton.

Apart from performing shows and transits to the next showsite, a minimum of two practices per week were scheduled. Lead would simply pick out an area and conduct a practice, perhaps on a shoreline or line of trees. There was never any formal NOTAM or anything of the sort to warn other air traffic. To my knowledge, there was never a complaint registered. The practices provided an excellent opportunity for an impromptu show at someone's hometown and I specifically recall a partial practice at my hometown in Nova Scotia and a full practice at Lloyd Hubbard's in Alberta.

Throughout their five year history, the Golden Hawks generated an enormous amount of goodwill on behalf of the RCAF. F/L Al Young obliges a photographer as he signs an autograph for a local Princess on 30 Sep 63. This was to be the last public appearance with the entire team together. (RCAF SH63-233 via Al Young)

In Regina to participate in the annual Buffalo Days Exhibition, the 1963 Golden Hawks are joined by another famous troupe, "Don Messer and His Islanders." Public Relations Officer Jim Giles, seated in the centre, organized the shot. (via Al Young)

Shows/Events Remembered

Gander, Newfoundland – The team left Goose Bay on June 11th in 200 & ½ weather and flew to Gander where a show was scheduled the next afternoon. On the morning of the show, we made an appearance at the local arena where the school children of the town had been assembled. The team members were individually introduced to the crowd and upon stepping forward each was applauded loudly. However, when our PRO, F/L Jim Giles, was introduced as a native Newfoundlander, the applause became a sustained roar which must have lasted five minutes. Those grand people brought a tear to Jim's eye.

St. John's, Newfoundland – We flew to St. John's on June 13th, the morning following the Gander show. The weather was excellent on arrival at the Torbay Airport. The St. John's show was scheduled for the next day so most of the team went to the local golf course for some relaxation. Shortly after the round began we were summoned from the course as the show had been advanced to that afternoon since the weather was forecast to be poor the following day. Thus, on about two hours notice, the show was on! We did not expect much of an audience under those circumstances. To our surprise, a vast crowd

of around 20,000 appeared for the show. I've always wondered how such a large crowd was turned out on such short notice. Those wonderful Newfoundlanders again!

Ottawa, Ontario – The annual National Air Force Day airshow was held at Rockcliffe in the east end of Ottawa near the Ottawa River on June 8th, 1963. The team's launch base

S/L Lloyd Hubbard guides the Hawks' seven-plane "arrow" formation cross-country in mid-1963. (DND PCN 7020)

Diamond bottomside silhouette at Gimli AFD, 21 Aug 63. (Hank Siemens)

the best bomb burst and crossover that we ever did, with four Sabres crossing at 90 degrees to each other exactly at the same time. For the crossover, lead set the altitude and was low man. For me, on a good cross all other aircraft disappeared at the same time as I was at the highest altitude just above No. 4, who was just above No. 3, with lead on the bottom. One could hear and feel the other aircraft at the cross point. The idea was to take separation from the aircraft on one's right, just missing it in altitude. There was a tendency to be descending at the crossover as Norm Garriock liked to shave lead who tended to be pushed down a bit. While we always had excellent R/T discipline, on this occasion discipline broke down and we all shouted on the radio.

The popular "bomb burst and crossover" was the Golden Hawks' show finale for all five airshow seasons. (via Al Young)

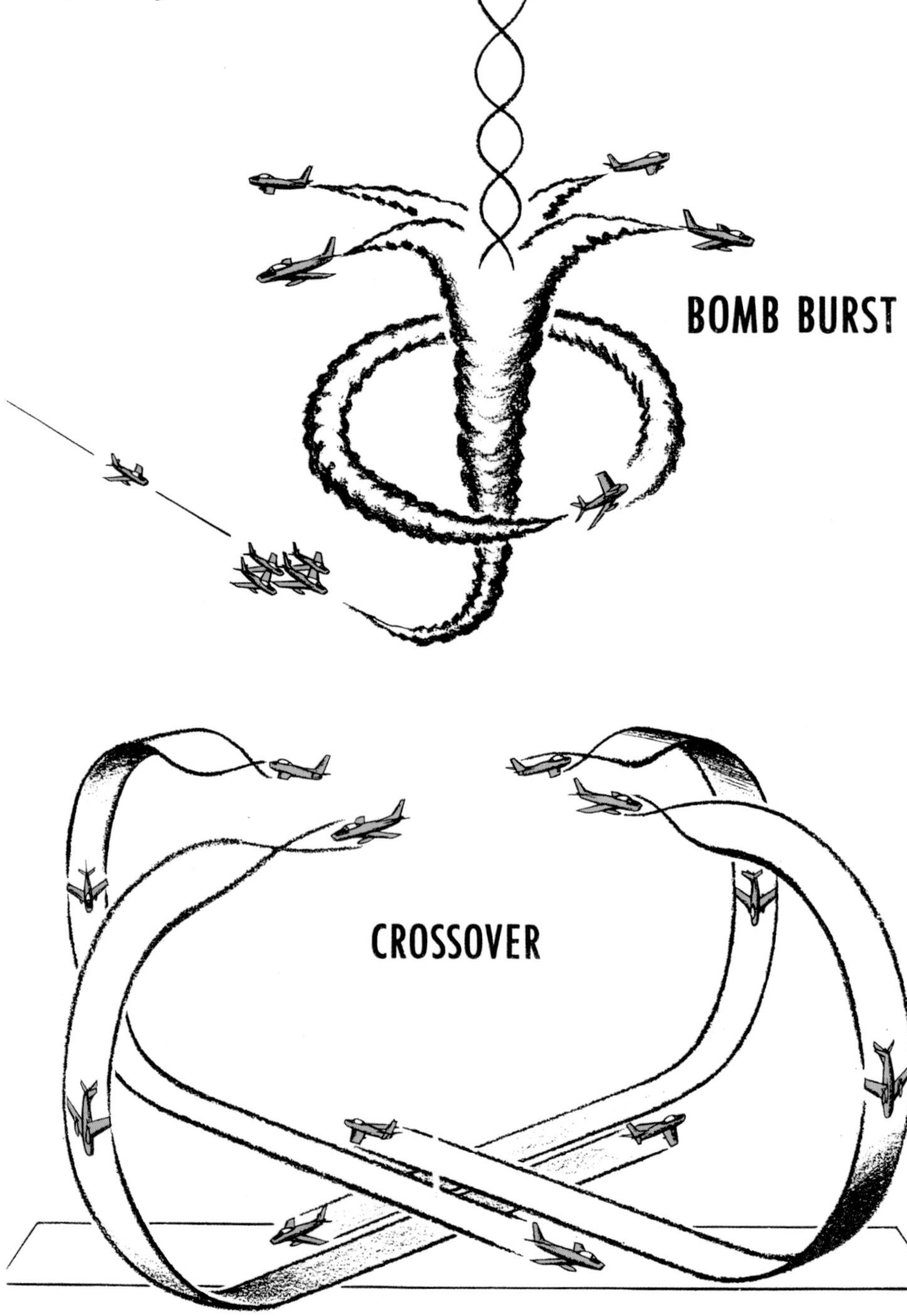

Preparations for a Sixth Season

Following a very successful 10 show tour in the USA and one last show in Canada, our 1963 season ended and we proceeded on a month's leave. We were losing Norm Garriock (left wing) and Ed McKeogh (lead solo) who were tour expired. Ed did perform one more service for the team by flying to Europe with Dave Barker to select additional Mk 6s for the 1964 season. Lloyd Hubbard was also scheduled to be replaced as he had completed three years but was extended to lead again in 1964. I was named deputy team leader and would become team lead in 1965. On reflection, Lloyd's extension should have alerted us that there was something amiss in the wind.

BOMB BURST

CROSSOVER

was Uplands and a full show was performed. However, we landed single ship at Rockcliffe (due to the short runway) in order to sign autographs and attend a formal reception at the Officers' Mess on the escarpment above the airfield. Shortly after arriving in the mess, I found myself in the washroom line next to the Russian air attaché. He remarked that the F-86 was 'a good airshow airplane but not much good for anything else.' I always regret not having the presence of mind to respond to his uncalled for remark by pointing out the F-86 kill ratio of 14:1 over the MiG-15 during the Korean War. The F-86 by 1963 was of course 'yesterday's best fighter aircraft.'

Winnipeg, Manitoba – My logbook records the Winnipeg show on July 13th with one word, 'fiasco.' The weather was terrible – low cloud and poor visibility. We attempted a flat show in which we had a flat bomb burst and crossover in our repertoire based on timed turns. After the break, I don't believe I saw another gold F-86 till back at the parking ramp! I cite this example to illustrate the very real 'the show must go on' attitude which perhaps at times was carried to excess in those days. It also illustrates the absolute discretion afforded the team lead and the complete confidence we all had in his judgement.

Toronto, Ontario – The Canadian International Air Show always drew large crowds and on the final day (August 31st) there were some 100,000 spectators lining the shore. The team was fortunate that day to perform

Golden Hawks 1963

The 1963 Golden Hawks were the fifth (and last) edition of the team to perform public airshows in Canada. (RCAF Photo via Ed McKeogh)

In November 1963 the tryouts for the 1964 team began. Four candidates had been selected, one of whom voluntarily withdrew midway through the trials. In the end, Brian Grover and Beau Warrian were selected as the second and third solos respectively. Both were very fine pilots; Brian in particular had been extremely aggressive during the tryouts. With Lloyd, C.B. and myself remaining in our positions, Bill Grip moved to the left wing and Dave Barker took up the role of lead solo. We were all looking forward to another great year.

The Team's Demise

As the old saying goes, February 7th, 1964 will forever remain 'a day that will live in infamy' for anyone who ever served with or watched the Golden Hawks. The training for the 1964 season was going well and we had flown 57 practice sorties. Lloyd was leading with as much enthusiasm and dedication as ever, although it must have been getting to be old hat. He did not slacken in his efforts to maximize use of every flight minute. Deseronto was again used by the formation and Mountain View by the solos. Muscles which may have atrophied somewhat during the off season built large again.

On the morning of February 7th, a Friday, with no prior warning or discernible indication to members of the team, the Golden Hawks disappeared from the RCAF organization chart. As we were preparing for our first practice of the day, Frank Hatton and Lloyd came out of the CO's office and into the pilot's lounge and broke the news. The CO indicated that he had received a phone call from Air Defence Command advising the team to 'cease and desist' immediately. We never set foot in our golden Sabres again."

Al Young

News of the sudden disbandment of the Golden Hawks disappointed thousands of Canadians and left many team members bitterly disappointed. The news quickly spread across the country. Commanding Officer Frank Hatton was as surprised as anyone. As recorded in his last historical report, he had heard a few rumblings over the previous month but had dismissed them since training for 1964 was so far advanced. New manoeuvres were coming along well, including a downward bomb burst and the solo's "pretzel and reverse calypso pass." Requests for PR visits had also been particularly heavy and had taken team members as far afield as Vancouver, Edmonton, Portage and Toronto in the previous two weeks.

Rumours of disbandment had not filtered down to the majority of team personnel who had no idea whatsoever that the team was in jeopardy. Indeed, the Friday morning of disbandment, the unit had just received another totally refurbished Sabre 6 in Golden Hawk colours for the upcoming season. It was being prepared for a test flight when the groundcrew were told to close up all of the aircraft on the line. Puzzled by this unusual order, canopies were quickly closed and each aircraft was double chocked at which time the technicians made their way into the hangar to receive the shocking news. The air of disbelief was evident on every face. As engineering officer Carl Peterson remembers, "To such a cohesive unit, splitting up the crew was like splitting up a family. To many, it marked the end of an era."

The team that never was! In spite of having completed 57 practices, the 1964 Golden Hawks were abruptly cancelled on 7 Feb 64 before the airshow season began. Pictured here with W/C Frank Hatton (centre) are the 36 technicians and team pilots (kneeling) that formed the sixth edition of the team. The RCAF's last Golden Hawk pilots were, L to R – F/L Dave Barker, F/L Beau Warrian, F/L Al Young, S/L Lloyd Hubbard, F/L Bill Grip, F/O Brian Grover and F/L C.B. Lang. Both newcomers, Warrian and Grover, were solo pilots under Barker's tutelage. (RCAF Photo via Bill Briggs)

The Winds of Change

The cancellation of the RCAF's most famous unit was but one result of tumultuous activity that had been taking place in the higher echelons of the Canadian government over the previous year. Sadly, it also signalled the end of the glory years for the RCAF. Funding and politics were about to change the air force forever.

The country had struggled over the issue of deploying American owned nuclear weapons on Canadian soil and on RCAF aircraft, both at home and in Europe. The issue had seen a crisis develop in Prime Minister John Diefenbaker's cabinet that ultimately led to the resignation of his Minister of National Defence, Douglas Harkness. The federal election in April 1963 saw the end of the Diefenbaker era as the Liberals came to power under Lester B. Pearson. He had changed his stance on accepting nuclear weapons just prior to the election. The Cold War was very much alive, thanks largely to the Cuban missile crisis only a few months earlier. Pearson appointed Paul Hellyer as his Minister of National Defence and it was confirmed that the government would allow the deployment of American owned nuclear weapons on Canadian stations in Europe for use on the RCAF's newest fighter bomber, the CF-104 Starfighter. Although controversial, this decision was in concert with the stance taken by the majority of the NATO allies in an effort to further strengthen the West against any possible aggression from the Soviet Union. Meanwhile, plans were also made for the deployment of "special weapons" on selected

RCAF stations. With great secrecy and under the blanket of darkness, the first nuclear warheads had arrived at RCAF Stn North Bay on December 31st, 1963.

Ironically, while the Liberal government initially agreed to strengthen the combat capabilities and viability of Canada's NATO contribution in Europe, it also began to seek ways to reduce overall defence expenditures. By the fall of 1963, the government, through the Minister of National Defence, had served notice to the commanders of its three military services that significant cuts to the country's defence budget were to be affected. There would be station and unit closures across the country. None of the commanders of the day in 1963 could have imagined that the days of the Royal Canadian Navy, Royal Canadian Army and Royal Canadian Air Force were numbered, a prospect that would have been (and soon became) much more sobering than simply a reduction in expenditures.

Nevertheless, in September of 1963 the budgetary axe fell and the Chief of the Air Staff, Air Marshal C.R. Dunlap, was ordered to slash some $30 million from the RCAF's budget for the 1964/65 fiscal year. In relative terms, this was an enormous sum of money and seemed an impossible task. If there was any effort by the senior military leadership to have the budget cuts made more palatable, such initiatives evidently fell on deaf ears. The government had a new agenda and military spending was going to be on a significantly reduced footing. Thus, A/M Dunlap tasked his Chief of Plans and Intelligence, Air Commodore G.S. Austin, with the unenviable

job of reviewing all aspects of RCAF expenditures and making recommendations where cuts could be made to save the prerequisite funds. His report was due by the middle of December.

As the budgetary crisis was unfolding in the hallways of air force headquarters, the Golden Hawks were flying the Canadian flag south of the border in the final swing of their fifth enormously successful season. They flew 10 shows at nine American locations between the 8th and 22nd of September to very enthusiastic audiences. Who could have imagined that the season ending show in Montreal for the Canadian Fighter Pilot's Association, the team's 317th public performance, would also be their last?

The message announcing the cancellation of the Golden Hawks was officially released to the media from the Minister of National Defence's office in the early afternoon of February 7th, 1964 after the team had been advised by phone. That phone call had been precipitated by a confidential message from AFHQ to the AOC Air Defence Command earlier that morning. It read:

"THE MINISTER HAS AUTHORIZED THE IMMEDIATE DISBANDMENT OF THE GOLDEN HAWKS. REQUEST CO GOLDEN HAWKS BE ADVISED OF THIS DECISION PRIOR TO PRESS RELEASE WHICH WILL BE ISSUED FROM MINISTER'S OFFICE EARLY AFTERNOON 7 FEB 64. INFORMATION REGARDING DISBANDMENT MAY BE DECLASSIFIED AFTER PRESS RELEASE HAS BEEN ISSUED. CO IS TO GROUND ALL AIRCRAFT UPON RECEIPT OF INFORMATION FROM YOU. DISBANDMENT ORDER WILL FOLLOW AS SOON AS POSSIBLE. FOLLOWING MESSAGE FROM CAS TO BE PASSED TO CO GOLDEN HAWKS. QUOTE, ALTHOUGH THE DISBANDMENT OF THE GOLDEN HAWKS WILL CAUSE DISAPPOINTMENT THROUGHOUT THE SERVICE, THE MEMBERS OF YOUR TEAM CAN BE JUSTLY PROUD OF THE EVERLASTING FAME THAT THEY HAVE BROUGHT TO CANADA AND THE RCAF. THE SUPERLATIVE FLYING SKILLS AND INCOMPARABLE MAINTENANCE STANDARDS HAVE BEEN ADMIRED BY MILLIONS OF PEOPLE THROUGHOUT NORTH AMERICA AND THE GOLDEN HAWKS HAVE EARNED AN HONOURED PLACE IN THE HISTORY OF THE RCAF, UNQUOTE."

The statement by the Honourable Paul Hellyer stated that "the decision to disband the team was based on the necessity to use the expenditures (approximately three quarters of a million dollars per year) required to operate the team for more vital defence needs, particularly new equipment." It also implied that the Sabre might somehow become unsafe and "will soon be very costly and difficult to maintain." Not surprisingly, these reasons did not sit well with either the Hawks or thousands of other members of the RCAF that the team had represented so well. While it was difficult to refute the cost of running the team, the RCAF had boasted that the Hawks were generating a million dollars of publicity each year. Were public relations no longer important to the military and civilian hierarchy?

The suggestion that the Hawks' Sabre 6 aircraft were no longer considered safe due to their age was nonsensical due to the large numbers of aircraft the team had to choose from. Although the Sabre had recently been retired from its operational role in the Air Division, as Al Young recalls, there were many Mk 6s "with as little as 1200 to 1500 hours on them and, apart from anything else, the show aircraft were completely stripped and inspected for structural problems after each season at 6 RD in Trenton. Certainly, none of us were ever concerned about the safety of the aircraft we were flying." Indeed, all of the aircraft for the 1964 season were already in place in Trenton when the disbandment order came and the Sabre continued to serve a vital role at the Sabre Transition Unit in Chatham for several years. The last formal flypast and retirement of the grand old lady did not take place until November 29th, 1968.

Another theory held by some ex-servicemen is that the unprecedented popularity of the Golden Hawks had strained the relationship of the RCAF with her sister services, the navy and the army. It has been suggested that both were having difficulty recruiting quality candidates in the wake of the flashy aerobatic team's appearances across the country. Judging by the millions who showed up to watch the Hawks perform each year, the RCAF public relations machine was in high gear and working very well. Although no evidence has surfaced to suggest that either of Canada's senior services lobbied to have the RCAF's pride and joy disbanded, the *Ottawa Journal* did

```
HOURLY HEADLINES

        U R G E N T

    (OTTAWA)---IT WAS LEARNED IN OTTAWA TODAY THE FAMED GOLDEN
HAWKS--THE AIR FORCE'S AEROBATIC TEAM---ARE BEING RETIRED.  AN OFFICIAL
ANNOUNCEMENT IS EXPECTED TO BE MADE SHORTLY BY DEFENSE MINISTER
HELLYER.


    (OTTAWA)---AN ANNOUNCEMENT IS EXPECTED FROM DEFENSE MINISTER PAUL
HELLYER SHORTLY CONFIRMING REPORTS THE ROYAL CANADIAN AIR
FORCES AEROBATIC TEAM, "THE GOLDEN HAWKS", ARE TO BE RETIRED.  INFORMED
SOURCES IN OTTAWA SUGGEST THE REASON FOR THE RETIREMENT IS THE AGE OF
THE AIRCRAFT.  THE SOURCES SAID THERE WILL BE NO REPLACEMENT BECAUSE THE
TWO JET INTERCEPTORS THE AIR FORCE NOW POSSESSES--THE CF-101 VOODOOS
AND THE CF-104 STARFIGHTERS--ARE BOTH TOO FAST AND NOT MANOUVERABLE
ENOUGH FOR AEROBATIC FLYING. (6)

UPI-49
    MORE SECOND WORLD ROUNDUP XXX U-S FIRM.

    (GOLDEN HAWKS)
    THE GOLDEN HAWKS ARE BEING RETIRED.
    THE FAMED AIR FORCE AEROBATIC TEAM--WHICH FLIES KOREAN-WAR
VINTAGE SABRE JET FIGHTERS--WAS FORMED IN 1959...THE GOLDEN YEAR
OF FLIGHT IN CANADA...AND THE 35TH ANNIVERSARY OF THE AIR FORCE.
ITS PRIME PURPOSE WAS PROMOTION OF THE R-C-A-F.
    THE RETIREMENT--EXPECTED TO BE ANNOUNCED SHORTLY BY DEFENSE MINISTER
HELLYER--WAS RECOMMENDED BY THE AIR FORCE FOR SEVERAL REASONS.  THE
AGE OF THE PLANES, AND THE MORE DIFFICULT PROBLEMS OF MAINTAINING A
NON-OPERATIONAL AIRCRAFT FOR THE HAWKS, CAUSED CONCERN FOR THE SAFETY
OF THE TEAM.
    UPKEEP AND MAINTENANCE OF THE AEROBATIC TEAM COST SOME 750-
THOUSAND DOLLARS A YEAR. (2)
```

As rumours began to leak out about the disbandment of the Golden Hawks, news wires marked "URGENT" flashed across the country. (via Bob Brown)

report the day following disbandment that the navy and army "were irked at the annual expenditure of about $1,000,000 on the Hawks for RCAF publicity."

The real reason behind the cancellation of the Golden Hawks lies in the aforementioned budget cuts. As often happens however, the true cost of running the team was somewhat exaggerated. In response to an opposition inquiry in the House of Commons following disbandment, the Defence Department revealed that the actual total cost of running the team in 1963 was $712,000. Perhaps more fundamental questions are why the Golden Hawks were deemed expendable and who ordered their disbandment? For years, many veterans of the RCAF have blamed the Minister of National Defence of the day, Paul Hellyer, as being the villain who ordered the cancellation of the team. To this day, Mr. Hellyer denies that notion, a stance that is backed up by an interesting ally, none other than Bill Lee. Lee's flair for public affairs

DEPARTMENT OF NATIONAL DEFENCE

DIRECTORATE OF PUBLIC RELATIONS

CANADA

AFN NO. 8   IMMEDIATE RELEASE

STATEMENT BY THE HONOURABLE PAUL HELLYER

MINISTER OF NATIONAL DEFENCE

After careful consideration of all the factors involved, it has been decided to disband the RCAF's air-show
aerobatic team, the RCAF "Golden Hawks". The team will not
perform this year.

Since they were formed in 1959 to celebrate the Golden
Anniversary of Flight in Canada, the Golden Hawks have performed
before millions of spectators in the United States and Canada,
and they have gained much favourable publicity for their service.

The decision to disband the team was based on the
necessity to use the expenditures (approximately three quarters
of a million dollars per year) required to operate the team for
more vital defence needs, particularly new equipment. In addition, the F-86 Sabre flown by the Hawks is no longer in operational service with the RCAF and will soon be very difficult
and costly to maintain. The performance of aerobatic manoeuvres
in close formation makes it mandatory for demonstration aircraft
to be maintained in near-perfect form to ensure the safety
of the pilots who fly them. The Sabre, which flew well in the
Korean conflict and for many years in NATO, is reaching the end of
its life expectancy.

In agreeing to the disbandment of the Golden Hawks, I
would like to congratulate all the pilots and groundcrews who have
been associated with the team over the years. The thrilling
performances of the Golden Hawks will long be remembered by all
who saw them in action.

7 Feb 64

The official statement released by the Minister of National Defence on 7 Feb 64. The Golden Hawks never flew again.
(via Directorate of History, NDHQ)

had been noticed by Hellyer while the former was serving as director of public relations at AFHQ. Lee, who ultimately joined the Hellyer political camp as a civilian lobbyist, also maintains that the MND did not order the cancellation of the Golden Hawks, adding that "I thought it was a huge mistake."

An Air Force in Dilemma

The answer to the demise of the Golden Hawks is found in the minutes of the RCAF Air Council meetings which took place between September 1963 and March 1964 during the height of the budget crisis among Canada's military services. They provide a fascinating glimpse into the inner workings of the RCAF during the period and the personalities and pressures that were being brought to bear. An important meeting of the council, which normally met at least weekly, took place in the Air Council room at AFHQ at 0900 hours on December 18th, 1963. Agenda items included the "40th Anniversary of the RCAF – NAFD Ceremony 1964, Golden Hawks Tour – 1964" and most importantly, "Reduction of RCAF Activities – Report by Co-ordinating Committee."

During this meeting, considerable discussion took place concerning the scope of celebrations that would be appropriate to commemorate the 40th anniversary of the RCAF. The CAS, A/M Dunlap, felt it would be most appropriate to hold the principal event in Ottawa and it was subsequently decided that June 6th would be the date for a combined 40th anniversary salute and National Air Force Day airshow at RCAF Stn Rockcliffe. The Golden Hawks would be the premier attraction as in the previous five years. The proposed itinerary for the Golden Hawks' 1964 season was also tabled by the Acting Air Member for Personnel (AMP) and examined in detail; it included some 70 shows. The Air Council agreed to the itinerary in principle but noted that it would have to be revised and retabled "in light of recent programme changes and economies which must be effected in FY 64/65" and also since it included some stations which would "soon be closed on the direction of the Minister." Nevertheless, the Golden Hawks were a "go" for 1964. It was also decided that the Red Knight program would continue under the command of the AOC of Training Command.

While the above decisions sounded favourable, there were ominous overtones to the meeting. AMP was tasked to confer with the Comptroller on savings with respect to air displays which had been shown in the revised 64/65 budget document and "to table detailed recommendations on how these savings can be achieved." However, the most controversial report of the day came at the end of the meeting via the "Co-ordinating Committee for Reduction of RCAF

Activities." This was A/C Austin's committee and they were assembled to brief the Air Council on the extent of actions taken to date in coordinating various reductions following "the Minister's announcement regarding a cut-back in RCAF activities." In addition to the Chief of Plans and Intelligence (A/C Austin), the team included the Assistant to the CAS and the Director Air Policy. Among 35 recommendations to save millions of dollars in the next fiscal year was a suggestion to cancel the Golden Hawks Air Display Unit. The Hawks were near the top of the list due to their high public profile and it may have been surmised that such a move might persuade the government to reconsider the extent of the announced budget cuts. If so, it was a gamble that failed.

Announcements of the closure of several RCAF stations had already been made and further recommendations included the disbandment of numerous units of the Air Reserves and many of the Auxiliary RCAF squadrons. Although the minutes of December 18th do not reflect any further decisions concerning these recommendations, they were to precipitate great emotional debate among the members of the Air Council and ultimately with the commanders of Air Defence Command and Air Transport Command. With a myriad of other important issues at hand, this was now an air force in dilemma.

Following the traditional Christmas break, the first meeting of the Air Council in the new year took place on January 8th, 1964. An all day meeting, it was decided that the RCAF "Gap Filler" radar program was to be cancelled and that 410 and 414 AW(F) Sqns would be shut down with the implementation of the "Bomarc Special Weapons Agreement" with the United States. There was no recorded discussion of the Golden Hawks or NAFD. However, at meeting 2/64, which took place one week later on January 15th, there is compelling evidence that the recommendation to disband the Golden Hawks had indeed been forwarded to the MND by the Air Council. In a discussion pertaining to the disposal of over 300 aircraft deemed surplus to RCAF requirements, the minutes recorded that:

"Recent proposals to the Minister concerning the Golden Hawk air display team were discussed, together with the impact their acceptance would have on the surplus of Sabre VI aircraft. Air Members were of the opinion that all Sabre VIs should be declared surplus if the proposals are approved, and that the declaration for disposal should be timed to coincide with the dates contained in the proposals made to the Minister."

By the end of the meeting, the Air Council had approved the immediate disposal of 165 aircraft, including six CF-100 Mk 3s, nine CF-100 Mk 4s, 44 Harvards, 43 Sabre 5s and 63 T-33s and directed that prompt action be taken to dispose of dozens more, especially those in storage on stations earmarked for closure. Of special significance, headlined under "Decisions," the Air Council also agreed that:

"Subject to Government acceptance of proposals recently made regarding the future of the Golden Hawks, the entire inventory of Sabre VI aircraft is to be disposed of. The timing of this proposal is to be in consonance with the recommendations made to the Minister respecting the Golden Hawks."

These clearly worded statements leave little room for interpretation. Thus, by January 15th, 1964, the die had already been cast with respect to the future of the Golden Hawks. Unless the MND rejected the recommendation, the team would be cancelled and savings diverted to other requirements. That decision was not long in coming. Although it is not known exactly when the Minister gave his final approval, Mr. Hellyer recalls that "The RCAF recommended closing down the team and I realized at once that there would be some political repercussions. I was somewhat reassured by the explanation that it was a cost-saving decision and by the undertaking that a new Tutor team would be established in the not too distant future. Under the circumstances, I concurred." Although a press statement dated February 4th, 1964 was prepared for release the next afternoon, it was delayed for unknown reasons. The announcement came the day following a meeting between the Minister and his Chiefs of Staff on February 6th regarding the "Long Range Defence Programme."

There is evidence, however, that the actual date of disbandment of the Hawks was debated. In view of the extensive preparation that had already taken place, and presumably to allow them to participate in 40th anniversary celebrations, it was initially proposed that the Hawks would not be disbanded until June 30th, 1964. This date appeared in a message from Air Materiel Command to Air Defence Command requesting revised requirements for Golden Hawks' support based on that phase-out date. Unfortunately, in what appears to have been a very sudden decision, it was subsequently decided to disband the team immediately as reflected in the press release of February 7th. By doing so, the government/air force effectively stifled any opportunity for rebuttal or debate, either internal, political or from airshow organizations that would suffer as a result. As one former Hawk member recalls, the decision was as "brutal and swift as the cancellation of the Avro Arrow program."

At the Air Council meeting that took place the morning of February 7th, the CAS expressed the opinion that financial restrictions would preclude any large scale air display activity in 1964. However, it was felt that National Air Force Day should be held in spite of the cancellation of the Golden Hawks. The Air Member for Personnel was therefore directed to table a new airshow policy with the guidelines that there would be no RCAF or foreign aerobatic team participation in Canada in 1964, nor would there be any large formation flypasts staged by the RCAF. These decisions would not stand up to the test of time.

In the aftermath of that fateful day, the decision to disband the Golden Hawks did not sit well with the Commander of Air Defence Command, Air Vice Marshal M.M. Hendrick, as evidenced by a carefully worded message he sent to his immediate superior, the Vice Chief of the Air Staff, on February 20th, 1964. In part, it read:

"REFERENCE GOLDEN HAWKS DISBANDMENT. I SHARE WITH YOU THE REGRET WHICH ALL AIR FORCE PERSONNEL FEEL AT THE DISBANDMENT OF OUR EXCELLENT DISPLAY TEAM. I APPRECIATE HOW DIFFICULT MUST HAVE BEEN THE DECISION TO CLOSE THE SUCCESSFUL CAREER OF THE RCAF'S MOST TANGIBLE CONTACT WITH THE CANADIAN PEOPLE ..."

Faced with a host of air display commitments at ADC stations in 1964, A/V/M Hendrick went on to request authorization to form a small T-33 section of three aircraft at St. Hubert to fulfil them. His plan was to use three former Golden Hawk pilots to provide at least solo displays or a synchronized aerobatic pair. They would not be advertised as a team. His request was unanimously rejected

The end of an era. Although the Golden Hawks were cancelled in February 1964, the Sabre 6 continued in service with the Sabre Transition Unit until November 1968. This photo shows the delta formation in a superb low pass circa 1962 over RCAF Stn Chatham, the team's original home. (RCAF Photo)

by the members of the Air Council who felt that any display team would reduce the economies attained by the cancellation of the Golden Hawks. On the surface, this position seemed understandable.

The discussion of a revised airshow policy continued in Air Council meetings between March 4th and April 22nd, 1964. Surprisingly, members became mired in minute details concerning the NAFD flying program, even going so far as to adjust the order of partici-

pating aircraft. This reflected an obvious concern for how the RCAF was to be perceived during its 40th anniversary. A plan to have a large scale flypast of T-33 aircraft forming the number "40" was approved on March 4th as an exception to the previously stated policy, only to be cancelled on April 22nd. Pressure was also coming from the CIAS in Toronto as to what participation would be provided for their internationally respected show. Yet, one member of the council voiced the opinion that "the publici-

ty and recruiting returns from Air Force Day celebrations are not of sufficient magnitude to justify the continuation of previous levels of effort devoted to these activities." Considering the fame that the Golden Hawks had brought the RCAF, this was a remarkable statement which contrasted sharply with the view held by the air force's public relations team. It also failed to recognize the lasting effects that teams like the Hawks had on youngsters who saw them perform. Many would seek air force careers years down-

stream following high school or university as a result of such exposure.

There is an ultimate irony in the cancellation of the Golden Hawks. By the time the air-show season in 1964 had commenced, Training Command was not only flying the Red Knight across the country but had also received approval for the "Gimli Smokers" to continue flying selected shows with eight T-33s in a non-aerobatic routine. Most extraordinary of all is that the "Moose Jaw Harvard Aerobatic Team," sporting seven

ending and they undoubtedly deserved better, the decision to cancel the team was not taken lightly. In fairness to the Air Council, the pressure to reduce costs by the government was overwhelming and the Golden Hawks were not the only ones to suffer. By April 1st, 1964, in addition to previously mentioned closures, four radar stations had been closed along with five of 11 auxiliary squadrons (403, 406, 424, 442 and 443). The RCAF Auxiliary was reduced from approximately 2,260 to 860 personnel. By that summer, 500 RCAF aircrew would also lose their

ments, however, was the stigma of radical change in Canada's military services as integration and unification loomed ahead. By the middle of the decade, a pervasive gloom had settled over the air force. The days of the RCAF were numbered but, like the Golden Hawks, the legacy would live on forever.

All told, over 15,000,000 North Americans saw the Hawks perform in five years. For Canadians, the team came to symbolize a form of national pride, a thrilling sight most would cherish and never forget. Thousands

The memory lives on. There are several monuments to the legacy of the Golden Hawks still on display in Canada. Examples include the aircraft at top left which was a gate guard for many years at the team's original home at RCAF Stn/CFB Chatham, New Brunswick. With the base closure, the aircraft was eventually obtained by the Atlantic Canada Aviation Museum in Halifax, Nova Scotia where it is now a prize possession. At left, Sabre 23651 as it appeared in the Museum of Science and Technology in Ottawa in 1969. The aircraft is now owned by the Canada Aviation Museum in Ottawa but is on loan to the Canadian Warplane Heritage Museum in Hamilton, Ontario. (DND, John Lameck, Dan Dempsey)

bright yellow Harvards (a.k.a. "The Goldilocks"), was resurrected suddenly in April to perform at major shows across the country. Not only did they perform at NAFD at Rockcliffe on June 6th, 1964, they also represented the RCAF at the Canadian International Air Show in Toronto on September 4th and 5th. Although the Goldilocks were a very fine team, Canadians who had thrilled to the sight of the Golden Hawks for the previous five years missed the speed, noise and excitement of their show.

And so it was that the Golden Hawks' chapter ended. Although theirs was an inglorious

jobs and thousands of technicians and support personnel would soon follow.

In retrospect, the early '60s had been good years for the RCAF. There had been significant capital expenditures associated with the procurement of the CF-104 Starfighter, CF-101 Voodoo, C-130 Hercules, Caribou and CH-113 Voyageur/Labrador helicopters. All of them had been introduced to Canadians at airshows across the country. A new Canadian designed and built jet trainer, the Canadair CL-41 Tutor, would begin operational service in 1964 and more Hercules would be ordered. Now overseeing all of these positive develop-

of youngsters in every corner of the country had sought their autographs – spellbound by a smile, a handshake or a kind word from the men in the blue flying suits. Indeed, true to form, the last function of the Hawks was a presentation to a cub and scout "father and son" banquet – a commitment honoured even though the team had been disbanded two weeks earlier. But it would not be long before another superb national aerobatic team would grace Canadian skies, this one also formed in celebration of a special anniversary. This team would be the last hurrah for the RCAF – they would be known as the Golden Centennaires.

No More Of This...

Their Wings Are Folded Forever

Golden Hawks Will Fly No More

Serving Progress

The Trentonian
AND TRI-COUNTY NEWS

Incorporating The Trenton Courier-Advocate (Estab. 1853) and The Brighton Ensign (Estab. 1871)

In Three Counties

VOL. 8 — No. 17 — 12 Pages   THE TRENTONIAN, Monday, February 10, 1964   Price Per Copy 7c.

...Or This

The Minister of National Defence, Hon. Paul Hellyer, announced Friday that the RCAF Golden Hawks precision aerobatic team is to be disbanded immediately. Mr. Hellyer's statement follows:

"After careful consideration of all the factors involved it has been decided to disband the RCAF's air show aerobatic team, the RCAF quote Golden Hawks. The team will not perform this year.

"Since they were formed in 1959 to celebrate the golden anniversary of flight in Canada, the Golden Hawks have performed before millions of spectators in the United States and Canada, and they have gained much favorable publicity for their service.

"The decision to disband the team was based on the necessity to use the expenditures, approximately 3 to 4 million per year required to operate the team, for more vital defence needs, particularly new equipment. In addition, the F-86 Sabre flown by the Hawks is no longer in operational service with the RCAF, and will soon be very difficult and costly to maintain. The performance of aerobatic manoeuvres in close formation makes it mandatory for demonstration aircraft to be maintained in near-perfect form to ensure the safety of the pilots who fly them. The Sabre, which flew well in the Korean conflict and for many years in NATO, is reaching the end of its life expectancy.

"In agreeing to the disbandment of the Golden Hawks, I would like to congratulate all the pilots and groundcrews who have been associated with the team over the years. The thrilling performances of the Golden Hawks will long be remembered by all who saw them in action."

HISTORY

The Golden Hawks, at present based at RCAF Station Trenton, started in 1959 at Chatham, N.B. They were formed to help commemorate the 50th Anniversary of Powered Flight in Canada and also the 35th Anniversary of the RCAF.

RCAF GOLDEN HAWKS TEAM LEADERS

S/L Fern Villeneuve (centre) was the first leader of the Golden Hawks precision aerobatic team. He led the team in 1959 and 1960. S/L Jim McCombe (left) was leader in 1961. S/L Lloyd Hubbard (right) led the team in 1962 and 1963. He was the leader at the time the team was disbanded.   — RCAF Photos

Finis

Economy and the changing face of defence have made a casualty of the Golden Hawks. This precision flying team has been, for the peacetime RCAF, a means of displaying in public the skills acquired in training. It is of a part with Air Force days, where armed services people get a chance to show what they have, and what they can do.

It was to be expected that in the drive to economize and divert money to improving the defence needs of the force, such "frills", if we can call them that, would be the first things lopped off. There was some recent evidence that bands may fall under the same axe. We hope not, since some such things are needed for morale.

As for the Golden Hawks, the men who flew the Sabres and maintained them can take pride in a job well done. The Sabres are now going, and that is part of the reason the aerobatics team is being disbanded. We doubt that the public will ever fully appreciate the skills involved. But every man who had a part in it can take a fierce pride in having shown what Canada can do in this respect, second to nothing in the world in sheer flying skill. And that includes the people who maintain the aircraft.

It is doubtful that we shall ever have anything like this again. Modern aircraft do not lend themselves to such displays.

But at least we can reflect that the skill which sent the Sabres hurtling through the skies in a kind of poetry of motion is continued in the more prosaic role of getting the peacetime job of the RCAF done. We hope that Canadians will feel the same pride in their armed forces that the Golden Hawks must have engendered in all who saw them.

ROYAL CANADIAN AIR FORCE

Farewell to the Hawks

"ALTHOUGH the disbandment of the Golden Hawks will cause disappointment throughout the service, the members of your team can be justly proud of the everlasting fame that they have brought to Canada and the RCAF. Their superlative flying skills and incomparable maintenance standards have been admired by millions of people throughout North America. The Golden Hawks have earned an honoured place in the history of the RCAF."

This message from the Chief of the Air Staff was delivered to the Golden Hawks Commanding Officer at RCAF Stn. Trenton on 7 Feb. 64, minutes after the official announcement of their demise had been made in Ottawa by the Minister of National Defence.

Public tributes in the press of the nation from coast to coast have followed in recent weeks. Thus, after five years, this *Sabre*-equipped aerobatic team has joined such distinguished formations as the Siskins, Blue Devils, Fireballs and Sky Lancers in the Canadian flying hall of fame.

The Golden Hawks were formed in the spring of 1959 as part of the RCAF's contribution to the commemoration of Canada's Golden Jubilee of Flight. Their first permanent home was RCAF Stn. Chatham, from which they operated for four years. At the conclusion of their 1962 tour, the team moved to Trenton and operated from that base during their longest and, as it turned out, last season in 1963.

Both Canadians and Americans thrilled to the precision flying of the Hawks who appeared in 317 public shows over the past five years. Now the pilots and ground personnel have dispersed to other assignments. Their once-proud gold and red *Sabres* have been retired. But their prestige lives on in the memory of millions. ◉

The Red Knight solo aerobatic show thrilled millions of Canadians nationwide over a 12 year span from 1958 to 1969. The unique paint scheme made the aircraft a readily identifiable symbol of the RCAF and later the Canadian Armed Forces. Shown here is the 1965 Red Knight, F/O Tex Deagnon, in one of the most famous photos ever taken of the aircraft. (DND PCN 5590)

And the Show Goes On

Although the Golden Hawks were formed as the RCAF's official aerobatic team in 1959, they were by no means the only airshow team born in that anniversary year. The national celebration was a major event for the RCAF and units across the country were eager to do their part. Training Command would make a large commitment in terms of resources, primarily with T-33 aircraft based at RCAF Stns Gimli and Portage la Prairie, Manitoba. The command's most lasting contribution however, would be a solo performer – the legendary Red Knight. The CF-100 community would also form two regional teams, one in the west and one in the east. Unlike the Golden Hawks, these teams were strictly part-time affairs as squadron members continued to devote the majority of their time to regular duties. Nonetheless, they made a valuable contribution to the aura of the RCAF. Some even survived the austerity program that brought about the demise of the Golden Hawks in early 1964, bridging the gap until circumstances permitted the formation of another national aerobatic team.

The "RCAF 35-50" Team

Training Command in the 1950s and '60s became famous for its large formation flypasts. Harvards flown by Training Command instructors had been used to spell out the letters "R C A F" at Air Force Day celebrations as early as 1948 at the CNE in Toronto. These large-scale formations necessitated an enormous effort, both in terms of logistic planning and maintenance support. Every detail had to be covered carefully to maximize safety – forming a single number or letter in the sky was one thing – having several flying formation with each other at the same time presented a whole new range of challenges. Of course, having sufficient numbers of aircraft airborne to do the mission was mandatory and this had to include spare aircraft which could quickly move into any position if a technical problem forced another aircraft out of the formation.

To celebrate the 35th anniversary of the RCAF and 50th anniversary of powered flight in Canada in 1959, S/L Bill Bliss of No. 3 Advanced Flying School came up with the idea of forming the numbers in the air using the school's T-33 trainers. What could have been more appropriate?

Bliss had rejoined the RCAF in November 1948, having served a tour overseas with 412 Sqn flying Spitfires during WWII. He had been known as "Junior" on the squadron and had served under some famous flight commanders during his tour, including the likes of Buzz Beurling, George Keefer and Don Laubman. He had also been among the RCAF's first jet pilots on the Vampire, gaining particular fame as the slot pilot of the Blue Devils from 1949 to 1951. He had learned his lessons well and now found himself in a position where HE was the wise veteran who his charges looked up to for leadership.

After his idea was passed up the chain of command and approved by the AOC Training Command, A/V/M Bryans, Bill Bliss found a ready pool of volunteers at 3 AFS from which to build his formation. However, since it was obvious a lot of practice would be required, it was decided that the task would be shared with the T-33 instructors at No. 2 AFS in Portage so as not to undermine either school's principal task of training jet pilots for the RCAF. Since the annual Air Force Day had been changed to

S/L Bill Bliss of No. 3 Advanced Flying School at RCAF Stn Gimli, Manitoba. His initiative led to the creation of some of the largest formations ever flown by RCAF pilots at Canadian airshows. (RCAF Photo via Bill Bliss)

different dates across the country to accommodate appearances of the Golden Hawks, the Training Command formation would also be able to make similar appearances at some of the larger shows. This meant cross-country flights – a godsend for instructors normally engrossed in the rigours of training. In fact, the idea was so popular they called themselves "Suntan Formation" and the team became Bill Bliss' pride and joy.

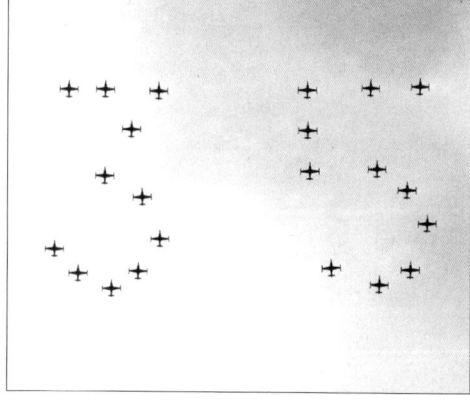

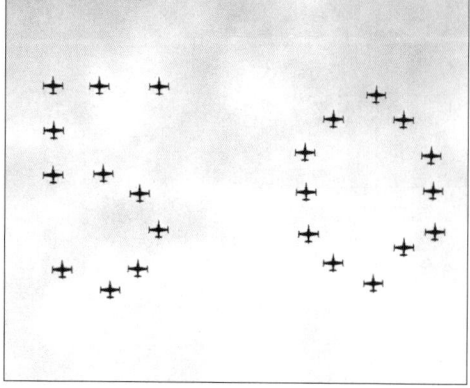

Training Command's contribution to the 35th anniversary of the RCAF and 50th anniversary of powered flight in Canada included these formations flown by T-33 instructors stationed at Gimli and Portage la Prairie, Manitoba. (RCAF Photos via Al Brown/George McAffer)

After working out the "35" and "50" formation positions on paper, S/L Bliss decided he would lead the "3" and "5" respectively. This meant that the Portage contingent would always be on the right and form the "5" in the first formation and "0" in the second. All told the "35" would need 22 aircraft and the "50" one extra at 23, plus spares and a spotter. The Portage contingent would be led by another highly respected fighter pilot, F/L Les Price, who had completed a tour with 444 Sqn at 4 Wing in Baden-Soellingen, West Germany.

The two contingents worked up their respective numbers separately at their home stations initially and put the numbers together for the first time on May 29th when Les Price led his formation to Gimli to rendezvous with Bill Bliss' gang. After a successful practice flypast, the team soon set out en masse for Ottawa for the litmus test – a flypast for the Chief of the Air Staff, Air Marshal Hugh Campbell, slated for June 6th at National Air Force Day in Ottawa. NAFD proved to be a great success as thousands of Canadians turned out on a beautiful day to watch the best the RCAF had to offer. It was a proud CAS that watched the "35" pass overhead in perfect formation in advance of demonstrations by almost every aircraft in the inventory. The show culminated with superb performances by the Red Knight and the Golden Hawks.

Having won the blessing of the air force's top brass, Bill Bliss' team returned to Gimli and Portage and the daily routine of instructional flying. However, they continued to practice for what was to be a hectic schedule of shows in July and August across Western Canada. Les Price's logbook reveals that between July 2nd and August 15th no less than 15 shows were completed, including performances at Gimli, Portage, Edmonton, Calgary, Moose Jaw, Vancouver, Cold Lake, Saskatoon, Regina, Prince Albert, Lethbridge, Winnipeg, Lakehead and Penhold. For the most part, these shows were flown on the weekends, the instructors fulfilling their normal duties during the week. This led to a frenetic lifestyle which left most of the staff exhausted by the end of the tour.

In spite of the hundreds of flying hours that were devoted to the tour, there was only one accident which occurred, that being in Saskatoon on July 25th. Following each flypast the "numbers" would split up into sections of four aircraft which would then do a standard overhead break at 1,000 feet AGL to individual stream landings. With 25-odd aircraft over the runway in close succession, it

The RCAF formation in all its glory was flown from 1960 to 1963 utilizing 38 T-33 Silver Stars. (DND PCN 3262)

was an impressive sight. On this particular afternoon however, few spectators were present as the flypast had taken place over the exhibition grounds on a blustery day. The wind was 25 knots out of the north as Al Young prepared to touchdown in turn on runway 27 when his aircraft was suddenly slammed to the runway. Unbeknownst to him, the lead aircraft of the section behind had lost sight of Young in the final turn while correcting for the strong crosswind and had landed on top of him. It wasn't until he got out of his cockpit that Young realized how lucky he was. Both pilots walked away from the accident to fly another day, leaving the incredible sight of one aircraft piggy-backed on the other …

Although the "35" and "50" formations took many hours of practice to perfect, they left airshow crowds in Canada marvelling at their ability to hold these large groups of aircraft together. But in terms of difficulty, this was nothing compared with what was still to come.

The "RCAF Letters" Team

The popularity of the "35" and "50" formations of 1959 led directly to the rebirth of another tribute which hadn't been seen in years in Training Command, the forming of the letters, R C A F. The part-time endeavour would last for four years, becoming a familiar and awe-inspiring sight at Air Force Days and the Canadian International Air Show between 1960 and 1963.

The architect behind the revival of the tradition was again the commander of the Standards Flight at Gimli in 1960, S/L Bill Bliss. Once again the instructors at Gimli and Portage would be used to stage the event. The first two letters, "RC" were formed by the

group from Portage under the command of F/L Neil "Big Daddy" Burns using the callsign "Suntan formation." Bliss led the "AF" contingent from Gimli under the callsign "Westwin formation." As with the previous year's experience, the two groups worked up their formations separately starting in May 1960. Before long "RCs" and "AFs" were being seen regularly over the two stations. As Bill Bliss laughingly recalls, "The Roman Catholic padre in Portage never had so much publicity!"

Putting the formation together was no easy task since it was almost one mile wide. Relative formation references had to be determined for each aircraft within each letter. The most challenging were the curved portion of the "R" and the "C." As a result, it was soon decided that the lead should be flown from the front of the "C" rather than the tip of the "A," so Bliss and Burns swapped letters. Ultimately, the RCAF formation itself comprised 38 T-33 aircraft and eventually became known as "Showtop Formation." A vital part of the team included two "spotters" whose job it was to look down on the formation from above and advise how the spacing looked within each letter and between the let-

ters themselves. Sam Firth and Ollie Fritsch were the first to fulfill this role, Firth's logbook showing many "spotter" sorties. Also airborne would be four spare aircraft in case of any malfunction within the formation.

The adventure started right from takeoff, each section of aircraft taking off in turn in three-plane vic or four-plane finger formation. Bill Bliss loved lining up the whole team on the runway at once if it was long enough – it was an incredible sight, but did make for some interesting takeoffs at the back of the pack! Once airborne each section of aircraft would move into box formation, one following the other in loose lineastern for each letter until the key commands came from the leader "Squadrons go line-abreast" followed shortly thereafter by "Squadrons go letters." S/L Bliss always took an extra pilot in his back seat with him to help out with the navigation and timing, which were critical. The letters were not actually formed until established on the final run-in to the target. At this point, even minor changes in airspeed and especially heading became very challenging for the team. Notwithstanding, minor changes were usually inevitable as corrections were made

As close as it gets! Both pilots walked away from this landing accident in Saskatoon on 25 Jul 59. (DND 20302-3)

by the leader for wind drift or timing, those famous words "just a skosh left (or right)" always leading to a grimace in every cockpit as Bliss made heading corrections. This resulted in a constant jockeying for position, especially on the outside of the letters as every pilot held on for dear life.

Of course, with so many drivers having been involved with so many aircraft, the tales of adventure (or misadventure) are legion! Mention the formation to someone who was there and you'll either get a ready smile or his eyes will roll back into his head …

The most hair-raising of all of the stories undoubtedly occurred on May 24th, 1960 at Gimli when the two formations came together for the first time over the station. The incident is now looked back upon with humour but had the potential to be disastrous. It is now euphemistically referred to as "The Day

thing I knew I was flying formation in a shadow! As I looked up I was horrified to see a T-33 wing a few feet above my canopy and a tip tank appeared directly in front of my windscreen – there was nowhere to go as another wing and tip tank also appeared under the nose of my aircraft. The "R" had inadvertently converged with the "C." This all transpired within a few seconds just as we were coming over the base! When everyone realized what had happened we just froze and the respective leaders slowly moved apart. Not a word was said for what seemed like an eternity, until a lone baleful voice came over the RT exclaiming 'Jessuuuus!!' I recall a few shaky hands signing in aircraft that day …"

Al Brown

Having miraculously survived the potential disaster, and with "lessons relearned" firmly planted in the minds of all, Bill Bliss decided it would be best to get right back in

mitment. A vital part of that task fell onto the shoulders of the large contingent of groundcrew from both Gimli and Portage that had arrived separately with a vast array of equipment – from aircraft ladders to start carts. By lining up the aircraft in two long rows on the ramp, one start cart was able to start four aircraft in a reasonably expeditious manner to ensure that a minimum of fuel was burned on the ground.

The system worked well and Air Force Day in Trenton on May 28th was a great success – and a good warm-up for National Air Force Day in Ottawa. Notwithstanding, the team conducted three more practices prior to the June 4th show, all of which were staged out of Trenton since it was the only RCAF station in the vicinity with enough ramp space to park all of the T-33s at once.

It was following one of the aforementioned practices that Bill Bliss decided to fly the RCAF formation over the Kingston Penitentiary en route to Trenton – one of those "seemed like a good idea at the time" gestures which unfortunately was not appreciated by the authorities. It was on the same sortie that the formation had "a little yellow airplane" pass between the "C" and the "A" going in the opposite direction. Recalls Al Brown, "All I remember seeing were two big eyeballs as he went past. I don't know whatever happened to him – he probably sold his airplane after that!" With these adventures behind them, National Air Force Day at RCAF Stn Rockcliffe also went off without a hitch. Bill Bliss had once again motivated his troops to excellence with a short comment over the RT one minute back from the field, "Make 'er sexy guys, there's a hundred thousand eyeballs watching you!" And so there were, none prouder than the Chief of the Air Staff, A/M Hugh Campbell, who had welcomed tens of thousands of visitors to the station that day. Their work done for that weekend, the team returned to Trenton to refuel and split up for the journey home to Gimli and Portage to resume their instructional duties Monday morning.

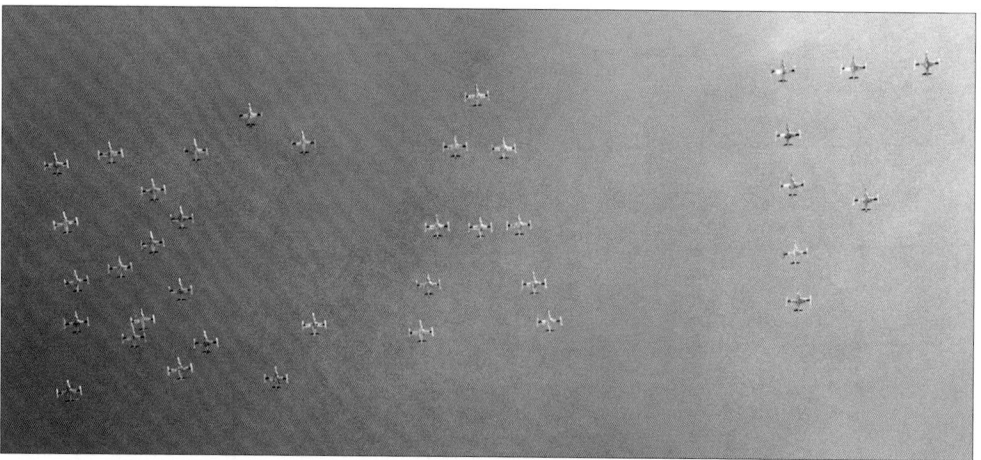

Lady Luck prevented a disaster when the distraction of an unidentified aircraft caused the "R" to drift into the "C" on 24 May 60 as the formation passed over the flight line at RCAF Stn Gimli, Manitoba. (RCAF Photo via Al Brown)

the RCs Crossed Themselves." Among the many who survived to tell the tale was F/L Al Brown, one of the great air force story tellers who went on to a long and stellar career, becoming affectionately known as "Red Lead." Young Mr. Brown was flying in the middle of the "C" that day and picks up the story:

"We were on the final run-in to Gimli in our big gaggle spelling out 'RCAF' when someone called a bogey at 12 o'clock. Of course, only the leader was supposed to be looking out front for other aircraft while the rest of us concentrated on holding position in the letters. However, when there was no immediate 'tally' call from lead indicating he had seen the aircraft, EVERYBODY decided to take a peek. Several seconds elapsed and the next

the air again and do it right. And so, with the blessing of the Gimli Station Commander, G/C B. Studer, away they went again for another one hour and 30 minute sortie. This time the formation went flawlessly and it was a relieved group that launched off to Trenton with the Gimli Smokers in tow for the first show of the summer two days later. As cross-country flights go, this entourage was spectacular and raised eyebrows due to its sheer size. As "Chops" Viger recalls, when a disbelieving controller at Lakehead asked S/L Bliss to confirm the number of aircraft in his formation, his casual reply was, "That's right, there's 50 of us up here!"

Once on the ground in Trenton the team had only one day to refine the logistics that would be required to get all 50 aircraft started and airborne to meet their airshow com-

In July 1960, Bill Bliss bade a fond farewell to Gimli and those "wonderful years" as he was posted to Toronto. As he recently reminisced about those bygone times, he eloquently put into words sentiments with which many ex-air force personnel would concur about their service careers in Canada:

"Those were glorious days in our unforgettable air force – days filled with excitement, fun and a way of life only a few lucky souls commonly share in our military careers. It was a fantastic era and I was proud to share it with a talented bunch of guys dedicated to what we all loved - FLYING. I can only hope that young people today will continue to have the desire and opportunity to join the service, enjoy a career in flying and share in the brotherhood of fellow airmen."

Bill Bliss

With Bill Bliss' departure, the interim lead of the RCAF Letters team was passed on to S/L "Pappy" Gibbs briefly and then to S/L Bud Lawrence when he arrived on the station as the new Standards' flight commander. On August 29th, the team was back in the air to practice for the upcoming CNE in Toronto. The annual show became the highlight of the year in terms of crowd size and number of shows flown in each of the four summers the team flew. Bud Lawrence retained lead of the team until May 1962 when he was appointed OC 3 AFS. At that time F/L Neil Burns took over as leader and it was he who led the team on its last appearances in the summer of '63 at National Air Force Day on June 8th followed by the CNE on August 31st.

The CNE, more properly known as the Canadian International Air Show, prided itself on "zero" timing between acts. This was quite challenging and the potential for miscalculation was always present, "Murphy's Law" prevailing more than once to make things exciting. The RCAF team worked out an arrangement whereby they would start their run-in from the east with the Gimli Smokers in trail. Then, prior to reaching the showsite, the Smokers would accelerate ahead of the formation and pull up into their Prince of Wales split. As the smoke cleared, the RCAF formation would suddenly appear overhead in all its glory. For the most part, this worked very well. However, members of the formation one summer will remember sharing centre stage with the Golden Hawks one afternoon, much to the delight of the local radio announcer. While watching the giant RCAF emerge from the smoke at centre stage, he suddenly shouted "Look at all the airplanes" as the Hawks pulled up from the south into their opening manoeuvre! Fortunately, these conflicts were few and far between and never amounted to more than a few rattled nerves.

F/L Mike Nash was another veteran instructor who flew on the team and has vivid memories of the experience:

"I had the great pleasure on more than one occasion of flying in the large RCAF formation that opened the CNE Air Show for a number of years. I led a section of four that made up the right side of the 'R'. Notwithstanding the seriousness of the task, it was at times hilarious and gave us much to talk about. We all remember, I'm sure, a particularly memorable training session out of Gimli – the time that Pappy Gibbs, with that massive formation behind him, decided to call for speed brakes to adjust his timing! It took a while to get the formation back in order after that …

The takeoffs were always something to behold. With the main formation, spares, spotters and Smokers, we occasionally had up to 52 T-Birds

The Gimli contingent prepares to practice their "AF" in August 1961 in preparation for the CNE in Toronto. With the letter "A" out front, this shot shows F/O C.B. Lang's view from the gaggle that formed the letter "F." (Tom Gigliotti)

running up on the button. Due to the jet wash at the back of the pack, our airspeed indicators would be indicating 90 knots – while still standing still with the brakes on! Everyone would always pray the night before for a generous crosswind. I recall struggling down the runway at Trenton on one occasion with not a lot of separation from the preceding formation when the lead of the number three vic ahead thought his bird was a bit sluggish on the controls and decided to abort his take-off quite late in the run. At just-before-liftoff-speed we had an exciting time trying to dodge Bill McMurray as he tried very hard to stop before the end of the runway. He made it … and so did we. (That damned aileron boost handle, it was always hard to tell whether it was on or off!)

I recall another occasion taking off for the CNE opener from Trenton when the weather conditions for a large formation takeoff were

not ideal. It was very hot, with not a breath of wind, and 52 T-Birds were churning up the air at the end of the runway. As the huge formation moved off section by section, the jet wash had no place to go. The turbulence over the runway at the surface was something else and with the high ambient temperature and full fuel load we used most of the runway to struggle off the ground into the mushy air. I'll never forget the face of the chap standing on his car bumper at the end of the runway holding a child as I wallowed past. I swear we were at eye level!"

Mike Nash

For all of the potential pitfalls and hours flown between 1960 and '63, the fact that there were no serious incidents speaks highly of the skill and professionalism of the instructors that flew in the RCAF formation and the technicians who maintained the aircraft day in and day out. By the time the spectacle ended in 1963, a "cast of thousands" had been involved as the old saying goes. Certainly, there were not many T-33 instructors or groundcrew from Gimli and Portage who had not been involved in one capacity or another. These years truly had represented the glory days of the RCAF. The formation had been an awe-inspiring sight for hundreds of thousands of Canadians, one which gave the average citizen great confidence in the men and women who were serving in the air force, all of this against a backdrop of heightened political and military tensions between east and west. The formation team also served another equally important purpose as it roared overhead – it instilled a great sense of pride in the 51,000 members serving in the RCAF at the time, a worthy tribute in itself to those working behind the scenes to preserve the operational effectiveness of Canada's air force.

The RCAF Red Knight

You only had to see him once – and you never forgot him. For 12 years this RCAF icon thrilled millions of Canadians with his exciting repertoire of solo aerobatics. Of all the paint schemes that have adorned aerobatic aircraft in Canada, the Red Knight's was perhaps the most striking. Whether silhouetted against an endless blue sky, the billowy white clouds of summer or the darkest thunderstorms, he was impossible to miss. Even the name was magical …

The 17 RCAF pilots who carried the mantle of the Red Knight never considered themselves heroes, although many of us who were young at the time certainly revered them as such. Each was a fine pilot who was selected for his ability to take an aircraft and fly it safely to the edge of the envelope. In comparison to an aerobatic team which can shape its performance to take advantage of multiple aircraft, the solo performer is on his own. From the time he starts his show until he taxis back in front of the crowd, all eyes are on him. Only a gifted commentator can help fill in the gaps that are inevitable as the performer repositions for his next manoeuvre. Thus, the onus is on the demonstration pilot to keep his show as tight as possible without exceeding either his own physical limitations or that of his aircraft. It is a tall order which takes a special breed of pilot and extraordinary discipline.

The Birth of a Legend

The roots of the Red Knight go back to 1957 and the Canadian International Air Show, the venue for Canada's largest annual flying display. The RCAF had no official display team at the time, instead presenting mass flypasts and solo aerobatic routines with various aircraft in the inventory. Unfortunately, it was during practice over the CNE waterfront that one such performer, W/C Howie Norris, lost his life along with his navigator when their CF-100 suffered an engine failure and stalled during a looping manoeuvre on September 5th, both officers failing to eject in time. The show officially opened the next day, but the featured performers were an American team, the USAF Thunderbirds flying five F-100C Super Sabres. The US Navy Blue Angels had fulfilled the role the year before, albeit alongside a fine team of Banshee fighters from VF 870 of the Royal Canadian Navy.

Watching the show along the Toronto waterfront in 1957 were a group of instructors from Central Flying School in Trenton. Among them was a veteran instructor by the name of F/L Roy Windover. He was concerned about the lack of a larger Canadian presence in Canada's national show – the last straw was when one of the "RCAF's" demonstrations was flown by an American pilot on exchange duties in Canada. Although the American did a fine job, Windover took exception to the fact that the RCAF was missing another opportunity to promote its own image. He therefore resolved that for the following year at the CNE, *he* would be flying a solo demonstration.

One of the advantages of being a senior instructor in the air force is that you occasionally have the opportunity to meet and fly with senior officers with whom you otherwise would never have occasion to rub shoulders.

This can be good for both parties, or perhaps not so good depending on the personalities involved! As it so happened, one of Roy Windover's "students" in Trenton at the time was the AOC Training Command, A/V/M J.G. Bryans. Bryans needed an instrument rating checkout on the T-33 and Windover had been the man appointed to guide him through the course. The timing could not have been better. Windover flew nine sorties with A/V/M Bryans following the Labour Day CIAS show and it was during this time that he enunciated his concerns to the AOC … and volunteered himself as the solution!

A/V/M Bryans gave Windover the go-ahead to work up an aerobatic routine in the T-33 and practices soon began in the fall of 1957. By the spring of 1958, Windover had worked up a very tight low-level show which was getting the attention of a lot of people, not the least of which were the station mechanics who were keeping a watchful eye on the G meters of the school aircraft Windover was using for practice. It was subsequently decided that the situation would be easier to monitor if a single aircraft was assigned to Windover for his practice sessions – thus began a long association for T-33 21057 as an aerobatic performer. On June 14th, 1958, F/L Windover flew his first official airshow in 057 at RCAF Stn Trenton's Air Force Day.

From Silver to Day-glo Red

At the time of Roy Windover's first T-33 show, the aircraft he flew was still in the standard silver/aluminum finish of Training Command. What transpired thereafter was a watershed in

F/L Roy Windover, the RCAF pilot responsible for the birth of the Red Knight show in 1958. He is pictured at RCAF Stn Trenton with T-33 21057, the first of four Canadair built T-Birds to serve in the role. (DND PCN 679, Cpl George Hardy)

the evolution of the Red Knight story, arguably the most important development in the creation of what was to become an RCAF trademark. Windover sought and received approval to paint one aircraft to distinguish it from the standard T-33s in use at CFS. As he recalled back in 1989, the colour chosen was "the day-glo reddish orange that was the normal paint on the tip tanks of the training aircraft. There was no special reason for this choice, except I wished the aircraft to stand out amongst foreign aircraft (at the CNE) and there was no money in the budget to purchase special paint."

On August 26th, the refinishers at Trenton rolled 057 out of the paint shop. She was stunning and the entire station was eager to show her off. Several PR photos were taken for posterity and it was the photographer from TCHQ in Trenton, Cpl George Hardy, that dubbed the name "The Red Knight." To him, the aircraft had apparently conjured up images of Manfred Von Richthofen, "The Red Baron" of Germany who had downed many allied pilots over the skies of Europe in WWI in his all-red triplane. Whatever the motivation, the name stuck and now holds an honoured place in RCAF history. As for George Hardy, he would go on to become the first official photographer of the Golden Hawks the following year.

Roy Windover fulfilled his ambition to represent the RCAF as a solo aerobatic performer at the CNE in 1958, flying shows on September 4th and 5th alongside the RCN Banshees from VF 870 and the US Navy Blue Angels. Against the hazy Toronto skyline, his red aircraft had stood out like a beacon. And although it was unfortunate that low cloud and rain the next day washed out the Saturday show, the precedent had been set. In attendance at the Friday show had been the Chief of the Air Staff, A/M Hugh Campbell, and he had liked what he had seen of the red jet …

F/L Windover returned to full-time instructional duties for the balance of 1958 but was rewarded with authorization to continue the Red Knight program in 1959 as Training Command's principal contribution to the special anniversaries of that year. He flew alongside the newly formed Golden Hawks at Air Force Day Trenton at the end of May and again at National Air Force Day (NAFD) at Rockcliffe on June 6th. However, he had been placed on notice that a posting to Europe on the F-86 Sabre could be

Roy Windover takes his freshly painted T-33 through a loop for Cpl George Hardy's camera. (DND PC 3137 via Greg Bruneau)

Don Connolly, a native of Kingston, Ontario, created this famous painting several years ago as a tribute to F/L Roy Windover. It depicts the Red Knight performing in front of the CNE Grandstand at the Canadian International Air Show in Toronto where the Knight played a starring role for 11 consecutive years. (courtesy Don Connolly)

expected in mid-summer. In the hope that the program would continue after his departure, he recruited F/L Bob Hallowell as a back-up pilot who would also fly a spare aircraft to the shows.

The Torch is Passed

If Roy Windover was the architect of the Red Knight legacy, then Bob Hallowell was the first of several saviours to keep the show alive. Having been recruited by Windover in the spring of '59 as the heir apparent, he flew his first dedicated high-level aerobatic practice on May 12th (in the Red Knight aircraft) at which time he received special written dispensation from the OC CFS, W/C Don Laidler, to commence low-level aerobatic training. Interestingly enough, all of his training was done solo in-between instructional trips in the T-Bird and C-45 Expeditor, with the odd Sabre trip thrown in for good measure. His logbook records seven low-level aerobatic practices prior to a flight to Rockcliffe on June 5th where he practiced the routine for NAFD and then flew back to Trenton non-stop. He returned to Ottawa the next day with Roy Windover and watched him perform his show.

F/L Windover performed his last show as the Red Knight at the International Freedom Festival in Windsor, Ontario on July 3rd, 1959 at which time he passed the torch to Bob Hallowell. The month of July was a busy one for CFS as they moved their operation to a new home at RCAF Stn Saskatoon, Saskatchewan. This also became the new home of the Red Knight and on August 2nd the residents of Prince Albert, Saskatchewan became the first western Canadians to marvel at the sight of the bright red jet when Hallowell flew his first official show.

Bob Hallowell went on to fly six more shows in the summer of 1959, all in eastern Canada, starring alongside the Golden Hawks at the CIAS in Toronto, Centralia and Windsor. At these shows he was accompanied by a crew chief, LAC Ferguson, who was first introduced to the realm of low-level aeros on August 25th. Ferguson was the first of a series

In July 1959 the Red Knight torch was passed to F/L Bob Hallowell as Central Flying School moved from RCAF Stn Trenton to RCAF Stn Saskatoon. Hallowell and his second crew chief, LAC Jack Woodhouse, were the first team to take the Red Knight across Canada from coast-to-coast in 1960. They also designed the Red Knight logo for the side of the aircraft and the first Red Knight crest. (DND PCN 1976)

of technicians who would play an indispensable role in the success of the Red Knight program. The last Red Knight show of the year took place on September 20th as the special celebrations of 1959 drew to a close. It had been a wonderful year for the RCAF and aviation in general in Canada. Much had been made of the accomplishments of the past 50 years and Canadians across the country had embraced the RCAF and its proud history with vigour. But, thought Bob Hallowell, why stop now?

Hands Off my Airplane!

By the end of September 1959 it appeared that the Red Knight program was to be relegated to history alongside the milestones it had helped celebrate. There was no plan which forecast a continuation in 1960 and as a result the station aircraft engineering officer at Saskatoon planned to remove the red paint from 057 and return the aircraft to line service. Determined that this should not transpire, F/L Hallowell took pen in hand on October 1st and wrote an impassioned letter to his boss, W/C Don Laidler, requesting that consideration be made to allow the Red Knight to fly again in 1960 as a symbol of prestige for Central Flying School. As Don Laidler recently recalled:

"My support, apart from wanting to promote aerobatics anywhere, was to say that CFS could continue to provide the required maintenance support for the Red Knight within existing resources. If I remember correctly, TCHQ, which had relocated to Winnipeg, arranged scheduling in conjunction with Bob. Both Bob, and Roy before him, had a pretty free hand in designing the flying displays, and no doubt had the advantage of flying rules that were more flexible than those of today. The displays I saw were crowd pleasers and showed very good judgement. If I had a hand in keeping the program going in the early days, it was just the natural thing to do."

Don Laidler

Ironically, only two days before Bob Hallowell had penned his letter, the Golden Hawks stand down parade had taken place in Trenton. On that occasion, the CAS had personally pledged his intention to do everything in his power to keep the Hawks alive as a permanent fixture and source of pride for the RCAF. What followed was a massive campaign by the public relations team at

55-00-01(CFS)

MEMORANDUM

1 Oct 59

OC CFS

Red Knight Display Aircraft - Retention

1   It is understood that the SAEO, RCAF Station Saskatoon, plans to dispose of the Red Knight T-33. The undersigned would like to vigorously protest this action.

2   In the two years that this aircraft has appeared in displays it has received much favourable comment. Due to its distinctive colour, and despite the restriction's on solo aerobatics, every performance has received high praise. As a result of the displays at Toronto and Centralia during Sep 59 congratulatory remarks have been received from such persons as G/C J Johnson (RAF) and G/C AG Kenyon, CO RCAF Station Centralia.

3   As well as gaining favourable publicity for the RCAF in general, the aircraft has become known as Central Flying School's specific display, and as such adds to the School's prestige.

4   If this aircraft is disposed of, it is dubious that authority could be obtained to paint another. The undersigned was present when 21057 went through its birth pains as the Red Knight, and authorization had to be obtained from AFHQ. With a little maintenance, 057 could easily be restored to display condition.

5   As pilot of the Red Knight the undersigned has had the opportunity of taking part in several displays, and from the point of view of personal satisfaction he would like to see this aircraft and its flying role retained.

(R Hallowell) F/L
CFS Research
349

F/L R Hallowell/ls

The letter that helped create a legacy. F/L Bob Hallowell's letter to W/C Don Laidler, the officer commanding CFS in Saskatoon in 1959, paved the way for the continuation of the Red Knight solo show. (via Bob Hallowell)

AFHQ to do just that. In the end, both initiatives succeeded – Bob Hallowell's even beyond his expectations. Not only would the Red Knight program continue, he was about to become a full-time aerobatic pilot, setting the stage for the next 10 years.

F/L Bob Hallowell and LAC Jack Woodhouse set out from Saskatoon on another adventure in the summer of 1960. (Jerry Vernon)

Air Force Headquarters requested a publicity photo of the Red Knight and Bob Hallowell obliged with this fine study of his aircraft over Saskatoon on 23 Nov 60. It was taken by an RCAF photographer perched in the open door of a C-45 Expeditor. (DND PCN 2268)

1960 – A Banner Season

The following year was a banner season for F/L Bob Hallowell and the Red Knight as the display was taken coast-to-coast for the first time – from Sydney, Nova Scotia to Vancouver, British Columbia. One simple but distinctive change he and his new crew chief made to their aircraft was the addition of a knight's helmet etched in black on either side of the nose of 057. It was nothing fancy, but was effective and added a further touch of flair to the image. Hallowell even found himself on the cover of *Star Weekly* at the end of the season, pretty heady stuff for the young man born and raised in small towns in southern Ontario. He recalls how the 1960 season unfolded:

"On March 10th, 1960, I flew 057 to Winnipeg for a conference on the Red Knight show season. It was decided that for major shows I would work with the Hawks as part of the RCAF aerobatic team, but was on my own for smaller shows. I started training the next day. On May 18th, I gave a checkout ride to my proposed crew chief for the year, LAC Jack Woodhouse. We got along famously and still keep in touch over 40 years later.

By May 20th, I had accumulated 22 hours and 20 minutes of practice (in 30 minute increments) and flew my first show of the season at Gimli with the "Smokers" team. Five months later we had flown 45 shows and had been all over North America!

At the bigger shows, I used to work a routine with the major teams whereby they would take off immediately in front of me. I would then take off and go right into my routine as they conducted their warm-up out of sight of the crowd for 10 to 15 minutes. Then as I landed, they would reappear and commence

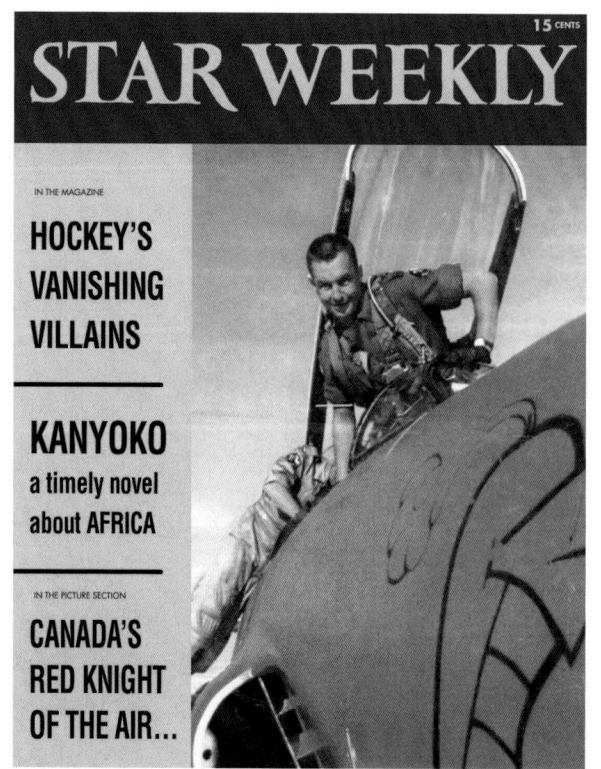

15 CENTS
STAR WEEKLY

IN THE MAGAZINE

HOCKEY'S VANISHING VILLAINS

KANYOKO
a timely novel about AFRICA

IN THE PICTURE SECTION

CANADA'S RED KNIGHT OF THE AIR...

their show. It made for a more continuous show for the spectators. I did this with the Golden Hawks at several shows, with the Blue Angels at the Pacific Northwest Airfair and with the Thunderbirds at Nellis AFB. I also flew several shows as a solo along with Bob Hoover. We did a nice beat-up at Paine AFB in Washington with an American named Ben Hall leading in a green and orange Mustang – Hoover on left wing in an F-100 Super Sabre and myself on right wing in the Knight. The FAA didn't like us much!

There is another famous story concerning the Blue Angels which has been distorted over the years. We were doing a bunch of shows at Paine AFB, billeted in a hotel in Everett. The 24 hour party room was just below mine! I dropped in for a while, but had an early air test the next morning so went up to bed. The Angels were there and knew that I had a 'Texas Mickey' of Canadian Club with me for an upcoming party with the Hawks. I woke up when two sweet young things climbed into the sack with me – fully clothed! They were followed by the Angels who had obviously staged the set-up. Each filed in laughing and poured themselves a drink of my CC. They then toasted the bed and occupants

A fitting tribute to a stellar season – the Red Knight made the cover of the *Star Weekly* in December 1960. (via Bob Hallowell, Peter Mossman)

and marched out. Then the girls promptly left and I laid there wondering if it had really happened. The next day the 'Red Knight' was known as the 'Pink Dink' – and I hadn't done anything!

On the post-season wrap-up it was decided to let me have a spare aircraft and I chose 21574. Both aircraft were ferried to Northwest Industries at Edmonton for overhaul and paint, and from there emerged the stylized Knight emblem with the white background and the yellow plume. While doing shows at the Red River Exhibition in Winnipeg, 'Woody' and I had a badge maker in a booth make up some shoulder patches and crests for us. I drew these and we paid for them ourselves – a far cry from the Hawks and the classy outfits they obtained in 1960!

In March 1961 I started training again when a short-notice posting overseas arrived. Since it carried a promotion to the rank of squadron leader with it, I wasn't too unhappy. At any rate, no one at CFS wanted my job – they'd seen too much of the previous season – on the road all the time, no special TD rates like the Hawks, running my own schedule and all the difficulties that went with it, etc. So F/L Ray Goeres at Portage volunteered for the job. I flew 574 down there on March 16th, 1961 and showed him the routine as he had already been approved as the next Red Knight. I went back on the 23rd to watch him practice and then returned to Saskatoon to prepare for my posting to Chatham and 4 Wing. This marked the end of my Red Knight career."

Bob Hallowell

Portage la Prairie adopts a Knight

Bob Hallowell had laid the foundation for the continuation of the Red Knight program and Ray Goeres was thrilled to be given the opportunity to keep it alive. An instructor at No. 2 Advanced Flying School, he was already a veteran of 15 years in the RCAF, having started his career with 101 Bomber Sqn of the RAF in World War II where he had won the DFC while flying the Lancaster bomber. Having been released after the war at the ripe old age of 24, it was six years before he could get back in as a so-called "retread," doing so on his 30th birthday. The Korean War and the expansion of the RCAF due to NATO had suddenly made experienced pilots popular again, especially as

F/L Ray Goeres, the 1961 Red Knight, is flanked by the team's crewmen, LACs Les Matthews and Jack Woodhouse. They were soon joined by a new alternate pilot, F/O Dave Barker. Below, Goeres takes his scarlet T-Bird over the top of a loop in the summer of '61. (DND PL 97218, RCAF photo via Ray Goeres)

A second T-33 in Red Knight colours was introduced into the program for the 1961 season. F/L Ray Goeres and F/O Dave Barker show off the aircraft in this rare formation shot. (DND PCN 3369)

instructors. Now, at 39 years-of-age, Ray Goeres suddenly found himself the proud "owner" of two red T-Birds adorned with the famous Red Knight helmet and flowing yellow plume.

Like the previous year, 1961 was also an extremely busy one, with Goeres completing 55 shows during the six month airshow season. He flew his first show of the season on May 5th, 1961 for the Vancouver Trade Show and finished up at *Trois-Rivières* on October 22nd. Jack Woodhouse continued as the Red Knight crewman, providing the continuity as the bright red jet traversed the country back and forth throughout the summer. An alternate Red Knight was also brought back into the picture to fly the spare aircraft and fill in where necessary, F/O Dave Barker taking on the role. With his dedicated crewman, LAC Les Matthews, the Red Knight was now a four man team. This arrangement worked well and would form the cornerstone of all future T-33 Red Knight operations.

F/O Dave Barker moved into the primary Red Knight role for 1962, building upon the well-established reputation the show had garnered across North America. His crew chief for the season was LAC Grant Harrison who was initially supported by Moe Foote and then Paul Boucher. As fame grew, so too did the demands for personal appearances by the Red Knight at functions outside normal airshow activities. Banquets, school and hospital visits and special autograph sessions all became part of the routine. Barker thrived in the role – he was a natural with children and spent many hours in pre- and post-show PR activities on behalf of the RCAF. Although the Red Knight continued to perform alongside the Golden Hawks at the nation's largest shows, his forte was really "small-town" Canada which rarely, if ever, had the opportunity to see the RCAF

in action. In many cases, these appearances became the highlight of the summer in out-of-the-way rural communities, leaving a favourable impression with local citizens for years to come. It was money well spent.

It takes a special breed of aviator to hurl an aircraft around the sky at low-level for the enjoyment of others. The high G forces, heat and perspiration can make it decidedly uncomfortable for the pilot at times, yet there is great satisfaction in a show well flown and appreciated. For those who enjoy this kind of work, you can never get enough. And so it was not surprising that Dave Barker had grand aspirations to fly with the Golden Hawks with whom he had performed at

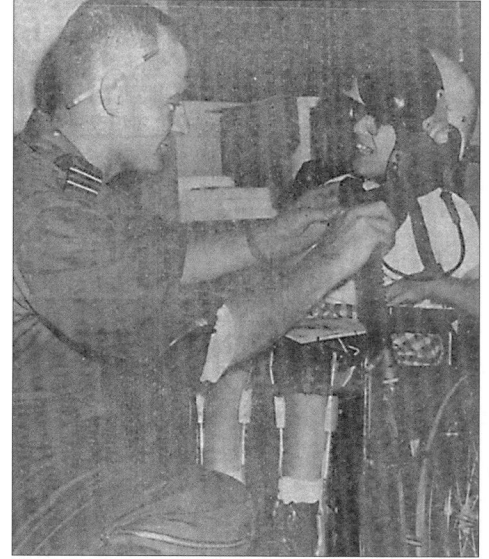

School and hospital visits became a popular public relations activity for the Red Knight team and were much in demand. In this touching photo, Dave Barker thrills a young patient in Battle Creek, Michigan during a visit in Sep '62. (via Bill Fraser).

The 1962 Red Knight team on the ramp at Portage la Prairie on 5 Apr 62. L to R – LAC Grant Harrison, F/O Bill Fraser (Alternate), F/O Dave Barker (Red Knight) and LAC Moe Foote. (DND PCN 3727)

Patrons of the Space Needle got their money's worth when Dave Barker and Bill Fraser announced their arrival in Seattle for the World's Fair in 1962. They performed alongside the Golden Hawks during Canada Week. (via Bill Fraser)

several shows in 1962. As his two year tour with the Red Knight drew to a close, he got his wish when he was selected to try out for the Hawks for the 1963 season. He subsequently made the team, not surprisingly being chosen as opposing solo to Ed McKeogh who moved into the lead solo position that season. Having already mastered the intricacies of aerobatics "on the deck," all Barker had to do now was miss his "boss" coming at him from the opposite direction at a closing speed of between 700 and 1,000 mph. Piece of cake ...

Personal Perspectives 1962-1963

For those RCAF instructors who enjoyed the challenge of multiple aerobatics in the demanding low-level environment, selection as the Red Knight was something to aspire to. Another young pilot who earned the privilege was F/O Bill Fraser. Although his tour was cut short by higher demands for his talents, his memories are vivid and capture the essence of what it was like to be involved in such a unique profession:

"I was in the Red Knight business in 1962 and 1963. For my first season on the road, I was Dave Barker's back-up but did eight shows on my own. I was the Red Knight in '63 and got in nine shows before leaving Portage la Prairie in early June of that year. Being transferred out in the middle of the season was very unusual considering the expenses in training and publicity that had

F/L Bill Fraser inherited the reins of the Red Knight at the start of the 1963 season. He is shown here in a typical PR shot with his crew chief, Cpl Pat "Stretch" Dunn. (RCAF photo)

already been invested. However, I had been selected to become the executive assistant to the AOC of Air Div HQ in Metz, France, A/V/M D.A.R. Bradshaw. He had been commandant of the Royal Military College in Kingston, Ontario during my time there until graduation in 1956.

My crewman in 1962 was LAC Paul Boucher who knew more about the T-33 than anyone in the air force. In 1963, Cpl Pat Dunn took over and we covered a lot of ground together – he was the most constructive critic I had. He would debrief me after each show and was instrumental in keeping the show quality exact – one of the unsung troops. As I have said before, the pilots get most of the attention, but without the hard work of the administrative and maintenance personnel, there would be no show.

In two years I did 17 official shows. There were several other unofficial ones, mostly practices authorized over Portage, done for such things as flying course graduations and

station visitors. My logbook also records many, many practices, starting each of the two years at high level and working down to show level. Most of these were done over the Assiniboine River, southwest of Portage. There was a wide bend in the river with a small meadow for an aim point, and the canyon was deep enough to provide a safety measure when the surrounding prairie was used as ground level. There was a farmhouse on the edge of the canyon, right on the bend. That family probably saw more of my Red Knight shows than the rest of my audiences combined.

During the show season practices were normally done at Portage after day flying was over. We lived in a PMQ where the kitchen window faced the hangar line so my wife Lee could watch my practice as she prepared dinner. She would comment on my vertical line in relation to the hangar roofs when I got home.

The Red Knight was uniquely Canadian – a solo military display. As with all of the RCAF teams, the positive publicity achieved was tremendous, and all for what was, even in those days, a very small budget. We did some 'openers' for the Golden Hawks and took part in some large Canadian and American displays but most of our shows were singles in out-of-the-way places that did not rate a team. We were away from home a lot. On arrival back at Portage, normally after hours, we would do a pass over the PMQs to let everyone know we were back.

My new posting was grand but I was sad to leave the Red Knight job, particularly in mid-year. It was a very special experience and certainly the sublime point of my flying career. The thrill of performing low-level aerobatics with the confidence that comes from knowing you can do them safely, flying the aircraft to its limits during aerobatics and cross-country flights, and the satisfaction of independent operations – in the boonies, without normal support, and having to deal with the locals are some of my fond memories. And the learned personal things – the discipline of practice and routine, and the self-confidence gained from those independent operations stood me in good stead for the rest of my career, both as a pilot and as a man. I have tried, I believe with some success, to pass these values on to my son who is also a pilot."

William C. (Bill) Fraser

A Fallen Knight

The Red Knight understudy at the start of 1963 was 25-year-old F/L Bud Morin who comfortably slid into the role when Bill Fraser left Portage for his overseas tour in June. He was looking forward to a further five months of airshow performances, especially now that he had inherited the mantle of Red Knight himself. Like Fraser, Bud Morin also had a fighter background, having flown Sabres with 430 (F) Sqn at 2 Wing, Grostenquin on his first operational tour. He had returned to Canada to instruct at 2 AFS in Portage following a ground tour in Metz, France.

F/L Bud Morin moved into the primary Red Knight role in June 1963. Tragically, he was killed during his Air Force Day performance at Gimli, Manitoba on 21 Aug, the only Red Knight to die during a scheduled public performance. (DND PCN 4570)

Ironically, Morin had also served with his new crew chief, Cpl Pat "Stretch" Dunn on 430 Sqn. Although they had not known each other well at the time, after two months of criss-crossing North America together they formed a special bond and respect for each other. Watching from the backseat can be both an exhilarating and terrifying experience during a practice or arrival show, and Stretch soon became accustomed to getting his "eyes watered." What was worse was that Morin had the benefit of "chaffs" as Dunn called them, a G-suit. "He used to kid me when I had difficulty handling the G from the back seat!"

One of Stretch Dunn's most memorable recollections was a cross-country trip from Winnipeg to Regina on the 14th of July 1963. The Red Knight had partici-pated in Winnipeg's Air Force Day the previous day along with the Golden Hawks and Moose Jaw's upstart team, the Goldilocks. Having survived the festivities of the night before, all three teams were heading westward on the quiet Sunday morning. Surprisingly enough, the merry band of men known as the Goldilocks had been the first to get underway and were flying back to Moose Jaw at a relatively low altitude, straight and level no doubt being the order of the day! The two Red Knights departed in formation sometime after-wards for Regina, followed by the Golden Hawks.

As Stretch Dunn recalls, the Knights were quietly minding their own busi-ness somewhere west of Portage when a shadow filled their cockpit and a Sabre passed close overhead, inverted to boot! "Got ya Bud" was the call from the Golden Hawk pilot as he zoomed past. Of course, no self-respecting fighter pilot could take this sit-ting down and the fight was on. Then someone suddenly spotted the Goldilocks down below and all hell broke loose as they were attacked from above. So much for the quiet Sunday jaunt!

What followed was a full blown "furball" reminiscent of the greatest traditions of down-town Europe in the glory days of the Sabre – eight yellow Harvards, two red T-Birds and eight golden Sabres mixing it up in a multi-bogey fray. "It was mayhem" recalls Dunn … and what a sight that must have been for the prairie folk all decked out in their Sunday best down below!

By mid-summer, Bud Morin had earned the respect of all who watched him perform his tight 12 minute routine. Not only was he fly-ing well, but he had a flair for public rela-tions which was an important part of the job. June and July were busy months as he appeared at many events across the country. He had completed a show in Kamloops, B.C. on the 11th of August and was making his way east to the CIAS in Toronto when tragedy struck and he was killed at RCAF Stn Gimli's Air Force Day celebration on

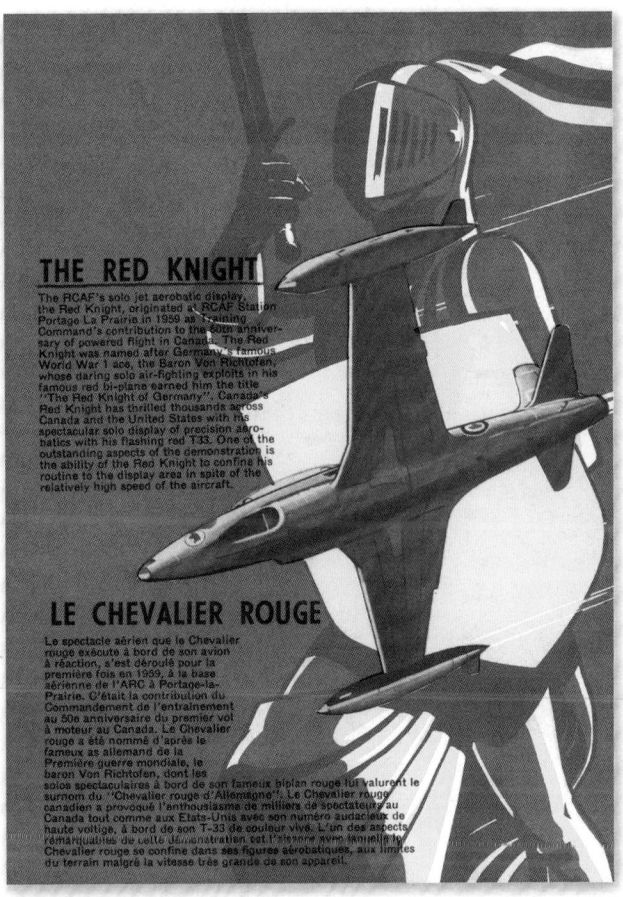

The Red Knight was known as "le Chevalier Rouge" to French speaking Canadians, as noted in this RCAF advertising brochure from the early 1960s. (author's collection)

August 21st. It was Morin's 49th show of the season and the first accident in the six year history of Red Knight performances.

Of many factors an airshow performer must take into account, the weather is more often than not the most challenging. It is *always* a consideration – even on a cloud-free day strong winds can play havoc with your show-line necessitating large corrections at slow airspeeds. Of course, on cloudy days the weather can be a real nemesis to performers, spectators and organizers alike. The fateful day that Bud Morin was killed was one of those prairie summer days when scattered to overcast cloud drifted across the field, occa-sionally giving way to glimpses of sunshine as the afternoon wore on. The first act of the

day was the Gimli Smokers whose repertoire normally included a number of bursts and rejoins with their nine-plane T-33 formation. A weather check by "Smoker 9" just after takeoff had reported an overcast layer at 2,500 feet above the aerodrome, certainly not high enough for their vertical bursts. However, conditions were slowly improving from the west and 30 minutes later as Bud Morin sat at the end of the runway in his Red steed (T-33 21057), he would have been struggling with the decision of whether the cloud base was high enough for his high show. It was definitely marginal. The Goldilocks had just finished their show and the Golden Hawks had just taken off for their warm-up. When asked by the control tower what his intentions were, Bud Morin asked for a weather check and was told the cloud was 3,000 to 4,000 feet scattered to broken. Based on that assessment, he advised that he would attempt a high show. This was not an unusual deci-sion, particularly since the weather was improving. When the weather is close, performers will often try a looping manoeuvre to see if there is enough room and if not switch to their medium (rolling) show.

Sitting alongside F/L Morin in the sec-ond Red Knight aircraft (T-33 21574) was his understudy, F/O Wayne MacLellan, another fine young instruc-tor from 2 AFS who had volunteered and been selected as Morin's alternate. He had already done 17 shows himself as the alternate Red Knight in 1963. Since he was going to be an airborne spare anyway at Gimli, Morin had decided to incorporate MacLellan into the act by briefing a "co-ordinated" routine whereby MacLellan would fly approximate-ly 1,000 feet abreast of Morin and mirror the standard show manoeuvres. This had been done previously in practice. However, when two Red Knights reappeared on stage togeth-er at the allotted time, it was "quite a sur-prise" as the station commander, G/C George "Red" Sutherland, recently recalled.

Within a scant few minutes, surprise gave way to horror when Bud Morin failed to recover from the first half of a Cuban-eight manoeuvre and crashed on the west side of the airfield. On their looping pull-up into the manoeuvre, both aircraft had entered cloud, likely at a lower altitude than expected. Morin called for the pair to tighten up the

F/O Wayne MacLellan started out his 1963 Red Knight tour as the alternate but quickly moved into the lead position with the loss of Bud Morin. He completed the 1963 season with his crew chief, LAC Bob Casey. (DND PCN 4568)

loop to reduce the time in cloud, but in doing so would have apex'd over the top at a lower altitude than normal. This loss in vertical altitude proved to be critical. Not liking what he saw, Wayne MacLellan wisely broke off the manoeuvre. Bud Morin exited the cloud with his nose well below the horizon. Unfortunately, his split-second assessment was that he had enough altitude to complete the manoeuvre and so he did a rapid half-roll to the upright position and began to pull out of his dive under high G. Stretch Dunn was watching from the ground and knew immediately that it was going to be close. Morin almost made it … but tragically there was not enough altitude remaining and he crashed into the runway in a near level attitude, a shocking end to an unfortunate set of circumstances.

Although the station commander's first inclination was to cancel the remainder of the show, by the time he got to the control tower, G/C Sutherland realized that the alternate Red Knight had decided to complete his show, being unsure of what to do under the horrific circumstances. Since the Golden Hawks were also already airborne, they too were permitted to put on their 25 minute display to end the show.

The death of Bud Morin was a sobering reminder of one of the pitfalls of high performance demonstration flying, pushing the

weather. It also underscored the importance of safety measures designed to protect both performers and spectators. Fortunately, the measures in force at the time had precluded any injury to spectators on the ground. To his considerable credit, F/O Wayne MacLellan finished the 1963 Red Knight season under what must have been trying circumstances. However, aside from two or three cancellations in the immediate aftermath of the accident, he completed all remaining scheduled performances – 20 in total. He was joined by a new staff member from 2 AFS, F/O Bill Slaughter, who had arrived fresh from an eventful Sabre tour with 421 (F) Sqn at 2 Wing where he had "ejected from Sabre 374 while on a radar approach into 3 Wing (Zweibrücken), wrote off a car and had two daughters!"

Bill Slaughter had already expressed interest in the alternate Red Knight position for 1964 but now found himself being measured for a red suit much earlier than anticipated. He officially became the alternate on September 3rd and flew a checkout with Wayne MacLellan one week later. On the 18th he was off to Northwest Industries in Edmonton to pick up a replacement Red Knight aircraft, 21620, in which he began practicing immediately. His only public show of 1963 took place at Steinbach, Manitoba on October 13th. However, between the four Red Knight pilots that year, they had completed 96 shows across North America.

1964 – A Year of Change

There were ill winds blowing for Canada's military services as 1964 dawned, enormous budget cuts having already been announced by the Liberal government of Lester B. Pearson. Integration of Canada's three services was introduced, to be followed four years later by unification. For the RCAF, one of the most tangible cuts occurred on February 7th with the unexpected cancellation of the Golden Hawks. That the Red Knight actually survived the tumultuous year of cutbacks was quite remarkable, although the number of scheduled shows was reduced significantly.

Wayne MacLellan would ordinarily have continued into his second year as the Red Knight but found himself a victim of the "famous 500" aircrew that received their pink slips from the government, so off he went to Air Canada. Fortunately, Bill Slaughter was already in the fold and became the anointed one to carry on the show for a seventh season, receiving the go-ahead on April 20th.

Another significant change to the program in 1964 involved the appointment of a commanding officer to oversee the operation and remove much of the administrative burden previously handled by the Red Knight pilots themselves. He would also double as narrator when he accompanied the team on the road and, if considered necessary, act as advance man for the team for the next scheduled showsite. The first senior instructor to fulfill this position was F/L Jack Des Brisay, a colourful character who had benefited from previous airshow exposure 10 years earlier as a member of the CF-100 team of Prairie Pacific. Joining the team as alternate for 1964 was F/O Tex Deagnon, another Sabre pilot who had flown in the Air Division with 430 (F) Sqn. With their two crew chiefs, LACs Ellis Gauthro and Paul Boucher, the Red Knight team now comprised five personnel.

Following the tragedy of the previous season, it was vital that the Red Knight have a good, safe season and under Bill Slaughter and Tex Deagnon that was accomplished. However, by any definition, this was still a shoe-string operation and as Bill Slaughter recalls, it was not always as smooth as one would have liked:

T-33 21620 was the third aircraft to receive the distinctive paint scheme of the Red Knight courtesy Northwest Industries of Edmonton. (author's collection)

shows across the nation, a significant reduction due to the aforementioned austerity program. However, the one constant in the airshow business being the need to practice regularly, he was scheduled for many "practice" shows across the country in the summer of '64. For those watching from the ground, it mattered not that these were not official shows – the thrill of watching the red jet twisting and turning through the sky was the same. And besides, with the Golden Hawks no longer flying, the Red Knight received top

"Of course there are many stories associated with my short tour as Red Knight, like the time I had the only serviceable T-33 in the air force and was scheduled for a show at Grand Prairie, Alberta. As Jack Des Brisay was in charge of logistics, and as there was no jet fuel at Grande Prairie (the closest being at either Cold Lake or Edmonton), I repeatedly confirmed with Jack that he had arranged for JP-4 fuel. And so he had – all in 45 gallon drums behind a shack where they had been unceremoniously unloaded. I did two practices and the airshow, taking turns with my crewman, LAC Ellis Gauthro, wobbling fuel from the drums to the aircraft for each flight. Good arm exercise …"

Bill Slaughter

Between his first show at RCAF Stn Portage on May 1st and his last at Moose Jaw on October 16th, Bill Slaughter did 19 major air-

This modest postcard was distributed by the Red Knight team during autograph sessions across Canada and the United States. (author's collection)

The 1964 Red Knight team. L to R – LAC Paul Boucher, F/O Tex Deagnon (Alternate), F/L Jack Des Brisay (OC), F/O Bill Slaughter (Red Knight) and LAC Ellis Gauthro. (DND PCN 5143)

Bill Slaughter's Red Knight was in good company during this stopover at RCAF Stn St. Hubert on 20 Jun 64. (Graham Wragg)

billing wherever he appeared. When Bill Slaughter shut down and stepped over the canopy sill of his Red Knight for the last time that October, he had no way of knowing what an important role he would play on Canada's next national aerobatic team three years later. The real fun was yet to come …

Into an Eighth Season

Tex Deagnon provided the continuity in 1965 for the Red Knight as all previous members were posted to new assignments. This meant a new OC as well, with F/L Jim Stothard being appointed the new man in charge. F/O Terry Hallett became the new alternate and two new crew chiefs, LACs Tom Lupton and Jack Rathwell, rounded out the team. The only other significant change in 1965 was the location of home base which switched from Portage la Prairie to "Canadian Forces Base" Moose Jaw. With the final retirement of the mighty Harvard, Moose Jaw became an all jet base utilizing the new CT-114 Tutor as the basic trainer with the T-33 now being utilized as an advanced jet trainer which would take all RCAF pilots to wings standard.

Canada adopted a new flag in 1965, and it wasn't long before the Red Knight was showing off Prime Minister Pearson's red maple leaf. The predominance of the flag on the tail of the aircraft underscored another important feature of military aerobatic performers – showing off the national colours for all to see. Also preceding the Red Ensign into the history books were two regional teams which had enjoyed popular support, particularly from western Canadians – the Gimli Smokers and the Goldilocks. Thus, the Red Knight became the sole performer from Training Command and the RCAF's only dedicated airshow act. Demands for the scarlet jet remained high across the country and Deagnon and Hallett often found themselves hundreds of miles apart doing different shows. As Terry Hallett recalls, when there was a scheduling conflict, "Tex took his pick of the shows he wanted to do and I did the

other ones – most people didn't realize there were two Red Knights." Indeed, having two Red Knights was the only way to satisfy the majority of requests which were coming in annually from every corner of the country.

The following year Terry Hallett got his pick of shows as he took over the reins from Tex Deagnon. Joining him was a new OC, F/L Ken Sheppardson, who was a strong advocate of the Red Knight program. F/O Roger Cossette, one of the RCAF's early Voodoo pilots with 416 AW(F) Sqn in Chatham, was selected as the new alternate. Such were the demands of the Red Knight in 1966 that the schedule was divided between the two demo pilots. Hallett did Central Canada and the west, Cossette primarily the eastern end of the country.

Unfortunately for the RCAF, Cossette was presented an opportunity to join Air Canada midway through the 1966 season, an opportunity which he felt he could not pass up. This development would have left Hallett as

the RCAF's sole aerobatic performer, a manageable situation except for the fact that he too had been advised that his tenure would end early – receiving a posting to the CF-104 Starfighter which would take effect before the end of the airshow season. This unwelcome news had infuriated Ken Sheppardson as it put the entire operation in jeopardy, not to mention the RCAF's reputation that he and his team had been carefully nurturing since May.

It wasn't long after this revelation in late July that Sheppardson ended up bending the ear of one of his staff instructors about his dilemma at the local watering hole known as the lower bar in the Moose Jaw Officers' Mess. Of course, as any pilot who has trained in Moose Jaw will attest, many of the world's problems have been solved in this august location. As F/L Jake Reilly recounts the story today (with appropriate humour), Ken Sheppardson "was livid" and couldn't get over the fact that someone would post the Red Knight out from under his nose before the end of the season. After some time listening to his tale of woe, aided by a few sarsaparillas, an exasperated Reilly finally declared "Okay, stop your whining and I'LL do it!" Sheppardson quickly replied "Okay, you're it!" Thus, in the finest traditions of crisis management was born another Red Knight. No fuss, no paper, no higher authorization – just get on with the job. And this is precisely what Jake Reilly did.

This photo depicting the 1965 Red Knight team was included in the CIAS program where the Red Knight was the feature RCAF performer. L to R – LAC Jack Rathwell, F/O Tex Deagnon (Red Knight), F/L Jim Stothard (OC), F/O Terry Hallett (Alternate), LAC Tom Lupton (courtesy CNE Archives)

Reilly already had plenty of flying experience under his belt when he was handed his new job as alternate Red Knight. Having graduated from Royal Military College in 1958, his first flying assignment following wings graduation had been on Sabres in the Air Div followed by a tour at FIS in Portage prior to arriving in Moose Jaw. This was a good thing, as he had the benefit of only one trip with Terry Hallett prior to starting solo practices for his new job on August 2nd, 1966. Over the next week he got in eight aerobatic practices prior to joining the team for their western swing, starting with Kelowna on August 9th. Meanwhile, Roger Cossette had completed his eastern swing and prepared to leave the RCAF. He had flown 20 official shows from Victoria, British Columbia to St John's, Newfoundland to Baie Verte, Quebec, flying his last Red Knight show at CFB Bagotville on August 6th. Thus, averting what had first appeared to be an insurmountable problem, Ken Sheppardson ended up with a seamless transition and the program continued unabated.

Autograph sessions were an important part of the job. The 1966 Red Knight, F/L Terry Hallett, responds to a child's curiosity as his crew chief shows off the cockpit to airshow fans at Pat Bay Airport (Victoria) on 4 Jun 66. (DND ET PL 66-01)

F/L Roger Cossette and his crew chief, LAC Chip Lake, toured eastern Canada in the summer of 1966. (DND 66-031-3 via Roger Cossette)

Veteran instructor F/L Jake Reilly was serving in Moose Jaw when he volunteered to fulfill the role of the Red Knight for the last half of the 1966 season. (RCAF photo via Jake Reilly)

For Jake Reilly, T-33 630 became his primary aircraft and LAC Chip Lake his crew chief. Along with Terry Hallett's crewman, LAC Jack Rathwell, the team proceeded on to Abbotsford and Comox, eventually ending up in Vancouver for the Pacific National Exhibition where Jake Reilly did his first four official shows.

September was a very busy month, starting with the annual Canadian International Air Show which Terry Hallett flew. By the 13th of the month his tour was over, his logbook revealing he had flown 59 shows that summer. Jake Reilly took over the lead role for the balance of the season. There was still a lot of travelling to be done, as far east as Lunenburg, Nova Scotia and as far south as Wichita, Kansas. As there was no longer an alternate pilot available, Chip Lake and Jack Rathwell split the crewman duties.

Terry Hallett cleans up his T-33 (21620) following a slow-speed silhouette at the Abbotsford International Airshow on 13 Aug 66. (Jerry Vernon)

The 1966 Red Knight season ended on October 14th with one last practice over the station at Moose Jaw. This was to be the end of Jack Reilly's short Red Knight career, although he had hoped to have the opportunity to fly the following season as well. He was posted to "Standards Flight" where he upgraded to an A1 instructor category. However, by this time a new "Canadian Armed Forces" aerobatic team had been formed at CFB Portage la Prairie for Centennial Year and had already been practicing for over a month. The anticipation of the new team quickly overshadowed the indispensable role that the Red Knight had played in keeping the airshow legacy alive in Canada during the lean years following the cancellation of the Golden Hawks. Indeed, it appeared that the Red Knight program was dead. As the end of 1966 drew near, there had been no favourable word in spite of newly promoted S/L Ken Sheppardson's persistent efforts.

A Centennial Red Knight

Canada's new centennial aerobatic team for 1967 was appropriately named the Golden Centennaires. The officer selected to command the team was W/C O.B. Philp, a fighter pilot by profession but also a graduate of the Empire Test Pilot School. "O.B." was well known in the fighter community as an excellent planner as well as a no-nonsense, straight shooter. This latter trait did not always enamour him with some subordinates or superiors, but at least you always knew where he stood on any given issue.

When planning had commenced for the Centennaire team with Philp's appointment in the spring of 1966, there had been no plans to include the Red Knight. O.B. had chosen some key personnel to help shape his team, all ex-Golden Hawks. S/L Lloyd Hubbard (the Hawk's last leader) would be his right-hand man and the team's public relations officer and commentator, S/L C.B. Lang the new team leader and F/L Dave Barker the new lead solo of what was to be a nine-plane team. It wasn't until dozens of requests from every corner of Canada started to flood in for appearances by the new team that Philp realized that his team could not possibly fulfill all of the requests. Only then was it suggested that the Red Knight be resurrected to fill the gaps. Since it was still only mid-December, there was time to act.

Getting authorization to add the Red Knight to his team was not a problem for O.B. Philp – he had a forceful personality and, while always remaining respectful of his bosses, had a way of convincing them that his way was the best way! Having received the appropriate go-ahead to add two more aircraft and four more personnel to his flying circus, word spread quickly. Addition of the Red Knight to the team meant that the citizens of Portage would get an early Christmas present, the *Daily Graphic* declaring in a feature article on December 23rd, *"Red Knight's coming home"* in response to a press release from Training Command Headquarters in Winnipeg. O.B. then set about his next challenge – deciding who his Red Knight pilot and alternate would be.

In February 1967 when O.B. Philp was making his final decision about the Red Knight, there were many fine pilots in the RCAF with T-33 experience who could have fulfilled the role, not the least of which was Jake Reilly who had done the RCAF a great service by stepping in to complete the 1966 season with virtually no notice. However, with time running out and so much administrative work yet to be accomplished for the centennial tour, O.B. decided he wanted someone he knew personally and had worked with before. He thus offered the job

Canada's Centennial Red Knight team. Back row, L to R – F/O Rod Ellis (Alternate), F/L Jack Waters (Red Knight). Kneeling, L to R – Cpls Vince Kavic, Bob Hawes. The team performed a record 101 shows across Canada and the United States in 1967. (RCAF photo via Jack Waters)

The classic lines of the Red Knight T-33 are evident in this photo as Jack Waters zooms overhead in the summer of '67. (via Jack Waters)

to F/L Jack Waters, another veteran fighter pilot and A1 instructor that had come to know Philp in Zweibrücken while on staff at the Wing Training Flight. Waters no doubt regarded this as a gift from heaven since he was on a ground job in Kitchener as a recruiting officer at the time – he instantly accepted the offer.

To compliment Waters' experience, the pilot chosen as his understudy was a tall, young man who had demonstrated a lot of promise in Moose Jaw. F/O Rod Ellis was 23 years-old at the time and had instructed on Harvards and Tutors in Moose Jaw after receiving his wings on the T-33. He was a base test pilot when he received the congratulatory call from O.B. Philp in mid-February. He had actually been one of dozens of volunteers who had hoped to join the new team, a wonderful opportunity for a relatively inexperienced pilot. Ellis would act as commentator for Waters and fill in when required during the long season. Selected to join the two pilots were two more fine technicians, Cpls Bob Hawes and Greg Moore. Cpl Vince Kavic came on board to replace Moore in late June when the latter was posted.

Jack Waters started practicing in Portage in early March for what promised to be a very busy season of airshow performances. His only previous low-level aerobatic experience had been watching his FIS instructor at Trenton practice a routine in the T-33 about 10 years earlier for the 1957 CNE. There were two ironies involved in this scenario, the first being that his instructor was a USAF exchange pilot by the name of Capt Charles Rose, the one and same pilot that Roy Windover had watched perform in 1957. The second was that Rose often practiced his show in a T-33 then painted in "primer yellow" – none other than 057, the aircraft

which became the Red Knight the next season. As Waters recalls, "I was Charlie's captive audience for a few of his practices. However, he inspired trust and I was always comfortable …"

The Red Knight Show

The 15 minute routine which Jack Waters developed for centennial year was not unlike the shows which his predecessors had flown in hundreds of previous Red Knight performances, although every solo performer likes to add one favourite "specialty" manoeuvre. He recalls some thoughts about his glory days as the Red Knight and provides a description of the show he flew for hundreds of thousands of Canadians as they celebrated the nation's 100th birthday:

"The Red Knight T-33 aerobatic show was a demonstration of all of those characteristics which made it an ideal advanced jet trainer for Canadian and American military pilots during the '50s and '60s. The demonstrated manoeuvres were those familiar to any modern military pilot, especially one engaged in combat operations, where the essential characteristic was, and is, performance at the 'edge of the flight envelope.'

The show commenced with the standard low-level takeoff in front of the audience prior to climbing to 5,000 feet. The next several minutes were devoted to a reconnaissance of the showsite and aircraft control checks with a consequent reduction in fuel load to the point where tip tanks registered empty – a requisite for a safe show. When all was well, I confirmed with the control tower that the showsite was clear of aircraft and then began a long shallow dive at 100 percent power to arrive over the airfield at the designated time.

My arrival from stage right was announced by F/O Rod Ellis, the Red Knight alternate and commentator. Rod also provided a running commentary throughout the show over a public address system. For my first manoeuvre, I flew the length of the runway at 500 knots and 300 feet and then commenced a 7 G pull-up and vertical climb to an altitude of 4,000 feet. At this point, I did a vertical reverse manoeuvre by rolling 180 degrees and immediately commencing a pull through in order to descend and approach the showsite from the left at 320 knots and 300 feet. Upon reaching the centre point of the airfield, I pressed the gun trigger switch on my control column to activate the smoke generating system and executed a full loop, exerting a force of 4 G. As I completed the loop at the centre point and arrived once again at 300 feet, I released the trigger to deactivate the smoke and turned sharply left 70 degrees away from the spectators and, while climbing steeply, rolled left inverted to reverse the turn to the right, to re-approach the airfield from the right at 330 knots and 100 feet.

I then raised the nose of the aircraft and at 300 feet, performed a slow roll along the entire length of the runway. Just as I completed the slow roll at 100 feet, I initiated a sharp 4 G pull-up to another vertical reverse to set up for my next pass. My next manoeuvre was a Cuban-eight traced in smoke entered from the left at 350 knots from 200 feet. It commenced with three-quarters of a loop and, when diving inverted at 45 degrees nose down to the ground, I rolled the wings level, descending to the centre point and 200 feet. The second half was executed in the same manner.

On smoking off I turned sharply to the left away from the spectators, and initiated a steep climbing left turn followed by a full right roll at the apex, and a steep descending left turn to approach the airfield head-on to the spectators at a speed of 350 knots and an altitude of 300 feet. Then, a quarter mile away from the centre point, I sharply pulled up to the vertical while triggering the smoke. The effect for the spectators was a dramatic full plan view of the Red Knight aircraft trailing white smoke in a vertical climb. They had to raise their eyes to follow me to a point where I rolled slowly right and continued to roll to a point where the nose slowly dropped as I started a slow descending left turn and rapidly increased speed, still turning and descending, to once again approach the air-

Another fine study of the Red Knight in landing configuration. (via Jack Waters)

field head-on to the spectators at a speed of 350 knots at 300 feet. Just before centre point, I released the trigger to cease the smoke. Because of the lazily slow reversal at the top of the manoeuvre and the slow descending left turn, gaining speed, this was my favourite part of the show. It gave me a brief period of mid-show relaxation. After about seven minutes of fairly heavy G forces in which my body often had an effective weight up to 1,100 pounds, my G suit was almost continually compressing my lower extremities to prevent blackout due to blood pooling away from the brain.

Arriving once again at centre stage, I banked sharply left into a full power 360 degree turn under a constant 6 G. On completing the high-speed turn, I exited the showsite heading stage right. Following another reversal came an inverted pass down the length of the runway, feeling the weightlessness of negative G forces. As I reached the end of the airfield, I rolled to the upright position, climbed abruptly to the vertical position and, at 4,000 feet, performed a half roll and pull through to re-approach the airfield travelling left to right at 300 knots and 100 feet.

On reaching the centre point, I turned sharply to the left, away from the crowd, and climbed to 800 feet while reducing power to 65 percent and extending the speed brakes. Upon reaching 800 feet and a speed of 200 knots, I continued turning left and extended the landing gear and flaps, then descended in a continuous left turn to arrive at the centre point at a speed of 160 knots and 100 feet. (My airshow narrative made only scant reference to throttle settings. Needless to say, the throttle was in constant motion but mostly at the 100% thrust setting - good old Rolls Royce Nene 10!)

The next manoeuvre was a 360 degree left turn at 100 feet with full power and landing gear, flaps and speed brakes extended. As I completed this turn, I waggled my wings (a crowd favourite) and retracted speed brakes and flaps and raised the landing gear. Then rolling level, I exited the showsite travelling to the right and accelerating to 300 knots. Then it was back in again for a four-point roll, hesitating momentarily at the 90 degree point, the inverted position and 270 degree point before recovering at approximately 100 feet.

Gaining airspeed during the next reversal, I arrived at centre stage to perform my own 'signature' manoeuvre – an abrupt 7 G pull-up to an absolutely vertical position followed by a full upwards roll and a pull over the top at 4,000 feet to an absolutely vertical dive and a full downward roll – to arrive at the centre point heading to stage right at 350 knots and 100 feet.

As I exited this manoeuvre, I raised the nose sharply and, at full power, executed two climbing victory snap rolls before a high rolling reversal designed to bring me back to the airfield at a speed of 400 knots at 100 feet. Now came my fighter pitch and landing. By this time I would be sweating profusely so immediately after landing I would open the canopy to cool down. Taxiing back in to the flight line, I was always met by our two crew chiefs, Bob Hawes and Vince Kavic, who would marshal me to my parking spot and then commence the post flight checks."

Jack Waters

The Red Knight team performed 101 official shows in 1967. Although Jack Waters did the vast majority of the official shows, Rod Ellis did split away for one swing on his own when the busy schedule so dictated. This saw him perform seven official shows and a host of practices in eastern Canada. Indeed, practice was a constant companion throughout the tour in order to keep skills honed and the show safe. The final show of the season was to have been number 100 at the closing ceremonies of *Man and His World* in Montreal on October 27th. However, that same afternoon a panic call came in from Schenectady, New York requesting a show on October 29th following a fatal crash of one of the USAF Thunderbirds. W/C Philp helped out by sending his Red Knight team down to do a show for them. Thus ended a highly successful season. Well, almost …

As an interesting footnote, O.B. Philp took his eight-plane Tutor team on a short US tour following the end of their last Canadian swing. Rod Ellis was invited to ride side saddle with S/L Red Dagenais during the Centennaire shows and thoroughly enjoyed the experience. While in the Bahamas, O.B. thought it would be a wonderful thing if his young Red Knight were to put on a solo show for the tourists in Freeport. This was done entirely under O.B.'s own auspices and is a heretofore little known adjunct to the Red Knight legend. Since there was no Red Knight aircraft with the entourage at the time, Ellis used S/L Lloyd Hubbard's T-33 (21592) which was painted in Golden Centennaire colours to put on public displays on November 11th and 12th. Although "unofficial," these were the only "Red Knight" shows ever flown in "Golden Centennaire" colours!

A Change of Aircraft

There would be another wholesale change of personnel for the 1968 airshow season, Jack Waters having been promoted to squadron leader and Rod Ellis posted to a highly desired tour on the Starfighter, via the legendary Sabre to boot. Once more, the Red Knight survived the axe to fly again, even though the Centennaires did not. The Red Knight was now the only air force airshow performer left to carry on the finest traditions of the RCAF, in spite of the fact that the RCAF itself was relegated to the annals of history on February 1st, 1968 when it ceased to exist along with its sister services. Unification had been officially adopted and with it came a universal green uniform to replace the traditional colours of the navy, army and air force. Also gone was the unique

rank structure of the navy and air force, army ranks having been adopted across the Canadian Armed Forces. Thus began an era of great anguish for Canada's military services as personnel struggled to maintain the pride and identity that had earned them worldwide respect.

Capt Dave Curran was a highly regarded FIS instructor at Portage la Prairie in 1968, holding an A1 instructor category on both the T-33 and Tutor. He too had completed a Sabre tour overseas on 430 Sqn and had checked out several of the successful Golden Centennaire candidates in 1966. He was now eager to carry on the traditions of the Red Knight and

Capt John Reid was selected as the alternate Red Knight in the spring of 1968. His strong desire to fly with the team ended in tragedy when he was killed at Portage la Prairie on 22 May 68. (DND Photo via John Corrigan)

quickly won the job. His alternate would be Capt John Reid who was being posted to Portage fresh off of a tour on Starfighters in the Air Division. Jack Waters had been promoted and returned to FIS as the T-33 flight commander; for all intents and purposes he became Curran's principal point of contact and supporter on the base.

As Dave Curran recalls, the overwhelming success of the Centennaires meant that CFB Portage remained cooperative in providing support to keep the Red Knight legacy alive. However, all other funding seemed to dry up, including from the Department of Exhibitions and Displays at NDHQ. However, this rapidly became the least of his problems.

John Reid had only been in Portage a few weeks when he was killed during an impromptu flight over the field. On May 22nd, a pre-arranged public relations team from Winnipeg had arrived at the base to take photos of the new Red Knight team for publicity purposes. When they requested some

airborne shots, Dave Curran was happy to oblige. However, as there was only one Red Knight T-33 in Portage at the time (21620), he invited John Reid to take the aircraft up to do a few simple flypasts for the benefit of the photographers. The aircraft had a full fuel load, a 577 load as it was called, meaning that both the internal and tip tanks were full. Although it was well known that the T-33 was not capable of performing looping aerobatics safely with fuel remaining in the tips, John Reid attempted to do so following two flypasts, much to the dismay of Dave Curran watching from the ground. Reid crashed onto the runway and died several hours later in hospital.

The untimely death of John Reid did not deter Dave Curran from his goal of keeping the Red Knight alive. He flew his low show (due to cloud) in T-33 21630 at the base's Armed Forces Day on June 9th. This would be the last T-33 show for the Red Knight. At the time, Curran had felt that the Tutor was better suited to the role since it was much lighter, didn't have the quirks of the T-33 hydraulic boost system and could perform a tighter show. He had requested the use of two of the old Centennaire aircraft for the Red

Knight since they were already fitted with smoke systems – now he got his wish. His request was passed from Training Command to the newly formed Canadian Forces Headquarters in Ottawa. Air force operations now came under the purview of the Director General Air Forces which would soon be commanded by BGen David Adamson. However, at the time, the senior pilot in the headquarters was a newly promoted lieutenant colonel in charge of fighters, trainers and tactical helicopters, none other than Bob Hallowell. His involvement with the Red Knight had come full circle. He quickly approved the request, again doing his part to keep the operation alive.

The new operations order outlining the guidelines for the use of two Tutors in the Red Knight role was signed by Col G.R.M. Hunt on June 24th, 1968. He was the deputy chief of staff for flying training at Training Command Headquarters. Although the Red Knight operation was an entity of the Central Flying and Navigation School (CFNS) in Winnipeg, the commandant of the school delegated much of the "hands on" responsibility to his detachment in Portage, then commanded by Major Bob Crouch.

The Red Knight switched to the CT-114 Tutor in July 1968. Standing L to R – Capt Dave Curran (Red Knight 1968), Maj Jack Waters (Red Knight 1967), Capt Joe Houlden (narrator). Kneeling L to R – Cpls Larry Hunt and John Hilts. (DND Photo via Dave Curran)

However, for the balance of 1968, in order to provide some continuity in the transition from T-33 to Tutor, Jack Waters was delegated as authorizing officer and coordinator of all practice sessions. This made sense given the fine working relationship that had already been fostered between Jack Waters and Dave Curran. The only change to the Training Command directive was that the minimum altitude for conducting aerobatics be raised from 100 to 200 feet above ground.

The Red Paint Saga

On July 15th, 1968, the Red Knight team finally received their Tutor aircraft (26153 and 26154) courtesy 6 Repair Depot in Trenton who had pulled them out of storage in Mountain View and ferried them to Portage. They were still in Golden Centennaire colours. Dave Curran had already designed a paint scheme for the new jets with assistance from Jack Waters. Eager to get them painted, a major obstacle was encountered when the base advised there was no money available to have the aircraft finished in Red Knight colours, this being an unforecast expenditure. Besides, no "official" design had been approved! This was a stunning disappointment as the support from the base had been excellent up to that point.

In a true testament of dedication to the cause, Dave Curran jumped in his car, drove to Winnipeg, found a commercial paint shop and personally bought enough red acrylic paint to finish both Tutors. It cost him $660 out of his pocket, no small sum for someone that was earning less than $10,000 a year at the time. (After tax, this represented an entire month's pay! It wasn't easy getting the money back, although he eventually did at the end of the season after several months of wrangling with the accountants … in-between shows of course.) Racing back to Portage that Friday afternoon, Curran proceeded to the hangar line and presented the refinishers with his "official" drawings and a trunk full of paint. The refinishers worked all weekend to put it on, giving a whole new look to the diminutive Tutor. The show was on!

With the blessing to convert to the Tutor also came a new teammate in the person of Capt Joe Houlden, who was designated as Dave Curran's commentator. A former Sabre pilot, Houlden had recently rejoined the RCAF and had just checked out on the Tutor in Moose Jaw. Jack Waters knew of his interest in, and aptitude for, public affairs so broached the

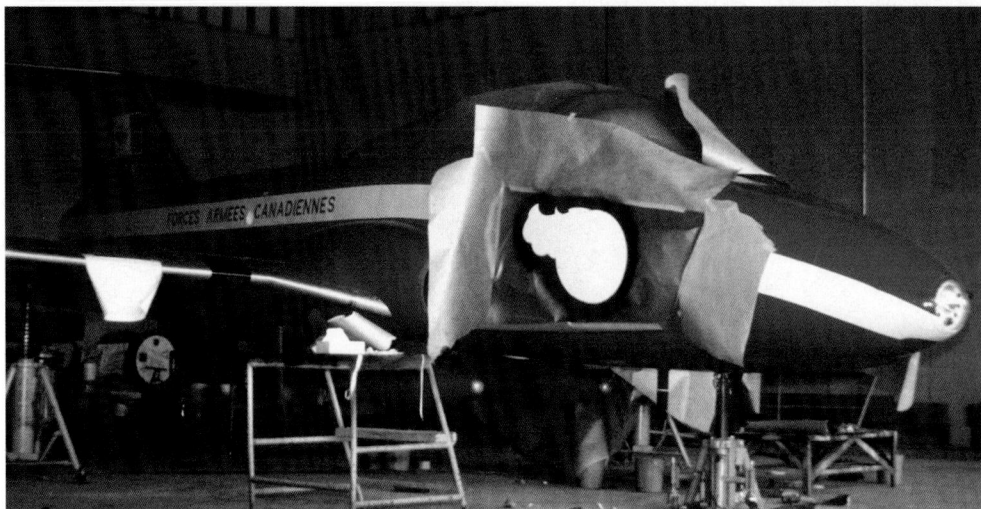

The anatomy of a new Red Knight. Stripped of its previous Golden Centennaire colours, Tutor 26154 is transformed into the Red Knight by the refinishers at CFB Portage. (via Dave Curran)

subject with Dave Curran prior to offering the job to Houlden. He was there within days … The two new volunteer groundcrew for the team were another two stalwarts, Cpls Larry Hunt, who had flown with the Golden Centennaires, and John Hilts.

It was up to Dave Curran to adapt his Red Knight show to the Tutor and he only had a little over two weeks to do so. Although he

discussed various aspects with Bill Slaughter, Jim McKay (ex-Centennaires solos) and Jack Waters, there was no formal training. Curran proceeded cautiously in designing a safe and effective show. One unique specialty that he was able to work up for his routine was a "loop to landing." This required a lot of skill, judgement and practice. Curran became an expert at the manoeuvre and did it whenever his show was over an

Capt Dave Curran shows off his new steed in the summer of '68. The Red Knight show in the Tutor was considerably tighter than that flown in the T-33. (Garth Dingman via Graham Wragg)

The scene at Mount Hope Airport in Hamilton, Ontario on 8 Sep 68. The Red Knight drew a crowd wherever he appeared. (via Dave Curran)

airfield and the prevailing conditions were suitable. However, he heeded closely the most valuable piece of advice he had received from Jack Waters, "Set your sequence and DO NOT vary it!" Many a demo pilot worldwide has lost his life because he failed to follow this basic axiom of demonstration flight. A low-level show environment, when both adrenaline and ego are at a peak, is no place for experimentation or impromptu improvisation. Even the great WW I ace Billy Barker had learned this lesson the hard way in 1930.

On August 1ˢᵗ, the Red Knight team finally hit the road for their six week tour under the callsign "Canforce Red Knight Flight." Dave Curran flew his first public show in the Tutor on August 2ⁿᵈ in Powell River, British Columbia. Two weeks later he had traversed the entire country, putting on a show at Charlottetown, Prince Edward Island. On September 13ᵗʰ, an historic flight took place over CFB Portage and the adjacent city when S/L Jack Waters in his former Red Knight T-33 (21630) led Dave Curran and Joe Houlden in their Tutors on a symbolic flypast. The next day, Curran flew his last show at Sky Harbour, Ontario at a memorial dedication to the British Commonwealth Air Training Plan of World War II.

In the end, after all of the trials and tribulations, Dave Curran performed a total of 22 shows in 1968. Once on the road, the team

An aviation photographer's dream. The Red Knight joins an RAF Vulcan strategic bomber in a rare flypast for airshow fans at the Abbotsford International Airshow in Aug '68. (via Dave Curran)

was entirely on their own, reminiscent of the old "barnstorming" days as he likes to recall. Innovation and initiative were the order of the day. He was the only Red Knight to ever fly shows in both the T-33 and Tutor, although the vast majority were in the latter.

The End of an Era

In the spring of 1969, approval was granted for a 12ᵗʰ consecutive season of airshow performances by the Red Knight who remained under the operational control of Major Crouch at the CFNS Detachment. Unfortunately, Dave Curran was on the move to an exchange posting in the United States and there was no obvious replacement for him. There were no experienced instructors of the class of previous candidates who were prepared to spend the long periods of the summer season on the road away from their fam-

ilies. For many pilots, the downside of the job outweighed the fame and glory. Nevertheless, there were two young instructors from Moose Jaw who were very keen to take on the role.

While each of the two pipeline instructors demonstrated excellent piloting skills, both were very young and neither had any operational experience to fall back on. One seemed to have a slight edge in the tryouts that ensued in Portage and subsequently was selected by Training Command Headquarters in Winnipeg. Lt Brian Alston, at 23 years-of-age, gained the distinction of being the youngest pilot ever appointed as the principal Red Knight. Throughout his flying training as a student and instructor, he had demonstrated superior flying skills which belied his relative youth. It was these skills combined with an aura of confidence which

The changing of the guard. In July 1968 the Red Knight's venerable T-33 was retired in favour of the CT-114 Tutor. The three aircraft flew together only once – on 13 Sep 68 in a ceremonial salute to the personnel of CFB Portage and citizens of Portage la Prairie. (via Terry Leversedge)

led Training Command to approve his quest to become the Red Knight. Considering he had only earned his wings two years earlier, this was a remarkable development.

Once Brian Alston started his practice regimen in Portage, Joe Houlden stayed on for the first few weeks of Alston's workup but had no interest in actually flying the Red Knight show himself. That led to him being replaced before the start of the tour by Capt Bob Cran, another Moose Jaw instructor who had expressed an interest in becoming Alston's commentator and alternate. Although he had a maritime operational background, Cran was in his 14th year in the air force and had two years instructional experience on the Tutor. Being nine years older than Alston, as well as senior in rank, he was a good mentor for the young bachelor and was able to take much of the administrative load off of Alston, leaving the young pilot to concentrate on his show. Also of invaluable assistance was the return of Cpl Larry Hunt for his second year with the Red Knight and Cpl Bob Hawes after a one year hiatus. Both veterans of airshow touring, there weren't too many showsites in Canada they hadn't seen!

Saturday, June 14th was a great day for the 1969 Red Knight team – their first public show in Shilo, Manitoba for Armed Forces Day. The next day the show was in Portage la Prairie, and once again thousands turned out to watch the familiar bright red Tutor perform. Alston sparkled – as far as he was concerned, he had the best job in the air force,

A Salute to Portage Areas Goodwill Ambassador "The Red Knight"

The name of Portage la Prairie has been synonymous with the "Red Knight." Throughout the year, all across Canada and the United States, Portage la Prairie has been brought to public attention through the ability and skills of this ambassador of Good-Will.

At the close of another season, we extend our thanks for a job well done and offer our best wishes for many more seasons of accomplishment.

Portage la Prairie, Manitoba was home to the Red Knight for seven of the 12 years the solo aerobatic performer flew. In a fitting tribute, the merchants of the city sponsored a two-page salute to the Red Knight and personnel of CFB Portage in the *Daily Graphic* newspaper at the end of the 1968 season. It is reproduced in part, courtesy the *Daily Graphic*.

but with the job came a lot of visibility and pressure. When asked by a reporter to describe his feelings for the role, he was quoted as saying "It's a kind of emotional thing. You just can't put it into words."

Pilots with years more experience were surprised at the way Alston handled the Tutor – his was a very aggressive show. He explored the full range of the Tutor's capabilities, from maximum positive G (7.33) to maxi-

---

THE PORTAGE LA PRAIRIE DAILY GRAPHIC, SATURDAY, OCTOBER 19, 1968

A salute to the Red Knight
Famous from coast to coast

Familiar sight all across Canada

When a flaming red air force jet streaks across any part of Canada these days, it's immediately recognizable as the Red Knight from Portage la Prairie.

Over the years the Red Knight has visited practically every corner of the country, sometimes in a solo show, other times as a feature of a full-scale demonstration of flying with craft of many other types.

But no matter where, the Red Knight stands out above all others — first in the T-33 Silver Star and now the Tutor which has replaced the original jet craft.

The trim jet has become a familiar part of the airforce scene all across the land — and may it continue.

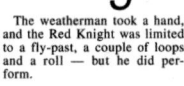

Thousands locally have seen the Knight

Practically everyone in Portage and distrtrict has seen the Red Knight in action at some time or another — either in practice or in actual shows.

A count of 14,200 people swarmed onto CFB Portage in early Junes this year for the annual forces' show and the Knight. The show finally had to be postponed until October.

These were only a few occasions locally when the flaming red plane was on hand for public view, but it gives an indication of the many thousands of people who have watched the Knight perform in this immediate area.

The weatherman took a hand, and the Red Knight was limited to a fly-past, a couple of loops and a roll — but he did perform.

In 1967 — in July — the weather "fouled up" again with more than 6,000 on hand to see the Knight.

DAVE CURRAN, the 1968 Red Knight, has to be regarded as one of the country's best-known commuters. His "here today, gone tomorrow" appearance is completely justified, since the armed forces veteran was involved in some 35 air shows this summer.

"FOLLOW ME, BOYS" . . . that seems to be the cry in this formation of Red Knights past and present. In the lead is the time-honored T-33 which, as Red Knight for the past decade, has thrilled air show audiences from coast to coast. In its wake are its successors, the flaming red Tutors which began Red Knight duties this year. The T-33 returns to normal duties this fall, leaving the Tutor to carry on the Red Knight tradition.

The 1969 Red Knight team had their advance publicity photos taken at CFB Portage on 23 Apr 69. Lt Brian Alston was the youngest pilot ever to be designated the Red Knight. L to R – Cpl Bob Hawes, Cpl Larry Hunt, Lt Brian Alston, Capt Joe Houlden. (DND PCN 69-104)

mum negative (-3.0), underscoring the attributes that had made the little trainer so popular with the Golden Centennaires. His *outside* Cuban-eight was, in a word, *eye-watering* to people in the know – a manoeuvre in which he pushed at least three negative G for an extended period of time, straining the very limits of the aircraft. Negative G can be excruciatingly uncomfortable, and in this manoeuvre Alston got a double dose of it.

The next weekend the road tour resumed with two shows in northern British Columbia. Then it was back to Manitoba for four shows prior to heading out to Penhold, Alberta and then on to Calgary for the big Stampede. The Calgary Stampede was one of the bigger shows of the year, Alston performing in front of the grandstand on July 11th. There was no rest for the team however, as they immediately departed eastwards to set up for a show the next day in Selkirk, Manitoba.

It was the day of the team's second show in Selkirk that disaster struck. Following the show, the team had recovered in Portage and then launched off to Moose Jaw. Upon landing late that Sunday afternoon, July 13th, they had been welcomed by base officials who had enquired whether Alston would be able to put on a short display for a group of visiting Italian officers, including the Italian Air Force Attaché. Alston readily agreed, jumping back into his refuelled aircraft for a short display. Unfortunately, while rolling out downwind from one of his manoeuvres, he experienced a serious engine problem in Tutor 154. In attempting to do a 180 degree turn back to the field for an emergency landing, his aircraft stalled and crashed onto the runway – Alston was killed instantly.

In the aftermath of the tragedy, Training Command decided to cancel the remainder of the 1969 tour. Two fatalities in two years was more than the system could cope with. To compound the disaster, Bob Cran was killed during an unrelated routine training sortie in the Tutor only 17 days after Brian Alston's accident. Cran had already applied to take over the Red Knight role from Alston in 1970; his loss put the future of the Red Knight in further jeopardy.

But A Legend Never Dies

By the spring of 1970, another budget crunch had hit the Canadian Forces, again courtesy the federal government. More large scale personnel cuts were pending and Canada's NATO contribution was to be severely reduced. To make matters worse, unification was not sitting well with many veterans of the three previous services. The growing pains were not over … It was in this climate that a short press release was issued from Winnipeg that spring:

Red Knight aerobatics axed – The defence department's economy program has axed the Red Knight and his solo displays of precision aerobatics. A department spokesman said Thursday there will be no Red Knight in performances in 1970 and there has been no decision on whether the crowd-thrilling performances will be reintroduced in future years.

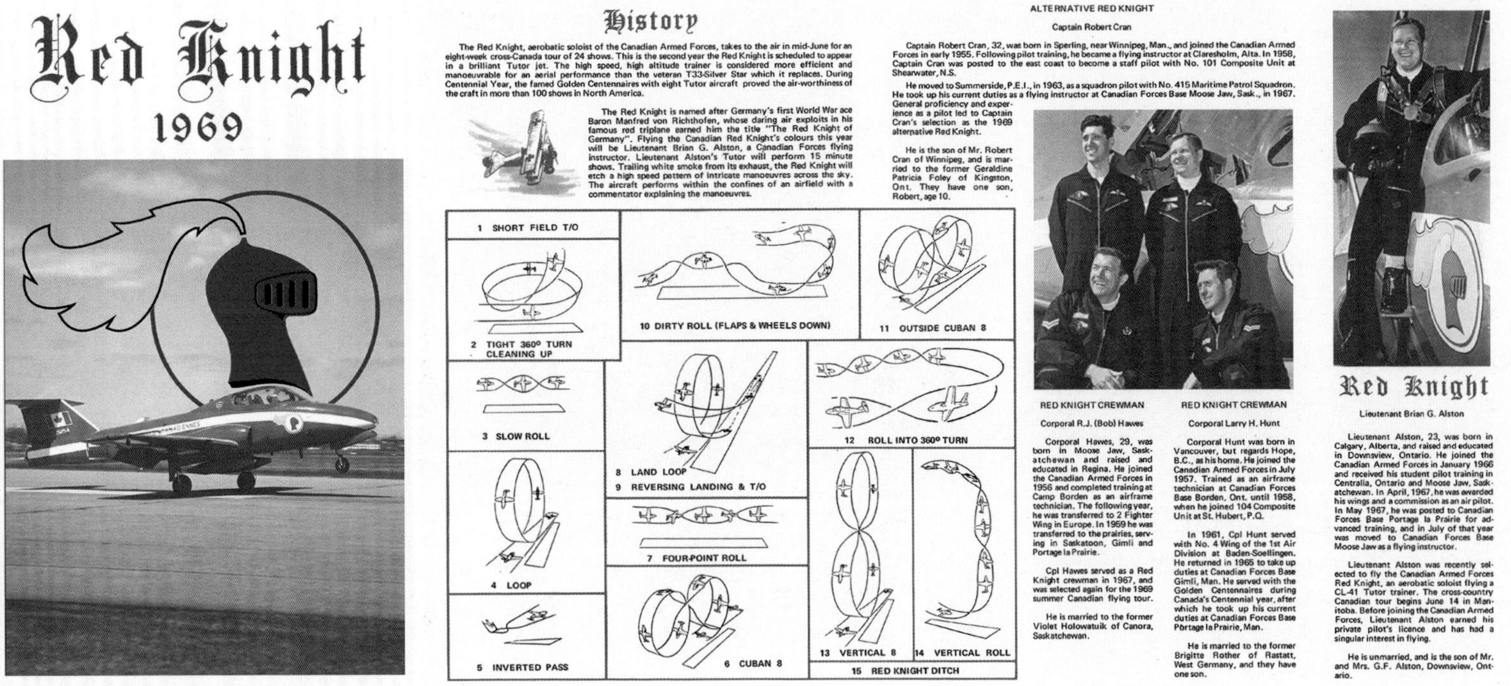

Red Knight
1969

History

The Red Knight, aerobatic soloist of the Canadian Armed Forces, takes to the air in mid-June for an eight-week cross-Canada tour of 24 shows. This is the second year the Red Knight is scheduled to appear in a brilliant Tutor jet. The high speed, high altitude trainer is considered more efficient and manoeuvrable for an aerial performance than the veteran T33-Silver Star which it replaces. During Centennial Year, the famed Golden Centenaires with eight Tutor aircraft proved the air-worthiness of the craft in more than 100 shows in North America.

The Red Knight is named after Germany's first World War ace Baron Manfred von Richthofen, whose daring air exploits in his famous red triplane earned him the title "The Red Knight of Germany". Flying the Canadian Red Knight's colours this year will be Lieutenant Brian G. Alston, a Canadian Forces flying instructor. Lieutenant Alston's Tutor will perform 15 minute shows. Trailing white smoke from its exhaust, the Red Knight will etch a high speed pattern of intricate manoeuvres across the sky. The aircraft performs within the confines of an airfield with a commentator explaining the manoeuvres.

1 SHORT FIELD T/O
2 TIGHT 360° TURN CLEANING UP
3 SLOW ROLL
4 LOOP
5 INVERTED PASS
6 CUBAN 8
7 FOUR-POINT ROLL
8 LAND LOOP
9 REVERSING LANDING & T/O
10 DIRTY ROLL (FLAPS & WHEELS DOWN)
11 OUTSIDE CUBAN 8
12 ROLL INTO 360° TURN
13 VERTICAL 8
14 VERTICAL ROLL
15 RED KNIGHT DITCH

ALTERNATIVE RED KNIGHT
Captain Robert Cran

Captain Robert Cran, 32, was born in Sperling, near Winnipeg, Man., and joined the Canadian Armed Forces in early 1955. Following pilot training, he became a flying instructor at Claresholm, Alta. In 1958, Captain Cran was posted to the east coast to become a staff pilot with No. 101 Composite Unit at Shearwater, N.S.

He moved to Summerside, P.E.I., in 1963, as a squadron pilot with No. 415 Maritime Patrol Squadron. He took up his current duties as a flying instructor at Canadian Forces Base Moose Jaw, Sask., in 1967. General proficiency and experience as a pilot led to Captain Cran's selection as the 1969 alternative Red Knight.

He is the son of Mr. Robert Cran of Winnipeg, and is married to the former Geraldine Patricia Foley of Kingston, Ont. They have one son, Robert, age 10.

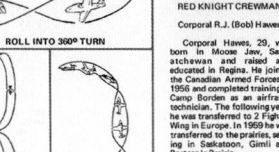

RED KNIGHT CREWMAN
Corporal R.J. (Bob) Hawes

Corporal Hawes, 29, was born in Moose Jaw, Saskatchewan and raised and educated in Regina. He joined the Canadian Armed Forces in 1956 and completed training at Camp Borden as an airframe technician. The following year, he was transferred to 2 Fighter Wing in Europe. In 1959 he was transferred to the prairies, serving in Saskatoon, Gimli and Portage la Prairie.

Cpl Hawes served as a Red Knight crewman in 1967, and was selected again for the 1969 summer Canadian flying tour.

He is married to the former Violet Holowatuik of Canora, Saskatchewan.

RED KNIGHT CREWMAN
Corporal Larry H. Hunt

Corporal Hunt was born in Vancouver, but regards Hope, B.C., as his home. He joined the Canadian Armed Forces in July 1957. Trained as an airframe technician at Canadian Forces Base Borden, Ont. until 1958, when he joined 104 Composite Unit at St. Hubert, P.Q.

In 1961, Cpl Hunt served with No. 4 Wing of the 1st Air Division at Baden-Soellingen. He returned in 1965 to take up duties at Canadian Forces Base Gimli, Man. He served with the Golden Centenaires during Canada's Centennial year, after which he took up his current duties at Canadian Forces Base Portage la Prairie, Man.

He is married to the former Brigitte Rother of Rastatt, West Germany, and they have one son.

Red Knight
Lieutenant Brian G. Alston

Lieutenant Alston, 23, was born in Calgary, Alberta, and raised and educated in Downsview, Ontario. He joined the Canadian Armed Forces in January 1966 and received his student pilot training in Centralia, Ontario and Moose Jaw, Saskatchewan. In April, 1967, he was awarded his wings and a commission as an air pilot. In May 1967, he was posted to Canadian Forces Base Portage la Prairie for advanced training, and in July of that year was moved to Canadian Forces Base Moose Jaw as a flying instructor.

Lieutenant Alston was recently selected to fly the Canadian Armed Forces Red Knight, an aerobatic soloist flying a CL-41 Tutor trainer. The cross-country Canadian tour begins June 14 in Manitoba. Before joining the Canadian Armed Forces, Lieutenant Alston earned his private pilot's licence and has had a singular interest in flying.

He is unmarried, and is the son of Mr. and Mrs. G.F. Alston, Downsview, Ontario.

Canadair Ltd of Montreal, the manufacturers of the Tutor, sponsored an attractive brochure for the 1969 Red Knight team. Thousands were distributed across Canada prior to the untimely end of the Red Knight legacy. (via DND DHist, John Corrigan)

Thus ended the longest running aerobatic display in the history of the RCAF and Canadian Forces to that time. The Red Knight program never was resurrected, although the professionalism of those who had persevered against the odds would soon be emulated again. Several monuments to the legendary show still exist across the country. They stand in solemn tribute to the 17 young men and their crewmen who thrilled North Americans in over 600 shows in the gleaming red jet during the 12 year history of the program. Those fortunate enough to have witnessed the dynamic performance of the Red Knight have memories that will last forever – true testament that a legend never dies …

Brian Alston thrilled the crowd at the Calgary Stampede with his show performance on Friday, 11 Jul 69. Tragically, he was killed two days later at CFB Moose Jaw when he attempted to save his aircraft following an engine failure during a practice demonstration. (Glenbow Archives, Calgary, Alberta NA-2864-18182-39)

The Red Herring

Although the Red Knight name was certainly dominant in airshow circles across Canada during the 12 year tenure of the program, airshow patrons from the Maritimes in the mid-to-late 1960s will remember another aerobatic soloist who left his mark in Canadian naval aviation history. Lt Ian Ferguson, the officer-in-charge of the T-33 Jet Flight at VU-32 in Shearwater, Nova Scotia gained renown for a very fine display in the T-33 between 1966 and 1971. Today, he is fondly remembered as the "Red Herring," the moniker under which he flew in an obvious naval parody of his RCAF counterpart. Ferguson had actually joined the RCAF himself in 1952 and flew an operational fighter tour on the F-86 Sabre with 413 Sqn at 3 Wing Zweibrücken prior to transferring to the fleet air arm of the RCN in 1958. He reflects back on those invigorating days that carved him a niche in Canadian airshow folklore:

"Back in the 1960s the RCN never put too much emphasis on aerobatic performances. There were certainly formations put together over the years for the CNE and other airshows which involved Sea Furies, Avengers, Banshees, Trackers, various helicopters and the T-33 flown by line pilots from the various squadrons. However, after the disbanding of the Grey Ghosts Banshee team early in 1960, there was little interest shown by naval squadrons in airshow activity. The RCAF with their famous Golden Hawks flying F-86 Sabres and the Red Knight in his crimson T-33 were the central attraction in the aerobatic department.

In 1966 some of our naval aviators grew tired of constantly hearing about the antics of the Red Knight and decided to make a move. Heads were put together and a plan formulated resulting in the navy's own, what else, Red Herring! Since VU-32 had the only fixed wing jets in the RCN, Commander Doug Ross, our commanding officer, authorized the Red Herring to perform in the T-33 with appropriate tail markings to be applied and a smoke generator installed in the aircraft. As the OIC of Jet Flight with a number of years experience in an assortment of jet aircraft, I was authorized to work up a solo aerobatic display. We also formed a four-plane T-Bird team of staff pilots led by myself.

The standard Red Herring solo show consisted of a 400 knot entry to centre stage, pulling up into a two-and one-half turn vertical roll, then back down into a fairly tight slow-speed loop. Then, using reversals, I performed a series of low-level rolls, a Cuban eight, a four-point roll, an inverted pass, a flat 360 degree max rate turn followed by a landing. I could also commence my solo show after our formation display by breaking from the lead position into the vertical roll and then, on completion of my show, rejoining the team to carry out a formation landing.

The inaugural show for the Red Herring was slated for Armed Forces Day at Shearwater on June 11th, 1966. Practices were carried out at the old Maitland air strip on the south shore of Minas Basin. Lt Hugh Fisher flew with me in a second aircraft to judge my manoeuvres for accuracy and to offer helpful advice. T-33 number 21631 was given its 'Fishy Tail' paint job and all preparations were completed for the big day. Unfortunately, the weather proved to be too low for my aerobatic display and 631 went unserviceable, so T-Bird Flight took to the air and demonstrated some low-level formation and later took part in an army mock battle providing simulated low-level rocket attacks. Other than a flypast for 'Naval Day' in September, there was no other requirement for the Red Herring that year.

With 1967 being the Canadian Centennial, it was a banner summer for the Red Herring and T-Bird Flight as we combined for 27 displays around the Maritimes, primarily in Nova Scotia. We flew over airfields, picnic grounds, churches, schools, railroad stations and even crossroad intersections and wharves. On a couple of days during the summer two performances were carried out at different locales. Some shows were done in the early evening which made for a long day for the pilots and groundcrew because we also had to carry out our daily commitment of target towing for the navy's surface ships.

The maritime weather was always a concern and on occasion we really had to stretch things to get the show in. One such occasion

Lt Ian Ferguson of the Royal Canadian Navy climbs aboard his T-33 in preparation for another show as the Red Herring during Canada's 1967 Centennial year celebrations in the Maritimes. (RCN Photo)

was for the arrival of trumpeter Bobby Gimby and his troop at the Truro railroad station one morning. The weather was 'on limits' so I briefed the team to tune their ADF radios to the Truro commercial radio station and then follow me line-astern on a bearing to the railroad station hoping to see some ground! The radio station was broadcasting the event live and we could hear our aircraft going over the station but we never did see much. At least the radio announcer acknowledged our passes! For all of our shows, we did what the elements allowed within the parameters of safety. We flew our first formation show April 18th over Church Point, Nova Scotia and I did my first solo display that same afternoon over Parsboro. Naturally, our largest show was the big Centennial show at Shearwater on June 3rd and we finished our season at Charlottetown on October 20th.

The Red Herring tail logo appeared only in 1966 on T-33 21631. It was replaced with the Centennial Maple Leaf logo in 1967. (via Ian Ferguson)

By comparison to 1967, the following summer was pretty quiet with only four shows flown in June and in 1969 I was posted to VS880 to fly Trackers. F/L Wayne 'Butch' Foster filled in as the Red Herring at the 1970 Armed Forces Day and I was resurrected again in 1971. Although I was then employed as a Tracker pilot with VS880, LCol Dave Tate, our squadron commanding officer, authorized me to workup my old T-Bird show again and I ended up doing nine displays that summer. My last show as the Red Herring was flown at Mahone Bay, Nova Scotia on August 7th, 1971.

The Armed Forces Day shows we flew in were attended by crowds of up to 20,000 and it always struck me that the static displays

The VU-32 Jet Flight Formation Team of the RCN performed 19 shows in support of Centennial celebrations in 1967. Four members of the team included, L to R, Standing – Lt Gus Youngson, Lt Ian Ferguson (team leader); Kneeling – Lt Gerry Willis, F/L Tony Nichols (RCAF). (RCN Photo via Gus Youngson)

and airshows were much appreciated by the general public. I recall one year during the advertising and media blitz about the forthcoming airshow that Capt (N) Bob Cocks, our base commander at Shearwater, was heard lamenting, 'The damn Red Herring is getting more publicity than the CO!'

Most of the team members with whom I flew had little or no jet time prior to joining

VU-32 so they were checked out in-house and built up their time towing targets. As a result, we had to work hard to put together an appealing show. Our formations may not have been as tight as other teams or gone as fast or as low, but we did our duty and were proud of our efforts."

Ian Ferguson

Three members of VU-32 display fine form over Halifax Harbour in the summer of 1967. The "NAVY" insignia on the side of the aircraft gradually disappeared following unification of Canada's three services on 1 Feb 68. (RCN Photo)

Chipmunk Synchronized Aerobatic Team
The Centralia "Smoke-Eaters"

The de Havilland Chipmunk first appeared on the scene with the RCAF in 1948 on a trial basis but it was not until 1958 that a semi-official demonstration team was formed in Centralia after the aircraft had become the RCAF's primary trainer. Before that year, there were many solo aerobatic demonstrations at airshows, performed by senior instructors who had been specifically cleared to do low-level aerobatics. Naturally, these performances were not as glamorous as those put on by much faster fighter aircraft, the Gipsy Major engine only cranking out 145 brake horsepower for a top speed of 140 mph (225 km/h). However, for the *ab initio* pilot just learning how to fly the diminutive little machine, or for those who aspired to do so, watching it loop and roll effortlessly got the heart pumping – soon they too would be doing the same thing, thankfully at much higher altitude.

The de Havilland DHC-1 Chipmunk

The Chipmunk was another Canadian success story. Conceived, designed and built at de Havilland Canada's Downsview plant in Toronto under the tutelage of chief designer W.J. Jakimiuk, the little trainer injected new life into DHC's design office following significant post-war layoffs. From a dead start in October 1945, the prototype trainer (CF-DIO-X) took to the air on its first test flight on May 22nd, 1946 in the hands of test pilot W.I.P. Fillingham. Just under two years later the RCAF took delivery of three aircraft (18001-18003) to evaluate them as spotter aircraft. They were assigned to 444 Sqn at the Joint Air School in Rivers, Manitoba which flew the three aircraft between April 16th, 1948 and the squadron's disbandment on April 1st, 1949. (Of interest, 18001 was eventually purchased by famed American aerobatic pilot, Professor Art Scholl. Following extensive modifications including a retractable landing gear, Scholl reregistered the aircraft as N13Y and dazzled North American airshow fans for many years prior to his untimely death while filming the movie "Top Gun" in another aircraft.)

The Chipmunk aircraft proved to be an agile performer but it was several years before the RCAF would acknowledge the need for a primary trainer for air force pilot recruits.

The de Havilland DHC 1 Chipmunk was the RCAF's primary trainer between 1956 and 1971. Chipmunk 18043 was flown by F/O B.K. Doyle of the Centralia Smoke-Eaters in 1961. It was photographed at 15 Wing Moose Jaw on 10 July 99 where veteran performer Bud Granley put it through its paces in a graceful display at the Saskatchewan Air Show. (Dan Dempsey)

The Harvard had been an overwhelming success in the BCATP and was well ensconced as the RCAF's principal training aircraft. However, the advent of the Cold War and resultant formation of NATO led Canada and her allies into an aggressive expansion program. In October 1950, the RCAF announced a scheme designed to create a pool of 600 civilian staff pilots and flying instructors for use in an emergency. A total of 34 Chipmunks were purchased and loaned to 20 member clubs of the Royal Canadian Flying Club Association across the country for this purpose.

As the RCAF expanded its pilot training to include foreign NATO students, an unacceptably high attrition rate began to develop among pilot trainees – by 1951 it had risen to 30 percent. As a result, the decision was taken to conduct an experiment with several pilot courses at No. 1 FTS Centralia, Ontario between July 11th, 1952 and December 14th, 1953 to determine if a simpler initial aircraft would address the problem. The selected courses began their flying training with 25 hours on the Chipmunk and then moved onto the more challenging Harvard. At the end of the experiment, the Chipmunks were transferred to No. 6 Repair Depot in Trenton where they were put in storage pending further analysis and a decision by the air force brass.

Although 10 Chipmunks were delivered to No. 3 FTS at Claresholm, Alberta in late 1954, it was not until October 9th, 1956 that the RCAF finally adopted the Chipmunk as its "official" primary trainer. The fact that it remained in the role for the next 14 years speaks highly of its design and durability. It was not replaced until 1971, having been used to teach thousands of RCAF and Canadian Forces pilots how to fly. The last Chipmunk

was struck-off-strength from the Canadian Forces inventory on February 3rd, 1972.

A New Team for Centralia

It was F/O Merv Billings of the Primary Flying School at RCAF Stn Centralia who received authorization to form the first Chipmunk aerobatic team in 1958. His wingman was F/O Jim Jotham, another A1 Standards instructor who had been posted into the training world immediately following wings graduation in 1956. He had already received some airshow exposure as part of a three-plane synchronized Harvard aerobatic team representing No. 1 FTS earlier that year. He explains how it all came about:

"In May of 1958, F/O Merv Billings, myself and another staff instructor (whom I unfortunately cannot recall), began to work up a three-plane aerobatic routine in the Harvard for Centralia's annual Air Force Day. Although the Chipmunk was the station's primary trainer at the time as we had many foreign students undergoing flying training under NATO, we still had three Harvards attached to the school. In June we performed at Centralia and London. In August, we decided to switch to a two-plane synchronized aerobatic show using the Chipmunk, again with Merv leading and me as his wingman. Our act made its debut in Toronto at the CIAS on September 3rd to 5th as part of the RCAF contingent participating in the show. Merv was posted later that year to 412 Sqn to fly the de Havilland Comet jetliner, leaving me the reins for the following year.

In April 1959, I approached the chief flying instructor at Centralia, S/L Al Piroth, with a

The original Smoke-Eaters. L to R – F/O John Thomas, F/O Rene Croteau, F/O Don Sinel, F/O Hal Schweyer, F/O Jim Jotham, F/O Pete Giles. RCAF Stn Centralia, June 1959. (RCAF 4820 via Jim Jotham)

request to continue the team for the upcoming air display season. After working up the routine again with F/O Don Sinel as my wingman, Al Piroth flew with us on May 5th, after which he officially approved our team. I then approached the maintenance engineering section to see what they might be able to do for us in the way of smoke. This led to our aircraft being modified with red wing tip smoke canisters. Also at this time, a four-plane Chipmunk formation led by F/O John Thomas was added to our show. These aircraft were fitted with a pressurized oil tank in the back seat to make white smoke. F/L Jack Leach was the Deputy CFI who arranged our schedule and support. Between May and September he had organized our appearance at 13 airshows. Towards the end of the season, F/Os Rene Croteau and Bob Caskie both flew on my wing in place of Don Sinel who was posted out."

Jim Jotham

Given their inability to fly very far on a tank of gas, the Chipmunk team never strayed too far from home base. However, with the two largest shows in the nation in Ontario, they didn't need to! The team appeared at the big National Air Force Day in Ottawa on June 6th, 1959 and of course at the CIAS in Toronto in September. In fact, it was two Chipmunks that kicked off the RCAF extravaganza each afternoon over the Toronto waterfront with a sky writing display to lead off the display which featured 15 different aircraft types then on the air force's inventory.

The main Chipmunk show commenced with Thomas' four-plane doing several flypasts and chandelles in front of the crowd at which time Jotham and Sinel would arrive overhead

from behind the crowd. Their synchronized show consisted of loops and rolls beautifully executed in close formation but also included some breathtaking head-on crosses which were flown at very close quarters. With the slow speed of the Chipmunk, it was relatively easy to judge crossing distance as the two aircraft approached each other, although drift caused by crosswinds had a profound effect on the aircraft and had to be taken into account. Just as the duo was finishing their routine, the four-ship would reappear for one more pass to conclude the show. The whole thing lasted about seven minutes.

The Chipmunk Synchronized Aerobatic Team demonstrates a co-loop at National Air Force Day at RCAF Stn Rockcliffe on 9 Jun 62. (DND PL 139650)

With Centralia having been home to several Harvard aerobatic teams in the late '40s and '50s, the benefits of having such a team were well known to all. Following a very successful season, and with F/O Jotham continuing as leader, the team was rejuvenated for the 1960 airshow season. F/O Bob Caskie, a Sabre veteran from 416 and 430 Squadrons, returned as his wingman and reflects back some 41 years to his season of airshow performances:

"I was posted to Centralia in May 1959 (along with F/O B.K. Doyle) after a tour in

the Air Div and subsequent graduation from instructor training at the Harvard FIS course in Trenton. In 1960 I was selected as wingman to Jim Jotham and we flew about 10 shows in the southern Ontario region and Michigan. We covered the area from Windsor – Toronto – Trenton – Ottawa – North Bay to Centralia. Partway through the season, Jim was posted and I took over the lead position with B.K. Doyle as my wingman and F/O Keith (Casey) Chapman as our alternate. We successfully carried on into 1961 at which time several new pilots joined the team. These included F/L Peter Caws and F/Os Ed McKeogh and Ron Donovan. The team covered the same general area but with fewer shows, the principal ones being Centralia, London, Toronto and St. Hubert.

I left Centralia in the fall of 1961, and returned in July 1963 as the OC of the Primary Flying School. During the time I was away, there was still some airshow team activity with F/L Peter Caws at the helm. Austerity measures in 1963-65 pretty well killed any organized show activity but we managed to sneak in some local 'practice' sessions. Although the team had official sanction from Training Command, we never had any special funding and really never had an official name. We had three modified aircraft that were fitted with wingtip pods that housed red smoke canisters that were triggered through the nav light switch. We also had a portable, pressurized oil tank strapped in the rear seat and piped through the front cockpit to the engine exhaust which gave us a white smoke capability. Most of our shows were on weekends and were within a few hours flying time from Centralia."

Bob Caskie

The Centralia Smoke-Eaters of 1960/61. L to R – F/L Bob Caskie, F/O Keith Chapman, F/L B.K. Doyle. (DND PMR 89-184 via Gwen Kerr)

In mid-1961 three new faces appeared on the team, F/O Ron Donovan, F/L Peter Caws and F/O Ed McKeogh. (RCAF Photo via Ed McKeogh)

F/O Ed McKeogh receives a pointer from veteran team member F/O K.C. Chapman. A few months later McKeogh won a solo position with the Golden Hawks. (RCAF Photo via Ed McKeogh)

The Smokers trailed red and white smoke when they performed at the 1961 Canadian International Air Show. (courtesy CNE Archives)

Since the team never had an official name, it was generally referred to as the Chipmunk Synchronized Aerobatic Team in reference to their close formation aerobatics. Another humorous label attached to the team was the "Centralia Smoke-Eaters." Given the amazing amount of smoke that the two little aircraft generated at their relatively slow speed, the motivation behind the name was apparently well founded. Two of the team members took their airshow experiences on to new heights in subsequent years, Ed McKeogh earning a position on the Golden Hawks for 1962 – 1963 and B.K. Doyle landing a spot with the Golden Centennaires in 1967.

Air Defence Command CF-100 Teams

Anyone who has worked within an air force fraternity will know that the fighter pilot is (and certainly considers himself to be) a breed apart – the guys at the so-called "pointy end of the stick." Their very job dictates a certain amount of bravado – the trick is to have the skill to back it up. Some would call their attitude arrogant, some egotistical, but in times of conflict it is often the fighter pilot who is among the first to throw his body into harm's way. Regardless of which aircraft the fighter pilot is assigned to fly, his job is to turn it into the best fighting machine possible given the available resources. In real combat, he may only get one chance to test his skills – if he fails, either he or a comrade will pay the ultimate price. Those who survive in the toughest conditions will be the most aggressive and relentless in the pursuit of their adversary. Billy Bishop had these essential character traits – so did Collishaw, Barker, Beurling and a host of other Canadian fighter aces of renown.

Given these basic premises, it is not surprising that a strong rivalry exists not only between fighter pilots themselves, but also amongst squadrons and most certainly aircraft types – and we're just talking about the good guys! This rivalry existed in the CF-104, CF-101 and CF-5 era of the RCAF/Canadian Forces and most certainly existed in the 1950s and '60s between those pilots assigned to the F-86 Sabre and CF-100 Canuck. In fact, they didn't like each other much!

When it was procured by the RCAF in 1952, the Sabre was the best day fighter in the world and had proven it in the Korean War. When the Canadian-designed and much heralded Avro CF-100 entered service a few years later, it became an instant rival as proponents and critics debated the relative merits of single seat, single engine vs dual seat, twin engine fighting machines. However, in spite of its power, the "Clunk" was no match for the agile Sabre in a dogfight. Move the fight into cloud however, or at night, and it was a different story. After all, the CF-100 was really designed as a long range, all-weather interceptor versus a pure fighter in the classic sense. And with program maturity it served the RCAF in Canada and Europe very well with its pilot and navigator team.

Given this healthy rivalry, when the RCAF announced in the fall of 1958 that it would form a new aerobatic team utilizing the F-86, some members of the CF-100 fraternity began to ponder how they too might get involved. The Golden Hawks were soon getting a lot of publicity across the nation, so two CF-100 units decided to form their own "regional" teams, one in the west and one in the east to get in on the celebrations.

The Bald Eagles

The Bald Eagles display team was formed at No. 3 AW(F) OTU at RCAF Stn Cold Lake, Alberta in the spring of 1959 and was the first formal team to be established since the unit had relocated to Cold Lake from North Bay in 1955. The driving force behind the team was F/L J.W. (Bill) Stewart, one of the senior instructors at the school. He had joined the RCAF in 1951 and following wings graduation completed a tour as an instructor on the Harvard prior to his first operational tour. This tour saw him serve on both 428 Ghost and 410 Cougar AW(F) Sqns based at RCAF Stn Uplands in Ottawa following conversion and combat training on the CF-100. It was his strong performance in the air defence environment which subsequently landed him back in Cold Lake as an instructor.

With all of the hoopla surrounding the 35th anniversary of the RCAF, W/C Ed Smith, the OC of 3 AW(F) OTU approached Stewart in early 1959 to enquire whether he would take on the task of putting together a formation team to handle the high demands for airshow participation that the unit was receiving. Stewart readily agreed and by early spring had put together a team.

On May 21st the team took to the air for their first practice in their standard Mk 4A CF-100s. Stewart had recruited F/O John Kuzyk as lead navigator – his role would be to assist with the navigation and timing in getting to the various show venues and then to act as an extra set of eyes and ears during the team's air display. Rounding out the team were pilots F/L Fred Hastings, F/O Don Lamont, and F/O Stu Pollock who were supported by their respective navigators – F/Os Keith Bottoms, Glen Emerson and Al Runge. F/O "Whipper" Watson was an additional navigator who flew with the team in the summer of '59.

With the Golden Hawks and Red Knight already having been formed, it wasn't long before the new CF-100 team wanted a distinctive identity as well. Bill Stewart explains how the fledgling team got its unique name – which had little to do with the feathered bird:

"Once we had organized our four-plane team, a discussion took place amongst ourselves to decide a suitable name. Someone jokingly suggested the 'Bald Eagles,' reflecting on W/C Smith's lack of hair. 'Big Ed,' as he was affectionately known, fortunately also had a good sense of humour and the name stuck!"

Bill Stewart

A rare colour shot of the Bald Eagles taken near RCAF Stn Cold Lake on 21 Jul 60. (PCN 1966)

The original Bald Eagles of No. 3 All Weather (Fighter) Operational Training Unit in 1959. L to R, Front Row (Pilots) – F/L Bill Stewart, F/L Fred Hastings, F/O Stu Pollock, F/O Don Lamont. Back Row (Navigators) – F/Os John Kuzyk, Al Runge, Keith Bottoms, Glenn Emerson. (RCAF Photo via Bill Stewart)

By the time the team was ready to go on the road, an impressive schedule had been organized which would take the team through Alberta, Saskatchewan, Manitoba and as far east as Lakehead, Ontario. They opened their season on June 13th at Lloydminster and finished up eight weeks later at Penhold on August 15th. All told, the team put on 15 shows as they criss-crossed the Prairies, the majority on weekends as Canadians flocked to shows large and small to see their air force in action. At the larger locations, the team performed alongside the Golden Hawks and Red Knight.

The Bald Eagles show routine was non-aerobatic but featured some aggressive manoeuvring in various formations. After a few practices, it was decided to remove the wing tip mounted radar reflector pods to permit higher G forces. Bill Stewart would bring his team in low and fast across centre stage in their opening line-astern pass, pulling up into a steep wingover as the team changed to box formation. The wingovers were designed to keep the aircraft easily within sight of the crowd at all times. Like any fighter display, one of the most impressive aspects as the four jets flashed by in different formations was the thunderous noise generated by the eight Orenda 9 engines, each aircraft capable of generating 13,000 pounds of thrust. The last manoeuvre of the show involved a tight 360 degree turn in box formation at centre stage. As the team rolled out with a speed of 400 knots, F/L Stewart pulled the formation sharply up into a steep climb, an impressive sight as the four aircraft rocketed skyward as one. The team would then return for a low-level fighter break in echelon formation to set up for landing, usually in pairs. For shows away from the operating airfield, spectators would be treated to one more low pass with gear and flaps down prior to the team's departure. By the time the five to six minute show was over, spectators were well aware of the performance capabilities of the CF-100, altitudes having ranged from 100 to 12,000 feet.

F/L Bill Stewart leads his team skyward in this graceful public relations shot taken near Cold Lake. (RCAF Photo via Bill Stewart)

(Right) "Soaring with Eagles" is the title of this rare work by veteran Canadian artist Graham Wragg. It depicts the Bald Eagles over RCAF Stn Winnipeg during Air Force Day 1960. (courtesy Graham Wragg)

The 1960 Bald Eagle team. L to R, Front Row (Pilots) – F/L Bill Stewart, F/O George Wilson, F/O John Parker, F/L Paul Diamond, F/O Sam Cramb. Back Row (Navigators) – F/Os John Kuzyk, Nick Chester, Lorne Jokinen, Peter De Smedt, Ken Miller. (RCAF 5821 via Bill Stewart)

The Bald Eagles re-formed in 1960 due to public demand and were once again a prominent feature of the annual Air Force Day which was a highlight of the summer in Cold Lake. Bill Stewart retained command of the team but took on a new set of wingmen eager to partake in the display flying. F/O John Parker took over as right wing, F/L Paul Diamond on the left, F/O Sam Cramb in the box and F/O George Wilson joined the team as a spare. The navigators were F/Os John Kuzyk, Lorne Jokinen, Pete De Smedt, Ken Miller and Nick Chester. The routine remained much the same as the previous year but the cross-country time was significantly reduced as the team stuck to appearances in Alberta for all but one show in Winnipeg. It was a relatively short season with the Cold Lake AFD kicking things off on July 16th. The town of Vermilion was the last to witness a show by the Bald Eagles. Although the CF-100 would continue to appear at airshows across Western Canada for many years, these were mainly in the form of static aircraft and simple formation flypasts.

Another glorious RCAF photo of the Bald Eagles showing the distinct lines of the Canadian designed and built Avro CF-100 Mk 4A. (RCAF Photo via Bill Stewart)

The Golden Gigolos

The first question to come to mind about this CF-100 team formed in Eastern Canada in 1959 by 433 AW(F) Sqn is how in the world they got their name. At first glance it might seem that the team chose the name simply as a parody on the Golden Hawks who were getting most of the fame and glory at the time as the showpiece of the RCAF. This was in part true, but the name originated from the squadron's radio callsign of the day which happened to be "Gigolo" – thus, every pilot on the squadron had a Gigolo callsign! Since the team was formed to celebrate the golden anniversary of powered flight in Canada, "Golden" was added to the squadron callsign and yet another airshow moniker was born!

Home base for 433 Sqn at the time was RCAF Stn North Bay which was destined to become headquarters of the Northern NORAD Region in October 1963. The North American Air Defence Command (NORAD) had been established on May 12th, 1958 between Canada and the United States and led to the establishment of a powerful air defence network comprising three separate radar lines and hundreds of interceptor aircraft. Indeed, 433 Sqn in 1959 was one of nine RCAF CF-100 squadrons stationed across the country. But while the role was very serious – Canada maintained a quick reaction alert (QRA) force on a 24/7 (24 hours a day, seven days a week) basis – there were sufficient resources to allow for the odd weekend of airshow fun!

F/L Pat Patterson was the squadron pilot designated to form the team with the capable assistance of lead navigator F/L Howie Sweet. The additional crews were F/Os John Rose and Gerry Takach on right wing, F/Os Terry Harris and Gerry Trudeau on left wing with F/Os Dave Rutka and Doug Chase flying the box position. Like their counterparts in the west, the Gigolos worked up a short but intense routine designed to emphasize the strengths of the nation's front line all-weather interceptor. They concentrated their shows in Central Canada but are known to have made at least one foray south of the border to perform at Schenectady, New York. As John Rose recalls:

"Most of the RCAF squadrons of the day received many requests during the summer from various communities to provide a flying display for their summer fair or other occasion. So we regularly got some guys together to beat up someone's ferris wheel or

RCAF Stn North Bay's contribution to the anniversary celebrations of 1959 was 433 AW(F) Sqn's Golden Gigolos. L to R, Front Row – F/O Gerry Trudeau, F/L Pat Patterson (team leader), F/L Howie Sweet, F/O Doug Chase. Back Row – F/O Terry Harris, F/O Gerry Takach, F/O John Rose, F/O Dave Rutka. (RCAF Photo via John Rose)

fair ground. In my time in North Bay, Cold Lake and Bagotville, there was a continuing call for formation flying for airshows."

John Rose

The Golden Gigolos flew only during the 1959 season but did their part in helping the RCAF celebrate its 35th anniversary. At the end of the season, the crews resigned themselves to a return to reality and the mundane world of sitting alert at all hours of the day and night until the alert siren sent them scrambling off into the murk in search of some unidentified aircraft penetrating Canadian airspace. However, this was by no means the end of 433 Sqn's participation in the Canadian airshow scene. As former squadron pilot Gary Richards recalls, the squadron would continue to provide aircraft on an ad hoc basis to fulfill airshow requests and also participated in some very large formation flypasts, as they had done in July and September 1959 when 60 CF-100s had filled the skies of Ottawa and Toronto respectively. Richards was a young flying officer at the time and still fondly recalls his airshow experiences in the Clunk – like many fighter pilots, he loved to fly formation, the No. 4 box position being his favourite. And also like most pilots, he has one extra special memory of his brief airshow career – on July 15th, 1961 at Timmins, Ontario. It was one of those glorious summer days, a perfect day for an airshow flown in front of an appreciative audience, and Richards recalls screaming in close to the crowd and then pulling his CF-100 straight up into the vertical until he was out of sight – a perfect way to end a memorable afternoon.

The Red Ravens

The last of the CF-100 teams to form during the front-line operational days of the aircraft were the Red Ravens of the Electronic Warfare Unit based at RCAF Stn St. Hubert, Quebec, the home of Air Defence Command at the time. The EWU's primary role was to provide electronic counter-measures training to ADC and NORAD fighters and radars. One of the team members was navigator Len Jenks, one of the so-called "scope wizards" who were a pilot's best friend during an intercept in cloud or at night. Jenks had joined the RCAF in 1954 and attended pre-flight school in Centralia with another young recruit who would become the leader of the Red Ravens, F/O Keith Simonson. Following flying training, Simonson had flown the CF-100 with 419 and 425 AW(F) Squadrons before being posted to the Electronic Warfare Unit. Jenks, meanwhile, had spent his first

The last CF-100 team to fly in the RCAF was the Red Ravens of the Electronic Warfare Unit based at RCAF Stn St. Hubert, Quebec. (RCAF SHA 50-6 via Len Jenks)

operational tour on the CF-100 with 409 AW(F) Sqn in Comox. He then embarked on an interesting journey, becoming the first RCAF jet navigator to attend the USAF Electronic Warfare School at Keesler AFB in Biloxi, Mississippi. Following graduation from Keesler (where there were some 23,000 students in various electronics training programs), Jenks was posted to the RCAF's Electronic Warfare Unit which put him in a position to join the Red Ravens:

"The Red Ravens were formed in April 1961 in response to an Air Defence Command tasking to provide air displays in the Province of Quebec on an 'as requested' and 'ADC approved' basis. The idea of a dedicated team came from discussions between our unit and ADC, both at the squadron level and at the Officers' Mess bar!

Our CO at the time was S/L Gord Fowler and he authorized a dedicated team of four CF-100 aircraft and crews to carry out these taskings. The lead position was flown by F/O K.O. Simonson and F/L Earl 'Shorty' McFarland, No. 2 was F/O Len Couture and F/L John Kilby, No. 3 was F/O 'Chalky' Leblanc and F/L Len 'Bud' Jenks, and No. 4 was F/O Bob McCraney and F/L Russ Jenkins. On some occasions, the rear seat was crewed by an alternate navigator.

We flew numerous practices and air displays over a period of approximately 16 months, at which time ADC air display policy was amended to restrict the number of air displays and participants. We flew the Mk 5D version of the CF-100 but with the wing extensions removed to accommodate tip tanks, the aircraft was more similar to the Mk 4 configuration. Notwithstanding any deferential references to the venerable 'Clunk', the CF-100 was a good, stable aerobatic aircraft.

Our airshow routine of about 20 minutes opened with a high-speed pass, and proceeded with various manoeuvres which included up to 120 degree wingovers, high drag profiles, tight turns and formation changes within close proximity of centre stage. The team was not authorized to do full formation aerobatics, such as loops and rolls. Nevertheless, judging from the generous feedback received, the Red Ravens were well received as an air display team. Among the air displays that we performed were the 50th anniversary of the Town of La Tuque, Joliette, Sherbrooke, Trois-Rivières, National Air Force Day (Ottawa) as well as many airshows at St. Hubert.

As our leader, 'K.O.' Simonson has noted, 'The Red Ravens were a very professional team and I was very pleased and proud to have three such excellent pilots flying on my wing, not to forget the super guys in the back seat. I have a lot of fond memories of the Red Ravens – although we were not a full-time dedicated air display team such as the Golden Hawks and the Snowbirds, we did a lot of practice and a fair number of displays, and enjoyed every minute of it – it was a fun time.' Indeed, it was!!"

Len Jenks, with K.O. Simonson

The end of the 1962 display season marked the end of formalized CF-100 teams in Canada. Starting in 1962, the aircraft was phased out of its front line interceptor role in Canada, replaced by the CF-101 Voodoo which would attract a strong following on the North American airshow scene over the next 22 years. However, the Clunk soldiered on in the electronic warfare field for many years, continuing to appear at airshows across the country until it was finally retired in 1981 at North Bay.

Aviation artist Geoff Bennett paid tribute to the RCAF's CF-100 demonstration teams in 1987 with this stirring work depicting the Bald Eagles taxiing in show formation circa 1960. (courtesy Geoff Bennett)

The Gimli Smokers

As Bill Bliss was putting together his large "35" and "50" formations in 1959, the seeds for a separate T-33 display team in Gimli had already been planted at No. 3 Advanced Flying School. From its humble beginnings, the Gimli Smokers would grow into a nine-plane formation team by 1961 and would participate in several major shows through the end of 1964.

The Gimli Smokers adopted their formal name in 1959, although the roots of the team go back one year earlier. The architect of the team was S/L Ken Lett, chief flying instructor at 3 AFS. In the summer of '58 he was tasked to lead a four-plane of T-33s to represent the school at RCAF Stn Winnipeg's annual Air Force Day on July 19th. Rather than satisfy himself with simple flypasts, he decided to work up a "bomb burst" manoeuvre that would inject a little excitement into the show for both the spectators and his pilots. This went over well and he was subsequently able to convince the station's engineering officer to install smoke systems in the T-Bird's ammo can area in anticipation of future displays. By mid-September, Lett conducted smoke generator tests on T-33s 483 and 349 and the groundwork was laid for airshow activity the following summer.

Fast forwarding to June 19th, 1959 found Ken Lett practicing formation again with five aircraft that all trailed thick white smoke – the Gimli Smokers had been born. As expected, requests for additional displays filtered their way down to Ken Lett's desk as the nation prepared to celebrate the 50th anniversary of powered flight in Canada. Two were of particular interest, Ottawa and Detroit, so naturally there was no shortage of volunteers. To add a little pizzazz to the act, a variation of the bomb burst known as the "*Fleur de Lis*" was introduced. Another variation came to be known as the "Prince of Wales Feather".

Additional pilots involved with the Smokers show in 1959 included F/Os Tony Bosman, Ollie Fritsch, Al Young, John England, Bob Webber, Bill Arthurs and S/L Bill Bliss. But as Ken Lett explains, there were no designated team pilots or assigned positions per se:

"We used any instructor who was available when performing or practicing at Gimli. It was only our expedition to Ottawa for July 1st Dominion Day ceremonies over Green Island, followed by Detroit for July 4th Independence Day, that we used the same players for two consecutive shows. The Prince of Wales split was not a difficult manoeuvre for an experienced pilot to handle competently with a minimum of training. The most demanding element was the timing required to 'burst' at the correct time given speakers at the ceremony who were as unpredictable then as they are today.

The Green Island ceremony at Ottawa was a large, complicated ground and air activity that was to be witnessed by Her Majesty Queen Elizabeth and the Duke of Edinburgh on Dominion Day. It was master-minded by G/C Cam Mussells who was CO of Uplands at the time. This was my first association

with a legend in the RCAF who was famous for 'demanding' many rehearsals for any activity he was responsible for. He insisted we arrive days early for many practices so we ended up flying to Uplands on June 22nd for a July 1st ceremony! After three practices he and I had a confrontation – in so far as a squadron leader can confront a group captain. I have a distinct recollection of telling him that we were capable of performing to the second and that we were wasting flying time – 'tell us what time you want us on stage and we'll be there!' Much to my surprise, he accepted, so we all went home for the weekend.

The Gimli Smokers pass overhead in perfect formation circa 1959. (via Terry Leversedge)

After returning to Ottawa, I did a timing run on June 30th to ensure I could back up my promise to 'Muss.' Needless to say, the timing of our show got revised. As luck would have it, the final person at the microphone was the padre who got carried away – with one minute to pull-up G/C Mussels was on the radio saying 'delay one minute.' We, as always, were resilient enough to do a very tight 360, re-form and arrive onstage at the new TOT. Fortunately, our team that day was composed of ex-Sabre jocks who were able to 'hang on.'

On July 2nd we flew to Selfridge Air Force Base near Detroit, Michigan for a performance on the 4th of July in a 'Hands Across the Border' ceremony. I recall that we stayed at the Brook Cadillac Hotel. During our stay, A/M Roy Slemon, then Deputy Commander-in-Chief of NORAD, joined us for a drink in the bar but forgot to pay, so Willie Suthers ended up with the bill. He and I had made a bet – if I would invite the air marshal to join us, Willie would pay if A/M Slemon didn't. Slemon's reputation was such that Willie was bound to be a loser!

The show in Detroit was routine and due to its close proximity we were able to sneak in a flypast at Windsor prior to the show. We

S/L K.C. Lett, CFI at No. 3 Advanced Flying School and founder of the Gimli Smokers. From his five-ship in 1959, the team grew to nine aircraft by 1961. (RCAF Photo via Ken Lett)

returned to Gimli the same day, thus ending my association with the Gimli Smokers. The system had decided that I needed some education, so I spent the next year at the RCAF Staff College in Toronto."

K.C. Lett

S/L Bill Bliss stepped in to help out with the Smokers in the summer of '59, seen here conferring with a teammate prior to departure for another show. (via Bill Bliss)

Following the Ottawa and Detroit shows, F/O John England joined the team, recording a flurry of activity in his logbook. Shows led by S/L Bill Bliss were flown in Lethbridge and Lakehead in August. The focus then switched to preparation for the CNE, with no less than eight practices taking place in Gimli and Trenton before the Canadian International Air Show in Toronto on September 11th and 12th. One week later the team was back in Ontario for five more shows, flying three in one day at Centralia, London and Windsor. The season ended the next day in Windsor on Battle of Britain Sunday as the Gimli Smokers joined thousands across the nation in paying tribute to those who had paid the supreme sacrifice during the famous aerial battle of World War II.

The Team Expands

With the extraordinary success of the 1959 airshow season led by the Golden Hawks, the RCAF was on a roll. A/M Hugh Campbell's successful initiative to re-form the Golden Hawks in Chatham as a permanent unit helped the Smokers also gain approval to mount a display for the 1960 season as well. F/L G.N. "Gin" Smith took over as leader and promptly increased the team's complement to eight aircraft, almost doubling its size from the previous year. Now, with additional aircraft flying in the formation, a more permanent group of instructors flying regular positions was highly desirable to enhance consistency and safety.

Additional members of the team in 1960 included F/Ls Bill Mitchell and John England plus F/Os Tony Bosman, George McAffer, Martin Sommerard, Ken Kensick, Fred Hope and Brian Dixon. Once again the "Prince of Wales" was the principal manoeu-vre flown by the team, but now as a seven-plane formation. And once again, the CIAS in Toronto became the focus of the team in September. With the contingent of T-33s flying the "R C A F" formation for the first time at the show, Training Command had an enormous complement of men and machines deployed in Trenton.

The 1960 CIAS opened with the United States Navy Blue Angels at precisely 4:00 p.m. on September 9th and ended just under two hours later with the Golden Hawks. However, the Gimli Smokers had an honoured, if brief, place in the show, opening the RCAF portion of the show with their Prince of Wales split followed by S/L Bud Lawrence's monster RCAF formation. The Saturday show was a mirror image of Friday and was the last for the 1960 version of the Smokers.

Thousands of spectators jam the Toronto waterfront for the annual Canadian International Air Show each year, as evidenced in this scene from 1961. (courtesy CNE archives)

The 1960 Smokers. L to R – F/O George McAffer, F/O Martin Sommerard, F/O Ken Kensick, F/L Gin Smith (Team Leader), F/O Fred Hope, F/O Brian Dixon, F/L Bill Mitchell, F/O Tony Bosman. Missing from photo is F/L John England. (RCAF Photo via Gin Smith)

The 1961 Smokers. L to R – F/O Elmer Dow, F/O Larry Mosser, F/L John England, F/O Pete Trott, F/L Gin Smith (Team Leader), F/O Robbie Robinson, F/O C.B. Lang, F/L Bill Mitchell, F/L Hugh Rose. Missing from this photo are F/L George Shorey, F/L Chops Viger, F/O George McAffer and F/O Len Mann. (RCAF GM-4560 via Gin Smith)

And One Makes Nine

In 1961 Smith took the show one step further by adding a ninth aircraft to the show to fly solo aerobatic manoeuvres in-between the formation's passes. The first instructors to fulfill this role were F/L George Shorey and F/O Hugh Rose who were joined by several additional new faces on the team flying in the formation – F/L Larry Mosser along with F/Os Elmer Dow, Pete Trott, Robbie Robinson, C.B. Lang and Len Mann. F/L Chops Viger also got involved during the season and another frequent staff member accompanying the team was Capt Dean Cling, the USAF exchange instructor with 3 AFS who frequently flew in the back seat with veteran team member John England.

As Gin Smith recalls, the first show of the '61 campaign was responsible for the birth of a new "tradition" in the jet fraternity which had nothing to do with flying:

"One of our most memorable shows was in Churchill, Manitoba. The Americans had a large detachment there so our show took in the July 1st and July 4th celebrations. It was there that Larry Mosser introduced the 'Dead Ants' society that spread throughout the fighter pilot community – from the Golden Hawks in Chatham to the CF-104 OTU in Cold Lake and ultimately to the Air Division in Europe."

Gin Smith

For the uninitiated, "Dead Ants" was something that had to be seen to be believed. It became primarily a jet jock tradition in the air force and could usually be seen late on Friday nights in messes across the country as the boys let their hair down after a hard week of intense training. It became part-and-parcel of the games of skill and cunning, the songs and the general partying that were (and still are) an effective way of relieving stress in a

high stress environment. A prerequisite of this particular little game was an abundance of liquid refreshment to alleviate one's trepidations of looking silly, the name of the game being when "Dead Ants" was called to hit the deck as fast as possible with your legs sticking straight up in the air. Hence the name - and woe was he who did not participate – a round for the house being the penalty imposed if caught standing around with your mouth flapping! Little did Larry Mosser know that his little joke would last for over 25 years and span two continents…

The weekend following the Churchill affair, the Smokers were in good company at RCAF Stn Cold Lake's Air Force Day, performing alongside the Red Knight (F/L Ray Goeres)

Above, the Smokers practice their formation in standard 3 AFS T-33s early in 1961. Below, now in smoke-equipped aircraft, F/L Gin Smith rolls in to his target as he descends to show altitude to set up for the team's spectacular bomb burst. (Tom Gigliotti)

and the '61 edition of the Golden Hawks led by S/L Jim McCombe. Smaller venues filled the gap until the annual CIAS where the Golden Hawks gave the Smokers coloured smoke to make a red, white and blue circle which they then penetrated with their Prince of Wales split to open the airshow. The team wound up its season in Hamilton on October 21st. It was en route to this show that the much celebrated "Dead Ants" was called *while in the air* for the benefit of the Golden Hawks who were also transiting in at the same time – no sooner was it called than the Hawks were treated to the sight of nine T-Birds – all flying along upside down beside them!!

The Smokers took to the air for their fourth season with F/L Larry Mosser replacing Gin Smith as team leader. By now the escapades of the team were well known – the flying was fun and the parties were great so more young instructors aspired to get involved. With a relatively high turnover of instructors in Gimli each summer, it was possible for those who had patiently been waiting in the wings to get a slot on the team. For 1962 this included first-timers F/Os Barry Dixon, Rick Flavelle, Brodie Partington and Harry Kelly. The taste of airshow flying could easily get into one's blood and it was natural for many pilots to begin to look beyond the Gimli Smokers to the possibility of getting a tryout with the Golden Hawks, as Harry Kelly explains:

"We performed with the Smokers only as an adjunct to our regular duties on the base associated with pilot training. During most of my tour at Gimli I was a 'standards officer' and one of the base instrument check pilots. I also had the delightful chore of being OIC 'Other Things' from Standards Flight, which included the 'Bug Smashers'

The 1962 version of the Smokers. L to R – F/Os Elmer Dow, Barry Dixon, C.B. Lang, Rick Flavelle, F/Ls Larry Mosser (Team Leader), George Shorey (rear), F/Os Harry Kelly, Robbie Robinson, Brodie Partington. (via Harry Kelly)

Meteorologist Tom Gigliotti was a frequent flyer with the RCAF in both the Air Division in Europe and while serving at RCAF Stn Gimli. Here he captures a close-up shot of the Smokers as they prepare for a show over Gimli on 18 Aug 61. (Tom Gigliotti)

(C-45 Expeditors), aannnd … the F-86 Sabres!!! We had three of them at Gimli at that time, for 'instructor motivation.' I felt it was incumbent on me to fly the Sabres as frequently as possible to ensure that they were absolutely serviceable at all times (heh, heh)! Some of us, while flying the Sabres at Gimli, had a remote area where we would emulate the manoeuvres of the Golden Hawks – honing our skills in the hope of getting a head start in the selection process for the Hawks. Some, like C.B. Lang, were successful in this endeavour. Thankfully, none of the Gimli Sabres were 'bent' in the course of our aerobatic flying from there."

Harry Kelly

The Final Two Years

The 1963 version of the Gimli Smokers saw F/L Brodie Partington take the helm, joined by newcomers F/Ls Walt Scott and Brian Evans along with F/Os Barry Dixon, Brian Burke and John Kennedy. Success got in the way of Walt Scott's tenure with the team as he got promoted to squadron leader half way through the season and was posted to Central Flying School. Although he was "very disappointed about leaving the Smokers," he departed with enough memories to last a lifetime and was replaced by F/L Larry Dyer.

No one really expected the Gimli Smokers to re-form in 1964 following the budget crunch that had seen the Golden Hawks relegated to

The 1963 Smokers. L to R, Front Row – F/O John Kennedy, F/O Rick Flavelle, F/L Walt Scott. Back Row – F/O Barry Dixon, F/L Brian Evans, F/L Brodie Partington (Team Leader), F/O Brian Burke, F/O Robbie Robinson. Missing is F/L Larry Dyer. (RCAF Photo via Walt Scott)

The 1963 Smokers taxi out on the Gimli ramp led by F/L Brodie Partington. (RCAF Photo GM-63/83 via Walt Scott)

the history books – but they did, and amazingly still with a large formation of nine aircraft. With the Hawks gone, the Smokers were now the only jet demonstration team in the country. Along with the Red Knight and "Goldilocks" from Moose Jaw, they would carry the mantle for the 1964 airshow season in Canada.

As in previous years, the 1964 team saw almost a wholesale change of players. F/L Russ Bennett was appointed team leader and built his team around three holdovers from the previous year, Larry Dyer, Brian Burke and John Kennedy. Rounding out the team were F/Os Don Ripley, "Tommy" Thompson, Ross Mayberry, Jim Shirley, Dale Horley and

Al Stuart. On occasion, F/O Doug Dargent also did some T-33 solo aerobatic work at some of the Smokers' shows.

The pattern of 1964 closely mirrored previous years with the Smokers performing in front of their largest audiences at National Air Force Day in Ottawa and the CIAS in Toronto, where they both opened and closed the show. However, of their 10 shows that season, the most enjoyable show may have been in Moose Jaw where they were hosted by the Goldilocks, their piston-engined counterparts flying the Harvard trainer. As

Russ Bennett recalled a few years ago, the Goldilocks were quite taken when the Smokers arrived overhead in the "crazy" formation which had become the Goldilocks' hallmark manoeuvre. That evening, the two teams put on a show in the Officers' Mess that rivalled their shows in the air!

The end of the 1964 season marked the end of the road for the Smokers and RCAF Stn Gimli's six year run as home of a Training Command airshow team – the Gimli Smokers would not fly again in 1965. Although they probably never received the credit they

The final version of the Gimli Smokers in 1964. L to R, Front Row – F/O "Tommy" Thompson, F/O John Kennedy, F/L Russ Bennett (team leader), F/O Don Ripley, F/L Brian Burke. Back Row – F/O Ross Mayberry, F/O Al Stuart, F/O Jim Shirley, F/O Dale Horley, F/L Larry Dyer. F/L Russ Bennett went on to greater glory as the slot pilot with the Golden Centennaires in 1967. (RCAF GM 64137 via Dale Horley)

Each new season brought a requirement for practices to safely indoctrinate new team members. Here T-33 130 breaks away following the "split now" call from the leader during the upward bomb burst. (Tom Gigliotti)

A rare souvenir plaque preserves memories of the Smokers. (via John England)

Staff members of the FIS Advanced Detachment, Portage la Prairie in 1963. Most saw service on the Viking Smooth over the three year duration of the station team. L to R, Front Row – F/Ls Tom Bebb, "Mac" McLachlan, Alan Brown, Capt Dick Burpee (USAF), F/Ls George Shorey, Reg Stuart. Back Row – F/O Bob McCord, S/L Cam MacDonald (FIS Det Cmdr), F/L Bill Bayley, W/C Wiley Spafford (OC FIS), F/L Culley Erlendson, F/L Jim McCullough, F/O Vince Magnus. (via Jordy Krastel)

deserved, the team had provided a lasting source of pride and motivation, excellent training and great camaraderie to all those who had been associated with them. And in spite of flying in the shadows of the flashy Golden Hawks up until their last year of operation, the Smokers had demonstrated to Canadians that the country's military flying schools were in the hands of some very talented instructors who would continue to produce first-class pilots as the RCAF entered its twilight years.

The Viking Smooth

Although the Gimli Smokers were the most famous T-33 team to grace prairie skies in the early 60s, there was another team which flew between 1962 and 1964 that also deserves a footnote in history. It too was made up of a collection of seasoned jet pilots, all A1 instructors assigned to the Flying Instructors

School Advanced Detachment based at RCAF Stn Portage la Prairie. Like many of the smaller teams, it too was born of a desire to be able to respond to requests for air force participation by citizens organizing local fairs and special celebrations that could not be accommodated by the Golden Hawks. By now the Hawks were in very high demand all over North America and couldn't possibly perform at all of the requested venues.

Many staff members of FIS participated in the seven-plane formation which was initially led by F/L Bill Bayley, commander of the FIS Advanced Detachment. He eventually gave way to F/L George Shorey who brought a season's experience with the Gimli Smokers to the team. F/L Al Brown participated in all three years of the team and remembers fly-

pasts at some rather unique festivities, such as the June 1962 National Ploughing Championships! This particular event however, was most memorable for the decrepit weather on the day of the event – pouring rain. Nevertheless, the team arrived overhead at the requested time in spite of the weather. Recalls Brown, "I think I saw one guy under a tree as we flew past!"

Notwithstanding the odd occasion when mother nature didn't cooperate, the small venues that the team did appear at always provided excellent training for the pilots flying the formation. The proof is in the photographs that were taken over the years as teams such as the Viking Smooth did their part to enhance the reputation of the RCAF in the eyes of the Canadian populace.

Although little known outside of southern Manitoba, the spacing on these seven-plane formations reveals that the Viking Smooth were a highly proficient group of formation pilots. (via Jordy Krastel)

Harvard Aerobatic Teams of the West

While the Gimli Smokers were getting underway with the T-33 in 1959, there was also a movement underway 375 miles to the west in Moose Jaw, Saskatchewan to form a display using Harvard trainers assigned to No. 2 Flying Training School. The Harvard was of course no stranger to airshow fans across Canada, the aircraft having made hundreds of appearances in airshows in the post-war era of the RCAF. It had already earned an honoured place in history as one of the world's best and most widely used trainers. Originally opened as 32 Service Flying Training School of the Royal Air Force on January 29th, 1940, the Moose Jaw station had made a valuable contribution to the training of hundreds of allied aircrew during WWII until the school was disbanded in mid-October 1944. In May 1953 the rebuilt station reopened to welcome the transfer of 2 FTS from RCAF Stn Gimli during *Operation Gimjaw*. The Moose Jaw school alone would subsequently train over 2,000 pilots on the Harvard by September 1964 under the auspices of NATO.

During its heyday as a Harvard training station, Moose Jaw was constantly abuzz as course after course of RCAF and foreign stu- dents were processed through 2 FTS. Although the instructor workload was heavy, it was important to occasionally get away from the student milieu and get in some pro- ficiency flying on one's own or with a fellow instructor. Solo aerobatics or formation fly- ing were the preferred escape mechanisms for many staff instructors, simply because they were challenging and fun to do. A select few staff instructors would get the opportuni- ty to strut their stuff at the annual Air Force Day in Moose Jaw or by providing flypasts at summer fairs in the surrounding rural communities.

2 FTS Harvard Team

One group of enterprising instructors at 2 FTS decided in the spring of 1959 that they did not want to be left behind when it came to airshow activities in that anniver- sary year. Thus, they convinced the school commandant to allow them to form a four- plane Harvard team that would represent 2 FTS regionally throughout the summer. The team was led by F/L Jim Stacey with F/Os Dave Bagshaw, Dave Baker and Bob Smith rounding out the team. The designat- ed solo performer on the team was Bob Smith, who briefly summarizes the team's activities:

"The four of us were all pipeline instructors at 'Moose Juice' so none of us had any opera- tional experience at that point. The CO of the station at the time was G/C Dunlop – in any case he was nicknamed SIR to me! For lack of a better name, we called ourselves the 'Yellow Chickens,' although this was not a name used for public consumption or in front of our supe- riors. We did airshows from Lethbridge to the Lakehead to celebrate the 35th anniversary of the RCAF. I vividly recall a large gaggle of T-Birds that performed with us on the 9th of August at Lakehead, forming a huge number 35 (or was it a 50?) in formation as they flew overhead.

Our routine in the 'yellow peril' comprised nothing unusual as we were restricted from doing loops close to the ground. As a result, all of the looping manoeuvres were turned into a rollout and pull-up down the back side. My solo show included four-point rolls, barrel rolls, chandelles, a roll-off-the-top, Cuban-eights and inverted flight (a challenge in the Harvard) while the other three aircraft in vic or line-astern formation did their thing back and forth over the crowd. We only flew in the sum- mer of '59 but it was a great experience and a lot of fun."

R.E. (Bob) Smith

The RCAF took delivery of its first Mk I Harvard on 20 Jul 39 from North American Aviation. In the summer of 1999, an old friend returned to CFB Moose Jaw and "The Big 2" to help 15 Wing cel- ebrate its 50th anniversary. It is shown here flanked by its successor, the Canadair Tutor, which has now also been retired from service. (Dan Dempsey)

When it came to airshows, there was no shortage of volunteers as this enthusiastic group of instructors from No. 4 FTS Penhold reveals. L to R, Front Row – G. McGowan, R.W. McKay, R.E. Ehrne, J.J. LaPointe. Back Row – R.O. Jacobs, T.W. Harris, A. Leiter, M.E. Fairley, W.G. Bullock, B.M. Ferris, J.B. Peart, E.A. Chonko. (via Bud Granley)

Harvard Aerobatics at Penhold

In the years following the big celebrations of 1959, Harvards of Training Command continued to appear at Canadian airshows, predominantly on the Prairies where three of the four basic flying schools were located. For the most part, these were ad hoc efforts employing instructional staff and were usually associated with the respective station's annual Air Force Day celebration. RCAF Stn Penhold, Alberta was the home of No. 4 Flying Training School and a proud sponsor of such teams in the early 1960s.

Formation flying is an important facet of military flying and with experience becomes second nature for most instructors. Thus, with an abundance of flying hours and aircraft, it was never difficult to find volunteers to put together a four-ship to perform routine flypasts when the situation so dictated. A low-level aerobatic demonstration however, was an entirely different matter and even then required both specific training and authorization before a pilot could engage in such activities.

Mastering the Harvard – F/O Bud Granley

In the fall of 1960, a young flying officer arrived at 4 FTS from the Air Division who was destined to make an indelible mark on the North American airshow scene – F/O N.S. "Bud" Granley. He had earned his RCAF wings in 1957 along with a posting overseas to 444 Squadron where he had served his first tour flying the best day fighter in the world, the F-86 Sabre. Granley had

been a member of the Canadian team that had won the Guynemer Trophy for finishing first in the NATO gunnery competition in the summer of '60, a most prestigious award among the North Atlantic Treaty's best fighter pilots. He had flown his last sortie and 1,000[th] hour on the Sabre in early October 1960, faced with repatriation to Canada and the dreaded instructional tour that awaited most fighter pilots after their first operational tour. It was time to pay the piper …

As it transpired, Granley arrived in Penhold only to find himself in a two month holding pattern awaiting his flying instructor's course which would not begin until early February 1961. What was a man to do? Go flying, of course! These were the heady days of the

F/O N.S. "Bud" Granley, still performing in the Harvard after 41 years. (via Bud Granley)

RCAF when the threat of Soviet expansionism in Western Europe ensured there was no shortage of flying hours on either side of the Atlantic. Granley was offered the opportunity to take a Harvard flying as often as he wished to reacquaint himself with an aircraft which he had heretofore only flown in training. He made the most of it – by the time he finished his FIS course and received his "official" unit checkout with F/O Pete Wooding on May 3rd, Granley was handling the machine like a seasoned veteran.

That Granley had flown with Wooding earlier was fortuitous as he was the station's designated demonstration pilot at the time. Wooding was obviously impressed with Granley's flying skills and undoubtedly related this sentiment to his boss in Standards Flight when consideration was being given to selecting his replacement as display pilot for Air Force Day 1961. S/L Ken Thorneycroft, himself a veteran of the Sabre era, concurred with Wooding's assessment and Granley won the job even though he'd been a line instructor for less than six weeks. This was impressive stuff … Practices over the next two months resulted in a very polished performance at the end of July, Granley's first official solo demonstration.

Penhold Harvard Aerobatic Team

In 1962, the OC of 4 FTS, W/C F.P. Clark, authorized the expansion of the demonstration to a two-plane synchronized aerobatic show to perform alongside the school's formation team and the Golden Hawks on Air Force Day. Joining Bud Granley in the rou-

F/O A.F. "Kip" Chaput formed the second part of the Penhold Harvard Aerobatic Team in 1962. (via Bud Granley)

Bud Granley's Golden Hawk Harvard, as depicted by Canadian artist John Rutherford of Kamloops, B.C. (courtesy John Rutherford)

tine was F/O Kip Chaput, a standards' testing officer who had worked his way to the top of the instructional ladder at 4 FTS. Like Granley, he was a gifted pilot and the two immediately hit if off. However, it was to be a short-lived relationship.

Having worked up an appealing show over several months, the team was looking forward to Air Force Day on June 3rd, 1962. Everything was in place and the Golden Hawks had arrived, always stirring great excitement on and off the station. However, when the day dawned the weather was well below limits for any type of aerobatic demonstration – in fact, "instrument flight rules" were the order of the day due to a very low cloud ceiling. *Nobody* flew ... *except* for our two intrepid aviators who decided to "take a look." When the two Harvards droned off the end of the runway at ultra low-level everyone expected them to reappear for landing a few minutes later. At least something had got airborne ... and the noise was always impressive! Instead, the two aircraft reappeared from opposite ends of the field heading straight at each other

"in the weeds," to coin an aviator phrase. As they reached centre stage, they immediately went into an opposing 360 degree turn which they had mastered over many practices. It wasn't an aerobatic manoeuvre per se, but was more than dynamic with their wingtips only a few feet off the infield as they crossed each other three times, generating a gasp from the crowd each time. The crowd loved it – the OC of 4 FTS did not! As Bud Granley recalls:

"Our two-plane team didn't last long. We may have had the shortest team career ever after the OC grounded us following the Penhold show. I spent the weekend writing a 2,000 word essay on the importance of aerobatic discipline, though I was able to carry on with solo demonstrations after that, on occasion with the formation team.

I remember being on one flight to an air-show when Brian Ferris, who was flying in the box, said 'Lead, I've just cut off your tail wheel.' I think that is the only incident the group ever had. It didn't do any more dam-

age than cutting up the tire. It was pretty easy to land the Harvard and keep the tail off the ground with the brakes until nearly stopped. Brian was a character that we all loved as the president of the single man's club on the station. He turned up at my house along with Ron Ehrne one Christmas in a bathing suit. He later became part of the 500 given their pink slips in 1964, joined Flying Tigers and was killed when their 'Connie' hit a mountain in Colorado around 1967."

Bud Granley

Losing their two-plane aerobatic team status was a tough lesson for Granley and Chaput, particularly for Granley as it precluded him from getting a tryout with the Golden Hawks prior to their disbandment. However, he took the lesson to heart and today remains one of the most professional and highly respected aerobatic performers in the world. He never forgot his dream of flying with the Golden Hawks, so in July 1977 bought into a Harvard which soon sported the Golden Hawk paint scheme. It has been over 41 years since his first show in Penhold, he is still going strong ...

Moose Jaw Harvard Aerobatic Team - "The Goldilocks"

With the Golden Hawks blazing a trail of glory across the nation in the early 1960s, no one would have expected the venerable Mk 4 Harvard to become a major factor on the Canadian airshow scene again. Time was running out for the grand old lady, her fate sealed by the jet age and a new basic jet trainer, the CL-41 Tutor, already well into its flight test program at Canadair Limited of Cartierville, Quebec, just outside of Montreal. However, in 1962 another new regional aerobatic team was born in Moose Jaw, one which would garner a great deal of admiration among airshow aficionados across the nation.

The notion of a new aerobatic team featuring an old aircraft was first proposed by veteran pilot F/L Murray Neilson, a staff instructor at the Flying Instructor School. In the fall of 1961 he had been granted a tryout with the Golden Hawks, no mean feat in itself considering the dozens of outstanding RCAF pilots who were vying for the job. Neilson had returned to Moose Jaw unsuccessful in his quest but with a new appreciation for low-level aerobatics and formation flying – both were a lot of fun! Knowing the capabilities of his fellow instructors at FIS, he was confident they could put together a show using many of the same manoeuvres flown by the Hawks, but in a tighter display due to the Harvard's slower speed.

F/L Neilson broached the subject with the OC of FIS, W/C "Wiley" Spafford. After some consideration, Spafford decided the idea had merit and began to consider who might be the best leader for the team among his highly talented staff. He decided on one of his most senior instructors, F/L Jerry Davidson, who had been instructing in the school for several years and also had a full Sabre tour in the Air Division under his belt with 414 Sqn. As Davidson explains, the proposal for a new team came out of the blue one afternoon:

"In the early spring of 1962 my boss, Wiley Spafford, walked into the crew room and asked me if I would select some of the guys to make up a formation display for the upcoming Air Force Day at Moose Jaw. I recruited fellow FIS instructors Murray Neilson, Bernie McComiskey, Glen 'Red' Willett, Bernie Lapointe, Denny Lambert and Mike Matthews and we began to work

F/L Jerry Davidson, the original leader of the Goldilocks, climbs into his Mk 4 Harvard on the Moose Jaw ramp in the summer of 1962. (RCAF Photo)

up a routine in our spare time, often late in the day after regular flying duties, or on the occasional Saturday.

At the time, of course, the Golden Hawks were getting well-deserved top billing at all the airshows in the country and we thought it would be a bit of a lark to do something of a parody on the Hawk's routine with our Harvards. Hence the name 'Goldilocks' was born. At this point everything was terribly unofficial, of course, and we were restricted in our manoeuvres by a dictum from Training Command HQ that specified 'no full looping manoeuvres, and no rolling a formation.' This made it rather challenging to come up with an interesting routine so we had to push the letter of the law to the extreme limits. When our boss questioned the occasional practice over the field, we would explain that that particular manoeuvre was not a loop, really, it was just the start of one, or it was a 360 degree turn sort of bent upwards …

After considerable practice, our routine consisted of an initial seven-plane pass in front of the crowd after which we split into a section of four in various formations, two coordinated solos and a single solo to fill in the gaps. We eventually rejoined and usually concluded the show with a seven-plane 'crazy formation' pass which became our trademark. The length of our show was about 14 minutes. Our first actual performance in front of a crowd was on June 16th, 1962 at Moose Jaw Air Force Day where we performed alongside the Golden Hawks! For this auspicious occasion my wife Shirley and Murray's wife Gloria both dyed their hair

A fine portrait of the 1963 Goldilocks, most of whom were holdovers from 1962. L to R, Front Row – Mike Matthews, Bob Dobson, Bernie McComiskey, Murray Neilson. Back Row – Moe Campbell, Bernie LaPointe, Roger Patey, Denny Lambert, Jerry Davidson. (DND MJ 64-2330 via Terry Leversedge)

The Goldilocks in their seven-plane arrow formation near Moose Jaw on 15 May 63. What started as a joke turned into a popular national team. The blind flying hoods used for instrument training are clearly visible behind the back seats. (DND PCN 4547)

goldy-blond. At the mess reception that night the visiting air commodore from TCHQ in Winnipeg asked to be introduced to 'the two Goldilocks' wives with the blond hair.'

Following the Moose Jaw show, we immediately began to receive requests for shows and flypasts at local events in southern Saskatchewan. At some of these local shows (usually small-town rodeos and fairs) there was little coordination between the event planners and our team other than an agreement that we would show up at such and such a time over the site. I remember on one occasion we flew around the outer edges of the town to let them know we were in the area – then for a bit of an attention-getter we fell into loose line-astern and did a seven-plane stream pass over the fair grounds at rather low altitude. The sudden appearance of seven Harvards in full fine pitch and max throttle stirred things up a little more than anyone had expected – the trailing aircraft caught glimpses of horses bolting and people running in all directions. That particular show got mixed reviews!

Additional shows in our first year were performed for Air Force Days at RCAF Stns Portage la Prairie on June 30th and Winnipeg on September 15th. For these shows we took along our station engineering officer,

F/O Roger Patey, and a small contingent of groundcrew led by Sgt Moe Lyons. It was following the Winnipeg show that we began to receive some rather favourable press and attention, much to the chagrin of the Golden Hawks! In fact – although we never found out who complained – we received a rather snotty directive from Ottawa that we were to cease and desist from using the name 'Goldilocks' in any official release. We were of course delighted to receive such attention, even if it was in the form of a mild reprimand. Since we were by now already well

known by the press and public alike as the Goldilocks, we took pains to never use the name 'officially.'

In late September of 1962 (we had never expected to last a full season), F/L Glen Willett got word of a much coveted transfer to the Starfighter to be replaced the following year by F/L Moe Campbell who flew as No. 7 (Denny Lambert moved into the No 4, box position). Also that November, I was granted a tryout with the Golden Hawks in Chatham and Trenton. Six of us tried out for

The smoke-makers! Team engineering officer F/O Roger Patey hands a can of oil to crew chief Sgt Rollie Muloin. The addition of smoke added a whole new dimension to the Goldilocks show. (via Rollie Muloin)

F/L Bob Dobson gets a close-up view of the signature manoeuvre of the Goldilocks – the crazy formation. (DND 4553)

four positions on the team that year, but regrettably I did not survive the final cut. I was back in FIS Moose Jaw in January 1963 and reassumed the lead of the Goldilocks.

Year Two and Going Strong

After a successful first season we were fortunate to get clearance to continue practicing and were back in the air as a team on March 11th, 1963. We began to polish our routine and Roger Patey and our groundcrew came up with a smoke system – the canisters holding the AVTUR oil were strapped in the back seat! This added a lot to our show, as did the addition of F/L Bob 'Dobber' Dobson. Dobber became our dedicated commentator, making his debut for the hometown crowd on April 26th. Following more local events, we made our inaugural trip east to do Air Force Day at RCAF Stn Trenton on June 1st followed by the National Air Force Day show at RCAF Stn Rockcliffe on June 8th. This was my last show with the team as I prepared for a transfer to the CF-101 Voodoo OTU at Bagotville, Quebec. I turned over the lead of the Goldilocks to Murray Neilson."

Jerry Davidson

F/L Geoff Bennett was a staff instructor at Moose Jaw during the Goldilocks' era and occasionally complemented their act with a "little old lady" comedy routine. Obviously a man of many talents, he is today renowned as one of Canada's finest aviation artists. (courtesy Geoff Bennett)

The 15 members of the "Moose Jaw Harvard Aerobatic Team" as of mid-June 1963. L to R, Front Row – F/Ls Roger Patey, Bob Dobson, Mike Matthews, Moe Campbell, Barney Hopkins. Back Row – Sgt Rollie Muloin, LAC Denny Lank, Cpl Joe Tyers, F/Ls Al Kucinskas, Bernie McComiskey, Murray Neilson, Denny Lambert, LACs Al Jordan, James Fitzhenry, Bill Heal. (RCAF Photo via Rollie Muloin).

The invitations in 1963 for the Goldilocks to perform at two of the RCAF's biggest annual shows in Trenton and Ottawa were also accompanied by an invitation to perform at the CIAS in Toronto, the biggest show of them all in terms of exposure. The team had hit the big times and the personnel of the station threw their full support behind the team. S/L Clyde Ferguson was the station supply officer and doubled as the public relations officer as well – good PR for the team meant good PR for Moose Jaw, so he ensured they got what they needed.

Murray Neilson wasted no time in getting his troops ready. F/L Al Kucinskas had already been selected to move into Neilson's former left wing position and received his low-level checkout from Neilson on June 17th as per Training Command directives. Also joining

the team as manager and commentator was F/L Barney Hopkins which allowed Bob Dobson to move into the opposing solo position temporarily vacated by Bernie Lapointe. The solo show featuring three of the Goldilocks provided some thrilling moments for spectators, particularly on the head-on crosses. The principal architect of this part of the show was F/L Mike Matthews who flew as lead solo from start to finish:

—————————

"The thing that stands out in my mind about the lead solo job was getting the timing right to allow for that prairie wind. In order to get our head-on crosses at centre stage during a strong wind, on the stall-turn reversals it would mean that one of us was just pulling up when the other was already on the way down! To get our pull-ups into looping

manoeuvres synched, we installed G meters in the solo aircraft for our last season. They didn't seem to make much difference, but we were surprised to see 5+ G on the clock."

Mike Matthews

—————————

With the dynamic solo show and crazy antics of the formation, the Goldilocks act was regarded as something of a barnstorming circus. By the summer of '63, their road show comprised nine Harvards and an Expeditor support aircraft to carry spares and some of the six man groundcrew team supervised by Sgt Rollie Muloin. Between NAFD at Rockcliffe and the CIAS in Toronto, Al Kucinskas' logbook records shows at Swift Current, Portage la Prairie, Winnipeg, Edmonton, Gimli and Kitchener-Waterloo – not a bad cross-country tour for a part-time

Solos Mike Matthews and Bernie Lapointe thrilled crowds with their head-on crosses between 1962 and 1964. Bob Dobson got into the opposing solo act in 1963 and Moe Campbell provided solo aerobatics during the three ring circus. (DND PL 99065, via Murray Neilson)

The Goldilocks patent another unusual formation in the summer of '63. (DND PCN 4609)

team. Team members on the whole were a relaxed group – they never took themselves too seriously on the ground and fully enjoyed their brief celebrity status, taking every opportunity to kid the Golden Hawks about the popularity of the Goldilocks show. Airborne however, it was serious business, notwithstanding what some of the crazy formations may have looked like from the ground. Behind the nonchalant appearance were seven highly qualified instructors working very hard at their craft. On August 31st, 1963 the Goldilocks season ended with their last performance over the Toronto waterfront. With all-jet training slated to begin the next summer in Moose Jaw, this very special day marked the end of the era for the Harvard at the CNE … or so everyone thought.

1964 – A Year of Irony

It was a proud group of aviators that returned to Moose Jaw in early September 1963 to resume their full-time instructional duties. It had been a gratifying airshow season and the team had been warmly received wherever they performed. In spite of their tongue-in-cheek relationship with the Golden Hawks, the fact is the two shows complemented each other very well. Canadians who saw the two teams perform together witnessed the best of old and new, both teams displaying precision flying second to none in the world.

Although the team had hoped to do a swan song in 1964 just before the retirement of

the Harvard, the news of the sudden cancellation of the Golden Hawks that ricocheted across the RCAF on the afternoon of February 7th, 1964 put an end to all such aspirations. Everyone at Moose Jaw shared in the loss of the Hawks, a team that many considered the finest aerobatic team in the world. But this was more than just the loss of a team – it was the loss of tradition, a tradition of excellence so carefully nurtured over many years, a tradition which had instilled enormous pride in Canadian servicemen everywhere. It also painted a foreboding future for airshow organizers in Canada who would once again have to rely on the American jet teams to draw crowds to the biggest shows north of the border.

The Phone Call!

Given the depressing circumstances of an air force suddenly downsizing due to budget cuts, imagine Murray Neilson's surprise at receiving a no-notice phone call in April 1964 telling him to re-form his Harvard aerobatic team and get back in the air! In making their gut-wrenching decision to cancel the RCAF's showcase team, the Air Council had underestimated the reaction of a civilian airshow industry now living their worst nightmare – the prospect of not being able to advertise an aerobatic team to draw crowds to their shows. Since the Harvard was far more economical to operate than the F-86 Sabre, the decision was made to re-form the Moose Jaw Harvard Aerobatic Team for one more season. So too would the Red Knight and Gimli Smokers be revived for the 1964 airshow season, albeit with a very limited schedule in comparison to previous years.

Reborn to fly again – the 1964 Goldilocks. L to R, Front Row – F/O Gerry Gelley, F/Ls Moe Campbell, Barney Hopkins, Bernie Lapointe, Al Kucinskas. Back Row – Cpl Joe Tyers, Sgt Rollie Muloin, W/C W.H. Spafford (OC FIS), F/Ls Denny Lambert, Murray Neilson, Mike Matthews, LACs Al Jordan , Denny Lank. Joining their crew chief for their moment of glory on the right are additional crewmen – LACs Heal, Schmidt, Bishop and Fitzhenry. (RCAF Photos via Al Kucinskas)

Moose Jaw's Harvard Aerobatic Team

F/O Bernie Lapointe (Solo)
F/L Mike Matthews (Lead Solo)
F/L Moe Campbell (Solo)
F/L Denny Lambert (Slot)
F/L Murray Neilson (Lead)
F/L Al Kucinskas (Left Wing)
F/L Barney Hopkins (Right Wing)

Those incredible fellows . . .

Photos by Ranson

RCAF Stn Moose Jaw was proud to once again highlight their aerobatic team in their Air Force Day program in 1964. (via Murray Neilson)

Moose Jaw artist Dale Cline was moved to produce this tribute to the Goldilocks following their last performance for the hometown crowd on 27 Jun 64. (courtesy Dale Cline)

With only six weeks to get into airshow form again, the Goldilocks had to move quickly. Fortunately, the majority of the team members were still instructing in Moose Jaw. Gone however were F/Ls Bernie McComiskey and Bob Dobson who had been posted out – they were replaced by F/L Barney Hopkins who moved into the No. 2 right wing position and F/O Bernie Lapointe who returned to his familiar No. 6 opposing solo position after his brief absence the previous summer. The only new face on the team was F/O Gerry Gelly who joined the group as team commentator. Once again the technicians under Sgt Rollie

Muloin rose to the occasion in getting the team's eight Harvards tweaked for demonstration flying, reinstalling the smoke systems and even adding an attractive blue cowl paint scheme emblazoned with numbers 1 thru 7 to complement the standard bright yellow airframes. For all intents and purposes, the Goldilocks had now become THE aerobatic team of the RCAF.

Farewell Old Friend

After several weeks of hard work rebuilding their show after hours, the team was ready

for National Air Force Day in Ottawa on June 6th, 1964, this time having the honour of performing two shows for the appreciative audience. For the first time ever, the Goldilocks closed the RCAF's annual extravaganza as the feature attraction. Eight more shows followed that summer – Moose Jaw AFD, Calgary International Airshow (two shows), North Bay AFD, International Air Cadet Day (Moose Jaw), Namao AFD (Edmonton) and finally their swan song at the CNE Air Show in Toronto on September 4th and 5th where they rubbed shoulders with the USN Blue Angels flying their F11A

The view from the back of the pack. The Goldilocks roll in for a low pass down the Moose Jaw ramp as depicted by Geoff Bennett. (courtesy Geoff Bennett)

All eyes were on the Goldilocks as tens of thousands of Canadians turned out for National Air Force Day at RCAF Stn Rockcliffe on June 6th. Shown on static display are three RCAF stalwarts of the day – Canadair's CL 28 Argus and CL 66 Cosmopolitan, joined by the Lockheed C-130 Hercules on the right. (DND PL 144602)

Tigers. Thus ended another chapter in the RCAF's aviation heritage as the Harvard was bid another fond farewell at the nation's largest and most famous airshow. In retrospect, the legendary aircraft could not have received a more fitting send-off than that provided by the exciting Goldilocks display. Accolades resonated across the country, the Goldilocks place in history secure.

Shortly after returning to Moose Jaw, four of the Goldilocks (Neilson, Kucinskas, Matthews and Lambert) wrote one more bit of little known history, becoming the first pilots ever to fly a formation aerobatic display in the Tutor. This they accomplished on October 2nd, 1964 in front of a captive audience of staff and students at 2 FTS. Students new to the station buzzed with the anticipation of getting their hands on the sleek jet so early in their careers. No one could have even begun to imagine that the aircraft would still be flying airshows 37 years later as the Snowbirds started their 2002 airshow campaign.

Stars of the Namao Air Force Day in 1964 were the RCAF Red Knight and the Goldilocks who closed the show. (author's collection)

Although the Tutor replaced the Harvard in Moose Jaw in mid-1964 as the RCAF's basic trainer, the last Harvard graduation in the RCAF took place at 4 FTS in Penhold on

May 21st, 1965. By then, more than 6,000 RCAF and NATO pilots had been trained in Canada on the Harvard since the early days of the British Commonwealth Air Training Plan. That spring the RCAF's *Roundel* magazine paid tribute to the Harvard, making special mention of the unique droning sound of the old Pratt and Whitney that had propelled the mighty beast. This of course had been a major signature of the Goldilocks show:

It has often been asked why a great number of Harvards in the air make no more noise than one Harvard in the air by itself. The answer, presumably, is that there is no more noise in the world than that made by one Harvard, and that it is physically and mathematically impossible to multiply infinity. Therefore, when you have heard one Harvard you have heard them all!

RCAF Roundel – May 1965

To some it may have been noise, but to many who flew her, and many of us that watched, it was just another form of music, one that would long be missed on the Canadian airshow scene …

Farewell old friend. The Goldilocks gave the Harvard a fitting send-off after a quarter century of service with the RCAF. (DND MJ 64-160-3 via Murray Neilson)

F/L Murray Neilson makes history as he leads three of his teammates through a formation display in the Tutor in October 1964. (via Murray Neilson)

The Golden Centennaires' nine-plane Tutor team photographed near Comox, British Columbia in early February 1967. The Canadian Forces team performed 112 official shows during Centennial year. (Canadair photo)

The Canadian Armed Forces Golden Centennaires

In 1967 Canada opened its doors to the world as the country came of age, marking 100 years of nationhood. It was a year of unprecedented celebration for Canada – from the time the Centennial Flame was lit on Parliament Hill in the wee hours of January 1st by Prime Minister Lester B. Pearson until the last day of the year, Canadians rejoiced in the knowledge that they were among the most fortunate citizens in the world, living in a land of boundless beauty and seemingly unlimited potential. For thousands of Canadians, the focus of the year-long celebration became Expo 67 in Montreal. "Man and His World" opened its doors on April 28th and by the time the sun had set over the *Ile Ste-Hélène* and *Ile Notre Dame* site on October 27th, over 50 million visitors from around the world had passed through its turnstiles.

For the newly integrated "Canadian Armed Forces," the year of celebration presented a whole new range of challenges as personnel from all three services across the country participated in behind the scenes logistic support and security. For millions of Canadians however, the skill and professionalism of their military personnel were exemplified in a highly visible manner by an extraordinary aerobatic team formed specifically for the Centennial – they were appropriately named "The Golden Centennaires."

Expo 67 in Montreal was a focal point for Centennial celebrations in Canada. The Centennaires made their debut at the opening ceremonies on April 27ᵗʰ as 11 aircraft flew overhead *Place des Nations* on *Ile Notre Dame*. (DND REC 67-475)

The Golden Centennaires opened and closed Expo 67 and over the course of six months performed 103 shows from coast-to-coast in Canada. Their dynamic show, which highlighted the grace and beauty of formation aerobatics with a stunning contrast in technology introduced over 50 years of military aviation in Canada, was widely acclaimed across North America. And although the Centennaires would not survive beyond 1967, the team set the stage for a whole new generation of flyers yet to come …

Fulfilling a Promise

The birth of a new aerobatic team in Canada had its genesis in the demise of the RCAF's most famous team, the Golden Hawks, in the winter of 1964. Two other significant events made the transition to a new team possible, the introduction of the Canadair CT-114 Tutor as the RCAF's first basic jet trainer and of course the celebrations that would take place to recognize 100 years of nationhood in 1967. With the upheaval surrounding the unexpected cancellation of the Hawks, Minister of National Defence Paul Hellyer had promised to consider a new aerobatic team in the future following introduction of the Tutor into the Canadian Forces flying training program. That achieved, when the proposal to form a new team to celebrate Centennial year was presented to the Minister in early 1966, he readily approved the plan.

Canadair Designs a Winner

The Canadair Tutor was destined to become the mainstay of Canada's air force aerobatic teams for over three decades. It owed its longevity, however, not due to its fine aerobatic characteristics but simply due to the fact that it was an outstanding basic jet trainer. With Canadair assembly lines turning out F-86 Sabres and T-33 Silver Stars at a prolific rate in the early 1950s, it was only a matter of time before the old mainstay, the Harvard, would also be replaced by a jet aircraft. Design engineers Karl Irbitis and Bob Lindley were the first visionaries to predict the transition over a decade before it happened. Although the RCAF showed little interest in a new trainer at the time, the ground work was laid upon which a strong partnership would later be forged.

Canadair was so convinced that the future of military basic flying training would be in jet aircraft that it won approval from the RCAF in September 1956 to design, build and test two prototype jet trainer aircraft. Karl Irbitis remained a dominant figure in the preliminary design stage giving way to Fred Phillips late in 1957 who took over as project engineer and was responsible for the final design of the CL-41, the company's designation for the new aircraft. Another instrumental player among a strong cast was test pilot Ian McTavish who also designed the cockpit layout for the side-by-side seating arrangement in the trainer.

The senior leadership of the Canadian Forces who made the Golden Centennaires a reality in 1967. L to R, Honourable Paul Hellyer (Minister of National Defence), General J.V. Allard (Chief of the Defence Staff), Air Marshal F.R. Sharp (Vice-Chief of the Defence Staff), Air Marshal E.M. Reyno (Chief of Personnel), Lieutenant General L.G. Lilley (Chief of Technical Services) and Vice Admiral R.L. Hennessy (Comptroller General). (*Sentinel*, January 1967)

On 16 Apr 66 rumour became reality when the formation of the Centennial Aerobatic Team was formally announced. An eight-plane Tutor display led by S/L C.B. Lang became the heart of the team. Following Lang through a six-ship loop are Tom Hinton (right wing), B.K. Doyle (outer right wing), John Swallow (left wing), "Red" Dagenais (outer left wing) and Russ Bennett (slot). (DND WGC 67-100-1)

From conception to production, part of the team that helped design the CL-41 admires an early wind tunnel model of the trainer with the cruciform tail. Designer Fred Phillips (top centre) subsequently moved the horizontal stabilizer to the top of the vertical fin resulting in the production model seen at right. (Canadair CL5536, Canadair 60350 via Bill Johnson)

It was Ian McTavish who made history when he smoothly lifted off the Cartierville, Quebec runway on the Tutor's first test flight on January 13th, 1960. Impressed by their subsequent evaluation, and by now having been convinced that "all-through" training on jet aircraft was the way of the future, the RCAF chose the Tutor as its next generation trainer over competitors from the United States, Great Britain and France. It designated the new aircraft the CT-114 Tutor and ordered 190 of them in September 1961, a major victory for Canadair who only six months earlier had rolled out the first of 200 CF-104 Starfighters built for the RCAF under licence from Lockheed. In May 1962, Orenda Engines was awarded the government contract to build the engine for the new trainer under licence from General Electric. It would be the GE J-85 CAN 40 with 2,700

Two views of the deceptively small General Electric J85 CAN 40 built by Orenda. The little engine can propel the Tutor to a top speed of 412 knots (772 km/h). (via Dave Curran)

The original Tutor prototype, CF-LTW-X, wings its way on a test flight near Montreal in the hands of test pilot Ian McTavish. The aircraft was later donated to the Canadian Forces, painted in Centennaire colours and mounted at the entrance to CFB Portage la Prairie, the home of the Golden Centennaires. It was officially dedicated on October 7th, 1971 as a tribute to the Centennaires and lasting memorial to F/Ls Tom Bebb and Dave Barker who lost their lives while training with the team. (Canadair 24566 via Bill Upton)

pounds of static thrust. The future of the RCAF and its defence partners was looking bright indeed.

The Tutor went on to become the longest serving basic trainer in Canadian history, serving in the role for over 35 consecutive years. But while every RCAF and Canadian Forces pilot between 1965 and 2000 flew the aircraft during their training, it was the little aircraft's role as an aerobatic performer that made it famous around the world. It all started with the Golden Centennaires …

Building a Centennial Team

With the RCAF having been completely out of the formation aerobatic team business for well over a year, the decision to mount a new team meant literally starting from scratch. Certainly, there were plenty of highly qualified pilots around that could do the flying part of the job, many with previous team experience, but it was the logistic side that was of principal concern as plans for the team were formulated. It was clear from the outset that a strong leader with superior organizational skills would be required to make the program a success. With the job would also come an enormous amount of pressure to live up to the reputation established by the Golden Hawks and their contemporaries for a dynamic, safe performance that would enhance the image of not only the RCAF, but indeed all of the Canadian Armed Forces, the mantle under which the team would operate.

A decision was quickly taken by senior staff at Canadian Forces Headquarters in Ottawa to run the team under the same philosophy as that used by the Golden Hawks, that is with a commanding officer of wing commander rank and squadron leader as team lead. The first step was to decide who was available and had the prerequisite experience to command what was to become the most visible public relations unit of the Canadian Forces in Centennial year. It did not take long to identify the right man for the job – Wing Commander Owen Bartley Philp – known across the air force simply as "O.B." W/C Philp had just completed a tour as the first commanding officer of 434 Strike/Reconnaissance Sqn at 3 Wing Zweibrücken, West Germany in the Starfighter era. When he handed over command of the "Bluenose" squadron on December 3rd, 1965 to W/C F.G. (Fern) Villeneuve, the original leader of the Golden Hawks, little did either man realize the irony of that handshake. Philp's destiny was about to change – and he had absolutely no inkling of what lay ahead.

To his annoyance, Philp found himself initially posted to supernumerary staff at Canadian Forces Headquarters awaiting reassignment at a later date. He never got to Ottawa however, instead being assigned to Canadian Forces Base Trenton as a temporary base operations officer. Twenty-five years later, long since retired from the Canadian Forces, O.B. Philp recorded his memoirs and related the story of how he became involved with the Centennaires. He subsequently passed away in 1995, but his story is reproduced here in part, courtesy of the Philp family:

The 1967 Golden Centennaires Officers. L to R, Front Row – F/L John Swallow (left wing), F/O Jim McKay (opposing solo), S/L Lloyd Hubbard (public information officer/commentator), W/C O.B. Philp (commanding officer), S/L C.B. Lang (team leader), F/L Tom Hinton (right wing), F/L Bill Slaughter (lead solo). Back Row – F/L Gord Brown (504K), S/L Bob Dagenais (outer left wing), F/L Denis Gauthier (personnel officer/commentator), F/L Jake Miller (CF-101 pilot), S/L B.K. Doyle (outer right wing), F/L René Serrao (CF-104), F/L Charlie Grant (engineering officer), S/L Russ Bennett (slot), F/L Rob McGimpsey (CF-101 navigator), F/L George Greff. Missing are the Red Knight, F/L Jack Waters, and his alternate, F/O Rod Ellis. (DND CAT 67/100, Cpl Bob Imre)

A rare nine-plane shot of the Golden Centennaires looping near Comox in February 1967. (Canadair 3671 via Larry Milberry)

"In the New Year (1966), I returned to Trenton and started to fit in to the temporary job. Both the Base Commander, Group Captain Ernie Butcher, and the Air Officer Commanding, Air Commodore Gord Diamond, attempted to find out what my future might be. The only answer from the chief of personnel was that I would be transferred in due course.

About the same time, rumours started to circulate that a new aerobatic team was to be formed as the air force's contribution to Canada's 1967 Centennial. We had been without a precision flying unit since 1964 when the Golden Hawks were disbanded for political reasons on the grounds of economic savings. Breaking up the Hawks had been a sad experience for the RCAF because the team had established a first-class international reputation and we were all justifiably proud of their achievements. Consequently, rumours of a new team caused a wave of hope and excitement throughout the service and there was a good deal of 'bar talk' about who might be involved.

Although I had organized and participated in many airshows, I had never been directly associated with a formation aerobatic team. I had been a fighter pilot, a graduate of the Empire Test Pilots School with several years test flying experience and an aircraft accident investigator, but the closest I had come to the Hawks had been to rub shoulders socially. Therefore, I had to assume that from my temporary posting I would be moved to a position using some of those qualifications. As the rumours drifted around, I was definitely not thinking aerobatic team.

In April 1966 I flew to the West Coast to spend a few days with my family over Easter. On my return to Trenton April 15th, an excited F/L Dave Barker met me with the news. 'Sir O.B.,' he hollered, 'the official word is out. The decision's been made. We're going to have a new aerobatic team for the Centennial caper. And the hot rumour is that O.B. Philp is the new commanding officer. How does that grab you?' I replied, 'Interesting if true.'

Barker was an ex-Golden Hawk, filling in as housing officer at Trenton. He was determined to escape and become a part of this new aerobatic world, and wanted to be the first to discuss his chances with me. The following day rumour became reality and it was officially

confirmed when I was called in by the base commander and handed a message. I was posted to the station at Portage la Prairie, Manitoba to create and command the Centennial Aerobatic Team. Fittingly, the job was to commemorate both Canada's Centennial and the 50th year of military aviation in Canada. I never did see the official documentation that authorized the formation of the aerobatic team, but remember it being reported in the newspapers as 'By Order in Council of the Federal Government.' Before reporting to Portage, I was to proceed to Canadian Forces Headquarters in Ottawa for a briefing by the Chief of Personnel, Air Marshal Ed Reyno.

The air marshal and I were not strangers. I had met him before at other meetings, and socially, where he was generally the dominant figure. However, this was the first time I had stood before him, one on one, or had been in his office which was impressively large and appropriately furnished, complete with RCAF wings woven into the air force blue carpet.

Expecting detailed instructions, I received 10 minutes of the air marshal's time. I was told the air force would supply the aircraft, manpower and logistics. All other funding would be provided by the Federal Centennial organization. In due course, headquarters would provide details. I was to proceed immediately to Portage and start weaving an organization. He was primarily interested in a well-disciplined unit which would provide good public relations for the RCAF. The mandate was to organize, train and fly demonstrations through 1967 and disband the unit when the year was over. End of briefing.

The Golden Centennaires era had been born, and it in turn would ultimately create the Snowbirds several years later, but this evolution would have its ups and downs. The whole Centennaires idea had to be thought out thoroughly; there were volunteers to be selected, tested and trained. Aircraft had to be flown to the limits of their capability in a search to capture the originality, precision and courage that symbolized the best of the RCAF.

Three days after my interview with A/M Reyno I was in Portage, only to find that G/C Vic Stuart, the base commander, knew little more than I did. Training Command Headquarters in Winnipeg had simply advised him that the team would be based at Portage. No further details were available. No team had been selected and a deadline

W/C O.B. Philp, DFC, CD

was looming. It looked like the old 'hurry up and wait' exercises we had all experienced during the last war. Since I had been told the team would be using CL-41 Tutor jet trainers – an aircraft I had never flown – I spent a useful couple of weeks while waiting for direction getting checked out on the little airplane, putting it through its paces, finding out how it could perform. This was interrupted when the system started to fall into place.

Right away a challenge was dumped in my lap. My mandate was to put a team together from scratch, trained and ready to perform, at the opening of Expo 67 in Montreal on April 28th. That was less than a year away and I had no operating base – half a hangar at Portage was all that was placed at our disposal. It would take a few weeks to organize. I set up a temporary office in my living quarters in the barracks and started from there.

Selecting a Leader

In May I had a call from Personnel. They had three pilots who were interested and qualified to be the team leader, but only one of them, S/L C.B. Lang, had previous aerobatic team experience. From 1963 until they disbanded in 1964 he had been with the Golden Hawks, flying the slot position. I did not know C.B. personally but I did know the other two hopefuls and they were doubtful starters. A couple of quick telephone calls to two of my fellow squadron commanders confirmed a hunch that C.B. was the man for the job. At that time he was serving at Maritime Headquarters in Halifax as air cadet liaison officer and was undoubtedly just as restless to get back to real flying as were the rest of us.

Events began to snowball when Personnel advised they had 76 pilots throughout the service who had applied to join the team! Now we had a job to do and we could not afford to waste a day. C.B. was driving from Halifax to Portage; I arranged to meet him in Ottawa. We had to find an experienced aerobatic pilot to be lead solo. At that point I remembered Dave Barker who was still kicking his heels at Trenton as the housing officer. We got him back in the air again where he belonged. The three of us, C.B., Dave and I became the nucleus of the Golden Centennaires. Eventually, the 76 eager volunteers were reduced down to 16 possibles.

S/L C.B. Lang (left), team leader of the Golden Centennaires and F/L Dave Barker, lead solo. Their previous experience with the Golden Hawks was invaluable in building Canada's Centennial team. (RCAF photos via Jack Waters and Maeve Philp)

Something else happened in Ottawa when C.B. and I got to know each other. It was the start of a deep, sincere and lasting friendship. After a second day of planning, we were a bit tired and thirsty. Leaving headquarters we stopped by the grog shop. C.B. picked up a bottle of rum – my choice was scotch. Back at the motel where we had connecting rooms, we loosened our collars, tossed away our jackets and had a couple of drinks. We talked about the future, our past service, discussed flying and the job of aerobatics which revived legendary anecdotes the way pilots have always done over the years.

We went out to dinner but could not get off the subject. I had to submit recommendations to headquarters for approval, including a rationale for the number of aircraft and composition of the team. Here we differed – C.B. was adamant that we should perform with an even number, either six or eight – I was equally convinced it should be an odd number of aircraft and had decided on nine. By the time dinner was over, I had managed to persuade C.B. to agree that he could work with nine. It took some convincing but I had something else going in the debate – I outranked him!

I brought up another aspect of formation aerobatic shows which I had never found particularly pleasing as a viewer. The use of high performance aircraft often left glaring gaps in the show. Speed and noise are fine up to a point, a feature of the Americans in many

routines. But these aircraft take so much airspace to turn and manoeuvre into position for the next pass, that the spectators have nothing to look at for awkward intervals. With nine aircraft and the right sequence of manoeuvres and formations, and with the advantage of a slower aircraft like the Tutor, something could be taking place in front of the spectators at all times.

This, to my mind, was what we needed to accomplish – something different, distinctive and uniquely Canadian. The object was not to impress other pilots with daring flying, but to please the viewing public with a safe, albeit spectacular, well choreographed show. Other pilots would appreciate the skills required.

C.B. listened to me expound my theories and then took it from there in a way that surprised me. Generally he agreed, but he went on with ideas of his own. He had always admired the European teams like the Red Arrows. If we could combine the best impressions of the European and American teams, we could probably come up with something distinctly Canadian. It was a relief to discover that we were on the same frequency and I felt confident he would gain the support of the other team members. Together C.B. and I could work it all out on the blackboard, and then go to work, which meant practice, practice and practice!

Philp and Lang – high spirits and a late night created the blueprint for a nine-plane formation show. (via Bill Johnson)

The Late Nighter

We returned to our rooms pretty steamed up and bubbling with fanciful ideas. There we settled down to the serious job of planning and sketching routines and formation changes. It should be remembered that at that time neither of us had more than 20 hours flying on the Tutor and were certainly not 'proficient on type.' Nevertheless, once we had agreed on each formation, change or manoeuvre, we sketched it on paper and moved on to the next one. I have to admit we also kept working on our bottles and the liquor most certainly helped to fortify our daring and to broaden our vision.

The following morning, both our rooms looked as though a prairie wind had swept through and scattered the contents of several large waste paper baskets. We had some good laughs as we gathered up our night's work, sorted out and then reviewed some 25 pretty original aerial choreographs.

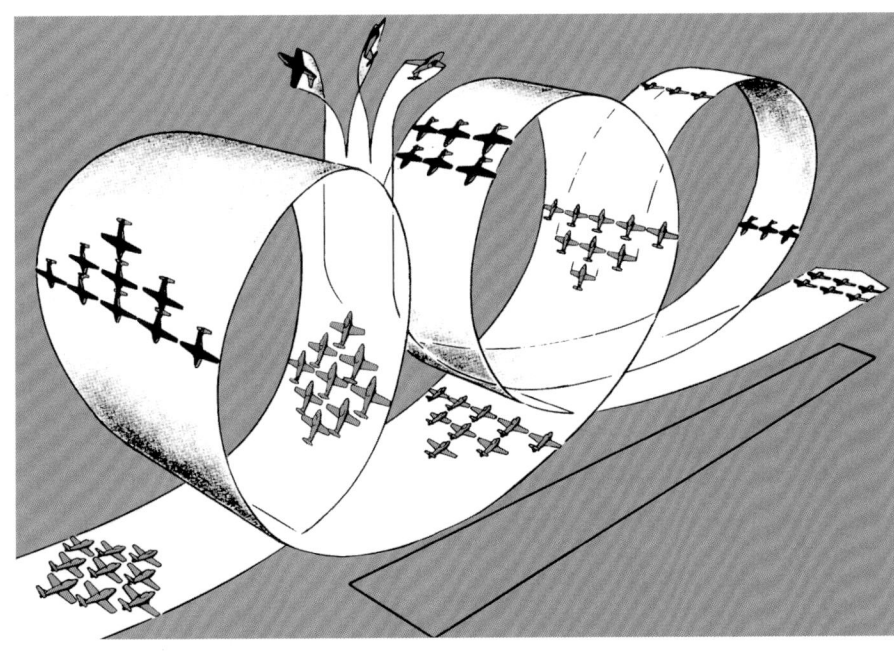
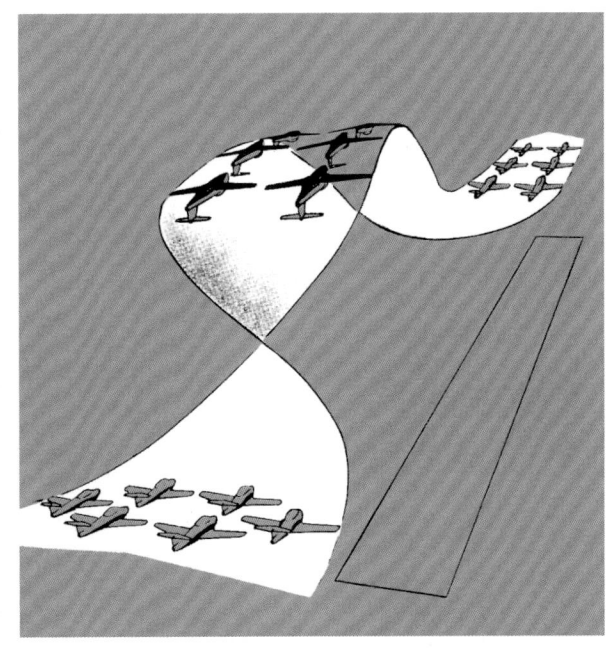
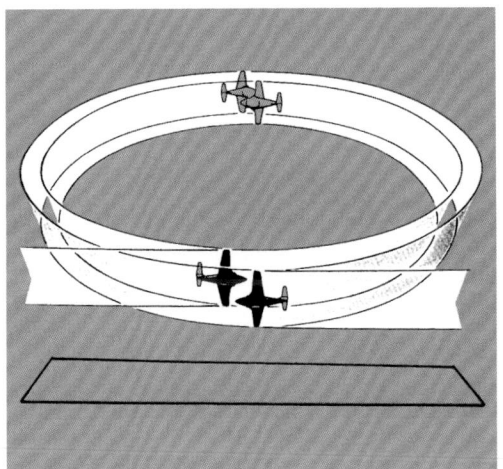
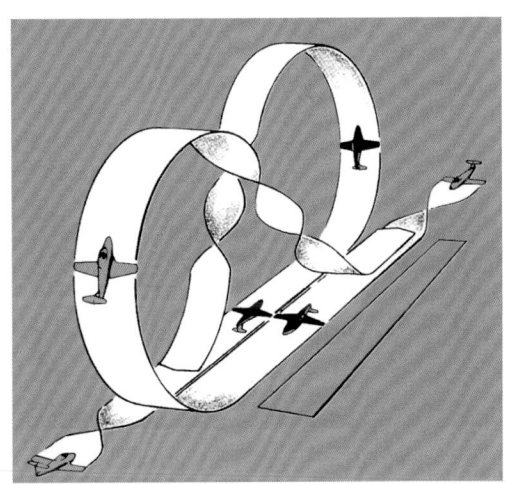
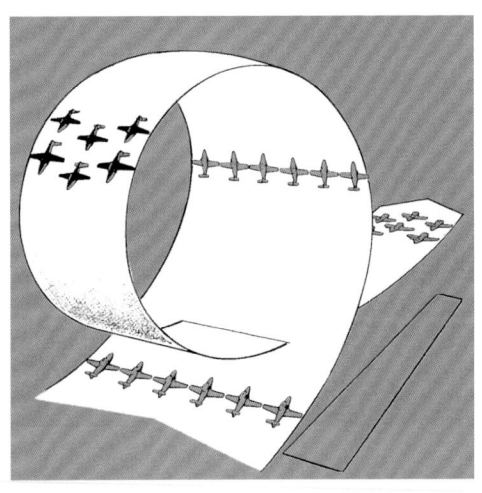
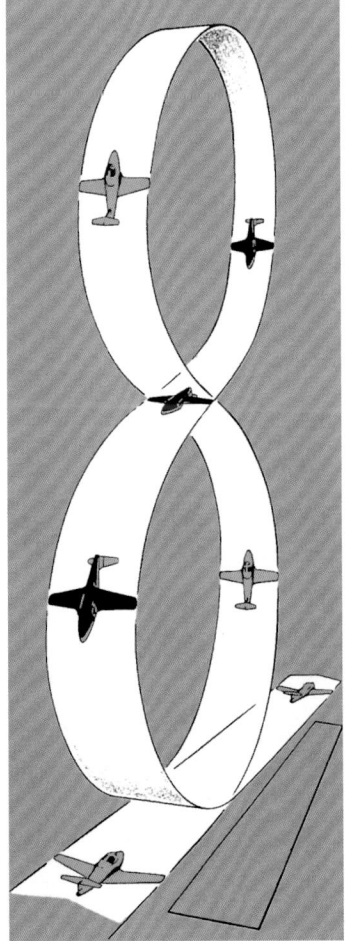
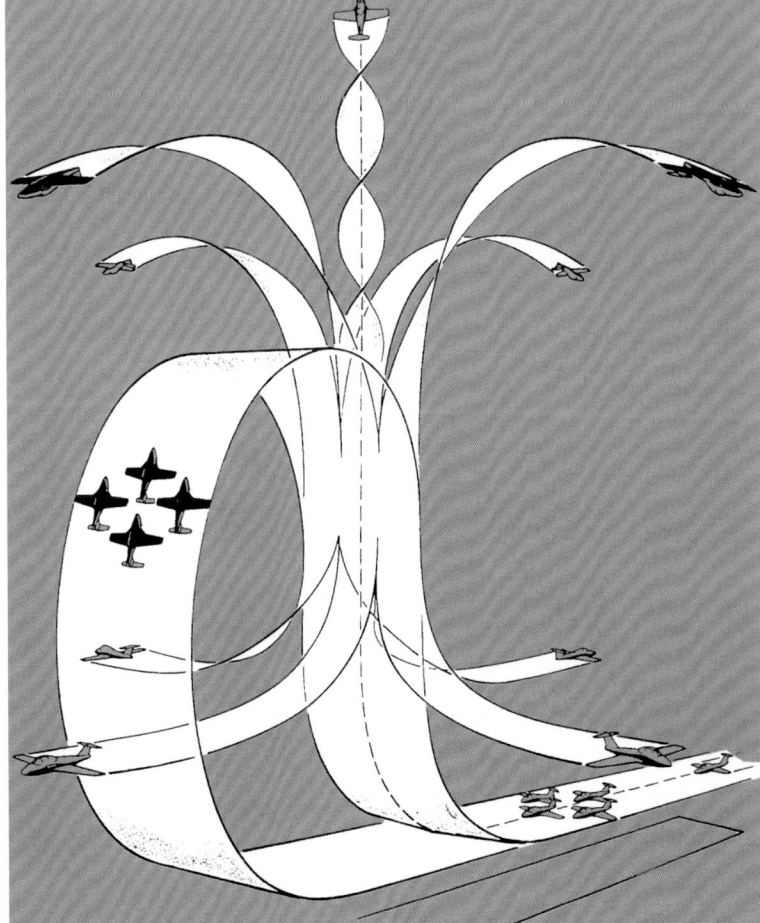

Seven of the 25 show manoeuvres conceptualized by O.B. Philp and C.B. Lang. From top to bottom, left to right – the nine-plane double loop to solo split, six-plane double delta to card six roll, solos co-360° turn, solos opposing outside Cuban-eight, six-plane line abreast to double-vic loop, solo inside-outside vertical eight and the show finale, the nine-plane upward-downward bomb burst. The original nine-plane manoeuvres were modified to eight aircraft in February 1967, following an accident which took the life of F/L Dave Barker. (Canadair graphics)

Out of the lot only one, a nine-plane twinkle roll, was discarded. In the cold light of day neither of us had the intestinal fortitude even to discuss it again, let alone try the trick. At a later date, one other formation had to be modified – a six-plane line-abreast roll had to be reduced to five. If we had clocked more time on the Tutor, we would have known the little aircraft did not have the power for the outside aircraft to stay in position.

The remainder of the night's work was carefully preserved and with 'sober' refinements most were used in the final show routine. Time would prove that C.B. was an excellent choice for team leader of what was to become an internationally known and respected unit. I only wish he were here today to contribute, with his own humour, his part in all this. He also had a hand in assisting me in getting the Snowbirds on their way. I lost this great buddy in 1985 when he died after a lingering illness.

Let the Tryouts Begin

We were busy and scattered for the rest of June, 1966. C.B., Dave Barker and I visited the training bases where the 16 selected hopefuls were located. Each candidate flew five hours of basic two-plane formations and two hours solo aerobatics. I flew a trip with each and was looking for stick and rudder ability – nothing else. As a result, we cut two more pilots and decided to take the remaining 14 to Portage in July for 10 days of intensive flying and togetherness. Of the 14 remaining, we would select seven which, with C.B. Lang and Dave Barker already on board, would make the unit of nine.

We were already satisfied with the candidates' flying ability and motivation to be part of the team. What we had to find out was how they would individually stand up to the pressure of flying three trips a day, five days a week as they trained to hone their skills to perfection. Nor did we know anything about their social behaviour, how they handled alcohol, if they had any family problems. We had to assess their ability to discuss a variety

The Golden Centennaires demonstration pilots that took their eight-plane Tutor show on the road in 1967. L to R, Front Row – S/L C.B. Lang, F/L Tom Hinton, F/L Bob Dagenais, F/L John Swallow, F/L Bill Slaughter. Behind – F/O Jim McKay, F/L Russ Bennett, F/L B.K. Doyle. Dagenais, Bennett and Doyle were all promoted to the rank of squadron leader during the show season. (DND WG 67-104-3C, Cpl Bob Imre)

Team Selections

The announcement that a new Centennial aerobatic team was to be formed spread rapidly across the RCAF, including the Air Division in Europe from which O.B. Philp had departed only a few months earlier. The result was an unprecedented flurry of messages and memorandums from pilots wishing to be considered for the team. This immediately presented Philp and Lang with the monumental task of trying to fairly assess each candidate. Since the majority of requests had come from the three main bases in Training Command (Portage, Moose Jaw and Gimli), a decision was taken early to select the team from within the Training Command environment. The only exceptions were the team leader and lead solo, the two most critical positions on the team.

An additional participant who played an important role in assisting Philp and Lang through this process was F/L Russ Bennett, then the career manager for all pilots of flight lieutenant rank and below assigned to Training Command. He explains why the decision was taken to utilize Training Command pilots and how the selection process worked:

"With regard to the selection of team members for the Golden Centennaires, it was a stroke of genius that C.B. Lang and Dave Barker were named to the team early as the leader and lead solo respectively. They were both excellent at what they did and given their experience and capabilities, I don't know where we would have been without them.

The remainder of the pilots for the formation team were selected from throughout Training Command. At the time, TC was still a big organization and there were many suitable pilots from which to choose. To have opened up the selection to all RCAF pilots at that time was certainly not necessary and would have needlessly compounded the process, making the selection very difficult. For example, how could you compare several CF-104 applicants who were about the same age, with the same

Selection to a national aerobatic team represents the ultimate accomplishment in a military aviators' flying career. It also represents a source of great pride and inspiration for family members. S/L Russ Bennett is joined by his parents in Saint John, New Brunswick prior to the team's performance in Jun '67. (via Bill Slaughter)

experience, and who had been similarly recommended, with each other and with similar groups of pilots from other environments such as the CF-101 world? It was a big air force back then. Moreover, since the Tutor was still relatively new on the inventory, very few pilots from outside TC had flown the aircraft and in fairness any short-list candidates would have had to have been given a checkout and some flying hours before the tryouts. Not that previous Tutor experience was essential, but it would have delayed the process and added to the bill. So, while I believe the decision to go air force-wide to select the team leader and the lead solo was the correct one, I also believe that the decision that was subsequently made to select the other seven pilots from within Training Command was also correct.

After that decision had been made by senior management, I was directed to send a message to all TC units inviting pilots of the rank of flight lieutenant or flying officer to apply for the team. There were a few other qualifiers such as jet experience since there were still some pilots around at that time who had none. After the applications were received by the given date,

I pulled the files of those who met the given criteria and O.B. and C.B. came to TCHQ in Winnipeg to review them. As I remember it, we ended up with 35-40 applicants from Training Command. It turned out that, with a few exceptions, neither O.B. nor C.B. knew much about the pilots who had volunteered. Since I knew them all to varying degrees as their career manager, I was able to fill in the blanks for them as required. O.B. of course had the final say, but it was quite obvious who should be given tryouts so I don't recall much discussion and little, if any, disagreement. By the time the decision was made to conduct final tryouts at Portage, the list had been pared down to 14 final candidates, twice the number of pilots required for the seven positions available.

I believe that all of those selected for tryouts had Tutor experience with the exception of B.K. Doyle and myself. However, we both had previous airshow experience, he with the Centralia Smoke-Eaters and I with the Gimli Smokers. B.K. was also stationed at TCHQ at the time so we drove the 50 miles to Portage for a Tutor checkout and a couple of weeks of intensive formation and solo aerobatic flying. The Tutor was a pretty easy aircraft to adapt to so I don't think we were under any disadvantage at all when the tryouts started, and we both ultimately earned a spot on the team.

The final tryouts in Portage consisted of six formation and three co-solo flights. C.B. led the formation trips with one of the prospective team members on each wing. I must give credit to O.B. for doing one trip with each candidate during the formation phase as some of it was pretty hairy stuff. During the solo assessments, candidates flew as the number two solo to Dave Barker in a relatively simple coordinated solo routine. The final seven pilots selected were all ex-Sabre pilots. Jim McKay, who joined the team after Tom Bebb was killed, was a pipeliner but a superb pilot who did an excellent job as the number two solo during the show season."

Russ Bennett

Canadair engineers prepare to modify one of the Centennaire Tutors. Cross-cockpit modifications were essential to allow pilots flying on the left side of the Centennaire formation to fly solo from the right seat. This involved the installation of a second landing gear handle, canopy ejection handle and emergency hydraulic hand pump on the right side of the cockpit. (via Dave Curran)

Engineering and test support provided by the Central Experimental and Proving Establishment (CEPE) at CFB Uplands was crucial to the success of the Golden Centennaires. Under senior test engineer Dave Heaks and senior test pilot Dave Wightman, CEPE staff were ultimately tasked to conduct some 17 projects on the Tutor to prepare it for the aerobatic role. These projects ranged from the testing of aircraft batteries to asymmetric tail loading analysis to extended negative G flight to determine inverted limits. As test pilot Bud White recalls, the latter test was the most interesting of all as staff test pilots deliberately remained upside-down pushing minus 3 G in an outside turn until the engine flamed out from fuel starvation. The rationale of this exercise was not just to determine the inverted limits, but also to test the aircraft's engine relight capability at low altitude. Shown in the photo above is another of CEPE's projects – the testing of the coloured smoke system for the Tutor. (DND RNC-1562-44)

of subjects intelligently and easily within the civilian world – they would be our ambassadors. This was not only 'show business,' it was an RCAF public relations job. These pilots would be front and centre in the air and on the ground. We had to study their self-discipline and their ability to get along with each other. For six solid months this unit would be living in each other's hip pocket. We could not afford to make one mistake in our final choice.

It was an interesting 10 days. One of the hopefuls decided at the end of the first week that he was not cut out for this type of operation. Another excellent pilot turned out to be a loner – he neither mixed well, nor was he comfortable in any discussion unless it involved flying. And there was always one in such a group who had never been involved in formation aerobatics, yet spent a good deal of time trying to convince us how to put the formations together! At the end of the trial, it was clear we were down to 10 successful applicants, from which to select seven. The three of us, being the selection board, were unanimous in our choice for the first six, but could not agree on the seventh member. 'C.B.,' I said finally, 'You are the team leader. You make the decision and we will live with the consequences.' C.B. did so and we had our team plus a spare who agreed to be on standby in the event we encountered unforeseen circumstances. The successful seven were F/Ls Tom Hinton, John Swallow, B.K. Doyle, 'Red' Dagenais, Russ Bennett,

Bill Slaughter and Tom Bebb. Now we had work to do. Training was to start in earnest on September 6th, 1966.

Golden Tutors

There was much to be done before the team started daily drills. Since the CL-41 Tutor is a two seat, side-by-side jet trainer, several cross-cockpit modifications were necessary so the aircraft could be flown safely from either cockpit by one pilot. Canadair Limited in Cartierville, Quebec not only engineered the necessary modifications quickly, their field service representative, Mr. Richard Armour, provided first-class support throughout the team's existence. Mini ammunition tanks were converted to carry 20 gallons of smoke oil each and provided 25 minutes of continuous smoke.

The aircraft colour scheme – gold on the upper surfaces, dark blue on the underside, with a red stripe along the side of the fuselage separating the two main colours, was conceived by Geoff Bennett, an officer serving with Training Command Headquarters in Winnipeg. Approval for this paint scheme came about in an unsolicited manner.

Geoff Bennett had painted a model of the Tutor in the design we finally agreed to, which was sitting in my office. The Defence Minister, Paul Hellyer, visited the team and I showed him the model – which he so admired that I presented it to him. He in turn

presented the model to 700 Wing of the RCAF Association in Edmonton a couple of days later at which he remarked: 'These are the official colours of the Golden Centennaires.' I do not suppose the Minister realized that this public statement was the official approval for the paint scheme. It certainly by-passed the normal channels of command.

The gold paint had been used by the Golden Hawks and the red was standard RCAF, but there was no dark blue in the inventory to meet our requirements. One of our technicians had some experience working in an automotive refinishing shop and thought there was a blue auto-body paint that was the right colour. We checked and it was suitable but since it had never been used on aircraft, Air Materiel Command said it might not stand up and would have to be tested.

Time was running out. We bought the paint with a local purchase order, charged it to Centennial funds and started painting! By the time the uproar died down the aircraft were all in their new colours and I made the point that the auto-body blue would get a good testing on the upcoming tour. The result was that the expensive gold paint was continually being touched up and repaired while the inexpensive blue turned out to be essentially maintenance free. As will be seen later, the gold paint with its faults eventually contributed to making the 'Snowbirds' name famous.

F/L Geoff Bennett's original model of the Golden Centennaires' paint scheme in Jul '66 and the end result ready for Expo 67 opening ceremonies in Montreal on 27 Apr 67. The colour scheme received quick approval from Minister of National Defence Paul Hellyer. (DND EN 66-258-38, REC 67-470)

The first Avro 504K to test fly at CFB Trenton drew a crowd when its engine failed shortly after takeoff on 6 Oct 66. (RCAF photo 66235-6 via Jack Waters)

Reliving History

To commemorate 1967 as the 50th anniversary of military aviation in Canada, headquarters decided to acquire and refurbish two vintage Avro 504K aircraft and display them statically wherever the Centennaires would be performing. I was not in favour of this static idea. If we were going to the trouble, time and expense to get these aircraft in shape, we should also fly them. The argument against this was that spare parts, particularly for the *le Rhone* rotary engines, would prohibit extensive flying. We would not give up and in a short time spare parts, including engines, dribbled in. Donated from various sources, they included one brand new engine from the museum in Halifax, Nova Scotia.

One interesting story concerning these spare parts was the acquisition of a 504K undercarriage. One of our groundcrew on leave in Peterborough, Ontario noticed a farmer pulling a cart which he was sure had 504K wheels! He was right and the farmer also had some other 504K bits and pieces in his barn. All were liberated in exchange for a brand new cart built by 6 Repair Depot at Trenton, Ontario. Both parties were satisfied with the deal.

Obviously these antiques would not stand up to a lot of cross-country flying, so we devised a way to take the wings off and have a C-130

Hercules transport them from one show to the next, one always leapfrogging ahead, to be reassembled and ready at the next location. No. 6 Repair Depot renovated both aircraft and did a superb job as the support base for this operation.

One problem to be faced was to find pilots willing to fly and demonstrate the 504K kites which the service had used in its infancy. Two flight lieutenants, Gord Brown and George Greff, volunteered and were accepted to play the part of aviators from the past, complete with uniforms of the period. Where the radio callsign for the Centennaires was GOLD, it was appropriate that the Avros were designated OLD GOLD!

Old Gold – Flying the Avro 504K

Another challenge in tackling those ancient biplanes was the absence of 'handling notes' and the scarcity of experience in flying behind a *le Rhone* rotary engine, with its air mixture controls, which was like a Model T Ford. Fortunately, my father Bart Philp had flown in both World Wars and had been a bush pilot in-between. He had an excellent memory for technical information on all aircraft types he had flown over the years. Dad reverted to instructor and had several sessions with George and Gord, specifically drilling them on how to use the engine controls. By

the time the first kite was ready for its test flight at Trenton, the young aviators were as knowledgeable as they were going to be, until they actually flew. We decided that in the event we had a problem, the first test flight should take place shortly after dawn, without the curious and the press. It turned out to be a good decision. A coin was tossed and George Greff won the right for first flight.

The aircraft rolled down the grass, picked up some speed and became airborne. Everybody cheered. Then at about 500 feet, the engine quit. George landed dead stick and I drove to where he stopped with a feeling of some misgiving. He looked down at me ruefully, 'Your Dad was right. He told me the engine would quit at about 500 feet if the mixture controls were not used correctly!'

With that episode behind us, George and Gord proceeded to get better acquainted with the old machine. Unlike modern carburetors which automatically compensate for fuel/air ratio, the *le Rhone* rotary engine controls consisted of two levers in the cockpit, one for air and the other for fuel. To obtain the correct mixture and thus power, fuel had to be adjusted manually to mix with the air – a delicate operation which, if not done correctly, would cause the engine to quit.

"Geez, O.B. is not going to like this!" might have been the second thought to go through F/L Gord Brown's mind when he pulled his bruised face out of his instrument panel following this little setback. It was caused when the wooden skid between the main landing gear broke and dug into the ground, causing the 504 to flip up on its nose. Flying the ancient machine was not without its problems – both Brown and Greff became experts on forced landings! Brown and CYCK were soon in the air again. (DND photo via John Bradley)

Old Gold – F/Ls George Greff and Gord Brown, two fighter pilots who stepped back four decades in history to give Canadians an appreciation of their aviation heritage. (Canadair photos)

Adding a Supersonic Duo

It now became apparent to me that we needed some further contrast between the Avro 504K and the Tutor to demonstrate fully the advance in aviation technology over the intervening 50 years. The CF-104 Starfighter was being flown by 1 Air Division in Europe in the nuclear strike/recce role and the CF-101 Voodoo by Air Defence Command as a supersonic all-weather interceptor. At Cold Lake, Alberta, F/L René Serrao, a native of Port of Spain, Trinidad and a superb demonstration pilot, was flying the Starfighter. At Chatham, New Brunswick, F/L Jake Miller, an equally fine pilot, and his navigator, F/O Rob McGimpsey, were flying the Voodoo. I got in touch with both crews and told them what I had in mind. They agreed wholeheartedly to participate, IF I could get approval. I made a pitch to headquarters to incorporate this plan into the routine.

Realizing the logistics problem we were building, I waited with bated breath while Ottawa considered the difficulty of our organization. Therefore, we were more than pleased when headquarters and the two Commands agreed to support the operation. Finally we had 'Philp's Flying Circus,' as it was called in some circles, complete. The trick now was to put it all together into a well-coordinated operation and make the air display both pleasing and exciting for the viewing public.

What a chain of command to be handled with tact and diplomacy! We now had five Commands involved – Air Division, Air Defence Command, Air Materiel Command, Air Training Command and Transport Command. To make this tour work, there had to be team spirit and a lot of support. There was tremendous backing, which made my

F/L René Serrao (CF-104 Starfighter) and F/L Jake Miller (CF-101 Voodoo) performed one of the most exciting fighter aerobatic displays ever flown. (DND PCN 67-303, PCN 67-192)

job that much easier. I was left in control without having to answer explicitly for everything I did or for every dollar I spent, although I am sure there were watchdogs who raised eyebrows occasionally. But the RCAF got on side to make the venture a success.

The Red Knight joins the Team

At Trenton back in 1959, the RCAF had officially created a solo jet aerobatic display as Training Command's contribution to the 50th anniversary of powered flight in Canada. The Red Knight had performed annually since that date. When the itinerary for the Centenaires was being designed, there were far more requests for performances than could be accommodated by the team, which was committed to 100 demonstrations. The Red Knight was therefore recruited to fill the gaps. To ensure the operation would be coordinated and that the Red Knight and his groundcrew trained to the same standard, the operation was put under my command. It was an additional administrative headache, but a logical decision.

The next step was to find a Red Knight and back-up. F/L Jack Waters, an experienced pilot who was running the recruiting unit at Kingston, Ontario was prepared to take on the job. F/O Rod Ellis, an instructor and maintenance test pilot at Moose Jaw, Saskatchewan became the alternate Red Knight as well as coordinator and commentator. Corporals Bob Hawes, Greg Moore (and later Vince Kavic) constituted the servicing crew for the two red T-33s.

Both Dave Barker and Bill Slaughter were ex-Red Knights so with their experience and help, Jack Waters devised an aerobatic rou-

With René Serrao glued to their side, Jake Miller and navigator Rob McGimpsey taxi out for their performance at the Abbotsford International Airshow on 11 Aug 67. (Jerry Vernon)

The Centennial version of the Red Knight team flew 101 shows across Canada and the United States in 1967, only seven of which were performed with the remainder of the Centennaires. L to R, Front Row – Cpls Vince Kavic and Bob Hawes. Back Row – F/O Rod Ellis and F/L Jack Waters. (RCAF photo via Jack Waters)

tine that was practiced and critiqued by Bill and Dave, until this segment was ready for the 1967 tour. Throughout 1967, the Red Knight detachment was seldom in the same part of the country as the Centennaires. However, Jack Waters, in addition to being an excellent pilot, was a good administrator and directed his operation with a firm hand. His section ran smoothly and what few problems he had that he could not solve, we resolved them courtesy of Bell's invention.

F/L Jack Waters takes his red steed up into the vertical in this Canadair public relations photo used in the Golden Centennaires' souvenir booklet. (Canadair photo courtesy Bombardier Aerospace)

The Snappy Dresser

During the fall of 1966 we had discussed what the team would wear as 'social attire' throughout the tour. There was a lot of discussion and general agreement that something quite conservative would be appropriate. I selected 'Red' Dagenais, who was the snappy dresser in the group, and sent him forth to find something suitable we could recommend to Command. With that broad mandate, 'Red' went off to Winnipeg to discuss our requirements with the big city haberdashers.

When he returned he walked into my office carrying a hefty garment bag. 'I'm not sure you are going to like this,' he said as he unloaded the contents. Rather than the conservative dress we had suggested, he produced a pair of dark blue slacks, white shirt, dark blue tie – and a GOLD JACKET, very craftily put together in my exact size! I had to try the outfit on and of course I liked it. So did the rest of the team, but could we sell it to the brass?

The five aircraft types that comprised the Golden Centennaires – the Canadair CL-41 Tutor, CF-104 Starfighter and T-33 Silver Star plus the McDonnell CF-101B Voodoo and Avro 504K. (Canadair graphic)

It was necessary to get approval and obtain funding. I went to higher authority, presented the outfit to A/V/M R.C. Stovel and some of his senior officers at Training Command Headquarters in Winnipeg – reactions were mixed … The only one to come out with a firm opinion was army Brigadier Stu Graham, a nice guy but brusque and a trifle

Being a breed apart, two sets of solos have a little fun showing off their snappy dress during a little "cross training" at an informal airshow reception. L to R, Standing – Lead solos Lt Norm Gandia of the Blue Angels and F/L Bill Slaughter of the Centennaires. Practicing their inverted flight are opposing solos F/O Jim McKay (Gold 8) and Lt Hal Loney (Angel 6). McKay won the handstand contest! (via Bill Slaughter)

stuffy. He said we should wear our RCAF uniforms for all social events! A/V/M Stovel expertly passed the buck by saying that if I could sell the Chief of Personnel, A/M Reyno, on the gold jacket, he would support it. So off to Ottawa I flew on yet another foray. I had phoned ahead for an appointment, but was running late and knew I had to squeeze the meeting in between more important matters on the air marshal's mind.

Landing at Uplands air base in Ottawa in the T-33, I did not bother to change out of my flying suit but jumped into a staff car and headed downtown. When I arrived at the office, the air marshal's secretary asked me to be seated. I told her that if it should bother her, to turn her back as I started to peel out of the flying suit, climb into the pants, gold jacket and accessories. When the buzzer sounded she turned around, speechless, and waved me into the air marshal's office. Resplendent in the new clothes, shoeless as flying boots were not appropriate in the halls of higher authority, I marched across the deep carpet and stood at attention before the great desk.

He took one long look – 'Christ, is that the best you can do?' I stood there, frozen, couldn't think of a word to say, but I thought, 'Hell, it was a good try!' Then A/M Reyno surprised me, 'If that's what your people want, I'll approve it, but I don't like it.' Then he added that Centennial funds would pay the bill – this never happened, we ended up paying for the outfits ourselves! In the end it was worth all the hassle. The team looked smart on the right occasions and 'Red,' the snappy dresser, had come up with a winner.

The Team Takes to the Air

In September 1966, the aerobatic team began practicing at Portage la Prairie. We started the Tutors in a three-plane formation, doing basic loops and rolls. After two weeks, we added the box aircraft and a month later included

An early practice south of Portage la Prairie in the fall of 1966 as four of the Centennaires follow C.B. Lang "over the top" in the first Tutor painted in Centennaire colours. Loose formations flown at high altitude were the order of the day until all members became comfortable in their respective positions. It took months of dedicated practice to perfect the complex routine that the Centennaires presented to the Canadian public. (DND RNC 1589-6 via Jack Waters)

PHILP'S FLYING CIRCUS
The Performers

S/L C.B. Lang - *Gold 1*

F/L Tom Hinton - *Gold 2*

F/L John Swallow - *Gold 3*

S/L Russ Bennett - *Gold 4*

S/L "Red" Dagenais - *Gold 5*

S/L B.K. Doyle - *Gold 6*

F/L Bill Slaughter - *Gold 7*

F/O Jim McKay - *Gold 8*

F/L George Greff - *Old Gold 1*

F/L Gord Brown - *Old Gold 2*

F/L Jack Waters - *Red Knight*

F/O Rod Ellis - *Red Knight Alternate*

F/L René Serrao

Gold 104

F/L Jake Miller and
F/L Rob McGimpsey

Gold 101

(Photos via Russ Bennett)

269

CANADIAN FORCES SENTINEL

JANUARY 1967

The Canadian Forces *Sentinel* magazine featured the Centennaires in their first issue of 1967. In the photo below, C.B. Lang takes his diamond through a practice loop. On his right wing is Tom Hinton, on the left John Swallow and in the slot, Russ Bennett. (via Bill Briggs)

THRILLS IN THE AIR FOR CANADA'S BIRTHDAY

The Avro 504 team deployed to Pat Bay Airport in Victoria in November 1966 to conduct operations in weather more conducive to "open cockpit" sorties. Many technical snags were ironed out during the deployment, including the replacement of engine magnetos following a rash of engine failures and forced landings. (via Bill Johnson)

by the loss of a solo pilot, one of our best. Tom Bebb, while on a solo training sortie crashed and was killed. Accidents like this one, particularly where the cause is not readily apparent, are not only upsetting but lead to some doubt in the other pilots' minds. They may wonder whether or not there is something basically wrong with the aircraft they are flying that we did not know about. It took some old wartime squadron discipline to keep us going, but being dedicated and professional airmen, they quickly returned to normal.

Besides being an excellent pilot, Tom Bebb was artistic and had designed a badge for the Golden Centennaires. This badge we all wore proudly on our flying suits as members of a distinguished unit. I doubt that any member of the Centennaires looked at that badge without thinking of Tom Bebb. The standby pilot we had previously selected, F/O Jim McKay, was called up to take Tom's place.

While the Tutors were working out at Portage, the CF-104 was practicing at Cold Lake, the CF-101 at Chatham and the Avro 504s were initially at

Trenton, then moved to Portage. However, as winter approached it was apparent that the open cockpit 504s were not going to get much air time. We made arrangements to move them to Victoria's Patricia Bay Airport on Vancouver Island, where the weather was expected to be more suitable for their operation.

Canada's new aerobatic team: The fun and the tension. And sudden death

The Canadian / STAR WEEKLY
PLUS A CHRISTMAS GIFT SECTION
DECEMBER 3-10, 1966

News of the formation of a Centennial aerobatic team travelled fast across Canada, as did reports of the accident which claimed the life of F/L Tom Bebb. The team was featured on the cover of *Star Weekly* in December 1966, along with a five page article. *Star* reporter David Carmichael was airborne with the team the day Bebb was killed. (Don Newlands photo courtesy *Toronto Star*)

the outer wingmen. Finally, in January 1967, we put the nine aircraft up together.

Training had been going along smoothly until October 1966 when we were shattered

Three crests used by the Centennaires. The first prototype incorporated the Centennial crest with an obvious link to the Golden Hawks. Of historical note is the original spelling of the team name. The original prototype gave way to F/L Tom Bebb's more familiar designs, his lasting contribution to the team. (via Bill Slaughter, B.K. Doyle, Joe Chermisnok)

F/L C.D. Grant, CD, Engineering Officer

A neat line-up of six Golden Centennaires shot for the Canadian Forces *Sentinel* magazine in the fall of 1966. The team eventually mastered a six-plane line abreast loop and five-plane line abreast roll. (DND CAT 66-059-5)

By the time February 1967 rolled around the nine-plane formation was shaping up well and the routines were beginning to smooth out. The volunteer groundcrew, under F/L Charlie Grant, our engineering officer, was complete and also working smoothly. Administration and logistic support arrangements from all the Commands involved were in place. We had a schedule of 100 airshows to face between the opening ceremonies of Expo 67 at Montreal on April 27th and its closing on October 27th, 1967.

The Comox Connection

Before we faced our first real test, it was imperative to practice the job of deployment, bringing all the elements together for complete dress rehearsals and also to test the administrative and logistic support systems. On January 21st we moved to CFB Comox, British Columbia on Vancouver Island.

This deployment also provided very necessary training for Charlie Grant and the 42 groundcrew technicians who would travel with the team. This small complement of men would be responsible for ensuring that not only the Tutors but also the CF-104, CF-101 and two Avro 504s were maintained in top condition at all times. This training was invaluable to all involved, particularly in establishing lines of communication and support procedures from the various commands and parent bases of the aircraft.

While all this was taking place, two other members of the unit were touring the country. We had added S/L Lloyd Hubbard, the last leader of the Golden Hawks, as our public information officer. He would do the English commentaries; F/L Denis Gauthier, our administrative officer, would handle the French commentaries. They were now visiting each showsite, making advance arrangements for ground transportation, accommodations and public appearances by the team members. The RCAF Association was the primary sponsor at most site locations across Canada and their members were of great assistance to Lloyd and Denis in coordinating our various requirements at each stop on the schedule.

It is interesting to note that Denis, dubbed 'Officer Ox' by the team, wore the wings of a navigator at that time. Later he applied for pilot training and eventually became a leader of the Snowbirds. It is also interesting to note that Denis, purely by chance, became an expert aerial photographer. We had our own RCAF photographer for ground shots but no one qualified for aerial work. At both Portage and Comox we were continually pestered by various news media people for photographic

Even in black and white, the nine Tutors of the Centennaires made a striking pose. (DND CAT 67-004-2 via Maeve Philp)

Part of the Golden Centennaires' Tutor groundcrew that kept the team in the air. L to R, Front Row – Cpl Johnson, Cpl Pollon, FS Gibson, F/L Grant, FS Hayward, Cpl Greene, Cpl Trimble. Back Row – Cpl Charlebois, LAC LePine, Cpl Anderson, Cpl Lapalme, Cpl Steckler, Cpl Restorick, Cpl Harding, Cpl Critch, Cpl Heal, Cpl Yeske, Cpl Murray, Cpl Cougle, Cpl McAskill, Cpl Haas, Cpl Ouellet, Cpl Leathem, Cpl Millard. (DND CAT 67-9)

trips. Invariably these flights became aborted missions because the cameraman, not used to G forces and aerobatic manoeuvres, quickly became nauseated and invariably deposited the contents of his last meal in the aircraft.

This left the individual embarrassed, the groundcrew mad as hell because they had to clean up the cockpit and me annoyed because the team was getting very little airborne photo coverage for the effort expended.

Denis solved the problem one day at Comox. A reporter who was scheduled to fly a photo mission was actually sick BEFORE he left the ground. He asked in a weak voice if we had anyone who could use his camera and 'Officer Ox' said he would give it a try. He turned out to be a natural – G didn't bother him, he didn't get airsick (which certainly pleased the groundcrew), and he managed to take excellent pictures. From that time on all the aerial photos of the Centennaires were taken by Denis Gauthier with a variety of cameras, notwithstanding the various media people who took the credit!!

Practices at Comox were going well. The CF-104 and CF-101 had established a 10 minute routine in concert that was noisy, exciting and very professional, flown by the incomparable René Serrao and Jake Miller. The Avro 504 had an eight minute routine which included not only aerobatics but also a 'falling leaf' manoeuvre. The Tutor routine of 30 minutes completed the show.

In those days there was no such thing as video, which in this modern day is a common and useful training aid. We did take some 16 mm film of the practices but they were not very successful. So I became the 'video' by watching the practice from the ground, making notes and then debriefing the team. For those who have ever tried to tell an experienced pilot that he is doing something wrong and suggest ways to correct the shortcoming, you will appreciate that while he may say, 'Yes Sir, I understand Sir,' he is probably

W/C O.B. Philp, S/L Lloyd Hubbard and F/O Denis Gauthier are greeted by former test pilot Al Lilly during a visit to Canadair in the winter of '67. The Centennaires' two flashy T-33s are visible in the photo. (Canadair 51829 via Larry Milberry)

Variations of six. Some of the most spectacular photos of the Centennaires were taken towards the end of their Comox deployment. Shown here, top and bottom left, are two versions of the Double Delta and below, the Double Astern (also known as the Card Six). (Canadair photos 3972, 92500, 92507)

Practice Show Saturday

On Saturday afternoon, between 1500 and 1545, the air above CFB Comox will be overcast with Tutors, a CF-104 and that new high speed addition to Canada's defences, the Avro 504, as the members of the Centennial airshow team get together in a pratice airshow that will approximate that which they will put on to thrill millions of Canadians from coast-to-coast throughout the summer.

All dependents are cordially invited to view this show, which will take place if weather permits. It must be noted that this is not an open-house type of effort, and sections of the station will not be opened so that the little monsters can see where daddy spends his coffee breaks.

All dependents are welcome to come and see the show. Don't miss it.

The Golden Centennaires spent five weeks at CFB Comox perfecting their routine in the winter of 1967. As reported by the base newspaper, the *Totem Times*, the team put on a special show for base personnel and their dependants in early February to thank them for their support. The show received much favourable comment from the enthusiastic crowd, the newspaper later reporting, "Centennaires' skill delights spectators." (via Russ Bennett)

thinking, 'Hell, the old man doesn't know what he is talking about. I know what I am doing is right.' On the other hand, show him a picture of what he is doing wrong and he immediately becomes his own best critic. Unfortunately, we did not have many pictures to help us. As a result, we had many painstaking arguments and discussions on the finer techniques of flying some of the formations.

A Second Tragedy

Just as practices and routines were reaching the peak of performance, we were shattered by another accident on February 15th that took the life of Dave Barker. Our lead solo – a member of the 'selection board' of three who had helped put the team together, was gone. He crashed in Tutor 176 following a low-level mid-air collision in the nine-plane formation.

I was back at Portage when C.B. called to give me the bad news. 'Boss, we lost Dave,' he said, then went on to explain the details as he knew them. 'How is the rest of the team?' I asked. 'I don't think the shock has set in yet,' he replied. I realized that it was still early afternoon in Comox and the team was normally scheduled to fly another practice before the end of the day. 'You should consider getting back in the air on schedule,' I suggested. 'Nothing complicated, just basic formation flying. I'll jump in the T-33 and be in Comox about the time you are back on the ground.'

I told G/C Stuart what had happened, phoned A/V/M Stovel at Training Command Headquarters, discussed the accident, told him my plans and departed for Comox, arriving late afternoon on the coast. C.B. met me and reported that the investigating team would arrive the next day. We proceeded to the Officers' Mess to face a very quiet group of Centennaire pilots. In addition to the shock of Dave's death, there was now concern that the team might be compelled to pack up. I assured them that I did not think that would happen but they were to be prepared for some bad press, particularly from those papers which had criticized the program from the beginning.

C.B. and I left the team in their state of uncertainty and went to my room for a private planning session. We agreed it was too late in the program to train a replacement pilot while waiting for any input from higher authority. We made plans to go with an eight-plane formation. Bill Slaughter would take over as lead solo.

F/L Dave Barker was a master of inverted flight. Prior to his untimely death, he had perfected an outside 360 degree silhouette pass with fellow solos F/L Bill Slaughter (flying Tutor 175) and F/O Jim McKay (flying Tutor 122). In later years, many Snowbird solos would emulate variations of this manoeuvre. (Canadair photo via René Serrao)

Next morning the accident investigation team arrived. Our time was getting short. We had to change the routine and needed all the practice time that we could get. The investigation team agreed with my concerns and conducted their investigation with a minimum of interference in the team's training program.

Having briefed A/V/M Stovel that we were prepared to go with eight aircraft, and that I was fully confident we would still have a successful operation, I waited for his decision with a bit of apprehension. He phoned me a couple of days later. 'Get on with it,' he said. I do not recall that I ever did receive an official message – just the phone call – but that was good enough and we pressed on relentlessly.

A pilot's view from inside the cockpit as the Centennaires make a low pass during the latter part of their training. The wings of the aircraft are overlapped approximately eight feet in this swept echelon position. (via Graham Wragg)

Nine golden Tutors taxi back to the ramp at CFB Comox, British Columbia following a practice in the winter of 1967. (Canadair photo)

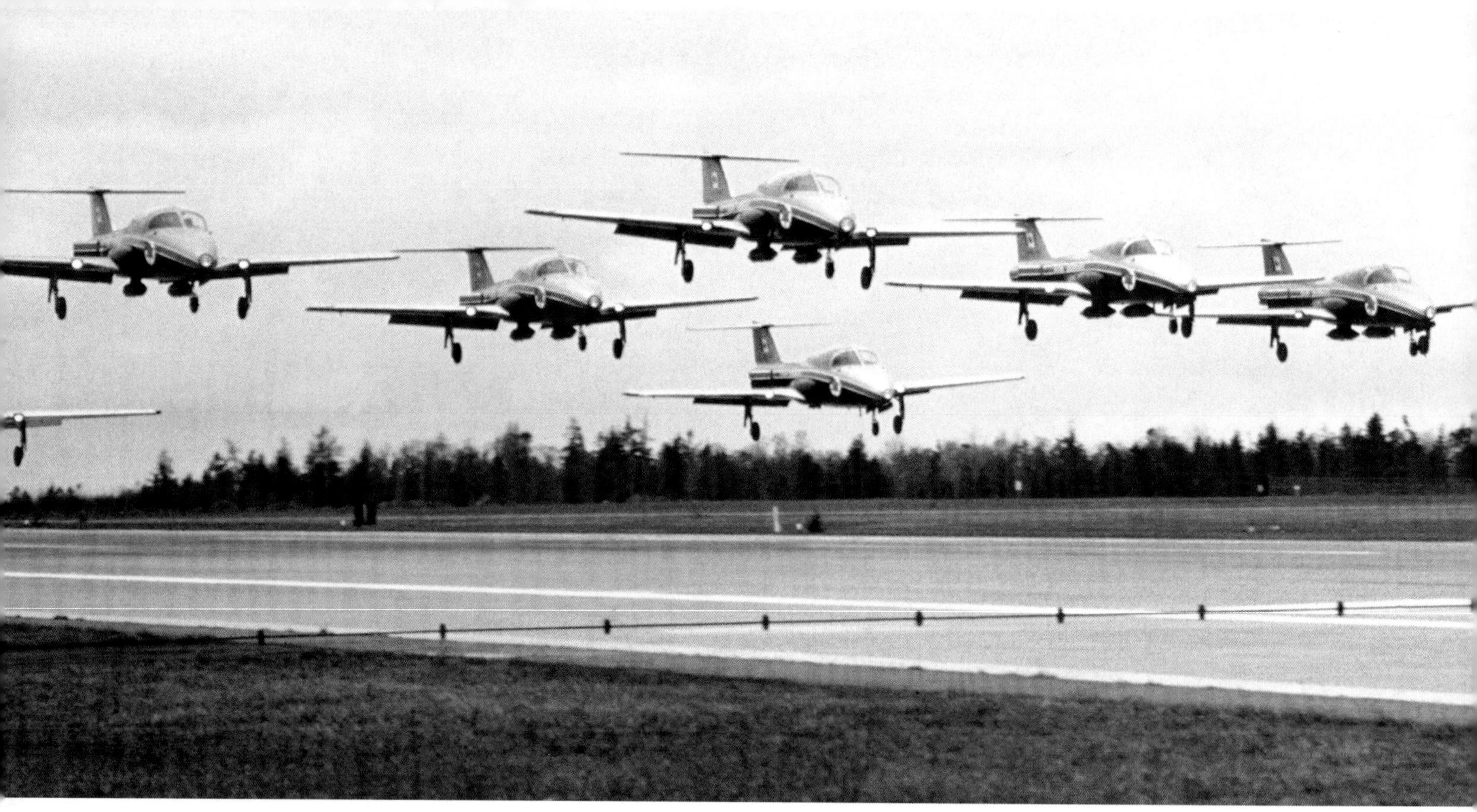

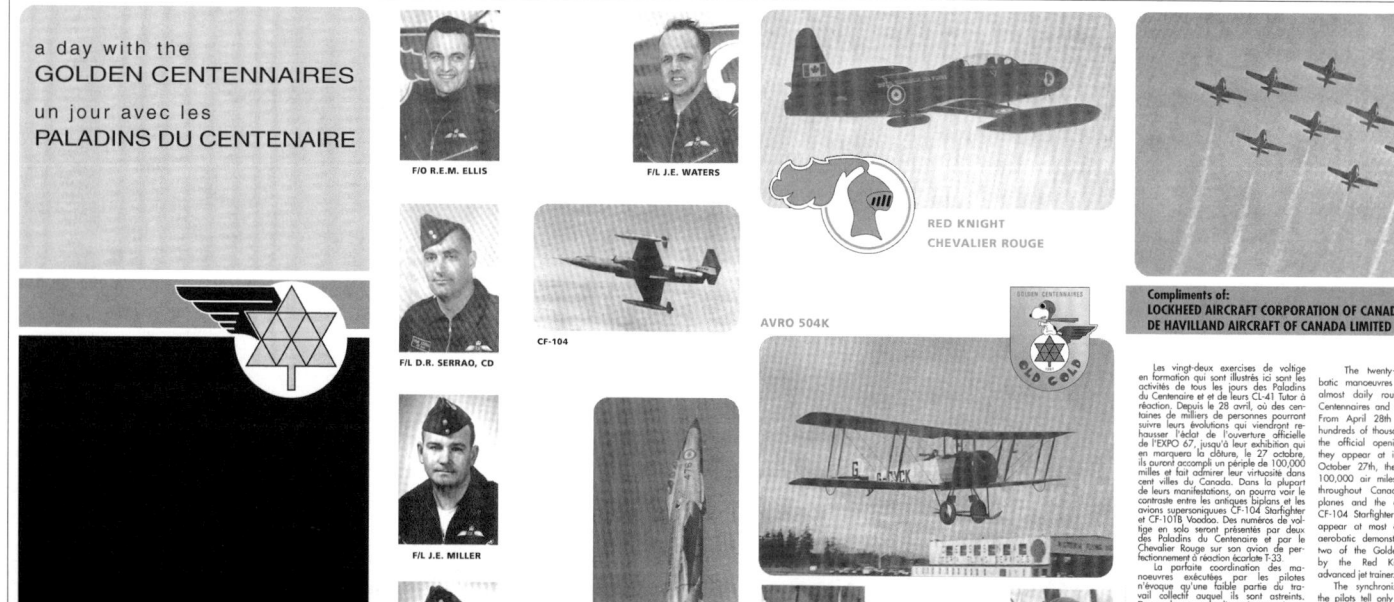

S/L C.B. Lang guides his team to a seven-plane formation landing during workups in Comox. Following slightly behind is one of the solos in a standard RCAF Tutor. Once the formation pilots were comfortable with the landing technique, the solos were added to the formation. An additional consideration for S/L Lang was to ensure that all aircraft landed beyond the fighter emergency arrestor cable clearly evident in the photo. (RCAF photo via Glen Miller).

The Tour Begins

On March 12th, the 'circus' returned to Portage for the final polish and to work out the deployment bugs learned from the Comox stint. By April 25th, although nobody admitted to being ready, we were all anxious to get going. We departed for Montreal to open Expo with a flypast on April 27th, followed by the first of the 100 scheduled demonstrations in Canada the next day.

Although the first few shows had some rough spots, in my opinion all were surprisingly successful and crowd pleasing. The team improved steadily with a precise, skilful, professional and innovative program. We criss-crossed Canada four times and performed before an estimated five million people. Only one show had to be cancelled, that was at Port Alberni on Vancouver Island, where low visibility caused by smoke from a forest fire scrubbed that performance. We added four additional shows as a result of political pressures, bringing the total to 103.

O.B. Philp

S/L Jean Boulet was the information coordinator for the Department of National Defence Centennial Planning Staff for 1967. His previous experience promoting the RCAF's Golden Hawks proved invaluable in producing a wide range of bilingual promotional material for the Golden Centennaires, including the brochure shown below which was jointly sponsored by Lockheed and de Havilland Aircraft corporations. (author's collection)

a day with the
GOLDEN CENTENNAIRES
un jour avec les
PALADINS DU CENTENAIRE

Un hommage des Forces armées canadiennes au Canada pour son centenaire. Des démonstrations effectuées par des avions d'entraînement de la première guere mondiale, par des avions de chasse et d'interception supersoniques à réaction et par le Chevalier Rouge complètent la manifestation.

An Armed Forces aerial salute to Canada's centennial year. Demonstrations by World War I trainers, supersonic tactical and interceptor jets, and the Red Knight complete the display.

F/O R.E.M. ELLIS

F/L J.E. WATERS

F/L D.R. SERRAO, CD

F/L J.E. MILLER

F/L R.M. McGIMPSEY

CF-104

CF-101B

RED KNIGHT
CHEVALIER ROUGE

AVRO 504K

GOLDEN CENTENNAIRES

OLD GOLD

F/L G. GREFF,CD

F/L G.A. BROWN, CD

Compliments of:
LOCKHEED AIRCRAFT CORPORATION OF CANADA LIMITED
DE HAVILLAND AIRCRAFT OF CANADA LIMITED

Les vingt-deux exercises de voltige en formation qui sont illustrés ici sont les activités de tous les jours des Paladins du Centenaire et et de leurs CL-41 Tutor à réaction. Depuis le 28 avril, où des centaines de milliers de personnes pourront suivre leurs évolutions qui viendront rehausser l'éclat de l'ouverture officielle de l'EXPO 67, jusqu'à leur exhibition qui en marquera la clôture, le 27 octobre, ils auront accompli un périple de 100,000 milles et fait admirer leur virtuosité dans cent villes du Canada. Dans la plupart de leurs manifestations, on pourra voir le contraste entre les antiques biplans et les avions supersoniquues CF-104 Starfighter et CF-101B Voodoo. Des numéros de voltige en solo seront présentés par deux des Paladins du Centenaire et par le Chevalier Rouge sur son avion de perfectionnement à réaction écarlate T-33.

La parfaite coordination des manoeuvres exécutées par les pilotes n'évoque qu'une faible partie du travail collectif auquel ils sont astreints. De nombreux mois d'entrainement intensif ont précédé la tournée qu'ils vont entreprendre et cet entraînement va se poursuivre pendant la tournée, les jours où ils ne feront pas de démonstrations. Bien que leurs prouesses aériennes soient stupéfiantes, ce ne sont pas des pilotes de voltige professionnels. Ce sont des pilotes militaires de carrière bénévoles qui ont été choisis pour montrer au public la valeur des Forces Armées canadinnes.

The twenty-two formation aerobatic manoeuvres illustrated depict an almost daily routine for the Golden Centennaires and their CL-41 Tutor jets. From April 28th when they entertain hundreds of thousands as a highlight of the official opening of EXPO67 until they appear at its closing ceremonies October 27th, they will have travelled 100,000 air miles visiting 100 centres throughout Canada. The vintage biplanes and the contrasting supersonic CF-104 Starfighter and CF-101 Voodoo appear at most of the displays. Solo aerobatic demonstrations are given by two of the Golden Centennaires, and by the Red Knight's scarlet T-33 advanced jet trainer.

The synchronized performances of the pilots tell only a small part of their collective story. Many months of concentrated training precede this tour, amd practices continnue on days when no demonstrations are scheduled. Although this aerial show is breath-taking, the performers are not stunt pilots. They are professional military flyers who volunteered and were selected to demonstrate to the public the competence of the Canadian Armed Forces.

Imprimé au Canada

Printed in Canada

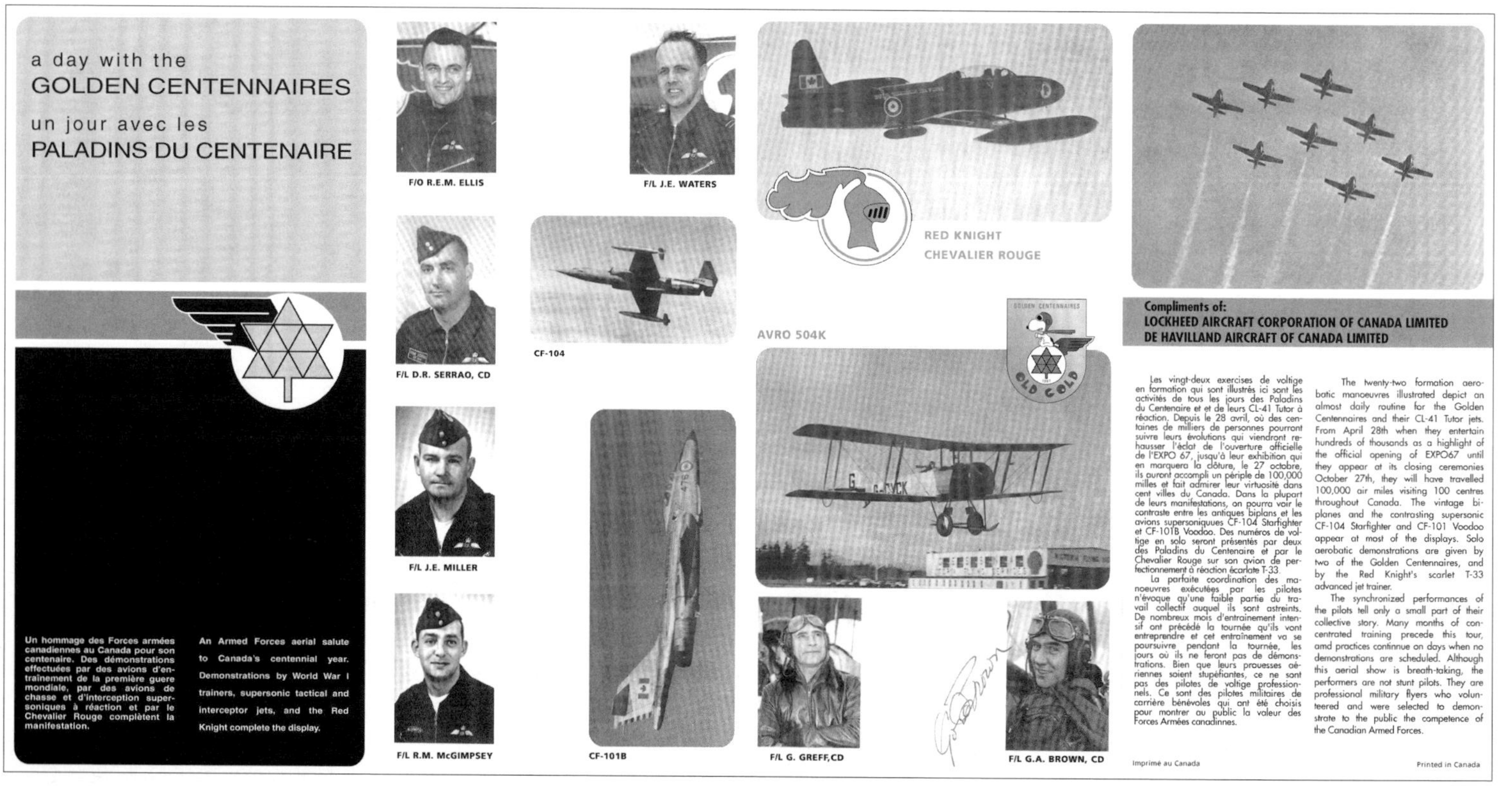

THE GOLDEN CENTENNAIRES
LES PALADINS DU CENTENAIRE

CANADA 1967

Produced in support of THE GOLDEN CENTENNAIRES by
Cette brochure LES PALADINS DU CENTENAIRE une gracieuseté de

CANADAIR

1967 AIR DEMONSTRATION SCHEDULE   **PROGRAMME DES DEMONSTRATIONS AERIENNES 1967**

	SHOW DEMONS- TRATION		SHOW DEMONS- TRATION		SHOW DEMONS- TRATION		SHOW DEMONS- TRATION
APRIL AVRIL		25 CORNWALL	9	50 PORTAGE	22	74 SUDBURY	8
1 PORTAGE	15	26 OTTAWA	10	51 WINNIPEG	23	75 SAULT STE MARIE	10
2 EXPO 67	28	27 MANIWAKI	11	52 BRANDON	24	76 KIRKLAND LAKE	13
3 ST. JEAN	29	28 CORNER BROOK	14	53 REGINA	26	77 TIMMINS	14
4 MONT TREMBLANT	30	29 GANDER	15	54 CALGARY	29	78 DRUMMONDVILLE	16
		30 ST. JOHN'S	16	55 LETHBRIDGE	30	79 QUEBEC	17
MAY MAI		31 SUMMERSIDE	17			80 TROIS RIVIERES	19
5 SARNIA	4	32 CHARLOTTETOWN	18	**AUGUST AOUT**		81 SWAN RIVER	24
6 LONDON	6	33 MONCTON	19	56 MEDICINE HAT	1	82 MELVILLE	26
7 WINDSOR	7	34 SYDNEY	21	57 EDMONTON	3	83 YORKTON	27
8 OWEN SOUND	8	35 NEW GLASGOW	22	58 SASKATOON	6	84 MELFORT	29
9 OSHAWA	10	36 HALIFAX	24	59 RED DEER	7	85 PRINCE ALBERT	30
10 NIAGARA FALLS	12	37 GREENWOOD	26	60 KELOWNA	10		
11 HAMILTON	14	38 GRAND MANAN IS	29	61 ABBOTSFORD	12	**OCTOBER OCTOBRE**	
12 PETERBOROUGH	15	39 SAINT JOHN	30	62 ABBOTSFORD	13	86 NORTH BATTLEFORD	4
13 ORILLIA	18			63 COMOX	14	87 GRAND PRAIRIE	5
14 BARRIE	19	**JULY JUILLET**		64 NANAIMO	16	88 LLOYDMINSTER	6
15 TRENTON	20	40 FREDERICTON	1	65 PORT ALBERNI	18	89 COLD LAKE	8
16 KINGSTON	21	41 WOODSTOCK	2	66 PRINCE GEORGE	21	90 ST. PAUL	9
17 VILLE D'ALMA	26	42 CHATHAM	3	67 KAMLOOPS	23	91 KENORA	14
18 CHICOUTIMI	27	43 BATHURST	4	68 VANCOUVER	25	92 FORT WILLIAM	15
19 SHERBROOKE	28	44 EDMUNSTON	5	69 VANCOUVER	26	93 ROUYN/NORANDA	17
20 THETFORD MINES	30	45 GIMLI	11			94 VAL D'OR	18
		46 MOOSE JAW	13	**SEPTEMBER SEPTEMBRE**		95 SEPT ILES	21
JUNE JUIN		47 CRESTON	14	70 TORONTO	1	96 RIMOUSKI	22
21 GRANBY	1	48 NEW WESTMINSTER	15	71 TORONTO	2	97 BAIE COMEAU	23
22 PETAWAWA	3	49 VICTORIA	19	72 KITCHENER-WATERLOO	6	98 EXPO 67	27
23 RENFREW	4			73 NORTH BAY	7		
24 HAWKSBURY	5						

Printed in Canada   Imprimé au Canada

the canadian armed forces
GOLDEN CENTENNAIRES
LES PALADINS DU CENTENAIRE
des forces canadiennes

The bilingual advertising poster of the Golden Centennaires. Some 25,000 posters were distributed across North America to herald the arrival of the team prior to each show. (via Maeve Philp)

Canadair Limited, as manufacturer of the Tutor and builder of the CF-104 and T-33, had more than a passing interest in the success of the Golden Centennaires. They produced a handsome, fully bilingual souvenir booklet on the team which is now a rare collector's item. By the time the season started, 100 shows had been scheduled across Canada – 103 were eventually flown in Canada plus an additional nine in the United States. (via B.K. Doyle)

THE GOLDEN CENTENNAIRES • LES PALADINS DU CENTENAIRE

W/C O.B. PHILP, DFC, CD

S/L L.J. HUBBARD, CD

F/L J.L.D. GAUTHIER

S/L C.B. LANG

F/L R.W. SLAUGHTER

F/L T.P. HINTON

F/L J.M. SWALLOW

F/O J.M. McKAY

S/L R.C. BENNETT, CD

S/L B.K. DOYLE, CD

S/L R.C. DAGENAIS

The Golden Centennaires Airshow

The aerial extravaganza created for Canada's Centennial was the largest aerobatic team of its kind in the history of the RCAF and consisted of 12 "show" aircraft when the entire team performed together. However, in trying to accommodate as many of the hundreds of show requests as possible, the Red Knight team of Jack Waters and Rod Ellis and their crewmen were usually off in another part of the country. This left the Centennaires' Avro 504, Voodoo/Starfighter duo and Tutor display as the feature attraction of virtually every show they performed at.

Advance billing for the team was high – news of its formation had swept the country thanks in large part to two front page articles in Canada's leading newspaper magazines which were distributed across the country at the time. On December 3rd, 1966, *Star Weekly* ran a beautiful cover photo by Don Newlands which showed the Tutor team inverted over the Manitoba prairie, still in standard RCAF colours. The title proclaimed "Canada's new aerobatic team: The fun and the tension. And sudden death," – the last storyline referring to the unfortunate accident which had taken the life of Tom Bebb two months earlier. This article was followed up by a stirring tribute by *Weekend Magazine* which highlighted the

Communities across the nation went to great lengths to welcome the Centennaires as they crossed Canada, as evidenced by the program cover of the Regina Airshow flown on July 26th. The show was jointly sponsored by the City of Regina and 600 (Regina) Wing of the RCAF Association. (via Jack Waters)

Uictoria Daily Times

weekend MAGAZINE VOL. 17, No. 17 APRIL 29, 1967

STRAIGHT UP FOR THE CENTENNIAL

see page 2

The timing was perfect when *Weekend Magazine* arrived on Canadian doorsteps on Saturday, 29 Apr 67, the day following the first full show of the Golden Centennaires at Expo 67 in Montreal. (Bruce Moss photo via Maeve Philp)

team on April 29th, 1967 to coincide with the opening of Expo 67. Its cover headline read "Straight up for the Centennial" and was accompanied by some even more stunning photos by staff photographer Bruce Moss who had also flown with the Golden Hawks. These fabulous photos sent the blood rushing in many a youngster across the country, mine included, and I can still vividly remember the day my mother put the magazine in my hands for the first time.

By the time the Centennaires hit the road in 1967, everyone who knew *anything* about aviation in Canada knew exactly who they were. Anticipation and expectations were high! From their opening flypast at Expo 67, the team did not disappoint. "It was Pomp and Circumstance All The Way …" was part of the headline the Montreal

Gazette ran to signal Canada's entry into the realm of international expositions, remarking that the Centennaires "had sparkled across the sky and rocketed upward standing on tails of white smoke." As the team criss-crossed the country during its 184 day Canadian tour, they were embraced with equal enthusiasm everywhere they performed. Characteristic headlines in Western Canada included: "Golden Jets Streak the Sky in Centennial Spectacular" (*Winnipeg Free Press*), "Huge Crowd Jams Field For Golden Centennaires" (*Lethbridge Herald*), "Thousands Watch As Jets Scream Over Namao Base" (*Edmonton Journal*), "Centennaires Zoom In At All Angles" (*Kelowna Daily Courier*) and "Centennaires Dazzling" (*Abbotsford News*). It was difficult not to get swept up in the euphoria that celebrated the team's show.

Avro Escapades

It is common practice in the airshow industry that organizers like to save one of their best acts for last to bring their show to a climax in style. Thus it was not surprising that the Golden Centennaires were asked to perform last at most of the shows in which they participated in 1967. They did so as a "package" wherever possible, but flexibility was key as some showsites demanded that the different components of the show operate from different airfields. For example, the fast movers could not operate out of Downsview Airport in Toronto whereas the Tutors and Avro 504 could.

Under ideal circumstances, O.B. Philp's circus started off with a salute to Canada's aviation heritage. Taking centre stage overhead was the Avro 504K, alternately flown by F/Ls George Greff and Gord Brown. The intent of this part of the show was simply to underscore how far aviation had come since the early barnstorming days of leather helmets and flying goggles. A total of 62 Avro 504Ks had been gifted to the fledgling Canadian Air Force by Great Britain in 1919 following the end of the Great War. This allowed Canada to introduce a Provisional Pilot Officer Programme at Camp Borden, Ontario designed to train university students for an aviation career. Eventually 155 K and N models of the aircraft were used by the RCAF as trainers until 1928. Neither Greff or Brown, both former fighter pilots, had ever flown anything as ancient as the 504 – at 40 and 38 years-of-age respectively, the aircraft had been retired from the RCAF inventory before Brown had even been born. Nevertheless, the opportunity to fly a vintage biplane in front of millions of airshow fans was a unique opportunity which both aviators were eager to exploit.

For Gord Brown, the opportunity also allowed him to escape an instructional tour on the Tutor following a stint as a staff officer at Canadian Forces Headquarters in Ottawa. Prior to his staff assignment, his flying career had taken an unusual twist when, as a pilot with the Central Experimental and Proving Establishment in Ottawa, he had spent four years flying the CF-100 interceptor on observation missions in support of the U.S. Space Program. These missions had taken him from Cape Canaveral in Florida to Ascension Island off the southwest coast of Africa. The contrast between that high tech assignment and the one he was about to

F/L Gord Brown gives the crowd a close-up view of his Avro 504K while (inset) F/L George Greff demonstrates some aggressive manoeuvring with his machine during another show. (Rae Simpson)

embark upon could not have been more marked.

The real challenge came after he and George Greff had been checked out on the rebuilt machines. It wasn't enough to just get airborne, do a few flypasts in front of the wildly waving crowd and then land in one piece – O.B. wanted them to do aerobatics! And so they did – starting at high altitude and working their way down to show altitude, just as every professional demonstration pilot must do.

Gord Brown recalls that they tried everything they could in the old machine after finally figuring out how to keep it flying. "We used to think it was a really successful flight if the engine kept running and nothing fell off!" Little wonder – six of the first seven takeoffs resulted in forced landings due to engine failures. This gave the Avro technicians (led by

Back at home plate, the technicians assigned to the Avro 504 made final preparations prior to sending their flying history book on tour. (via Bill Johnson)

Sgt George Carpenter) fits as they struggled with engines that hadn't been used in almost 40 years and in the best case were only good for about 25 hours each. The problem was eventually solved by removing the original magnetos and replacing them with more modern, reliable versions.

While the Avro would loop easily enough, albeit with its 110 horsepower *le Rhone* straining all the way, trying to roll the big machine at low altitude was a character-building exercise which had the potential to shorten one's lifespan. Most of these little discoveries were made during winter workups in Victoria. The two intrepid aviators took turns droning around the scenic countryside adjacent to the Pat Bay Airport, a welcome sight to many aviation buffs. Feeling particularly rambunctious one morning, Brown decided it was time to try some inverted flying to determine whether this might be possible in the show: "No sooner did I roll upside down than the engine promptly quit and the aircraft started to skid sideways as I was staring down at the barn on Michell's Farm, a well known landmark on the Saanich Peninsula. I managed to roll upright – fortunately the engine relit and I pressed on." Inverted flight did not become a feature of the Avro 504K show!

One impressive manoeuvre that did become part of the show however, was the "falling

Fired up and ready to go. George Greff and Gord Brown prepare for a little formation practice at CFB Portage on 8 Apr and then leap into the air at St. Hubert on 27 Apr, the day of the opening ceremonies at the Expo 67 site. (via John Veevers, DND REC 67-469)

leaf." This was a combination of incipient spin entries commenced at approximately 1,000 feet above ground to open the 504 segment of the show. The large rudder on the Avro 504K was very effective, so as the nose was raised to stall the aircraft, a combination of rudder reversals just prior to entering a spin would cause the aircraft to swish back and forth as it slowly descended. Combined with the relative silence of the idling engine, this gave the impression of a falling leaf in autumn as it gently fell towards the ground. As Gord Brown recalls, he and Greff would allow one full spin turn at the end of the manoeuvre which climaxed with a mighty roar as spin recovery took place and a burst of power was applied to pull out of the ensuing dive at 300 feet. Considering the age of

The old and the new. Its day's work over, the Avro 504K sits majestically in the setting sun as the Centennaire solos fly past in their mirror pass. Some 36 years elapsed between the retirement of the Avro 504 and introduction of the Canadair Tutor as the RCAF's newest trainer in 1964. (via Bill Johnson)

the two machines, this was sporty stuff! However, it underscored how confident Brown and Greff came to be with both the aircraft and the RCAF technicians who maintained them throughout the tour.

The balance of the eight minute Avro 504K show comprised loops, wingovers and low passes in front of the airshow audience. As Greff and Brown took turns flying the show, the extra aircraft was being positioned by C-130 Hercules at the next showsite. This was no easy task and required a very dedicated groundcrew team who had to remove the two sets of wings from the aircraft in order to fit the aircraft into the Hercules. Forethought during the rebuild process had made this possible and special jigs had been built in which to fit the wings for transport. Although many hours were spent ferrying the Avros around Canada, the end result was that millions of Canadians were introduced to some of the country's early aviation heritage, a noble cause well worth the effort.

In a Class of Their Own – Jake Miller and René Serrao

No sooner had the Avro touched down than one of the team's two commentators, S/L Lloyd Hubbard or F/L Denis Gauthier, would direct the spectators' attention to stage left and two seemingly distant dots on the horizon. It only took a fraction of a second for straining necks to realize that there was a smoky trail attached to the dots – and that they were getting larger quickly, very quickly! Enter the legendary Miller/Serrao team …

F/Ls Jake Miller and René Serrao are responsible for creating a fighter duo that is still regarded in many airshow circles as the finest of its type ever flown. Individually, both the CF-101B Voodoo and CF-104 Starfighter were incredible airshow machines, their distinctive profiles, raw power and howling noise making them an instant hit with North American airshow audiences. Both aircraft could easily break the sound barrier, the 104 having the distinction of being able to fly as fast as Mach 2 – twice the speed of sound. Together, the two aircraft put on an aerobatic show that was simply unforgettable!

Jake Miller was a highly experienced CF-101 pilot employed as the base maintenance test pilot at Chatham, New Brunswick in the fall of 1966 while keeping "combat ready" with 416 All-Weather Fighter Sqn. He had a reputation as an outstanding "stick and rudder" man and was chosen by O.B. Philp to demonstrate his prowess over many other fine candidates. His partner in the Voodoo was F/L Rob McGimpsey, an airborne intercept navigator who subsequently cross-trained to pilot himself. Evidently, he had a good teacher in Miller whom he fondly remembers "as the finest pilot I have ever seen in my life." McGimpsey recalls that the pair of them jumped in a T-33 on November 3rd, 1966 and raced out to Portage (well, sort of) to meet O.B. and find out what he had in mind for a Voodoo show for the Centenaires. Armed with the knowledge that they would have about 10 minutes to demo the big bird, many "air tests" at

Chatham subsequently also became aerobatic training sessions after the test flight phase of the sortie was complete. McGimpsey's logbook reveals that the first of these took place on November 9th but with the busy flying schedule, opportunities for dedicated training were sporadic. However, in March 1967 things got serious as the opening of Expo 67 drew near. Commencing on March 3rd, airshow practices became almost a daily affair. By the end of the month, Jake Miller had his impressive show well in hand when he put on his first official show for the Commander of Air Defence Command, A/V/M Mike Pollard, at CFB North Bay. With blessing in hand, they were off to Portage on April 2nd to join the rest of the Centenaires to fine tune and integrate their respective shows. Once they started the airshow season, the Voodoo team used three aircraft – 17459, 17395 and 17483.

F/L René Serrao had a similar reputation to Jake Miller and in fact was subsequently touted by legendary Lockheed test pilot "Snake" Reaves as the best Starfighter demonstration pilot in the world – this from a pilot who himself had watered many a fighter pilot's eyes with his own F-104 demonstrations. Serrao's talents were well known to Philp, having served under O.B. during a CF-104 tour with 434 Sqn in Zweibrücken. Serrao was back instructing on the machine at 6 Strike/Recce OTU in Cold Lake, Alberta when he was presented the opportunity of a lifetime. In fact, he may well have been a master of his own destiny when he ran into his old boss in the fall of

F/L René Serrao and F/L Jake Miller prepare to start engines alongside the team's eight Tutors. Their high performance co-solo show may well have been the most exciting fighter display ever flown. (via Bill Johnson)

1966. He explains how he got involved with the Centennaires and some of the intricacies and problems associated with high performance aerobatics:

"After the formation of the Centennaires had been announced, I ran into O.B. in Toronto and expressed my keen interest in joining his team as a demo pilot for the CF-104 should he obtain approval from CFHQ to add a fighter element to the show. At the time, I received only a smile as he casually mentioned that he had already thought of someone for the job. 'The Scamp' waited until the end of the year to have W/C Ken Thorneycroft, who was the CO of 6 S/R OTU at Cold Lake, tell me I had been chosen for the job … if I still wanted it! With the offer came authorization to begin designing and working up a 10 minute low-level, fully aerobatic solo display.

I accepted on the spot and immediately went to work designing a display to show off the Starfighter. After about a dozen practice days in-between regular instructional trips, I settled on the following demo routine in a clean-clean (no tip tanks or pylons), single-seat CF-104:

1. A high-speed (Mach .98) knife-edge silhouette pass from left to right along the length of the showline followed by a rapid deceleration (throttle to idle and speed brakes) in a 6 G climbing turn so as to lower manoeuvring flaps at 450 knots. I then applied full throttle and afterburner while executing a 6 G turn reversal back to the showline for:
2. A minimum altitude, classic slow roll at 500 knots with flaps again raised, followed by 6 G vertical pull-up into:
3. A 6 G Cuban-eight with manoeuvring flaps and afterburner. This was followed by another 6 G climbing 90/270 degree turn, descending back to the showline for:
4. A four-point roll (500 knots, flaps up) followed by a 6 G vertical pull-up into:
5. A low-level loop using manoeuvring flaps and afterburner followed by a reversal and:
6. An inverted low-level pass along the entire showline. Reversing, I set up for:
7. A 500 knot, 7.33 G minimum-radius combat turn (360 degrees) decelerating in a second 360 degree turn for:
8. A dirty, slow-speed flypast (undercarriage down, speed brakes out, full

F/L René Serrao rockets past stage centre during his Centennial show. The CF-104's small (21 foot, 11 inch) wingspan is clearly evident in this plan view. (via Glen Miller)

flap, '3' on the automatic pitch control indicator) followed by a full afterburner acceleration into a vertical reverse back for:
9. A high speed (Mach .98) low-level pass with full afterburner climaxing with a 6 G pull-up to:
10. A vertical exit with continuous aileron rolls to the contrail level (hopefully) for a tail slide and spin recovery.

This was the routine I put together for O.B.'s approval which he granted after watching the show just prior to going to Comox in February 1967 for further practice with the Centennaires. I initially had approval to operate from only 10,000 foot runways but as the airshow year progressed, I was able to win approval to operate into many more airfields – down to 6,000 feet which of course always necessitated the use of the drag chute on touchdown in order to stop before the end of the runway.

Throughout my workups and subsequent tour I was well supported by various personnel at Cold Lake including several with the Central Experimental and Proving Establishment Detachment. The assistance

Flying just above the stall, F/L Serrao "wing walks" past the crowd in a slow speed dance. (via Russ Bennett)

started at the top with 100 percent support from my boss, W/C Thorneycroft. The base maintenance aircraft engineering officer was also a great help to me, although he drew the line when I presented him with a set of blueprints to have 744 painted in Golden Centennaire colours! F/L Cuttance was the main engineering coordinator at Cold Lake, assisted from time to time by F/O Donovan, and these two very busy chaps bent over backwards in their support.

Once on the road, I used primarily two 104s for my display, 12744 and 12769, although there were at least half a dozen other tail numbers that appeared as spares during the course of the season. My crewchiefs were Flight Sergeant Hal Richardson who was later relieved by Warrant Officer Lorne McLean. They supervised a team of nine technicians from Cold Lake assigned to the team. During the airshow season, deployed operations were occasionally carried out without the benefit of my support crew when last minute program changes required me to carry out my own flight inspections (daily inspections, before and post-flight inspections, etc).

Repeatedly flying the CF-104 to the edges of the flight envelope in such an aggressive manner did create some maintenance headaches for my crew. The rapid accelerations and decelerations in both airspeed and G of my routine resulted in some 'regular' afterburner shroud failures (cracking) which necessitated the modification and beefing up of the shroud brackets. Early in the practice period, these cracks at times caused overheat and/or fire warnings so I became most proficient in flying precautionary forced landing patterns! (These were flown at 230 knots IAS in the CF-104 until landing was assured). However, once the modifications were approved and carried out, the cracking ceased and my aircraft were trouble-free in the afterburner area while on the actual airshow circuit.

Additional snags experienced during the season included fuel leaks from the auxiliary fuel cell during high-speed, high G manoeuvring, as well as a nagging tendency for my lap belt to inadvertently uncouple in rough air or during aggressive manoeuvring. The groundcrew readily attacked all of these problems on the road as well as handling all of the normal maintenance requirements associated with a high performance fighter. Cpls 'Red' Wishart and Ernie Poitras were

With manoeuvring flaps selected, René Serrao pulls up into a loop – one of very few pilots ever to loop the Starfighter at low-level. In full afterburner, the Orenda-built J-79 developed 15,800 pounds of thrust. (Bill Johnson)

two of my outstanding crewmen who accumulated many hours climbing into fuel tanks to trouble shoot, de-rig and re-rig them with all of the fuel fume hazards, etc. However, the fuel tank problem finally required a dedicated flight test/engineering investigation by CEPE after S/L Suds Sutherland (a very knowledgeable CF-104 engineering officer) insisted that it was a lack of sustainable air pressure at the wing tip vent valves, and not violent air manoeuvring, that was causing the fuel leaks. This phenomena only occurred with the wing tip tanks removed due to the different wing tip vortices that resulted. I subsequently flew the initial test flights at Cold Lake in an instrumented clean CF-104 which showed that as speed and G forces built up, air pressure at the wingtips decreased and was insufficient to keep the wing tip vent valves closed. Thus, "Suds" had been right! A fix was finally designed and installed towards the end of the season – namely a small wing tip fence just outboard of the wing tip vent to prevent pressure depletion. This now meant that the groundcrew had to install and remove the wing tip fences before and after every show as I needed the tip tanks reinstalled for most cross-country transits between shows.

The Dynamic Duo

Our Starfighter team deployed from Cold Lake to Comox to join the remainder of the Centenaires on Thursday, February 16th, the day after Dave Barker was tragically killed while flying with the Tutor team. After adjusting to that shock, we spent the next nine days practicing and integrating our show. Timed passed quickly with the intensity of our practices and February 25th was a sad day – the end of the Comox deployment. It was back to Cold Lake for five weeks for our Starfighter team. I resumed regular instructing at the OTU and continued solo practices until the first week in April when we deployed to Portage. It was here that I met Jake Miller for the first time and saw his 10 minute routine in the Voodoo with Rob McGimpsey in his back seat. I guess our individual 10 minute solo routines were deemed by O.B. and C.B. Lang to be 'stealing the Tutor thunder' because on April 4th Jake and I were instructed/asked to combine our shows into one 10 minute tandem formation routine.

The Starfighter Diary

It is nothing more than a large black notebook, but within the pages of the Starfighter diary kept by F/L René Serrao and his crew during 1967 is a fascinating glimpse into the behind the scenes workings of a dedicated team. The challenges of putting on a safe, professional show are many both in the air and on the ground, day in and day out throughout the airshow season. But behind the spell-binding show are simple human beings who differ from most only in that they truly understand the meaning of motivation … and the penalties associated with failure in their chosen profession. Some selected excerpts from the 1967 diary, amplified with notes from René Serrao:

Saturday, February 18th – Comox. Flew two practice shows (solo) – aircraft good. Fuel pump change.

Sunday, February 19th – Flew two practice shows. Valade found severe crack upper portion of (afterburner) shroud. Commenced change then found feedback cable tension too high – 98 lbs. Decided engine change. Aft section removal and engine change in progress. Cooperation from Comox excellent (equipment and hangar space).

Wednesday, May 10th – Confusion. Change in plans – twice. Show number 6 at Oshawa – 1800 hrs. Aircraft remains serviceable. Richardson – Rochon – Greter – Reception. Everyone very enthusiastic about entire aerobatic team.

Saturday, May 27th – Weather very good. Show number 15 at Bagotville. Swell day for airshow. Hercules with JATO power assist. Old Gold really good. Aircraft serviceable on return. (Cooperation *plus* from Bagotville)

Friday, June 9th – Group picture 1100 hrs, practice 1400 hrs, show number 19 at Cornwall 1830 hrs. Beer Call at Officers' Mess after show – needed stiff drink! *"The Cornwall airshow was flown at an open air park on the St. Lawrence River. A very still,*

The CF-104 Starfighter rolls out as the CF-101 Voodoo continues a second 360 degree turn to set up for a high-speed, head-on pass by the Starfighter. (Jerry Vernon)

That night, while the rest of the troops partied, Jake and I crawled under the table with our rum bottle and designed our 10 minute formation and integrated solo routine – which we were expected to execute the next morning! Jake thought I should lead with the CF-104 and he would tag along with his CF-101. Our first formation effort the next day did not go too well – two areas required immediate change!

During our practice together we learned that the CF-101 could not stay on the CF-104's wing at Mach .95 and 7 G, that the 101 out-accelerated the 104 up to 400 knots but that the 104 then out-accelerated the 101 at and above the 400 knot range. This necessitated that Jake take over leading as it was far easier for me to stay with the Voodoo no matter what Jake did, than he try to keep up with me in the 104 at high speed. The only exception was the takeoff. Formation takeoffs with Jake leading required Rob McGimpsey to monitor me and advise Jake at the first sign of me dropping back in full afterburner. Jake would then reduce power slightly or even crack his speed brakes momentarily using Rob's commentary to allow me to stay with him. In effect, we were sort of flying formation on each other.

The second item we eventually changed in our show was a formation pass with both of us

inverted – we both lacked practice at this delicate manoeuvre and it proved to be 'a bit too close for comfort and long life' a couple of times. We just dropped it from the routine, but did sneak it back in a few times later in the year.

By the end of our Portage deployment, the CF-104/CF-101 Tandem Formation routine consisted of:

1. High-speed, close line-astern entry from left to right at Mach .98 and minimum altitude. Simultaneous afterburner selection in front of the crowd as both aircraft rolled into a 6½ G, 360 degree left turn in line-astern. Starfighter split off at the end of the 360 degree turn in front of the crowd.
2. Voodoo continued with a second 360 degree turn, decelerating to a slow-speed dirty flypast left to right as the Starfighter did a 90 degree right, 270 degree left reversal to return back for a head-on pass at Mach .98 as the Voodoo slowly flew by the crowd just above the stall.
3. Starfighter decelerating 360 degree turn to exit left for a deadside (behind the crowd) racetrack.
4. Voodoo slow roll left to right to a deadside racetrack pattern.
5. Starfighter multiple rapid rolls from right to left to a deadside racetrack.

Miller and Serrao made this inverted formation pass look easy, but the manoeuvre was initially thrown out due to its difficulty – a true measure of professionalism. After much practice, the manoeuvre was displayed publicly for the first time at Abbotsford on 13 Aug 67. (Jerry Vernon)

F/L Jake Miller slowly rolls his big Voodoo upside-down for his inverted pass in front of the Abbotsford crowd in August 1967. (Bill Johnson)

6. Voodoo inverted pass left to right to a deadside racetrack.

7. Starfighter entered right to left for a low-level loop (500 knots, full afterburner, 6 G) followed by a dumbbell turn in full afterburner.

8. Voodoo slow-speed dirty pass left to right with Starfighter high-speed overtake at stage centre at Mach .98 pulling up into dumbbell turn.

9. Voodoo accelerated and cleaned up while pulling up into a 6 G Cuban-eight. Voodoo exited right into a racetrack pattern behind the crowd.

10. Starfighter four-point roll right to left followed by a vertical reverse to rapid rejoin with the Voodoo stage left into close line-astern.

11. Tandem formation roll from left to right exiting into a 270 degree left turn to run in head-on to the crowd at stage center.

12. Full afterburner line-astern pull-up into the vertical with a rolling exit to end our part of the show.

humid, grey hazy day with no horizon made me say to myself, as I started up into my loop – 'Look René, you've had a rough time picking up Jake on the head-on passes in this murk, give yourself a bit of extra height in this loop.' This I did – up I went an extra 500 feet over the top. As I got past the vertical on the way back down the backside of the loop, having 'allowed' for the extra height I had to lose, the world very rapidly began getting too close as my speed hit 500 knots. I pulled back hard on the stick, deep into stick shaker and as close to 4.5 on the APC as I dared. As I recall, the G meter was in the +9 range and Denis Gauthier froze in his commentary on the ground. I came as close to terra firma as I ever want to come in a low-level loop. Denis later said my tailpipe was only a couple of feet from the river surface as I pulled out. I saw the rooster tail off the river in the rear view mirrors.

That extra 500 foot zoom almost ended a great flying career. Had I executed this loop the same way I had done time and time before, I am sure this close call would not have happened. I include this episode for all future low-level loopers – Stay with your proven and well practiced routine! Make sure you can duplicate it in all conditions and stick with it. Don't go trying to learn a new pattern on a day you don't have good visual clues to help you through a strange pattern! (recommend quadruple rum and coke to calm nerves after such an experience.)"

Saturday, June 10th – Show number 20 at Rockcliffe (1645 hrs) for Canadian Armed Forces Day – Good Show.

Monday, July 10th – Accommodation very good, but crowded – four to a room! (Gimli, Manitoba)

Friday, August 11th - Sunday, August 13th – Shows 44 to 46 at Abbotsford Airport, 1700 hrs.

Saturday, September 2nd - Sunday, September 3rd – Shows 52 and 53 at Canadian National Exhibition. Weather hot and sunny.

Thursday, September 14th – Show number 59 scheduled at Kirkland Lake – 1830 hrs. *"It was at these Northern Ontario shows that the CF-104 LN3 inertial navigation saved the day. The smog at Kirkland Lake showsite was like pea soup, yet we were able to operate out of North Bay – find the showsite without delay, start our show right on time, to the second, and return to base without running out of fuel."*

Friday, October 20th – Show number 78 at Val d'Or – 1230 hrs. Tip tank and vent valve mod installed for show. Aircraft serviceable on return – tip tank and vent valve mod removed. Very enthusiastic crowd watched a very impressive show - especially the 104. *"Following my split from Jake after our initial 360 degree entry manoeuvre, while I was doing*

In retirement René Serrao took up sketching. He penned this tribute to honour the memory of Jake Miller who passed away in August 2000. (René Serrao)

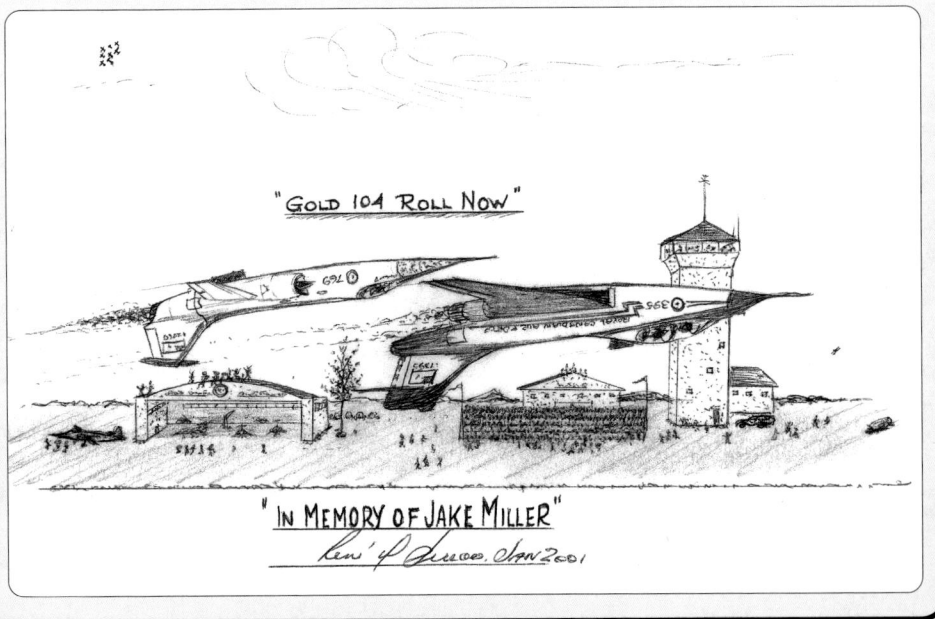

"GOLD 104 ROLL NOW"

"IN MEMORY OF JAKE MILLER"

F/L Jake Miller shows off the bottom of his Voodoo at Abbotsford '67. (Bill Johnson)

my reversal to set up for our head-on pass, Jake called me to slow up my turn as he was having a bit of after-burner trouble and had to slow up his turn rate. So I slacked up the Gs in my turn. The next thing I realized I was supersonic and watched the Val d'Or Hospital go zipping by below. The CO of CFB Val d'Or did not appreciate having a big bill for broken windows!"

Sunday, October 29th – Final Show – total airshows for the year – 82. Both 104 and 101 crews disappointed that States' shows cancelled for the CF-104 and CF-101. Excellent pass over station by 104 and 101 on return from show. Should have had a good bash tonight with 101 crew because all plans for tomorrow went astray. *"The Hercules support flight arrived a day early and I had to forego the celebration and fly home to Cold Lake on Monday so the support crew could pack up and board the Herc."*

Monday, October 30th – St. Hubert – 1000hrs – Final thanks and farewell from W/C O.B. Philp. F/L Serrao departed for Cold Lake at 1400 hrs. Beautiful pass over station. Crew departed for Cold Lake at 1610 hrs … All over except the memories … *"I finally arrived home in Cold Lake in the wee hours of Tuesday morning, October 31st, after the long flight from St. Hubert. Finally got into my own bed at home and slept the clock around to Wednesday. I guess the body finally said 'I need a rest.' It was a great year.*

A few weeks later, both Jake Miller and I attended the Centennaires' tour of American airshows at Cannon AFB, New Mexico and Nellis AFB in Las Vegas, Nevada (though we were not authorized to fly airshows). C.B. Lang led his team through their best performances of the year at both Cannon and Las Vegas."

Saturday, November 18th – The sad news of disbanding the Centennaires was announced at Las Vegas after the last performance.

When we were finally ready to hit the road for the Centennial celebration everyone met in St. Hubert. However, things got off to a shaky start with our accommodation. On April 25th, the day after our arrival, the team had to play 'musical motel' after O.B. got his 'backside' scalded from steaming hot water in his toilet. The entire motel (hastily built for Expo 67) was wired and plumbed wrong – nothing worked! Frantic last minute motel changes took place … and O.B. had a sore rear-end for a few days!!

On Thursday, April 27th, official opening ceremonies took place at Expo and we participated with a team flypast (less the Avro 504K) at 1600 hrs (4:00 p.m.). C.B. Lang led the Tutor team over the Expo site with Jack Waters close behind in line-astern in his Red Knight T-33, Jake and I on either wing. Just

A month in the life of the great Miller/McGimpsey Voodoo team as recorded in Jake Miller's meticulous logbook. With partner René Serrao flying the Starfighter, they put on 17 official shows in the month of August alone. (via Glen Miller)

YEAR 1967		AIRCRAFT		PILOT, OR 1ST PILOT	2ND PILOT, PUPIL OR PASSENGER	DUTY (INCLUDING RESULTS AND REMARKS)	SINGLE-ENGINE AIRCRAFT				MULTI-EN		
							DAY		NIGHT		DAY		
MONTH	DATE	Type	No.				DUAL (1)	PILOT (2)	DUAL (3)	PILOT (4)	DUAL (5)	1ST PILOT (6)	2ND PILOT (7)
—	—	—	—	—	GOLDEN	CENTENNAIRES					TOUR	1967	
						TOTALS BROUGHT FORWARD							
AUG	2	CF-101B	395	SELF	F/L GAUTHIER	#39 MEDICINE HAT Co-104						1:00	
"	3	"	"	"	"	YC-ED 104						:35	
"	5	"	"	"	F/L McGIMPSEY	SOLO PRACTICE						:30	
"	5	"	"	"	"	#40 NAMAO Co-104						:30	
"	6	"	"	"	"	ED-XE 104						:45	
"	6	"	"	"	"	#41 SASKATOON Co-104						:20	
"	7	"	"	"	"	XE-YC 104						:45	
"	7	"	"	"	"	#42 RED DEER Co-104						:45	
"	9	"	"	"	"	YC-ABBOTSFORD 104						1:00	
"	10	"	"	"	"	#43 KELOWNA Co-104						:55	
"	11	"	"	"	"	#44 ABBOTSFORD Co-104						:40	
"	12	"	"	"	"	#45 " " "						:40	
"	13	"	"	"	"	#46 " " "				— RCVR VR —		:55	
"	15	T-33	490	"	"	VR-QQ-VR					:30		
"	16	CF-101B	395	"	"	#47 COMOX-RCVR - Co-104						:40	
"	17	"	"	"	"	QQ-VR 104						:30	
"	18	"	"	"	"	#48 NANAIMO Co-104						:50	
"	19	"	"	"	"	#49 SIDNEY Co-104						:40	
"	19	"	"	"	"	#50 VICTORIA Co-104					REPLACES PORT ALBERNI DUE TO FOREST FIRE	:45	
"	23	"	"	"	"	#51 KAMLOOPS Co-104						1:00	
"	25	"	"	"	"	#52 PNE Co-104						:40	
"	25	"	"	"	"	#53 " Co-104						:40	
"	26	"	"	"	"	#54 " Co-104						:40	
"	26	CF-101B	395	SELF	F/L McGIMPSEY	#55 PNE Co-104						:40	
"	27	"	"	"	"	VR-OD					395 GOES U/S IN OD AFTER 48 CONSECUTIVE TRIPS	1:05	
"	29	T-33	490	"	"	ZD-CH			1:35				
"	30	"	"	"	"	CH-ZD			2:00				
		TOTALS											
		T-33	1334/45										
		CF-101	1304/45										
		CF-100	694/50										
		F-86	10/15										
		JET	3338/20										

certified correct by
Commanding Officer
GOLDEN CENTENNAIRES

SUMMARY FOR: AUG 1967
Golden Centennaires
DATE: 30 AUG 67
SIGNATURE:

The most famous Miller/Serrao shot of them all – the tandem roll captured by Bill Johnson at Abbotsford in 1967. (Bill Johnson)

after we passed over the VIP dais at the opening ceremony, C.B. Lang pulled his Tutors up into a 'Prince of Wales' feather. Two seconds later, Jack Waters pulled up into a steep climb and called 'burners now' at which time Jake and I plugged in our afterburners and accelerated straight up into the vertical as the Red Knight followed with his smoking climb and steep wingover. Expo was officially open!

The next morning we did a practice at St. Hubert followed by our first official show at Expo that afternoon, Friday, April 28th when the gates opened to the world. Over the course of the summer there were many adventures with Jake and I opening many of the major shows across Canada, doing so 82 times. The Litton LN3 inertial navigation system in the CF-104 was a great help in getting to and from remote showsites and finding them in a timely fashion. Though Jake led the formation with Rob helping navigate from his back seat, we made full use of the 104's navigation system throughout the year, especially in marginal weather. Not once did Jake and I miss our

'on stage time' by more than plus or minus five seconds. We would probably have not been able to maintain this record without the LN3 system, especially at airshows that were far from home bases. Our 10 minute show normally followed the Avro 504K show by George Greff or Gord Brown and preceded the team's Tutor display.

For our part, many believe Jake Miller and I wrote history with our CF-101/CF-104 tandem formation routine during Centennial year. We demonstrated that a coordinated airshow with very dissimilar high performance aircraft was both feasible and most effective. I am proud to have done so with such a high calibre pilot as Jake Miller."

René Serrao

One airshow aficionado who recorded his impressions of the show was aviation author and photographer extraordinaire, Bill Johnson, later destined to become the Snowbirds' first official photographer. In his book *Airshow* published in 1971, he charac-

terized Serrao's show as one which "was flown with as much *verve and élan* as the law allows." And as for the routine with Jake Miller, Johnson recorded these sentiments:

"The Voodoo flown by F/L Jake Miller with navigator Rob McGimpsey aboard (what a ride that must have been!) and the Starfighter with F/L René Serrao, flew at, over and around each other for several deafening minutes and then joined in an absolutely gorgeous tandem roll. To see the howling Starfighter tucked in under the stabilizer of the big Voodoo for this vigorous *pas de deux* was a once in a lifetime experience."

Bill Johnson

Not only was Bill Johnson correct, he got the photos to prove it! And even though over three decades have passed since Jake Miller and René Serrao left airshow fans smiling in awe, the visions of the Voodoo and Starfighter tearing up the sky just below the speed of sound still linger on.

The Golden Centennaires Tutor Show

Within a minute or so of the Voodoo and Starfighter's drag chutes deploying after touching down from their show, the audience's attention was again directed to stage centre – they hardly had a chance to catch their breath before they were confronted by eight aircraft swooping in directly at them, landing lights on. This was the grand finale to the Golden Centennaires show – S/L C.B. Lang's Tutor team. As they smoked on and pulled up into the vertical on their opening manoeuvre, airshow fans across the country got their first plan view of the largest formation aerobatic team that had ever been formed outside of western Europe.

In spite of the pre-season losses of Tom Bebb and Dave Barker which ultimately reduced the Centennaires Tutor show from nine to eight aircraft, the show that went on the road in late April 1967 was a model of grace and precision. Collectively, the team had put in hundreds of hours of practice, refining the routine "right up until we went on the road" as Russ Bennett recalls. With the exception of only one pilot, all of the team members had flown the F-86 Sabre operationally in Europe with the RCAF's No. 1 Air Division. More importantly, several members of the team had significant airshow experience – C.B. Lang and Dave Barker as slot pilot and opposing solo respectively with the Golden Hawks, Russ Bennett as leader of the Gimli Smokers and Bill Slaughter as the Red Knight.

Naturally, C.B. Lang and Dave Barker had used the Golden Hawks show as a foundation upon which to build the Centennaires show in the early stages of the team work-ups in Portage. However, although the Hawks had planned a fully integrated seven-plane show prior to their disbandment in 1964, Canadians were most familiar with the four-plane diamond and two (latterly three) solos that comprised their routine. Now they were treated to eight aircraft twisting and turning as one before the two solos split off leaving a basic formation of six Tutors.

Technically, the Centennaires show was complex with some of the most intricate formation changes during aerobatics ever flown anywhere. It was the formation changes during multiple loops and rolls that were the most challenging to master. A case in point was the eight-plane "double loop" manoeu-

Three views of the eight Golden Centennaire Tutors during their opening sequence – sweeping in to commence their show, the pull-up into their first loop and the bottomside silhouette from right to left. (Top, Jerry Vernon, below via Russ Bennett).

The six-plane Line Abreast loop was one of many picturesque manoeuvres flown by the Centennaires. Since the pilots had to use an overall sight picture to judge their position relative to the next aircraft, this manoeuvre was very challenging, particularly in turbulence. (via Glen Miller)

Slot man Russ Bennett splits away from leader C.B. Lang to complete a cloverleaf followed by the dynamic six-plane opposing cross at stage centre. (via John Veevers)

S/L C.B. Lang prepares to pull up his Double Delta formation for a roll. (via John Veevers)

vre in which the two solos split off from the main formation. The third manoeuvre of the show, it started from stage left as S/L Lang pulled the team up in diamond formation using 3½ to 4 G. As the vertical was reached he called for "tee formation" which required the inner and outer wingmen and two solos at the back to apply full power and move up into a line-abreast formation off of the leader and number 4 respectively. The team maintained this formation over the top and then down the back side and straight into another loop. This time at the vertical however, when Lang called "double abreast go" (also known as card six), the two solos eased out of the formation and once clear Bill Slaughter pushed and Jim McKay pulled to establish separation from each other. Meanwhile, the

main formation, now in double abreast, completed their second loop low to the ground, entered a high wingover and came back in for a formation roll, changing from double abreast to wedge formation during the roll.

As the formation triggered their smoke off from that manoeuvre, the two solos had already rolled upside down from 3,000 feet and pulled through at opposite ends of the field to set up for their first of many exciting "head-on" manoeuvres. The tension among the audience was palpable as heads swivelled to watch the two aircraft approach and then flash past each other in a heartbeat. The aerial ballet then continued as the main formation and two solos alternated manoeuvres at centre stage, in turn filling the sky with trails

of red, white and blue smoke. The entire Centennaires show lasted approximately 30 minutes and looked like this:

1. Formation takeoff (eight-plane, wind permitting) to warm-up during the Miller/Serrao show
2. Diamond entrance loop head-on to crowd to downward cloverleaf to bottomside silhouette (right to left)
3. Diamond roll (eight aircraft, left to right)
4. Double loop (eight-plane diamond to tee to solo split to double abreast)
5. Double abreast to wedge roll (six aircraft)
6. Solos half-roll-and-pull-through to opposing Cuban-eights

The Golden Centennaires were the first team in the world to take off and land eight aircraft all at once in close formation. Once airborne, they put on a clinic of precision flight. (top photo via John Veevers, all others by Bill Johnson)

7. Wedge to double delta loop
8. Solos opposing level roll
9. Double delta to wedge roll
10. Solos opposing co-loop
11. Wedge to double delta loop
12. Solos opposing four-point roll
13. Double delta to card 6 roll
14. Solos co-360 opposing turns
15. Card 6 to six-plane line abreast loop
16. Solos opposing "outside" Cuban-eights
17. Line abreast roll (five aircraft)
18. Solos inside-outside mirror 360 (with lead solo inverted)
19. Line abreast to double vic loop (six aircraft)
20. Solos flip-flop
21. Formation double vic split (six aircraft) to opposing cross-over
22. Solo "inside-outside" vertical eight
23. Double bomb burst (upward-downward) and solo vertical rolls
24. Rejoin to eight-ship low-level break and landing

The solo show by F/L Bill Slaughter and F/O Jim McKay featured all of the head-on crosses the Golden Hawks had made famous, plus some. The relatively slow speed of the Tutor in relation to the Sabre meant that loops were tighter and therefore much lower over the top than those of the Sabre. However, the biggest difference was in the use of negative G in the solo show. Jim McKay's "inside-outside" vertical eight, for example, was unique among military jet teams worldwide – no other jet team had ever performed this manoeuvre before, or since. Yet, with careful practice over several months, McKay "perfected it to a tee" according to Bill Slaughter, in spite of the excruciating "plus 7 and minus 4" his G meter often registered by the time his smoke was triggered off out the bottom of the second loop. These solo manoeuvres provided a strong testament to the strength and durability of the Canadair Tutor.

Inverted flight had been Dave Barker's specialty and his untimely death on February 15th

For most airshow fans, the "heart stopping" part of the show is provided courtesy of solo aerobatic pilots whose primary mission is to demonstrate the maximum capability of man and machine, all the while ensuring that safety is never compromised. Bill Johnson captured the drama of the solo routine with these Abbotsford shots in the summer of '67. Top, F/O Jim McKay (left) flashes past lead solo Bill Slaughter (right) in a very close cross on the backside of the dynamic co-360. During the manoeuvre the two solos crossed each other three times. Pictured below is the final cross in front of the crowd. (Bill Johnson)

necessitated some significant adjustments, as Bill Slaughter explains:

"On February 19th, Jim and I went to work and started putting together our co-solo routine. This proved relatively easy to do since Jim was an exceptional pilot and was already familiar with the manoeuvres. He therefore moved into the opposing solo position with no difficulty at all. I flew from the left seat as Gold 7 and did all of my head-on rolls to the left – Jimmy flew from the right seat as Gold 8 and did his rolls to the right.

For me, taking over as lead solo included performing the daunting outside 360 degree turn which I approached with some trepidation. Only through many repetitions did I learn that at minus 3.5 G (or so), one had to resist the natural instinct to tense up for the manoeuvre and instead learn to hang fully relaxed in the straps while upside-down. Otherwise, the effects of the negative G were compounded. As Jim did the formidable inside-outside vertical eight, he and I (as had Dave), wore a pad across our thighs and under the lap belt straps to prevent the inevitable bruises and welts.

During our formation part of the show, we flew at the back of the eight-plane either side of number 4, slot man Russ Bennett – I on the right and Jim on the left. This was also our position in the eight-plane takeoff and landing. When we took off, landed or flew as two four-planes, I led the second section with Bob Dagenais on the left wing, B.K. Doyle on the right and Jimmy in the slot. For the double bomb burst at the end of the show, I flew slot in the lead (upwards) section and pushed out of the formation on the split call from C.B. Lang. I recall some really close splits with Russ' three-ship coming down at us from above. Once the seven aircraft had split, Jimmy did vertical rolls up through the smoke and the show was over."

Bill Slaughter

While the team was turning the summer sky into ribbons of coloured smoke during Centennial year, the tandem of Lloyd Hubbard and Denis Gauthier were providing informative commentary over the public address system (and frequently local radio stations). A gifted commentator can often turn a good show into a great one, using tone and inflection to variously describe the show manoeuvres, aircraft technical infor-

Two contrasting views of the front cross of the co-360. As lead solo, Bill Slaughter's job was to set the staging and timing of the manoeuvre and make the radio transmission calls. Jim McKay's job was straight forward – make the cross without hitting the boss! (via Bill Slaughter, Jerry Vernon)

Below, the inside-outside 360. Bill Slaughter rolls upside-down and then pushes all the way around the turn while hanging in his straps. Negative G can be very uncomfortable – flying an aircraft accurately under such conditions demands a great deal of practice and discipline. (via John Veevers)

The Centennaires used two flashy T-33s for logistic support and transport, one flown by W/C Philp, the other by S/L Hubbard. (Larry Milberry)

mation and backgrounds of the team members. Gauthier demonstrated a flair for commentating and ended up doing the lion's share of the commentary as a result. This allowed Hubbard to concentrate on the organization and logistics of the many public relations appearances made by the team over the course of the season.

By the time the Centennaires show had ended, spectators had seen a world-class performance which landed the team on the front page of newspapers everywhere they performed. However, after taxiing in and shutting down the job was not over – autograph sessions were an essential element of the team's public relations mandate, whether along the fence immediately following the performance or during additional visits to hospitals or schools in the spring and fall. As for the groundcrew, the shutting down of the team's aircraft simply signalled the start of the second half of their work day!

The Groundcrew

The Centennaires employed a 42 man technical team from Portage to keep the team's Tutors and Avro 504s in prime condition, most of whom deployed with the team across the country during the Centennial tour. They were joined by additional specialized crews from Chatham and Cold Lake for the CF-101 and CF-104 respectively. Three more crewmen saw service with the Red Knight over the summer of '67.

Commanding the groundcrew operation was F/L Charlie Grant, a 25 year veteran of the RCAF who had worked his way up through the ranks and received his commission as an engineering officer in 1962. He had seen service at 4 Wing Baden-Soellingen in that capacity and had joined the team from his most recent tour in Cold Lake. His two senior supervisors, to whom a great deal of responsibility was delegated, were Flight Sergeants J.M. Gibson and N.L. Hayward.

Throughout the season as the team moved across the country, eight crewmen took turns flying with the team pilots from showsite to showsite, a definite benefit of the side-by-side seating in the Tutor. The balance of the groundcrew team were transported via C-130 Hercules courtesy of a host of crews from 426 and 435 Transport Sqns based at Trenton and Namao (Edmonton) respectively. The vital role these support teams played in the success of the Golden Centennaires was largely invisible to the general public, but without their dedication there would simply have been no show.

Days for the groundcrew were very long due to the requirements associated with routine maintenance and snag rectification. Combine this with the constant travelling over almost six months and it is a wonder that anyone looks back at the experience with anything other than contempt. Yet for most of the groundcrew, the tour represented the finest year of their air force careers, a sentiment

Ground support is vital to every aerobatic team, whether provided by dedicated team technicians or, as in this case, logistic support courtesy Air Transport Command. The C-130 Hercules was used to transport technicians and spare parts to every showsite in the summer of 1967. At remote locations it was also used to refuel the Centennaire Tutors. (RCAF photo via John Veevers)

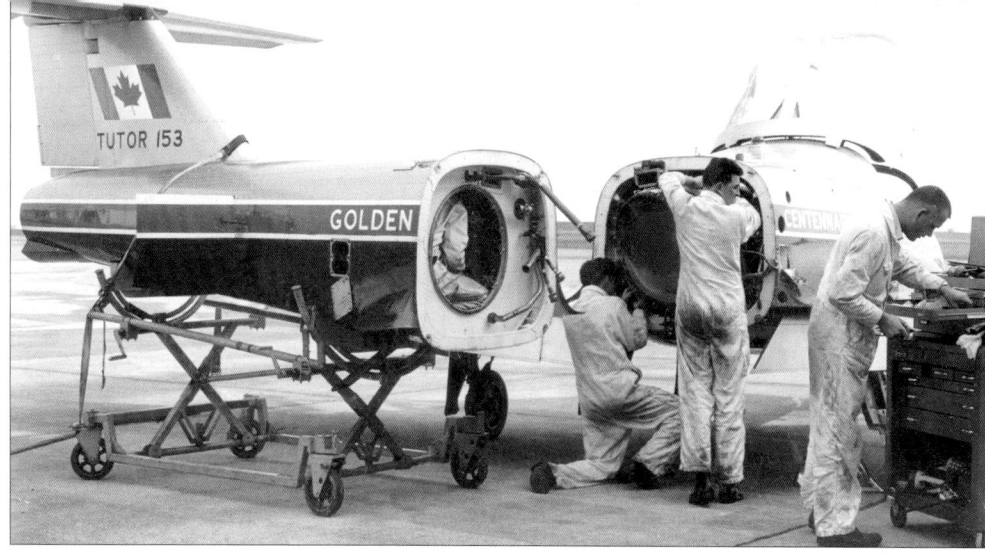

There was no such thing as regular working hours when it came to engine changes on the road. (RCAF photo via Keith Johnson)

Four of the nine CF-104 Starfighter technicians from CFB Cold Lake prepare René Serrao's aircraft for another show. (RCAF photo via René Serrao)

echoed by Corporal Keith Johnson who was an instrument/electrical technician doing "acceptance checks" on the Tutor in Gimli when he was selected to join the team in July of 1966. He was one of the select few technicians who had the opportunity to travel in the Tutor from showsite to showsite for part of the season, a welcome relief from the boring flights crammed inside a Hercules. Between

the two aircraft, Johnson logged over 118 hours in the air transiting from show to show with his colleagues during 1967, earning $511 per month for his efforts plus $6.50 a day for meals while he was "on the road."

For every member of the groundcrew team there are many anecdotes – special memories that have survived the passage of time. Two

stick out in Keith Johnson's mind. There is the humorous recollection from a mid-June cross-country flight of the Centennaires eight Tutors from Chatham, New Brunswick to

Jake Miller and the dedicated team from Chatham that kept his Voodoo flying through a gruelling airshow season. (DND CAT 67-99)

The Avro 504K techs assigned to the Golden Centennaires. L to R, Cpl Trimm, Sgt Carpenter, Cpl Chermishnok, Cpl Doherty, Cpl Brooks, Cpl Ewing. Kneeling is F/L George Greff. (DND 67-14)

As one of the two senior NCO supervisors attached to the Tutor technical team, Flight Sergeant Jerry Gibson accepts a presentation on behalf of the groundcrew. (RCAF photo via John Veevers)

Stephenville, Newfoundland when, after the fact, the crewmen discovered they had "all been flying the aircraft at the same time!" Over the course of the summer some of them got to be pretty good on the controls – a sidelight of the great adventure. Then there was that unforgettable low-level trip from Kelowna to Abbotsford on August 11th riding side-saddle with Jim McKay. It was a glorious flight through the Rockies as the golden Tutors in trail formation weaved their way through some of Canada's most spectacular scenery, topped only by the thrill of "looking up at the cars" on the last part of the journey through the Fraser Canyon, past Hell's Gate and Hope and on to the eagerly waiting welcome committee at Abbotsford … For those crewmen who weren't able to escape the rigours of travel in the back of the Herc, their memories and satisfaction derived from the pride associated with being part of an unforgettable team that was truly appreciated by the people of Canada in 1967.

Reflections of a Commander

That the Centennaires had strong public support was evidenced by the widespread publicity the team enjoyed as it crossed Canada back and forth over the summer. Many communities experienced the largest traffic jams in their history as citizens thronged to showsites to see Canada's new aerobatic team, scenes reminiscent of earlier airshow years. To truly appreciate the spectacle however, one had to be in close touch with the team on a day-to-day basis to see the magnitude of the reaction firsthand. The one person in the best position to take it all in was the commander of the team himself, O.B. Philp. He concludes the story of the Centennaires by reflecting back on his experience:

"From the time I was named to command the unit until we started on the road, I was completely engrossed in the job, enjoying the challenge of organization, training and creating. I was determined that come hell or high water, this flying circus would be first-class. We achieved our goal because right from the start, all Commands gave us excellent support. Orders had been given in true RCAF style – clear and concise. The unit was to be formed, organized, trained, perform during 1967 and disband by December 15th of that year.

Initially I did not think beyond this disbandment date or consider any future for the team, but as the tour progressed, I became

The Centennaires were in high demand for photographs wherever they appeared, seen here posing with a local beauty queen in the spring of 1967. Note the CF-104 ejection seat spurs worn by René Serrao.(via Bill Slaughter)

more aware of its significance. Day after day it seeped into my mind that the RCAF, by showing its colours, was sending a message to the people – Canadians in all walks of life. At every show we stirred up memories of the Golden Hawks and reminded the public that we produced some of the finest pilots in the world.

I made a point of walking up and down each showline, talking to the spectators, many of whom could not understand why the Hawks had been disbanded. At accompanying social events, many strangers expressed appreciation for 'their' aerobatic team. It was apparent the Centennaires had been accepted as a national identity, just as the RCMP Musical Ride had been over the years.

I also talked with recruiting units and I found that after each performance there were many

F/O Jim McKay brightens up a youngster's day during a hospital visit by the team. (via Russ Bennett)

Radio announcer Jack Turnbull interviews George Greff and Gord Brown, both dressed in period garb, prior to a demonstration by Brown in the Avro 504K. (via Bill Slaughter)

more inquiries about the possibility of joining the military for air and ground duties. Then there were the letters – hundreds of them – not simply complimentary but urging and hoping the team would continue on a permanent basis. The clear message was: 'Don't let the Centennaires follow the fate of the Hawks!'

Towards the end of the summer I decided to make a pitch to keep the unit in existence, convinced it had not only succeeded in doing a good PR job but had also instilled a sense of pride in so many Canadians. I forwarded a submission to Ottawa. The week before we performed our last Canadian show, closing Expo on October 27th, I was advised the request was being actively reviewed. It is not common knowledge that it almost succeeded!

Flying the flag. Many Canadians wanted the Centennaires to continue to represent the country beyond 1967. It was not to be … (courtesy CNE Toronto Archives)

The Golden Centennaires were a big hit south of the border and were welcomed in style, as evidenced by this shot taken in sunny Texas in November 1967. (via Bill Johnson)

At the same time, I received my new posting to Cold Lake, Alberta to command another new unit for operational training on CF-5 fighter aircraft which were about to be introduced into service. Personnel at headquarters were so confident the Centennaires would continue to exist, that my replacement had been selected. W/C Bud Lawrence, who was attending Staff College in the U.K., would take over the team. Naturally, hopes were high among C.B. Lang and the team that they might be able to continue for at least another year.

Heading South to the USA

The tour was drawing to a close, but because we had received such great press, there was a surprise in store. We were invited to the United States to perform at seven locations with our Tutor team plus another two at Freeport in the Bahamas. The final show would be at Nellis Air Force Base, Las Vegas, Nevada, home of the USAF Thunderbirds. The decision whether to accept or not was left up to me. We had been on the road without a break for six months and were tired, with short tempers just beginning to show.

I put it to the team and found that both pilots and groundcrew were enthusiastic about going south to display their level of competency, of which they were justifiably proud. Since the adrenalin was still flowing, I made my decision. I thought, 'What the hell, it's a good way to finish off the celebration!' We headed south …

On October 31st, 1967 we left Montreal, arriving at Maxwell AFB, Montgomery, Alabama, for a show on November 2nd. The following day we flew to Florida for a show

at Kissimmee on November 5th, McCoy AFB on November 8th and Holmstead AFB on November 9th. The next day we transited to Freeport in the Bahamas, a short hop, to put on two shows November 11th and 12th. On November 13th we departed for Randolph AFB in Texas for a show on the 14th. Next day it was off to Cannon AFB for a show on the 16th and then to Nellis for the last show which was flown on November 18th.

The team was treated royally at all stops en route. It seemed that people had heard about the Golden Centennaires and wanted to see these upstarts from Canada. If there was one highlight during these final shows, it had to be Freeport. The number of Canadians living there went out of their way to make us welcome. It was a good decision to make this mini-tour south of the border – it put the icing on the cake leaving good memories for all members of the unit.

The End of the Line

While at Nellis for the final performance of the year, I received a telephone call, followed by a telex message, which read as follows:

The caption on this US Army photograph reads "Never before and never again." It was taken on the ramp of Nellis AFB in Las Vegas, Nevada on 18 Nov 67 to commemorate the gathering of some of the world's finest aerobatic teams and performers. In front are the British Parachute Free Fall Team, the Red Devils, and the US Army Parachute Team, the Golden Knights. The centre row fea-

GOLDEN CENTENNAIRES. DUE TO CURRENT BUDGET RESTRICTIONS THE MINISTER OF NATIONAL DEFENCE HAS RELUCTANTLY REVERSED THE EARLIER DECISION AND ORDERED THE DISBANDMENT OF THE GOLDEN CENTENNAIRES AEROBATIC TEAM FOLLOWING COMPLETION OF THIS YEAR'S TOUR.

I accepted this crushing news with deep regret, but kept it to myself until the team was airborne. Nothing like this should handicap the concentration demanded for their final aerial display. S/L Hubbard made the announcement during his commentary. The team received the news on landing. We were scheduled to depart for home the next day but under the circumstances and by popular request from the team, we decided to stay an additional day in Las Vegas.

Needless to say we had one hell of a party with our American friends from both the Blue Angels and the Thunderbirds and later amongst ourselves at our hotel. I do not remember all the details about that night except I ended up playing roulette and winning $2,700. It was a good thing I had won since several of the boys had lost; with my winnings I was able to bankroll the losers. We sadly made our way back to Portage la Prairie.

Although it had been an eventful and very satisfactory year, everyone involved, from the various headquarters to air and ground members, was deeply disappointed with the decision to disband. It seemed that we were the only ones who appreciated how the five million Canadians felt who had seen the team perform. I could only hope there might be another opportunity to start up again. At that time it appeared impossible, but barely 18 months later, by pure chance, fate provided the means.

As I reflected on the past year I realized that we had become a very close-knit group. Collectively the aircrew and groundcrew had moulded together, in a matter of months, a unit to which they were all completely dedicated. It was a gratifying thought, but what kind of men were these who volunteered for this type of duty, which required a high degree of skill, strict attention to detail under constant pressure and tremendous self-discipline?

Their tour required absence from wives and families for long periods, always in front of the public, for flying was only part of the job. A good deal of time was taken up with social commitments which required a further sense of showmanship. If only the public could understand these men who loved life and the opportunity to fly – who considered membership in an aerobatic team, such as we had created, the highest achievement in their professional careers!

There had been many set-backs and disappointments, the worst being the tragedies of losing Tom Bebb and Dave Barker in training. We might have faltered but the team members continued, devoted to the task and met their commitments undaunted. I remember thinking at the start, there might be some initial stage fright, but not from these men. They started out as excellent performers and steadily improved. It had been a long, hard and exhausting schedule that demanded 100 percent from both men and equipment – and both had produced.

Every team must have a leader and in C.B. Lang we had a great one. Granted he could not see very well without his prescription glasses which he always took off before leaving the aircraft, but he had the confidence of the team and was precise and faultless in the air. Back on the ground however, he appeared to have great difficulty parking the formation as he had been briefed. It was a standard comment among the groundcrew: 'I wonder where he is going to put them today?' they would say with affectionate grins. It took me a while to realize that although C.B. had made a couple of mistakes, he was playing a game with us and 'goofing up' on purpose. He was in fact a perfectionist who richly deserved all the tributes that came his way for excellent leadership.

I thought of Gord Brown and George Greff dressed like old-time barnstormers, scarfs flying over their shoulders as they demonstrated the antique Avros and how they developed delightfully clear complexions. This was caused by the oil thrown back into the open cockpit by the *le Rhone* engines. Yes, it was pure castor oil!

It reminded me of the time in Gander, Newfoundland when late one evening, at a cocktail party, I was told the old kite would

tures the USAF Thunderbirds, legendary American performers Bob Hoover, Bill Fornoff and Dick Schram and the US Navy Blue Angels. In the rear is the entire complement of Golden Centennaires aircrew, one of the few photos ever taken with the entire group together. (SFC Joe Gonzales, US Army via Maeve Philp)

A fitting tribute to the Golden Centennaires by artist Geoff Bennett, the former RCAF pilot who designed the team's paint scheme. (courtesy Geoff Bennett)

not be able to fly the next day. Our supply of castor oil had not arrived and none could be found. I left the party, went to the local hospital, introduced myself to the matron and asked her how much castor oil she had. It took a while to convince her that I had not had too much 'Newfie Screech' and did not qualify for a straightjacket. For two hours we worked together, pouring six ounce bottles of the precious oil into a five gallon can. The Avro flew on schedule!

I thought of René Serrao and Jake Miller flying the CF-104 and CF-101 with flawless precision and accuracy to the extent that even other professionals were amazed. René, on occasions when he had a point to make with me, after he had had a few drinks of Trinidadian rum, would waggle his great finger at me and say, 'Skipper, stand up, pay attention and don't answer me back!' Big, barrel-chested Jake Miller on the other hand, would pick me up in a crushing bear hug and say, 'Owen baby, you listen to me!' Two great, unforgettable individuals.

As I reflected on each and every one in this noble group of players, I realized it was a tribute to their skills that had made the Golden Centennaires and 'Philp's Flying Circus' so successful. Just as important had been the groundcrew who were as dedicated as the pilots, who worked long hours with

diligence, tenacity and ingenuity to ensure aircraft and equipment worked to perfection and we did not miss a performance. Strong, motivated men standing in the background, ensuring that all needs were met.

It reminded me of the time we were in transit to Chatham, New Brunswick when one of the Tutor aircraft developed engine problems. Information was passed back to the Hercules, our support aircraft, to alert the groundcrew on board, that there would be an engine change on arrival. A spare Tutor engine was in a can on the aircraft but without all the accessories attached. While still in flight, the groundcrew took the engine out of the case, built it up as far as they could and two hours after landing at Chatham, the aircraft was on a test flight with a new engine, ready for the evening performance. That was dedication, ingenuity and initiative!

There were other incidents, less pleasant, that took place during this eventful year. Long before the tour started, in the early part of 1967, I had visited each province to meet with provincial Centennial committees. With the exception of Quebec, these visits were all very cooperative.

We had scheduled 15 appearances in Quebec, all to the satisfaction of the local committees. But the chairman of the provincial committee,

who refused to speak English and addressed me through an interpreter, opened the meeting with the statement, 'Since Quebec has 25 percent of the population in Canada, we expect 25 percent of the scheduled airshows.' I had to answer through Denis Gauthier – while I have forgotten the name of this person, his attitude astounded and annoyed me. As I was not known to back off when confrontation was obvious, I replied in kind. Our schedule was firm, we could not commit to additional shows and the schedule had been approved by Ottawa. I further told him, quite bluntly, that if he wished to pursue the matter, it would have to be within the political net and suggested he contact Mr. Hellyer, the Minister of Defence.

With that he got up from the meeting, took his interpreter with him and left the room to make a phone call. Some time later the interpreter came back and said I was wanted on the telephone. Expecting to speak with an aide, I was surprised to find myself speaking to the Minister himself. He said that he had told the chairman he supported my decision and while I might accommodate changes in locations, we could not be expected to arrange additional performances based on a percentage of the population. The Minister wished me success with the tour and that was that. I never did meet the chairman again but I appreciated this support from the top.

On the other hand, when I arrived in Newfoundland for the liaison job, there was a different scenario. The committee had laid on a small luncheon which was attended by Premier Joey Smallwood. When we were introduced he was a bit cool. His welcome to Newfoundland was tinged with the attitude it was not really Newfoundland's Centennial, but the rest of Canada's so why should he get excited? I remember thinking to myself there was no point in getting the Premier's back up, so I kept these thoughts to myself. Sitting next to him at lunch and wondering how to handle the situation, the Premier broke the ice. 'Would you be knowing my boy Bill?' he asked.

I was pretty sure he was referring to Bill Carr, a Newfie boy who had made good in the RCAF and whose current rank was air commodore. I was happy to tell Mr. Smallwood that the air commodore and I had known each other for several years and that I considered Bill Carr a friend. The whole atmosphere changed, even to the point that if he could do anything personally while we were in Newfoundland, I was to call him direct. Once again I realized that it's not what you know, but who you know, and Bill Carr had unknowingly opened another door.

And then there was the 'Drat,' a mysterious team trademark. It was left on the ceilings of every hotel, motel, mess and any other accessible location, including some ladies' washrooms, in our travels. Made by heating a piece of cigarette foil with a match or lighter until the tissue paper backing pulled away, this tissue was rolled into a ball and put in the mouth to wet it down while fashioning a wine glass shape from the silver foil. The wet wad of tissue paper was then packed into the base of the 'wine glass' and with a rapid, underhand motion, thrown against the ceiling and presto, the Drat would stick to the ceiling upside down. These Drats became the unofficial calling card of the Golden Centennaires and became a team symbol more by accident than by design.

A Team Like No Other

It was now time to put all these thoughts behind me and get on with the job of disbanding the unit. While this was in progress letters of praise were pouring in from near and far. In my opinion the most gracious tribute came from Bob Hoover, probably the best demonstration pilot ever produced by the United States and a man accustomed to

justified international acclaim for his own deeds.

Before we completely disbanded it was necessary to have a parade for the presentation of Centennial medals. I had been told that our old friend Brigadier Stu Graham would be in attendance and that A/V/M Stovel would present the medals. Nobody wanted a parade. No member of the unit could remember when he had been on parade the last time. Marching – what was that? Nonetheless we had a couple of half serious practices which were, to say the least, ragged.

The final farewell. *Sentinel* magazine paid a final tribute to the Centennaires in January 1968. On January 12th, Air Vice Marshal Richard Stovel, Commander Training Command, and a staunch supporter of the team, presented O.B. Philp and his team with Centennial medals during their stand down parade. (via Tony Edmundson, Maeve Philp)

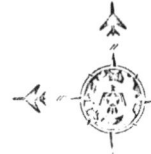

THE UNITED STATES AIR FORCE *Thunderbirds*

U.S.A.F. AIR DEMONSTRATION SQUADRON. NELLIS AFB. NEVADA 89110. PHONE 702.382.1800

5 December 1967

[Stamp: MINISTER'S OFFICE / 161-02 / DEC 7 1967 / DEPT. N.D. OTTAWA]

The Hon Leo Cadieux
Minister of National Defense
Ottawa, Ontario
Canada

Dear Mr. Cadieux,

On behalf of all the Thunderbirds, both past and present, and all Americans who have had the opportunity to see them fly, I want to express my admiration and appreciation to the RCAF Golden Centennaires. The demonstration they performed at our 1967 Thunderbird Reunion was by far the finest exhibition of precision flying any of us had ever seen. All of us received the news of their disbanding with heavy heart for their exhibition is a great tribute to your country and to aviation throughout the world.

The reunion show was our first opportunity to see our Northern neighbors fly and it reminded all of us, and our civilian friends, of the fact that the Canadian forces are still one of the most professional, dedicated and skilled existing in the free world. We saw these men, both in the air and on the ground, working together as an outstanding team made up of officers and airmen from all over Canada. Each of them reflected the highest standards of military bearing, dedication and diplomacy. It was saddening for all of us that we will not be able to fly with them in the coming year, for they represent that which is the finest of the Canadian military.

Please pass on to Wing Commander O. B. Philp, Squadron Leaders Lang and Hubbard, and all the Centennaires, our sincere thanks for their wonderful show and we all wish them well in their new assignments. We hope that all of our Canadian friends will stop and see us whenever they are in the Las Vegas area.

Best wishes from all the Thunderbirds,

Sincerely,

Neil L. Eddins, Major, USAF
Commander

The USAF Thunderbirds flew the North American F-100C Super Sabre in 1967. (USAF Photo)

The Golden Centennaires enjoyed a special camaraderie with their counterparts to the south, the United States Navy Blue Angels and United States Air Force Thunderbirds. Upon learning of the Canadian government's decision to disband the Centennaires, the Thunderbird Commander wrote this eloquent letter to the Honourable Leo Cadieux, Canada's new Minister of National Defence. (via Maeve Philp)

Between 1957 and 1968, the USN Blue Angels flew 6 Grumman F11F Tigers. (US Navy Photo)

BLUE ANGELS

THE BLUE ANGELS
NAVAL AIR STATION
PENSACOLA, FLORIDA

24 November 1967

Wing Commander O. B. Philp
Commander, Golden Centennaires
Canadian Forces Base
Portage, Manitoba, Canada

Dear Wing Commander Philp:

A short note to let you and your fellow "Golden Drats" know that, despite the underhanded and cunning tactics employed by you on the evening of 19 November, the U. S. Navy Flight Demonstration Team arrived home safely on the afternoon and evening of 20 November.

Since our return, we have been attempting to decide on a suitable means of repayment for your gracious hospitality. A suggestion for a strong note of protest delivered to your government through diplomatic channels was discarded as too time-consuming. At the present, it appears that our most popularly accepted idea is at a temporary impasse awaiting investigation into the legality (and sportsmanship) of sending high-explosives through the mails.

Seriously, our only regrets are that we shall not be meeting you again as a demonstration team. In your single year of existence, you have reached a level of ability and performance seldom achieved. We are proud to have known the Golden Centennaires and will treasure the memories of our relationship.

We look forward to an early reunion.

Sincerely,

Bill

B. V. WHEAT
Lieutenant Commander, U. S. Navy
Officer-in-Charge

U. S. NAVY FLIGHT DEMONSTRATION TEAM

But on the day of the presentations, January 12th, 1968, the showmen came through right on the money. I hollered orders as if I knew what I was doing and the officers and men looked like they had been on the drill square every day of their military lives. Brigadier Graham, as the resident senior army officer in Training Command, was charmed out of his socks. He summed up by saying, 'They not only maintained and flew their aircraft in an exemplary manner, they can march!' From him, that was a real compliment. In making his speech to the audience of military and invited civilian dignitaries, A/V/M Stovel said the team displayed 'the highest example of professional skill' in the air and on the ground. 'To the Centennaires and all who supported them, we want to say thank you for a tremendous contribution to Canada's Centennial year … We have all been enriched by association with this first-class team.'

Typical of numerous messages from the Commands associated with this effort in the Centennial year, was this one from the Commander of Air Defence Command at North Bay, A/V/M Mike Pollard:

Their place in history secure, the Golden Centennaires fly into the prairie sunset in this fine portrait by John Rutherford of Kamloops, B.C. (courtesy John Rutherford)

FROM AIR VICE MARSHAL POLLARD TO BASE COMMANDER FOR WING COMMANDER O.B. PHILP. ON THE OCCASION OF THE DISBANDMENT OF THE CENTENNAIRES, LET ME CONGRATULATE YOU AND YOUR TEAM ON AN OUTSTANDING PERFORMANCE THROUGHOUT YOUR TOURS, ON CONSISTENTLY HIGH STANDARDS OF AIRMANSHIP, ON THOROUGHNESS OF PLANNING AND EXECUTION IN SUPPORT AND STAGING AND ON THE BREATHTAKING PLEASURES WHICH YOUR SHOW INVARIABLY ACCORDED. WE IN AIR DEFENCE COMMAND WERE PROUD TO BE ASSOCIATED WITH THE CENTENNAIRES. MY VERY BEST WISHES TO EACH OF YOU IN YOUR NEW ASSIGNMENTS.

A/V/M M.E. Pollard
Commander ADC

It was all over and we dispersed to other assignments. In January I took up new responsibilities at Cold Lake and spent the next year and a half organizing my old squadron from overseas, 434, as it started operational training with the new CF-5 fighter.

In August 1969 I was promoted to group captain, now changed to the rank of colonel with unification of the Forces. Posted then to Canadian Forces Base Moose Jaw, I became base commander. I was ready for another challenge. It was not long in coming …"

O.B. Philp

A Salute to the Past – A Foundation for the Future

Although the Golden Centennaires flew under the banner of the Canadian Armed Forces in 1967, the team also represented the swan song for the Royal Canadian Air Force which ceased to exist when unification of Canada's three military services took place on February 1st, 1968. The team had epitomized the proud traditions of the RCAF established over 44 years of war and peace, their accomplishments motivating untold numbers of young Canadians to join the Canadian Forces in ensuing years as pilots, technicians and other support personnel. Many would be exposed to the joys of aerobatics on the Tutor during flying training. Others would learn highly skilled trades and later maintain the aircraft that was destined to serve Canada for another 33 years as the Forces' basic jet trainer and platform for the successors to the Golden Centennaires – the Snowbirds. It was only a matter of time until the legacy continued …

The Canadian Air Force Heritage Flight was formed in 1998 and flew across the nation the following summer in celebration of the 75th anniversary of Canada's Air Force. The team paid tribute to three classic aircraft upon which thousands of Canadian and allied pilots earned their wings – the Harvard, T-33 Silver Star and CT-114 Tutor. The team is shown here front and centre at the Quinte International Air Show which was flown under perfect conditions on 13 Jun 99 at 8 Wing Trenton, Ontario. (Mark Munzel)

The Motivators

Among every air force in the world there is a special group of aviators whose mandate is to impart their expertise to the chosen few who have been selected to undergo military flying training. In Canada they are known as Qualified Flying Instructors (QFIs) or Instructor Pilots (IPs). While there is considerable reward in seeing a young person fulfill his or her dream of earning their wings, many instructors over the years have also had the satisfaction of flying on various school formation demonstration teams. Aircraft on these regional teams ranged from Chipmunks and Harvards to T-33s and Tutors. This tradition continued into the 1970s and 80s with several new teams leaving their marks on the airshow circuit – among them the Musket Gold, Dragonflies and Vikings. Another aerial demonstration team that earned official recognition as the army's counterpart to the Snowbirds was the Canadian Forces Parachute Team – the SkyHawks. All of these teams played an important role in demonstrating the professionalism of Canadian Forces personnel to thousands of citizens across the country while simultaneously motivating young students to strive for the perfection so clearly evident in their displays.

The T-33 Teams 1970 - 2001

With its final retirement from active duty as an electronic warfare and combat support aircraft in April 2002, the venerable T-33 Silver Star joined the ranks of several legendary aircraft to have seen service with the RCAF, RCN and Canadian Forces. None however could match the old T-Bird for its longevity. Including the 20 Lockheed T-33As initially borrowed from the USAF in 1951 and the 636 Canadair-built Silver Stars subsequently delivered to the RCAF commencing in 1953, the T-33 saw over 50 years of active service in Canada, a remarkable record for an aircraft that had its genesis in the late 1940s.

As described in some detail earlier, the Canadian version of the T-Bird made its inaugural appearances at airshows in the summer of 1953 as a semi-official Training Command aerobatic team under the leadership of S/L Lou Hill. Several formation teams followed in the footsteps of the Central Flying School "Silver Stars" as they were then known after they participated in *Operation Prairie Pacific* in 1954. Canadians in Central and Western Canada will remember the Gimli Smokers who flew from 1959 to 1964 as the best known of the "prairie teams" that complemented the famous RCAF Red Knight solo pilot. Residents of central Ontario may remember one of the more humorous teams, a three-ship formed by the 414 Sqn T-33 detachment at North Bay that unofficially called themselves "The Pink Dinks" during Canada's Centennial celebrations, "since all of the good colours were gone." Maritimers

The No. 1 FTS Formation Team started the 1971 airshow season based in Gimli, Manitoba but finished up at their new home in Cold Lake, Alberta. L to R, Kneeling – Capt Dave Thom, Capt Bobbi-Joe Hart. Standing – Capt Bill Lynch, Lt Brian Allen, Lt Wayne Adair, Capt Jim Gale. Missing from photo are Capt Gerry Hermanson and Lt Guy Dutil. (DND MJ 71-550)

however, will conjure up memories of the Red Herring and his aerobatic T-33 show that saw the Royal Canadian Navy out in style the same year.

1 FTS T-Birds Formation Team

Of several T-33 teams that would subsequently be formed to celebrate special occasions in Canada in the aftermath of the official cancellation of the Red Knight solo program, the first was the 1 FTS T-Birds of Gimli, Manitoba which were formed in 1970 as a regional team. Comprised of five aircraft, the team was created for the express purpose of assisting the province of Manitoba celebrate its centennial that summer. Capt Dave Thom, who had the distinction of being the last pilot to fly a T-33 out of Gimli, led the team and explains how a rather innocuous beginning led to some major airshow activity the following year under the tutelage of none other than Col O.B. Philp:

"The 1 FTS T-Birds team was formed in the last year of flying operations at CFB Gimli (1970) along with teams from Portage and Moose Jaw to provide public air displays indicative of the flying proficiency required during pilot training. We were essentially a stop gap measure to fill the void left after Centennial year in order to satisfy the many public requests for air displays. Our shows were mainly on a local or provincial basis with a couple of notable national exceptions such as the Abbotsford and CNE airshows. Our authorization to form a team may also have been due in part to an American cutback in providing teams and individual aircraft to Canadian shows due to the ongoing Vietnam War and political pressure.

In designing our show, we had to adhere to some rigid guidelines. There were to be no individual or formation aerobatics, our limits being 60 degrees of pitch and 120 degrees of roll. We could also have no more than four aircraft in formation and all manoeuvres had to be indicative of present pilot training practices. This made for a somewhat dull airshow from a pilot's perspective but we followed the letter of the law, performing in 1970 at Moose Jaw, Abbotsford and Winnipeg for the Manitoba Centennial. This particular show included a mass flypast of nine Dakotas, one Argus, four T-Birds, four Tutors, four CF-101s, four CF-104s and four CF-5s. Following the flypast, we performed a display at St. Andrews Airport.

Following some suggestions from Col O.B. Philp and Maj Phil Perry, we managed to introduce some positive changes for 1971

Capt Dave Thom leads the 1 FTS Formation Team across centre stage at Abbotsford '71 in box formation. At left are the shoulder patches worn by members of the school until the unit moved from Gimli to Cold Lake. With the subsequent replacement of the T-33 by the CF-5 as the new advanced jet trainer, the school was renamed 1 Canadian Forces Flying Training School. (Bill Johnson)

This beautifully restored Canadair T-33 made waves on the North American airshow circuit in the late 1980s when Frank Sanders and his team from Chino, California paid tribute to the RCAF Red Knight. A historic meeting took place at the St. Hubert airshow in Montreal in 1989 when Sanders presented photos of his aircraft to the original Red Knight, F/L Roy Windover. On hand to take part in the event were Bill Upton (Canadair), Robert St. Pierre (Montreal Airshow), Roy Windover, Frank Sanders and George Miller who had performed alongside the Red Knight as a member of the RCAF Golden Hawks. (via Robert St. Pierre)

while still staying within the rules. We introduced the Gimli Goose, a formation change from a traditional box which saw Nos. 2 and 3 sliding back to formate on No. 4. We then flew the formation in a 360 degree turn in front of the crowd, a formation also adopted by the Snowbirds that same year. We also introduced a climbing, 60 degree Prince of Wales Plume (taken from the Siskins) which we added as a closing manoeuvre. Comments from the above two gentlemen were much more positive after the 1971 Abbotsford show.

Since we became part of O.B.'s Canadian Forces travelling road show in 1971, we did several big shows across the country while moving the school from Gimli to our new home in Cold Lake. These included the Homecoming Air Show at Moose Jaw, Abbotsford, Trenton and the CNE. For one show at the CNE, our four T-Birds also flew in formation with four Snowbird Tutors. Unfortunately, this only occurred once as the subsequent shows were cancelled due to poor weather.

The team was not re-formed in 1972 as 1 FTS bid a fond farewell to the T-33 and converted to the CF-5 as our new advanced jet trainer."

Dave Thom

From Red Herrings to Tracer Reds

When the air force's "Red Knight" solo show was relegated to the history books in 1969 followed by the navy's "Red Herring" counterpart in 1971, no one ever really expected either name to surface again – except as a distant memory of past glories from the pre-unification years. However, both names would make a comeback on the North American airshow circuit in distinctly different ways, the Red Knight as an American civilian performer flying a Canadian T-33 and the Red Herrings as a rejuvenated T-33 formation team.

In keeping with their naval roots, two T-33 utility squadrons using naval nomenclature, one on each coast, remained active in the post-unification era to support operational training of the navy's surface fleet, often in the role of target towing. Initially, VU-33 remained in its original home at Pat Bat in Victoria, British Columbia but eventually moved north to Comox as the Canadian Forces struggled to consolidate and preserve as many assets as possible in an era of escalating cutbacks. On the East Coast, VU-32 fulfilled the same role for the Atlantic fleet from its traditional home at CFB Shearwater, Nova Scotia, formerly HMCS Shearwater.

With a "naval air" presence having long ago been established in the Halifax/Dartmouth area, requests for air displays in the summer months were a matter of routine, whether in support of bonafide airshows or community fairs and exhibitions around the Maritimes. One enterprising young pilot who took an opportunity to restore a little naval history to Atlantic Canada was Capt John Roulston, who explains how an innocent request for information resulted in the rebirth of a name that hadn't been heard in six years:

───────────

"When I became the T-33 flight commander in VU-32 in 1977, it was not uncommon for

one or two of our T-33s to participate in fly-pasts or small air displays around the Maritimes. On July 18th, 1977 however, we were tasked to provide a 'series of flypasts' in support of the annual Halifax Naval Day with four aircraft. The organizers contacted me and wanted to know what the name of our 'team' was for their advertising campaign. Thinking back to the late 60s, I knew there had been a 'Red Herring' solo T-33 demonstration pilot from VU-32, an obvious navy take-off of the RCAF's Red Knight, so I replied, 'The Red Herrings' thinking that this name would only be applied for the one show.

The name also seemed to fit the distinctive day-glo red paint scheme on our aircraft and one of our frequent roles – towing gunnery targets for the navy and army. The theory behind the bright paint was that it helped the gunners determine which was the target and which was the tow plane! This did not always work, as I found out one day at the Shilo, Manitoba range when one army gunnery crew got off six or eight rounds on my aircraft before the range officer could stop them. Fortunately, the obsolete Bofors gun they were using at the time was not a great anti-aircraft weapon (they did not hit one of our targets in a week-long exercise) and I returned to Winnipeg unscathed. But I digress ...

A beautiful portrait of a VU-32 T-Bird in standard day-glo finish flown by the Red Herrings when the name was resurrected in 1977. Ironically, the same aircraft had been flown by the VU-32 team 10 years earlier during Centennial year. (DND photo, Sgt Vic Johnson)

The Tracer Reds were the last airshow team formed by VU-32 and had a strong following in the Maritimes. The last team members were Capts John Black (team leader), Rick Wilson, Dave Amberly and Maj Tony Roeding (Sqn CO). (DND photo via Larry Milberry)

For Naval Day we were cleared to perform over the city down to 300 feet for 15 minutes doing 'whatever we wanted.' The show was obviously a big hit as the Red Herrings were quickly invited to perform at airshows in Summerside, Shearwater and Greenwood within the next couple of months. Over the next three years the team became quite well known on the East Coast and we performed approximately 10 shows a year. As we often performed at the same shows as the Snowbirds as well as formations of CF-5s, CF-101s and CF-104s, we knew we could not match the precision of the former nor the speed and noise of the latter. I therefore developed a routine that provided 'something different.' A commentator on the ground would describe to the audience the sequence of training that a student pilot would receive at Moose Jaw. For our first pass my wingmen would play neophyte students, bobbing and weaving all over the place – all in startling proximity to my aircraft! For our next pass their remarkable improvement allowed them to fly in a stable if uncoordinated fashion with cross-controlling of aileron and rudder reminiscent of the famous Goldilocks Harvard formation team. Of course, on the last pass we would try to look our best. This

last pass was often followed by the popular 'Herrings, three-second break for trail' call which preceded the four-ship 'beat-up' phase of the show – for however long the organizers wanted! Sometimes, such as at CFB Cornwallis graduation parades, it could be 15 minutes or more until the next act showed up to take over and we were asked to ad lib until they arrived. This was some of the best flying we ever did as noise complaints had not yet been invented - not that the T-Bird made a lot of noise anyway!

Eventually, our circuit consisted of annual airshows in Halifax, Dartmouth, Summerside, Chatham, Cornwallis and Greenwood as well as a wide variety of smaller events. We were definitely a 'down east' team – however, one which built quite a reputation in three years. Although, the team composition changed slightly from time-to-time, depending on who was on leave, on temporary duty, posted, and so on, the team usually consisted of myself as lead and Capt Bob Banks, Capt Bob Deane and Lt Yvon Bourdeau as my wingmen. Others who flew with us until my departure in 1980 included Capts Hugh Fisher, Wayne Wilhelm, Ben Marcotte, Ed Beth and Lt Al Hutton.

By the time of my departure from VU-32 in 1980, I had flown roughly 30 shows as Red Herring lead. By this time, our show had grown into a fairly complex 10 minute routine (could be adjusted from six to 15 minutes) involving various cross-controlled and precision formations, solo sequences and the like. Although not as spectacular as the Snowbirds, we were very proud of our team as we felt that the T-33, with fuel in the tip tanks and an engine that was slow to spool up, was as difficult to fly in these types of manoeuvres as any aircraft involved in airshows of the day."

John C. Roulston

The Red Herrings continued to provide airshow support for several more years until the name was finally retired for good. Maj Wayne Halliday renamed the team the Tracer Reds in the fall of 1983 to reflect the squadron's "Tracer" callsign. The team performed periodically over the next several years until VU-32 was disbanded in 1992 and absorbed by 434 Combat Support Sqn which took over the naval support role. Even the last commanding officer of VU-32, Maj Tony Roeding, couldn't resist the satisfaction that comes with air-

Residents of Atlantic Canada have been treated to some magnificent airshows over the years at CFB Shearwater, home of the Nova Scotia International Air Show. Static displays are a popular aspect of any airshow but when the aerial display begins the aim for most fans is to get as close to the action as possible, as the shot on the right clearly shows. (courtesy NSIA)

show flying, performing with the team for three consecutive years. The last edition of the Tracer Reds included Capts John Black, Rick Wilson and Dave Amberly with Roeding flying the slot and solo position. Over the next 10 years, the Bluenosers of 434 Sqn continued the tradition of airshow support with flypasts and static displays from Shearwater and Greenwood until they too were disbanded in April 2002, bidding a fond farewell to the T-33.

VU-33 Formation Team

Coincident with the rebirth of the Red Herrings in Shearwater in 1977, VU-32's sister squadron on the West Coast also formed a four-plane T-33 team under the command of Capt Pete Wittich. Although they did not adopt an informal name like their eastern counterparts, the show put on by the VU-33 team was every bit as pleasing. Their repertoire included a variety of formations and tight turns in front of the crowd but the *coup de gras* came near the end of the show with a formation cross-over split aimed directly at the spectators stage centre. With the T-Bird's long wings and day-glo red tip tanks, the visual illusion created by the four aircraft meshing together was simply heart stopping and never failed to gain a reaction from the crowd. In subsequent years the team was reduced to two aircraft until VU-33 was also relegated to the history books in 1992, being replaced by 414 Combat Support Sqn. The last veteran fighter pilot to lead the team from 1990 to 1992 with characteristic gusto was former Snowbird Capt Harry Chapin whose professional show ensured that VU-33's contribution to Canada's airshow team heritage would not soon be forgotten.

To mark the end of an era, VU-32 and VU-33 both painted up airshow birds in 1992 to pay tribute to their squadrons before they were re-named as 434 and 414 Combat Support Sqns respectively. (DND Photo)

The Silver Stars

The historic "Silver Stars" name attached to the RCAF's first T-33 aerobatic team in 1953 by S/L Lou Hill was resurrected 30 years later in the spring of 1983 by another veteran instructor and former Snowbird solo, Capt Eric "Speedy" Fast. Posted to the Base Flight section at Cold Lake, Alberta, he was placed in charge of the unit's fleet of 12 T-33s. Never one to pass up an airshow, when offered the opportunity to form a three-plane formation team to support airshow requests, Fast leapt at the challenge.

With an establishment of T-33s, Dakotas and Huey helicopters serving a wide variety of support roles at Cold Lake, Base Flight was manned by a mixture of seasoned veterans and young pilots fresh out of wings training in Moose Jaw. For these young pilots the unit provided an excellent opportunity to gain experience in "real world" military flying – being afforded the opportunity to gain that experience under the tutelage of a veteran like Speedy Fast was an

added bonus. Nowhere were his years of experience more evident than in the professional displays he presented in the T-33 in 1983 and 1984. These were highly motivational exercises for the two young wingmen fortunate to fly under his watchful eye and both learned their lessons well. Lt Al Benell was destined to later command 417 Sqn (the successors to Base Flight) and retire the T-33 from service in 2002 while Capt Mike Skubicky applied his experience to the Snowbird tryouts in the fall of 1984, winning the coveted opposing solo position as Snowbird 8. Evidently, he had learned more from Speedy Fast than just formation flying, much to the delight of both …

The Silver Stars had worked up another show for the 1985 season and had completed one display for the residents of Fort McMurray, Alberta when their season was abruptly terminated. A mid-air disaster in nearby Edmonton involving two C-130 Hercules transports at the end of March resulted in the cancellation of virtually all of the regional airshow teams across the Canadian Forces.

The Silver Stars 1983-1984. L to R – Capts Al Benell, Eric "Speedy" Fast (team leader) and Mike Skubicky on the ground and in the air. Thousands of Canadian pilots climbed up the ladder into the tight confines of the T-33 cockpit during the aircraft's 50 years of service in the RCAF, RCN and Canadian Forces. (via Al Benell)

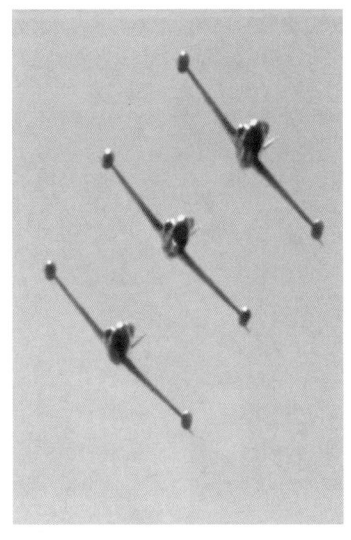

The Black Knights strike a handsome pose in the summer of 1984. Team members were Capt Stu McAskill (team lead), No. 2 Capt John Lahey, No.3 Maj Bob Jones/Capt René Robert and No. 4 Capt Lou Glussich. (DND Photo via John Lahey)

The T-33 had an aesthetically pleasing plan view, as shown in this vic formation pass flown by the Black Knights at the CFB Trenton Airshow in 1984. (Mike Valenti)

The Black Knights

In 1983 the Black Knights of 414 Electronic Warfare Sqn in North Bay, Ontario also formed a part-time formation team to participate in regional shows. Leading the team was a former Starfighter pilot and an original member of the Snowbirds, Capt Bob Sharpe. Building on the popularity of the '83 campaign, the team was reformed in 1984 under a new leader, veteran instructor Capt Stu McAskill. Additional practice time was dedicated to polishing the four-plane routine and an expanded schedule led to Canadian shows in London, North Bay, Sault Ste Marie and the CIAS in Toronto. However, the uniqueness of the T-Bird routine also led to invitations to perform at two large American shows that summer, the Dayton Air Fair in Dayton, Ohio and a USAF Open House at K.I. Sawyer AFB, Michigan. Although the team planned to fly again in 1985, the aforementioned accident in Edmonton led to the demise of the Black Knights formation team as well.

Although the Black Knights were never formed again in any kind of official capacity, solo aircraft were provided in later years to support airshows in Western Canada after the squadron was moved to its final home in Comox, British Columbia. It was from that location that the last commanding officer of the squadron, LCol Yves Bossé, received authorization to lead a four-ship of Black Knights in their last flying appearance at an airshow on July 29th, 2001. Fittingly, the final flypast took place over home plate at 19 Wing Comox where they opened the show for the benefit of thousands of residents of the Comox Valley. Joining Bossé in the final farewell salute were Capt SteveWormsbecher, Capt Larry Summers and Maj Terry Hoffart.

Farewell to the T-Bird

In the spring of 2002 the T-33 Silver Star was retired from the Canadian Forces, 49 years after the RCAF's first production T-Bird (21001) had made its maiden test flight at Canadair on December 22nd, 1952. That aircraft now sits majestically on display at the Edmonton International Airport for all to see. Millions of airshow fans on both sides of the Atlantic will long remember the distinctive silhouette of the aircraft as it whistled overhead at hundreds of airshows, but only one country, Canada, will ever be able to claim bragging rights for having flown the aircraft the longest. It truly was a classic and versatile aircraft to the end.

Some of the many colours of the T-Bird. In its 50 year service to Canada, the T-33 appeared at over 1,000 airshows in a variety of paint schemes, serving as both a performer and support aircraft to some of the nation's pre-eminent aerobatic teams. Clockwise from top left – the Golden Hawks (Rae Simpson), Golden Centennaires (Larry Milberry), Red Knight (Rae Simpson), 50th anniversary T-Bird (Mike Reyno), 414 Sqn four-ship in the typical livery of the 1980s (Larry Milberry), the Black Knight of 414 Sqn (Mike Reyno), Snowbirds (Rae Simpson), and former RCAF pilot Ormond Hayden-Baillie's Black Knight photographed at RAF Duxford in Jun 1975 (via Turbo Tarling). Centre – the classic lines of the T-33. (Mike Reyno)

The Musket Gold

In 1970 a new generation of primary trainer entered service with the Canadian Forces to replace the de Havilland Chipmunk. As beloved as the Chipmunk had been, the Beechcraft CT-134 Musketeer was an easier aircraft to take-off and land and featured side-by-side seating which offered the advantage of being able to watch a student manipulate the controls of the aircraft.

The de Havilland Chipmunk was a familiar scene in airshows across Canada for decades, both in military formations like this one or in civilian livery such as that flown by legendary performer Art Scholl. It was replaced by the Musketeer in 1970. (via Cajo Brando).

The arrival of any new aircraft in the air force inventory is a cause for celebration and as luck would have it the Musketeer made its debut as part of the Canadian Forces airshow extravaganza that performed at the nation's three largest airshows in 1971 – Moose Jaw, Abbotsford and the Canadian International Air Show in Toronto. In keeping with tradition, the new trainer was painted the same bright gold-yellow that had adorned both the Chipmunk and Harvard. It was therefore impossible to miss, so what it gave up in speed to other acts it gained with its dazzling colour and ability to stay very close to the crowd. Capt Gary Swiggum was the first instructor from 3 CFFTS to design and lead a four-plane Musketeer show that was to last for 14 consecutive years.

It would take an aviator to appreciate how difficult it was to fly a light aircraft in formation the way the Musket Gold did. With a gross weight of only 1,100 kg (2,350 pounds), the aircraft was very susceptible to summer turbulence and team members had to work exceptionally hard to maintain smooth formation. Yet, the Musket Gold made it look easy. Although they were not

The 1973 Musket Gold team consisted of a two-plane demonstration flown by Capts Cajo Brando and Bill Vermue. (DND photo via Cajo Brando)

authorized formation or solo aerobatics, the team did conduct some aggressive "up and down" manoeuvring that pushed the aircraft's 180 horsepower Lycoming engine to its limits. All of the standard formations were flown and over the years some imaginative splits and crosses were introduced to enhance the show.

For the novice pilot taking training in Portage la Prairie, the Musket Gold provided an inspirational insight into what hard work could accomplish. Many a wishful aerobatic pilot, including the author, first bore witness to the exhilaration of formation flying while riding along with the Musket Gold during a practice. Combining this experience with the "hands on" loops and rolls that were taught to students during the second phase of flying training at 3 CFFTS provided the confidence

that one needed to move on to the next step in flying training – conversion to the Tutor in Moose Jaw – jet flying at last!

It would be hard to find a prairie town in Canada that didn't welcome the Musket Gold during their 14 years of performances. The team also flew in many American airshows as far south as South Dakota. Team members ranged in experience from seasoned leaders like Capts Don McLeod and Pete Francis to young "pipeline" instructors who earned the right to fly with the team after building up hundreds of hours of experience teaching others how to fly. In 1980 the team honoured one of its stalwart exchange pilots, Capt Leo Jespers of the Royal Netherlands Air Force, by allowing him to lead the Musket Gold for his third and last year with the team. For longevity however, no one could touch veteran technician Sgt Wayne Vrooman who spent nine consecutive years with the team through three promotions in rank – from corporal to master corporal to sergeant.

Although the 1984 season was destined to be the last for the Musket Gold, the team did enjoy a brief renaissance in 1992 when authorization was granted to re-form the team for a final farewell appearance at Portage la Prairie. Back to lead the team through its final swan song to coincide with the closure of the base was its former com-

By the mid-1970s the Musket Gold had become fully ensconced on the Canadian airshow scene as a four-plane formation team. The 1976 team comprised, L to R - Capts Dick Reid, Bob Gottfried, Pete Francis, Bob Jones and Glen Buchanan (team lead). Below, the Primary Flying School crest and Musket Gold badges over the years. (DND Photo via Glen Buchanan, badges via Henry Devison)

One of the finest portraits of the Musket Gold ever taken over southern Manitoba near their prairie home of Portage la Prairie. (DND PCN 72-286)

The 1978 Musket Gold. L to R – Capt Leo Jespers (RNLAF - slot), Lt John Valade (left wing), Lt Mark Hollman (right wing), Capt Pete Francis (team lead). (DND Photo)

Crewman John Richkun contributed these photos of the 1982 Musket Gold en route for another weekend of demonstration flying. Getting to the show was half the fun – it was after landing that the crewmen's work began, in this case refuelling the aircraft at The Pas, Manitoba. (John Richkun)

The 1980 Musket Gold. L to R, Front Row – MCpl Gord Bugden, Sgt Wayne Vrooman, MCpl Rick Adams. Back Row – Capt Leo Jespers (RNLAF - team lead), Capt Bill Collier, Lt André Deschamps, Capt Steve James, Lt Chuck Pym, Capt Ron Sarich. (DND Photo via Bill Collier)

The 1981 Musket Gold. L to R, Front Row – Capt Marc de van der Schueren, Cpl Don Edwards, Cpl Henry Devison, Cpl John Richkun. Back Row – Capt Rob Slinger, Capt Greg McQuaid, Capt Paul Baldasaro, Capt Bob Struthers, Capt Charles Pym. (DND Photo via John Richkun)

The 1982 Musket Gold. L to R, Front Row – Capt Ryan Lepalm, Pte Barry Bracegirdle, MCpl Rod MacKinnon, MCpl Henry Devison, Cpl John Richkun. Back Row – Capt Jim Manton, Capt Greg Newmarch, LCol Don Macht (Commandant 3 CFFTS), Capt Greg McQuaid (team lead), Capt Marc de van der Schueren, Capt Bob Struthers. (DND Photo via John Richkun)

The 1984 Musket Gold. L to R, Front Row – Pte Barry Bracegirdle, MCpl Henry Devison, Cpl John Richkun, MCpl Rod MacKinnon, MCpl Gord Bugden. Back Row – Capt Grant Griffiths, Capt Ab Jagat (team lead), Lt Kevin Stewart, Capt Jim Manton, Capt Ryan Lapalm. Missing are Capts Steve Hale and John Haazen. (DND Photo via Henry Devison)

mander from the 1982 and 1983 seasons, Maj Greg McQuaid. He was joined by Capts Linton Sellen, Russ Williams and Rob Carter, all veteran instructors of 3 CFFTS. Together, the foursome had the distinction of being the last primary flying school team to ever fly in Canada.

The Manitoba Airshow 1992 staged on June 20th and 21st marked the end of another era in Canada's air force history – the 52nd and final year of operation for Portage la Prairie as a military base. Formed in 1940 as the RCAF's No. 14 Elementary Flying Training School to support the BCATP, the base saw 15,000 aircrew trainees pass through its gates. It was therefore appropriate that the base played host to some of the earliest participants in the program during their final airshow as delegates of the 6th Commonwealth Wartime Aircrew Reunion joined thousands of Manitoba residents who converged on the base for the last military show.

Fittingly, crystal-clear prairie skies prevailed over the weekend and a first-class show was staged by show chairman LCol Ken Carr and his team. Joining the Musket Gold and Dragonflies for the final farewell were a wide ranging group of performers that included the Snowbirds, Skyhawks, CF-18 demo, CF-5 demo, representation from the American military and three long time friends of the Canadian Forces – Bud Granley, Al Pietsch and Frank Ryder.

As I sat in the audience that day watching the last show of the Musket Gold, it was obvious that the team had put a great deal of effort into their practices as they flew a flawless performance. With their formation landing at

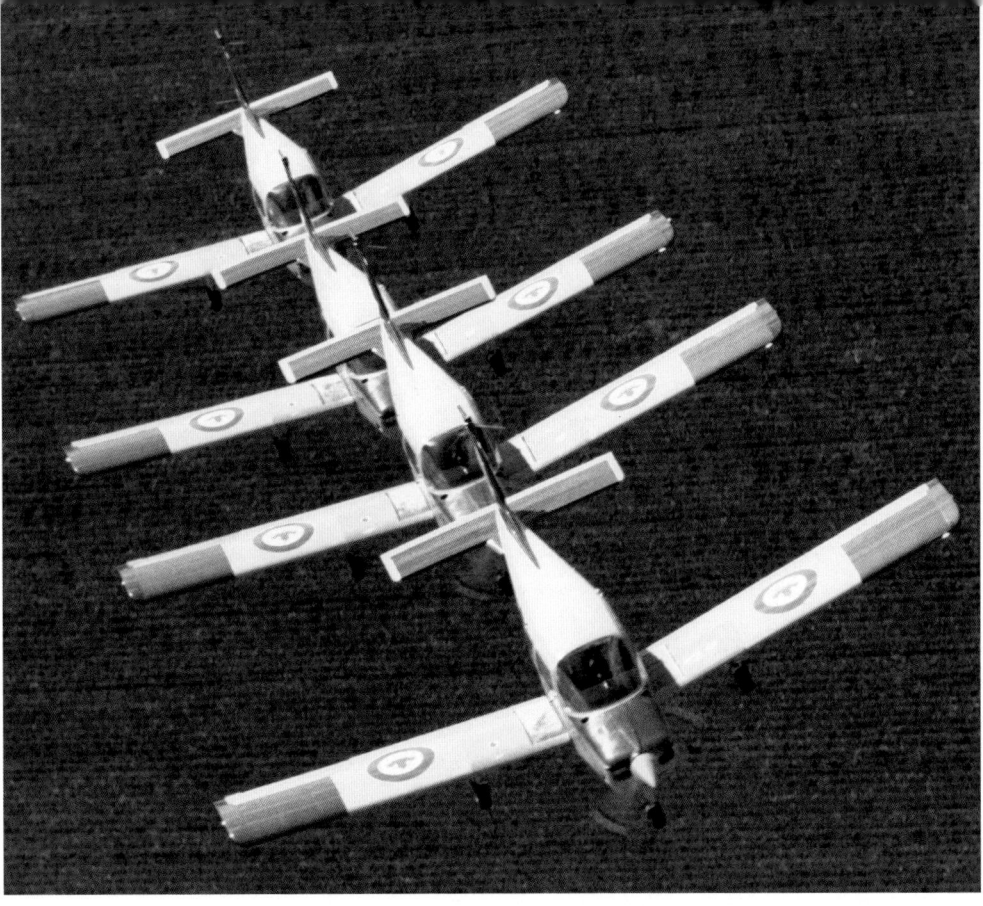

It took some fine flying to attain this kind of precision. Flying behind Capt Pete Francis are Lts Mark Hollman, John Valade and Capt Leo Jespers of the Royal Netherlands Air Force. (DND IWC 78-115)

the end of their show, another milestone was reached as the Musketeer's 22 year tenure as the primary trainer for the Canadian Forces came to a close. On September 1st, 1992 ownership of the base was passed to Southport Aerospace Centre and a new era of contracted flying training under a team led by Bombardier/Canadair began on the base

using a new aircraft, the Slingsby T-67C Firefly. Many of the Canadair staff who continue the legacy of excellence and professionalism for which Portage has always been renowned are retired members of the Canadian Forces, still passing on the gift of flight to the lucky few selected for flying training.

The last of the Musket Gold – the team performed for the last time at the Manitoba Airshow 1992. L to R – Capt Linton Sellen, Capt Russ Williams, Maj Greg McQuaid (team lead) and Capt Rob Carter. (DND Photo)

Rotary Wing Teams

As airshows gained popularity in the post-war years of the late 1940s, a new phenomenon arrived on the scene in Canada when the RCAF took delivery of its first helicopter on March 5th, 1947 at RCAF Stn Trenton. In the ensuing years the revolutionary machine would change the face of aviation around the world. The Sikorsky S-51/H-5 (serial No. 9601) was the first of several variants introduced to the air force inventory but had a less than spectacular debut when only three weeks later it suffered its first of many crashes when its tail rotor disintegrated on takeoff. Fortunately its pilot, S/L Tom Wallnutt, walked away from the crash and the little machine was repaired and flew again. Such were the tumultuous early days of introducing

Solo helicopter demonstrations have been a feature at airshows across Canada since the early days of the RCAF. Here a Labrador helicopter demonstrates its hover capability at the Abbotsford International Airshow in 1965. (via John Spronk)

The RCAF's first helicopter, the Sikorsky S-51, struts its stuff at NAFD 1962. Taken on strength in 1947, the aircraft was retired in 1965. (Rae Simpson)

this radically new technology to the RCAF. In time, all technical difficulties were rectified and the S-51 went on to serve Canada's air force until 1965, principally as a training and search and rescue platform. Naturally, the little machine was a big hit when it made its first airshow appearances at Air Force Days as spectators marvelled at the machine's ability to take-off and land vertically and hover in mid-air right in front of them.

The successful development of the helicopter is generally credited to Russian-born American, Igor Sikorsky, whose VS-300 first accomplished a vertical takeoff and landing in September 1939. While the shaky lift-off recorded for posterity on movie film looks more humorous than practical, it was from this humble beginning that the small 1,100 pound "whirlybird" with a top speed of 50

mph was transformed into one of the most versatile flying machines in the world.

As the Sikorsky line of helicopters advanced in technology the RCAF took advantage of the new capabilities by taking delivery of several new types, notably the S-55 in 1954 and S-58 a year later. The numbers were relatively small, 15 and 6 respectively, but both versions proved to be invaluable workhorses with their increased range, payload and hoisting capability that were a godsend to those in need of rescue. Also joining the inventory in 1954 was the first of 20 Piasecki/Vertol H-21s, the first twin-rotor helicopter to enter service with the RCAF, affectionately known as the "Flying Banana" due to its curved airframe design.

Canada's navy also benefited significantly from the new technology when it took delivery of a naval variant of the S-55 in 1955 known as the HO4S, an anti-submarine warfare helicopter fitted with a dipping sonar that was assigned to a new squadron designated HS 50. Another Piasecki/Vertol machine, the HUP-3 also joined the RCN in October of that year and by the spring of 1956 both new helicopters had joined the navy's Avengers and Sea Furies aboard HMCS *Magnificent*. By far the largest helicopter purchase of the era took place when

the RCN began to take delivery of the CH-124 Sea King in 1961 for service aboard HMCS *Bonaventure*, the modified Majestic Class ASW aircraft carrier that was the RCN's most formidable warship until it was paid off on July 3rd, 1970. The turbine-powered Sea King possessed an all-weather and night dipping capability that the HO4S did not, thus making the machine an invaluable addition to both the carrier and the navy's fleet of modified destroyer escorts (DDHs). A total of 41 Sea Kings were eventually purchased for the navy and were assigned to two operational squadrons, HS-423 and HS-443, as well as a training squadron, VT-406. The aircraft is still in service some 40 years later.

As each of these helicopters and their successors were introduced into service, they were paraded in front of Canadians from coast-to-coast at Air Force and Naval Day celebrations, adding a new and enjoyable dimension to the flying demonstrations. Although these demonstrations were largely conducted by individual helicopters highlighting their manoeuvrability and roles such as search and rescue, some imaginative exhibitions involving different types performing together began to appear in the late 1950s.

The Sikorsky S-61/CH-124 Sea King helicopter has been a regular feature at countless airshows since it was introduced to the RCAF inventory in 1961. This 440 Sqn aircraft was decorated to salute the 75th anniversary of the RCAF in 1999. (Mike Reyno)

Here's something you don't see every day. These H-21s and an S-58 are conducting an aerial square dance on 9 Jun 62. They got into the spirit of things by having cowboy hats painted on their fuselages before the annual RCAF extravaganza that was held each year at RCAF Stn Rockcliffe. The aircraft taxiing is a Grumman Albatross. (DND PL 139652 via John Bradley)

The Hillers

The Royal Canadian Army Service Corps' new tactical reconnaissance and training helicopter, the Hiller CH-112 Nomad, began appearing at airshows alongside its RCAF and RCN counterparts in 1962. Deployed to Europe in the mid-60s in support of the 8th Canadian Hussars headquartered at the Canadian Army Base in Soest, West Germany, the helicopter troop (Four Troop) helped celebrate Canada's Centennial by hosting the inaugural helicopter "Fly-in Breakfast and Airshow" for its allies in 1967. With typical Canadian flair, the entire event was a huge success. The troop took great pleasure in demonstrating the manoeuvrability of the Nomad to an appreciative audience and, as former army aviator Jon Pellow recalls, they capped off their performance by completing a stunt no fixed aircraft could accomplish – they lined up in a hover in front of their audience and dipped their noses to take a bow - after a square dance demo!

While the Hiller also performed at many airshows in Canada during the 1960s, the first vestiges of a semi-official team began with a move of the Rotary Wing Training School from Rivers, Manitoba to a new home at CFB Portage la Prairie in July 1970. There, the rotary wing operation was amalgamated with the Primary Flying School equipped with the new Musketeer to form No. 3 FTS. The following summer veteran Hiller pilot Capt Walt Morris was authorized to design and lead a four-ship Hiller show that laid the framework for future rotary teams that would perform for over a dozen years. Invited to take part in the large Canadian Armed Forces flying exhi-

Chief of the Air Staff, A/M Hugh Campbell, inspects one of the Royal Canadian Army Service Corp's new Hiller helicopters during NAFD 1962. The CH-112 Nomad was deployed with Canada's NATO forces in West Germany. (RCAF Photo)

Accompanied by two of their technicians (centre), the pilots of the 1971 Hiller team were, L to R - Capts Walt Morris, Ross Craddock, George Fawcett and Ron Aumonier. (DND Photo via Peter McKeage)

bition that summer of 1971, the Hiller team was complemented by two Voyageur helicopters that also put on a most impressive performance as a dancing duo. Although the Hiller was retired from service in 1972, Walt

Morris was not finished with airshows just yet he had the privilege of forming the first airshow team on the Canadian Forces new tactical reconnaissance and training helicopter, the Bell CH-136 Kiowa.

Two rare views of the 1971 Hiller formation team lead by Capt Walt Morris. On the leader's right is Capt Ross Craddock, on his left Capt George Fawcett and in the box Capt Ron Aumonier. (DND Photos)

The 1971 Canadian Armed Forces Airshow Team included these two army Voyageur helicopters that put on an impressive synchronized duet. (*The Plainsman*)

The Kiowa Arrives

The first of 74 Kiowas to be taken on strength by the Canadian Forces began to arrive in 1971. In its tactical support role, the nimble little machine served as an artillery spotter, reconnaissance platform and liaison aircraft. At its peak, in addition to 3 FTS, the Kiowa saw service with five regular force squadrons – 403, 408, 427, 430 and 444 Sqns, the latter based at CFB Lahr, West Germany in support of Canada's 4th Mechanized Brigade Group (4 CMBG). Commencing in 1982, Reserve Force squadrons in Toronto and Montreal were also equipped with the Kiowa.

Green Gophers

While the Kiowa would gain its greatest airshow fame as part of a 3 FTS team, one of Canada's tactical squadrons also formed a team in 1975 and 1976. Based at CFB Gagetown, New Brunswick, 403 Tactical Helicopter (Operational Training) Sqn was responsible for teaching pilots assigned to 10 Tactical Air Group the art of tactical helicopter flying on both the Kiowa and Huey helicopters. In response to airshow requests, squadron commanding officer LCol Bob Chisholm authorized Capt Jim White to put together a four-ship airshow routine to accommodate these requests in 1975. Calling themselves the Green Gophers, White and his team put on several shows that summer, adding a bit of pizzazz by strapping smoke grenades to the skids of their Kiowas to generate a few minutes of coloured smoke. The following year Capt Dave Winmill took the helm to work up another show with a new group of volunteers who flew a very tight (half a rotor width), stepped-down formation. As team member Grant Whitson's logbook reveals, the team flew their 12 minute show in each of New Brunswick, Nova Scotia and Prince Edward Island that sum-

mer, impressing airshow crowds with not only their tight formation flying, but also head-on crosses flown in pairs. The highlight of the season was a command performance for Queen Elizabeth II on July 16th during a visit to CFB Chatham. Although the team did perform for 422 Sqn's Colours presentation in May 1977, operational priorities combined with postings and courses made the continuation of any kind of a regular team impractical.

From Otters to Kiowas The Hummingbirds

Canada's small Air Reserve force in the 1970s was largely confined to the cities of Montreal and Toronto where squadrons in each city were equipped with the venerable single Otter in a support role. Two of Canada's oldest squadrons, 400 and 411 Sqns, were based at Downsview Airport in the heart of the city, the same location at which de Havilland had staged Canada's first post-war airshow in 1946. Given the squadron's historic past, staff worked hard to preserve their heritage by participating in many municipal activities which frequently included flypasts at the CNE. Achieving operational status with the Kiowa helicopter in June 1982 when the Otter was retired, the squadron was eager to show off its new aircraft at Canada's largest airshow. As team member John McClenaghan recalls, this was a welcome respite from living in tents in Petawawa where squadron personnel often found themselves deployed by 10 TAG in support of army exercises:

"With the acquisition of the Kiowa, Capt Dave Miller, a regular force support officer that had served with 403 Sqn in Gagetown, received authorization to form a helicopter team to support the annual CIAS. Since the Toronto Air Reserve units had participated

411 "City of North York" Sqn poses in front of Toronto's most famous landmark. Leading the formation is the founder of the squadron's formation team, Capt Dave Miller. On his left are Maj John McClenaghan and Capt Al Camplin. (DND IOC 83-165)

for many years at the show with the Otter, we were invited back as participants in 1982. Capt Miller put together a 10 minute show using three aircraft which included an aggressive manoeuvre that appeared to be a loop but was actually an optical illusion, since the Kiowa was incapable of zero G. We also performed stepped-up criss-crossing breaks, join-ups from full speed (100 knots) into the hover and several formation changes. We called ourselves the Hummingbirds that first season, an apt name considering the flying characteristics of the Kiowa. In 1983 smoke was added to our show using flares strapped to our skids. Unfortunately, the spring of 1985 we received word that 10 TAG had prohibited parade formation in its rotary wing squadrons so we reluctantly ended the brief history of the Hummingbirds."

John McClenaghan

Although the Green Gophers enjoyed only fleeting fame, they did perform before Royalty in 1976. L to R – Capts Dave Winmill (team lead), Grant Whitson, John McWhirter and Jim Thompson. (DND Photo via Grant Whitson)

The Toronto Air Reserves participated in the Canadian International Air Show between 1982 and 1984. Here, the 1983 "Lazer Blues/Hummingbirds" await their turn to fly while watching the show from a unique vantage point – the Toronto Island Airport. (via John McClenaghan)

The Dragonflies

Canada's most famous helicopter demonstration team were the Dragonflies which had their genesis at CFB Portage in 1972. The precedent for a team had been set by the Hiller airshow team of the previous season and it was Capt Walt Morris who had the pleasure of continuing the tradition by assembling the first Kiowa team in the Canadian Forces. Although the manoeuvres flown by the new team were almost exactly the same, the more streamlined shape of the Kiowa combined with its bright yellow and green livery made for a more aesthetically pleasing show.

Capt George Fawcett, a member of Morris' 1971 Hiller team, was awarded command of the team in 1973 and by that June had settled on Capts Jim Kendall and Gary Flath as two of his wingmen, offering the final spot on the team to the school's USAF exchange pilot, Capt Bob Johnston. Collectively, the quartet developed a short but dynamic 15 minute routine building on the previous year's display. With so many fixed wing teams having adopted a name, the team pondered an identity over the course of the season that would highlight the manoeuvrability in their show. They finally settled on "Dragonflies" in 1974 under their new leader, Jim Kendall.

Dance of the Dragonflies

One advantage that the Dragonflies had over their fixed wing counterparts is that they could start, take-off and launch into their routine all within immediate view of the spectators. With the crowd's attention directed to the team parked on the infield just left of centre stage, it was only a matter of seconds before the rotors were wound up and the team lifted off together into a low hover in perfect line-abreast formation facing the

Top – Canada's first Kiowa team was formed in 1972. L to R, Standing – Capts E.R. Schmidt, Ron Aumonier and Fred D'Amico. Kneeling is team leader Capt Walt Morris. Above – The "thread the needle" manoeuvre shown here in 1973 was the Dragonflies' equivalent to a bomb burst and provided a dramatic finale to the Dragonflies show. (via Fred D'Amico)

crowd. Moving forward and then executing simultaneous left turns put them into line-astern formation as they slowly passed left-to-right in front of their audience. From there the show was on! The team made several close passes in various formations trailing smoke before ending up pointed at the spectators again for a formation hover demonstration. This was a popular part of the show since the pilots were clearly visible to the crowd as they deftly rotated their helicopters in unison using their rudder pedals – all without going anywhere! Spacing between the whirring blades of each helicopter was set at one rotor diameter (approximately 10 metres) which was plenty close considering the certain disaster that awaited any infringement into another chopper's airspace. At the end of this sequence, Dragonflies lead, 2 and 3 moved off to the left leaving centre stage to the team's solo, Dragonfly 4. All eyes were then on him as he demonstrated why helicopter pilots believe they have the best job in the world. Aggressively manoeuvring his helicopter through a range of dizzying spirals, climbs and descents to within a few feet of the ground, the solo's job was to demonstrate the tactical mobility of the helicopter. Invariably, he left spectators truly impressed by the time he had finished.

The show finale was also a real crowd pleaser. Aptly coined "thread the needle," the manoeuvre was set up as the solo finished his routine and accelerated on the deck away from the crowd to be met by his three teammates advancing at high-speed directly towards him (and the crowd). Just prior to meeting head-on, the lead called for smoke on and then "Break Now" as he pulled up aggressively into a cyclic climb with No. 4 immediately following suit after passing under his lead. Simultaneously, No.'s 2 and 3 broke hard into each other, crossed and then completed individual 360 turns. The result

The 1975 Dragonflies. L to R – Capts Gary Flath, Jim Carnegie, Bill Matthews and Jim Kendall (team lead). (DND Photo via Gary Flath)

The 1976 Dragonflies. L to R – Capts Gary Flath (team lead), Bill Matthews, Fred Holtslag, John Zuurbier (RNLAF). (DND Photo via Gary Flath)

was the team's version of a horizontal bomb burst. Then came the finesse part of the manoeuvre – as Dragonflies 2 and 3 were finishing their 360° turns, lead and 4 aimed to rapidly descend straight down so that the four-ship ended up in box formation again flying towards the crowd. Stopping short just in front of stage centre, it was time for the popular "formation bow" at which time a right turn was executed and the team exited in line-astern formation once again. All that remained then was the "wild applause" of the adorning fans …

Following the routine practice of handing over the team to a current team member, Gary Flath took the helm in 1976 for his fourth and final year on the team. Unlike the Snowbirds which were given a full time mandate as an aerial demonstration team, staff instructors on the Dragonflies retained their principal instructional role, volunteering their time to practice after hours and do demonstrations on weekends. In 1976, Gary Flath's logbook recorded a dozen shows flown between Moose Jaw, Saskatchewan and Dryden, Ontario plus a show at Minot, North Dakota. The show of the year however, was reserved for the last of the season when LGen W.K. Carr, Commander Air Command, proudly showed off the team in Portage to the visiting VIPs of the Wartime Pilots Association brought together for a reunion.

By the mid '70s, the Dragonflies had firmly established themselves as the premier helicopter display team on the North American continent and among the best in the world. This popularity translated into invitations to travel further afield, including such exotic places as Abbotsford and the CIAS in Toronto along with numerous appearances in the northern United States. Each successive team upheld the traditions of their predecessors and no major airshow in Canada was complete without the presence of the

Capt Gary Flath leads the Dragonflies in a surprise greeting to Maj Denis Gauthier's Snowbirds sitting on the ramp at Minot, North Dakota in 1976. (via Gary Flath)

Dragonflies. For successive team members, the team represented the best flying of their careers. One who certainly relished the experience was Capt Jim Hunter who went from Dragonfly 2 in 1978 to team leader the following year. His logbook reveals 120 sorties associated with Dragonfly practices, transits and shows in the two years he flew with the team. Witnessing first-hand the positive public relations that the team generated prepared him well for his assignment in later years

The 1978 Dragonflies continued the tradition of their predecessors with another exciting show. L to R – Capts Mike Wansink (team lead), Jim Hunter, Dennis Carey, Bill Michael. Missing is Capt John Zuurbier. (DND Photo)

when, at the rank of colonel, he was selected to command 15 Wing Moose Jaw. This ultimately made him responsible for overseeing the Snowbirds and allowed him to play a strong supporting role in the formation of the Canadian Air Force Heritage Flight in 1998.

From Dragonflies to Snowbirds

Another team member who can claim a rare distinction is Capt Ron Carter who was selected to fly right wing with the Dragonflies in 1981. Only a few months later he found himself being measured for a red flying suit when he was selected as the new 1982 coordinator/narrator for the Snowbirds, a position he had long coveted. His success story is one which underscores the intrinsic value that airshows play in attracting young people to aviation careers:

"My personal connection with the Dragonflies and the Snowbirds actually began with the author of this book. In the summer of 1971, Dan Dempsey and I were military college cadets undergoing basic officer training at CFB Chilliwack, British Columbia, just a few miles east of Abbotsford which just happened to be the location of one of the best annual airshows in the world.

As we were scheduled to have the airshow weekend off, a number of cadets (led by Dan, as I recall) planned to attend the Saturday show. This airshow was to be a first in that it heralded the Abbotsford debut of the Snowbirds, a new seven-plane Tutor demonstration team from Moose Jaw. As many of our group of cadets wished to become pilots in the air element of the new Canadian Armed Forces, we were all eagerly awaiting flying training and looking forward to getting onto Tutors ourselves. We therefore really enjoyed the Snowbirds' performance, although that type of flying was still only a dream for us. I must admit however, that the Snowbirds' debut at Abbotsford was somewhat overshadowed by the presence of the USAF Thunderbirds who were then flying F-4 Phantoms in a fully aerobatic show. The sheer size and power of this machine made for a truly impressive airshow routine,

A famous portrait of the 1977 Dragonflies photographed near their home base of Portage la Prairie. (DND IWC 77-360)

An unusual view of the 1978 Dragonflies gives a pilot's perspective of the tight formation flown by the team. Leading this formation is Capt Mike Wansink with Capts Jim Hunter and Dennis Carey in echelon left formation. The photograph was taken from the cockpit of Dragonfly 4, Capt John Zuurbier of the Royal Netherlands Air Force. (DND IWC 78-110 via Ron Carter)

especially for impressionable young cadets like us. So impressed were we, that a die-hard core of enthusiasts returned the next day for a repeat performance.

A number of those cadets, including Dan and I, eventually ended up at Moose Jaw for flying training after earning our university degrees at the Royal Military College of Canada and *Collège Militaire Royale* respectively. Following wings graduation, Dan became an instructor pilot on the Tutor at Moose Jaw, which eventually led to his becoming a solo pilot for the Snowbirds, CF-104 fighter pilot and finally the Snowbirds' team leader in 1989 and 1990. As for myself, I had so enjoyed my familiarization flight in a Kiowa helicopter while taking primary flying training at CFB Portage la Prairie, that I asked for and received rotary wing training following wings graduation at Moose Jaw. At that point in time, I thought that I had left fixed wing flying forever as I really enjoyed flying helicopters and there were limited opportunities in the air force for crossing back and forth between the two.

My personal connection with the Snowbirds began some years later, when I found myself well into my first operational tour flying Sea King anti-submarine helicopters with 443 Sqn at CFB Shearwater, Nova Scotia. I had become a Sea King crew commander and was the operations officer for the Helicopter

Air Detachment assigned to HMCS *Nipigon*. A Canadian Forces message in the summer of 1979 requesting volunteers for the bilingual team coordinator position with the Snowbirds became for me one of those defining moments in life when I decided to apply for the position.

Unfortunately, my initial attempts to land the position met with frustration for two consecutive years when Capts Denis Mercier and Wally Peters were selected for the job. I had known both Denis (a fellow cadet) and Wally (a squadron commander and the college's football coach) at CMR and I realized that I'd been beaten out by two excellent individuals. After having given it my best shot twice, I decided that being on the Snowbirds

The 1980 Dragonflies. L to R, Back Row – Capts Pete Campbell, Rene Morrissette, Gary Miller (team lead). Front Row – Capt Dennis Carey, MCpl Cal Jefford, Capt Ed Ukrainetz. Missing are Capt Marcel Belzil and additional team groundcrew, Privates Rick Pay and Steve Morden. (DND Photo via Ed Ukrainetz)

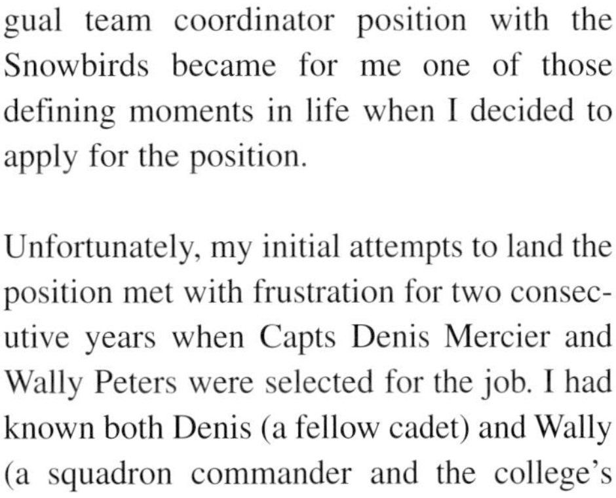

just didn't seem to be in the cards for me and looked forward to my next assignment as a rotary wing instructor at 3 CFFTS in Portage.

While still on my instructor's course, I was approached by Captain Gary Miller, team leader of the Dragonflies, about possibly flying with the team. As I had enjoyed the formation phase of flight training the most, I was definitely interested. Events took their course and I was eventually nominated to the team for the 1981 season flying the No. 2, right wing position.

In looking back, it's amazing how much the operation of the Dragonflies mirrored that of the Snowbirds in their formative years. Team pilots and commentators came from the cadre of instructors assigned to the school while groundcrew were drawn from the base maintenance organization. Operations were funded from within normal budgets and practices were scheduled after normal working hours. Team insignia, public relations materials and clothing for social occasions were largely funded by team members. Display locations were assigned by higher headquarters and often included small events of a local nature which could not be accommodated by the Snowbirds.

By the end of April 1981, I was well into the routine of flying daily instructional trips

The Dragonflies performed for thousands of northern Alberta residents during the CFB Cold Lake Airshow in Jun 79. (Rae Simpson)

The 1981 Dragonflies: Capt Gary Miller, Team Leader; Capt Ron Carter, Right Wing; Capt Wayne Norris, Left Wing; Capt Ed Ukrainetz, Solo; Capt Richard Archambault, Commentator; MCpl Cal Jefford, Crew Chief; MCpl Rick Therrien, Crewman; Pte Paul Blinn, Crewman; Pte Steve Morden, Crewman. (DND Photos via Ron Carter)

interspersed with Dragonflies practices. The flying was challenging and fun, and I was enjoying both aspects of my tour immensely. Then opportunity came knocking when I was offered the long-awaited Snowbirds job. I simply couldn't pass it up. Official word came very quickly and I was to be posted to 431 Sqn that September. However, by mutual agreement, I was permitted to finish the summer airshow season flying with the Dragonflies.

Our work-ups were completed after 16 practices at which time we performed our acceptance show for the base commander. Our work-ups were typical of what could be expected in any demonstration team. We flew basic formations at first to improve our proficiency in flying four-plane formations. Manoeuvres from the show routine were gradually added as the team's overall proficiency improved. The rate of progress was usually dictated by the individual progression of the new team members. On some occasions, experienced Dragonflies flew dual with the new pilots for training

purposes. In my case, Capt Wayne Norris and I were the new team members and we flew with Captain Ed Ukrainetz, a returning team member and the solo pilot for the 1981 season.

The 1983 Dragonflies. L to R, Back Row – Capts Pete McKeage, Stu Metcalfe, K.A. Jamieson, Greg Reiser (team leader). Front Row – Cpl Rick Pay, Pte Rick Chevere. Missing are Capts Bernie Faguy and R.J. Payette and Cpl Steve Morden. (DND Photo via Peter McKeage)

In due course we developed a tight routine of formation and solo manoeuvres enhanced by a rudimentary smoke system consisting of standard military smoke flares attached to a locally designed mounting on the skid cross tubes. Our highly sophisticated trigger system consisted of the pilot pulling a rope to trigger the flare! Our commentator for the 1981 season was Capt Richard Archambault who did an excellent job in choreographing our show to music. The overall effect was a very compact and unique show which was well appreciated by our audiences.

Of the 12 shows we flew at nine locations in 1981, the Canadian International Air Show was the highlight of the season. We flew a team photo mission around the CN tower in Toronto and flew two shows at the CNE on September 6th and 7th. These were my last trips with the Dragonflies and my last trips in a Kiowa. On completion of the CNE we turned our Kiowas over to the Air Reserves at Downsview since 3 CFFTS was to receive new Jet Rangers for the basic training role.

The 1992 Dragonflies pose majestically in echelon left formation. (DND Photo)

My connection with the Dragonflies was over, but my tour with the Snowbirds was about to begin.

Formation of a Different Sort

Being one of the Snowbirds' team coordinators for the 1982-83 seasons was definitely the highlight of my aviation career. Although the Dragonflies and other similar Canadian demonstration teams emulated the Snowbirds, there was simply no other unit like it in Canada. They were, and are, unique, and it was a privilege to be selected to serve with them.

Although the coordinators' job in itself was very rewarding, there is no doubt that I missed being in the formation from time to time. To compensate somewhat, there was plenty of formation flying for the coordinators during transits, as the first year coordinator generally traveled with the nine-plane formation. As well, the coordinators played a significant role in the photographic and media flights conducted by the team. However, flying formation in a helicopter was completely different from formation flying in the Tutor and I had a steep learning curve to get up to Snowbirds' standards. As my proficiency improved over the course of the season, I began to pitch out with the formation when traveling in sections as a four-plane, and eventually as a 10-plane. It was a demonstration team after all, and even though I wasn't part of the airshow routine, we were always in the public

eye. I therefore worked very hard to measure up and look like I belonged.

There were many stories that came out of that year of traveling with the team, but the most rewarding personally was an arrival at Nellis AFB, home of the Thunderbirds, late in the 1982 season. We had been trying for two days to make it to Reno, Nevada from the east coast, and had been delayed by severe thunderstorms in the American Midwest. The second day found us detouring a good deal south to get around the systems. The fourth flight of the day found me flying in the box of a four-ship with lead, 2 and 3 from Gallup, New Mexico to Nellis. Given the waiting audience, I tucked it in really tight as the 'Boss' led the formation down the main runway for the pitch. I pitched with the formation and then dropped back on downwind for a solo landing. Positive comments from the Thunderbirds watching with the rest of my teammates who were already on the ground really made my day. Although it was only a small accolade, it was probably the flying highlight of that year for me. With the Nellis arrival, my hard work had paid off and I felt that I truly belonged to the Snowbirds at that point. My transition from Dragonfly to Snowbird was finally complete.

I feel very fortunate and honoured to have been the only Canadian Forces pilot to have been a member of both teams. It was all great

flying and a wonderful experience I wouldn't have traded for anything."

Ron Carter

Passing into History

The Dragonflies did indeed convert to the CH-139 Jet Ranger for the 1982 season. The first public airshows with their new mount took place at the "Maple Leaf Airshow" staged at Gimli, Manitoba on June 12th and 13th. Other major airshows that summer included Moose Jaw, Portage, Brandon and Grand Forks, North Dakota where tens of thousands of American citizens also applauded the team. For the most part however, the 1982 season was spent demonstrating the skill and professionalism of the Canadian Forces to the residents of "small town" Canada at locations across Manitoba such as Miami, Elphanstone, Ethelbert, Killarney, Baldur, Elkhorn, Minto, Swan River and Winkler. For the residents of these small communities, the opportunity to watch a first-class airshow and then shake hands with the crews was among the highlights of their year. Unfortunately, the tradition came to an end following the 1984 campaign which was led by veteran instructor Capt Greg Reiser. His solo pilot for that last season was Capt Peter McKeage, who reflects back on the team's demise:

"I could go on for hours reliving adventures I experienced flying with the Dragonflies.

The manoeuvres the team mastered were absolutely at the maximum envelope of the aircraft and the pilots flying them. Yet, with our professional approach and strict adherence to safety guidelines we were able to put on a show that was both entertaining and widely appreciated. I fear it is a period in our air force history that will never be duplicated. You can rest assured that the decision to disband the team prior to the 1985 season was a terrible blow to the morale of the school and a great loss to the Canadian Forces. Over its history, the team probably had a more positive effect on recruiting young people to military careers than we will ever know. When I think of all the small towns we visited that would never have been privileged to see any military presence, I am truly proud of the job we did and all of the people associated with the team over the years. I have never been associated with a closer, more professional group of people."

Peter McKeage

Like their fixed-wing counterparts at Portage, the Dragonflies were revived in 1992 for a final farewell salute to CFB Portage la Prairie at the Manitoba Airshow prior to the base's transfer to civilian ownership. Capt Jacques Girard led the team through its last performance, bringing back fond memories for the thousands of spectators in attendance. This brought to a final close the era of the formation helicopter team in Canada. While solo performances using the full range of operational helicopters still flying with the Canadian Forces are a regular feature at most airshows, visions of four tiny Dragonflies performing as one seem destined to remain only a fleeting memory for those fortunate to have seen them perform.

Canada's last helicopter demonstration team, the Dragonflies, performed for the last time on 20-21 Jun 92. L to R – Capts Jacques Girard, Miles Mozel, Gab Pomerleau and Brian Wicks. (DND Photo)

The "Heavies"

Although the preponderance of airshow teams to have flown in Canada over the years have involved fixed wing trainers or jet fighters, those aircraft affectionately referred to as the "heavies" have always been an integral part of any airshow. Curious spectators young and old alike climbed into the cavernous hulls of aircraft like the Lancaster, Flying Boxcar, Yukon, Argus, Buffalo, Hercules and Boeing 707 for years at airshows that stretched from Comox to Greenwood. In more contemporary times, the Argus sub-hunter gave way to the Aurora and the 707 transport to the A-310 Airbus. For years each of these aircraft appeared in the air as well, either in flypasts or in the hands of a senior squadron pilot who amazed all by standing these big machines on their tails in impressive solo demonstrations. Who will ever forget the sight or sound of an Argus thundering over the field on the deck with props in full fine pitch, or the magnificent JATO (jet assist) take-offs, para jumps involving dozens of army paratroopers or LAPES (low-altitude parachute extraction system) drops of those giant bulldozers by the mighty Hercules that always wowed the crowd?

Tactical Tigers Air Demonstration Team

Of all these larger aircraft, only one can boast membership on a semi-official formation team. In 1982 the Tactical Airlift School based at CFB Edmonton (Namao) formed a four-plane team of C-130 Hercules transports manned by the instructors responsible for teaching advanced tactics to line crews across the country. By 1984 the team under the leadership of Maj Frank Fay had incorporated many of the crowd-pleasing manoeuvres seen in earlier years as solo demonstrations. The team started off their show by passing in review in box formation, subsequently switching to line-astern and line-abreast formations. Following a vic formation pass the team split up with the leader and number 2 setting up for a formation LAPES drop. As their cargo strapped on skids slid to a halt in front of the crowd in a cloud of dust, Tiger 3 appeared overhead with 40 members of the Canadian Airborne Regiment pouring out of the back in a tactical paradrop demonstration. Then, as the last jumper floated to the ground, Tiger 4 was on final for a high-speed pass that belied the size of the aircraft. To end the show, all four aircraft joined up and then

The Tactical Tigers pass in review during CFB Edmonton's Armed Forces Day in 1983. (Steve Hale)

reappeared over the base for a low-level battle break to landing.

The battle break was traditionally a fighter manoeuvre but was also most impressive when flown by a section of Hercules approaching the field in a high-speed, low-level tactical formation. As the formation reached the centre of the field, each aircraft would in turn pull up into a 180 degree climbing turn to position downwind for landing. It was an exciting way to end an aerial demonstration. Tragically, it was from a similar formation flown by local Hercules crews the following March at CFB Edmonton that a mid-air collision occurred between the lead and number 2 as they rolled out on downwind. What had started out as a motivational flypast designed to heighten the spirits of squadron personnel in celebration of the formation of the air force, instantly turned into a disaster of unprecedented proportions as 10 squadron members on the two aircraft lost their lives. Although there was thankfully no one hurt on the ground, the repercussions of the accident were to reverberate across the air force as virtually all non-operational formation flying was cancelled. This resulted in the grounding of the majority of the regional formation teams that were preparing for another airshow season in 1985 and for many marked the end of an era.

LAPES drops conducted by C-130 crews were popular with airshow crowds across Canada. (via J.W. Jones)

The introduction of the CT-114 Tutor in 1964 as the new basic jet trainer of the RCAF eventually spawned the birth of the Golden Centennaires and a number of regional teams that ultimately lead to the formation of the Snowbirds in 1971. Shown here is a unique four-ship from the early days at Portage la Prairie when the aircraft was sporting "day-glo" colours. (RCAF Photo)

Tutor Teams

From the time the Canadair Tutor was introduced into the RCAF inventory in 1964, it was clear that the diminutive little jet would become a favorite with air force instructors. It was far lighter on the controls than either the Harvard or T-33 which made formation flying and aerobatics a relative breeze. The aircraft made its airshow debut at the 1964 CNE in Toronto flown by staff members from Training Command's Central Flying School, although not in an aerobatic capacity. The distinction of the first formation aerobatic display went to four of the "retired" Goldilocks led my F/L Murray Neilson a month later in Moose Jaw. From 1965 onwards the Tutor became a regular feature at airshows across the country flown by many different instructors. It was even demonstrated at the International Air Salon in Paris that year by F/L Tom Hinton who also flew his aerobatic display at the CNE. The subsequent formation the next year of the Golden Centennaires to prepare for Centennial year marked the start of a lasting legacy for the aircraft as an airshow performer.

While the Centennaires and Snowbirds can rightfully lay claim to having made the Tutor famous, there were other teams that played an important role in helping motivate young men and women to seek military careers. In its prime, the base at Moose Jaw, Saskatchewan was the busiest airfield in Canada and one of the most active in all of North America in terms of aircraft movements. So, while the city may have had a bit of a sleepy reputation, the airfield located some six miles to the south was anything but.

Like all military flying schools, 2 FTS was divided into a number of flights (normally four) to which were assigned an equal number of staff instructors and students. The numbers varied, but at its peak the school was graduating up to 150 pilots a year with a new course of 25-30 students starting every six weeks or so. Such were the demands of the course that the washout rate was high, with occasionally only half of those who started the course marching off the flight line with pilot's wings 11 months later. However, *esprit de corps* and camaraderie were high among the troops and even the older RCAF veterans who arrived "on station" kicking and screaming after being fingered for an instructional tour eventually got caught up in the exuberance of youth that pervaded the base. Indeed, many revelled in it over time.

Flying with other instructors, known as "mutual flying," has always been an essential element of an instructional tour as it allows staff to keep their own flying skills honed to the lofty standards demanded by the profession. The missions vary but include everything from aerobatics to low-level navigation to cross-country trips in order to practice instrument procedures. One of the more popular mutual sorties that has always placed high on the agenda is formation flying. Whether in a simple pair or section of four aircraft, flying formation is one of the most challenging aerial disciplines to master and requires extensive practice.

B Flight Jesters

Every flying training school breeds a healthy rivalry among its distinctive flights. While the pride associated with being a member of a particular flight can be manifested in many ways, one measure that is readily obvious is the precision displayed in formation flying. Thus, a nicely flown low-pass (when duly authorized by the commandant) or even a standard overhead break from echelon formation always garnered an audience on the flight line during the Tutor era, just as it had in the Harvard and T-Bird days. Whether the callsign was Argos, Buzzards, Cocktails, Dragons or several others that appeared over the years, staff and students alike always strived to look their best when flying overhead the base. Special tasking from Training Command from time-to-time allowed 2 FTS instructors to showcase their formation talents further afield at special events or airshows. With this in mind, one group of enterprising B Flight instructors concocted a plan to form their own very unofficial "formation team" in the summer of 1969, managing to convince their boss that this was a good idea. As if to acknowledge that they were not about to threaten the reputation of the Golden Centennaires, they call called themselves the "B Flight Jesters!"

The Jesters' two principal shows flown in Saskatchewan in 1969 were for the opening of the Diefenbaker Dam and the Moose Jaw Armed Forces Day. However, they were also destined to receive "international" exposure. One young instructor who took advantage of

the opportunity to fly with the team was Lt Wayne Ralph, a future editor of *WINGS* Magazine and author of the internationally acclaimed biography, *Barker VC*. He provides some anecdotal memories from his brief foray with the Jesters:

"I was a very junior sprog instructor in B Flight when the Jesters were formed by our flight commander, Maj Neil Pringle, who appointed himself team leader. He put a number of his C category and junior B category instructors in the right seats of the Tutor for the experience, always ensuring that every seat was filled – hence the relatively large number of names that crop up in relation to what was never more than a four machine show. I did very little of the actual 'over the crowd' flying that summer, instead acting as a back-up to Claude Thibault flying right wing or Robie Robichaud in the box. Although we did a number of shows, our biggest claim to fame was the Air Force Day at Minot AFB, North Dakota in July '69 where we were sent off to represent the school, much to our delight. Since the Red Knight, Lt Brian Alston, was also there as the Canadian Forces classy solo performer in his scarlet red Tutor, his commentator Capt Joe Houlden offered to also narrate our show.

We flew all of the standard formations but Robie also performed 'student formation' stunts as part of the routine, pretending not to know how to fly formation at all during a few passes, of course with Joe Houlden playing his part on the microphone below. The USAF Thunderbirds in their F-4 Phantoms were the featured attraction to close the show that day and happened to see the Jesters' antics while driving onto the base. They were never quite sure whether Robie was legitimately a student formation pilot or just some nut performing crazy manoeuvres in close proximity to other aircraft. I must admit that from my perspective hanging on in the right seat, it was a rough ride and a bit unnerving for this inexperienced military pilot. In any case, our show was well received by the 10,000 spectators in attendance and we did get introduced at the banquet that evening as the 'famous Jesters from Moose Jaw.' We had a lot of fun rubbing shoulders with the Thunderbirds that evening, who by the end of the night must have been convinced that we were complete lunatics!"

Wayne Ralph

The Viking Reds

While the Jesters and other smaller school teams may have enjoyed only fleeting fame, one prairie team that did enjoy a longer existence was the Vikings, descendants of the Viking Smooth from T-33 days. Formed at the Flying Instructor School in Portage la Prairie in 1969, the first of the FIS Tutor teams became known as the Viking Reds. Capt Tom Byrne was a member of the team and provides an overview of the team's activities:

"The Viking Reds were a six-plane team flown out of FIS Portage in 1969 that helped fill the gap between the Centennaires and the first Snowbird team. The team was led by Maj Ron Beehler with Capts Tom Bugg, Gerry Thorneycroft, Clancy Scheldrup, Guy Childress (USAF), Tom Hinton, Pat Barrett and myself taking turns flying the wing positions, depending upon who was available. Naturally, we all still carried our normal load of students, just as the first Snowbird team did two years later.

We did most of the fairs in western Ontario, eastern Saskatchewan and Manitoba that summer, normally behind Lt Brian Alston

The Viking Reds were among the first of the post-Centennaires' teams that helped fill the void left by the disbandment of the team at the end of the 1967 season. L to R, some of the staff instructors who took turns flying in the six-plane formation show – Maj Ron Beehler (team lead), Capts Tom Bugg, Gerry Thorneycraft, Clancy Sheldrup, Guy Childress (USAF) and Tom Byrne. (via Tom Byrne)

who was the Red Knight throughout most of the period until his untimely death in July. We flew virtually all of our shows out of Portage and as a consequence maintenance was uncomplicated as breakdowns then occurred at the home drome. It was a cheap but efficient operation. All in all, it was a great summer enjoyed by everyone – pilots and spectators. Since we were non-aerobatic, our show was always close to the crowd and consisted of a lot of 'welded' formations with heavy G using variations of standard formations taught in the school.

Another thing that made our team stand out is that most of our shows were flown using white aircraft, old Centennaires that had been stripped of their gold and blue paint and then re-painted white as a result of skin corrosion. These aircraft were subsequently transferred to Moose Jaw when we moved FIS there in July 1970 after the decision was made to consolidate all of the Tutors in one location, a move driven by Col O.B. Philp. It was from Moose Jaw that the white aircraft were introduced to Abbotsford for the first time in August 1970 led by Maj Bing Peart."

Tom Byrne

The Vikings Formation Display Team

With the formation of the Snowbirds in 1971 in their seven white Tutors (as described in Chapter 12), the need for a second smaller team at Moose Jaw seemed redundant. However, as the new team gained fame and achieved formal status in the ensuing years, it was inundated with invitations from across Canada to perform at a wide variety of events large and small. The fact that the Snowbird schedule could simply not accommodate all of the requests helped lead to the re-birth of the Vikings in 1976. The proposal for the new team came from former Golden Hawk, Maj Ed Rozdeba, who had been seconded to FIS as the deputy commander under Maj Dick Lidstone. Rozdeba quickly gained support for a small regional team from both Maj Lidstone and the commandant of the school, LCol George Miller, another former Golden Hawk and more recently the leader of the Snowbirds. Having made great strides in promoting the Snowbirds, Miller knew more than most that there was a niche that the Vikings could also fill on behalf of the Canadian Forces. All three senior officers enjoyed an excellent rapport with their base commander, Col Dave Tate, who himself had

The most dynamic manoeuvre in the Vikings' repertoire was this head-on double astern cross known as the Carousel Cross. This rare shot was captured by another FIS pilot flying with Viking 2 in the summer of '78. (via Dick Bos)

flown airshows at the CNE back in the early '50s in a navy Sea Fury. Thus, with the appropriate overtures to Air Command in Winnipeg, the Vikings Formation Display Team was born.

Eventually assuming command of FIS, Ed Rozdeba developed a first-class four-plane formation show over the next three years using hand-picked wingmen from among his staff. There was no shortage of talent or volunteers to choose from. Like Standards Flight at 2 CFFTS, all FIS instructors had earned "A" category instructor status after several years of line instructing, a prerequisite for posting to the unit and in itself a major accomplishment. FIS was discharged with three responsibilities – teaching prospective instructors posted to 2 CFFTS the art of instructional technique, conducting jet refresher training for all pilots coming off a ground tour to resume flying duties and preparing all off-base pilots selected for a Snowbird tryout utilizing a 25 hour specially designed refresher course on the Tutor. With formation and aerobatic proficiency being so high among the FIS staff, the standing tongue-in-cheek joke was that the resident instructors had taught the Snowbirds how to fly, a theory which actually had some merit.

By their second year of operation in 1977, a senior group of FIS instructors had been selected to fly on the Vikings in Moose Jaw. L to R – Capt Jean-Guy Beaumont, Capt Roy DeWolfe, Maj Ed Rozdeba team lead), Capt Ray Hansford and Capt Don McLeod. (DND MJ 1977-1970 via Dave Rozdeba)

The 1978 Vikings. L to R – Capt Don Mcleod, Capt Speedy Fast, Maj Ed Rozdeba, Lt Dick Bos (RNLAF) and Capt Jim Fowler. (DND MJ 1978 2382 via Dick Bos)

More than one successful Snowbird candidate can attribute his success to the tips he learned at FIS in the frenetic three weeks or so before the annual tryouts began. And for several staff members who had paid their dues in Moose Jaw as instructors over several years, the Vikings became a stepping stone to winning a position on the Snowbirds.

Although the Vikings' show was strictly non-aerobatic with formation limits set at 30 degrees of pitch and 60 degrees of bank, the experienced staff flying on the team were certainly capable of handling much more. Dave Tate recalls with a smile that "Roz" was continually "pushing the envelope" and needed a gentle reminder from time-to-time to keep everyone happy. The team's repertoire included all of the standard formations plus a four-plane line-abreast silhouette that was particularly challenging. All were packed into a tightly choreographed show that lasted 15 minutes and included a running commentary by a fifth

Former Snowbird Maj Murray Bertram led the Vikings through their routine at Paine Field, Washington in the summer of 1982, capturing the crowd's attention with this four-plane cross leading into the Carousel. (Nancy Johnson)

responsible for ensuring safe separation. Turning as soon as they crossed allowed the team to complete the 360 degree horizontal circle in which the four aircraft crossed at the far side of the circle and then again directly in front of the spectators. An immediate hard turn by Number 3 then led to a high-speed rejoin and one last diamond bottomside silhouette followed by a formation landing to close out the show.

The winter of 1978 marked the end of Ed Rozdeba's air force career when he reached

compulsory retirement age. Fittingly, his last trip was leading the Vikings in Tutor 114050 in a salute to Canada's latest wings graduates and their proud families on December 1st, 1978. Leadership of the team was passed to the team's left wingman, Capt Speedy Fast, an ex-Snowbird solo who continued to lead the team with the same spirit and enthusiasm as its original founder. Under Fast and successive leaders in Moose Jaw that included Roger Maltais (ex-Saguenay Expo) and Dave Burroughs (ex-Deadeye Zip), the popularity of the team continued to grow.

The spring of 1979 saw a changing of the guard as several new faces appeared on the team. L to R, Front Row – Capt Speedy Fast (team leader), Capt Dick Bos (RNLAF). Back Row – Capts Bob Drake, Don Hollington and Dan Dempsey. (DND Photo MJ 1979-708)

member of the team. The team's signature manoeuvre was a formation co-360 introduced in the team's first year which Rozdeba named "The Spirit of 76," renamed the following season as the Carousel. It began with all four aircraft flying straight towards the crowd. At two miles back the team split into two elements that turned away from each other and then reversed direction to facilitate an exciting head-on cross at stage centre. Lead and number three led the two elements and were

Members of the 1983 Vikings that continued to impress airshow audiences with their precision formation show. L to R – Capt Guy Trudeau, Capt Jim Turner, Capt Tom Taylor, Maj Murray Bertram (team leader), Capt Roy Wansink, Capt Bill Carswell and Capt Mel Warren (DND Photo via Guy Trudeau)

The Vikings flew for the last time in 1984 under the command of another ex-Snowbird, Maj Ken Carr. Shown in this photo is an upward burst introduced to the show. (Mike Valenti)

Following his tour at FIS, Capt Bill Carswell received an exchange posting to the RAF to instruct at Central Flying School on the Hunting Jet Provost Mk 3A and 5A. While there he was also privileged to fly on the team known as "The Vintage Pair." The team consisted of a de Havilland Vampire Mk T11 and Gloster Meteor Mk 7, Carswell being checked out to demonstrate the latter. Of his unique experience, he recalls, "I was on the team for 1984 and 1985 and performed 50-60 displays each season. Our performance comprised a seven minute aerobatic and formation flying display, including limited formation aerobatics. The manoeuvring was limited to 350 knots and +2.5/0.0G so as to conserve fatigue life on the airframes. Still, the two aircraft were a thrill to fly. They were impressive performers, visually unique, and generally very well received by both the spectators and the other airshow performers. All in all, I am extremely privileged and proud to have been involved with the Vintage Pair - it remains one of the highlights of my flying career." What made Bill Carswell's participation on the team most interesting is the fact that the Meteor was also the first jet aircraft to fly in Canada in 1945. Team members were, L to R - F/L Dave Marchant, F/L Chris Whitbread, S/L Bruce McDonald, F/L Mike Wood (all RAF), Capt Bill Carswell (Cdn Forces). (via Bill Carswell)

A reorganization of 14 Training Group saw FIS move to CFB Portage in August 1981 at which time the commander of the new Central Flying School Detachment, Maj Murray Bertram, took the helm of the Vikings. Following an early appearance by the team in February 1982 at the annual Sourdough Days in Whitehorse, Yukon, Maj Bertram led the Vikings through 10 shows that summer, the largest being those flown at Portage la Prairie (a two day show) plus Ellsworth AFB, South Dakota and Paine Field, Washington. The next spring the team was invited to perform at Williams AFB in Phoenix, Arizona and Castle AFB in Meridian, California where they were warmly received. Maj Bertram led his last show at Thompson, Manitoba on July 9th, 1983, handing over the CFS Det to Maj Ken Carr with whom he had shared the Snowbird spotlight in 1975. Ken Carr had the honour of leading the Vikings through the balance of 1983 and the team's last season in 1984, giving the majority of his staff a chance to fly with the team. Nine shows were flown in their last year of operation. Venturing as far west as CFS Baldy Hughes, British Columbia for the remote station's Armed Forces Day, the team also performed two major shows in Ontario that summer – June 16th at the Canadian Warplane Heritage Airshow in Hamilton, Ontario and August 25th at the CFB Trenton Airshow. As it transpired, the residents of the radar station at CFS Dana, Saskatchewan were the last to ever see the Vikings perform on September 30th, 1984.

Although the Vikings will be remembered by many small prairie communities from Manitoba to Alberta, the number of invitations the team received to perform in the United States was impressive. Many came from NORAD bases where Canadian personnel were temporarily posted. The demonstrable support to these personnel was most welcome as evidenced by a letter of appreciation sent from the deputy commander of the 24th NORAD Region (a Canadian brigadier general) to Air Command in August 1978 regaling the success of the "Big Sky Day Open House" hosted by Malmstrom AFB (Great Falls, Montana). In lauding the performance of the Vikings from Moose Jaw and Rut Zulus from Cold Lake, the general stated, "These two Canadian flying teams were the feature attraction of the day and their high degree of flying skill and professional conduct both in the air and on the ground certainly enhanced the Canadian Forces image while giving high visibility to the individual aircrew and to their home units … I very much appreciate this outstanding support and consider it a significant accomplishment when the Canadians perform the only live flying at an American Open House which has a military population that equates to one tenth of our total armed forces strength."

Given the tangible appreciation that the Vikings received for their efforts over the years and the exhilaration that team members felt in performing in front of thousands of spectators, many will consider their time spent on the team as one of the highlights of their career.

Raven One

Although the demise of the Vikings along with virtually all of the regional teams in 1985 was a major disappointment, continued public demand for Canadian Forces support at special events and airshows across the country did ensure the continued presence of static aircraft and simple flypasts at many airshows across North America. One aircraft that garnered a lot of attention in 1989 and '90 was an all-black Tutor belonging to Central Flying School which had been reformed in August 1981 at Winnipeg, Manitoba as a component of 14 Training Group. To celebrate the 25th anniversary of the Tutor, the commandant of CFS, LCol Jerry Elias, used his initiative to "quietly" have a single CFS Tutor (114078) painted in a striking all-black paint scheme which became known as "Raven One" after the

Central Flying School's "Raven 1" stood out among her contemporaries during this historic flypast at the 1989 Saskatchewan Air Show celebrating the 25th anniversary of the Tutor as Canada's basic jet trainer. The honour of flying the aircraft was bestowed upon long time instructor and former Snowbird, Maj Jim Fowler. (DND Photo)

The Canadian Air Force Heritage Flight officially took to the air in the summer of 1998 led by F/L Bill Lamon. The T-33 shown in this 1999 photo (133500) had a proud heritage indeed. It was the first Canadair-built T-Bird taken on strength by the RCAF in January 1953 and flew in the colours of the Golden Hawks between 1961 and 1963. (William Gilson)

unit's callsign. The fact that the unit had no permission, no paint shop and no money to complete the scheme was not permitted to impede the brilliant plan he had concocted with ex-Snowbird Maj Jim Fowler. The end result however was a great motivator for the unit which generated considerable publicity. Sitting directly across the field from Air Command Headquarters, the black aircraft was not hard to spot among the rest of the unit's aluminum-skinned Tutors. Not surprisingly, it became the focus of considerable attention everywhere it appeared on static display. It was also used to lead various fly-pasts in support of community events as staff members were proud to show off the aircraft.

Air Force Heritage Flight

In 1998 a new airshow team officially took to the skies to pay homage to three of Canada's most famous training aircraft – the Harvard, T-33 and Tutor. What made the team particularly unique however was the fact that it was a combined military/civilian team which owed its formation not to an initiative from within the Canadian Forces, but rather to one of the foreign beneficiaries of the RCAF pilot training system. The connection lay in the roots of the NATO flying training program of the 1950s and 60s that saw thousands of allied pilots trained in Canada, including a young Belgian by the name of Bill Lamon who took his training at RCAF Stns Centralia, Moose Jaw and Portage la Prairie. Of all the pilots who came to Canada to learn how to fly, it would be difficult to find one more appreciative or passionate about his Canadian experience. Through his infectious enthusiasm, Bill Lamon, now an American citizen and lieutenant colonel in the USAF Auxiliary (Civil Air Patrol), became the driving force behind a tribute to Canadian flying training in the late 1990s:

"To some people, an airplane may be nothing more than a mode of transportation constructed of steel and aluminum; to others the airplane is a treasure to be cherished for its accomplishments in man's quest to conquer the sky. For me, the Harvard, T-33 and Tutor not only represent three of these treasures, they also evoke an era of wonderful memories and a deep affection for their history. Those of us who flew the Harvard all agree that just listening to the roar of its radial engine not only invigorates the tranquility of a peaceful sky, it also invigorates one's soul. Hence, it should not be a surprise that the genuine endearment for these aircraft is not only common among Canadian pilots but is also felt by the thousands of pilots from around the globe who took their training on them in Canada. While 1999 was the year during which Canada's air force celebrated the 75th anniversary of the Royal Canadian Air Force, it was also the year during which the 'Heritage Flight' paid tribute to the rich heritage and history of pilot training in Canada.

The 1999 Heritage Flight comprised, L to R – Capt Mike Ayling, Lt Darcy Molstad, F/L Bill Lamon, Capt Sheldon Tuttosi and Capt Pat Boyle (inset). (via Bill Lamon)

The team comprised three aircraft: Harvard 20436 (bearing the civilian registry N436WL); T-33s 133500 and 133119 from 4 Wing Cold Lake and 19 Wing Comox respectively (which alternated shows) and Tutor 114102 from 2 CFFTS Moose Jaw. Harvard 20436 was one of 270 Harvard Mk IV's built in Canada and taken on strength by the RCAF for advanced flying training, starting her career at RCAF Stn Penhold in 1953. She was assigned to No. 2 Flying Training School (2 FTS) at Moose Jaw in 1956 and remained there until she was retired in September of 1967. That same year, she was purchased by her first civilian owner who flew her out of Calgary until December 1988 when she came into my hands. Since her arrival at my home in Oregon, she has been fully restored to her original RCAF colours. Making her 'first U.S. appearance' during the 1989 airshow season, she has since participated in many airshows in California, Oregon and Washington as well as Canada. In 1992, I flew her to the National Aviation Museum in Ottawa where she was honoured by both Canadian and Belgian Air Force officials for her service in the training of Belgian military pilots. As a result of that event, I dedicated her to both the 88 Belgian Air Force pilot cadets who had taken their training in Canada and to 2 CFFTS at Moose Jaw where I made my first acquaintance with a Harvard in 1960.

In view of my profound affinity for my Canadian air force experiences, I took it upon myself to pursue my deep desire to make this Harvard a member of a formation which would constitute a tribute to all of the instructors and students who took their advanced training on Harvards. After much negotiation with Canadian air force officials, I was delighted in 1995 to have the privilege of leading her first dissimilar formation flight with a T-33 and a Tutor (flown by

Capts Larry Summers and Ed Baraniecki respectively) at the Eugene Air Show in Eugene, Oregon. The next summer we flew a 'Vic' flypast which I led in the Harvard with Col Jim Hunter, Base Commander CFB Moose Jaw, to honour the 50th anniversary of the 'Big Two' (2 CFFTS). The T-33 was flown by Capt Moe Girard with the Tutor being piloted by LCol Bert Doyle. On September 8th, 1997 we joined forces again and did an 'in trail' formation flyby at McChord AFB in Washington, this time with Capt Chris Brown, Capt Bob Roberge and myself as the respective aircraft commanders. While our performance there was meant as a tribute from Canada to the 50th anniversary of the USAF, it evoked such strong emotions when I listened to the Canadian national anthem and the announcer's referral to 'air force heritage,' that I was inspired to suggest to Canada's Chief of the Air Staff, LGen Al DeQuetteville, that he create a special Heritage Flight. The outstanding support I received from LGen DeQuetteville and his senior staff officer for heritage and history at 1 Canadian Air Division, Mr. Don Pearsons, led to the official approval of the flight on November 14th, 1997.

As the Harvard was designated the lead aircraft due to its relatively slow speed, it was decreed that a Canadian air force pilot also be on board, thereby satisfying Canadian Forces and Transport Canada regulations related to formation flying in Canada. Capts Ian Searle and Tim Rawlings became the first Canadian Forces pilots to join me in the Harvard for the 1998 airshow season, also taking turns flying the Tutor. Capt Brehn Eichel of 417 Sqn flew a T-33 adorned with a large '50' on the nose to denote the 50th anniversary of the aircraft. The following season, Ian and Tim were replaced by Capt Mike Ayling, another young man that I simply cannot say enough about – he was a delight to fly with. The team approach that we developed in leading the formation provided both of us with a wonderful and most memorable experience. While the Harvard

Both the aircraft and their respective colours made the Heritage Flight a much photographed formation during the 75th anniversary of Canada's Air Force in 1999. (via Bill Lamon)

got a lot of accolades as the lead aircraft, the importance of the T-33 and Tutor as members of the team cannot be underestimated. Two T-33s were selected for the team in 1999 from among the 53 operational T-33s which then remained in service in the Canadian Forces, one from 417 Sqn Cold Lake and the other from 414 Sqn stationed at Comox. Capt Sheldon Tuttosi flew 417 Sqn's T-Bird in the Alberta and Saskatchewan airshows. The 414 Sqn aircraft was painted in the squadron's 'Black Knight' colours and was piloted by Capt Pat Boyle who flew in the Ontario, Manitoba and British Columbia airshows. Finally, the Tutor was flown by Lt Darcy Molstad who flew all of the airshows in which the Heritage Flight participated. His aircraft bore the same paint scheme designed

in 1995 to celebrate the 50th anniversary of pilot training in Canada.

Each aircraft of the Heritage Flight represented the aircraft on which thousands of Canadian military pilots earned their wings. The first era on Harvards stretched from the beginning of the Second World War to the early '50s. Then, from the early part of 1954 to June 1974, the first generation of jet pilot trainees got their wings on T-Birds. Aside from a brief experiment with CF-5 wings training in 1974, all fixed wing pilots from 1975 until 1991 got their wings on the Tutor prior to the introduction of the three-tier wings system now in place. The Tutor was finally retired in 2000. Since hundreds of Commonwealth and NATO pilots also got their training on one or more of these aircraft, the Heritage Flight was a salute to the accomplishments of all of them.

As a Belgian by birth, an American by citizenship but a Canadian at heart, I was not only proud to have been able to represent NATO and the Belgian Air Force in this tribute to Canada, but I am especially proud to have had, at my age of 61, the privilege of flying with some wonderful young men of the Canadian air force who joined me in paying homage to the wonderful world of Canadian pilot training."

William E. Lamon

The silvery Tutors that could once be seen glinting in the skies over Portage, Winnipeg and Moose Jaw on a daily basis are gone now, having been retired from active service as training aircraft. However, the diminutive aircraft soldiers on with the Snowbirds, Canada's world-famous aerobatic team. Theirs is a story of incredible dedication and perseverance that merits special examination in Chap 11. Airshow fans across North America can look forward to seeing the Tutor painting the sky with plumes of white smoke in Snowbird colours for several years to come.

The Harvard in all its glory. Bill Lamon's aircraft is an honourary member of "The Big 2" in Moose Jaw, Saskatchewan. The aircraft was affectionately known as "The Yellow Peril" to those who learned to fly on her. (Jeff Foss, via Bill Lamon)

The SkyHawks

It is fitting that this chapter entitled "The Motivators" end with a tribute to the Canadian Forces Parachute Team – the SkyHawks. Like their air force counterparts, the SkyHawks have been an integral component of Canada's military forces since they were first formed in 1971. Discharged with the responsibility of representing the Canadian Forces at a wide range of events, the SkyHawks have participated in every major airshow in the country as well as a host of national events in their 31 years of service – from the Olympics to the Molson Indy to the Grey Cup. They have also performed in the United States, Europe and Australia, their worldwide viewing audience having now exceeded 60 million spectators.

The SkyHawks are made up of volunteers serving with Canada's Regular and Reserve Forces. The team normally comprises 17 personnel but with the number of volunteers far exceeding the slots available each season, prospective new members are carefully screened not only for their professional skills but also for their potential as public relations ambassadors, one of their most important mandates. Using physical fitness, teamwork and professionalism, the team strives to present themselves as role models for youth everywhere. They have been lauded for their work with the RCMP and local police forces in promoting an anti-drug lifestyle, frequently visiting schools to promote this message. All team members are expert jumpers with

The de Havilland Buffalo has been a frequent and invaluable companion of the SkyHawks since the team's inception in 1971. Relatively few adventurers will ever know the exhilaration of jumping out of the back of an aircraft into free fall flight. (via the SkyHawks)

experience ranging from several hundred to over 1,000 aerial descents.

The team traces its roots to the Canadian Airborne Centre formally located at Canadian Forces Base Edmonton, Alberta. While army paratroopers have been a regular feature at airshows for decades, demonstra-

tions normally included tactical paradrops only, sometimes involving hundreds of personnel who used the opportunity as a valuable training tool. Jumping platforms for such massive jumps were normally the C-119 Flying Boxcar and its successor, the C-130 Hercules. With sport parachuting in Canada growing in popularity in the late 1960s and

Advances in parachute design have allowed the SkyHawks to demonstrate some impressive multi-jumper formations over the years. (DND Photo)

The Canadian Forces SkyHawks have been flying the Canadian Flag with pride for over three decades. (DND Photo)

early 1970s, a group of parachute instructors with the Canadian Airborne decided to form a team for the 1971 airshow season as part of a larger Canadian Forces aerial display. In part, they drew their motivation from the famous US Army Golden Knights parachute team that was known around the world for their intricate aerial manoeuvres. The growing success with each season led to the SkyHawks being made a permanent demonstration unit of the Canadian Forces. The team is now based at the Canadian Forces Parachute Centre in Trenton, Ontario where they rely on the transport resources of 8 Wing for airlift support.

The SkyHawks Show

Like all aerial acts, the Skyhawks routine has matured over time as team members have gained experience in the art of free fall and both individual and formation flying. An important factor in the team's evolution has also been the development of the steerable parachute. While the team started with more traditional round parachutes when they were formed, they soon switched to the familiar rectangular chute which enabled them to

steer their chutes with far greater precision. Having their custom made chutes designed in the image of the Canadian flag has been an immensely popular feature wherever they perform.

The SkyHawks show typically features several jump passes, typically starting at an altitude of 10,000 feet or approximately three kilometers. As the team narrator directs the attention of spectators to high overhead, thousands of necks crane skywards searching the sky for the jump aircraft and the telltale smoke that will signal that the first jumpers have exited the aircraft. To enhance the spectators' ability to see the jumpers so far up, each are fitted with smoke canisters attached to their boots. What few spectators anticipate however, is that the jump aircraft will rarely be directly overhead, instead being displaced upwind from the target area on the ground to take into account the prevailing winds at the time of the jump. This is where the cooperation of the aircrew flying the aircraft and the jumpmaster who tells the jumpers when to go comes into play. A miscalculation by either can make it all but impossible for the jumpers to hit their target in the centre of the display area.

The free fall demonstration that kicks off the SkyHawks show is high in drama. Exiting the aircraft together, they immediately "fly" their bodies into formation, grasping arms to form a star shape. At a predetermined altitude, the formation leader calls for the release at which time the jumpers rapidly split apart to form a starburst effect, usually in red smoke. The free fall portion of this manoeuvre can last up to 45 seconds before the jumpers deploy their main canopies, with speeds as high as 320 kilometres per hour being attained. Chutes are normally deployed not lower than 2,200 feet following free fall. Another breathtaking demonstration that has always generated significant audience reaction, particularly from those who cannot hear the show narration, is the deliberate cutaway of a main chute by one of the team's senior members. This manoeuvre is designed to demonstrate the importance of training and discipline in reacting to a critical, life-threatening emergency – the failure of one's main parachute. In performing the stunt, the jumper deliberately releases his main chute as he would in a real emergency, free falls for a few more seconds and then deploys his reserve chute. As this is a delib-

The aptly named "Candy Cane" is a crowd favorite which leaves a swirling kaleidoscope of colour as the jumper approaches the ground. (DND Photo)

erate demonstration, the jumper in question actually wears two reserve chutes for this part of the show.

Subsequent demonstrations by remaining jumpers are designed with great precision and involve formation flying that leads to various intricate manoeuvres, from a seven-jumper stack to a three-jumper splayed formation highlighting their Canadian flags. As each formation approaches the ground, the command to separate is given and the solo part of the show begins. As each jumper

In carrying out their public relations mandate on behalf of the Canadian Forces, team members like Captain Julie Brazeau become role models for young people across the nation. (via the SkyHawks)

The seven-jumper stack is an amazing manoeuvre that necessitates careful planning to execute. Shown here are six members of the 2000 team obviously enjoying themselves as they are photographed by the helmet-mounted camera of the seventh jumper. (DND Photo)

approaches the ground, various twists and spiralling turns are executed to illustrate the impressive manoeuvrability of their steerable chutes, each leaving swirling plumes of smoke behind. These require great skill in their timing and execution as the aim of each jumper is ultimately to land on the "cross" laid out on the ground denoting the target. Using a small flag planted in one corner of the jump zone to assess the surface wind, each jumper will in turn manoeuvre his parachute to effect an "into wind" landing, just as an aircraft does. Crowd reaction is spontaneous as each jumper touches down, the greatest applause reserved for those who land precisely on target. For each member of the SkyHawks, a perfect landing creates a rush of euphoria, even after hundreds of jumps.

Practice Makes Perfect

The polished performance that Canadians have come to expect from the SkyHawks is the result of a long training season that begins each winter and lasts until the team deploys for their first show of the season, usually in early spring. Working up each new team is a methodical process that necessitates a high level of dedication and professional approach to safety to ensure that no jumper is ever endangered by the team's aerial manoeuvres. As the team has never had the luxury of a dedicated jump aircraft, they have always relied on the support of their air force colleagues to provide the airlift support necessary for their training and show performances. As a result, team members have gained experience jumping from a variety of Canadian Forces aircraft, from Otters to Hercs to their preferred jump platform, the venerable de Havilland Buffalo that continues to be an invaluable asset to the Canadian Forces in many roles.

A Canadian Symbol of Pride

Like all those who serve on a precision demonstration team, there is a special camaraderie that exists among members of the SkyHawks, a bond that transcends simple friendship. It is created in part by the ethereal knowledge that you are accomplishing something truly unique and important, an adventure that the vast majority of those who marvel at your accomplishments can only ever dream of experiencing. Yet, for those willing to take up the challenge, the Skyhawks are living proof that desire and dedication can lead to the fulfillment of ambitions that at first glance seem unattain-

Each SkyHawks team is unique with several new members welcomed to the fraternity every season. Shown here are 14 members of the 2001 team. L to R, Front Row – Sgt Tom Duke, Sgt Martin Lodder, Sgt Doug Sheppard, WO Ed McLean, Cpl Terry Gough, Master Seaman Jay Berry. Back Row – WO Andy Hulan, Cpl Kenny Downton, Sgt Dave Wagner, Cpl Michel Bolduc, Sgt Rock Levesque, Cpl Dave Thistle, Capt James Sebe, Cpl Chris Kariganis. Missing are Capt Hugh McReynolds and Cpl Danette Frasz. (DND Photo via the SkyHawks)

able. It is a message the team has delivered to millions of spectators from coast-to-coast in Canada in over 3,800 official appearances spanning three decades. And it is a message the team will continue to project as proud ambassadors of the men and women who continue to wear the uniform of the Canadian Forces in service of their country.

The maroon beret has been a symbol of pride for Canadian paratroopers for decades. In saluting their audience following each show, the SkyHawks also help perpetuate the memory of those soldiers who have lost their lives serving their country in both combat and peace keeping missions. (via the SkyHawks)

Aerial Artistry

The Art of Peter Mossman

Canadian military pilots have been flying airshows for over eight decades, their aerial exploits having entertained millions of spectators spanning two continents – North America and Europe. Since the Royal Canadian Air Force formed its first official demonstration team in 1929 there have been many teams, national and regional, utilizing a wide variety of fighter and training aircraft and sporting many different paint schemes.

What follows is a unique collection of art that represents the wide range of Canadian military aircraft and schemes that have flown with Canada's airshow teams throughout the period. Where standard squadron aircraft were used, as with most of the regional teams, the collection is not all-inclusive but rather includes one or more representative versions of an aircraft type. However, all of the special paint schemes that have adorned Canada's

national teams are included. Specific tail numbers have been selected to add authenticity and historical perspective to the collection, as have pilot/crew names for a particular aircraft in a given year. Of special interest is the fact that the teams have been based from coast-to-coast in Canada, the young men and women who have served on them having hailed from every province in the country. The names of

all known team members that flew or maintained these aircraft can be found in the team member annex at the back of the book.

Canada is blessed with some very fine aviation artists who have done much to preserve the history and traditions of the nation's air forces, from the Royal Canadian Air Force and naval air element of the Royal Canadian Navy through to the modern day Canadian Forces. This rare collection has been created over a two year period by Peter Mossman of Toronto, Ontario. His enthusiasm for military aircraft and love of art are evident in the exacting detail and realism he brings to each piece of work. It is unfortunate that each cannot be reproduced here in their original size, for they are truly magnificent.

Like many of his contemporaries, Peter Mossman's love affair with aircraft began at an early age. He explains how it all started and the technique he uses to create his masterpieces ...

'This is the plane your big brother flies in, and she is a honey. Love, Jimmy'

"This simple note, scrawled on the back of a photo of an RCAF Halifax bomber, began a life-long love of airplanes.

I subsequently devoured any publication featuring aviation for years until the founding of the Canadian Aviation Historical Society which gave me an understanding of the many choices of study. As an artist, I enjoyed as many 'gubbins' hanging from an aircraft as possible, so I selected military as my primary interest. Eventually, I narrowed my study to Canadian military aircraft as a specialty.

A dream job in the art department at A.V. Roe Canada at Malton had me working hands-on with the CF-100, the Arrow and the Avrocar. This experience helped my non-technical brain absorb some of the intricacies of aircraft and flight.

I have been fortunate over the years to indulge my passion illustrating aircraft for various publishers, the Royal Canadian Mint and private commissions as far-flung as Australia. However, a telephone call from the author started me on an assignment from heaven (pardon the pun) – to portray the aircraft of Canada's military airshow teams.

All paintings are rendered in gouache (opaque water colour) on illustration board. I use an airbrush to establish the general paint scheme, cast shadows and perspex, while all details are rendered with a No. 3 sable brush. I generally try to show the aircraft in bright sunlight, upper left, while making a low-level, high-speed pass. Most of the time it's fun to scruff up the aircraft and make it look operational. However, in the case of demonstration flights, a good polish would be the norm. With the present livery of the Snowbirds, I took the liberty of reflecting a big western sky in the highly polished paint scheme.

My thanks to all those who contributed to my research efforts and to Dan Dempsey for inviting me to contribute to this magnificent project. I will proudly add it to a rapidly growing library on the history of the Royal Canadian Air Force and Canadian Forces."

Peter Mossman
Toronto

SISKIN EXHIBITION FLIGHT   1929-1932

Armstrong Whitworth Siskin Mk IIIA
Royal Canadian Air Force
Camp Borden, Ontario   (1929-1930)
St. Hubert, Quebec   (1931)
RCAF Station Trenton, Ontario   (1932-1934)

Pilot Officer R.C. Hawtrey
(Trans Canada Air Pageant 1931)

417 (FR) SQN AEROBATIC TEAM   1947-1948

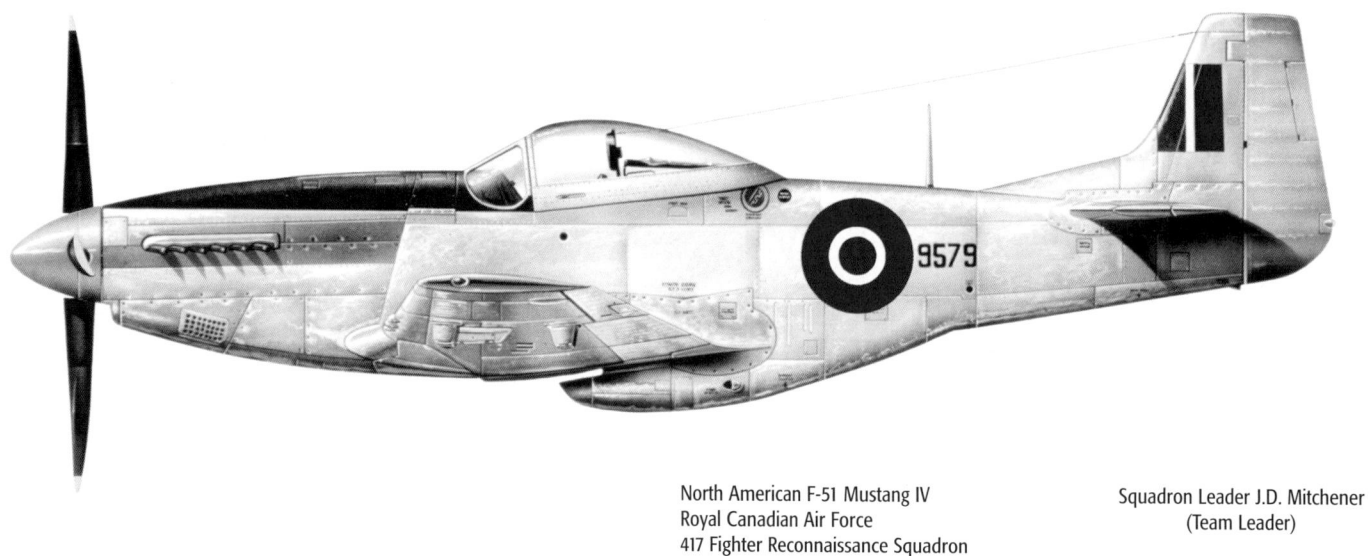

North American F-51 Mustang IV
Royal Canadian Air Force
417 Fighter Reconnaissance Squadron
RCAF Station Rivers, Manitoba

Squadron Leader J.D. Mitchener
(Team Leader)

BLUE DEVILS / AIR DEFENCE GROUP AEROBATIC TEAM   1949-1951

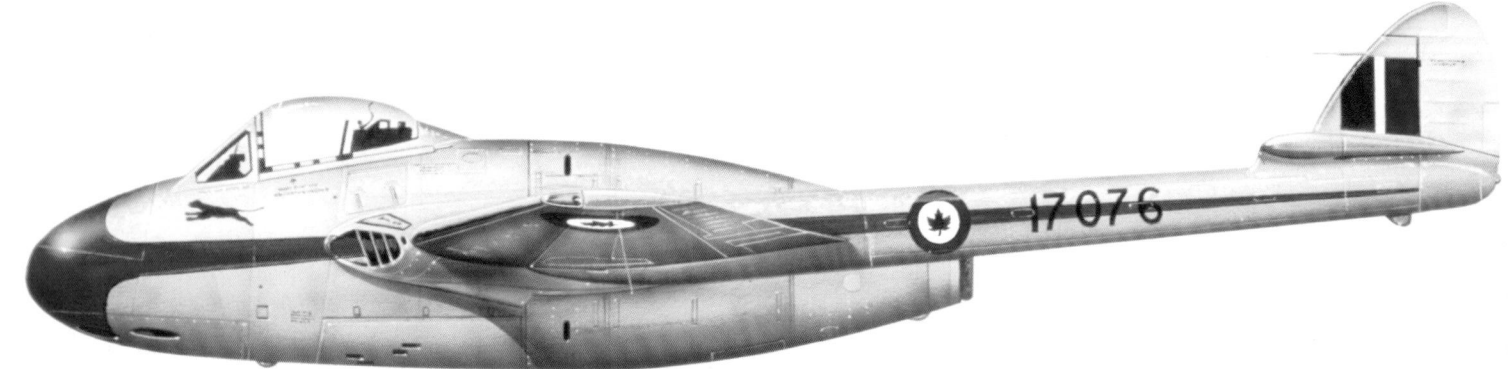

de Havilland Vampire Mk 3
Royal Canadian Air Force
410 Fighter Squadron
RCAF Station St. Hubert, Quebec

Flight Lieutenant D.C. Laubman
(Team Leader)

RCN SEAFIRES 1946

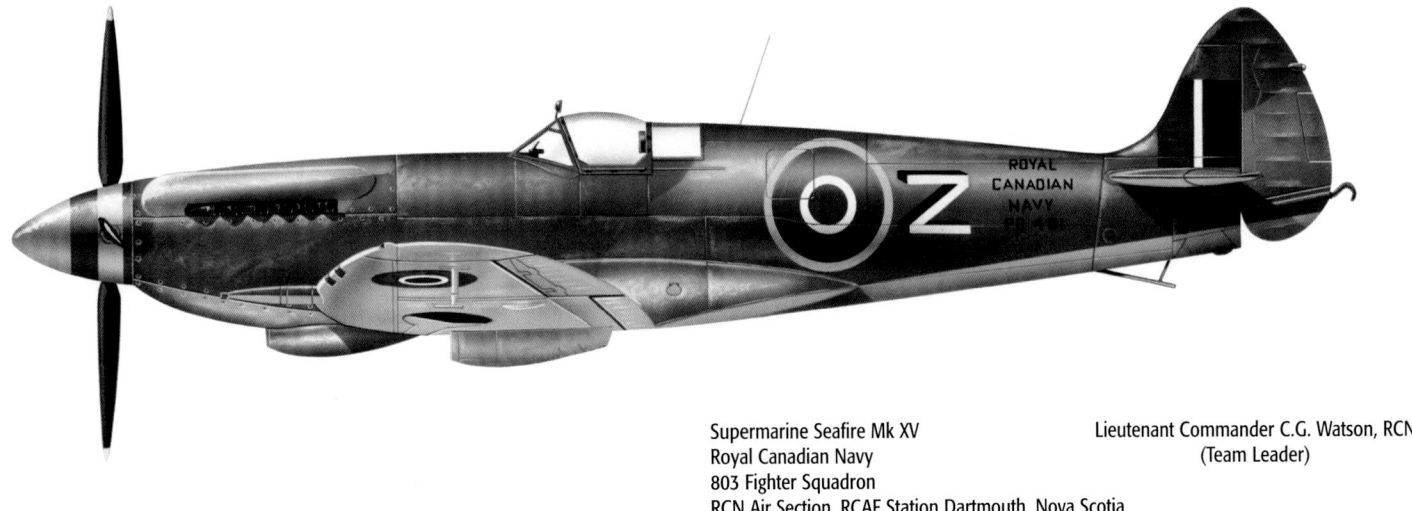

Supermarine Seafire Mk XV
Royal Canadian Navy
803 Fighter Squadron
RCN Air Section, RCAF Station Dartmouth, Nova Scotia

Lieutenant Commander C.G. Watson, RCN
(Team Leader)

RCN SEA FURY TEAM 1952-1953

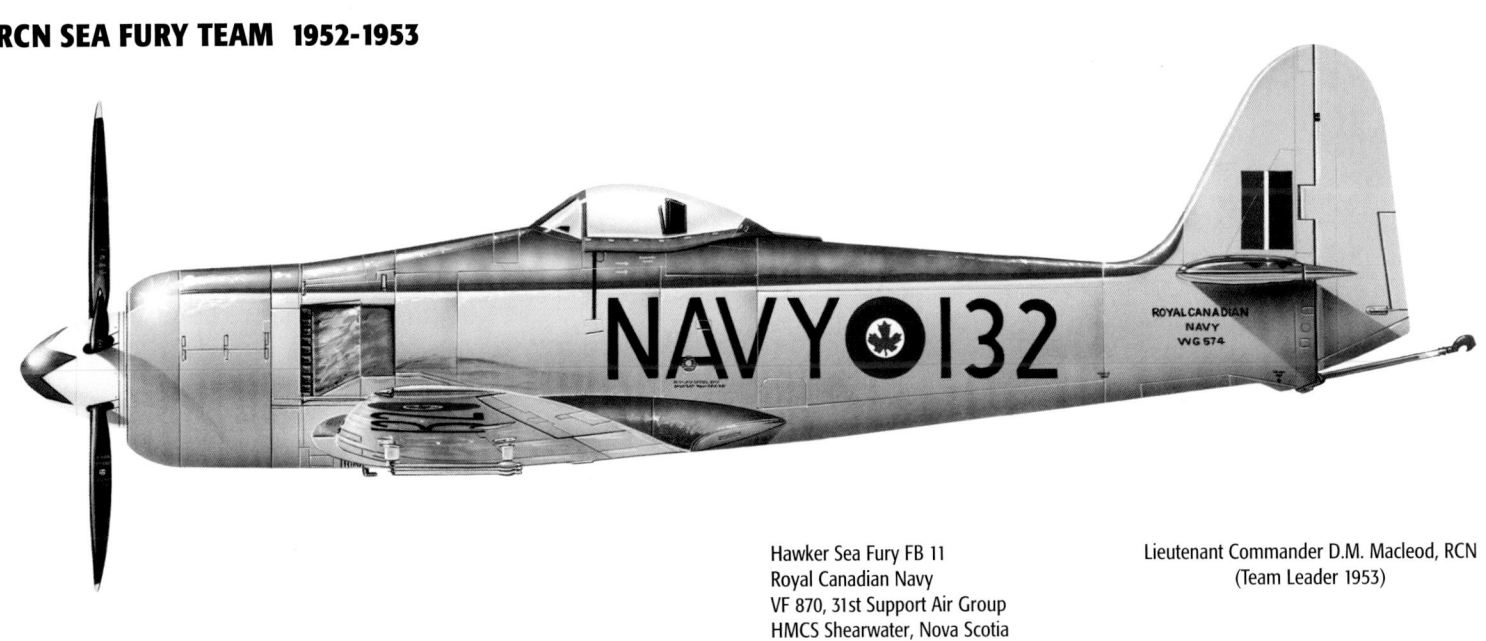

Hawker Sea Fury FB 11
Royal Canadian Navy
VF 870, 31st Support Air Group
HMCS Shearwater, Nova Scotia

Lieutenant Commander D.M. Macleod, RCN
(Team Leader 1953)

GREY GHOSTS 1958-1960

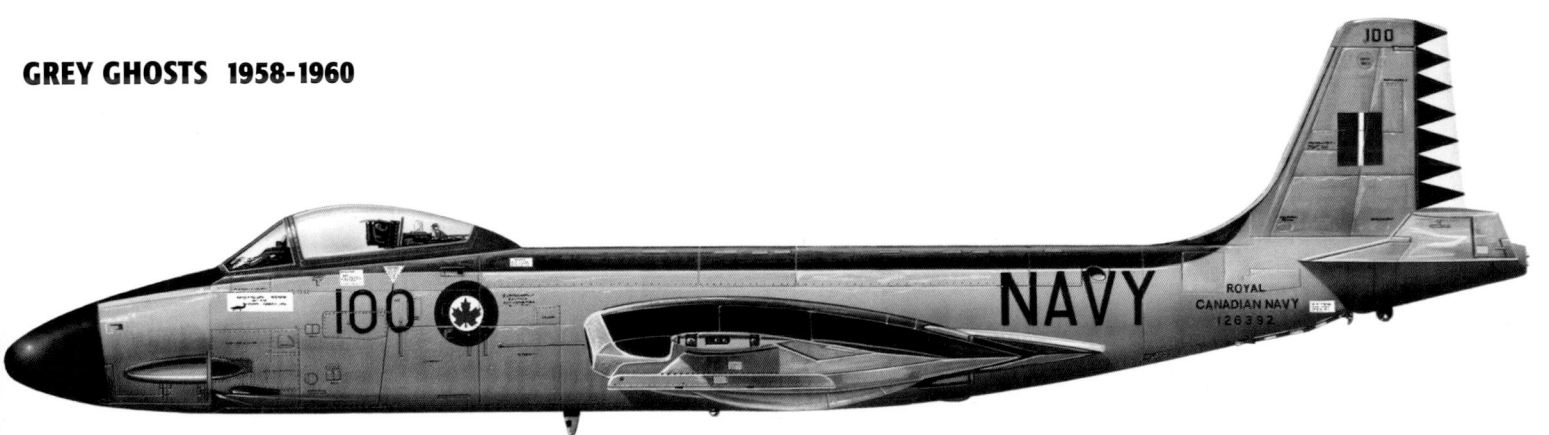

McDonnell F2H-3 Banshee
Royal Canadian Navy
VF 870
HMCS Shearwater, Nova Scotia

Lieutenant Commander W.J. Walton, RCN
(Team Leader)

410 (F) SQN AEROBATIC TEAM   1952-1953

North American / Canadair F-86 Sabre Mk 2
Royal Canadian Air Force
410 Fighter Squadron, No. 1 (F) Wing
RCAF Station North Luffenham, England

Flight Lieutenant G. Nichols
(Team Leader)

441 (F) SQN AEROBATIC TEAM   1953

North American / Canadair F-86 Sabre Mk 2
Royal Canadian Air Force
441 Fighter Squadron, No. 1 (F) Wing
RCAF Station North Luffenham, England

Flying Officer G. Brine
(Team Leader)

439 (F) SQN AEROBATIC TEAM   1953-1954

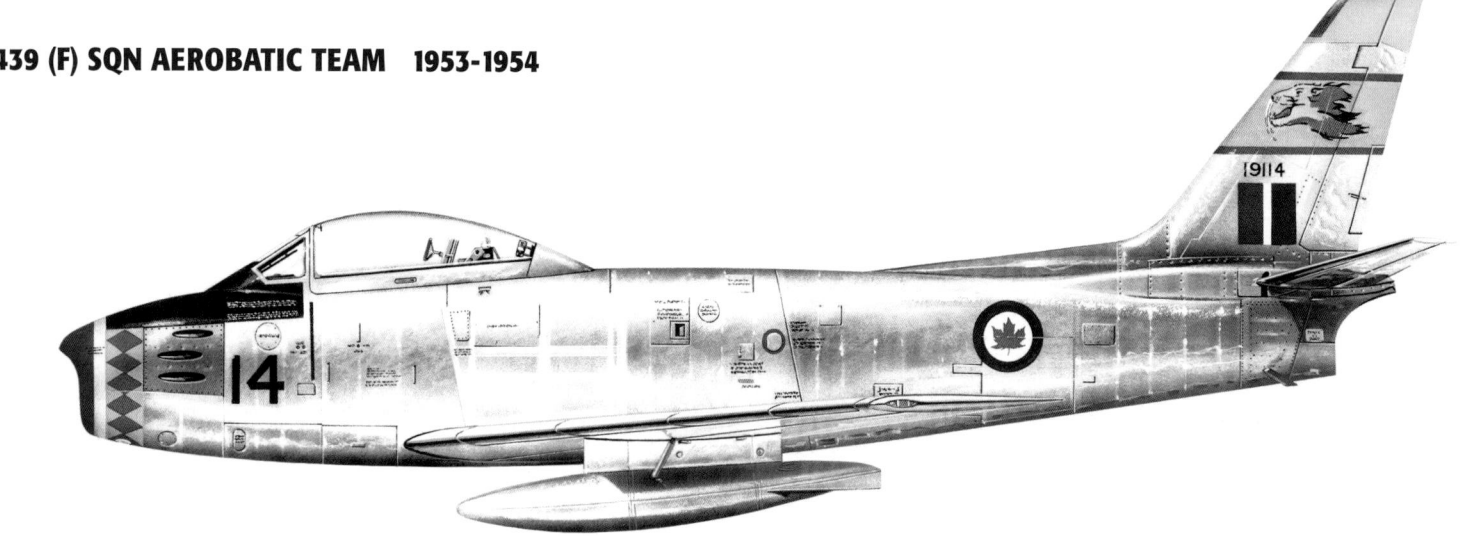

North American / Canadair F-86 Sabre Mk 2
Royal Canadian Air Force
439 Fighter Squadron, No. 1 (F) Wing
RCAF Station North Luffenham, England

Flight Lieutenant H. Wenz
(Team Leader)

SILVER STARS 1953-1955

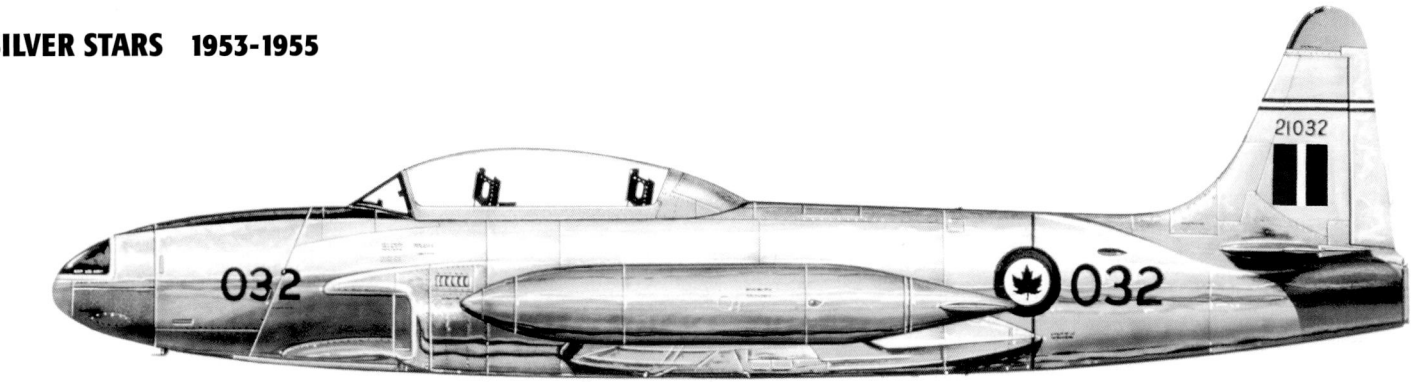

Lockheed / Canadair T-33 Silver Star
Royal Canadian Air Force
Central Flying School
RCAF Station Trenton, Ontario

Squadron leader L.J. Hill
(Team Leader)

431 (F) SQN AEROBATIC TEAM 1954

North American / Canadair F-86 Sabre Mk 2
Royal Canadian Air Force
431 Fighter Squadron
RCAF Station Bagotville, Quebec

Flying Officer F.G. Villeneuve
(Team Leader)

423 AW(F) SQN FORMATION TEAM 1954

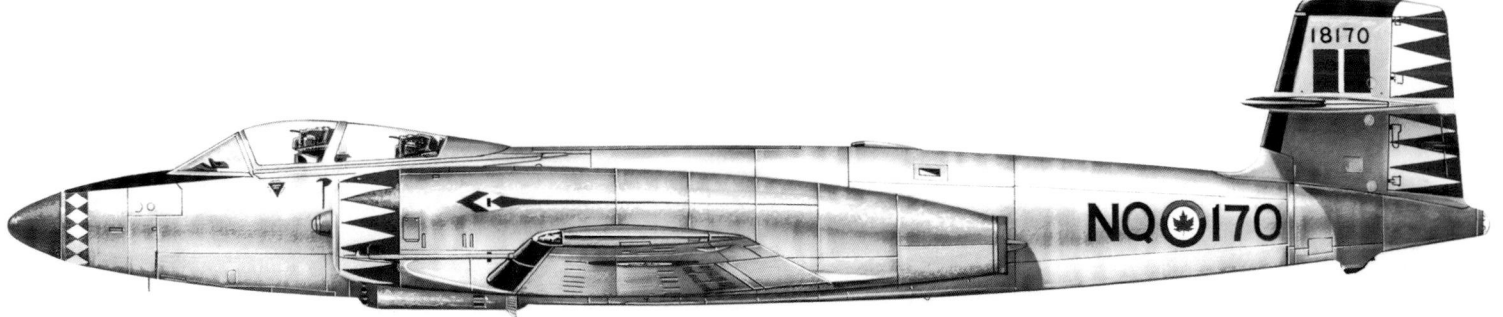

Avro CF-100 Canuck Mk 3B
Royal Canadian Air Force
423 All Weather Fighter Squadron
RCAF Station St. Hubert, Quebec

Squadron Leader L.P.S. Bing
Flying Officer P.A. Hawkes
(Team Leader)

3 (F) WING "FIREBALLS" AEROBATIC TEAM   1954

North American / Canadair F-86 Sabre Mk 2
Royal Canadian Air Force
RCAF No. 3 Fighter Wing
RCAF Station Zweibrücken, West Germany

Flight Lieutenant C.E. Keating
(Team Leader)

2 (F) WING "SKY LANCERS" AEROBATIC TEAM   1955

North American / Canadair F-86 Sabre Mk 5
Royal Canadian Air Force
RCAF No. 2 Fighter Wing
RCAF Station Grostenquin, France

Flight Lieutenant T. Hannas
(Team Leader)

4 (F) WING "SKY LANCERS" AEROBATIC TEAM   1956

North American / Canadair F-86 Sabre Mk 6
Royal Canadian Air Force
RCAF No. 4 Fighter Wing
RCAF Station Baden-Soellingen, West Germany

Flying Officer J.D. McLarty
(Team Leader)

LANCERS AEROBATIC TEAM   1955

(Note: The Lancers never flew a public display. The team was cancelled following a fatal mid-air collision in the landing circuit in May 1955. Only one aircraft had been painted in team colours at the time of cancellation.)

North American / Canadair F-86 Sabre Mk 5
Royal Canadian Air Force
No. 1 (F) Operational Training Unit
RCAF Station Chatham, New Brunswick

Flight Lieutenant D.G. Cinnamon
(Team Leader)

GOLDEN HAWKS   1959-1960

North American / Canadair F-86 Sabre Mk 5
Royal Canadian Air Force
Golden Hawks Display Unit
RCAF Station Chatham, New Brunswick (1959-1962)

Squadron Leader F.G. Villeneuve
(Team Leader 1959)
LAC W.B. Briggs
(Crew Chief Gold Lead)

GOLDEN HAWKS   1961-1964

North American / Canadair F-86 Sabre Mk 6
Royal Canadian Air Force
Golden Hawks Display Unit
RCAF Station Trenton, Ontario (1963-1964)

Squadron Leader L.J. Hubbard
(Team Leader 1963)
LAC E.R. Harnum
(Crew Chief Gold Lead)

RED KNIGHT 1958-1968

Lockheed / Canadair T-33 Silver Star (1958-1968)
Royal Canadian Air Force / Canadian Armed Forces
RCAF Station Trenton, Ontario   (1958-1959)
RCAF Station Saskatoon, Saskatchewan   (1959-1960)
RCAF Station Portage la Prairie, Manitoba   (1961-1964)
Canadian Forces Base Moose Jaw, Saskatchewan   (1965-1966)
Canadian Forces Base Portage la Prairie, Manitoba (1967-1968)

Red Knight 1960
Flight Lieutenant C.R. Hallowell
Crewman – LAC J.A. Woodhouse

BALD EAGLES   1959-1960

Avro CF-100 Canuck Mk 4A
Royal Canadian Air Force
No. 3 All Weather Fighter Operational Training Unit
RCAF Station Cold Lake, Alberta

Flight Lieutenant J.W. Stewart
Flying Officer J. Kuzyk
(Team Leader)

GIMLI SMOKERS   1959-1964

Lockheed / Canadair T-33 Silver Star
Royal Canadian Air Force
No. 3 Advanced Flying School
RCAF Station Gimli, Manitoba

Flight Lieutenant B. Partington
(Team Leader 1963)

CHIPMUNK SYNCHRONIZED AEROBATIC TEAM (SMOKE EATERS)   1959-1962

de Havilland DHC 1 Chipmunk
Royal Canadian Air Force
Primary Flying School
RCAF Station Centralia, Ontario

Flight Lieutenant B.K. Doyle
(1960-1961)

GOLDILOCKS / MOOSE JAW HARVARD AEROBATIC TEAM   1962-1964

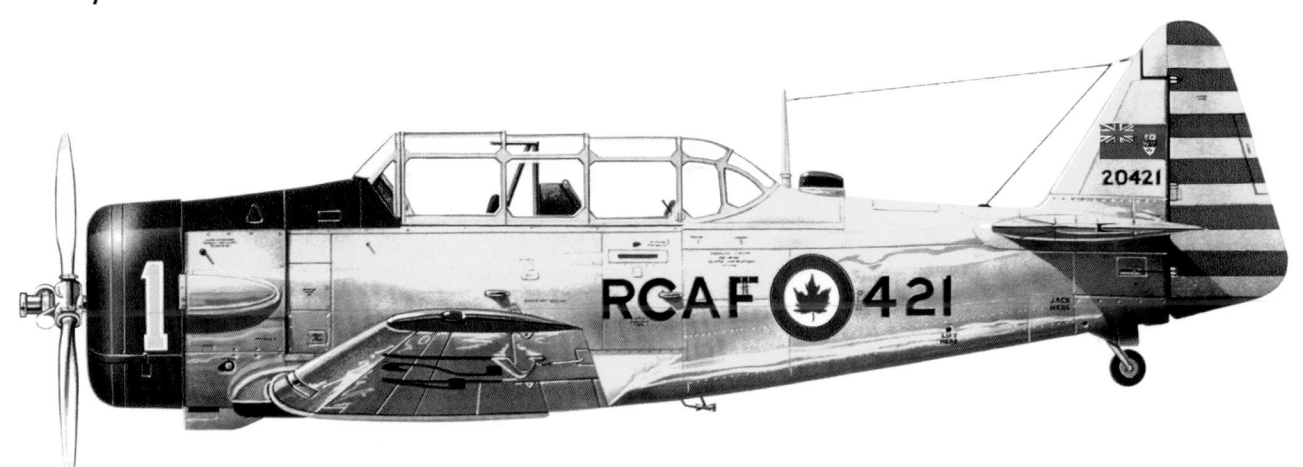

North American Harvard Mk 4
Royal Canadian Air Force
Flying Instructor School
RCAF Station Moose Jaw, Saskatchewan

Flight Lieutenant M.B. Neilson
(Team Leader 1964)

RED HERRING   1966-1971

Lockheed / Canadair T-33 Silver Star
Royal Canadian Navy – Canadian Armed Forces
VU 32
Canadian Forces Base Shearwater, Nova Scotia

Red Herring 1966
Lieutenant I.R. Ferguson, RCN

GOLDEN CENTENNAIRES 1967

Canadair CT-114 Tutor
Royal Canadian Air Force
Canadian Armed Forces Centennial Aerobatic Team
Canadian Forces Base Portage la Prairie, Manitoba

Squadron Leader C.B. Lang
(Team Leader)
Corporal G. Harding
(Crew Chief Gold 1)

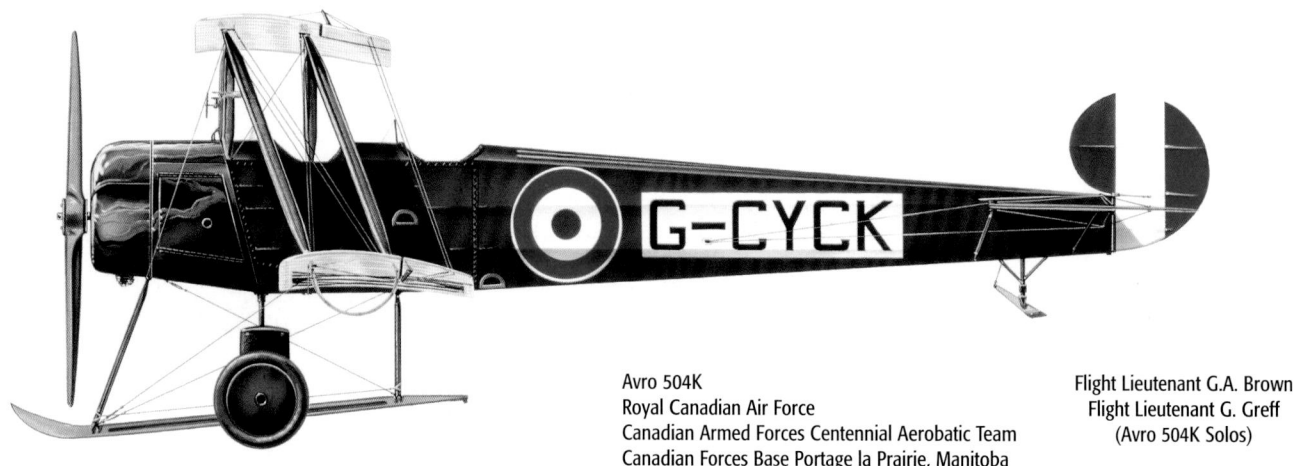

Avro 504K
Royal Canadian Air Force
Canadian Armed Forces Centennial Aerobatic Team
Canadian Forces Base Portage la Prairie, Manitoba

Flight Lieutenant G.A. Brown
Flight Lieutenant G. Greff
(Avro 504K Solos)

Lockheed / Canadair T-33 Silver Star (Red Knight)
Royal Canadian Air Force
Canadian Armed Forces Centennial Aerobatic Team
Canadian Forces Base Portage la Prairie, Manitoba

Red Knight 1967
Flight Lieutenant J.E. Waters
Crewman – Corporal R.J. Hawes

GOLDEN CENTENNAIRES 1967

(Note: Although illustrated from actual RCAF blueprints,
Starfighter 744 was never painted in Golden Centennaires'
colours. It was flown on part of the tour by F/L René Serrao
in standard RCAF livery as depicted on 769 below.)

Lockheed / Canadair CF-104 Starfighter
Royal Canadian Air Force
Canadian Armed Forces Centennial Aerobatic Team
6 Strike/Reconnaissance Operational Training Unit
Canadian Forces Base Cold Lake, Alberta

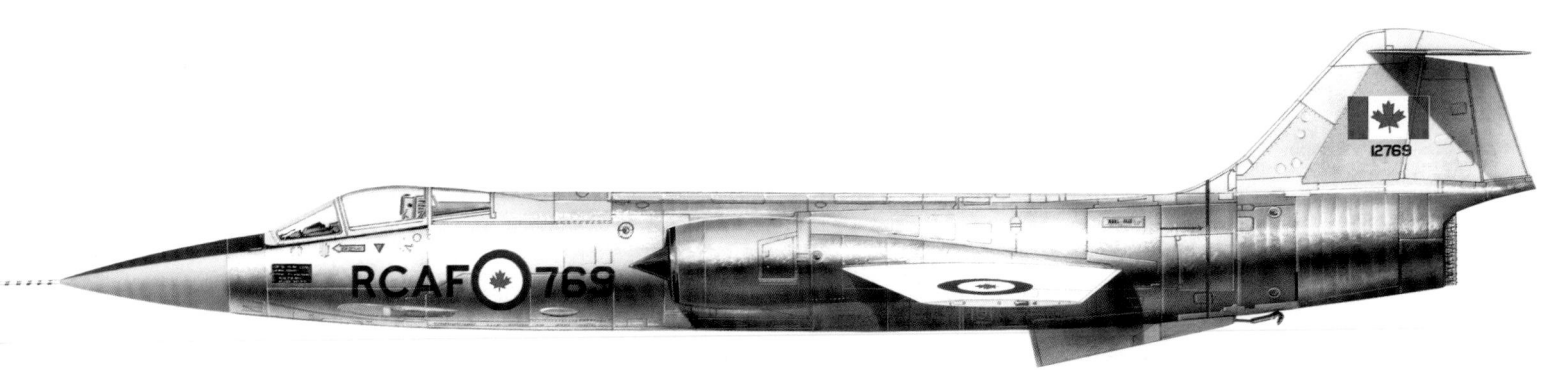

Lockheed / Canadair CF-104 Starfighter   Flight Lieutenant D.R. Serrao
Royal Canadian Air Force   (CF-104 Solo)
Canadian Armed Forces Centennial Aerobatic Team
6 Strike/Reconnaissance Operational Training Unit
Canadian Forces Base Cold Lake, Alberta

McDonnell CF-101B Voodoo   Flight Lieutenant J.E. Miller
Royal Canadian Air Force   Flying Officer R.M. McGimpsey
Canadian Armed Forces Centennial Aerobatic Team   (CF-101 Solo)
416 All Weather Fighter Squadron
Canadian Forces Base Chatham, New Brunswick

MUSKET GOLD   1971-1984, 1992

Beechcraft CT-134 Musketeer
Canadian Armed Forces
3 Canadian Forces Flying Training School
Canadian Forces Base Portage la Prairie, Manitoba

Capt G. Swiggum
(Team Leader 1971)

DRAGONFLIES   1972-1984, 1992

Bell CH-136 Kiowa, Bell CH-139 Jet Ranger III
Canadian Armed Forces
3 Canadian Forces Flying Training School
Canadian Forces Base Portage la Prairie, Manitoba

Captain F.D. Holtslag
Crew Chief – Corporal R. Black
(Team Leader 1977)

THE STARFIGHTERS   1973-1983

Lockheed / Canadair CF-104 Starfighter
Canadian Armed Forces
1 Canadian Air Group
Canadian Forces Base Baden-Soellingen, West Germany

Major E.G. Thurston
(Team Leader 1980)

SAGUENAY QUÉBEC   1980-1983

Northrop / Canadair CF-5 Freedom Fighter
Forces Armées Canadiennes
433e Escadron tactique de combat
Base des Forces Canadiennes Bagotville, Québec

le major Y. Bossé
(Chef d'équippe 1983)

RUT ZULUS   1976-1985, 1993

Northrop / Canadair CF-5 Freedom Fighter
Canadian Armed Forces
419 Tactical Fighter (Operational Training) Squadron
Canadian Forces Base Cold Lake, Alberta

Captain R.A. Lake
(Team Leader 1970)

CF-5 SOLO   1989-1994

Northrop / Canadair CF-5 Freedom Fighter
Canadian Armed Forces
419 Tactical Fighter (Operational Training) Squadron
Canadian Forces Base Cold Lake, Alberta

Demo Pilots 1990
Captain S.D. Green
Captain T. Jordan

DEADEYE ZIPS   1976-1982

Lockheed / Canadair CF-104 Starfighter
Canadian Armed Forces
417 Tactical Fighter (Operational Training) Squadron
Canadian Forces Base Cold Lake, Alberta

Captain J.D. Bagshaw
(Team Leader 1977)

HAWKS   1965-1984

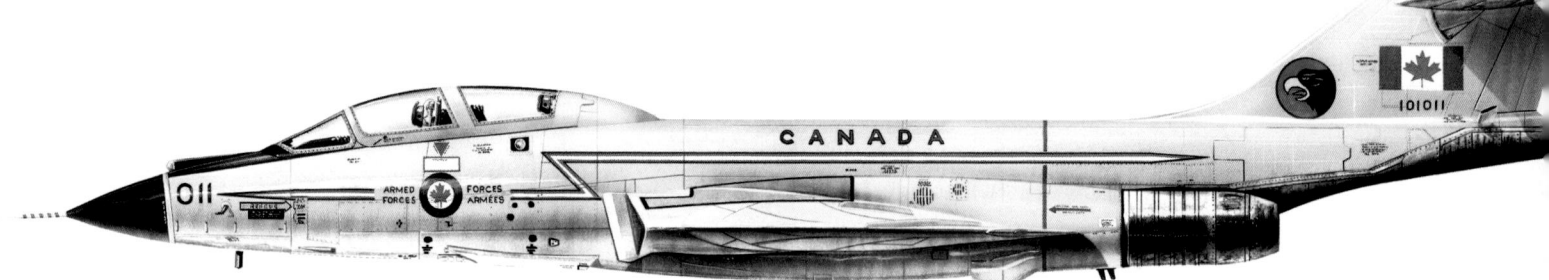

*(Note: The 409 Sqn Hawks were but one display team
in the Voodoo era. Each of 410, 416 and 425 Sqns also
formed CF-101 teams that gained widespread recognition
for the RCAF and Canadian Forces for over two decades.)*

McDonnell CF-101B Voodoo
Royal Canadian Air Force – Canadian Armed Forces
409 All Weather Fighter Squadron
Canadian Forces Base Comox, British Columbia

Captain T.L. Hunt
Captain G. MacPherson
(Team Leader 1981)

CF-18 SOLO   1983-Present

McDonnell Douglas/Boeing CF-18 Hornet
Canadian Forces
410 Tactical Fighter (Operational Training) Squadron
4 Wing Cold Lake, Alberta

Demo Pilots 1999
Captain R. Mitchell
Captain M. Mirza

RED KNIGHT 1968-1969

Canadair CT-114 Tutor (1968-1969)
Canadian Armed Forces
Red Knight Display Unit
Canadian Forces Base Portage la Prairie, Manitoba

Red Knight 1969
Lieutenant B.G. Alston
Crewman – Corporal R.J. Hawes

SNOWBIRDS 1971-1973

*(Note: In 1973 the new Snowbird logo
replaced the "Big 2" on the tail.)*

Canadair CT-114 Tutor
Canadian Armed Forces
2 CFFTS Formation Team - Snowbirds
Canadian Forces Base Moose Jaw, Saskatchewan

Major G.E. Younghusband
Crew Chief – Sergeant W. Holloway
(Team Leader 1972)

SNOWBIRDS 1974-Present

Canadair CT-114 Tutor
Canadian Forces
431 Air Demonstration Squadron (April 1978)
15 Wing Moose Jaw, Saskatchewan

Major J.G.R. Painchaud
Crew Chief – Sergeant J. Flach
(Team Leader 2000)

From the time the RCAF entered the jet age in September 1945, Canadian airshow audiences were spellbound by the revolutionary advances in technology that led to the development of jet fighter aircraft. While it was the deadly serious business of aerial combat that precipitated the advance of these machines, their appearances at airshows provided pure entertainment, introducing an element of high speed and noise their piston engine counterparts could not match. Initial displays by the Meteor and Vampire created great excitement which soon mushroomed with the introduction of the F-86 Sabre, homegrown CF-100 interceptor and F2H Banshee into the inventories of the air force and navy respectively. Teams like the Blue Devils and Golden Hawks brought great fame to Canada's military services with their thrilling displays of precision and power, earning themselves a revered place in the nation's aviation history. In late 1961 however, a new era began as Canada prepared to take delivery of its first supersonic fighters since the demise of the Avro Arrow – the CF-101 Voodoo and CF-104 Starfighter, distinguished members of the so called "century series" club of fighter aircraft. Within a few years they were joined by the CF-5 Freedom Fighter. All three aircraft could break the sound barrier at low level with ease. In the hands of Canadian fighter pilots, they brought an electrifying element to the North American airshow scene which those fortunate enough to have witnessed will not soon forget. Today, their classic lines have been replaced by one aircraft, the CF-18 Hornet, with its impressive manoeuvrability at all airspeed ranges. Even after 20 years, it remains one of the world's most formidable airshow performers ...

The Fast Movers

Capt Jordy Krastel leads a section of four CF-104 Starfighters from 417 Tactical Fighter (Operational Training) Sqn along with four CF-5 Freedom Fighters from 434 Tactical Fighter Sqn to open Abbotsford 1971 in spectacular fashion. Both squadrons were then based at CFB Cold Lake, Alberta and provided the high performance element of the Canadian Forces impressive '71 airshow team. (Bill Johnson)

Acceleration Plus! Two graphic illustrations of the power of the CF-101 Voodoo – at left a Nighthawk on takeoff; at right, an Alouette accelerates to supersonic speed. (Ron Miller, Kevin Psutka)

Voodoo Magic –
The McDonnell CF-101

The introduction of the McDonnell F-101B Voodoo into the RCAF inventory was a direct result of the controversial cancellation of Canada's Avro Arrow project on February 20th, 1959 as the RCAF prepared to celebrate its 35th anniversary. The demise of the Arrow had been in the works for some time, rumours having escalated dramatically when the Canadian government had announced plans in September 1958 to acquire limited numbers of the Boeing IM-99 Bomarc B surface-to-air missile. Nevertheless, the cancellation of the Arrow left Canada without sufficient countermeasure to the formidable manned bomber threat posed by the burgeoning Soviet air force as the Cold War between East and West continued unabated. The Avro CF-100 Canuck, Canada's first indigenous all-weather interceptor, was no longer deemed acceptable as a deterrent as it did not have the dash speed nor weaponry deemed necessary for a timely intercept of Soviet bombers over the Canadian north. With its supersonic speed and ability to carry both nuclear tipped Genie rockets and infra-red Falcon missiles, the Voodoo did. The tandem seat, all-weather version of the aircraft had made its maiden test flight in March 1957. In total, 480 F-101Bs were built for the USAF, equipping 17 interceptor squadrons at peak strength.

In a subsequent pact negotiated with the American government within the framework of the Continental Air Defence Integration (CADIN) program, it was later announced that Canada would assume responsibility for the manning, operation and maintenance of the Pinetree radar line under *Operation Queen's Row*. The Pinetree line comprised an umbrella of 33 radar sites constructed primarily along the Canada/United States border, largely at American expense. In exchange for this commitment, the United States would provide the RCAF with 66 F-101 Voodoo interceptors deemed surplus to USAF requirements. Although the official handover ceremony of the aircraft took place at RCAF Stn Uplands in Ottawa in April 1961, it was not until October that the first operational aircraft arrived at RCAF Stn Namao, on the northern outskirts of Edmonton, for conversion training. The Voodoos delivered to the RCAF were among the last batch of 93 built at the McDonnell plant in St. Louis, Missouri and consisted of 56 CF-101Bs and 10 CF-101Fs, the trainer variant which included flight controls in the back seat as well as the front. The last airframe to be delivered to the RCAF was also the last Voodoo to come off the McDonnell assembly line – serial number 59-483 which was renumbered CF-101B 17483.

With its new high-speed interceptor, the RCAF's Air Defence Command under the leadership of Air Vice Marshal M.M. Hendrick ultimately replaced its nine CF-100 squadrons with five CF-101 squadrons. The majority of the "Clunk" crews made the transition to the new machine. This included the CO of 432 Sqn (and former Blue Devil), W/C R.D. "Joe" Schultz. He led an initial cadre of nine pilots and eight navigators to the United States where they completed their flying conversion to the Voodoo with the USAF at Hamilton AFB in California. This nucleus of aviators then became the instructors who conducted all further squadron conversions at Namao which was at the time one of four Strategic Air Command refuelling bases in Canada and a good location for the training. Notwithstanding the Alberta winter, it had one of the longest runways in North America at 14,000 feet. This came in handy as pilots made the adjustment to the big machine which had a much higher takeoff and landing speed than the CF-100. Like the Lockheed F-104 Starfighter which would soon be introduced at RCAF Stn Cold Lake some 180 miles to the north-east, the Voodoo also used a drag chute on landing to decelerate.

The five squadrons to stand up on the Voodoo were, in order of conversion, 425 *Alouette* Sqn, 410 *Cougar* Sqn, 416 *Lynx* Sqn, 409 *Nighthawk* Sqn and finally 414 *Black Knight* Sqn. The Alouettes became the initial training squadron for the first year of operation, handing that responsibility to No.

| 17402 | 17410 | 17400 | 17409 | 17477 |
| 425 Alouette Sqn | 410 Cougar Sqn | 416 Black Lynx Sqn | 409 Nighthawk Sqn | 414 Black Knight Sqn |

The squadron colours of the RCAF Voodoo squadrons as they stood up in 1961-1962. (Peter Mossman, James Jones)

3 AW(F) OTU in Bagotville in October 1962. Although 410 Sqn was later disbanded in the spring of 1964 as an operational unit due to fiscal cutbacks, it was re-formed four years later under the newly unified Canadian Forces, replacing 3 OTU as the repository of all airborne intercept training for the balance of the Voodoo era.

The initial paint scheme adopted by the RCAF for the new interceptor distinguished each squadron by employing different colours on the striped rudder which adorned each aircraft – black and silver for 425; red and white for 410; black and yellow for 416; blue and yellow for 409; and black and red for 414. In later years the stripes were removed as large squadron emblems on the tails took precedence, but the pride in the squadron colours never waned among aircrew or groundcrew, an essential ingredient in the *esprit de corps* of each unit.

Considering the complexity of the aircraft, the pilot's instrument console in the Voodoo was remarkably simple. The console had a true airspeed gauge (knots) and a very small machmeter within the main airspeed indicator. (via Ron Berlie)

The CF-101B Voodoo in post-1965 RCAF colours displaying Canada's new flag. This aircraft from 416 AW(F) Sqn was made famous by the crew of F/L Jake Miller and F/L Rob McGimpsey during their 1967 tour with the Golden Centennaires. (Peter Mossman)

Airshows Voodoo Style

In the 22 years it served the RCAF and Canadian Forces, the Voodoo made hundreds of public appearances at airshows across North America. Its impressive size and booming "hard burner light" quickly made it a favourite among airshow audiences across Canada. By most fighter standards it was a huge machine – certainly no airshow static display was complete without its looming presence as patrons marvelled at its size – it dwarfed many aircraft of its generation. It stood 18 feet (5.48 m) high, had a length of just over 71 feet (21.66 m) and a wingspan just shy of 40 feet (12.09 m). Powered by two Pratt & Whitney J57-P55 turbojet engines, each rated at 10,200 pounds of thrust at military power and 16,000 pounds in afterburner, the aircraft could climb to 35,000 feet in 2 minutes 20 seconds in full burner. Once at that altitude, it had a maximum advertised airspeed of Mach 1.73 (or 700 knots indicated airspeed). And being capable of attaining over 600 knots on the deck, "one-o-wonders" had to be very careful not to break the sound barrier during high-speed manoeuvring at airshows. This was not as easy as it sounds, as former formation team member, soloist and

test pilot Capt Ron Berlie recalls:

"There were large errors in the airspeed indicating system of the Voodoo due to the effects of compressibility in the transonic speed range. To illustrate, there was a chart in the Aircraft Operating Instructions for conversion of 'indicated' Mach number to 'true' Mach number. For example M0.8 indicated was actually 0.85 true; M0.9 indicated was 0.97! If you saw M0.92 indicated you were very close to supersonic and M0.95 indicated meant you were really doing M1.05 – time to get your cheque book out, practice your marching (hat not required) and find some friends – you'd just broken windows for miles around! Similarly, there was also a note in the AOIs advising that even in the primary mode, the servo altimeter was subject to large position errors at high subsonic speeds. Of interest, once you pushed through the sound barrier, instrument indications became reliable again, though a little too late if you were doing an airshow!"

Ron Berlie

The first public appearances of the Voodoo in Canada took place in the summer of 1961

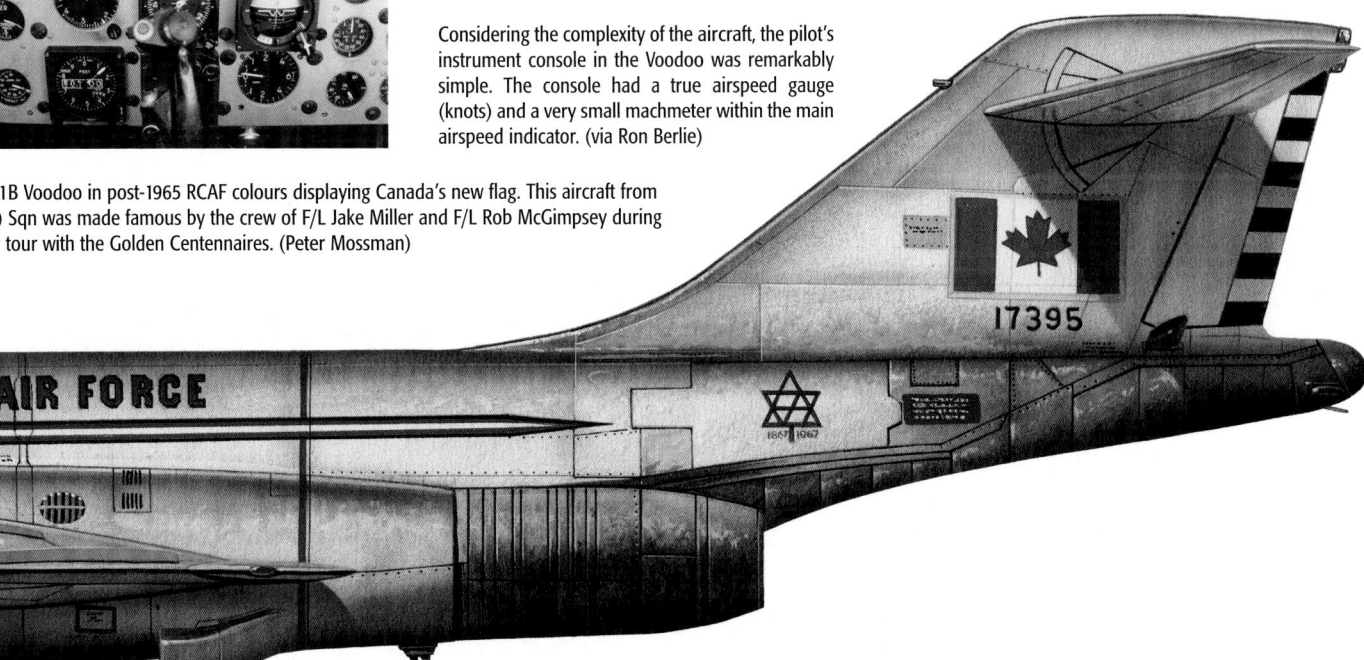

A fine study of a "second batch" Canadian Forces CF-101 as it taxis in following a performance in Comox in 1984. The replacement 66 Voodoos delivered in 1971-1972 were easily identified by the infra-red sensor on the nose. (Ron Miller)

The badges that distinguished the pilots and airborne intercept navigators of Canada's CF-101 interceptor force from 1961 to 1984.

shortly after the official handover ceremony at RCAF Stn Uplands. The two aircraft accepted in the ceremony were numbered 17101 and 17102 for public relations purposes and toured the country bearing those registrations. They were subsequently renumbered 17410 and 17440 prior to entering

operational service that fall. As each squadron transitioned to the new aircraft over a period of several months they returned to their assigned bases to take up their air defence responsibilities as part of the NORAD alliance – 425 to Bagotville, 410 and 416 to Uplands (Ottawa), 409 to Comox and 414 to North Bay.

While there was never any question that the primary responsibility of the squadrons was as combat ready interceptor units, squadrons did go out of their way to try and accommodate a heavy demand for public

appearances over the summer months. This eventually translated into part-time airshow teams for most of the squadrons, each taking pride in showing off their colours and prowess to appreciative audiences across the country. The first of the five squadrons to put together the semblance of an airshow team was 416 Sqn, doing so in 1962.

The RCAF's Air Defence Command of the 1960s was redesignated Air Defence Group with the formation of Air Command in 1975. The five squadrons that comprised ADG continued to participate in airshows from coast-to-coast, four of them with the CF-101 Voodoo. (DND NBC 78-1798)

416 AW(F) Sqn Demonstration Teams

The first year of operation for 416 Sqn in the Voodoo era was anything but stable as the squadron moved "homes" three times. The squadron was stationed in Uplands from January to July 1962 and then spent the next four months in Bagotville (with 425 Sqn) prior to arriving at their permanent home of Chatham, New Brunswick. Given this frenetic schedule of moves and the intense training activity that was required to obtain operational combat capability, it would seem somewhat surprising that the squadron had any time for airshow activities. Yet, 416 was among the first to establish a semi-official demonstration team, Lynx Formation, which years later would come to be known as The Bobcats.

The Voodoo's entry into the realm of airshows was the result of several factors. Firstly, airshows were immensely popular across the country with millions of Canadians attending "Air Force Days" each year. Although the RCAF Golden Hawks were thriving into their fourth year of operation as the RCAF's showcase team, the Chief of the Air Staff, Air Marshal Hugh Campbell, believed it was important that the full capability of the RCAF be demonstrated to Canadian citizens. Big dollars were being spent to revitalize the air force with highly sophisticated supersonic fighters and it was important that Canadian taxpayers understand what they were getting for their money, and why. Therefore, airshow participation by all operational units on a rotational basis became a fact of life.

The fact that 416 was able to embrace airshow tasking so quickly was largely due to two individuals with extensive airshow experience, W/C Dean Kelly (CO 416 Sqn) and F/L Al Robb. Kelly wasted no time in picking up on the Voodoo where he had left off with the Sabre, impressing all with a precision display that pushed the envelope of the big machine. His largest audience of the summer was at RCAF Stn Rockcliffe (only a few miles away from Uplands) for National Air Force Day on June 9th, 1962 where he led a contingent of squadron Voodoos for a fly-past followed by his solo display. A similar display dazzled the spectators at Bagotville's AFD on August 6th. Squadron historical records at 416 are full of praise for W/C Kelly's airshows, just as 441 Sqn's are of his F-86 performances.

As for Al Robb, he had been a member of the first Sabre aerobatic team at 410 Sqn in North Luffenham, England 10 years earlier, making him a natural for selection as 416 Sqn's first demonstration team leader on the Voodoo. Joining him as lead navigator was F/O Chuck Verge. The other crews were F/O Stu Whalley with F/L Ray Jefferies, F/O Roger Cossette with F/O Don Parker and F/O Pete DeLong with F/O Gord Larsen. For Al Robb, two shows that summer stand out:

"The Voodoo shows that hold the most vivid memories for me took place within two days of each other, at Sept Isles, Quebec on August 4th followed by Air Force Day at our home station of Bagotville. At Sept Isles we really tore the airfield apart. Following several formation passes, we rolled out after a reversal and set up in four-plane line-astern formation. This allowed us to come in very low and very fast – just under the speed of sound. As we approached stage centre right in front of the crowd, we pulled straight up individually into vertical climbs, lighting our afterburners just as we pulled up. We then culminated our show with vertical rolls. In spite of our rather low altitude and high airspeed, the crowd loved it and not a single complaint was received. This led to a repeat performance in Bagotville, the exception being that we ran in for our vertical finale in a two second trail formation. The result was equally spectacular, although a combination of our wing tip vortices and jet wash as we pulled up unfortunately sent swirling clouds of dust into part of the crowd. By contrast, the shows I led two summers later at Dow AFB south of the border and then at our home station in Chatham were quite tame, yet still a lot of fun to fly."

Al Robb

Crew members of one of the RCAF's first Voodoo teams to perform airshows in the summer of 1962. L to R – F/L Al Robb/ F/O Chuck Verge; F/O Stu Whalley/ F/L Ray Jefferies; F/O Don Parker/ F/O Roger Cossette; F/O Gord Larsen/ F/O Peter DeLong. (via 416 Sqn)

The 416 formation team of 1970 was led by former Golden Centennaire, Maj B.K. Doyle, shown at left leading his team through a show at CFB Chatham, New Brunswick in September of that year. Above, the team's solo display was flown by the CO of the Sqn, LCol Don MacCaul. (via 416 Sqn)

Performances from Chatham

The squadron's arrival at its final destination, RCAF Stn Chatham, on November 15th, 1962 coincided with the departure of the Golden Hawks for RCAF Stn Trenton, Ontario. Local residents used to seeing the diminutive Sabre dancing in the skies over the Miramichi now had a much larger and faster neighbour to marvel over as well. (Well okay – there were a few noise complaints.) Like all of the operational Voodoo squadrons, 416 maintained a Quick Reaction Alert (QRA) facility at the end of the runway in Chatham. Two armed Voodoos sat alert 24 hours a day, seven days a week throughout the Cold War,

The 416 Sqn airshow team that enhanced the Canadian presence at the 1972 William Tell weapons meet at Tyndall AFB in Florida. L to R, Kneeling – Capt Ivan Morrell, Capt Bob Jones, Maj Harry Stroud (team leader), Capt Mike Blair, Capt Don Schmidt. Standing – Capt Jim Thompson, Capt John Allison, Capt Joe Sharpe, Maj Brian Smallman-Tew, Capt Ray Harpell, Capt Des Larock, F/L Dave Trotter (RAF) (via 416 Sqn)

poised to be scrambled and airborne within minutes of the alert horn sounding. Local residents soon became accustomed to having the still of night shattered by the alert birds as they rocketed off the runway in full afterburner in response to an order from NORAD to identify unknown aircraft penetrating the Canadian Air Defence Identification Zone.

Finally established in Chatham, the squadron participated in many community events, sending aircraft to perform flypasts on request when operational circumstances permitted. Roger Cossette's logbook reveals several shows in the summer of '63, none more mem-

Members of the Canadian Forces Voodoo team that performed at the Canadian International Air Show in 1972. L to R, Kneeling (pilots) – Lt Stu Holdsworth, Capt Bob Cote, Capt Murray Bertram. Standing (navigators) – Capt Al Ruttan, Lt Ron Hysert, Capt J.P. Paquette, Lt Dave Buggie. Missing is the team leader, Maj Bill Grip, of 409 Sqn. (via 416 Sqn)

Capt Ivan Morrell demonstrates some fine timing as he overtakes the Lynx formation at stage centre during one of the team's performances at Tyndall AFB. (via 416 Sqn)

Lynx Formation 1974. L to R – No. 1 Maj Mike Nash/ Maj Karl Robinson; No. 2 Lt Bob Craig/ Capt Paddy O'Sullivan; No. 3 Capt Jim Thompson/ Capt J.L. Clark; No. 4 Capt Dwayne Lung/ Capt Craig Given; No. 5 Capt Bert Doyle/ Capt Harry Redden. (via 416 Sqn)

orable than the one flown with Dean Kelly at RCAF Stn St. Hubert on September 27th, Battle of Britain Sunday. Following several passes in formation, the duo landed and the commanding officer's aircraft was refuelled with a partial load. Along with everyone else on the base, Cossette then watched his boss leap back in the air to put on his solo show:

"I had never seen a 101 twist and turn and make as much noise as W/C Kelly did that day. He was one hell of a good pilot and squadron commander. When tasked to put on my own solo show for the press back in Chatham on October 18th, I did my best to copy the boss, burning 1,042 gallons of fuel in 18 minutes!"

Roger Cossette

With four of the five Voodoo squadrons stationed in eastern Canada, appearances at the major annual shows, National Air Force Day in Ottawa and the Canadian International Air Show in Toronto, were shared amongst them. S/L D.R. Blucke with lead navigator F/L J.R. Wheeler led a contingent of five aircraft to Ottawa for NAFD celebrations on June 12th, 1965 and when the squadron's turn came up for the CNE show in September of that year, S/L S.A. "Sam" Millar crewed with S/L Ron Bell did the honours with a similar number of aircraft. By this time, the so called "fast movers" had become a well established and popular addition to the annual CNE show and for this occasion the Voodoos helped open the extravaganza directly behind the CF-104 Starfighters from 6 Strike/Recce

OTU in Cold Lake. Sam Millar, who joined 416 as a flight lieutenant and left as a wing commander six years later, still has vivid memories of the squadron's first foray at the show in the Voodoo era:

"Our job was straightforward – we were to arrive at centre stage at an exact time going as fast as we could – without going supersonic. Operating out of RCAF Stn Trenton, we took off at the predetermined time and headed west along the shore of Lake Ontario. As we approached Toronto, I moved the five-plane formation into trail with about five seconds between aircraft and pushed up the speed to 600 knots indicated airspeed, just below Mach 1. We were right on the beach as we hit stage centre in front of the crowd and pulled up individually into the vertical,

selecting full afterburner as we did. We did a roll-off-the-top something over 20,000 feet and rejoined to head back to Trenton. A large crowd was waiting our return so we spent several minutes putting on a show for them prior to landing. We had a lot of fun."

S.A. Millar

The following summer was fairly quiet in terms of airshow activity for 416, although at least one two-ship led by the crew of F/L Brian Phipps and F/O Rob McGimpsey was dispatched to CFB Shearwater to enlighten Nova Scotians with the Voodoo's capabilities. Centennial year in 1967 was another matter – it brought requests for flypasts and airshows from all over the Maritimes as Canadians everywhere celebrated Canada's 100th birthday. The squadron was also tasked to participate in the Centennial Airshow in Ottawa and make a repeat appearance at the CNE in September, doing so with their usual vigour – once again under the leadership of S/L Millar. The 416 crew that engendered the most fame for the Voodoo that year however, was the team of F/Ls Jake Miller and Rob McGimpsey supported by a contingent of squadron groundcrew that were seconded to the Canadian Armed Forces Centennial Aerobatic Team, the Golden Centennaires. F/L Miller was given special permission to work up an aerobatic solo routine which was integrated into the Centennaires' show, usually in tandem with the CF-104 Starfighter flown by F/L René Serrao. In total, Jake Miller's logbook records a host of practices and 83 official shows flown by the Voodoo team between April 28th and October 29th, 1967, a testament to both the crew's stamina and the groundcrew's hard work.

A study in concentration. This photo demonstrates the precision for which Canada's Voodoo teams became famous. The photo was taken by the navigator of the aircraft flying the left wing. (via Dan Morley)

A 416 Sqn CF-101 Voodoo in all its glory. (via Dan Morley)

It was another former member of the Golden Centennaires, Maj B.K. Doyle, who led 416 to a return engagement at the CNE in 1970, ably assisted by lead navigator, Capt Pete Ott. This five-plane team featured a four-plane formation display interspersed with a solo performer. Taking a page from Dean Kelly's past, the CO of 416 Sqn, LCol Don MacCaul, appointed himself as the solo demo pilot. Capt Dave Lennox kept an eye on his boss from the back seat as the tandem flashed up and down the Lake Ontario waterfront in-between B.K. Doyle's formation passes.

In 1972, air force leaders decided to experiment with a composite display team for the annual CNE show to represent each of the CF-101 and CF-5 fighter communities. The Voodoo team was led by former Fireball (1954) and Golden Hawk (1963-1964), Maj Bill Grip of 409 AW(F) Sqn in Comox. He had already been leading their Voodoo team, the Hawks, around western Canada earlier that summer. However, the balance of the four-plane CNE team was made up of 416 Sqn aircrew. A separate 416 airshow team was formed for the biannual William Tell weapons meet hosted by the USAF's Air Defence Command at Tyndall AFB in Florida in September of 1972. Although the national representative that year was 425 Sqn, 416 Sqn was determined not to miss out on the fun, following the example of 410 who had formed the first "Willy Tell" airshow team two years earlier. Maj Harry

Stroud led a five-ship team through two shows which suitably impressed the predominantly American crowd gathered to help celebrate the competition's silver anniversary.

The province of Newfoundland became the focus of attention in 1974 as it celebrated its 25th year in the Canadian confederation. Among several shows, Maj Mike Nash led a four-plane team to a huge celebration in Gander where the local citizens ensured that all in attendance had been suitably "screeched in" before they left the province. On balance, the squadron continued to field teams every year for airshow performances in eastern Canada, sharing appearances at the CNE with the Bagotville based squadrons. Capt Jim Shirley led a four-ship in 1975 while Maj Dave Curran of Red Knight fame led the Lynx formation in 1976. His left winger was Capt Doug Moore who would later join the Rut Zulus CF-5 team in 1979. Moore's logbook reveals that the team did a combination of 11 airshows and flypasts in the summer of 1976, including a "Royal" airshow for Her Majesty Queen Elizabeth II on July 16th during her visit to CFB Chatham. One of his more humorous recollections includes a particularly memorable flypast in Moncton, New Brunswick. It underscored the old air force axiom "flexibility is the key to air power," most often recited when things weren't going quite as planned:

"It was during our taxi to the runway in Chatham when Lynx 4, Capt Ed Kuhar, ground-aborted. We didn't have time to wait for him so departed as a three-ship even though as we were doing so Ed radioed that he was returning to the ramp for the spare and that he would catch up to us if we could just slow down a bit! Maritimers will know that Moncton is only about 45 nautical miles from Chatham and we had a hard TOT (time on target) to boot, so there wasn't much loiter time for us to play with. Nonetheless, we listened to Ed's progress on the radio with growing interest. We heard him call for taxi and then call for takeoff. As soon as he was airborne he asked where we were and his nav quickly found us and locked us up on his radar. Shortly thereafter, Ed casually tells us that he has a 200 knots-plus overtake on the formation – we're going as slow as we can – about 350 knots – to help him out with his join-up. As we approach our TOT over Moncton, Dave Curran is committed and begins his mileage countdown to overhead: 'Lead's five back, four back, three back,' etc. Then just as we're over the target, we HEAR and observe Ed go scorching past us at a great rate of knots. Up until that moment our pass had been planned as a four-ship flypast. However, to the people on the ground (and to us other 'observers' as well), it was a great high speed-low speed pass … and it certainly must have appeared from the ground that we knew what we were doing!"

Doug Moore

The 1979 Bobcats led by Maj Renaud Bellemare pose for a base photographer in a T-33 chase plane with the city of Chatham, New Brunswick in the background. (via Doug Cushman)

The Bobcats are Born

Maj Ben Macht led the Lynx team through 1977, handing the team over to Maj Renaud Bellemare for 1978. With 1978 came a new name for the team – the Bobcats. Having worked up another fine show, their season got underway in mid-June with performances at CFBs Chatham and Summerside … and then promptly came to a grinding halt! The discovery of fuel line problems grounded the entire Voodoo fleet for several weeks; even then the operational squadrons were slow to recover to full strength. Naturally, the top priority went to NORAD, including resuming QRA commitments with the first available aircraft. This was a bitter disappointment for team members who had been looking forward to a full schedule of airshows over the summer. As it was, they did not manage to squeak in another show until August 5th at Grande-Anse, New Brunswick. Thankfully, by the end of August squadron strength had been restored to sufficient strength to allow the Bobcats to make a grand appearance at the CIAS where they flew shows on each of September 2nd, 3rd and 4th.

Undaunted by the previous summer's disruptions, Maj Bellemare received authorization to form another team in 1979 with a new cast of colourful characters. Included was Capt

Doug Cushman who delighted many an airshow reveller in many a back bar with his "bug smasher" routine reminiscent of his younger days flying the venerable Expeditor trainer (affectionately known as "the bug smasher"). Such grandiose performances *après show* were all part and parcel of the airshow scene which underscored the tremendous *esprit de corps* which permeated Canada's air force at the time. And so members of Lynx squadron continued to spread their good name around the Maritimes and into Maine where the team was a welcome addition to Loring AFB's Air Force Day in mid-August. The 1979 season ended with a final performance at CFB Greenwood, Nova Scotia on October 14th.

"Roy's Boys"

The squadron fielded another high-spirited team in 1980 which adopted the moniker "Roy's Boys" after their popular leader, Maj Roy Mould. Lead navigator was Capt Steve Peach with the additional team members as follows: No. 2 Right Wing – Capt Terry McKenzie/Lt Ron Cooney; No. 3 Left Wing – Lt Dan Morley/Capt Jim Christie (left wing); No. 4 Slot/Solo – Capt Tom Sabean/Lt Dan Michailiuk and No. 5 Deputy Lead and Alternate – Capt Lance Carroll/Lt Bob Biggart, the latter occasionally spelled off by Capt Hank Dielwart. For Roy Mould, the 1980 Bobcats represented his third airshow season on the Voodoo, having flown with the Warlocks in 1977 and 1978. Sabean, Peach and Biggart had all flown on the '79 team which provided all important continuity to the operation. Similarly, Lance Carroll was no stranger to the airshow circuit, having flown with the 1973 Larks, but as lead navigator. He was one of a number of Voodoo "scope wizards" (as Voodoo navs were known) to have cross-trained to pilot and graduated from the back to the front seat of the interceptor.

Over the years the 416 Voodoo airshow routine developed into a finely tuned and tightly choreographed performance. Unlike the

Roy's Boys! The Bobcats of 1980. L to R – Capt Jim Christie (Navigator), Lt Dan Michailiuk (Navigator), Capt Tom Sabean (Pilot), Capt Lance Carroll (Pilot), Capt Steve Peach (Lead Navigator), Maj Roy Mould (Team Lead), Capt Dan Morley (Pilot), Capt Terry Mackenzie (Pilot), Capt Hank Dielwart (Navigator) and Capt Ron Cooney (Navigator). (DND Photo via Steve Peach)

Snowbirds who had a full-time mandate to develop a complex aerobatic routine, airshow performances by operational squadrons were a secondary duty only with the priority squarely placed on operational commitments. Therefore, strict guidelines had been put in place across the Canadian Forces years earlier to enhance flight safety among all airshow participants. For the high performance teams, this included maximum bank and pitch angles (120 degrees of bank except at the end of an afterburner climb, 90 degrees of pitch above the horizon and 30 degrees below it), a maximum speed of Mach 0.95 true airspeed and minimum altitude of 300 feet above ground. Aerobatics were no longer permitted and the aircraft were restricted to a 1,500 foot showline in front of the viewing public. Long gone were the days of zooming in on the deck until you saw the whites of the spectators' eyes! Nevertheless, the Voodoo was a formidable airshow machine even with a few restrictions and teams across the country never failed to delight their audiences with their power, speed and noise.

The 1980 team developed a number of scenarios for the season which included both arrival and departure shows in addition to the normal show sequence. In unrestricted weather conditions, it consisted of:

1. An arching four-plane diamond topside silhouette (360 KTAS, 70 degrees of bank), dropping Bobcat 4 (the solo) at centre stage.
2. Solo full afterburner max rate 360 degree turn at 6.5 G and 500 + KTAS

3. Three-plane line-astern pass.
4. Solo knife-edge pass (450 KTAS with 90-120 degrees of bank).
5. Three-plane dirty vic formation (landing gear and flaps down) with burners at centre stage; Bobcat 3 split off and reversed for slow-speed pass.
6. Solo high-speed overtake (Mach 0.95 TAS, approx 600 KTAS) on Bobcat 3 with vertical exit at stage centre.
7. Two-plane dirty split (landing gear, flaps, landing lights on) head-on to the crowd (230 KTAS) through 180 degree turn, burner light on roll-out.
8. Bobcat 3 touch-and-go right to left to high angle climb out with flaps down.
9. Two-plane head-on dirty cross (230 KIAS) along the showline, exiting away from crowd with burner light.
10. Solo flip-flop pass – 120 degree roll left, then right, at 450 KTAS

11. Four-plane high-speed pass in trail with vertical climb to 15,000 feet with afterburner.
12. Rejoin in box for battle break pitch followed by formation landing in pairs.

This is the show the team took on the road in the summer of 1980 following their hometown debut at CFB Chatham's Armed Forces Day on June 28th. Other venues included Cambellton, Dalhousie, and Moncton, New Brunswick (Atlantic Airshow), CFS Goose Bay, Newfoundland, Bangor, Maine and three shows in Toronto at the CIAS. The team also developed a two-plane contingency show should operational circumstances prevent deployment of the team's normal complement of five aircraft. Fame of the Voodoo show, 416 style, spread all the way to the southern states and a late request came in at the end of the season for a show in Birmingham, Alabama. A two-ship was approved and Capts Lance Carroll and Terry McKenzie happily headed south accompanied by Hank Dielwart and Steve Peach. This was the last formation show of the season for the Lynx squadron – rumour has it they left quite an impression on airshow folks down south!

The End Draws Near

By the end of 1980 the writing was on the wall for the CF-101 as the McDonnell Douglas F-18 had been announced as the new fighter aircraft for the Canadian Forces. Eager to further cement the legacy of the Voodoo on the Canadian airshow circuit, approval was given for the squadron to field teams in each of 1981 through 1984. Former team members from 1980, Capts Tom Sabean and Dan Morley, were given the honour of leading the last squadron four-plane teams in

The Bobcats announce their arrival for Armed Forces Day at CFB Trenton with a low pass in September 1982. (via Graham Wragg)

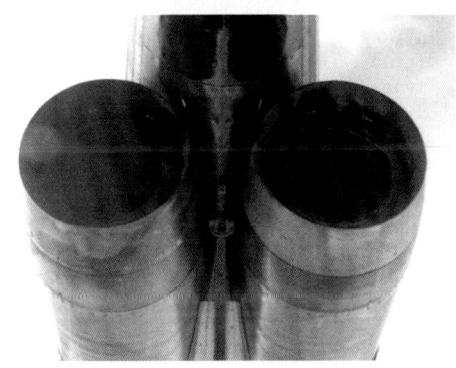

Top – The 1982 Bobcats led by Capt Dan Morley pose for the photographer with Toronto's downtown and waterfront as the backdrop during the Canadian International Air Show. The red coloured wings were a unique feature introduced to assist crews in "enemy" recognition during air combat manoeuvring (ACM) work-ups in preparation for transition to the CF-18 Hornet. Centre left – Showtime! 416 Sqn crews inspect their aircraft prior to strapping in. Above – a Voodoo crew's view of the world from the line-astern position. Practitioners of the art on this day were Capts Seldon Doyle and Darrell Synnott. Left – the entire 1982 Bobcat team on the ramp at Pearson International Airport. (via Dan Morley)

Now there's perfection for you. Two members of the Bobcats demonstrate textbook line astern at 360 knots for the masses at CFB Trenton. (via Graham Wragg)

1981 and 1982 respectively. Their shows mirrored the show of 1980. Lead navigator for the 1982 campaign was Capt Hank Dielwart, one of Canada's most experienced Voodoo navigators. This was the fourth airshow team he had flown with, the first having been with the 409 Sqn team back in 1969. Through dozens of shows from one end of the country to the other, he had just about seen it all! Like their counterparts from Bagotville, the Warlocks, the 1982 edition of the Bobcats was the last squadron team to fly with four aircraft. They performed shows at CFBs Greenwood, Chatham and Goose Bay as well as Loring AFB and the CIAS in Toronto. Their last show of the season took place on September 26th, 1982 at CFB Shearwater.

There was one additional special airshow that took place in 1982 in Ottawa, the official unveiling of the first CF-18 Hornet on October 25th. To commemorate this most auspicious occasion, it was decided that four solo shows would be flown featuring the three current serving fighters (the CF-101, CF-104 and CF-5) followed by a demonstration of the CF-18's capabilities. Capt Ron Berlie of 416 Sqn, who had flown Bobcat 4 in the last show in Toronto, was given the privilege of demonstrating the power of the Voodoo before an international audience of government and military VIPs at CFB Uplands. While his steed could not match the turning radius of the Hornet, Capt Berlie's impressive performance provided a fitting reminder that Canada's Voodoos had been the guardian of Canadian sovereignty and an important link in the NORAD alliance for over two decades.

The Last Voodoo Team in the World

In 1983 the 416 formation team was reduced to two aircraft even though the squadron was to remain at full strength until the end of 1984. Maj Bob Olson led the '83 team with lead navigator Capt Paul Zorz and then hand-

ed the reins to Maj Hayden Henwood for the final appearances of the Bobcats in 1984. Capt Bob Bouchard was his navigator with the crew of Capts Dennis Watson and Andy Graham flying on his wing. The team's spare aircraft was flown by the crew of Lt Larry Martin and Capt Carl French. With the 409 Sqn Hawks flying their last show in July, the Bobcats became the last Voodoo team to perform anywhere in the world. Maj Henwood was able to accommodate appearances at 11 locations where the team flew a total of 14 performances. The team flew their first show of the season at CFS Gander on May 29th. From there the summer airshow circuit took them to Hamilton, Chatham, Niagara Falls (New York), Goose Bay, Greenwood, Summerside, the CIAS in Toronto, Portage la Prairie, St. Hubert and finally the Shearwater International Air Show in Nova Scotia. In spite of the passage of 18 years since the Voodoo graced a Canadian airshow for the last time, the thrill of demonstrating the aircraft remains a vivid memory for Hayden Henwood:

Members of the last Voodoo team in the world model their "formal" flying suit attire prior to attending a reception in September 1984. L to R, Front Row – Capt Andy Graham, Maj Hayden Henwood (team leader), Capt Bob Bouchard. Back Row – Capt Dennis Watson, Lt Larry Martin, Capt Carl French. Below, the two pilots who flew the last show, Capt Dennis Watson and Maj Hayden Henwood. (via Bob Bouchard)

"Thinking back on the final year of Voodoo airshows, two specific manoeuvres come to mind for different reasons. I remember the challenge of performing a 360 degree, 5-6 G turn (*sans* G-suit) at 300 feet and 500 knots while keeping the aircraft within the confines of the show area. I also recall the sheer exuberance of that final pass, in trail, flying as fast as you could go without slipping 'super,' pulling back on the stick to 6 G, rocketing skyward and then rolling off-the-top at 20,000 feet only a few seconds later. At that point two thoughts always ran through my mind; there really was 'no life like it' – and what a carnival ride this would have been if one could have found a way to capture the thrill and acceleration of the Voodoo's hard burner light …"

Hayden Henwood

Since 1984 represented not only the phase-out of the Voodoo but also the 60th anniversary of the RCAF, authorization was granted for each of the remaining squadrons to paint a single aircraft in squadron colours. Voodoo 101043 became "Lynx Squadron Canada" in a striking black and white scheme that drew favourable response from all those who had been associated with the big machine. Today she resides at the Atlantic Canada Aviation Museum in Halifax, Nova Scotia, having been flown there on her final flight on February 7th, 1985 by former Bobcat, Capt Rick Boyd.

And so the aircraft went out in style with 416, both in the air and on the ground, ending a proud 22 year legacy of airshows for the squadron in the Voodoo era. On December 31st, 1984 at the stroke of midnight, the squadron's alert commitment ended on the Voodoo and by early February they were all gone, several destined to pedestals and museums. The skies over Chatham would never be the same again.

410 AW(F) Sqn Demonstration Team – The Cougars

The Cougars of 410 Sqn have one of the longest and most distinguished histories of any Canadian squadron in the airshow business. It was on 410 (F) Sqn that the RCAF Blue Devils were formed in 1949 on Canada's first jet fighter, the Vampire. The squadron also had the distinction of being the first to form an F-86 Sabre team in Europe from its home base at North Luffenham, England in 1952. Several Voodoo teams also flew under the banner of 410 in the CF-101 era and the red and white squadron colours are still an annual sight at airshows featuring the CF-18 Hornet.

The squadron was the second to convert to the CF-101 Voodoo at RCAF Stn Namao commencing in November 1961. However, its role as an operational interceptor squadron was to be brief. A little over two years after settling in to its new home at RCAF Stn Uplands in Ottawa, the squadron was disbanded on March 31st, 1964 in the wake of significant military budget cuts by the Canadian government. However, it would be reborn again four years later at CFB Bagotville when the CF-101 OTU, No. 3 AW(F) Operational Training Unit was rechristened 410 AW(F) Operational Training Squadron in April 1968. The Cougars were back in business.

Notwithstanding their relatively short lifespan at Uplands, 410 Sqn did manage to accommodate requests for several airshows in 1962 and 1963. The distinction of showing off the aircraft for the first time in Cougar colours went to F/L Tom Murray who handled most of the squadron's airshow commitments in that first year of operation. He had been on the initial cadre of instructors to convert to the Voodoo in the United States and eventually found himself at Uplands putting Canadian crews through the Voodoo simulator which was installed there. When all of the squadrons had completed initial sim qualifications, the CO of 410 Sqn, W/C Ken MacDonald, recruited Murray to join his squadron rather than proceeding to Bagotville. He subsequently happily accepted the challenge of demonstrating the new aircraft, accompanied by his navigator F/L Dave Mitton. His logbook reveals that he flew his first show for Air Force Day at RCAF Stn Trenton on July 21st, 1962, another at Val d'Or on August 8th. At the end of the month it was off to Toronto as leader of the first two-plane team to display the new jet at the CIAS. The much anticipated appearance at Canada's

In what can only be described as an amazing photo, Maj Carl Bertrand times his overflight of Parliament Hill perfectly with his fast movers as they overtake three Huey helicopters in a salute to the 25th anniversary of VE Day – May 8th, 1970. The fighters were flying at a speed of about 450 knots, the helicopters about 80. (DND BN 755223 via W. Gladders)

premier showcase of aviation technology was combined with an inaugural appearance by Canada's other new, highly touted fighter, the CF-104 Starfighter. Joining Murray in the other Voodoo was F/O Ted Climenhaga while the Starfighters were flown by staff pilots of the Central Experimental and Proving Establishment, then also based at Uplands. Together, the foursome took turns dazzling the audience with high and low-speed passes punctuated with deafening afterburner booms.

In 1963, 410 Sqn was again offered the opportunity to fly their colours in front of the hometown Ottawa crowd during NAFD at Rockcliffe on June 8th. This they did with great aplomb, F/O Krall impressing the crowd (and rattling windows) with a near supersonic pass culminating in a vertical departure that quickly made him a receding dot high overhead. The opportunity to perform during NAFD would not come again as rumour became fact late in the year when it was announced that the squadron was to be disbanded. The last three crews to hold alert at Uplands stood down on March 31st, 1964 at the stroke of midnight.

Flying the Flag

The rebirth of 410 Sqn as a training unit in 1968 at CFB Bagotville began a tradition which has continued unabated for over three decades. Charged with the responsibility of training all Voodoo crews for the remainder of the aircraft's lifespan, the frenetic activity prevented much in the way of airshow activity in comparison to the operational squadrons. An exception occurred in 1970 when the squadron commanding officer, LCol Hal Pike, decided the squadron should have a team to commemorate the 25th anniversary of VE-Day on May 8th. He selected Maj Carl Bertrand to put together a five-plane team. Practices began at the end of March and the team ended up performing shows at CFS Val d'Or, Senneterre and La Baie prior to a home base show on June 13th.

The 410 Sqn airshow team of 1970. L to R, Front – Cougar Lead Capt Earl McCurdy/ Capt Chuck Wierelejchyk; Right – No. 2 Capt Dave Hickman (USAF)/ Capt Doug Hillstrom (USAF); Left – No. 3 Capt Jim Speiser/ Capt Charlie Gladders; Rear – No. 4 Capt John Rose/ Capt Jim Lauder. Below is the solo crew of LCol Hal Pike (right) and Maj John Houghton. (via W. Gladders)

Although this was originally to have been the last show for the team due to Carl Bertrand's departure for staff college in July, the team was permitted to continue under the command of Capt Earl McCurdy for another special occasion. Joining the team to fly the slot position was Capt John Rose, who explains the circumstances:

"We formed the second edition of the Cougar Formation Team in September 1970. The decision to have another team was sparked by an invitation from the USAF for Canada's CF-101 squadrons to send a team to the William Tell weapons meet at Tyndall AFB that October. The USAF had not had a William Tell meet since 1965 as no competitions were conducted from 1966 to 1969 due to the Vietnam War.

As the meet offered realistic training for aircrew and groundcrew alike with live weapons firing, it was decided to have a competition to determine which of our squadrons would rep-

The instructors of 410 Sqn demonstrate some very low-level formation for the Callshot 1970 participants at CFB Chatham. (via 410 Sqn)

resent Canada at 'Willy Tell.' When 410 Sqn put up a team for the 'Callshot' competition (as it came to be known), other squadrons cried foul complaining the squadron was overqualified! Since it was true that all of our staff were highly qualified Voodoo veterans, we compromised by agreeing not to compete but instead to send a formation team to perform during the meet.

We started workups on September 30th and flew about 10 practices, deploying to Tyndall a month later for our show on October 31st. The team was composed of four formation aircraft plus a solo. Earl McCurdy with Chuck Wierelejchyk flew lead, Dave Hickman and Doug Hillstrom (our USAF exchange types) flew as No. 2, Jim Speiser and Charlie Gladders were No. 3 and I filled the box with

The Cougars made a rare but welcome appearance at the 1974 Saskatchewan Air Show. (DND MJC74-948)

Jim Lauder. Our CO Hal Pike accompanied by John Houghton performed the solo duties.

The day of the performance was brilliantly clear and warm and a very large crowd had assembled on the grass areas adjacent to the expansive flight line. We were placed in the display sequence so as to not 'show up' the Thunderbirds in their F-4Es who put on their normal, start to park, precision display. In contrast, we must have looked rather worn at the edges that day as we climbed into our aircraft, having enjoyed the abundant hospitality offered the night before.

Our display sequence was fairly straightforward. For those who know the Voodoo, the

limitation was wing loading which reduced the turning radius. Notwithstanding, Earl did a fine job leading the four-plane through several turning passes with a bomb burst and rejoin to a final diamond flyby. Hal Pike, a prince of a gentleman and a fine pilot, did a variety of solo manoeuvres – an inverted pass, point rolls and tight turns in burner, entertaining the spectators while the formation manoeuvred for the next pass. I'm sure our efforts were appreciated. After completing the show and while taxiing in to the flight line, we formed a line abreast formation with all five aircraft as we approached the front of the crowd. We had briefed a final salute to the crowd as we reached our parking spots.

By way of explanation, our original batch of Voodoos were acquired in late 1961, and

although we never had a requirement to use the device, still had the refuelling probe connected and operational. The probe was faired behind doors on the upper side of the nose just forward of the cockpit. When extended, it reared up menacingly forward and above the nose. It is difficult to explain to someone who has never seen the barber-pole painted probe extended, but suffice to say that some saw it as obscene!

As we stopped in close proximity to the crowd, we simultaneously raised our probes in salute. I remember looking forward at the huge crowd filled with many 'stars' (i.e. generals) and their ladies. The five probes went up and there was an immediate, shocked look

that swept across all of the faces – followed by total laughter as the probes retracted. Needless to say, we had a huge response when we climbed down out of our jets. We retreated back to Bagotville the next day …"

John Rose

The opportunity to perform in front of an international audience was a satisfying experience for the crews fortunate enough to participate on the Cougar team and was a welcome distraction from the constant stress of never ending training that was the life of the airborne intercept (AI) instructor. Sadly, the fond memories of their weekend jaunt to Tyndall were marred only a month later when two members of the team were killed during routine AI training. While converging on a low-level target, USAF exchange pilot Capt Dave Hickman and Canadian navigator Jim Lauder were killed when their Voodoo

crashed inexplicably on November 20th. The remaining team members flew a missing man formation on November 25th over the base chapel to honour their comrades during memorial ceremonies.

Attempts to revitalize another 410 Voodoo team the next summer were soon dashed when engine problems grounded the Voodoo fleet for several months. Recalls Earl McCurdy, "Voodoo formations were not to be seen at 410 after about March 19th, 1971 due to a general grounding for engine problems. I didn't fly the 101 again until toward the end of May – and only then strictly for training purposes. In the meantime, thanks to the good graces of Warrant Officer Kilburn, we had the tip tanks removed from three T-33s. Along with brothers Dave and Jim Speiser, we got a pretty good airshow team going. We flew about 10 shows that summer, including Armed Forces Day at CFB Bagotville."

425 AW(F) Sqn Demonstration Teams

The Alouettes of 425 Sqn had the distinction of being the first RCAF squadron to convert to the CF-101 in October 1961. As such, it was also designated the training unit for all succeeding crews for the first year of Voodoo operations. This necessitated an extended stay at Namao as the four remaining Voodoo squadrons qualified to "combat ready" status. In July 1962 the squadron flew into its permanent home at RCAF Stn Bagotville where it still resides today 40 years later.

Once the squadron transitioned from a training to an operational role it became easier to accommodate requests for flypasts and airshow appearances. The first pilot to command the squadron in the operational era was W/C Grant Nichols who had earned the distinction of being the leader of the RCAF's first F-86 Sabre aerobatic team in 1952. Although 425 Sqn did not form a dedicated Voodoo airshow team in the initial years of operation, he recalls that squadron members did take the opportunity to wave the flag at local celebrations whenever operational circumstances permitted. W/C Nichols often did the honours himself as he did in 1964 when he led a three-ship to several venues with lead navigator F/L Brodie Templeton in his back seat. Eventually, four-plane formations became the norm. These missions could be both motivational and challenging as formation leaders were usually required to arrive overhead the designated viewing area at an exact time, often with little understanding from ground coordinators of the complexities of wielding around a formation of fighters at 400 knots-plus. From time-to-time the flypasts led to some rather interesting tales and

more than a few raised eyebrows! Lead navigator on one such occasion was F/L Nick Chester who had been a member of the 1960 Bald Eagles CF-100 formation team:

"In June '66, 425 Sqn was flying out of North Bay while our runway at Bagotville was being extended. Nevertheless, it was decided that Air Force Day would go ahead on June 11th and the squadron was tasked to do a four-plane flypast to open the show. F/L John Gray was designated as leader and the flypast was uneventful. Two days later, we were tasked to do a 'welcome' flypast for visiting air attachés from around the world. As we approached the field for our pass, the tower radioed that we had been too high during our opening pass on Air Force Day!! This surprised us, so John made sure there would never be any complaints of that nature again!"

Nick Chester

F/O Dick Lidstone, who was flying the slot as number 4 in the above mentioned flypast, got a running commentary from his nav, F/O Reg Howard, as the low pass developed – it was of the 'Jeeesusssss … HOLY @#!&%!' variety as their aircraft continued to sink ever closer to the runway. Lidstone later remarked that he should have 'had the gear down,' a sentiment reinforced when he saw the photograph …

In September 1966, the Alouettes made their debut at the CNE Air Show led by S/L Don Hutchinson, opening the show with four Voodoos racing in at 500 knots-plus in one mile trail, trailed by four Starfighters doing the same thing. Following their high-

speed passes, each formation rejoined in box formation for a second pass. The weather on the day was marginal and the show was later marred by the death of one of the Blue Angels solos who crashed into the breakwater. The next day was a weather cancellation.

With operational priorities taking precedence on the squadron it wasn't always easy to find practice time or available bodies for "formation" teams. One way around the dilemma was to use crews that were used to flying with each other for operational taskings such as the Callshot weapons competition between Canada's three operational Voodoo squadrons. The squadron used the 1967 team led by F/L Earl McCurdy to good advantage in this manner, ensuring that as many as possible of the Centennial requests for flypasts and shows were fulfilled.

Following unification on February 1st, 1968, airshow fans couldn't help but notice the metamorphosis of Canada's air force aircraft on static displays as the customary Royal Canadian Air Force that had adorned the side of aircraft was replaced by Canadian Armed Forces on one side, *Forces Armées Canadiennes* on the other. By the time Maj Bob Flynn led a six-ship of Voodoos over CFB Bagotville in June '69 for Armed Forces Day, all vestiges of the RCAF had been relegated to the history books. The standard issue green uniform of the unified Canadian Forces was now a common sight across the country, the remaining air force "hangers on" having been ordered to closet their beloved RCAF blues. Thus, the decade of the 1970s became a critical one in the development of airshow teams in Canada as the air force, like the

The Alouettes that performed on Air Force Day 1964 at Bagotville. L to R – F/O Pete Dzulinsky, F/L Doug Stuart, F/L Mike Hobbs (RAF), F/L Brodie Templeton, W/C Grant Nichols (team leader), F/L Stan Perry (RAF). (via Brodie Templeton)

army and navy, struggled to preserve the traditions of the former services. Notwithstanding the unwelcome change in appearance on the ground, everyone was determined to maintain the reputation for excellence in the air upon which the foundations of Canada's air force had been built.

Like her sister squadron in Bagotville, 425 Sqn also formed a team in 1970 led by Maj Al Sundvall with Capt Don Parker navigating from the back seat. Among three young lieutenants eager to fly on the team was Lt Lowell Butters who was selected to fly the slot or No. 4 position for two years running:

"In 1970, we mustered together a four-plane that performed a number of local shows that summer. Our furthest excursion took place on September 25th when we flew to Winnipeg via two refuelling stops at USAF bases. The next day we did a practice show at Gimli and

The 1971 Alouettes led by Maj Bryce McDonald flew several shows around Ontario, shown here at Carp on August 15th. The team solo was Capt Ross Betts whose repertoire included aileron rolls, a four-point roll and an inverted pass. (Graham Wragg)

Mon Dieu may well have been what the French Air Attaché was thinking as he peered through his instamatic camera to capture a shot of this 425 Sqn flypast at RCAF Stn Bagotville on 13 Jun 66. Leading the formation was F/L John Gray – flying the fine line between his leader's jet wash and terra firma was F/O Dick Lidstone. (via Nick Chester)

The Alouette Reds entertained airshow audiences across Ontario and Quebec in 1972. Crews in this shot are: Red Lead – LCol Ron Hayman/ Maj Earle Spencer; Red 2 – Capt Ted Jackson/ Capt Lance Carroll, Red 3 – Capt John Duncan/ Maj Fred Brittain; Red 4 – Capt John Stiver/ Capt Fraser Barnes, Red 5 (solo) – Capt Jim Sorfleet/ Capt Rick Alp. (DND Photo via Ron Hayman)

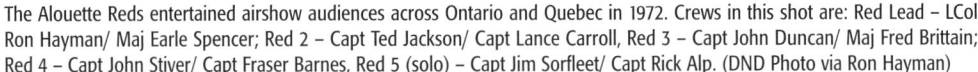

An interesting view of the Larks as team leader Maj Gene Lukan rolls into a "dirty" flat turn at the Canadian International Air Show in Toronto in 1973. The shot was snapped by navigator Capt John Evans in Lark 4. (via John Evans)

the air force teams were flying out of Trenton that year and on September 2nd we all did a mass gaggle, for their Air Force Day as I recall. It was a disaster! The weather was very hazy and the airshow (boss) control left a lot to be desired. We ended up maintaining separation from the CF-104 section ahead of us by using our air intercept radar ... and when we came across on our final high-speed burner pass, we met the Snowbirds coming across the airfield the opposite way! This was probably quite impressive from the ground ... The weather stayed very hazy all weekend and we ended up being able to fly only one CNE show on September 5th."

Lowell Butters

then two flights on the 27th – a flypast and then an airshow at Winnipeg. One of our more noticeable routines was our takeoff. All four aircraft lined up together on the runway and then Alouette lead and two would do a 'military power' takeoff and Ray Paul (flying No. 3) and I would go into full afterburner about 10 seconds later. We got airborne before the first pair and then it was burners out, speedbrakes out and we could usually join up in our box formation just after the end of the runway!

As everyone knows, the Voodoo was great for airshows and flypasts. It was big, smoky and noisy. We always incorporated lots of burner action in the show and usually always ended with a high-speed burner climb straight up! The crowd loved it. The jet was fabulous to fly in formation; very stable and the flight controls and throttle response were

very precise. On landing, we usually pitched out in two elements and landed in formation. Again, the CF-101 was very stable on a formation landing with full elevator, rudder and even aileron control on the runway down to an airspeed of about 100 knots.

The next year, 1971, I again flew slot with a more formal 425 Sqn formation team led by Maj Bryce McDonald with Lt Rick Phoenix in his back seat. We also added a fifth solo aircraft flown by Capt Ross Betts. We did a number of shows around Bagotville in May and June including Armed Forces Day on June 20th. Operating from our alert facility at Val d'Or, we flew in Ottawa on July 1st for Canada Day followed by another show later that day at Kirkland Lake, Ontario. Following a few shows in August, we deployed to Trenton early in September for the Canadian International Air Show. All of

Due to popular demand, LCol Ron Hayman formed another five-plane team in 1972 using the callsign "Alouette Reds." While the vast majority of the shows were flown in support of community events in Quebec (10 in total), the team did have the honour of flying over Parliament Hill in Ottawa during annual Battle of Britain ceremonies in September to conclude their season of airshow activities.

From Alouettes to Larks to Skylarks

With 425 Sqn's rotation at the CNE coming up again in 1973, a new team was formed in late spring under the command of Maj Gene Lukan, again utilizing five Voodoos but now calling themselves the Larks. The team put on six displays leading up to the CNE, even adding their own narrator in the person of Capt Andy Campbell to spruce up the show. By all accounts, the team put on a fine display, but the new name did not survive the test of time.

The selection of a new airshow team is always an exciting development and pleasant distraction from normal squadron duties. For those so inclined, display flying, while very challenging, also provides an element of satisfaction that other types of flying cannot match. There is nothing that brings out the best in an individual more than the knowledge that someone else is not only watching what you are doing, but wishing they could trade places. Thus, there was never any shortage of volunteers to join a demonstration team in the Voodoo era and 425 was no exception. Why would you want to be sitting around "holding five" minute alert in the QRA all weekend when you could be out at

The Skylarks 1975. L to R, Front Row (the pilots) – Capt Tim Harper, Lt Bill Ruppel, Capt Fred Harrington, Maj Dave O'Blenis (team leader), Capt Rick Engler, Capt Jean Michel Comtois. Rear Row (the navs) – Capt Mike Lemay, Lt Al Hunter, Capt Pat Nicholson, Capt John McDonald, Lt Andre Tremblay, Capt Gilbert Dubé. (DND BNC 75-3109)

some airshow with the boys turning JP-4 into noise … and having thousands of people thank you for it!

It was with this spirit that another team was born in the spring of 1975 to demonstrate the prowess of 425 Sqn. Under their new leader, Maj Dave O'Blenis (a future Deputy Commander-in-Chief of NORAD), the team adopted a new name, Skylarks, and began preparing for a busy season that would once again culminate at the Canadian International Air Show at the CNE in Toronto. Unfortunately, an in-flight fire on May 14th, 1975 forced the crew of Capts Tim Harper and Mike LeMay to eject from their stricken aircraft. The ensuing investigation revealed an engine problem which grounded the Voodoo fleet while all aircraft were inspected. This disappointing development put a definite damper on what had promised to be an enjoyable summer as aircraft resources were severely limited over the next several months. This necessitated the cancellation of the team's Toronto appearance and CNE patrons had to do without the presence of the Voodoo in the show for the first time in many years.

The Birth of the Warlocks

In 1976 a new team was formed in Bagotville that would enjoy seven years of longevity. Under the leadership of Maj Larry Lott (with Capt Bob Borland assisting as lead navigator), the four-plane team enjoyed unusual continuity with all four demonstration aircraft being crewed by the same personnel for two years running. Also unusual given the previous track record of changing names for the squadron team was a label that finally stuck, becoming the most recognizable symbol of the squadron for thousands of airshow fans in eastern Canada. The name was "The Warlocks." Larry Lott explains its origin: "The name Warlocks actually came from J.J. St. Pierre's wife, Marion. Since 'witch' has always been an aspect of 'voodoo,' and since a male witch equals a warlock – *voila*! We had a new name."

The Warlocks flew a number of regional shows in 1976 venturing as far east as Goose Bay, Labrador. They were disappointed when they were unable to perform at the William Tell meet that fall. It seems that someone in the USAF chain of command had decreed that if their air force could not put a team together for the meet, the Canadians couldn't either! The following season featured many flypasts by the team

A magnificent plan view of the Warlocks as they skim over the Saguenay River east of CFB Bagotville, Quebec. Glued to team leader Larry Lott are Bob Robichaud (right wing), Mike Hardie (left wing) and John McNamara (slot). The photo was taken from a CF-5 photo reconnaissance fighter. (433 Sqn photo via Larry Lott)

and several large shows, including *le Spectacle Aérien* in Bagotville, a prominent role in Loring AFB's Air Force Day in Maine and a triumphant return to the CNE where the team opened the CIAS for three straight days under blue skies. The season culminated in September with the Warlocks leading a 16-ship flypast of Voodoos and CF-5s based in Bagotville (425, 410 and 433 Sqns) over Ottawa to welcome the Queen on an official

The original Warlocks of 1976. L to R, Front Row (the pilots) – Capt Jacques Nadeau, Capt John McNamara, Maj Larry Lott (team leader), Capt Mike Hardie, Capt Bob Robichaud. Back Row (the navs) – Capts Rick Sponder, Blair Morrell, Bob Borland, J.J. St Pierre, Doug Brown. (via Larry Lott/Doug Brown)

Capt Don Brodeur, Warlock 3 in 1979, practices a little line-astern as he inspects his lead's "burner cans". The unknown comic in the back seat couldn't bear to watch … (via Don Brodeur)

Members of 425 AW(F) Sqn that flew with the Warlocks in 1978. L to R, Front Row (pilots) – Capts Don Brodeur, Don Bosworth, Rick Galashan, Maj Romeo Lalonde (team leader), Capts Jacques Nadeau, Greg Mortimer. Rear Row (navigators) – Capts Serge Roy, Terry Cuthbert, J.P. Paquette, Chuck Langtry, Kevin Psutka, Bona Sennechal. (DND BNC 782270, via Kevin Psutka)

visit to Canada. Thus ended two highly successful years for the Warlocks. Airmen across the country were deeply saddened six weeks later when two former stalwarts of the team, Capts "Robie" Robichaud and Bob Borland were killed when their Voodoo "pitched up" and crashed during takeoff for a routine squadron training mission.

For the 1978 and 1979 seasons, veteran fighter pilot Maj Romeo Lalonde took the helm from Larry Lott, crewing up with navigators Capt Kevin Psutka the first year and Maj Art Armstrong the second. In addition to their normal complement of shows, the team was once again honoured to be selected to lead another flypast for a special visitor to Canada in 1978, President Ronald Reagan of the United States. Residents of southern Ontario had the opportunity to enjoy the Warlock show on two separate occasions in 1979, at the up-and-coming Hamilton Air Show in mid-June as well as the CIAS in September. Also getting into the act in 1979 was the new boss of 425 Sqn, LCol Rhiney Koehn. He had flown the slot position with the 409 Sqn team 10 years earlier and had an obvious flair for demonstration flying. Taking off with only a partial fuel load that would allow him to pull maximum G right after takeoff, LCol Koehn raised many an eyebrow with his spectacular show – he had few rivals when it came to putting the Voodoo through its paces. Of these bygone days he recalls:

"I had a lot of fun doing the solo aircraft demonstrations in the Voodoo. In each of 1979 through 1981, I flew the annual air-

shows at London and the Dayton Air Fair. There were also one or two day shows at Bagotville, Trenton, Peterborough and others, including Ellington AFB at Houston, Texas, and also a two day show at Namao in September 1980 to celebrate the 75th anniversary of Alberta joining confederation. The memories from those glory days are still alive."

Rhiney Koehn

In 1980 former Snowbird Maj Keith Coulter assumed command of the Warlocks, leading the team through several shows that summer. They weren't always the mega shows that he had previously experienced while patrolling the outer right

wing of the Snowbirds in 1977 and 1978, but they were nevertheless important opportunities for the Canadian Forces to demonstrate the highly honed skills of its fighter crews to the taxpayers of Canada. Coulter continued to lead the Warlock's formation display into the beginning of 1981, including shows at London and Bagotville, until a higher calling caused him to relinquish command to a fellow supervisor on the squadron, Maj Jim Gregory. Maj Gregory had the distinction of being the last leader of the Warlocks, a role which he relished. He relates some of his experiences from the time he took over the team until his last show, revealing the challenges and rewards of leading a high performance demonstration team:

LCol Rhiney Koehn (seen here being presented the first clasp to his Canadian Forces Decoration by LCol Fern Villeneuve) thrilled many airshow patrons on both sides of the border with his solo Voodoo displays between 1979 and 1981. At right, the lead crew of the last Warlock four-plane formation team in 1982, Maj Jim Gregory (pilot) and Capt Denis Guerin (airborne intercept navigator). (DND Photos)

Top – Two members of the Warlocks taxi for takeoff at CFB Trenton for a performance at the CIAS at Toronto in 1980. Centre – LCol Rhiney Koehn demonstrates some impressive aerodynamic braking following his show at the London International Air Show in June. His solo show that summer took him as far west as CFB Edmonton (Namao) where he helped the province of Alberta celebrate its 75th anniversary of confederation with a major two day airshow. Below, a beautiful portrait of his aircraft prior to the show. At right, an impressive view of a 425 Sqn Voodoo. Few civilians ever get a chance to experience the thrill of high performance flight. Amateur photographer (and professional airline pilot) Bob McIntyre experienced the incredible power of the Voodoo in a familiarization flight that most airshow fans could only dream of. This shot was included in McIntyre's fine profile series on Canada's fighter aircraft published in 1984. (Paul Peters, Sherrall Chapman, DND photo all via Rhiney Koehn, photo top right Bob McIntyre)

The 1981-1982 Warlocks Show

"I was posted back on Voodoos in 1980, my previous CF-101 tour of duty having been with 416 AW(F) Sqn at CFB Chatham from 1966 to 1970. My association with the Warlocks began in August 1981 when I assumed command from Maj Keith Coulter following his appointment as squadron operations officer of 425 Sqn. At that time I had about 1,100 hours on the CF-101.

When the lead change occurred, the team already had a well established 20 minute routine and it was a very good one. It started with four Voodoos in close formation for a couple of passes, at which time Warlocks 2 and 3 would break off and accomplish solo routines while Warlock lead and 4 remained a two-plane. The finale was all four aircraft coming in from left to right at high-speed (close to the sound barrier) and pulling up into the vertical. I studied the routine thoroughly as I needed to ensure that I was familiar with not only lead's routine, but also that of the two solos.

My first practice session occurred over the runway at CFB Bagotville on August 11th, 1981 with Lt Mike Kyne as my back-seater. Our lead navigator, Maj Joe Sharpe, was not available that day but I needed someone in the back seat who was familiar with the routine and could help me visualize the show from the air. We took off following our briefing and immediately switched to our discrete frequency for a brief warm up. We then headed back to the base to begin the routine.

The first pass included all four CF-101s in a box formation arriving at centre stage from right to left. This pass was designed to provide the audience a 'canopy view' of the team. Following this pass, I reversed the turn and while the four aircraft were still in box formation, passed centre stage with the belly of the aircraft towards the crowd. Both of these opening passes provided good photo opportunities. As the formation arrived at centre stage, Warlock 3 flown by Capt Paul Washington would break away from the formation from his inside position, select afterburners and commence a high-speed 360 degree level turn. This manoeuvre demonstrated the level turn radius of the aircraft in a clean configuration (gear and flaps up). Even though pulling 5 to 6 G, the Voodoo ate up a lot of real estate doing this turn.

The Warlocks roll in for a tight topside silhouette. (via Jim Gregory)

Warlock 2, flown by Capt Jean-Luc Sinave, departed the formation to the right shortly after number 3 began his 360 degree turn. As number 3 was returning to centre stage completing his level 360 degree turn and exit, number 2 would arrive at stage right, moving right to left, to demonstrate the maximum rate turn of the aircraft. After selecting flaps down, the afterburners were used to achieve the required turn rate. This manoeuvre was in direct contrast to the high-speed 360 as much less airspace was required to complete the turn.

Following Warlock 2 and 3's split from the formation, Warlock lead and 4 (flown by Lt Greg Peters) would reverse our turn to the right to get set up for a line-astern flat pass from right to left. (It would be pointed out to the crowd by the airshow narrator that there was less than three feet vertical separation between us during this pass). As this first practice was progressing, I was becoming more and more confident that my study of the routine was paying off. Although I may not have always had 2 or 3 visual at the appropriate time, Mike's indication that he had them visual and that we were in the correct position allowed me to continue.

As lead and number 4 exited stage left from the flat turn pass, number 3 approached from the right for a climbing and descending 360 degree turn. Paul Washington would accelerate to about 400 knots (using afterburners) and at centre stage begin a 5 G pull-up to 6,000 feet while commencing a right hand turn. He would then return to centre stage in a descending turn and exit to the left. Meanwhile, with number 4 moving into ech-

The Warlocks were among three Canadian Forces airshow teams that parked on the Wardair ramp at Toronto International in 1981. L to R – Maj Jim Gregory (team leader), Capt J.P. Dionne, Lt Mike Kyne, LCol Roger Maltais (CO 425 Sqn), Lt Greg Peters, Capt Réjean Bossé, Capt Jean-Luc Sinave, Maj Joe Sharpe. Missing are Capt Paul Washington and Capt Ben Toenders. (Wardair *Super Jet News*, Oct 1981)

Geoff Bennett created this fine portrait of the Warlocks in action – the dynamic high speed-low speed pass. (courtesy Geoff Bennett)

elon right, I reversed our turn to the right and positioned us to line up heading straight at the crowd, perpendicular to the showline.

As Warlock 3 departed centre stage to the left, lead and 4, heading right at the crowd, performed what was called a slow-speed cross or dirty split. With gear and flaps down and landing lights on, I would call 'split now' over the radio about one mile back from the showline. At about 250 knots, I turned right and number 4 turned left giving the crowd the impression that the two aircraft momentarily merged. The trick was to plan the turn so that the two aircraft would not bust the showline nor be too far away. As both aircraft turned away from the crowd, I would call 'burners go' at which time both aircraft would select afterburners and raise their gear and flaps. The plan here was to have the afterburners light just as the tail of the aircraft was pointing towards the crowd. This yielded maximum effect of the 'boom, boom' of the afterburners – a definite crowd pleaser!

As we continued our turns, I would call 'reverse' at which time we would both turn to parallel the showline and meet head-on for another cross. It was critical to have a visual on number 4 for this manoeuvre to work. This being the first practice for me, I

could not, for the life of me, get my eyes on Warlock 4. Mike was trying to talk my eyes onto the aircraft but I just could not see him. It was at this point that I had to make a decision – continue the manoeuvre and hope to visually find number 4 before the head-on or depart the scene now. I decided to depart the scene! My situation awareness at that instant was not what I wanted it to be and I was blind to the aircraft that I was about to meet head-on for the next pass! I called 'Lead's breaking it off' and the practice was abruptly halted.

During our debriefing, I apologized to the team for the abrupt halt in the practice session and explained that I was not comfortable continuing with the manoeuvre. I was very impressed with the professionalism displayed by the other team members in recognizing and supporting my decision. This was probably one of the most difficult events during my time as lead of the Warlocks because I had come into an established air display team and on the first practice was the one who caused the practice to abruptly stop. However, I suppose that's what practices are for. The key to the smooth flow of the display was just that – to know when and where to look for the other aircraft to ensure safe separation.

I was bound and determined to not let the team down again and subsequent practices went very well, each lasting 50 to 60 minutes. Throughout our formation practices, we tried to fly the same aircraft. This was important because each aircraft has its own idiosyncrasies. This was especially true with the CF-101 afterburners. When afterburners were selected in the cockpit, you took the two throttles, advanced them to the full military power position (full forward) and then moved them outboard and forward again for full afterburner. As both engines were totally independent of each other, it was not uncommon for one afterburner to light off before the other. In order to get the maximum effect of the ignition of the afterburners for the crowd, after having been accustomed to a particular aircraft, you could compensate for the uneven afterburner light by selecting the slower afterburner first. This resulted in one very loud 'BOOM' rather than the usual 'BOOM BOOM.' Changing aircraft each time you flew meant a new feel each time you went flying.

Each year Air Defence Command would task CF-101 squadrons with flypasts or airshows. The major airshow in Eastern Canada was of course the Canadian International Air Show which occurred each

September on Labour Day weekend at the CNE. The next biggest airshow was the London International Air Show. In 1981, it was our turn again to perform at the CIAS. Knowing that the airshow took place over the waters of Lake Ontario in front of Ontario Place, I was concerned with the over water performance knowing that haze was often a problem in the Toronto area. The fact that we might be manoeuvring over the water in haze meant that there would be no horizon to rely upon. I was particularly concerned in this regard with my numbers 2 and 3 when they accomplished their level 360 degree turns. Most of the turning would have to be done with reference to the VSI (vertical speed indicator) and altimeter to ensure that they did not unknowingly descend during their high G turns. I therefore wanted to expose the team to over water conditions in a practice beforehand and found the perfect location. Lac St Jean is a large lake located 35 to 40 miles west of CFB Bagotville and provided the ideal training site. A small sandbar at the northeast corner of the lake became our showline. I decreed that during this practice our minimum altitude would be 500 feet above the water. I also insisted that the navigators closely monitor and provide their pilots with vertical awareness, especially while Warlocks 2 and 3 performed their level 360s. I needed to be assured that the crews were exposed to the same kind of visual conditions we were expecting in Toronto and they had developed an appreciation and procedures that would allow them to cope with this 'no horizon' display. Unfortunately, on the day of the practice the weather was severe clear!

As show day approached we finally got an opportunity on September 1st to expose the team to haze conditions. As this would be our last practice before the main event, I emphasized that the conditions over Lac St Jean were the exact conditions the team would be facing at the CNE. This practice was to be the test! We used the same sandbar on the northeast corner of the lake. True to form, there was no horizon looking to the southwest over the lake – perfect! We were all very happy with this practice and therefore felt ready for the CNE.

As it transpired, our deployment to Toronto was an event in itself. Our attempt to deploy on September 3rd had to be cancelled due to the weather in Toronto. We therefore planned to deploy the next morning with the hope of arriving early enough to be able to

fly in the show that afternoon. The flight from Bagotville to Toronto was uneventful and the four aircraft landed after a 1.3 hour flight. Arrangements had been made for the team to park our aircraft at the new Wardair hangar. A small group of groundcrew from 425 Sqn were waiting for us on arrival. The groundcrew support unit was made up of a warrant officer supervisor and usually one technician from each of the trades such as aero engine, airframe, instrument and electrical and safety systems. It was always a relief to have our own groundcrew in place at a deployment base – too many times I landed at airfields where the Voodoo was an unknown to the local groundcrew. This always meant that the aircrew became responsible for all the required servicing of the aircraft. This was not an easy feat on the CF-101, especially if the appropriate ground equipment wasn't available.

Unfortunately, the weather was not improving at all so the CNE airshow committee decided to cancel the airshow for day one. I must say, although everyone is always disappointed when an airshow is cancelled, this was the right decision. This was not the end of our problems for the day however. During the early evening reception at the hotel put on by the CNE, the NCO in charge of the groundcrew came over to me and explained that his crew had been extremely busy since our arrival. It appeared that one of our engines had ingested FOD (foreign object damage), damaging several compressor blades and rendering the engine unserviceable. The warrant officer had made arrangements to have a new engine trucked in from Bagotville which would arrive on scene sometime very early the next morning. Having spent hours removing the damaged engine, all of our groundcrew were back at the airport waiting as the flatbed truck arrived on the Wardair ramp early the next day. Using borrowed engine cranes they had managed to find, the new J57 engine was serviceable and ready for a test flight by 0900 hours! I was not only very pleased that I had all four aircraft ready for the airshow on day two, but I was also very proud and appreciative of the excellent work our crew had accomplished. They were true professionals! Needless to say, we were all very disappointed when weather again forced the cancellation of the show on September 5th. Somehow it didn't seem fair!

The weather finally showed signs of improving for day three. Although there were low

patches of cloud in and around the airport, the reported conditions on the waterfront were improving rapidly. It was decided to fly the show. I had the usual briefing with the team but I needed to make adjustments because of the weather. Under normal circumstances, for our takeoff all four CF-101s would line up on the runway and the formation would depart as two two-ships. The second pair of aircraft would join up with the lead pair usually within a mile or so from takeoff. However, this time we didn't have the luxury of a lot of visibility with the low cloud and haze – I needed the second pair joined up near the end of the 10,000 foot runway! To accomplish this, we planned that the lead pair would come out of burner as soon as possible after takeoff and reduce power in order to reduce our acceleration rate. The second pair led by Paul Washington would take off with a minimal time interval behind us and keep their afterburners selected in order to catch us. It worked beautifully and all four Voodoos were tucked into box formation just a few hundred feet off the departure end of the runway!

Although I wanted to remain in contact with the ground as we flew northeast to our predetermined holding point, the cloud and visibility steadily got lower and lower so I decided to pull up into the cloud with Toronto radar providing advisory service. We broke clear of cloud around 7,000 feet into a beautiful clear bright sky. Our holding point was over Lake Ontario about 30 or so miles to the northeast of the showsite, stage centre being the Ontario Place waterfront grandstand. Approaching the hold, Maj Joe Sharpe, our lead navigator, established radar contact with other aircraft in the holding area. The show had begun and although weather over the showsite was good, we were still above a solid layer of cloud and our on stage time was getting near. I decided that it was now time to break through the cloud layer so that we might be able to visually pick up our holding point and the initial run-in flight path. Using our aircraft radar to our advantage, we broke out of cloud about 1,000 feet above the water. We ended up on stage on time.

As we hit stage centre, I was happy that we had trained over the waters of Lac St Jean because over the water on this day, there was no horizon! In fact, the haze was so thick that it was difficult to see a horizon anywhere. The entire show was accomplished with many, many glances inside the cockpit to

maintain situation awareness. The last sequence of our display was a high-speed dash along the showline with a vertical departure. Of course, liberal use of afterburners impressed the crowd. Instead of rejoining in a four-plane formation, we landed back at Toronto as two two-planes. Under the weather conditions that we experienced that day, it was a lot more manageable to split the formation and land in pairs.

The last scheduled day of the CNE airshow (September 7th) was an outstanding day weather wise. It was about time! The Warlock team attended the main airshow briefing which occurred before each show. It was presented by the airshow staff and attendance was mandatory for all participants. Items such as weather, a list of participants, display schedule and so on were reviewed and discussed. Also reviewed was the previous day's activity. During this particular briefing, I vividly recall the captain of the Canadian Forces CC-137 (Boeing 707) aircraft standing up and presenting an air-to-air refuelling certificate to one of the CF-100 crew. Now, we all know that the CF-100 does not have an air-to-air refuelling capability, but during the process of holding for the previous day's airshow (remember the weather wasn't the greatest), apparently the CF-100 passed right through the 707's airspace while he had a couple of CF-5s in tow for a refuelling demonstration! As the captain of the Boeing said during the presentation, 'The CF-100 was close enough to us to qualify for the air refuelling certificate.'

Our last show over the CNE waterfront was a great success and we even managed to accommodate a special request for a few flypasts over Kitchener prior to landing. The next day it was home to Bagotville to prepare for our next show. Another event that I personally wasn't going to miss was the 'Defunct Clunk Club' retirement of the Avro CF-100 Canuck being held at CFB North Bay during the weekend of September 12th, 1981. An airshow was planned and I wanted the Warlocks to participate. However, CFB Trenton had also scheduled their Quinte International Air Show on the same day. I was constantly getting phone calls from the Trenton airshow coordinator wanting me to take the Warlocks to Trenton rather than North Bay. Personally, I had no allegiance to Trenton – I did, though, to North Bay! It was the home of Air Defence Command, Voodoos had once been stationed there, the CF-100 was an air defence interceptor, I had

been stationed at North Bay, flown T-33s with 414 (EW) Sqn and so on.

As a result of lengthy negotiations, I made a deal with the organizers in Trenton which would allow us to do both shows on September 12th. The Warlocks would deploy to North Bay on September 11th, open their show on the 12th, land and quickly refuel, depart North Bay for Trenton and open the second half of the Trenton airshow. After landing, two aircraft would remain in Trenton and two would go back to North Bay. I was assured by the Trenton people that the servicing and refuelling personnel at Trenton would be ready and waiting to quickly refuel and start the two Voodoos returning to North Bay.

We departed Bagotville for North Bay on September 11th as advertised, arriving with enough fuel to carry out the traditional

over the radio that one of my speedbrakes was not fully open and appeared to be damaged. Sure enough, inspecting the area after climbing down from the cockpit, the hydraulic speed brake jack had punctured itself right through the speed brake structure and skin. This aircraft wasn't going to go flying anytime soon!

Fortunately, our squadron CO, LCol Roger Maltais, had flown another Voodoo to North Bay. Unknown to him, he was about to lose his jet because I needed four serviceable aircraft for the airshow in Trenton! We were soon airborne again and arrived at our prearranged hold point in Trenton on time. My back-seater, Joe Sharpe, wasn't just another pretty face! He was tasked to get us there on time and that he did. Once again, the show went off without a problem … until we landed. My first clue that something was not going according to plan was when the park-

Another portrait of the Warlocks by Geoff Bennett, this time seen in the diamond formation. (via Larry Lott)

'beat-up.' We parked the aircraft in the old Quick Reaction Alert (QRA) area of the base and left to join the 'Defunct Clunk Club' party. The next day was a beautiful day for an airshow – clear, blue skies. The Warlocks opened the airshow which went without a flaw. Everything worked as advertised and I was very pleased with the team's performance. Following our usual vertical departures, the team quickly rejoined into a box formation for an overhead break. As I rolled into the 60 degree, 3 G turn through 180 degrees I popped the speedbrakes as usual. As I did, I felt a slight yaw which was unusual, but since it had gone as quickly as it had arrived, I didn't think more of it. After the landing and as we were taxiing in as a four-ship, one of the team members called

ing spots for the four aircraft were nowhere to be seen. No marshallers – no groundcrew – no nobody amongst 50,000 people!! Finally, a marshaller arrived but only to park the two aircraft that were to return to North Bay as planned. 'Now, where's the fuel bowser that I was promised would be here waiting for us?' Of course, the groundcrew knew nothing of the plan! The flexibility of air power now came into play. To make a long story short, all four aircraft eventually ended up back in North Bay that evening, thanks to the outstanding cooperation of our groundcrew who set aside their own party aspirations to meet the last two aircraft which arrived late. The next day it was back to Bagotville, thus concluding the 1981 season for the Warlocks.

Final Glory

It became a tradition between the two operational CF-101 squadrons in the east (425 and 416) to alternate Voodoo participation each year between the CNE in Toronto and the London International Air Show. In 1982, it was our turn to perform at London. We were authorized to once again form a four-plane team, as it turned out the last Warlock four-ship in history. In addition to my lead navigator, Capt Denis Guerin, I chose the following team members: Warlock 2 – Capt Doug McLennan (pilot), Lt Gerry Lalonde (nav); Warlock 3 – Capt Daniel Pelletier (pilot), Lt René Cousineau (nav); and Warlock 4 – Capt Chuck McCrea (pilot), Lt Michel Latouche (nav).

The 1982 air display was designed to echo that from the previous year's successful routine. Our first practice was flown on May 5th, 1982, logging 0.9 hours flying time. Six subsequent practices were flown before the end of the month. It was during one of these practice sessions that air force PR photographer (then sergeant) Vic Johnson took a series of photos of the team, one of which graced the cover of *Airforce* magazine. He and former Warlock pilot Greg Peters flew in a spare squadron Voodoo to get the shots.

Our first public flying display for the airshow season occurred at CFB Bagotville during the 410 Sqn Reunion on May 25th, 1982. This was a real test for the Warlocks as most everyone who attended the reunion had been a Voodoo pilot or navigator. This was a tough audience!! I do remember, though, that this display went over very well and a few people allowed later on that evening that the display had brought a few tears to their eyes. That was the best review a display team could receive.

Our next public displays were to be at the London International Air Show. We deployed our four CF-101s on June 3rd via CFB North Bay, arriving with sufficient fuel on board to complete a mini 'arrival' airshow. Unfortunately, the flying displays on the first day of the show were cancelled due to terrible weather.

Day two, June 6th, started out with very marginal flying weather but the show went as scheduled with some modifications. One of the advantages of our Warlock show was that it was possible to fly the complete routine under varying cloud ceilings by simply flattening out the performance. One advantage of the very humid weather was that it provided us with an opportunity to have our aircraft fully engulfed in vapour cloud as the aircraft flew past at high speed. This vapour cloud would become more pronounced if the aircraft was pulling G at the same time, making for crowd pleasing results.

The manoeuvre of greatest concern under the conditions was our high-speed vertical departure. If we were to complete the final manoeuvre, I needed to be assured that the sky above the airport would be clear of other aircraft up to about 15,000 feet because we would most likely be punching up into a cloud layer. Before the show began, I had called Toronto Centre and made arrangements with the Air Traffic Control London sector to be prepared for four Voodoos arriving on top of cloud via a vertical departure from the airshow. I gave ATC a time window of when to expect the four aircraft and indicated that it was quite possible that we would need an IFR clearance to get back down through the cloud for a landing in London.

Once the show got underway, the sequence of acts was fractured because of the weather and the air display director was trying his best to make the show flow without too many gaps. Once we were established in the holding area, our time on stage was advanced. Because the two solo acts needed a lighter fuel load to begin their sequences, I called

Another fine photo of the Warlocks, this one taken the hard way as the chase aircraft rolled over top of the formation for the photographer in the back seat. (DND IOCT 82-101, Sgt Vic Johnson)

for afterburners and speedbrakes on all four aircraft to reduce our fuel weight. This must have been pretty impressive (and noisy) for the people on the ground below our holding area – eight J57 engines blazing away in afterburner several hundred feet above their heads! We couldn't go much higher because of the low overcast layer of cloud.

As a team leader begins his final run-in to arrive on stage at a designated time, there is a point in time when you are committed. In other words, you cannot turn, slow down (with much effect), or accomplish any other manoeuvre to lose time. As the formation approached the airfield for our first pass, the previous act (a very manoeuvrable bi-plane) was still in the midst of his closing manoeuvre – a loop. Fortunately, the pilot was on the same frequency as we were and assured us that he would get out of our way. He did!

Our demonstration went very well considering the low cloud. As the demonstration progressed, I could see a few breaks in the overcast layer to the northeast of the field. Just prior to the last pass, I advised the formation that we would do the vertical departure and rejoin on top of cloud. The anticipated vapour cloud surrounded each aircraft as the Voodoos pulled up and disappeared vertically through the overcast layer of cloud, much to the delight of the crowd.

It was a beautiful bright day above the layer of puffy white stratocumulus cloud. All aircraft were in the expected position after this manoeuvre and I called the Warlocks into a box formation and switched the formation over to the prearranged Toronto Centre frequency. Toronto Centre was expecting us alright, but they had their hands full with other aircraft trying to get an IFR clearance to break through the cloud layer for their show. There was a formation of F-4 Phantoms and another of A-10 Thunderbolt IIs trying to convince Toronto Centre that they needed to get down as soon as possible. Toronto Centre issued us holding instructions over the London VOR-TAC in order to allow them some time to sort out the traffic. The CF-101 was only equipped with a TACAN for IFR navigation (and an ILS that we didn't trust) and holding overhead a VORTAC was a bit of a challenge because the TACAN lost all course guidance directly overhead the facility. Rather than try and negotiate another holding pattern with Toronto Centre (which I knew they weren't about to approve), I set up a holding pattern that was close to the one issued in the IFR clearance by using cross

In a final salute to the Warlocks, the team was featured on the December 1982 cover of *Airforce* Magazine. (courtesy *Airforce*)

bearings from other VORTAC facilities and having the navigator scan the airborne radar to keep a radar eye out for other traffic. By the time we landed in pairs we were all getting low on gas.

Following one last practice together, the CFB Bagotville airshow was flown on June 27th, 1982. The last flight of the Warlocks went off without a hitch and was well received by all. The airshow was also to be my last flight in the CF-101 Voodoo. I was posted to the newly formed Fighter Group Headquarters in North Bay and left 425 Sqn within days of the airshow. I had accumulated 1,409 hours on the Voodoo.

The Warlock experience was, for me, a thrilling one. I can truly say I've been there – done that – got the T-shirt!"

Jim Gregory

So ended the Warlocks demonstration team. Although the squadron continued to fly the Voodoo until July 1st, 1984, it was reduced to half strength in the summer of 1982 as many squadron pilots and technicians were posted to the Hornet operational training squadron in Cold Lake, Alberta. With this development, the squadron also saw its 24/7 alert status changed from five minutes to one hour. Under *Operation Cold Shaft*, two Voodoos could still be scrambled to Gander, Newfoundland where they would refuel and then be directed to a combat air patrol station in the north to intercept Soviet bombers that continued to test NORAD air defences. This scenario was played out for real on several occasions during the squadron's last two years of operation with the Voodoo. It would not be long however, before 425 AW(F) Sqn would be reborn with a new, much more capable fighter aircraft, one they would also be proud to show off at airshows in central and eastern Canada.

409 AW(F) Sqn Demonstration Teams

409 Nighthawk Sqn was the only Voodoo unit to operate in western Canada and over two decades became synonymous with the Abbotsford International Airshow. The squadron already had a proud legacy dating back to the Second World War when it was reactivated at RCAF Stn Comox, British Columbia on November 1st, 1954 equipped with the Avro CF-100. The squadron's last commanding officer in the CF-100 era would also be the first to take it into the new age of supersonic intercept, W/C E.G. "Irish" Ireland. Fourteen crews of pilots and navigators underwent conversion training on the CF-101 at RCAF Stn Namao in February and early March of 1962 while a contingent of squadron personnel remained in Comox to continue to uphold Canada's West Coast alert commitments within the 25th NORAD Region. As the first crews became qualified on the new interceptor, they immediately returned to Comox to accept the first squadron Voodoos (17445 and 17446) which arrived from Hamilton AFB, California on March 2nd. It was just over two weeks later, on March 19th, that two Voodoos replaced the CF-100 on alert. A scant four days later they conducted their first scramble to intercept and identify an "unknown" aircraft.

In the formative years of CF-101 operations, 409 Sqn's airshow activity, like that of its counterparts in eastern Canada, was sparse as full-time training and alert commitments kept squadron personnel preoccupied. The Cuban missile crisis of October 1962 had taken the world to the brink of World War III, adding new impetus to the importance of being able to react quickly and decisively to unknown incursions of North American airspace. The incident had also raised awareness among the Canadian public of the nation's military capabilities as more and more people came to appreciate the vital role the services played in defending Canadian sovereignty. This in turn further generated public interest in airshows. Although RCAF Stn Comox did not host an independent Air Force Day in 1963, it did join forces with the village of Comox to hold a "Comox Day" on August 13th which featured the RCAF Golden Hawks and Red Knight as well as flying demonstrations by 407 Sqn Neptunes and the Nighthawks of 409.

Memorable Experiences

As partners in the NORAD alliance, Canadian Voodoo crews worked with their American counterparts on a regular basis just as their predecessors on the CF-100 had done, plying their trade on both sides of the border. Exercises designed to test radar sites, crew reaction times and intercept tactics between aircraft of both nations were a regular feature of day-to-day life. Given this close working relationship, it became the norm for a Canadian squadron to be tasked to participate in significant NORAD ceremonies such as a change of command between senior commanders. 409 Sqn's turn to do so came in March 1965 when a four-plane under the command of S/L Sid Popham was dispatched to

CFB Comox on Vancouver Island, now known as 19 Wing, was the home to 409 AW(F) Sqn for almost three decades, the last 22 years of which represented the Voodoo era. (DND Photo via Terry Leversedge)

S/L Sid Popham (top) and F/L Pete Pellow started a tradition of 409 Sqn Nighthawk appearances at Abbotsford in 1965 that lasted 19 years. (via Sid Popham)

1968 was a year of transition for Canada's air force as evidenced by this photo as 409 Sqn passes in review at Abbotsford led by Capt George McAffer. On the nearside, CF-101444 is sporting the new Canadian Armed Forces livery; the other two aircraft are still in RCAF colours. (Bill Johnson)

Colorado Springs to partake in a mass flypast of NORAD aircraft over the assembled dignitaries below. While not an airshow *per se,* these events were attended by many high ranking military officers and political officials and were thus very high profile occasions. However, it is no simple matter to put a large number of dissimilar aircraft flying formation over a target at an exact time and the pressure on the designated leader on the day can be considerable, as all involved soon discovered. Accompanying S/L Popham on the day in question was his navigator, F/L Pete Pellow, who explains how the best laid plans can sometimes go wrong:

"For the mass flypast we were the second section of four aircraft behind the lead section of F-106 Delta Darts. Following us were four-ship flights of USAF F-101 Voodoos, F-104 Starfighters, F-102 Delta Daggers and F-89 Scorpions – a total of 24 aircraft in all. The two or three practices we had before the event were bad enough, but come showtime it really came apart! The lead 106 driver had great difficulty in finding the parade location and as a result stayed very high on the initial run-in. When he finally spotted the target very late, he started a rapid right turn towards the dais. Sid yelled over the radio, 'Lead, don't touch your power!' Too late – lead came back to idle in the turn and all hell broke loose. Sid hung-in somehow without pitching up and we crossed stage centre almost underneath the 'sixes. The 104s broke right out of the formation and returned to base! The rest were all over the place – except the F-89s bringing up the rear – they selected full burner to close the huge gap behind us left by the vacating aircraft. The

last word from the leader was, 'Sorry guys, guess I'll be heading back to 'Nam!'"

Pete Pellow

Abbotsford welcomes the Voodoo

The next big adventure for the squadron in 1965 took place at the Abbotsford Airshow, not far from home base. No one at the time could have envisioned the relationship that would develop in the ensuing years between the squadron and the small community. The rapidly escalating popularity of their show over its first three years demanded an RCAF presence, especially since it was now billing itself an "international" airshow. In response to overtures from show executives, the base operations officer of RCAF Stn Comox, W/C "Smoky" Drake, was flown to Abbotsford on board a C-45 Expeditor on July 27th, 1965 to meet with show executives. At the controls was S/L Sid Popham who had volunteered to lead the Voodoos in the show for the first time accompanied once again by his navigator, F/L Pete Pellow. Together they became the resident airshow authorities on the squadron until mid-1967. With the show only being two weeks away, it was agreed that the first appearance of the new interceptor would be limited to a few "straightforward" fly-pasts. One minor inconvenience noted in the meeting was that the civilian air traffic controller would be directing the show on a VHF frequency even though military fighters only had UHF capability. Not a problem for a sterling interceptor crew – just give them a "hard TOT" to be overhead and they'll be there. However, Popham and Pellow were given a hand-held VHF receiver as an emergency

back-up radio to carry with them in their aircraft, just in case …

On the day of the first show, the three-ship took off from Comox to make good their TOT – which they promptly did. The problem was, about 20 seconds back on their run-in (roughly three miles from the field), a garbled voice came over the VHF radio stating the show was behind schedule and advising them to "delay your pass." Too late! As he bore down on the field with an aircraft on either wing, Sid Popham spotted a P-51 Mustang pulling up into a loop. He simply avoided him by easing over to "tickle" the crowd, "rather low and rather fast" as he recalls. Those spectators who hadn't seen the smoking trails approaching from the right got the shock of their lives. As the three air-craft rocketed off into a wide turn to set up for their next pass, S/L Popham relayed a message back to the controller, "Sorry, your show's back on time!" Meanwhile, the Mustang beat a hasty retreat onto the ground as the three-ship rolled in for their next pass in echelon formation, with thousands of wide eyes now firmly glued to their distinctive profile. However, the Voodoos weren't finished yet. The spectators were in store for one more pass which was to be the highlight of the show, one never before seen at Abbotsford. Now separated into a loose trail formation, each aircraft turned back towards the airfield and accelerated to high-speed, just below the sound barrier. As they hit stage centre they executed a classic, maximum G pull-up to afterburner climb. With the pull-up, each aircraft was enveloped in a mist of white cloud as air moisture in the low pressure area above the wings condensed instantaneously. It was a spectacular sight.

The Abbotsford International Airshow

As 409 Sqn was engrossed in the rigours of combat ready training with its new interceptor in the summer of 1962, another genesis was taking place at a small airport east of Vancouver. Abbotsford, British Columbia is the home to western Canada's largest annual airshow extravaganza, a show which is widely recognized as one of the finest in North America. Situated in the lush Fraser Valley some 60 km east of downtown Vancouver, the show has attracted some of the world's greatest aerial acts to what was once an RCAF training base.

No. 24 Elementary Flying Training School opened on September 6th, 1943 at the newly constructed RCAF Stn Abbotsford, formed as part of the British Commonwealth Air Training Plan. It was equipped with almost 100 Cornell trainers until it stood down in August of 1944. However, the station was soon redesignated as a "heavy bomber" station to train crews destined for combat duties in Southeast Asia and Burma under the RAF's "Tiger Force." No. 5 Operational Training Unit (5 OTU) had already been established at nearby Boundary Bay under the command of W/C D.J. McKay and Abbotsford now became a detachment of the OTU responsible for the operational training of the 11-man crews of giant, four-engined B-24 Liberator bombers that were soon droning over the countryside. At its peak, over 2,500 service personnel were based at Abbotsford and in June 1945 alone, 5 OTU crews logged 5,629 hours of flying time.

The RCAF's First Open House

On February 26th, 1945 a new commanding officer took over No. 5 OTU, W/C D.J. "Blackie" Williams. Decorated with a DSO and DFC for his exploits on the Mosquito in the European theatre, Williams was responsible for holding the RCAF's first "open house" at Abbotsford on August 8th, 1945. Over 12,000 people descended onto the station in more than 3,000 cars, an exciting portent of things to come. Only six days after the show, the Japanese surrendered to end World War II.

With war's end all units established for "Tiger Force" were ordered to cease training and by early September all had been disbanded. The station at Abbotsford was soon put on a maintenance basis as the RCAF continued to downsize, brought back to life only when the Royal Canadian Air Cadets would arrive for summer

camp or the Abbotsford Lions Club would stage an airshow. It was indeed at this location that the first major post-war airshow in the area was staged for the local populace in July 1948, a three day affair opened by the AOC of North-West Air Command, A/V/M K.M. Guthrie. Those attending the last day of the show were treated to their first jet performance by a de Havilland Vampire flown in from Edmonton. In 1958, the Department of Transport took over the station, converting it to an alternate airport for international flights diverted by weather or emergency.

The Legacy Begins

The modern day Abbotsford show traces its roots back to 1962. Like all great shows that have withstood the test of time, it took a special group of dedicated volunteers to get the show started and keep it alive and growing over the years. The idea for the show came from a member of the Abbotsford Rotary Club, Mr. W.J. "Bud" Lloyd who came to be known as "Mister Airshow" in the formative years. He believed that the wide open spaces

framed by the majestic Mount Baker to the south could be developed into a world-class showsite given its close proximity to Vancouver, one of the world's most beautiful cities. Lloyd solicited the help of the fledgling local flying club (which counted in its ranks at the time a grand total of 17 private pilots) to get the ball rolling. He rapidly found a strong ally in Mr. John Spronk, president of the Abbotsford Flying Club which became a joint sponsor of the first show that was coined the Rotary Air Show. It was a modest start, featuring skydivers, a few civilian aerobatic displays and a flypast of the oldest registered aircraft in Canada – a Fleet Model II. The show was officially opened by Air Commodore Walter Orr although RCAF participation at the first show was limited to a para-rescue demonstration. But if the show was modest, the unflagging enthusiasm of the local community was not. No fewer than 75 local businesses from the municipalities of Matsqui, Sumas and the village of Abbotsford jumped on the bandwagon to support the show, attracting a total of 14,000 people for their efforts.

Encouraged by the results of their first show, Bud Lloyd as chairman and John Spronk as events coordinator forged ahead for plans for a larger 1963 show. Spronk even got in on the act himself with a comedy "How Not to Fly" routine. Having the show opened by the Honourable George R. Pearkes, VC, CD, DSO, MC, a Victoria Cross winner, former Minister of National Defence, and then-Lieutenant Governor of British Columbia was a step in the right direction. Although the show was still too small to compete for the presence of the much in demand RCAF Golden Hawks, organizers were delighted when the RCAF

On the heals of the first Abbotsford Airshow 10-11 Aug 45, AVM F.V. Heakes, AOC Western Air Command, and G/C R.S. Turnbull, OC 5 OTU, welcomed the citizens of British Columbia to a victorious static and air display at Boundary Bay on 15 Aug 45. This was the day following Japan's surrender to end World War II. (via Syd Burrows)

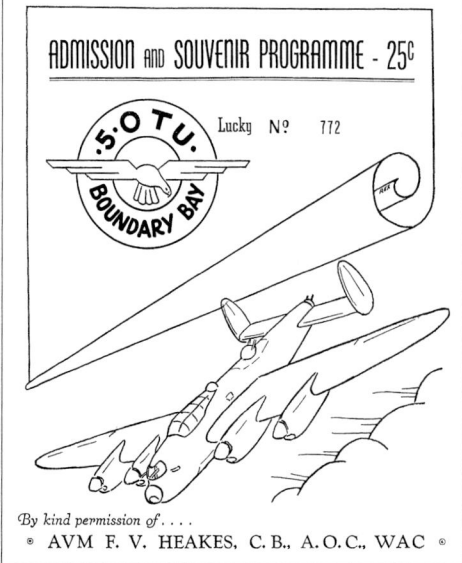

ADMISSION and SOUVENIR PROGRAMME - 25¢

5 O.T.U. BOUNDARY BAY

Lucky N° 772

By kind permission of . . . .
⊛ AVM F. V. HEAKES, C.B., A.O.C., WAC ⊛

5 O.T.U. LANCASTER DISPLAY

August 15, 1945 - 2 p.m.

DISPLAY

Nothing is held back — This is "Pukka"

You are going to get the inside story of the intense preparations and training given operational aircrew at this, the biggest operational training station in Canada.

On the Apron (See Map, Point No. 3) are battle-scarred Lancasters direct from England that have proved their worth in the bombing of Germany. They are open for inspection, with a veteran crew that flew these ships on their bombing missions, ready to explain the complicated piece of mechanism of a modern bomber.

Also on the Apron is the plywood marvel the Mosquito Fighter Bomber together with the Spitfire, the fighter saviour of the Battle of Britain. On exhibition too is a Tiger Moth — the first aircraft they are taught to fly; Harvard and Anson, the intermediate trainers. Then come the Mitchell and Lockheed which are medium bombers used mainly for Coastal work. Then the DC-3 used for transport troop carrier and supply, followed by the Beachcraft Expediter used for training Pilots on Radio Range procedure. Alongside these is the famous day bomber, the Liberator. Experienced aircrew will be on hand to describe and explain these aircraft.

In the Synthetic Building (See map, Point No. 2) is all the equipment actually used in the training of operational crews, together with the mid-upper, rear and ball turrets. Work them yourself, and examine the bombing teachers.

Watch the demonstrations of Air-sea Rescue evolved from the Channel battles during the Battle of Britain to its present high state of perfection for the rescue of these highly trained personnel. See the actual Instructional Films shown to these crews. See the Photographic Display of the actual photos of the bombing that brought Germany to her knees.

REMEMBER THIS IS THE REAL STUFF AND
YOU CAN TRY THEM YOURSELF

In the Link Trainer Building (See map, Point No. 5) are the wonderful pieces of mechanism which teach flying under all conditions without ever leaving the ground.

TRY A FLIGHT YOURSELF — you may be another Bishop
ALL PROCEEDS TO RCAF BENEVOLENT FUND

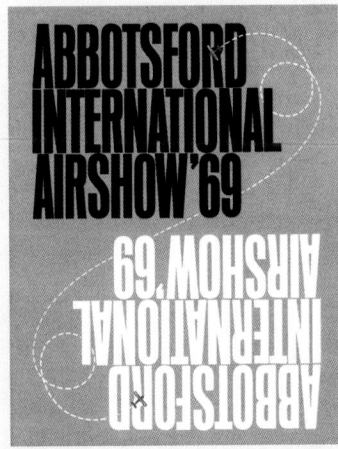

The increase in popularity of the Abbotsford show was evident in the evolution of its airshow programs. Shown here are the years 1962-1970 plus the program from 1999 when the show helped the Royal Canadian Air Force celebrate its 75th anniversary. In 2002, Abbotsford celebrated its 40th anniversary as one of North America's leading airshows. (via John Spronk)

offered to have their famous Red Knight open both shows in his scarlet T-33. F/L Bud Morin had the honour of being the first RCAF jet pilot to fly in the show, dazzling audiences on August 10th and 11th with his carefully orchestrated routine. All Abbotsford staff and airshow patrons were shocked to learn of his untimely death only 10 days later while performing at RCAF Stn Gimli, Manitoba.

The 1963 show also began a popular tradition amongst airshow fans, a large static display of aircraft ranging from small civilian trainers to relative giants like the RCAF's Neptune antisubmarine warfare aircraft and H-21 Piasecki twin-rotor search and rescue helicopter. This too would become a major drawing card for the show, within a few years developing into one of the largest static displays in the world.

John Spronk took over chairmanship of the show in 1964, expanding the flying display to over three hours. However, many fans went away disappointed with a total void of RCAF participation in the show – not a single aircraft. Canada's military services were being downsized by the government, a move which left hundreds of aviators jobless until many were snapped up by the airline industry on both sides of the border. The only jet aircraft to fly in the show were a privately owned de Havilland Vampire expertly flown by Calgary

lawyer Milt Harradence and three F-106 Delta Darts which did a flypast from McChord AFB in Washington courtesy of the USAF. Given that the RCAF's new CF-101 Voodoo interceptors had been operational at RCAF Stn Comox for over a year (and were less than 15 minutes flying time away), the situation could only be described as embarrassing for all concerned.

The RCAF Returns

The notable absence of the RCAF at Abbotsford in 1964 had left a bitter taste in the mouths of many, especially when it was learned that an uproar created by the Canadian

International Air Show in Toronto had resulted in the hasty re-forming of the Goldilocks Harvard team in Moose Jaw which had represented the RCAF in the show, along with the Red Knight. (It had earlier been decreed by the RCAF that, in the face of significant government budget cuts, there would be no air force participation in ANY civilian airshows in 1964.) The 1965 Abbotsford committee was led by co-chairmen Peter Sikora and Jerry Lloyd (son of Bud) who were determined to correct this wrong and did so through a plan to salute the 25th anniversary of the Battle of Britain, a fact the RCAF could hardly ignore. Even still, their participation was limited to a few static aircraft, helicopter search-and-rescue demonstration and a long awaited appearance by three of the country's new interceptors from Comox, albeit a spectacular debut!

Taking the Battle of Britain salute at the 1965 show was Group Captain E.A. McNab (Ret'd). G/C McNab had been the Officer Commanding of Canadian No.1 (Fighter) Sqn when the battle began and was the first RCAF pilot to engage the enemy in his Hawker Hurricane, successfully shooting down a Dornier 215 on that first operational mission. Appropriately, the airshow salute was made by a Hurricane rebuilt and flown by Robert Diemert of Carman, Manitoba and the show ended with a mass flypast of World War II fighters. Also of significance to airshow fans was the fact that G/C McNab had been an inaugural member of the RCAF's first official aerobatic team, the Siskins, having flown with

the team for all four years of its existence.

Another major feature of the 1965 show was the arrival of the United States Air Force en masse, as John Spronk recalls: "Thanks to the efforts of Col Coverley from McChord AFB, who fancied the Abbotsford show, he arranged the first ever major static display of US aircraft on the North American continent. It included a brand new C-141 Starlifter, B-52 Stratofortress, C-124 Globemaster II, A3D Skywarrior (USN), F-102 Delta Dagger, F-106 Delta Dart, F-89 Scorpion and F-4C Phantom. Since it was the first time the Starlifter had ever been on static display, the village of Abbotsford decided to adopt it and painted the town name on either side of the nose."

All in all, the Abbotsford committee's planning and hard work paid off with over 100,000 visitors and 700 aircraft flying in to the 1965 show. It was deemed a "smashing success" and the future looked bright. The success of the show also served to reinforce to the hierarchy of the newly integrated Canadian Forces the important role that airshows could play in recruiting and public relations, not just for the RCAF but also for the navy and army. Thus, in 1966 Chairman John McGowan saw a refreshing change in attitude towards the Abbotsford show with the Canadian Forces providing a much increased presence, in the air and on the ground. The RCAF contribution included another magnificent flypast by the Voodoos from Comox as well as a formation of 407 Sqn Neptunes, another air-sea rescue demonstra-

tion by 442 Sqn and the unveiling of four relatively new RCAF aircraft – the C-130 Hercules transport, CP-107 Argus submarine hunter, CT-114 Tutor and brand new CF-5 tactical fighter. The navy provided a flypast of four of its Tracker submarine hunters and the army put on a demonstration of its CH-112 Voyageur helicopter which had been transported to the show inside the Hercules in a demonstration of tactical mobility. The grand finale to the four and one-half hour show saw the triumphant return of the Red Knight, this time flown by British Columbia's own F/L Terry Hallett of Powell River who drew top billing for the show.

Centennial Expansion

There is an old saying that "success breeds success," an axiom that certainly held true for "Canada's Centennial International Abbotsford Airshow" as the show was dubbed in 1967. This truly put the Abbotsford show on the world stage. For the first time, the show drew federal and provincial support with messages of welcome from Prime Minister Lester B. Pearson and Premier W.A.C. Bennett respectively. Corporate sponsors, including the likes of Northwest Industries Limited, de Havilland Canada, Pacific Western Airlines, Canadian Pacific Airlines, Air Canada, Imperial Oil Limited and Shell were joined by American heavyweights Northrop and Boeing in supporting the show.

Now into his sixth year as director of events, John Spronk was able to recruit some valuable

While promoting aviation heritage and the latest advances in technology, airshows also provide rare opportunities for recruiting for a nation's military services and advertising for civilian corporations. In 1965 while celebrating the 25th anniversary of the Battle of Britain, the Department of National Defence was busy selling the concept of integration of the "Canadian Forces" introduced the previous year. Full unification followed in 1968. (via John Spronk)

1965 Abbotsford International Air Show

Aug. 14, 1940 : Flight Lieutenant E. A. McNab, left, talks with Air Marshall Billy Bishop, V.C. at Northholt near London, England.
AUGUST 14, 1965 : Group Captain E. A. McNab (Retired) will accept and return the salute of a lone Hawker Hurricane as it passes in slow flypast on this, the 25th Anniversary of the Battle of Britain.

Integrated For Strength

Now you have greater opportunity to serve...learn...and travel with the Canadian Armed Forces

See your Canadian Armed Forces Career Counsellor at 547 Seymour Street, Vancouver 2, B.C., Phone 684-7341

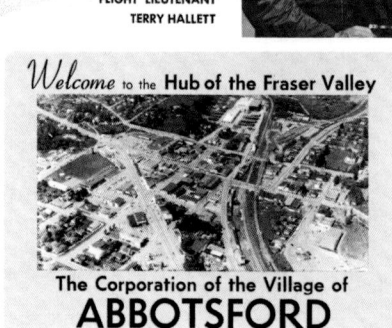

The 1966 Abbotsford International Air Show Presents . . .

The Red Knight

FLIGHT LIEUTENANT TERRY HALLETT

Welcome to the **Hub of the Fraser Valley**

The Corporation of the Village of
ABBOTSFORD

Jet Aerobatics

See the famed Red Knight during the Air Show. Thrill to the precision aerobatics performed at close quarters. F/L Terry Hallett, The Red Knight, enlisted in the RCAF in 1958 and by 1960 was flying F-86 Sabres in France. He is a jet instructor, the son of Mrs. D. Carter of Powell River, B.C., is married and has one son. The Red Knight Aircraft is a T33 Silver Star jet trainer capable of speeds up to 580 miles per hour.

New Role   New Equipment   New Opportunities

The Super F-5 is just one of the many new, exciting things that's happening in the air, on the ground and at sea in the Canadian Forces.
Fast, versatile and rugged the Super F-5 is an ideal partner for our ground forces. Operating from sod fields it's deployed right up front where the action is, ready to step in and back up Canadian troops — with authority.
Join the Aircrew in Canada's new Global-

Mobile force. Get into the most exciting, rewarding, most adventurous flying of all — Aircrew in the Canadian Forces.
Get in right now — it's the chance of your lifetime!
Your Canadian Forces Recruiting Counsellor will give you all the enrolment details. See him today at:
The 1966 Abbotsford Air Show or
547 Seymour Street, Vancouver 2, B.C.,
Phone 684-7341

Join the Canadian Forces

new attractions to the show – the first appearance of an international aerobatic team in the form of the famous US Navy Blue Angels led by LCdr Bill Wheat, the arrival of the RAF's giant Avro Vulcan nuclear bomber and the first performances by Professor Art Scholl in his modified de Havilland Chipmunk trainer. But for the 300,000 spectators who took in the three day spectacle, the highlight was the Canadian Forces Golden Centennaires who stole the show with their salute to the past, present and future of Canadian military aviation. This included Abbotsford's first look at the CF-104 Starfighter.

At the end of 1967 the Abbotsford International Air Show Society was formed to organize all future events. It was a sign of permanence for the show. Even though everyone expected a letdown in attendance in 1968, it did not materialize and good weather brought out another 300,000 spectators. Although disappointed by the disbandment of the Golden Centennaires, the crowds were entertained by another four hour show that featured new acts such as wingwalking, more Warbirds (notably Bob Hoover in his P-51 Mustang), a return engagement by Art Scholl and finally another fine performance by Canadian Forces aircraft that culminated with the Red Knight (Capt Dave Curran) in his new mount, the CT-114 Tutor.

Abbotsford closed out the decade in 1969 with their 8th annual show and the inclusion of two new acts for the first time, a four-plane CF-104 Starfighter formation team from 417 Sqn at CFB Cold Lake and the USAF Thunderbirds flying their new F-4E Phantom IIs. By popular demand, both teams would make many return engagements in the ensuing years.

The '70s and Beyond

With the dawn of a new decade the enthusiastic group of volunteers that ran the Abbotsford show continued to look for ways to improve their show, and did. Both the Canadian Forces and American military became integral partners in the show, in the air and on the ground, helping Abbotsford gain a reputation as one of the finest airshows in the world. With the formation of the Snowbirds in 1971 and the continued presence of one of the American jet teams on an alternating basis, the show was one of the very few that could boast two military aerobatic teams every year right into the mid-1990s. Even rarer was the appearance of five national aerobatic teams in 1986. And with these teams came a host of other dynamic military performers – the high performance Canadian fighter teams such as the Hawks, Deadeye Zips and Rut Zulus, Canada's own Skyhawks and the US Army Golden Knights parachute teams, as well as a wide variety of solo demonstrations.

Over 39 years the show has also attracted some of the world's finest civilian aerobatic performers, including the likes of Art Scholl, Bob Hoover, Milt Harradence, Freddy Ludtke, Joe Hughes and his wingwalkers John Kazian and Gord McCollom, the Canadian Reds which begat the Ray-Ban Gold, Jerry Billing, Bud Granley, Joann Osterud, Leo Loudenslager, Jimmy Franklin, Gene Soucy and wingwalker Teresa Stokes, Team America, Wayne Handley, Patty Wagstaff, Julie Clark, Sean Tucker, Manfred Radius, Air Combat Canada, the Northern Lights, Jim Leroy, Eric Beard, Bill Carter, Kent Pietsch and a wonderful collection of classic aircraft from the Confederate Air Force and the Canadian Warplane Heritage.

Hosting military and civilian performers of the calibre noted above is an expensive proposition for any airshow. Costs can only be offset through corporate sponsorship and large crowds each year. When it comes to drawing crowds, airshows are very much at the mercy of the weather and Abbotsford has not been immune to some less than ideal weather over the years. Following a disappointing year in 1997, show executives had to make the difficult decision to cancel the 1998 show, leaving thousands of airshow enthusiasts without the highlight of their summer. However, under the leadership of managing director Ron Price and his dedicated staff, the show was reborn in 1999 just in time to help celebrate the 75th anniversary of Canada's Air Force and the birth of the RCAF on April 1st, 1924. Also celebrating an anniversary at the 1999 show, his 30th, was veteran airshow announcer Bob Singleton. He has been an integral part of the success of the Abbotsford show over the years, his easy going style and smooth delivery making him one of the most sought after airshow announcers in the business.

Back-to-back fine showings in the years 2000 and 2001 launched the new millennium for the Abbotsford show which celebrated its 40th anniversary in 2002. Given its current direction and popularity, the show will continue to attract the best acts from within the thriving North American airshow industry.

A typical day at the Abbotsford Airshow – thrilling audiences with some of the best aerial acts in the world since 1962. One of the world's finest show announcers, Bob Singleton, returned to Abbotsford for his 33rd year in 2002. (Mike Valenti)

A glimpse from the past. The Nighthawks that performed on Comox Day and the Abbotsford Airshow in 1968. L to R – Capts Brodie Templeton, Barry MacLeod, Al Cooper, George McAffer (team leader), Les Putland, Fred Williams. (via Brodie Templeton)

Naturally, once airshow fans had regained their composure, the Voodoos became the talk of the town for weeks. Indeed, that first appearance in 1965 started a tradition that, with few exceptions, lasted for 19 years. There was nothing quite like the sound of eight J-57 afterburners being lit simultaneously when you weren't expecting it or happened to be looking the other way when the aircraft suddenly appeared overhead. The crews participating in that first Abbotsford show came away with their own stories and the distinct impression that this was good sport! Thus, there was no shortage of volunteers to do it again the following year.

One crew that got into the act for the next two years was that of F/Ls Dave Walker and Jim Dale, usually flying the slot position. Walker's logbook reveals at least a dozen airshow appearances or flypasts in 1966 and 1967, with the odd solo show thrown in for good measure. Most were led by S/L Popham or S/L Arnie Leiter (with his nav F/L Len Dodd). Centennial year was to be a hectic one for airshows in Canada and the residents of the Comox Valley were the first to receive a glimpse of Canada's new aerobatic team with the arrival of the Golden Centennaires in January for a seven week training period. It was a big year for the Nighthawks as well as they made three appearances in Victoria surrounding Centennial celebrations, helped send Canada's "Centennial train" on its way from Vancouver to Expo 67 in Montreal and opened both CFB Comox's Armed Forces Day and the Canadian Forces dazzling 90 minute presentation at Abbotsford on each of the three day show in August.

In 1968 Capt George McAffer did the honours by leading a three-ship of Voodoos at both the Comox Armed Forces Day and the Abbotsford shows with Capt Al Cooper navigating from the back seat. Like the previous year, some 300,000 spectators enjoyed

watching the CF-101's flash past to open another impressive military show.

High Stake Consequences

Although it was frequently the same group of volunteers who chose to give up their weekends to participate in airshows, positions within the formation were interchangeable as it was generally considered that all squadron pilots were capable of flying close formation since they did so as part of their operational flying almost every day. This attitude changed somewhat as the result of an accident on May 29th, 1969 when a midair collision between the slot man and the leader of a four-plane formation occurred near Denman Island during an airshow practice. The navigators of the two aircraft, Capts John Emon and Laurie Bastie, were both killed when the two aircraft collided during a formation rejoin, a grim reminder that the consequences of error in high performance flying could be very tragic. Following the subsequent Board of Inquiry, the CO of 409 Sqn, LCol G.F. "Hammy" Hammond, decided to give the team a fresh start and selected Maj Sam Skinner to build a new team from scratch. Assisted by lead navigator Capt Bill Bland, Skinner led the team for the balance of the year. Bill Bland's logbook reveals that the new team flew their first of three successive practices on June 11th, 1969 prior to participating in Comox's Armed Forces Day on June 14th. Their next public appearance was not until July 30th but was for an international audience at Colorado

Springs for the change of command of the Commander-In-Chief of NORAD. By the time Abbotsford rolled around again their routine was finely tuned and the shows flown from August 8th through 10th were the highlight of the season.

With the season having ended on a much higher note than it started, approval was given for the squadron to form another airshow team for 1970. Moving back to his familiar lead position was Capt George McAffer joined by Capt Fred Williams as lead navigator. Capt Doug Stuart followed suit in 1971 with Capt Don Middleton in his back seat. Disappointingly, engine problems plagued the Voodoo fleet in 1971 and the team was relegated to two aircraft and a much reduced airshow schedule.

New Improved Voodoos

The arrival in 1971 of a "new" consignment of Voodoos for the Canadian Forces brought an improved intercept capability to the fleet. Under *Operation Peace Wings*, the remaining 56 original Voodoos were replaced by another 66 F-101s that had been placed in long term storage by the USAF at Davis Monthan AFB in Arizona. Although the replacement airframes were several years older than the current CF-101s, they had accumulated significantly fewer hours flying time and were refitted with a new fire control system for the Voodoo's weapons complement of two McDonnell Douglas AIR-2A

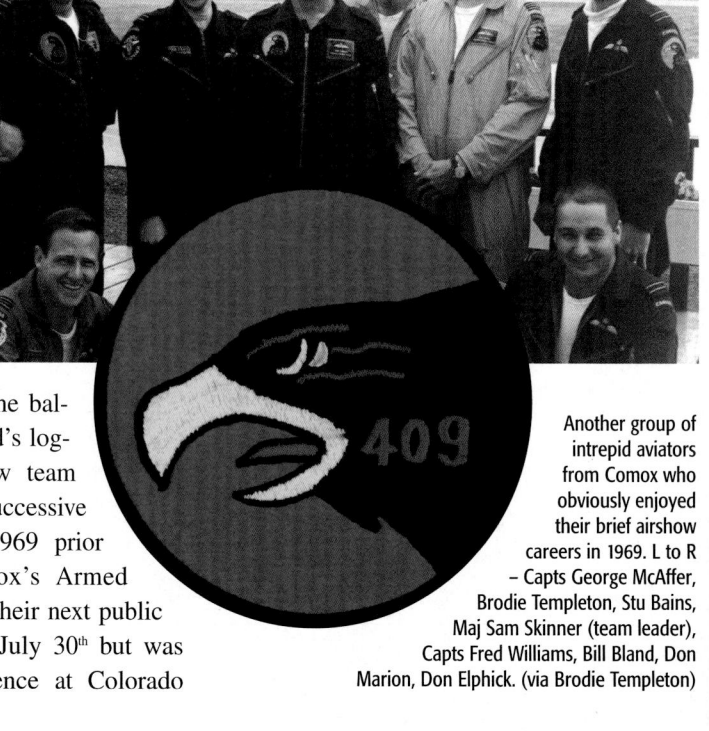

Another group of intrepid aviators from Comox who obviously enjoyed their brief airshow careers in 1969. L to R – Capts George McAffer, Brodie Templeton, Stu Bains, Maj Sam Skinner (team leader), Capts Fred Williams, Bill Bland, Don Marion, Don Elphick. (via Brodie Templeton)

The 1973 Nighthawks. L to R – Capts Gary Raindahl, Tom Murray, Tony Brett, John Pew, Gus Hay, Roger Lamothe, Ken Carr, Paul Gill. (Dan Baker via Tony Brett)

Genie rockets and two Hughes AIM-4D Falcon missiles.

Having been taken out of their cocoons in the desert, all of the replacement Voodoos were first flown to Bristol Aerospace Limited in Winnipeg. Bristol was the prime contractor for major overhaul and repair work on all RCAF and Canadian Forces Voodoos for over two decades. In their plant on the east side of the city's international airport, Bristol swapped the engines and modified the ejection seats, navigation and communication equipment prior to painting all 66 aircraft in their new Canadian Forces colours. The aircraft with the improved Hughes MG-13 fire control system installed were easily identified by the infra-red semi-hemispheric sensor mounted on the nose of the aircraft. In order to install the sensor, the aircraft's refuelling probes had been removed. The newly modified Canadian aircraft were also distinguishable by a new numbering system which saw registration numbers starting with 101001 through 101066. Of these, 56 were again CF-101Bs and 10 were CF-101Fs.

The last of the original Voodoos to perform at Abbotsford did so on August 14th and 15th, 1971 courtesy of Capts Doug Stuart and Harry Chapin with their navigators Capt Don Middleton and Lt Roger Lamothe. The first of the new Voodoos allocated to 409 Sqn (101018) arrived at CFB Comox the very next day, although it would be early October before it would see operational service. For the next 11 successive years, the Nighthawks formed a four-plane demonstration team to fly their colours at airshows throughout western Canada and the United States.

The 1972 team was led by veteran fighter pilot Maj Bill Grip, one of the last members of the RCAF Golden Hawks in 1964. His 409 team ventured as far east as the Saskatchewan Anniversary Air Show, then hailing itself as the largest one day airshow in North America – and proving it with a daunting display of precision and power by Canadian and American military aircraft alongside many outstanding civilian acts. Maj Grip also led a composite Voodoo team of 416 Sqn aviators at the CIAS in Toronto during the Labour Day weekend that September.

Capt Tony Brett took command of the 409 demo team for 1973 with a very experienced team that employed three pilots that had flown with the team the year before, Capts John Pew, Gus Hay and Ken Carr. Like all members of his team, he thoroughly enjoyed demonstrating the capabilities of the Voodoo in public and his team worked hard to perfect their show. If there was one overriding characteristic of a four-plane Voodoo show, most observers would label the ear-splitting noise of the performance as being the most memorable. Now, for those wishing to be "entertained" in this fashion, the sound of the J57 in afterburner was pure magic – for those not so enamoured, it could be purgatory personified as Tony Brett explains:

"For our 1973 airshow workup we conducted several airshow practices over the base, often doing two shows in one flight. Capt Ken Carr, our solo, could really haul the Voodoo around and part of his itinerary was to complete a very tight, low-level 360 degree turn in full afterburner in front of the showline. In doing so he passed right over a large mansion on Point Holmes, just outside the base limits. The owner was not enamoured with Voodoo operational noise at the best of times but Ken's first pass over his house was the last straw. He phoned the base and was put through to the mess where some

WAG answered and told him: 'Wait ten minutes and they'll be right back!'

I learned of this incident in the mess after the flight. To counter the negative effects I rounded up the whole team, still in our sweaty flying suits, piled them in a couple of cars and drove right over to the mansion. The owner answered the doorbell rather timorously. I introduced myself, indicated that I had the whole team with me and wanted to explain what we were doing. Still a little unsure of us he invited us in, drinks were offered and the stiff atmosphere soon melted. He was quite taken with our personal approach and subsequently became one of our biggest fans and supporters.

Several single, two and four-ship flypasts and airshows were approved for local towns and cities in support of various festivals and celebrations that summer – Port Alberni comes to mind. They requested a single T-33 to do a few flypasts in support of a parade at the Legion. All the city bigwigs were to be there, including the editor of the local paper. I volunteered to do the flight but when the day arrived there were no serviceable T-Birds, just Voodoos. I called the parade organizer, explained the situation and offered the Voodoo but warned that it was considerably noisier. He was very enthusiastic and advised he would love to have the Voodoo. Off I went, found the parade grounds and had a great time beating the place up. The misgivings set in on the way home – what if I had caused any heart attacks and the like, and how many phone calls would the base get?

The calls started before I got back and I waited to be called 'front and centre' for my beat-up. Then the mayor called praising my flypast and telling the base to ignore all those 'cranks' who called to complain. The editor of the Port Alberni newspaper also wrote up a great editorial and I came out smelling like a rose. Some days you come out a winner.

We later put on a full airshow at the Ladysmith airport, just south of Nanaimo. The CFB Comox Base Commander, Col Don McNichol, was there. The last pass of the show was a high-speed pass, the four aircraft separated in line-astern, each lighting burners in front of the showline. We put it down pretty low and raised a fair dust cloud. The VIP next to the base commander turned and asked if we weren't rather low. Col McNichol replied, 'They know what they are doing.' It was nice to have that kind of support.

The beautiful symmetry of this pass was in sharp contrast to the structural failure of Nighthawk 2 only minutes later during a high-speed burner climb. (via Tony Brett)

A Brush with Disaster

Unfortunately, that support would soon be put to the ultimate test. Having completed major shows at CFBs Cold Lake and Moose Jaw, the team was performing at the Abbotsford Air Show on August 12th, 1973 when we suffered an accident on our last high-speed pass.

The day had dawned with a 17,000 foot overcast layer of cloud which was lower than the normal recovery altitude from our final individual passes to vertical pull-up, a popular tradition of all Voodoo teams. I briefed the team that rather than pulling up through the layer, I would flatten my final pull-up to 60 degrees rather than the normal 80 degrees. Unfortunately, my No. 2 lost sight of me on their pull-up and tried to regain visual contact by bunting and simultaneously initiating the aileron roll that was the exiting signature of our show. The combination of slight negative G, rapid roll rate and high-speed resulted in a phenomena known as 'inertial roll coupling' followed almost immediately by a violent, negative G 'pitch-up.' This in effect threw the aircraft onto its back relative to its direction of flight. The aircraft was grossly overstressed with negative G causing both engines to rip out and the airframe to come apart.

Both the CF-101 Voodoo and CF-104 Starfighter were susceptible to pitch-up, a stall condition in which the controls are no longer responsive and therefore non-recoverable, with the single exception of deploying the drag chute. With these aircraft, pitch-up could occur in both the positive and negative G regimes and at any speed by increasing the angle of attack into the stall condition. Roll coupling could be a cause of

pitch-up with these aircraft. To understand this, consider the aircraft at zero G – there is zero angle of attack and the direction of flight is parallel with the fore and aft axis of the aircraft. The aircraft can safely perform a rapid rate of roll because it is very close to a point roll. Now consider the aircraft at one or more Gs – there is now a definite angle of attack and the direction of flight is no longer parallel to the fore and aft axis. When the aircraft rolls it is no longer a point roll. Rather, the nose and tail are swinging around a significantly large arc and centrifugal force comes into play trying to increase the size of the arc and therefore the angle of attack. Should the angle of attack be increased to the stall, then roll coupling has become the cause of pitch-up.

The 1974 Hawks made a triumphant return to the North American airshow circuit. L to R – Lt Ed Campbell, Capt Mike Spooner, Maj Mike Mahon, Capt Tom Potter, Capt Jon Pew, Lt Mike McKay, Capt John Molloy, LCol Ev McKay (CO 409 Sqn), Lt Bart Wickham, Capt Gerry MacIntosh. (via Bart Wickham).

As I pulled over the top of the climb and looked back to pick up my wingmen, I was horrified to see that my No. 2 had disintegrated into several balls of flame. Miraculously, both crewmen survived their ejections through the fireball and recovered to fly another day. Thankfully, no one on the ground was injured when the debris plummeted to earth just over the Washington state border to the south of the Abbotsford airport."

Tony Brett

The Nighthawks returned to the airshow scene in 1974 with LCol Ev McKay leading his charges to a highly successful season. Airshow fans throughout Western Canada were equally pleased to see the team back in Abbotsford for three full shows, thankfully with less spectacular finales. Another highlight for the team that summer was an invitation to participate in the Winnipeg Centennial Air Show where they performed two shows on August 17th and 18th.

Coping with the Unknown

On July 5th, 1976 the Nighthawks suffered the loss of two teammates when the team's solo aircraft crewed by Capts Les Cox and Roy Smith inexplicably flew into the water just off the base towards the end of the team's very first practice for the upcoming airshow season. After an emotional farewell, it was decided that the team would continue and practices resumed under team leader Capt Tom Potter. Most airshow patrons look-

At left, Maj Dave Koski leads the 1977 Hawks past the entrance to NORAD Headquarters in Cheyenne Mountain, Colorado flying "Hawk One Canada" in commemoration of 409 Sqn's 25th anniversary. At right, a finely executed flat turn shows off the bottom of the CF-101 Voodoo. (DND PCN 77-407, Sgt Vic Johnson via W. Gladders, Bill Johnson)

ing forward to seeing the team perform again were oblivious to the tragedy, for which no cause was ever established. The Nighthawks did not disappoint, going on to a fine season thanks in part to Capts Lou Glussich and his navigator Rich Littler who had volunteered to join the team to replace the lost crew.

Hawk One

The year 1977 was a special one for the Nighthawks as it marked their 25th anniversary as a squadron. In keeping with tradition, plans had been made to award the unit with her Squadron Colours to mark the occasion. At the suggestion of Maj Dave Koski, recently returned from flying Starfighters in West Germany, a decision was made to design a special paint scheme for one of the squadron aircraft to also commemorate the event. The result was "Hawk One," arguably one of the most famous paint schemes to ever adorn a Voodoo. The aircraft (CF-101012) made its maiden flight on June 17th, 1977 and was soon on a cross-country tour to promote the squadron and pick up the new Squadron Standard from the nation's capital in Ottawa. LCol George Herbert and Maj Russ Hellberg did the honours.

With such a unique paint scheme, it only made sense that Hawk One would find its way onto the airshow circuit with the 1977 version of the Nighthawk team. Although Maj Dave Koski led the team with Russ Hellberg in his back seat, the privilege of flying the specially painted aircraft went to the team solo, Capt Ron Coleman. Airshow patrons therefore got the opportunity to see Hawk One from almost every angle. Coleman was joined by veteran navigator Charlie Gladders after at least one other navigator decided the solo routine was not for him! One manoeuvre that was unique to the

'77 team was a touch-and-go to burner climb-out by Hawk One as Maj Koski led the rest of the team in an opposing dirty pass, the idea being to cross at stage centre just as Hawk 4 was touching down on the runway. This no doubt made for some interesting throttle jockeying to get the timing right, but the end result was very impressive. One of the special highlights of the season was the Alberta Airshow staged at CFB Cold Lake, Alberta. Here the Hawks had the opportunity to strut their stuff in front of the "mud movers" (ground attack pilots) of 417 and 434 Sqns along with thousands of spectators who made their way to the base from hundreds of miles around.

Ron Coleman was rewarded for his fine flying in 1977 by being anointed as team lead the following season, handing the solo duties over to Capt Doug Evans. The 1978 season was interrupted temporarily in late July when the entire fleet of Voodoos was grounded due to a fuel line problem. One of the challenges of operating sophisticated high performance fighter aircraft is that the constant exposure to high G forces and multiple selections of afterburner do invariably put enormous stresses on the airframe and engine. From time-to-time, these stresses can result in aircraft failures which can be catastrophic if not immediately rectified. All fighter aircraft, regardless of their generation, have experienced technical problems in the course of their operational lifespan and the Voodoo was no exception. In this case, extensive investigations were launched into fuel line clamps and afterburner sensing lines. Having identified the problem, outstanding dedication by Voodoo technicians fleet-wide saw the aircraft back on operational duty within two weeks. This in turn allowed the team to make their annual sojourn to Abbotsford to once again open the show in style.

Promoted to the rank of major, Doug Evans took over the team in 1979 with lead navigator Capt Mel Ferraby. By now the team's dynamic demonstration had become well known across the western United States as well as Canada. In 1979, the state of Washington welcomed the team for performances at the Spokane Air Fair, Portland Rose Festival and McChord AFB open house near Tacoma. An additional five Canadian locations as far away as Winnipeg made for a busy season. For the 1980 season, Capt Lynn Housworth and veteran navigator Bill Books led the Hawks to several major shows highlighted by two performances at Paine Field, Washington, the standard three shows at Abbotsford and the Alberta 75th Anniversary Airshow at CFB Edmonton.

Balancing the squadron's operational responsibilities to NORAD with demands for constant readiness training and airshow appearances by the Hawks was ultimately the decision of the squadron's commanding officer. As a former team member, LCol George McAffer had provided strong support to the team from 1978 through the end of 1980 and was replaced by an equally strong proponent in LCol Larry Lott. He would be the last commanding officer of 409 Sqn in the Voodoo era, holding the position from December 1980 to July 1984. Of his support for air demonstration teams he reflects, "I was (and remain) very keen on airshow involvement as I believe it's the biggest bang for our recruiting buck. Since I had already had my share of the fun, I generally let the Hawks get on with the job, believing it was a major's job at squadron level." LCol Lott selected Maj Terry Hunt to lead the 1981 version of the Hawks assisted by his navigator Capt Gord MacPherson. Having just completed a tour with the Snowbirds in 1978 and 1979 as the first line astern pilot, Terry Hunt was well versed in the

The 1977 Hawks introduced a novel touch-and-go opposing pass with the main formation (left) to complement their fine formation flying. (DND Photos, Cpl Chris Hosford via Jim Reith)

airshow business and was a natural to lead the Hawks. In fact, he would be fortunate to do it twice, in 1981 and 1984:

"In addition to being big, fast and noisy, the Voodoo was a good formation platform, once you got used to the very sensitive pitch control. (I think that is why most of the Snowbird first line astern pilots in the early years were all ex-Voodoo pilots – we had developed a fine touch in pitch control after flying the Voodoo). Our four-plane show lasted about 12 minutes. Our two most popular manoeuvres were the high speed-low speed pass and the finale – a four-ship, in-trail, high-speed pass with a vertical departure. During the

high speed-low speed pass, the three-plane flew past the crowd at a paltry 220 knots with everything hanging. The solo would aim to do the overtake at show centre and varied his speed to do so. As I recall, the limiting mach number used by the solo for this pass was Mach 0.9 indicated. The reason was the Voodoo mach meter would hang up in the transonic range – about M0.9 indicated and then jump to M1.1 once through the sound barrier. Sooo, as you approached the speed of sound, you had no way of knowing exactly how close you were. As breaking the sound barrier at airshows was frowned upon (to say the least), we built in a margin of error. Even transonic, the aircraft would lay down a pretty damaging shock wave at low-level. On an

average summer day, M0.9 was probably in the neighbourhood of 550 knots so the solo could generate some pretty impressive overtake. Of course, the manoeuvre would be built up by the commentator, so by the time the 'dirty' three-ship was approaching stage centre, the whole crowd would be 'urging on' the solo aircraft that was still a small speck on the horizon. It was a hit or miss thing. However, Ed Campbell made it work more often than not in 1981. Regardless, late or early, it always drew a round of applause for the solo (they always relished that, while we poor formation types sweated it out in the trenches!).

The Abbotsford Airshow and the Hawks were synonymous for many years as the Hawks had the distinction of being the show openers for the flying portion of the day. We prided ourselves in the fact that you could set your watch by our opening pass – precisely at 1300 hours. Woe betide anyone on the airshow microphone who went overtime. In our first show in 1981, a dignitary was delivering an opening speech for the show – to be finished by 1300 hours. As with most such dignitaries, he failed to finish on time. His speech came to an abrupt end as the clock struck the top of the hour as our four-ship blew in from stage right behind the crowd at 300 feet and 400 knots for an opening topside pass. Once the noise had died down our commentator, Bill Motriuk, took the microphone out of the dignitary's hand and glibly stated 'the show's on.' No one went overtime on the second or third day of the airshow that year!"

Terry Hunt

There was one additional duty completed by the Hawks in 1981, a solemn but special one.

There was never a shortage of volunteers to join the Hawks airshow team. The 1979 team, L to R, Kneeling (pilots) – Maj Doug Evans (team leader), Lt Andy Dobson, Capts Bill Cleland, John Wiggin, Glen Buchanan. Standing (navigators) – Capts Mel Ferraby, Dave Taylor, Larry Russell, Gerry McCluer (USAF), Ron Neeve. (DND Photo via Andy Dobson)

A surreal photograph of the 1981 Hawks at Paine Field, Washington on a moisture-laden day. Leading the team is Capt Terry Hunt with lead navigator Capt Gord MacPherson. On his right is the crew of Capt Joel Clarkston/ Capt Bill Kolupanowicz, on the left Capt Barry Kennedy/ Capt Bill Ricketts and in the slot Capt Ed Campbell/ Capt Bill Books. (Ron Miller via Terry Hunt)

This is what airshow fans came to see in the Voodoo era, a "one-o-wonder" pulling G. (Bill Johnson)

At left, Capt Dale Erhart has his Voodoo wound right up as he flashes past the Abbotsford crowd (and Blue Angels) prior to his vertical exit in the summer of '80. At right, Capts Eric Matheson and Howard Tarbet execute a dynamic head-on dirty cross at Comox in '83. (via Dale Erhart, Dave Reyenga)

On July 2nd, Maj Hunt led the team in two flypasts during the funeral of Terry Fox, a 22-year-old, one-legged young man from Port Coquitlam, British Columbia. He had fought his way into the hearts of millions during his "Marathon of Hope" run across Canada in 1980 to raise money for cancer research. He was halted by the disease on the 143rd day of his odyssey, finally succumbing to it 10 months later. The team flew a "missing man" formation as a tribute to his courage, a tribute usually reserved for fallen comrades. It was a special honour for the extraordinary young man whose legacy is still remembered each year when thousands of Canadians participate in the annual Terry Fox Run across the nation.

The year 1982 was a frenetic one for 409 Sqn as it was the last year the squadron retained a full complement of aircrew and groundcrew. As such, it was also the last year for a full-time four-plane Hawk team. Taking over as leader from Terry Hunt was another veteran airshow performer, Maj Ray Dunsdon. He had flown with the famous "Deadeye" teams of 417 Sqn on the CF-104 Starfighter in 1973 and 1974, the latter as team leader. This gave him the distinction of being the only Canadian Forces pilot ever to lead both a Starfighter and Voodoo demo team. Capt Gord MacPherson stayed on as lead navigator for the 1982 season, seeing the team through 11 airshows that summer. If being famous in North America was not enough, the team also found itself featured in *Aviation Journal* of Japan, courtesy of some fine camera work by renowned aerial photographer Katsuhiko Tokunaga who has made a career of flying with just about every airshow team in the world!

On July 1st, 1983 the Nighthawks of 409 Sqn officially downsized in strength from 273 officers and men to 193. The squadron was also reduced to 12 Voodoos with only eight flyable at any given time due to the reduction in maintenance personnel. These reductions also necessitated the downsizing of the Hawks to a two aircraft team. The team was led by Capt Eric Matheson with Maj Jon Main as lead navigator and flew a reduced schedule of seven shows that summer. The 1983 Abbotsford show was dedicated to the Voodoo along with another popular performer appearing for the last time, the Royal Air Force's mighty Vulcan bomber. To commemorate the event, a grand finale flypast of the veteran perform-

"Hawk One Canada" in full chute at Paine Field in 1981. (Ron Miller)

The 1982 Hawks earned some welcome recognition for the Canadian Forces. L to R – Capts Jay Jongerius, Dave Mosher, Lt Andy Anderson, Capts Tim Strocel, Dan Trynchuk, Bob Slack (USAF), Gord MacPherson, Maj Ray Dunsdon (team leader). Missing are Capt Joel Clarkston and Lt Mark Forseille. (Katsuhiko Tokunaga)

ers was conducted on the last day of the show for the benefit of the Abbotsford faithful.

Farewell to the Hawks

In March 1984 authorization was granted for 409 Sqn to form one last Hawk team to see the CF-101 out of operational service on the west coast. Like her counterpart 416 Sqn, located some 2,700 statute miles (4,300 km) to the east, the authorization was initially limited to a two-plane team only. However, with the strong support of Col W.R. "Bob" Dobson, Base Commander of CFB Comox, timely permission was received for the Nighthawks to assemble a four-plane team for two hometown appearances, Armed Forces Day on April 14th and the 409 Sqn Reunion and Voodoo farewell on June 29th, 1984. The caveat was that the show was to be structured in such a way that minimal practice would be required to incorporate the two additional aircraft into the show.

Those honoured with selection to the last Hawk team were Hawk 1 – Maj Terry Hunt with lead navigator Capt Dave Reyenga; Hawk 2 – Capt Gary Soule/Capt Bernie Hughes; Hawk 3 – Capt Dave Pullan/Maj Jon Main; and Hawk 4 – Capt Tom Chester/Capt Doug Neill. All of the two-plane shows were flown by Hunt and Chester. As with all Canadian Forces teams, an official Operations Order spelled out the authorized manoeuvres for the Hawks. The repertoire of the last four-plane CF-101 team in history comprised 15 manoeuvres as follows:

1. Hawks 1 & 4 demonstrated a formation takeoff followed by a dumbbell turn to set up for an opening angled pass right to left in front of the crowd.
2. Hawk 2 demonstrated a maximum performance takeoff and afterburner climb.
3. Hawk 3 demonstrated a slow speed-high angle climb to rejoin with Hawk 2 and hold.
4. As Hawk 3 was lifting off, Hawk 1 and 4 surprised the crowd from behind at 1,000 feet AGL descending to perform a cross-over split upon reaching 300 feet AGL stage front.
5. Hawk 1 – solo afterburner 360 degree high performance turn.
6. Hawk 4 – solo knife-edge pass left to right at 450 KIAS.
7. Hawk 1 – solo touch-and-go to afterburner high angle climb at stage centre.
8. Co-solo high speed-slow speed 360. Hawk 4 entered from stage right in a slow-speed dirty configuration being overtaken by Hawk 1 at high-speed. At stage centre both aircraft initiated a 360 turn to the right demonstrating the minimum and maximum turning radius of the aircraft.
9. Upon completing his 360, Hawk 1 exited stage left to join up with Hawks 2 & 3, Hawk 4 performed an additional 360 turn, accelerating from 220 KIAS to 550 KIAS and exiting stage left.
10. High speed-slow speed pass. The Hawk three-plane formation then approached from stage left in landing configuration (speedbrakes extended, landing gear and flaps down) and was overtaken by Hawk 4 at stage centre at high-speed.
11. Solo rejoin. As the formation completed an oval turn liveside, Hawk 4 rejoined into box formation.
12. Four-plane bottomside silhouette pass left to right to high angle dumbbell turn.
13. Four-plane topside silhouette right to left followed by a right turn liveside to reposition head-on to the crowd at stage centre.
14. Four-plane fan break towards the crowd from box formation, exiting over the crowd at 1,000 feet AGL stage left and right.

Two contrasting views of the 1982 Hawks led by Maj Ray Dunsdon. Note the large trailing edge flaps and speed brakes of the landing configuration on the right. (Bill Johnson)

409ers will recognize the perch on the left as being the VIP viewing area for CFB Comox airshows over the years. At right, one of the Hawks checks "his score" from a high-spirited group of Canadian Forces technicians as he taxis back to the "hot side" at Abbotsford – straight "9"s for the day's work. (Ron Miller)

15. Following in-place turns deadside, the team re-entered from left to right in five second trail for individual high-speed passes to high-angle afterburner departures to conclude the show.

Of all of the solo manoeuvres flown by the Voodoo at airshows, the knife-edge pass was one of the more difficult. Capt Tom Chester was one of the last pilots to demonstrate the manoeuvre and explains how he mastered it:

"Prior to having the privilege of demonstrating the Voodoo with my navigator Capt Doug Neill, I had flown with our USAF exchange pilot Capt Bob Slack in 1982 when he was the solo pilot on the Hawks. He had demonstrated his method for doing the knife-edge by raising the nose slightly, rolling to approximately 110 degrees of bank and then pushing negative G to maintain altitude. When it came time for our own workups, Doug and I tried various ways to try and maintain as close to a 90 degree bank angle as possible. I found success by generating asymmetric thrust on my engines. We would begin the manoeuvre by starting our run-in from stage left at 450 KIAS and 300 feet AGL. Nearing the showline, I would simultaneously roll right, push full left rudder and select full right afterburner. As the burner kicked in, I retarded the left throttle to near idle. By doing this I could maintain a 90 degree bank angle and control my altitude by modulating the left throttle. If I needed to gain altitude, I would retard the left throttle further causing greater asymmetric thrust and the aircraft would climb on its side. Conversely, if I needed to descend I would increase the power to the left engine. Recovery from the manoeuvre was accomplished by simultaneously rolling left, releasing the rudder and selecting mil power on both engines. In preparation for a show, I would have to adjust the rudder pedals to the full aft position in order to be able to achieve full deflection while in the knife-edge since Doug and I would be hanging sideways in the cockpit against the canopy railing.

While the knife-edge was technically the most challenging manoeuvre of the show, the high speed-slow speed pass was certainly the most fun. The trick was to arrive at stage centre at the same time as the formation. I found that if I drew an imaginary line from my aircraft through the formation to show centre during the run-in, I could judge the pass with reasonable accuracy. If the formation remained stationary in my windscreen in relation to show centre as I closed distance on them, then we would all be lined up as we passed the reviewing stand. If the formation appeared to be moving ahead of show centre, then we would have to speed up. Doug provided much input during this pass. He would monitor the true airspeed to ensure we didn't break the speed of sound and would act as a backup in the assessment of how well we were doing. In Doug's opinion, we always needed to be faster! As we approached the formation, we would reduce power so that we could select afterburner to get that nice crowd pleasing burner light as we hit stage centre. It was during our final show in Cold Lake that I heard Doug shout for the first time to slow down! During the final stages of the run-in the true airspeed meter hit 638 knots. I think we must have been as close to the sound barrier as we could be without breaking it. If we had, we would have been without plausible denial as the only other

The final farewell. Sunday, August 14th, 1983 was a nostalgic day when airshow fans bid a fond farewell to two icons of the Abbotsford International Airshow, the CF-101 Voodoo and Avro Vulcan. Above, the Hawks who performed in the show for the last time. L to R – Capt Eric Matheson / Maj Jon Main, Capt Howard Tarbet (far rt)/Lt Kurt Saladana. (Ron Miller)

Aviation photographer Bill Petro captured these rare shots of Hawk 1 during two memorable photo missions out of Comox. At right, former Snowbird Capt Terry Hunt leads some old friends through the Comox Valley as Petro's chase pilot rolls over top of the formation. Below, farewell to Comox. LCol Larry Lott flying Hawk 1 leads a nine-ship of Voodoos from Comox to Cold Lake on 6 Jul 84. This photo by navigator Dave Reyenga shows the squadron sliding into big vic formation with four aircraft either side of the lead. Note the red and blue wings on two of the aircraft for ACM training. (Bill Petro, Dave Reyenga)

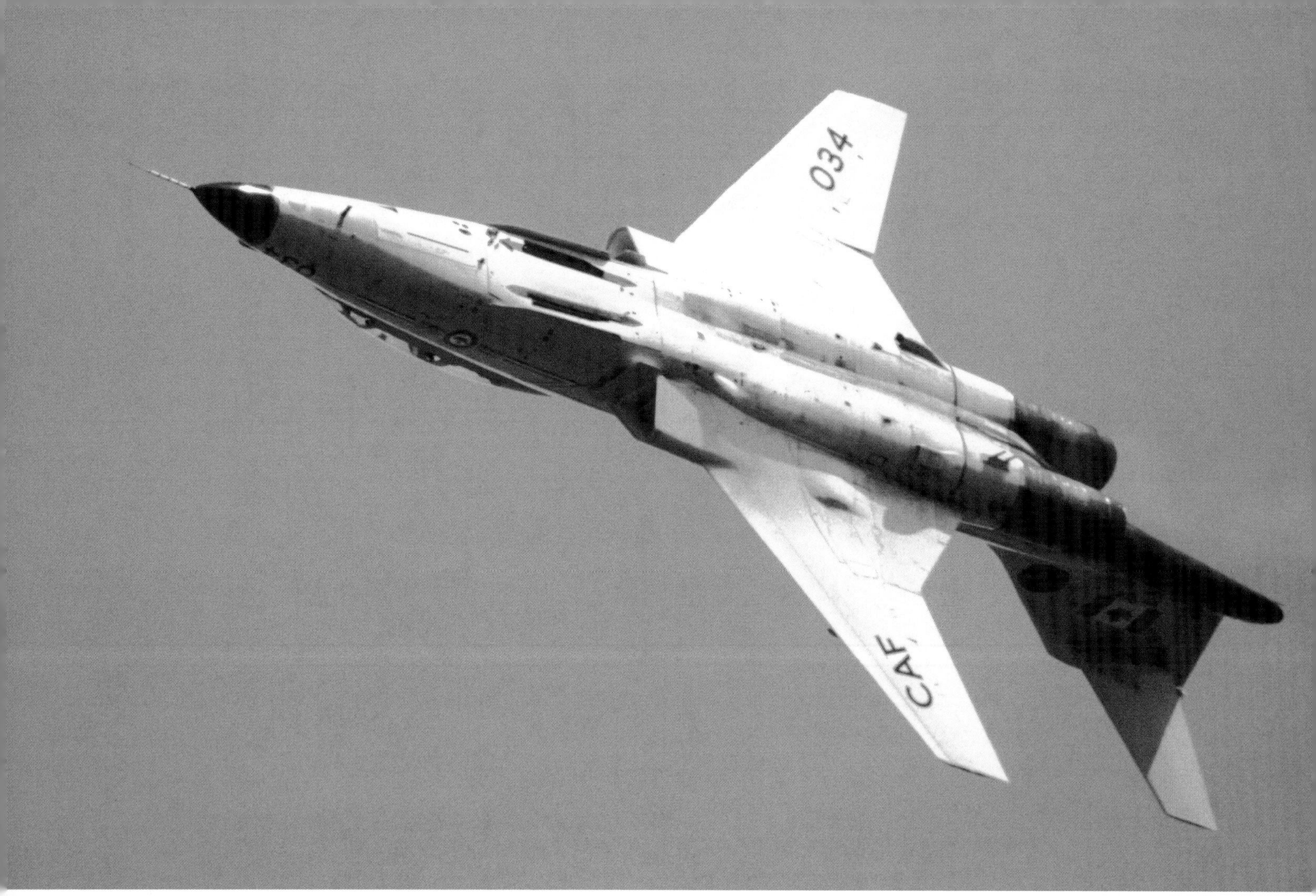

Capt Eric Matheson and Maj Jon Main streak past the Abbotsford crowd for the last time in 1983. (Bill Johnson)

Voodoos flying in Western Canada at that moment had their gear and flaps down!"

Tom Chester

In addition to the four-plane shows, the Hawks flew three two-plane shows in 1984, one each in April, May and June. Of these, the most significant was that flown at CFB Namao in Edmonton on May 13th, the same location where the majority of the original Voodoo crews had taken their conversion training 22 years earlier in 1962.

On June 28th, 1984 the last two 409 Sqn crews to hold alert on the Voodoo left the QRA hangar in Comox for the last time, joining the remainder of their squadron mates for a champagne toast to salute the end of a distinguished era in Canadian air force history. It would be one of many toasts over the next two days as over 800 reunion attendees converged on the base for the final farewell. The Hawks would kick it off the next morning with their last show in the Comox Valley.

While everyone expected the reunion airshow to be the last for the team, they were called upon to perform one last time after LCol Lott led a nine-plane to CFB Cold Lake a week later to help celebrate the rebirth of the Nighthawks as a tactical fighter squadron on the CF-18 Hornet. The Hawks therefore flew their last show on July 7th after which eight of the Voodoos were dispersed to places far and wide in Canada. The one exception was Hawk One (101057) which was flown by Larry Lott and Jay Jongerius back to Comox where it still proudly guards the entrance to the base.

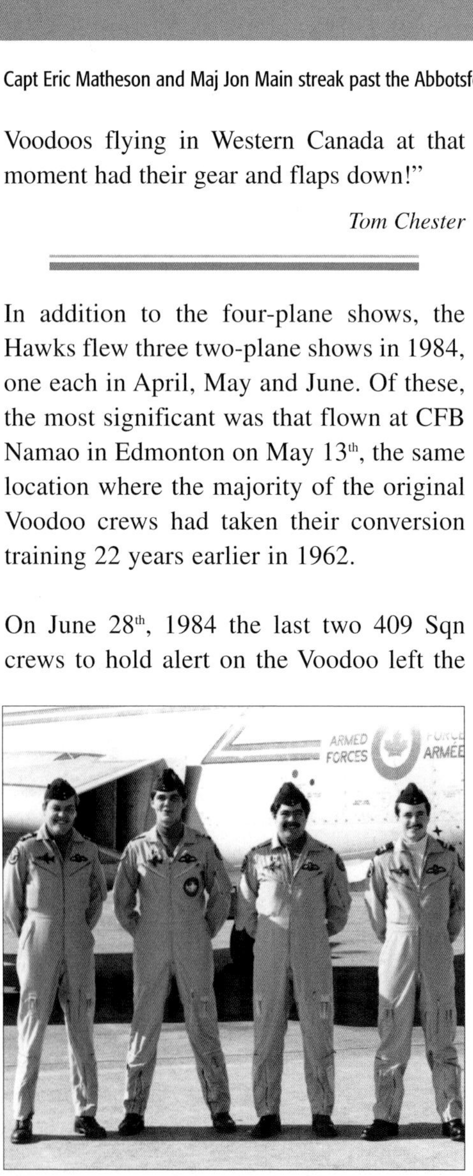

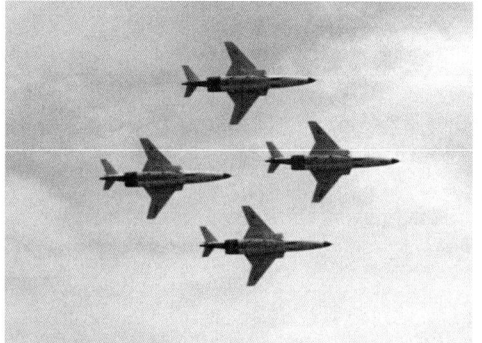

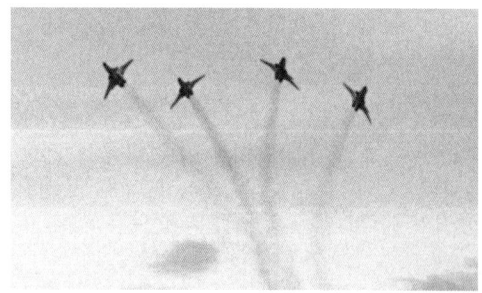

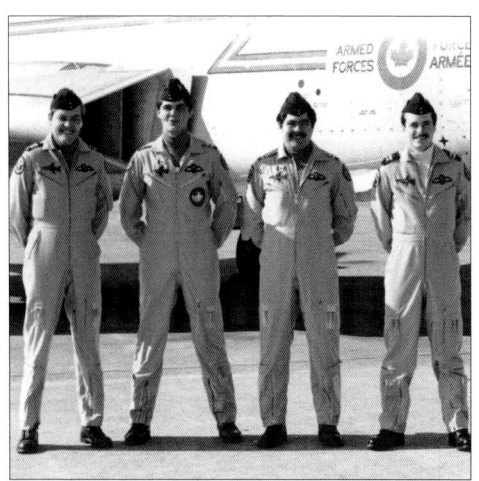

The last Hawk team flew in 1984, officially as a two-ship. L to R, Hawk Lead – Maj Terry Hunt/Capt Dave Reyenga; Hawk 2 – Capt Tom Chester/Capt Doug Neill (DND CX 84-501)

One for the history books – the last Voodoo four-ship in the world. The crews for this final show at Comox, B.C. were: Hawk Lead – Maj Terry Hunt/ Capt Dave Reyenga; Hawk 2 – Capt Gary Soule/ Capt Bernie Hughes; Hawk 3 – Capt Dave Pullan/ Maj Jon Main; Hawk 4 – Capt Tom Chester/ Capt Doug Neill. The show was narrated by Capt Kurt Saladana. (S. Chester)

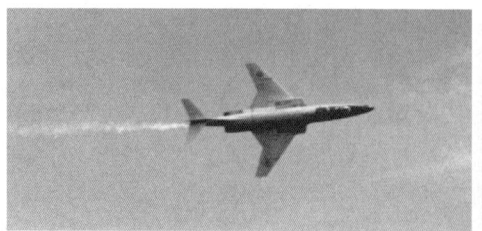

Swan song for the Voodoo. To commemorate 22 years of CF-101 operations in Canada, authorization was granted for each of the last four squadrons to paint a single aircraft in squadron colours, most of which appeared at airshow static displays. The 414 Sqn aircraft (EF-101067) was specially equipped to conduct electronic warfare training with NORAD crews. Along with EF-101006, the aircraft conducted a final flypast over the Voodoo memorial at CFB North Bay on April 4th, 1987. (courtesy Graham Wragg)

Farewell old friend. Millions of Canadians bore witness to the Voodoo magic at airshows from coast-to-coast during its operational lifespan. The aircraft was an impressive sight from any angle, in the air and on the ground. (Ron Miller)

Canada's Starfighter Teams

It holds a revered place in the annals of fighter aviation in the western world, one of the true classics that flew in Canadian and European skies for over two decades. Canadian pilots clamoured to get a posting on her, in great measure because she was a joy to fly, but also because a posting to a CF-104 Starfighter squadron meant an operational tour in Europe. It was an assignment of the greatest contrasts during the Cold War, on one hand the opportunity to enjoy the idyllic setting of the West German or French countryside – on the other the tension of sitting alert as part of one of the most formidable military forces ever assembled on a continent where NATO stared down the Warsaw Pact for over four decades.

Conceived in 1952 by mastermind Clarence "Kelly" Johnson at the Lockheed "Skunk Works" design facility tucked away in a secluded mountain valley near Burbank, California, the F-104's profile was unmistakable. What made it so distinct was not its streamlined 54 foot, 9 inch (16.69 m) fuselage, but rather its tiny wingspan of only 21 feet, 11 inches (6.68 m), the razor sharp leading edges of its wings sloping downwards at a negative dihedral of 12 degrees. Johnson had designed the aircraft as a lightweight air-superiority fighter in response to inputs received from American fighter pilots during a visit to Korea in December 1951. They wanted an aircraft with unmatched speed, rate of climb, ceiling and manoeuvrability – the F-104 was Johnson's response to those demands.

The prototype XF-104 (53-7786) made its highly secretive first flight on March 4th, 1954 from Edwards AFB, California in the

The Starfighter had a shape all its own and was one of the most recognizable fighters of its generation. (DND Photo)

hands of Lockheed test pilot Tony LeVier. He would later assume a "larger-than-life" reputation after being one of the few pilots to ever successfully "deadstick" a 104 to landing. Critical emergency "red page" procedures for failure to relight a dead engine would later be summarized by one word – EJECT! With its small wingspan, the Starfighter glided like a rock.

Although the USAF decided to purchase 17 service test aircraft under the designation YF-104A in July 1954, it was not until February 16th, 1956 that the YF-104A was unveiled to the public for the first time in a highly lauded media event at Lockheed's Burbank factory. The aircraft looked fast just standing still! In the air it truly was a speed demon – in April 1956 the Starfighter became the first fighter aircraft to exceed Mach 2 in level flight and in May 1958 it became the first aircraft in history to hold both the world speed and altitude records simultaneously (1,404.19 mph and 91,249

feet). That December it set six more time-to-climb records, including 82,020 feet (25,000 metres) in four minutes, 26.03 seconds from a standing start on the runway at NAS Point Mugu, California. But America's engineers and test pilots were not finished yet. One year later, an F-104C (the initial tactical strike version of the Starfighter) attained a speed of Mach 2.36 and zoomed to 103,389 feet on December 14th, 1959. This marked the first time that the 100,000 foot altitude was exceeded by an aircraft taking off under its own power.

Ironically, in spite of its accomplishments, the F-104A lost favour with Tactical Air Command (TAC) even before it was scheduled to enter service in 1956, largely because of a lack of endurance, limited weapons load and teething problems that had resulted in a relatively high accident rate. The initial 153 production F-104As were redirected to Air Defense Command as a stopgap measure to fill in until the arrival of the F-106 Delta Dart. Subsequently, TAC recanted for a time, pressing 77 F-104Cs into service. It was the F-104C variant assigned to the 479th Tactical Fighter Wing that was among American forces deployed on combat alert during the Cuban missile crisis of October 1962. The same wing later flew combat missions out of Da Nang, South Vietnam and Udorn, Thailand during the Vietnam War. Ultimately however, it was foreign-built F-104G and CF-104 Starfighters that generated the enduring legacy for the aircraft. A total of 2,580 Starfighters of all types were eventually produced, seeing service with the air forces of Canada, West Germany, Belgium, Denmark, the Netherlands, Norway, Greece, Turkey, Spain, Italy, Jordan, Pakistan, Taiwan and Japan in addition to the United States.

The CF-104 Starfighter's J-79 engine generated 15,800 pounds of thrust in full afterburner, enough to propel the fighter to twice the speed of sound. Residents of Cold Lake, Alberta soon became accustomed to hearing the eerie wail of the engine at night during maintenance checks. (DND PRMC 83-279)

CAF

732

Bob McIntyre

The contenders. The RCAF narrowed its search for a nuclear strike fighter-bomber to two aircraft in early 1959. Above, the Grumman F11F-1F Super Tiger test flown by F/L Jack Woodman and S/L Bob Middlemiss (in cockpit) at Edwards AFB. Below, members of the RCAF evaluation team at Palmdale with the F-104 Starfighter. L to R – F/L John Murray (engineer), test pilots S/L Bob Middlemiss and F/L Jack Woodman and F/L Pierre Bussieres (engineer). At right, S/L Bob Christie in early test pilot days. (via Bob Middlemiss, Bob Christie)

The Canadian CF-104 Story

Canada's involvement with the Starfighter began in the late 1950s when the RCAF began to contemplate a future replacement for its F-86 Sabres on NATO duty in Europe. With NATO doctrine having shifted to a "limited nuclear warfare" strategy in 1957, the suggestion was eventually made that Canada consider adopting the role along with several of her allies. The Conservative government of Prime Minister John Diefenbaker accepted the role for the RCAF's Air Division and the search was on for a new aircraft to do the job, bearing in mind that the Avro Arrow test program was in full swing and would take care of the country's air defence needs well into the future, or so everyone thought.

The Air Council charged the Chief of Operational Requirements, Air Commodore Wilf Bean, with the responsibility of forming an evaluation team of specialists in fighter requirements, air defence and strike operations along with aeronautical engineers specializing in electronics, armament, logistics and command and control systems. The director of operational requirements was responsible for the coordination of both operational and technical staffs that were to perform the evaluation on the various weapons systems under consideration with periodic reports to the Council through the Vice Chief of the Air Staff.

The team coordinator was S/L Bob Middlemiss, a veteran of Spitfire operations

in WW II and more recently a Sabre squadron commander with Canada's NATO Air Division based in France and Germany. After careful review, the team drafted the paperwork outlining the desired capabilities of the new aircraft. The RCAF ideally wanted a twin engine aircraft with a two man crew, low-level radar optimized for terrain following/avoidance and short takeoff and landing capability, all at a cost of not greater than one million dollars per aircraft. However, an overriding criteria was that the aircraft selected had to be available by December 1962 to assume NATO duties in Europe.

Assisting Middlemiss's team in their evaluation was S/L Bob Christie of the Directorate

of Air Defence and Strike Operations (DADSO). One of the first graduates of the USAF's Experimental Test Pilots School at Edwards AFB in 1951, Christie was a veteran of 10 years test experience on the Sabre and CF-100. He had been chief test pilot while serving with the Central Experimental and Proving Establishment (CEPE) at Rockcliffe and was subsequently appointed commander of the Air Armament Evaluation Detachment (AAED) of CEPE at RCAF Stn Cold Lake from 1954 to 1957. As such, he had been heavily involved in all aspects of the CF-100 test and evaluation program during which time the Primrose Lake test range was built.

Once underway, the team considered virtually every aircraft potentially available with their NATO partners. As Bob Middlemiss recalls, aircraft subsequently eliminated from contention included the Dassault Mirage IIIC and Mystere, Blackburn Buccaneer, Fiat G-91, Saab Drakken, Chance Vought F8U Crusader, Douglas A4E Skyhawk, McDonnell F-101 Voodoo, Northrop N-156 Freedom Fighter and a proposed ground attack version of the CF-105 Avro Arrow. The team heavily favoured the McDonnell F-4 Phantom but it was not only deemed too expensive, it could not meet the timeline for introduction into the RCAF inventory. Thus, the two aircraft that subsequently made the Canadian short list for the new strike role in the "cost vs capability vs availability" debate were the Lockheed F-104 Starfighter and Grumman F-11F-1F Super Tiger, both powered by the J-79 engine.

S/L Middlemiss had flown the Super Tiger twice in June of 1958 at Edwards AFB. However, it was not until January 15th, 1959 that he and Bob Christie finally got their first familiarization trip in a dual seat F-104B (# 7321) out of Palmdale, California. Following this introduction, the team continued the process of touring various aircraft and component systems companies. Unexpectedly, S/L Christie and part of the team were dispatched to the United Kingdom to re-evaluate the available candidates, including the Buccaneer. European aircraft manufacturers had brought political pressure on Ottawa, contending that their aircraft had not been given due consideration in the selection process.

While in the UK, Christie's team was ordered back to Canada on very short notice, without explanation. It was only over the mid-Atlantic the next day that they were informed that the government had cancelled the Avro Arrow project. The haste in the team's departure was to ensure that none of the team members could be questioned about the future direction of the selection process. Middlemiss received the same news directly from A/C Bean.

With the Arrow cancelled, A.V. Roe and Orenda struggled to find some possible use for components of the cancelled project. Christie recalls that the entire process was so political that Orenda came up with the idea of fitting the Republic F-105 Thunderchief with their Iroquois engine, still an unproven item at the time. However, the team considered the Thunderchief to be a heavy, cumbersome beast and quickly dismissed it.

With the RCAF team having definitively narrowed the choice to the Starfighter or Super

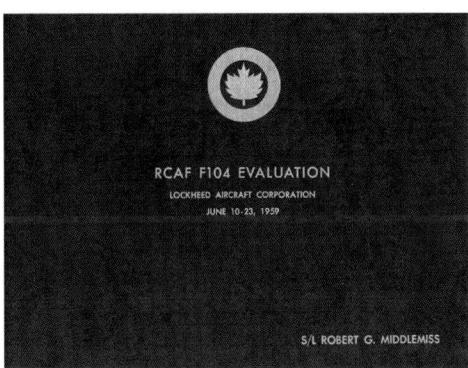

LOCKHEED F-104 STARFIGHTER PERFORMANCE RECORDS

• WORLD SPEED RECORD	1404 MPH (M-2.15)
• WORLD ALTITUDE RECORD	91,249 FT.

• WORLD TIME TO CLIMB RECORDS

3,000 m (9,843 FT.)	0 MIN. 41.85 SEC.
6,000 m (19,685 FT.)	0 MIN. 58.41 SEC.
9,000 m (29,528 FT.)	1 MIN. 21.14 SEC.
12,000 m (39,370 FT.)	1 MIN. 39.90 SEC.
15,000 m (49,213 FT.)	2 MIN. 11.10 SEC.
20,000 m (65,617 FT.)	3 MIN. 42.99 SEC.
25,000 m (82,021 FT.)	4 MIN. 26.03 SEC.

• USAF TIME TO INTERCEPT RECORD
8 MIN. 59.9 SEC. FROM BRAKE RELEASE TO 35,000 FT. INTERCEPTION OF TARGET 150 N. MI. FROM BASE. AVERAGE SPEED-1000 KNOTS.

A smooth sales pitch, some impressive statistics and support from NATO allies helped win the day for the F-104 Starfighter. (via Bob Middlemiss, Bob Ayres)

Tiger, Middlemiss prepared a brief test program to further evaluate the two aircraft in June of 1959. F/L Jack Woodman, a 1952 graduate of the Empire Test Pilots School and the only RCAF pilot to have test flown the ill-fated Arrow, joined the evaluation team from CEPE in Cold Lake. The Starfighter evaluation took place at Palmdale on the F-104C. Middlemiss and Woodman took turns flying each of eight sorties in various configurations. Woodman flew one sortie in a pressure suit and helmet, zooming a "clean-clean" Starfighter to 90,000 feet, something he would have dearly loved to

have accomplished in the Arrow had the program survived. Another encounter, this time during a maximum weight takeoff, also got his heart pumping when he blew a tire just before rotation. He managed to get airborne and did an unscheduled test of the bomb and pylon tank jettison system prior to returning for an uneventful landing. Bob Middlemiss repeated the test on June 20th, flying his fully loaded Starfighter on a simulated low-level strike mission that lasted two hours and ten minutes.

Plans to immediately begin final testing on the Super Tiger up the road at Edwards AFB were delayed by five days when the last prototype of the aircraft received an unscheduled "bath" caused when the sprinkler system in its hangar was accidentally set off by the engines of a B-52 outside. By the time the aircraft dried out, the test phase was reduced to a total of three days, culminating on June 27th. Middlemiss and Woodman each flew four test flights on the Super Tiger.

Although Bob Middlemiss personally favoured the handling characteristics of the Super Tiger, Bob Christie had come to the conclusion that the Starfighter had more potential with its cutting-edge technology. It was only days later, on July 2nd, 1959, that Minister of National Defence George Pearkes rose in the House of Commons to formally announce that Canada would replace its Sabres in Europe with the F-104

A USAF F-104A on the ramp at RCAF Stn Uplands on 26 Mar 61 reveals the fighter's distinctive tricycle landing gear. At right, the Canadair production line in full swing as a dozen CF-104s near final assembly in early 1962. (DND PL 132300, Canadair 30353)

Starfighter in the low-level nuclear strike and reconnaissance role. The decision caught some by surprise and was the beginning of the final death knell for the Super Tiger, the US Navy having long since decided the aircraft was not suitable for carrier operations, West Germany having earlier opted for the Starfighter in October 1958 and the Japanese soon to follow in November 1960.

The formal adoption of the new NATO doctrine represented an entirely new role for Canada's fighter pilots as the country joined her allies in the high stakes game of nuclear deterrence. Lockheed had won the day with a powerful lobbying campaign that featured considerable industrial benefits, not the least of which was a license agreement that would permit the fighter to be manufactured in its entirety in Canada. Additional benefits would also include the manufacture of parts for many of the other nations that would also opt for the F-104G as their next generation fighter.

Canadair Gets the Nod

In August 1959 it was announced that Canadair Ltd. of Montreal would continue its predominant role as the leading supplier of fighter aircraft to the RCAF by building a fleet of 200 CF-104 single seat fighters for the air force under license from Lockheed. Similarly, in a partnership that had worked well with the F-86 Sabre production, Orenda of Toronto was awarded the contract to build the 104's powerful GE J-79 engine that could propel a cleanly configured Starfighter from the end of a runway to twice the speed of sound at 35,000 feet within six minutes. Airframes and engines would come together at the Canadair plant in Cartierville, just as they had for the fleets of Sabres and T-33s in the early 1950s.

After the formal announcement of the Starfighter selection, things moved quickly to get the program underway and Canadair began the complicated process of "tooling up" to manufacture the aircraft. The CF-104 would be a variant of the F-104G optimized to Canadian specifications. One difference was that the North American Search and Ranging Radar (NASARR R-24A) on the Canadian model was optimized solely for ground mapping navigation in conjunction with the Litton LN-3 Inertial Navigation System and CAE's Position and Homing System. Another was that the cockpit layout was designed by many of the same people that had been involved in the selection process, with appropriate liaison with the Institute of Aviation Medicine in Toronto. Having experienced the "disastrous placement" of the CF-100 cockpit, Bob Christie was certain that the CF-104 had to be better. It was therefore with considerable gratification that the final design became something of a standard, the European allies accepting the Canadian layout with little change.

From an operational standpoint, another major difference with the CF-104 was that it had the standard M-61 Vulcan rotary cannon removed in favour of additional fuel cells that increased the internal fuel load by 101 imperial gallons. Thus, the CF-104's only defence was its speed. In strike configuration, the aircraft would carry an additional 200 gallon jettisonable drop tank under each wing to supplement its wingtip tanks of the same size, thus giving the aircraft the range it needed to reach its wartime targets within the Warsaw Pact. All tanks would be jettisoned as their fuel was used, leaving only its lone "special" weapon on the centreline pylon for the high-speed dash to target.

While preparations were underway to build the Starfighter in Canada, the RCAF announced the selection of the commanding officers who would command the eight CF-104 squadrons that would make up the four Canadian fighter wings in Europe. Heading the list was newly promoted W/C Bob Middlemiss who would command 427 Sqn, the first CF-104 squadron deployed in the European theatre. Bob Christie was also promoted and posted to SHAPE headquarters in Paris where he joined the *arbeitenden* F-104G program that had been initiated by the West German Air Force. From his new desk Christie assisted a host of NATO countries with the introduction of the Starfighter into their defence plans, flying with all of them prior to taking command of the RCAF's 1 (F) Wing in Marville, France in 1965. Meanwhile, F/L Jack Woodman was seconded directly to Lockheed at Palmdale as the RCAF's point man for the Starfighter. In an analysis of the Starfighter published soon after it had been selected he concluded, "One thing is certain – when the airplane is fully operational, the RCAF will truly have a flexible and potent weapon. It is the writer's guess that a CF-104 squadron will be the most sought-after posting in the RCAF." Woodman left the RCAF in 1963 to become Lockheed's chief test pilot for the F-104, watching his predictions come true from Palmdale, California.

Another RCAF test pilot who saw early service on the 104 was F/L Bob Ayres, a 1956 graduate of the Empire Test Pilots School in Great Britain. He was dispatched to the United States in May 1960 to get a formal checkout on the F-104A then in operational service with the USAF, joining the 337th Fighter Interceptor Sqn at Westover AFB, Massachusetts. After building up some valu-

able flying experience, he joined the NATO F-104G Joint Test Force staff at Edwards AFB later that December. Woodman and Ayres were among the first of a distinguished group of Canadian test pilots who would oversee the acceptance, test and development of all modifications and weapons clearances involving the Starfighter fleet during its 25 year service flying the Canadian roundel. For his part, Bob Ayres' logbook reveals flights in 105 different Canadian CF-104s, plus an additional 11 USAF and 26 German Air Force Starfighters over an 11 year period. Little wonder he was the first RCAF pilot to crack the 2,000 hour mark on the aircraft. He also had the distinction of "deadsticking" a Starfighter to landing during his test pilot career, not once, but twice!

No. 6 Strike/Reconnaissance OTU

The initial cadre of eight instructors for the CF-104 operational training unit, No. 6 Strike/Recce OTU at Cold Lake, were carefully selected and underwent a Sabre refresher in January 1961. They eventually proceeded to Palmdale for an F-104 checkout after completing a weapons course on the F-100 Super Sabre at Nellis AFB. S/L Bill Paisley, the unit's designated chief flying instructor, followed shortly thereafter by W/C Ken Lett, Canada's first CF-104 commanding officer, each led a contingent of four pilots to Palmdale. By September the eight "originals" were back in Cold Lake to begin the onerous task of building the training syllabus that would eventually see 75 courses comprising over 700 Canadian fighter pilots graduate from the program between 1962 and 1983.

As the originals were keeping themselves preoccupied in Cold Lake, their new mounts were being manufactured in Cartierville, Quebec. March 18th, 1961 dawned a glorious, sunny day in Montreal, a fitting start for the rollout of a new supersonic flying machine. Canadair's first production CF-104 (12701) was a stunning beauty in RCAF colours as she was rolled out into the light of day for the first time. However, this was just the beginning of an extensive test program – she would soon join the CF-104 prototype (12700), a USAF F-104A modified by Lockheed in its Palmdale plant. Apart from having contracted Lockheed to build the 38 dual seat CF-104Ds that would be used to train RCAF pilots, it had also been agreed that the first two production singles would be test flown out of the Palmdale facility. Thus, 701's first flight was in the back of an RCAF Hercules for the trip west. However, she was soon reassembled and rocketed into the blue at Palmdale in the hands of Lockheed test pilot Ed Brown on May 26th. Eventually, 701 was flown to Cold Lake by F/L Garth Cinnamon to join airframes 702 through 705, not at the OTU but rather at the CEPE Detachment whose mandate was to test all new systems and weapons that would be assigned to the Starfighter for the duration of its operational service.

The first CF-104s to fly in Canada (12703 and 12704) took to the air two hours apart on their maiden flights from Cartierville on August 14th, 1961 in the hands of test pilots Bill Kidd and Glen "Snake" Reaves. Reaves was a Lockheed test pilot who enjoyed legendary status with all Canadian fighter pilots who flew the machine, not only because of

History in the making. Canadair's first CF-104 gets plenty of attention as it rolls off the assembly line on 18 Mar 61. (Canadair photos - 25302 (top right), C1101 (below) via Bill Upton)

The first five production CF-104s were assigned to the CEPE Detachment in Cold Lake as test beds. CF-104702 was later placed on a pedestal in Grand Centre, Alberta where it still resides as a lasting tribute to the classic aircraft. (RCAF LA 3141 via Chris Grasswick)

his acknowledged expertise on its systems but also because of the incredible manner in which he handled the aircraft. Those Canadair staff gathered to witness the return of the two aircraft for landing after their first test flights marvelled at the high-speed pass flown by Kidd as he screamed over the runway and punched up into the low overcast almost vertically. But they were aghast at Reaves' return two hours later as he "wing walked" his way across the field in a super slow pass, his Starfighter hanging just above the stall. Considering this was the aircraft's first flight, Reaves' audacity not only demonstrated his finesse at flying the aircraft but also his complete confidence in the Starfighter, its J-79 engine and the technicians at Canadair who had built the machine.

Meanwhile, the maiden flight of the first Lockheed-built dual earmarked for Canada had taken place on June 14th, 1961 at Palmdale. Following its test flight phase, it was released to the RCAF and was the first

CF-104D to be delivered to Cold Lake, an exciting day for W/C Lett and S/L Paisley who did the honours in January 1962. The station had already seen its first single seat Starfighter (12709) delivered earlier in November but it was destined for No. 10 Field Technical Training Unit (10 FTTU) as a training platform for the initial cadre of technicians. The first single seater to reach the OTU (12707) finally arrived on March 1st directly from the Canadair plant in the hands of Bill Paisley. It was several weeks behind schedule due to the inevitable snags that every new aircraft encounters. Before long, the Canadair plant was churning out 14 singles a month and training at the OTU was in full swing. Between April and July 1962, 63 singles were delivered to Cold Lake. By the time the last CF-104 (12900) rolled off the RCAF production line in June 1963, 82 singles and 22 duals had been delivered to the remote station. The balance were delivered to Europe for the eight operational squadrons.

Early Appearances

From the moment the Starfighter entered service with the RCAF, it was destined to become a magnet at airshows across the country. There was nothing quite like it – its relatively small size combined with its tremendous speed and the banshee wail of its engine created a mystique that was unmatched by any other fighter of the day. However, its first appearance in Canada for a select audience had a rather auspicious beginning. F/L Bob Ayres had just checked out with the 337th Fighter Interceptor Sqn of the USAF when he was tasked to accompany one of the squadron's pilots to Ottawa for a special mission:

"On May 15th, 1960 I accompanied Capt George Schulestad from Westover AFB to RCAF Stn Uplands at the Ottawa International Airport for the purpose of demonstrating the F-104's capabilities to a group of senior air

officers from several nations interested in acquiring the Starfighter aircraft. We each flew into Ottawa in a single seat F-104A, the original interceptor version of the aircraft which had a downward ejection seat.

On the morning of the demonstration flight (which George was designated to fly) the weather was poor – low visibility, high humidity, with a low cloud ceiling. Capt Schulestad took off at the designated time and did a long sweeping turn to do a pass down the hangar line where the dignitaries were gathered. However, due to the poor visibility he was not lined up properly so the control tower cleared him for a second pass, the goal being to stay in closer in order to be better seen. George did just that, but in order to turn in more sharply he selected afterburner and pulled hard around the corner with higher G. Trouble was, as he rolled out he left the burner in too long. The low pass was spectacular … but he was supersonic!! The result was a thundering boom which caused glass from the 'almost completed' new terminal building to pour out from the structure onto the ground. All of the windows in the control tower, which was situated on top of the new terminal building, were also blown out. Total damage – a stately three quarters of a million dollars!

Needless to say, many people were embarrassed, but since the Canadian government had requested the demonstration to show off "their" new fighter, the damage was quietly repaired with as little fanfare as possible. Meanwhile, George was shortly thereafter promoted to the rank of major and the rest is history. Oh, I think he did receive a tongue-in-cheek reprimand from the commanding general at Air Defence Command, but that's all. He retired years later with general's rank himself …"

George R. Ayres

Another disbelieving spectator on the day of the Starfighter debut was Bob Christie, whose memories of the event also remain vivid:

"I had arranged to meet the base commander and G/C Len Birchall, CO of North Bay, to watch the show. We were standing between the RCAF hangars (two of them in a row – CEPE and 412 Sqn) and the new air terminal. The run was made northwest to southeast along Runway 14. A public address system was set up to provide a running commentary for the large crowd of base personnel and visitors on hand. As the announcer said 'Here it comes,' we looked down the flight line to the north and suddenly noticed the ceiling inside CEPE, then 412 Sqn, disintegrate in a shower of asbestos that was used as a fire retardant; it appeared at first as if the roofs had fallen in. Then the sonic boom hit! We followed the aircraft and as it passed the terminal, one got the impression that someone had taken a giant water hose to the building. We suddenly realized that what appeared to be water pouring down the side of the building was in fact glass, falling like rain! In the next micro-second we realized that there wasn't a piece of glass left in the place. From that moment forward, the day became known as 'The Big Bang.'"

Bob Christie

What a debut – raised eyebrows all around! However, the incident did serve to underscore just how easily the Starfighter could slip through the sound barrier at low level, something all future 104 demo pilots would have to monitor very closely in the interests of safety … and self-preservation. The incident also added to the mystique and notoriety of the aircraft. Thus, when another American F-104 appeared at National Air Force Day (NAFD) in Ottawa the following month (courtesy this time of Lockheed), the aircraft garnered more than a passing interest as it rocketed by – this time remaining below the speed of sound.

Once 6 Strike/Recce OTU was up and running at RCAF Stn Cold Lake there was precious little time for anything but training as all those associated with the early days of Starfighter service remember all too well. These were exciting days for the RCAF with two new fighter aircraft on the inventory – but the days were long and seven day work weeks were the norm. Thus, early public appearances of Canadian 104s in eastern Canada such as at NAFD were courtesy of RCAF test pilots attached to CEPE at the Uplands air base or its detachment at the Canadair plant. Included among the latter category was F/L Frank Gilland. His logbook reveals that he was one of the first RCAF pilots to show off the Canadian version of the Starfighter with a flypast at the spectacular NAFD airshow at Rockcliffe on June 9th, 1962 along with four other fellow test pilots. As Gilland laughingly recalls, "The formation was probably led by F/L Lorne Tapp. We used to put Lorne out front because he couldn't fly formation worth a damn!" Gilland returned to Ottawa the following summer for a return engagement and also performed at the CNE in Toronto with fellow test pilot F/L Clive Loubser at the end of August, demonstrating the popular high speed-slow speed pass.

It was not until 1964 that 6 Strike/Recce staff made their airshow debut at NAFD celebrating the 40th anniversary of the RCAF. S/L Bill Paisley led an impressive four-ship flypast on June 6th in "strike" configuration – an MN1A practice bomb dispenser on the centreline (simulating a 2,000 pound "special weapon") with large pylon fuel tanks slung under each wing along with wingtip tanks. On the ground, thousands of curious onlookers surrounded another Starfighter on static display manned by F/L Lyle Kettles. As the

The inaugural appearances of Canadian-built Starfighters in eastern Canada were conducted by CEPE staff pilots based at Uplands in Ottawa and the Canadair plant at Cartierville, Quebec. This flypast took place at RCAF Stn Rockcliffe, Ontario during National Air Force Day on 9 Jun 62. (DND PL 139668)

In a tradition that continues today, tens of thousands of airshow fans crammed the shores of Lake Ontario in the early 1960s to watch the aerial extravaganzas staged by the Canadian International Air Show. The largest attraction was the RCAF showcase which featured the Golden Hawks, Red Knight and early appearances by Canada's newest high-performance fighters, the CF-101 Voodoo and CF-104 Starfighter. Key to a smooth flowing show was the airshow announcer whose task was to keep the eager spectators both informed and entertained as the spectacle unfolded. Since 1974, the man behind the microphone at "Boss Control" in Toronto has been Stu Holloway (inset), a veteran pilot himself and one of Canada's finest airshow announcers. (courtesy CNE Archives)

runway at Rockcliffe was far too short to accommodate the 104, one was hauled over on a flat bed truck from Uplands the night before the show. Looking at its long nose and stubby wings, it was easy to see why the press had dubbed the aircraft "the missile with the man in it" and curious onlookers surrounded Kettles and the aircraft:

"In addition to a steady flow of people around the 104 during the show, there was also a steady flow of questions of all kinds, from young and old alike. One gentleman asked where the gun was located – he didn't believe me when I told him that we did not have a gun but that they could be installed. He then looked at the needle-nosed pitot head and asked what it was. When I tried to tell him how it worked, he just broke into a big grin, gave me a big wink and said,

'That's okay, it's one of those secret ray guns isn't it?' With that, he then walked away content that he had it all figured out. I let him go with his new-found knowledge."

Lyle Kettles

Following the Ottawa affair, the Starfighter gradually made inaugural appearances at many Air Force Days across the country. This included the show at RCAF Stn Namao on August 23rd, where Edmontonians were wowed with a near supersonic pass in sharp contrast to the droning Harvards of the Goldilocks that performed in lieu of the disbanded Golden Hawks.

In early September 1964, S/L Len Fitzsimmons led a four-ship of 104s from Cold Lake to participate in the CNE in Toronto. S/L Fitzsimmons, who hails from

the Toronto area himself, recalls that Cold Lake sent an army of some 50 technicians to RCAF Stn Trenton which was to be the staging base for the duration of the show. Indeed, Trenton became an integral component of the success of the CNE show as it hosted the popular "fast movers" contingent every year. However, "popular" was not exactly the description the station commander in Trenton would have used to describe the arrival of the Starfighter contingent, as Len Fitzsimmons explains:

"The station commander in Trenton was G/C Butcher and he was very proud of his station. They had just resurfaced their runway the week before our arrival to prepare for the CNE. Our first practice over the Toronto waterfront took place on September 3rd and upon landing I was met by the group captain

S/L Bill Paisley, chief flying instructor at No. 6 Strike/Recce OTU at RCAF Stn Cold Lake, led the first contingent of staff instructors to appear at NAFD Rockcliffe in 1964, the aircraft appearing in "strike" configuration. At right, the 6 OTU contingent that flew at the CNE a few months later. L to R – Capt Bob Noak (USAF), F/L John Lauritsen, F/L Hugh Grasswick, F/L Len Fitzsimmons (leader). (RCAF photos via Bill Paisley, Len Fitzsimmons)

in his staff car. 'I want to show you something,' he allowed. The next thing I knew we were driving to the end of the runway in his staff car. When we got out it was pretty obvious what had happened. We had lined up in echelon for a single-ship takeoff with five seconds spacing. While performing our run-ups to full power prior to our takeoff roll, each aircraft had slipped forward about two feet in the relatively fresh asphalt, thus creating no less than 12 deep tire ruts in the beautiful new runway surface. I could only apologize to the group captain as we had followed our standard pre-takeoff procedures. I must admit he was most pleasant about the whole affair but was particularly relieved when I offered the solution whereby we would conduct our subsequent engine run-ups on the concrete holding pad immediately adjacent to the end of the runway and thus avoid a repeat performance.

We flew another practice the next day prior to the big weekend shows on Saturday and Sunday. Our routine was pre-planned by the DND/CNE organizers and was pretty simple. It included passes in four-plane box formation and concluded with a high-speed pass at minimum altitude in trail formation with two to three seconds spacing between each aircraft – a great crowd pleaser. After that we rejoined and headed back to Trenton.

By the time the next summer rolled around the OTU had undergone a large turnover of staff so the new boss, W/C Bob Middlemiss, allowed me to lead the CNE contingent again in '65. The 1965 show was very similar to the previous year except that we took five aircraft and were followed in by Sam Millar and his Voodoo team from 416 Sqn in Chatham. We flew each day from September 2nd through 5th inclusive, winding our way

westward along the northern shore of Lake Ontario in the murky visibility to make good our TOT over the showsite. The shows all went off as advertised and it was a thoroughly enjoyable experience."

Len Fitzsimmons

With the Starfighters having been such a big hit with fairgoers and airshow fans alike at the CNE, it was a given they would be invited back in the ensuing years. S/L Grant Baker returned with a five-ship in 1966 to dazzle the crowds and F/L Al Seitz did the honours in 1967 with five more OTU instructors determined not to be outdone by the Golden Centennaires at Canada's largest show. Of course, it was hard to beat the very impressive performance put on by René Serrao during his fully aerobatic Starfighter show, but that did not deter his colleagues from the OTU from trying! Another

The 6 Strike/Recce OTU CNE formation teams of 1965 and 1966. L to R, Kneeling – F/L Ken Maley, S/L Len Fitzsimmons (leader), F/L Moe Morrison. Standing – F/L Lyle Kettles, Maj Bud Jamesen (USAF). At right, the 1966 team – L to R, Kneeling – F/L 'Pogo' Hamilton, S/L Grant Baker (leader), F/L 'Buster' Kincaid. Standing – Maj Don Gerlinger (USAF), F/L 'Gin' Smith. (RCAF CK 65-531-1 via Lyle Kettles, CK 66-407-1 via Grant Baker)

F/L René Serrao, one of the most famous Starfighter demo pilots of all time, flew 82 public displays as a member of the Golden Centennaires in 1967. Here he executes a series of rapid rolls at Abbotsford. (Bill Johnson)

interesting twist to the Starfighter show in '67 was the inclusion of not one, but two, USAF pilots on the team, Capts Jamie Denard and Cebe Habersky. It was common practice among many of Canada's airshow fighter teams to extend an invitation to foreign officers on exchange duties to participate on squadron teams. This of course was very gracious and for the individuals concerned afforded an opportunity for some unique flying they otherwise would not likely have experienced within their respective air forces.

As the Starfighter gained popularity as an airshow performer, it frequently adorned the covers of airshow programs as witnessed by these examples from 1966, 1969 and 1971. The photo at right shows a strike training configuration with Mk 106 practice bombs designed to simulate the ballistics of the special weapon that was carried by the CF-104 until the end of 1971. (author's collection)

Capt René Serrao puts his Starfighter through its paces during the 73rd of 82 shows he flew with the Golden Centennaires in 1967. This particular show took place over home plate at CFB Cold Lake, Alberta on 8 Oct as the season drew to a close. The CF-104 Starfighter was the fastest aircraft ever to serve operationally with the RCAF and Cdn Forces. With its tiny wingspan of 6.68m (21 ft, 11 inches), the aircraft was capable of speeds over twice the speed of sound. The paint scheme shown here was the same as that employed in the nuclear strike and reconnaissance role in the Air Division overseas with the exception of the red horizontal stabilizer. (Rae Simpson)

Top - Instructors from 6 Strike/Recce OTU at Cold Lake pass in review at Cold Lake's Centennial Airshow in 1967. F/L Al Seitz had the honour of being the last CF-104 demo team leader in the RCAF. On 11 Mar 68, No. 6 Strike/Recce OTU became 417 Tactical Fighter Training Squadron following unification of the Canadian Armed Forces the month before. Below - Following the move of 1 Wing from Marville, France to CFB Lahr, West Germany in March 1967, 439 Sqn continued in their photo reconnaissance role. Shown here in 1968 is a rare shot of four Tigers in their photo recce suite during Armed Forces Day, "armed" with the Vinten Vicom recce pod especially designed for the Starfighter. Even after converting to the conventional ground attack role two years later, 439 Sqn retained a limited recce capability, the last CF-104 Sqn to do so. (Rae Simpson)

The Centennial Zoom

During 1967, the CF-104 became the focus of a major national centenary project within the RCAF that was to gain much publicity, albeit after the fact. The goal was to assault the Russian-held world altitude record and to capture this prestigious record during Canada's Centennial year. The world altitude record – one of only six "absolutes" in the aviation record book of the *Fédération Aéronautique Internationale (FAI)* – had been captured from the Americans by the Russian test pilot Mosolov flying a highly-modified and rocket-boosted MiG-21 (the E-66A) to 113,892 feet. Although the Aerospace Engineering & Test Establishment (AETE) at CFB Uplands was given the prime task, the project would ultimately involve some 5,000 military, Defence Research Board and Ministry of Transport personnel. W/C R.A. (Bud) White, a 1960 graduate of the Empire Test Pilots School and AETE's senior test pilot, was designated national and project leader. The AETE team based their challenge on the highly-modified and stripped-down CF-104 prototype (12700), the use of a highly up-rated but life-limited engine, speed augmentation by utilizing jet stream winds and a unique "zoom" manoeuvre. Major support was provided by the USAF's loan of three Gemini full pressure "space" suits, special training at Edwards AFB and by two additional CF-104s borrowed from the AETE detachment at Cold Lake, 448 Test Sqn.

All told, 42 flights, including 26 "zooms" (12 of them above 96,000 feet) were flown in S/N 700 from Ottawa. Of these, three were authenticated before the FAI. Authentication involved microwave tracking by the Defence Research Tracking Establishment at Shirleys Bay – the first time that FAI record approval had ever been achieved by a non-optical system. The high prevalence of the jet stream over the Ottawa Valley, and the fact that most of the flights had to be conducted in the area of the busiest civil air traffic in Canada, meant that extraordinary support and coordination by MOT air traffic controllers was required to vector civil and IFR aircraft out of danger without revealing the confidentiality of the "zoom" flights.

Although the Centennial team fell short of the world record, AETE gained valuable technical insights that were to prove highly valuable for subsequent CF-104 maintenance and operations. W/C White did attain a paint-blistering speed of Mach 2.45 – the fastest ever attained

High flyers. W/C Bud White (left) set a new Canadian altitude record towards the end of Canada's Centennial year, generating significant publicity for the RCAF on the eve of its disbandment due to unification of Canada's military services. *Sentinel* was the new magazine of the Canadian Armed Forces. S/L Bob Ayres and F/L Jack Woodman were two other veteran RCAF test pilots who earlier zoomed the Starfighter to dizzying heights wearing pressure suits. (RCAF Photos)

by any Starfighter – and his authenticated altitude of 100,110 feet achieved on December 14th, 1967 still stands as the official Canadian altitude record. Much was made of White's record following the flight with extensive press coverage across the country as Centennial year drew to a close. The aircraft continues to be proudly displayed at the Canada Aviation Museum at Rockcliffe, just a few miles from where it made its record-breaking attempts almost 35 years ago. For his leadership of the Centennial team, combined with his earlier contribution to the USAF and NASA Mercury and Gemini Space Programs, W/C White was later awarded the McKee Trophy and inducted into Canada's Aviation Hall of Fame.

The Tradition Continues

As it transpired, the 1967 Canadian International Air Show marked the last airshow appearance ever made by 6 ST/R OTU. On March 11th, 1968 the unit disbanded to be reborn as 417 Tactical Fighter (Operational Training) Sqn. It was a bittersweet transition as the memories of the hard won battle honours between 1942 and 1945, especially the campaigns in North Africa and Italy, were revived even as the RCAF and its traditional rank structure had been disbanded under unification scarcely a month before.

Capt Al Seitz led the first CF-104 team in the 417 Sqn era, the major show once again being the two day CNE affair. Abbotsford got top billing the next year with ex-Golden Hawk Maj Norm Garriock leading a four-

The stylistic 417 Sqn shoulder badge that was adopted soon after the squadron was re-formed in 1968 contrasted the squadron's historic heraldic badge. At right, the shoulder badge that distinguished Canadian 104 pilots from all other aviators. (author's collection)

Top - Maj Norm Garriock leads Maj Bill Worthy in a slow-speed pass during their show opener at Abbotsford '69. The lead aircraft is configured with the high resolution Vinten Vicom photo reconnaissance pod. CF-104711 made many appearances over the years at Abbotsford, including as lead aircraft of the 1982 Deadeye Zips when the Starfighter made its last appearance at the show. Above - four zippers demonstrate the art of symmetry at Abbotsford. (Bill Johnson)

try's Voodoos and the new CF-5 tactical ground support fighter. The impressive shows put on by the Canadian Forces in the immediate post-unification years helped keep morale and *esprit de corps* alive in the aftermath of severe budget cuts and a 50 percent reduction of Canada's Starfighter squadrons in Europe. In each of 1970 and 1971, the headline act was a combined 10-plane show by the CF-104s and CF-5s based at Cold Lake, wonderfully choreographed to keep spectators' heads swivelling as the separate four-plane formations were interspersed by a solo performer in each of the CF-104 and CF-5. This was great stuff … and airshow fans loved it!

The former leader of the Bald Eagles CF-100 team, Capt J.W. (Bill) Stewart, led the 104 contingent in 1970 with wingmen Al Heston of the USAF and fellow Canadian instructors John Callahan and Phil Engstad. The symmetry of the formation show was punctuated by powerful solo performances by Capts Jordy Krastel and Garry Sanderson in two additional Starfighters. Deciding this was too much fun to pass up, Krastel took command of the team in 1971 taking a similar act to Moose Jaw, Abbotsford and the CNE in Toronto.

plane show. Joining Garriock for his second year on the team was Capt Bob Morgan who flew the slot position. Morgan was no stranger to airshows, having performed in many displays as early as 1951 when he had flown Mustangs with 416 Sqn. He flew three successive years on Cold Lake's Starfighter team, practicing after hours and performing on weekends. He was one of hundreds of RCAF pilots who had joined the air force with no ambition other than to fly airplanes – which he proudly did as a "senior captain" for 36 years. His last performances in the Starfighter took place at the three day Abbotsford Airshow in August of 1969, but he would go on to perform later airshows in the C-130 Hercules and Twin Otter, even getting in on the act by dropping the Canadian Forces SkyHawks parachute team on numerous occasions.

The Starfighter teams of the 1970s are still fondly remembered by airshow patrons who watched them perform. Although the aircraft would lose its strike role in 1971 when the Trudeau government elected to drop

Canada's nuclear strike commitment to NATO, a new conventional ground attack mission would keep the aircraft in Canadian skies for another dozen years.

By 1970 the CF-104 had become engrained as an airshow regular alongside the coun-

Canada's 1971 Starfighter team. At left, Capt Jordy Krastel in the tight confines of the CF-104. At right he is joined by his formation teammates, L to R – Capts Eric Saunders, Krastel, Bill Nesbitt and Ed Rozdeba (standing). Missing is soloist Capt Bill Stewart. (DND CK 711540 and 711536)

The Starfighter could crack the sound barrier with ease at low level. High-speed passes just below the speed of sound culminating with rolling vertical departures were immensely popular with airshow fans everywhere. (Bill Johnson)

The Canadian Forces combined CF-104 and CF-5 shows in 1970 and 1971 were some of the most exciting fighter displays ever flown. Above, former Golden Hawk Capt W.C. (Bill) Stewart put on a sterling aerobatic performance as part of the fighter package in 1971, including an inverted pass and a dirty roll following a touch-and-go. (Jerry Vernon) At right, Capt Jordy Krastel rockets past the 434 Sqn section of CF-5s led by Capt Don Bergie at Abbotsford 1970. (Nancy Johnson) Below, same venue one year later, Krastel (773) leads Eric Saunders (772), Bill Nesbitt (787) and Ed Rozdeba (789) in a neat eche-lon pass. Bottom, a glimpse of raw power frozen in time, the show opener in 1971. (Bill Johnson)

B.C.'s Centennial Dash

The year 1971 also saw another rather unusual public relations event staged by 417 Sqn in commemoration of the province of British Columbia's Centennial. The squadron kicked off the year of celebrations on January 1st with two CF-104s piloted by Majs Bill Worthy and Glen "Red" Willet re-tracing a route through the Rockies first surveyed by the Canadian Pacific Railroad between 1871 and 1875. A similar route flown by the Canadian Air Force in 1920 on a national mail flight had taken three-and-one-half days – Worthy and Willet did it in just over 49 minutes from the time they left Cold Lake until they arrived over Victoria's inner harbour. The highly publicized event was carried live on CBC radio as the duo traversed the province in a fitting salute to 100 years of technological progress on land, sea and air.

The following summer, 1972, saw the boys from 417 return to the familiar airshow venues using the moniker "Deadeye Whiskeys" under the leadership of Capt Gord Todd. The solo pilot that summer was Capt Delwood "Yogi" Huyghebaert, a bundle of energy who would soon find himself being fitted for a red flying suit and an initial two year tour with Canada's newest aerobatic team, the Snowbirds:

"In April of 1972 I was selected as the CF-104 solo demo pilot to perform alongside

Majs 'Red' Willet (left) and Bill Worthy following their arrival in Victoria to kick off the British Columbia Centennial on 1 Jan 71. Accepting letters for the Premier is Commander Tom Murphy of MARPAC. (via Bill Worthy)

Capts Gord Todd, Dave Bartram, Terry Humphries and Ed Folks who flew the formation part of the show. We had a five-plane opening sequence, then as the solo I would break off to continue with a coordinated four-plane and solo show. We flew the five-plane show at Cold Lake, Moose Jaw, Abbotsford, Trenton and the CNE at Toronto. In addition, I did a solo show at Summerside. The CF-104 was a great machine for airshows with its noise, speed and stability. It was also, however, a bit challenging to keep some activity at stage centre at all times during a solo show. It would take 50 seconds to go by stage centre, turn around and return – a lot of time in airshow jargon. All in all, it was a great year with an abundance of experience gained in the airshow business. This served me well during the Snowbird tryouts late in '73 when I was selected as Snowbird 9 for the 1974 and 1975 airshow seasons."

Yogi Huyghebaert

The "Deadeye" teams of 1973 to 1975 were notable in several regards. Firstly, they continued to comprise five-plane shows in a highly polished routine reminiscent of their predecessors. Secondly, each of the teams saw a return of a foreign exchange pilot to the team, a member of the Royal Air Force in 1973, Royal Australian Air Force in 1974 and one of each in 1975. Also of interest is the fact that each of the leaders from this period would go on to lead a second high performance team later in their air force careers – Capts Eric Thurston (1973) and John David (1975) leading Starfighter teams in Europe and Capt Ray Dunsdon (1974) leading the Hawks Voodoo team eight years later. Each team leader came away with many memories of their airshow days in the Starfighter, but for Ray Dunsdon, his most vivid "airshow" memory came at the hands of another, rather famous, 104 pilot:

"On April 27th, 1972 Al French and I were tasked to fly down to Palmdale in a couple of duals to pick up Lockheed test pilots Tony LeVier and 'Snake' Reaves and fly them back to Cold Lake the next day to help us celebrate the 10th anniversary of Canadian Starfighter ops. Of course, they were going to fly in the front seat no matter what – even though Tony hadn't flown a 104 for over seven years and Snake only on occasion to do his five minute 'sequence.' Anyway, after a rather rambunctious night, we got airborne the next day with a terrifying formation take-

Two more contrasting views of CF-104 precision formation flying, both captured at Moose Jaw. At left, Gord Todd's 1972 team in a "slow-speed" line-abreast pass. At right, Capt Eric Thurston leads the 1973 Starfighter team through their opening pass during a return engagement the following summer. (Bill Johnson, Nancy Johnson)

The 1972 Deadeye Whiskeys in review. Top – soloist Yogi Huyghebaert went on to fly two tours with the Snowbirds as a solo (73,74) and team leader (85,86). Centre – the team takes off in finger-four formation at the Saskatchewan Anniversary Air Show in Moose Jaw on 16 Jul 72. Below – the team taxis in show formation for takeoff at CFB Cold Lake. Following team leader Capt Gord Todd are No. 2 Capt Ed Folks, No. 3 Capt Dave Bartram and No. 4 Capt Terry Humphries. (Bill Johnson)

Two CF-104Ds taxi to the ramp at Moose Jaw during the 1973 Saskatchewan Air Show. Note the extended leading edge flaps and large speed brakes. (Bill Johnson)

off out of Palmdale and the two of them flew all the way to Cold Lake. Unfortunately, it was a little late by the time we got there. Nevertheless, I advised Snake that he was cleared to do his routine so Tony and Al landed and we set up for the run-in. Snake had 'er wound up to 420 knots as we reached the airfield boundary – 20 feet off the ground. He then raised the nose about 20 degrees and commenced a perfect eight-point roll. As we rolled to the inverted I was sure we were dead – but I couldn't eject upside down! Then, just as quickly, we were back level again – at 20 feet! As he completed his sequence he noticed there didn't seem to be many people rushing out to the flight line. 'Where is everybody?' was his obvious ques-

tion, but as it was now just before 6:00 p.m., most of the pilots had adjourned to the Officers' Mess to start the party.

As we carved off the runway I pointed out the Mess to Snake. 'Oh, I see them,' was the next comment and there we were again – right in the weeds as he lined up. As I was happily waving eyeball-to-eyeball to friends on the front balcony as we flashed past, up came the nose again and I suddenly found myself in a series of rapid rolls – four in all I think. I thought I was dead again … but Snake wasn't finished – for his patented landing he flew around final turn in 'stick shaker' all the way, pulled the drag chute before touchdown and then commenced to

turn off the runway after less than a thousand foot ground roll – smooth as silk. After finally arriving at the Mess, Tony and Snake 'held court' all night at the lower bar. Needless to say, it was crammed full of fighter pilots."

Ray Dunsdon

If there was one constant among pilots of the Starfighter community over the lifespan of the aircraft it was their bravado and love of life in general. The old axiom "work hard – play hard" certainly rang true in the 104 era and was applied with vigour by Canada's Starfighter demo teams. Like all fighters, the Starfighter had her challenges and could be quite unforgiving, particularly in the low-

Royal Australian Air Force pilot F/L Dave Leach (left) was one of several exchange pilots who had the privilege of flying on Canada's Starfighter teams over the years. Joining him in this photo are his 1974 Canadian teammates – Capts Ray Dunsdon (team leader), Ron Clarkson, Frank Thorne and Gord Todd. At right, Leach in 1975 just prior to opening a show with S/L Bill Worthy flying a CF-5D. (via 417 Sqn, Doug Swanson via Bill Worthy).

speed regime. Woe was he who inadvertently got slow in the 104. The role of the aircraft, initially nuclear strike and reconnaissance which gave way to conventional ground attack, demanded great precision in the low-level arena where final ingress to targets was normally conducted at 540 knots ground-speed (or nine nautical miles per minute) as low as you could stand it. Constant practice was necessary to allow Starfighter pilots to develop the skills necessary to execute wartime tasking in what would have been decidedly unfriendly Central European skies had the Warsaw Pact ever decided to test the mettle of NATO. This same degree of skill was necessary to display the aircraft safely in front of the viewing public and 417 Sqn instructors, all veterans of at least one tour in Europe, did so with aplomb.

The 1975 team pose outside their digs at 417 Sqn. L to R – F/L Rojer Wholey (RAF), Capt Frank Thorne, Capt Dave Bligh, Capt John David (team leader) and F/L Dave Leach (RAAF). (via 417 Sqn) Top, a gorgeous silhouette pass in diamond formation. (Bill Johnson) Above, the team taxis in following a show at CFB Trenton. (Larry Milberry)

The performance of airshows is a voluntary duty on most squadrons, but the discipline required to do so safely comes from a rigid training regime learned early in one's career. Here, two 417 Sqn students get some close formation practice on their way home from the Jimmy Lake bombing range just north of CFB Cold Lake – on a perfect day for flying. (DND REC 75-777, MCpl Vic Johnson)

The Deadeye Zips

By 1976 there was still no replacement for any of Canada's fighter aircraft on the immediate horizon and with budgets tight the decision was made to reduce the Starfighter demo team to two solo aircraft plus a spare. Even with a reduction in numbers however, Capts Ron Doyle, Dave Burroughs and John Bagshaw still managed to impress airshow patrons wherever they performed, even introducing a flashy new name, the Deadeye Zips. For the most part, Doyle and Burroughs flew a fully aerobatic co-solo show with John Bagshaw providing a running commentary. As Dave Burroughs recalls, they flew the full gamut of manoeuvres, including a "loop, inverted pass, four-point rolls, Cuban-eight, slow-speed 'at the edge of the kicker' wing walk and high-speed passes culminating with each aircraft doing a vertical departure with multiple rolls." Shows in 1976 included Comox, Edmonton, Winnipeg, Cold Lake, Moose Jaw, Colorado Springs, Abbotsford, Toronto and Shearwater.

John Bagshaw would stay on to lead the 1977 edition of the Zips, not quite with the same *carte blanche* of the year before initially, but with three aircraft in the show. The team flew 11 airshows, not a bad summer's work for a part-time team. An initial pre-season show was flown on March 19th in Meadow Lake, Saskatchewan but the real fun was to begin at the end of April. The 1977 Zips wasted no time in making a name for themselves, as Laurie Hawn recalls:

The first of the famous "Deadeye Zip" teams flew a fully aerobatic co-solo show in 1976. L to R – Zip Lead Capt Ron Doyle, Zip 2 Capt Dave Burroughs and Zip 3 Capt John Bagshaw. (DND Photo, Sgt Vic Johnson via 417 Sqn)

"Well, after watching all the fun that Ron Doyle, Dave Burroughs and John Bagshaw had flying airshows in 1976, I decided that the Deadeye Zips were for me. The 1977 version of this supersonic trio was to include John Bagshaw as Zip lead, myself as Zip 2 and Dave Bligh as Zip 3. Like garlic-breath, we couldn't get rid of Burroughs entirely, and he was to figure prominently in one of

The knife-edge dance flown by Capts Laurie Hawn (top) and John Bagshaw (bottom) is one of the more dynamic manoeuvres ever flown by a fighter team, as this rare photo reveals in 1977. (Harald Riedel via Laurie Hawn)

our more spectacular 'feets'. I use the word 'feets' intentionally, because that's what we stuck in our mouths more than once.

After our warm-up at Meadow Lake, we got down to some serious practice trying to perfect what, for us, were a couple of unique moves. These included coordinated dirty/clean 360 degree turns, with the clean aircraft doing two of them at 6 to 7 G around the dirty aircraft doing one with gear and land flap hanging. We were inspired by the Blue Angels doing clean/dirty loops in their A-4 Skyhawks, but decided that it would be easier in the 104 if we turned the manoeuvre on its side. We also tried hard at doing a mirror pass with lead and two in canopy-to-canopy knife-edge passes. It wasn't too bad except when each guy tried to correct to the other, and then we looked like a mirror pass of two windshield wipers. With three aircraft, the intent was to keep someone in front of the crowd all the time ... well, most of the time, alright occasionally. After a few other passes, we'd finish off with opposing high-speeders and a rejoin to a bomb burst head on to the showline. For part of the year

The Deadeye Zips were renamed the Alberta Arrows for the province's biggest airshow at CFB Cold Lake in the summer of 1977. Veteran DND photographer Vic Johnson captured this publicity shot of the team during a practice flight over northern Alberta on May 20th. L to R – Capt Dave Bligh (left wing), Capt John Bagshaw (team leader), Capt Laurie Hawn (right wing). (Sgt Vic Johnson, via 417 Sqn)

Capt Dave Bligh breaks out of the line abreast formation to set up for his first solo manoeuvre of the show at Abbotsford '77. (DND Photo)

we were allowed aerobatics and we included rolling manoeuvres and a roll-under break. We subsequently decided that it was dumb to alternate aerobatic and non-aerobatic shows, so we took a little fighter pilot licence as to where and when we did the aero shows. I'm not sure why we didn't get fired once or twice.

Did I mention Burroughs? On April 28th, we were to take four aircraft to Comox to put on a show for the Royal Roads graduation parade. Showing a distinct lack of judgment, we asked Burroughs to be number four. Due to aircraft availability problems, we proceeded to Comox in dribs and drabs. 'Baggy' went first so that he could do a quick recce trip down to Roads. Then all went well until, on the way back to Comox, he espied one of Her Majesty's Canadian Boats cruising the coast. Ever the benevolent one, 'Baggy' decided to brighten the poor fishheads' lives with a touch of the sound of freedom. Make that several touches, with a sledgehammer. As he pulled off from his last pass, he realized that they were really getting into the spirit of the whole thing by setting off smoke charges for his reciprocal enjoyment. The fact that he was par-

taking of their 'live-fire' exercise only became clear on return to base when he was met by an adoring base operations officer who had just gotten off the phone with one of Her Majesty's Senior Canadian Boat People. No sense of humour, those fishheads.

We didn't stop there. Burroughs and I were next to depart Cold Lake and, unbeknownst to us at the time, we would nearly top 'Baggy's' stunt in spectacular fashion. We had filed off just in time to make it to Comox before the airfield closed for a practice by the Snowbirds. En route at altitude, Burroughs had an inadvertent kicker and lost his hydraulic generator. He turned off the automatic pitch control (designed to prevent pitch-up), but didn't say anything to me. Why be a wimp? As we approached Comox, we had just enough time for one low pass. Not knowing about his previous problem, I put Burroughs in line-astern and lined up on the ramp. Ahead lay the line of nine Snowbirds with engines running, and 'Baggy' now in 'Cat' Beaulieu's other seat. Beyond the 'Birds was a line of 409 Sqn Voodoos and several Argus sub hunters from 407 Sqn. We approached at a stately 540 knots … or so, and a couple of hundred feet …

or so. 'Take that, you dog-whistles,' I say as we scream overhead with burners cooking. 'Very impressive,' comes the very sarcastic voice of Gord Wallis, who is Snowbird lead and an ex 104 driver himself. 'Just jealous,' I think to myself. Then tower comes up and says, 'Zip two, are you OK?' 'Hey, what's going on back there? I'm lead; I have a right to know.' I look down at the shadow and, to my shock, I see only one aircraft silhouette. 'Burroughs, check in – are you okay?' Burroughs finally comes up, a little shaken, rejoins and we proceed to initial and land. To back up, just as we approached the Snowbirds, Burroughs either got into my jetwash or had the kicker fire. Afterwards, 'Baggy' said that if we could harness that pitch rate, we wouldn't have to take crap from any of those F-5 pukes anymore. He said that one second we were in line-astern; the next he was looking at Burrough's top planform; the next he was looking at the bottom planform, and then at the top again. 'Baggy' still doesn't know how he missed me. Anyway this little act caught the 'Birds just as lead had called the brake release for taxi. 'Baggy' said it was the greatest bomb burst he had ever seen, even if it was only in two dimensions! There were Tutors scattered

everywhere. Burroughs, in the meantime, was riding out the gawdamndest pilot induced oscillation (PIO) he had ever seen, when everything went black. He could faintly hear voices around him and came to the immediate conclusion that he was, in fact, dead. Not a totally unjustified conclusion really. After a few more seconds, the voices persisted and Dave realized that they were talking through his nose. So he took his helmet off, rotated it 90 degrees, put it back on, and did up the chin-strap. Whereupon, we proceeded to land and be met by the same adoring BOpsO.

We're not done yet. That night in the back bar, we're reliving the day's adventures with a couple of Golden Throat Charmers (the beer, not the Snowbirds). There are a bunch of other troops around, when in walks the Minister of National Defence, Barney Danson. Geez, I didn't realize we were in that much trouble! No sweat. Barney's on a visit to the coast and has wandered away from the base commander's reception in search of some real company. He is soon on a first name basis with everyone there. About 30 minutes later, a panicky, distraught, and subsequently livid base commander comes charging into the back bar looking for his lost Minister. Accusing us of contributing to the delinquency of a Minister of the Crown, he led Barney away, at the latter's protest.

Not done yet. The next day we're set to do the thing at Roads. Remember Roads? We do, and it's blessedly uneventful until we return to base. In one of his more lucid moments the night before, 'Baggy' has promised Terry Hallett (an ex-Red Knight) that we'll do a flyby over his house. Well, Terry's house is in the middle of Courtenay. But 'Baggy' is a man of his word and we did the deed, much to Terry's delight and his neighbours' not-so-delight. For good measure, we also do a pass over the Mess, as it's now past bar-time. What we forget here, of course, is that the base hospital is right across the road. Anyway, to make a long story short, our season is off to a great start. The base commander calls our commanding officer, Pete DeSmedt, to dis-invite the Deadeye Zips to the Comox Airshow later in the year and requests that we never darken his doorway again.

A couple more shows follow in Portage and Alsask. Just before Moose Jaw, we find out that for the Cold Lake Airshow, we are to be renamed the Alberta Arrows. It seems that someone wanted a CF-5 aerobatic team for this show, but 419 Sqn couldn't make it hap-pen. What a name! But at least we'd be allowed to do some aeros. Moose Jaw was good, and then we had one week to become aerobatic. We used the excuse to generate a couple of practices each day, and felt ready to go. I don't think the Red Arrows were threatened, but three 'Aluminum Death Tubes' going the speed of heat pushed by three screaming J-79s managed to get a few folk's attention.

The next weekend it was back to non-aerobatics again, and we were off to Minot for their airshow, which had been called Northern Neighbours Day (remember that name). With the exception of four F-106s and four T-38s flying by once each at 'Flight Level Nosebleed,' the entire show was Canadian.

Many of the social events were organized by Al Pietsch, a veteran of many years on the airshow circuit. His airfield, 'Pietsch Patch,' is only a few miles south of Minot and made an excellent place for altimeter checks. Except for Bligh forgetting his flaps on one turning pass and violating the showline by a mere mile, the flying went very well. The parties, on the other hand, were exceptional. Between Al Pietsch's beer truck, a receptive O'Club and a rowdy bunch of Canucks, we managed to make our mark. The base commander seemed genuinely interested in how we could keep up the pace. We assured him that it was just a matter of practice and opined that, perhaps next year, he should consider inviting the Mexican Air Force and calling it Southern Neighbours Day. He allowed as how that idea might have some merit.

The late Al Pietsch (right), a veteran civilian airshow performer, was a staunch friend of Canada's military teams. He is shown here with former Snowbird leader George Miller in 1990 at Moose Jaw. (Jacquie Perrin)

Comox next. With a Change of Command parade, we were back on the list of invitees. As mentioned, we had decided that switching back and forth between show types was a pain in the ass. Our boss, Pete DeSmedt, was there doing a board of inquiry, so we thought we'd try the unauthorized aero show on him. What we forgot to do, however, was give the aero script to John Glover, who had offered to do the commentary. John would announce a 'dirty pass,' and someone would come by in a slow roll – or a four-point roll instead of the announced 360 degree level turn. After a couple of passes John caught on, and instead of announcing what we were about to do, he would comment on what we had just done. After the show, we waited for the axe to fall from the boss, but all he said was 'nice show' and bought us a beer. Licence to steal …

Abbotsford was the final show, and what a great place to finish off. With the weather and the display, it's got to be the best airshow in the world. It sure brought our summer of great flying and fun to a fitting climax. The average trip that summer was .7 hours and a lot of logbook pages were filled with not much total time. But the Zipper was a great airshow airplane and I don't think I have ever had more fun out of a summer's flying."

Laurie Hawn

With their approval to once again conduct low-level aerobatics, the Deadeye Zips 1977 show took on a new and exciting dimension. At high-speed, the 104 rolled beautifully so crisp four-point rolls, majestic slow rolls and inverted flight were easily accomplished. Multiple full deflection aileron rolls were another story due to the risk of encountering roll coupling which could lead to pitch-up and certain disaster at low-level. Another manoeuvre introduced by John Bagshaw also got the attention of many fighter pilots – a standard landing approach to a touch-and-go, dirty roll, and another touch-and-go – all within the length of the runway. Bagshaw is the only Canadian pilot ever to do the manoeuvre (at least intentionally). Aside from requiring a long runway, the manoeuvre demanded a lot of finesse and a perfectly operating aircraft: "The boundary layer control was critical for the 'touch-and-roll-touch' manoeuvre. Through trial and error, I found Starfighters 753 and 731 had very nicely synchronized systems with no roll-off as the land flap came down. They therefore became my preferred aircraft – and fortunately they always stayed serviceable."

The approval of the 1977 team to conduct aerobatic manoeuvres was not to be repeated in subsequent years, presumably because it was felt that there were not sufficient hours available to devote to specialist practices that would help ensure the safety of such a show. The air force hierarchy at Air Command, under considerable financial duress, had fought hard to keep the Snowbirds alive as the official "Canadian Forces Air Demonstration Team" with a full-time mandate for 21 team members, including the nine demonstration pilots. Nevertheless, fighter teams like the Zips continued to play a vital role in demonstrating the military capabilities of the Canadian Forces to the nation's citizens while also attracting the youth of the country to service careers.

Once one has had a taste of airshows as a performer, the sheer enjoyment and adrenalin rush gets in your blood. Although strictly a secondary duty for most, many pilots welcomed the opportunity to continue to participate in shows and flypasts throughout their careers. After the 1977 season and a new posting to AETE, Capt Dave Bligh volunteered to fly weekends whenever one of the local communities requested "one of them jets" to do a flypast. On occasion, this resulted in some rather interesting developments, such as the day he unwittingly became parade marshal of a real stampede of horses and wagons, created when he "arrived below the roof tops" down the main drag of Lloydminster on the Alberta/Saskatchewan border during their "Western Days" parade – precisely on time mind you.

As for Laurie Hawn and John Bagshaw, both would continue to be strong supporters of airshows and each later played significant roles in the transition to the CF-18 Hornet, ultimately commanding their own squadrons. In the interim, they continued to apply the same spirit and sense of humour they had displayed as members of the Deadeye Zips to their operational training. John Bagshaw recalls one such incident in a humorous anecdote from the fall of 1977 when 417 Sqn deployed to Nellis AFB, Nevada to partake in the massive "war games" exercise known as Red Flag:

"On October 22nd, we went to Red Flag for the very first time – for any Canadians. I had been pestering Ray Dunsdon in Air Command to get our jets camouflaged for this illustrious event, but sigh, with no luck.

Since the adults wouldn't camouflage our jets, we decided to do it ourselves – with poster paint. The art teacher at the Cold Lake school showed me the recipe, and we bought the powder in Las Vegas with our own money when we got there. We asked the art store owner how much he thought we would need to paint eight jets and he told us, '... about half a pound.' You should have seen the look on his face when we told him, 'No, no – these are REAL jets we are going to paint.' I think we ended up with about 300 pounds of the stuff! Somehow the concoction was named 'Bagshaw Beige.' I recall that as we were in the process – up on the jets with buckets and mops – an American 'One Star' came driving by – stopped   got out – and yelled 'What the *&%*#* do you guys think you are doing? You are all on charge!' – or words to that effect. When we explained that we were Canadians, these were our jets, and this was all a poor country could afford, he just walked away muttering and shaking his head, never to be seen again. It did work wonders though. Everyone complained how hard the Zip was to see during the exercise. The leading edges had to be retouched each trip – the amount dependant on how much hair the pilot had on fire that trip. And if anyone flew through rain, the rule was you had to re-do your jet by yourself. I don't recall anyone flying through rain. And the colour scheme turned out to be the basis on which we (actually Laurie Hawn) designed the CF-18 camouflage scheme."

John Bagshaw

The Deadeye Blues

The next young man to take the helm of the 104 team from Cold Lake was Capt Lloyd Campbell, a graduate of CF-104 course 37 in June 1971. He had subsequently completed an operational tour with the "Red Indians" of 421 Sqn in Baden-Soellingen followed by a staff assignment at the headquarters of the 4th Allied Tactical Air Force in Ramstein, West Germany prior to repatriating to Canada.

"In 1978, I was an instructor pilot and major (elect) on 417 Sqn. When I was offered the opportunity to lead the CF-104 team that year, I accepted with enthusiasm, thinking back to the glory days of the previous two years and the 'Deadeye Zips' (as well as other great 'Zipper' programs of years gone by). Unfortunately, for whatever reason, the circumstances in '78 were different. Perhaps it was because we lost a Snowbird in May of that year, a good friend and ex-104 pilot, Gord de Jong (a.k.a. Liquid Man), tragically killed when the horizontal stabilizer of his Tutor failed during an airshow at Grande

LGen Lloyd Campbell, Canada's Chief of the Air Staff, was leader of the 1978 Deadeye Blues. He is shown here following a flight in the BAE Systems Hawk 115 advanced jet/fighter trainer now employed at 15 Wing Moose Jaw, Saskatchewan and 4 Wing Cold Lake, Alberta under the NATO Flying Training in Canada (NFTC) program. (DND Photo)

Prairie. In any event, what followed was a bit of a crack-down by the powers that be and the decision was made that teams other than the Snowbirds would not be so acknowledged. So our 'non-team' took form – myself as lead, Ted Lee as No. 2, Harv Wregget as No. 3 and 'Buzz' Burroughs as solo. Nobody was allowed to call themselves anything identifiable as a team, nor were we allowed to have promo pictures, brochures or what have you. So, rather than being 'Deadeye Zips,' in our case we were relegated to using one of our routine squadron formation call signs, 'Deadeye Blues.' Not too glamorous, but on the other hand, what's in a name?

As for the season, however, it was also to be relatively constrained that year, perhaps for the same reason. We started with two practices in May (overkill, I expect, given our skill and cunning) before departing for Winnipeg on May 27th (also my wedding anniversary but we won't talk about that). The show was relatively straightforward, relying in general on the fact that the Starfighter looked and sounded great no matter what. A four-plane diamond from behind the crowd (stage left) at about 540 knots followed by a split into a three-ship plus one. 'Buzz,' our solo, had previous experience and was able to do a pretty impressive job – tight 360s, knife-edge passes and so on. As for the rest of us, we did high-speed passes, low-speed passes (relative, of course, given the CF-104's flying characteristics) plus sundry other passes over a 10 minute period. The whole program ended with a manoeuvre called the 'Prince of Wales,' a sort of 'bomb burst' in which I, as lead, exited in a vertical roll. The first time I performed this manoeuvre for real was in Winnipeg. I recall being very impressed with myself – rolling my way merrily up to about 18,000 feet or so to impress the crowd (much beyond the point where anyone could actually see me, of course) until I finally ran out of airspeed and ideas. While in my own opinion I didn't come *that* close to pitching up, the thought certainly crossed my mind as I floated inverted over Winnipeg International Airport (keeping the 'APC gauge' below one) and it did occur to me that it would be ever so embarrassing for a soon-to-be major to jettison a CF-104 over the city. Fortunately, such was not the case – particularly since the Commander of Air Command was looking on!

The rest of the season was less exciting, at least from my perspective. We did Moose Jaw in June, a show that went very well –

until the departure. Our 'departure show' followed a simple formula: low, fast and noisy. Unfortunately, it was also flown about tower height, on a northerly heading and apparently directly over the base commander's office! Back at Cold Lake, post-attack 'bomb damage assessment' from our spies at Moose Jaw had the base commander spilling his coffee and ordering all subsequent departure shows cancelled. Fortunately, Col Les Price, our own base commander, was a great guy and treated us very gently. From then on, things went quite smoothly. We did a number of fly-pasts, flew airshows at Wetaskiwin and Ft. McMurray and, in my own case, opened the airshow at Trenton on September 23rd as a 'single.' My high-speed pass and vertical departure took place just in advance of Oscar Boesch and his sailplane – and while I couldn't see or hear either, I was told the noise, power and speed of the Starfighter contrasted well with the grace and solitude of Oscar's aerobatic sailplane demo. And thus ended the one-and-only season of the Deadeye Blues."

Lloyd Campbell

The aforementioned departure pass on June 26th, 1978 was witnessed firsthand by the author and I can attest that, in the 35 years since I started watching airshows in earnest, this particular pass remains one of the most spectacular I have ever seen. The airshows of the 1970s at Moose Jaw were a thing to behold, and if the show itself was not enough, the day after would see the flight line full of students and instructors alike waiting for visiting aircraft to head home in the hope that they would have enough gas for a "departure show." Few failed to deliver and we always knew we could count on the 104s from Cold Lake to outdo everyone else. They did so on this day in spades. After taking off to the west they turned south to set up for their individual passes in a wide "fighting wing" formation. We all watched in great anticipation as the four aircraft actually disappeared from view momentarily below the "dirt hills" to the south, mere pimples on the flat prairie landscape. When they reappeared as rapidly growing dots coming straight at us, it was obvious to all that this was going to be something to behold. It was! As they crossed overhead there was only a shrill whistle before the shockwave and thundering noise that followed seemed to lift us off the tarmac, hands flying instinctively to ears. Following the momentary shock it was smiles and laughter all around amongst the

boys on the ramp. There was simply nothing more motivating than seeing (and feeling) a Starfighter moving at the speed of heat.

Although team members of the famous Deadeye teams would have happily gone from airshow to airshow all summer, not even a 104 pilot could be in two places at once. Thus, as demands dictated, other squadron members filled in as solo performers to satisfy requests for appearances across the country. One who did so in June of 1978 was Maj Walt Pirie who did a swing through the Maritimes, flying shows at Shearwater, Greenwood and Chatham Armed Forces Day airshows. He would also figure prominently when CFB Cold Lake celebrated its silver jubilee the next summer.

Cold Lake's Silver Jubilee

417 Sqn launched 13 Starfighters led by Maj Walt Pirie to help CFB Cold Lake celebrate its 25th anniversary in 1979. A similar number of CF-5s integrated into a tightly choreographed routine made for a spectacular airshow. (Ron Berlie)

Although the name sounds rather foreboding, all Canadian fighter pilots have a soft spot for Cold Lake, Alberta, the home of fighter aviation in Canada. This is where they really learned how to fly. The base opened on March 31st, 1954, welcoming its first operational squadron, 433 (All Weather) Fighter Sqn, in the fall and winter of that year. By May of 1955, No. 3 (AW)F OTU had been relocated from North Bay to RCAF Stn Cold Lake to take advantage of the station's massive air weapons range in training all future CF-100 fighter crews. They would soon be followed by more budding fighter pilots who would take advanced jet training on the T-33 and later the CF-5 prior to commencing tactical conversion on the CF-104, CF-5, CF-101 or CF-18. Today, the chosen few take lead-in fighter training on the BAE Systems Hawk 115 prior to sliding into the cockpit of the CF-18.

The Zips made a triumphant return to Abbotsford in 1979. Above, some of the finer details of the bottom of the CF-104 are revealed during this close pass, including the flap and aileron hinge lines and twin antennae of the radar homing and warning system on the tail of 763. Below, team soloist Capt Don Robinson executes an impressive "dirty roll" with every-thing hanging. (Bill Johnson)

The 1980 Deadeye Zips were the last four-plane Starfighter team to perform public airshows in Canada. L to R – Hauptmann Harald Riedel (GAF), Capts Cash Poulson, Gus Youngson (team leader) and Dan Bouchard. Missing is narrator Capt Dudley Larsen (USAF). (via 417 Sqn)

It was on June 11th, 1955 that the station held its first Air Force Day. Considering its remote location, station officials were surprised when over 30,000 spectators converged on the base, at one point creating a traffic jam stretching 15 miles from the gates of the new station. Since that day, dozens of popular shows have been held on the base featuring, at one time or the other, every aircraft that has flown in the RCAF and Canadian Forces inventories.

Given this backdrop, it was only natural that CFB Cold Lake plan a major airshow to celebrate its Silver Jubilee in 1979. They spared no expense in doing so, lining up all of the major Canadian acts for the June 16th extravaganza as well as representation from the USAF, USN and RAF. Given the occasion, 417 and 419 Sqns pulled out all the stops as each squadron put up a 13-ship flypast of CF-104s and CF-5s led by Maj Walt Pirie and LCol Bill Taylor respectively. While the flypasts in themselves were impressive, the 26 individual high-speed passes that followed from both ends of the field – the 104s from one end and F-5s from the other – were a sight to behold. Also making their debut in the show were the 1979 Deadeye Zips led by Capt Wally Peirson. Airshow fans got their money's worth that day and the four-ship team went on to perform at Abbotsford in August.

The last four-ship team of zippers to do the airshow tour in Canada would come the following summer, veteran fighter pilot Capt Gus Youngson having the honour of leading the troops. Sadly, Gus passed away before his time in September 2001, leaving these thoughts on his Starfighter demo days:

"I returned from Europe to join 417 Sqn in late '79 and was invited to lead the Zips in '80. We had a real international team: Dan Bouchard was No. 2 (nobody was sure where Dan was from because he couldn't be understood in either English or French); Cash Poulson was No. 3 ('nuff said); Harald Riedel, our German exchange officer, was No. 4 and our solo; and Dud Larsen, our USAF exchange officer, flew the spare and did our announcing. Our groundcrew contingent varied somewhat over the summer but Sgt Mike Middleton was the crew chief and they all did a great job keeping our five jets serviceable. We flew four well known Canadian shows in four provinces that summer – London, Saskatchewan (Moose Jaw), Portage and Edmonton (Namao) but were disappointed that we didn't get to

Abbotsford. Nevertheless, we really enjoyed ourselves – 'clean/cleans' for all of the shows, made a lot of noise and thrilled a lot of people. We were proud to be able to show off such a beautiful aircraft."

Gus Youngson

As 1981 rolled around the writing was on the wall for Starfighter operations in Canada. With the New Fighter Aircraft selection to replace the three existing fighter fleets now in full debate, it was only a matter of time before the OTU would shut its doors forever. Still, the CF-104 was to soldier on in Europe for another five years, thanks to a Depot Level Inspection and Repair (DLIR) program that saw the fleet refurbished and equipped with a new navigation/attack system, the Litton LW-33. Unfortunately, it was a lack of resources due to the ongoing DLIR program that prevented the squadron from generating a demonstration team in 1981. Instead, squadron commanding officer, LCol Jake Newlove, supported airshow requests by sending single ships to either fly in shows or grace static displays on the ground. One veteran CF-104 instructor who did so was Maj John Laidler. Having exceeded the coveted one thousand hour mark on the Starfighter, he opened the large Trenton shows in each of 1981 and 1982, wringing out his aircraft and "turning JP-4 into noise."

The last full year of operations for 417 Sqn was in 1982 as the last three courses comprising a total of 26 intrepid aviators got underway in turn. With this being the Starfighter swan song as far as the Canadian airshow scene was concerned, there simply had to be a team – and so there was – a two-ship flown by Capts Dave Owen and Keith Robbins who had both flown on teams in

As the principal operator of the CF-104 in Canada, 417 Sqn often relied on staff instructors to perform solo displays when the squadron formation team was not available. Here, two stalwarts who did so in the latter part of the 104 era, Maj Walt Pirie (left) and Maj John Laidler. (DND Photos)

The final Deadeye Zip airshows were flown in 1982 by Capts Dave Owen and Keith Robbins, captured here during their last appearance at Abbotsford in the camouflage paint scheme that would see the aircraft through the end of its NATO service in Europe. (Ron Miller)

Germany. They did the squadron and the 104 legacy proud, flying a dynamic and entertaining show before thousands of appreciative fans. All told they flew 15 official shows at eight locations, including Fairchild AFB, CFB Edmonton, CFB Moose Jaw, K.I. Sawyer AFB, Abbotsford, CFB Cold Lake, Toronto (CIAS), CFS Suffield and Red Deer, Alberta. Although not officially sanctioned to do aerobatics, "Gronk" (as Owen was affectionately known) managed to steal a dirty roll in his last Abbotsford appearance, one for the history books. Fittingly, the last public appearance of the team was in their home province on September 12th. The 104

community was stunned and saddened when only three months later Dave Owen and another stalwart of the squadron, Andre "Mex" Tremblay, failed to return from a staff formation mission on a blustery winter day only a few days before Christmas. It took a heart-wrenching five weeks before the accident site was found west of the base on January 24th, 1983.

Following the graduation of the last CF-104 course in May 1983 (Course 75), attention turned to preparing for the squadron Standard's presentation and shutdown. The colours ceremonies took place on June 4th

with a host of former squadron alumni attending the gala weekend. One of the highlights was the appearance of a team put together to salute the Starfighter one last time in Cold Lake. As an added attraction, it was decided that three of the graduates of the final CF-104 Fighter Weapons Instructor's Course would fly on the team led by Capt Phil Murphy of 417 Sqn. Representing 441 Sqn was Capt Rob Martin, 439 Capt John Roulston and 421 Capt Jim Grecco. With the conclusion of their show and the mandatory high-speed passes, Canadian Starfighter airshows faded into the sunset forever.

Ron Miller

To commemorate the stand down of 417 Sqn, a specially painted CF-104 was done up in Canadian colours. It now resides at the Reynolds-Alberta Museum in Wetaskiwin, Alberta, home of the Canadian Aviation Hall of Fame. (courtesy Graham Wragg)

Starfighters in the Air Division

By the time CF-104 Starfighters began to arrive in Europe, Canada's NATO Air Division had already been in operation for 11 years, No. 1 Fighter Wing having been formed at North Luffenham, England in November 1951. The eight squadrons of F-86 Mk 6 Sabres and four squadrons of CF-100 Canucks extant in 1962 would be replaced by a total of eight CF-104 squadrons, two operating out of each wing. No. 3 Wing in Zweibrücken, West Germany was the first to re-equip with the new jet with 427 Sqn commencing operations on December 16th, 1962 followed by 434 Sqn in April 1963. They in turn were followed by 4 Wing Baden-Soellingen, West Germany (444 and 422 Sqns), 2 Wing Grostenquin, France (430 and 421 Sqns) and 1 Wing Marville, France (441 and 439 Sqns). In November 1963 the last of the RCAF's Sabre 6s in Europe were disposed of and by March of 1964 eight squadrons were operational with the CF-104. Of these, six were assigned the strike/attack role while two (441 and 439) specialized in photo reconnaissance.

There would be many changes to the structure of the Air Division in the ensuing years, starting with the closure of 2 Wing in Grostenquin early in 1964 as an economy measure. Politics would rear its ugly head again in 1966 when France announced that all NATO operational units based in the country would have to accept French command or leave France. There was a mass exodus from the country. The RCAF closed No. 1 Air Division Headquarters in Metz along with 1 (F) Wing at Marville in March 1967, relocating both to Lahr, West Germany. The Air Division was also reduced to six squadrons with the disbandment of 444 and 434 Sqns on March 31st and April 1st, 1967 respectively. Ironically, Lahr was being run by the French Air Force at the time, being situated just a few kilometres east of the Rhine River, not far from Strasbourg. After a brief period of co-habitation, the RCAF officially took over the Lahr base on September 6th, 1967.

The spring of 1969 saw further reductions as the Canadian Forces bade farewell to Zweibrücken, the keys to the base being handed over to the United States Air Force. The Air Division was now "consolidated" on the two remaining bases at Lahr and Baden-Soellingen. Yet, even more radical changes were just around the corner. On September 19th, 1969 the Liberal government announced a major reduction in the land and air components of Canadian Forces Europe (CFE). The operational CF-104 squadrons would be cut in half, reduced to just two strike and one reconnaissance squadron with the closure of 430, 427 and 422 Sqns, all three disbanded by July 1st, 1970. With this drastic reduction, 1 Air Division passed into history and was replaced by 1 Canadian Air Group (1 CAG) with its headquarters co-located in Lahr with CFE Headquarters and the army's 4 Canadian Mechanized Brigade Group (4 CMBG) comprising 3,300 personnel. The final change to the Starfighter order of battle took place at the end of 1971 when the government of Canada elected to abandon its nuclear strike commitment to NATO, switching to conventional ground attack with the three remaining squadrons. The last Canadian nuclear strike alert duty took place on December 31st, 1971. Following the change in combat roles, the last three CF-104 squadrons were all based in Baden for the next 13 years. It was these three squadrons (439, 421 and 441) that saw the Starfighter through to the end of its distinguished service in Europe, 441 Sqn being the last to retire the aircraft on March 1st, 1986.

Initial Offerings

As with initial Starfighter operations in Canada, it took the European squadrons considerable time to get comfortable with their new aircraft and in particular low-level flying in the notoriously poor European weather. Flying around a few hundred feet off the ground at 450 knots in only three miles visibility was hard work but came to be pretty standard fare for RCAF pilots as they scorched around France and Germany on daily training missions. However, when the weather was good, the flying was magnificent. And when the weather was simply too poor to fly, there were plenty of other distractions to build camaraderie. Morale was high … and Jack Woodman's predictions were proven to be true.

Although there were no formal CF-104 air demonstration teams in the formative years of Starfighter ops in the European theatre, there were plenty of flypasts conducted by the Canadians in support of both airshows and local community events. These were important in that they demonstrated both Canada's commitment to, and physical presence among, the integrated forces of NATO during a period of high tension in the Cold War. The numbers were significant. Although reduced from 12 day fighter/interceptor squadrons to eight CF-104 squadrons, Canada still had well over 100 Starfighters on the ground in Europe by 1965.

The magic of flight has always been a fascinating subject for children. Here a group of Canadian school children from the station at 4 Wing, Baden-Soellingen, West Germany get a close look at an RCAF CF-104 Starfighter circa 1965. (RCAF Photos)

Official Heraldry in Europe – CF-104 Squadrons

STALK AND KILL

PRO PACE ARMATI

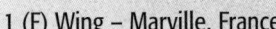

FANGS OF DEATH

1 (F) Wing – Marville, France

CELERITER CERTOQUE

AD CUSTODIENDAM EUROPAM

BELLICUM CECINERE

RCAF No. 1 Air Division – Metz, France
2 (F) Wing – Grostenquin, France

FERTE MANUS CERTAS

AGMEN PRIMUM LIBERTATIS

UN EXCELSIS VINCIMUS

3 (F) Wing – Zweibrücken, West Germany

STRIKE SWIFT STRIKE SURE

AUF WACHT

THIS ARM SHALL DO IT

4 (F) Wing – Baden-Soellingen, West Germany

No. 1 Air Division organization as it was originally planned when the last of eight CF-104 squadrons became operational in March 1964. Grostenquin was closed early in 1964, Metz and Marville in 1967 (HQ and 1 Wing moved to Lahr) and Zweibrücken in 1969. The Air Division was disbanded on 1 Jul 70 and replaced by 1 Canadian Air Group, comprising two strike and one reconnaissance squadron.

During the early years of CF-104 operations at No. 1 Air Division, public appearances of Canadian Starfighters were generally confined to flypasts for special events or airshows using available squadron pilots. On 9 Aug 67, 430 Sqn, 3 (F) Wing Zweibrücken carried out a flypast over Dieppe to commemorate the ill-fated WW II raid. At right, the pilots who performed the flypast – L to R, F/L Ed Zaluski, F/L Tom Storey, F/L Joe Gagnon, F/L Willy Anderson, F/L Dave Wallace and in front, S/L Grant Baker (lead). (via Grant Baker)

Another venue that afforded an opportunity for formation flypasts were the frequent NATO weapons meets designed to hone combat skills to a fine edge. Squadrons regularly sent between four and eight aircraft each to such meets along with a strong contingent of groundcrew to keep the aircraft serviceable. The arrival of the respective squadrons over the host base was almost as important as the competition itself, national pride being at stake. At times, arrival day took on the air of an airshow, with hundreds of civilians surrounding the base perimeter to witness each nation's arrival. These typically took the form of a formation flypast followed by individual low passes ... if the pilots could get away with them.

Departure days also usually afforded an opportunity for a final farewell pass to the base and surrounding area. On occasion, these included some rather novel apparitions, usually concocted the night before in a moment of cerebral brilliance as the boys let their hair down following the completion of the intense competition. "Hey, why don't we …" One such example occurred following the 4th Allied Tactical Air Force weapons meet at Chaumont, France in 1964. F/L Willy Floyd joined forces with fellow RCAF pilot F/L Doug Nicholson and two American fighter pilots to do an impromptu four-ship flypast consisting of two CF-104s and two F-100 Super Sabres. However, it wasn't just Chaumont that was the recipient of "the sound of freedom." Recalls Floyd, "We managed to beat up 11 NATO airbases before we ran out of gas. Some unhappy general threatened court martial, but I never heard any more about it."

As demands increased for "more than a single pass" at various events in Western Europe, Canadian squadrons slowly started to lean towards keeping the same pilots together if possible to facilitate continuity and make the most of training sessions. Usually, one or two senior pilots in the squadron might be designated as leaders of such formation displays. One of the earliest squadrons to do so was 430 Sqn in the spring of 1966 when deputy commanding officer, S/L "Mo" White, led a four-ship in a series of displays at Rimschweiler, Ensheim and CFB Soest, then home to the Canadian Army's Infantry Brigade Group. The latter was considered the most important as the May 26th show marked the visit of Her Majesty Queen Elizabeth II and the Duke of Edinburgh to the base.

The following year, 1967, saw a flurry of activity as the RCAF celebrated Canada's Centennial across Europe with participation in several large airshows such as the one staged in Brussels, Belgium. A section of Tigers led by F/L Bill "Digger" Graves did the honours at that particular show. As former slot man Guy Fabi recalls, "It was one hell of a weekend. I don't know what everyone else thought, but we sure thought we were great!"

Tiger Meet 1968

Within the NATO fraternity, the most well known and eagerly anticipated tactical air meet that brought allied forces together during the Starfighter era was the Tiger Meet. The Tiger Meet began in 1961 when the 79th Tac Ftr Sqn of the USAF, based at RAF Woodbridge, England, formed an association of fighter squadrons bearing the Tiger as their emblem. Their initial meeting on July 19th, 1961 brought together the first three squadrons to join the club but the concept was so popular it quickly spread throughout NATO. By the next summer, six of the 15 NATO nations had joined in and eight squadrons met at Woodbridge, including Canada's 439 "Tiger" Sqn. From that point forward, Tiger squadrons based across Western Europe took turns hosting the meet which saw it shift from England to Belgium, France, Germany and Scotland. In 1968, 439 Sqn based at 1 Wing Lahr was honoured with its first opportunity to host its allies.

The highlight of the annual meet was an airshow put on by the participating nations. In 1968 these included 31 Sqn – Belgian Air Force (Kleine Brogel), JABO G 43 – German Air Force (Oldenburg), 79th TFS – USAF (Woodbridge), 53rd TFS – USAF (Bitburg), AG 52 – German Air Force (Leck), 21 Sqn – Italian Air Force (Cameri) and 1/12 Sqn – French Air Force (Cambrai) in addition to the host Canadians. The opening act of the show flown on September 19th was a 16-ship trail beat-up involving two aircraft from each nation, many sporting various 'Tiger' paint schemes. The Canadians then took over with a combination of four-plane and two-plane CF-104 manoeuvres designed to keep the roar of afterburners at an appropriately high level.

439 Sqn grabbed the spotlight when they arrived at the 1969 Tiger Meet at RAF Woodbridge, England led by this colourful rendition of a Starfighter. By the time Canada hosted its third Tiger Meet at Baden-Soellingen in 1983, there were 18 Tiger squadrons in the NATO fraternity plus an additional three squadrons from France, Switzerland and Australia. CF-104833 was the first of several squadron aircraft to be painted in Tiger colours, a tradition later adopted after the squadron converted to the CF-18 Hornet. (courtesy Graham Wragg)

The highlight of the show was the aerobatic demonstration put on by Capt René Serrao as he put a 1 Wing Starfighter through the act he had perfected with the Golden Centennaires the year before. As he touched down, seven more Starfighters arrived overhead to conduct a tactical battle break and landing to end the show.

It was the following year, 1969, that 439 Sqn eagerly joined what had become something of a tradition amongst the Tiger community by painting one of their aircraft in stripes for the annual meet. As it transpired, the ninth meeting of the Tigers was to take place back at the birthplace of the meet, Woodbridge, England. Starting from scratch on August 1st with a group of squadron volunteers, CF-104 12833 was transformed from a rather weather-beaten warplane to a striking black and yellow Tiger. Three days later, the Canadians made a sensational appearance at Woodbridge led by their new Tiger bird, beating up the field in a series of four-ship passes to the delight of the assembled masses.

From Air Division to Air Group

The onset of the 1970s brought troubling cuts to Canada's military forces in Europe notwithstanding the formidable threat still posed by the Warsaw Pact. Much to the dismay of her NATO partners, Canada disbanded three more CF-104 squadrons. Now only three remained to carry the Canadian torch. But in spite of the understandable disappointment in the additional reductions, Canada's fighter pilots continued to put their best foot forward both operationally and in flying the Canadian flag publicly whenever possible.

Those who follow the airshow scene worldwide will know that Europeans, like their counterparts in North America, have traditionally been enthusiastic airshow fans. The modern-day leader among airshow displays in Europe is unquestionably Great Britain which has been hosting aerial spectacles since the advent of powered flight. Some would even argue that the British "invented" the art of low flying. Given their historical ties to the Royal Flying Corps and Royal Air Force in war and peace, it was only natural that the Canadians would continue to receive invitations to participate in virtually every major airshow in the United Kingdom. They invariably accepted.

One such event that the Canadians never missed was the annual Battle of Britain memorial held each fall. On September 19th,

Following major cutbacks to Canada's NATO forces in 1970, 1 Air Division was replaced by 1 Canadian Air Group.

1970 a major airshow was held at RAF Coningsby to mark the victorious battle. Canada put together a five-plane from 421 Sqn led by Maj Brian Titterton to participate in the show. The solo performer for that particular show was Maj Ed McKeogh, no stranger to airshows as a former solo pilot with the RCAF's famous Golden Hawks. Indeed, many of the Hawks went on to fly the CF-104 and all participated in flypasts or airshows with various squadrons. For his part, McKeogh went on to lead "Red Indian" formations to various venues in 1971, including some mass formations of nine or even 12 aircraft. These missions had an important training aspect to them. In the days of nuclear strike and reconnaissance, the CF-104 had been employed in a single aircraft mission scenario. Now, as 1 CAG moved into the conventional ground attack role, formation flying became an integral component of attack tactics as pilots ingressed and egressed from their targets.

Queen's Colours

The year 1973 will long be remembered by all those serving in 1 CAG at the time as it marked the 25th anniversary of active service for each of 421, 439 and 441 Sqns. In a ceremony that was to be repeated across Canada by many squadrons marking the same milestone, the three 1 CAG squadrons were presented their Queen's Colours on May 4th. Hundreds of spectators were on hand to witness the gala affair which, in addition to 450 officers and men on parade, included the Canadian Forces Central Band, CFB Ottawa Pipe Band and gunners of The Royal Canadian Horse Artillery who fired a 21 gun Royal Salute. The fact that the presiding officer for the ceremony was His Royal Highness Prince Philip the Duke of Edinburgh created some unique circumstances. One pilot who was selected to perform a special flypast in conjunction with the ceremony was Capt Willy Floyd, the Group's maintenance test pilot and solo demonstration pilot:

"On the day of the Colours' presentation there was no airshow as such because of a Royal decree which placed a restriction of a minimum of 1,000 foot altitude and no inverted flying for participating aircraft. Thus, I was delegated to make a solo pass for the first Royal Salute when the Prince arrived on parade. Subsequently, as he presented each squadron with its Colours, a 12-ship of Starfighters flew overhead. The grand finale was a 36-ship diamond led by LCol Sam Firth, timed perfectly to end the parade with the last Royal Salute.

For my opening gambit, it was obvious that I could not remove the royal bonnet from 1,000 feet, so I arrived at the exact moment (plus or minus half a second) doing Mach .98 from behind the audience in attendance to watch the parade. The Prince, on the dais at the time, never even blinked an eye. This according to Col Arnie Bauer, the base commander, who was standing in front, saluting and ordering, 'Royal Salute … Present Arms.' Swoosh! I quickly pulled into the vertical and did aileron rolls all the way to about 25 grand … this done to escape the Royal Wrath!

Later, when presented to the Prince in the Officers' Mess, he asked what altitude I had been at when I flew overhead. I answered, with the correct response, 'At one thousand

His Royal Highness The Duke of Edinburgh takes the Royal Salute as 36 CF-104s overfly the 450 personnel on parade for the squadron Colours presentation at 4 (F) Wing Baden-Soellingen on 4 May 73. (DND BSC 73-876)

feet, Sir.' He paused, fixed me with those penetrating eyes and declared that I was a bloody poor liar … but probably a bloody good pilot and bought me a drink. The Prince had always been a great friend of the RCAF, occasionally sharing an ale with the boys at North Luffenham in the early Sabre days. Fond memories from a long time ago …"

Willy Floyd

The celebrations surrounding the Colours' presentation to 421, 439 and 441 Sqns continued the next day with a major airshow that was open to the public. In addition to a repeat performance of Sam Firth's 36-ship flypast and an aerobatic display by Willy Floyd, 1 CAG was honoured by the attendance of two of the world's finest aerobatic teams, the Red Arrows of the Royal Air Force and *Patrouille de France*, both teams putting on a dazzling performance. The following month, 421 Sqn repaid the favour in Great Britain when Maj John England led a four-ship of 421 pilots to The Embassy Air Tattoo staged at RAF Mildenhall on June 7th and 8th. Capt Willy Floyd accompanied them to put on his solo aerobatic display.

The 421 Sqn team that performed at the Embassy Air Tattoo at RAF Mildenhall, England in 1973. L to R – Capt Willy Floyd (solo), Capt Ed McGillivray (No. 2), Maj John England (team leader), Capt Cec Hume (No. 3), Capt Brian Allen (No. 4). (DND Photo via Ed McGillivray)

A Change of Command to Remember

With the approach of the mid-1970s, ongoing budget cuts continued to put the financial squeeze on Canada's military leaders who were under considerable pressure to reduce costs in every conceivable way – while still meeting their operational commitments. Much had changed from the free-wheeling days of the early '60s. This of course was of little consequence to the average fighter pilot who was content to jump in his jet, race around with his hair on fire ("two missions today please, not over lunch hour … and could you make sure one of them is to the range?") and retire to the bar for a few ales, leaving the mundane problems of the world to the "adults." It was only when the problems started to cramp their style that the line operators would sit up and take notice. George Landry was a veteran fighter pilot in the CF-104 and CF-5 era who looks back with humour on one little crisis that created some grief among the troops in 1975.

"When I arrived in Baden in 1974 we were in the midst of a worldwide fuel crisis. Fuel was so short that even driving cars was restricted. For example, on weekends only cars with even numbered licence plates could drive on even days and odd plates on odd days. As a result, when Don Miles handed over command of 441 Sqn to John Hutt on May 23rd, 1975, it was decreed by the gods that there

The infamous 441 Sqn Change of Command flypast of 1975. Having duly captured everyone's attention on the parade square with their unscheduled appearance in vic formation, this dynamic trio came back for a second pass in line-astern. Demonstrating their superior initiative (and total disregard for their careers) are self-anointed demo pilots Capts Ian Struthers, George Landry and Gerry Hermanson. (Rod Sword via Ian Struthers)

would be no flypast (because of the fuel shortage???). Prior to this, we had done flypasts for everyone, even maintainer and administrator handovers. I suspect we may have so honoured even the *putzfraus* or the spy named 'Sputnik' who drove the squadron bus! The thought of taking over a fighter squadron without a single plane in the air was so offensive to the line pilots that three of us decided to go to the local flying club and rent some light aircraft to properly mark the event (unofficial and unapproved of course). Ian Struthers led the charge in a Cherokee 140 (he had to lead because he had never flown light aircraft before and we wanted him up front where we could keep an

eye on him! We started it for him, gave him a few speed references and told him to set 2200 RPM and lead us to greater glory). I was number 2 in a Cessna 172 and Gerry Hermanson number 3 in an L-19 Birddog – complete with a large checkerboard flag tied to the strut. During the flight the flag tied itself into a knot and beat the crap out of Hermie's right flap. We took off in vic formation and cranked over the centre marg – Struts' timing over the parade was excellent and Rod Sword recorded the event on film. We did another pass in line-astern for the Queen – and our moment in the sun was over. Total flight time – six minutes. The event was very well received by everyone below the rank of lieutenant colonel … but not so popular above that level!"

George Landry

The 1 CAG Teams

Whether the result of the initiative described above or a diminishment of the fuel crisis, flypasts for changes of commands were soon back in, as were continuing demands for the presence of Canadian Starfighters at European airshows. Another Canadian team that made a name for themselves during this period were the Tiger Romeos of 439 Sqn. After a suitable number of practices, Maj Bill Fuoco led the team to four performances at the RAF's Greenham Common Air Tattoo in 1976, one of the largest shows in Europe

The Tiger Romeos – this stirring tribute to the 439 Sqn demonstration teams of the mid-70s was created by former RCAF pilot Geoff Bennett. (courtesy of Geoff Bennett)

The Tiger Romeos. L to R, 1976 – Lt Marty Abbott, Maj Bill Fuoco (team leader), Capt Keith McDonald, Capt Guy Dutil and "Fang." In 1977, Standing – Maj (elect) Keith McDonald (team leader), Capt Brian Bainbridge. Kneeling – Capt Lawrence Sianchuk, Capt Keith Robbins. Note the Tiger emblem on the tail of the aircraft and individual helmets, a common practice that builds *esprit de corps* among NATO fighter squadrons. (DND Photos via Keith McDonald)

that summer. So popular was their appearance that they were invited back the following summer for three more shows with Maj Keith McDonald moving into the lead position. The year 1977 was also a banner year for change of commands, with the Romeos performing four shows for commanding officer handovers that included 421 Sqn, Canadian Forces Europe, CFB Lahr and 1 CAG.

By this time, there was sufficient demand for appearances that each of the three squadrons formed their own demonstration teams and/or appointed solo demo pilots to perform at one or more of the larger shows being staged that summer. Naturally, there was no shortage of volunteers, the inescapable fact being that being a performer in an airshow was even more fun than being just a spectator on the ground. Maj George Landry had come to this conclusion long before and led the 441 Sqn Check Whiskey team that was assigned to grace another mega show in the summer of '77 – Mildenhall, England.

While those discharged with the responsibility of performing airshows tend to make light of the challenges involved, they are considerable – especially so in the realm of high performance demonstrations. With speeds ranging anywhere from 190 to 600 knots, mastering a co-ordinated show that includes a formation presentation interspersed with a solo act requires a lot of planning and aerial practice to both perfect the sequence and ensure it is safe for the viewing audience. However, in spite of the "set" routine, performers often have to contend with variables such as weather and air traffic control inputs, as George Landry explains:

"As we took off at Mildenhall, the tower advised me that our slot time had been reduced by two minutes (thanks for the warning!). Since the takeoff and landing were part of the show, there was no convenient place to cut out two minutes without destroying the whole flow, so I tightened up the show by cranking the formation tighter (shaving 15 seconds per pass should do the trick). Gus Youngson and Bob Wade hung in on my wing but it threw off our solo's timing (Bruce Reid) and he was a year late on the high speed-low speed pass. Realizing he was going to be a little tardy, Bruce lit the torch and was in danger of catching up to us when he astutely noted two significant facts. Firstly, he was about to enter into a major glass replacement program as he rapidly approached Mach 1. Secondly, he was in a pilot induced oscillation (PIO) at 100 feet (or so) off the deck. The Zip could be very unstable at high transonic speeds if you didn't trim nose down – like trying to fly formation with nose-up trim. In response, Bruce sucked the power to idle and managed to ride the ragged edge between ground strike and pitch-up for the full length of the runway. This might have been the first whisper, PIO pass recorded in that part of England. It was apparently quite spectacular … and fortunately out of my view! By the way, we completed the show in the allotted time."

George Landry

Refusing to be left out of all the fun, 421 Sqn was also well represented at airshows across the continent. Capt Don Leonard was given "the keys" to a 104 to do solo shows from

1976 through 1978, performing in France, Germany and England. And in each of 1977 and 1978, the Red Indians formed a formation demonstration team led by Capt Jim Graham. The highlight of 1978 was a return to the squadron's roots in England, as left wingman Paul Deacon recalls:

"In May 1978 the team flew to RAF Manston to participate in the Biggin Hill airshow. It was the first appearance of 421 Sqn Starfighters near the airfield at Maidstone, Kent where the squadron had been formed during World War II. We were hosted in grand style by 127 Wing of the RAF Association which carried on exchanges with the squadron in each of the following years until the demise of Canadian Forces Europe. This was also the only occasion I ever met the flight engineer from my father's Halifax crew assigned to the RCAF's No. 6 Bomber Group, a little Englishman by the name of Harry 'call me Bomber' Harris (not to be mistaken with 'The' Bomber Harris).

As for the airshow, the weather was atrocious but we made the show with a 560 knot afterburner opening pass as Jim Graham led us in from behind the crowd in line-abreast. Our commentator, Capt Ed Karpetz, said it was just beautiful watching the reaction of the crowd. Everyone loved it – except for the folks in the nearby hospital that 'Omar' Leonard infringed upon while avoiding the worst of the weather. The only other downside was the drive from Manston back to the reception at Biggin in the Volkswagon van our hosts had provided – Norm Shaw was determined to drive down the wrong side of the road. I don't

think he fully grasped the concept of driving 'on the other side' and every roundabout was a whole new experience as we watched our lives flash before our eyes! By the time we got to Biggin the party was well underway, so there was some serious catching up to do. But, with national honour at stake, we attacked with gusto! Oh yes, just before we left, Col Arnie Bauer of the Canadian Defence Liaison Staff in London presented us with boxes of what seemed like thousands of 'first day covers' we were to sign to mark the occasion. Every one of them was duly signed. We almost didn't get out of there for another day."

Paul Deacon

With 1 CAG Headquarters receiving requests for flypasts and airshows from far and wide, 441 Sqn's 1978 tasking included a straight-forward flypast over Strasbourg, France but also a rare opportunity to fly a show at Aviano, Italy. Capt Rick Martin was appointed team leader of the five-plane team. His logbook reveals the team did five practices prior to launching off on their adventure to Italy on June 30th. Once on location, the team conducted a practice on July 1st prior to participating in the big show the next day. Their show, which also commenced with a five-plane vic formation surprising the crowd from behind, was equally well received. Of course, the Italian home crowd was already well indoctrinated to the ultra-low altitudes from all directions flown by their national team, the *Frecce Tricolori*, so the Canadian arrival was not quite as shocking as it tended to be in other countries. And as Rick Martin recalls, part of the fun included meeting other teams for the first time:

"All of the performers were hosted at a reception the night before the show and we ended up in a circle talking to the Austrian team, the 'Karo As' who flew the Saab 105 jet trainer. They looked very sharp in their full team blazer and slacks outfit while we, of course, were in flying suits. Early in the evening, their leader, who was very upright, very tall and very Austrian, looked down at me and asked what position I flew on the team. I looked up and said, 'I'm the lead.' From the look on his face, I could tell he was somewhat taken aback by this revelation, perhaps because everyone else on our team was tall like him, while I was 'of average stature.' So, with a straight face I added, 'I have to be the lead, I can't fly formation!' I don't think he quite knew how to take that. He actually approached Dave Owen (our solo) later to ask

The "Red Indians" of 421 Sqn established an airshow team in 1976 to carry on the tradition of promoting the squadron and Canada throughout NATO, just as this photo of a squadron Starfighter had a few years earlier. The olive drab paint scheme of the early 1970s gave way to the more familiar camouflaged livery that saw the Starfighter out of service in 1986. (DND Photo)

him whether I was serious. We ended up having such a good time with them over the weekend that they offered to save us the flight home around Switzerland by taking us on their wing through Austria and dropping us off at the German border. It was tempting – but we declined. Good thing!"

Rick Martin

The Canadian Reds

By mid-1978 a decision was taken to move towards a single Starfighter team that would represent Canada at all future European airshows. The objective of this decision was to reduce the flying hours necessary to work up a team. The move also ensured more resources were available to meet operational tasking during the spring and summer months when manpower was at a premium due to leave and the standard rollover of personnel during the posting season.

As Capt Jim Graham had acquired the most experience leading the Red Indians since early 1977, he accepted a higher calling to be team leader. No doubt as a result of his squadron affiliation, the team adopted the name Canadian Reds for this first "official" 1 CAG demonstration team. With recommendations from the three respective commanding officers, Graham was joined by five additional veterans of 104 operations – Brian Bainbridge from 439 Sqn, Bob Wade from 441, Gus Youngson, a former 441er then running the simulator training program and

finally Nev Symonds from 421 Sqn. The team flew a modest four shows that summer. As Youngson recalls:

"The highlight of our season was the Mildenhall show flown on August 26th and 27th. We also flew an additional show at Leicester (out of Mildenhall) on the second day. Mildenhall was a big show with a large static display and several hours of military flying displays, which in my experience always included at least a couple of the big European aerobatic teams (Red Arrows, *Patrouille de France*, *Frecci Tricolori*). It was during one of the shows at Mildenhall that a member of the *Frecci* drove himself into the ground coming out of cloud following a bomb burst. The team pressed on and finished their show without him! On September 2nd, 1978 we flew a large show at Baden commemorating the 25th anniversary of the base. The weekend also included the dedication ceremony associated with placing the F-86 Sabre on the pedestal that adorned the main gate until the base was closed."

Gus Youngson

The 1 CAG Starfighters

For the 1979 season the team reverted to a more representative name, the 1 CAG Starfighters, that would remain with the team through to the conclusion of Starfighter shows four years later. The leadership of the

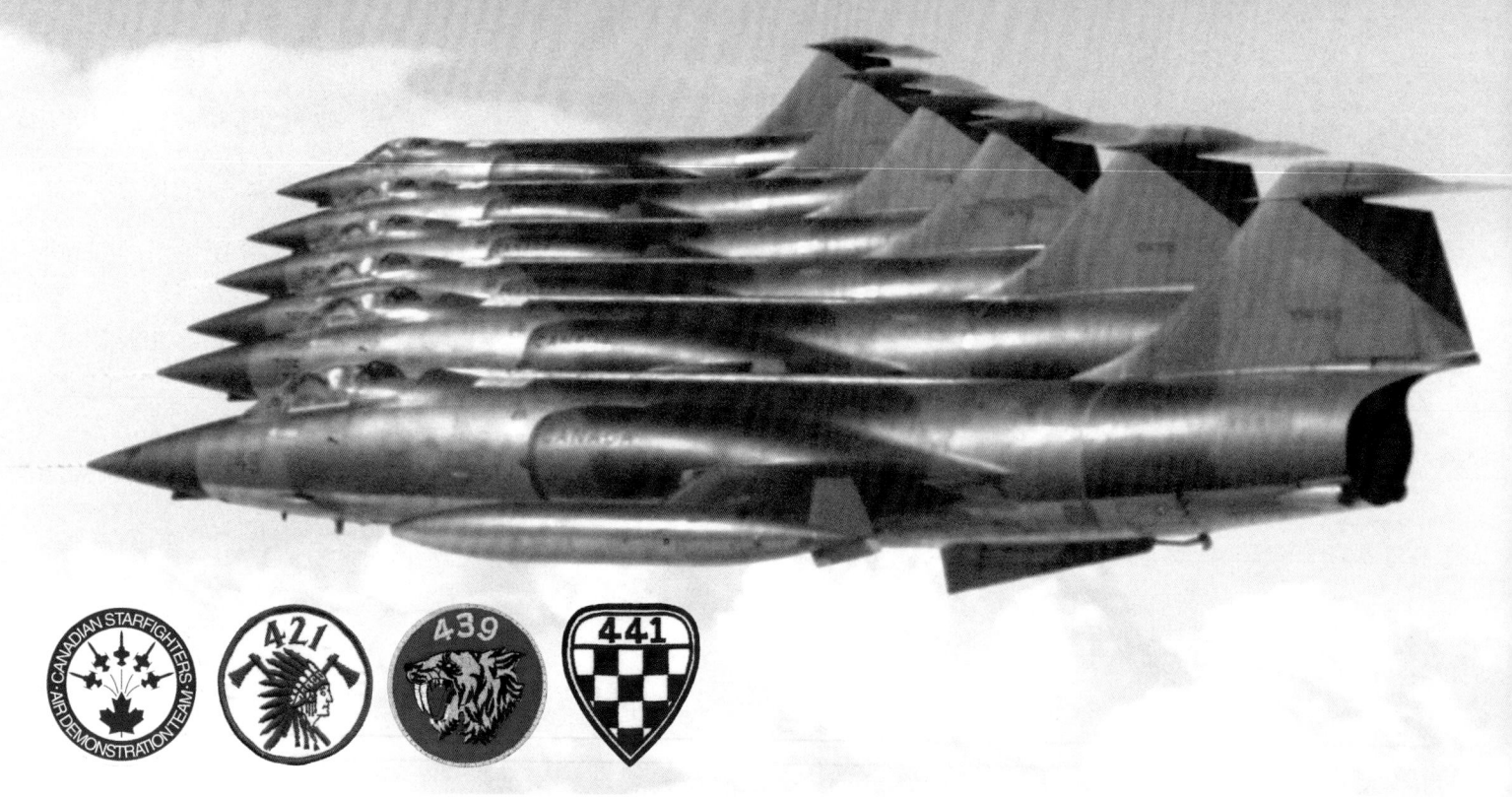

A beautiful aerial portrait of the 1979 1 CAG team captured by CF photographer Sgt Wayne Gordon using a Hasselblad with an 80 mm lens. The aircraft are being flown by, from the far side, Maj John David, Capt Stan Jones, Capt Norm Shaw, Capt Henry Van Keulen, Capt Dave Owen and Capt Clive Ken. The chase CF-104D was flown by Maj Greg Bruneau of Snowbird fame. Inset is the Canadian Starfighters Air Demonstration Team badge eventually adopted by the team along with the shoulder patches from the three tactical fighter squadrons from which team members were drawn at CFB Baden-Soellingen. (DND Photo PCN 79-153, Sgt Wayne Gordon)

team was handed to Maj John David of 441 Sqn, by this time on his fourth CF-104 tour having served previously with 427, 421 and 417 Sqns. Now on his way to over 3,000 hours on type, David was also joining his third Starfighter team. He had gleaned his first airshow experience in 1970 as the designated Air Division CF-104 demonstration pilot, putting the Starfighter through a fully aerobatic show that included an opening inverted pass across the length of the airfield followed by a Cuban-eight, four-point roll, loop and so on. This experience made him a natural selection to fulfill the solo role on the 417 Sqn team in 1973 prior to leading the team himself through its 1975 season. His latest team followed the model started in 1978, with two members from each squadron being selected to put on a five-plane display which included a four-plane formation integrated with a solo performer. The latter was flown by Capt Dave

Owen, a holdover from the '78 team.

Notwithstanding the directive for a single 1 CAG team, 439 Sqn managed to preserve tradition by gaining authorization to form a "single-show" team for the 1979 Tiger Meet airshow in Cambrai, France. With Capt Brian Bainbridge leading a four-ship, Capt Dan Bouchard did the solo honours in the latest version of the squadron's Tiger bird (104862) and the hard-earned reputation of the Canadian Tigers remained intact.

With a new decade came a new Starfighter team led by another veteran of airshow performances, Maj Eric Thurston, leader of the 1973 Starfighter team in Canada. He explains some of the unique challenges of doing shows in Europe where weather and language differences were often factors in conducting operations:

The 1979 1 CAG Air Demonstration Team was presented a large CF-104 model by King Baudouin of Belgium in appreciation for their outstanding performance at the Florennes International Airshow on 23 Jul 79. Team members, L to R – Cpl Ron Pinke, Maj John David (team leader), Capt Stan Jones, Capt Norm Shaw, Capt Henry Van Keulen, Capt Dave Owen, MCpl Jim Craik and Cpl B. Hayman. (DER KANADIER via Norm Shaw)

"We developed the 1980 show along the same lines as previous years. The solo (Gary Lacroix) always flew a clean-clean Starfighter whereas the rest of us flew with a standard tip tank configuration. The advantage for the solo was that he could pull up to a maximum of 7.33 G during his show whereas we were restricted to 5 G. The disadvantage was that he was always short of fuel!

To get around this problem on practices, the four-plane formation would always take off early to do a preliminary work-up and then return to the base for a hard TOT. At this time, with the airspace closed for the pick-up, the solo would be lined up on the runway and ready to go. As we approached the end of the runway in 'finger-four left' formation at about 100 feet, Gary would start his takeoff roll. As soon as he was airborne, he would join up on the right side of the formation. We got pretty good at the timing as the summer progressed and Gary, on a good day, would be in formation before we hit the Hügelsheim highway off the end of the runway. We would then set up for a full show practice, usually using a tree line near a well known 'hack' point at Büchelberg, about 30 km north of the base.

We had five dedicated groundcrew assigned to the team who did great work making sure the team was never late nor missed a practice or airshow. These were MCpls Ken Wiebe,

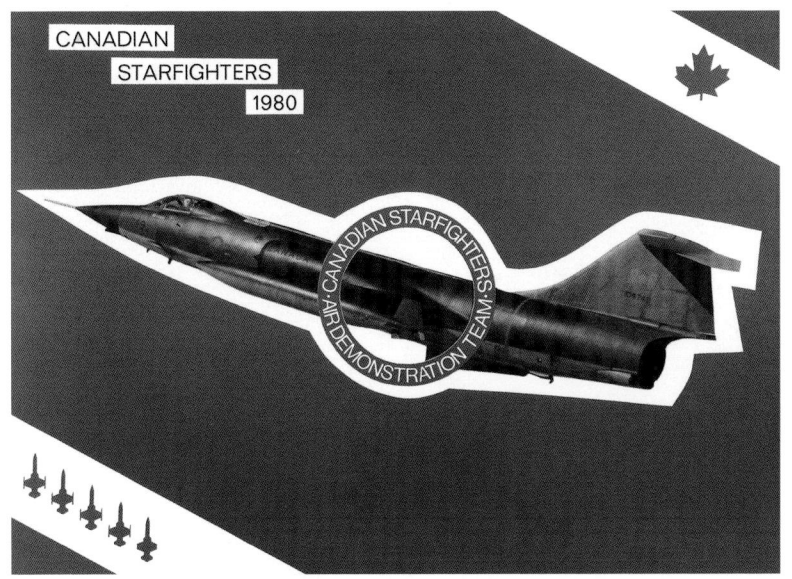

CANADIAN STARFIGHTERS 1980

CANADIAN STARFIGHTERS AIR DEMONSTRATION TEAM

The 1980 Canadian Starfighters are joined by a special guest during a visit to Baden. L to R – Capts Gary Lacroix, Al Camplin, Scott Bowes, Rick Gelinas, Rick Bollinger, Maj Eric Thurston (team leader). At right, MGen Pablo Mackenzie (Chief of Air Doctrine and Operations at NDHQ) accompanied by Col Tony Bosman and LCol Herb Sievert. (DND Photo)

J.C. Tremblay, Bob Nitschke, Ed Moore and Cpl Larry Kostyal. Unfortunately, for shows far from base we had to restrict ourselves to only two crewmen who usually accompanied us via two T-33s (which then went on static display). For shows closer to home, the team pre-positioned ahead of us via ground transport if we planned to land there. Our first big show of the season at Biggin Hill also represented our first logistic challenge. Due to the short runway and the lack of start equipment, we had to operate from RAF Manston. Rather than travel to and from Biggin Hill by bus (a tortuous and long trip via the English country roads), the organizers provided a Cessna Citation to ferry us back and forth. Consequently, we had no problems with timing and actually got to see most of the other performers.

The Newbury Airshow was held at Greenham Common, a two day show on May 31st and June 1st. This airshow was superbly run by the organizers and the operators with very tight timing between acts. However, about two hours before our start time on the first day of the show, we were advised that the fuel bowser that had refuelled us the previous day might have had contaminated fuel. Samples were taken and sent via helicopter to a lab for analysis. As our start time approached, we were all strapped in and ready to go but the results of the analysis had not been received. Finally, with only minutes to spare, we got the word that the fuel was fine and we made our takeoff time. Another few minutes and the organizers would have had to cancel our performance.

Our next show was not until June 29th in Aviano, Italy. Half the fun was just getting there as we had to contend with the rigid Italian 'procedural IFR' air traffic control system. However, an estimated crowd of 200,0000 took in the show, clogging the roads around the base with about the same number of Fiats! Shows on the same weekend at Ramstein and Leipheim were the next challenge for the team, the biggest problem coming in the early planning phase to determine whether it was feasible to do the Ramstein show, recover and refuel at Lahr (Baden was closed for runway repairs) and still make the Leipheim show on time. As it turned out, Ramstein scheduled us early in their show and Leipheim altered their schedule to make sure we would be available as the closing act. Everything went according to plan – except for the weather! Our recovery in Lahr had been fairly uneventful, other than the fact that Gary Lacroix ended up somewhat short of fuel. Our maintenance team from Baden was waiting for us and, consequently, the turn-around and flight planning were accomplished very quickly. Unfortunately, between Stuttgart and Bavaria

The 1980 team pause for a photo with some of their groundcrew prior to getting down to business. (via Eric Thurston)

the cloud was on the trees. Therefore, en route to Leipheim we had to contact Rhein Radar and go IFR as a five-plane vic. I told the controller where my initial check point was for the show (in the Krumbach valley south of Leipheim) and sure enough, he gave us a cloud-break right over top of the IP and on time. Considering the circumstances, it could not have worked out better.

Having mastered the 'two shows per day at different locations' routine, it was back to England for shows at both Mildenhall and Leicester on the weekend of August 22nd to 24th. Our last performance in Baden took place on September 5th for the benefit of the Chief of the Defence Staff, Gen Ramsey-Withers, and the local school children. Unfortunately, the weather was very poor – had it not been for the familiar landscape at Baden, I doubt we could have completed the show.

Our 1980 season concluded with a show at Goppingen, a tiny German soaring airfield in the Schwabish Alps just southeast of Stuttgart. The planning was a nightmare as

All former CF-104 pilots will recognize both the terrain and symbology on this map. The 1:500 scale map depicts the run-in to show centre at Baden-Soellingen flown by team leader Eric Thurston on one of the last shows of the 1980 season. The two solid black lines represent two route choices – over the Schwarzwald (right) if the weather was good, or up the Rhine Valley (left) if the weather was poor. He used the latter! Time checkpoints for a precise time on target (TOT) are clearly marked. (via Eric Thurston)

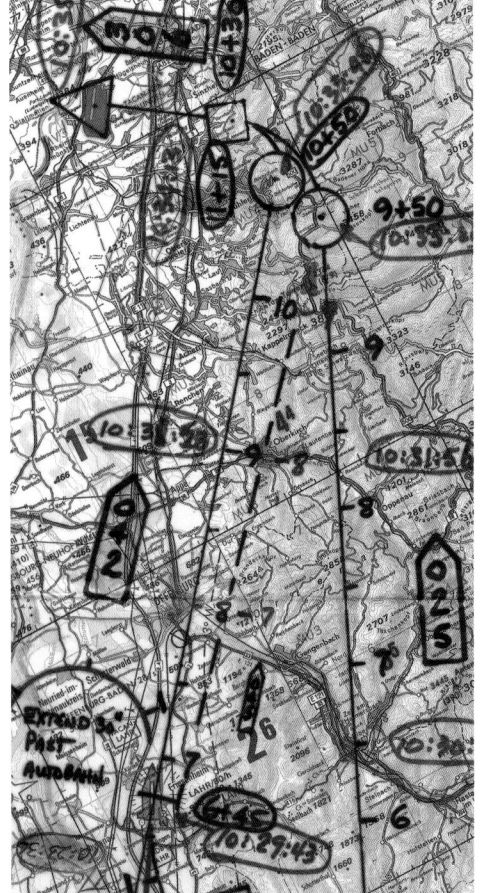

Capt Bob Saunders couldn't pass up the opportunity for a little humour when he came across this vendor's sign at an airshow in England in 1981. L to R, Standing – Capt Bob Saunders, Maj Chris Tuck (team leader), Cpl Jacques Caron, Cpl Jim Dunham, Capt Curt Johnston, MCpl Ed Holloway, Cpl John Gough, Sgt Frank Kennedy. Kneeling – Capt Ron Platt, Capt Kerry Cranfield, Capt "Mex" Tremblay, MCpl Pete Turgeon. (via Bob Saunders)

no one there spoke English, so we used the services of the base translator. The hardest part of that performance was performing the show in the hilly terrain without scraping off poor No. 4 (Scott Bowes) on the hills at both ends of the runway. In fact, we named the hill just west of the airfield "Bowes Bulge" in memory of the great view he had of the tree foliage.

All-in-all it was a great summer. It's hard to believe it was 22 years ago – still seems like yesterday! Everybody on the team worked hard … we had some great trips and good performances … travelled with the best – the *Frecci Tricolori*, *Patrouille de France*, Red Arrows, *Karo As* (the Austrian four-plane aerobatic team flying Saab 105s in a very tight and exciting show) and some exciting solo aerobatic performers – a couple of whom unfortunately did not make it through the season. But probably the best part was working with a team made up of members of all three squadrons and the 1 CAG maintenance organization."

Eric Thurston

With many positive accolades filtering back to Canadian Forces Europe about the fine public relations work accomplished by the Starfighter team, workups commenced on April 23rd for the 1981 season with a brand new cast of characters. Taking the helm was former Snowbird Maj Chris Tuck who had spent two seasons (1975-1976) travelling the North American airshow circuit. He led the team through 11 practices prior to putting on a very polished acceptance show on May 13th for the Comd 1 CAG, BGen P.D. Manson. To keep the team in top form, an additional

19 practices were flown during the season, either at an airshow site or in the local area around Baden.

The 1981 season again featured participation in some of Europe's largest airshows with the team visiting five countries. Following their first official public show at Frankfurt-Main on May 17th, the team represented the Canadian Forces at Mildenhall, Metz, Prestwick, Baden-Soellingen, Greenham Common, Aviano and Ramstein prior to completing their last show on August 12th at St. Mawgan, England. Unfortunately, two additional West German shows at Karlsruhe and Hahn AFB were cancelled due to weather.

In addition to Canada's own Starfighters Demonstration Team, Canadian Forces Day 1981 at Baden-Soellingen featured two of the world's most famous aerobatic teams, the *Frecce Tricolori* and *Patrouille de France*. (author's collection)

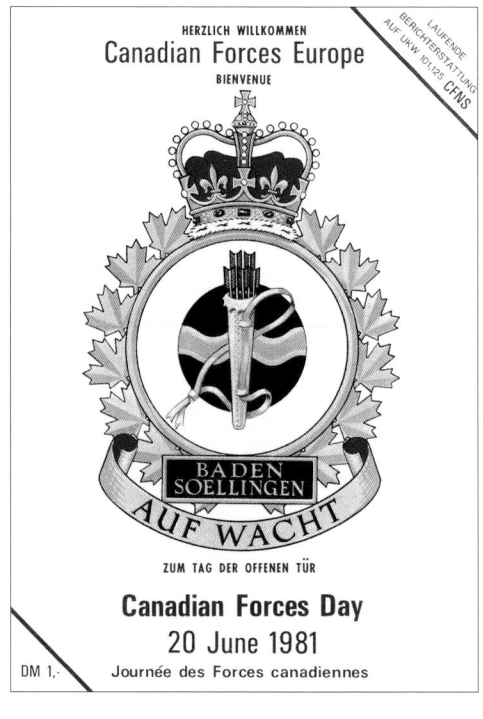

HERZLICH WILLKOMMEN
Canadian Forces Europe
BIENVENUE

LAUFENDE BERICHTERSTATTUNG AUF UKW 101.125 CFNS

BADEN SOELLINGEN
AUF WACHT

ZUM TAG DER OFFENEN TÜR

Canadian Forces Day
20 June 1981
Journée des Forces canadiennes

DM 1.-

The 1 CAG Starfighters of 1982. L to R – Maj Fred Mueller (team leader), Capt Tom Lawson, Capt Bob Saunders, Capt Scott Ritchie, Capt Doug Erlandson. Missing is Capt Mike Hoch. (via Bob Saunders)

After the opener, our show was relatively simple and straightforward with our solo, Capt 'Mex' Tremblay, alternating passes with the four-plane. Since the team was ostensibly non-aerobatic, the best we could manage was 'slanted 360s' during our turnarounds which became progressively steeper as the season progressed. Our one moment of fame, as it were, occurred at the RAF Greenham Common Air Tattoo where awards were given for airshow performances. We received an honourable mention for having the 'tightest box.' Incidentally, Sir Douglas Bader, as patron of the Air Tattoo and in one of his last public appearances before he passed away, also proffered public congratulations to 'those Canadians'."

Chris Tuck

After a number of years on the European airshow circuit, the Canadian Starfighter show had become very popular, especially for its stunning arrival. Chris Tuck explains how the manoeuvre was set up:

"The opening sequence was probably the most impressive manoeuvre in the show, all the more so in light of current regulations which are much more restrictive than \those we enjoyed in the early '80s. We commenced our show in a five-plane vic

formation at show centre, but from behind the crowd. The intent was to achieve as much surprise and generate as much noise as possible. About 20 seconds back and with takeoff flap down, we selected speed brakes and then went into afterburner. Speed brakes came in at the last moment and the crowd was overflown as low as we thought we could get away with. A rather aggressive pull-up was then required to avoid overspeeding the flaps at 520 knots. Our commentator, Capt Bob Saunders, referred to this as 'the sound of freedom.'

Leadership of the 1982 version of the Starfighters passed to 439 Sqn with veteran fighter pilot Maj Fred Mueller taking the reins of the team. It was another busy season with the team completing 18 practices and 12 shows between April 29th and September 25th. Major shows were flown at Dijon and Toulouse, France; Mildenhall and Leicester, England; Jever, Belgium; and Landau and Norvenich, Germany. As fate would have it, this would turn out to be the last full season for the team.

The Canadian Starfighters were an impressive sight on the ground as well as in the air, seen here in England in 1982. (Bob Saunders)

Canada's Last Starfighter Team

Canada's last Starfighter team was formed in 1983 with Capt Rick Martin of 441 Sqn taking command once again. The team perfected their show through 11 practices commencing on April 14th prior to launching south down the Rhine River to Colmar, France for their first show on May 8th. Unfortunately, the show was reduced to four aircraft when No. 4 hit a bird on the run-in and was forced to abandon the show as a safety precaution. After a short delay in order to assess the damaged aircraft, the remainder of the team completed their show, much to the appreciation of show organizers and the thousands of spectators on hand.

Following an on-base practice on May 20th, the team recovered in Frankfurt to prepare for the massive Rhein-Main airshow two days later. It was during this show that the team suffered a season ending accident when the solo aircraft suffered a low-level pitch-up during a high G turn, forcing the pilot to eject to safety. Sadly, part of the aircraft wreckage spilled across the nearby *autobahn* striking two cars and fatally injuring their occupants. The only Starfighter airshow accident in over 20 years of appearances, the tragedy left team members in stunned disbelief as they had worked hard to develop a professional and safe show. Although all team members quickly returned to their normal combat training duties, the ensuing accident investigation kept the team on the ground. By the time the investigation was concluded, a decision was taken not to work up the show again for the remaining few shows of the season.

Notwithstanding the terrible misfortune at Rhein-Main, 1983 was a year of celebration

NATO's Tiger squadrons converged on CFB Baden-Soellingen for their annual tactical flying exercise in May 1983. In keeping with tradition, 439 Sqn painted this flashy Tiger, the last rendition of a rare breed. The first CF-104 in Tiger colours (104833) had appeared almost 23 years earlier at RAF Woodbridge on 7 Aug 69. (author's collection)

at Baden-Soellingen as it marked the 30th anniversary of Canadian operations at the base. Befitting such an important milestone, a large airshow was planned on June 12th to thank the surrounding German and French

communities for their support over the years. A large static display of NATO aircraft was complemented by three specially painted CF-104s done up in the squadron colours of 421, 439 and 441 Sqns. Maj Greg Bruneau

The pilots of Canada's last Starfighter team photographed at CFB Baden-Soellingen just prior to the start of the 1983 season. L to R – Capt Al Stephenson, Capt Dave Anderson, Capt Rick Martin (team leader), Capt Steve Green, Capt Neale Nowosad. Missing is Capt Glen Huxter. (DND Photo)

CFB Baden celebrated 30 years of Canadian fighter presence in the Rhine Valley with a major airshow in the summer of '83 which featured many acts, including this flypast of CF-104s. This was the base's last airshow in the 104 era. (author's collection, via Rick Martin)

narrated the show which featured some of Europe's finest performers. Foremost among these were the *Patrouille de France* and *Frecce Tricolori* aerobatic teams, both sporting new advanced jet trainers, the Alpha Jet and Aermacchi MB 339 respectively. Although the Starfighter team was unable to perform, there was plenty of CF-104 activity in the show which featured a simulated mass attack on the airfield and mass flypast displaying the numbers 3 and 0 in a salute to base personnel. Although Maj Wally Peel had been the architect of the formation,

in a classy move he insisted that Rick Martin lead the formation as the final act of the Starfighters.

The End of An Era

With the dawning of 1984 came the full realization that the days of the Starfighter were truly numbered. The process of training fighter pilots on the CF-18 Hornet, Canada's new state-of-the-art multi-role combat aircraft, was well underway at Cold Lake and its arrival in theatre was imminent. With a number of 1 CAG pilots and technicians having already repatriated to undergo conversion and 439 Sqn slated to stand down in November, CF-104 manning reached minimum levels. Thus, the decision was made that 1 CAG would not field another airshow team. Static displays at larger airshows

would be supported as much as operational commitments would permit.

Following the stand down of 421 Sqn on October 30th, 1985, the last CF-104 pilots to fulfill NATO duties were the "Silver Foxes" of 441 Sqn, doing so with their usual professionalism right up until their last day of operation in theatre. Capt Rich Lancaster, whose future would include a tour as a CF-18 demo pilot and Snowbird solo, was the last Canadian pilot to show off the CF-104 on static display. With England having been the birthplace of Canadian jet fighter operations and the benefactor of more Canadian airshow demonstrations than any other NATO partner, it was fitting that the International Air Tattoo at RAF Fairford be graced with the last presence of a CF-104 Starfighter in the summer of 1985.

From its controversial roots, the CF-104 served the RCAF and Canadian Forces amazingly well over almost a quarter of a century. As a low-level, high-speed nuclear strike bomber and reconnaissance platform, the aircraft was second-to-none. Although its deterrent value was later reduced by its limited capacity to carry a large load of conventional weapons, Canadian fighter pilots were renowned for their prowess in reaching their assigned targets precisely on time and in the most marginal VFR weather conditions. This

To help celebrate Baden's 30th anniversary, Canada's last three operational CF-104 squadrons each painted an aircraft in squadron colours, with impressive results. (artwork courtesy Graham Wragg, DND BSC 85-565)

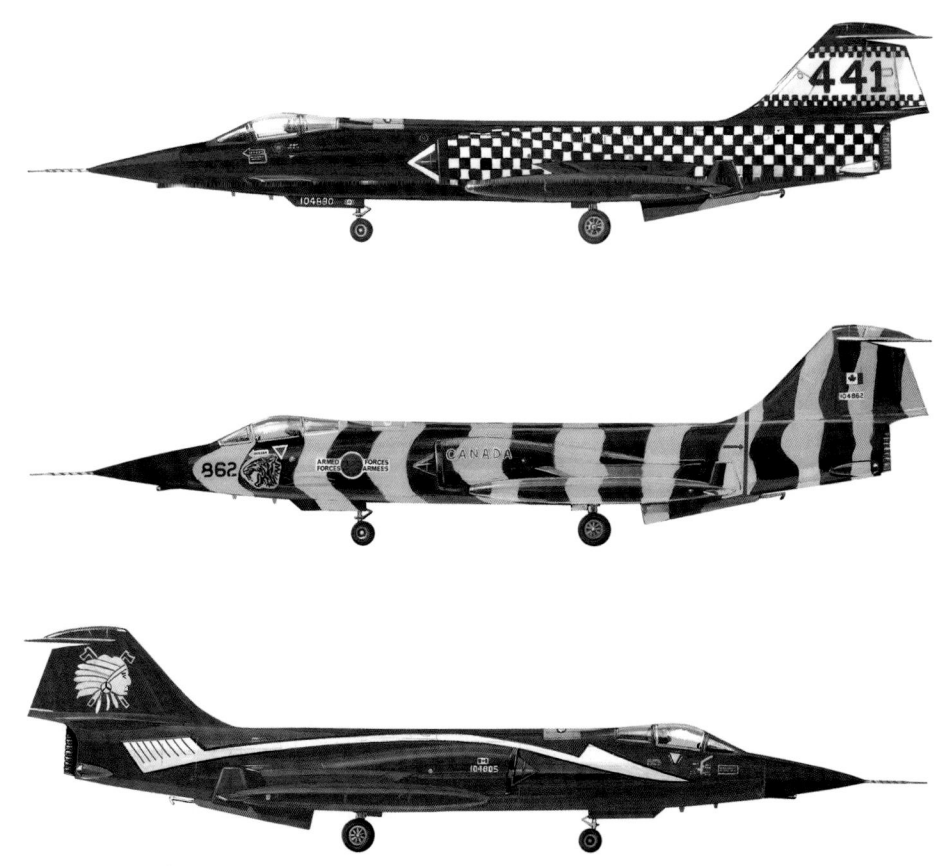

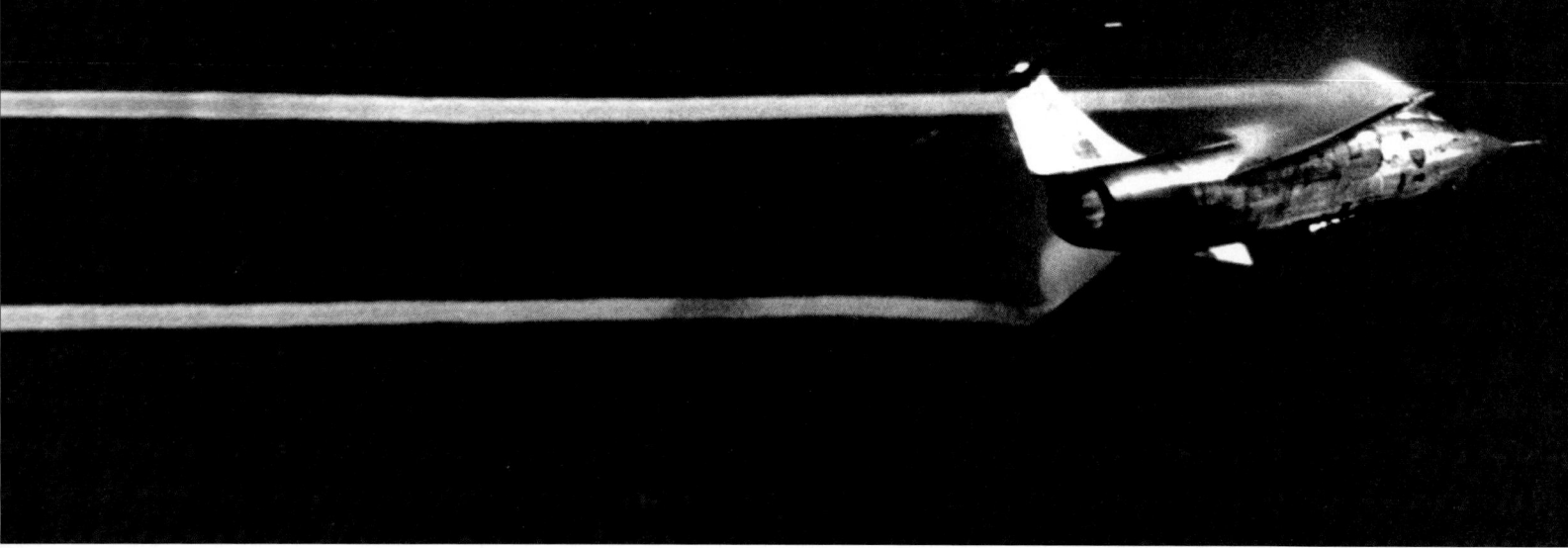

Gone but never forgotten – the shockwaves created by a Starfighter at high speed. (Nancy Johnson)

reliability, whether in pairs, sections of four or as members of a 36-plane "force package," made them an important and respected ally within the NATO partnership that had adopted a doctrine of "flexible response."

On March 1ˢᵗ, 1986 the pilots of 441 Sqn, led by their commanding officer LCol George Adamson, took off for one last nostalgic jaunt across the Schwarzwald into southern Bavaria. They soon turned back into the Rhine Valley, tightened their 12-plane formation and roared over Lahr as they headed north to Baden-Soellingen for the final farewell. As they emerged from the familiar haze silhouetted by a golden sun, hundreds of spectators watched the aircraft pass into history. They had come from all over Canada to pay their last respects to a truly classic flying machine. Even today, long after the last flypast, the CF-104 still evokes a powerful feeling of admiration and sentiment among those who were fortunate enough to have flown her. And for veteran airshow fans in the West, the indelible image of a Starfighter ingressing on the deck just under the speed of sound will long constitute one of their most vivid and memorable airshow experiences.

The final layout of the CF-104 cockpit photographed at CFB Baden in 1985. (DND BA 85-3767)

The newspaper of the Canadian Forces in Europe
L'Hebdomadaire des Forces canadiennes en Europe

VOL XVII NO. 9, 7 300 COPIES   ISSN 0175-6346   26 FÉVRIER 1986

CF-104 Starfighter-the end of an era

Celebrations begin at CFB Baden-Soellingen today, Wednesday, 26 February, to mark the end of an era in the history of the Canadian Forces — the close-out of the CF-104 and the stand-down of the last Starfighter squadron, 441 Tactical Fighter Squadron.

«The missile with the man in it» as the CF-104 became known, has served the Canadian Forces faithfully for nearly 25 years and, in the words of BGen David Huddleston, commander 1 CAG, «She has, in our hands, upheld the reputation of Canadian airmen in NATO which we inherited from our predecessors and has done so with distinction in the three different roles to which she has been committed.»

Many of the hundreds of people who have been associated with the Starfighter during its operational years will attend the close-out ceremonies which will continue until 2 March. «The men and women who have been associated with the CF-104 era over the last quarter century can take immeasurable pride in the fact they were part of something intangible that only those who have been there can truly relate to,» said Col Al DeQuetteville, commander of CFB Baden-Soellingen.

Since April 1980, when the CF-18 was announced as the new fighter aircraft and as replacement for the CF-104, the Starfighter's days have been numbered. «The Starfighter is hanging up her spurs and making way for the Hornet era; however, I am confident that the order of Starfighter pilots will keep the memories and esprit de corps alive for many years to come,» said LCol George Adamson, commanding officer of 441 Squadron.

The CF-104 saw Canadian military aviation from postwar technology through several generations of fighter development as a bridge to the present. The long period of service was not without cost. Of the original fleet of 238 aircraft, 110 were lost in crashes with 37 aircrew fatalities.

«Unfortunately the CF-104 era was not without its sad times — I am thinking of all those who lost their lives while flying the aircraft. If they could be with us for this historic event, they too would probably echo the warm sentiment that we all share for the 104,» said LCol Adamson.

As part of the close-out ceremonies there will be a bus tour of former Canadian bases, including Marville, Metz, Grostenquin and Zweibrucken, and a visit to Choloy Cemetery, between 26 and 28 February. Other events include an all-ranks mixed beer call at the base recreation centre on 28 February at 1600 hrs; a parade to mark the official stand-down of 441 Squadron at 1300 hrs on 1 March followed by an open house; an all-ranks dinner-dance at 1900 hrs on 1 March in the shared premises of the officers' mess and the WOs' and sergeants' mess, and services to dedicate stained glass windows, in memory of those who died while flying or maintaining the CF-104, in both the Protestant and Catholic Chapels on 2 March.

The Starfighter was selected as replacement for the Canadair Sabre in July 1959. On 14 August of that year Canadair was chosen as the manufacturer for the CF-104. Two hundred singles and 38 duals were contracted for

(Continued on page 3)

Farewell to the Silver Foxes and the CF-104

DER KANADIER
Baden-Soellingen

VOL XVII NO. 9 7 300 COPIES   ISSN 0175-6346   SECTION 3   26 FÉVRIER 1986

The CF-104 reconnaissance years

The end of an era. Entitled "Farewell to the Silver Foxes and the CF-104," this photograph accompanied one of many articles published in the Canadian Forces Europe newspaper, *DER KANADIER*, that traced the history of the Starfighter in RCAF and Canadian Forces' service. It depicts the pilots of Canada's last Starfighter squadron, 441 Tac (F) Sqn, who conducted the last official CF-104 flypast shown below on 1 Mar 86. (DND Photo) The 441 Sqn pilots participating in the last flypast were, by section, L to R – Lead Maj Mike Savard, No. 2 Capt Craig Halliwell, No. 3 Maj Al Hunter, No. 4 Capt Harry Mueller/BGen Fred Sutherland; Lead LCol George Adamson (CO 441 Sqn), No. 2 Capt Gord Zans, No. 3 Maj Dan Dempsey, No. 4 Capt Ron Smith; Lead Maj Bert Doyle, No. 2 Capt André Deschamps, No. 3 Capt Kelly Kovach, No. 4 Capt Bill Huckstep. Spotters – Capt Jim Sullivan/Captain Wally Niemi. (DND Photo)

Journey into the past

By Janice Cowan

Saturday's 12-aircraft flypast during close-out ceremonies at CFB Baden-Soellingen, although wonderfully impressive, was not as poignant as a flypast of CF-104s that took place last Wednesday in Northern France.

As 50 Canadians, standing in knee-high snow and freezing temperatures, watched, Maj Wally Peirson, deputy commanding officer of 441 Squadron, led a flypast of four Starfighters high above the headstones of Choloy Cemetery in a final tribute to those who died while flying or maintaining the CF-104 during its operational years.

Many of the 50 Canadians who witnessed the event were paying their own tributes to friends they had once known and had worked alongside. Over there, among the row upon row of gleaming headstones, a whole aerobatic team of 21 and 22 year old pilots was buried . . . over here the young pilots of two aircraft flying in formation as a salute to a departing buddy are laid to rest . . . nearby the pilot of a fighter that crashed into the hospital at Grostenquin with resulting terrible consequences.

The visit to Choloy Cemetery was all part of the close-out ceremonies and just one small segment of a bus tour organized by 441 Squadron. It was called a «former bases tour» but it turned out to be much more than that . . . a trip down memory lane that can only happen once in a lifetime.

The three-day tour took two busloads of people to the former 1 Air Division Headquaters in Metz; Marville, the former home of 1 Wing; Grostenquin, the home of 2 Wing; and Zweibrucken, where 3 Wing was located.

Among the passengers were LGen Paul D. Manson, Assistant Deputy Minister (Personnel) who flew CF100s for two years with 440 All-Weather Fighter Squadron based at Zweibrucken, and who was also at Metz where he served at 1 Air Division Headquaters; MGen (Ret.) K.C. Lett, who was BOpsO at Zweibrucken and SOpsO at 1 Air Division; BGen (Ret.) R.G. Christie, who was commander at Marville when it closed in 1966; Hugh Grasswick, now a pilot with Canadian Pacific Airlines, who married his wife Sheelah while he was a squadron pilot in Marville; BGen Paul Argue, commanding officer, Canadian Support establishment, Kolsas, Norway, who was in Metz as part of 1 Air Division tactical evaluation team from 1962 to 1966, and his wife Sheila (who gave birth to the very last baby born at the Canadian hospital in Grostenquin!)

There were many other interesting passengers all with fond and not-so-fond service memories of the places they visited.

Pictures of the trip and the stories that were recalled as the buses drove through the snow covered countryside of France and Germany will appear in next week's Der Kanadier.

SATURDAY'S CEREMONIES to mark the close-out of the CF-104 and the stand down of 441 Tactical Fighter Squadron ended with this spectacular 12-aircraft flypast by the last Canadian squadron to fly the Starfighter, led by the commanding officer, LCol George Adamson.   (DER KANADIER PHOTO BY MELAINE OSOLINSKY)

DER KANADIER
Baden-Soellingen

VOL XVII NO.10 7 300 COPIES   ISSN 0175-6346   SECTION 3   5 MARCH 1986

DER KANADIER

The newspaper of the Canadian Forces in Europe
L'Hebdomadaire des Forces canadiennes en Europe

| VOL XVII NO. 12, 7 300 COPIES | ISSN 0175-6346 | 19 MARCH 1986 |

LETTRE DU PREMIER MINISTRE

"... tout à leur honneur et à celui de l'Aviation ..."

Major-général D.P. Wightman, CMM, CD
Commandant
Forces canadiennes en Europe
Ottawa K1A 0A2

Le 27 février 1986

Cher général Wightman,

Au nom de tous les Canadiens, je tiens à vous féliciter et, partant, à féliciter les hommes et les femmes du 1er Groupe aérien du Canada au moment où vous vous apprêtez à vous réunir pour rendre hommage à ce vénérable appareil qu'est le CF-104.

Le Starfighter a servi le Canada avec distinction pendant 25 années. Bien qu'il ait été injustement dénigré par les critiques, je me suis laissé dire que le CF-104 était et demeure considéré comme un classique du genre par ceux qui ont eu le privilège de le piloter et d'en assurer l'entretien.

Le procès-verbal, récemment publié, d'une réunion du cabinet du 30 juin 1959, au cours de laquelle fut prise la décision d'approuver l'achat de l'appareil, révèle que le programme visant à doter l'Aviation royale de nouveaux appareils devait durer cinq ans, et que cinq années plus tard, le CF-104 de Lockheed serait inopérationnel. On estimait donc que les CF-104 seraient remplacés graduellement en 1969.

Le fait que le CF-104 ait continué à servir dans de si nombreux rôles jusqu'en 1986 est tout à l'honneur de l'appareil lui-même et du personnel de la 1ère Division aérienne et du 1er GAC. Même s'il cesse de servir le Canada, il n'est que des plus approprié qu'il continue à servir la cause de la liberté au sein de l'aviation turque.

Je m'en voudrais de ne pas profiter de cette occasion pour rendre également hommage à tous les pilotes de CF-104 et à ceux qui ont assuré l'entretien de l'appareil durant ses 25 années de service. Leur contribution au maintien de la liberté qui nous tient à coeur est tout à leur honneur et à celui de l'Aviation et du Canada. Nous sommes tous fiers de la tradition d'excellence que notre aviation s'est acquise en Europe. Maintenant que vous entrez dans l'ère du CF-18, je suis convaincu que vous saurez maintenir cette fière tradition.

Au moment où vous vous réunirez à Baden pour célébrer vos accomplissements et rendre hommage au Starfighter, je vous demande de vous recueillir un instant à la mémoire de ceux de vos camarades qui ne sont pas là pour partager votre fierté, votre joie et vos souvenirs. Je parle respectueusement au nom de ceux qui ont donné leur vie pour leur pays aux commandes du CF-104. Ils sont morts en temps de paix; néanmoins, leur sacrifice et leur honneur n'en sont pas moins grands que ceux de nos compatriotes qui ont perdu la vie au combat. Je vous demande en leur mémoire de vous employer à sauvegarder les idéaux pour lesquels ils ont sacrifié leur vie.

En terminant, permettez-moi de vous redire le profond sentiment de fierté et de gratitude qu'éprouvent tous les Canadiens pour le magnifique travail que vous avez accompli et continuez d'accomplir au service du Canada.

Avec tous mes respects

GEN DAVID HUDDLESTON lands at Diyarbakir, Turkey, to deliver CF-104 to Turkish Air Force.
LE GEN DAVID HUDDLESTON atterrit à Diyarbakir en Turquie pour le transfert des CF-104 à l'aviation turque.
(PHOTO DES FORCES CANADIENNES PAR LE SGT RICK SANSCHAGRIN)

BGEN GOKER welcomes BGen Huddleston to Diyarbakir, Turkey.
LE BGEN GOKER souhaite la bienvenue au bgén Huddleston à Diyarbakir en Turquie.
(PHOTO DES FORCES CANADIENNES PAR LE SGT RICK SANSCHAGRIN)

MAJ ERIC THURSTON and Capt Wally Niemi sign in their aircraft for the last time. Capt Cetin Akkaya, a member of the Turkish Air Force's 181 Squadron, observes the procedure.
LE MAJ ERIC THURSTON et le capt Wally Niemi signent une dernière fois le livre de bord de leur avion. La capt Cetin Akkaya, membre du 181e Escadron de l'aviation turque, observe l'opération.
(PHOTO DES FORCES CANADIENNES PAR LE SGT RICK SANSCHAGRIN)

"... very proud of ... our Air Force in Europe"

PRIME MINISTER — PREMIER MINISTRE

Major General D.P. Wightman, CMM, CD
Commander
Canadian Forces Europe
OTTAWA K1A 0A2

27 February 1986

Dear General Wightman,

I am writing to express, on behalf of all Canadians, congratulations to you and, through you, to the men and women of 1 Canadian Air Group as you gather . . . to honour the venerable CF-104 aircraft.

The Starfighter has served Canada well during its distinguished 25-year history. Although unfairly maligned by the critics, I am advised that the aircraft was and is viewed as a «classic» by those who had the privilege to fly and to maintain her.

A review of recently released minutes from the Cabinet meeting of 30 June 1959 at which the decision to approve the purchase of the aircraft was made, indicates that the programme to re-equip the Air Force would take five years and that five years thereafter the Lockheed CF-104 would be ineffective. Thus the aircraft was expected to be phased out in 1969.

The fact that the CF-104 has continued to serve in many roles until 1986 is a further tribute to this magnificent aircraft and to the personnel of 1 Air Division and 1 CAG. It is only fitting that, even as the aircraft leaves Canadian service, it will continue to serve the cause of freedom in the Turkish Air Force.

I would be remiss if I did not use this occasion to also pay tribute to all who have flown, maintained and supported the CF-104 during its 25-year career. Their contribution to the preservation of the freedom we cherish has brought credit upon themselves, the Air Force and Canada. We are all very proud of the tradition of excellence which has characterized our Air Force in Europe. I am confident that, as you embark on the era of the CF-18 aircraft, you will continue to operate in that fine tradition.

As you gather in Baden to celebrate your accomplishments and to pay tribute to the Starfighter, I would ask you to pause and reflect and to remember those of your comrades who are not here to share your pride, your happiness and your feelings of nostalgia. I speak with special respect for those who gave their lives, during the era of the CF-104, in the service of their country. They died in time of peace; nevertheless their sacrifice and their honour is no less than those who gave their lives in time of conflict. I would ask you to use the honour of their memory to re-dedicate yourselves this weekend to the ideals for which they so unselfishly gave their lives.

In conclusion, may I reiterate the profound sense of pride and the debt of gratitude of all Canadians for the magnificent job you have done and continue to do for Canada.

Yours sincerely,

Home again. Two old friends made a return visit to Cold Lake in 1999 during the nation's largest military airshow in celebration of the 45th anniversary of the base and 75th anniversary of Canada's Air Force. CF-104850 (below) and CF-104632 (a dual) are now a privately owned airshow team in the United States. Former Starfighter pilots and technicians joined thousands of airshow fans who travelled from hundreds of miles away to take in the duo's appearance. The team also performed in Trenton and Abbotsford. (Dan Dempsey)

Canada's CF-5 Teams

The third Canadian fighter aircraft to make an appearance on the North American airshow scene in the 1970s and 80s was the CF-5 Freedom Fighter. Although it did not have the reputation of the Voodoo or Starfighter as a demonstration aircraft, it nevertheless generated a positive image of the Canadian Forces and was capable of putting on an exciting show. It was not uncommon to see all three aircraft types in the larger Canadian airshows over the 15 years that they were employed simultaneously. Having been introduced to the Canadian Forces in 1968, the CF-5 outlasted both the Voodoo and Starfighter teams, finally sharing the airshow stage with the aircraft that replaced all three combat aircraft, the CF-18 Hornet.

One similarity the CF-5 had with its counterparts was that it was easily capable of supersonic speeds and high-speed subsonic dashes therefore became standard fare for all CF-5 aerial demonstrations. It was an aesthetically pleasing aircraft in both solo and formation flight and its camouflage paint scheme gave it a decidedly "combat look." In some ways this belied its overall effectiveness as a tactical fighter, the common complaint being that the relatively small size of the aircraft limited both its conventional weapons load and combat radius.

Like the introduction of the Starfighter and its nuclear role earlier in the decade, the selection of the F-5 as a tactical combat aircraft for the RCAF was also steeped in controversy. Initially designated the N-156, it had been dismissed early in the selection process that eventually led to the procurement of the Starfighter. By the time the search began for a new ground support tactical fighter, the CF-104 assembly line at Canadair had ended. At the time, no one in the RCAF considered the F-5 a worthy candidate for the new tactical fighter for the same reasons it had been dismissed some six years earlier – it was simply too small for the RCAF's stated requirements and did not have the capabilities of its contemporaries. The RCAF still coveted the McDonnell F-4 Phantom II, a much larger and far more capable multi-role combat aircraft.

History of the Northrop F-5

Northrop engineer Welko Gasich had designed the F-5 as a lightweight, inexpensive supersonic fighter that, in theory at

least, could operate from shorter runways and secondary airstrips. The aircraft's final design included a streamlined "area rule" fuselage to facilitate supersonic airflow over the aircraft, thin wings with a span of 25 feet, 10 inches (7.87 metres) and an all-flying horizontal tailplane mounted low on the fuselage underneath twin engines. The power plant for production models consisted of two J-85-GE-13 turbojet engines, each having a maximum thrust of 4,080 pounds in afterburner designed to give the aircraft a top speed in the Mach 1.3 to 1.5 range. Aircraft armament was designed to incorporate two 20-mm M39 cannons in the upper nose plus the capability of carrying an AIM-9 Sidewinder heat-seeking missile on each wingtip along with a variety of conventional munitions on a centreline pylon and two pylon stations under each wing.

Northrop's overtures to the USAF and US Navy for its new fighter in 1955 met with disappointment as neither service perceived a need for such a lightweight fighter. However, in a prudent move that was to reap rich rewards, Northrop had also decided to propose a tandem seat supersonic trainer version of the aircraft under the designation N-156T with similar performance characteristics to the fighter version. In June 1956, the USAF announced that it would purchase the new supersonic trainer, designated the T-38 Talon, to replace its T-33 Silver Stars in the advanced training role.

Buoyed by this commitment, Northrop decided to also continue development of the fighter version as a private venture and on July 30th, 1959 the maiden flight of the N-156F took place at Edwards AFB in the hands of Northrop test pilot Lew Nelson. In spite of the fact that the prototype engines were non-afterburning, the aircraft still went supersonic on its first flight. Throughout the development and test phase, the company continued to seek foreign allies who might have a need for a more cost effective solution to their defence needs. Their efforts were rewarded by the new Kennedy administration in 1962 which pledged to support all American allies "in the

support and defense of freedom." The ensuing Military Assistance Program (MAP) and additional foreign military sales yielded a bonanza for Northrop as it went on to build 1,871 variants of the F-5. A further 776 aircraft would ultimately be manufactured under licence in Canada, Spain, Switzerland, South Korea and Taiwan. On August 9th, 1962 the N-156F was anointed the F-5A Freedom Fighter, with its tandem seat combat trainer counterpart being designated the F-5B.

Late in 1964, Northrop selected its eighth production model F-5B dual seat trainer (63-8445) as a demonstrator aircraft that began a tour of Europe and the Middle East in an attempt to attract new customers. The delegation to NATO was lead by senior test pilot Dan Darnell along with retired US Navy Capt Bob Elder who did much of the demonstration flying. By this time W/C Bob Christie was well ensconced in the NATO F-104G Starfighter program at SHAPE headquarters in Paris. He recalls that the

The first RCAF pilots to fly the Northrop F-5 both flew the same demonstration aircraft, W/C Bob Christie (top) in September 1964 and S/L Walt Niemy in January 1965. (RCAF Photos)

F-5B took the familiar hopscotch route to Europe via Goose Bay, Bluie West 1 (Greenland), Iceland, Scotland and into the USAF base at Evreux, France. It was at Evreux that Christie became the first RCAF pilot to fly the F-5B with Bob Elder on September 19th, 1964. Later asked to evaluate the F-5 and compare its merits as a combat fighter to the F-4 Phantom, Christie's assessment was that the F-5 paled in comparison! Apparently the major European NATO allies had drawn the same conclusion, Britain and West Germany opting for the F-4 and France sticking with its Mirage series of fighter bombers.

Of interesting historical note to the F-5 story is the fact that the aircraft did undergo a combat evaluation with the USAF in South Vietnam commencing on October 20th, 1965. Designated the *Skoshi Tiger Program*, a total of 18 F-5Cs (an upgraded, air refuelable version of the F-5A) conducted 3,500 combat

The first official PR shot of the Canadian government's choice for a new tactical fighter, the Northrop F-5, was taken in the company of Canadair's CL-41 Tutor basic jet trainer on 10 Sep 66. By this time, almost 190 Tutors destined for the RCAF had come off the Canadair assembly line. (Canadair C3343 via Bill Upton)

sorties in South Vietnam over a six month period. Based at Bien Hoa, the missions included close air support, interdiction and reconnaissance. In spite of some teething problems, the program was deemed a success with the relatively small size, speed and agility of the aircraft being credited for the loss of only two aircraft during the campaign. At the conclusion of the trial, the aircraft were handed over to the South Vietnamese Air Force. However, this did not mark the end of USAF involvement with the F-5. Between 1975 and 1987 a later and much improved variant of the aircraft, the F-5 E/F Tiger II, gained fame with aggressor squadrons of the USAF, US Marine Corps and, in particular, the USN Fighter Weapons School, "Top Gun."

Freedom Fighters for Canada

It was in July 1965 that the Canadian government announced that it had selected the Northrop F-5A as Canada's new tactical fighter aircraft. Although directly in opposition to the recommendations made by the RCAF selection team which favoured the Vought A-7 Corsair II as a fallback position to the F-4, the government decided to com-

promise performance for a lower cost fighter that would still reap industrial benefits for the country. To that end, just as had transpired with the F-86, T-33 and CF-104, the government announced that Canadair would be the primary contractor to build the new fighter under license from Northrop. In total, some 60 subcontractors shared the 215 million dollars earmarked for the program, including Orenda of Toronto which was awarded the contract to build the aircraft's engines. Designated the J85-CAN-15, they were up-rated to 4,300 pounds of static thrust in afterburner. To distinguish the Canadian-built aircraft from those manufactured by Northrop, the Canadian versions were designated the CF-5A and CF-5D (dual seat trainer).

Although the RCAF had identified the need for 200 aircraft, only 125 were initially ordered due to the fiscal restraints of the day. This number was subsequently reduced to 115 airframes due to inflation, made up of 89 CF-5As and 26 CF-5Ds. Having been given their marching orders, the RCAF resolved to make the best of an undesirable situation by working closely with Northrop and Canadair engineers to improve the Canadian version of the aircraft. For the most part, the prototype engi-

neering and test program to accomplish airworthiness certification was accomplished by Northrop in close consultation with a Canadair team headed by senior test engineer Jack Greeniaus. Canadair's program manager Frank Francis and production manager Andy Throner then wrestled with the production engineering challenges associated with the improvements. And the improvements were many. Taking full measure of the lessons learned in Vietnam by the USAF evaluation, improvements designed into Canadair's CF-5A included, in addition to the up-rated engines, a detachable inflight refuelling probe on the starboard side of the aircraft, auxiliary louvered air intake doors on either side of the rear fuselage to increase airflow during takeoff, a strengthened windshield for added protection against bird strikes, windscreen and engine inlet anti-icing, jettisonable underwing pylons, an arrestor hook for emergency landings, additional armour plating, an improved avionics package, an 87% increase in electrical generating capacity and a lead-computing Ferranti gyro-optical gunsight. To overcome the lengthy takeoff distances experienced by bomb-laden F-5s in Vietnam, the engineering team was able to reduce the distance by 25 percent through the introduction of an

Having previously manufactured and assembled the entire RCAF inventory of F-86 Sabres, T-33 Silver Stars, CF-104 Starfighters and CT-114 Tutors, Canadair Limited of Montreal was well placed to build the CF-5 for the Canadian Forces. The CF-5D assembly line in Plant 2 was in full swing in October 1968. (Canadair C4636 via Bill Upton)

increased to 240 to replace aircraft sold to Venezuela). The Dutch purchase also directly led to a strengthening relationship with the Canadian Forces when it was later announced that the Canadian Forces would train Dutch air force pilots from primary selection to the completion of advanced jet training on the CF-5. This highly successful program lasted 12 years, from 1971 until the end of 1983.

February 6th, 1968 was another memorable day for the engineers and technicians at Canadair as the first CF-5A (14701) rolled off the Cartierville assembly line. Like its CF-104 predecessor seven years earlier, the first prototype was also transported to Edwards AFB to undergo its test program. Northrop test pilot Hank Chouteau did the honours for the inaugural flight of the new fighter on May 10th, the aircraft having been reserialed as 116701. Unfortunately, the aircraft was subsequently lost in a crash on December 3rd. The third CF-5 off the assembly line was a dual-seat trainer (116801) which was the first to take off from Cartierville on August 28th, 1968.

Squadron Reductions

The deliveries of the first production model CF-5As had barely begun when operational planners of the newly unified Canadian Armed Forces were beset by the troubling news of further cuts to the national defence budget by the recently elected government of Prime Minister Pierre Elliott Trudeau. For the CF-5 fleet, this ultimately resulted in only 54 aircraft being put into service of the 115 originally built by Canadair. With the loss of a few aircraft during testing, some 55 brand new CF-5s were placed in storage in Trenton and North Bay after their initial flight testing, to be later rotated into operational service.

extendable nosewheel strut that increased the angle of attack on the wings by three degrees during takeoff, thus reducing liftoff speed. Finally, to enhance the flexibility of the aircraft in a combat environment, provision was also made for an interchangeable reconnaissance nose housing up to three 70-mm Vinten Model 547 high definition cameras.

Subsequent to the Canadian decision to equip with the CF-5, the government of the Netherlands announced on February 1st, 1967 that it too had negotiated a contract to have Canadair build 105 F-5s under the designation NF-5A and NF-5B. This was welcome news for Canadair as it brought the total number of F-5 orders to 220 (eventually

The first Canadian-built CF-5 to take to the skies above Montreal was a dual-seater, 116801, which lifted off from Cartierville on 28 Aug 68.

434 Sqn in Cold Lake, Alberta was the first of two operational CF-5 Sqns to be equipped with the new fighter. Shown here is a heavily laden CF-5A in an unlikely, but impressive pose – climbing vertically in afterburner configured for air-to-ground weapon's training – two "Station 85" fuel tanks with a SUU-20 practice bomb/rocket dispenser on the centreline. (Bob McIntyre)

Although the RCAF had originally envisioned at least four operational CF-5 squadrons, following the cutbacks only two squadrons were equipped with the new fighter under 10 Tactical Air Group of Mobile Command – 434 "Bluenose" Sqn in Cold Lake and 433 "Porcupine" Sqn in Bagotville. In addition to its operational role, 434 Sqn was also tasked with the training role for both squadrons. As such, it was the first to stand up with the new aircraft under the command of LCol O.B. Philp, fresh from his highly successful tour as commanding officer of the Golden Centennaires. The squadron was reactivated on February 15th, 1968. While their aircraft were being manufactured at Canadair, an initial cadre of 10 pilots proceeded to Williams AFB for 30 hours of F-5 training with the 4441st Combat Crew Training Squadron. However, it would be December before the first squadron CF-5D (116804) was flown into Cold Lake by LCol Philp and Maj M.D. "Johnny" Johnson. In the interim, the instructors honed their skills on the T-33. The first CF-5 training course, a pre-104 course, got underway in April 1969.

In Support of NATO

With the first course well underway, 433 Sqn pilots arrived at Cold Lake in May 1969 to commence their conversion training. They began receiving their own aircraft in Bagotville in August. Ultimately, both squadrons were earmarked as "rapid reactor" squadrons, to be deployable to Norway and the northern flank of NATO on short notice. The ability to deploy rapidly had been made possible when the Canadian Forces purchased five Boeing 707-320 strategic transport aircraft in 1972 and modified them to include an air refuelling capability. Over the years this resulted in many deployments to the northern flank by both squadrons where integrated operations with other NATO allies provided invaluable training. The CF-5 had the distinction of being the first Canadian fighter to utilize air-to-air refuelling to extend its operational range, the first such deployment of eight fighters from Bagotville to Andoya, Norway taking place on June 6th, 1973 during *Exercise Long Leap 1*.

From 1 CFFTS to 419 Tac Ftr (Trng) Sqn

In 1974 another important milestone took place in the evolution of the CF-5 in Canadian service. The venerable T-33 had

The three squadrons that flew the CF-5 tactical fighter during the aircraft's 27 years of service with the Canadian Forces.

been in service as an advanced jet trainer for over two decades when it was decided to replace it with the CF-5D in a similar role. No. 1 Canadian Forces Flying Training School (1 CFFTS) which was co-located in Cold Lake thereby became the bastion for conversion training to supersonic flight for pilots selected for advanced jet training after earning their wings. This helped relieve the pressure on 434 Sqn which up to that time had been responsible for both the conversion and tactical training. That pressure was relieved totally when 419 "Moose" Sqn, having been reactivated on November 1st, 1975, ultimately assumed the training roles of both 1 CFFTS and 434 Sqn. With its last basic fighter course graduating in early April, 434 Sqn was able to concentrate solely on its tactical fighter role.

Under a succession of fine commanding officers commencing with LCol Al "Red Lead" Brown and a very experienced staff, 419 Sqn became a highly spirited unit and vibrant member of CFB Cold Lake and the nearby communities of Grand Centre and Cold Lake. At its peak, the squadron establishment included over 40 CF-5s making the early morning and late evening flight lines an impressive sight. Sharing the skies with the CF-104s of 417 Sqn and fellow CF-5 pilots from 434 Sqn ensured there was plenty of squadron rivalry and "bar talk" on any given day.

Over a period of 20 years, the CF-5 proved to be an excellent transitional platform between the relatively benign CT-114 Tutor basic jet trainer and the high performance fighters then in use in the Canadian Forces – the CF-101 for air defence, CF-100 for the electronic warfare role and the CF-5 and CF-104 for conventional ground attack. From basic fighter manoeuvres (BFM) to dissimilar air combat training (DACT) to conventional weapons deliveries using bombs, rockets and guns, the CF-5 did it all. With the introduction of the CF-18 Hornet in 1982, air-to-air refuelling also became an important part of the training syllabus on the basic fighter course conducted by 419 Sqn.

The rigorous training regime and high G environment began to take a toll on the CF-5 fleet by the mid-1980s. To extend the life of the aircraft by several thousand hours, a major upgrade program was initiated in 1988 which saw 33 duals and 23 singles provided with strengthened wings and vertical stabilizers, new horizontal tailplanes, control surfaces and landing gear to extend the

Two views of the Northrop F-5B demo aircraft in RCAF colours in Sep 66. At left, test pilot S/L Walt Niemy (front seat) prepares for a flight with Northrop demo pilot Casey Finnegan. They are parked adjacent to Canadair's Plant 2 where the Canadian machines were later manufactured and assembled. Right, the aircraft touches down at Cartierville, Quebec. (Canadair Photos via Bill Upton)

service life of the aircraft. Then, in November 1990, in a move which seemed prudent and logical at the time, a decision was taken to put the same duals and 11 of the singles through an avionics upgrade program (AUP) that would make the CF-5 cockpit compatible with the CF-18, thereby reducing more expensive training hours on the latter. This was a complicated program which involved the installation of a heads-up display (HUD)/weapons-aiming system, inertial navigation system, HOTAS (hands on throttle and stick) controls, new air data computer and VHF radio all tied into a digital data bus. Both contracts were awarded to Bristol Aerospace Ltd. of Winnipeg.

The AUP program proved challenging as engineers and test pilots worked out the bugs of what was, for all intents and purposes, almost a new aircraft. Although the first AUP aircraft was not released to 419 Sqn for operational use until October 1993, by mid-1994 the squadron had 21 aircraft on strength. Long-time CF-5 instructors, most of whom had also flown the CF-18, immediately took to the revitalized aircraft and were pleasantly surprised to find that the HUD, upgraded inertial navigation and weapons system provided even better accuracy than the Hornet. The new aircraft were quickly integrated into the training syllabus and the first basic fight-

er pilot course of 1994 was able to complete the entire course on the new aircraft.

Then, in a paradox that has been the bane of Canadian military planners for decades, the roof fell in when more budget cuts befell the Department of National Defence. Early in 1995 it was announced that Fighter Group would be reduced by 25 percent. This forced a substantial number of operational CF-18s to be placed in storage with a resultant significant reduction in the number of cockpits available for Canadian fighter pilots. To preserve as many operational CF-18s as possible, the difficult decision was made to ground the entire CF-5 fleet and remove it from active service. By this time, 37 AUP aircraft had been completed and the program was suspended. The end came quickly – 419 squadron ceased CF-5 operations on March 31st, 1995 and was deactivated on June 25th, the Moosemen proceeding to new assignments. Although approximately a dozen of the upgraded CF-5s were subsequently sold to a foreign interest, the remainder seem destined for eternal storage. Thus, the CF-5 era in Canadian military service ended as it began, cloaked in controversy.

The CF-5 as an Airshow Performer

Once the Canadian government announced its decision to purchase the CF-5, airshow

organizers were quick to place requests for an inaugural public appearance of the new fighter. However, it would be the summer of 1970 before Canadian-built CF-5s would make their grand appearance. Prior to that time, appearances were at the courtesy of Northrop Corporation.

In the summer of 1966 the Northrop demo aircraft, now emblazoned with RCAF on its nose and a large Canadian flag on its tail, made a few select appearances in Canada. By this time Northrop had identified 19 international customers, mainly smaller nations, primarily through the US Military Assistance Program. The demonstrations in 1966, which included the country's largest shows at Abbotsford and Toronto, were designed to emphasize the speed and manoeuvrability of the aircraft and were flown by Northrop demo pilot Casey Finnegan. Accompanying Finnegan from Edwards AFB on this first F-5 demo in Canada was S/L Walt Niemy, the lead CF-5 test pilot from CEPE in Ottawa and a member of the F-5 evaluation team who had first flown F-5B 63-8445 on January 21st, 1965. The F-5 returned to Abbotsford in 1967 for the centennial extravaganza and was used as the lead-in act for the Golden Centennaires who closed the show on all three days. It was then once again on to the CNE for a repeat performance. By this time, a Northrop-built CF-5 single-seat test prototype (63-8421) had been adorned with RCAF colours for promotional purposes until Canadair's own CF-5s began coming off the assembly line in the summer of 1968.

The first Northrop-built CF-5A prototype (38421) was adorned in RCAF colours for Canada's Centennial year in 1967 and replaced 38445 as a test and demonstration aircraft. Note the trademark "X" on the tail denoting it as an experimental aircraft and the CEPE heraldic badge under the cockpit. (DND via Walter Niemy/Bill Upton)

A CF-5D from CFB Cold Lake made its first public appearance at Armed Forces Day Namao (Edmonton) in the summer of 1969. (Dan Dempsey)

The Schooner Formation Team 1970-1971

Capt Don Bergie (inset) leads Canada's first CF-5 demonstration team from 434 Tac Ftr Sqn, CFB Cold Lake in the summer of 1970. On his right wing is Capt Ken Mowbray, left wing Capt Tom Tilghman (USAF) and in the slot Capt Jake Miller. At right, a close-up of the team and a unique perspective of the eight-ship fighter package that got the 1970 Abbotsford Airshow off to a roaring start. (DND Photo via Terry Leversedge, AE 70-177-1, AE 70-177-2 via Don Bergie)

It was LCol Steve Gulyas, the second commanding officer of 434 Sqn in the CF-5 era, that received permission to form the squadron's first display team in the summer of 1970 under the leadership of Capt Don Bergie. Joining Bergie on the four-plane team were Capts Ken Mowbray on right wing and Tom Tilghman of the USAF on the left, Capt Jake Miller of Golden Centennaire fame flying the slot position. Bergie led the team through the first of seven practices on July 20th in preparation for their inaugural appearance at the Abbotsford Airshow on August 7th through 9th. Known simply as Schooner Formation, their show manoeuvres closely mirrored, and were integrated with, the finely tuned repertoire that had been established by the CF-104s of 417 Sqn in previous years. The end result was a spectacular debut for the benefit of Abbotsford patrons.

A similar 10-plane routine was repeated again the next year with a new set of players from 434 Sqn, as former team member George Adamson recalls:

"In the summer of 1971 the squadron flew another combined CF-5/CF-104 show at both Moose Jaw and Abbotsford as part of the large Canadian Forces display organized by Col O.B. Philp, then base commander at CFB Moose Jaw. The 434 team consisted of lead Capt Ron Clayton, No. 2 Capt Wally Peel, No. 3 Capt Barry Krall, No. 4 'yours truly' and No. 5, our solo, Capt Jake Miller. The 104 demo pilots were Capts Jordy Krastel, Eric Saunders, Bill Nesbitt, Ed Rozdeba plus Bill Stewart as the solo. This was a highly polished show which commenced with a combined big arrow formation after which we split up into our individual four-plane formations with the two solos filling the gaps. You can imagine that despite the big turning radii of these fast movers, there was always something at centre stage. I recall that we received many compliments about our act that summer."

George Adamson

The 1971 Schooner Formation team demonstrates the line-abreast formation and "dirty" diamond during their coordinated show with the Starfighters of 417 Sqn at Abbotsford. At right, the team taxis in following their performance at Moose Jaw. (Jerry Vernon, Dan Dempsey)

433 Sqn shows off their brand new CF-5 tactical fighters to the residents of Chatham during Armed Forces Day 1970. (DND CM70-2018)

The Saguenay Manics Formation Team

Having officially stood up on the CF-5 on September 26th, 1969 under the command of LCol Claude LaFrance at CFB Bagotville, 433 Sqn busied itself training to combat ready status as its new aircraft arrived from Canadair. The tactical mission scenarios assigned to the new fighter were many and varied, including ground attack, close air support, anti-shipping, photo reconnaissance and air superiority.

It was the summer of 1970 before the squadron had the opportunity to show off their new aircraft to the surrounding populace. In addition to flying flypasts as far away as Chatham, New Brunswick during Armed Forces Days, Capt Romeo Lalonde was authorized to put on solo performances at Bagotville and nearby Sherbrooke, Quebec. In comparison to the much larger Voodoos that local citizens were accustomed to seeing, Lalonde's performances in the CF-5 looked agile indeed as he darted about the sky.

Aside from simple flypasts requested for a variety of events, the first 433 Sqn formation demonstration team was assembled in 1971, calling themselves the Saguenay Manics. They performed a multitude of demonstrations over the summer. Venues in the province of Quebec included CFB Bagotville, Lac St Denis, *Man and His World* at Montreal, *Trois Rivières*, Quebec City, *Collège Militaire Royale de St Jean*, St. Agapit and Bromont. Forays outside the province saw the team perform shows at CFB Trenton and the CIAS in Toronto, two shows in New Brunswick (CFBs Chatham and Gagetown) and a very well received performance at Loring AFB in Maine. Like their counterparts at 434 Sqn in Cold Lake, this too was a five-plane team led by Capt Joe Gagnon. Right wing was flown by Capt Cole Harvey, left wing by Capt Romeo Lalonde with the slot being occupied by Capt Jean-Guy Beaumont. The solo for the team was Capt Denis Gauthier who would go on to become one of the squadron's most seasoned airshow pilots. Promoted to the rank of major, Gauthier put together a three-plane show for appearances in eastern Canada in the summer of '72 which stretched from Borden, Ontario (the birthplace of the RCAF) to the big maritime patrol base at Summerside, Prince Edward Island. The airshow season was just underway when Gauthier received a higher calling from his old boss from the Golden Centennaires, Col O.B. Philp.

Canadian Forces CF-5 Demonstration Team

Once again anointed the director of Canadian Forces airshows for 1972, Philp had continued to press his superiors to relax restrictions pertaining to formation aerobatics for his charges. Unbeknownst to many, his efforts were not directed solely for the benefit of his new demonstration team at Moose Jaw, the Snowbirds. Capt Wally Peel, a holdover from the 1971 434 Sqn CF-5 team explains:

"For the 1972 season, Col Philp gained approval to form an aerobatic CF-5 demonstration team as part of a bigger and better Canadian Forces airshow extravaganza that would be featured at four major Canadian shows that summer. The previous season's 'Slanted Snowbirds' became partially aerobatic this year with the addition of two aerobatic solos, although team leader Glen Younghusband was still officially restricted to wingovers and slanted loops with the formation. However, our CF-5 team was authorized to do four-plane formation rolls. The team was politically driven by including members from both 434 and 433 Sqns. We continued to perform an integrated show with the 417 Sqn CF-104 team (now led by Capt Gord Todd) as had been done in the previous two years. For unknown reasons, our CF-5 team was the only one authorized to do rolls. Our show consisted of a four-ship take-off, box roll, arrowhead roll, dirty box with high-speed solo overtake and a final box pass

Formed in 1971, the Saguenay Manics were the first of many CF-5 display teams formed by 433 Sqn. L to R – Capt Joe Gagnon (team leader), Capt Cole Harvey (right wing), Capt Romeo Lalonde (left wing), Capt Jean-Guy Beaumont (slot), Capt Denis Gauthier (solo). (DND Photo via Romeo Lalonde)

flown towards the crowd. Our landing recovery was from a low-level echelon, one second break for landing.

The 433 Sqn contribution to the team comprised the team leader, Maj Denis Gauthier, and Capt Jean-Guy Blouin who flew as No. 2. Selected to the team from 434 Sqn were Len 'Igor' Harding as No. 3, myself as No. 4 and the incomparable Jake 'The Snake' Miller as our solo. Consequently, the individuals or 'team-halves' were required to practice at their separate bases and then meet for a few days to prepare as a four-ship prior to an airshow appearance. As our show included formation rolls, some naysayers believed we were an accident looking for a place to happen. At Bagotville, preparation was relatively straightforward as Blouin was practicing on the real leader's wing. At Cold Lake, however, Igor and I practiced with Jake leading, Igor on the left wing with me in line-astern. Now, when was the last time anyone had seen Jake leading guys through rolls? It had been over four years since his aerobatic duet with René Serrao during Centennial year and Jake had been flying the much heavier Voodoo at the time. As it turned out, Jake was an outstanding lead but was much slower in the execution of his rolls than Denis turned out to be. In fact, Jake loved leading us on cross-countries and even more so to put me on the right wing for an occasional vic roll at any airport where he could gain approval. Ultimately, Igor and I found it easier to do the airshow manoeuvres with Denis' faster roll rate which significantly reduced the risks created by not having much practice time with him.

A brief anecdote from the first 'full team' practice illustrates the difference between the

The 1972 Canadian Forces CF-5 display team was authorized formation rolls in addition to a fully aerobatic solo show. L to R – Capt Jake Miller (434 Sqn), Capt Jean-Guy Blouin (433 Sqn), Capt Wally Peel (434 Sqn), Maj Denis Gauthier (433 Sqn), Capt Len Harding (434 Sqn). (via Wally Peel)

roll techniques flown by Denis and Jake. The '433 half' came to Cold Lake in preparation for our first show at Moose Jaw. After the first roll, it was obvious that hanging onto Denis was considerably easier than onto his proxy, Jake. Jake used a much slower roll rate which necessitated a slight bunt through the inverted portion. After a few rolls, Denis asked Jake to lead the four-ship so Denis could sit back behind the formation and see how we looked. Igor and I were obviously anxious to see how Jean-Guy would do when confronted with his surprise; so here we go – a slight pull-up, the roll starts, approaching inverted – and suddenly only Igor and I are left as the regular Cold Lake three-ship, the phantom No. 2 reappearing again on the right wing down the backside of the roll. After a few more rolls with Jake, Jean-Guy was able to hang on just fine. Notwithstanding these initial trials, the team got its act together and performed beautifully at Moose Jaw (July 15th-16th), Abbotsford (August 11th-13th),

Moncton (August 18th-19th) and Toronto (September 1st-4th). My logbook shows a total of 62.8 hours of flying time in support of airshows in the summer of '72.

Indeed, as we fighter guys saw it, the 1972 airshow circuit was the culmination of Col O.B.'s persistent drive to have the Snowbirds rightfully become the dedicated demonstration team to represent the Canadian Forces. The involvement of the CF-5, CF-104 and CF-101 in any kind of a combined fighter team was seen by us to conclude at the end of '72. Consequently, at the CNE in Toronto, we saw an opportunity to do something unique after the last show with the three fighter teams and the C-130 Hercules that was also participating in the show. We proposed a plan to the Herc crew (whose names I regret not recording) and they readily agreed. The result of this 'conspiracy' was to have the Hercules lead the three fighter teams in box formation over Trenton in lov-

Maj Denis Gauthier leads his very tight diamond through a roll during the summer of '72. Seemingly welded to him are right winger Jean-Guy Blouin, left winger Len Harding and slotman Wally Peel. At right, Jake Miller screams past the Paine Field crowd venting fuel as he pushes negative G in a close pass. (Jake Miller, Bill Johnson)

A CFB Trenton based C-130 Hercules leads the fighter component of the Canadian Forces 1972 airshow team in this "one-of-a-kind" flypast on 4 Sep 72 in tribute to their boss, Col O.B. Philp. (DND Photo via Wally Peel)

ing honour of Col O.B. However, using great fighter-pilot logic, we decided that we would not ask for approval, rather keeping our flypast a surprise by suddenly flying down the runway in this grand formation. After our last show on September 4th, we joined up and staggered down the runway at a speed more conducive to the Herc than any fighter. Upon our arrival at the mess for the customary post-show debriefing, we were commanded onto the parade square for 'farewell' remarks from the boss. During that memorable occasion, Col O.B. made those members who had participated in the unapproved pass wonder if our careers were in jeopardy. As he concluded his lecture however, and given no incident had transpired, he did find a smile, allowing that 'the pass did look good.'"

Wally Peel

The year 1972 did indeed mark the end of the combined CF-5/CF-104 shows as predicted. So too ended the experiment of the combined 433 and 434 CF-5 team with its unique aerobatic authorization. In 1973 the Snowbirds were granted permission to conduct nine-plane formation aerobatics under their new team leader, Maj George Miller, thus becoming the only military aerobatic team in the country. However, with the airshow business in North America booming and the demands for Canadian Forces participation remaining high, there was still a requirement for so-called regional teams to fill many of the public relations requests that the Snowbirds could not accommodate. With the two CF-5 squadrons becoming increasingly involved with training deployments all over North America and frequently to Europe, it became increasingly difficult for the squadrons to

generate part-time airshow teams. This was particularly true for 434 Sqn which became something of a political football, enduring moves from Cold Lake to Bagotville and finally to Chatham, New Brunswick during the CF-5 era. As a result, from 1975 onwards CF-5 airshow appearances were generally handled on an east-west basis when operational circumstances permitted, with 433 Sqn fulfilling requests from Ontario east and 1 CFFTS, latterly 419 Sqn, taking care of airshow requests from Manitoba west.

The Incomparable Soloist

As any airshow performer will attest, it is the pilot behind the machine that really defines the success of a solo airshow performance. Military or civilian, they come in all shapes and sizes, not always in the "steely-eyed" image airshow fans might visualize. The one common denominator among all performers however, is a love of flight that motivates them to display their passion week-in-and-week-out during the long airshow season. For many it is a mere snapshot in their lives; for others it becomes a way of life.

It had been the summer of 1970 before 434 Sqn was able to form a part-time CF-5 display team to perform at selected airshows. The pilot who would come to be designated the squadron's solo display pilot was Capt Jake Miller who had gained considerable fame for his CF-101 displays with the Golden Centennaires. Given his previous airshow experience, Miller was authorized a fully aerobatic display in the CF-5. Those familiar with his flying abilities were not surprised when he came up with a sterling routine that many regard as the finest CF-5 display ever flown. If exceptionally tight loops and Cuban-eights were not enough, Miller's low-

Soloist Capt Jake Miller is congratulated by the CO 434 Tac Ftr Sqn, LCol Pete Howe, on the completion of his 1,000th hour in the CF-5 on 5 Jul 72. Miller is sporting the standard fighter pilot attire of the day – parachute, Mae West and G-suit. At right, he closes the gun bay of his CF-5A in preparation for a performance at Paine Field, Washington. (DND EN72-328-2 via Glen Miller, Nancy Johnson)

CANADIAN FORCES BASE COLD LAKE COURIER

Weatherman Cooperates to Make the Day a Success
CFB Cold Lake Welcomes 10,000 Visitors for Armed Forces Day 76

BY RON SMART

Saturday, June 26th saw CFB Cold Lake open the doors as they presented Armed Forces Day 76. Approximately 10,000 persons took in the shower-marred action as the stream of onlookers edged on to the hangar line for the static displays which opened at 11 am. At 12 Noon, airshow organizer Maj J. Callaghan gave the "Go Ahead" and the flying events got underway at 1:30 pm commencing with a superb 16-plane flypast led by LCol A. Bossman, Commanding Officer of 417 Squadron. The flypast consisted of 4 CF-104s of 417 squadron, 4 CF-5s each from 434 and 419 Squadrons, and 2 T-33s each from Base Flight and AETE.

Although skies were threatening most of the afternoon, the weatherman managed to have it hold out long enough for the highlights of the show. The inclement weather marred the Skyhawks' free fall jumps from 10,000 feet, however team leader Capt Phil Campbell, 27, of Edmonton gave the jump order and the 'Hawks' made two jumps from just below the base of the cloud at 2,500 feet in an impressive display of parachuting. With red smoke canisters attached to their ankles the Skyhawks floated to precision landings in front of the display area.

Capt Jake "the Snake" Miller put on a superb CF-5 solo to surpass all others. Although limited by overcast conditions, Capt

Miller managed to push the aircraft to its limits, and himself also. In his opening manoeuvre, Jake rolled (into a) 7 G load force as he put the aircraft into a 360 degree turn finishing with a continuing outbound spiral.

One of the most thrilling highlights of the afternoon was the bombing display put on by Capts Frank Thorne and Bruce Watson in CF-104s and Capt Don Esperson and Maj Ray Sawchuck in the CF-5s … When it looked as if the world was going to fall in, along with an ensuing storm, somebody must have said a prayer, because a huge gaping hole appeared in the heavens just in time for the stage performance of the Armed Forces "Snowbirds." The 'Birds led by Maj Denis Gauthier seem to supersede their previous efforts every time they fly. This year's programme of loops and turns is the result of many hours of work by both pilots and their groundcrew. Compliments go out to both crews and solos Ken Carr and "Speedy" Fast for another exciting, flawless performance.

Many thanks go out to all sections involved for a super airshow and to the organizing committee led by Maj Callahan …

Cold Lake *Courier*, July 1976

An excerpt of the glowing report on Armed Forces Day 1976 by Cold Lake's base newspaper, the *Courier*. (via Glen Miller)

level inverted passes and series of rapid rolls (as many as eight in succession) flown the length of a showline were high testament to his flying skills. As fellow CF-5 airshow pilot Denis Gauthier later recalled, "The man didn't need many dials to fly!" And fly Miller did. With the airshow bug in his blood he had begun practicing an airshow routine in the summer of '69 in the hope he might be able to get back onto the airshow circuit. Although the training demands of the squadron would prevent that from happening that year, in a parting gesture of respect from his old boss, O.B. Philp designated Miller to pick up the first single seat CF-5A from Canadair (116707) and fly it to Cold Lake on October 29th. From that point forward the "single seater" became Miller's aerobatic aircraft of choice. It was also in one of his favourite airshow aircraft (116724) that Miller later set a

new west-to-east Canadian speed record on May 2nd, 1970 during *Operation Bluenose* when he flew from Vancouver to Halifax (with re-fuelling stops in Gimli and Val d'Or) in an amazing 4 hours, 23 minutes and 53 seconds. His average speed during the 2,800 mile (4,480 km) flight was 636 mph (1,018 km/hr). Also establishing another impressive record going the other way on July 1st was fellow squadron pilot Capt Pat Pattison who covered the distance westbound (into wind) in 5 hours, 34 minutes and 21 seconds.

Jake Miller went on to dazzle airshow crowds across Canada at shows large and small for four successive years in the CF-5 (1970-1973), performing as far west as Comox, British Columbia and as far east as Moncton, New Brunswick. Following his last show of the '73 season at Minot, North

Dakota, most of Miller's flying was devoted to the art of teaching students the intricacies of air-to-ground and air-to-air combat, dozens benefiting from his expertise. He did manage to squeak in a few more airshow performances for old times sake – Cold Lake in 1976, El Toro, California in 1978 and Whitehorse, Yukon in 1979 during that city's famous week of fun known as "Sourdough Days." Eventually, Father Time caught up with the man who loved to fly upside-down. Jake Miller flew his last trip in the CF-5 on March 27th, 1981, his meticulously recorded logbook revealing exactly 2,836 hours flown on the CF-5 of the more than 6,500 hours he logged on military jet aircraft during his career – more than enough to make any fighter pilot proud. Jake passed away in the summer of 2000 near the base he loved, his airshow legacy secure.

The Bagotville Teams

The Saguenay Manics

Given the popularity of their inaugural team in 1971, 433 Sqn continued to field airshow demonstration teams virtually every year through 1983. Although the teams appeared under a number of different guises, each reflected the affinity all air force personnel who have served at CFB Bagotville felt with the beautiful Saguenay region of the province of Quebec. Maj Denis Gauthier continued to lead the Saguenay Manics in 1973 and 1974 but on a smaller scale with only two aircraft. Nevertheless, the team still performed 13 shows in 1973 and Gauthier performed several shows the following summer prior to leaving the squadron for points west, namely Moose Jaw, Saskatchewan. His extensive CF-5 airshow experience had led to his selection to replace George Miller as team leader of the Snowbirds for the 1975 and 1976 seasons.

The Saguenay Manics took to the air again in 1973 with a two-ship team flown by Capt Mike King (left) and team leader Maj Denis Gauthier. (DND Photo via Romeo Lalonde)

The Saguenay Expos

For the 1975 season the decision was taken to once again expand 433 Sqn's demonstration team to five CF-5As under the command of Maj Roger Maltais. Joining him were Capts Claude Thibault (right wing), Ray Ferguson (left wing), Bill Boucher and later Richard Brosseau (slot) and George Hawey (solo). Although the team flew only eight shows at four venues that summer, one of the most interesting characteristics of the personnel involved is that five of the six would continue their involvement with airshows for a good part of their careers. Roger Maltais would go on to lead the Vikings Tutor team in Moose Jaw and become a strong supporter of both the Snowbirds and "his" own Warlocks Voodoo team after he later took command of 425 Sqn. Ray Ferguson went on to instruct at

419 Sqn and would later lead the Rut Zulus CF-5 team. Similarly, Richard Brosseau, who came to be affectionately known as "Bross" throughout the fighter world, would fly on five different CF-5 teams during his stints with 433 Sqn and later 419 Sqn. Claude Thibault was also a future leader of the Rut Zulus in Cold Lake and most importantly a pivotal supporter of the Snowbirds during his tenure as base commander at Moose Jaw from 1988 to 1990. Finally, George Hawey, having already spent two seasons flying with the Snowbirds, would return to lead the team in 1983-1984, even then staying on to render his support as the base operations officer at Moose Jaw under Claude Thibault.

Aside from the serious business of demonstrating high performance aircraft in close proximity to spectators which demands rigid discipline to effect a safe performance, there is another lighter side that makes participation on an airshow team something special.

It is the camaraderie established among team members that creates a bond that is unique among aviators. These bonds are solidified on the ground after the pressures of the show are over and it is time to reflect on one's good fortune (or prowess as the case may be) in a more relaxing environment. Humorous situations also often develop unexpectedly which contribute to lasting memories, as Claude Thibault explains:

"Our main shows in Quebec in the summer of '75 were of course the Bagotville airshow and another big show at St Jean which we flew from Dorval Airport in Montreal (since St. Hubert was closed for runway repairs). On the day of the Bagotville show, we got our show in over the base and then rejoined with a 707 tanker. We were to make a pass over the airfield with the tanker but the deteriorating weather got so bad that we proceeded to St Jean for a low pass followed by a landing at Dorval. With Bagotville now closed, we of course found ourselves with no travel bags! It was St Jean Baptiste weekend and we dearly wanted to go into town. We therefore called Bagotville and had Bob Bruce deliver us some clothes in a single once the weather had cleared up. While we were waiting impatiently, I related a story to the others about how I had once had my wife pack my bags when I was running late for a trip. When I reached the other end, I had everything required, except a pair of pants. As I don't quite dress 'off the rack,' it was not easy to find a substitute pair. Well, when Bob showed up we all anxiously checked our bags. We were all okay – except for George Hawey who had everything he needed – except pants (much to his chagrin)! Having learned my lesson, I was the only one with two pairs, so I lent one to George. Well, the waist was fine, but the bottom of the legs came halfway to his knees, a fact which we did not hesitate pointing out for the rest of the evening ..."

Claude Thibault

In 1975 the 433 Sqn demo team adopted a new name, the Saguenay Expos. Team members were, L to R – Lead Maj Roger Maltais, No. 2 Capt Claude Thibault, No. 3 Capt Ray Ferguson, No. 4 Capt Bill Boucher, Solo Capt George Hawey. (DND Photos via Claude Thibault)

The Saguenay Expos of 1976 and 1977 were led by a new leader, Maj Len Couture. The 1976 season was a great success with the five-ship performing at nine locations including inaugural appearances at the London International Air Show and a large American show at Plattsburg AFB, New York. The following season was to be one of mixed success however. The team performed a four-plane show at CFB Bagotville and then ventured to the East Coast where they appeared at Sydney, Nova Scotia and Summerside, Prince Edward Island. Now in his third season with the team, Capt Richard Brosseau started off the show in his regular slot position but then broke off to conduct solo manoeuvres in-between the formation passes. In preparation for the annual CNE show in Toronto, higher priorities resulted in the team being reduced to two aircraft. Brosseau was tasked to lead the team with Larry Kinch (formerly Expo 3 in the four-ship) as his wingman. Then, on August 10th, 1977, disaster struck when Kinch's aircraft

Capt Richard Brosseau flew on five CF-5 display teams during his career and was 433 Sqn's solo pilot in 1977. (DND Photo)

inexplicably plunged into the St. Lawrence River off of Forestville, Quebec during a practice. No cause for the accident was ever determined. With insufficient time to work up a new wingman, Rick Brosseau finished the season as a solo performer, upholding the squadron's reputation at shows in Bagotville and Goose Bay, Labrador as well as the four shows he flew at the CNE, all to very positive reviews.

The year 1978 saw *les porcupics* revive another four-ship team initially led once again by Len Couture. His lasting contribution to the team was a new manoeuvre which was euphemistically labelled the "Caca Formation." Designed to characterize the formation flying of student pilots, it involved his four wingmen flying with significant cross-control of aileron and rudder which gave the formation a most unusual

appearance, an obvious off-shoot of the crazy old formation flown by the Goldilocks Harvard team in the early '60s. Still, the symmetry achieved by the wingmen was quite remarkable considering the very sensitive rudder of the CF-5 which was easily capable of rapidly rolling the aircraft 360 degrees around its lateral axis, a lesson taught early in the CF-5 training syllabus at Cold Lake. Shortly after introducing the manoeuvre, Couture handed the reins of the team to Capt Denis Rivard for the bulk of the airshow season. Rivard led his team to all of the traditional airshows in eastern Canada but was also tasked to put on displays for some unusual visitors to Canada that summer – a military delegation from China and another from the Vietnamese Air Force.

One young fighter pilot who spent three seasons flying with the 433 Sqn demonstration team prior to being rewarded with a two year exchange tour to France on the Mirage III fighter/bomber was Lt Jacques Thibaudeau. He recalls some fond memories from over 20 years ago:

Maj Len Couture leads the Saguenay Expos in their celebrated "Caca" formation over another CF-5A Freedom Fighter. The pilots flying this challenging formation are, L to R – Jacques Thibaudeau, Jean Egan, Len Couture, Chuck Caron and Mag Dumais. (DND Photo via Jacques Thibaudeau)

The Saguenay Expos on the ramp at CFB Trenton on 23 Sep 78. L to R – Lt Jacques Thibaudeau, Capt Jean Egan, Capt Denis Rivard (team leader), Lt Mag Dumais. (DND TN 78-5261 via Jacques Thibaudeau)

June 16th and 17th was a relatively new "international" show at the Mount Hope Airport in Hamilton, Ontario. With the airport being home to the Canadian Warplane Heritage collection, the CF-5 display added a sharp contrast to the beautiful array of restored warbirds that took to the air over the weekend. One week later, another special show

The 1979 Saguenay Pogos carried on the fine traditions of their predecessors. L to R, Top – Maj Rick Bastien (team leader), Capt Mitch Boivin. Bottom – Lt Jacques Thibaudeau, Capt Chuck Caron. (DND Photos via Jacques Thibaudeau)

"My introduction to air displays took place in 1978 when I was posted to 433 Sqn as a pipeliner, my first operational posting after completing fighter training. In those days, every operational fighter squadron had a dedicated airshow team which performed at five to 10 showsites each summer and of course the Snowbirds were very popular across the country. I had been motivated from a young age to join the air force after watching these teams perform and I can recall being very impressed with the way Capt Rick Brosseau handled the CF-5 during his solo demonstrations. Therefore, as soon as I got a chance, I volunteered to fly with the 433 Sqn team, doing so during each of the 1978, 1979 and 1980 airshow seasons.

Our show on the CF-5 was very similar to those I had watched the Rut Zulus perform at Cold Lake during my basic fighter training. It consisted of several high-speed passes in various formations, including a four-ship echelon, diamond and line-abreast pass. At this stage No. 4 would break off, complete a manoeuvre and then set up to chase down the three-ship 'V' formation which had slowed to minimum speed with the gear and flaps down. The solo would also usually perform a high G, minimum radius 360 degree turn in front of the crowd and a knife-edge pass the length of the showline. Our final manoeuvre of the show was an upward bomb burst head-on to the crowd followed by a rejoin and fan break to landing.

To get the maximum benefit from each sortie, we often conducted a low-level tactical mission prior to our shows which was carefully planned to have us arrive at the showsite precisely at the predetermined time. One local show which lent itself very well to this option was the annual air display at the nearby Chicoutimi marina each June. It was always a special pleasure doing a full air display over the Saguenay River in front of downtown Chicoutimi and thousands of local residents. I can also recall doing extended missions which involved air-to-air refuelling with one of our B-707 tankers followed by an airshow. On these occasions, normally associated with larger shows such as Trenton and Ottawa, we would do a low flypast with the tanker which was also very popular.

These were wonderful years for me and paved the way for future airshows when I later converted to the CF-18 Hornet."

Jacques Thibaudeau

The Saguenay Pogos

Another new four-plane team was born in Bagotville in 1979 under the leadership of Maj Richard Bastien. Known as the Saguenay Pogos, they enjoyed a very successful season with eight shows completed at six locations. One show that was particularly pleased to welcome the CF-5 contingent on

took place at CFB Bagotville to commemorate 10 years of operational service for the CF-5 with the Canadian Forces. The Pogos ended their season on October 14th in Nova Scotia at the CFB Greenwood Airshow.

The Saguenay Québec

In 1980 the 433 Sqn CF-5 team adopted a new and final name that would see the team through to the end of the CF-5 airshow era for the squadron. Maj Marc Dumontet was the first leader of the Saguenay Québec and was succeeded by Maj Jean Boyle who led

A CF-5A of the Saguenay Québec presents an interesting size comparison with the CF-101 Voodoos of the 425 Sqn Warlocks, both teams having flown in the 1983 Trenton airshow. Clearly evident on the CF-5 are the fluorescent strips on the nose, tip tanks and vertical fin which enabled the aircraft to fly close formation at night. (Larry Milberry)

The 1980 Saguenay Québec were also featured on a public relations poster to advertise their shows in eastern Canada. L to R – Maj Marc Dumontet, Capt Reg Décoste, Capt Dan Leboeuf, Capt Mitch Boivin. (DND Photos via Jacques Thibaudeau)

his team to several shows, including the 1981 Canadian International Air Show in Toronto. Maj Bob Archambault was the last to have the privilege of leading a four-ship version of the team around eastern Canada in 1982. In 1983, the team was reduced to two aircraft as 433 Sqn yielded some of the airshow spotlight to their colleagues at 434 Sqn. Nevertheless, former Snowbird Maj Yves Bossé still led the 433 contingent through a total of seven displays flown at three major airshows – the CIAS in Toronto, CFB Trenton Armed Forces Day and the Shearwater International Air Show in Nova Scotia. Aside from a few single-ship shows flown in 1984, this ended 433 Sqn's airshow appearances in the CF-5. However, the squadron would soon return to the forefront with a shiny, new performer – the McDonnell Douglas CF-18.

The Schooner Bluenose

Having given up their CF-5 training responsibilities totally by April 1976, 434 Sqn became engrossed in their full-fledged role as a tactical fighter squadron, handing most of the airshow tasking in western Canada to 1 CFFTS, latterly 419 Sqn. This did not take the "Bluenosers" totally out of the limelight however. Aside from a myriad of exercises

and deployments, the squadron made the news on November 7th, 1976 when two CF-5s flew non-stop from Comox, British Columbia to Shearwater, Nova Scotia with the assistance of a B-707 tanker from 437 Sqn. It was the first such non-stop flight of Canadian fighters in history and necessitated three mid-air refuellings to make the distance. LCol Scott Clements and Capt Rod Sword covered the distance in 4 hours, 29 minutes and 17 seconds, an impressive demonstration of tactical mobility that was greeted with appropriate fanfare in Halifax. By producing a first-day flight cover in conjunction with the mission, the squadron was also able to publicize 25 years of active service for 434 Sqn which received its Queen's Air Standard the following summer.

Following their move from CFB Cold Lake to Bagotville in July 1982, the Bluenosers returned to the airshow scene with a demonstration team for the 1983 airshow season. Squadron commanding officer LCol George Macdonald appointed veteran fighter pilot (and former Snowbird) Capt Dave Wilson to lead the team. As it transpired, this would be the last four-plane team for the squadron, notwithstanding a very successful season which saw the team perform in London, Gimli, Moose Jaw (much to the chagrin of the Rut Zulus), Bagotville, Bangor and Kitchener.

With the exception of the Snowbirds, airshow activity across the Canadian Forces was severely curtailed for display teams in 1984, although Maj George Landry did manage a few two-ship shows with wingman Capt Steve Whitely. Hopes to form a team in 1985 did not materialize due to continued restrictions which saw the authorization of only one CF-5 demo team, the Rut Zulus of 419 Sqn winning that honour. Besides, 434 was on the move again, this time to

Capt Dennis Beselt was the last 434 Sqn pilot to demo the CF-5 in 1985. (via 419 Sqn)

Chatham, New Brunswick to fill the void on the base left by the retirement of the CF-101 Voodoo from operational service. However, 434 Sqn was authorized a solo demo pilot to help fulfill airshow requests in eastern Canada that continued to inundate Air Command. These were flown by Capt Dennis Beselt, another ex-Snowbird who was later destined to return to lead the team. Beselt's logbook records a total of nine shows in 1985. Aside from the two shows flown at the ever-popular London International Air Show, the remainder were

Public relations are by no means confined to airshows. Capt Rod Sword and LCol Scott Clements (CO 434 Tac (F) Sqn) pause for a photo in Comox prior to their historic non-stop flight across Canada in 1976. At right, the first-day cover that was flown coast-to-coast. (via Rod Sword)

all military shows hosted by the Canadian Forces at Trenton, Bagotville, Goose Bay, Greenwood and Shearwater.

The conclusion of the 1985 airshow season in Canada marked the end of the road at airshows for CF-5s bearing the "Bluenose" tail stripe. The last commanding officer of the squadron in the CF-5 era, LCol Tom Henry, explains:

"For the last two years of the squadron's life as a tactical fighter squadron, from August 1986 to July 1988, we did not field a demonstration team. The Fighter Group appetite for airshows at that time was pretty weak given the serviceability problems the fleet had encountered and the overriding necessity of maintaining our operational commitments. Even after our serviceability increased, we still fought hard to achieve our training requirements. We were able to fly a couple of flypast-type displays in the Maritimes but did not work up a team or do any solo aero displays. Our last claim to fame was a nine-plane diamond flown over all of the major centres of New Brunswick for public relations and morale purposes in July 1988 – one final salute to over 20 continuous years of CF-5 tactical operations for the Bluenose Squadron."

Tom Henry

At right, Capt Dave Wilson leads the Schooner Bluenose through their dynamic routine in the summer of '83. (via 434 Sqn)

Below, the Schooner Bluenose demonstration team flew four standard CF-5A tactical fighters, the squadron emblem clearly visible on the tail fins of the aircraft. (DND Photo via Terry Leversedge)

The Cold Lake Teams

The Cobras

Having taken over the role of advanced jet training for Canadian Forces pilots from the T-33 Silver Star, it did not take the new CF-5 instructors at 1 CFFTS long to get their feet wet on the airshow circuit. Selected to lead the unit's demonstration team was Maj Bill Worthy, a veteran of two tours on the Starfighter with 444 and 417 Sqns, the latter having included membership on the 1969 Starfighter demo team. Joining him were Capt Dave Wilson, having moved over from 434 Sqn, and three additional wingers who had all served in the Air Division on the CF-104 with 430 Strike Attack Sqn, namely Capts Al Currie, Glenn Heaton and Maj Gord Hatch. The team simply adopted the moniker used by the school, The Cobras, and were supported by a contingent of five groundcrew personnel.

Although training requirements had clear priority, the team was able to work up a fine routine using four CF-5D dual seaters that was popular with airshow fans and highly motivational for the budding fighter pilots eager to join the ranks of Canada's opera-

1 CFFTS was quick to form its first CF-5 demonstration team in 1974. Standing beside a school aircraft are the team pilots, L to R – Capt Al Currie, Capt Dave Wilson, Capt Glenn Heaton, Maj Bill Worthy (team leader), Maj Gord Hatch. Accompanying them are some of the dedicated technicians that kept the team flying safely throughout the summer. (DND Photo via Bill Worthy)

tional CF-104, CF-101 and CF-5 squadrons. The team continued into 1975 with Bill Worthy at the helm but with a new set of wingmen and groundcrew to give as many staff instructors and groundcrew as possible

The shoulder badges worn by the staff and students of 1 Canadian Forces Flying Training School in 1974 and 1975 until the school was disbanded and replaced by 419 Tac Ftr (Trng) Sqn. (author's collection)

Maj Gord Hatch captured this beautiful portrait of the Cobras led by Maj Bill Worthy in the summer of '74. Right wing is being flown by Capt Dave Wilson, left wing by Capt Al Currie and the slot by Capt Glenn Heaton. The Rut Zulus formed in 1976 at 419 Sqn were a direct descendent of this team. (Gord Hatch)

The standard conversion training configuration of Canada's CF-5D fighter trainers is revealed in this 1974 shot of the Cobras. The CF-5D was weapons capable with bombs and rockets but did not carry the 20 mm cannon, the space being required for the second seat. (Gord Hatch)

The Rut Zulus

Having taken command of 1 CFFTS in the summer of 1975 following a tour of duty on 434 Sqn, LCol Al Brown was honoured to stand up 419 Tactical Fighter Training Squadron only a few months later as its first commanding officer in the CF-5 era. Like many of his compatriots of the day, Brown fully understood the importance of "Armed Forces Days" in fostering a professional image and understanding of military roles for the nation's citizens. Thus, when Maj Doug Stuart, his deputy commanding officer and operations

The shoulder badges proudly worn by all 419 Sqn personnel and the Rut Zulus during the CF-5 era. (author's collection)

the opportunity to partake in this most enjoyable "secondary" duty. Major shows in 1975 included the large military shows at Moose Jaw, Edmonton and North Bay. However, this was to be the end of 1 CFFTS's brief foray with the CF-5. In a move designed to preserve the history and heritage of Canada's operational squadrons, it had been decided that the famous "Moose" squadron of Fulton and Mynarski fame would be reactivated and replace 1 CFFTS. But while this development led to the demise of the Cobras, it marked the beginning for a new demonstration team, the Rut Zulus.

The second (and last) edition of the Cobras CF-5 demonstration team flew in 1975. L to R, Standing – Maj Bill Worthy (team leader), Maj Doug Stuart, Maj George Adamson. Kneeling – Capt Paul Deacon, Capt Ted Delange. Majs Stuart and Adamson formed the nucleus of the Rut Zulus in 1976. The unsung heros behind any demonstration team are its technicians. They work largely unnoticed behind the scenes with little of the fanfare and none of the glory. At right, the road crew that kept the Cobras flying safely in Edmonton and Moose Jaw. L to R, Standing – Cpl J.L. Boudreau, Pvt Kostyan, MCpl J.R. Hunter. Kneeling – Cpl C.W. Hills, Pvt J.D. Martin. (DND Photos via Bill Worthy).

officer, approached him with the request to form a squadron airshow team, Brown lent a sympathetic ear. As the two veterans proceeded to the base commander's office to seek his approval, Brown had only one demand, "Keep us out of trouble!" Col Steve Gulyas approved the plan and a new team was born. Doug Stuart picks up the story:

═══════════════════════

"The Rut Zulus, as our CF-5 formation team came to be known, first flew in 1976 and performed at airshows throughout Canada and

the United States for many years thereafter. Prior to being selected as team lead for the 1976 and '77 airshow seasons, I had flown the box and solo positions with the 1975 edition of the Cobras under Bill Worthy. I was therefore very comfortable with what we could do with the CF-5 in an airshow environment given the restrictions of the day.

After the stand up of 419 Sqn in the fall of 1975, all of the 1 CFFTS dual-seat CF-5Bs were assigned to the squadron and the FTS was disbanded. Along with the duals came 22 single-seat versions of the aircraft, giving the squadron a total of 42 jets – a number that would be reduced to 36 a year or so later. With this many aircraft, along with a complement of 33 instructor pilots, we had the resources to form a formation team to help represent the Canadian Forces during airshow seasons – thus the creation of the Rut Zulus.

The name of the team, according to the gospel of one Capt Bob 'du Lac' Lake, was chosen because it represented the prowess and strength of the most elite of the phonetic alphabet letters – the letter 'Z.' I believe he also threw something in there to do with the power of Zeus as well. In reality, I simply decided to use the last letter of the alphabet so as not to conflict with any other formation call signs that began each day's training with Alpha. I knew that even the mighty 419th couldn't muster 26 formation missions in one day! I must admit though, I liked 'du Lac's' grandiose description much better. As for the 'Rut' part of the name, it simply represented the tactical callsign that had been bestowed on the squadron by LCol Bob Dobson, the base operations officer at CFB Cold Lake at the time. Since our squadron crest featured a bull moose as its centrepiece, the selection of Rut was a 'no brainer.' So, with the blessing of 'Red Lead' (Al Brown), we started our workups. Rut Zulus we used for practices, transits and airshows – and Rut Zulus it would remain throughout the years that 419 Sqn was equipped with the CF-5.

In addition to myself, our 1976 team was comprised of Capts Stu Holdsworth and Bob Archambault as Zulus 2 and 3 respectively with Maj George Adamson flying the slot and solo as Zulu 4. We used the single-seat version of the aircraft versus the dual for two reasons. Firstly, it looked better in formation because of it's shape and combat colour scheme and secondly, the nose area (*sans* ammo cans) was large enough to carry extra drag chutes and our luggage, something the dual was incapable of doing. The 1977 Zulus saw Stu Holdsworth move to the No. 4 position with 'du Lac' joining the team as the right winger. During the two year period in which I was lead, we performed at many locations that included large and small shows such as Moose Jaw, Abbotsford, Lloydminster and Minot, North Dakota. Our show lasted about nine minutes and was essentially the same for both years.

The Zulu Routine

The opening manoeuvre of the show involved a four-plane entrance from the left in Canada Goose formation (No. 2 and No. 3 flew off No. 4's wing vice the lead's) and arrived at show centre at 300 feet AGL in a right turn, 420 KIAS, canopies towards the crowd. At show centre, a climbing left turn was initiated. While in plan view on the back side of the turn, the formation changed to diamond while continuing a descending turn for a bottomside pass at show centre. A climbing turn was continued to the left, followed by a dumbbell turn to the right and a descent to once again pass in front of the crowd. At show centre, No. 4 broke right out of the box, selected full afterburner and performed a 6.5 G, 360 degree level turn at 450 KIAS, the corner velocity of the CF-5. While this was taking place, the three-ship continued a climbing left turn, slowed to 190 KIAS and selected gear and flaps down. A right descending reversal placed us about one mile

The Rut Zulus join the Deadeye Zips on the "hot line" following a performance at Abbotsford '77. "Fat Albert," the C-130 Hercules support aircraft of the US Navy Blue Angels is in the background. (Bill Johnson)

The 1978 Rut Zulus were a welcome addition to any airshow, shown here on the ramp at Fairchild AFB near Spokane, Washington. (Les Koski)

back from show centre at 300 feet AGL, passing left to right. This gave the No. 4 solo aircraft time to complete the 360 and position his aircraft and set up for a high-speed run that would pass the slow moving formation at show centre. His speed was not to exceed Mach .92. This was a tricky manoeuvre but when timed exactly (the airshow Gods had to be on your side) gave the crowd a spectacular view of the speed differential. As the formation arrived at show centre, No. 3 broke left, selected full afterburner and completed a 'dirty' 360 degree turn culminating in a steep climb away from the crowd. While climbing, the aircraft was 'cleaned up' and departed stage left to set up for the final pass – a high-speed low pass and pull-up, followed by a series of vertical rolls and a roll-off-the-top. While this was taking place, the No. 4 aircraft reversed after his left-to-right high-Mach pass and set up for a knife-edge from right to left. Timing was such that he flowed in behind No. 3. The remaining two aircraft, lead and No. 2, were also setting up to follow No. 4 and passed by the crowd from right to left in line-astern. Both aircraft then positioned themselves for the final run-in and vertical departure. The flypast order was No. 3, No. 4, No. 1 and No. 2. Once the final pass was complete it took only a short time to rejoin, descend and complete a low break from diamond formation with each aircraft breaking in alternate directions, lead to the left, No. 2 to the right, etc. The aircraft landed individually, taxied in formation and shut down in unison. The aim of our show was to have something happening in front of the crowd at all times. Judging by the remarks passed on to us by both spectators and peers, I think we achieved our aim.

Although the team never encountered any major problems throughout its existence, we did experience a few minor problems and amusing occurrences during my tenure:

In 1976, we were tasked to do a full show at Saddle Lake, Alberta. The commemorative historical event involved the re-enactment of the signing of an original peace treaty between the First Nations and the government. First Nations participants in full dress regalia, the RCMP, government leaders and the Lieutenant Governor were all to be in attendance. The day before the event, I flew a single-ship recce mission, surveyed the area and picked out a showline. I could see that large, bough-covered structures had been erected at the site and that a big crowd would probably be in attendance. Show day arrived and we took off to arrive overhead at the pre-determined time. As we approached show centre on our opening pass, I suddenly realized that most of the First Nations

Two views of the Zulus showing the diversity and effectiveness of the camouflage schemes employed by the squadron. The lighter coloured aircraft were extremely difficult to see during air-to-air combat manoeuvring whereas the camouflage schemes rendered the CF-5 almost invisible over terrain when looking down on it from above. In addition to providing excellent training to budding fighter pilots, 419 Sqn staff proved to be highly skilled adversaries during annual Maple Flag war games over the expansive Cold Lake training range. (DND Photo, Rae Simpson)

Capt Bob Lake leads the Rut Zulus in an aesthetically pleasing line-astern pass at Cold Lake with Capts Roy DeWolfe, Bob Archambault and Les Koski following. (Ron Berlie)

attendees had added historical realism to the event by arriving via non-motorized vehicles (i.e. horses) and had corralled them right in the middle of my well planned showline! After our first pass, I quickly briefed a new showline and we carried on for a nine minute period that was filled with airplanes zooming, horses stampeding and people waving anything they could get their hands on. It was hard to tell if they were waving in anger or just having fun. The show ended, we returned to Cold Lake, and I waited for the inevitable phone call. For whatever reason, none came – nor, by the way, did any letters of appreciation saying 'thanks for a great show.' Later that summer we suffered our only setback in my two years on the team. We were preparing for the Abbotsford Airshow when Bob Archambault broke his leg while dirt biking. Luckily, Paul Deacon from the 1975 CFFTS team was still instructing on the CF-5. He was recruited to fly his old position and after a few practices performed admirably.

Without doubt, our most amusing tale transpired at the Minot Airshow in 1977. We had flown down south two days prior to show day due to a Canadian holiday. This gave our groundcrew at Cold Lake a well deserved long weekend. Four other Canadian Forces teams had the same idea – the infamous Deadeye Zips from Cold Lake (notice they used Z as well), the Vikings Tutor team from Moose Jaw, the Musket Gold Musketeer team and the Dragonflies Kiowa helicopter team from Portage la Prairie all arrived on the same day. For our arrival, an old friend of Canadian aviation, Mr. Al Pietsch, had laid on a welcome party at his hangar at the downtown airport and a good time was had by all. Later that evening, Al and I returned to the base to find several Military Police vehicles in front of our assigned quarters, complete with all lights flashing. As I entered the building, I was confronted by a rag tag group of Canucks, the air display director and the wing commander. It seems the boys had been a little noisy and the desk clerk had called the authorities to have the noise stopped so that other people in the

Above, Capt Bob Lake rips over the head of Bill Johnson as he snaps this impressive shot in 1978. Below, the 1982 Zulus led by Maj Roger Ayotte demonstrate some fine Canadian precision for their friends at Paine Field, Washington. Right wing is being flown by Capt Jack Orr, left wing by Capt Ray Ferguson and the slot by Capt Reg Décoste. Note the "low vis" and camouflaged aircraft with Soviet-type numbering on Lake's aircraft plus Zulus 2 and 4 in the lower shot. (Bill Johnson, Nancy Johnson)

quarters could sleep. The fact that there were no other people staying in the quarters had fully escaped him. As the senior officer on scene, I was immediately charged by one of the Zips to represent our entourage. After a brief talk with the wing commander, all was near settled when one of the Zips approached him and asked, 'Sir, don't you call Sunday's show Northern Neighbors' Day?' When assured this was indeed correct, he looked the wing commander straight in the eye and said, 'Sir, I have a suggestion. Next year call the show Southern Neighbors' Day and invite the Mexican air force. You will have far fewer problems.' At this the wing commander broke up, told us to carry on, have 24 hours of rest and fly safe. And that we did!

My three years flying the CF-5 on the airshow circuit are three that I will never forget. Although members of the team were all volunteer staff pilots and groundcrew who sacrificed our weekends to fly airshows, not one of us ever regretted this commitment. We were proud to represent our air force and our country – and we had fun doing it."

Doug Stuart

Above, a fine view of the Rut Zulus and their camouflaged CF-5Ds near Cold Lake. The team was a popular attraction on the North American airshow circuit for nine consecutive years, from 1976 to 1984. Below, among many superb airshow artists from the United States that have established strong friendships north of the border are the Pietsch family of Minot, North Dakota who first performed at the Saskatchewan Homecoming Air Show in 1971. The trio performed in Ottawa in 1990 where they were photographed with two long time friends and fans of their show. L to R - Kent Pietsch, Doug Stuart, Al Pietsch, Warren Pietsch and George Miller. At right, one of the amazing feats that made the Pietsch show so popular - an opposing ribbon cut perfectly executed by Al and Warren. The tight-knit airshow community mourned the loss of one of the fraternity's great gentlemen when Al tragically lost his life in a weather related flying accident in August 1995. (DND Photo, bottom via the Pietsch Family)

For the next six years, the Rut Zulus became a fixture at airshows across western Canada, thrilling millions of Canadians with a safe and exciting show. Not surprisingly, there was no shortage of volunteers to serve on the team and each year the commanding officer of 419 Sqn was able to draw from a wealth of airshow experience in selecting a team leader to work up a four-plane demonstration. Between 1978 and 1984, these leaders included Bob Lake, Roy DeWolfe, Roger Ayotte, Claude Thibault, Ray Ferguson and Reg Décoste – all well known names in the Canadian fighter community. The team was also highly regarded in the United States and was frequently welcomed to some of the largest shows in the northern states, including those at Paine Field as well as USAF "Open Houses" at Fairchild, Malmstrom and Minot Air Force Bases.

In later years the team moved from the single-seat to the dual-seat CF-5D as their primary mount, in part because they were the most plentiful on the squadron but also because they afforded the opportunity for groundcrew to fly with the team to respective showsites. Also immensely popular with airshow crowds were the aggressor-type paint schemes that were applied to the aircraft in a variety of camouflage schemes.

The legacy of the Rut Zulus came to an end with the completion of the 1984 airshow season. Faced with uncertainty over the future of the aircraft and frequent unserviceabilities that were becoming more than a minor nuisance, all available resources had to be preserved for the training of Canada's fighter pilots. As had transpired with many of Canada's previous fighter teams, the last edition of the Rut Zulus was truly an international team. Led by Capt Reg Décoste, the team included *le capitaine* Christian Aubré of France, Capt Frans Blosser of the Netherlands and Capt Rick Zyvitski who flew the slot and solo position. With the completion of his exchange tour to Canada in mid-season, Aubré reluctantly gave up his position to Capt Don Brodeur, a former member of the Warlocks Voodoo formation team who would later earn a position on the Snowbirds.

As if to signal the end, the 1984 airshow season was the busiest ever for the Rut Zulus who flew 19 shows at eight locations

between May 14th and September 8th. Special honours included farewell appearances at Abbotsford, the Canadian International Air Show in Toronto (formerly the exclusive territory of 433 Sqn) and a particularly satisfying appearance at Randolf AFB in San Antonio, Texas, the home of one of the USAF's largest jet training bases.

The culmination of the 1984 season was a poignant one for Canadian airshows in that it spelled the end of fighter demonstration teams in Canada. Along with the Rut Zulus, the Hawks and Bobcats of Voodoo fame also disappeared from the North American airshow scene that summer, relegated to the annals of history along with the Deadeye Zips and Warlocks which had flown their last shows in 1982. This left a void for airshow organizers since teams of "fast movers" had always been a major attraction for airshow fans – a guaranteed hit at any show. Fortunately, CF-18 solo demonstrations would continue to be approved for major shows in the future.

419 Sqn Solo Demo Pilots

While 419 Sqn continued to support static displays at airshows over the next several years, flying activity was restricted to the occasional flypast until the spring of 1988 when the squadron gained approval to appoint a solo demonstration pilot to conduct non-aerobatic demonstrations at major airshows across the country. The first fighter pilot selected to do so was Capt Steve Charbonneau who flew his acceptance show for the base commander in Cold Lake on June 2nd and then headed east for one of his biggest shows of the year – the London International Air Show. A total of nine locations were included on the airshow itinerary that summer stretching from Comox on Vancouver Island to Hamilton on Lake Ontario.

Flying the Maple Leaf

The following year, 1989, marked the 25th anniversary of active service of 419 Sqn. Its distinguished record included service as a World War II bomber squadron, all-weather interceptor squadron with both NORAD and NATO and finally a tactical fighter training squadron. In a series of initiatives to commemorate this special occasion, squadron commanding officer LCol Murray Bertram received authorization to adorn one of his squadron's CF-5 single-seaters in a striking red and white scheme. The brainchild of Maj Marty Tate, the design featured a motif of a

"Moose" squadron's specially painted CF-5A was a popular attraction at North American airshows between 1989 and 1994 inclusive. This PR photo shoot (above and facing page) was flown by Capt Seldon Doyle, his last flight with 419 Sqn prior to commencing an exchange tour with the USAF flying the F-15 Eagle. (DND PMRC 90-184)

Following the retirement of the CF-5 from operational service in 1988, all CF-5 demo pilots were selected from the ranks of staff instructors at 419 Tac Ftr (Trng) Sqn. (DND Photos via 419 Sqn)

| Capt Steve Charbonneau – 1988 | Capt Raimo Kujala – 1989 | Capt Steve Green – 1990 | Capt Tim Jordan – 1990 | Capt Bob Painchaud – 1991 |

| Capt Dave Deere – 1992 | Capt Greg Carlow – 1993 | Capt Sylvain Larue – 1993 | Capt Ron VanderVoort – 1994 | Capt Marcus Walton – 1994 |

From the time it first hit the airshow circuit, 419 Sqn's coloured bird became a favorite of airshow photographers across the country. From top right, it is captured by Mike Valenti in 1989 and then Larry Milberry and Tony Cassanova in 1990. Below, designer of the paint scheme, Maj Marty Tate, captured the dynamic shot at home base in Cold Lake, Alberta. (DND PMRC 90-178)

Capt Bob Painchaud, the 1991 Canadian Forces CF-5 demo pilot, shows off the pride and joy of 419 Sqn. (DND Photo via Bob Painchaud)

large bull moose head on the tail and a striking red maple leaf on the bottom of the aircraft. As the squadron celebrated its roots dating back to Mildenhall, Suffolk, England where the squadron was formed in 1941 as a Wellington bomber squadron, Bertram assigned the aircraft to the squadron demonstration pilot to promote the squadron's heritage. The aircraft was an instant hit with airshow audiences everywhere it appeared that summer, Capt Raimo Kujala doing the honours. With the large red maple leaf symbolizing the Canadian flag, the most popular manoeuvres of the solo demonstration became the knife-edge pass and the high-speed vertical departure at the end of the show. So popular was the red and white CF-5 on the airshow circuit that public demand and squadron pride kept the aircraft flying for the next four years. In fact, three CF-5As appeared in the special livery – 116703, 116740 and 116721.

In 1990 two pilots shared demonstration duties on the red and white jet, Capts Steve Green and Tim Jordan who opened many an airshow with a blistering high-speed pass just below the speed of sound. The following season saw former 1 Canadian Air Group Hornet demo pilot Capt Bob Painchaud take the aircraft on the airshow circuit, a shade of things to come for the quiet-spoken young man who would go on to fly two tours with the Snowbirds, as a solo and then team leader. His successor for the 1992 season, Capt Dave Deere, would also later aspire to fly with Canada's showcase team, winning

the No. 4 first line astern position in the fall of the next year. In the interim, he thoroughly enjoyed the 27 displays he put on in the summer of '92, many in celebration of the 50th anniversary of the Alaska Highway.

In 1993 a special ceremony took place in Kamloops, British Columbia, 50 years after the city had "adopted" 419 Sqn in honour of a native son, W/C John "Moose" Fulton, who was the first commanding officer of 419 Bomber Sqn. Fulton and his crew had lost their lives when they failed to return from a mission over Hamburg in July 1942. In addition to a memorial dedication at the city's airport, Fulton Field, commanding officer LCol Doug Erlandson was proud to announce the appointment of the Honourable E. Davie Fulton as the first Honorary Colonel of 419 Sqn. The Canada Day ceremony and parade attended by 130 squadron personnel and a host of dignitaries saw 419 Sqn granted the Freedom of the City in an

age-old tradition. As the squadron marched proudly through the streets of Kamloops, four squadron CF-5s made their presence well known to all. To underscore this special relationship, permission was granted to reform the Rut Zulus for one last show during the city's big airshow on August 4th, 1993. Led by Maj Les Koski, this final edition of the team, which had brought 419 Sqn much acclaim, included Capts Bill Brown, Ben Lavergne, Ron VanderVoort and Sylvain Larue as solo (flying 740). The next day the squadron's other designated solo pilot for 1993, Capt Greg Carlow, took the popular jet to Abbotsford for three more displays.

With 740 becoming "time-expired" the following year, it made one more flight to Kamloops where it was mounted on a pedestal at Fulton Field, an eternal reminder of the special relationship that exists between the city and the squadron. The year 1994 also marked the end of airshow appearances for

The flagship aircraft of 414 Combat Support Sqn and 419 Tactical Fighter Training Sqn made a handsome pair on the CFB Comox ramp in Aug 94. CF-5 Demo Pilot Capt Marcus Walton was on hand to participate in the closing ceremonies of the 1994 Commonwealth Games in Victoria and took the opportunity to capture this rare shot. Both aircraft are sporting emblems saluting the 70th anniversary of the RCAF. (Marcus Walton)

the CF-5 in Canada. One last CF-5 was adorned with the special paint scheme for this final year of appearances in tribute to the 70th anniversary of Canada's Air Force, the RCAF having been formed on April 1st, 1924. The last Canadian Forces pilots to have the privilege of demonstrating the aircraft to airshow audiences in Canada were Capts Marcus Walton and Ron VanderVoort. The aircraft they performed in, 116721, is now proudly displayed at the RCAF Memorial Museum at 8 Wing in Trenton, Ontario.

Saying Goodbye

The retirement of the CF-5 in 1995 in the face of relentless governmental budget cuts that precipitated ongoing reductions of personnel strength in the Canadian Forces came as a great disappointment to those who had spent thousands of hours seeing the aircraft through a complicated upgrade program to extend its service life. It was difficult to justify these budgetary decisions as simply a sign of the times, given that Canadian CF-18s had flown combat missions as part of the international coalition in the highly publicized Gulf War only four years earlier.

As a gathering of past and present Canadian Forces personnel made their way to Cold

On 17 Jun 95, a contingent of 419 Sqn personnel deployed to Kamloops, B.C. to dedicate CF-5A 116740 to the city which had adopted the squadron in 1943 during World War II. Pictured above with the mounted aircraft at the city's airport ("Fulton Field") are the four 419 Sqn pilots who conducted the flypast commemorating the event. L to R – Capts Brad Sinclair, Marcus Walton, Sylvain Larue and Dave Stone. (via 419 Sqn)

Lake to bid the CF-5 and 419 Sqn a final adieu in June 1995, there was much to reflect upon. For all of the controversy over its initial selection, the CF-5 did serve the Canadian Forces very well over 27 years. She brought a new capability to the air force with an air refuelling capacity that significantly enhanced her operational effectiveness … and an entire generation of fighter pilots learned to ply their trade from the confines of her cockpit.

As for the deactivation of 419 Sqn, outgoing commanding officer LCol John Laidler echoed the sentiments of all in attendance with his farewell remarks, reproduced here in part:

"The traditions of 419 Squadron are well entrenched in its 31 years of active service. It has served its country well in war and peace, and I am saddened to see those traditions come to an end. On the one hand, I hope once again to see the Colours paraded proudly by a reactivated 419 Squadron. On the other hand, I hope the need never arises for the squadron to be recalled for war-time duty."

John Laidler

LCol Laidler's remarks turned out to be somewhat prophetic. On July 1st, 2000 the mighty Moose bellowed again as 419 Sqn was reactivated to resume its role as an operational training squadron for Canadian and allied fighter pilots under the NATO Flying Training in Canada program. Under its new commanding officer, former Snowbird commander LCol Steve Hill, the squadron is once again conducting fighter lead-in training, now using the state-of-the-art BAE Systems Hawk 115 fighter trainer.

With this fine portrait, Canadian artist John Rutherford captured the sense of national pride that went into the creation of 419 Sqn's patriotic colour scheme. (courtesy John Rutherford)

CF-18 Hornet Demos

"Ladies and gentlemen, on behalf of the Canadian Forces and 410 Sqn Cold Lake, we are proud to present to you Canada's newest fighter aircraft – the CF-18 Hornet."

With these words a new era began on the Canadian airshow scene in 1983 as the much celebrated McDonnell Douglas Hornet was introduced to millions of Canadians for the first time. Here, at last, was the state-of-the-art combat aircraft that Air Command had impatiently been waiting for. It presented a quantum leap in technology and firepower over the three operational fighters it replaced – the CF-101, CF-104 and CF-5 – and was a true multi-role fighting machine. Soon the aircraft would be gainfully employed with Canada's NATO and NORAD forces. But in the interim, there was still much to learn about the jet and its truly incredible capabilities, and dozens of Canadian fighter pilots were standing in the wings waiting their turn to convert to the highly publicized aircraft.

The Right Solution

The selection of new military hardware is always a painstaking and lengthy process, no more so than in Canada, a country that has been immune to foreign intervention on its soil and as a result only begrudgingly provides new funding for military equipment – and only then when it can't squeeze any more serviceability out of its existing resources. Examples have been plentiful in all branches of the Canadian Forces for decades.

In the case of the procurement of the Hornet, it was at least the right solution for Canada's

Air Force and, unlike the government's selection of the CF-5, was the aircraft that Air Command wanted to replace its ageing fighter trio. That in itself was a major victory. The complicated process had its genesis on November 20th, 1975 when a cabinet decision was made to maintain Canada's existing defence contributions to NORAD and

NATO, the latter including a fighter commitment to both the Central Region of Europe and the Northern Flank of Norway. As much as some might have wished otherwise, it had become increasingly clear that Canada could not separate its desire for foreign trade from its alliance to the European members of NATO. In the context of NORAD, pressures were also being brought to bear on Canada to take an increased responsibility for its own air defence. Whatever the background politics, the announcement constituted a refreshing change for the Trudeau government which had demonstrated little real interest in the Canadian Forces in the late sixties and early seventies. The decision set in motion a 16 month study by the Department of National Defence to explore detailed options for the replacement of the existing fighter fleets, including timelines and cost estimates, while simultaneously determining what measures would be required to main-

The CF-18 Hornet, seen here on its inaugural test flight with its distinctive false canopy bottom, has been the mainstay of Canada's fighter force for 20 years. (Courtesy The Boeing Company, C22-308-5)

The welcome government announcement that the Canadian Forces would be equipped with a new fighter aircraft generated intense competition within the aerospace industry. In 1978, *Wings* magazine completed a seven month study featuring each of the competitors and the fighters they were to replace. (courtesy *WINGS*)

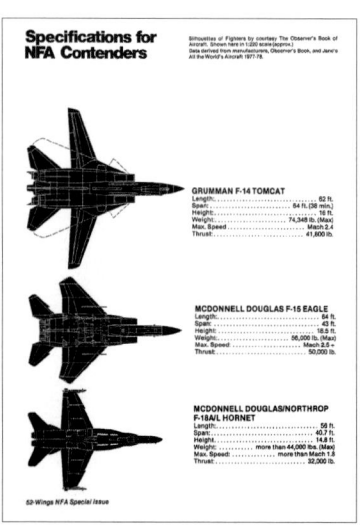

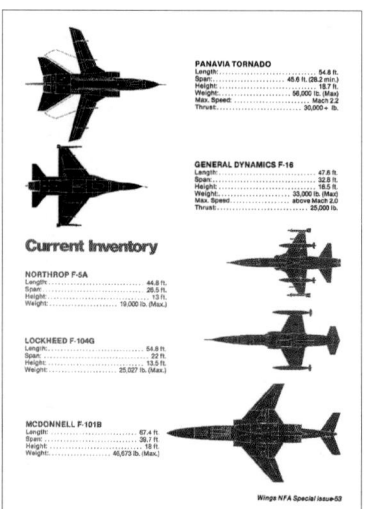

The Hornet's unprecedented manoeuvrability made it an instant hit with Canadian airshow audiences commencing in 1983. Shown here is 410 Sqn's contribution to the celebration of the 75th anniversary of the Royal Canadian Air Force in 1999. (Mike Reyno/Skytech Images)

tain the current level of combat capability until a new aircraft could be delivered.

The conclusions of the study were presented by the Minister of National Defence in March 1977. Of no surprise to anyone serving in Air Command, it predicted serious difficulties in maintaining operational commitments with the CF-101 and CF-104 beyond 1983 while observing that the CF-5 would have to be removed from operational service and dedicated to a training role by 1985. Moreover, the study recommended that an attempt be made to replace all three aircraft with a single multi-role combat aircraft capable of both air-to-air and air-to-surface operations, thus making it suitable for use in both North America and Europe. Five allied aircraft were initially identified as potential candidates that warranted detailed consideration and whose manufacturers would be formally invited to submit bids – the Grumman Aerospace F-14 Tomcat, McDonnell Douglas F-15 Eagle, General Dynamics F-16 Fighting Falcon, McDonnell Douglas/ Northrop F/A-18 Hornet and the Panavia Tornado. Northrop entered the competition with its YF-17 prototype (Cobra) and Dassault Breguet was invited to bid the F-1E aircraft. The French company decided instead to offer their new Mirage 2000, still on the drawing board, but they subsequently withdrew from the competition without submitting a bid.

Based on allocated resources at the time, it was deemed that 130 to 150 new fighters would be required to fulfill existing commitments. This included 54 aircraft for basing in Central Europe, 36 earmarked for air defence in Canada, 12-24 for contingency operations on the Northern Flank of NATO, 21-26 for operational training and finally, 7-10 aircraft that could, statistically, be lost to attrition during the phase-in period. To meet the timeline for initial operational capability, a contract with the winning bidder would have to be signed by the end of 1978 to ensure initial deliveries by mid-1981. The total cost – a maximum of $2.34 billion Cdn (1977 dollars).

In keeping with the government's policy on defence procurement, the "total military system procured was to provide no more than the minimum military capability needed to accomplish the assigned task." However, the acquisition criteria also dictated that the winning contractor would have to make provision for substantial industrial benefits to Canadian industry, a standard

BGen Paul Manson, Project Manager NFA (left), and Adm Robert Falls, Chief of the Defence Staff (right), listen in as the Honourable Barney Danson, Minister of National Defence, announces the short list of Canada's NFA competitors in November 1978 – the F/A-18 Hornet and F-16 Fighting Falcon. (DND Photo via P.D. Manson)

caveat on all such Canadian contracts. While this has traditionally been a source of great frustration to foreign manufacturers, it is generally accepted as the cost of doing business with the Canadian government. Thus, while it might seem like a simple military matter to the uninitiated spectator, the process of military acquisition is in fact a complicated mosaic that includes major diplomatic, economic and industrial factors as well. The decision to purchase a new fighter for the Canadian Forces came on the heels of other expensive re-equipment programs – $1 billion Cdn for the purchase of 18 new maritime patrol aircraft (the Lockheed P-3 Aurora) to be based in Canada and $187 million Cdn for new battle tanks (the German Leopard II) to be based in Lahr, West Germany.

The NFA Program

The senior air force officer selected to oversee the evaluation and recommendation for the New Fighter Aircraft (NFA) was newly promoted BGen Paul Manson. A former CF-104 commander of 441 Sqn in West Germany during the strike/recce era, he had most recently completed a tour as base commander of the Air Defence Command base at Chatham, New Brunswick, thus also making him very conversant with Canada's NORAD

commitments with the nuclear-capable Voodoo interceptor. Gen Manson's team was formed early in 1977 and over the course of its three year mandate grew from 30 personnel to some 190 during the comprehensive evaluation phase. The team included members from the Departments of National Defence, Supply and Services and Industry, Trade and Commerce.

Faced with the enormous challenge of evaluating some of the world's most formidable combat aircraft while putting into place a detailed procurement program with very stringent deadlines, BGen Manson has often been lauded for his meticulous approach to detail and scrupulous guidelines that ensured that there was no undo influence in the final selection of Canada's new fighter aircraft. A "Request For Proposal (RFP)" was issued on September 1st, 1977 to the manufacturers of the competing companies which defined the requirements of the project in great detail. Each was given five months to submit their bids to supply the new fighter, including all logistics support and proposed industrial benefits. This set off a flurry of activity as competing teams descended on Ottawa, most setting up dedicated offices to prepare their bids. On February 1st, 1978, over 1,300 kilograms (3,000 pounds) of documentation landed on the NFA team's doorstep.

Deputy Chief of the Defence Staff, LGen G.C.E. Thériault (left), was the first senior officer from NDHQ to receive a familiarization flight in the F/A-18 Hornet by McDonnell Douglas test pilot Jack Krings on 10 Mar 79. A few hours later, the exhilarating experience was shared by BGen P.D. Manson (right). (Courtesy The Boeing Company C12-9086-51, C12-9086-70)

The Canadian Forces F-16 Flyers
CFB OTTAWA • CFB WINNIPEG • CFB COLD LAKE
APRIL — MAY 1979

Once the short list of NFA contenders was announced, General Dynamics spared no expense in ensuring the senior leadership of the Canadian Forces and Air Command were well aware of the capabilities of the F-16 Fighting Falcon. In visits to CFBs Ottawa, Winnipeg and Cold Lake, 19 pilots were given familiarization rides in 1979 – from the Chief of Defence Staff to the military's senior test pilots. The F-16 subsequently lost out to the F-18. (via P.D. Manson)

In November 1978, Minister of National Defence Barney Danson announced that the short list of finalists in the competition would be the F-16 and F-18. Over the next 16 months every conceivable aspect of the two competing programs was re-evaluated on a side-by-side, comparative basis. Following this exhaustive study, the NFA team concluded that the CF-18 was best suited to Canada's defence needs and that McDonnell Douglas had also offered the better industrial offset package. Following further detailed scrutiny by various government cabinet committees, Canada announced on April 10th, 1980 that it had selected the CF-18 as Canada's new fighter aircraft. BGen Manson continued as program manager until the summer of 1980, at which time he was rewarded with a posting back to Lahr, West Germany to command 1 Canadian Air Group. He would not be out of the country for long however, later returning to command Air Command and ultimately all of the Canadian Forces as Chief of the Defence Staff.

Manson Reminisces

General Manson, recalling a few of the highlights of the NFA program over 20 years later, relates some interesting stories about those intense days:

"We insisted from the beginning that there was to be no social contact whatsoever between representatives of the bidding companies and members of the Program Office. As it happens, this decree was warmly welcomed by the manufacturers because it gave all of them an assurance that their competitors were not unduly influencing the NFA team. Moreover, it saved them a lot of marketing money!

It is interesting to note that, from the outset, we identified three particularly tough decisions which had to be made, each of which involved choosing between one or two of something. First, there was the fundamental question of whether we should acquire one or two fleets of fighters. (Some observers – and at least one competitor – believed that a high-low mix was what Canada needed, given the wide diversity of the Air Force's roles in Europe and Canada.) Secondly, there was the choice between one or two engines. Finally, and this was a really difficult one, we had to choose between a one-man vs. two-man crew. After months of intense analysis on these three questions, we opted for one fleet, two engines and a majority of one-seaters. Subsequent experience has convinced me that we made the right choice in each case.

The prohibition on socializing didn't prevent the various competitors from pulling out all the stops to win this contract, at the time the largest capital procurement in the history of the federal government, and a lucrative contract even for the giants of the aerospace industry. Politicians were subjected to all sorts of pressures and we had to be very careful to ensure that government decision-makers were given 'straight gen' about the competing bids. I personally was called upon to brief the Prime Minister and cabinet ministers on numerous occasions throughout the course of the program. When it came to the final days, it looked as though the whole business was going to come crashing down over the question of industrial benefits, and especially industrial benefits for Quebec, at that time in the throes of political upheaval. The right decision was made however, and it was one that demanded no small amount of political courage. The system worked, and the Air Force was the winner. The CF-18 has since proven itself to be the superb multi-role fighter we expected it to be."

Paul Manson

The Hornet Takes Off

One of the most exciting aspects of the CF-18 selection was the fact that Canada would take delivery of its new aircraft in parallel with the US Navy, in effect making it a joint launch customer. In accepting the carrier-based version of the aircraft "off-the-shelf," extensive modification costs were avoided. Indeed, the only basic differences between the F/A-18A and CF-18 were the replacement of the automatic carrier landing system (ALCS) with a standard instrument landing system (ILS) and the installation of a 600,000-candlepower spotlight on the port side of the CF-18 for night identification of intercepted aircraft. Provision was also made on the Canadian Hornets for carriage of LAU-5003 rocket pods (each carrying 19 CRV-7 rockets) and BL-755 cluster bombs, part of the CF-104 war stocks already in storage in West Germany. All up, the Hornet remains an impressive weapons platform, capable of carrying over 7,700 kilograms (17,000 pounds) of ordnance (bombs, missiles and rockets) on nine weapons stations in addition to its nose-mounted 20mm M61 cannon. Like its navy counterpart, the CF-18 is powered by twin GE F404 turbofan engines producing a total of 32,000 pounds of thrust.

A rare photograph of the Northrop YF-17 prototype piloted by Northrop test pilot Hank Choteau as it appeared in 1978 in pseudo-Canadian colours. During the NFA competition, it was dubbed the "CF-18L prototype" for promotional purposes. Only two YF-17s were ever built, Northrop later joining McDonnell Douglas to produce the larger F/A-18 Hornet. (Northrop Photo)

The final production F/A-18 was in fact a derivative of the Northrop YF-17 that had initially been developed as a contender for a new fighter aircraft for the USAF. Although General Dynamics' YF-16 had edged out the Hornet in that competition in January 1975, only four months later the Navy announced it had opted for a Northrop/McDonnell Douglas proposal to develop the YF-17 as a new generation multi-role fighter to complement the fleet air defence of their F-14 Tomcats. The Navy preferred a twin-engined fighter for the enhanced safety it offered during operations at sea, a factor which also made sense for Canada given the remote expanses of the north and the country's extensive coastlines.

The collaboration between McDonnell Douglas and Northrop in developing the YF-17 prototype proved a winner. Although three variants were originally envisioned, fighter and attack versions were combined to produce the F/A-18A. On January 22nd, 1976 McDonnell was awarded a contract to build nine single-seat and two dual-seat full-scale development aircraft, with Northrop retaining an integral role as the principal subcontractor. The first test flight of the new fighter took place in November 1978. The rest, as they say, is history. Today, the US Navy operates some 37 F/A-18 squadrons from stations worldwide as well as from 12 aircraft carriers. Of course, airshow fans worldwide are most conversant with the Navy's Hornets as the mount of the Blue Angels Flight Demonstration Squadron, the longest serving aerobatic team in the world. They converted to the F/A-18 during their 40th anniversary in 1986. In addition to the US Navy and Marine Corps, the F-18 is today in service with the air forces of Canada, Australia, Spain, Kuwait, Finland, Switzerland and Malaysia and is regarded as one of the most versatile combat aircraft ever produced.

Canada's Hornets

The Canadian contract with McDonnell Douglas ultimately called for the production of 98 single-seat fighters (designated the CF-188) and an additional 40 combat capable dual-seat trainers (the CF-188B) for a total of 138 airframes. This made Canada not only the first foreign customer for the aircraft but also the largest operator of the F-18 outside of the United States. Like their counterparts from the US Navy, all of Canada's new fighters were assembled at the McDonnell Douglas plant in St Louis, Missouri.

The first production CF-18 was naturally a dual-seater (188901) which took to the skies of St Louis on July 29th, 1982 in the hands of McDonnell Douglas test pilot Jack Krings. Its highly successful test program took only three months. The first two aircraft (901 and 902) were delivered simultaneously to the Canadian Forces in Ottawa where a highly publicized ceremony on October 25th saw the aircraft accepted by Minister of National Defence Gilles Lamontagne and Chief of the Defence Staff Gen R.M. Withers. To commemorate the event, an airshow was staged for the large gathering of government officials and dignitaries which featured nostalgic solo performances by each of the CF-101 Voodoo, CF-104 Starfighter and CF-5 Freedom Fighter. Remarked one smiling observer after the airshow, "Were the passes supposed to be (at) 400 feet each, or add up to 400 feet?"

The honour of being the first commanding officer to stand up the CF-18 in Canadian service went to another popular fighter pilot who was also later destined to command Air Command. LCol Al DeQuetteville was another veteran of the RCAF and Cdn Forces who had also flown his first fighter tour on the CF-104 Starfighter in the strike attack role with 422 "Tomahawk" Sqn at 4 Wing in Baden-Soellingen. A subsequent tour with AETE in Cold Lake had given him a

The first and last Canadian Hornets to come off the McDonnell Douglas assembly line in St Louis were both dual seaters. On the left, 188701 takes shape in Apr 1982; on the right 188940 (the 138th CF-18) nears completion in Sep 1988. By this time, Canada had eight squadrons equipped with the new fighter, five in Canada and three in Europe. (Courtesy The Boeing Company)

Canada's first CF-18 was officially unveiled at a roll-out ceremony at McDonnell Douglas Corporation in St Louis on 28 Jul 82 in the presence of Prime Minister Pierre Elliott Trudeau. As Canadian and American guests surrounded the new fighter, cockpit tours were conducted by McDonnell Douglas test pilot Jack Krings. (Courtesy The Boeing Company)

solid background for overseeing the introduction of the most technically advanced aircraft ever to enter Canadian service. DeQuetteville had the privilege of flying the first aircraft from St. Louis to Ottawa and then on to Cold Lake the following day for the official acceptance ceremony which took place on October 30th, 1982 The aircraft were accepted by the Commander Air Command, LGen K.E. Lewis, who was accompanied by the Commander Fighter Group, MGen W.G. Paisley.

With the formalities over, 410 Tac Ftr (Operational Training) Sqn set about the business of training a strong cast of hand-picked pilots from across the spectrum of fighter experience in Canada to form the initial cadre of instructors on the squadron. The long-established traditions of the Cougars as a training squadron in the Voodoo era would now continue on the Hornet.

Unmatched Performance

With all of the publicity surrounding the selection of the Hornet in the face of some very stiff competition, it was important that the aircraft be exposed to Canadians as soon as possible. To that end, LCol DeQuetteville received authorization to appoint a demonstration pilot to work up a show that would accentuate the impressive handling characteristics of the Hornet at as many airshows as possible in 1983. As demonstration flying is always done on a volunteer basis, it did not take long for word to filter through the squadron that the commanding officer was looking for a suitable candidate. Capt Gary Liddiard was ultimately selected for the job. Although he had not flown any solo airshow demonstrations in the past, Liddiard's credentials included a four year operational tour

The start of a new era in Canadian military aviation, the formal acceptance of the CF-18 in Cold Lake on 30 Oct 82. (DND CKC 82-4276)

The first and the last! Jack Krings gets airborne on CF-188901's first test flight on 29 Jul 82. At right, the aircraft uses a mobile arrestor cable to make its last landing on the 3,300 foot runway of Ottawa's Rockcliffe Airport on 18 Oct 2001 prior to being donated to the Canada Aviation Museum. Flying the aircraft into the former RCAF station were LCol Gord Zans, Commanding Officer 410 Tac Ftr (OT) Sqn, and former Chief of the Air Staff, LGen (Ret'd) Al DeQuetteville. LGen DeQuetteville was the first and last Canadian Forces pilot to fly this particular aircraft. (Bottom photo courtesy The Boeing Company, all others DND Photos)

with 409 Sqn on the Voodoo after graduating from the RCAF's first Tutor course in 1965 (Course 6406), followed by a total of eight years instructional experience on the T-37 (USAF Exchange), Voodoo (with 410 Sqn) and the CF-5 (with 419 Sqn). His meticulous approach to detail would yield a highly professional and entertaining demonstration.

Liddiard set out to design his show by consulting with the resident expert on the aircraft, test pilot Pete Pilcher of McDonnell Douglas who had been seconded to 410 Sqn to assist with their conversion to the aircraft and indeed had his own F-18 demo show with which he had "watered many eyes" during the official acceptance ceremonies. Using the old philosophy "walk before you run," Liddiard's initial routine did not include full blown aerobatics. However, he was authorized a vertical pull-up at slow speed immediately after takeoff to a roll-off-the-top. With a cleanly configured CF-18 being capable of getting airborne in only about 1,700 feet in full afterburner, this was a very impressive way to commence a show and highlighted both the awesome power and tight turning radius of the aircraft. That characteristic alone allowed Liddiard to fly a show easily within the confines of the airfield, something a generation of airshow fans had never seen, certainly not from the Hornet's predecessors.

As his logbook reveals, Liddiard had only 100 hours on type when he performed his first official show at the CFB Cold Lake Airshow on May 12th, 1983. He had already completed his "acceptance show" for the base commander, an important milestone that every military demonstration pilot must go through to receive the stamp of approval from his superiors – an approval process that evaluates the safety, professionalism and

---

CF-18 High Show 1984

Full AB Min Roll Takeoff Loop
Knife-edge Pass (600 knots)
Head-on Clover Leaf to Aileron Roll
Hi Alpha Pass (120 knots)
Square Immelman (Split S)
Max Rate 360 Turn (7 G at 325 knots)
Loop to Vert Reverse to Aileron Roll
Vertical Rolls to 25,000 feet
High-speed "Whisper Pass" (600 knots)
Idle Power Barrel Roll
Minimum Roll "Carrier" Landing

---

overall appeal of the show. With blessing in hand, Capt Liddiard went on to fly a dozen shows across Canada in the summer of 1983 with inaugural appearances at three major shows – Abbotsford, Toronto and Shearwater. The aircraft was a major draw across the country with millions of Canadians flocking to shows to see Air Command's latest acquisition. As both Liddiard and Fighter Group became more comfortable with the show, authorization was granted to conduct what would become a signature manoeuvre for the Hornet – a full loop on takeoff. Thus, Gary Liddiard made history by being the first Canadian Forces pilot to ever conduct such a manoeuvre in a modern-day fighter. He would later have the distinction of also being the first Canadian to demonstrate the aircraft in Europe and would play a pivotal role in training all subsequent demo pilots in that theatre.

Following Gary Liddiard's inaugural airshow season, the decision was made to designate two demonstration pilots to share the duties in 1984 over the long summer. Having seen firsthand, or heard through the airshow grapevine, what the CF-18 could do, there wasn't an airshow in the country that did not

want it among its headline performers. The two young men anointed with the magic wand came from different fighter backgrounds – Capt Dale Erhart from Voodoos and Capt B.J. Ryan from Starfighters. While Erhart had been posted to 410 Sqn straight from his operational tour with 409 Sqn in Comox, Ryan had only to switch hangars on the base at Cold Lake as he had been a Starfighter instructor at 417 Sqn. He had just managed to reach the coveted 1,000 hour mark on the Starfighter prior to being selected as a member of the initial cadre of Hornet instructors. Dale Erhart explains how the Canadian Forces Hornet display evolved in one short year:

"My first real airshow experience dated back to 1980 when I flew left wing with the 409 Sqn Hawks on the CF-101 Voodoo. Capt Lynn Housworth led the team that year and Capt Don Thornton was my navigator. Don would later 'cross train' to pilot and become a Hornet demo pilot himself in Europe.

Having already experienced the thrill of the North American airshow circuit, I was delighted to be selected along with B.J. Ryan to split the 1984 Hornet demo season. Thanks to the dedicated and highly professional work of Gary Liddiard the year before, we were fortunate to be authorized a fully aerobatic show from the outset. Therefore, with the guidance of 'Lid' and Pete Pilcher of McDonnell Douglas, we were able to put together quite an impressive show.

After considerable discussion and practice, we came up with two shows, a 'high show' for good weather and a 'low show' when there was a restrictive ceiling. The high show was very dynamic and took full advantage of

Since the CF-18 Hornet arrived on the Canadian airshow scene in 1983, it has been featured on airshow programs across the nation. (author's collection)

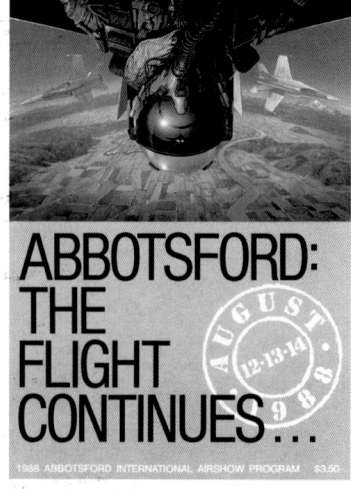
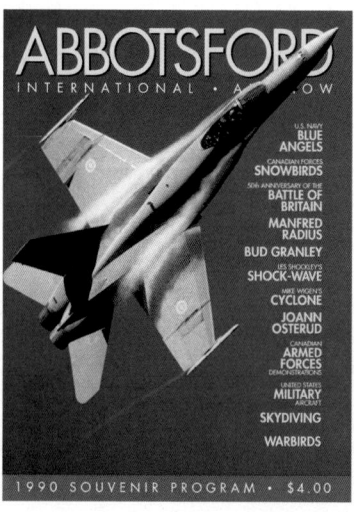

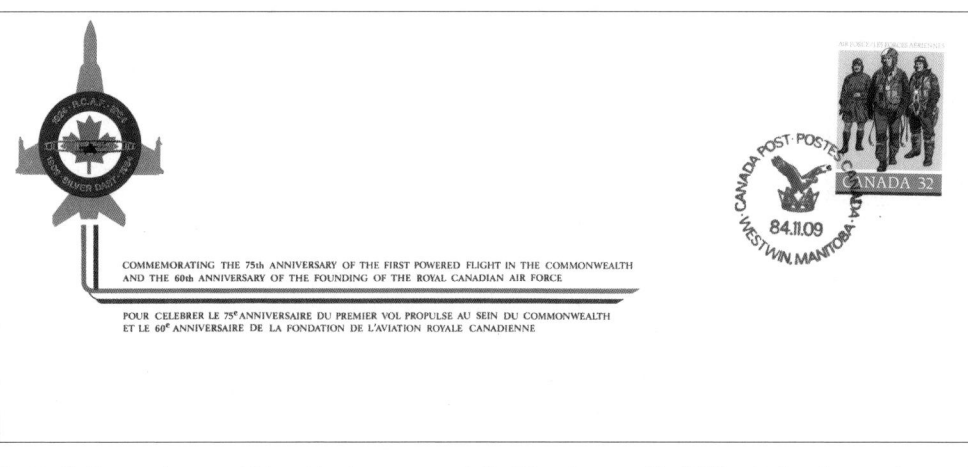

In 1984 Air Command approved this emblem to commemorate the 60th anniversary of the RCAF and 75th anniversary of powered flight in Canada. The first-day cover was released at Air Command Headquarters on 9 Nov 84 by the Commander Air Command, LGen P.D. Manson. In contrasting the evolution of aviation from the Silver Dart to the CF-18, he wrote in part:

"This is a year for celebration and for reflecting upon the important role played by aviation and the Air Force in the development of our nation. May this fine new stamp remind all Canadians of the significance of the RCAF's motto: PER ARDUA AD ASTRA – 'Through adversity to the stars.'" (author's collection)

the Hornet's power and turning radius. The low show started with a dirty roll on takeoff and included a slow-speed dirty pass with the tail hook down and refuelling probe deployed. After that it included a lot of high G turns to the base of the cloud layer with rolling manoeuvres. The airplane had no 'G limiter' at the time and a '35 alpha' limit was available for most of the season.

Of interest, B.J. and I made a pact not to fly with each other in the same aircraft while working up our shows, basically for two reasons. Firstly, there is nothing more hair-raising than 'watching' low-level aerobatics from someone else's back seat and secondly, we had some concern with the dual's stability during this kind of aggressive manoeuvring at low level (unfounded, as we found out with more experience). So, rather than flying with each other, we watched each other practice from the ground, reviewed our HUD tapes and compared notes. Equipment like the HUD, inertial nav system (with a show centre waypoint) and a compass we could adjust to any cardinal point for any runway, all made our job much easier than previous fighter demos, not to mention the fact that the Hornet could *really* turn!

As B.J. Ryan got busy with the first European deliveries to Baden-Soellingen, I was able to scoop the majority of the shows. However, he felt privileged, as did I, to get in several shows, including some big ones like London and the CIAS in Toronto. I lucked in and was able to do Edmonton, Moose Jaw, Comox, Abbotsford, Mirabel, Chatham, Bagotville and a final demo for the brass at the USAF's *William Tell* weapons meet in October at Tyndall AFB, Florida.

I learned so much that summer of '84 – from B.J., from the American demo pilots who flew the F-15 and F-16 and, of course, from the Snowbirds. Way back in 1978 one of the first Red Knights, Bob Hallowell, had told me that he attributed his success (and survival) to 35 hours of hard practice doing aerobatics at higher altitude before he worked his routine down to show altitude. I took his advice to heart and it worked. The year went past all too quickly and, like most skills that aren't practiced regularly, that magic ideal of flying a perfect show quickly vanished as the instructional routine at 410 once again took precedence.

The following season, Capts Guy Dutil of 410 Sqn and Chuck Caron of 425 took over the Hornet demo duties. Chuck was the first pilot from one of the operational Hornet squadrons in Canada selected to perform shows in eastern Canada. Although I never had the chance to see his show, I did watch Guy fly his fine show at Winnipeg in September 1985 as I manned the static display aircraft. I never really had a hand in 'teaching' these guys how to fly their shows. As we had done, they asked questions, but in general the 'new blood' developed their own routine. Speaking of a different routine, in March 1986 Bob Wade asked me to fly in his 'trunk' (ergo, the dreaded back seat) to critique his proposed routine. What a hellish ride! Now I remembered why B.J. and I had agreed not to fly together. Bob had many good ideas and a few others I critiqued in debriefing. As everyone knows, he went on to have a great airshow season.

Even now, 18 years later, my mind still frequently drifts back to that wonderful sum-

mer, most often I guess to my last show. That last show at Tyndall was my finest hour. What a great pleasure it was to perform in front of the USAF, especially since some felt 'we' had betrayed them by buying a navy aircraft. The Eagle and Falcon demo pilots had to reach a minimum 5,000 foot apex during looping manoeuvres in their routine whereas we only had a 3,000 foot minimum. So, even though their turn performance is similar, our show stood out because our loops were much tighter. Upon landing I stepped out of the jet to be greeted by the Commander Air Command, LGen Manson, and his deputy, MGen McNaughton. They were clearly thrilled … McNaughton, who towered over me, looked down on me with his low, loud voice and said, 'Do you know how many 'stars' were watching you today, son?' I said, 'No sir.' He replied with a laugh, 'Enough to make the Milky Way!!'"

Dale Erhart

Both Guy Dutil and Chuck Caron had flown airshows prior to taking on the Hornet solo role in 1985, Dutil in 104s in Europe and Caron with the CF-5 in Bagotville. When they handed the responsibilities over to Bob Wade and Tristan deKoninck in 1986, it was to two ex-Snowbirds who had truly been around the North American airshow scene and had seen Canada and much of the United States from every imaginable angle. Bob Wade shares his experience as he relates how he built his show, and how a disastrous accident wound up putting him on the road for the entire summer:

Whether explaining the finer details of his aircraft to airshow enthusiasts or the varied roles of Canada's military aircraft to parents and students, public relations activities are an integral part of the demonstration pilot's responsibilities. Capt Bob Wade was one of several such ambassadors for the Canadian Forces in 1986. (DND Photos)

"During the spring of 1986, I was instructing on the CF-18 at 410 Sqn in CFB Cold Lake. The squadron commander, LCol Terry Humphries, invited me to fly the CF-18 demonstration for the 1986 airshow season. The North American airshows were separated into Eastern and Western regions, with the dividing line running through Winnipeg. Capt Tristan deKoninck, from 425 Sqn, had been selected to conduct the eastern shows and I was to fly the shows in the west. This division of effort was utilized to relieve the burden on one squadron from having a pilot and aircraft away every weekend. Tragically, Tristan was killed very early in the season during his post airshow departure from Summerside, Prince Edward Island. The weather was poor and it is believed he suffered from spatial disorientation during a steep climb into cloud after takeoff. This presumably resulted in the aircraft entering an unrecoverable attitude and impacting the ground a short distance from the airfield. As a consequence, I was requested to conduct all of the CF-18 airshows for the remainder of the season.

The Hornet was still new in the inventory at this time. We were taking delivery of two new aircraft from the McDonnell Douglas assembly line every month at 410 Sqn. I flew many of the acceptance flights and frequently used these aircraft for displays as they still had that 'factory-new' look. Even after three years of service, the Hornet had its armchair quarterbacks in the media who were very critical of the fact that it was designed to US Navy specifications. The pundits believed that the CF-18 would not be suited to Canada's requirements for both air defence in NORAD and ground attack in NATO. Having flown the CF-104 for 10 years, I knew we had a winner in the CF-18 and

was eager to demonstrate its full performance capability to the public.

I designed my show to give the audience a means of direct comparison between the CF-18 and all other fighter aircraft performing on the airshow circuit. I knew that if the public could see a tangible difference, it would go much further than having politicians and military spokespersons tout its attributes. My display was aggressive and included some new manoeuvres that had not been previously demonstrated. I was diligent in ensuring safety throughout each manoeuvre and wrote an operations order specifying the altitude and speed criteria for each sequence. My first obstacle was getting the display approved by Fighter Group and then by Air Command. That approval was soon forthcoming however, and my airshow season commenced on April 26th, 1986.

I flew my display with a centreline fuel tank installed as I required the extra fuel for transiting between showsites. The routine started with a take-off loop, as the Canadian Hornet continued to be the only fighter demonstrating this manoeuvre. Exiting the loop, I would pull the nose up to 70 degrees of pitch and then execute a max rate roll to the inverted position. I would then immediately pull back down to complete a half Cuban-eight and re-enter stage centre for multiple level rolls. I later modified this manoeuvre on a recommendation from Bob Hoover, an old friend from Snowbird days, and a master civilian aerobatic performer. He suggested completing several max rate rolls while at 70 degrees nose up attitude to add more crowd appeal to the turn around. He was definitely right, as the manoeuvre could still be accomplished without the aircraft leaving centre stage by more than a mile. The multiple level rolls dispelled the myth that the CF-18 had a roll rate problem.

From a Square Loop to a High Alpha 360

My next sequence of manoeuvres included two firsts for a fighter aircraft – a square loop and a high alpha 360 degree turn. The square loop was executed to demonstrate the superior pitch rate of the CF-18 over other competitive fighters such as the F-15 and F-16. Then, after completing a level 360 degree turn at 7.8 G and 325 knots, I re-entered from stage left at 200 feet above ground in level flight. Reducing speed to approximately 100 knots and a flight attitude of 28 to 33 degrees angle of attack, I could demonstrate the superior slow-speed handling characteristics of the CF-18. This was my signature manoeuvre, and one which could not be duplicated by any other fighter. I would complete a 360 degree level turn in front of the crowd at this angle of attack and appear to be hanging in the air by a thread. It was not difficult to fly as one simply maintained attitude with stick pressure and altitude with thrust. The turn was actually accomplished with rudder since the fly-by-wire system washed out the ailerons at 25 degrees angle of attack. The crowd loved it and it convinced the world that this jet had a slow-speed capability second to none. The advantages in a gun fight were obvious.

Upon completion of the 360 degree high alpha turn, and back at centre stage, I selected full afterburner and pulled the nose up to 80 degrees of pitch. The aircraft had better than a one-to-one thrust-to-weight ratio and would accelerate in this near-vertical attitude. I climbed in this attitude in full afterburner to 3,000 feet and completed a 'split S' to reposition back to show centre. From show centre at 550 knots, I would pull the aircraft to the vertical and complete continuous rolls until reaching about 25,000 feet. That was the end of my demonstration and it usually convinced even the most sceptical that this was a fighter in which Canadians could be confident and proud.

I conducted 56 performances across North America in the summer of 1986. It felt great to be flying a fighter that performed better than all its competitors. This was something Canadian fighter pilots had not experienced for decades. Everyone associated with the aircraft was delighted, as of course was McDonnell Douglas. However, a senior ranking officer at NDHQ, who was not intimately aware of the Hornet's capabilities, expressed concern after he watched the show

Canadian demo pilots flying the CF-18 have gained fame for their loops on take-off, dirty rolls, square loops, multiple rolls and "high alpha" slow-speed passes. White mist forming instantaneously in the low pressure area above the wing is usually a telltale sign that the pilot is pulling G – lots of it! (Mike Valenti, bottom right William Gilson)

Once the bastion of CF-100s, T-33s, CF-104s and CF-5s, 4 Wing Cold Lake is now the home of three of Canada's five CF-18 Sqns (410, 416, 441), the CT-115 Hawk fighter conversion squadron (419) and a combat support squadron (417). Shown overflying the base during the annual Maple Flag war games is Capt Miguel Bernard, the western demo pilot for 1998. (Mike Reyno/Skytech Images)

at CFB Trenton. As a result, the show was grounded temporarily until he could be convinced that it was safe. Surprisingly, it was also suggested that some of the manoeuvres be changed so as not to upstage the F-15 Eagle of the USAF. LCol Laurie Hawn came to the rescue with some great staff work from his position in Fighter Group. He convinced the senior leadership of the Canadian Forces that the show was not only safe, but *essential* in order to raise the credibility of the CF-18 to the people of Canada. His logical argument was accepted and I never missed a show – or changed any manoeuvres.

In all of my performances and arrival shows, there were only two occasions where I experienced a malfunction with the aircraft. At the CFB Bagotville show I had one throttle stick in full military power. I was able to complete the show, although the high alpha 360 degree turn could only be slowed to about 20 degrees alpha because of the excess power. Once the show was over, I simply shut the engine down prior to landing. This was the beauty of having two engines! During another arrival show, while pulling up after a high-speed pass at around 580 knots, the drive for the right leading edge flap broke. This caused the left flap to drive down while the right flap remained up. After a few very exciting moments, I was able to slow down and hold the wings level. The aircraft was then landed without further incident and the spare static display aircraft used for the show.

Being on the road for most of the summer left me with a wealth of memories. My most memorable flypast took place at Expo 86 in Vancouver when I flew a high alpha pass along the length of False Creek and past the Expo site. Without question, my most memorable show was at Abbotsford which saw five national military aerobatic teams perform that summer. Teams from the United States, France, Italy, Brazil and our own Snowbirds were in attendance. This was an extravaganza never accomplished before or since in North America. Due to obvious time constraints with so many teams performing, the CF-18 was the only aircraft to fly on each of the three days at the show – a great honour. My most touching personal moment occurred after the show in Halifax, Nova Scotia when the airshow announcer had 60,000 people sing Happy Birthday on my 40th.

I flew my last official CF-18 show on March 11th, 1987. It was for an audience of one at CFB Cold Lake when Rick Hansen visited on his around-the-world *Man in Motion* tour. I enjoyed this year immensely and was very proud to have had the opportunity to show the Canadian public that their tax dollars had been well spent on the CF-18."

Bob Wade

THE 3-4 MAY AIRSHOW AT MCAS EL TORO WAS ITS USUAL SUCCESS, VERY LARGE CROWDS AND LOTS OF ACTION. THIS YEAR A SLEEPER STOLE THE SHOW. TWO CANADIAN CF-18'S FROM CFB COLD LAKE, 410 SQN, CAME FOR THE SHOW. THOUGH NOT ON THE SCHEDULE, ONE OF THE AIRCRAFT PERFORMED IN THE SHOW EACH DAY. THE PERFORMANCE CAME ABOUT MIDDAY THROUGH THE SHOW AND EVERYTHING FOLLOWING WAS AN ANTICLIMAX. THE ENTIRE AEROBATIC PERFORMANCE WAS DONE IN FRONT OF THE SPECTATORS AND LEFT THE FLYING TYPES WITH THEIR MOUTHS AGAPE. THE MOST SENSATIONAL MANEUVER WAS A "HARRIER CIRCLE" IN FRONT OF THE CROWD. HOWEVER, IN THIS CASE IT WAS AN F-18 DOING THE CIRCLE! IF YOU HAVE NOT SEEN THIS MANEUVER, IT GOES SOMETHING LIKE THIS. APPROACH THE GRANDSTAND AT LOW AIRSPEED, HIGH ANGLE OF ATTACK, AND LOTS OF POWER. A SLIGHT BANK TO THE LEFT AND HOLD ATTITUDE/ALTITUDE WITH THRUST WHILE THE AIRCRAFT DRIFTS THROUGH 360 DEGREES IN A $1/4$ MILE CIRCLE. WOW! THEN ACCELERATE INTO A CLIMB. WE HAVE A LOT TO LOOK FORWARD TO WHEN THE "BLUE'S" BEGIN FLYING THIS BIRD.

A message from an American aviator that found its way back to Cold Lake following the airshow at Marine Corps Air Station El Toro, California in 1986.

All Canadian Hornet shows since 1986 have been derivatives of the shows developed over the first four years of CF-18 operations with

the Canadian Forces. Each passing year has brought one, and usually two, new faces to the North American airshow community, each welcomed to a new fraternity of colleagues in a profession which demands the highest precision and discipline. For each one of these demonstration pilots pictured in this chapter, their airshow experience remains one of the highlights of their aviation careers. In the year 2002, 410 Sqn celebrated its 20th anniversary of airshow performances by the Hornet. Although 425 Sqn fielded its first CF-18 demo pilot in 1985 in Capt Chuck Caron, it was 1989 before 433 Sqn introduced Capt Richard Duguay as its first demo pilot for Eastern Canada. Since that time, eastern performances have generally alternated between the two Bagotville-based squadrons.

While designation as an airshow solo pilot is a rare honour that typically lasts for only a single season (aside from a tour on the Snowbirds), there have been exceptions

Passing the torch. Capt Neale Nowosad (left) was selected as 410 Sqn's demonstration pilot for the 1987 airshow season, taking over from Capt Bob Wade. (Mike Valenti)

in the fighter community. One notable exception in the CF-18 era was Jacques Thibaudeau. Seven years and two postings after he had flown his last airshow in the CF-5, he was selected as the 1987 eastern demo pilot. He explains how he prepared for the season and how the sudden departure of a colleague gave him the opportunity to spend two summers on the CF-18 airshow circuit:

"I was introduced to the Hornet airshow scene in 1987 after being transferred to 425 Sqn. At that time, I had roughly 700 hours on the CF-18 attained as an instructor pilot at 410 Sqn. Once selected for the job, I met with Bob Wade in Cold Lake for a few training flights and then proceeded with my own training back in Bagotville. Prior to commencing my practices in the actual aircraft, I found the simulator invaluable in getting a feel for the routine and establishing critical

airspeeds and altitudes for the various manoeuvres. Once I transitioned to solo training in the Bagotville military flying area, I established a rigid training regime whereby I began my practices at 2,000 feet AGL and then gradually lowered the altitude through stages – 1,000 feet, 500 feet, 300 feet and finally directly into the show commencing with the famous takeoff loop. I always used the same configuration, a clean aircraft except for an empty centreline tank and a maximum of 6,500 pounds of fuel for takeoff directly into the show. As this was my first year as a Hornet demo pilot, I pretty much stuck to 'the Bob Wade routine.'

Success Through Teamwork

The eastern demo team has been organized along similar lines since 1986. The team consists of the demo pilot (selected for one year and acting as team leader), a static pilot, a sergeant NCO acting as crew chief and up to seven master corporals/corporal technicians. In my time, only the selection of the demo pilot had to be approved by Fighter Group, the others being at the discretion of the squadron commanding officer. Of course, airshow duties were of secondary importance with all team members having to continue with their primary duties at the squadron or wing level.

I would also be remiss in not mentioning that a reserve captain by the name of Jean-Charles Perreault had a very positive influence on our efforts to promote the Canadian Forces. Back in 1986 he offered to seek private civilian sponsors to enhance the public relations of our Hornet demonstrations in Eastern Canada. His offer to explore the possibilities was made to our commanding officer who ensured that the private sponsorship was sought strictly in accordance with existing Canadian Forces regulations and orders. Capt Perreault also offered his services as a PR person for the demo team.

The biggest private sponsorships came from companies headed by aviation buffs. Our largest sponsor operated a large car dealership while another important sponsor owned an industrial clothing facility. Both were located in the Quebec City area. These sponsors provided custom made flight suits for the demo pilot and sporty polo shirts for the supporting groundcrew who took just as much pride in their own appearance while on the airshow circuit.

Prime Minister Brian Mulroney, the guest of honour at the *Trois-Rivières* airshow on 24 Jun 87, took the opportunity to congratulate Capt Jacques Thibaudeau on his exciting Hornet demonstration.

In preparation for a major airshow, the team's technicians would travel by road and leave the base one or two days in advance. Their Canadian Forces vans (normally two of them) were loaded with spares, main landing gear tires, toolboxes and the like. The PR team members, Capt Perreault and other reserve personnel, would use a privately sponsored van to transport themselves and squadron public relations paraphernalia such as badges, squadron/base crests, T-shirts and CF-18 photographs to the respective showsites. These were always popular with airshow fans. Overall, the efforts of our groundcrew and Capt Perreault to improve public relations for the Canadian Forces were very positive and they were invaluable members of our team.

The 1987 season turned out to be highly successful with 34 demonstrations completed at 23 locations between May 19th and September 19th. With the sole exception being a show at Hanscom Field in Boston,

Capt Yves Tessier of 433 Sqn conducts a little PR from the cockpit of his Hornet at the CFB Bagotville Air Show in 1990.

The 433 Sqn team that worked behind the scenes to keep Capt Yves Tessier's 1990 Hornet display on schedule. L to R, Front row – Cpl Alain Boulianne, Sgt Denis Cormier, Capt Yves Tessier, Maj Jean-Charles Perreault, Cpl Kathleen Lemieux. Back row – France Forgues, Cpls Michel Dufour, Sylvain Marcouiller, Eric Henry, Antoine Bansept, Lucie Després. At right, the squadron's 1997 demo team. L to R - Cpl Chrétien, Capt Langille, MCpl Maldemay, Cpl Fortin. Tail art on the team's 1997 jet paid tribute to Canada's 130th birthday. (DND Photos via Yves Tessier, 433 Sqn)

Massachusetts, all of my shows were flown in Eastern Canada and of these, only two were flat shows due to low cloud or visibility. Meanwhile, Capt Neale Nowosad of 410 Sqn had an equally successful season demonstrating the Hornet in Western Canada.

Capt Pierre Blais was chosen as my replacement for 1988. Pierre and I flew two flights together at which time he proceeded to train himself for low-level aerobatics. His routine was essentially the same as mine and many positive comments were received about his excellent show. In 1989 things got interesting. With 433 Sqn having stood up on the Hornet on January 4th, 1988, Capt Richard Duguay was the first squadron pilot selected to become the next CF-18 airshow pilot from Bagotville. However, after completing his training and flying a couple of shows, Richard decided to retire from the CF to join Air Transat. This put the base in an awkward position and I was asked if I could work up my airshow routine again in minimum time. This was indeed a golden opportunity for me. I had just been promoted to the rank of major and been transferred to a ground job in wing operations.

With now over 1,300 hours on the Hornet, I felt very comfortable with both the machine and low-level aerobatics. So, in a matter of a couple weeks I was back on the airshow circuit. In early July, I phoned Col Terry

Humphries who was in charge of operations at Fighter Group in North Bay to ask him if I could integrate the first manoeuvre of my low show (a ¾ tuck-under roll) with the first manoeuvre of my high show (the take-off loop). Col Humphries had no objections to this combination. I subsequently used two maintenance flights combined with airshow practices to try the new manoeuvre. Since I had done both manoeuvres independently from brake release before, I began at 1,000 feet above the runway initially, then did two simulated runs at 500 feet AGL and 300 feet AGL respectively and, finally, did it from the ground up.

The other manoeuvres introduced in the summer of '89 were a 270 degree 'John Derry' roll before every turn and an inverted turn 'whisper' pass – roughly 60 degrees of heading change in front of the crowd while upside down with idle power from one end of the runway to the other. I also reduced the entry speed of the square loop from 325 knots to 280 knots and introduced an aileron roll just before the loop. The roll was initiated at 220 knots and was done in full afterburner. This roll not only provided good entertainment, but from a safety perspective ensured that both afterburners were lit before initiation of the square loop (occasionally, one afterburner would ignite one-half to one second after the other which was not ideal for the initiation of the square loop).

Needless to say, ample use of the Hornet's impressive one-to-one thrust-to-weight ratio was made to provide what I believe was an exciting show for the Canadian public. Combined with its ability to sustain a 5 G turn at only 280 knots due to its advanced aerodynamic design, this meant the show could easily be kept within the confines of the airfield while safely manoeuvring in front of the public.

In 1990, Capt Yves Tessier of 433 Sqn took over as the eastern Hornet demo pilot after we flew several low-level aerobatic sorties together. This marked the end of my airshow career. Overall, flying air displays with the Hornet was a blessing for me. The flying was short but intense – a high show sequence would easily consume 5000 pounds of fuel, yet the entire sequence would last only 10 minutes from takeoff to touchdown. Looking at my logbook, I count 120 low-level aerobatic sorties related to airshow practices or actual air demos. In both 1987 and 1989, I was able to fly three practice sessions per week before proceeding to a showsite. In my mind, this is the only way to stay proficient (and safe) in that type of work."

Jacques Thibaudeau

In later years Maj Thibaudeau put into words many of the lessons that have been learned by airshow performers over the years in a comprehensive article for the Canadian

Team players. Behind every demonstration pilot is a dedicated crew that ensures show aircraft remain safe for public performances. Shown here are two teams that, although separated by 10 years and some 2,600 kilometers, shared a common bond of professionalism – the 1989 team from 425 Sqn in Bagotville, Quebec and the 1999 team from 410 Sqn in Cold Lake, Alberta. (DND Photos)

Forces *Flight Comment* magazine. Covering everything from selection and training to weather and aircraft limits, it was a practical essay on the "do's and don'ts" of display flying. And although designed for a military audience, his practical considerations are just as appropriate to civilian performers – as is his bottom line: *"To organize and fly a safe and crowd pleasing air display is the mark of a true professional. Armed with knowledge, common sense and dedication, you will experience a highly successful season and please hundreds of thousands in the process."*

Speaking of pleasing airshow fans, Abbotsford 1989 afforded a unique opportunity to witness history in the making when the Soviet Air Force made its first appearance at a North American airshow. Highlighting their presence was the MiG 29 Fulcrum which put on a magnificent solo display to complement the best of what the West had to offer – the A-10, F-15, F-16 and CF-18 displays. To bring the show to a truly

In 1990 two MiG-29 Fulcrums returned to Canada and were escorted from Alaskan airspace to Winnipeg by 441 Tac (F) Sqn. En route to Ottawa for the National Capital Air Show, the MiGs were led on the final portion of their journey by members of 433 Tac (F) Sqn. Joining them to capture the event for posterity on 30 Jun 90 was CF photographer WO Johnson who took these historic shots, unimaginable only a few years before. Note the distinct similarity in design in many areas of the two fighters. The eastern escort team included, L to R, Capt "Moe" Girard, LCol Ray Levasseur, Maj Serge Boudreault, Maj Yvan Blondin and WO Vic Johnson. (DND Photos)

memorable close on August 13th, some last minute diplomatic overtures and the spirit of *glasnost* resulted in Maj Bob Wade becoming the first western pilot to fly in a Soviet fighter. Wearing a borrowed Russian helmet and G suit, Wade put the aircraft through its paces with chief Mikoyan test pilot Valery Menitsky riding shotgun in the back seat.

Given the implausible events of that weekend, and with Marshal of the Soviet Air Force Skomorokhov in attendance, it is little wonder that only a year later the Russians formed their first demonstration team utilizing six Fulcrums. The *Strizhy* (Swifts) put on their first public display six months later in France.

Canada's Hornet Demonstration Pilots 1983-2002

Capt Gary Liddiard
410 Tac (F) Sqn 1983
409 Tac (F) Sqn 1985

Capt Dale Erhart
410 Tac (F) Sqn
1984

Capt B.J. Ryan
410 Tac (F) Sqn
1984

Capt Guy Dutil
410 Tac (F) Sqn
1985

Capt Chuck Caron
425 Tac (F) Sqn
1985

Capt Bob Wade
410 Tac (F) Sqn
1986

Capt Tristan deKoninck
425 Tac (F) Sqn
1986

Capt Neale Nowosad
410 Tac (F) Sqn
1987

Maj Jacques Thibaudeau
425 Tac (F) Sqn
1987, 1989

Capt Terry Shortt
410 Tac (F) Sqn
1988

Capt Pierre Blais
425 Tac (F) Sqn
1988

Capt Rich Lancaster
410 Tac (F) Sqn
1989

Maj Mark Holmes
410 Tac (F) Sqn
1990

Capt Yves Tessier
433 Tac (F) Sqn
1990

Capt Louis DeGagne
410 Tac (F) Sqn
1991

Capt Jon Graham
425 Tac (F) Sqn
1992

Capt Keith Moore
410 Tac (F) Sqn
1993

Capt Marc Charpentier
433 Tac (F) Sqn
1993, 1994

Capt Kevin Stewart
410 Tac (F) Sqn
1994

Capt Mike Woodfield
410 Tac (F) Sqn
1995

Capt Jean-Marc Bzrezinski
433 Tac (F) Sqn
1995

Capt Duane Lecaine
410 Tac (F) Sqn
1996

Capt Greg Morris
425 Tac (F) Sqn
1996

Capt Doug Carter
410 Tac (F) Sqn
1997

Maj Norm Gagne
410 Tac (F) Sqn
1997

Capt Steve Langille
433 Tac (F) Sqn
1997

Capt Steve Nierlich
410 Tac (F) Sqn
1998

Capt Miguel Bernard
410 Tac (F) Sqn
1998

Capt Bill Moffat
425 Tac (F) Sqn
1998

Capt Rob Mitchell
410 Tac (F) Sqn
1999

Capt Mike Mirza
410 Tac (F) Sqn
1999

Capt Scott Greenough
410 Tac (F) Sqn
2000

Capt Patrice Hervieux
433 Tac (F) Sqn
2000

Capt Lee Vogan
410 Tac (F) Sqn
2001

Capt Rick Williams
410 Tac (F) Sqn
2001

Capt Gary Schwindt
433 Tac (F) Sqn
2001

Capt Doug Clements
410 Tac (F) Sqn
2002

Capt Scott Shrubsole
425 Tac (F) Sqn
2002

Missing:
Capt Richard Duguay
433 Tac (F) Sqn 1989

Capt Grant Cossey
425 Tac (F) Sqn 1994

European Demo Pilots 1986-1990

Capt Paul Noack
409 Tac (F) Sqn
1986

Capt Ron Platt
439 Tac (F) Sqn
1986

Capt Billie Flynn
409 Tac (F) Sqn
1987

Capt Grant Youngson
439 Tac (F) Sqn
1987

Capt Don Thornton
409 Tac (F) Sqn
1988

Capt Bob Painchaud
421 Tac (F) Sqn
1988

Capt Chris Glover
421 Tac (F) Sqn
1989

Capt Kirk Leuty
439 Tac (F) Sqn
1989

Capt Mal Macnair
409 Tac (F) Sqn
1990

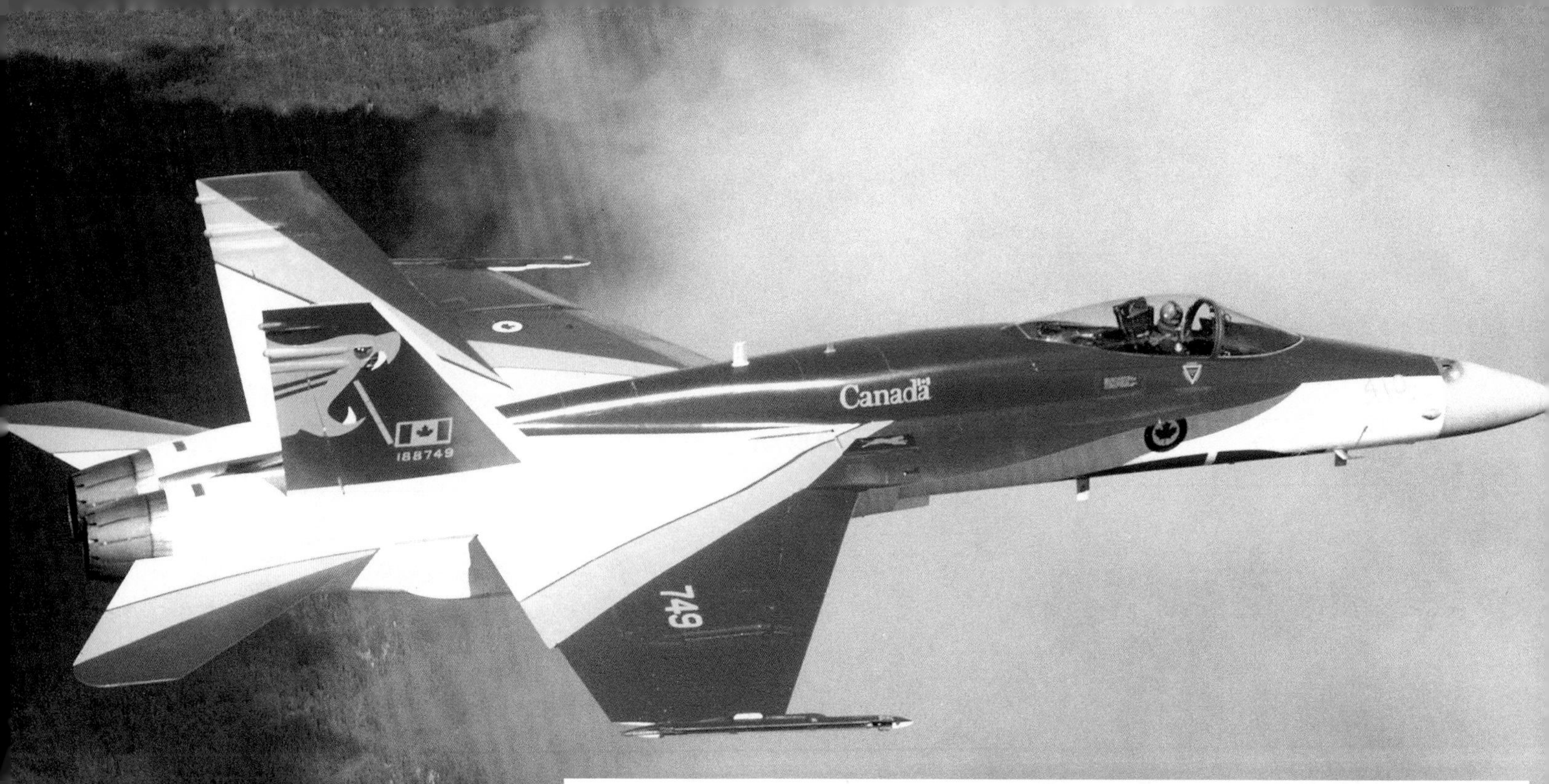

DND 1990

DND 1993, Cpl Jim Templeton

Hornet Art – Canada's High Performance Airshow Aircraft

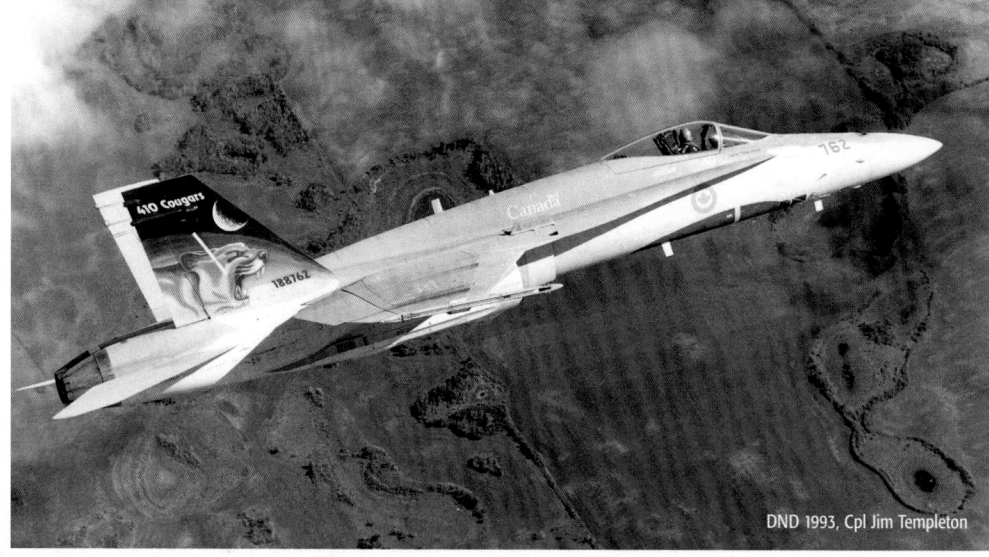

Civilian graphic designer Jim Belliveau of 410 Sqn Cold Lake has an interesting hobby – painting jets! Since 1990 he has worked with a team of dedicated military volunteers who have devoted thousands of hours to create the masterpieces that have graced Canadian airshows from coast-to-coast. Belliveau's creations are often designed to commemorate a special event in Canada's aviation history. His assistants over the years have included refinishing specialists MCpl Don Sutherland, MCpl Greg Brown, Cpl Dan Morvillo, MCpl Doug Hennessey, Cpl Terry George, Cpl Brian Victor, MCpl Pat Trainor, MCpl Ray Morawietz, Cpl Craig Price and Cpl Brent Johnston, as well as the staff of 1 Air Maintenance Sqn. As these pages graphically illustrate, the team's artwork has varied from tail art to complete aircraft refinishing. (DND Photos courtesy 410 Sqn.)

DND 1994

DND 1996

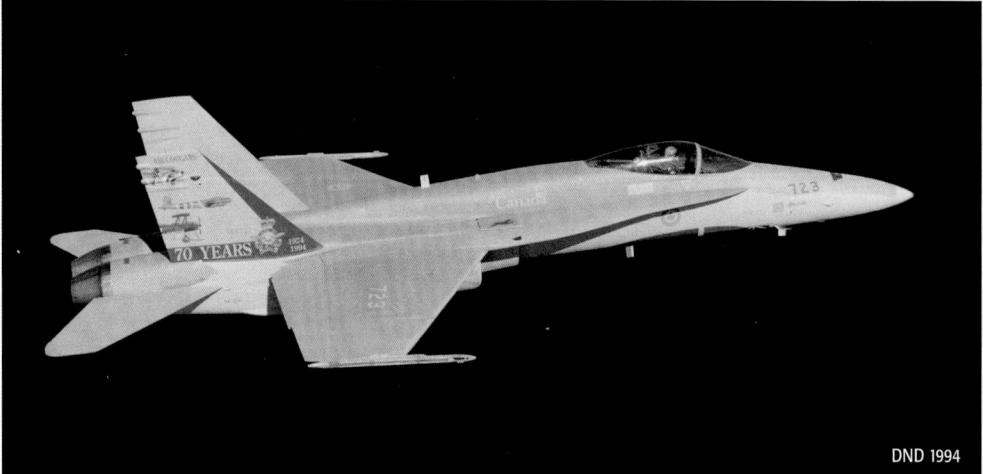

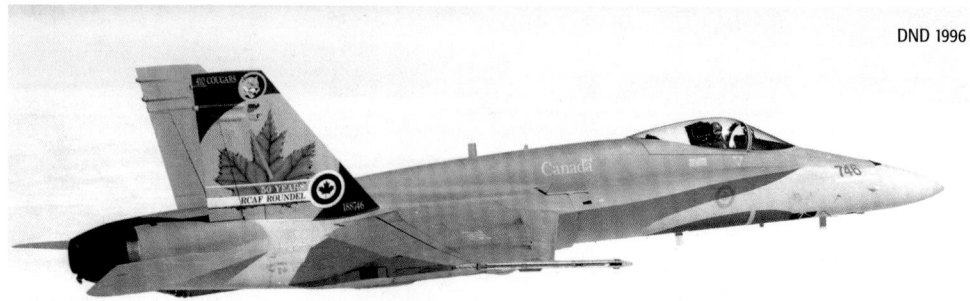

DND 1997, Cpl D. Bernier

DND 1995, Cpl Chris Bentley

1998, Mike Reyno/Skytech Images

DND, 1998

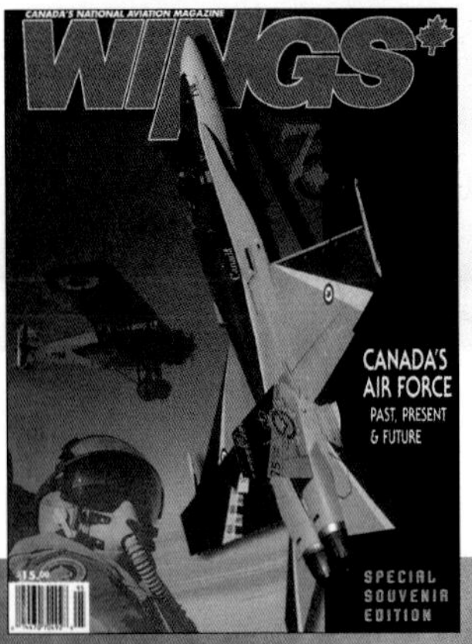

Above and immediately below – 410 Sqn's eye-catching 75th anniversary Hornet was one of the most popular schemes of all time. It was featured in a special edition of *WINGS* magazine which saluted the heritage and history of Canada's Air Force in 1999. (Mike Reyno/Skytech Images, cover courtesy *WINGS*)

Below – Although the majority of CF-18 coloured birds have been associated with 410 Sqn, the Silver Foxes of 441 Sqn Cold Lake were among many squadrons that painted an airshow aircraft to salute the 70th anniversary of Canada's Air Force in 1994. (The invasion stripes were added in memory of the 50th anniversary of D-Day, 6 June 1944, and the Canadians who paid the supreme sacrifice during the epic battle.) At right is the "checkerboard" squadron's tribute to the 75th anniversary of the RCAF five years later. (Mike Reyno/Skytech Images, William Gilson)

DND 2000

Mike Reyno/Skytech Images 2000

Two more colourful designs from 4 Wing in Cold Lake, Alberta graced the Canadian airshow circuit in 2001 and 2002. The scheme above recognized the 60th anniversary of the formation of 410 Sqn in 1941 while the 2002 edition paid tribute to 20 years of Hornet operations in Canada. (Mike Reyno/Skytech Images)

3 Wing at Bagotville, Quebec has also done its part in promoting the Canadian Forces over the years. Low visibility "airshow" schemes introduced in 1993 have evolved over time into the spectacular example below which appeared in 2002 to celebrate the 60th anniversary of the formation of 425 Sqn. The mastermind of this scheme was Cpl Dan Raymond with assistance from Capts Scott Shrubsole and Marty Roesler-Yue. The dedicated refinishers who took turns working overtime for five weeks to prepare and paint the aircraft included MCpl Yves Cliche and Cpls Jean-Guy Blanchette, Marc Charette, Joe Tappin, Vicky Bardslokken, Patrick Viau, Daniel DeCourval, Dany Buckingham and John Twaddle. (Richard Girourard – above and below left, Mike Reyno/Skytech Images – below right and bottom)

Hornet Demonstrations in Europe

With Canada having been the first foreign nation to purchase the Hornet after the United States Navy, and therefore the first to deploy the aircraft to the NATO theatre in Europe, there was immediate interest in having the aircraft perform at airshows across the continent. The arrival of one of the most formidable fighting aircraft in the world gave the Canadians a renewed status in the alliance, one they hadn't enjoyed since the early 1950s and 1960s when they had been among the first of the allies to deploy the Sabre and Starfighter respectively to that theatre.

For McDonnell Douglas, the prospect of having the Hornet so capably demonstrated in the hands of Canadian pilots was a welcome endorsement of their product. Although the immediate future of the fighter forces of Britain, West Germany and Italy were firmly tied to the joint venture Panavia Tornado fighter bomber, and smaller nations such as the Netherlands, Belgium, Denmark and Norway had opted for the lighter, single-engine General Dynamics F-16 to replace their F-104 and F-5 squadrons, there were still several nations hanging in the balance with respect to their future defence needs. Spain had been the first European country to join the F-18 consortium in December of 1982 but had still not taken delivery of their first aircraft when the Canadians arrived in Europe with their formidable new machines. Subsequent Canadian demonstrations of the aircraft in Switzerland and Finland helped play a role in the selection of the aircraft by their respective air forces in 1988 and 1992 respectively.

The Nighthawks Arrive

The first CF-18s to arrive at Baden-Soellingen to commence a new era of Canadian fighter operations were not Tigers as expected but the Nighthawks of 409 Sqn, having bid farewell to Comox and over two decades of service to NORAD almost a year earlier. This had not been the original plan, but when a combination of fatigue problems within the vertical fins of the new aircraft and bad weather delayed the 439 conversion course, the decision was taken to send 409 Sqn to Europe instead. This was of only minor inconvenience to the Tigers but a heartbreaker for the Silver Foxes of

Commencing in mid-1985, the skies of Western Europe bore witness to the arrival of a new Canadian fighter to bolster NATO's 4 ATAF – the Hornets of 409 Tac (F) Sqn. On hand to record the event was veteran Canadian Forces photographer WO Vic Johnson who captured this tight four-ship of Nighthawks over southern Germany. (DND ISC 86-560)

441 Sqn as it meant their long association with Europe would come to a close with the retirement of the Starfighter.

Operation Baden Nighthawk I saw the first four-ship arrive at Baden on June 7th, 1985. However, these were not the first Hornets to have crossed the Atlantic non-stop. The first visitors had arrived in the spring of 1984 during *Operation Rhine Hornet* led by Al DeQuetteville in order to assess the compatibility of the fighter with the existing infrastructure at Baden and Lahr. It was this trip that had paved the way for the Hornet's eventual arrival. Thus, fully loaded with three external fuel tanks and four missiles each, the Nighthawks had left Cold Lake on June 5th and flown non-stop to Goose Bay utilizing air-to-air refuelling. After an overnight stop they launched into the darkness late the next night to time their arrival at Baden for 0930 hrs the next morning, again using a Boeing

707 tanker to make the non-stop journey across the Atlantic. Topping up twice to ensure they could always make landfall in the event of an emergency, the flight from Goose took exactly 5.5 hours. It was a memorable morning as the tight diamond led by Maj Gary Liddiard dropped out of the overcast and thundered overhead the base to herald their arrival. As the four grey fighters taxied to parking in their new home in the south dispersal, they were welcomed by a large contingent of staff led by Col Dave McIntosh, Base Commander CFB Baden.

Watching the four smiling pilots quickly disembark and happily peel out of their cumbersome immersion suits was a bittersweet moment for those of us still upholding Canada's NATO commitments with the Starfighter. While we were all delighted to see the new aircraft finally entering operational service, the arrival of the newcomers meant that our tours in the idyllic *Schwarzwald* region would soon come to a close. Yet, while it was true that the new steed had capabilities far surpassing those of our ageing aircraft, could this rookie squadron to the NATO theatre ever surpass the camaraderie of the Starfighter family? We thought not – and went to great lengths to prove it over the seven remaining months of CF-104 operations until 441 Sqn's distinguished service in Europe came to an end on March 1st, 1986.

The 409 Sqn team led by Capt Billie Flynn that made the first Canadian Hornet appearance at the Paris Airshow in 1987. (DND Photo)

Although 409 Sqn faced a formidable challenge in adapting to an entirely new theatre of operations with the new aircraft, demands to show off the "magic jet" around Europe were inevitable and were soon forthcoming. However, affording the squadron an opportunity to get used to its new surroundings, an official welcome ceremony by NATO was not scheduled until the end of October to coincide with a visit by Canada's Minister of National Defence. In order to properly show off the new aircraft, authorization was granted to work up an aerobatic demonstration for the October 31st ceremony.

Let the Show Begin

Since Gary Liddiard had become the first of Canada's Hornet demo pilots two scant years earlier, he was a natural choice to fly the inaugural demonstration in Europe. Given his previous experience, it took him only four dedicated practices to work up a fully aerobatic show. Although this would be his last official performance as a demonstration pilot on the Hornet, Liddiard fulfilled an integral role in the on-going demonstration program right through the summer of 1990 when his European tour ended. In total, he oversaw the training of nine pilots in the art of high performance aerial demonstration. During this period, with the return of 439 and 421 Sqns from their conversions in Cold Lake, the squadrons took turns selecting volunteers for the demonstration role with two pilots sharing shows each summer commencing in 1986. The first two Canadians to demonstrate the CF-18s capabilities to airshow audiences in Europe were Capts Paul Noack of 409 Sqn and Ron Platt of 439 Sqn. Both have vivid memories of their European tours.

Capt Paul Noack of 409 Sqn was the first to show off Canada's newest fighter outside Baden-Soellingen and offers some thoughts

When not performing airshow duties in 1986, Capt Paul Noack carried out normal combat training with 409 Sqn. He is shown here briefing with Maj Gord Todd, the first Canadian Forces pilot to check out on the F/A-18 Hornet at the US Navy test pilot school. (DND ISC 87-493, WO Vic Johnson)

CF-18 European Shows 1986-1987

1986		1987	
Gerona, Spain	24-26 Apr	Mildenhall, England	3-24 May
Mildenhall, England	23-25 May	Liege, Belgium	23-24 May
Sion, Switzerland	13-15 Jun	Stavanger, Norway	30 May
Hannover, Germany	13-16 Jun	Aviano, Italy	30-31 May
Metz, France	20-23 Jun	Skrydstrup, Denmark	13-14 Jun
Kleine Brogel, Belgium	27-29 Jun	Paris, France	16-21 Jun
Ramstein, Germany	8-11 Aug	Montijo, Portugal	27 Jun
Baden-Soellingen, Germany	18 Sep	Twenthe, Netherlands	3-4 Jul
Eindhoven, Netherlands	20 Sep	Bex, Switzerland	21-22 Aug
Baden-Soellingen, Germany	27 Sep	Ramstein, Germany	1 Aug
		Baden-Soellingen, Germany	19 Sep
		Leuchars, Scotland	20-21 Sep
		Baden-Soellingen, Germany	5 Nov

By the end of the 1987 airshow season, four Canadian demonstration pilots had completed demonstrations in 12 European countries.

on his European tour in the summer of '86 which saw him perform in four countries:

———————

"There was nothing quite like it! There I was: 25 years-old; single; and given the newest, hottest fighter in the world to fly and demonstrate around Europe! Maj Gary Liddiard had provided invaluable assistance in preparing my show and I was soon raring to go. My first venture away from home base was to Gerona, Spain on April 24th with Maj Paul Deacon. Although this show was only originally planned as a static display, it quickly turned into a flying demo after the Spanish Air Force made a plea to our headquarters in Lahr while we were on site. At the time, the SAF had not yet received their first F-18 and obviously wanted to see more than simply a static aircraft. I was happy to oblige once the appropriate approval came through. King Juan Carlos was in attendance and paid us a visit to personally thank us for coming.

As I was sharing airshow duties with Ron Platt of 439 Sqn, he did his first show of the year at the big show at RAF Mildenhall, England in May. Then in June, he headed off to Sion, Switzerland while I headed north to Hannover, Germany for a weekend show. Arriving on Friday afternoon, I thought I would only be flying one demonstration the next day. However, the organizers rapidly made it very clear they wanted a demo every day – starting right now! The following weekend I was off to Metz, France where we experienced some unforeseen problems. As I recall, there had recently been a flying accident in Belgium and as a result, during our in-brief, the French Air Force officer in charge of the show demanded that the minimum demo altitude for all performers be raised to 1,000

feet! As the standard was 300 feet, this created great consternation among the performers in attendance and the demo pilots banded together in protest to achieve a compromise of a 500 foot show altitude. The show went on as advertised.

Two more major showsites rounded out my tour. A show at Kleine Brogel was a typical Belgian event with both spectators and participants enjoying the weekend to the maximum. Ramstein, Germany, by far the largest show in Europe, was truly an incredible experience with all NATO countries being well represented. My last show of the season was back in Baden on September 27th for the 'hometown' crowd as Ron Platt had flown his last show the weekend before to a very appreciative crowd at Eindhoven in The Netherlands. Although I had anticipated this would be my last demo on the Hornet, I was asked to do one more over the base the following February for a group of travelling Canadian parliamentarians. This truly brought to a close my short but very memorable tour as an F-18 demo pilot."

Paul Noack

———————

Capts Ron Platt (top) and Marty Tate (bottom) were escorted into Switzerland in Jun 86 by a pair of fellow Tigers from 11 Sqn flying their F-5 fighters. Platt was the first Canadian Forces pilot to dazzle Swiss spectators with a high performance Hornet show. (via Marty Tate)

Capt Ron Platt was equally enthusiastic about his airshow experience but for him, one weekend stood out from all others. Taking off from Baden on June 13th with wingman Capt Marty Tate in tow, it was only minutes before the duo were met at the German/Swiss border by a pair of Swiss Air Force F-5 fighters from Sion that led them on a low-level tour of the Swiss Alps, something no other foreign fighter pilot had ever had the privilege of experiencing in "neutral" Switzerland. What was particularly special for the two Canadians was that their "guides" were from the Swiss Tiger squadron, 11 Sqn, based in Sion. The two Hornets garnered more than a passing interest that weekend from spectators and officials alike as the aircraft had been announced as a preliminary contender to replace the F-5. Platt did his part to impress all with a stunning performance the likes of which had never before been seen in Swiss skies … and, with repeat performances by Capts Kirk Leuty in 1989, Mal Macnair in 1990 and Louis DeGagne in 1991, the Hornet was ultimately selected as Switzerland's next generation fighter.

In the ensuing years, Canada's CF-18 pilots continued to fly the Canadian flag at almost every major airshow in Western Europe, doing both 1 Air Division and their country proud. While these encounters always generated exciting experiences for the crews involved, some were truly memorable. One such example took place in 1989. Capt Chris Glover of 421 Sqn and Capt Kirk Leuty of 439 were selected to split the airshow duties that summer and used that age-old tradition, the coin toss, to decide who would go to Paris – Leuty won, much to Glover's chagrin! This victory set the stage for an extraordinary experience. While at the Paris show Leuty met Anatoly Kvotchur, a Mikoyan test pilot who was to demonstrate the MiG 29 Fulcrum at the show. In fact, the two shared lunch just before setting off to prepare for their individual shows. Leuty flew first, with Kvotchur immediately following. After putting on his own stellar high performance show, Leuty was taxiing in as the MiG 29 rocketed into the sky and immediately launched into its twisting and turning demonstration of raw power. No sooner had Leuty stepped out of his cockpit to watch the remainder of the Soviet's show, the MiG experienced a catastrophic engine failure

With the revival of 1 Air Division to replace 1 Canadian Air Group in Europe, a new heraldic badge was approved by the Governor General of Canada in 1988.

while in low-level, knife-edge flight and immediately nosed over vertically due to the asymmetric thrust generated by the other engine. Staring death in the face, Anatoly Kvotchur did the only thing he could do – "pull the handles" as his stricken aircraft needle-nosed into the ground like a lawn dart. The photographic footage is some of the most spellbinding ever taken of an aerial disaster. In a remarkable testament to the ejection system of the MiG 29, Kvotchur's parachute opened just in time to save his life. Sprinting towards the downed pilot in full stride, in spite of the searing heat of the fireball, Kirk Leuty was the first to reach the Soviet pilot. As crash vehicles converged on the scene, Leuty was with Kvotchur just long enough to get a "thumb's up" from the Russian before he was rushed away to hospital.

The fact that no one on the ground was injured by the explosion spoke volumes about the safety measures and show restrictions that were extant in Western Europe following the horrific airshow disaster at Ramstein, Germany only the year before. Kvotchur's injuries were minor in nature and he returned to the airfield before the end of the show to be welcomed by his fellow performers. Kirk Leuty was among the first

to greet him and the two Cold War warriors shared a toast to Kvotchur's successful ejection. What tragic irony then, that having impressed hundreds of thousands of European spectators in the summer of 1989 with his Hornet demonstration, Capt Kirk Leuty lost his life in April 1990 following a head-on mid-air collision with a fellow 1 Air Division pilot during a routine air-to-air combat training exercise just north of Baden-Soellingen. It was a great loss … and the beginning of what was to become an ominous year.

As it transpired, that summer of 1990 would be the last a dedicated Hornet demo pilot would be appointed in Europe, Capt Mal Macnair of 409 Sqn doing the honours, as he explains:

"I was scheduled to fly 12 shows in the summer of 1990 but my last airshow was cancelled when our squadron was selected to deploy to the Persian Gulf on *Operation Scimitar*. Of the shows I performed, the Italians definitely had the most exuberant fans, the Dutch had the most (130,000 per day) and the French were the most thoroughly gracious hosts possible. However, my greatest personal honour of the year did not come during those shows but rather during an 'on field practice' over Baden-Soellingen before the official airshow season began. Although in reality it was my acceptance show by the 4 Wing commander, we had some special VIPs in the audience – original members of the Nighthawks from WW II who had returned to the base for a reunion. I therefore felt the honour of 409 Sqn on my shoulders that day more than any other. All in all, it was an exceptional final year for the Canadians on the European airshow circuit, in spite of the cancellation of our last show. I'm sure we were missed in subsequent years given the wonderful feedback the fans gave us at each and every show."

Mal Macnair

Understandably, when the winds of war blew across the Middle East in the summer of 1990, all further consideration of airshow participation came to a grinding halt for most of the NATO allies. At the time, no one could have anticipated the historic conflict that was about to unfold.

A formidable deterrent. A Canadian Hornet on combat air patrol during *Desert Storm* in 1991. Carrying three external fuel tanks to extend its loiter time, the aircraft is armed with four AIM-9 Sidewinder missiles and three AIM-7 Sparrows. The Iraqi Air Force elected not to participate in this particular airshow. (Craig Halliwell)

From Airshow to Air Power

For Canadians serving at 4 Wing, rapid changes to their peacetime posture took place soon after the Iraqi invasion of Kuwait on August 2nd, 1990. With the ensuing strife in the Middle East threatening to plunge the entire region into war, a United Nations Security Council resolution led to the deployment of a coalition of military forces to the region to encourage the Iraqis to retreat from Kuwait and its rich oilfields. In addition to Canadian naval forces, 409 Sqn soon received word that they would be deployed to Doha, Qatar as part of the USA led *Operation Desert Shield*. Intensive preparations began in September and on October 4th the aircraft took to the skies and headed east to the Persian Gulf to join the massive allied air force deploying to the region. Two months later, the Nighthawks were replaced by the Tigers of 439 Sqn. Supplemented primarily by pilots from 416 "Lynx" Sqn based at Cold Lake, the Canadian contingent became known as "The Desert Cats." When diplomacy failed to dis-

lodge the invaders, *Desert Shield* became *Desert Storm* and the Canadians joined the allied war effort commencing on January 17th, 1991. Initially employed in the CAP role (combat air patrol), the Canadian contingent later also conducted fighter escort for coalition strike packages and air-to-ground bombing missions against the Iraqi Republican Guard. All told, the 25 Canadian Hornets deployed to the Gulf conducted 2,700 sorties, including training and combat missions. It was the first time Canadians had dropped bombs since the Second World War. It would not be the last …

The Gulf War understandably affected airshows in Europe and across the Atlantic with many shows being cancelled or significantly scaled back in scope as more and more assets were assigned to the Middle East. Ironically, within a few months of the Iraqi defeat, 409 Sqn was disbanded at 4 Wing on June 24th, 1991. This downsizing effectively ended all future flying displays at European airshows for the Canadians, although 4 Wing continued to support static displays when opera-

tional circumstances permitted. It was only three months after the disbandment of 409 Sqn that the Canadian government signalled its intention to close Baden-Soellingen by 1994, a decision that surprised and disappointed many on both sides of the Atlantic.

The End of a European Presence

The end came sooner than expected with a decision to repatriate the last of Canada's Hornets early in 1993. To signal the end of a most distinguished era in Canadian air force history, hundreds of personnel from across Canada made their way to *Flugplatz Soellingen*, the original birthplace of 4 (F) Wing in April 1953, to give the base a resounding send-off from November 20th to 23rd, 1992. The Tigers of 439 Sqn were the last to conduct a 16-plane flypast over the closure ceremonies parade on November 23rd. Two months later, in January 1993, 24 CF-18s "slipped the surly bonds" over the base for the last time and headed home.

Although the heritage forged over 40 years of Canadian fighter presence in Europe had come to an end, it would not be forgotten. Approving a staff initiative at Air Command Headquarters in Winnipeg, LGen David Huddleston, Commander Air Command, ordered the repatriation of 4 Wing to Canada's largest fighter base, CFB Cold Lake. The wing stood up again on June 26th, 1993 with her sister wing, 3 Wing from Lahr, finding a new home at Bagotville shortly thereafter. It was Gen Huddleston's leadership that subsequently led to the renaming of all air force bases in Canada under the "wing" concept. And it is from 3 and 4 Wings that Canadian Hornet pilots have continued to amaze millions of airshow spectators across Canada and the United States year after year, upholding the traditions of all those who have gone before them.

The last of the Tigers. Whether on the ground or in the air, 439 Sqn's last Tiger bird was an attention getter. At left, it pays a farewell visit to a familiar landmark in southern Germany, Hohenzollern Castle. At right, the last Canadian fighter pilots to serve in Germany. In spite of having participated in the Gulf War only two years earlier, the squadron was disbanded and the aircraft repatriated to storage in Canada in January 1993. The Sqn was later re-formed as a combat support squadron in Bagotville, Quebec. (DND Photos via Craig Halliwell)

The View From Within

Since watching the inaugural Hornet shows in Europe in 1985 and 1986, I've been witness to dozens of high performance fighter demonstrations. While touring with the Snowbirds in 1989 and 1990, it was a privilege to share the airshow stage with the likes of Capt Rich Lancaster, Maj Jacques Thibaudeau, Maj Mark Holmes and Capt Yves Tessier. Each of them, and all who have gone before and after, have been excellent ambassadors for the Canadian Forces.

One of my personal regrets is that I never had the opportunity to witness firsthand the expertise of any of our own Hornet demo pilots from their back seats. However, among many memorable Hornet flights, the one that stands out the most is the day I went flying with lead solo Lt Lee Grawn of the USN Blue Angels in a full practice over NAS Pensacola, Florida. As the Snowbirds were in the area winding up our 1990 season, we had dropped in to pay our respects to "the Blues." Taking their entire team on a practice over their home station was a great thrill for all concerned, as was the opportunity for me to see their entire show from the air. Several sequences that day remain indelibly etched in my memory – I was really looking forward to the dirty roll on take-off – but what really put a smile on my face is when Lee, having just rolled out a few feet above terra firma, jammed the stick straight back into his gut and turned the jet into a white ghost of condensation as we almost instantaneously pitched to the vertical and accelerated – straight up – raising the gear as we climbed. Watching the runway recede at a great rate of knots through the twin tails in the rear view mirror was really something to behold. That smile I mentioned came off during the sustained 8 G max performance turn later in the show (there's that white mist

Blue 5, the lead solo of the US Navy Blue Angels, prepares to execute the dynamic "dirty roll" on takeoff. (Blue Angels Photo)

again) as Lee did his best to send me to *never never land*. He didn't and my smile soon reappeared. It became permanent with the solo "sneak pass" – which was probably as low as I've been in any fighter without the wheels down! Yes, the grass is still green at Mach .98. All in all, it was a wonderful experience. So, to all those airshow fans who have ever marvelled at the raw power and manoeuvrability of the Hornet, I can honestly say, "You should see it from *inside* the cockpit!"

Hornets and the Future

Leaping ahead to 2002, its been exactly 20 years since Canada took delivery of the first of its 138 CF-18s in 1982. Although not without its maintenance headaches, the aircraft has served the Canadian Forces exceptionally well in war and peace over the past two decades. Commencing in the summer of 2002, the last 80 aircraft to come off the assembly line will finally commence a major upgrade program stretching over the next five to six years to revitalize their structural integrity and internal systems which have fallen into obsolescence over the last decade. Particularly critical from a systems standpoint will be a much improved radar, the APG 73, new multi-function colour displays

Canada's Fighter Wings

Following the disbandment of Canada's three European-based CF-18 Sqns (409, 421 and 439) with the closure of 1 Air Division, 3 and 4 Wings were re-formed in Canada. Today they are the home of the nation's five remaining fighter squadrons.

Highlighting the dramatic zoom capability of the CF-18, Canadian artist Paul Tuttle created this fine work in 1997 using CFB Shearwater, Nova Scotia's international airshow as a backdrop. In full afterburner, the twin engines of the Hornet generate 32,000 pounds of thrust. (courtesy Paul Tuttle)

former republic of Yugoslavia. Had NATO intervention not taken place, it is almost certain that the massacre of thousands of innocent civilians would have continued. Closer to home, who could have imagined the prospect of fully armed Canadian warplanes scrambled across the country in the wake of the horrific terrorist attacks on the United States that forever changed our sheltered world on September 11th, 2001.

All of the above events have underscored the fact that the utopian world for which we all long shows no signs of materializing anytime soon. Therefore, Canada, like all nations who value freedom and democracy, must do more to keep all of its military forces – land, sea and air – modernized and capable of responding to the unforeseen threats that continue to arise. Thus, while updates have been long in coming for Canada's Hornets, they are finally imminent and will extend the planned life of the aircraft to 2017, even as Canada now ponders continued partnership with its closest allies in the development of the Hornet's potential replacement – the Lockheed Martin F-35 Joint Strike Fighter (JSF). On February 7th, 2002 Canada became the third country to allocate funds (initially $150 million) jointly shared between the Defence Department and Industry Canada to get in on the ground floor of what will be the largest fighter development project in history. Development of the JSF is expected to reach US $200 billion or more. Government officials have estimated that Canadian companies could reap as much as $10 billion in high technology business if they were able to compete successfully to produce parts or systems for the new aircraft. Regardless of whether or not Canada eventually purchases the new fighter to replace its CF-18s, one thing is certain. When this latest engineering marvel from the aerospace industry finally does arrive, it too will be the subject of great attention at airshows around the world.

and stores management system, a new electronic warfare suite and new secure radios and real-time data link that will make the aircraft fully compatible with its most technologically sophisticated allies. The Boeing Company, which merged with the McDonnell Douglas Corporation on August 1st, 1997, will oversee the integration of the new systems into Canada's Hornets while actual installation will take place at Bombardier Aerospace's plant in Mirabel, Quebec. Delivery of the upgraded aircraft to 410 Sqn will begin in 2003 at the rate of two aircraft per month, with the four operational squadrons to be so equipped in turn.

These are essential improvements to ensure the combat effectiveness of the Hornet. Technology stands still for no one, especially in the field of defence. If a country's armed forces are to remain viable as a deterrent force and fully effective if called upon to conduct combat operations, they must receive regular updates to keep them compatible with allied forces with which they will operate. Indeed, Canada's CF-18s have been called into combat twice in the last 11 years – in 1991 in the aforementioned United Nation's sponsored coalition to repulse the Iraqi invasion of Kuwait and again in 1999 during the equally devastating events in the

Canadians from coast-to-coast are treated with some of the world's finest airshow acts at dozens of shows across the nation every year. Whether reminiscing to the unmistakable drone of the Pratt and Whitney Wasp on Bud Granley's famous "Golden Hawks" Harvard, or marveling at the technological wizardry of Canada's Hornets, there is something for young and old alike at every show. (Dan Dempsey)

Canada's CF-18 demo pilots for 2002, Capts Doug Clements of 410 Sqn (below) and Scott Shrubsole of 425 Sqn (opposite page), proudly show off their flashy machines that thrilled millions of airshow fans across North America during the 20th year of Hornet operations. (Mike Reyno/Skytech Images)

While official military teams have received much of the publicity surrounding airshows, hundreds of largely anonymous military personnel and dozens of civilian performers have also played an equally important role in furthering the development and popularity of airshows in Canada. Military aircrews have participated in hundreds of flypasts and solo demonstrations since the earliest days of military aviation in Canada, helping establish and maintain a positive image with the citizens whom they serve. In the glory days of the RCAF, mass flypasts often opened major airshows across the country, setting the stage for an exhilarating afternoon of flying entertainment. For the ground-crew who serviced these aircraft and the thousands of workers who toiled behind the scenes, there was and is no prouder moment than seeing "their" aircraft pass in review. Canada has also spawned some world-class civilian per-

from many quarters. While this some of the flypasts, and a few it is dedicated to all of the military who have helped make airshows affair over the years.

formers over the years who have earned accolades pictorial salute illustrates only a small sample of of Canada's well known civilian performers, personnel and their civilian compatriots such a vibrant and inspiring family

The Canadian Warplane Heritage's magnificent Avro Lancaster and the McDonnell Douglas/Boeing CF-18 Hornet represent two generations of aircraft that have served Canada with distinction – in war and peace. Both have been popular attractions at airshows across Canada for many years. The restored Lancaster in the colours of 419 Bomber Sqn's serial VR-A is dedicated to the memory of Pilot Officer Andrew Mynarski, a mid-upper gunner who lost his life after trying to save his tail-gunner colleague from their burning aircraft over France on June 12th, 1944. He was posthumously awarded the Victoria Cross and is a member of Canada's Aviation Hall of Fame. (Mike Reyno/Skytech Images)

Canadian Classics
A Pictorial Salute

Airshow Escapades

There are few military aviators in Canada who have not had the opportunity to participate in an airshow during their careers, either as part of a flying display or by manning one of dozens of static aircraft that give the general public an opportunity to see a nation's aircraft at close quarters each summer. For those in the air, there is no greater adrenalin rush than putting one's reputation on the line for all to see. Yet, for all the satisfaction in doing so, the fact remains that demonstration flying is one of the most demanding of disciplines, requiring an extremely high level of concentration and awareness to ensure that safety is a constant companion.

Canadian airmen have been participating in flypasts at airshows and special events since the dawn of Canada's flying services. While most have been flown in Canadian skies, hundreds more took place across the Atlantic during Canada's 40 year presence in Europe with NATO. The most famous took place on July 15th, 1953 over RAF Odiham, England during the Coronation of Queen Elizabeth II. On that auspicious occasion, 641 military aircraft saluted the new Queen in a mass flypast that took 27 minutes to complete. Of the 197 piston and 444 jets that participated, the RCAF's No. 1 (F) Wing at North Luffenham contributed 36 Sabres led by F/L Neil Burns, 12 from each of 410, 439 and 441 Sqns. By 1955 the RCAF had formed 4 wings of 12 squadrons overseas in the defence of European skies and flypasts were a common occurrence. An infamous incident during a 4 ATAF flypast at Trier, West Germany on April 2nd, 1955 is still remembered by those who participated as a near catastrophe when an ill-advised speed brake call resulted in an unplanned "bomb burst" as Sabres scattered to avoid hitting each other. Fortunately, fast reflexes left behind only bruised egos in the air … and a rather irate Air Div commander on the ground! The lesson was well learned however, and only a month later the air division redeemed itself with a flawless flypast of 144 Sabres (all 12 squadrons) led by a new leader, S/L Bud Lawrence, OC of 444 Sqn. The celebration on this occasion was a fond farewell to the outgoing Chief of the Air Staff, Air Marshal C.R. Slemon.

Every aviator has a favourite airshow story. Ask any who have participated in a formation flypast, whether it be at an airshow, country fair, sports event or for a military parade, and one is sure to elicit a smile along with plenty of stories. There are many variables that go into planning and executing a successful flypast. Of these, the weather is often one of the most challenging factors which can lead to some rather character-building moments. One member of the RCAF who spent his fair share of time flying in front of crowds was Maj Mike Nash who commenced his operational career flying CF-100 Canucks and ended it on CF-101 Voodoos. He reflects back on the heady days of his youth with a fondness and sense of humour that is typical of those who have been fortunate enough to share in this special kind of adventure:

"Just mention of the word 'airshow' brings back a pleasant flood of memories of those delightful events and the people involved. While I never had the pleasure of flying much in the aerobatic team style, I, like many of my comrades of the day, had much fun and learned a great deal doing our 'thing' on Air Force Days or whenever the opportunity arose. Although all of the exercises, the gunnery camps, the meetings, the various postings and positions, the routine of training, the staff work and all the things that occupy one over 35 years of service are well remembered, the beginning of a smile among a group of ageing pilots most likely reflects the tickle of a well worn memory of this or that airshow.

My 'airshow' career got off to a shaky start in 1954 when, as a teenaged flight cadet, I was 'volunteered' to stand in front of a fantastic Mustang fighter on public display during Air Force Day at the London Airport where officer training was then conducted. 'Yes ma'am, that is the front end, that's the tail and that's where the pilot sits.'

My first airshow *embarrassment* came only two years later, way back in August of '56, with a task to lead a two-plane formation of 440 Sqn CF-100s from Bagotville to Moncton. We had pre-positioned at Chatham the day before the show but never had time for a practice run over Moncton. I recall being determined to do all the right things and put on a good display because the squadron commander was a guest at the Moncton Airport for the show. Well, the formation was great and the flypast on time but I couldn't figure out why there weren't more people on the ground. I thought maybe the Boss was putting on a private showing for some friends. It couldn't be the wrong airport ... *could it?* Later, back home, we discussed the matter in private!

The most memorable airshow that I ever participated in was one that took place in Europe at Twenthe Air Base of the Dutch Air Force on July 5th, 1958. It was in celebration of some special anniversary and was to be a grand affair with participation by all of the NATO air forces in Europe – the British, French, German, Italian, Norwegian, Danish, American and, of course, the RCAF with both F-86s and CF-100s. By now 440 Sqn was based at 3 Wing Zweibrücken, Germany and we got the call to provide the CF-100 contingent. We put up three sections for a total of 12 aircraft. We also had the honour of leading the formation as the 'Lead Sleds' were considered somewhat less manoeuvrable than the other fighters in the show. Besides, who could we hurt if we were out in front!

It was noteworthy that there would be no practice runs simply because there were too many aircraft involved. A low-level route was established to provide each air force a suitable pinpoint to locate the formation and to have good opportunity to join up in their allotted positions. We in the CF-100s would pre-position at Twenthe and on the day of the show would navigate a triangular track, gradually picking up each air force in turn. Finally, we would lead the whole gaggle on the triumphant flypast at Twenthe after which we were to recover there and join in the anniversary celebrations. This was a grand plan!

As it happened, on the day of departure the weather was spectacular in the Zweibrücken area, clear skies and gentle breezes everywhere *except* to the north where one could see a well defined layer of middle cloud across the horizon about 50 miles away. There was a slight bump on top of the middle layer almost due north. Well, Twenthe was also due north of Zweibrücken about an hour's flying time. We departed 'Zwei' in two-plane elements two or three minutes apart to get a little separation so we wouldn't bunch up over Twenthe which was reporting overcast sky conditions. I was number two in the squadron commander's lead section and, as I got into my venerable Clunk, I thought to myself 'that bump couldn't be over Twenthe, could it?'

Well, the closer we got to Twenthe, the bigger and uglier that thunderstorm got and the higher we climbed to try and get over it. I couldn't believe the damn thing was directly over Twenthe when we arrived and, worse, I couldn't believe that the Boss was going to take me down directly into it. But he did … and I followed for about the two seconds it took for

him to disappear in the soup. I was then left to untangle my inner ear from my bellybutton and recover on instruments in the middle of a thunderstorm. I struck out for Zweibrücken to let the weather improve but in looking back towards Twenthe there was a most remarkable sight – straight arrow CF-100 contrails from the south leading right into that giant thunderstorm and then coming back out a little lower down going in all directions. It looked like a giant mushroom with hair!

But that's not the good part. On the day of the show, we took off at the appointed time and began our triangular sweep to gather our friends one by one. Our flight altitude was to be 2,500 feet with the other flight elements joining from 500 feet above and below as we progressed along our triangle. It wasn't long into the flight that it became obvious something was amiss as the lead wasn't responding to some calls … and later to any calls – even calls from my close-in wing position and from others in the formation. So on we went with the lead oblivious to the radio chatter and apparently oblivious to everything else as I and our number three frantically tried to get his attention with hand signals, bouncing around in formation and eventually flying in front of his wing. So engrossed were they that they never noticed the wispy cloud layer that was taking shape right at our altitude. By the time we got to the rendezvous points for the British and French formations, the cloud, though wispy, had thickened to limit visibility somewhat. The radios got pretty busy when the French Mysteres passed through the formation belly up in a turn and the British Hunters flew by at 90 degrees from the right just below us, never to be seen again!! By this time, someone had had the good sense to cancel the whole thing. It wasn't 'til we were back at Twenthe having completed a flyby with a much reduced formation that the lead became aware of his radio problems. It was and is the biggest foul-up I've ever been part of. But we had a great time at the party that night when we recreated the fiasco with the Boss in a wheelbarrow!

On returning to Canada, I had the great pleasure on more than one occasion of flying in the large T-33 'RCAF' formations that opened the Toronto CNE Air Show for a number of years (as described in Chap 5). Then, in 1964, I was part of the first Tutor formation to appear at the CNE along with colleagues from Training Command's Central Flying School. The Tutor was brand new to us and to the air force. It was just coming into service fresh off the

assembly line at Canadair's plant at Cartierville near Montreal to replace the Harvard in the basic pilot training role. The T-33 Jet Flight at CFS was tasked to ferry the new Tutors out west to the training schools while the Basic Flight guys (Harvards and other proppy things) got checked out on the Tutor. Since we had no flight manuals yet, we flew the Tutor much like we flew the T-33, quickly learning that the Tutor didn't go very far using T-Bird speeds and power settings!

Then along came CNE time and with our new expertise we were tasked to take a four-plane to Toronto for the Canadian International Air Show. The Tutor had side-by-side seating and was engineered to be flown from the left seat when solo. However, except for the undercar-

Maj Mike Nash and his navigator Maj Karl Robinson of 416 Sqn. Airshow memories to last a lifetime … (via 416 Sqn)

riage control on the left edge of the panel, just about everything was accessible from either seat. S/L Jack Kaiser, head of Basic Flight and newly checked out on the Tutor, was leading our effort. I was flying on the left and had to keep a close eye on the pitot tube on my right wing that was necessarily close to the lead's left aileron. I decided one day to fly my position from the right seat rather than the left. It was a much more comfortable seat from which to fly the left side of the formation and allowed me to keep the pitot tube where

I wanted it without the distraction of peering across the cockpit from the left seat. The first time I tried it we were doing great until lead called for wheels up. Without looking, I grabbed for the undercarriage handle in the left corner of the cockpit – but the first thing I hit was the other control column. Jack later wondered why I had left the formation so quickly and so early.

In Toronto, the weather was glorious, hot and dusty but quite turbulent at low altitude as was often the case at the CNE at that time of year. As was usual, we undertook some practice flights over the waterfront before the actual event. Prior to our first practice, someone decided that we should introduce some aerobatics into our routine but limit them to vertical manoeuvres just to be safe since we hadn't tried any up to this point. I guess everybody thought that we could just follow the T-Bird protocols so we had our little Tutors cranked up to 350 knots as we hit centre stage. At that speed with such a lightly loaded wing and with the hot and dusty weather conditions, the turbulence was so bad I couldn't read the lead's aircraft numbers. Our attempt at a loop was not lost on the observers at centre stage and our contribution was quickly scaled back to a nice vic formation. But it was fun …

Later in life, in 1974, I had the pleasure of leading a Voodoo team from 416 Sqn in Chatham back to Toronto. The CF-101 was a great show aircraft, very stable for good position keeping and very noisy, particularly when the hard-lighting afterburners were engaged. It was a crowd pleaser. We alternated over centre stage with a solo aircraft between passes of a four-plane box and left the stage vertically at the end of our contribution. 'Boss Control' claimed we were a minute late at centre stage on one practice (difficult to do with four 'backseaters' checking timing during our racetrack and on the run-in) and was intent on awarding us the 'Horse's Ass' trophy at the subsequent safety de-brief that followed every practice. (The 'Horse's Ass' trophy was designed to introduce a little levity into an otherwise serious briefing.) I wouldn't acknowledge such an error on our part so when 'Squadron Leader' Mike Nash was asked to stand to accept the award, the whole crew stood and all displayed the same Mike Nash name tags. The identity of the 'real Mike Nash' remained safe for the duration."

Mike Nash

A Salute to the Past

Spitfires of 417 Sqn participate in a victory flypast near Udine, Italy in May 1945 as the RCAF's contribution to the famous "Desert Air Force." Some 400 aircraft repatriated to England following VE Day. (DND PL 60703)

Right – the Canadian Warplane Heritage's Lancaster proudly flew the RCAF Ensign across Canada during a cross-country tour that ended up at the Abbotsford International Airshow in 1990. (Jerry Davidson)

Below – This magnificent flypast took place over RCAF Stn Trenton on 30 Sep 51 during the presentation of the BCATP Memorial Gates. Leading the formation is a Lancaster accompanied by B-25 Mitchell bombers of the locally based Air Armament School. The F-51 Mustangs were provided by 416 Sqn who flew in from Ottawa (Uplands) to participate in the highly publicized event. (DND PL 52821)

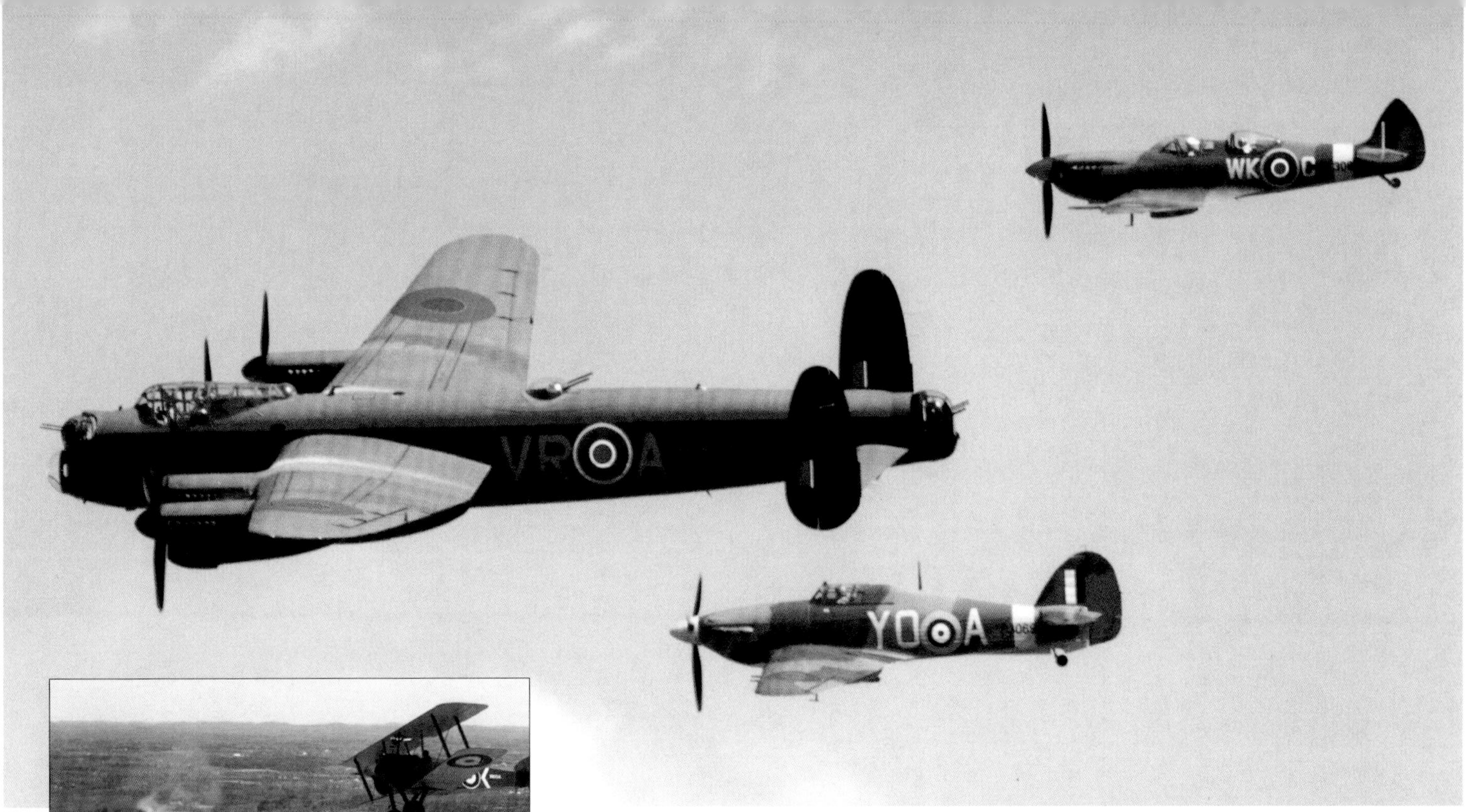

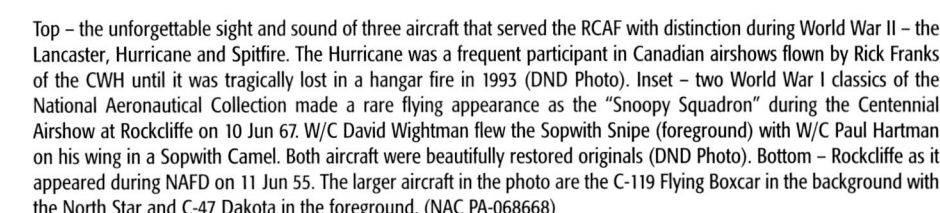

Top – the unforgettable sight and sound of three aircraft that served the RCAF with distinction during World War II – the Lancaster, Hurricane and Spitfire. The Hurricane was a frequent participant in Canadian airshows flown by Rick Franks of the CWH until it was tragically lost in a hangar fire in 1993 (DND Photo). Inset – two World War I classics of the National Aeronautical Collection made a rare flying appearance as the "Snoopy Squadron" during the Centennial Airshow at Rockcliffe on 10 Jun 67. W/C David Wightman flew the Sopwith Snipe (foreground) with W/C Paul Hartman on his wing in a Sopwith Camel. Both aircraft were beautifully restored originals (DND Photo). Bottom – Rockcliffe as it appeared during NAFD on 11 Jun 55. The larger aircraft in the photo are the C-119 Flying Boxcar in the background with the North Star and C-47 Dakota in the foreground. (NAC PA-068668)

Flypasts at the Canadian National Exhibition

The Canadian National Exhibition in Toronto was a showcase for large military flypasts from the late 1940s right through to the mid 1960s. Pictured at the top are heavy bombers that filled the sky in 1952. The famous "RCAF formation" first appeared at the show in 1948 flown by Harvard instructors from Centralia, Ontario led by F/L Russ Murray. Below, a neat seven-plane arrow flown in 1956 by instructors from the Sabre OTU in Chatham was a precursor of things to come with the Golden Hawks. (Centre photo via Bob Ayres, others courtesy the CNE Archives)

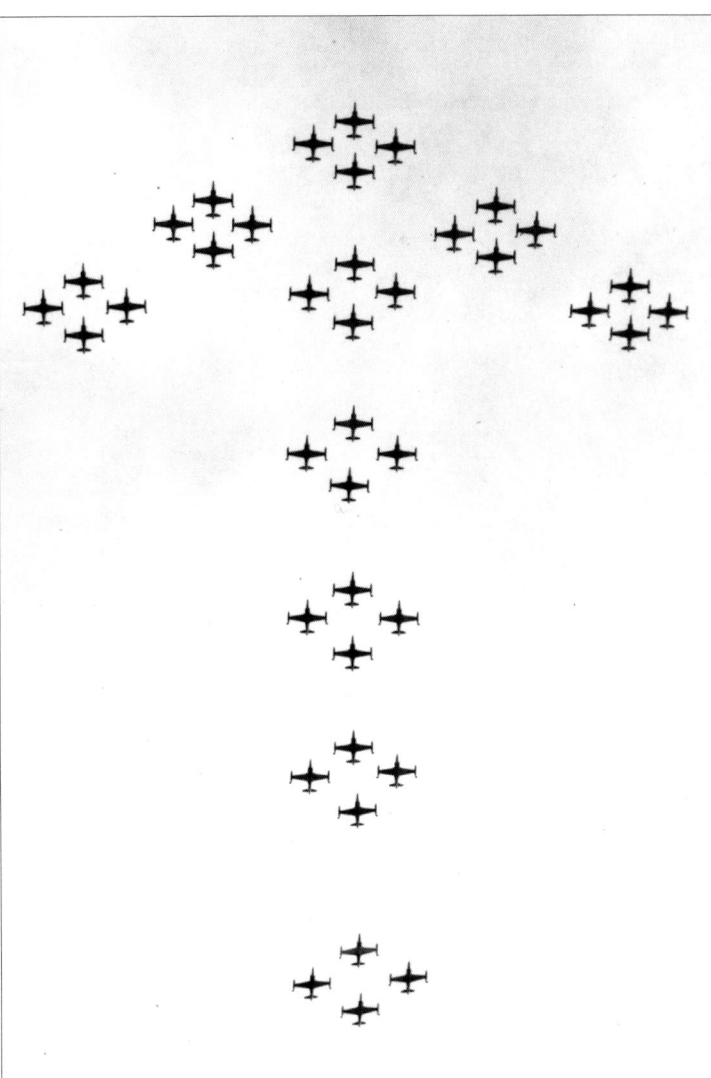

A combination of T-33s and Sabres flew over the Princess Gate to welcome visitors in 1957 (via Graham Wragg). Top right and bottom – Instructors from Gimli and Portage la Prairie, Manitoba joined forces in the early '60s to create impressive formations like these led by S/L Bud Lawrence – a giant arrow and another rendition of the famous "RCAF" formation. (via Walt Scott)

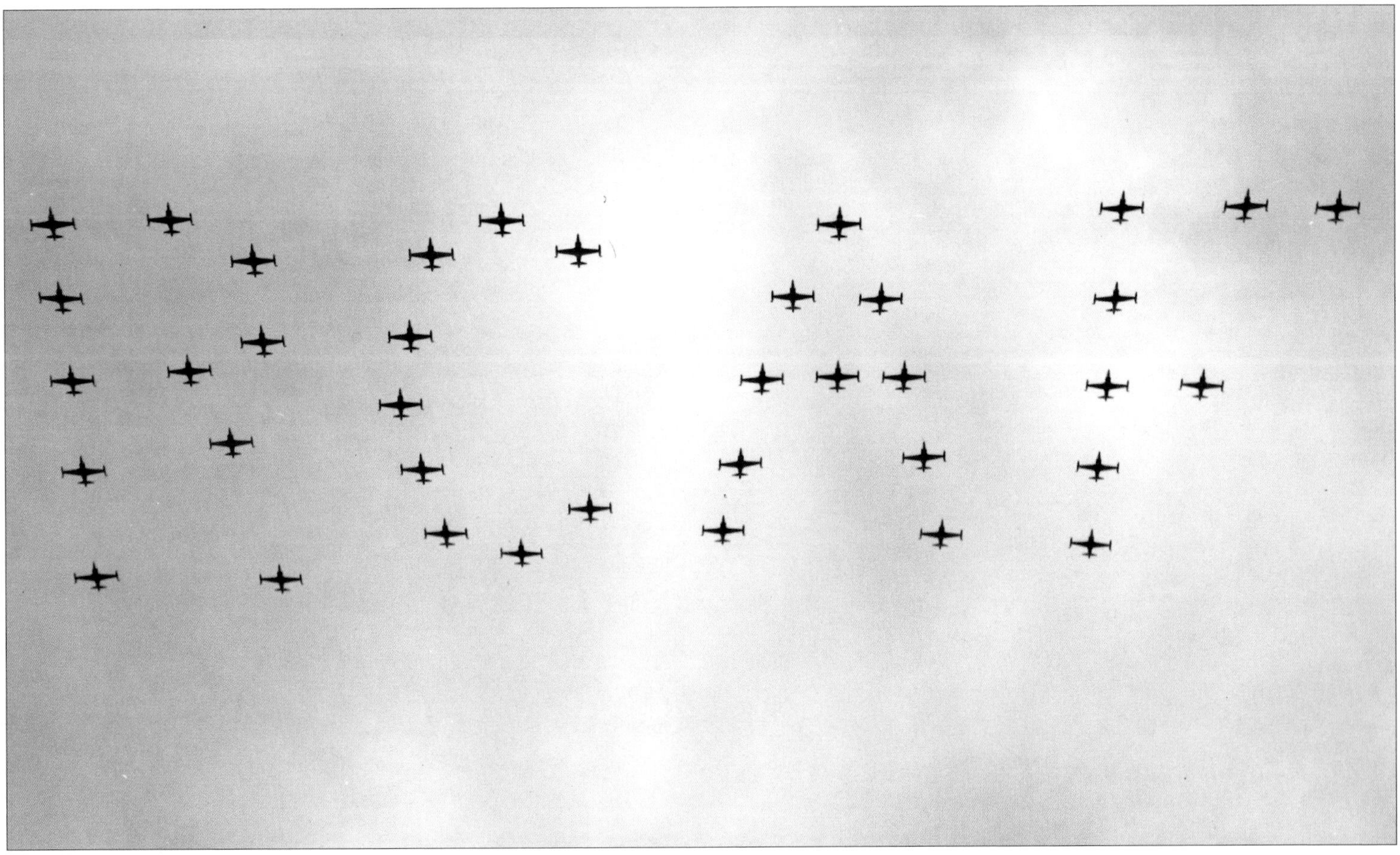

Heavy Lifters

The C-130 Hercules has been the transportation workhorse of Canada's air force since the early 1960s, providing plenty of dramatic flair over the years. Above, the ever-popular JATO takeoff, this one captured at Abbotsford in 1972 (Rae Simpson). Far left, a 435 Sqn trio salutes their new commanding officer, LCol Mark Dodd, during a change of command parade in 1978 (via Jordy Krastel) while at right, LCol Jim Jotham leads a three-ship from CFB Trenton over Exhibition Stadium on 20 Jun 84 to open a Toronto Blue Jays home game. (via Jim Jotham)

The Boeing 707 doubled as a long-range transport and strategic refueller for Canada's CF-5 and CF-18 fighters for over 20 years. A frequent visitor to Cold Lake for training, it was always a popular addition to base airshows where it simulated a refuelling exercise (Rae Simpson). The Airbus A-310 shown on the right replaced the 707 in 1992 and always draws a crowd, inside and out. (Dan Dempsey)

Below – The NATO AWACS, a derivative of the Boeing 707, is an infrequent visitor to Canadian skies but made a special appearance in Aug 99 in celebration of the 50th anniversary of the alliance. The aircraft was piloted by two Canadians, Col Terry Chester (commander of operations for the NATO Early Warning Force in Geilenkirchen, Germany) and Capt Jim Mars who commanded a multinational NATO crew. Escorted by a 410 Sqn Hornet and 414 Sqn T-Bird, this rare photo was captured near the Comox glacier. (Mike Reyno)

Sub Hunters and Maritime Patrol

Facing Page
The P2V-7 Neptune was an integral component of the RCAF's impressive ASW force in the 1950s and early '60s, complementing the Argus and the RCN's CS2F Trackers and S-61 Sea Kings. Top – a striking low pass by a Neptune at the Mount Hope Airport in Hamilton on 3 Sep 61 (Jack McNulty). Inset, 404 Sqn in fine form at the CNE in 1956 (courtesy CNE Archives). Centre – The Tracker performed at Canadian airshows for over 30 years (Rae Simpson). Below – the Sea King in its prime in a rare mass flypast over Shearwater. (DND Photo)

Right and centre
The CL-28 Argus entered operational service with the RCAF in 1958 and was a crowd favourite during airshows due to its sheer size and the sound of its four Wright piston engines. These dynamic flypasts took place at Rockcliffe in Jun 61 and Cold Lake in Aug 78. The big machine had a top speed of 467 km/hr (290 mph). (DND PCN 3284, Rae Simpson)

Bottom
The CP-140 Aurora replaced the Argus in 1980 and with an imminent upgrade will remain the mainstay of Canada's ASW and maritime patrol force. (Mike Reyno/Skytech Images)

Search and Rescue Demos

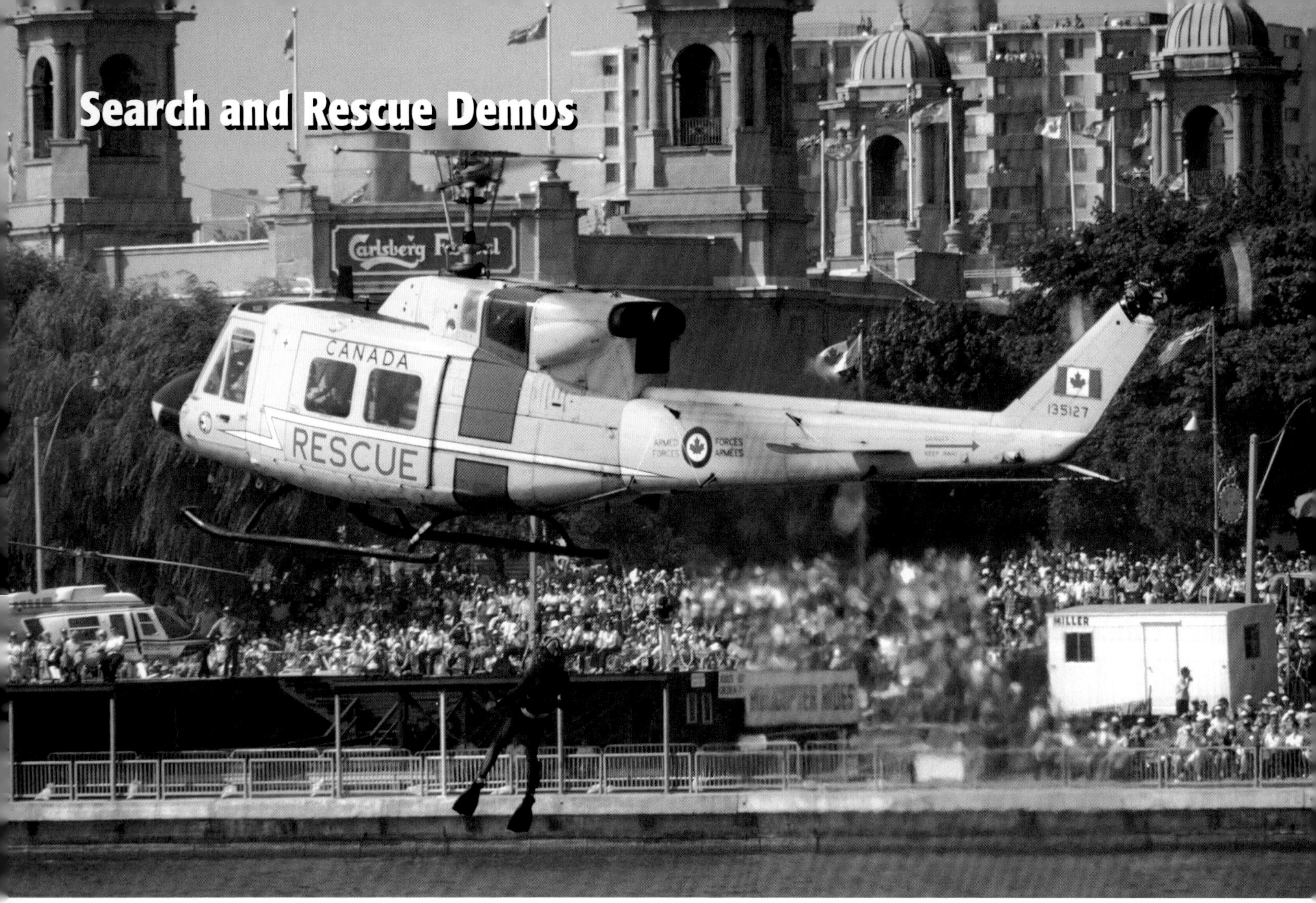

Search and Rescue demonstrations provide a first-hand look at the military personnel and equipment that have been saving lives in Canada for over 50 years. Top, the Lake Ontario waterfront in Toronto provides a unique opportunity to demonstrate water rescues, in this case by a Bell CH-135 Twin Huey (Rae Simpson). Above left and right – two workhorses from RCAF days, the Sikorsky S-58/H-34 and the Piasecki/Vertol H-21 (the "flying banana"). The H-21 became the RCAF's first twin-rotor helicopter when it entered service in 1954. It's unique design made it a popular attraction at airshows where it demonstrated everything from hovering to hoisting to a unique float adaptation (Rae Simpson, Larry Milberry). Below, the Boeing/Vertol CH-113 Labrador flew its last airshows in 2001 after 40 years of service. It is being replaced by the CH-149 Cormorant (DND Photo). At right, the de Havilland DHC-5 Buffalo celebrated its 35th anniversary of service to the Canadian Forces in 2002 and has made hundreds of airshow appearances over the years, both as a STOL demonstrator and jump platform for the Canadian Forces Parachute Demonstration Team, the Skyhawks. (Dan Dempsey)

Special Salutes

Since the dawn of manned flight, flypasts have been used to entertain and to motivate, to salute and to celebrate. Few sights are as inspiring as a large formation of aircraft passing overhead in noisy tribute. As the following pages illustrate, Canadian pilots have been engaged in this gratifying form of precision flying for decades. Top – a celebratory parade involving all three services in Quebec City on 13 Jul 69. Taking the Royal Salute from the 5th Combat Group and 425 AW(F) Sqn is His Excellency the Right Honourable Roland Michener, Governor General of Canada. The Voodoo flypast was led by Maj Bob Flynn with HMCS *Ottawa* tied up alongside the reviewing stand (DND Photo). At left, 30 years later Bob Flynn's son, LCol Bill Flynn of 409 Sqn, led a contingent of Hornets over Parliament Hill on Canada Day 1999 upon their return from the Balkan War in Europe. Canadian fighter pilots logged over 2,600 combat flying hours during the 79 day NATO campaign mounted to help restore peace in Kosovo (Vic Johnson). Below left and right – Two examples of Royal Salutes flown at opposite ends of the country. In the summer of 1959, CF-100s from 409 AW(F) Sqn formed an "E" for Elizabeth when Her Majesty visited British Columbia (via Bill Books). At right, four aircraft types combined for this Royal Salute on 16 Jul 76 over New Brunswick – Voodoos and T-33s from Chatham, CF-100s from North Bay and CF-5s from Bagotville (via Turbo Tarling).

Fighters in Europe

Top – No. 1 (F) Wing of the RCAF was called upon to conduct numerous flypasts and airshows following their arrival at North Luffenham, England in 1952. In this shot, all three squadrons (441, 439 and 410) are featured in a classic Sabre 12-ship taken on 11 Dec 52. All three squadrons had established aerobatic teams by the summer of 1953 (*Flight* magazine via Al Robb). Bottom left – All eyes are raised to take in a flypast over 3 Wing Zweibrücken in this famous photo. Bottom right – 439 (F) Sqn led by W/C Pete St Louis marks the end of an era with the last Sabre flypast over 1 Wing Marville on 1 Nov 63. Most of the Air Division Sabres suffered an ignominious ending in a scrap heap in Prestwick, Scotland and were soon replaced by brand new Starfighters based in France and West Germany. (RCAF Photos)

Top – Four RCAF aircraft that left their marks at airshows around Europe included the F-86 Sabre, T-33 Silver Star, CF-100 Canuck and CF-104 Starfighter. They were photographed for posterity near 2 Wing on 19 Nov 62 (DND PL 147903). Below left – Another impressive shot from 2 Wing days, this a *Croix de Lorraine* conceived by F/L F.X.R. "Chota" Belval as a dedication to the people of France. It was flown on several occasions in 1961 and 1962 by 423 AW(F) Sqn, this one led by W/C John Buzza over Metz on 18 Feb 61 with F/O Len Sturch snapping the shot from below (via Bill Books). Right – A gorgeous shot of a Starfighter nine-ship in 1971 led by former Golden Hawk, S/L Ed McKeogh. The shot was captured from a 104 recce bird flown by F/O Rod Ellis. (RCAF Photo via Ed McKeogh).

Fighters at Home

Canadian skies have been witness to dozens of unique formations over the years. To celebrate the arrival of the CF-104, a "Straight Flush" was flown on 3 May 63 by test pilots at CEPE in Cold Lake. Led by S/L Wilf Speck in 701, the others are F/Ls Norm Ronaasen, Larry Nelson, Fred Belliveau and "Johnny" Johnson (RCAF Photo). At right, there was plenty of nostalgia at the 1999 Cold Lake Airshow when three special guests from the south arrived – two former CF-104s and an F-86 Sabre now privately owned in the United States. (Mike Reyno) Below, the Silver Foxes of 441 Sqn led by LCol Ian Struthers show fine form in a rare nine-ship of Hornets on 28 Jul 87. Others in the formation are Capts Rob Chapman, Bill Ryan, Jim Christie, Chris Sponder, Mike Erikson, Curt Johnston, Maj Stu Holdsworth and Maj Jack Orr. (DND photo via Bob Wade).

The Voodoo community provided its own version of a "Straight Flush" with this highly publicized 410 Sqn photo taken on 22 Aug 75 near Bagotville. The crews were – No. 1 Maj Gary Clay/LCol Don Mackay, No. 2 Capt Barry Watkin/Capt Don Wenzel, No. 3 Capt Robin Deturk (USAF)/Maj Ron Pratt, No. 4 Maj Tony Brett/Maj Jim Dale, No. 5 Capt George MacDonald/Capt Dave Lennox, No. 6 Capt Lowell Butters/Capt Roger Lamothe (DND BNC 75-3774). Above left – CF-100 formations made many airshow appearances during their day, these the first wave of a 36-ship that thundered over Rockcliffe during NAFD in 1961. Above right – LCol Larry Lott leads 409 Sqn over Comox on 10 Feb 83 in an impressive demonstration of serviceability following the squadron's Tac Eval. (via Terry Hunt). Right – "Red Lead and Company." LCol Al Brown leads a seven-ship of 434 Sqn CF-5 tactical fighters over a 1,000 man parade at Cold Lake on 1 Apr 74 in celebration of the 50th anniversary of the RCAF. The photo was taken by a recce CF-5 flown by Capt Les Koski. Below, a flypast of a more sombre variety as 434 Sqn forms a cross in the sky during Remembrance Day ceremonies conducted by Base Commander Col Steve Gulyas on 11 Nov 76. (via Al Brown)

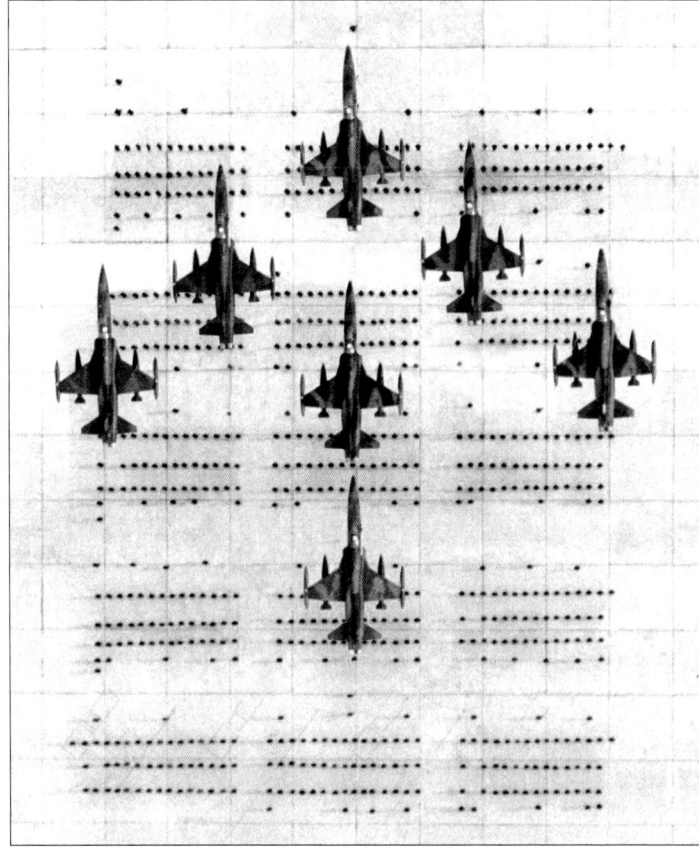

Final Farewells

The final farewell is always a nostalgic affair. Depicted here are eight jet aircraft that served Canada admirably during their tenures, each seen out in style at reunions or airshows as they passed in salute for the last time. Although their classic lines are now gone, those who flew or maintained them will keep a generation of memories alive for decades to come. Above – LCol George Adamson leads 441 Tac (F) Sqn in the last CF-104 flypast over CFB Baden-Soellingen on 1 Mar 86 (K.C. Lett). Below – Banshees of the Royal Canadian Navy make their last pass over HMCS *Shearwater* on 8 Oct 62, marking the end of naval fighter aviation in Canada. In spite of the 40 years that have since passed, the bond among naval aviators in Canada remains strong (DNS 29439 via Graham Wragg). At right – LCol Tom Henry marked the end of CF-5 operations on 434 Tac (F) Sqn with final flypasts over two countries – Norway during their last deployment to NATO's Northern Flank and then back home in the Maritimes with this nine-ship. (via Tom Henry).

Canada's Voodoos were given a colourful send off when the last four units operating the aircraft each painted a CF-101 in squadron colours. This rare shot was taken on 19 Jun 84 – top to bottom, Hawk 1 (409 Sqn Comox), Lynx 1 (416 Sqn Chatham), Lark 1 (425 Sqn Bagotville) and Bat 1 (414 Sqn North Bay) (DND NBC84-1339, WO Dave Willard). Centre – two generations of fighters that maintained a healthy rivalry during the Cold War. Below, Maj D.H. Riddell leads the last F-86 Sabre flypast over home base at Chatham on 29 Nov 68 (DND CM68-164/2, W.R. Johnson). On the right, the CF-100 ended its long service in 1981 with a farewell airshow tour across the country by two Clunks, one painted in the original black prototype scheme and the other in the

camouflage livery employed in Europe (DND IOC81-082, Sgt Vic Johnson). Bottom – The "Big 2" bade a fond farewell to 35 years of basic training on the Tutor at the 1999 Saskatchewan Air Show with this 16-ship flypast led by Col Marc Ouellet (Dan Dempsey). At right – the latest military jet to be retired in Canada was the T-33 which boasted over 50 years of service in various roles. The Black Knights of 414 Sqn made their last airshow appearance when they opened the Comox Airshow on 29 Jul 01 led by LCol Yves Bossé. (Michael Head, *World Airshow News*)

Civilian Performers

Chevalier Jerry Billing

Just mention of the word "Spitfire" will evoke a flood of memories for all those airshow fans who have ever had the pleasure of watching this majestic aircraft perform. For many, certainly those who flew her, Reginald Mitchell's masterpiece is considered the most beautiful aircraft ever built. Her elliptical wing and unique sound gave her a signature all her own and she will forever remain one of the most recognizable and cherished fighters of the World War II era. For over 22 years, the name Jerry Billing was synonymous with Spitfire airshows in Canada as the veteran World War II pilot put a Mk IX through a fully aerobatic display. Throughout this period he had a unique relationship with "Z5•J" and her owner, movie actor Cliff Robertson. A featured performer at the Canadian International Air Show in Toronto, Jerry took his display as far west as the Abbotsford Airshow, doing the legendary Spitfire proud wherever he appeared.

Jerry's relationship with the Spitfire began in May 1942 when the young RCAF pilot from Essex, Ontario climbed aboard a Spitfire in England for the first time. His superior flying skills led to authorization to do his first "public" airshow for station personnel before he had even graduated from the course! As a member of 19 and 185 Sqns of the RAF and later 401 Sqn of the RCAF, Jerry flew the Mk I, II, V and IX during two combat tours that spanned England, France and Malta. His credits include fighter ops during the Blitz of Malta in 1942 and D-Day in 1944.

Following the war Jerry flew Vampire airshows as a staff instructor with Central Flying School prior to joining the famous RCAF Blue Devils for their final shows in 1951. He later went on to also perform

many shows flying the F-86 Sabre. His reunification with the Spitfire was every pilot's dream and he developed a low-level aerobatic routine that was an exhibition of grace and beauty. No matter where the Spit's engine sprang to life, all eyes were on the sleek machine as Jerry lifted off into a max performance climb. Minutes later he would open his show with a high-speed pass on the deck at a speed of 310 mph. Whether climbing, diving or executing low-level rolls, Jerry's show was precise and graceful, each manoeuvre accentuated by the wonderful sound of the Merlin engine. For 22½ years, Jerry Billing and his Spitfire were

one. He flew his last performance at Windsor, Ontario in 1994, bringing to a close a 53 year flying career.

In April 1995 Jerry received one of his greatest honours when he was informed that the President of France had conferred upon him an appointment as *Chevalier dans l'Ordre National du Merité*, a Knight of the National Order of Merit, in honour of his contribution to the liberation of France during World War II. In recognition of that prestigious decoration, his hometown created a mural on one of the city's buildings as a lasting tribute to one of the city's most famous sons.

Top, Jerry Billing shows off his magnificent Mk IX Spitfire along the CNE waterfront in the mid-1980s (photo courtesy the CIAS). Above, a study in contrasts: Jerry's official portrait and the reflective fighter pilot just before flying his last airshow in 1994 – at the age of 73 … (Spike Bell). Below, part of the mural that forms a tribute to the local hero in Essex, Ontario.

Milt Harradence

Well known Calgary lawyer Milt Harradence, later appointed a Judge of the Alberta Court of Appeal, was a unique figure on the North American airshow circuit in the 1960s. A war time RCAF Bolingbroke pilot and post-war Air Reserve P-51 pilot, Milt gained recognition for his airshows in three ex-RCAF fighters – a P-51 D Mustang, a Vampire and an F-86 Mk 6 Sabre in the colours of the famed Golden Hawks. Milt acquired the Mustang (CF-LOR) in 1960 as payment in kind for services provided by ferrying surplus 403 "City of Calgary" Sqn Mustangs to a buyer in the United States. He subsequently joined the Texas-based "Confederate Air Force."

Milt Harradence had the rare privilege of flying his P-51 Mustang alongside the Mk 6 Sabres of the Golden Hawks during this rare photo shoot in 1963, showing off two of the world's most famous fighter aircraft. After procuring a Vampire (bottom left) for a short period, he later purchased and flew several airshows in the last flying Golden Hawk Sabre. (top photo DND Photo, others plus text via Al Young)

Milt performed his first show in the Mustang at Grande Prairie, Alberta in 1961 and showed at various locations in Alberta and Saskatchewan over the next few years. Famed for operating at very low altitudes, his 15 minute show consisted of a high-speed low pass, aileron roll, Immellmann, Cuban-eight, loop, vertical roll and loop off a low-level roll. His reputation as a premier P-51 demonstration pilot led to an invitation to perform at the Wright Patterson AFB Airshow in Ohio in 1966, the first Canadian pilot to be so honoured.

In 1964 the Mustang was sold and Vampire CF-RLK purchased in the United States where surplus military fighters were more warmly welcomed by regulatory authorities than in Canada. Although he displayed the Vampire only once in Calgary, the aircraft became a factor in the acquisition of the Sabre (CF-AMH) in 1966, still resplendent in Golden Hawk colours from its 1963 tour. Airshow fans were thrilled to see the Golden Sabre in the air again and Milt was honoured to be invited to open the 1967 Centennial Airshow at Abbotsford, performing with the likes of the Golden Centennaires, Red Knight and Blue Angels. Unfortunately, the on-going costs associated with proper maintenance and repairs, spare parts, fuel and storage became prohibitive and ultimately led to the sale of the aircraft, thus ending Milt's brief but spectacular airshow career.

When later asked why he had decided to perform in airshows, Milt Harradence replied, "I found the challenge to perform low-level aerobatics in a high performance aircraft irresistible. The satisfaction of accepting the risk of pushing your aircraft to it's mechanical and structure limits and yourself to the limit of your physical abilities, flying skill and managing to survive, added a zest to life that only those who have accepted the challenge can appreciate."

The Canadian Reds

In 1972, a new two-plane civilian team destined to become one of the most popular shows of its kind in North America took to the skies in Canada. Using two S-1 Pitts Special biplanes especially designed for high performance aerobatics, partners Bill Cowan and Don Farion became known as the Canadian Reds. Devoting most of their spare time to perfecting their show routine over the next three years, the duo developed a dynamic show that received widespread acclaim. In 1975 Bill Cowan took on a new partner, another former member of the RCAF who had joined CP Air as an airline pilot. Whereas Bill Cowan had gained his initial airshow experience flying with a Tutor four-ship out of 2 CFFTS, Rod Ellis had been a member of the Golden Centennaires flying the alternate Red Knight throughout 1967. With Ellis taking over the lead position of the Canadian Reds, Cowan was able to concentrate on new techniques to improve their show, notably becoming an expert in one of the most difficult aerial stunts of all – inverted formation flying. Flying new dual-seat S-2As, the duo took the Canadian Reds show and reputation to new heights for eight straight years, earning themselves high praise from airshow sponsors for both their show in the air and the outstanding contribution they made to the airshow industry.

The Canadian Reds entertained North American airshow audiences with their precision flying as a two-ship for 11 consecutive years. Partners Rod Ellis and Bill Cowan then formed the nucleus of the Ray-Ban Gold Aerobatic Team they formed in 1983. (Jerry Davidson)

The Ray-Ban Gold

Between 1986 and 1989, Canada's Ray-Ban Gold presented one of the finest four-plane civilian aerobatic displays in the world. Team members (above right) were, L to R – Gold 4 Al Hauff (slot and solo), Gold 3 Bill Cowan (left wing), Gold 2 George Kirbyson (right wing) and Gold Lead Rod Ellis (team lead). (Centre right photo by Bob Brown, all others by Jerry Davidson)

In 1983 the Canadian Reds took on a new sponsor, Bausch and Lomb, and a new name as a result – The Ray-Ban Gold. With the new name also came a new image as the aircraft appeared in a striking new paint scheme of black and gold. Most importantly, a third aircraft was added to the routine flown by another CP Air pilot, George Kirbyson, whose credentials also included extensive fighter experience on the CF-104 Starfighter. The highly polished performance of the Ray-Ban Gold attracted one more veteran airshow pilot to the team in 1986, Air Canada pilot Al Hauff. He too had learned to fly with the RCAF, flying a variety of aircraft including the CF-100 and CF-101 Voodoo. Most importantly, he had extensive airshow experience in his own home-built Pitts Special with which he had captured the Canadian National Aerobatic Championship in 1977 and 1978. As a foursome, the members of the team

shared a love of aerobatic flight that was clearly evident in their exciting display. Developing a choreography which highlighted their cumulative wealth of flying experience, the repertoire was expanded to include some radical manoeuvres including a formation outside loop along with a variety of intricate synchronized manoeuvres traced in smoke.

The Ray-Ban Gold flew as a four-ship until the end of the 1989 season when Rod Ellis retired from the airshow business, handing over the lead responsibilities to George Kirbyson. The following season however would be the last for the Ray-Ban Gold. Like all great teams, there comes a time when the constant sacrifices to career and family begin to take on a different light and the unanimous decision was made to retire the most successful civilian team in Canadian history at the end of the 1990 season.

Bill Carter

Bill Carter has been a well-known name on the Canadian airshow circuit for 14 consecutive years. One of aviation's best ambassadors, he takes great pleasure in demonstrating the joys of flight through a highly dynamic show in his S2B Pitts Special. A resident of Guelph, Ontario, Bill earned his wings in 1966 and has accumulated over 25,000 flight hours, largely at Air Canada where he is presently a captain on the Boeing 767.

Bill joins a long list of aerobatic pilots who have selected the Pitts as their aerobatic aircraft of choice. His custom-built 260 HP engine gives the little aircraft a top speed of 212 mph, more than enough power and speed to thrill any airshow audience. Bill wastes no time in doing so – from the time he receives takeoff clearance it is one spectacular manoeuvre after another – starting with a half-roll to inverted pass on the deck just after getting airborne. From then on it is a dizzying array of tailslides, torque rolls, multiple snap rolls and a mile-long, knife-edge pass to salute his audience. But the one manoeuvre that always causes an audience to hold their breath a little longer is Bill's trademark ribbon cuts which he executes both upside-down and during knife-edge flight.

Bill's dedication to the airshow industry is always evident on the ground, whether it be through media flights, autograph sessions or goodwill visits dealing with children at schools and hospitals.

Bill Carter and his famous inverted ribbon cut in his Pitts Special.

Team Extreme

Canada's newest entry to the realm of team aerobatics was known as Air Combat Canada when it first started entertaining airshow fans with its high intensity aerial demonstration in 1997. The brainchild of former Canadian Forces CF-18 Hornet instructors Paul Molnar and Paul Ransbury, the team expanded the following year, introducing an innovative emergency manoeuvre training course for pilots of all experience levels plus an introduction to air combat flying for those with a real sense of adventure.

In 2001 the team took on an international component when it introduced a branch in the United States, also using the team's high performance Extra 300L aircraft as their mount. Today, the show presented on both sides of the border is a dynamic combination of formation and solo manoeuvres using one of the most manoeuvrable aerobatic aircraft in the world. Of their show repertoire of dazzling stunts, none is more spectacular than the "Inverted Cyclone" entry that kicks off each show. Commencing at 10,000 feet AGL, the two aircraft are put into an intentional inverted spin to corkscrew down thousands of feet before they separate for their first head-on pass. Whether demonstrating the maximum performance capabilities of their aircraft during a simulated dogfight or canopy-to-canopy formation flying, Team Extreme offers something unique for every airshow fan while proudly displaying their Canadian heritage.

Paul Ransbury and Paul Molnar, founders of Air Combat Canada and Team Extreme with the Extra 300L.

Northern Lights

The void left by the disbandment of the Ray-Ban Gold following the 1990 season was filled in 1995 when an exciting new Canadian team was introduced to the North American airshow scene, this one masterminded by ex-Snowbird André Lortie. Calling themselves the Northern Lights, the team used up to five brilliantly coloured Extra 300s to perform a show that received widespread praise. In their first year of operation, Lortie was joined by fellow Snowbirds Glenn Kerr and Michel Cliche as they presented their dynamic new show at 27 shows across North America. The next year saw Snowbirds Mario Hamel and Ménès Pierre-Pierre join the team followed by Dave Deere for the 1997 season, additional positions being filled by a variety of talented pilots, including Michele Thonney from Switzerland, Mike Mancuso and Eric Haagenson from the United States and Azat Zaydullin from the Ukraine. Taking advantage of their previous aerobatic experience, many of the team's manoeuvres mirrored those of the Snowbirds, notably the inverted portions of the show that included the challenging "Double Take" roll. The popularity of the team led to appearances across North America as well as Europe, South and Central America and Asia.

In July 2001 a bold new step was taken when the team converted to jet aircraft by introducing four L-39 jet trainers from the Czech Republic, their desire being to eventually field an even larger team. Significant financial, regulatory and personnel issues were resolved to make the transition with Lortie and Hamel remaining as business partners. They were joined by two newcomers with plenty of jet experience, former Canadian Hornet demo pilot Greg Morris and American Dan McCue. Although being awarded the prestigious Bill Barber Award for Showmanship in 2001 bode well for the future, difficulties in the wake of the terrorist attacks of September 2001 kept the team on the ground in 2002. The airshow community and the millions of spectators who enjoyed the Northern Lights during their first seven years of operation are hopeful the team will be back in the air soon. Team leader André Lortie is optimistic that will be the case.

The Northern Lights teamed up with 3 Wing Bagotville's CF-18 Hornet to achieve this spectacular photo prior to the annual CIAS in Toronto in 1997 (Rick Radell). Centre – a unique perspective during the same photo mission and an L-39 jet trainer done up in team colours (Ken Lin). Below – The only civilian jet team in the world as it appeared during the 2001 airshow season. (Mike Reyno)

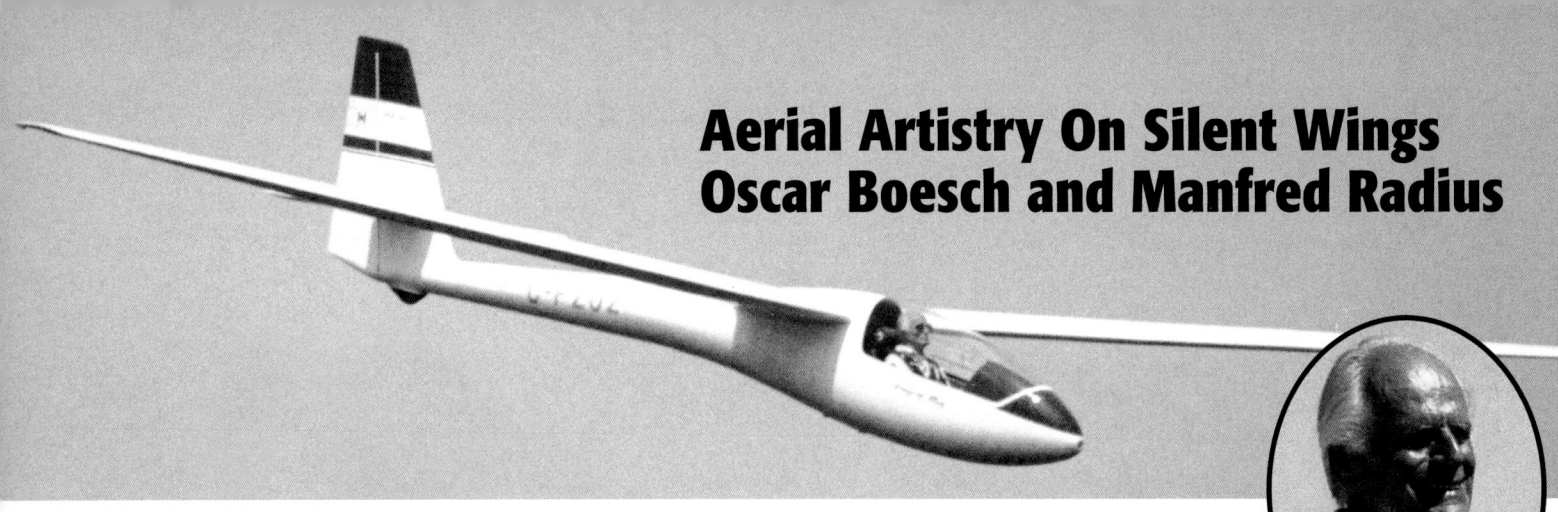

Aerial Artistry On Silent Wings
Oscar Boesch and Manfred Radius

For many years, two of the world's foremost sailplane demonstration pilots have made Canada their home since emigrating from their native homelands. Oscar Boesch and Manfred Radius have captivated millions of spectators with their beautiful displays of aerobatics, each carving his own niche in Canada's airshow heritage.

Oscar Boesch has been gliding for some 60 years, having been inspired to fly as a teenager while watching eagles soar in the Austrian Alps, his homeland. Since arriving in Canada in 1951, he has continued to demonstrate his passion for flight at hundreds of airshows in his Schleicher AS-W15 sailplane nick-named "Wings of Man." Flying to the theme song from the movie *Born Free*, Oscar's routine demonstrates the magic and majesty of pure flight through a series of loops, rolls and clover leafs traced in white smoke trailed from his wingtips. In 1977 he was featured in an IMAX film entitled *Silent Sky* which is still being shown around the world, including the Smithsonian Institute in Washington, D.C. A timeless performer, Oscar has the distinction of having flown 65 airshows at the Canadian International Air Show in Toronto where he was again honoured to perform in 2002, spreading his wings once more for the hundreds of thousands of fans who attended the spectacle.

Manfred Radius has gained worldwide fame for his graceful yet daring soaring display that has taken him from his home in Canada to as far away as Australia. He too was a teenager when he started flying sailplanes in 1961 in his childhood home of Hamburg, Germany. Now with more than 50 years in aviation, his personal soaring achievements include an altitude of 35,000 feet over the Rocky Mountains and a personal distance record of 375 miles during a flight that lasted 8 hours and 45 minutes. His world championship-level aerobatic routine flown to classical music includes outside loops, snap rolls, tail slides, rolling turns, inverted spins, a vertical eight and a spectacular grand finale – his inverted ribbon cut. Manfred also has the distinction of being the only glider pilot in the world to have executed an inverted simultaneous double ribbon cut, doing so in Melbourne, Australia in February 1999 with the two ribbons set at only 25 and 31 feet above the ground. Manfred performs his show in an H101 Salto sailplane which he calls "The Ultimate." It is stressed to + 7 and – 5 G and is capable of speeds of up to 280 km per hour.

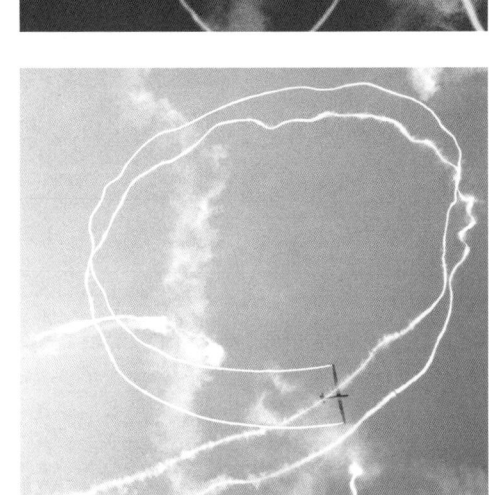

Oscar Boesch (top) and Manfred Radius (below) have earned recognition as two of the world's finest sailplane aerobatic pilots. Above right, Oscar's graceful artistry over Lake Ontario. Below, Manfred's always spectacular inverted ribbon cut and low-level manoeuvring. (via Oscar Boesch, Larry Milberry, Manfred Radius).

Bud Granley

Bud Granley is among the finest and most respected civilian performers to ever grace the North American airshow circuit. With over 40 years in the airshow business, Canada's most prolific civilian performer has become a fixture at numerous shows, including Abbotsford where he has often performed four times in a single day in his T-6/Harvard, Yak-55/52, Fouga Magister or any number of warbirds.

Fascinated with flight at an early age, Bud learned to fly with the Royal Canadian Air Cadets and subsequently joined the RCAF in 1956. Posted to the highly coveted F-86 Sabre which he flew at 4 Wing Baden-Soellingen in West Germany, Bud was a member of the third consecutive RCAF team to win the annual Gunnymer Trophy as the best gunnery team in NATO. His repatriation to Canada to instruct on the Harvard at RCAF Stn Penhold, Alberta led to the commencement of his airshow career when he was selected as the station solo demonstration pilot in 1961.

Bud's airshow credits include fully aerobatic performances in an impressive collection of aircraft. While his much beloved and famous Harvard adorned in the livery of the RCAF Golden Hawks remains his signature aircraft, over the years he has also performed aerobatic demonstrations in the P-40, Supercub, P-51, Cessna-195, T-28, Glasair, Spitfire, Fouga Magister, Yak-55, Yak-52, AN-2, Yak-50, Glastar and Chipmunk. His logbook also reveals flypasts performed in a replica Japanese Zero, Skyraider, Corsair, Wildcat, Avenger and several ultra-lights and frequent participation at the Reno Air Races.

For all of the enjoyment and adulation he has received from the airshow business, Bud's greatest pride is derived from his family, many of whom have followed in his aviation footsteps. Two of his sons, Chris and Ross, were accomplished fighter pilots in the Canadian Forces and both earned positions on Canada's famed Snowbirds aerobatic team. Today, Ross frequently performs with his father in a spectacular demonstration of precision flight using two highly aerobatic Yak aircraft. Given the obvious aviation talents that run deep in the Granley family, airshow fans can look forward to seeing the Granley name around North American airshows for many years to come.

Canada's master showman, Bud Granley, shown with two of his sons, Ross (below left, courtesy Peter Hulbert, *The Province*) and Chris (below right), each of whom served a tour with the Snowbirds. With over 40 years of airshow experience, Bud has performed in everything from his famous T-6 to the Yak-55 to the Spitfire. (Photos via Bud Granley)

The Snowbirds' trademark "Big Diamond" formation seen here at the Abbotsford International Airshow – the only nine-plane team flying in North America today. (Bill Johnson)

The Snowbirds
Canada's Aerial Ambassadors

In 1971 an unofficial seven-plane formation demonstration team took to the air for the first time at Canadian Forces Base Moose Jaw, Saskatchewan, the home of Canada's busiest military flying base. Initially known as the 2 CFFTS Formation Team, the display developed from a diamond of four aircraft flown in 1970. It was the success of this group that led to the formation of the expanded team in 1971, one that grew in size and popularity in the ensuing years. The Canadian Forces Snowbirds are today officially designated 431 Air Demonstration Squadron. For over three decades, this highly professional team has been demonstrating its aerial magic across North American skies to the delight of airshow audiences. They are recognized as among the best in the world at precision formation aerobatics, employing nine jet aircraft in a stunning show of precision and grace. As ambassadors for Canada, the Snowbirds have flown the Canadian flag from the far reaches of the Canadian north to the Gulf of Mexico for a total audience that now exceeds 100 million spectators. In preserving the proud traditions of their predecessors, the Snowbirds have become a highly visible symbol of national pride.

Snowbirds Through the Years

Since 1973, the Snowbirds have been producing an attractive brochure for public relations and recruiting on behalf of the Canadian Forces.

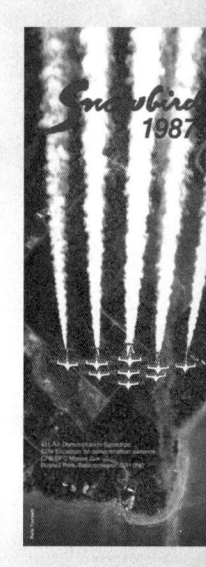

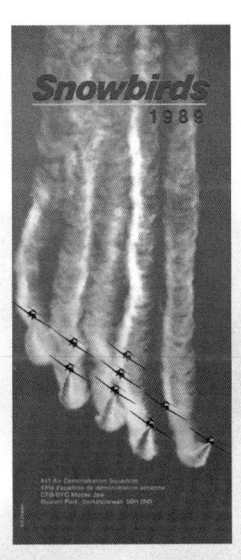

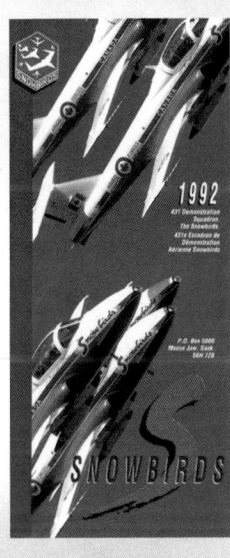

The Snowbird story really begins where the Golden Centennaires left off in the fall of 1967 following their disbandment at CFB Portage la Prairie at the end of centennial year. There had been widespread disappointment that the Canadian government had not permitted the team to continue given the phenomenal popularity of the show. No one had been more disappointed than O.B. Philp, the team's commander who had carefully nurtured his talented group to new heights never before seen in North America. It was perhaps fate then, that saw Col Philp posted to CFB Moose Jaw in the summer of 1969 as the new base commander. Located in the middle of the Canadian prairies, Moose Jaw was (and remains) the gateway to "wings" for all aspiring pilots in the Canadian Forces. By the time O.B. Philp took over, the base already had a long legacy of training pilots for the RAF, RCAF, Canadian Forces and a host of NATO allies dating back to 1941. Now, assisted by some like-minded visionaries, Col Philp was about to make history again.

The White Tutors

Armed with the conviction that there was still underlying support for an aerobatic team in Canada, the wheels started turning virtually from O.B. Philp's first day on his new base. Following a brief introductory meeting with his branch heads, the first order of business was a base tour, starting of course at the flight line. The tour was conducted by the commandant of "The Big 2" (as 2 CFFTS had come to be known), LCol Bill Bliss, who had also been wearing the mantle of "acting base commander" until Philp's arrival.

By the late 1960s, the early morning flight line in Moose Jaw had become an impressive sight with over 100 Tutors gleaming in the early morning sun. The young trainees about to embark on "the first launch" would soon grow to love the little machine, their instructors already having mastered its intricacies. By the time Philp and Bliss made their way down to the flight line that morning in August 1969, the sky was full of Tutors, the blend of noise and jet fumes still intoxicating to both veterans in spite of years of flying jet aircraft. The flight line itself was a beehive of activity with aircraft taxiing in and out as quickly as the groundcrew could turn them around. Within a few days of his first tour, the new base commander noticed a number of Tutors sporting an overall white paint scheme with red trim

Canadian Forces Base Moose Jaw, Saskatchewan – the home of the Snowbirds and the scene of some magnificent airshows since 1971. (Garry Cotter)

that stood out among the aluminum-skinned aircraft on the flight line. Later seeking the reason, it was explained that the white aircraft were ex-Golden Centennaire aircraft that had been returned to training duty at the

Colonel O.B. Philp, DFC, CD "Founder of the Snowbirds"

school. In removing their gold paint, it had been discovered that some minor corrosion had occurred and thus, as a safeguard, the decision had been made to refinish the aircraft with a white, anti-corrosive paint. Philp quickly ascertained that there were five of the aircraft on the base, several more flying with FIS in Portage la Prairie, with the remainder in storage at Mountain View, Ontario – along with the smoke systems that had been designed by Canadair. The internal plumbing for the smoke system and wiring for the cross-cockpit modifications the Centennaires had used were still intact. Armed with this knowledge, it wasn't long before the wheels were turning in O.B. Philp's mind, the sight of the white aircraft triggering fond memories of the Golden Centennaires …

By the end of 1969, Philp felt comfortable with his new surroundings and had made the changes he thought necessary to improve the overall efficiency of the operation. He had also come to the conclusion that the base had more men, materiel and

One of the white Tutors that Col O.B. Philp found at CFB Moose Jaw upon taking command of the base. (Jerry Vernon, Abbotsford 15 Aug 71)

flying hour resources than those required for the forecast training scheme, largely due to ongoing uncertainty over what the final pilot manning level would be under the unified Canadian Forces. He decided the time was ripe to approach his superiors with the notion of forming another aerobatic team, with the understanding that all funding and resources would come from within his existing establishment in Moose Jaw – he was disappointed in the response. While there was sympathy for Philp's plan, there was insufficient support as he explained in his memoirs in 1989:

"The underlying trouble was the unsettled state of national defence. Integration and unification of the armed forces had, perhaps unwittingly, created a sphere of possessive jealousy among the senior brass. Naturally they had to ensure that their branches of the service would be treated equally and their own judgement would be considered fair.

The senior air force officers felt that any such move on the air side (to create a new team) would be seen by the army and navy as rocking the boat and not required in support of the defence roles being formulated. Such a move might create other problems, unsettling to the offspring which was emerging as the new Canadian Armed Forces. This was not a view I shared but without the support of my seniors, the prospects of forming an aerobatic team in the near future looked bleak indeed."

O.B. Philp

Those who worked with O.B. Philp during his career will attest to the fact that he was not a man easily swayed from his convictions – a polite way of saying he was downright stubborn! When he believed in a cause, no stone would go unturned and abandoning his vision was unacceptable until every last possibility was exhausted. Mulling over his desire to create another team, it was in the spring of 1970 that LCol Bill Bliss provided him the opportunity he needed to further his cause. Over the previous year, Bliss had been able to accommodate several requests for flypasts to open home football games for the Saskatchewan Roughriders in neighbouring Regina, only 40 miles east down the Trans Canada Highway. These straightforward flypasts had been authorized by Training Command Headquarters and proved a worthwhile public relations exercise, helping solidify a strong bond between the base and the citizens of Saskatchewan. In these flypasts, Philp saw an opportunity to further his cause.

With tongue in cheek, Philp decided that the instructors of The Big 2 needed more formation practice; he therefore worked out a plan with Bill Bliss to set up an "in house"

training program to enhance the formation flying skills of his pilots. Bliss was happy to oblige although he never saw the final fruits of his labour, taking early retirement to accept a civilian position in the flight simulator business. Nevertheless, the program provided excellent results and by that summer polished four-plane formations from Moose Jaw were providing flypasts at special festivals and fairs, in addition to the annual Armed Forces Day at the base on June 27th, 1970. Philp was careful to keep Training Command "duly informed of these operations" but made a point of not asking specific permission to do each flypast. They were in the public interest, and besides, why invite someone to say no?

2 CFFTS Formation Team "The Tutor Whites"

The next key figure to enter the scene was Maj Bing Peart, the senior flight commander at 2 CFFTS and the officer appointed acting commandant of the school for the balance of the spring and summer of 1970 until the new commandant arrived. Peart was an enthusiastic supporter of the formation program and wasted no time taking charge. To give the formations a little extra pizzazz, a white Tutor was introduced as the lead aircraft for the Roughrider home games starting in July. However, as O.B. Philp recalled in 1989, "When we were allowed to

The scene at Abbotsford in August 1970 when 134,000 spectators took in the weekend show, revealing strong public support for the formation of another Canadian aerobatic team. At left, two commandants of "The Big 2" that helped lay the foundation for the creation of the Snowbirds, LCol Bill Bliss and LCol Tom Reid. (*The Plainsman*, CFB Moose Jaw, 13 Aug 70; DND Photos)

Lieutenant Colonel W.H. Bliss, CD

Lieutenant Colonel T. Reid, CD

The voice of Canadian Forces air demonstrations in 1970 and 1971 was Capt Joe Houlden, a staff instructor at "The Big 2" in Moose Jaw and former Red Knight narrator. At left, Minister of Transport Don Jamieson (who officially opened the 1970 Abbotsford show) and Maj Bing Peart, leader of the 2 CFFTS Formation Team. (DND Photos)

accept an invitation to participate in the prestigious Abbotsford Airshow, I decided to take off the wraps. We sent a formation of four white Tutors led by Maj Bing Peart."

Peart and his team did their part by putting on an impressive formation display. Dubbed "The Tutor Whites" by Canadian Forces airshow announcer Capt Joe

Houlden, Peart's show was very tight and featured excellent station keeping by his wingmen – Lt Doug Zebedee (right wing), Capt Bill Cowan (left wing) and Capt Fred McCague (slot). Philp accompanied the team to Abbotsford but was quick to downplay any notion of a new Canadian aerobatic team following the show, deadpanning that this was strictly an unofficial base team. Nonetheless, this was exactly the type of scuttlebutt that Philp was hoping to generate – all part of his grand scheme.

Back at home, Philp pulled out all the stops in advertising the success of the 1970 Abbotsford show which had billed itself

"Canada's National Airshow." He instructed the editor of *The Plainsman*, CFB Moose Jaw's bi-weekly newspaper, to run a special edition saluting the Abbotsford show. Capt Rod Sword and his staff of 10 volunteers produced an outstanding tribute to the show, strategically placing photos of the four white Tutors ("Moose Jaw's Fearless Four") on the front and back cover of the 20 page paper. Between these pages were a wide variety of articles and photographs covering every aspect of the three day show, extolling the fact that 134,000 spectators had taken in the show which had included a solid hour of entertainment by 30 Canadian Forces aircraft each day.

Maj Bing Peart leads the "Tutor Whites" in a slow speed "dirty" pass in box formation. On the left, the landing gear is just starting to extend. At right, the extended speed brakes, flaps and landing gear are fully visible. (Jerry Vernon, Wayne Ralph)

Support Behind the Scenes

The senior airmen working within the Canadian Forces structure were well aware of the success of Abbotsford and justifiably proud of the accomplishments of their "air force." Carefully watching from his office in Winnipeg was the Commander of Training Command, MGen William K. Carr, an astute leader who knew exactly what O.B. Philp was up to. Formerly the Director General Air Forces at CFHQ between 1966 and 1968, Gen Carr had been involved with the formation of the Golden Centenaires and therefore knew O.B. Philp well. While he had to exercise prudence given the politics of the day, he wasn't about to stifle Philp's initiative. The next opportunity for the Tutor foursome to increase their visibility came from Carr's headquarters itself. CFB Moose Jaw was directed to provide a flypast in Winnipeg at the first Canadian reunion of World War II aircrew slated for September 26th, 1970. A wartime Spitfire recce pilot and winner of the Distinguished Flying Cross, MGen Carr hosted the reunion and was quick to praise Maj Peart's team for their contribution. A bonus included a performance at the St. Andrews Airshow on the city's outskirts the same day which also received many accolades.

Although O.B. Philp was unquestionably the driving force behind the movement to revive a new aerobatic team, he had many

Major General W.K. Carr, DFC, CD
Commander Training Command

Our own Tutors performed flawlessly at Abbotsford and, by request, opened the Chilliwack Airport on Thursday.

THE PLAINSMAN
Saskatchewan's Military Newspaper
CFB Moose Jaw, Sask.

A SALUTE TO ABBOTSFORD   ...CANADIAN AVIATION'S FINEST HOUR

VOL. 2, NO. 19   AUGUST 13, 1970   C.F.B. MOOSE JAW

OUR NATIONAL AIRSHOW

Canada's First National Airshow is over. It was a fantastic success. 130,000 people passed by the gates to see the airshow that just nine years ago drew only 1400 people.

INDUSTRIAL DAY — A Beginning

Thursday was Industrial Day, a first for Abbotsford which up until now has never attempted to court the big industry that has the money to make a big airshow an even bigger success. Some of the giants were there, including Lockheed, Douglas, Boeing, Canadair and de Havilland. A giant step forward was the announcement that three major companies would use this year's show to introduce new aircraft.

FRIDAY — "I guess that means the show is open."

Friday the first flying day, dawned cloudy with the threat of rain, and the crowds stayed home. However, 17,000 did attend to witness Transport Minister Don Jamieson's opening speech and seven hours of sheer enjoyment. Unfortunately, the Minister was still rambling on at 1:00 pm when six screaming jets passed by, opening the show on their own. The Minister, still speaking on the 'great north', then officially opened the Airshow with the now famous statement, "I guess that means the show is open.".

Going unmentioned was the cairn comemorating this year as Canada's first National Airshow. It had been made up of rocks from 27 countries (including the absent Russia) and a capsule with messages from the Prime Minister and Opposition Leader.

SATURDAY — A Sunny Spectacle

Saturday morning's rain must have influenced the prospective crowd nevertheless 47,000 turned out to see our own Armed Forces open the second day's flying. By early afternoon the skies had cleared and the crowd was treated to a flawless show including the sixty minute military show demonstrating the air element's every role. The crowd gasped and stood with their mouths open as over 30 Forces aircraft were flown to maximum performance. No one single act can be singled out as the best, there is as much merit in the first act as in the last. In one instance, there

may have been a lack of noise and speed, but it was more than made up in grace and agility. Other acts featured power and size, here the observer must have been impressed with the pilot's concentration and fast reactions. Borrowing from an article in last year's program, we must make one point very clear. The low level aerobatic pilots, demonstrating unerring precision are not 'daredevils'. They are true professionals who have spent countless hours of planning and practicing and to label them 'daredevils' is a libellous slight on their professionalism.

SUNDAY — 70,000 Saw Something Extra

Sunday's show was best of all. That is if you got in to see it. There were over 70,000 people in attendance with every parking lot filled to capacity. By 2:30 pm the RCMP reported that cars were lined up at a dead stop, for 21 miles back towards Vancouver. Those who did get in were treated as no other Abbotsford crowd has ever been. Every performer seemed to be putting on that little extra. Art Scholl for example, went through a display in his modified Chipmunk that cannot be described. It was based on his sequence that won him the world's aerobatic championship, but that was not all. The extras that were thrown in (including two world's firsts, one an inside-outside vertical eight) left everyone speechless.

THEN THE MEMORIES

But then suddenly it was over.

The Abbotsford Airshow, Canada's first National Airshow had come to an end. What a letdown. Everyone had been working for so long, planning and co-ordinating all the work that goes into a show of that calibre. . . and now it was suddenly over. . . . . . . .it just did not seem right that it should end. Minutes earlier everyone had been going in high gear and now all that was left were a few lost children, tons of garbage, a few hundred uneaten hot dogs and many, many memories. . . . .Memories of unexcelled, polished flying; of loud howling jets; hasty lunches of a coke and a hamburg'; and of some of the nicest people in the world. That was Abbotsford 1970.

MOOSE JAW'S
FEARLESS FOUR.

Maj. Peart leads the Moose Jaw Tutor formation back to the line at Abbotsford. The Tutors were a real hit, we can be very proud. Maj. J.B. Peart was lead, Lt. Doug Zebedee was No. 2, Capt. Bill Cowan was No. 3 and Capt. Fred McCague flew the box.

The screamers at Abbotsford. Real crowd pleasers.

$600 Worth Of Junk

Diane Parsons of Seattle, a performer and aerobatic star herself, watches her husband, Chuck Driskell complete a normal landing. Chuck flies a pile of junk. (See story Page 14.)

Col O.B. Philp ensured that the 1970 Abbotsford Airshow and his four-plane Tutor team got plenty of press after the show. (*The Plainsman*, CFB Moose Jaw, 13 Aug 70)

supporters who played important roles in seeing the dream materialize. LCol Tom Reid joined Philp's staff as the new commandant of 2 CFFTS in October and immediately became a strong ally. Another who would come to play an indispensable role was LCol Larry Rudosky. His accounting skills as base comptroller allowed Philp to manage his financial resources to maximum effect. By the end of 1970, the remainder of the white Tutors mysteriously appeared back in Moose Jaw, ostensibly to allow for the possibility of an expanded flying training program on the Tutor following the retirement of the venerable Expeditor.

Also quietly pulled out of storage, thanks to the assistance of two important supporters at NDHQ, Lew Crutchelow (Chief of Supply) and Gerry Meuser (Assistant Deputy Minister for Materiel), were the old Centenaire smoke systems which had been lying dormant for three years. The next step in the evolution of the new team was a critical one. Although Philp was satisfied that steady progress was being made, he also believed it was too early to seek formal permission again to form an official team. He therefore decided on his own initiative to quietly expand the 2 CFFTS Formation Team for 1971 to seven white Tutors.

Snowbirds 1971

The Dawn of a New Era

LCol Tom Reid's arrival in Moose Jaw to assume the dual roles of commandant and base operations officer was no accident. Apart from bringing a wealth of experience to 2 CFFTS from his days flying the Sabre, T-33 and CF-104, Reid's love of formation flying was well known to O.B. Philp, a fact which would make him an important ally in the progression towards a new demonstration team. Indeed he was, participating in every facet of the operation – from helping select the team members from within his pool of instructors to providing full administrative support and attending many of their shows. Of the vision created by his old boss, Reid recently reflected:

"In the beginning, before the name 'Snowbirds' arose, O.B. created a synergism – an ideal shared by a number of dedicated officers. Each thought that their vision of how a new team should be developed was being pursued – and each believed that they were causing it to happen. To a degree this was correct, which simply underscored the tremendous commitment that was in place at the time. However, the final accomplishment must be attributed to a single name – Col O.B. Philp."

Tom Reid

Maj Bing Peart had done an excellent job with the 2 CFFTS team and was appointed Reid's deputy until a well deserved promotion saw him posted out the following summer. In the interim, Philp needed to identify a new leader for his planned seven-plane team. Thus began a process that has become a bi-annual ritual ever since – the selection of a new team leader for the nation's aerobatic team. Skill and charisma were not enough – the officer chosen for the job had to have the desire to lead a large group of aircraft and make the program work. After considerable discussion between Philp and Reid, the field was narrowed down to two of the school's senior staff. Ultimately, it was decided that Maj Glen Younghusband, the training and standards squadron commander, should be offered the position. Col Philp would make the pitch to Younghusband himself. If in agreement, responsibilities within the school would be shuffled to give him time to do the job.

Maj Younghusband accepted O.B. Philp's overtures to take on the new "secondary" duty as leader of the 2 CFFTS team and played a key role in the evolution of the Snowbirds. He was the first of 17 leaders who have been selected to guide the Snowbirds through their 32 year history to date. He recounts his experiences from one of the most gratifying periods of his 38 year air force career:

"It was just prior to Christmas 1970 that Col O.B. called me into his office and suggested in his own inimitable way that I should consider volunteering to lead a seven aircraft formation display team that he planned to form for the summer of 1971. For the time being, the job would entail a number of restrictions – the team was not to perform any aerobatic manoeuvres, limits were placed on degrees of pitch and bank, formation changes were not allowed along the showline and all of the resources necessary to support the team would have to be provided by CFB Moose Jaw. Accepting the job was an easy decision as the chance to be in at the start of what was hoped would eventually be a new formation aerobatic team was a once in a lifetime opportunity. While I had not previously flown on an aerobatic team, I was a highly experienced fighter pilot and flight leader with tours on the F-86 Sabre, CF-104 Starfighter and Hawker Hunter. At that point, I had been flying the Tutor for about 18 months.

That it was possible to support a formation team from base resources was largely due to a fortuitous set of circumstances. As the former commanding officer of the Golden Centennaires, O.B. was determined that the air force would have another formation aerobatic team – and he was prepared to take responsibility for the decisions that would make it happen. He had a strong supporter in LCol Tom Reid, Commandant of 2 CFFTS, and CFB Moose Jaw was blessed with many highly capable and experienced aircraft technicians who worked for the Base Aircraft Maintenance Engineering Officer, Maj 'Suds' Sutherland. He also believed in the need for a team and was willing to stick his neck out to support it. The key however, was in the type of flying instructor serving at Moose Jaw. There were a number who had recently completed tours in West Germany flying the CF-104 and as a result of limited openings on operational squadrons there was also a core of talented first tour instructors with three to five years experience on the Tutor. Not before or since have there been many occasions where such a large pool of experienced and capable pilots served on the same unit at the same time.

When word got out, there were many volunteers for the team and those chosen to try out were put through a short, but rigorous selec-

The originals. In Jun 71 the 2 CFFTS seven-plane formation team was renamed the Snowbirds and comprised 11 instructors from the school. L to R, Standing – Capts Fred McCague, Chester Glendenning, Laurie Illingworth, George Hawey, Michael Marynowski, Lloyd Waterer, Tom Gernack, Bob Sharpe, Doug Zebedee. In the cockpit – Capt Gord Wallis, Maj Glen Younghusband (leader). (DND Photo)

tion program during the month of February 1971. The selection process consisted of up to three formation trips of gradually increasing difficulty, building to formation flying while manoeuvring in excess of 3G. All selection flights were flown with one of three people: myself, LCol Tom Reid or Maj Terry Thompson. Terry had flown with an English Electric Lightning team (The Firebirds) while serving on exchange with 56 Sqn of the RAF. The Tutor had been designed to provide limited control of systems functions from the instructor's seat on the right side of the cockpit and as a consequence it could only be flown solo from the left seat. The cockpit modifications used by the Centennaires to allow solo flight from the right seat had been removed when the aircraft were returned to normal use. The aircraft flown by the 1971 team, former Centennaire aircraft that had been repainted white and red, required two pilots in the cockpit of those that were to be flown on the left side of the formation. Therefore, to allow a variety of formation patterns to be flown, it was necessary to have 11 pilots in the seven aircraft.

The volunteers who made up the original Snowbird groundcrew in 1971. L to R – Cpl "Andy" Anderson, Cpl Wayne Adams, Cpl Al McFadden, Sgt Dick Gaff, Cpl Ed Torfasen, Cpl Bob Nixon, Cpl Mike Thompson. (DND MJ 71-0621, 29 Jun 71 via J.P. Baraton)

As it turned out, pilots selected for the 1971 team were evenly split between those with a previous tour on the CF-104 and those who were on their first flying tour. In addition to myself, successful candidates for the first Snowbird team were: from a CF-104 background – Capts Tom Gernack, Laurie (Inch) Illingworth, Gord Wallis (Team Lead 1977-78), Fred McCague and Bob Sharpe; first tour pilots were – Capts Chester Glendenning, George Hawey (Team Lead 1983-84), Lloyd Waterer, Mike Marynowski and Lt Doug Zebedee.

Technical support during 1971 was somewhat unsettled as it was provided by base maintenance and the numbers and names changed to some degree throughout the year. For major airshows, maintenance support was assigned to an organization tasked with supporting all Canadian Forces participation. Most other performances were flown in western Canada and being of one day duration rarely required dedicated technical support on site. Also, the need to carry 11 pilots meant there was little capacity to take tech-

nicians along. Notwithstanding, Sgts Dick Gaff and Lorne Foster along with Cpls Anderson, Adams, McFadden, Torfason, Nixon and Thompson all worked with the team in some capacity during the team's first year of operation. Another base technician who played a key role was MCpl Ron LaGrange who supervised the installation of the smoke systems back onto the old Centennaire aircraft. Fortunately, most of the techs involved in 1971 volunteered to join the 1972 team.

Two famous Snowbird formations developed in 1971 and still flown today, the Double Diamond and the Canada Goose. In the formative years, the team flew formations with wing tip separation and 10 feet nose-tail separation. (Bill Johnson)

There was plenty of military hardware on the flight line at Abbotsford in 1971. Lined up alongside the USAF Thunderbirds in their F-4 Phantoms are part of the Canadian Forces contingent – the Snowbirds, CF-5s, CF-104s, T-33s, Tracker and Buffalo. (DND Photo via Terry Leversedge)

While pilots were assigned to the 2 CFFTS team, it was a secondary duty and we were all still required to carry out our normal instructional duties, although these were reduced where possible. This meant our formation training flights were generally flown at the end of each work day or on the weekend. We practiced an average of about 10 times a month from March to June with a lesser number of practices in the following months as the number of shows increased.

Due to the limited time for practices, it was necessary to keep the routine fairly short and simple. Essentially, it consisted of a number of formation patterns with changes made during what could best be described as dumbbell turns at each end of the showline. The time for the display varied but it usually lasted around 15 minutes, not including takeoff or landing.

The first limited display by the Snowbirds, although the name had not yet been selected, was flown at Saskatoon in support of a Saskatchewan government trade show called 'Index 71.' During 1971, one performance was flown in the Maritimes, a couple in Ontario and one in the USA; all other performances were in western Canada including the Saskatchewan Homecoming Air Show on July 11th and Abbotsford

Airshow from August 13th to 15th. A total of 25 performances were flown with the final one taking place on November 27th at Williams AFB on the outskirts of Phoenix, Arizona. This was perhaps the most memorable show of the year because of the positive response from the large crowd and the reaction from the USAF flying instructors based at Williams who operated in a very structured environment. They could hardly believe that a group of pilots on instructional tours of duty could put on a display of the standard and complexity they had just witnessed.

While the 1971 show sequence was relatively simple compared to the performances of the following years, it was flown in a highly professional manner, was well received by the viewing public and it helped create a demand for a full time, fully capable formation team.

There was strong belief among all those involved with the 1971 team that what had been started would both continue and grow. If that was to happen, the team needed a name, and it had to be something that was uniquely Canadian. Tom Reid came up with the idea to hold a contest and O.B.'s secretary, Lois Boyle, was tasked to organize a 'name the team' competition in the local ele-

mentary schools. She promptly did so with her usual efficiency. A large number of possible names were submitted by the students and on June 25th, 1971 the team selected 'Snowbirds.' The winning name was submitted by Douglas Farmer, the 12-year-old son of the base Protestant Padre and a young girl from one of the Moose Jaw schools whose name has unfortunately been lost over time. 'Snowbird' was the title of an Anne Murray hit which was popular at the time. It fit well with the white aircraft flown by the team, had an association with Canada and suggested something with grace and beauty.

Subsequent Snowbird teams and all those who enjoy airshows owe a lot to Col O.B. Philp, the personnel serving at CFB Moose Jaw in 1971 and that group of pilots and technicians who gave up a lot of personal time to produce a high class formation display. It was a display that, despite imposed limitations, was pleasing to the public, impressed senior military decision-makers of the time and helped generate a broad base of support which was a major factor in gaining approval for the creation of a Snowbird team that has thrilled audiences in Canada and the United States for over 30 years."

Glen Younghusband

The Saskatchewan Homecoming Air Show 1971

Although exposure of the Snowbirds at the Abbotsford International Airshow in western Canada and the Canadian International Air Show in the east were vital in helping promote their reputation, it was a show at their home base in Moose Jaw in July 1971 that first generated the visibility the team needed within the Canadian Forces. This was a pivotal show, as without grassroots support from their own personnel at virtually every rank level, there was little chance of long term survival.

An additional level of support which played a valuable role in the success of the Snowbirds was that provided by the province of Saskatchewan. Indeed, it was Premier Ross Thatcher who started the ball rolling during the New Year's Eve Ball at the Officers' Mess in Moose Jaw in 1970 with a simple question, "O.B., what are you going to do for Homecoming '71?" This was a provincial government initiative to stage a major celebration the following year designed to bring the sons and daughters of Saskatchewan back to the province to commemorate their heritage. After giving the Premier's question some thought for a few days, Col Philp made a courtesy call to Regina early in January and pitched the idea of a major airshow for that summer. There were two caveats – the proposal would have to be approved by Training Command and the provincial government would have to chip in some financial support. Philp figured about $12,000 donated to the base non-public funds account would allow him to secure some top-notch civilian performers and advertise the event across Saskatchewan. A cheque arrived on his desk two days later!

With the Saskatchewan government clearly on board, Philp took his plan to Winnipeg and MGen Bill Carr whose support would make or break the plan. Of this meeting, O.B. Philp has recorded:

"I discussed the proposal with Gen Carr, pointing out that I thought this would be an excellent opportunity to further cement our good relationship with the province of Saskatchewan and the city of Moose Jaw. I pressed the point that the profits from the show would go to our non-public fund which we could certainly put to good use and, if approved, the airshow would be in lieu of the annual Armed Forces Day.

Gen Carr said he had no difficulty with the proposal, but since we would be creating a third major Canadian airshow requiring the appropriate support, he would have to discuss this scheme with headquarters before giving me a green light. As the conversation eased I mentioned that we would increase the number of aircraft in our unofficial team to seven. The answer was that as long as I didn't ask for any additional resources or financial support, I could carry on.

When the decision from the top came back to me there was a provision, on a take it or leave it basis: 'It's agreed you can have the support providing you take on the responsibilities of Director, Canadian Armed Forces Airshows at both Abbotsford and the CNE (Toronto) as well as Moose Jaw for 1971.' Understanding the old adage that you never get something for nothing, I hastened to agree but added the seven-plane team would perform in all three shows."

O.B. Philp

With blessing in hand, Philp appointed Tom Reid as air operations director for the overall Canadian Forces airshow package. Former Golden Hawk Maj Dave Tinson was heavily involved promoting the spectacle and Maj Phil Perry, a former engineering officer with the Hawks, was recruited from Cold Lake to organize the technical support. Col Philp promptly collared two captains from the school who would also play prominent roles in the success of the show. Capt Rod Sword had been doing a superb job as editor of the base newspaper (a secondary duty he was about to lose) and Capt Joe Houlden had already distinguished himself as a smooth talking airshow announcer the previous year. He would once again fulfill that role in 1971 at the three major Canadian Forces displays in Moose Jaw, Abbotsford and Toronto. He still fondly remembers those heady days:

"The summer of 1970 had been something else, especially at Abbotsford. Enthusiasm and morale were sky high at the 'Jaw' under O.B.'s leadership. He called in all of his cards in 1971 and put together a first-class show at Moose Jaw built around his Canadian Forces travelling extravaganza. He lobbied for a package that, for flight safety reasons, would remain intact and do all of the major shows. In my mind, this was a good idea. Once O.B. had grabbed Rod Sword and I, we were each given an office and told to get to work! From then on, our primary duties on the base shifted to organizing the airshow."

Joe Houlden

As planning for the show gained momentum, the planners soon realized that this had the potential to be one of the largest one day airshows in terms of aircraft participation on the North American continent that summer. They decided this was a good advertising ploy

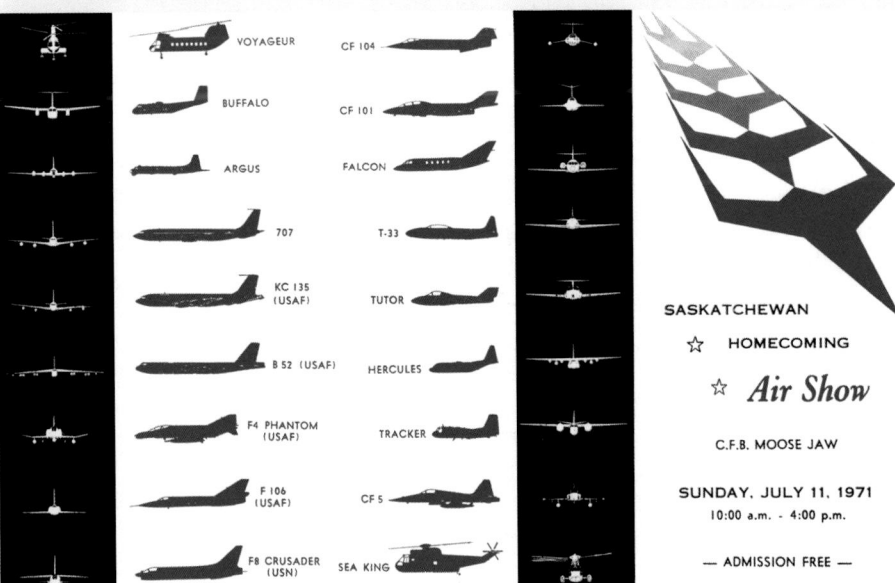

(Top) The logo which first featured Capt "Badger" Berger-North's stylized sheath of wheat became the Snowbird "Speedbird" the following year. Below is the advertising brochure that heralded the biggest airshow in Saskatchewan history. (via B. Berger-North)

VOYAGEUR
BUFFALO
ARGUS
707
KC 135 (USAF)
B 52 (USAF)
F4 PHANTOM (USAF)
F 106 (USAF)
F8 CRUSADER (USN)

CF 104
CF 101
FALCON
T-33
TUTOR
HERCULES
TRACKER
CF 5
SEA KING

SASKATCHEWAN
☆ HOMECOMING
☆ Air Show
C.F.B. MOOSE JAW
SUNDAY, JULY 11, 1971
10:00 a.m. - 4:00 p.m.
— ADMISSION FREE —

and went the extra mile to ensure that it was! A total of 52 Canadian Forces aircraft would be involved with the show supported by 65 technicians. Another 15 aircraft from the USAF would round out the military portion of the display. And with the provincial monies, some of the best civilian acts in the world were brought to Moose Jaw – the legendary Art Scholl in his highly modified de Havilland Chipmunk, the wing-walking act of Joe Hughes and John Kazian using a 1942 Super Stearman, Scotty McCray in his Schweizer 2-22 glider, Jim McDonald in his Champion Citabria and Al Pietsch in his custom-built Starduster Too.

The 1971 Snowbirds set up for landing from this very challenging seven-plane line-astern formation. (Bill Johnson)

The local newspaper, the *Moose Jaw Times-Herald*, started a daily advertising campaign some 30 days prior to the July 11th date and soon every newspaper in the province was running advertisements as well. News of the show spread all the way to Ottawa – even the Russians could not pass up this opportunity to see some western hardware in action and they dispatched their air attaché to Moose Jaw. Unfortunately, someone failed to tell Mother Nature about the big shindig. In the days leading up to the event, southern Saskatchewan was inundated with torrential

rain that caused widespread flooding. Organizers could only hope that the weather would let up, but on the morning of the big day, grim-faced base personnel woke up to more pelting rain. The show was in jeopardy. Then suddenly, as if by an act of God, the rain stopped in mid-morning and the cloud started to break up, the weatherman taking full credit for this good fortune. Over the years this phenomena has come to be known as the "Snowbird hole," some seemingly divine intervention that often parts ominous clouds to let sunshine stream through in time for an airshow.

When the weather broke, it seems that everyone and his dog headed to Moose Jaw. That was the good news – the bad news was that the rain had turned fields on the base designated as parking lots into quagmires. Of 12,000 prospective spaces, only 2,000 were useable. This created one of the largest traffic jams in Saskatchewan history as thousands of vehicles converged on the base from every direction. I know – I was there!

Philp and his staff had expected as many as 50,000 spectators would attend and had attempted to make provisions for that number. Realizing that even in good weather parking would be a challenge, a widespread advertising campaign urged airshow fans to "Take the Bus." This seemed sound advice but soon became a nightmare as not even the buses could contend with the thousands of airshow fans who wanted to board. Even those who did soon found themselves mired in the same traffic jam with everyone else. Thus, the key was not how you got there, but how early you had departed to make your way to the base.

Everyone who set out to attend the airshow at Homecoming '71 will never forget the experience. I had been on vacation in Regina visiting family and we departed the city in two cars at 9:30 a.m. for the drive west, a drive which would normally take less than an hour. Two hours later, I distinctly recall the panicky feeling in the pit of my stomach as we watched a USAF B-52 bomber darken the skies as it swooped over the base in a warm-up to the show. We were stuck dead in our tracks on Hwy 2 south of Moose Jaw, still three miles from the base, and the traffic behind us was lined up bumper to bumper as far as the eye could see. There was only one thing to do – abandon the car and walk! We finally made it to the flight line on the base just as the official opening of the show took

place at 1:00 p.m. We never did see anyone else in our family for the rest of the day – they had abandoned their car in the city and taken the bus! They never made it to the show …

Those who did were rewarded with a formidable display. The Commander of Training Command, MGen Carr, officially opened the show to the roar of eight Canadian fighters as they passed in front of the crowd low and fast in perfect formation, a magnificent start to the afternoon. The combined CF-104 and CF-5 teams from Cold Lake would later return to put on a thundering display to end the three-and-one-half hour airshow. The Canadian military display began with 11 paratroopers (soon to be named the

The Saskatchewan Homecoming Air Show staged at CFB Moose Jaw in 1971 marked the start of an annual tradition that lasted over two decades. The show attracted some of the best aerial acts in the world to the prairie home of the Snowbirds. It also created the biggest traffic jam in Saskatchewan history. (author's collection)

Skyhawks) from the Canadian Airborne Centre in Edmonton. They were followed by a wide array of aerial demonstrations representing each of the functional commands in the Canadian Forces. This included teams of Musketeers, T-33s, helicopters such as the Hiller, Huey and Voyageur, the Hercules, Buffalo, Argus and Tracker, and of course the seven-plane Tutor show. Joe Houlden introduced Moose Jaw's own "Snowbirds" to Canadians for the first time that afternoon and the team put on a beautiful display trailing billowy white smoke. Oblivious to the genesis of an aerial legacy which shared the name of her hit song, Anne Murray was thousands of miles away in her hometown of Springhill, Nova Scotia. Ironically, just the

THE LEADER-POST

VOL. LXII—No. 161　30 PAGES　　REGINA, SASKATCHEWAN, MONDAY, JULY 12, 1971　　***** SINGLE COPY　10c

Thousands thrilled by Homecoming air show

Saskatchewan newspapers were quick to praise CFB Moose Jaw's efforts in staging the biggest event in the province's history. The Canadian Forces put on an impressive display both on the ground and in the air. (courtesy the Regina *Leader Post*)

previous evening she had performed her own outdoor concert for 20,000 Maritimers to commemorate her first gold record – she had just sold one million copies of "Snowbird."

It is estimated some 45,000 spectators eventually made their way onto the base for Homecoming '71 while as many as another 40,000 were stuck in a 10,000 car traffic jam. As a result, the sleepy streets of Moose Jaw were flooded with 15,000 airshow hopefuls who couldn't even get out of the city. From his vantage point on top of No. 3 Hangar, Capt Joe Houlden reported that he could see thousands of cars clogging roadways in all directions, none moving. The traffic jam

stretching from the base along Hwy 2 to Moose Jaw and then east on the Trans Canada Hwy was still 11 miles long by mid afternoon. Notwithstanding the enormous logistic problems, the dazzling display won high praise from those fortunate enough to see it, as did Houlden's colourful and descriptive commentary. The stage was set for the next year …

The Road to Acceptance – Selling the Snowbirds

Following the highly successful inaugural season of the Snowbirds in 1971, O.B. Philp decided to again seek formal endorsement of his unofficial team. He had come to appreciate the predicament of his air force bosses as the senior leadership of the three former services struggled to make the new Canadian Forces system work. His memoirs reveal that he decided on a new tactic, one that was potentially fraught with risk and therefore required careful planning:

"It was time to test the waters at the higher echelon again but this time, rather than approach the senior airmen first, I decided to lobby senior army and navy people. First on my list was MGen Jim Tedlie, at that time Deputy Chief of Force Development. I had known Jim since he was the CO of the station at Churchill, Manitoba back in the late 1940s and hoped he might be sympathetic. Besides, he held the purse strings when it came to recommending funding for programs. He had the ear of the Vice Chief of Defence, LGen Mike Dare. Tedlie, as a senior

army officer, had no objection to a Canadian Armed Forces aerobatic team, even to the extent of providing additional funding. Well aware of the impact the Centennaires had made, he brought our conversation to the attention of the Vice Chief, which turned out to be most helpful.

I then called on Rear Admiral Bob Falls, Deputy Chief of Personnel and picked up some more support. Next stop was MGen Mike Pollard, Chief of Technical Services, a fine airman who, while AOC Air Defence Command, had supported whole-heartedly the Centennaire operation in 1967.

I was hopeful once again but checked myself when I remembered an important lesson I had learned from Air Vice Marshal J.L. Plant in the 1950s. He told me, rather directly on one occasion, 'Never put your boss in an indefensible position.' So I circled the target by calling on MGen Dave Adamson. While he was not my

Airshows are often dedicated to worthwhile community causes. In 1972, the benefactor of some welcome support was the Saskatchewan Council for Crippled Children and Adults. The famous photo above featuring Easter Seal "Timmy" Danny Musgrove and Maj Glen Younghusband of the Snowbirds became a strong endorsement for "Camp Easter Seal." In the past 31 years, the Snowbirds have participated in scores of similar charitable causes. (DND Photo)

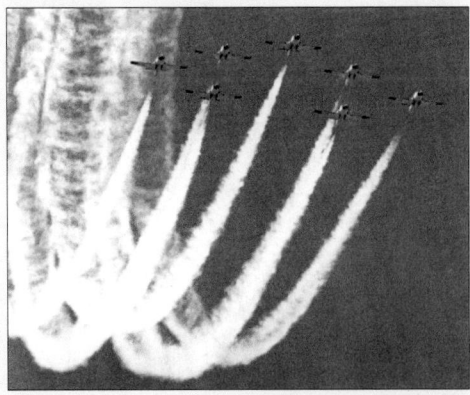

Although it took time and perseverance, by the summer of 1972 Canadians were being thrilled by sights like this as their own Snowbirds left pillars of white smoke against a backdrop of blue. (R. Van Tilbourg)

immediate boss, he was then Deputy Chief of Operations and Reserves and would have something to say about my future. I apprised him of my discussions with the other senior officers and told him that since Gen Sharp (an airman) was now Chief of the Defence Staff and since the key senior officers appeared to support my ideas, I would be putting an official request for aerobatic team status through my commander. The pendulum was swinging and seemed to be moving forward, although far more conservatively than I liked.

The official request for aerobatic team status was duly drafted and forwarded to Department of National Defence Headquarters, through Training Command Headquarters, in the latter part of 1971. I hoped that this time, having lobbied all of the right people in the proper places, that authorization would be forthcoming. Not so. Authorization came back to add two solo aircraft which could perform aerobatic manoeuvres. But the formation was still limited to 120 degrees of bank, 60 degrees of pitch nose up and 30 degrees nose down. No formation changes were allowed except in straight and level flight. Stymied again, I was disgusted with the decision but rationalized that half a loaf was better than none.

That Was Fun – Let's Do It Again The Anniversary Air Show 1972

The lessons of 1971 were well learned and another mega airshow was planned at Moose Jaw for 1972, this time with the blessing of the new Commander of Training Command, MGen W.A. Milroy. This affair was coined The Anniversary Air Show to commemorate the 20th anniversary of the reopening of the base in 1952 and was dedicated to the Saskatchewan Council for Crippled Children and Adults.

To organize the Canadian Forces package for 1972, O.B. Philp once again put together

The cover of *The Plainsman* said it all on July 20th, 1972. (via 'Badger' Berger-North)

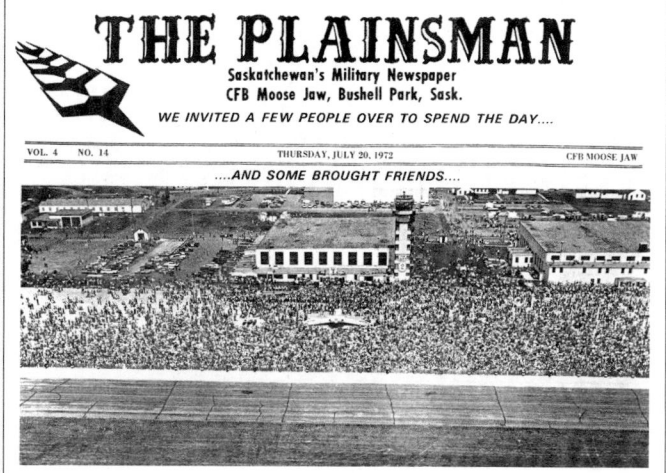

THE PLAINSMAN
Saskatchewan's Military Newspaper
CFB Moose Jaw, Bushell Park, Sask.
WE INVITED A FEW PEOPLE OVER TO SPEND THE DAY....

VOL. 4   NO. 14   THURSDAY, JULY 20, 1972   CFB MOOSE JAW

....AND SOME BROUGHT FRIENDS....

another winning team led by LCol Tom Reid and Maj Phil Perry who was this time brought in from Comox to act as the technical support coordinator. Capt John Hackett of the Snowbirds became the airshow information officer and Capt Gord Brown (of Centennaires fame) handled the administrative duties. Airshow announcer responsibilities were now handed to Lt Doug Wilson from CFB Uplands in Ottawa. With the principal team now responsible for organizing military participation at four major shows, Col Philp appointed Maj Don Williams as the base coordinator to oversee the massive Moose Jaw program which was highlighted by a four hour airshow culminating with the Snowbirds. His fine work paved the way for dozens of successive shows in the years to follow. Yet again, his staff had given O.B. Philp much to be proud of:

"The Anniversary Air Show at Moose Jaw on July 16th, 1972 was an overwhelming success. Again we billed it as the 'Largest One Day Air Show in North America' and it more than lived up to its name. The event was well advertised and drew 140,000 spectators from Saskatchewan, Manitoba, Alberta and North Dakota.

Gen Fred Sharp, Chief of the Defence Staff, accepted our invitation to attend and officially open the show. The Armed Forces part of the display was spectacular, comprised of some 41 aircraft and flew the same series of demonstrations that we would put on at the other three shows – Abbotsford, Moncton and Toronto. The Snowbirds' routine was flawless and included Younghusband's questionable 'slanted 360.'

After the show I had an opportunity to talk to the General privately about the future of the Snowbirds. I explained my frustration at not receiving authorization for full aerobatic team status and reminded him of the good press the team had been receiving across the country: 'We have created a national identity not dissimilar to that of the RCMP's Musical Ride and I think the time is right to establish the Snowbirds as a permanent unit in the Canadian Armed Forces.' Gen Sharp looked at me intently. I had his full attention and he told me to go on. 'We should open the team selections to volunteers across the service,' I said, 'to compete for the available positions. It requires the status of a permanent unit, and needs its own budget.' 'I am not aware of any major opposition to the Snowbirds,' he said, 'I'll have the program reviewed.'

I could not ask for any more. I had finally had my say to the man at the top. But there was no time to relax, we had to keep the momentum moving. The following day as the various participating aircraft were departing to their home bases I received a message. It was from MGen Dave Adamson, Deputy Chief of Operations and Reserves, at headquarters. He had been in attendance at the show but had returned to Ottawa the same night – 'Only one word to describe your air display – outstanding!'

This was all I needed, along with the knowledge that the Snowbirds had been the centre-piece in the largest one day airshow in North America."

O.B. Philp

Maj Glen Younghusband leads the Goose formation down the backside of his famous "slanted 360," looking for all the world like a loop! (Bill Johnson)

Snowbirds 1972

"With the enthusiastic reception that the public accorded the 1971 team, along with strong support from a number of senior military officers, Col O.B. Philp felt the time had come for the air force to have another aerobatic team. Early in the fall of 1971, he formally requested approval to form a nine aircraft team which would include opposing solos. When the response came back just prior to Christmas, it was positive for the nine aircraft, including the two solos, but once again placed pitch, bank and formation change limits on the formation portion of the performance. On the positive side, the two solos were authorized opposing aerobatics with only the normal showline restrictions.

Again on his own initiative, a decision had been made by Col O.B. to modify 11 aircraft for solo flight from either seat. Had the modifications been delayed until the team was approved by NDHQ, it would not have been possible to have the aircraft ready in time to start the show season. Once again MCpl Ron LaGrange was put in charge of the modification program and he soon became one of our full time technicians. Ron not only installed the cross-cockpit system, but also made a number of key improvements and with the support of base maintenance had all the aircraft ready by the time the team was ready to practice as a nine-plane.

As in the previous year, pilot selection started at the beginning of February and was completed by the end of the month. Although around 20 pilots applied to join the team, there was really only one opening available as eight members of the 1971 team had volunteered for 1972! The successful candidate was Lt Larry Currie, which said a lot for his ability to fly formation.

The year 1972 was the first year the Snowbirds operated in a manner that was much the same as that used today. Each pilot was now assigned a permanent position that he would fly within the formation. Capts Mike Marynowski and Lloyd Waterer were assigned the honour of working up the new solo aerobatic show as the lead and opposing solo respectively. Dedicated technicians were also assigned to the team under the very able leadership of Sgt Bill Holloway who was largely responsible for setting up a system of technical support which has changed little over the years. I and Sgt Holloway felt

The nine demonstration pilots of the 1972 Snowbirds. L to R, Kneeling – Capts Tom Gernack, Michael Marynowski, Laurie Illingworth, Fred McCague. Standing – Capt Lloyd Waterer, Lt Larry Currie, Capt Gord Wallis, Capt Chester Glendenning. Cockpit – Maj Glen Younghusband (team leader). (DND Photo)

strongly that a key to keeping the Snowbirds alive in the future would be the ability to carry all first-line technical support from showsite to showsite in the team aircraft, with CFB Moose Jaw providing backup support to recover aircraft with major unserviceabilities. Despite many in the air force who felt that a transport aircraft carrying spares and additional technicians was an absolute necessity, O.B. approved my request to let the team try and operate with the maximum of 10 technicians we could carry in the Tutors. To handle the workload, a number of the technicians were given basic cross-train-ing in a second trade, something the rest of the air force didn't adopt until a number of trades were combined many years later.

Along with dedicated technicians, the Snowbirds were allocated office, crew and briefing space, and a full time public relations officer/commentator. Capt John Hackett was Mr. Everything. He handled public relations, arrived at show locations before the team to make sure everything was organized, provided the spare aircraft, provided the show commentary and looked after a host of other matters. With boundless ener-

A rare shot of the first Snowbird nine-plane as it sweeps over the abandoned airfield at Mossbank, the original home of the RCAF's No. 2 Bombing and Gunnery School during World War II. (DND photo via 431 Sqn)

The Snowbirds demonstrated their "slanted 360" near Harrison Hot Springs for one ecstatic photographer on a glorious day in the summer of '72. (Bill Johnson)

gy and a never failing sense of humour, John did the work of at least two people.

Training for the 1972 season started at the beginning of March which didn't leave a lot of time. Fortunately, as mentioned previously, all the pilots except one were returning from 1971. Faced with the restrictions which had been imposed, it was a challenge to design a show which would approach the standard the public had come to expect after watching the Golden Hawks and the Golden Centennaires. The limitations made little sense from a safety point of view (the reason given for their imposition) and it became obvious that the Snowbirds would have to somehow massage them without raising the ire of NDHQ. The solution that I came up with was to offset the looping manoeuvres by about 15 degrees into wind and call them 'slanted 360s' and to use a dumbbell turn approximately 70 degrees above the horizon at the ends of the showline for formation changes and to replace a full roll. The 'Heart,' which was the signature manoeuvre of the 1972 team, could be explained as a double wingover. Although it was quite obvious to any airman that the formation sequence included aerobatics, loops and rolls were never mentioned except when describing the performance of the opposing solos. The end result was a show which was somewhat shorter, 22 minutes, and less spectacular than those flown by subsequent teams, but a show which had the beauty and precision for which the Snowbirds have become famous.

The famous Snowbird Double Diamond as it appeared in the summer of 1972. (Bill Johnson)

When O.B. first viewed the various manoeuvres and I told him that 'what looked like a loop was in fact a slanted 360,' he was silent for a few seconds and then replied, 'Right. It looks good to me. Keep it in the routine.' Later in the year when the colonel was queried about aerobatics by the Chief of the Defence Staff, Gen Fred Sharp, who had just watched a Snowbird performance, he used the same explanation and got much the same response.

The first full show sequence that included the opposing solos was flown on April 13th and the show was approved in an evening performance at CFB Moose Jaw on May 2nd. The first formal performance for a non-military audience was flown at Yellowknife in the Northwest Territories on May 13th. An indication of the crowd appeal of the Snowbirds, particularly in small town Canada, was gained in transit to Yellowknife when the team made a refuelling stop at Fort Smith. At the request of air traffic control, a couple of passes were made over the town and airport prior to landing. By the time the refuelling was complete, a crowd approaching 2,000 had converged on the airport. Needless to say, it was felt necessary to perform as many manoeuvres as fuel would permit before departing for Yellowknife.

From that first deployment it was obvious that a team of nine show pilots, at least one commentator and 10 technicians was the way to go. It made for a closely-knit group, provided the Snowbirds with a great deal of flexibility and kept the cost to the military and show sponsors to a minimum. It is fair to say that the ability of the Snowbirds to carry their technical support in the show aircraft has been one of the major reasons for the team's longevity.

The 1972 team was instrumental in setting the character of the Snowbirds which has been maintained throughout the years. The goal was to present a professional, but low key image, to have no 'prima donnas' and to respond in a positive, friendly and enthusiastic manner to requests from the public, show sponsors and the media. In other words, to present an image that the armed forces, and Canadians from all walks of life, could relate to, feel comfortable with and be proud of. The popularity of team members and the respect accorded the Snowbirds in Canada and the United States attests to how well that team character has been preserved.

Formation aerobatics on a day like this are a joy - the type of day airshow pilots and photographers like Bill Johnson (inset) live for.

Of his first chase flight with Bill Johnson aboard, Snowbird solo Capt Mike Marynowski later reported, "He giggled a lot!" At right, one of thousands of photographs that would be taken by the intrepid photographer during the team's first 20 years. Bill and wife Nancy were among the first to be inducted into the Honorary Society of Snowbirds in 1995. (Bill Johnson)

One important item missing from the Snowbird program was an appropriate team logo. A design incorporating a stylized Inuit snow goose was initially used, but the team was not very happy with its appearance. At the beginning of March, Capt David 'Badger' Berger-North, a talented amateur graphic artist, was asked to design a logo that would reflect and encompass the team *raison d'etre*, Snowbird name, the province of Saskatchewan and Canada all at once. After a number of attempts, Badger decided to base the design on the stylized ear of wheat in a logo he had designed for the 1971 Saskatchewan Homecoming Air Show. He placed the stylized ear of wheat, which also looked like aircraft in formation, on a stylized snowflake background and put the team name at the bottom. He presented his proposed logo to the team with both a red and a blue background. The team chose the red and white version and thus was born one of the most widely recognized logos in North America.

An unfortunate aspect about the start of new formation teams is that it seems, regardless of extensive training and the care taken to produce a safe performance, most teams have a serious accident during the early years. This happened to the Snowbirds when Lloyd Waterer was killed following a wing tip collision with Mike Marynowski during an opposing solo manoeuvre at CFB Trenton, Ontario on June 10th, 1972. Since there were no previous team solo members to call on, it was not possible to bring in a replacement for Lloyd. Thus, we flew with a single solo and seven or eight-plane formation for the remainder of the year.

1972 saw the start of two relationships that the Snowbirds would enjoy for many years. The first was with Bill Johnson, a world-class photographer, who with his wife Nancy would take many outstanding inflight pictures of Snowbird teams over the years. The second was with the Pietsch family of Minot, North Dakota who not only flew some great aerobatics but were also warm and generous hosts to many of the teams.

Among the many memories from 1972 are some of a less serious nature: John Hackett doing his commentary from the diving tower at the Kelowna Regatta and announcing after the performance that there was one more

A lovely shot of the Snowbirds' Arrow formation as Mike Marynowski rolls his Tutor over top of the formation. (Bill Johnson)

manoeuvre – then jumping off the tower fully dressed in his flying suit and hat. The Canadian International Air Show in Toronto, where our Snowbird aircraft were based across Lake Ontario at St. Catharines – visibility over Toronto was very poor in haze and low cloud due to an onshore wind. As a consequence, the Thunderbirds and other jets based at Toronto's International and Downsview Airports were unable to fly. Across the lake and over the showline the weather was acceptable, although there was still a lot of haze. We were able to fly on all four days and one of the Toronto papers referred to us as the 'Phantom Aerobatic Team' that appears out of the haze, puts on a show and then just as suddenly disappears. Then there was the show in Minot where the technical members of the team felt that the Blue Angels were taking their performance during start, taxi and shutdown just a bit too seriously. When we taxied to our shutdown location in front of the stands, I looked up to see not Bill Holloway directing me to the shutdown point, but an attractive young lady in hot pants and long leather boots. One of the team members, who was never named, had picked her out of the crowd and asked her to do it – the crowd loved it!

The Snowbirds graced the front cover of the CIAS Programme for the first time in 1972. Canadians were thrilled to see a team of their own back in the air again. (author's collection)

In comparison with later years when the Snowbirds were a fully supported separate unit, the 1972 team had a shorter season (May to early September) and a show that was somewhat less complicated and of shorter duration, but we set the standard for the outstanding teams that followed and played a large part in generating the public support that has kept the Snowbirds alive through many years of reduced military spending."

Glen Younghusband

In spite of the tragic death of Lloyd Waterer early in the season, the Snowbirds had rebounded well from the adversity and enjoyed strong public support as they carried their show across the nation. The team was on a roll – and O.B. Philp was determined to take it another step forward. He had envisioned from the outset that if the team continued, a new leader would be selected every two years as had been the general practice with the Golden Hawks and the plan for the Golden Centennaires, had they survived beyond 1967. Glen Younghusband's strong leadership was to be rewarded with a promotion to lieutenant colonel in the summer of 1973 and appointment as CO 434 Tac (F) Sqn in Cold Lake flying the CF-5. In the interim, he would assume the role of acting commandant of 2 CFFTS where he could continue to provide a strong supporting role to the new team leader.

In 1972 a dedicated team of groundcrew were assigned to the team. Standing behind the team pilots are, left to right, MCpl Ron LaGrange, Sgt Bill Holloway, Cpl Joe McCluskey, MCpl Larry Legault, Cpls Reg Bach, Dwight Vaughn, Claude Mikkelson, Pete Hennicke, Mike Thompson, Bob Nixon. (DND Photo via Glen Younghusband)

The birth of a famous logo. The matchbook cover that inspired the sketches that led to the final version of the Snowbird crest. Today, it is recognized around the world as a symbol of aerial excellence, Canadian style. (via B. Berger-North)

The Birth of the Snowbird Logo

The Snowbird logo has become famous around the world as the symbol representing Canada's aerobatic team. However, like the team itself, it had austere beginnings as its designer 'Badger' Berger-North, a veteran of both the RAF and RCAF recalls:

"When the idea of the Canadian Forces participating in the Saskatchewan Homecoming '71 celebration was proposed, Maj J.B. 'Bing' Peart was chosen as the Moose Jaw airshow coordinator. At the time he was also one of the *aides-de-camp* to the Lieutenant-Governor of Saskatchewan. While he was attending an official function at 'The Saskatchewan,' a Regina hotel, he happened to pick up a book of matches that featured on its cover a stylized ear of wheat.

As I had designed numerous logos and worked on base/mess entertainment functions, some with him, he came to me to see if I would design a logo suitable for the upcoming airshow. He then gave me the book of matches, wondering if a symbol like the ear of wheat on the cover, and representative of Saskatchewan, could be incorporated into a design. The design that I finally submitted to him was accepted for the airshow and was also incorporated into the heading of *The Plainsman*, CFB Moose Jaw's paper. Maj Peart was posted to Ottawa early in 1971 and handed the job of airshow coordinator to Maj Tom Spruston who saw it through to fruition.

With the naming of the team on June 25th, the next most obvious quest was to come up with a distinctive insignia that was unique to the unit. After the airshow on July 11th, it soon became clear that the Snowbirds were 'go' for the year 1972. While the team was giving an airshow in the north, team members came up with a design which consisted of a bird in the stylized Inuit manner. This was printed upon sticky-backed paper for distribution. Upon reflection later, the team was not totally

happy with this logo as it was deemed not to meet the need.

The Snowbirds first attempt at a team logo in 1972 featured the Canada Goose. It quickly gave way to a more stylistic logo which incorporated the symbol originally designed for the Saskatchewan Homecoming Air Show. (via Doug Marshall)

In the spring of 1972, on March 1st, Maj Glen 'Bone' Younghusband and Capt Laurie 'Inch' Illingworth asked me if I would come up with a suitable design that could be used as a distinctive shoulder patch. The aircraft used by the team were still the 2 CFFTS Tutors with the 'Big 2' on the fins. My initial attempts were to try to incorporate a bird into the logo, but it was obvious from the start that this would be difficult. After many attempts and using a stylized snowflake as the background, I decided to modify the logo that I had designed for Airshow '71 and place it into the snowflake. This produced a compact design for not only a shoulder patch, but also which could be used on programs, etc. I made up examples in both blue and red, with the team choosing the red version. The team wore the shoulder patch for the first time for the 1972 season, and the logo first appeared on the Tutor fin during the 1973 season.

I am extremely proud of having been involved with the Snowbirds in their formative years, all of us hoping the team would last past a couple of years, but little dreaming that it would become a national institution. I am somewhat awed when I realize that this logo is taken in the world of aviation, internationally, as a sign that the bearers of this insignia are paragons in this art of aviation."

D.V. 'Badger' Berger-North

Maj George Miller awaits clearance to taxi at Abbotsford. The new Snowbird crest adorned the tail of the team's aircraft for only one year (1973), giving way to a new paint scheme the following season. (Bill Johnson)

The 1973 Snowbirds (sporting their new flying suits) and their groundcrew, all volunteers. L to R, Standing – Maj George Miller (leader) Capts Larry Currie, Mike Murphy, Carl Stef, Lt Bob Wade, Capts George Hawey, Gord Wallis, Tom Griffis, Laurie Illingworth, John Hackett. Kneeling – Sgt Bill Holloway, Cpls John Doerkson, Ely Bowen, Ed Torfason, Chuck Wicks, Bob LeBlanc, Peter Hennicke, Claude Mikkelson, MCpl Larry Legault, Cpl Rusty Rutherford. (DND Photo)

Snowbirds 1973

As Col Philp began his search for a new leader, he knew exactly what he was looking for – another veteran pilot with a strong fighter background (and preferably aerobatic team experience) to take the Snowbirds to the next logical step – full aerobatic status. He knew most of the majors in the air force with suitable qualifications but wanted another opinion from a respected ally. He called on Maj C.B. Lang (then serving at NDHQ) for his thoughts. In reviewing the list of possible candidates, both came up with the same name - Maj George Miller. A former solo with the Golden Hawks, Miller was highly regarded in the CF-104 community where he was employed at the time. Therein lay the problem – he had not been in the European theatre long and pulling him off of a highly sought after tour might be difficult. However, this turned out to be inconsequential as Col Philp was able to spring Miller with a phone call to the Commander 1 Canadian Air Group, BGen Ken Lewis. As for George Miller, he leapt at the opportunity and picks up the Snowbird story:

"I often recall the 1973 Snowbird experience and the thrill and challenge, as a team, of preparing a nine-plane display in a time span of seven weeks, that is from first pilots' meeting to our first show. I arrived at Moose Jaw on March 12th, 1973 having accepted the very honoured position of team lead a week prior in Germany via a conference call led by my esteemed former squadron commander and Snowbirds' founder, Col O.B. Philp. From the moment I arrived, O.B., as base commander, offered the support, 'open door' and independence I needed to cover ground quickly. I still remember our first meeting in Moose Jaw which he summed up by saying, 'Your first show is in Yellowknife on May 15th. I don't care if it's a four or nine-plane and the speed you develop is up to you. Keep it safe and just let me know when you're ready to show me something and I'll be your eyes from the ground.' And that he was, and his observations proved a tremendous help and incentive to us as we cut corners to form and develop quickly.

Having never flown the Tutor aircraft, I had to quickly 'check out' and start flying with

selected team members immediately. The eight pilots joining me were the best of the 2 CFFTS instructional staff that had volunteered. They were graciously allowed the opportunity by LCol Glen Younghusband, who at the time was acting commandant of 2 CFFTS and the previous team lead over the introductory years.

We wasted absolutely no time. I decided to assign team positions based on one interview, one formation trip and intuition. With exhaustive briefings and debriefings and all of us fully focused in max learn mode, we cut directly to four-plane formation and solo work at 500 feet. Every day was a three trip day if the weather allowed it. I quickly found we had strength everywhere. At the difficult outer left wing, Capt Bob Wade's skill enabled us to rapidly develop the line-abreast work. Our two solos, Capts 'Inch' Illingworth and Tom Griffis, began building a safe but aggressive routine with no obvious sign of being tentative in the wake of the previous year's solo fatality. I had no cause to develop any real concern.

The Snowbirds' beautifully painted T-33 support aircraft (133275) was a favourite among airshow buffs. The advance team that manned the aircraft in 1973 were Cpl Rusty Rutherford (safety systems technician) and Capt John Hackett (team coordinator and narrator). (Denis Garand via Robert St. Pierre, via Rusty Rutherford)

The Johnson "support wagon" arrives to greet the Snowbirds following their show at Paine Field, Washington in 1973. Nancy Johnson congratulates Gord Wallis, Tom Griffis, John Hackett and Mike Murphy on their show. At right, the symmetrically pleasing Card 7 formation has been used frequently in the Snowbird show over the years. (Bill Johnson)

We tried a lot of original stuff as our 25 minute routine developed and as we worked on whittling our 'off stage' time down to 10 seconds. We faced few restrictions and I imposed none outside acceptable boundaries of team discipline and safety. Apart from first year restrictions of no bomb bursts or formation changes during an aerobatic manoeuvre, NDHQ and Training Command HQ gave little direct input to affect the team's operation. Organization of the season schedule and selection of showsites and promotion was done by the team. The going was not easy as we were so short staffed with so little time to organize the team and schedule from scratch. Evenings were spent on the telephone coordinating promotion and showsites. All of our team flight suits and social attire was voluntarily paid for by the pilots and groundcrew, as was a lot of our promotional material. O.B. provided great base commander support in the provision of assigned groundcrew and the dedication of rapid base response to team needs whenever required. He also provided financial support as best he could. His advice, moral support and his actions as intermediary with headquarters were invaluable. The transfer of a clerk typist from 2 CFFTS helped immeasurably as we did not have the additional staff positions of later years. Capt John Hackett's skills were again immediately applied in advance site preparation and media coordination. He also worked hard to develop a show commentary, a showsite public address interface system and a video taping procedure for recording practices and displays, using borrowed equipment. He was later ably joined by Capt Andy Bessette as French commentator for a few bilingual shows, although Andy became much more in demand the following year.

The assignment of team groundcrew led by Sgt Bill Holloway and the provision of a dedicated maintenance area on base truly gave the team the integrated spirit and means to do the job. Breaking new ground together every day in planning, organization and display development was extremely exciting and motivating. Within a few weeks of our first show, 2 CFFTS adjusted its afternoon schedule to allow us to practice over base. This

The 1973 Saskatchewan Air Show included a special salute to the 100th anniversary of the Royal Canadian Mounted Police. The show had garnered considerable fame as the largest one day show in North America and marked Col O.B. Philp's swan song at CFB Moose Jaw as he prepared to retire from the Canadian Forces. His lasting legacy – The Snowbirds. (author's collection)

provided the valuable audience reaction and critique together with O.B.'s comments. I chose the nine-plane double loop entry with solo splits to open the show and chose a

show 'action' highlight to close it. This involved putting three simultaneous manoeuvres on stage as part of the landing sequence that allowed a four-plane box landing followed immediately by the rest in trail. We included a four-plane loop to downwind, a three-plane roll-around break and solos' low-level tuck-under break, all at the same time. It proved to be a real crowd pleaser.

Our opening show at Yellowknife went very well. It was the first of 38 in 1973, seven of which were in the United States. This took the team from coast to coast twice. The revival of a full aerobatic display team representing the air force, the Canadian Forces and indeed Canada, evoked a great response wherever we performed.

On July 14th, 1973, Capt Carl Stef had to eject from his aircraft following an engine compressor stall due to a bird strike. Due to the subsequent back injuries he received from a very hard parachute landing, he was unable to return to the team until September. To the team's credit, it was able to modify its formations within a few days and carry on as an eight-plane team until Carl's return.

I was extremely proud of the 1973 team and how well it rose to the challenge in such a short time frame and under considerable financial and administrative restraints. It launched initiatives in every area of team operations and support and established standards and procedures that would enable the growth of a national team to achieve the vision foreseen by Col O.B. Philp in getting it all started a few years prior."

George Miller

By the end of the 1972 season, many instructors in Moose Jaw were considering trying out for the Snowbirds and those already on the team certainly had colleagues in mind that they would like to see join them. It wasn't a

Two views of modified formations that were flown when a bird ingestion forced Capt Carl Stef to eject prior to a practice for the 1973 Saskatchewan Air Show. At left, the modified Double Diamond and at right, the Arrow. Note the tight wing overlap that the team adopted in 1973. (Bill Johnson)

Capt Tom Griffis was one of many Tutor instructors in Moose Jaw motivated to try out for the team by both the challenge and close friends. From winning a slot as Snowbird 8 in 1973-1974, he returned to command the team in 1979-1980. (Nancy Johnson)

petitive nature and the desire to fly solo now pushed me to go for the one open solo spot for the '73 season. Being a solo pilot is not everyone's desire but for me it was an easy decision. I didn't think I was all that good at formation flying and now that I was on the team, I did not want my cover blown! Thus, in part for self-preservation, I worked hard at earning the solo spot.

Enter George Miller. I immediately liked his style and flair. His first job was to select the solo pair and when he and Inch Illingworth eventually selected me I was relieved. Thus my initial three months with the team taught me two important lessons which were put to good use for my future role with the team. First, if you really put your mind and effort into the task at hand, you might surprise yourself with the results. The second and possibly the most important lesson was that pilots on the team do not necessarily reflect the best stick and rudder candidates available – those with the desire and willingness to learn would surface as successful pilots with the Snowbirds. When I later came back as team leader in '79 and '80, I remembered my own experiences from '73 and when it came time to select new members, my input into the selection process emphasized, and was greatly influenced by, my initial experiences with the team.

During my two years as one of the solo pilots, George Miller as 'Boss' was to become my second mentor. George had a tremendous amount of experience as well as skill and a flair for 'the show.' He knew what our job was and he knew how to execute it. Even though he and I did not always see eye to eye on specific issues, particularly with respect to the solo routine, he ingrained in

Maj George Miller signs autographs in a ritual that has not changed in over 30 years – meeting the public along the fenceline after the show. (Bill Johnson)

me the importance of putting forward an aggressive but safe show for the public. George redefined what 300 foot minimums and 1500 foot showlines meant and anyone who witnessed one of George's shows always left with a smile on their face and a certain pride in the excellence of the Armed Forces of Canada. Although it is always difficult to quantify the results of a Snowbird show, I am sure that many of today's pilots and members of the armed forces got their first taste of the military at one of George's shows."

Tom Griffis

By the summer of 1973, Col O.B. Philp had been base commander in Moose Jaw for four years. This unusually long period of time had allowed him to take his dream of having another display team in Canada from a four-plane school team in 1970 to a nine-plane aerobatic team by 1973. He had set the stage for the future and now handed over the reins of power to an equally strong proponent, Col Ralph Annis. Like Philp, Annis would go on to play a pivotal role in keeping the Snowbirds alive. As the original lead solo of the RCAF's Golden Hawks in 1959-1960, Annis had a full understanding of all aspects of airshow operations. In him, George Miller had another powerful ally in which to take the team the next step forward:

job for everyone, and for those who were interested there was always that nagging thought of self-doubt, "What if I try out and don't make it?" This facet of human nature is something that every Snowbird hopeful has had to come to terms with since the beginning of the team tryouts. One instructor that struggled with that decision was Capt Tom Griffis, a cross-trained navigator from the maritime world on his first tour as a pilot. Given his background, he perhaps had more reason than others at that stage of his career to be concerned about competing with seasoned fighter pilots serving at 2 CFFTS:

"Going back to the fall of 1972, when tryouts were approaching for the 1973 team, I can recall my good friend and mentor, Gord Wallis, convincing me to throw my hat into the ring. At the time I think the prospect of failing when faced with competition probably played a bigger role in my initial reluctance to try out than I would like to admit. Constant prodding and encouragement from Gord finally convinced me I should have a go at it and the die was cast for my future involvement with the team.

When the final selections were made for the 1973 team, I can clearly remember that my com-

Col O.B. Philp presents Maj George Miller and the 1973 team a farewell memento from his Golden Centennaires' days in advance of his retirement. The team is sporting their trademark red dinner jackets. (DND Photo via 431 Sqn)

Snowbirds 1974

The entire Snowbird team was outfitted in red for the 1974 tour. L to R, Kneeling – Capts Tom Griffis, Murray Bertram, Carl Stef, John Shaw, Maj George Miller (leader), Capts Mike Murphy, Bob Wade, Harry Chapin, Yogi Huyghebaert. Standing – Cpls Peter Hennicke, Mike Thompson, Rusty Rutherford, Ray Lund, Sgt Doug Marshall, Cpls Ely Bowen, Al Boyce, MCpl Cal Wanvig, Cpl Ed Torfason. (DND Photo)

"The 1974 team continued setting many milestones and the pattern for the future. The restrictions that previously prevented bomb bursts and formation changes during 'aero-batic' manoeuvres were lifted and the team took every advantage of it. Our opening nine-plane bomb burst became a signature of the team and formation changes were incorporated into nearly every on-stage manoeuvre. Nine-plane formation takeoffs and landings were incorporated wherever runway width and prevailing wind conditions allowed.

The new pilots and groundcrew we took on were exceptional and soon proved the value of our intensive selection process. We need-ed to fill both line astern positions but, to my relief, they were superbly filled by Capts Murray Bertram and Harry Chapin. Capt John Shaw was a natural at inner right wing and Capt 'Yogi' Huyghebaert came on to do a great job as opposing solo with Capt Tom Griffis. Another great addition was Sgt Doug Marshall to head the groundcrew as crew chief. His ability to coordinate and lead a quick response to maintenance problems 'on the road' and to work near miracles to keep all nine aircraft flying instilled great confidence among team members. It especially allowed a degree of operational independence granted by headquarters that permitted the team to extend its reach to austere areas.

Being able to take the Snowbirds to northern sites was particularly gratifying. Displays of this kind were a first for most northern communities and they went all out to host the team – certainly everyone came out to watch. The show at Inuvik, Northwest Territories was a first for aerobatic teams in that it was performed at midnight, in perfect daylight conditions. The citizens turned out in full and were boosted by busloads from Tuktoyaktuk. It prompted an all-night festival. In those early years, taking the team north presented unique challenges, especially navigating. As the team Tutors were only equipped with TACAN (tactical air navigation), we could not access the NDB (non-

Team coordinator Capt Greg Bruneau departs Moose Jaw in June '74 to make advance arrangements for the arrival of the team. The coordinators play a vital role in the team's operation, ensuring all administrative and operational details are in place prior to each and every Snowbird performance. Capt Bruneau's parting gift to airshow organizers in 1975 was the first "Airshow Handbook" which imparted useful guidelines in organizing a show – from smoke oil requirements to airshow safety. At right, the Snowbirds' first postcard. Team coordinators Greg Bruneau and Andy Bessette are centre left and right respectively. (Graham Wragg, author's collection.)

The first official photograph of the 1974 Snowbirds in their new colours. (DND Photo.)

A contrasting look at the top and bottom of the new paint scheme as George Miller leads his inner wingmen through the Wineglass Roll. (Bill Johnson)

directional beacons) network serving the north. This largely necessitated low-level visual navigation when transiting between showsites and we had to be very careful with weather. This sometimes meant formating en masse with the team's T-33, flown by our public relations officer and commentator, Greg Bruneau, as it had the on-board navigational equipment needed. Greg experienced an extremely serious bird strike near Fort Smith (southeast of Great Slave Lake) when flying the T-33. He momentarily lost consciousness when hit by the bird and pieces of the shattered plexiglas. He did an outstanding job of recovering the aircraft and landing safely.

The 1974 team now looked great in its first full paint scheme. The familiar design we know today has changed little since 1974 although contemporary styling of some lines, lettering and numbers have kept apace. I sketched the basic paint scheme with the assistance of Cpl Rusty Rutherford, our safety systems technician. The fore to aft lines were adapted to somewhat reflect the acknowledged impact of the Golden Centennaire design. From the beginning, I wanted to see a full underbelly design incorporated. I admit the beautiful paint scheme of the USAF Thunderbirds was an influence in this direction. With Rusty, I roughly drew an underbelly design incorporating the Snowbird 'sheaf-of-wheat' logo. We took

this to the base graphic design artist, Bob Thompson, who did a superb job in rounding it out in presentation form. Subsequently, Training Command and NDHQ rallied a rapid approval process ending with Tom Griffis flying the first newly-painted aircraft into Moose Jaw to an ecstatic gathering of team members and families prior to season start. The rest of the aircraft were completed shortly thereafter.

In all, the team completed 79 performances in 1974, traversing the country three times. The farthest afield were a number of shows in Newfoundland to celebrate its 100th birthday. Team members would likely recall the hosting of the first Aerobatic Team Pilots' Reunion at Moose Jaw as being the occasion of our most memorable performance that year. The team worked extremely hard to coordinate the weekend reunion for May 31st and June 1st and it resulted in a large and boisterous number of past aerobatic team members attending. To the absolute delight of everyone, including local and national media, four of the original Siskin pilots from the 1929-1932 team attended. When the Snowbirds received the approving comments of these and the rest of past team members, we knew we had achieved a standard of formation aerobatics that we were proud to perform for any audience, anywhere."

George Miller

From Siskins to Snowbirds. The last surviving members of the RCAF's inaugural aerobatic team joined the Snowbirds at the first aerobatic pilots' reunion in 1974. L to R – Ralph C. Hawtrey, E.A. "Mac" McGowan, Fowler M. Gobeil and Ernie A. McNab. (DND Photo)

Building an Identity

The achievement of full aerobatic team status was a major milestone in the history of the Snowbirds but it was the new paint scheme in 1974 that generated the most excitement for airshow fans across Canada and the team members themselves. The new look gave the team an aura of both acceptance and permanence. From that day forward, every team member realized that they were part of something extraordinarily special, not the least of whom was Cpl Rusty Rutherford who had helped design the scheme:

"One of my most cherished memories of my two years on the Snowbirds was standing at the corner of the hangar with George Miller and Bob Wade at dusk that day as our first Tutor in the new paint scheme did a low pass across the ramp. It was a very emotional moment.

From the groundcrew perspective, another milestone in 1974 was obtaining our own show uniform. Until 1974, the groundcrew had worn white coveralls with a red T-shirt and the appropriate crests. These were very hot and difficult to keep clean. In the spring of 1974, we had red uniforms made at our own expense using the design of the cur-

rent CF work dress. They were made by a Chinese seamstress down on River Street without the knowledge of the pilots. Needless to say, when they returned from a practice one day there was a blaze of red on the tarmac! Since there seemed to be a lot of petty jealousy among the base maintenance staff towards the team at the time, after work that night we decided to get all of the remarks out in the open and went to the Corporals' Club in all of our red splendour. We expected a hard time, but were pleasantly surprised by a very positive reaction from our peers."

Rusty Rutherford

Back Door Politics

When Col Ralph Annis assumed command of CFB Moose Jaw on August 17th, 1973 he knew it was going to be an uphill battle to keep the Snowbirds alive. While there were a growing number of supporters for the team, there remained many detractors who still saw an aerial team as an extravagance the Canadian Forces could not afford. As a result, there was a great deal of politicking going on behind the scenes to educate those who did not understand the role and effectiveness of the Snowbirds. One senior offi-

cer who was close to the action was the Base Operations Officer, LCol Terry Lyons, who underscores the role that Ralph Annis played in keeping the team alive:

"While everyone close to the Snowbird story knows the critical part that O.B. Philp played in getting the team off and running, I wonder how many team members and outsiders know the true role that Ralph Annis played in the team history? From my observations on the sideline as BOpsO, Ralph was probably the next most important individual to affect the team in its entire time of existence. When I became associated, the team had to fight to justify itself every year. There was a faction in NDHQ who figured that the team cost too much to continue, did not give enough value for the buck and besides, was dangerous. Ralph was continually lobbying with the brass in headquarters, any influential civilians that he could get next to and every politician who came within the province. This was a continual battle for Ralph and he was completely dedicated to the team's survival. We discussed this subject many, many times – at work and after work (while having one of the very few pints we old types used to have).

The original blueprints of the new Snowbird design were created by graphic artist Bob Thompson from sketches provided by George Miller and Rusty Rutherford. At right, the specifications of the Tutor, now completing its 32nd year with the Snowbirds. (via R. Rutherford, 431 Sqn)

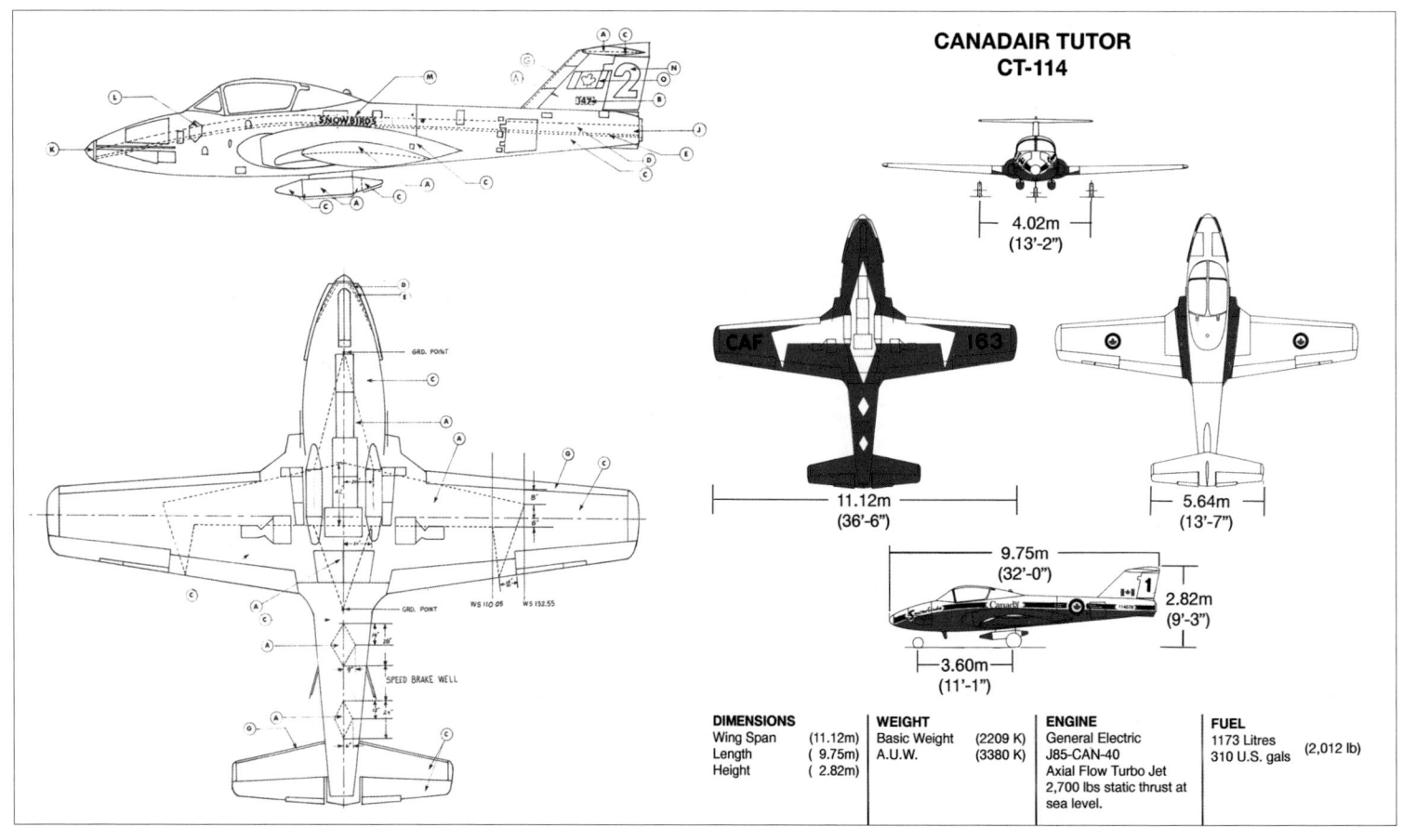

CANADAIR TUTOR CT-114

4.02m (13'-2")

11.12m (36'-6")

5.64m (13'-7")

9.75m (32'-0")

2.82m (9'-3")

3.60m (11'-1")

DIMENSIONS		WEIGHT		ENGINE	FUEL	
Wing Span	(11.12m)	Basic Weight	(2209 K)	General Electric J85-CAN-40 Axial Flow Turbo Jet 2,700 lbs static thrust at sea level.	1173 Litres 310 U.S. gals	(2,012 lb)
Length	(9.75m)	A.U.W.	(3380 K)			
Height	(2.82m)					

No matter where they went, the new look of the Snowbirds was popular. The 1974 team was welcomed to CFB Comox in style by a resident 409 AW(F) Sqn CF-101 Voodoo. (DND Photo via Doug Marshall)

In 1974 the team was all but kaput. The word was out that the team was to be cancelled after the season. That the team continued was because Ralph was the driving force behind the movement to save the team. He put out the word to retired air force brass and they wrote, telephoned, met with, lobbied, pleaded with every politician, serving officer of general rank, business executive, anybody who might lend support to the goal of keeping the team alive. The majority of his training flights were put to good use in headquarters lobby visits. I believe his bull-dogged determination and absolute dedication are the only things that kept the team in existence during the mid-seventies. It was his groundwork that got DND to purchase the pilots proper red flying suits for 1974 and finally led to the establishment of the team on a permanent basis in 1978, albeit after he had left the scene. To be sure, he had help from others; he could not have done it without the support of guys like Bill Carr, Bill Vincent and other like minded Generals, but from my viewpoint, if we had not had Ralph Annis as CO at the time we did – the team would have gone the way of the Hawks and Centennaires. He has never been given the honour and recognition he deserves for his outstanding contribution to the team. 'Nuff said about dear old 'Rotten Ralph' (RR), a true Snowbird alumni."

Colonel R.H. Annis, CD

Lieutenant Colonel
T. Lyons, CD

Terry Lyons

Ministerial Intervention

Col Ralph Annis had made some valuable inroads in getting support for the team by the time the Snowbirds started their 1974 season, the most obvious being the new paint scheme and red flying suits for the team pilots. The latter had been acquired by coercing the Chief of Supply, John Killick, to provide the requisite funds in the wee hours of a mess dinner in Trenton. Mr. Killick was a powerful (some would say feared) civilian in the DND hierarchy known for his no nonsense approach and sharp tongue, and when Annis decided to approach him he was warned to "be careful!" He accepted this sage advice and Col Annis' diplomatic approach, followed up by a letter later that morning (while nursing the effects of the previous evening's festivities), won over Mr. Killick. The Snowbirds got their red flying suits ... and Mr. Killick got a photograph.

As it transpired, of the dozens of individuals that Ralph Annis lobbied in 1974, no one was more important than Minister of National Defence James Richardson. Col Annis had met the Minister several times and diplomatically used each occasion to extol the virtues of the Snowbirds. During the show in Winnipeg that summer, he had been strategically seated next to the Minister and carefully described each manoeuvre to him, emphasizing how the pilots flew each formation, the safety built into the show and the public relations activities carried out by the team on behalf of the Canadian Forces. There wasn't much more that he could do in terms of direct contact with the Minister of National Defence. However, Col Annis could privately solicit the assistance of others to assist with his campaign – and did so in great measure!

Col Annis also found a staunch political ally in Senator Sidney L. Buckwold. Following a brief conversation with the Senator, Col Annis took pen in hand on October 11th and sent a personal letter to him. In part, it read:

"... All in all, it is safe to say that many millions of Canadians have watched the Snowbird Demonstration Team perform and the masses of letters I have received confirm the popularity of this group. I know that many airshow conveners have written directly to Mr. Richardson on our behalf and I am sure that he is aware of the popularity of the Snowbirds. What I am concerned about is that he may not be aware that the Snowbirds are finished when they return to CFB Moose Jaw on 22 October, 1974. When I say finished, I mean that there is no authority to continue their training, maintain the Snowbird aircraft or to replace the tour-expired pilots. 1975 will not see a Snowbird Demonstration Team unless approval for their retention is given in the very near future. Selection and training of tour-expired pilots must commence by December so that we will be ready to go on the road in May. Any delay can only postpone the opening of the tour season or force us into a semi-ready state which to me is unacceptable since we would not be fully trained, fully professional and in my opinion unsafe, to do the demanding job required of a demonstration team ..."

Extract from letter, Col R.H. Annis to the Honourable S. Buckwold of the Canadian Senate, October 11th, 1974

The letter written by Col Annis and Senator Buckwold's subsequent appeal to the Minister of National Defence in support of retention of the Snowbirds were timely. On December 3rd, 1974 a memorandum signed by the Chief of Defence Staff, Gen Jacques Dextraze, was sent to MND Richardson recommending the cancellation of the Snowbirds in the face of on-going budget cuts. News of this decision had swept through the headquarters and precipitated a flurry of activity as those who firmly believed in the team, primarily airmen, scrambled to see what could be done to alter the situation. A phone call to O.B. Philp (now retired) brought swift action from the founder of the team as he immediately cast his wide net of influence with several key phone calls of his own. The "old boy net" was on full alert! One intimately involved was former Golden Hawk LCol Al Young, then working as a senior staff officer in the NDHQ directorate responsible for air operations and training. He recalls that "there was a good deal of intrigue and scheming going on and I believe some high level in-service politics. It was I who was directed to draft the CDS to MND memorandum of December 3rd, 1974, which of course was contrary to my own view. I therefore tried to phrase it in such a way as to give the Minister some way out, yet still pass the CDS without being stiffened."

The back door politics worked – James Richardson saved the Snowbirds when he tactfully but firmly turned away the Chief of Defence Staff's recommendation in his reply which read "CDS – I am sure you can find some way to keep the Snowbirds flying. J.R." This was not the last time the team would be threatened with extinction, but was certainly one of the closest. Mr. Richardson has heretofore never received the credit he deserved for his bold decision. Past and present Snowbirds owe him and all those who worked behind the scenes a debt of gratitude for having had the courage to fight for the continuation of the team. History has proven they were correct.

The Minister of National Defence, the Honourable James Richardson (left), visited Moose Jaw in the summer of 1974. His "thumbs up" for the team later that fall kept the Snowbird dream alive. The Minister was accompanied by Maj George Miller (centre) and Capt Mike Murphy. (DND Photo)

✈ Snowbirds 1975

In the midst of his lobbying efforts throughout 1974, Ralph Annis had led the search for a new team leader for the 1975-1976 seasons, hoping that there would still be a team! The Forces wide search led to the selection of Maj Denis Gauthier as the next Snowbird leader. Maj Gauthier had gleaned his initial airshow experience from the ground as the personnel officer of the Golden Centenaires in 1967, learning many lessons from the master himself, O.B. Philp. A navigator at the time, he had cross-trained to pilot and earned his wings in 1969. Most importantly, he had flown the CF-5 fighter for five years with 433 ETAC in Bagotville, Quebec and had flown on several airshow teams during the period, as a solo, wingman and leader. He arrived in Moose Jaw in the fall of '74 eager to select his new team:

"I took over the Snowbirds as the third team leader and was blessed to have Col Ralph Annis as my base commander. He had plenty of aerobatic experience, common sense and was an excellent leader.

Let me say at the outset that without the dedicated participation and support of our technicians, my teams, like all others, would have suffered immensely. All of my technicians hold a big place in my heart and whatever accolades are written about them will never be enough. Sgt Bill Holloway led the groundcrew in 1975, ably assisted by MCpl Cal Wanvig as deputy crew chief.

Special mention must also be made of the total dedication of my coordinators/commentators, Capts Greg Bruneau and Jack

The 1975 Snowbird pilots pose with BGen G.A. MacKenzie, Director General Air Operations at NDHQ. L to R, Standing – Capt Greg Bruneau, Capt John Shaw, Maj Denis Gauthier (leader), Capt Chris Tuck, BGen MacKenzie, Capts Dave Wilson, Carl Stef, Murray Bertram. Kneeling – Capts Harry Chapin, Ken Carr, Yogi Huyghebaert. (DND Photo)

The 1975 groundcrew as they appeared on the team's PR brochure. L to R, Kneeling – Cpls Bud Peters, Ed Torfason, Peter Hennicke, MCpl Cal Wanvig. Standing – Cpls Wayne Swayze, Al Boyce, Garth Suitor, Fred Broderick, Ray Lund, Sgt Bill Holloway. (DND, Cpl L. Phillips)

Girard, who both served the team in many roles with great distinction. Both were excellent organizers and PR men in an era when public relations was critical to the team's survival. When we started the winter trials in Moose Jaw for the 1975 team, I elected from the outset to only accept pilots who had completed a previous operational tour, preferably on jets. My rationale was simple – I committed myself to always transit with the entire nine-plane in formation (occasionally more with the commentators along) and therefore I wanted pilots who thoroughly understood this challenge and

Warrant Officer J. Cochrane was one of several Canadian Forces photographers to capture the Snowbirds on film in the mid '70s. At left, a classic shot of Maj Denis Gauthier leading the Big Diamond as team coordinator Capt Greg Bruneau puts the photographer in perfect position to snap the shot. At right, a unique perspective of the five-plane line-abreast formation. (DND IEC 75-85, IEC 75-71 WO J.A. Cochrane)

MND James Richardson leads an entourage congratulating the Snowbirds following a performance in Abbotsford in 1975. (via 431 Sqn)

were best qualified to do so. I needed pilots that had gained experience, on their own, dealing with the challenges of unforecast deteriorating weather, inflight emergencies and the criticality of judging air safety versus mission accomplishment. In this respect I already had a strong nucleus from the 1974 team who were now joined by Capts Chris Tuck, Dave Wilson and Ken Carr who had all come from the fighter community.

Before starting the season, we were designated the "Canadian Forces Air Demonstration Team" thanks to the efforts of Col Annis and his superiors. We received a small public relations budget with which we were able to produce a small but attractive brochure to advertise the team at our showsites across North America. Once we hit the road, I treated the flying of airshows pretty well like combat flying. I had been given expensive resources to hit 65-70 targets every year at a certain time, and with maximum effect. Although I felt qualified to take the lead, I also felt a tremendous amount of pressure to maintain or better the record of my predecessors. I was also most careful not to do anything that could possibly endanger the future of the team. In the middle '70s, the life of the team was forever hanging on a thread.

We thoroughly enjoyed the 1975 season, especially the start of the schedule in the Northwest Territories. I am thankful for having met wonderful Canadians up there and for having had the opportunity to see the topography in a special part of our country. We started the tour at Hay River and then went on to Yellowknife. On May 11th

The Canadian Rockies have provided a spectacular backdrop for many Snowbird photos. This 1975 photo was used as a presentation photo by the 1976 team. (DND, WO J.A. Cochrane)

we flew a memorable midnight show at Inuvik, finishing on the 12th. From there it was on to Whitehorse and Watson Lake in the Yukon prior to heading south to pick up the schedule again in Victoria, British Columbia. In all we flew a total of 65 shows in my first year as team lead."

Denis Gauthier

An impressive shot of the 1975 Snowbirds in line-abreast formation. Aside from inverted formation, line-abreast is generally considered the most difficult formation to fly as a pilot must rely on an overall sight picture to maintain lateral position. (DND Photo)

The 1975 Snowbirds thrilled residents of "the land of the midnight sun" with manoeuvres such as the Double Bomb Burst, also known as the Upward-Downward Bomb Burst. (via 431 Sqn)

THE HUB

SERVING HAY RIVER & PINE POINT, N.W.T. 20¢   Volume 3   Number 14   May 14, 1975

Second Class mail registration number 3053.   Published weekly on Wednesdays

SNOWBIRDS DAZZLE HAY RIVER

The town of Hay River in the Northwest Territories is one of many northern communities that always welcomes the Snowbirds in style. (via 431 Sqn)

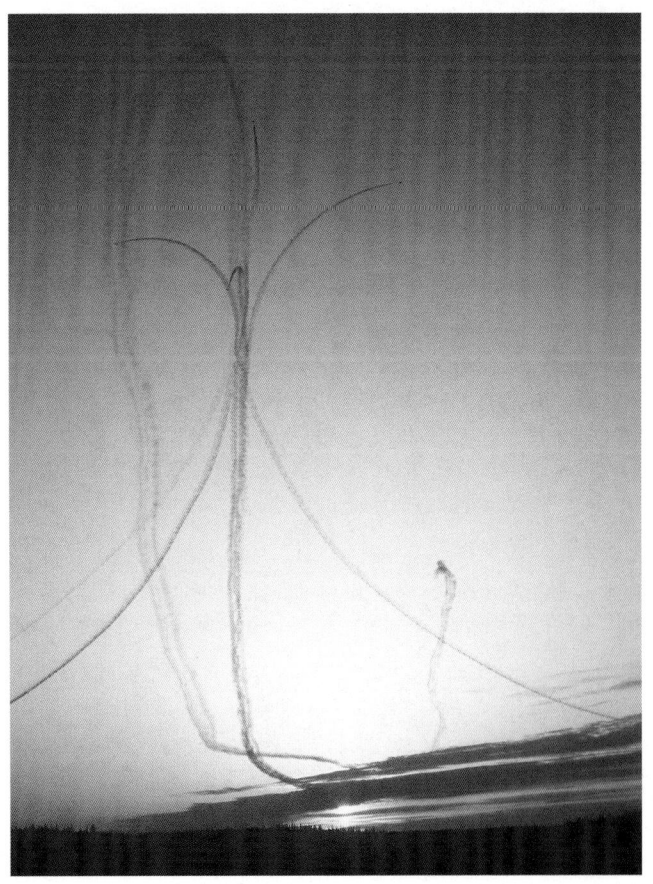

Maj Denis Gauthier, Leader; Capt Gerry Nicks, Inner Right; Capt Chris Tuck, Inner Left; Capt Dave Wilson, Outer Right; Capt Paul Beaulieu, Outer Left; Capt Jim Sorfleet, First line Astern; Capt Harry Chapin, Second line Astern; Capt Ken Carr, Lead Solo; Capt Speedy Fast, Opposing Solo; Capt Jack Girard, Coordinator; Capt Mike Jephcott, Coordinator.

Snowbirds 1976

"When it came time for the annual tryouts for the 1976 edition of the Snowbirds we were again fortunate to have many volunteers to choose from. However, I had a problem in that both of my line astern pilots had served two years on the team and were due to be posted out. I was therefore grateful that Harry Chapin, our second line astern, volunteered to remain for a third year thus preventing the simultaneous replacement of the two line astern positions. Following the tryouts, Capts Gerry Nicks, Paul 'Cat' Beaulieu, Jim Sorfleet and Eric 'Speedy' Fast were the successful candidates to join Capt Mike Jephcott who had already been selected as our new coordinator. Another key addition was Sgt Doug Marshall who rejoined the team as crew chief. Having served in that capacity in 1974, Doug brought a wealth of experience and was a gifted leader. He was loved by all and was not a bad co-pilot as well (in good weather and level flight).

The one recurring headache during my two years as team leader was the unreliability of the main UHF radios which were used exclusively in the military. Attempting to operate into high density civilian airports without VHF radios (used by every civilian aircraft in the world) was a real challenge. Only luck and the professionalism of all air and ground crews prevented catastrophes. At the end of my tour, a strong (and unpopular) report of this technical shortcoming to the Directorate of Flight Safety at NDHQ finally solved this problem.

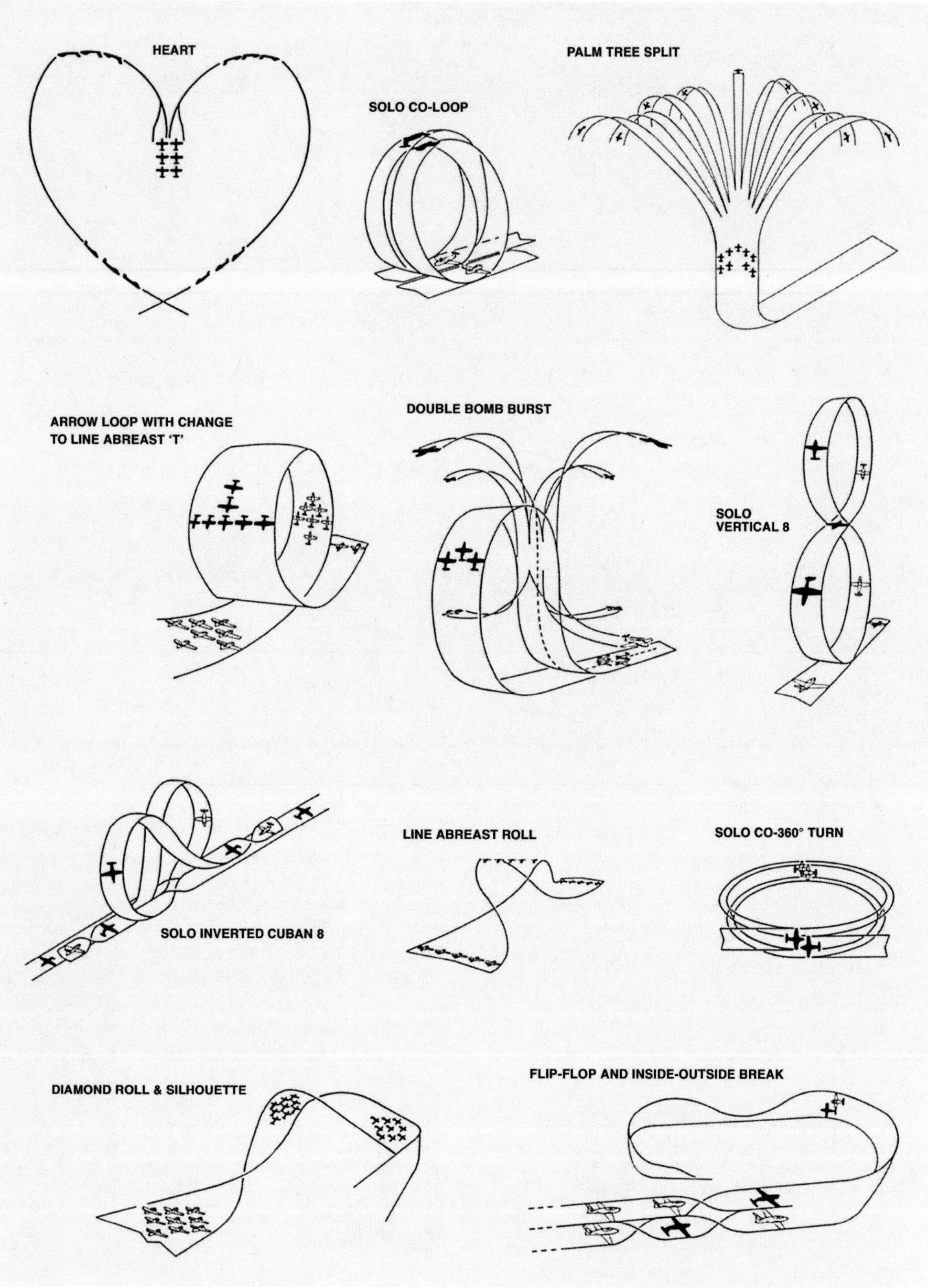

HEART

SOLO CO-LOOP

PALM TREE SPLIT

ARROW LOOP WITH CHANGE TO LINE ABREAST 'T'

DOUBLE BOMB BURST

SOLO VERTICAL 8

SOLO INVERTED CUBAN 8

LINE ABREAST ROLL

SOLO CO-360° TURN

DIAMOND ROLL & SILHOUETTE

FLIP-FLOP AND INSIDE-OUTSIDE BREAK

The 1976 Snowbird brochure included graphics of some of the more popular team manoeuvres.

Sgt Doug Marshall, Crew Chief; Cpl Wayne Swayze, Aero Engine; Cpl Moe Taylor, Airframe; Cpl Ross Chapman, Instrument Elect.; Cpl Gary Friesen, Airframe; MCpl Nick Nichols, Instrument Elect.; Cpl Chuck Wicks, Airframe; Cpl Vern Opperman, Aero Engine; MCpl Cal Wanvig, Deputy Crew Chief; Cpl Ian Neilson, Safety Systems.

to our show, we also flew our nine-plane diamond directly behind the Blue Angels six-plane delta for a 15-plane silhouette pass, canopy to the crowd. We landed the big nine-plane diamond in close formation. Following our team shut down in front of the audience, the crowd began applauding and never stopped until I spoke, after being asked to do so by the show announcer. Given the unbelievable reception we had just been afforded, words were difficult to find and feelings difficult to express. I will always remember this as a very special, if not the most memorable moment in my flying career."

Denis Gauthier

The Snowbirds and Blue Angels at Naval Air Station Willow Grove, Pennsylvania in 1976, the Liberty Bell formation and an appreciative audience after the show. (via 431 Sqn, Bill Johnson)

Opposing solo "Speedy" Fast nails the front cross of the dynamic Co-360 with lead solo Ken Carr. (Nancy Johnson)

Like the previous year, 1976 holds many fond memories from the 71 shows we flew. Although we opened the XXI Olympiad in Montreal on July 17th, our most memorable show took place south of the border earlier that month. We had been scheduled to perform at six locations in the United States as a Canadian salute to the US Bicentennial. As a result, we designed and flew a wine glass formation which we called the 'Liberty Bell.' It was delicate to lead and very difficult to fly, particularly for Paul 'Cat Balou' Beaulieu, the outer right winger. At the 4th of July Bicentennial Airshow at Willow Grove Naval Air Station near Philadelphia, 105,000 spectators were on hand to take in the spectacle. In addition

✈ Snowbirds 1977

By the end of the 1976 season, the Snowbirds had been flying for six years and had overcome every obstacle placed in their way. They now had a strong following not only in Canada, but in many parts of the United States as well. With the approach of a new season came a new evolution in the process of selecting future team leaders – selection of a leader from within the ranks of those who had already served a tour on the team. There were several advantages to this development, the most obvious being familiarity with the show choreography and manoeuvres.

The first to have the honour of returning to the team for a further two year tour was the late Gord Wallis, a former Starfighter pilot. He had flown one of the line astern positions for the first three years of the team's existence so was very familiar with the aerobatic profiles developed by the team. Promoted in the intervening period to the rank of major, he now returned to the team from a staff position at NDHQ. His easy-going style made him a popular choice.

The 1977 Snowbirds. L to R, Kneeling – Maj Gord Wallis (leader), Capts Gerry Nicks, Wayne Thompson, Jim Sorfleet, Jack Girard, Col Dave Tate (Base Commander), Capts Joe Molnar, Keith Coulter, Paul Beaulieu, Gord de Jong, Speedy Fast. Standing – Sgt Harold Breadner, Cpl Barry Dickson, MCpls Bob O'Reilly, Wally Corbin, Capts Mike Jephcott, Stu Morgan, MCpl Nick Nichols, Cpls Moe Taylor, John Zorn, Ross Chapman, MCpl Garth Suitor, Cpl Ian Neilson. (DND Photo)

Aesthetically pleasing silhouette passes are crowd favourites. Maj Gord Wallis leads the 1977 team in bottomside versions of the Double Diamond and Card 7. Of historical note, Snowbird positions were renumbered in 1977, Snowbirds 4 and 5 becoming the line astern pilots, 6 and 7 the outer wingers. (Bill Johnson, Nancy Johnson)

The Snowbirds have brought together some wonderful characters over the years. Capt Speedy Fast demonstrates his formation flying technique for fellow solos Capt Gord de Jong (Snowbirds) and Lt John Miller (Blue Angels) as Maj Gord Wallis looks on. (Bill Johnson)

The fall tryouts again brought a strong cast of candidates to Moose Jaw for the Snowbird tryouts and yielded an ideal balance of experience and youthful enthusiasm. Joining the team with fighter experience were Capts Joe Molnar (CF-104) as second line astern, Gord de Jong (CF-104/CF-5) as opposing solo and Stu Morgan (CF-101) as team coordinator. Joining them from 2 CFFTS were instructors Capts Keith Coulter and Wayne Thompson, the latter making history as the first pilot to join the team with a rotary wing background (Kiowas). Sgt Harold Breadner was selected to lead an equally enthusiastic team of groundcrew into the 1977 season. Those in the airshow industry continued to marvel at how the team could operate across North America without a support aircraft and only 10 technicians to take care of 11 aircraft on the road. The answer lay in the type of people who had volunteered for the team and the careful assignment of expertise. In addition to the crew chief, the groundcrew road team consisted of four airframe technicians, two aero-engine technicians, one instrument electrical technician and one safety systems technician, a balance which is still maintained today.

As it has for many Snowbird teams over the years, the 1977 season began in the Canadian north. This was predominately due to the fact that Snowbird appearances scheduled by the two team coordinators had to be built around the major shows of the summer which took place between June and September. This included large civilian sponsored shows such as London, Abbotsford and Toronto as well as major military shows at CFBs Bagotville, Shearwater, Comox, Trenton and so on. With the team having to criss-cross the country so many times to accommodate these showsites, it would have been difficult to make a long excursion north in mid-season. Therefore, the easiest way to show off the team to Canada's northern communities was to do so on the first swing of the season in May.

Hay River in the Northwest Territories has always been a favourite stop for the Snowbirds as the town virtually shuts down to welcome the team. It had the distinction of being the first official show of the season, taking place on May 6th. The balance of the first swing saw stops in Yellowknife, Norman Wells, Whitehorse and Fort Nelson. Unfortunately, Fort Simpson and Watson Lake had to be cancelled due to weather, the team making up the shows with return engagements in future years. The last show of the swing on May 17th was particularly memorable for Gord Wallis as it was performed in his hometown of Wetaskiwin, Alberta.

The season was progressing well when an unfortunate collision occurred during a routine formation change while performing at Paine Field in Everett, Washington in mid-July. Two pilots were forced to eject but were not seriously injured. Thankfully, no one on the ground was injured as the aircraft fell harmlessly into Puget Sound, the collision having occurred while the formation was off-stage. Vital lessons were learned from the mishap and only two modified shows had to be flown before the nine-plane was performing again.

For every team there are one or two particular shows that stand out during the season as having been the most satisfying. For the 1977 team it was the second day at Abbotsford, British Columbia on August 13th. Recalls lead solo, Capt Eric "Speedy" Fast, "That was the best show I've ever flown in. O.B. Philp gave us a 9.5 out of 10. Coming from him, that meant a lot." Landing following such a show puts the entire team, pilots and groundcrew alike, on a tremendous high. It was not to be the highest point of the season however. As the team had been threading their way across North America, the never-ending effort to secure a permanent future for the Snowbirds had been grinding on.

As the first Commander of Air Command, which was formed in 1975 to help restore some of the proud traditions of the RCAF, LGen Bill Carr was instrumental in securing a permanent establishment for the Snowbirds. Working behind the scenes with his Deputy Commander (and eventual successor), MGen Ken Lewis, a bold initiative had been taken to alleviate what had become annual battles to keep the team alive, as Gen Carr explains:

"The climate of cutbacks and reductions in which the Snowbirds were originally formed was the same climate in which we were able to form Air Command. A lot of people fought us, but blood being thicker than water, having friends like Jim Richardson and Barney Danson when they were Minister of National Defence helped us to fulfill destiny. We had encountered some difficulty finding money each year to support the team. We had to make sure no apparent incremental costs showed up to draw criticism while assuring the other services that the additional aircraft used by the team were merely a means to ensure that we had some expansion capability in our training program. There was merit to this argument – it is important to remember that in the back of everyone's mind was the belief that someday soon, again, expansion would be needed and would happen. Even the staunchest army officers of the day came to understand that although training pilots was expensive and had a long lead time, it was geared to support them!

Notwithstanding, with the high profile and growing popularity of the Snowbirds with each passing season, we eventually came to the conclusion that long term survival could best be achieved by awarding our aerobatic team squadron status, something that had never been done before. The problem was that in order to create a new squadron and protect it, we had to come up with establishment positions that did not appear to impinge on our ability to support the other service branches. We did so by convincing every Air Command base to donate a portion of the 21

positions we needed to create 431 (Air Demonstration) Squadron. Thanks to the efforts of Col Dave Tate in lobbying his counterparts, they all came through in spades, each believing in the worth of a permanent team."

W.K. Carr

Col Dave Tate, Base Commander of CFB Moose Jaw from 1976 to 1979 quickly picked up where Ralph Annis had left off in promoting the Snowbird cause. He too was no stranger to demonstration flying, having done weapons deliveries at the CNE Air Show in the early 50s from the cockpit of an RCN Sea Fury during the early days of his military career. His admiration for the Snowbirds and belief in their cause was both genuine and obvious. As an instructor in Moose Jaw at the time, I often witnessed the team come home from their airshow swings during the summer. One thing that soon became obvious was that each time the team shut down, there would be a staff car waiting at the end of the line of Snowbird Tutors. As the canopies came up, Col Tate would be front and centre to wel-

come the team home. What really impressed me as a young lieutenant however, was the fact that Col Tate didn't just greet the team leader, he went out of his way to slowly make his way down the whole line, making sure he shook the hand of every team member. For me, that indelible image has always defined the essence of outstanding leadership – an understanding that the most important asset in any organization is your people. Now, some 25 years since he played such a pivotal role in helping the Snowbirds gain squadron status, Dave Tate relates how this highly welcome news was relayed to the Snowbirds in the fall of 1977:

"Before the start of the 1977 season we had received strong representation from the chairman of the Reno Air Races in Nevada that they really wanted to have the Snowbirds perform down there. It was not unusual to get such requests, but we had to carefully pick

The Honourable Barney Danson
Minister of National Defence

and choose our shows south of the border to ensure maximum exposure for the team and the Canadian Forces. However, Reno was one of the more well known annual airshows in the United States and one in which the Snowbirds were keen to perform. After talking to Gen Carr about this, we had received his approval, and subsequently that of NDHQ, to schedule the Snowbirds at Reno for the duration of their airshow. Just prior to Terry Lyons and me joining the Snowbirds at Reno on September 15th, we received some great news – news that we had been praying to hear for quite some time. While taxiing out prior to takeoff for Reno, the Moose Jaw control tower relayed a message to us from Gen Carr that went something like this, 'Tell Col Tate that approval has been granted for the Snowbirds to receive squadron status which will become effective April 1978.'

This was some of the best news I had ever heard and Terry and I were proud to take this message to Gord Wallis and the team in Reno. It set the stage for a wonderful weekend and great party. Everyone was grateful for the work that had gone on behind the scenes to achieve this goal and especially for the support of LGen Carr, Admiral Bob Falls (the Chief of the Defence Staff) and the Honourable Barney Danson, Minister of National Defence. The Minister had only made one previous visit to Moose Jaw and had struck me as a gregarious, sincere individual who really had the best interests of the Canadian Forces in mind. This welcome development was certainly indicative of his support.

As for the Reno Air Races, I was later advised by Gerry Duty of the executive committee that the appearance of the Snowbirds increased his attendance by 25,000 spectators. I can certainly attest to the fact that the team was warmly received by the appreciative crowd, as I know they have been in successive appearances over the years."

Dave Tate

The Snowbirds have been warmly welcomed at the Reno Air Races since their first appearance in 1977, the start/finish pylon marking stage centre for the show. (Bill Johnson)

Snowbirds 1978

By the late '70s there was widespread interest in the Snowbirds among pilots in the fighter and jet trainer communities. The job presented a new and unique challenge for those who had already flown an operational tour and it was obvious to all that those fortunate enough to make the team were having the time of their lives. At the time, there had been a large influx of highly capable young pilots sent back to Moose Jaw to instruct fresh off of advanced jet training on the CF-5 fighter in Cold Lake. There simply weren't enough operational cockpits to go around and many who had demonstrated the potential to fly fighters found themselves back on the Tutor instead. Many of these young instructors soon aspired to fly with the Snowbirds. They had the talent and enthusiasm to master the aircraft within a relatively short time span and what they lacked in experience, they made up for in raw desire.

One young pilot whose smooth hands and feet won him the inner right wing position in the fall of 1977 was Capt Marc Ouellet. A graduate of the Royal Military College class of '74 who had barely been instructing for two years when he was granted a tryout, he was the only so-called "pipeliner" among the eight pilots chosen to try out for four open positions on the team. The 1978 team would record a monumental milestone in becoming the first Canadian aerobatic team to achieve independent squadron status, but as Ouellet recalls, it was to be a year of triumph and tragedy:

"You would never know from reading the year-end report by Maj Gord Wallis that the 1978 show season was anything but normal. However, that year was 'anything but normal' and I would venture goes down in Snowbird history as one of the most challenging in the first 30 years.

The Snowbirds were awarded full squadron status on 1 Apr 78, the 54th anniversary of the formation of the RCAF, the only aerobatic team in Canada to be so honoured. L to R, Kneeling – Capts Stu Morgan, Ray Hansford, John McNamara, Joe Molnar, Marc Ouellet, Wayne Thompson, Terry Hunt, Keith Coulter, Gord de Jong, Yves Bossé. Standing – Cpls Ian Neilson, John Zorn, MCpls Bob O'Reilly, Wally Corbin, Cpl Mike Poisson, Sgt Cec Keddy, Maj Gord Wallis, Cpls Gary Ward, Al Dillman, Kevin Buell, Fred Broderick. (DND Photo)

The tryouts commenced in mid-November with eight candidates, six from 2 CFFTS and two from the fighter community. What started quickly with two trips a day for each candidate suddenly ground to a halt with the onslaught of an early winter. Some tryout missions were simply crossed off as days without flying went by and in mid-December, with almost all the solo missions remaining, candidates were given the choice of opting out of the solo slot competition. Funny, not everyone wanted to be a solo, in spite of Gord de Jong's insistence it was the best job in the world! Those that wanted the high G abuse of the body continued and with only two days remaining to the Christmas break deployed to Cold Lake for good weather and their final missions and solo assessments. On December 21st, Christmas finally came early for four new Snowbird pilots - myself as No. 2, No. 4 Terry Hunt, No. 7 John McNamara and No. 9 Ray Hansford. Gord Wallis also selected seven new ground-crew to the team who would be led by our new crew chief, Sgt Cec Keddy.

The team gelled quickly in the new year, primarily due to the seasoned leading of Gord, but also aided by some harsh winter weather which accounted for three weeks on the ground. Despite not practicing much in the air, we had plenty of opportunities to develop our social skills and bond as a team. These social events were, of course, aided by

the spirit and, most important, sense of humour of our spouses. As we were behind in training, we flew a number of on-base practices to get the most out of every minute airborne; although it was too cold for the school to fly, we did!

Our most significant practice over the base took place on April 1st, 1978. Besides being the birthday of the RCAF, it marked the reactivation of 431 Sqn, originally a World War II bomber squadron, as 431 Air Demonstration Sqn, the Hatiten Ronteriios (Warriors of the Air). With CFB Moose Jaw Base Commander, Col Dave Tate, as the reviewing officer of the squadron stand-up parade, we marched proudly in the morning and flew our first mission as a new squadron that afternoon. The Snowbirds now had a proud history on which to build along with the clear acknowledgment from the Minister of National Defence and the Chief of the Defence Staff that there would be a future.

We deployed to Comox a few days later for the annual spring work-ups but could not shake our weather woes. We were only able to do three high show practices and had to redeploy back to Moose Jaw early for final workups prior to our acceptance show. On April 21st, still sporting the "baby-blue" flight suits from the previous year, we successfully performed our acceptance show in front of the Commander Air Command,

Two proud leaders, Col Dave Tate and Maj Gord Wallis, with the 431 Sqn Heraldic Badge which had been in retirement since 1954. At right, Gord Wallis presents a painting to Snowbird founder O.B. Philp to commemorate the achievement of squadron status. (DND Photos)

No. 431 Squadron

Heraldic Badge
An Iroquois Indian

Motto
The Hatiten Ronteriios
(Warriors of the Air)

Operational Dates
11 Nov 42 – 5 Sep 45
RCAF Bomber Squadron

18 Jan 54 – 31 Oct 54
RCAF Fighter Squadron

1 Apr 78 – present
Canadian Forces
Air Demonstration Squadron

431 Squadron Heraldic Badges

Like all RCAF squadrons formed during World War II, 431 (Bomber) Squadron was granted an official heraldic badge authorized by His Majesty King George VI following the stand up of the squadron in November 1942. The badge bore the Tudor Crown (as depicted above) which formed part of the King's Royal Cypher. Following the death of His Majesty on February 6th, 1952 and subsequent ascension to the throne of Her Majesty Queen Elizabeth II, it was decreed that the Tudor Crown would be replaced by the St. Edward's Crown as depicted in the Queen's Royal Cypher. Air Force Routine Order 405 dated 3 July 1953 stated that there would be a transition period that would gradually see the introduction of the new crown on all RCAF Heraldic Badges. The transition took several years.

Following unification of the Canadian Armed Forces on February 1st, 1968, it became necessary to once again change the badges. While the St. Edward's Crown remained, "Royal Canadian Air Force" was replaced with the word Escadrille. After 431 Sqn was re-formed on April 1st, 1978 a new squadron badge was therefore approved. In recent years, air force heraldic badges have been modified a final time, with Escadrille being replaced by Escadron, a more accurate french translation of the word Squadron. 431 Sqn's current heraldic badge is depicted opposite.

The Bomber Era

No. 431 (Bomber) Squadron was formed on November 11th, 1942 at Burn, Yorkshire, England. It was the 28th RCAF squadron (11th bomber) formed overseas during World War II and was initially attached to No. 4 Bomber Group of the RAF. It was subsequently assigned to No. 6 (RCAF) Bomber Group at Tholthorpe and No. 64 (RCAF) Base at Croft in Yorkshire. At the end of hostilities in Europe in June, 1945, 431 Sqn was selected to join "Tiger Force" for combat duties in the Pacific. Having repatriated to Canada to prepare for deployment to the Pacific theatre of operations, the squadron was in training with RCAF Eastern Command when the Japanese surrendered. The squadron was disbanded on September 5th, 1945 at Dartmouth, Nova Scotia.

Squadron Combat Record

Aircraft Flown	Vickers Wellington Mk. X (Dec 42 – Jul 43)		
	Handley Page Halifax Mk. V (Jul 43 – Apr 44)		
	Handley Page Halifax Mk. III (Mar 44 – Oct 44)		
	Avro Lancaster Mk. X (Oct 44 – Sep 45)		
First Combat Mission	2/3 Mar 43, mine laying by seven Wellington Xs		
First Bombing Mission	5/6 Mar 43, bombing run by three Wellington Xs		
Last Combat Mission	15 Apr 45, bombing run by 15 Lancaster Xs		
Total Wartime Sorties	2,584 including 11 sorties airlifting POWs back to England		
Operational Flying Hours	14,621 hours		
Non-operational Hours	8,986 hours		
Bombs Dropped	14,004 tons		
Air-to-Air Victories	6 enemy aircraft destroyed, 1 probable, 4 damaged		
Combat Casualties	72 aircraft lost, 490 aircrew		
	(313 KIA, 54 MIA, 104 POW, 18 safe, 1 injured)		
Non-operational Casualties	14 personnel killed		
Honours and Awards	1 DSO, 63 DFCs, 10 DFMs, 2 CGMs, 1 MiD		
Battle Honours	**Primary**	English Channel and North Sea	1943-1944
		Baltic	1943-1944
		Fortress Europe	1943-1944
		France and Germany	1944-1945
	Secondary	Biscay Ports	1943-1944
		Rhine, Biscay	1943-1944
		Berlin	1943-1944
		German Ports	1943-1945
		Ruhr	1943-1945
		Normandy	1944

The officers and men of 431 (Bomber) Squadron pose with one of the squadron's Halifax bombers circa 1944. (RCAF Photo via 431 Sqn)

The Fighter Era

No. 431 (Fighter) Squadron was formed as an interim F-86 Sabre squadron at RCAF Stn Bagotville, Quebec on January 18th, 1954. Attached to Air Defence Command, the squadron was formed due to delays in the production of the CF-100 all-weather interceptor. Squadron pilots engaged in air-to-air fighter training using the same tactics that had made the F-86 Sabre famous in Korea and the skies of Western Europe. The squadron formed a four-plane aerobatic team in the spring of 1954 under the leadership of F/O Fern G. Villeneuve. The squadron was subsequently assigned to participate in *Operation Prairie Pacific* designed to introduce western Canadians to jet operations in the RCAF. Between August 15th and September 11th, the team and an additional solo aircraft performed 10 airshows between Vancouver and Toronto before almost 500,000 spectators. The squadron was officially disbanded on October 1st, 1954 to be replaced the same day by 432 AW(F) Sqn equipped with the CF-100.

Aircraft Flown	North American /Canadair F-86 Mk 2 Sabre
First Fighter Training Sortie	3 Feb 54, RCAF Stn Bagotville, Quebec
First Official Airshow	12 Jun 54, National Air Show, Toronto, Ontario
Last Official Airshow	11 Sep 54, CNE Air Show, Toronto, Ontario

The Air Demonstration Era

431 Air Demonstration Squadron was formed on April 1st, 1978 under the authority of the Commander Air Command, LGen William K. Carr, DFC, CD. The squadron's mandate is to demonstrate the skill, professionalism and teamwork of Canadian Forces personnel for public relations and recruiting purposes.

Aircraft Flown	Canadair CL 41A (CT-114) Tutor
First Training Sortie	1 Apr 78
	CFB Moose Jaw, Saskatchewan
First Official Airshow	28 Apr 78
	Royal Roads Military College,
	Victoria, British Columbia
1,000th Official Airshow	20 May 90
(of the Snowbirds)	CFB Edmonton (Namao), Alberta

The first 431 Sqn pilots to conduct airshow performances were not Snowbirds but members of 431 (F) Sqn flying the F-86 Sabre in 1954. L to R, Kneeling – F/Os Fern Villeneuve, Rod MacDonald and Fred Rudy. Standing are F/Os George Fulford, J. Landreville and Al McIlraith. By the end of 2002, a total of 162 Canadian Forces pilots have followed in their footsteps, earning the right to wear the red flying suits that characterize them as Canada's aerial ambassadors. (RCAF Photo)

431 Squadron Commanding Officers

Bomber Sqn

Wing Commander J. Coverdale (RAF) Killed in Action	01 Dec 42 – 21 Jun 43
Wing Commander W.F.M. Newson, DFC Operational Tour Expired	26 Jun 43 – 10 May 44
Wing Commander H.R. Dow, DFC Prisoner of War	14 May 44 – 25 Jul 44
Wing Commander E.M Mitchell Operational Tour Expired	27 Jul 44 – 10 Jan 45
Wing Commander R.F. Davenport Killed in Action	14 Jan 45 – 11 Mar 45
Wing Commander W.F. McKinnon	18 Mar 45 – 15 Jun 45
Wing Commander E.M. Bryson, DFC	04 Aug 45 – 05 Sep 45

Fighter Sqn

Squadron Leader C.D. Barnett	18 Jan 54 – 31 Oct 54

Snowbird Sqn

Major G. Wallis, CD	26 Oct 76 – 12 Oct 78
Major A.T. Griffis, CD	12 Oct 78 – 08 Oct 80
Major M.B. Murphy, CD	08 Oct 80 – 15 Oct 82
Major G. Hawey, CD	15 Oct 82 – 19 Oct 84
Major D.F. Huyghebaert, CD	19 Oct 84 – 18 Oct 86
Major D.S. Wilson, CD	18 Oct 86 – 12 Apr 87
Major D.K. Beselt, CD	12 Apr 87 – 15 Oct 88
Major D.V. Dempsey, CD	15 Oct 88 – 20 Oct 90
Major R.W. Stephan, CD	20 Oct 90 – 17 Oct 92
Major D.R. Rainkie, CD	17 Oct 92 – 15 Oct 94
Major S. Hill, CD	15 Oct 94 – 19 Oct 96
Major D.S. Shyiak, CD	19 Oct 96 – 16 Oct 98
Major J.G.G.R. Painchaud, CD	16 Oct 98 – 19 Oct 01
Major S.P. Will, CD	19 Oct 01 –

Jerry Davidson

Snowbird Commanding Officers & Team Leaders – 1971-2001

Major G.E. Younghusband, CD
01 Jan 71 – 15 Oct 72

Major G.E. Miller, CD
12 Mar 73 – 22 Oct 74

Major D. Gauthier, CD
22 Oct 74 – 26 Oct 76

Major G. Wallis, CD
26 Oct 76 – 12 Oct 78

Major A.T. Griffis, CD
12 Oct 78 – 08 Oct 80

Major M.B. Murphy, CD
08 Oct 80 – 15 Oct 82

Major G. Hawey, CD
15 Oct 82 – 19 Oct 84

Major D.F. Huyghebaert, CD
19 Oct 84 – 18 Oct 86

Major D.S. Wilson, CD
18 Oct 86 – 12 Apr 87

Major D.K. Beselt, CD
12 Apr 87 – 15 Oct 88

Major D.V. Dempsey, CD
15 Oct 88 – 20 Oct 90

Major R.W. Stephan, CD
20 Oct 90 – 17 Oct 92

Major D.R. Rainkie, CD
17 Oct 92 – 15 Oct 94

Major S. Hill, CD
15 Oct 94 – 19 Oct 96

Major D.S. Shyiak, CD
19 Oct 96 – 16 Oct 98

Major J.G.G.R. Painchaud, CD
16 Oct 98 – 19 Oct 01

LGen W.K. Carr. The 1978 Snowbirds were ready to go!

It was just into our third show of the year at Grande Prairie, Alberta on May 3rd, 1978, that tragedy struck. The horizontal stabilizer of lead solo Capt Gord de Jong's aircraft suffered a structural failure during a triple level roll and we lost a great friend and natural leader. His loss had a tremendous effect on all of us on the team, as well as his many friends and colleagues air force wide.

As a result of the accident, the entire Tutor fleet was grounded. Air Command and base staff at all levels worked around the clock to identify the structural problem and engineer a fix. It was nearly three weeks before we flew again. During this time we reconstructed the entire show as an early decision was taken not to try and replace Gord – we would fly the remainder of the season as an eight-plane. New six-plane formations such as the hexagon and delta were developed to allow Capt Joe Molnar, our second line astern pilot, to do some opposing solo work with Capt Ray Hansford, our remaining solo. It must also be said that in spite of the loss of his partner and close friend, Ray did an admirable job in finishing the season with some very impressive single solo manoeuvres.

On June 15th, six weeks after the crash and following 19 show cancellations, we flew our new 1978 show in Quebec City. Our efforts to get back on the road as soon as possible placed a tremendous burden on our groundcrew. With the final stainless steel T-tail bracket still not installed, a full NDT (non-destructive testing) inspection was required after every fourth flight. In the process of these long inspections, two additional tail faults were discovered and corrected. As usual, we never heard a complaint from Cec Keddy and the boys who worked incredibly long hours.

Maj Gord Wallis and LGen Bill Carr, Commander Air Command, on the occasion of the team's 1978 acceptance show. (DND Photo)

Capt Ray Hansford (left) crosses lead solo Capt Gord de Jong over the top of the co-loop early in the 1978 season. (Nancy Johnson)

Despite the hardships and initial setbacks, the show did go on and we managed to perform in front of approximately 2.4 million people by the end of the season. Many traditions of seasons past remained unchanged – the best part of the job was still meeting the kids afterwards, we still complained that there weren't enough rental cars, nobody wanted to drive with the 'outers' and, on a few occasions, the team lead had to rein the boys in. The team had grown very close and we were all looking forward to a fresh start in 1979."

Marc Ouellet

Maj Gord Wallis deserves considerable credit for having kept his team focused during the traumatic year that was 1978. Losing a stalwart on the team like Gord de Jong meant Wallis had to exercise all of his leadership and managerial skills to make the season a success. This he did with great style. Fortunately, he was assisted by a very strong staff on the base led by Col Dave Tate. Although they had all seen it before, it didn't make the task any easier. Terry Lyons reflects back on the support he witnessed while serving as base operations officer in this crucial era of team development:

"The early '70s were good days for the team in terms of public response. Times were lean but the shows were gaining the Snowbirds a great reputation. The base was always fully behind the team because the base commander made it clear that HE was fully behind the team (both Ralph Annis and Dave Tate during my term). During those early days, either the base commander, George Miller (as commandant of the Big 2 in 1975-76 and former lead), I (as base operations officer) or a staff officer from Training Command Headquarters attended all shows. It was great for us and satisfied the big brass that someone was keeping an eye on the team. But who on us? We had a T-Bird to fly, or if it was down, we took a spare team machine. Sometimes we took parts, spares, an extra tech. We scrounged stuff – powered diesel pumps for the smoke tanks rather than the old hand pump for example, a trip for the wives to Comox during workups in an old Dakota on a 'training flight.' After many months of back and forth letters, visits, telephone calls and meetings with both RR and Dave Tate, we finally got flying pay for the groundcrew on a full time basis before I retired in 1980. I think I wrote more drafts of letters about that issue than any other operational matter while I was BOpsO!

Both of these COs were really behind the team. Dave Tate was elated when the team finally became 431 Air Demonstration Squadron and worked extremely hard to ensure it happened. I know I had a lump in my throat when Dave Tate, Gord Wallis and I signed the scroll making the establishment of the team a fact. Before the Snowbirds became 431 Sqn, the team leads (on paper at least) reported to the base commander through the base operations officer. In reality, they usually went direct to the boss, except when he wanted to give them a blast, then he would use me!"

Terry Lyons

At left, the 1978 Snowbirds in their "show" uniforms. At right, a close-up of the blue flying suits that the team pilots wore in 1977 and 1978. L to R – Capts Keith Coulter, Terry Hunt and Marc Ouellet. (Bill Johnson, Nancy Johnson)

An unusual view of the Big Arrow formation which has been looped, rolled and silhouetted over the years by various Snowbird teams. To achieve this formation, Snowbirds 6 and 7 slide back and over Snowbird 5, then drop down into their wing overlap position. (Bill Johnson)

Residents of the Fraser Valley in British Columbia are treated to sights like this every summer when the Snowbirds make their annual trek to the Abbotsford International Airshow. For this shot, Capt Stu Morgan filled in admirably on the right wing for departed colleague Gord de Jong while fellow coordinator Yves Bossé flew chase. (Bill Johnson)

The 1978 Snowbirds demonstrate their formation prowess with a tight Double Diamond silhouette. (Bill Johnson)

Maj Tom Griffis, Leader; Capt Marc Ouellet, Inner Right; Capt Graham Miller, Inner Left; Capt Terry Hunt, First Line Astern; Capt Jim Reith, Second Line Astern; Capt Frank Thorne, Outer Right; Capt John McNamara, Outer Left; Capt Larry Rockliff, Opposing Solo; Capt Ray Hansford, Lead Solo; Capt Jim Fowler, Coordinator; Capt Yves Bossé, Coordinator; Capt Ron Duckworth, Executive Officer

⚡ Snowbirds 1979

The next former Snowbird to return to the fold as commanding officer and team leader was Tom Griffis who had flown one of the solo positions as Snowbird 8 in 1973-1974. Following his first tour with the team, he had been posted to a staff position at defence headquarters in Ottawa. It was his strong leadership qualities and flair for public relations that had made him an early favourite to replace Gord Wallis, something he didn't realize at the time:

"My selection as team leader for 1979/1980 came as a total surprise to me. Not that I did not want the job, but I always felt there were many more qualified candidates than myself. Upon selection, I immediately looked to Gord Wallis (the incumbent lead) and George Miller for guidance and advice. As I later found out, my selection was due in large part to the efforts of these two individuals. I did not have the military rank of major to hold the position of team leader but through a strong lobbying effort by George, I was offered the position. I will always be grateful to these two individuals for giving me the honour and opportunity to be team leader of the Snowbirds.

After taking command at the conclusion of the 1978 season, we tried to convince the military powers to authorize inverted formation flying but to no avail. The incumbent members were convinced it could be safely implemented and we looked for outside guidance from Bill Cowan and Rod Ellis, two former military pilots making a name for themselves in the civilian airshow circuit.

Prior to the team workouts for the '79 season, the four remaining holdover pilots and myself travelled to Vancouver for some lessons on their Pitts Specials. We then applied the techniques learned on the Pitts to the Tutor. When I ran the prospect of inverted formation flying up the military flag pole, we were confronted with stiff opposition and the idea was quickly shelved. As the years moved on, it was gratifying to see the team introduce inverted formation flying, another distinguishing feature of the Snowbirds.

The Heart has been a perennial favourite with children since the team's inception. Thousands of them have been dedicated in practices and performances over the years. (Bill Johnson)

Every member of the team has vivid memories of their years on the team and I am no exception. If I go back 20 plus years and try to filter out one or two impact events, I always come back to our nine-plane formation looping over Mount Rainier in 1979 and our final show of the 1980 season. In the summer of 1979, Bill Johnson, our unofficial team photographer and an individual of exceptional talent, convinced me that we

could, under the right conditions, get a 'killer shot' of the formation looping over Mount Rainier, located south of Seattle, Washington. The team had tried unsuccessfully to do this in 1974. It was hard enough to fly nine aircraft in a looping manoeuvre that would top out at 17,000 feet or so, but how would anyone capture the event in a photo op?

Fortunately, the '79 team had an exceptionally gifted pilot as one of its team coordinators in Capt Yves Bossé. Without the prospect of positioning Bill for his 'killer shot,' such a manoeuvre would not have been contemplated. After several hours of discussions and planning with input from all the pilots, as well as Bill and Yves, we left Seattle's Paine Field for our photo flight. Typically, the lead aircraft of the Snowbirds will give his wingers anywhere up to 10 percent power to play with in a looping manoeuvre. But for Mt. Rainier, we decided the most the lead aircraft could afford was only one percent if we had any chance to execute the manoeuvre. We relied on the three slot pilots (two in the nine-plane formation and Yves and Bill in the chase aircraft) to 'stack' themselves on top of each other as we went over the top of the loop. This was the only way that we would still be in some semblance of formation on the backside of the loop with everyone except me at full power. Yves did a magnificent job of getting and keeping Bill in position. As it turned out, our very first attempt turned out to be the 'killer shot' we had all imagined. With all the intricacies of attempting the manoeuvre, I forgot to call for smoke on the initial pull-up and, as fate would have it, this mistake made for the real deal. Subsequent loops over Mount Rainier

Sgt Cec Keddy, Crew Chief; Cpl Michel Bernier, Airframe; Cpl Michael Roy, Instrument Elect; Cpl Fred Rockall, Aero Engine; MCpl Garry Ward, Deputy Crew Chief; Cpl Ed Gammon, Comm Systems; MCpl Kevin Buell, Airframe; Cpl Michel Poisson, Instrument Elect; Cpl Al Dillman, Aero Engine; MCpl Ian Neilson, Safety Systems.

One of the most famous shots ever taken of the Snowbirds as they crest the top of a loop at almost 17,000 feet above sea level, the majestic Mount Rainier in the background. Given the limited power of the diminutive trainer, few would have thought this achievement possible in a nine-plane formation at that altitude. Photographer Bill Johnson captured this shot from a Tutor chase aircraft flown by Capt Yves Bossé.

The Snowbirds appear suspended in space in another surreal photo taken near Colorado Springs in the summer of '79. (Bill Johnson)

with the formation smoking took away from the beauty and mystery of seeing nine planes inverted over the mountain.

By 1979, the Snowbirds were beginning to become a household name in Canada but much more work was required within the military hierarchy to establish the Snowbirds as a permanent fixture in the world of air-show performers. Every member of the 1979 and 1980 teams made significant contribu-tions towards this end. One of our key differ-entiators from the two American teams, besides the fact that they flew front-line fighters while we flew trainers, was the fact that we flew a nine-plane formation. This was one of our strengths but until 1979 had been an underexploited asset. The introduc-tion of five minutes of opening manoeuvres in the nine-plane formation was introduced in '79 due in large part to the efforts of Marc Ouellet, Terry Hunt, John McNamara, Ray Hansford and Larry Rockliff. They were the architects of the show profile for the '79 season that we carried through with minor modifications into the following season. With a nine-plane team you also have many more opportunities for 'split' or 'bursting' manoeuvres – a feature that we exploited throughout the '79 and '80 seasons."

Tom Griffis

 Snowbirds 1980

"The tryouts for the 1980 team saw another strong field of candidates vying for a position on the team, five from 2 CFFTS and three from off base with fighter backgrounds. Joining incumbents Graham Miller, Frank Thorne and Larry Rockliff were Chuck Gillespie, Bob Drake, Wally Stone and Dan Dempsey. Given his obvious formation talents, Yves Bossé was invited to step into the second line astern position when Jim Reith decided to accept a long awaited employment offer from Canadian Airlines. Denis Mercier joined Jim Fowler to round out another excellent coordinator tandem. Also among several fine groundcrew joining the team was Sgt Don 'Dutch' Simms, one of the all-time great Snowbird characters who taught us all the value of a sense of humour.

Like the previous season, everyone contributed to a tightly choreographed display which was very well received. We also worked hard at the public relations side of

The 1980 demonstration pilots pose for an impromptu photograph following a performance at the Reno Air Races. L to R – SB 8 Larry Rockliff, SB 6 Frank Thorne, SB 4 Bob Drake, SB 2 Chuck Gillespie, SB 1 Tom Griffis (leader), SB 3 Graham Miller, SB 5 Yves Bossé, SB 7 Wally Stone, SB 9 Dan Dempsey. Below are the team coordinators, SB 10 Denis Mercier and SB 11 Jim Fowler.

the job which I have always believed was an essential cornerstone of the Snowbird mandate. In this regard, one new milestone for the team, and a significant one, was the appearance of the team for the first time ever in New York City. Performed in front of the Coney Island Amusement Park over a two-day period, an estimated two million Americans took in the show, one of the

largest audiences in Snowbird history. The performances were followed by a very successful and highly publicized press ride over Manhattan. On our return to land at Republic Field, we were pleased to oblige a request for a low pass over JFK International Airport. The day's work was rewarded with a first-class dinner in Chinatown which included Ambassador Ken Taylor. There is no question the team (and all Canadians) benefited from his bold efforts during the rescue drama in Tehran earlier that year. It was a good year to be a Canadian in the United States.

The memories of our last show of 1980 will never leave me. Although it represented my final contribution to the team, more importantly, it represented two years of dedicated work by every member of both teams to achieve 24 months of accident free flying. During the period leading up to 1979, the team had experienced several accidents including the tragic death of Gord de Jong in 1978. Our mandate to criss-cross the continent and perform in 75 shows a year is a demanding objective in itself – to do it safely without incident is a daunting task. Every team leader's primary objective is to execute his mandate without an aircraft incident or accident. The 1979 and 1980 teams did so which for me represented a huge relief. Every member of these two teams worked and lived as a team in the full and true sense of the word. We worked

HELLO NEW YORK! New Yorkers were caught off guard when the Snowbirds led by Maj Tom Griffis swept in over Manhattan in May 1980, the team's first visit to "the Big Apple." These impressive views of the Empire State Building and World Trade Center were taken over the shoulder of Capt Chuck Gillespie by his crewman, Cpl Al McGrath. The team returned for an encore performance with 11 media personnel on board three days later after two million spectators had taken in their two day show at Coney Island. (Cpl A. McGrath)

The 1980 team prepares to taxi for another show. At right, the team groundcrew. L to R, Top row – Sgt Don "Dutch" Sims, Cpls Al McGrath, Rocky White, Mike Langevin, Jack Gariepy. Bottom row – Cpls Ed Gammon, Michel Bernier, Mike Roy, Fred Rockall, MCpl Gary Ward. (Bill Johnson, Sgt E.J. Hendricks)

The Dayton Air Fair honoured the Snowbirds with a commemorative cover flown at the show on July 20th, 1980. Earlier, Richards Gebaur Air Force Base in Kansas City had hosted "Operation Handshake" to thank Canadians for their support during the Iranian hostage crisis. (author's collection)

incredibly hard to build a legacy which we hoped would be, and was, improved upon. Oddly enough, the most satisfying single event for me after 24 months of leading the Snowbirds was the moment the last aircraft touched down on our last show in October 1980.

The history of the Snowbirds has always been one where the lessons learned from one year were put to good use by the succeeding team. This coupled with a team 'debriefing' format where every pilot was subjected to intense scrutiny from his peers has allowed the Snowbirds to build

Many hours of practice are required before the Snowbird solos (in this case the author (left) and Capt Larry Rockliff) get this close to each other. Although it may appear otherwise from the ground, there is ample safety built into each manoeuvre. Below, one of several magazine covers that featured the Snowbirds in 1980 in what was an excellent year for public relations. (Bill Johnson, via Tom Griffis.)

and become one of the premier formation teams worldwide."

Tom Griffis

The Big Diamond topside silhouette offers a rare glimpse into the cockpits of the nine jets as they slide by stage centre at 300 knots. Pilots on the topside of the formation looking down must learn to ignore the ground rush as it flashes past in a blur of colour. (Bill Johnson)

Canadian Forces photographer Vic Johnson first flew with the Snowbirds in 1980 and over several years captured many dynamic shots like this. This is the view from the cockpit of Capt Yves Bossé (SB5) as Capts Chuck Gillespie (SB2) and Frank Thorne (SB6) use their speed brakes to effect a station change from Mini-Concorde to Goose during a loop near Ottawa. (DND Photo, Sgt Vic Johnson)

1 Maj Mike Murphy
Sgt "Dutch" Simms

2 Capt Chuck Gillespie
Cpl Paul McKeen

3 Capt Dennis Beselt
MCpl George Beck

4 Capt Bob Drake
Pte John McCanna

5 Capt Sonny Lefort
Cpl Perry Luchia

6 Capt Dean Rainkie
Cpl Tony Vanderberg

Snowbirds 1981

Major Mike Murphy, Snowbird 3 in 1973-1974 and now a veteran of CF-104 operations in the NATO theatre, was slated to return to Canada following a staff tour at 1 Canadian Air Division when his name rose to the top of the list of ex-Snowbirds under consideration to replace Tom Griffis. He recalls the circumstances that led to his selection:

"I remember our conversation as if it were yesterday. LCol John Hutt was visiting Canadian Forces Europe in the fall of 1979, conducting annual career manager interviews. He popped the question early on in our session. 'How would you like to return to Canada to lead the Snowbirds for the 1981-82 seasons?' Not surprisingly, I had trouble focusing on anything else for the remainder of the interview. After receiving the blessing of the chief of staff (better known as my wife), it then became a matter of awaiting the final confirmation via posting message. Several months of waiting seemed like an eternity!

Upon returning to Moose Jaw after a six-year absence (five of those years in Baden and Lahr, West Germany), I quickly realized that a number of things had changed since I had hung up my red flight suit. Here was a well established team (now an air demonstration squadron in fact) that had come a long way in the intervening years. In essence, everywhere I turned I continued to be impressed by the organization and the myriad of improvements. No longer was it the year-to-year subsistence that was regrettably the modus operandi in the early days. Notwithstanding the fact that the team had never taken its existence for granted, it was quite obvious to one about to take charge that 431 (AD) Sqn was on a very solid footing indeed. I was all the more anxious to take up the challenge of commanding the squadron and leading the team into its second decade of operations.

The fall tryouts went well, with Capts Dennis Beselt, Sonny Lefort, Dean Rainkie and John Politis winning spots in the formation. Along with another superb group of groundcrew selected from among the best on the base, the Snowbirds welcomed our first female officer in Lt Heather Campbell who took over from Capt Ron Duckworth as executive officer. Building on the strengths of the newly expanded nine-plane opening sequence worked up by the 1980 Snowbirds, our 1981 edition opted to maintain a similar opening sequence format and choreography. The novel Concorde nine-plane topside pass continued to gain prominence. The double diamond loop and roll combination choreo-

The three-plane solo flip flop flown in 1981 was the precursor to several variations of the manoeuvre in future years. On the top, the view from liveside. Below is what spectators saw at Abbotsford in 1981. Pushing negative 3 G around the corner is the author (SB 9) with Capts John Politis (SB 8) and Sonny Lefort (SB 5) on the left and right respectively. (Bill Johnson)

Spring training in Comox usually affords the opportunity for some unique aerial footage. Below, a glimpse of the wing overlap in the Big Diamond. (Bill Johnson)

7 Capt Wally Stone
Cpl Dick Bennett

8 Capt John Politis
Cpl Bob Bauer

9 Capt Dan Dempsey
Cpl Al McGrath

10 Capt Denis Mercier
Cpl Barry Fremont

11 Captain Wally Peters

12 Captain Ron Duckworth

graphed to 'Ballad to Adeline' by pianist Richard Clayderman, became a trademark manoeuvre of the 1981 team. A total of 67 shows at 51 sites were originally approved but due to sponsor cancellations, we ended up with 61 shows on the books at 47 locations. Plagued by unacceptable weather at the wrong times throughout much of the season, only 79 percent of these were flown. Clearly we had some work to do to appease the weather gods if we were to avoid suffering the same fate the following year.

We were in Toronto to perform at the Canadian International Air Show over the Labour Day weekend and the following day, as we were preparing to depart and transit to our next showsite, we received the shocking news that the Thunderbirds had suffered a tragic accident. They had lost their team leader during a routine takeoff from the Cleveland, Ohio airport. LCol D.L. Smith had been unsuccessful in his ejection attempt following a bird strike and subsequent engine failure that occurred just after takeoff. In order to bid farewell to our fallen comrade, we dispatched a contingent of four pilots to represent the Snowbirds at his funeral service.

Although we might have been more fortunate weather-wise during 1981, we certainly were successful in gaining media benefit from a number of prominent Canadian and international visitors. These included: Ed Schreyer, the Governor General of Canada; Anne Murray, Canada's famous singing Snowbird; Mrs. Moya Lear of Learjet Corporation; golfing legend Arnold Palmer; Maurice Richard and Réjean Houle, Montreal Canadiens hockey stars; and Ken Taylor, our former Canadian Ambassador to Iran.

Allow me a short anecdote regarding an outing in downtown New York. The late Milton Berger, show sponsor for the Coney Island series of airshow performances, had invited Ken Taylor and the team to a special dinner in 'Little Italy.' Milton had planned this event to thank the former ambassador, and by extension Canada, for the initiative taken to safeguard and evacuate several American citizens during the Iranian crisis. Yes, Milton had even gone to the trouble of engaging a big male opera singer to kick off the dinner with an emotional rendition of 'O Canada.' Trouble was, after belting out the first verse, he forgot the words and was reduced to humming the rest. Needless to say, this was a rather embarrassing moment for poor old Milton Berger et al.

Below, a unique perspective of the Double Diamond. The chase aircraft for this mission was flown by Capt Denis Mercier. (Bill Johnson)

The 4-3-1 Split was a popular manoeuvre in 1981. It was immediately followed by a quadruple roll from stage right by Snowbird 8 as Snowbird 9 (at the top of this photo) dove down to set up for a 7 G vertical eight. (Rafe Tomsett)

who filmed at a number of our 1981 showsites. Use was made of some excellent formation footage shot from our rearward-facing AETE camera pod in addition to some dynamic solo manoeuvres from a cockpit mounted camera. The new 14 minute film was narrated by well known musician Tommy Banks of Edmonton and released in the spring of 1982.

Ever flown formation on a B-25 Mitchell bomber with eight other Snowbirds? Who could forget the photo sessions with the Walt Disney team conducted along the Straits of Juan de Fuca just prior to the Abbotsford Airshow weekend! The belly-mounted pod holding nine movie cameras, enabling 360-degree coverage, provided a unique and interesting formation challenge as the 1981 team judiciously placed each of nine jets in one camera's field of view. The simultaneous peel offs, rejoins and flypasts were all rather spectacular. We were fortunate to be able to visit the Canadian Pavilion in the Epcot Center at Disney World, Florida to view the final product the following year.

Thanks in particular to the determined efforts of deputy commanding officer, Maj Wally Peters, the team was successful in obtaining funding for a new 16 mm film to replace 'Flight of the Snowbirds' which was over five years old and in need of updating. The contract was given to Kicking Horse Productions of Edmonton,

The 1981 Snowbirds had reached an historic 10th anniversary milestone and I dare say, also set 'the standard' for those to follow in terms of organizing and running Snowbird anniversary reunions. This was a significant undertaking, especially considering that we had been on the road for almost six months. On Friday, October 9th, 1981 the team flew its final show of the season before an enthusiastic crowd of ex-Snowbirds as well as base military personnel and their dependants. Our keynote speaker for our formal dining-in the next night was none other than Col (Ret'd) O.B. Philp, our godfather and mentor. As expected, O.B. did a magnificent job of walking us through our rich aerobatic team heritage while at the same time, reminding us of our responsibilities and challenges of the future. As a finale, a champagne breakfast afforded the opportunity to gather the 'clan' once more, to renew friendships, to reminisce and to glance through squadron photo albums before we headed our separate ways. I recall thinking at season's end that it would be difficult to better the accomplishments of a very busy and highly successful 1981 season!"

Mike Murphy

The 1981 Snowbirds pose with the Walt Disney film team and crew of the specially modified B-25J Mitchell bomber following their unique photo trip. The B-25, owned by the Canadian Warplane Heritage Museum at the time, was originally built for the US Army Air Force under the acceptance number 458884A. Sporting post-war RCAF colours of 418 (City of Edmonton) Sqn, the aircraft was flown by Capt Joe McGoldrick (yellow cap). The gentleman on his right is Hollywood cinematographer Barry Herron, a well known former RCAF photographer whose work appears in Chapter 3. (via 431 Sqn)

✈ Snowbirds 1982

Postcards distributed during autograph sessions are popular items. The 1982 version highlighted the team pilots. L to R – Capts Ron Carter, John Politis, Dean Rainkie, Tristan deKoninck, Geoff Gamble, Maj Mike Murphy (leader), Capts Dennis Beselt, Sonny Lefort, Rob Chapman, Jon Graham, Maj Wally Peters. (Klaus Bohn)

Lt Heather Campbell joined the Snowbirds in late 1981 as the team's executive officer having been commissioned from the ranks. She also had the distinction of being the team's first female officer. (Sgt E.J. Hendricks)

"The off-season turnover brought five new pilots to the team (Geoff Gamble, Tristan deKoninck, Rob Chapman, Jon Graham and Ron Carter) as well as several new ground-crew led by a new crew chief, Sgt Alex Cameron. The workups were going well for us and we were operating ahead of schedule in January 1982 when we received word of another tragedy for the USAF Thunderbirds. They had lost two pilots in 1981 and had just lost four more in a formation training accident. The formation had failed to recover from a line-abreast loop during a practice session at Indian Springs, their training site near Nellis Air Force Base in Nevada. In order to pay our respects, we called a temporary halt to our training program and sent a four-plane to the memorial service. The service was an extremely emotional one. Our attendance was very much appreciated by the Thunderbird families and the entire Nellis community.

Our newly completed Snowbird film was released in February 1982. This 16 mm film and the seven minute VHS version were both excellent public relations vehicles. In addition, for the first time in the squadron's history, a historical yearbook was published. The venture, thankfully sponsored by GM Productions (Gary McMahon and Rick Grissom) and designed by renowned aviation photographer Bill Johnson of Seattle was well received by the public.

The 1982 season saw the introduction of a new fatigue monitoring program for the Snowbird fleet, thanks in part to trials conducted by two former team members. Our 1981 lead solo, Dan Dempsey, did some aggressive testing on a specially instrumented AETE Tutor at Cold Lake with former inner Gerry Nicks wearing his engineer hat to monitor and record the telemetry results. The subsequent evaluation enabled us to monitor and thereby reduce the low-cycle fatigue problems that we had been encountering. In addition, new Panasonic VHS equipment gave us a greatly improved reproduction quality, particularly in the freeze-frame replays, so valuable for debriefing purposes.

A successful spring training program in Comox was just concluding when I got a call from MGen Bill Paisley, Deputy Commander Air Command. My former boss from 1 Canadian Air Group days, he was keen to determine if we were sufficiently worked up and comfortable to perform a minor air display in front of Her Majesty Queen Elizabeth II and HRH Prince Philip. The occasion was the Proclamation of the Constitution Act and the date was April 17th, 1982. Although somewhat of a blustery (read bumpy) day, the event went off without a hitch. Wellington Street and the Parliament Buildings were not only graced by the presence of Her Majesty, but

also by nine of the shiniest red, white and blue jets that 431 Air Demonstration Squadron could muster. With special approval by the Commander Air Command for an eight minute show over Parliament Hill, we carried out a modified opening sequence consisting of the nine-plane big arrow loop and roll, Concorde topside silhouette and the seven-plane upward bomb burst, a fitting start to what was to be another action-packed year!

The 1982 Snowbird air display featured a first for the team when our two solo pilots rejoined the formation for what was to become our trademark nine-plane finale. The nine-plane downward bomb burst was used as the mini-finale for the opening sequence and ideally dropped the two solos on show-line for the first of their opposing manoeuvres. The five-plane line-abreast loop was added to the Snowbird patented line-abreast roll making this a double manoeuvre, a team first. Our finale concluded with the Concorde to big diamond loop and silhouette.

Although our 1982 list of prominent persons was not as diverse as that of 1981, we were fortunate to have our Minister of National

The 1982 groundcrew team. L to R – Sgt Alex Cameron, Cpls John McCanna, Barry Fremont, Dick Bennett, Harry Partridge, Bob Bauer, Perry Lucia, Marty Cornfield, Tony Vanderberg, MCpl George Beck, Cpl Frank Pineau. (Sgt E.J. Hendricks)

Defence, the Honourable Gilles Lamontagne, visit with the team on two separate occasions. He flew with Capt John Politis during a June 30th press ride in the nation's capital and one month later, during a visit to CFB Moose Jaw, the MND presented stripes to newly promoted Sgt George Beck, our deputy crew chief. The team also had the privilege of performing for the Air Command Colours' presentation held at CFB Winnipeg on July 31st, 1982.

The 1982 show season produced a Snowbird team record for scheduled shows flown. A total of 69 shows were planned and 66 were flown for a phenomenal 96 percent success rate, but I guess it all had to end sometime. After two seemingly meteoric show seasons including 114 official shows, quadruple that number of show practices, countless official receptions and public relations events, and a gazillion cross-country transits, it had all come down to the final show of the year. It was also the end of an air demonstration career for a number of us. Arguably, the final show was the most difficult one of all to perform. It is impossible to describe the flood of emotions that you experience as you climb out of your jet and shake hands with your fellow squadron mates for that final time. These are the people that you have trusted implicitly for the past two years of intense training

The Snowbirds climb over the crowd in a near perfect Big Diamond as part of their 1982 show. (Dan Dempsey)

The 1982 Snowbird solos strut their stuff for a critical audience of fighter pilots at CFB Cold Lake, Alberta. On the left is opposing solo Capt Jon Graham, on the right lead solo Capt John Politis (D/LSFL). (Dan Dempsey)

and air display execution.

It was terribly hard to let it all go so suddenly. The only saving grace, however, was in knowing that there was a hand-picked replacement standing in the wings, eagerly waiting to take up the challenge. It was with these emotions, coupled with a true sense of pride and satisfaction, that I handed over command of 431 (AD) Sqn to Maj George Hawey. It was October 15th, 1982, a day indelibly etched in my mind!"

Mike Murphy

Bill Johnson's telephoto lens captures the essence of the Snowbirds – nine aircraft flying as one as Maj Mike Murphy leads the 1982 team out the bottom of a loop. (Bill Johnson)

Snowbirds 1983

Maj George Hawey was another original member of the 1971 team selected to return to the Snowbirds to command the team. In the nine year period since he had left the team, he had completed two tours on fighters, one on the Canadair built CF-5 and the other a rare exchange tour flying the venerable McDonnell Douglas RF-4 Phantom with the USAF. Like those before him, he was determined to see the team prosper:

Maj George Hawey leads the Snowbirds over Comox in a practice in the spring of 1983. The Concorde is one of the Snowbirds' most famous nine-plane formations. (Bill Johnson)

"When I took command of the Snowbirds, the team had introduced an extensive nine-plane opening and closing show routine. I was eager to exploit the aptitudes of Capts Tristan deKoninck, Geoff Gamble, Jon Graham, Rob Chapman and Ron Carter as well as Sgt Alex Cameron and his technicians prior to changing the show routine substantially.

The evening ceremonies at the Heritage Inn in Moose Jaw on October 15th changed that sentiment when the guest speaker, O.B. Philp, made the strong suggestion that I should bring back the upward-downward bomb burst previously performed by the Golden Centennaires and some of the early Snowbird teams. Having formerly worked under the command of O.B., I knew that I better get some information on this manoeuvre ASAP and start planning on including it in the 1983 show sequence.

The team selection process was completed by November 14th and workups started the next day with Capts Bill Ryan, Holmes Patton, Richie Clements and Bob Stephan as the new wingers. The new team coordinator, Maj Norm Fraser, was back in the office with Capt Ron Carter working on the 1983 show

schedule alongside our administration officer, Capt Leslie Whan, and secretary, Marg Fowler.

On January 13th, Col Don Williams (BComd CFB Moose Jaw) and I flew to Calgary to meet with O.B. and C.B. Lang. C.B. had been the leader of the Golden Centennaires and was going to help me with the upward-downward bomb burst. To loosen the tongues and keep the information flowing, a bottle of Chivas for O.B. and Lamb's Navy Rum for C.B. were considered apropos. After a long night of discussions it was decided that a practice the next day was not a good idea.

The upward-downward bomb burst was first practiced as a two-ship on January 27th with myself and Snowbird 5, Capt Holmes Patton. As suggested by C.B., spacing was accom-

plished by SB 5 performing a loop and holding that spacing during the run-in to show centre. Following several repetitions, we concluded that we could effectively include this manoeuvre in our 1983 show package with fairly consistent results. O.B. witnessed a practice at Comox on April 14th and gave high praise to our show routine – in particular the upward-downward bomb burst he had proclaimed should be back in the show. This manoeuvre proved to be a real crowd pleaser for the 1983 and 1984 seasons.

1983 was marked by several highlights. Bill Johnson came out of semi-retirement to shoot the team from his familiar position in a chase aircraft. Bill snapped many rolls of Kodak and many of his superb shots were ultimately once again included as part of our annual team brochure.

The 1983 Snowbirds. L to R, Standing – Capts Ron Carter, Bob Stephan, Richie Clements, Tristan deKoninck, Geoff Gamble, Cockpit – Sgt Alex Cameron, Maj George Hawey (leader), Capts Bill Ryan, Holmes Patton, Rob Chapman, Jon Graham, Maj Norm Fraser. Kneeling – MCpl Bob Bauer, Cpls Marty Cornfield, Harry Partridge, Pat Messaoud, Mike Landers, MCpl Bill MacPhee, Cpl Georges Ménard, Pte Tim Payne, Cpl Ron Bernard. Missing – Capt Leslie Whan, Cpl Frank Pineau. (via 431 Sqn)

The northern swing included a practice at Juneau, Alaska and shows at Inuvik, Norman Wells and Yellowknife in the Northwest Territories. On the return journey south we did a show at Grande Prairie before proceeding to Cold Lake, Alberta. The show at CFB Cold Lake was performed in front of several hundred fighter pilots from various NATO countries participating in the annual Maple Flag exercise. The team was very reluctant to perform and dedicate the 'heart' manoeuvre to all these fighter jocks. A solution was suggested by an unnamed team member that all we had to do was cut the smoke just past the vertical line and before the bottom cross. The result would be what looked like a horse's behind. A suitable dedication was injected and the manoeuvre was received with considerable enthusiasm.

On July 1st, Canada Day, we performed in front of Prince Charles and Princess Diana at the Universaide in Edmonton. July 10th was the most turbulent show I ever experienced while flying a high show for the World Boy Scout Jamboree in Kananaskis, Alberta. Needless to say, that show was flown using much wider 'school' formation references with plenty of separation between our wing tips.

On July 22nd while transiting from Stephenville, Newfoundland to Saint John, New Brunswick, Bill Ryan experienced a flameout at 33,000 feet in overcast skies and over water. As expected, the Tutor wasn't going to relight at 33,000 feet so Bill set up a glide and I formated on his wing. The rest of the team continued to Saint John with Tristan deKoninck leading. While on discrete frequency, several team members suggested Billy donate his stereo to the Snowbird lounge while others wanted his car or additional personal items. Bill did not see the humour in this, as he was dead-sticking his

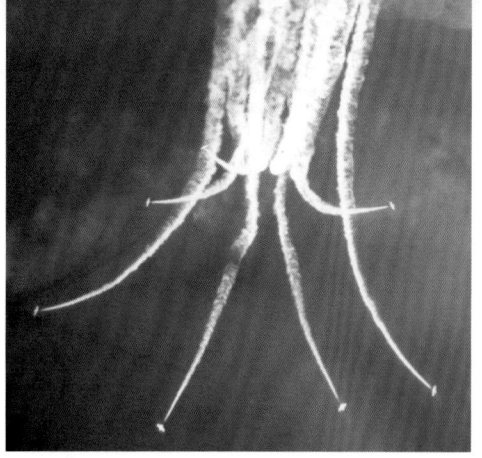

Capt Ron Carter banks steeply to allow this unique perspective of the downward bomb burst shot from above. The glassy water below illustrates why over-water shows require special training. (Bill Johnson)

way into cloud. Fortunately, as advertised, the Tutor relit at 25,000 feet and we landed uneventfully in low overcast and rainy weather at CFB Summerside.

The Chicago showsite flown on July 16th and 17th was difficult due to the skyscrapers on the dead side and the ill defined, grey horizon on live side which was over water. Due to some heading errors on my part combined with poor visibility and no horizon, what was programmed to be a high show turned out to be a low show. This had the double digits (our coordinators) scrambling to adapt at the last minute. That evening after a full debrief, some members got into a little Kabunga diving while another member experienced a spider bite to his throttle hand. All survived to perform a flawless full high show on the second day despite having to dodge the Sears Tower and other BFB's (big buildings) again.

August 3rd and 4th saw us perform at the legendary Oshkosh, Wisconsin airshow in front of hundreds of thousands of aviation enthusiasts. At one of the evening receptions, we were all fortunate enough to meet and listen to exciting tales from 'Pappy' Boyington of World War II 'Black Sheep' squadron fame. Our only weather cancellation of 1983

occurred at the end of the month on the occasion of the 75th anniversary of powered flight in Canada at Baddeck, Nova Scotia on August 26th. Despite giving it a valiant effort, all we managed to do was transit to and from the showsite. We promised the show organizers a 'rain check' although we all knew it wouldn't have the same meaning as performing for the anniversary of powered flight.

The team's annual media flight in Toronto on September 1st was highlighted by the fact that we did a nine-plane loop over Toronto International Airport along runway 15/33. The media personnel during that flight were all checking in 'green' (i.e. they hadn't been sick) and my passenger kept asking if we were going to be able to do a loop. Toronto terminal control couldn't get enough airspace for us to do any kind of vertical manoeuvring, so after what seemed like 33 times around the CN Tower, we returned to TIA as a nine-ship. The tower controller at TIA must have been monitoring our request for some airspace over the lake because as soon as I checked in with the tower, he cleared us for a '360 in the vertical' down runway 33. All media personnel were extremely pleased with their flight and the bird's eye view of Toronto International.

The latter part of the season included a show at Kitchener, Ontario during the famous Oktoberfest. On departure from Kitchener, I was asked to perform a flypast for the Oktoberfest parade. As this should have been a simple routine, I figured no map was required – I was sure I could find Main Street! As we approached Main Street, Bob Stephan informed me that the water tower we had just flown by had the letters G U E L P H written on the side … OOPS … so a free flypast for Guelph."

George Hawey

A dramatic view of the Double Diamond from the outside right wing reveals that the Snowbirds fly very close to each other. (Ed Drader)

With their groundcrew waiting, the Snowbirds prepare to turn in for their simultaneous park routine on the Abbotsford ramp. (Ed Drader)

A side profile of the Big Diamond helps reveal how team pilots fly the formation. Snowbirds 2, 3, 8, and 9 take their visual cues directly from the lead aircraft. Snowbirds 5, 6 and 7 fly off of Snowbird 4, the man in the middle surrounded by eight other aircraft. All manoeuvring of the main formation is called by the leader over a discrete radio frequency to help each pilot match the profile of the lead aircraft. (Bill Johnson)

The 1984 Snowbirds at work. On top, the Inverted Wedge has been the most commonly used formation to open the show over the three decades the team has been flying. Below left, when the wind conditions are right, the Snowbirds conduct a "smoke check" prior to taxiing out for their takeoff. Centre, Cpls Tim Payne and Pat Messaoud assist their teammates in rectifying a snag. At right, the team prides itself in its appearance on the ground and in the air. (Bill Johnson top, Ed Drader, Nancy Johnson bottom right)

🛩 Snowbirds 1984

"The 1984 team welcomed five new pilots and four technicians, including a new crew chief in Sgt Rick Harvey. The show routine added the card nine loop and big diamond roll as the major changes. The Comox deployment included photo shoots by Clay Lacey with his Lear Jet over Mount Washington ski area. The shoot was completed using an IMAX camera mounted in the nose of the Lear as well as a fixed camera at the top of the chair lift at the ski hill. The director wanted us to fly directly up the chair lift as low as possible and over his camera and sound recording system. This must have impressed the skiers! The director got what he needed but I never was made aware of what finally came of the filming sequence (perhaps the cutting room floor). The shots were to have been part of a documentary on flight to be released at the 1985 World's Fair in Japan.

The biggest disappointment of my two years leading the Snowbirds was not being able to perform the last show prior to the change of command to Yogi Huyghebaert. The weather had delayed our return to Moose Jaw with freezing rain, snow and everything else falling from the sky. Al Pietsch and family provided their customary hospitality to us in Minot, North Dakota as we delayed our arrival in Moose Jaw – the runway was closed with nil braking action. We eventually made it in the following afternoon after a 50 foot path on the runway had been sufficiently treated with urea to allow us to land. The change of command was carried out in No. 5 Hangar without the traditional last airshow."

George Hawey

A glorious shot of the Double Diamond in review at Abbotsford 1984. (Bill Johnson)

The 1984 version of 431 (AD) Sqn. L to R, Standing – Capts Leslie Whan, Mike Bell, Bob Stephan, Richie Clements, Dave Forman, Al Merrick, Maj George Hawey (leader), Capts Bill Ryan, Holmes Patton, Carl Shaver, Steve Wallace, Maj Norm Fraser. L to R Kneeling – Cpls Dan Jean-Marie, Doug Dennison, Pat Messaoud, Mike Landers, Sgt Rick Harvey, MCpl Bill McPhee, Cpls Georges Ménard, René Petit, Ron Bernard, Tim Payne. Missing is Cpl Frank Pineau. (Bill Johnson)

🐦 Snowbirds 1985

Veteran fighter pilot Yogi Huyghebaert was the second former Snowbird solo pilot to take command of the team, doing so on October 19th, 1984. His first airshow experience had been as a solo demonstration pilot with the 417 Sqn Starfighter team of 1972. His low-level aerobatic experience had made him a natural for selection as a solo with the Snowbirds two years later. Now, with subsequent tours on the CF-5 fighter, Yogi returned to inject his colourful brand of leadership into the Snowbird routine:

"Having completed refresher training on the Tutor at Portage la Prairie and moved back to Moose Jaw in August 1984, I joined the team in Toronto for the Canadian International Air Show and accompanied them for the rest of the season. Twelve days after taking command of the team, we started the team try-outs for the 1985 version of the Snowbirds. These were completed in 15 days with Capts Steve Purton (SB 3), Gino Tessier (SB 5), Steve Hill (SB 6) and Mike Skubicky (SB 8) being the successful candidates. Our ensuing workups went well and we were able to do a nine-plane practice by December 10th. We changed the show a great deal by bringing back some old manoeuvres and inventing a few new ones.

Our airshows during the season went very well although one might not agree from some of the debriefs. Since safety is paramount as the team continually strives for perfection, there are always areas that deserve

The upward-downward bomb burst utilizes seven Snowbirds and is most dramatic when flown against a blue canvas. (Bill Johnson)

discussion and we didn't hold back at all during debriefs. And these were not limited to airshows alone. One of the most challenging aspects of life as Snowbird lead actually came from the cross-country transits between showsites. The Tutor is range limited to start with, especially so with smoke tanks, and transiting in formation tends to use even more fuel. My first challenge in this

area came on our first cross-country to Houston, Texas.

Our first leg out of Moose Jaw saw us short of gas when Snowbird 4 called a 'November Sierra' bingo (300 lbs of fuel remaining) with some 60 odd miles remaining to Grand Forks, North Dakota. This wasn't all that bad until 40 nautical miles out when air traffic control closed the runway with a USAF T-38 right in the middle with a blown tire. As there were no alternatives we continued, split up into triple vic formation and set up for a visual approach. About one mile back on final approach the runway opened and we landed with the low fuel aircraft almost out of gas. Later that same day another encounter with ATC saw us vectored all over west Texas, or so it seemed. However, this was not a problem because the weather at Houston was CAVOK which meant no low cloud and good visibility. As fuel was getting short and dusk was upon us, I asked for updated weather. ATC replied CAVOK as earlier reported. However, as we approached the airport at 1,000 feet AGL, in the nine-plane, I couldn't see the ground. Being an astute fighter pilot, I knew CAVOK was not the real weather! Sheepishly, air traffic control came back with W0X0F (zero ceiling and zero visibility in FOG). Again, with no gas and no planned alternate, I asked for a snap vector to the nearest airport. Silence … After what seemed an eternity, I spotted a Boeing 737 which ATC finally came back and advised me to follow. We landed in triple vic with the most uncomfortable feeling of not

The 1985 Snowbirds. L to R, Standing – Maj Yogi Huyghebaert, Capts Al Merrick, Steve Purton, Dave Forman, Gino Tessier, Steve Hill, Carl Shaver, Mike Skubicky, Steve Wallace, Mike Bell, Eric Dumont. Kneeling – Sgt Rick Harvey, Cpl Mark Keller, MCpl Brian Herde, Cpls Bert Hargreaves, Al Herron, Doug Dennison, René St. Laurent, Dan Jean-Marie, John Mahoney, René Petit, Troy Canam. (Bill Johnson)

knowing what airport we had landed at! The fog rolled in as soon as we were on the ground … The airfield turned out to be Hobby Field at Houston.

April 1985 saw our annual trek to Comox for spring training, returning to Moose Jaw for the acceptance show. The weather turned poor and we had to do a low show for the acceptance show which I believe was the first time this had ever happened. Notwithstanding, our season started on time with the traditional northern swing. Once again the cross-country bug came to bite. En route from Whitehorse to Juneau, Alaska we were losing radio reception with Anchorage Centre. As the weather was forecast to be 4,500 feet scattered, variable broken cloud, I cancelled our IFR clearance and went down to a lower level to continue visually. Of course, the weather started to deteriorate to the point that we were below 1,000 feet above the water with conditions worsening. With no navigation aids and only an area map things were becoming a little tense. When I finally got a tacan lock at about 15 nm, I turned around a small mountain and picked up the strobe lights leading into the airport. I had never been into Juneau before so it was an interesting experience. We landed safely, but so much for the 4,500 foot broken cloud condition!

Another interesting incident happened at the Mirabel Airshow in Quebec. We were in our holding pattern prior to starting our show when Eric Dumont, SB 10, called to give us another 10 minute hold. As fuel gets critical during a show, I questioned the delay but Eric

The Snowbirds are the only team in the world that take off and land nine aircraft at once. To do so, they require a 200 foot wide runway and minimal crosswind. (Bill Johnson)

was just informed that we were to continue holding. Approaching the 10 minute mark, he again informed us there would be a further delay. As I could not accept a further delay without cutting short the show, I gave notice that I would be setting up for a landing. A couple of minutes later we were cleared in for the show. During the opening sequence, a loop followed by a clover leaf right to a silhouette in front of the crowd, a DC 9 airliner landed underneath us without notice! Needless to say, we had an extensive debriefing with the Ministry of Transport and airshow organizers after that episode.

One of the many highlights of the 1985 season occurred at Dayton, Ohio. Prior to the show, the coordinators informed me that mess kits would be required at Dayton for a formal reception. Oh really? As all familiar with the small confines of the Tutor are well aware, there is no room for any extra kit in the aircraft, so I declined the invitation to the dinner. As the show drew nearer I was again informed that we were invited to a black tie dinner and mess kits would be required.

However, arrangements had been made to have them flown to Dayton for us. Following the Saturday show, we were whisked away in a bus back to our hotel for a quick change into mess gear and a bus trip to a dinner. En route we debriefed the show and quipped about what joke I should tell if called upon to speak. We arrived at the dinner venue and were immediately awestruck. It was the American Aviation Hall of Fame annual dinner and, as it turned out, we were presented the 'Spirit of Flight' award. Rest assured there were no jokes. The award was presented by David Hartman and a lump came to the throat when President Ronald Reagan came on television from Washington, D.C. to congratulate the inductees, with a special congratulatory message to the Canadian Snowbirds. This memorable evening included the 'who's who' in aviation.

Although this was just one of many high points in the 1985 season, there were some low ones as well. The worst was at season's end when we arrived back at Moose Jaw and were informed that we could not perform our last airshow because someone, somewhere had decreed it wasn't on the schedule! Not only was it disappointing that we could not wrap up the season with a show for our families, but we were hosting a 15th anniversary reunion. Former team members had come from across the country to help us celebrate, but there would be no show on October 18th. In spite of this unfortunate development, the remainder of the celebration over the weekend went well."

Yogi Huyghebaert

The type of symmetry displayed by manoeuvres like this fan break can only be achieved through repeated practice and film analysis. Once the Snowbirds begin to put their show together each season, every practice is filmed from the ground. (Ed Drader)

The 1986 Snowbirds. L to R, Maj Yogi Huyghebaert, Team Leader; Capt Joe Parente, Inner Right Wing; Capt Steve Purton, Inner Left Wing; Capt Jim Fowlow, First Line Astern; Capt Gino Tessier, Second Line Astern; Capt Steve Hill, Outer Right Wing; Capt Howard Tarbet, Outer Left Wing; Capt Mike Skubicky, Lead Solo; Capt Don Brodeur, Opposing Solo; Capt Bob Curran, Coordinator; Capt Eric Dumont, Coordinator; Capt Leslie Whan, Administration Officer.

 ## Snowbirds 1986

"After a very short holiday we were back at it again with a new round of tryouts for the 1986 team commencing on November 1st. These were completed in record time and six days later Capts Joe Parente (SB 2), Howard Tarbet (SB 7), Jim Fowlow (SB 4) and Don Brodeur (SB 9) were named to the team. Season workups went well with a very challenging manoeuvre added – the nine-plane Concorde roll. We left for Comox a bit earlier than normal in '86 as there were two crews scheduled to film the team during spring work-ups. One film, The Real Stuff, was a television documentary narrated by music producer David Foster while a Japanese crew filmed another one hour special for JVC. Although these extra sorties put pressure on our new crew chief, Sgt Alex Bouzane, and his technicians, their unwavering dedication ensured we got the job done. All went well and two excellent public relations films were produced.

An early highlight for the team was the opening of Expo '86 in Vancouver. Although we got weathered out for Canada Day at Expo, we returned to the West Coast for Abbotsford and the closing of Expo. Abbotsford that summer hosted the largest gathering of military aerobatic teams ever to perform at one show in North America. A special honour for me was having the opportunity to lead a five-plane formation flypast consisting of the team leaders of the participating aerobatic teams: the Snowbirds, *Patrouille de France*, *Frecce Tricolori* of Italy, *Esquadrilha da Fumaça* of Brazil and the US Navy Blue Angels.

Expo 86 was a major event for the City of Vancouver and the Snowbirds were honoured to participate. This is the view from Snowbird 5 as the team announces its arrival over the site of the world exposition. (Cpl A. Herron)

The rest of the season went well as scheduled and we were kept very busy right up until the closing of Expo on October 13th. Five days later we did our final show of the season at Moose Jaw in front of a very special audience, a gathering of aerobatic pilots representing many of Canada's former teams dating back to the Harvard and Sabre days of the RCAF. As I was handing over the team to Maj Dave Wilson, I thought it very fitting that he should fly the last show with me. It was a very emotional experience when we landed and I relinquished command of the Snowbirds to him.

My tenure as commanding officer of the Snowbirds was undoubtedly the highlight of my flying career. I am grateful to all of the pilots and groundcrew who made these two years so memorable and to the hundreds of friends we made over the years. As I have stated so many times, a bond is formed amongst team members that cannot be explained. I see that evidenced as much today as when I had the reins of the team."

Yogi Huyghebaert

Japanese photographer Katsuhiko Tokunaga has photographed all of the world's premier aerobatic teams from the air. Here, a view of the Big Diamond from a Tutor chase aircraft flown by Capt Eric Dumont in 1986.

Sgt Alex Bouzane, Crew Chief; Cpl Mark Keller, Aero Engine; MCpl Brian Herde, Deputy Crew Chief; Cpl Don Brak, Safety Systems; Cpl Al Herron, Airframe; Cpl Mark Doane, Airframe; Cpl Gilles Dubé, Instrument Elect; Cpl Gord Neave, Aero Engine; Cpl John Mahoney, Instrument Elect; Cpl Bert Hargreaves, Comm Systems; Cpl Troy Canam, Supply Tech.

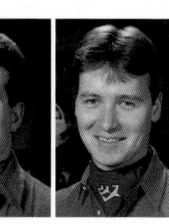

Maj Yogi Huyghebaert leads an historic flypast representing five of the world's aerobatic teams at Abbotsford '86. Top to bottom – the United States Navy Blue Angels, *Patrouille de France*, Canadian Snowbirds, *Frecce Tricolori* of Italy and *Esquadrilha da Fumaca* of Brazil. (Katsuhiko Tokunaga)

Katsuhiko Tokunaga captures the Big Diamond on the downside of a loop off the coast of British Columbia.

✈ Snowbirds 1987

Like his predecessors, veteran fighter pilot Maj Dave Wilson brought a wealth of flying experience to the Snowbirds including what he had gleaned as the outer right wing in 1975-1976 and leader of the 434 Sqn CF-5 demo team in 1983. The fall tryouts yielded four new demonstration pilots in Capts Paul Giles (inner left wing), Don Barnby (second line astern), Boyd Smith (outer right wing) and Wes MacKay (opposing solo). Early in the new year, Maj Wilson decided he had the talent to introduce some revolutionary manoeuvring to the Snowbird display. With the basic looping and rolling manoeuvres introduced to the new team members, the team set about an ambitious plan to put their own stamp on the Snowbird routine. Wilson decided he wanted to revisit the notion of introducing inverted formation flying into the show, something the 1979 team had wanted to try but could not get approved at the time. With an additional eight years of airshow experience as a team behind them along with the support of Col George Miller who was now commanding the base, Wilson got the nod to pursue the possibilities.

Inverted Formation Flying

Capts Joe Parente and Jim Fowlow were the second year wingmen flying in the Snowbird four-plane diamond in 1987 and would play a key role in taking the Snowbird display to a new level. Without their expertise and willingness to try inverted formation flying for the first time, the plan would have gone nowhere. Once they were convinced it could be done, it was then up to first year inner Capt Paul Giles to determine if he was comfortable enough to do it safely 100 percent of the time. Joe Parente explains how the new manoeuvre was introduced that came to revolutionize the Snowbird display:

<hr>

"During the 1986 airshow season we had welcomed the opportunity to display with the Italian *Frecce Tricolori* at a few showsites and had seen the crowd reaction to some of their more dynamic manoeuvres. Even though our altitude rules were far more restrictive than theirs, the Tutor slower than the Aermacchi MB-339 and we didn't have coloured smoke, we were determined to add a little panache to our show. There was plenty of resistance from ex-members on up to change the Snowbird aerial ballet, but we, the incumbent four plus

The Double Take introduced by Maj Dave Wilson revolutionized the Snowbird display by introducing inverted formation manoeuvring to the team's repertoire. The first step was getting the inner wing pilots comfortable flying formation while hanging in their straps upside-down. Below, a unique wide-angle perspective of the manoeuvre in 1996 from the cockpit of SB 3, Capt Greg Carlow. (Ed Drader, Roman Holowatyj)

our new lead 'Willie D' (Dave Wilson), were intent on giving the '87 show a whole new look and feel. Thus was born the idea to change the way the main formation did business.

One of our newly-planned manoeuvres was to have the inner box (Snowbirds 1 to 4) fly by in an inverted silhouette, so we started to work through the logistics of achieving this. Since the oil pump on the jets had not been modified, we were still limited to 15 seconds inverted at the time. Our problem was getting all four aircraft rolled inverted and then set into a box formation which would then be banked for the silhouette in front of the crowd – all in 15 seconds. In spite of our best efforts, it just wasn't going to happen!

Furthermore, no one on the team had any experience flying inverted formation. Although it may sound obvious, maintaining station upside down uses the same basic techniques as flying right side up. The problem is, the sight picture is so different and the feeling of hanging in the straps so

unusual that it is all a little confusing to start. It may sound simple enough, but when you're in the seat on the day, it is easy for something to get lost in the translation!

As our workups moved into March, the three inners were still struggling with inverted formation and lead was having some 'interesting' roll-ins. Coupled with the fact that we still didn't have a way to prevent breaking the 15 second limit, the manoeuvre was in serious jeopardy. Then, on March 20th, four weeks before our acceptance show and just a few days before we were about to throw the manoeuvre away, 'Brode' (lead solo Don Brodeur) came up with the idea of starting with two aircraft inverted and two aircraft upright and then doing a formation half roll to reverse positions. This was a very simple solution to doubling our 'smoke on' time for the manoeuvre and yet was still very effective. It also solved another problem. Now only two aircraft had to roll inverted to start the manoeuvre versus four and by reversing positions 15 seconds later the inverted restriction had been solved.

A graphic illustration of why the Double Take is appreciated by spectators and pilots alike. This particular example features the 1991 team led by Maj Bob Stephan. At the top is Capt Marc Robert (SB 3), bottom Capt Ross Granley (SB 2) and in the slot Capt Vince Jandrisch (SB 4). (Alice Drader)

Shortly thereafter, I agreed to be the guinea pig and give it a go. Jim Fowlow was flying with me the day we tried it for the first time. 'Willie D' called me into position, echelon left, then called for the roll-in. Once I was stabilized in position upside down, he pulled up and performed a shallow half roll with me on the wing. It worked! All that was left to do now was to put it all together as a four ship box …

Finally the 'penny dropped' and it wasn't long before the inners, Paul Giles (a.k.a. 'Tuttle') and I, were starting to 'hang in' position on a regular basis. The final manoeuvre became the four-ship entering from stage left with SBs 2 and 3 inverted, lead and SB 4 upright. From there, lead used a little over 2 G pull up, giving us something to play with to stay inside the –3 G aerodynamic limit, unloaded and performed a half roll. We exited stage right with lead and 4 inverted, 2 and 3 upright.

It turned out that the roll-in by the wingers was the secret to the manoeuvre. If the roll-in was a nice point roll, you didn't have to correct much so you could get into position fairly rapidly and stay there. If you blew the roll-in, you had your work cut out for you. To enter the manoeuvre, Paul and I flew cross-cockpit opposite to our normal sides at wing tip reference and stretched back slightly off of lead. Therefore, after the roll-in we would be 'on side' while upside down. We agreed that we would always have nose-tail clearance off of lead for the entry and not move inside wing tip until perfectly stabilized inverted.

Probably the best seat in the house for this one was from the box, in Jimmy's cockpit. He would fly stretched and deep to allow us some manoeuvring room. Lead would run it in at 300 feet, hmmm …, and then call for the roll-in. We would 'tweek the nose up' and use a maximum deflection roll to the inverted position. I can remember seeing out of the corner of my eye, Tuttle's aircraft plan form to me as I was to him with less than 50 feet between us – must have been cool from Jim's cockpit. He could sit back and watch it all happen in front of him, perhaps a little too 'in front of him' sometimes!

The first time we successfully completed the manoeuvre with video, we were sitting around reviewing the film and trying to think of a name. Tuttle did this hilarious impersonation, as only he could do, of a spectator taking a double look at the box formation flying by with two aircraft upright and two inverted. He dubbed it the 'double take' and the name stuck."

Joe Parente

The double take manoeuvre was flown by the Snowbirds for 12 successive years, from 1987 to 1998 and reintroduced in 2002. Although it involves only four aircraft, it may well be the most challenging manoeuvre ever flown by the team. Inverted formation flying is extremely difficult and for the two wingmen in the double take, the first half of the formation roll presents the ultimate challenge in formation flight. It is a manoeuvre that necessitates exceptionally smooth control by the leader and the utmost in judgement and discipline – attributes which demand that the manoeuvre be modified or eliminated in shows conducted in abnormal turbulence.

In perfecting the manoeuvre over many months of practice while preserving the essential element of flight safety, the 1987

Capt Richard Lapointe snapped this interesting perspective of a Snowbird loop while flying with Capt Jim Fowlow in the first line astern position. The other pilots in this shot are Capts Paul Giles (SB 3), Howard Tarbet (SB 7) and Don Brodeur (SB 9).

team created a new dimension to the Snowbird spectacle which future teams would exploit. Ironically, for all of the advances Dave Wilson introduced to the Snowbird show as team leader, he never had the opportunity to demonstrate his prowess publicly. In the spring of 1987, only six months into his command, unforeseen circumstances forced him to relinquish command of the team to Maj Dennis Beselt, a fellow CF-5 fighter pilot.

For Dennis Beselt, the opportunity to lead the Snowbirds came much earlier than he or anyone else could have imagined. Having only completed his first tour on the team as

Snowbird 3 five years earlier, he explains how he came to be the youngest leader ever to command the team at 29 years of age:

―――――――――

"From all accounts, 1987 started out in a fairly routine fashion under the leadership of first year team lead Maj Dave Wilson. The team had a very busy and ambitious winter with many new and innovative additions made to the display, despite having to deal with some particularly poor weather. Inverted formation with aircraft rolling in formation in close proximity to one another certainly appeared to push the envelope of our beloved Tutor, but the result was an

exciting and fast paced show even by Snowbird standards – a virtual three-ring circus. In addition to these significant display changes, the team introduced a modification to the familiar paint scheme and began to lay the groundwork for the use of coloured smoke. Although coloured smoke was not used during the 1987 show season, this work came in very handy one year later. In my opinion, the work done in this off-season led to some of the most dramatic changes in the history of the Snowbirds, and Dave Wilson and the entire team must be congratulated on their significant achievements. For a new lead, these were truly remarkable milestones.

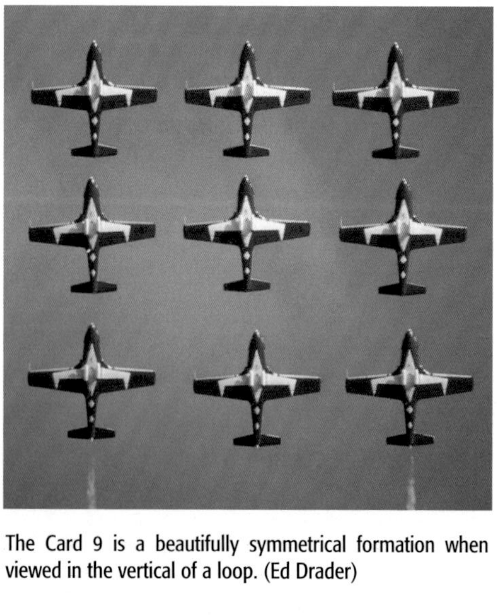

The Snowbirds attend hundreds of public relations functions on behalf of the Canadian Forces each year. Captured at a mid-season reception is the 1987 team. L to R, Standing – Capts Eric Dumont, Richard Lapointe, Don Brodeur, Wes MacKay, Howard Tarbet, Boyd Smith, Don Barnby, Jim Fowlow, Paul Giles, Joe Parente, Maj Dennis Beselt (leader). L to R, Kneeling – Cpls Brian Duivenvoorde, Serge Pilote, Gord Neave, Gilles Dubé, MCpl Mark Doane, Cpls Wally Marshall, Chris Detta, Mike Cook, MCpl Dan Bergeron, WO Alex Bouzane. Missing are Capt Ross Fetterly and Cpl Darren Schuszter. (via 431 Sqn)

The Card 9 is a beautifully symmetrical formation when viewed in the vertical of a loop. (Ed Drader)

It was during the spring deployment to Comox that the team went through its most significant change and where I came on the scene. Unfortunately, due to unforeseen medical reasons, Dave was forced to give up the team. With the start of the season only a few weeks away, the team was left in a precarious position which required quick thinking and decisive action. No better person to handle these problems than our own Col George Miller, Base Commander of CFB Moose Jaw and a former team leader himself. Although not privileged to all of the details of what went on during those few hours, I do know he made a short list of possible candidates in consultation with some former team members, carried out phone interviews, made his decision and had my promotion moved forward and in Moose Jaw before the team arrived home. Needless to say, it was a very exciting 48 hours and I remain grateful that my bosses in Cold Lake, Maj Rick Martin and Col Dave Kinsman (Base Commander of CFB Cold Lake), released me on such short notice. In exchange for this hasty departure Col Kinsman made me promise that the team would be back for the Cold Lake Open House, even if only for a simple flypast given the time constraints we now had to deal with.

I took command of the team on April 12th, 1987 and with the promise to be in Cold Lake by May 16th we set out to see what we could get ready. Although I commend each individual on that '87 team and Dave Wilson for the fine show they had prepared, I must single out two people in particular who helped immensely in those early days. First, we were fortunate to have third year coordinator Capt Eric Dumont to oversee all the administrative aspects of our changing status. Eric handled the many administrative matters: contacting sponsors; reproducing PR material; cancelling or re-scheduling shows, etc. It was a tremendous amount of work and, fortunately for me, I saw very little of it on my desk. He handled it all in an excellent manner which reflected well on the Snowbird operation and the Canadian Forces as a whole. The other major contributor was Capt Jim Fowlow who, as the second year first line astern pilot, offered the advice and criticism that only someone in the slot could provide. My aerobatic profiles were corrected quickly thanks to Jim and this allowed us to progress at a fast pace.

Following a short deployment to Prince Albert, Saskatchewan between April 27th and

29th, the team performed its acceptance show in front of LGen Larry Ashley, Commander Air Command, on May 7th. We deployed the next day. As previously mentioned, Cold Lake was at the top of our priority list but we felt we needed to get one show under our belt before we headed to the tough 'fighter base crowd.' With this in mind, we performed our first show of 1987 in Juneau, Alaska on May 10th. This quick handover and workup was a tremendous team achievement and one that we are all proud of.

After the excitement of the spring, the season went remarkably smoothly and was filled with many interesting and memorable events. We flew a total of 56 shows despite the fact that virtually the entire northern swing was

Photographer Rafe Tomsett was into his seventh year flying with the Snowbirds when he snapped this wide angle perspective in 1987.

cancelled. One of my first memories of that season was on our trip to 'The Rock.' I was fortunate during my tour to be able to fly by, over, or at the hometowns of virtually every member of the team. St. John's, Newfoundland was the first of these home-town events, and since the team had been weathered out the previous year we were under some considerable public pressure (i.e. team members Fowlow/Marshall family and friends) to perform. When we woke up on show morning we found a thick blanket of snow, low cloud, high winds and fog – a normal June morning in Newfoundland! I learned an important lesson that day, 'Never cancel until all options and time are expired.' On this occasion, on the advice of everyone – including weathermen and organizers – we cancelled the show in the early afternoon and headed back to the hotel. Needless to say, we hadn't made the short journey into town

before the sky cleared, the fog lifted, and the snow began to disappear. This was quickly followed by criticism from the Fowlow/Marshall family and friends! We never lived that down … and I never made that mistake again.

The team was also fortunate in 1987 to meet up with both the Thunderbirds and Blue Angels. These encounters were memorable for different reasons. We met the Thunderbirds in Colorado Springs, a display that had been placed on the schedule at the very highest of levels, at the request of the Canadian Deputy Commander of NORAD. However, it was obvious even during the planning stages that we were going to play second fiddle to the Thunderbirds, being somewhat

forgotten in the mass of USAF blue uniforms and silver stars. We also had to contend with our first high and hot show and on our practice day we certainly had our eyes opened by the limitations of our little jet. We needed a quick lesson in CHEAT, CHEAT and CHEAT, utilizing every trick in the book to keep our nine-plane formation together over the top of loops and rolls due to the high density altitude. As for the day of the show however, we didn't have to worry too much about the heat as we were scheduled to fly at 8:00 a.m.! The gates opened at 9:00 a.m. and I can remember driving up the back road to the participants' entrance in the dark to attend our brief, only to find the show organizers had not yet arrived to open the gate. Anyway, the ⅛th of a mile in morning fog kept us on the ground, and it was only through the assistance of local Canadian staff and Thunderbird lead Col Mike Riggs that we did eventually get to fly at the end of

The Snowbirds have been drawing crowds like this for over three decades. As the only nine-plane team outside of Europe, they are one of the most sought after airshow acts on the North American continent. (Ed Drader)

the show. And I mean the very end. We performed for the exiting crowd nearly nine hours after our scheduled time. In spite of all of the distractions, this show was a great achievement for the team as they performed brilliantly in tough conditions and under a great deal of adversity.

In contrast, our time with the Blue Angels was a fun and memorable occasion. Although not scheduled to perform in Pensacola, we were able to organize a visit while in Florida on our final swing, including an over-base 'practice' in association with the Blue Angels' weekly training. It was an exciting two days which started off somewhat on the wrong foot when the Blues' leader, Commander Denis Wisely, had to deflect the wrath of the station commander after I had convinced the young tower controller to approve our nine-plane overhead break – from IFR minimums at 200 feet!

The visit included the practice along with combined briefing and debriefings. It is really the briefing that comes to mind and what I'm sure everyone on our team remembers. I still smile when I think back – the Blues

around their big oak table, each of them in their assigned seat with Commander Wisely and his blue leather embossed briefing folder in hand. It was a picture right out of a navy recruiting movie. Needless to say, we were all caught totally off guard when Commander Wisely began to recite his way through each and every RT call, power setting and roll rate of their entire 45 minute show. This was a much more formal 'end of the season' approach than we were used to. I'm not quite sure what the Blues thought when it was our turn to brief, as I pulled my perspiration stained show card out of my pocket and essentially said to our lead solo Don Brodeur, 'Brode, outside of the runway, any questions?'

Through all of the busy activities of 1987, the sudden lead change, smoke trials and modified paint job, I must mention the excellent job done by our crew chief, Warrant Officer Alex Bouzane, and his entire ground-crew team. Alex had a lot to deal with during the year and after working for seasoned veterans like Yogi and Dave, breaking in a new, wet-behind-the-ears major like me must have

added to his work load. It's quite evident from the exemplary work of his crew and his quick progression through the ranks that he was an extra special NCO.

The year 1987 was a memorable one for the Snowbirds and certainly for me. I am grateful to all the members of that 'special' team for their hard work and dedication. I cannot over emphasize the respect and gratitude I gained for Col George Miller during this time. He was almost single handedly responsible for getting the team back on track quickly, by making the necessary decisions and worrying about any repercussions later. He was always ready to offer assistance or advice when asked, but at the same time allowed me to run my team. I felt truly privileged to have had the team under such a knowledgeable and supportive base commander."

Dennis Beselt

Snowbird 8, Capt Wes MacKay, signs autographs for some young admirers in the summer of '87. (Alice Drader)

The Snowbirds were honoured with the Art Scholl Memorial Showmanship Award by the International Council of Air Shows at the annual December planning conference in 1987. The legendary airshow performer lost his life filming a sequence for the movie *Top Gun*. Maj Dennis Beselt shows off the award with Col George Miller, CFB Moose Jaw Base Commander, in the Snowbird lounge (BB 56). (DND Photo)

Snowbirds 1988

"As is always the case with the end of one team, there comes a need to quickly create a new one. As the 1988 tryout session was my only opportunity to be part of this exciting and uniquely Snowbird audition, I found it to be a challenging and rewarding two weeks. As sad as it was to see the breakup of one team it was equally gratifying to see new people step up and meet the challenge. In 1988, the Big 2 was not flush with second tour experience and with CF-18 squadrons expanding it was not easy to attract outside talent. With the requirement to rely exclusively on base applicants and a Big 2 rule requiring staff to complete 18 months before being eligible to submit their names for the team, we were left tight for applicants. Despite these constraints, the tryouts went ahead smoothly and we were able to fill three of the four show positions plus a new coordinator with excellent people.

Unfortunately, at the end of the formal tryouts we did not feel we had a suitable pilot to fill the opposing solo position. We were able to overcome this predicament only with the help of the Commandant of 2 CFFTS, LCol Bill Reinhardt, who allowed us to run a second mini-trial with two second tour pilots who hadn't met the normal school embargo period. A special note of appreciation must go to Capt Jeff Jacques who performed admirably in these abbreviated and intense few days but lost out narrowly to Capt Ken Rae. Under slightly different circumstances, he would have made a fine member of the team.

There was to be one very significant addition to the normal workup program as the 1988 Winter Olympics were to be staged in Calgary and we had been approached to be part of the elaborate opening ceremonies. Participation was dependent on the team's ability to trail coloured smoke in the five colours of the Olympic rings. This would have been impossible had it not been for the extensive work done the previous winter. After much additional experimenting with nozzles, pressure, colour mixing and formations, we were able to make a favourable impression on Olympic officials at an informal over-base demonstration on January 18th. We were now officially part of what would be a once in a lifetime event.

That we were able to accept this invitation was due in large measure to the outstanding

The 1988 Snowbirds led by Maj Dennis Beselt helped open the Winter Olympics in Calgary when they swept in over McMahon Stadium trailing the colours of the Olympic rings. They subsequently turned the drab winter sky into a kaleidoscope of colour with several manoeuvres, including the Big Vic formation and the Canada Burst. (top - Rafe Tomsett; centre and bottom - Chris Templeton via J.P. Baraton)

service of our own groundcrew under the leadership of Sgt Jerry Unrau combined with the critical support the team received from base maintenance, in particular Maj Dave Dacyk. In addition to our normal aircraft maintenance cycle, the team aircraft were also being rotated through Northwest Industries in Edmonton to be upgraded with new VHF radios. Of course, we had a lot of extra work and flying associated with the coloured smoke preparations which led to an even more frantic juggle of aircraft than usual as we had the added pressure to have at least nine 'smokers' on the line in Calgary for the Olympics. This juggle went virtually down to the wire before magically coming together on the morning of the event. CFB Moose Jaw had all but taken over the Executive Aviation hangar in Calgary on the eve of the ceremonies, with at least two Hercules transports full of base personnel, test pilots and ferry pilots, many of whom worked through the night. This tremendous work and dedication left us with a flight line of nine jets plus a spare to fly this most historic event. On February 13th, 1988 the Snowbirds flew what must be the most highly visible flypast in the team's history, witnessed by billions of people around the world as the team trailed the Olympic colours. As we flew over McMahon Stadium, it was ablaze in all of its Olympic colour and pageantry. It was a tremendous thrill and a proud moment that still gives me

Capt Ken Rae straps into Tutor 023 prior to a practice flight. The perfectly aligned Snowbird team makes for a stirring sight on the ground. (Rafe Tomsett)

The 1988 Snowbirds. L to R, Standing – Maj Dennis Beselt (leader), Capts Shane Antaya, Paul Giles, Bjorn Kjaer, Don Barnby, Boyd Smith, Darryl Shyiak, Wes MacKay, Ken Rae, Richard Lapointe, Kevin Kokotailo, Ross Fetterly. Kneeling – Sgt Jerry Unrau, Cpls Mike Cook, Guy Fortin, Serge Pilote, Marc Cossette, Oswald Lindsay, Walter Marshall, Denis Fontaine, MCpl Dan Bergeron, Cpls Chris Detta, Darren Schuszter. (Ed Drader)

The Concorde Loop executed at stage centre was a popular feature of the 1988 Snowbird show. (Ed Drader)

goose bumps, especially as Calgary is my hometown. It was a truly unforgettable experience.

Following the Olympic excitement the team settled into its normal winter activities with very minor changes to the show. We deployed to Comox on March 29th and as this was my only spring deployment, I found it truly enjoyable. I came to understand how vital these two weeks are in the development of each year's team and its ability to get ready for the upcoming season. It was on the last day of this deployment that we flew what was possibly the best show of my entire two year tour. It was again a 'practice' but on this occasion it was a full dress rehearsal that happened to coincide with the SPAADS F-86 reunion at Comox on April 2nd, 1988.

The crowd included ex-Golden Hawks, Centennaires and Snowbird alumni along with many other very knowledgeable veteran aviators. Although we were definitely second in importance to the F-86 that flew in for the occasion, our display was much anticipated by the gathering. The team performed flawlessly under this scrutiny. The smoke was thick, white and billowed against the clear blue Comox sky. I don't remember being so much in sync with lead solo Wes MacKay at any other time; although we flew many good shows during the year, this one was special.

Following our traditional northern swing, the remainder of the season took us to many unusual venues, some very high profile shows and of course, all of the regulars. One of my personal favourites each year was the July 1st celebration in Ottawa where I believe we flew the last full downtown show over Lebreton Flats. From there our July 4th duty was in New York City, flying before millions of people along Coney Island followed by dinner in the 'Big Apple' with Honorary Snowbird Milton Berger.

Snowbird solos Ken Rae (left) and Wes MacKay (right) put on an exciting display of precision co-solo aerobatics during 1988. (Ed Drader)

Like all head-on crosses, the Upward-Downward Bomb Burst used visual illusion to dramatic effect. Snowbird 4 in 1988, Capt Bjorn Kjaer, executes a perfect cross as he meets team leader Maj Dennis Beselt coming down the backside of his loop. (Mike Cook)

In all we flew 58 shows in 1988, my last flight being a low show practice in Latrobe, Pennsylvania, on September 25th. It was with great shock and sadness that the team suffered a season ending tragedy that same evening when Capt Wes MacKay was killed in a car crash and Capts Ken Rae and Paul Giles were seriously injured. These were certainly the worst of days and a terrible way to lose such a valued teammate and friend while simultaneously bringing to an end what had been such a successful and memorable year.

As I reflect back, my days as Snowbird lead represented an extraordinary 18 months for me. The events of those days will forever be carried in my heart."

Dennis Beselt

Snowbirds 1989

Taking command of the Snowbirds from Dennis Beselt on October 15th, 1988 held special meaning for me as I had flown off his left wing in 1981 when he was Snowbird 3. Although all Snowbirds share a common bond, that bond is special between teammates who have flown together for an entire year. There may be similarities from year to year, but no two seasons and no two teams are ever the same, each defined by a unique set of characters and events that shape the Snowbird experience.

I had long aspired to return to the team and was deeply honoured to be back as part of this magnificent organization following a tour with Canada's last CF-104 Starfighter squadrons in West Germany and two long years on the ground. My elation was tempered however by feelings of compassion for the tragic manner in which the team's 1988 season had ended. As Dennis bade an emotional farewell to his team, I couldn't help but reflect on how far the team had come in the seven years since we had flown together … and on how important it was to continue in the spirit of those who had preceded us. I was determined to rebuild the team with the strong cast of characters that were left behind. There was no question we had the full support of the air force to do it, from LGen Larry Ashley, the Commander Air Command, on down.

My most pressing problem in taking command of the team had been rectified quickly when Capt Bob Stephan had agreed in a telephone conversation to set aside his much sought after tour in West Germany to return to Moose Jaw and fill in temporarily for injured lead solo Capt Ken Rae. As Bob had only just arrived in Germany, this said a lot for his dedication to the team. Sadly for Ken, he was unable to regain flying status in sufficient time to complete the workups which was a major disappointment for all. Base Commander Col Claude Thibault was instrumental in helping smooth out the administrative details associated with this abrupt change and proved to be a very strong ally for the team throughout his tenure in Moose Jaw.

With the tryouts completed following three final assessment flights on November 10th, we were able to announce the 1989 team by early evening. I was extremely pleased with the results as we welcomed two veteran fly-

The 1989 Snowbirds practice the Canada Burst in Comox as the remnants of smoke from the opening sequence waft across the showline. (Bill Johnson)

ers to the team along with three outstanding young instructors, two as demo pilots and one as a new coordinator. The groundcrew interviews had also been very enjoyable and it was satisfying to see so many young technicians eager to join the team. Not knowing any of them, I was particularly grateful for Sgt Jerry Unrau's sage advice as technical

crew chief in making our final selections. Rounding out the team were the office staff led by Capt Ross Fetterly. They never ceased to amaze me with their initiative and resourcefulness.

Having myself been inspired to join the Canadian Forces from watching the RCAF's legendary airshow teams as a youth, I was fully cognizant of both the importance and impact that the Snowbirds could exercise in Canadian society. These notions had certainly been reinforced watching Tom Griffis and Mike Murphy embrace the team's public relations mandate during my first tour and I was eager to do the same. Thus, I welcomed every opportunity to enhance the team's public image while motivating young people to chase their dreams – regardless of the field of endeavour or the odds of success. To help with this goal I solicited and received excellent support from DND Public Affairs at both the national and regional levels.

The 1989 season opened on May 1st with a show for the citizens of Thompson, Manitoba – not a regular stop on the Snowbird circuit but one where we were very warmly welcomed. From there we experienced many highlights. Whether it was helping the London International Airshow commemorate the 40th anniversary of NATO or celebrating the Windsor-Detroit International Freedom Festival, the Snowbirds were proud to represent the men and women of the Canadian Forces.

A rare opportunity for the 1989 team included being special guests at the Molson Indy Pre-Race Dinner in Toronto in July and then starting the big race off with a nine-plane line-abreast pass over the start line, much to the delight of the race fans below. Abbotsford, always a highlight in the Snowbird season, made history by welcoming the Russians to a North American airshow for the first time. Naturally, this drew a lot of attention from both sides of the border and the Russians did not disappoint. Their displays in the MiG 29 Fulcrum and An-225 Mriya (wingspan 290 feet with six engines developing over 300,000 pounds of static thrust) provided airshow fans with a formidable display of raw power set against the backdrop of Mount Baker. With the additional presence of the USAF Thunderbirds, with whom we were honoured to perform (and take flying with us during a practice), it was a banner year for Abbotsford.

Three contrasting views of the 1989 Snowbirds. Top – A dynamic view of the Canada Burst: Snowbird 5 is pushing out at minus 3 G; the solos (8, 9) have rolled 90 degrees and are splitting away; and Snowbirds 6, 7 and 2, 3 have rolled away from lead in turn to establish their separation. Snowbird 4 is the last to separate away from the lead aircraft. Centre – The Big Delta formation was used to open the show in 1989. Bottom – The lead element of the triple vic takeoff, used when runway width or wind conditions preclude a larger formation takeoff. (Ron Miller)

Snowbird groundcrew put in long hours to ensure the team is always ready to perform. At left, technicians Marc Cossette, Leo Jenkins and Guy Fortin do an engine run to investigate a snag. At right, the fruits of their labour as the team completes another successful practice. (Rafe Tomsett, Marc Cossette)

"East meets West" was the big attraction at the 1989 Abbotsford International Airshow. With the USAF Thunderbirds forming an impressive backdrop, Marshal of the Soviet Air Force Skomorokhov inspected Snowbird lead's aircraft after the show and then asked to meet each member of the team personally. (Alice, Ed Drader)

The 1989 Snowbirds at their home base in Moose Jaw, Saskatchewan. L to R, Standing – Capts Ross Fetterly, Dom Taillon, Les Racicot, Dale Hackett, Bjorn Kjaer, Shane Antaya, Maj Dan Dempsey (leader), Capts Steve Will, John Low, Darryl Shyiak, Bob Stephan, Kevin Kokotailo. L to R Kneeling – L/S Darcy Gallipeau, MCpls Doug Dennison, Oswald Lindsay, Cpls Jim Burton, Mario Deshaies, Sgt Jerry Unrau, MCpl Guy Fortin, Cpls Marc Cossette, Dave Scharf, Leo Jenkins, MCpl Denis Fontaine. (Ed Drader)

Flying with the Snowbirds
The Press Rides

Press rides play an indispensable role during the Snowbird season as they give media personnel a rare opportunity to relate to their audiences the thrill of flying in tight formation with nine aircraft while providing excellent advertising for the upcoming airshow. These media flights usually constitute a very positive experience as the benefactors of this "ride of a lifetime" are so impressed you can't help but feel good after the flight as you are inundated with their bubbling enthusiasm. Naturally, this always results in terrific exposure for the Canadian Forces in the press which of course is the reason for all of the effort. However, the caveat usually is used for good reason ...

Every once in a while the team takes up a passenger who soon realizes why he or she has chosen a profession with feet firmly planted on terra firma. Although press rides are very sedate as a rule, airsickness does occur from time to time with the odd individual who takes exception to breathing (and talking) through an oxygen mask while being cocooned into a seat complete with parachute and rocket catapult strapped to their posterior. Why would that make anyone uncomfortable? Although every passenger is methodically pre-briefed about the do's and don'ts, airsickness can become a very unpleasant experience for the individual and pilot alike, especially if the breakfast comes out before the mask comes off! Once airborne, to gauge how each of the guests are doing the team uses a simple colour code over the radio with each pilot relaying the status of his passenger to the boss: green for feeling fine; amber for not too swell (what am I doing here?) and red for ... too late! Fortunately, green is usually the order of the day and everyone comes down elated. When

Victoria *Times Colonist* photographer Bruce Stotesbury captured this dynamic shot of the Snowbirds over Victoria International Airport and the town of Sidney, B.C. on 18 Jul 98. It was taken from the cockpit of Snowbird 7 (Maj Ian McLean) using a 16-mm 2.8 Nikon fisheye lens. The manoeuvre being led by team leader Maj Darryl Shyiak is known as "an up and down left." Press rides such as this have put the Canadian Forces team on the front page of every major newspaper in Canada over the years while providing invaluable promotion for Canada's aviation industry. (courtesy the *Times Colonist*)

SUNDAY JULY 19, 1998

TIMES ✠ COLONIST

140TH YEAR · No. 218 ·   VICTORIA, BRITISH COLUMBIA $1.00 PLUS GST

Top of the world

a red is called, the aircraft in question must leave the formation and usually has to land.

This brings to mind one memorable press ride in Bagotville, Quebec on June 15th, 1990 which involved Snowbird 6, Capt Dale Hackett. A young journalism student had been selected to fly with Dale – this was going to be his first big story. As the takeoff time got closer, this young man got quieter and quieter. Although he wouldn't admit it to anyone, this was an assignment he wasn't looking forward to – in fact, he was just plain terrified of flying – in anything, let alone with nine aircraft in formation. Since some of our passengers are occasionally a little nervous, each time the team taxis out for takeoff on such a ride, each pilot talks to his passenger to allay any apprehension he or she may have since everyone wants this to be a positive experience. Unfortunately, Dale's reassuring words didn't work – no sooner had we raised the landing gear after takeoff than a disgusted call came over the radio, "Boss, six is red!" (See mask comment above!). I couldn't believe my ears –

this must have been the fastest red call in history – no precursor "I'm not feeling well" or "I think I'm going to be sick" from the young man in question – he cut straight to the quick! End of the trip for Snowbird 6 that day! As Dale later recalled, " I can't remember a more dejected looking individual in my life. He was literally tossing his cookies five seconds after takeoff." ... At least the rest of us got to enjoy the flight. Fortunately, occasions such as this are rare.

Of the approximately 2000 civilians that have flown with the Snowbirds since the team's inception, most have been so thrilled that they didn't want to land! Incidents during media flights, other than the occasional problem with airsickness, have been exceptionally rare. Unfortunately, the team's excellent record in this regard was diminished somewhat when an accident occurred in June 2001 forcing one of the pilots and his military passenger to eject to safety. Although the accident occurred away from the main formation, it served to underscore the importance of the team's pre-flight safety briefing.

The Canadian International Air Show in Toronto is one the Snowbirds always look forward to as it is one of the few locations where we are static long enough to have our families join us and partake in the excellent hospitality. I've always really enjoyed media flights and we had already completed rides in London, Windsor, Ottawa, Abbotsford and Paine Field, Washington when it came time for the annual ride in Toronto on August 31st. The morning of our press ride dawned a glorious day in Toronto with bright sunshine and clear skies. The next day, a large photograph was featured

in the *Toronto Star* as the team flew past the CN Tower and open Sky Dome where the Toronto Blue Jays were to play later that day.

It was during our second show at the CIAS on Sunday, September 3rd that disaster struck the 1989 team. Capt Shane Antaya, our second year veteran inner right wing pilot, lost his life when his aircraft collided with mine following the split in the upward-downward bomb burst. I was still upside down when a jolt from behind shook my aircraft as both aircraft descended towards

Lake Ontario below. Tragically, whatever had caused Shane to lose control of his aircraft in the split second that created the collision also prevented him from ejecting from his aircraft and the country lost a fine young man.

Like any family, there is nothing that hurts more than losing a teammate on the Snowbirds. It cuts to the very soul ... and there are simply no words to describe the anguish we shared with Shane's family in having lost him. Up until that point in the show, everyone had flown a near perfect

display in the calm air over Lake Ontario. Only days before Shane had been lauded for his professional presentation on teamwork and safety in the workplace to an audience at Dow Chemical in Kingston. Indeed, I had received so many positive responses about Shane from organizers that I had invited him to introduce the entire team at the dinner reception that evening. He impressed us all by not only introducing all 20 of us in turn with his infectious smile and enthusiasm, but by also including all of our hometowns which he had memorized.

In the aftermath of a tragedy it is human nature to gather strength from family members and friends and this is what the Snowbirds have always done on the rare occasions that disaster has struck. We on the 1989 team were certainly touched by the outpouring of grief and support that came from around the world following the accident. Hundreds of letters, messages and phone calls poured into the Snowbird office following our flight home to Moose Jaw on September 5th. They came from members of parliament representing their constituents, from ambassadors and military leaders, from mayors and reeves, from airshow organizations and police forces and from average citizens who had been touched by the Snowbird magic in some way over the years. We were grateful for this support, as we were from those media personnel across Canada that encouraged the team to continue. Among the leading articles in this regard was one written by MGen (Ret'd) Richard Rohmer, then military editor for *The Toronto Sun*. A former RCAF fighter pilot and well known author, he wrote an eloquent article in support of the team in the immediate days following the accident. Entitled "Snowbirds must fly again," he stated in part: "As a unit, the Snowbirds are highly visible, elite and proud representatives of the Canadian Armed Forces. They present a fine image and presence across the country that would be sorely missed if the group was disbanded." Those words are as true today as they were when they were written 12 years ago.

In the days following the accident, I felt very strongly that we should finish the season on a positive note by doing what we did best – meeting with the public we served. We had time and were unanimous that we should finish the season as a tribute to Shane. Fortunately, my overtures were supported all the way up the chain of command.

That the team was able to continue was largely due to the unequivocal support of two individuals, Minister of National Defence Bill McKnight and the Commander of Air Command, LGen Fred Sutherland. I remain grateful for the understanding these two gentlemen displayed and the influence they were able to bring to bear to allow us to get back in the air and finish our season. They were not alone – certainly none of us would have been able to continue without the support of our own families.

Thus, having bid a fitting farewell to our departed colleague, the Snowbirds quietly took to the air again on September 13th to rework a modified eight-plane show. Just over two weeks later we flew the first of our last six scheduled shows of the season. The response from the people of St. Catharines that day was heartwarming, as were the

reports from the media scrum that were in attendance to record our return to the airshow circuit.

The 1989 season ended on October 14th back in Moose Jaw in front of family and friends. For half of the team it was their last show, a bittersweet ending to what had been a difficult tour for them. Each of them, pilots and groundcrew alike, deserved immeasurable credit for overcoming the tragedy and finishing the season in such a professional manner. Some very fine public relations had been done on behalf of the Canadian Forces and the country as a whole over the course of the year. Those of us staying on now looked forward to seeing the Snowbirds into their 20th year of operations guided by the same spirit and unwavering belief in the team.

Dan Dempsey

Another fine shot of the Snowbirds during a media flight, this one over the nation's capital in 1988. Pre-show media flights over the team's next airshow venue always create tremendous excitement among the local populace. Over 100,000,000 spectators have watched the team perform over 32 years. (DND, WO Vic Johnson)

Honorary Snowbird Ed Drader stepped onto the Snowbird scene in 1980 by presenting the team with an 8 mm film of their show. He has been one of the team's strongest supporters ever since. In 1989 he asked permission to take a shot of the team's "triple vic" takeoff from the end of the runway at Kamloops. We were happy to oblige. (Ed Drader)

A tight shot of the team's performance at Paine Field, Washington in 1989. At right, Capt Shane Antaya (Snowbird 2) in a touching moment with a young airshow fan. (Bill Johnson, J.P. Baraton)

The Concorde Topside Silhouette was a popular edition to the 1989 Snowbird show. Following the loss of Shane Antaya, the team concluded the season by flying the formation with an empty right wing position in tribute to him.

Snowbirds 1990

Leading the Snowbirds into their 20th anniversary was a real privilege. Planning had actually begun a year earlier by laying the framework for a series of special activities to help commemorate the event. These activities included the filming of a new movie on the team, on-going support to two new books outlining the team's history, planning a major reunion at the end of the season and the introduction of coloured smoke into the show routine for the first time. As 1990 also represented the silver anniversary of Canada's maple leaf flag, an early decision was made to use red and white smoke in as many shows as possible to commemorate that national milestone as well.

To successfully accomplish all of these extra activities we needed a strong group of team members and a lot of cooperation from other base agencies. Completing the annual tryouts in only nine days took care of the first part as we welcomed some superb new pilots and groundcrew to the team. Among our enthusiastic new groundcrew was Sgt Dan Bergeron, the first crew chief to return to the Snowbird fold having done a previous tour on the team. With a significant increase to the workload of the groundcrew due to extra filming missions and introduction of coloured smoke to the show, Sgt Bergeron's previous experience proved invaluable.

The second part of the equation was taken care of by all of those base personnel who worked behind the scenes to help the team achieve one of the most successful seasons ever. From administrative to technical support, we could not have asked for more from the branch heads and their staffs at CFB Moose Jaw. Our show was their show as well.

Our fall workups got off to a fine start and on December 19th we looped and rolled the nine-plane diamond for the first time. Among several distinguished visitors during the winter, we were pleased to welcome Vice Admiral C. Thomas, the Vice Chief of the Defence Staff, who toured the squadron and lauded team members for the important work they did on behalf of the Canadian Forces. That work was much in evidence throughout the season, including a flypast over downtown Moose Jaw on March 30th as Mayor Stan Montgomery presented Col Thibault and 938 base personnel who had marched to city hall with the 'Freedom of the City.' The tradition, which dates back to medieval times in Europe, underscored the close relationship between the base and city while saluting the 66th anniversary of the RCAF.

The winter workups over the frozen prairie of Saskatchewan tend to drag on into March as the team puts the final touches on its carefully orchestrated routine. However, any trend towards monotony was certainly broken up by the arrival of a film crew from Yaletown Productions of Vancouver led by producer Mike Collier. I had initiated this project a year earlier to replace our well worn DND promotional movie shot in 1981. This new endeavour was destined to become a one hour television documentary (*Those Magnificent Snowbirds*) in partnership with CanWest Global Communications as well as a 14 minute short feature (*Come Fly with Us*) which played in Famous Players theatres and was later used for squadron motivational presentations. The unique script, won in competition through the federal Department of Supply and Services, looked at the Snowbirds through the eyes of a young boy who eventually grew up to join the team. We wanted to underscore every facet of our operation while stressing the public relations and recruiting mandates of the team. Naturally, the highlight of both productions was the stunning photography set to the original music of Steven Vitali, a young Canadian musician that had impressed us in 1989 with his stirring music.

The 20th anniversary Snowbirds. L to R, Standing – L/S Darcy Gallipeau, Capt Ross Fetterly, Capt Dale Hackett, Capt Dom Taillon, Capt Vince Jandrisch, Cpl Jim Burton, Maj Dan Dempsey (leader), MCpl Dave Fischer, Capt Rich Lancaster, Cpl Dave Scharf, Sgt Dan Bergeron, Capt Jeff Hill, Capt Brooke Lawrence, Cpl Leo Jenkins, Cpl Dan Séguin. On wing – Capt Les Racicot, Capt Steve Will. Kneeling – MCpl Doug Dennison, Cpl Rick Macnab, MCpl Mario Deshaies, Capt Ross Granley, Capt John Low, Cpl Tony Edmundson,. (Bill Johnson)

Principal photography was shot by Bob Gibson of Yaletown but was complemented with some outstanding aerial photography from our rearward facing camera pod and hand-held minicam footage by Cpl Marc Cossette. Marc was responsible for the phenomenal cockpit footage taken of the solo manoeuvres. Several key sequences were also shot from a specially equipped Learjet provided by CineExec Corporation of California. After eight months of filming across Canada, the last challenge was to find a suitable narrator. In this regard the team was fortunate that director Ken Jubenvill was a friend of veteran Canadian actor Leslie Neilsen who readily agreed to narrate the film. The end result was a pleasing effort that has been aired as far away as Asia and Europe and continues to appear from time to time on television documentaries 10 years later.

One of our more ambitious endeavours in 1990 was the introduction of coloured smoke to the Snowbird show. Ever since watching the big three European teams, the Red Arrows, *Patrouille de France* and *Frecce Tricolori*, fly their beautifully choreographed coloured smoke shows, I have been a strong advocate of enhancing the Snowbird show in this fashion. Notwithstanding the challenges of using coloured smoke and the headaches that come with it, my attitude was "If they can do it, so can we!"

I had many allies in this regard, including Col George Miller with whom I had first

Photographer Bob Gibson and director Ken Jubenvill had no shortage of subject material as they followed the Snowbirds across Canada during the 1990 season. The fruit of their labour is still being aired around the world.

discussed the prospects back in 1986. His enthusiasm for the proposal was matched by Col Claude Thibault, his successor. We knew from the Olympic experience in 1988 that it would be impossible to fly all of the shows in our schedule using coloured smoke since we did not have, and were not about to get, a dedicated support aircraft. Since the logistic problems were formidable, I suggested a compromise that we do the major shows in 1990 using coloured smoke and the balance using the traditional white smoke. LGen Sutherland, who ultimately had to approve the plan, was an

exceptional supporter and the end result was a significant enhancement to the show.

Accomplishing the task with limited resources was easier said then done. One of the key principals in making the scheme work was the Base Aircraft Maintenance Engineering Officer, Maj Terry Leversedge. A very strong proponent of the need for a national aerobatic team, Maj Leversedge afforded me everything I asked for. This included a six man "smoke team" to supplement our own groundcrew on the road at those showsites earmarked for coloured smoke displays. We treated these additional technicians as regular members of the team and it was gratifying to see that in subsequent years several of them joined the team for a full two year tour.

The addition of the red smoke gave the show a whole new look and was particularly effective on overcast days against the white (or black!) background of clouds. To complement it, the 1990 team added several popular new manoeuvres to the show. These included the maple leaf burst (traced in red) honouring the aforementioned anniversary of the Canadian flag and the Philion roll, dedicated to the courage of a young Ontario teen struggling to overcome severe burns suffered in a fire in his home. All were perfected in our annual sojourn to Comox which was punctuated with more shooting for the movie and a welcome invitation to promote the team on the CBC's *Front Page Challenge* television program.

The weather at the 1990 Saskatchewan Air Show on Saturday, July 7th provided a dramatic backdrop for the Snowbirds' coloured smoke display while creating difficult flying conditions for the team. At left, the author leads the team around the corner for the Double Diamond Bottomside Silhouette. In this shot, the team has moved to wider "wingtip" formation as a safety measure due to the turbulent conditions. The low show was cut short when lightning approached the field. The funnel cloud at right represents an airshow organizer's worst nightmare. Fortunately, only strong winds and torrential rain resulted as it passed over CFB Moose Jaw just after the Snowbirds had landed. Skies were clear for the Sunday show. (Ed Drader)

Painting the Sky Red

The 1990 Snowbirds introduced red smoke to their show to celebrate the team's 20th anniversary and the silver anniversary of the Canadian flag. On top, a unique perspective of the Downward Bomb Burst. Above, the Maple Leaf Burst. Below, the Roll-Back (left) and Concorde Loop (right), also with the new look. (Bill Johnson)

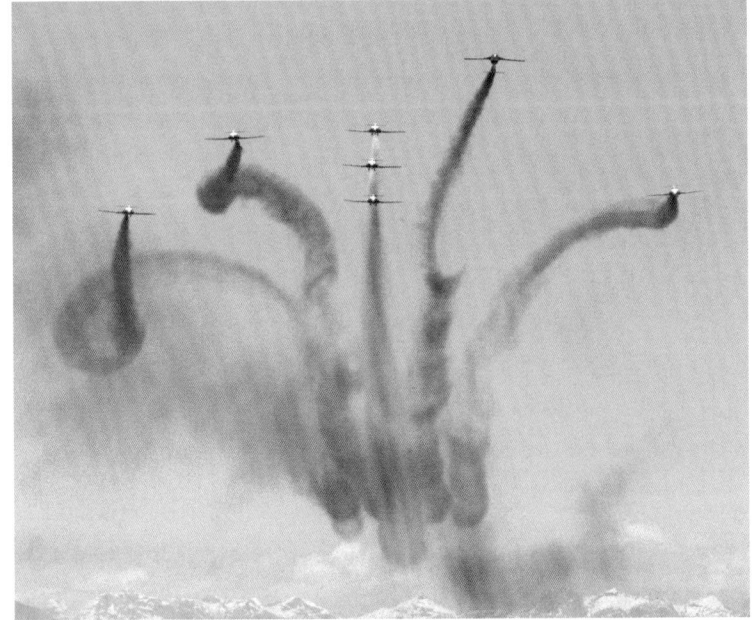

The Philion Roll added a new twist to the Snowbird show as Snowbirds 2, 3, 6 and 7 (just out of the frame) did simultaneous aileron rolls at stage centre trailing red smoke following their individual roll-backs. (Ron Miller)

Once we hit the airshow circuit in late April there were many highlights as communities large and small across Canada and the United States went to extraordinary lengths to salute the team's 20th anniversary. An early highlight was the flying of our 1,000 official airshow at CFB Namao in Edmonton on May 20th, the citizens of Alberta being among the first to witness our

This photograph gives a whole new meaning to the fighter pilot axiom "check six." Capts Bob Hill and Don Schofield of Air Canada bring the Canadian Warplane Heritage "Mynarski Lancaster" in for a close look at Snowbird 1 during filming for the team's 20th anniversary movie. The shot was taken from the ramp of a 424 Sqn Buffalo from CFB Trenton. (John McQuarrie)

coloured smoke show. We were also privileged to later perform the last military airshows at CFBs Portage la Prairie, Manitoba and Summerside, Prince Edward Island. Like Namao, these military air bases were destined to close due to budget cuts. So too was Royal Roads Military College in Victoria, British Columbia, the 1990 Snowbirds being the last to grace the skies above that great institution in celebration of its 50th anniversary.

The events surrounding the team's 20th anniversary activities in Ottawa in the summer of 1990 will certainly remain among my fondest memories. It all started with a gala dinner at the Chateau Laurier sponsored by the National Capital Air Show Association on June 27th. After a media flight and breakfast at the National Aviation Museum the next morning, we were afforded the rare opportunity to fly formation with the Canadian Warplane Heritage's Lancaster bomber as filming continued for our new movie. Our annual Canada Day flypast over Ottawa in the presence of Her Majesty Queen Elizabeth II was followed by a first for the team – the execution of our upward bomb burst over the Parliament Buildings. But in spite of all of these special memories, I believe the one that will be most vividly etched in the minds of 1990 team members will be the reception the team received during the Canada Day celebrations that evening on Parliament Hill. Mega producer David Foster had flown in for the nationally televised event as part of the entertainment extravaganza and played a stirring rendition of his theme song 'Flight of the Snowbirds' as giant screens showed aerial footage of the team. As David neared the climactic ending of his composition he announced our presence – as we joined him from behind stage, the tens of thousands of

In a rare occurrence, Col O.B. Philp was left speechless when presented with a stained glass Snowbird crest handcrafted by Maj Yves Bossé (right) at the 20th anniversary reunion dinner. In typical O.B. fashion, in later years he donated the work of art back to the squadron where it now proudly hangs outside the *Snowbird Hall of Fame* later named in his honour in 1995. (DND, Cpl C.H. Roy)

spectators jammed on the Hill erupted into a prolonged ovation that caught us all by surprise. It was the most humbling moment of my four year Snowbird career and, for me at least, underscored just how important the team had become as symbols of national pride for Canadians. I don't think any of us have ever stood taller than we did that evening …

The last half of the 1990 season mirrored the first with a multitude of public relations activities and very little time off in between. Yet with each location came fresh faces, new enthusiasm and wonderful hosting right across the country – from Abbotsford to Toronto to Shearwater. Our schedule in the United States afforded us many memorable visits which included the National Air Races at Reno, Nevada as well as the home bases of the Thunderbirds in Las Vegas and Blue Angels in Pensacola, Florida – where once again it was proven that the special bonds and camaraderie first established with these teams by the Golden Hawks and Grey Ghosts in the late 1950s are timeless.

I have always maintained that there are three facets to the Snowbird job – the exceptional flying, the opportunity to travel and take in some of the most spectacular scenery on the planet and finally, the opportunity to meet literally thousands of people during a tour of duty with the team. For me, it was an exhilarating experience made all the more special by the people I shared it with – my teammates, our families, other performers and some of the world's greatest photographers whose dedication has helped make the team famous. All came together at the end of the season for our final show of the year and 20th anniversary reunion. Just prior to the reunion, J.P. Baraton released his labour of love, a soft-cover compendium of Snowbird stories and historical data entitled *Snowbirds 1971-1990, a 20 year history*. It has proven a fine research vehicle on the team.

Family reunions are important, and the extended Snowbird family is no different. They are joyous occasions and the members of the 1990 Snowbirds, working as a team as they had all year long, staged a wonderful affair to conclude a wonderful season. The highlights of the weekend were the 20th anniversary slide show by Ed and Alice Drader and the release of O.B. Philp and Bill Johnson's magnificent tribute to the team, *Snowbirds from the Beginning*, a book of exceptional quality in a class of its own. As former team members leafed through its pages, eyes sparkled as long distant memories leapt to life through the camera lenses of Bill and Nancy Johnson. And more than one old Snowbird was probably thinking, "Hey, that's me, I once had the best job in the world."

Dan Dempsey

LGen Fred Sutherland, Commander of Air Command, accompanied by BGens Claude Thibault (centre) and Dave Kinsman congratulate members of the 1990 team following their last show of the season. At right, *Snowbirds from the Beginning*, a spectacular tribute to the team. (Jacquie Perrin, Bill Johnson)

🐦 Snowbirds 1991-1992

It was a pleasure to hand over command of the Snowbirds to Maj Bob Stephan on October 20th, 1990. With three years of Snowbird solo flying under his belt combined with a wealth of fighter experience on the CF-5, he was more than qualified to lead the team into its 21st season. As is evident from his recollections, Bob prided himself in his people:

"Reflecting on fond memories now ten years past proved to be a satisfying exercise, particularly because just a moment's reflection of my time as team lead immediately brought to mind what I most fondly remember of those two years – the people I worked with.

Just prior to becoming team lead, I was fortunate to have been only one year removed from being a team member, and as such, I was still relatively familiar with the team's operation, albeit from a distinctly different perspective. With the 1990 team still 'on the road,' I immersed myself at home in Moose Jaw with the task of getting somewhat up to speed with the myriad of tasks and administrative and logistical details the squadron is saddled with on a daily basis. I soon realized that any apprehension I may have had concerning my ability to come to grips with all this information was unfounded, due entirely to those squadron members often in the background but crucial to the operation – the office staff. There was the team's new logistics officer, Paul Richards – extremely knowledgeable and experienced (I didn't say old), he told me up front, 'Just sign where I tell you. I'll keep us out of trouble.' He

always did. There was Darcy Gallipeau, the team's supply technician, who could always be counted on to get his hands on anything and everything we required, just don't ask how he acquired it! And last but most assuredly not least, there was Marg Fowler aka 'Loni,' the team's secretary, who was never surprised because she'd seen it all! A favourite memory of mine was being able to truly take Marg 'on the road' for the first time. Having Marg in attendance at my last showsite was a definite highlight.

Apart from the squadron proper, but nonetheless an integral part of the success of the operation was the support rendered from various units on the base in Moose Jaw. Col Terry Humphries, Base Commander during my tenure, was consistently supportive and approachable. The Base Aircraft Maintenance Engineering organization and of particular note, Maj Terry Leversedge, always went the extra mile to ensure the team was

Base Commanders at CFB Moose Jaw have played a central role in Snowbird operations from the team's inception, each lending their own style of leadership to the success of the team. Gathered at the reunion in October 1990 were those responsible for overseeing the team for the first 21 years. L to R – O.B. Philp, Ralph Annis, Dave Tate, Gerry Van Ek, Don Williams, George Miller, Claude Thibault and Terry Humphries.

operationally fit, often under trying circumstances and impossible timelines. And finally, LCol Yogi Huyghebaert, Base Operations Officer, an old friend and mentor, was always available for both moral and operational support and sage advice – even if he was wrong about landing sequences! Yogi and his wife Phyllis are like family to me; having them around was truly an added bonus.

My change of command ceremony in the fall of 1990 was coincident with the 20th anniversary of the team. It was therefore especially satisfying and honestly quite humbling to address an audience comprised of former team members and my family. As I stated then, I hadn't felt as much pride as I did at that moment since my father pinned my wings on years earlier. Immediately following the anniversary festivities, it was down to the business of selecting new team members for the upcoming season. I've often described the tryouts as the 'best of times' and the 'worst of times,' because while it was always a thrill to welcome new aircrew and groundcrew members aboard, it was, on the other hand, incredibly difficult to inform others that they had unfortunately been unsuccessful. Another enjoyable aspect of the process was the pairing up of aircrew and groundcrew for the season. The crew chiefs in 1991 and 1992 and the individuals I transited with, were, respectively, Dan Bergeron and Joe Maillet. Dan and Joe were invaluable to me. They purposefully and meticulously managed every aspect of squadron maintenance and groundcrew personnel matters, and they were wonderful sounding boards and confidants. I thoroughly enjoyed working with them.

The 1991 Snowbirds. L to R, On wing – Capts Paul Richards, Réal Turgeon, Glenn Oerzen, Bill Watts, Vince Jandrisch, Ross Granley. In cockpit – Sgt Dan Bergeron, Maj Bob Stephan (leader). Capts Marc Robert, Nick Cassidy, Brooke Lawrence, Rich Lancaster, Jeff Hill. Standing – L/S Darcy Gallipeau, MCpl Dave Fischer, Cpls Rick Macnab, Rick Murray, Marco Asselin, Tony Edmundson, Dan Séguin, Doug Wray, MCpl Ed Dillon, Cpl Mac Gilchrist. (Bill Johnson)

I first flew with the Snowbirds in the 1983-1984 seasons, and I must digress momentarily to relate a story that occurred during those years. George Hawey was the team lead. The nine-plane was transiting one day from who knows where to NAS Glenview, located in the heart of Chicago, from where we were to stage and perform a show on the Chicago waterfront. The Tutor, fully loaded with fuel, holds just enough (including sometimes fumes) to barely get the job done. On this particular day, a typical mid-summer, muggy, hazy, marginal VFR afternoon, we arrived overhead Glenview with sufficient fuel to pitch and land, and perhaps even perform a short arrival sequence. But Chicago being very busy, we ended up being vectored everywhere except towards the airport.

Top, the Snowbird groundcrew are among the first to experience the tranquility of the Comox sunrise during spring workups each April. The calm is soon shattered when nine J-85 engines wind up for another training session as the team puts the final polish on their show. (John McQuarrie)

Frustrated (and we could always tell because his pubs ended up being hurled onto the dash), George explained that we now needed to land ASAP due to fuel. The controller somewhat sarcastically inquired if George was declaring an emergency, to which George immediately responded, 'No, but if you keep us on this heading, you will be creating one!' Needless to say, we were cleared directly to the airport. I often reflected that I would relish using that line if an appropriate situation presented itself – unfortunately one never did. In all seriousness, I was very impressed with George, his leadership skills, and the overall way in which he conducted business. It was a pattern worth repeating, and one that I tried to emulate.

The last to see Snowbird pilots off before a performance and the first to greet them on landing are their individual ground-crew. Engrossed in a 1991 practice are, left to right, standing – Sgt Dan Bergeron and MCpl Ed Dillon; seated – MCpl Dave Fischer, Cpls Dan Séguin, Rick Macnab and Rick Murray. (Rafe Tomsett)

Every transit, showsite, and performance was memorable, but over time, and with age, it seems that only specific, isolated memories of certain ones remain. Low-level transits were a favourite and we tried to include them whenever possible. Vince Jandrisch, first line astern in 1991, particularly enjoyed flying low-level. Although I was unable to see Vince during said transits due to the stretched trail formation (one behind the other) which we flew, I still felt it prudent to occasionally suggest over the radio that he raise his altitude a tad. Later in the year, Vince questioned my powers of vision and the fact that I couldn't possibly see him while flying these sorties. I remarked that while he was right, I nonetheless thought that I knew him rather well, and therefore, at appropriate times, I would simply make the aforementioned call – besides, he never questioned the request!

On another occasion, it was discovered that Ross Granley, inner right wing, was flying an aircraft with a possible engine snag because his aircraft was burning more oil during transits than the solos' aircraft were during shows. We finally ascertained however, that the excessive amount of oil being burned was due not to a faulty engine, but simply to the fact that Ross, like the rest of his family, enjoyed low-level aerobatics and inverted flying anywhere and at any time!

Early in the 1991 season, LCol Jim Kerr, representing Air Command, called and made an offer I readily accepted without consulting the rest of the team – I knew there was no need. Towards the end of the season we traveled by special invitation to Kissimmee, Florida where for three days we were hosted by the Disney Corporation as we waited and prepared to perform a flypast over the castle at the Magic Kingdom – in formation with the US Navy Blue Angels. While being guests of the Disney Corporation was top drawer to say the least, the flypast with the Blues was something I'll never forget. We rendezvoused over a lake some 20 miles from the Magic Kingdom and formed up directly behind the Blues' six F-18s. We employed all 11 aircraft, including the coordinators, and all of our groundcrew were on board. Just prior to starting the run-in, I asked Blue lead to push the power up slowly

This unique perspective of a tight turn led by team leader Maj Bob Stephan over the Comox runway was taken by pilot turned artist/photographer Jerry Davidson, the original leader of the RCAF Goldilocks aerobatic team in 1962. Team pilots typically experience between three and four times their normal body weight during turns such as this. (Jerry Davidson)

A picturesque shot of the 1992 team as they execute the Big Arrow Roll. (Garry Cotter)

so as not to leave us behind (the Tutor accelerates somewhat slower than an F-18!). The plan was for fireworks to be let loose immediately following the flypast. Well, we did lag behind slightly, and to our shock and surprise, we arrived over the castle in the midst of multi-coloured, exploding fireworks! So much for 'bombs bursting in air!'

(one slightly larger than the rest), instead of the normal nine!

I have always been an avid golfer. Fortunately for me, others on the team shared my enthusiasm and enjoyment of the game. There were opportunities to play some spectacular golf courses during the year and a number of us tried to take advantage whenever it was possible. Marco Asselin and Bill Watts were the other die-hard golfers on the team and the three of us spent many an early morning, coffees in hand (Pepsi for Marco), driving wherever we needed to 'get a game.' Invariably, there was wagering, but to this day, probably because we spent so much time kibitzing and laughing, I'll never remember who ended up on top – but I'll always remember the good times on the links.

Further about golf but also a flying tale involved a certain photo flight we flew out of

Salinas, California in 1992. Salinas is a stone's throw from Carmel Bay and Pebble Beach, the site of perhaps the most famous golf course in North America. I was determined to have a picture of the nine-plane with Pebble Beach in the background. Although the location was a rather noise sensitive area, we were able to make it happen. A beautiful photo of a nine-plane diamond loop taken from a chase plane above the formation, with the 18th hole of Pebble Beach below, now hangs in a place of honour in my home.

I don't often pull out old Snowbird videos and reminisce, but the odd time my 'almost' ten year old son thinks it's cool to put on Dad's old flying videos. When we do watch some of them together, I'm reminded of just how fortunate former team members are to have photographers Ed and Alice Drader's year-end tapes in their possession. Ed and Alice have been incredibly supportive of the

The 1992 edition of the Snowbirds. L to R, Kneeling – Cpls Rick Murray, Mike Ubell, Mike Crickmore, Sgt Joe Maillet, Maj Bob Stephan (leader), Capts Rob Martin, Marc Robert, Glenn Kerr. Standing – Cpls Earle Bourgeois, Kori Ibey, MCpl Ed Dillon, Cpls Marco Asselin, Doug Wray, Terry Spence, Vince Leather, Mrs. Marg Fowler, Capts Nick Cassidy, Bill Watts, Frank Bergnach, Glenn Oerzen, Bob Painchaud, Maj Réal Turgeon, Capts Mike Lenehan, Paul Richards. (Rafe Tomsett)

At Abbotsford in 1992, I was dismayed to learn from our team doctor that our stalwart second line astern pilot, Nick Cassidy, had fallen ill and was unable to perform. Just as I was about to canvass the group for suggestions on a modified show, the Doc remarked that we need not worry – we had a replacement pilot. I knew I'd been duped, and as I looked up, my eyes were met by a massive vision in red – one Dan McLaren, fully decked out in a form-fitting red flight suit, appropriately adorned with all Snowbird insignia, including a gold name tag with the position "5 Alt" (alternate) embroidered next to it! So there does exist a 'one and only' picture out there somewhere – 10 show pilots

The Snowbird version of the famous Goldilock's formation was a feature of the team's low show in 1991 and 1992. (Ed Drader)

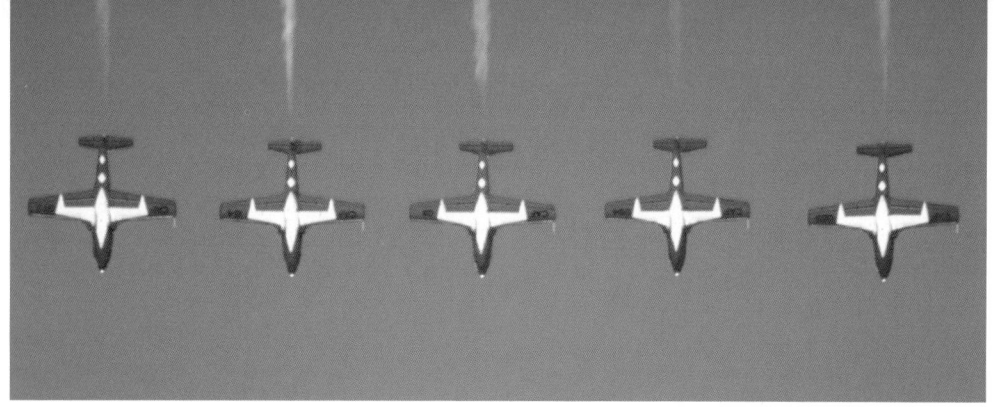

The symmetry of the line-abreast formation, seen here on the backside of a loop, is a favourite among photographers. (Garry Cotter)

Snowbirds over the years and they are two of the most unselfish people I have ever met. The year-end and anniversary tapes they have produced are truly pieces of art and I am always immediately taken back to memorable former times when I watch them.

I'll end as I started, remembering the people I worked with. More than the places and the shows, they will always be what I will think of when I reflect on my time as a Snowbird."

Bob Stephan

An hour off school to watch the Snowbirds practice is always a popular choice among children at CFB Comox and manoeuvres such as the breathtaking Lag Back Roll never fail to draw a reaction. Team members always take a few minutes to spend with the children prior to debriefing their practice as Capt Glenn Oerzen responds to a young lady's curiosity. (Garry Cotter, Rafe Tomsett, Ed Drader)

A Tribute to the Golden Centennaires

As the Snowbirds traversed Canada in 1992 they kept running into an old friend, one that hadn't been seen in Canadian skies for 25 years – a Golden Centennaires' Tutor. In a tribute to the team and all those who had served on it, a special ceremony had been held at the former home of the team, CFB Portage la Prairie, on April 16th, 1992. The Commander of Air Command had authorized the painting of Tutor 093 in the original splendour of the Centennaires and the aircraft was to make a cameo appearance at all of the major Canadian shows that summer. The aircraft was formally unveiled on April 16th by way of a flypast over Centennaire Park at the entrance to CFB Portage. In an eloquent speech to celebrate the occasion, the Base Commander,

Col Ray Henault, included this explanation of how the project got underway:

"… The flypast you are about to see will consist of a four-plane Tutor formation, with the lead aircraft sporting Golden Centennaire colours. The aircraft was painted specifically to honour the 25th anniversary of the Golden Centennaires and to rekindle the memory of an air display team that was the symbol of Canadian pride in this nation during Canada's centennial year. The painting project was initiated by Capt Don Barnby (an instructor at the CF Flying Instructor School at CFB Portage and a former Snowbird) and completed by CFB Moose Jaw with the willing cooperation of the Base Commander, Col Terry Humphries, and his Aircraft Maintenance Engineering organization. Most

appropriately, the lead aircraft is being flown by the Commander of Air Command, LGen Dave Huddleston, accompanied by the Commandant of the Flying Instructor's School, Maj Herb Paul. The Commander's participation in this commemorative flypast is a tribute to his all-embracing dedication to the air force and the preservation of its history, and adds immeasurably to the significance of the occasion … I invite you now to watch the flypast and to remember the glory of the Golden Centennaires."

Col R.R. Henault
April 16th, 1992

LGen David Huddleston (left) was a staunch supporter of Canada's aviation heritage during his tenure as Commander of Air Command. He led the flypast to commemorate the 25th anniversary of the Golden Centennaires with Maj Herb Paul, Commandant of FIS. (Ed Drader)

Tutor 093 on the Snowbird flight line in 1992 with the successors to the Golden Centennaires. (Terry Leversedge)

🐦 Snowbirds 1993

Maj Dean Rainkie found himself "short-toured" on his second CF-18 Hornet posting in August 1992 when he was offered the opportunity to return to the Snowbirds to lead the team through 1993 and 1994. He had already enjoyed two previous rewarding fighter tours – the first flying the CF-101 Voodoo with 416 Sqn at CFB Chatham, New Brunswick and the second with VFA 125 at Naval Air Station Lemoore, California. Dean was the first Hornet pilot to return to the Snowbird fold having learned to fly, and then instruct on, the highly sophisticated all-weather fighter while on exchange duties with the United States Navy. His recollections:

Cpl Marlene Shillingford made history by being the first female technician selected to join the Snowbird team in 1993. (Garry Cotter, Jerry Davidson)

School visits during the spring and fall are regular features at each Snowbird showsite as team members motivate youngsters of all ages to reach for their goals. Maj Dean Rainkie answers questions following a school assembly. (Bob McIntyre)

"The 1993 season marked two significant milestones for the team. The squadron performed for the first time outside of Canada and the USA, with three full demonstrations being performed in October at Zapopan Military Air Base located just outside Guadalajara, Mexico. Squadron members were hosted in an exemplary fashion during the six day tour of the country and met several Canadians resident in the local area. In addition, for the first time in the Snowbird team's history, a female technician of the Canadian Forces, Cpl Marlene Shillingford of Newmarket, Ontario was selected to join the elite cadre of Snowbird groundcrew. Supplementing the everyday duties throughout her two-year tenure with the squadron was a very high demand on the media front, with Marlene being highlighted in numerous television, radio and newspaper interviews.

The fall routine was disrupted early during the selection process in October 1992 due to persistent inclement weather in the Moose Jaw area. As a result, the eight pilot candidates and five remaining team members deployed to Naval Air Station Fallon, Nevada to conduct the annual pilot selection process. Following the standard winter workup period at Moose Jaw and Comox, the squadron embarked on its first tour of the season to Western Canada and the USA. Showsites included Norman Wells in the Northwest Territories; Prince Rupert, Smithers, and Kelowna, British Columbia; Yakima, Washington and Juneau, Alaska. The challenges and dramatic splendour associated with the snow-capped mountainous terrain in these areas made for spectacular viewing of the demonstrations. Other noteworthy sites which offered the beauty of waterfront aerial displays included Nanaimo,

1993 Snowbirds at their home base in Moose Jaw, Saskatchewan. L to R, Kneeling – Cpls Vince Leather, Denis Houde, Mike Ubell, Pierre Turgeon, Sgt Joe Maillet, Maj Dean Rainkie (leader), Capts Rob Martin, André Lortie, Glenn Kerr, Derek Mosher. Standing – Cpls Earle Bourgeois, Mike Crickmore, MCpl Jim Flach, Cpls Kori Ibey, Marlene Shillingford, Terry Spence, Mrs. Marg Fowler, Capts Chris Granley, Frank Bergnach, Michel Cliche, Bob Painchaud, Francois Cousineau, Mike Lenehan, Paul Richards. (DND 15 Wing Base Photo)

Maj Dean Rainkie glances over at Capt Rob Martin who is hanging in his straps in preparation for the Double Take Roll. (Jerry Davidson)

British Columbia; Grand Beach, Manitoba; Toronto and Leamington, Ontario; and Point au Pic, Quebec.

A new nine-plane manoeuvre was successfully added to the 26-minute aerial display, one of which formed the shape of a wedge and was appropriately named as such. Of our nine-plane manoeuvres, the maple leaf burst drew audience acclaim and quickly became one of the most popular sequences flown by the team in the recent past. Incorporation of another old formation, the card nine, was tried early in the winter workups but was abandoned – in spite of the persistence of some team members, including our lead solo pilot, Capt Bob Painchaud. When Bob (a.k.a. 'Cowboy') returned to lead the team for the 1999 season, he reintroduced the formation into his show.

The 1993 demonstration year was very successful with the team crossing Canada and

Only a few select individuals have withstood the test of time as Snowbird photographers. Their passion for photography and flying must often overcome significant physical discomfort to yield results as they literally put their lives in the hands of their pilot. Their reward is some of the most exhilarating flying imaginable as this self-portrait implies. (Garry Cotter)

the USA seemingly endlessly in performing 70 of the 76 scheduled demonstrations. July also saw the well-deserved promotion of Sgt Joe Maillet, the team's crew chief, to the rank of warrant officer while on the road at Red Deer, Alberta. During the Abbotsford

Airshow held in August, spectators witnessed the Snowbirds share the aerobatic skies with the Russian Knights flying their SU-27 Flanker fighter aircraft at what was appropriately dubbed the 'East Meets West' Airshow. Another memorable performance for the team was a concurrent air demonstration with the RAF Red Arrows and USAF Thunderbirds at the opening ceremonies of the new Denver International Airport. The season ended its formal display schedule at Point Mugu, California where pilots of the United States Navy Demonstration Team, the Blue Angels, had the good fortune of 'riding along' during the Snowbird practice performance on October 22nd. One other noteworthy passenger that day was Capt Craig Berryman (USMC), who had survived the unfortunate experience of becoming a prisoner of war during *Operation Desert Storm* in 1991."

Dean Rainkie

Abbotsford 1993 set the scene for another meeting of East and West. Members of the Russian Knights aerobatic team pose in front of their SU-27 Flanker with the USAF Thunderbirds and Canadian Snowbirds. (Ed Drader)

The Snowbirds flew the impressive Maple Leaf Burst with nine aircraft in 1993 and 1994. (Garry Cotter)

Sunrise and the Snowbird groundcrew are on the move once again. (Rafe Tomsett)

Snowbirds 1994

"The 1994 season was again inscribed with several notable events for both the squadron and the Canadian Forces as a whole. The year marked the 50th anniversary of D-Day and several ceremonies were held throughout 1994 to commemorate past duty and sacrifices for country. In tribute, the squadron displayed allied forces D-Day stripes on my lead aircraft.

Additionally, LGen (Ret'd) Fred Sutherland was formally inducted as the squadron's first 'Honorary Colonel' at a ceremony following the annual acceptance show on April 23rd, 1994. We remain forever indebted to him and his wife Heather for their allegiance and strong support of all squadron commitments and activities. A second ceremony was held on June 8th, 1994 at Canada's Aviation Hall of Fame to bestow on 431 Sqn the Belt of Orion Award for Excellence. The ceremony was attended in Wetaskiwin, Alberta by Hon Col Sutherland, LCol (Ret'd) Yogi Huyghebaert, Maj Steve Hill (Snowbird lead designate for 1995-1996), Capt Tana Beer (squadron logistics officer) and Cpl Earle Bourgeois (squadron supply technician).

431 Squadron paid tribute to the 50th anniversary of the D-Day landing on the beaches of Normandy by painting invasion stripes on Snowbird 1. The year 1994 also marked the 70th anniversary of the RCAF which was acknowledged with a special tail insignia. (Rick Radell)

His Excellency the Governor General of Canada, the Right Honourable R.J. Hnatyshyn, paid tribute to the Snowbirds during their 1994 tour. He is shown here with Snowbird 2, Capt Mario Hamel, and Snowbird 1, Maj Dean Rainkie.

In September, the squadron received the distinct honour of being named the first ambassadors of the Canadian Injury Prevention Foundation, a non-profit organization founded by heart surgeon Dr. Robert Conn of Toronto. The foundation aims to educate young children, teens and adults in their assessment of taking 'Smart Risk' and the association of risk with life's routine activities, a practice which the Snowbird team experiences on a regular basis.

One of the most satisfying aspects of the Snowbird job is the opportunity to meet thousands of people, young and old. In an average 70 show season, each Snowbird pilot will sign between 12,000 and 15,000 autographs. (Garry Cotter)

Two contrasting Snowbird views. Above – the majestic line-abreast loop with CFB Comox in the background. Below – nine Snowbirds in perfect line-abreast formation. (Rafe Tomsett, Jerry Davidson)

The 1994 winter workup session progressed steadily and on schedule with newly painted aircraft arriving at regular intervals. The show season commenced on May 1st at Yellowknife, Northwest Territories and terminated on October 9th in Kissimmee, Florida with 64 of the 72 scheduled performances being flown. Again, the team hosted several Canadian celebrities during the various media rides including Philipe LaRoche, gold medallist for the National Ski Team at the Winter Olympics and Darcy Downs, also a member of the Canadian National Ski Team. On July 1st, members of the Canadian Astronaut Program – Julie Payette, Bjarni Tryggvason, Dave Williams and Rob Thirsk occupied the vacant seats during the Canada Day Parliament Hill flypast ceremony. The squadron also performed a flypast to mark the opening ceremonies of the Commonwealth Games in Victoria, British Columbia on August 18th. Valerie Pringle of Canada AM was one of the more well known media to fly with us in 1994, doing so in advance of the Canadian International Air Show in Toronto.

Lastly, the team was afforded an 'unscheduled' photo session with then Vice President Al Gore, who was attending a political rally coincident with the arrival/departure of our 11 aircraft in Jackson, Tennessee. The echo of Tutor jet noise throughout the hangar in which he was conducting his speech regrettably drowned out much of his oration… that is, until the black-suited, communication device-in-his-ear, armed, Secret

The dynamics of close formation flying. Smooth control inputs are key to keeping the formation together. (Garry Cotter)

Service agent approached and 'persuasively corrected' the situation. The smile emanating from the face of Snowbird 3, Capt Andre Lortie, in the resulting photograph told the whole story.

There are of course many more events that remain treasured memories for myself and the other team members. The camaraderie and friendship, in and away from the aircraft and shows, and the family ties and

sacrifices are experiences that truly 'do last a lifetime.'"

Dean Rainkie

The 1994 Snowbirds. L to R, Standing – Capts Ménès Pierre-Pierre, Michel Cliche, Chris Granley, Will McEwan, Mario Hamel, Maj Dean Rainkie (leader), Capts André Lortie, Derek Mosher, Dave Deere, Norm Dequier, Mike Lenehan, Tana Beer. Kneeling – Cpls Gord Tulloch, Mike Crickmore, Denis Houde, Pierre Turgeon, Sgt Mark Doane, Cpls Rick Ouellette, Richard Jack, Marlene Shillingford, MCpl Jim Flach, Cpl Ron Kleim. Missing Cpl Earle Bourgeois. (Rick Radell)

🦅 Snowbirds 1995-1996

With the selection of Maj Steve Hill to command the squadron for the 1995 and 1996 seasons, another veteran CF-18 pilot took the helm of the Snowbirds. Following the completion of his first tour with the team as Snowbird 6 eight years earlier, Steve had joined the famous Tigers of 439 Sqn based in CFB Baden Soellingen, West Germany. Following the invasion of Kuwait in 1990, he had found himself assigned to the Canadian "Desert Cats," a composite CF-18 Sqn which flew out of Doha, Qatar during *Operation Desert Storm*. With 56 combat missions under his belt, he now rejoined four other veterans of the Gulf War on the squadron – second year outer Capt Dave Deere (45 missions) and first year inner Capt Greg Carlow (50 missions) on the flying side and crew chief Sgt Mark Doane and deputy crew chief MCpl Martin Singher on the maintenance side of the house. But by the time he rejoined the Snowbirds as the new boss, Steve Hill's thoughts were far removed from the stresses of armed conflict:

"In 1976 I was an aviation enthusiast attending Centennial College and working towards a commercial pilot's license with the hope of a flying career, but until I saw the Snowbirds my calling was unclear. The first time that I saw the Snowbird ballet was while driving south on the Don Valley Parkway in Toronto on the way to a flying lesson at the Toronto Centre Airport. The team was performing

The Snowbird show is tightly choreographed to keep heads swivelling as manoeuvres alternate between the solos and main formation. Above, solos Steve Dion and Jean Guibault demonstrate the mirror silhouette. Below, the 1995 Snowbirds are about to create a waterfall of smoke in Page, Arizona. (Doyle R. Buehler, Garry Cotter)

during the Canadian National Exhibition and the billowing white smoke carved a perfect heart in the cool blue sky over Lake Ontario. The beauty and skill required to accomplish this feat with so many aircraft in tight formation totally fascinated and impressed me to the point that I remember muttering, 'What I'd do to have the chance to try that!' Little did I know at the time that this story would

be repeated many times by many people over the next 20 years. During my first tour with the team in 1986 we made a movie with Canadian composer David Foster at Comox British, Columbia. This film was widely shown throughout Canada and the United States for the next 10 years. In fact, later during my first year as team lead in 1995 I was approached by a young, enthusiastic instructor in Moose Jaw who informed me that I was the reason he was in the air force. He explained how the film had turned his life around and focused him on the goal of becoming an air force pilot. I subsequently heard this same story many times during the next two years. It is ironic that I too could have told this story to the team of 1976.

However, the Snowbirds are more than just a recruiting tool for the Canadian Forces. The adage that the team demonstrates the teamwork and professionalism of the Canadian Forces is absolutely an understatement. The team promotes unity and pride to all Canadians, whether it is to 50 people on a snow bank in Watson Lake in the Yukon, or 100,000 folks watching the Canadian International Air Show in Toronto. The theme and level of effort is always the same – perform with pride and to the highest level of perfection possible. The elusive perfect performance (from a critical team member's perspective) is always so close but at the same time just out of reach. Look out though if the team does have a perfect show where all nine flyers plus the coordinators and groundcrew come together! These rare times are what the

The 25th anniversary edition of the Snowbirds in 1995. L to R, Standing – Capts Tana Beer, Ménès Pierre-Pierre, Steve Dion, Ian Searle, Will McEwan, Mario Hamel, Maj Steve Hill (leader), Capts Greg Carlow, Jeff Young, Dave Deere, Norm Dequier, Claude Lebel. Kneeling – Cpls Liz Vella, Éric Bissonnette, Gord Tulloch, Rick Ouellette, Daniele De Luca, Tony Solimine, Sgt Mark Doane, Cpls Tim Woodward, Richard Jack, Ron Kleim, MCpl Martin Singher (Rick Radell)

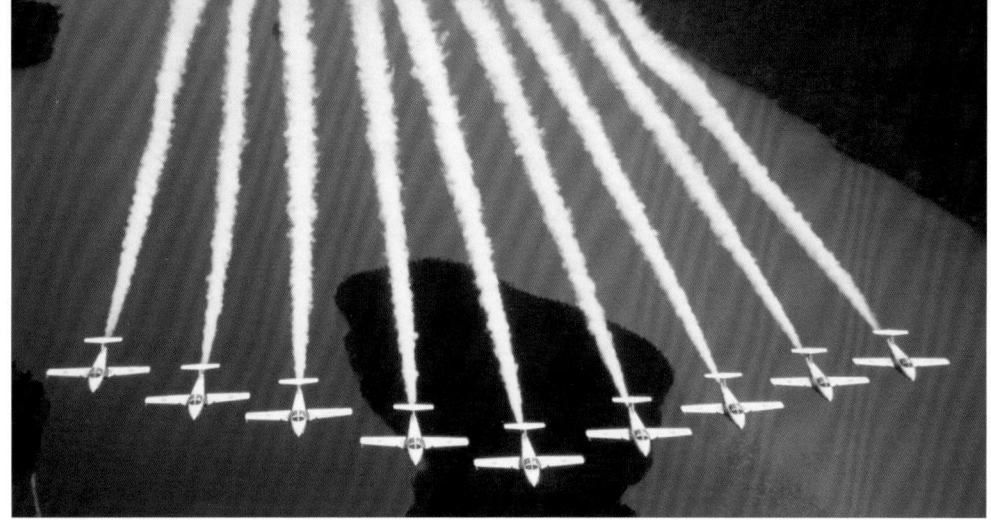

A rarely seen nine-plane formation is the Big Vic. This giant bird has a wingspan of some 95 metres (over 300 feet). (Bob McIntyre)

Snowbirds strive and live for; they make the frequent separations from family and friends, and the hard work, all worthwhile.

There were many memorable moments during my command that will stay with me forever. Performing with the Blue Angels and Thunderbirds in the United States and having the American public so warmly welcome us, both in person and in the press, was an eye opener, to say the least. I always insisted that the team be as down to earth as possible and that no one left the fence line until every last child got the autograph or photo that they came for. Accessibility is another trait that the Snowbirds are famous for and deserve to be proud of. We also had time for a good laugh now and then that relieved the tension associated with living and working together for extended periods of time away from home. One such occasion occurred at El Paso, Texas where we had Honorary Snowbird Dan McLaren, all 300 pounds of him, dress up in his number 5 red show suit, strap in and pretend to start, taxi and fly the performance. Little did the crowd know, 'Bernie' was hiding in the cockpit and did the actual start and taxi and once around the corner of the hangar line, let Dan out to return to his usual outstanding sound man duties.

The close relationship that was nurtured between the air and groundcrew of the Snowbirds is unique in the Canadian military. I insisted to showsite organizers that social events would be attended by all team members and that all members were to be treated equally. This was very much appreciated by our groundcrew and rightly so because without them the team would not be able to function. An example of the extraordinary effort put forth by our groundcrew under the stalwart leadership of my crew chief and close friend, Sgt Mark Doane, occurred at Point Mugu in 1995. While

pulling up for a nine-plane loop at 300 feet above ground we encountered a flock of ducks. I lost my right windshield, SB 5 lost his windshield and right gull door and SB 7 had a basketball size dent in the leading edge of his left wing. Following the recovery from the loop, I separated the formation and landed last. When I pulled into the chocks Mark calmly parked me and began carefully picking the shattered glass off of me and out of the cockpit. We were scheduled for two days off in Los Angeles. However, the groundcrew worked 36 of the next 48 hours repairing the jets to ensure that the show could go on and that their record of never cancelling a show due to maintenance remained intact.

Honours I will cherish include leading the team for the 25th anniversary, leading a flypast at Sidney, British Columbia to pay respects to our founder O.B. Philp when he passed away, establishing the Snowbirds Honorary Society and having the opportunity to proudly represent Canada's service men and women to Canadians and Americans from coast-to-coast. The bond that exists between Snowbird team members is real and timeless. As the team enters its fourth decade, it is important to remember the contributions made by our predecessors and to recognize the ultimate sacrifice that five of our teammates have paid while proudly serving Canada and doing what they loved to do."

Steve Hill

The Canadian flag has been flown to every corner of the continental United States by the Snowbirds, shown here in Page, Arizona. In the mid-90s the team added a final slow speed pass in front of the crowd with gear and flaps extended prior to landing, Maj Steve Hill leading the 25th anniversary team in this example. (Garry Cotter)

Formation aerobatics command a bond of trust among team members that is absolute. The only pilot watching the ground (or water) as the formation manoeuvres is the team leader. All other Snowbirds concentrate solely on keeping their aircraft within a tiny piece of airspace by focusing on specific references on the aircraft beside or in front of them. As this photograph graphically illustrates, all other cerebral inputs (including the view) must be ignored. (Jerry Davidson)

Methodical groundcrew inspections of team aircraft before and after every flight are vital to the safety of the team's operation. At left, Cpl Richard Jack checks the oil on Snowbird 5 prior to refuelling the aircraft in Moose Jaw. On the right, Cpl Tony Solimine records data from Snowbird 2's recording accelerometers installed to monitor the frequency of G accelerations (from –3 to +7 G). Snowbird shows in the Canadian north provide unique challenges. Single point refuelling at smaller airports such as Watson Lake in the Yukon necessitate clustering the aircraft around a single fuel hose. Regardless of the time it takes, the end result is always the same – 11 perfectly aligned aircraft on the ramp – a point of pride for the groundcrew since the inception of the team. (Garry Cotter)

The 1996 Snowbirds pose for a team shot at Pearson International Airport. L to R, Standing – Capts Shirley Grenier, Christopher England, Steve Dion, Ian Searle, Dan Robinson, Rod Ermen. In cockpit – Sgt Pete Henry, Maj Steve Hill (leader). Capts Greg Carlow, Jeff Young, Brock Andrew, Jean Guilbault, Claude Lebel. L to R, Kneeling – Cpls Margaret McPherson, Ken Marcicki, Tim Woodward, Daniele De Luca, Tony Solimine, Peter Dueck, Ian McLean, Éric Bissonnette, Mike Eubel, Greg Turcotte. Missing – MCpl Martin Singher, Cpl Liz Vella. (via 431 Sqn)

🐦 Snowbirds 1997

Major Darryl Shyiak became the 15th commanding officer of the Snowbirds when he shook hands with Steve Hill on October 19th, 1996 at the conclusion of the team's last show for that season. Another previous Snowbird outer winger, his background differed significantly from his predecessors in that his operational experience had been gained as a rotary wing pilot in the challenging search and rescue profession. However, having returned to Moose Jaw and the "Big 2" as a flight commander for the previous three years, he had had plenty of time to hone his aerobatic skills on the Tutor in preparation for this most challenging assignment. Known for his superb "people skills," the team flourished in its public relations mandate under his command:

"It was an honour to take command from Steve Hill with whom I had become good friends at the start of our military careers in the fall of 1979 during basic officer training in Chilliwack, British Columbia. I inherited a highly motivated and very well trained team.

The aircrew tryouts for the 1997 team started on October 30th, 1996. Blessed with excellent weather, the tryouts were completed in only seven days. While the aircrew tryouts were being conducted, interviews by myself and the crew chief, Sgt Pete

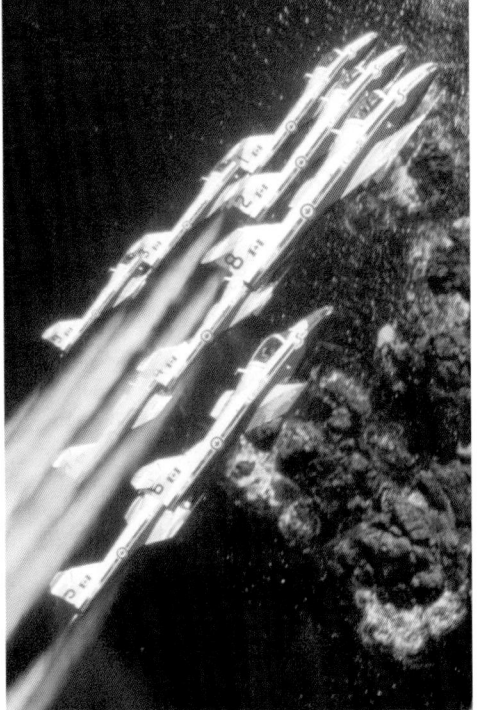

Maj Darryl Shyiak leads the 1997 Snowbirds in another fine aerial portrait over the west coast of British Columbia. (Garry Cotter)

Henry, were conducted to select the new groundcrew members for the '97 team. On November 5th, 1996 the new team for 1997 was announced.

Following the winter workups and an extremely successful spring deployment to Comox, we conducted a rare pre-season media flight in Moose Jaw to advertise the summer's Saskatchewan Air Show. Two special guests who joined the local media were Moose Jaw's Mayor, His Worship Ray Boughen, and our very own Marg Fowler, our long-serving squadron secretary who flew with the team for the first time. We flew our acceptance show two days later on April 18th. The operations order for the season was signed immediately after the show by LGen Al DeQuetteville, Commander of Air Command, giving the team approval to take its display on the road.

The highlight of the ground displays in Abbotsford '97 was unquestionably the full scale mock up of Canada's first Avro Arrow. Airshow fans were amazed at the size of the controversial interceptor. The program was scrapped on what came to be known in the Canadian aviation industry as "Black Friday," 20 Feb 59. (Garry Cotter)

The 1997 Snowbirds pose during spring training at Comox, B.C. L to R, Standing – Capts Shirley Greenwood, Chris England, Marcus Walton, Scott Shrubsole, Dan Robinson, Rod Ermen, Maj Darryl Shyiak (leader), Capts Derek Miller, Mike Ayling, Brock Andrew, Jean Guilbault, Richard Walsh. Kneeling – Cpls Margaret McPherson, Brian Doll, Peter Dueck, Greg Turcotte, d'Arcy Monaghan, Gary LeCourtois, Sgt Pete Henry, Cpls Ken Marcicki, Ian McLean, Troy Bartlett, MCpl Marco Asselin. (Garry Cotter)

The first airshow for the 1997 team was the biggest and most important of the season. Flown at Nellis AFB in Las Vegas, Nevada on April 25th and 26th, the "Golden Air Tattoo" was the largest military airshow in American history in celebration of the 50th anniversary of the USAF. Almost one-half million people, including more than 80 commanders-in-chief representing virtually every air force in the world, gathered for the two-day event. Flying displays were conducted by more than 80 aircraft with over 100 aircraft on static display. In addition to the Snowbirds, there were performances by four other military aerobatic teams: the Chilean Air Force Halcones flying Extra 300 piston-engine aircraft, the Brazilian Air Force Smoke Squadron flying turboprop T-27 Tucanos, the Blue Impulse of the Japan Air Self-Defence Force flying Kawasaki T-4 jet trainers and the USAF Thunderbirds flying their F-16 Fighting Falcons. For the Japanese Blue Impulse, the occasion marked the first time that they had performed on foreign soil; their performance with coloured smoke was extremely impressive. Other highlights of the event included: flypasts by the B-2 Spirit 'Stealth' bomber and vintage aircraft including the B-17 Flying Fortress, a B-24 Liberator, a B-25 Mitchell and an A-26 Invader; famed pilot Chuck Yeager performing combat manoeuvres in his P-51 Mustang named Glamorous Glenn III against a German Me-109G; F-86 Sabres dog fighting with a Russian MiG-15, a STOL demonstration by the USAF's new C-17 Globemaster III strategic transport; and an F-22A Raptor on static display.

These challenging first shows of the season flown at high density altitude and moderate turbulence kicked off what was to be a memorable year. Everywhere we went we were treated to first-class hospitality. The folks in Redding, California certainly led the way by assembling over 20 houseboats on Lake Shasta to host us on our day off, a rare occasion when many of our wives were able to join us. Winnipeg, Manitoba was another memorable stop, the citizens celebrating in the streets following the end of the disastrous Red River flood. They were eager to show everyone in the military how much they appreciated the Canadian Forces invaluable assistance during the crisis.

We were also pleased to be able to participate in two special events in the Maritimes in the summer of '97. The first was the Borden-Carleton, Prince Edward Island airshow which formed part of the celebrations commemorating the grand opening of 'Confederation Bridge.' This 13 km bridge joins Borden-Carleton with Cape Jourimain Island, New Brunswick and has the distinction of being the longest bridge over ice-covered waters in the world. After flying over the bridge during opening ceremonies on the morning of May 31st, the team flew a high show that afternoon as part of the festivities.

The airshows at Bonavista and Harbour Grace, Newfoundland were organized as part of the provincial celebrations to commemorate the 500th anniversary of John Cabot's voyage to the 'New World' on board the *Matthew* in June 1497. Queen Elizabeth II headlined an impressive guest list of dignitaries in attendance for the event. Although poor weather resulted in the cancellation of the show at Bonavista on June 24th, a modified show was flown the following day. Operating out of St. John's on June 28th, we used instrument departures to get above the ground-based fog and then flew a shortened show for the people of Harbour Grace, recovering in the same fashion.

The first two days of July were very busy days for the 1997 team. During the morning of July 1st, the team completed a 'Canada Burst' behind the Parliament Buildings in Ottawa in celebration of Canada's birthday. That evening the team went on stage for the Canada Day celebrations on Parliament Hill. The following morning the team proceeded to the Royal Canadian Mint for the unveiling of a new $20 Canadair CT-114 Tutor collector's coin. The coin features the Snowbirds in a big diamond formation with the squadron crest on one side. The gold cameo inset on the other side portrays Mr. Edward Higgins, a former vice-president of Canadair who was the program manager during the design and construction of the Tutor aircraft.

Our shows in Lethbridge, Alberta on August 16th and 17th had special significance for the team and me personally. Both were dedicated to the memory of Capt Wes MacKay, Snowbird 8 during the 1987 and 1988 seasons who had lost his life in a car accident. Capt MacKay's widow, parents, brothers and all spectators at the show were very moved by the tribute the Snowbirds made to honour our fallen comrade.

As it does every year, our 1997 season on the road ended with the team's traditional 'smoke-oil' party, on this occasion held in Battle Creek, Michigan on September 9th. Largely financed by smoke errors or other minor infractions which resulted in the levy of five dollar fines ('fivers') throughout the season, the smoke-oil party represents the last opportunity for team members to reflect on the season past one last time together in a relaxed atmosphere. With that we returned home to family and friends and flew our last show in Moose Jaw on September 13th."

Darryl Shyiak

The "last chance" check. In a tradition as old as the team itself, as each Snowbird aircraft taxis out for a practice or performance it is carefully scrutinized for any last minute technical snags. The thumbs up from the last crewman is a final signal to each pilot that his aircraft is ready to go. (Garry Cotter)

Although the Snowbirds have been flying the same aircraft for over 30 years, no two annual displays have ever been the same, a testament to the imagination of team members in their quest for aerial excellence. On top, a dynamic twist is added to the solo's head on cross by adding two additional aircraft, thereby giving both a horizontal and vertical dimension to the manoeuvre. On the bottom, the ever popular Twizzle Roll has been dazzling audiences since the mid-1970s. The spectacular backdrop for this shot was Kelowna, British Columbia. (Garry Cotter)

Two perfectly aligned views of the Snowbird stem. Snowbirds 1, 4 and 5 provide the backbone for all Snowbird formations. (Garry Cotter, Doyle R. Buehler)

Snowbirds 1998

"The aircrew tryouts for the 1998 team culminated on October 28th, 1997 and we welcomed three new pilots, a new logistics officer and six new groundcrew to the team. Among them was a new crew chief, Sgt Mark Keller, who had previously served on the team in 1985 and 1986 as an aero-engine technician.

Scheduling for 1998 became a major headache for our coordinators as several larger Canadian airshows were cancelled for a variety of reasons. These included CFB Trenton, CFB Bagotville and Edmonton initially followed by Abbotsford only a few days before the International Council of Air Shows (ICAS) annual convention.. To further complicate the issue, the tragic crash of Swiss Air Flight 111 in August off the shores of Nova Scotia resulted in the cancellation of Atlantic Canada's largest annual show at CFB Shearwater. The team was able to make arrangements to perform at Syracuse, New York instead.

In a departure from tradition for the Snowbirds, it was decided to incorporate a new technique of training and developing pilots selected to fly the line astern position. Beginning with the 1998 team, the new line astern pilot started off his two year tour in the second line astern position and then moved to the first line astern position for his second year. We felt the new process would provide improved stability in the critically important first line astern position while allowing the new second line astern pilot to be trained by someone who had actually flown that position for an entire season.

The first appearance for the 1998 team was to have been a flypast during the opening ceremonies at the 1997 Grey Cup in Edmonton, Alberta. Unfortunately, freezing drizzle, low cloud and fog prevented the team from getting airborne on the big day. However, all members of the team did enjoy being VIP guests during the game at Commonwealth Stadium!

The winter deployment for the 1998 team was to Portland, Oregon where all members of the team conducted school visits and other PR related functions hosted by organizers of the Portland Rose Festival. The deployment turned out to be an extremely successful one, an important opportunity for the team to develop its skills in public relations in addition to practicing its deployment procedures. We followed this up by conducting a highly successful media flight for reporters in the Comox valley area during our spring deployment to Vancouver Island.

BGen J.S. Lucas, Chief of Staff Operations at 1 Canadian Air Division Headquarters in Winnipeg gave us his approval to commence the airshow season on April 30th following our acceptance show. As usual, we were happy to get the show on the road and once again there were many memories.

One of our more unusual appearances took place in Pemberton, British Columbia on July 23rd in the heart of the Canadian Rockies. It was the first time in our 28 year

The first order of business when the team lands at each showsite is the "over-wing," an opportunity for the advance coordinator to brief the other 20 team members on the details pertaining to that specific location – from show times to public relations functions to media interviews. (Garry Cotter)

The tranquil beauty of this photograph illustrates why the name "Snowbirds" is so appropriate for Canada's aerobatic team. (Rafe Tomsett)

history that the team had ever performed in Pemberton, the reason being the topography which made it impossible to put on a full show. Nevertheless, our modified show was warmly received by the local citizens and vacationers alike and it was a pleasure to meet with them after our performance.

After being plagued with thunderstorms during its 1997 airshow, the performers and organizers at the Kamloops Airshow for 1998 were faced with an even more serious problem – a forest fire was burning out of control within 10 miles of the airport. To complicate matters, the wind was blowing the smoke from the forest fire directly over the airport. In true Snowbird fashion, the '98 team flew part of our low show so we were at least able to put on a limited performance for the numerous spectators in attendance.

The airshows performed in California during the 1998 season were very special for the team for a number of reasons. At Salinas it was once again a pleasure to fly alongside the Thunderbirds – we were extremely impressed with their consummate professionalism and many close friendships were made. Salinas was also unique from another perspective in that we flew a twilight performance in advance of the two regular weekend shows. On Friday, September 25th, just as the sun was setting, we performed our nine-plane low show opener and closer. With nine sets of navigation and landing lights on, we were told the team made for a spectacular sight. Prior to one of our final shows of the season, we were pleased to be able to take famed Canadian film director James Cameron flying with the team during its media flight at Travis AFB on October 2nd. Due to the resounding success of his epic

film *Titanic*, Mr. Cameron was inundated with media interviews after the flight to capture his impressions of having flown with Canada's national team.

The last show of the season at Moose Jaw is one every team looks forward to with mixed emotions, particularly for those second year members like myself whose tenure was about to end. Unfortunately, the last performance was not to be for the 1998 team. Poor weather on October 16th prevented us from flying one last show for family, friends and the personnel of CFB Moose Jaw. Although a major disappointment, it did not dampen the pride I felt in handing over the team to my good friend (and former student) Maj Bob Painchaud who would lead the team into its 30th anniversary."

Darryl Shyiak

The Snowbirds made their first appearance in Pemberton, B.C. in 1998, much to the delight of local residents and tourists from as far away as Australia. L to R, Standing – Capts Emmanuel Bélanger, Marcus Walton, Scott Shrubsole, Mike Ayling, Mike VandenBos, Maj Darryl Shyiak (leader), Capts Derek Miller, Jayson Miles-Ingram, Ian McLean, Ian James, Richard Walsh. Kneeling – Cpls Gérard Ménard, Mike Sanikopoulos, Brian Doll, Gary LeCourtois, Sgt Mark Keller, Cpls Travis Laslo, d'Arcy Monaghan, Troy Bartlett, MCpl Marco Asselin, Cpl Corey Stangeland. Missing – Capt Mike Perry, Cpl Ken Mick. (Garry Cotter)

Snowbirds 1999

In terms of airshow familiarity, Maj Bob Painchaud is one of the most experienced Canadian Forces pilots ever to lead the Snowbirds. His airshow career began in 1988 when he was selected to share 'demo pilot' duties on the CF-18 Hornet while serving with 421 Tactical Fighter Squadron at CFB Baden Soellingen in West Germany. Three years later his skills yielded a similar assignment with 419 Sqn while serving as an instructor on the CF-5 at CFB Cold Lake. These two years of low-level airshow experience were instrumental in winning him one of the coveted solo positions as Snowbird 9 for the 1992 and 1993 Snowbird seasons. Now, a scant six years later, he was back to command the team. Under Maj Painchaud's leadership, the Snowbirds have seen some of the most significant changes in their long and distinguished history:

"When informed that I had been selected to command the 1999-2000 Snowbirds, I knew that I would soon reach the pinnacle of my military flying career. I was fully aware that the next two years would perhaps be the most challenging, exciting and rewarding years of my life as a pilot. My dream had come true. Little did I know that I would be faced with a devastating and disturbing situation within a few weeks of taking command.

Shortly following the change of command parade and the selection of the new team members, we were privileged to perform a flypast over Winnipeg Stadium to commemorate the official opening of the 1998 Grey Cup game. The morale of the team was soaring and we had barely been together for a month. How could I ever have imagined that while I was away in Las Vegas for the annual ICAS convention, tragedy would strike as I was on

The year 1999 marked the 75th anniversary of the RCAF and 431 Squadron's 25th year as an active squadron. (Garry Cotter)

my return trip home. On December 10th, 1998 a training accident took the life of Snowbird 2, Capt Michael VandenBos, affectionately known as 'Woodboot' to his teammates. This was a very difficult experience to live through and left our entire team in disbelief and profound sadness.

Earlier that summer, I had selected Capt Ian Searle to return to the team as one of our coordinators. Everyone knew that Ian would serve the Snowbirds very well in his new capacity. However, we never imagined how fortunate we would be to have him on board. As a former outer right wing pilot with the 1995-1996 team, Ian quickly agreed to help out the team by relinquishing his new position to replace 'Woodboot' as Snowbird 2.

The months which followed were long, strenuous and quite often frustrating. The weather in the new year saw some of the most adverse weather conditions imaginable. The result was that flying continuity was non-existent and our progression insufficient, possibly the worst in our training history. Our struggle to move forward was dealt another severe blow in February when six out of our nine show pilots were grounded as a result of imposed parachute weight limitations for all Tutor pilots exceeding a weight of 185 pounds. For the next three weeks, only myself and the two line astern pilots were able to take to the air and work on the show profiles. Regrettably, due to his large stature, Capt Warren Wright

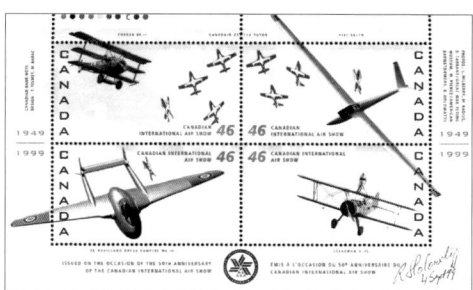

Canada Post helped the Canadian International Air Show celebrate its 50th anniversary in 1999 with this special issue that included the Snowbirds. (via Dr. R. Holowatyj)

Above – The 1999 training season got off to a tragic start with the loss of Snowbird 2, Capt Michael VandenBos, a young man who revelled in his role as an ambassador for Canada. (Rick Radell) Below – In September 2001, the citizens of Michael's hometown of Whitby, Ontario named Captain Michael VandenBos Public School in tribute to his memory. (courtesy Capt Michael VandenBos Public School)

Left – Professional photographer Warren Liebmann took this fine study of Snowbird 1 using a technique he has coined "silver reflections" – aircraft photographed at night on a water soaked tarmac. (Warren Liebmann via 431 Sqn).

There were several not so subtle reminders in 1999 that the Snowbirds and their aircraft have been around for awhile. The first was when Tutor 114006 joined the team for the first time – having come off the Canadair assembly line 35 years earlier in 1964. The oldest pilot on the team was four years old the day 006 flew her maiden flight; most team members had not been born! Even more telling was when Capt Tim Rawlings made the team, the son-in-law of former 1981-1982 Snowbird Capt Sonny Lefort. Ironically, both flew the No. 5 (second line astern) position. Finally, still not tired of taking Snowbird photographs, honorary Snowbirds Rafe Tomsett (left) and Ed Drader (right) were still taking pictures 19 and 20 years respectively after they snapped their first shots of the little red and white jets. (Canadair Photo, Ed Drader, Alice Drader)

(our new inner pilot) had to be removed from the team as a result of the new restrictions. Losing Warren at this point in the training season was another very depressing setback. After the unfortunate task of informing him that he would no longer be able to continue flying with the 1999 team, I remember returning home despondent, wondering aloud what I had done to deserve all that had transpired. Only my wife Terie had ever seen me like this and

knew how much I was now suffering. With her words of encouragement and another breath of courage, I elected to continue fighting even harder – I am glad and proud that I did. Following this latest setback, our team was very fortunate that Capt Norm Dequier, a former solo pilot during the 1994-1995 season accepted my offer to replace Warren as Snowbird 3 for the 1999 season. Fortunately, Warren was able to rejoin us for the 2000 season once the para-

chute problems had been resolved.

The next step was to find a new coordinator. After weeks of searching for a replacement, Capt Eric Pootmans, an instructor pilot with the 'Big 2,' volunteered to fill the position for the 1999 season. As a result, Capt Emmanuel Bélanger agreed to remain on the team as Snowbird 10 for an additional year through the 1999 and 2000 seasons thereby ensuring future continuity.

The 1999 Snowbirds visited the Canadian Warplane Heritage Museum at Mount Hope Airport in Hamilton, Ontario and met up with two famous aircraft that formerly served on 431 Sqn, the Lancaster bomber and F-86 Sabre (in Golden Hawk livery). L to R, top to bottom on the Golden Hawk – Capts Eric Pootmans, Tim Rawlings, Craig Brown, Mike Perry, Emmanuel Bélanger, Cpls Rich Slonski, Ken Mick, Capts Ian James, Jayson Miles-Ingram, Ian Searle. In the Lancaster – Maj Bob Painchaud (leader), MCpl Travis Laslo, Sgt Mark Keller. With the Snowbird – Cpls Corey Stangeland, Chris Hardy, Mike Sanikopoulos, Maj Ian McLean, MCpl Marc Elder, Cpls Brad Fulton, Paul Bourgoin, Gérard Ménard. On the wing – Capts Patrick Ouellet, Norm Dequier. (Rick Radell)

In spite of our extreme bad luck, we managed to successfully get the remaining pilots airborne again and by mid-April had assembled an appealing and unique show sequence. Our efforts paid off as we departed for a short deployment to Cold Lake, Alberta from April 7th to 10th as part of a mini squadron exchange with 410 Sqn. We then continued our journey to Comox for our spring training camp, returning home just over two weeks later for our acceptance show.

Throughout the 1999 season, it was refreshing to see that the entire team was doing well, morale was high and our shows were being well received. With over 70 performances in more than 55 locations across North America, we were busy. Often, we were required to perform four shows a week while conducting a myriad of public relations activities, many in commemoration of the 75th anniversary of Canada's Air Force. Flypasts to celebrate Canada Day over Parliament Hill in Ottawa and the opening of the Pan American Games in Winnipeg were among other highlights of the season.

Although the start of our 1999 season was tragic, challenging and uncertain, the airshow season was highly successful and ended on a very high note. At our year-end show on October 16th, 1999 the squadron was presented our Squadron Colours in a moving ceremony attended by many former Snowbirds. The day was made extra special by the presentation of the 1999 Golden Hawks Award by the Air Force Association of Canada for outstanding performance in the field of Canadian military aviation. It was indeed an honour for the team to have been recognized in this fashion during a difficult year which highlighted the 25th anniversary of 431 Sqn and its proud history."

Bob Painchaud

Two profiles of the famous Snowbird five-plane line-abreast formation, from above and below. (Rafe Tomsett, left; Russ Heinl, right)

Two new twists to the show included a wing rock by the solos immediately after takeoff and a tightly flown echelon parade which appeared from stage right behind the crowd. (Russ Heinl)

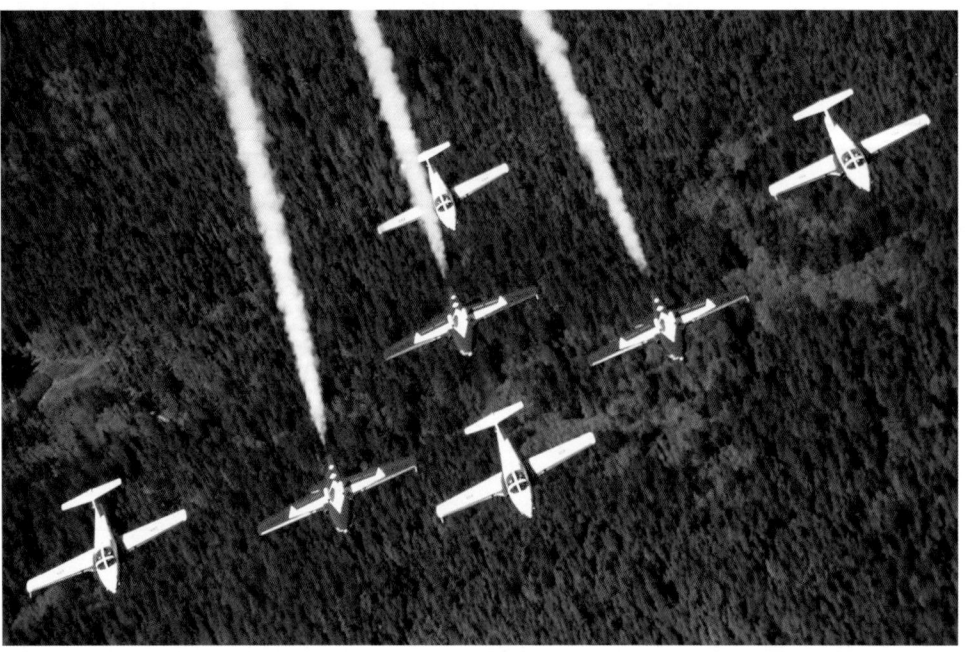
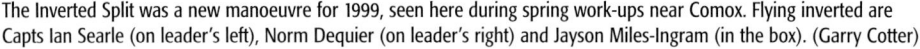

The Inverted Split was a new manoeuvre for 1999, seen here during spring work-ups near Comox. Flying inverted are Capts Ian Searle (on leader's left), Norm Dequier (on leader's right) and Jayson Miles-Ingram (in the box). (Garry Cotter)

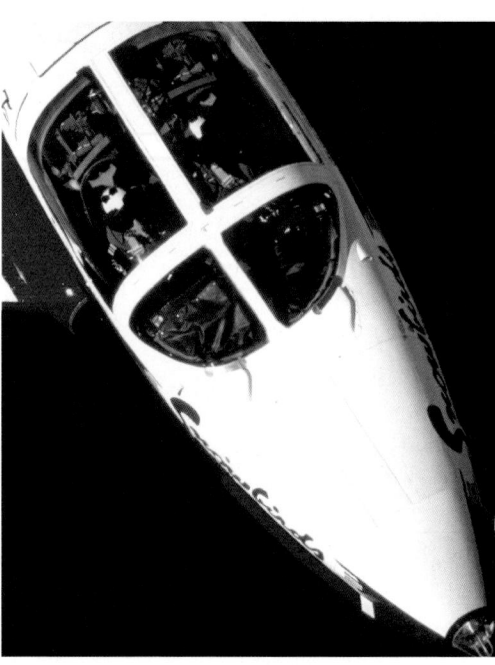

Maj Bob Painchaud tucks in close to the Buffalo photo ship to allow this unique perspective. (Ed Drader)

On 10 Apr 58 Her Majesty Queen Elizabeth II approved the awarding of Squadron Standards to operational RCAF squadrons upon achieving 25 years of cumulative service.

431 Sqn received its "Queen's Colours" on 15 October 99 denoting 25 years of service as a bomber, fighter and air demonstration squadron. The presentation of the Squadron Standard was made by the Lieutenant Governor of Saskatchewan, the Honourable J.E.N. Wiebe, on behalf of Her Majesty. Also in attendance were MGen Lloyd C. Campbell, CMM, CD, Commander of 1 Canadian Air Division and Col Marc Ouellet, CD, Commander of 15 Wing Moose Jaw.

The Colours were accepted on behalf of all past and present squadron personnel by Maj Bob Painchaud, CD, Commanding Officer of 431 (Air Demonstration) Sqn. The 431 Squadron Standard is a double silk flag, hand embroidered on both sides with a border composed of the floral emblems of the ten provinces of Canada. The unit heraldic badge is located in the centre of the flag surrounded by the 11 battle honours earned by squadron personnel during World War II. At right, LCol, the Reverend Stan Johnstone, consecrates the Squadron Standard in an age-old tradition as the Honourable J.E.N. Wiebe looks on. (Photos via 431 Sqn)

Into the New Millennium Snowbirds 2000-2001

1971-2000

"Just before Christmas of 1999, I was honoured to learn that I would have the opportunity to lead the Snowbirds for a third year through the 2001 season. However, I did not fully appreciate at the time that this decision would become increasingly important in the latter stages of 2000 as a result of the phase-out of the Tutor from the pilot training program at 15 Wing in Moose Jaw.

In a significant change to our previous operations, we received air force approval to implement a three-year rotation plan for the team demonstration pilots versus the traditional two year tour. Although new to the Snowbirds, similar plans have been used by several of the world's aerobatic teams such as the RAF Red Arrows, Italian *Frecce Tricolori* and FAF *Patrouille de France*. Although I realized there would be

A most historic event highlighted the 2000 show season – the 30th anniversary of the Snowbirds. As a result, over 90 airshows were scheduled to commemorate this milestone and the Millennium year. Our season got underway with a northern swing through the Yukon, Northwest Territories and Alaska. This was followed by a long excursion to Fort Lauderdale, Florida where an estimated crowd of three million spectators witnessed our performance over the course of three days. With an average of four weekly airshows scheduled, many flying hours were expended transiting from

and its 30th anniversary, brought the largest ever gathering of alumni, honoraries and friends back to Moose Jaw to celebrate. We were proud to show off our new office space renovated over the course of the summer and to re-dedicate the Col O.B. Philp Snowbirds Hall of Fame in the presence of so many former team members.

With the implementation of our new rotation plan, only two new pilots were required for the 2001 airshow season. Following the annual fall tryouts, the Snowbirds were in the public eye once again with the selection of Capt Maryse Carmichael as Snowbird 3, the first female pilot to win a position on the show team in 30 years and a first among the world's military aerobatic teams. Blessed with the ability, drive and personality to fulfil her new role, Maryse will undoubtedly benefit the Snowbirds from a public relations perspective and will serve as a role model and source of inspiration for many youth across North America.

Farewell to "56" Barrack Block 56 was the home of the Snowbird office and squadron lounge for over 25 years. Within the walls of that humble edifice a new team was born each year, one that would slowly grow and mature into a close-knit fraternity like no other. It was a place of work and play – one which no Snowbird who strolled down her historical hallway of memories will ever forget. She was relegated to the annals of history in 2000 in the name of progress, a new housing complex for student pilots rising over the hallowed site. (Jacquie Perrin)

some challenges to the validity of this plan, I was confident that it could benefit the Snowbirds by reducing the need to change half of the team each year, thereby increasing the overall experience level from year to year.

one showsite to another and a large number of public relations activities were once again conducted throughout the course of the summer. The year-end show, marked by the formation of an independent squadron maintenance organization for the Snowbirds

Today, business is much different on 431 Air Demonstration Sqn. Significant changes associated with the introduction of the NATO Flying Training in Canada program in Moose Jaw, a downsized air force and the significant expansion of the Snowbird main-

The 2000 edition of the Snowbirds represented the team's 30th anniversary. On the left, the officers. L to R, standing – Capts Robert Mitchell, Craig Brown, Maj Tim Rawlings, Capts Chris Van Vliet, Ian Searle, Warren Wright, Maj Bob Painchaud (leader). L to R, kneeling – Capts Dan Morrison, Andrew Cook, Emmanuel Bélanger, Bob Reichert, Patrick Ouellet. At right, the groundcrew – Cpls Nancy Anderson, Kevin Madower, Chris Hardy, MCpl Marc Elder, Sgt Jim Flach, Cpls Harold Duff, Paul Bourgoin, Brad Fulton (on right), Ken Mick, Dean Gullacher, Rich Slonski. (John McQuarrie, Ed Drader)

Over the years the Snowbirds have been photographed from almost every possible angle. This shot is unusual because Capt Emmanuel Bélanger is overtaking the formation on the outside of the loop, the result of pulling up with a much higher initial airspeed. Photographer Garry Cotter managed to capture the shot through the top of the canopy of Snowbird 10 as they whisked by. (Garry Cotter)

tenance organization have placed greater demands on the unit. In spite of the fact that the dual role of commanding officer and team lead has become increasingly more difficult, the job continues to offer the greatest professional rewards and experience.

When I look back over my three years leading the team, I realize that the squadron had to cope with much adversity. However, when I reflect on our success and accomplishments, I remain proud; proud that we successfully overcame the aftermath of a tragic accident and subsequently accomplished so much over the course of that period. As the 2001 season drew to a close, I felt blessed for the trust and confidence that was placed upon me. To have been given the opportunity to lead such a superb and unique team of professionals was indeed an honour. I know that it is teamwork, perseverance and dedication that allowed us to overcome the difficult times and succeed throughout. I wish to pay tribute to all of those who served under my command. They truly epitomized the skill, professionalism, and teamwork of all of those who serve in the Canadian Forces and exemplified the 31-year-old traditions of the Snowbirds."

Bob Painchaud

As a footnote to the end of the 2001 season, the Snowbirds were pleased to participate in the opening of a new public school in Whitby, Ontario immediately following their annual appearances over the Labour Day weekend in Toronto. Having made hundreds of school visits throughout their history, it was of special significance that this school was named in the memory of Capt Michael VandenBos who lost his life in a training accident in December 1998. The school was officially dedicated in the presence of Michael's parents and a host of dignitaries and special guests. The Chief of the Air Staff, LGen L.C. Campbell, presented a portrait of Michael to the school to honour his memory.

CAPT. MARYSE CA

October in Moose Jaw means the end of another Snowbird season and for a number of team members the culmination of the most rewarding flying tour they will ever have. But for every team member that departs, another fresh face will step forward to take their place. At right, Capt Maryse Carmichael became one of those new faces in the fall of 2000, making history as the first female pilot in the world to earn a position on a military aerobatic team. (Roman Holowatyj, Rafe Tomsett)

The Canadian Aerophilatelic Society has been a proud supporter of the Snowbirds for many years, producing first day covers on Canada Day (July 1st) each year. Here, the 30th anniversary issue in 2000 signed by the team pilots. (courtesy Maj Dick Malott, CAS)

Every photographer's dream is being able to shoot the Snowbirds from the open ramp of a Canadian Forces Buffalo courtesy of 442 Sqn at CFB Comox. Here, two fine examples of the results, the shadow in the lower photo telling a story in itself. (Garry Cotter, John McQuarrie)

The first Snowbird team of the new millennium. L to R, Front row – Capts Rick Thompson, Dan Morrison, Jean-Pierre Turcotte, Craig Brown, Maj Ian Searle, Capts Chris Van Vliet, Wayne Mott, Maj Bob Painchaud (leader), Capts Maryse Carmichael, Warren Wright, Robert Mitchell, Bob Reichert, Andy Cook, Eric Pootmans, Jayson Miles-Ingram.

2nd Row: MWO Randy Doan, Sgt Allan Ecker, MCpls Warren Hruska, Nancy Anderson, Cpls Mike Grimard, Martin Martel, Richard Pilon, Sgt Jim Flach, Cpl Kevin Madower, MCpl Dean Gullacher, Cpl Harold Duff, MCpl Mark Gegner, Cpl Jean-Pierre Bérubé, Mrs. Marg Fowler.

3rd Row: Cpl Chris Martin, MCpl Phil White, Sgt Dan Ross, MCpl Pat Gugel, WO Barry Silk, Cpls Mike Pelletier, Al Cole, MCpl Ken Mick, Cpls Dave Kopp, Greg Folliott, Sgt Al Beasley, Cpls Rob Oddy, Cindy Singleton, Ronald Robson.

4th Row: Cpls Dieter Kempter, Brian Phillips, Darell Fournier, Joel Charron, Dave Corry, Sgt Jean LaFramboise, Cpls Ian Rensby, Maryse LaFramboise, Bob O'Reilly, Sheldon Stotz, MCpl Dave Bell, Cpls Brad Fayant, Mickey Kelly, Donald Cathcart, Steve Bird.

5th Row: MCpl Tom Critchley, Cpls Ryan Willett, Terry Allain, Chris Hardy, MCpl Brian Herde, Sgt Bob Bauer, Cpl Rich Slonski, MCpls Dave Lott, Paul Silvey, Cpl Brad Fulton, MCpl Fred Martin, Cpl Mike Underwood, MCpl Sean Stone.

Missing from photo: Sgts Jerry Erickson, Mary Meier, MCpls Marc Elder, Dan High, Cpls Cheryl Beaulieu, Duane Benz, Paul Bourgoin, Dallas Cave, Lee Devine, Lisa England, Wanda Madower, Pat Marceau, Rick Probetts, Kam Singh. (DND, MCpl Senecal)

The publication of this book will coincide with the completion of the Snowbirds 32nd airshow season under a new commander, Maj Steve Will, a previous member of the 1989 and 1990 teams. A highly experienced CF-18 fighter pilot and veteran of the Kosovo conflict in the Balkans, Maj Will returned to the team with a renewed enthusiasm for the Snowbird mandate and an air of optimism for the future:

Over 30 years of Snowbird airshows has not dampened the enthusiasm of Canadians for their aerobatic team – there will always be autographs to sign and questions to answer after each show. (Ed Drader, Alice Drader, Dan Dempsey)

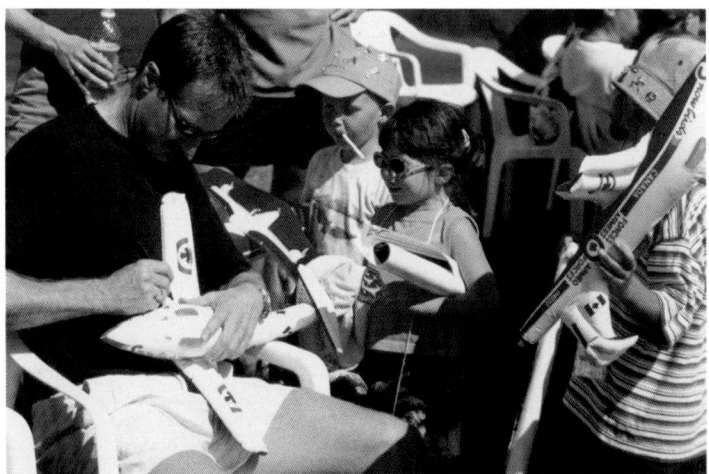

Snowbirds 2002

"When I learned that I would be appointed commanding officer of the Snowbirds for the 2002 to 2004 airshow seasons, it took some time for the enormity of that fact to sink in. It seems like only yesterday that I was flying the inner left wing on the team as Snowbird 3. To move up those couple of numbers to the Snowbird 1 position was literally a dream come true, not to mention a quantum leap in responsibility.

I contemplated my good fortune with a mixture of awe and anticipation. Even now as we travel across Canada, I remain awed by the history and continued popularity of Canada's longest serving aerobatic team. For over 30 years the Snowbirds have been regarded as a world-class demonstration team and have proven themselves worthy ambassadors of our great country. Many men and women before us have worked incredibly hard to create that reputation and I know all of us on the team today share a common desire to preserve both that reputation and the proud traditions of the Snowbirds and their predecessors.

During the 10 months since my change of command parade the time has literally flown by. Having been blessed with unusually good weather during the training season we managed 160 missions before performing our acceptance show. Of course, for the third year members the training period seemed endless (not another up-and-down!) – but I'm positive that the new arrivals would have gladly taken

Maj Steve Will's early exposure to the air force through the Royal Canadian Air Cadets has led him to a rewarding career that has taken him from the cockpit of the CF-18 Hornet to his second tour on the Snowbirds, this time as commanding officer and team leader for the 2002-2004 seasons. (DND Photos)

another 20 or so sorties before performing in front of their first real audience.

As usual, Comox was the highlight of the workups with challenging flying

The 2002 Snowbird Show Team. L to R, Front row – MCpl Martin Martell, Cpl Chris Martin, MCpl Mike Grimard, Cpl Mike Pelletier, Sgt Dan Ross, Cpl Richard Pilon, Cpl Harold Duff, Cpl Rick Probetts, MCpl Dean Gullacher (missing Cpl Jean-Marc Brien). Back row – Lt Jay Walker, Capt Lyle Holbrook, Capt Wayne Mott, Capt Andy Mackay, Maj Steve Melanson, Maj Maryse Carmichael, Maj Steve Will (team leader), Capt Chris Bard, Capt Warren Wright, Capt Rob Mitchell, Capt Bob Reichert, Capt Andy Cook.

Snowbird 2002 Home Team. Front Row (Left to Right) – Capt Jayson Miles-Ingram, Capt Dan Morrison, Cpl Darrell Fournier, Cpl Ian McIvor, Capt Arlene McGuire, WO Roger Arseneau, MCpl Russ Davies, Cpl Rick Yuke, Cpl Joel Charron, Cpl Sheldon Stotz, MCpl Dawn Williams, Capt Rick Thompson (Sqn SAMEO), CWO Randy Doan (Sqn CWO), Cpl Daniel McIntyre. Middle Row – MCpl Cindy Singleton, MCpl Paul Silvey, Cpl Micky Kelly, Sgt Mary Meier, MCpl Mike Underwood, Sgt Bob Bauer, Cpl Duane Benz, MCpl Brian Herde, Sgt Marc Elder, Sgt Al Beasley, WO Barry Silk, Cpl Ian Rensby, Mrs. Marg Fowler, MCpl Rich Slonski. Back Row – MCpl Shawn Stone, MCpl Glen Duvall, Pte Christian Lentz, Cpl Greg Folliott, Cpl Don Cathcart, MCpl Pat Gugel, Cpl Steve Hawkins, Cpl Eric Moisan, Cpl Brian Phillips, Cpl Jean-Pierre Berube, Cpl Alvin Cole, Pte Matt Faulkner, MCpl Nancy Anderson, Cpl Terry Allain, Cpl Wanda Madower, Pte Lynn Myers, Cpl Terry McLaren, Sgt Grant Beeber, MCpl Dwane Barcier, Cpl Kevin Madower. (via 431 Sqn)

Teamwork is the essence of the Snowbird operation, both on the ground and in the air. At Comox in the spring of 2002, while the groundcrew refined their "road maintenance" procedures, the pilots put the final polish on their aerial routines including an impressive nine-plane line-abreast formation. Back in Moose Jaw, the home support team completed major overhauls on several aircraft, reuniting them with their pilots in time for the show season. Inset, the official heraldry celebrating the 50th anniversary of the reign of Her Majesty Queen Elizabeth II adorned the Snowbird aircraft throughout the 2002 season. (Rafe Tomsett)

conditions and a great opportunity for the team to bond before starting the show season. We enjoyed some phenomenal flying, losing only one day to poor weather as we put the final polish on our show. Accompanying us to Comox last spring was a film crew shooting a new CBC documentary on the training of a Snowbird. Entitled *1800 Seconds*, it aired nationwide on Canada Day. Having the film crew around in Comox was an added bonus as our new arrivals quickly got accustomed to being in front of a camera. As usual, we also did our annual photo flights – the weather cooperated and photographers Rafe Tomsett and Garry Cotter, as always, came through with some spectacular shots.

Arriving back in Moose Jaw it was time to lay everything on the line and fly our acceptance show. The show on the 'practice day' before the big event was less than stellar in our eyes, and a lengthy debrief with some frank discussion ensued. The next day dawned clear and I could feel the enthusiasm in the briefing room – the pilots were chomping at the bit to get airborne. Once in the air, we knew the day would be a difficult one, with high winds and turbulence that created bumps all the way around the loops and rolls. Everyone performed brilliantly however and we came down feeling very good about our performance in such challenging conditions.

Three days later, after saying long goodbyes to our families we were finally on the road for our first swing. Redding, California was our first road show of the season on May 4th where we were again blessed with perfect flying weather. Nerves were understandably tight during our pre-flight briefing, but everyone was focused and keen to get that first show behind them. The crowd of over 30,000 was treated to a fine show and I was extremely proud of everyone on the squadron that weekend. We had trained hard for seven months and the fruit of that labour was obvi-

ous in the smiling faces of the children who clamoured for autographs at the end of the show.

Among many highlights of the 2002 season, we were very pleased to help Abbotsford celebrate its 40th anniversary along with the USAF Thunderbirds. We were also particularly happy to help welcome the RAF Red Arrows to Toronto for the first time ever over the Labour Day weekend. The weather during the three day Canadian International Air Show was some of the best ever seen at the show and we were honoured to fly with the Red Arrows during their Saturday show, reciprocating later that afternoon when we took their entire team flying with us to close the show. This may well have been the first time two national aerobatic teams have ever flown with each other during a public show. We flew one additional show with the Reds at the Nova Scotia International Air Show the following weekend at which time they began their journey back to England. All in all, our five-and-a-half month airshow season went very well and generated many fond memories.

As we now look forward, we face times of great change on the team. Our Tutor jet, which has faithfully served the Snowbirds for the past 32 show seasons, will be retired from the rigours of demonstration flight in the not too distant future. The passing of this nimble little lady will indeed mark the end of an era. While it will be sad to see the Tutor eventually go, the team will be at a true watershed as it transitions to a new aircraft. One of the contenders should be the BAE Systems Hawk, the same sleek trainer that we were privileged to fly in with the Red Arrows. This aircraft would certainly do the Snowbird colours proud and future team members would be privileged to continue anew the Snowbird legacy.

To command this fine squadron on behalf of the Canadian Forces is indeed an honour. In this time of transition, I will continue to lead the Snowbirds with an eye on the past … but a commitment to the future."

Stephen Will

Flying High with the Snowbirds

A common question posed to Snowbird pilots along the fence line following a show is how they are able to fly so closely together with such precision and grace, seemingly effortlessly. Imaginative theories from novice airshow spectators always bring a smile – the aircraft must all be controlled by the leader using radar, or they must all be tied together by some technological wizardry! And those two solo pilots – how can they come so close without hitting each other? The answer of course is that there is no special magic or technology in a Snowbird display – it simply boils down to hand-eye coordination, acute concentration to sharpen reflexes … and months of practice.

Those who aspire to fly with the Snowbirds must combine a burning desire with personality and flying skills as the road to selection is not easy. Time and again over many years it has been proven that 'desire' is often the difference between a pilot who makes the team and one that does not. Since all Snowbird pilots are volunteers, competitive tryouts are held each year, normally in early November, to select the best available pilots for the team from those names that have been forwarded to the team by career managers. Prospective candidates are first screened by their own units and must be specifically recommended prior to consideration by the team. In general, a two-to-one ratio has been used for the tryouts each fall, that is two candidates try out for each open position. Up until the end of the 30th anniversary of the team in 2000, this usually translated into eight candidates trying out for four positions. By changing half the team each season, a uniform level of expertise was maintained from year to year. However, these numbers will no longer be required with the introduction of a

For those young officers and non-commissioned members who aspire to join the Snowbirds, this symbolizes their goal. Making the team is not easy – for those fortunate enough to be selected, the rewards will last a lifetime. (Roman Holowatyj)

three year rotational tour. Notwithstanding, the team will continue to try and attract two tryout candidates for every position available. On paper at least, each of these candidates will have demonstrated the prerequisite personal and professional skills to make the team. The tryouts will soon separate those with the best skills and greatest desire.

The Tryouts

Although all those trying out for the team will have significant jet experience, either as an instructor or fighter pilot, they will be taught new techniques of formation flying which are critical to the Snowbird operation and must be mastered quickly by successful candidates. These include the use of aileron and elevator trim, power management and the use of rudder to maintain lateral position during aggressive formation flying.

Contrary to popular belief however, a Snowbird tryout is not about leaping into a jet aircraft and demonstrating how low you can fly or how much G you can pull. Rather, it is very much about learning, teamwork and self-critiquing honestly in front of peers. Candidates with expanded egos have generally not done well on Snowbird tryouts.

Similarly, many fine pilots have not made the team because they were not able to assimilate rapidly enough the specialized formation techniques that are crucial to the safety of large formation aerobatics.

By the time the actual tryouts begin, all candidates will have had the opportunity to fly with the team in a full show practice and co-solo demonstration in order to experience firsthand their ultimate goal. For most, especially those who have not had the opportunity to do so before, this is at once a breathtaking and eye-watering experience. Even seasoned fighter pilots have been known to proclaim they "had no idea" after coming down from one of these demonstrations. Invariably, most candidates come back grinning widely …

The tryouts are flown at high altitude, 3,000 feet above ground, and traditionally consist of 12 to 14 trips for each candidate. The first few two-plane formations are instructional trips in which the candidates are taught the aforementioned Snowbird techniques of formation flying. The next two trips are used to practice these techniques and then the fun begins – the four-plane phase. This phase is gruelling as each candidate must now demonstrate his prowess while being assessed constantly in the air and on the ground. The manoeuvres flown consist of set routines of pull-ups, wingovers, breaks and rejoins and eventually 360 degree flat turns utilizing up to 4 G. At no time are formation aerobatics flown by the candidates. Once on the ground, usually soaking wet from perspiration, self-debriefs by each candidate are an integral part of the selection process. Not only must they be able to tell everyone what they did wrong during the trip, they must be able to relate what they are going to do to improve on the next sortie. Candidates soon determine that combinations of "power

Snowbird tryouts place volunteer pilots in a competitive environment designed to determine who has the best flying skills and personal attributes to win a position on the team. The formation phase will comprise a maximum of four aircraft; the same box formation will constitute the building block upon which newly selected Snowbirds will take their flying skills to new highs. Eventually, after many practices, the formation will grow to nine aircraft and work their routine down to show altitude. (Terry Leversedge)

anticipation, trim and rudder" frequently figure into the self-critique vocabulary.

In addition to the formation phase, each pilot will fly several trips with the lead solo to have their solo aerobatic abilities assessed – again at high altitude. Up until the year 2000, one of the candidates was selected to fulfill the demanding role of the opposing solo, arguably the most difficult first year position on the team. Generally speaking, the lead solo got to pick his opposing solo providing the latter had shown strong formation skills during the tryouts. For the 2001 season onwards however, the opposing solo will be selected from pilots entering their second year with the team. The same pilot will then make the transition to lead solo in his third and last year. Although head-on co-solo aerobatics are not for everyone, many Snowbird manoeuvres now involve individual rolls at low altitude or inverted formation flying. It is therefore vital that each new team member be capable of performing these manoeuvres confidently and safely.

The last two days of the tryouts are very stressful as candidates fight to stay alive in the competition. Incumbent team members meet daily to discuss the progress of each candidate, knowing full well that they will have to live with their decision through a long summer of airshow performances. The discussions are frank, with each veteran having the opportunity to express his views about each candidate. Invariably, over the years at least five and often six of the candidates have been worthy of selection to the team, the final selection coming down to minor differences and occasionally personalities. It is always difficult for the team leader to break the bad news to a candidate who has flown well but been eased out of the final selection by the narrowest of margins. Today, as in the past, once the incumbents have selected the new pilots, the next task is to decide where each of the successful candidates will fly – inner wing, outer wing or line astern. This is always an interesting and lively debate.

Once the decision is made however, the news spreads like wildfire across the base and soon the Snowbird lounge is full of Snowbirds and members of the 'Big 2' alike eager to congratulate the new members of the team.

The Building of a New Team

For those candidates given the good news, the feeling is overpowering. In my own experience in the fall of 1979, it was the most euphoric moment of my flying career. Making the team as Snowbird 9, the new opposing solo, made the experience just that much more special. From my youngest days of watching the Golden Hawks and Red

The two solo pilots are the last to join the big diamond formation on the outside left and right wings. Having spent most of the early weeks of the workups concentrating on solo aerobatics, they have their work cut out for them. (Roman Holowatyj)

Knight, my childhood dreams had consisted of fanciful loops and endless rolls in F-86 Sabres and T-33s. To now have the opportunity to do it for real was almost too much to believe. Like all successful Snowbird candidates, I had much to be thankful for and many to thank. At the top of the list for me were "Speedy" Fast and Jim Sorfleet. Both were ex-Snowbirds then instructing at 2 CFFTS who taught me the intricacies of solo aerobatics and formation flying in the Tutor. Speedy is still passing along his passion for flying to young students in Portage la Prairie.

For every new team, the day following the tryouts is a special one. The grins are still wide as the new team gathers for the first words of wisdom from "the boss" who outlines his training plan for the next five to six months. There is much work to be done and no time to be wasted. In a methodical and carefully planned routine that has withstood the test of time, the team uses a building block process to work up the show. For the new formation pilots, this means being paired up with a second year pilot in a basic four-plane box formation to further solidify the techniques learned on the tryouts, except now much closer at wing tip formation. The first loops and rolls will soon be accomplished from this formation but not until the first year pilot has been deemed "ready" will he be permitted to fly aerobatic manoeuvres solo.

Gradually over several weeks the formation grows larger as new members are cleared to fly solo – first five, then six and finally seven

Snowbird positions within the big diamond formation are:

SB 1	Team Leader	SB 4	First Line Astern	SB 7	Outer Left Wing
SB 2	Inner Right Wing	SB 5	Second Line Astern	SB 8	Solo
SB 3	Inner Left Wing	SB 6	Outer Right Wing	SB 9	Solo

Of historical note, the line astern and outer wing positions were renumbered to the above designations in 1977. Up until that season the line astern positions were numbered Snowbirds 6 and 7, while the outer right wing was Snowbird 4 and the outer left Snowbird 5. (J.D. Dempsey)

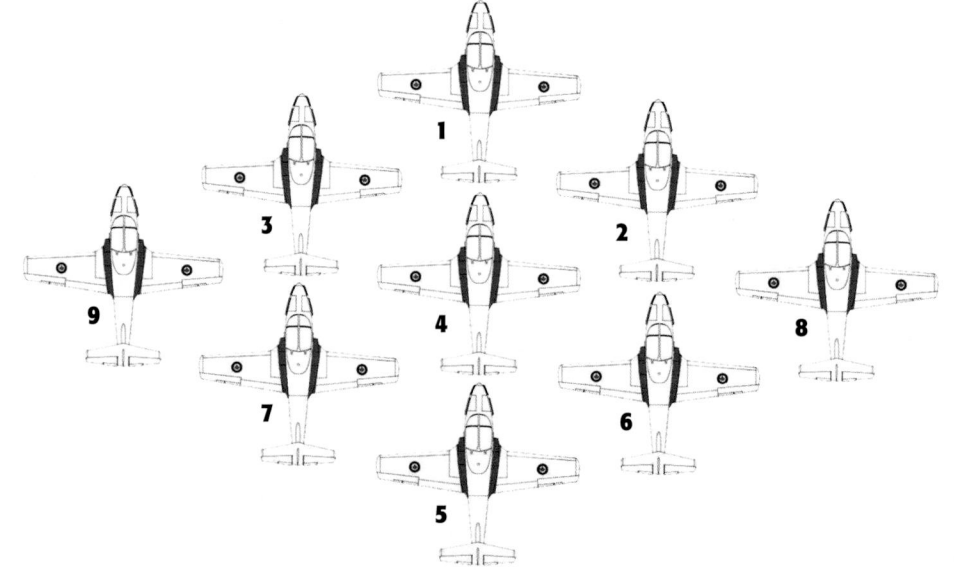

aircraft looping and rolling as one – at high altitude. Only when everyone in the seven-plane is fully comfortable will the solos join the formation to make it a nine-plane. Weather permitting, a common goal is to try and loop and roll the nine-plane before Christmas. As new manoeuvres are introduced in the new year, especially the complex splits and rejoins, first year team members again fly dual with their incumbent counterparts to learn the manoeuvre. As the comfort level of the team increases, the show steadily moves down towards show altitude.

Snowbird practices take place south of Moose Jaw in a small, restricted piece of airspace reserved specifically for the team, their practice field an abandoned World War II training station located just south of Old Wives Lake. Seen from altitude, the traces of the old triangular airfield are still visible at Mossbank where No. 2 Bombing and Gunnery School was formed as part of the British Commonwealth Air Training Plan.

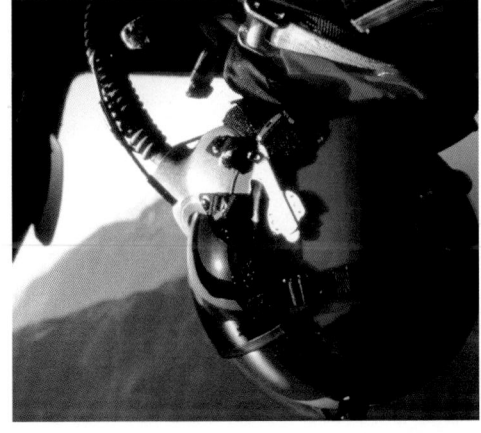

The world of the Snowbird pilot. Formation aerobatics demand a high degree of discipline and focus – there is little margin for error. (Rafe Tomsett)

From low-level however, only an ex-Snowbird might recognize the chunks of concrete now overgrown by prairie weeds as a former runway, its edges barely discernible. And if the remnants of the small, weathered old hangar that serves as "show centre" could talk, it would have a thousand stories to tell …

As the Snowbird show begins to take shape, smoke is introduced to the routine, each pilot turning it on or off at the leader's command through the use of the trigger on his control column. It is always a thrill for the new team to return to base for the first time for their standard overhead break (from 200 feet above ground) while trailing thick white smoke. The long plume will stretch two miles behind them. It is yet another sig-

nal of progress, another small step in the evolution of one of the world's greatest flying displays. There is an additional surge of adrenaline as the team leader makes the familiar radio calls as he approaches the end of the runway – "Snowbirds, smoke now … one back for the pitch … turning right (or left)… speed brakes, go." And no matter how long a person has served at the base, for that brief few seconds when the team flashes overhead all will come to a standstill as every head on the ground turns to watch the team roll into "the pitch" to set up for their landing.

This will be the routine two or three times a day, five days a week for over five months. When the winds of winter keep the team on the ground, weekend flying will become necessary. Once the nine-plane "show opener" has been put together, another key member of the team will begin to make a vital contribution to the show. Every year, one of the team's technicians is appointed as the video man. His job will be to film every full practice at Mossbank (and every show during the season) for review by the team pilots as part of their post-show debriefing ritual. This particular technician will become all too familiar with Mossbank and the harshness of prairie winters in Saskatchewan, often trudging through freshly fallen snow to make his way to "stage centre." And he will be the very first of the year to see the nine twinkling lights of the team's famous entrance that will herald the start of each performance.

Designing the Snowbird Show

Every Snowbird show over the past 32 years has been unique. More than 40 different formations and manoeuvre combinations have been utilized by the various teams over the years. Naturally, perennial favourites such as the Canada burst, heart, downward bomb burst and solo head-on crosses will forever remain an integral part of the show. So too will music, the selection of the same reflecting the unique character of each Snowbird team. The Snowbirds were the first team in the world to set their show to music and have done so with great effect in combination with live commentary from the cockpits of the pilots at various times in the show. Most avid airshow spectators would agree that the aforementioned team entrance head-on to the crowd, combined with music, live check-in and smoke-on, is one of the most stirring sights in aviation.

The fall harvest on the Canadian prairies is over when the Snowbirds begin their workups for the next season. Before long, the team will be practicing over a blanket of white as winter settles in. However, only very poor weather or extremely cold temperatures will keep the team on the ground as they build their show for the next season. (Roman Holowatyj)

One of the most stirring sights in aviation, the nine twinkling lights of the Snowbird nine-plane. This has been the trademark opener of the Snowbird show for over 30 years. (Russ Heinl)

The design of the show each season is left to the discretion of the team leader and his pilots and in this regard the team has enjoyed a great deal of autonomy. However, each manoeuvre must comply with strict safety guidelines in accordance with Canadian Forces regulations. As the Ministry of Transport in Canada and Federal Aviation Administration in the United States are the regulatory agencies for airshow safety in each country, the Snowbirds maintain a good working relationship with both. As one would expect, each and every formation and solo manoeuvre is designed with safety of the viewing public and pilots as the overriding criteria.

Ultimately, the team designs three shows – an unrestricted high show, a modified high show (no looping manoeuvres due to cloud) and a low or flat show, again necessitated by weather conditions. Once the various show routines are designed on paper, the formation and solos work independently to master new manoeuvres prior to integrating them into the show. Hours are spent in pre-practice and post-practice debriefings and not until every member of the nine-plane is fully comfortable does the team move into its final show position with more than a metre of wing overlap in the formation. By the time the team deploys to Comox, British Columbia each spring, only fine tuning adjustments are

Inverted formation flying takes many hours to master. Snowbirds 2, 3 and 4 will begin the long process early in the workup season. (Roman Holowatyj)

required to the show before the season begins. However, in addition to testing the squadron deployment procedures, Comox affords the opportunity for some essential specialist training – conducting aerobatics near mountains with obscured horizons, over-water training and nine-plane takeoff and landing practice. As well, some of the most dramatic photo missions by the team have been launched from Comox, often with the support of a 442 Sqn Buffalo aircraft.

Once the entire show has been designed and tested, a formal operations order detailing all

of the manoeuvres is forwarded to each of the above mentioned agencies for review. The final step in the approval process takes place each April when representatives of the three agencies are invited to Moose Jaw to witness a live performance of the team in what has come to be known as the "acceptance show." The show is approved on behalf of the Minister of National Defence by the Commander of 1 Canadian Air Division or his delegated representative of General officer rank. With approval in hand, the team then prepares to say goodbye to loved ones and embark on their six month airshow season.

Once the team has worked up the basic manoeuvres in their opening sequence, they will move onto the complicated "split" manoeuvres such as those pictured here. First year team members will once again "dual up" with veterans to be shown the techniques utilized for the different breakout patterns at high altitude. Split-second timing is the order of the day as groups of aircraft split out of the formation simultaneously on the cadence of the leader's command: Snowbirds – Split – Now! (Ed Drader)

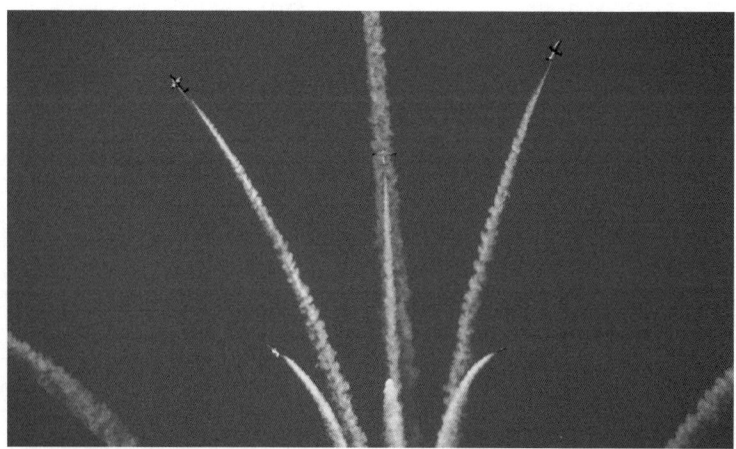

The Snowbirds' nine-plane takeoff and landing are unique among the world's aerobatic teams. They are precision manoeuvres which can only be performed under specific conditions. CFB Comox, with its 200 foot wide runway, provides the first opportunity for the team to work up this aspect of the show. At left, the pilot's perspective through John McQuarrie's wide angle lens as the airspeed reduces to 113 knots. Right, the impressive view from the back of a Buffalo. (Garry Cotter)

By the time the team leaves the smooth air of the Comox Valley, they will be set to take their show on the road for six months. (Jerry Davidson)

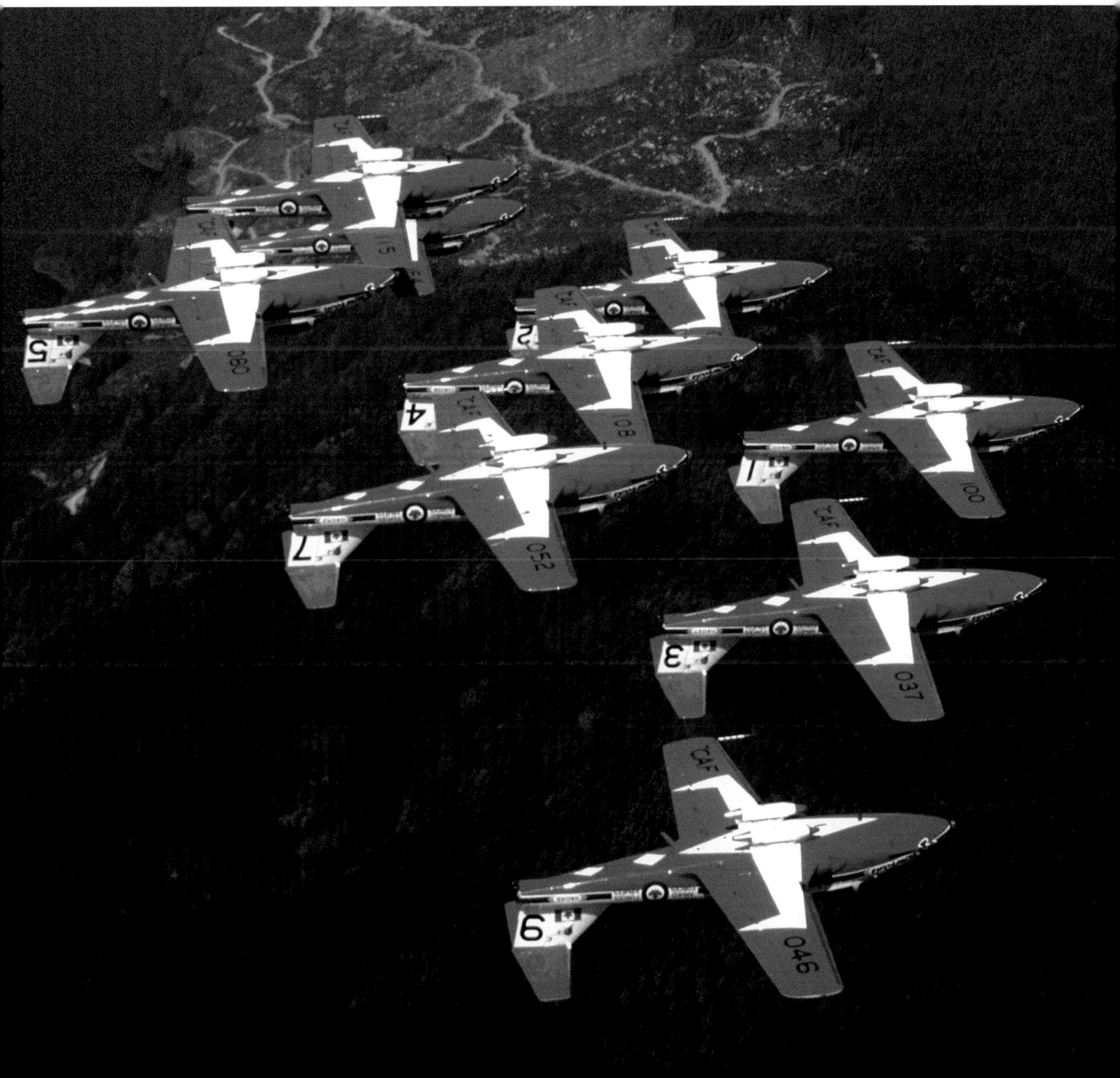

Snowbird Formations Through the Years

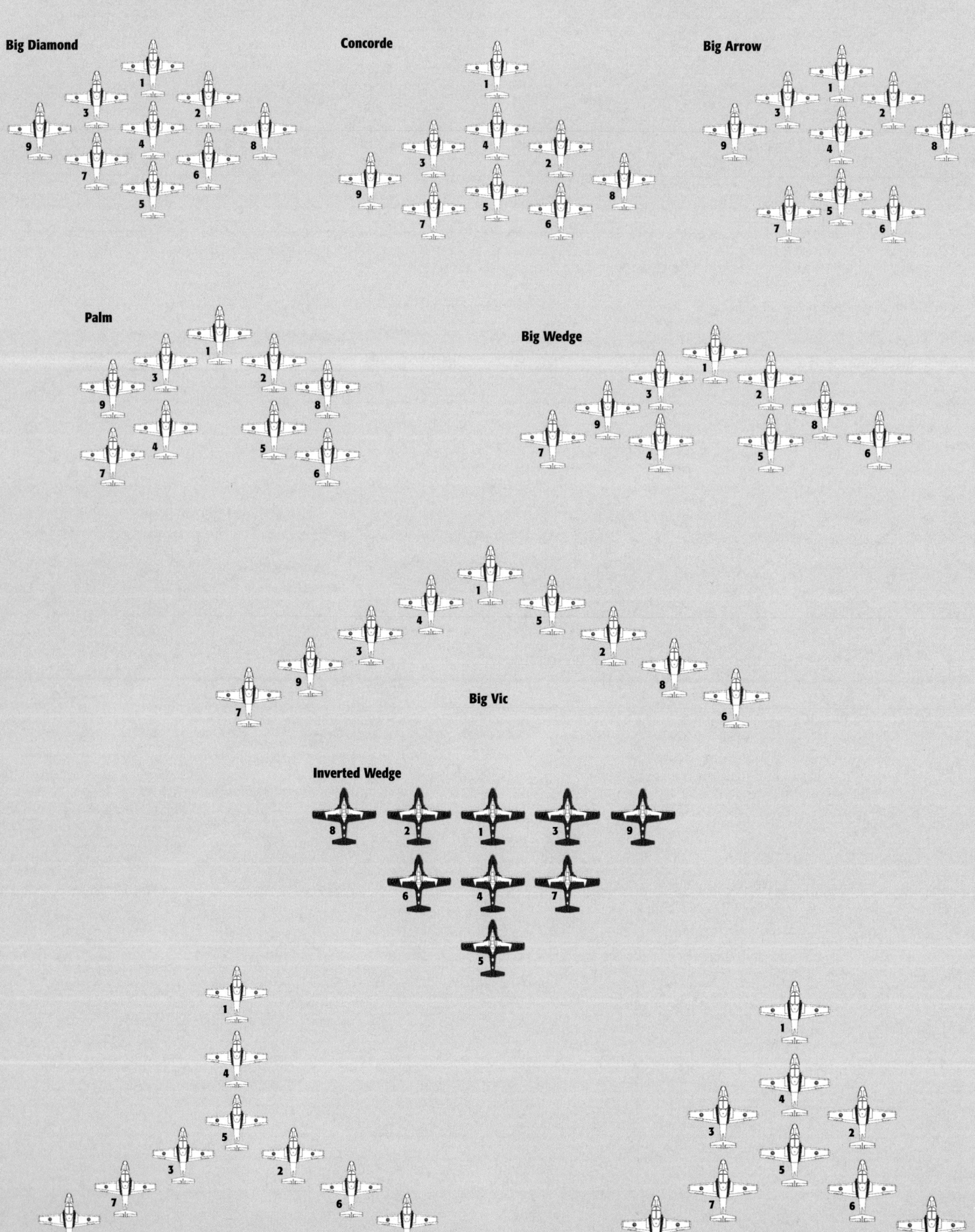

Big Diamond

Concorde

Big Arrow

Palm

Big Wedge

Big Vic

Inverted Wedge

Big Goose

Swept Delta

Viggen

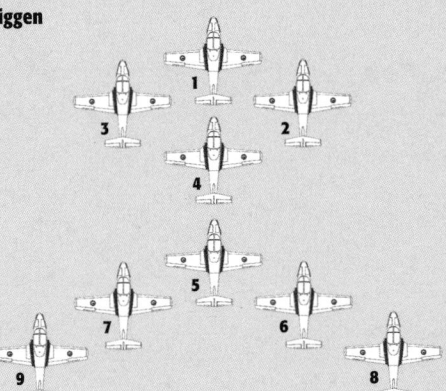

Card Nine

Drakken

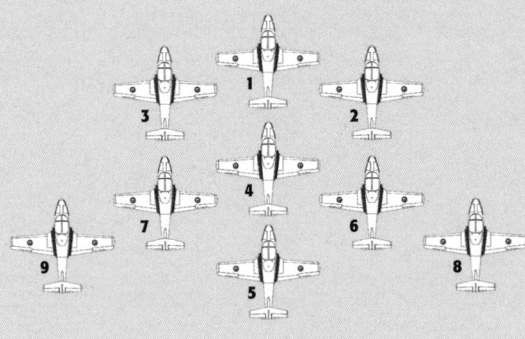

Big Delta

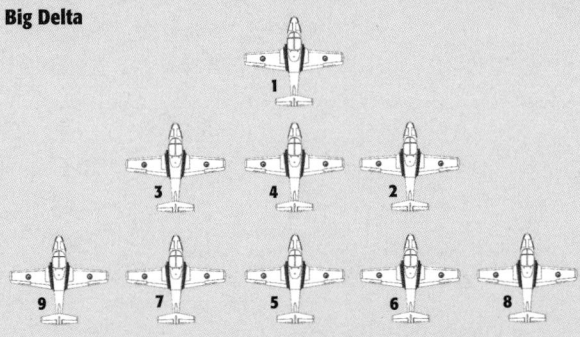

Vulcan

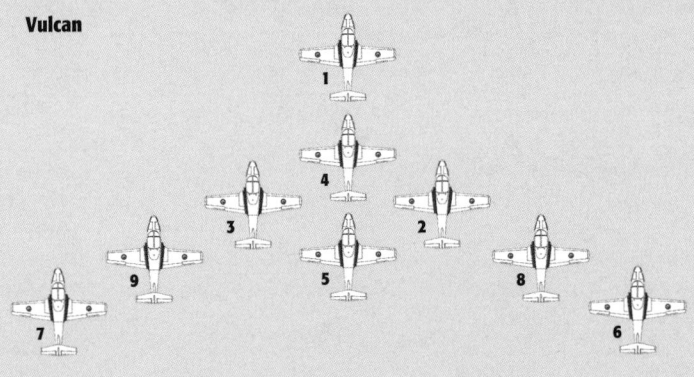

Nine-Plane line-abreast

Nine-Plane Wineglass

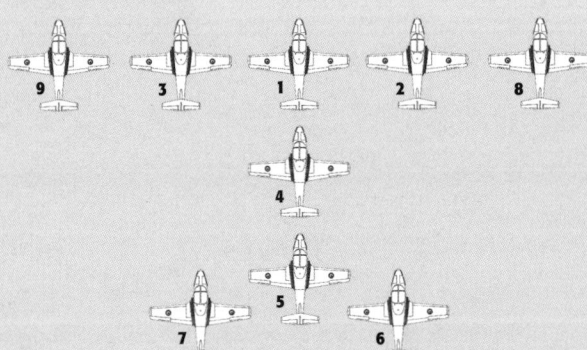

Eagle

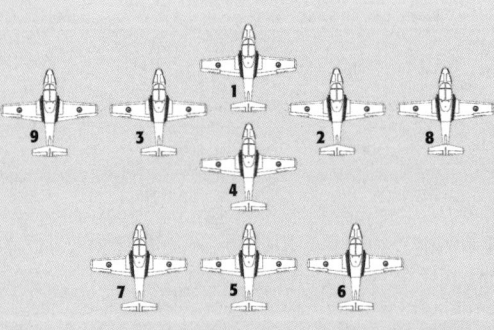

Double Diamond

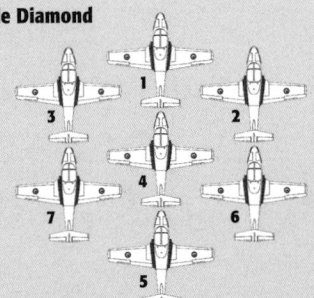

Mini Concorde

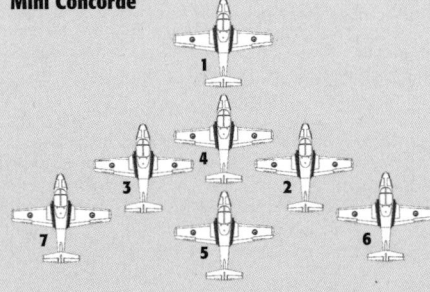

Arrow

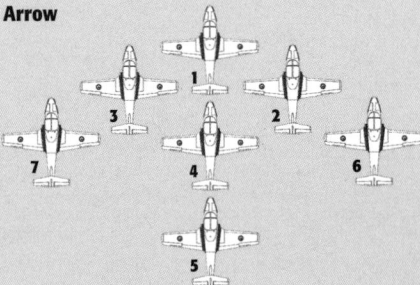

Liberty Bell (1976)

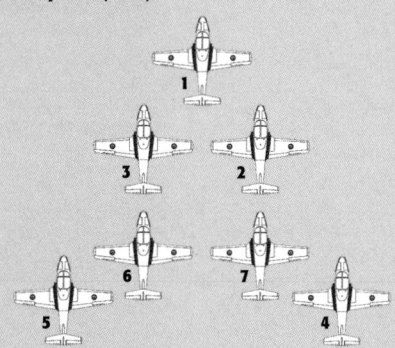

Inverted Wineglass

Dart

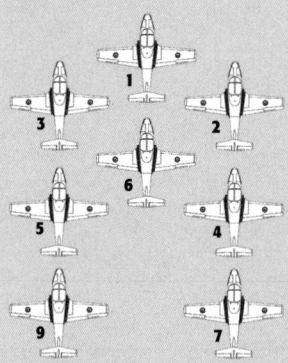

Card Six

Champagne

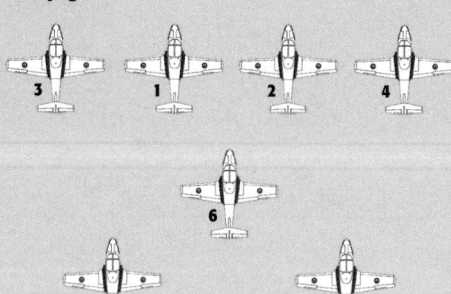

Card Seven

Note: Up until 1977 the line astern pilots flew Snowbirds 6 and 7.
They are now Snowbirds 4 and 5.

Salute

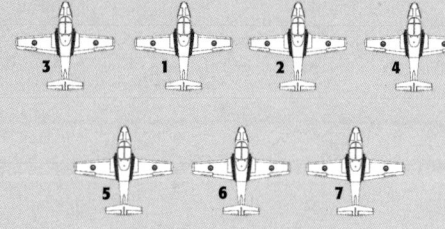

Speedbird

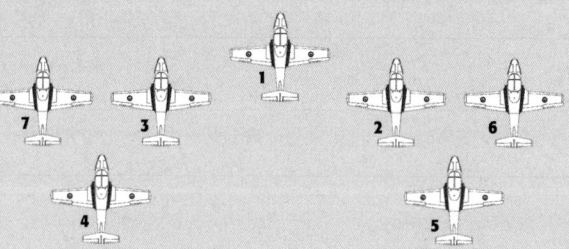

Vic

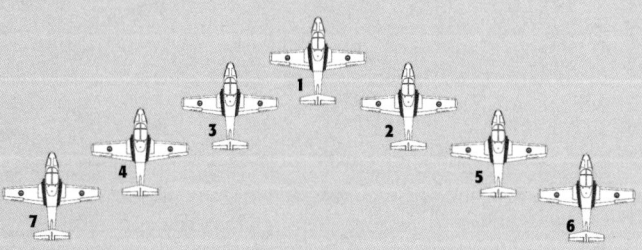

Wedge

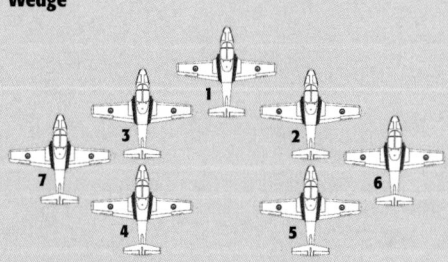

Delta

Inverted Split

Line-Abreast T

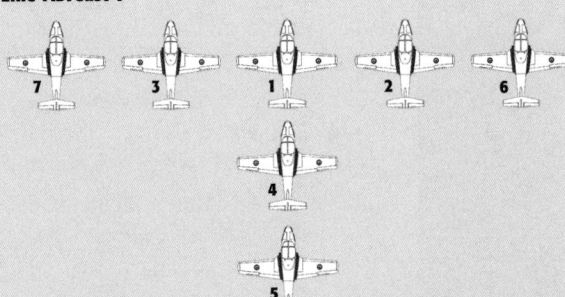

Cross

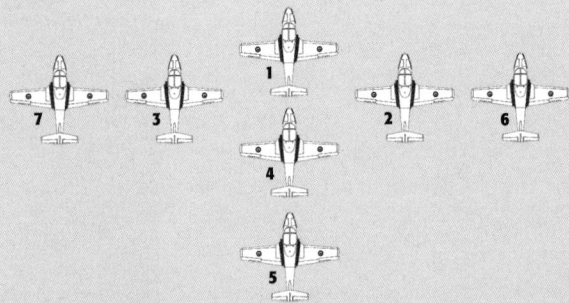

Swept Seven

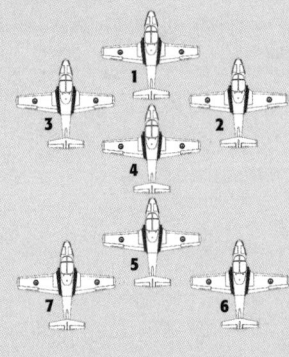

Canada Goose

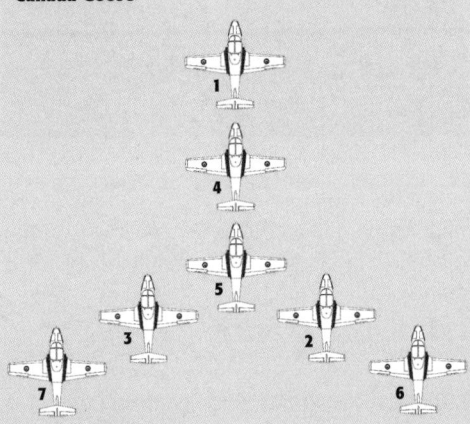

Feather

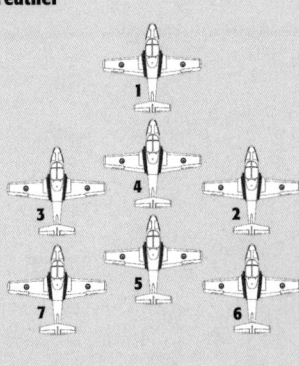

Heart 1

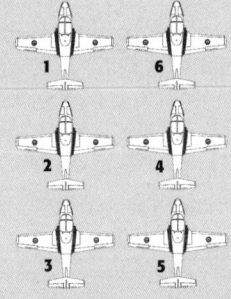

Heart 2

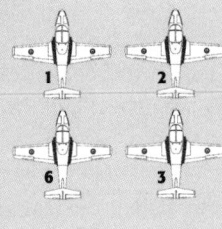

Hexagon

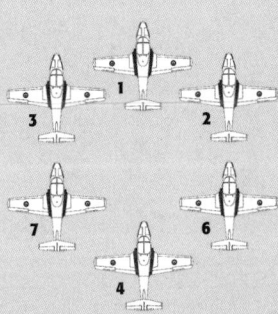

Inverted Box

Five Plane line-abreast

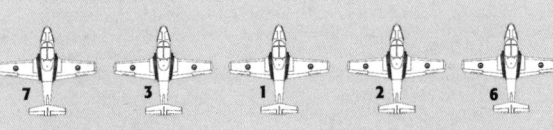

Double Take

Solo Double Inverted

Echelon In Review

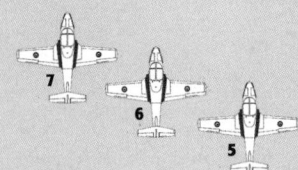

Flip Flop

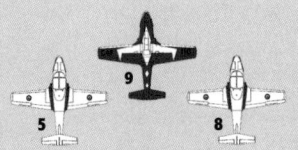

Note: Formation led by lead solo, Snowbird 8 or 9

Formation graphics
by J.D. Dempsey

649

The Snowbirds and Music

Music has been an integral component of the Snowbird show since it was first introduced in the routine in 1976. It was the initiative of two new members of the team, Gerry Nicks and the late Jim Sorfleet, that resulted in the implementation of a whole new dimension to the Snowbird experience. From the time the first rudimentary experiments were conducted to establish crowd reaction, it was evident that music was to play an important role in all future Snowbird displays. Indeed, it would now be hard to imagine a Snowbird show that was not set to music.

Numerous scores composed by a wide variety of artists have been used in Snowbird shows over the years. As Gerry Nicks recalls, in the formative years these included mainly classical scores from his personal collection – classics such as the *William Tell* and *1812 Overtures*, *Fifth of Beethoven*, *Blue Danube*, *Can Can* and Rimsky Korsakov's *Bumble Bee* (also known as the *Bumble Boogie*!). More contemporary tunes were also used, including *Nights in White Satin* and *Je t'aime*. Each was paired with an appropriate manoeuvre in the show to help set the mood for the audience – the *1812 Overture* for the "upward-downward bomb burst" for example, *Je t'aime* for "the heart," and so on. The process was refined in 1977 with several new and popular scores added to the show – the theme from *2001 – A Space Odyssey*, *Pomp and Circumstance*, *Linus and Lucy's Theme* and the *RCAF March Past*.

Although all of the above scores were easily recognizable, it was a relatively unknown melody that truly captured the imagination and rapidly earned the label as the Snowbirds theme song for first generation Snowbird fans. Few people had ever heard the tune composed by S. Haseley when it was featured in the Snowbirds first movie released in the spring of 1977, and most never did learn its name, *Southern Sun*. It wasn't even utilized in the Snowbirds repertoire in 1977 but by the end of the season, it had proven so popular in the movie that it became ingrained in the Snowbird psyche. For airshow fans, no matter when or where it was heard, it immediately conjured up images of nine little aircraft filling the sky with trails of smoke, climaxing with the "palm tree split." In later years, the 1981 team introduced *Ballad to Adeline* by Richard Clayderman, its graceful theme becoming associated with the "double dia-

David Foster

mond roll." It became a point of pride for the team coordinators to key the music in such a way that it would climax at the apex of the roll – and they invariably got it right.

In more recent times, it is fitting that the most popular songs associated with the Snowbirds have been written by Canadian artists, notably David Foster and Steven Vitali. David first came on the scene in 1986 when he wrote the score for (and narrated) the one hour CBC documentary *The Real Stuff* which was widely acclaimed. For Canadians, his instrumental *Love Theme from St Elmo's Fire* became as much a part of the Snowbirds as the movie for which it was written. Similarly, his spectacular tribute to the team, *Flight of the Snowbirds*, achieved immense popularity and became a regular feature of the Snowbird show.

Steven Vitali

For Steven Vitali, the Snowbirds became a springboard to a musical career when he forwarded a demonstration tape to the team early in 1989. It was captivating. Steven's own theme song written for the team was appropriately titled *In Flight*. The ultimate compliment to this work is the fact that it is still being used to open the show more than a dozen years after its release, its spine-tingling melody still generating goose bumps as those nine twinkling lights first come into view. Steven's music was featured in *Those Magnificent Snowbirds* and *Come Fly With Us* released in 1991, both narrated by Canadian actor Leslie Neilson. To celebrate the team's 25th anniversary in 1995, Vitali cut a new album, *Snowbirds*, featuring a compilation of the most popular music scores used by the team since their inception.

Like the design of the Snowbird show each season, the responsibility for selecting music rests with the team members themselves and becomes a reflection of their character. Once a majority consensus is reached, the team coordinators then engineer the audio tapes that will be keyed at specific times in the show. This becomes a real juggling act as one coordinator narrates the show while the other operates the sound board, all the while keeping one ear tuned to the discrete radio frequency the team is working on. Teamwork with airshow announcers and those responsible for the show's sound system help ensure a seamless audio presentation. In the end, it is the audience that comes away with a visual and audio production that makes great theatre, and is uniquely Canadian.

A Legacy of Memories

Every individual who has worn the Snowbird crest has memories that will last a lifetime. For the lucky few chosen to command the team or return as the technical crew chief, the opportunity to serve comes twice. For most however, this is a one shot affair. Whether the tour lasts two years or three, it is but a snapshot in one's life that comes and goes quickly. Capt John Politis flew with the Snowbirds in 1981 and 1982 as one of the team's two solo pilots. He did so with as much passion and dedication as anyone who has ever donned the trademark red flying suit. He relates his impressions of that memorable period in his life while outlining some of the challenges of flying formation and solo aerobatics with the team:

The Greatest Job In The World

"Some day when I look back and review my life I know that I will consider my two years on the Snowbirds as having been among my best years. Today, two decades after my tour on the team there is not a day that goes by that I don't cast my mind back and remember this happy period of my life. Invariably, I draw a surge of emotions from this reflection. Sometimes a feeling of disbelief will overwhelm me. There will be times, when I look over old photos or tapes of past performances, that I can't believe that I was a part of something so fantastic.

Making the cut and joining the Snowbirds was an exciting dream come true. Moreover, being selected as the opposing solo was intoxicating. On the night of my selection as a solo, once the feeling of disbelief wore off, a thrill overcame me. I was just 24 years old. I was bursting with the anticipation of flying at near ground level and performing head-on passes with an opposing aircraft. Additionally, the prospect of flying the outside right wing position of the big diamond formation as Snowbird 8 was daunting.

The unique beauty of the solo pilot's job is that it encompasses both worlds of display flying – formation aerobatics and solo aerobatics. Throughout the show the solos will join with the other seven members of the team to fly the various nine-plane formations. Formation flying requires each pilot to fly smoothly, never jerky or rough with the controls. While in formation, pilots should never come close to full-scale deflection with the control stick or rudders. To watch from the ground the nine-plane formations move as one in a fluid and poetic motion. However, when the two solos break out of the nine-plane and begin their series of head-on crosses, a totally different type of flying is then required. This is where the solo pilot's 'fangs' come out. To squeeze maximum performance out of the Tutor, the solo pilot needs to aggressively push and pull the controls and throttle through their full range of travel. Each solo will undergo up to + 7 and - 3 G during the co-solo routine. In fact, during an airshow a solo's adrenaline is pumping so hard he must rely on his G meter to keep from overstressing the airplane.

For the solo pilot, the road to achieving show standard is a long one. From his first day, the

Not all would-be Snowbirds aspire to be one of the two designated solo pilots on the team, Snowbirds 8 and 9. Although the role is physically punishing, it does offer the ultimate in exhilaration during head-on low-level aerobatics. Commencing in the year 2001, the opposing solo is selected from among second year members of the team. (Roman Holowatyj)

new Snowbird solo is taught to ease himself down to where he is comfortable flying lower and lower altitudes. The ability to fly low AND to perform aerobatics at near ground level must be mastered before he can learn to fly the head-on crosses, but this phase of training is not rushed. It begins at a reasonable height above the ground, flying various aerobatic manoeuvres, and working down to progressively lower altitudes as confidence is gained. This period of confidence training is

particularly challenging, but also a lot of fun.

What a pulse-racing kick this was for me! Compared to the years I had spent as a flying instructor within the rigid structure of Training Command, the challenges and boundaries on the Snowbirds seemed limitless. After just a few sorties, I discovered that it was the equivalent to being handed the keys to a racy sports car and told to 'indulge yourself.'

The Art of Formation Flying

Flying formation doesn't look hard. However, anyone who has ever flown close to another aircraft will attest to the fact that formation flying is not as easy as it looks. It is hard enough to do it well with only two or three aircraft. To put nine jets together, with wings overlapped, low to the ground, looping and rolling, is a phenomenal achievement. Flying his position on the outside of the large Snowbird formations is one of the hardest tasks for a new solo pilot to learn.

During the winter training months the seven members of the main formation spend the majority of their time practicing formation flying skills, while the new solo will spend most of his time under the guidance of the lead solo learning solo manoeuvres. The new solo spends comparatively little time developing his formation skills as he tries to learn how to fly the difficult 'outside wing' position. It is therefore not unusual for the new solo to initially hold back the development of the nine-plane formation as the new pilot grapples with learning the dual role of formation and solo flying.

To maintain your position in a large formation of jets while coping with the heaving summer turbulence found below 3,000 feet is a challenging task. As the turbulence increases in intensity, all nine aircraft begin to oscillate. Everyone is expected to keep their aircraft stationary within the confines of a small area referred to as each pilot's 'box.' These so-called boxes are small in dimension – about a foot or so (30 cm) for those pilots flying directly off of the lead aircraft and approximately two feet (60 cm) for the other five members of the formation. Keep in mind that this is all occurring while the wings of each airplane are overlapped and being affected by the airflow disturbance off each wing. If the turbulence induced bounces grow too large your teammate will begin to venture outside his 'box' and into your airspace (your box). If the turbulence becomes extreme, any one of the pilots can announce this by calling out 'wing tip.' This is the signal to everyone else that aircraft in the formation are beginning to move outside the normal limits (their 'box'). On the first 'wing tip' call (sometimes two or three excited 'wing tip' calls can suddenly come at once),

all pilots then move out and establish a looser position, changing their flying references to ensure that wing tip clearances are now established between aircraft.

The amazing thing is that no matter how bad the turbulence gets, no matter how big the bounces are, when viewed from the spectator's perspective, 99.9 percent of the oscillations don't even get noticed. Here's a tip for next time you're watching an airshow – watch the smoke trailing just behind the aircraft. If the smoke immediately behind the jets is straight and smooth there is probably very little turbulence. However, if the smoke trails are jerky and ragged, then look closely at the jets as they fly past and you will probably notice movement within the formation, especially the aircraft on the outside of the formation.

An element that regularly comes into play when flying on the outside of the formation is a phenomenon known as 'crack-the-whip.' This is when a small movement by an airplane on the inside of the formation results in a progressively larger bounce for

To overcome the effects of reduced thrust on a hot summer day, the Snowbirds have developed a technique called "stacking" over the top of loops. This involves Snowbirds 4 and 5 moving ahead of their normal "nose-tail" reference to effect overlap when the airspeed is lowest over the top of the loop (normally 110 to 115 knots). At this stage all pilots will have full nose down trim on their control columns to improve stability. As the formation comes down the backside, the line astern pilots will slowly slide back to normal reference, thus preventing Snowbird 5 from stretching at the back of the pack. Doing the stacking in this 1995 photo is Snowbird 4, Capt Will McEwan. The other visible aircraft are Snowbirds 2 (Mario Hamel), 6 (Ian Searle) and 8 (Steve Dion) along with leader Maj Steve Hill's tailpipe. (Roman Holowatyj).

The Big Diamond Roll on a glorious day in Comox in April 1999. Power management during the roll is critical, especially by the team leader and Snowbirds 5, 8 and 9 on the outside of the formation. On a hot summer day, even a one percent RPM error can cause a pilot to stretch out of position. (Garry Cotter)

the inner wingman, and ultimately an even bigger bounce for the outside wingman. On rare occasions due to extreme turbulence, this oscillation can become so violent it literally whips the outside wingman right out of the formation. To minimize this effect, I used to ride high on my references so that I could look beyond the inner wingman, who was flying directly beside me. I would try and see the team lead's tailplane or canopy. I then focused most of my attention on whatever I could see of the team lead, and less attention on the inner wingman. This way I could react immediately to a movement by the lead without the lag time that would otherwise develop if I solely focused on the inner wingman. This technique is called 'flying through' and greatly reduces the whipping effect. Even though the inner was only a few feet away, and our wings were overlapped, I could 'fly-through' as long as he stayed inside his 'box.' If he bounced outside his normal box, I would immediately kick the rudder and slide out. Once the oscillation dampened out, I would rudder back into position and refocus on the team lead.

Another difficulty flying large formations on the outside, especially in the little Tutor, is a lack of power. For example, in a big diamond roll to the left the solo on the inside of the roll (left side) has the formation turning towards him. This results in a smaller turning radius and therefore requires considerably less thrust. The solo on the outside of the roll (right side), flying a bigger circle, will need close to full power to keep from falling out of position. To complicate matters, at the halfway point of the roll both pilots experience a reversal. The pilot on the left side now finds himself on the outside of the turn requiring full power while the pilot on the right is now on the inside of the roll and requires much less power. To allow for spool-up time on the engine, a technique mastered by the Snowbirds over the years is for the inside pilot to deploy his speedbrakes for the first half of the roll to prevent having

to reduce his power to near idle to stay in position. At the halfway point he must select speedbrakes in and apply full power to stay in position. Missing the exact point of reversal means that one plane will fall out of the formation while the other plane will slide into the formation, necessitating a large aileron correction.

The team lead has to set an exact and relatively stable power setting for each manoeuvre. How much or how little is determined from months and months of never ending trial and error. This is where the Tutor's lack of power is a real hurdle. Power on a hot summer day is so critical that failure of the leader to reduce power slightly at the critical time will quite likely cause the outside plane to fall out of a rolling manoeuvre or the second line astern pilot to stretch back over the top of a loop.

The Tutor's limited thrust also makes formation changes difficult. Many of the formation changes the Snowbirds fly are assisted by physics. If during a loop, for instance, a pilot wants to change formation and move back, it is accomplished by reducing power and by dropping slightly below the reference aircraft. In physical terms this means flying a bigger circle than the reference aircraft and for the same speed, the aircraft flying the larger circle will therefore slide back. The opposite technique is used to move forward: a pilot will apply full power and also fly high on his reference aircraft. These combined actions (more power and flying a smaller circle) result in a movement forward. Needless to say, flying above or below the aircraft beside you as a means of changing position within the formation takes a great deal of practice to accomplish confidently and safely. It can be all the pilot has to rely on when full or idle power is not enough. A pilot is 'out of power' when trying to move forward but discovers that, even though the throttle is at max, the aircraft is still moving backwards. For an aircraft 'out of power,' the only way to catch up with the formation is for the

lead to either reduce power or turn toward the lagging airplane.

Mastering Head-On Aerobatics

In spite of the formation flying challenges, this is obviously not the solo pilot's main focus. A solo pilot's niche is the head-on cross. Flown properly, a head-on cross should give the illusion that the two aircraft are passing through each other. Spine tingling and heart stopping to get right – down right dangerous to get wrong!

The two solos begin 'the head-on' by lining up on each other about one or two miles apart, heading nose-to-nose. Initially each pilot looks for the opposing aircraft's nose-light and, to a lesser extent, its smoke trail. When there is a cross wind blowing, each solo will need to crab (angle) into the wind to track a straight line. This throws off the nose-light reference, as well as the smoke trail, rendering the lineup and crossing references harder to gauge. They will be flying at a combined closing speed of approximately 700 miles per hour (1,100 km per hour). As they get closer, it is the opposing solo's job to adjust his track slightly to create a miss with the lead. Out of the corner of their eyes they can see the crowd as they speed towards centre stage. When the two planes are at just the right closing distance, the lead solo will call 'Solos, Roll NOW' at which time both pilots will slam their control columns full deflection to effect the cross, the idea being to cross belly-to-belly.

Theoretically, the opposing solo is responsible for the miss and the lead solo is responsible for adjusting the timing of both aircraft to ensure the cross occurs at stage centre. The truth be known, however, a lead solo would never let a cross deteriorate to the point where there was a high risk of collision. If at any time the lead solo feels that the two aircraft are converging dangerously, a call 'Solos Break it Off' is made over the radio.

The spine-tingling excitement of the head-on cross courtesy the 1990 solos, Capts Les Racicot (SB 8) and Rich Lancaster (SB 9). (Bill Johnson, Rafe Tomsett)

A textbook solo cross by Snowbird 9 (left) and his partner Snowbird 8. As the two solos roll out on the showline, each will call "Contact" to acknowledge they see the other aircraft. The lead solo sets the line and calls the roll over the radio – the opposing solo makes the miss. (Rafe Tomsett)

On this command both solos immediately throw themselves into predetermined escape manoeuvres. Fortunately this doesn't happen too often, only twice for me over two years and hundreds of crosses!

How close do solos get? In reality, both pilots tighten, or loosen, the crossing distance between them to their personal comfort level. The comfort level grows closer with time. Early in the show season the miss distance might be as much as 60 feet (20 metres) belly-to-belly. As the season progresses, however, and the skill and confidence level of the two solos increases, the crosses become much tighter. Tight enough, in fact, that over the top of the co-loop for instance (when the closing speed is relatively slow), I would pass the other solo with as little as 20 or 30 feet (8 to 10 metres) between us – close enough to hear the other jet 'whoosh' as it passed by. This always put a smile on my face.

Some showsites are harder to fly than others depending on the characteristics of the surrounding terrain. Many shows take place away from an airport so that the first time you see the area is when you are flying inverted down the showline. A good map is essential and this is the team coordinator's job. If a map can be provided with a scale that offers a decent amount of relief (1:50,000 or better is what I preferred), the solos are in luck. Usually a map with poor relief or one with a large scale is all that is available at smaller showsites. An overhead

photograph of the showsite is a rare treat; I can count on one hand the number of times that happened for me. The solos need to spend a lot of time in pre-flight preparation studying the map (as does the boss), discussing prominent features that will be used as reference points. Memorizing as much as possible and mentally flying the run-ins is crucial because, once airborne, there is precious little time for map reading.

When shows occurred over a runway we felt really blessed. With a runway to line up on, I knew that the head-on set-ups would be a

Two more examples of perfection as the solos cross upside-down at 3,000 feet above ground with only 120 knots on the clock. On the top, Capts Bob Stephan and Steve Wallace in 1984; on the bottom, Capts Les Racicot and Rich Lancaster in 1990. (Bill Johnson)

piece of cake. Runways offer natural reference lines from which to gauge the run-in towards each other. Each solo can use the edge or the centre of the runway to initially line-up on. They can then confidently nudge the miss distance between them a bit closer providing they do not have to contend with a strong crosswind.

More often than not, however, the show takes place over a field or some other location with nondescript ground features, angled or curved roads, or worst of all over the water. Flying over the water is a particularly difficult task because in addition to the lack of lineup references, there is often extreme difficulty with depth perception, that is judging height over the water. This is a real danger. If the water is glassy and calm, it is almost impossible to tell whether you are flying upside down at 10 feet, 100 feet, or 1,000 feet. Over the water the solo must rely on his altimeter to survive, just as the team leader does in carefully guiding the formation through its aerobatic routine. For instance, a Tutor requires approximately 3,000 feet to complete a loop. At the top half of a loop, a solo needs to have at least 3,000 feet of height to safely start the second half, referred to as the 'pull-through.' If a pull-through is initiated below 3,000 feet, a solo tinkers with disaster. At the top of a loop I would always confirm that I was at least 3,000 feet high. Then as I started the pull-through, I would look down at the water through the TOP of the canopy. At this point I would always tuck a little early because the water looked very

close and it seemed as if I was about to dive into it!

For an airshow over water, organizers try to arrange to have unmanned boats anchored along the showline. Discernable objects on the water provide the necessary scale and backdrop to assist with depth perception. They make height determination easier by providing a scale of reference. The annual airshow site of the Canadian National Exhibition in Toronto is located along the shoreline of Lake Ontario. This is a typical water showsite where extra care and planning must take place prior to flying the airshow.

One of the most challenging aspects of the lead solo's job is the staging, that is planning and flying the head-on cross so that it takes place at stage centre, right in front of the crowd or VIP stands. The lead solo alone corrects for wind and staging using his stop-

The solo Twinkle Roll, later known as the Twizzle Roll, was a heart-stopping flash of wings and lights. Commencing in 1980, Snowbird 5 got in on some of the glory by leading the solos in a new manoeuvre dubbed the Roll-Back Cross (at right). Some nine years later it was modified and became the Lag-Back Cross, shown below in 1990. All three manoeuvres are very effective in achieving audience reaction as the aircraft appear to pass through each other. (Bill Johnson)

watch and mental gymnastics. He alone accepts the accolades when a well staged cross occurs, and he alone suffers the embarrassment when the cross takes place in an adjacent county! Each manoeuvre is set up by commanding the opposing solo when to turn before and after each manoeuvre. The commands are short and crisp – 'Solos, turn NOW' to commence a run-in, 'Solos, pull NOW' to commence a vertical reverse or 'Solos, smoke off NOW' to end a manoeuvre and signal a turn. The opposing solo will only fly predetermined tracks and run-ins, and will not manoeuvre towards the stage area until commanded to do so by the lead solo. As well as being responsible for staging the cross, the lead solo has to be careful not to turn the solos in too early which would conflict with the formation while they are 'on stage.' Ideally, the lead solo and team leader aim for seven to 10 seconds between their 'smoke on' and 'smoke off' calls.

A dynamic view of the roll back cross as seen from directly beneath the aircraft. (Bill Johnson)

Of all of the head-on crosses flown by the solos, the cross at the top of the co-loop is the most difficult to perfect. Any wing drop during the initial pull-up by either pilot will render it nearly impossible to get the cross over the top. But when the execution is perfect, the two aircraft can cross as close as six metres (20 feet) apart. In this example, opposing solo Larry Rockliff nails the cross as lead solo Ray Hansford flashes past below. Of this episode captured with a 15 mm lens in September 1979, Bill Johnson wrote: "For the passenger fortunate enough to be tagging along on one of these events, this is a surreal millisecond they will never forget … You can definitely hear the opposing aircraft when it passes, by the way." (Bill Johnson)

Any wind blowing along the showline will displace the solo cross left or right of centre stage. The lead solo constantly makes adjustments for this. For example, a manoeuvre begins with both solos crossing at centre stage, flying away from each other for a few seconds, completing a vertical reverse and then returning for an opposing head-on cross. If a 30 knot wind component were blowing down the showline, the lead solo corrects for this by calling for the opposing solo (if he had the tailwind) to begin his vertical reverse a full six seconds before the lead solo would begin his. Both solos end up flying their ver-

tical reverses asymmetrically at an interval of six seconds, but if the lead solo has judged the wind properly, they will ultimately cross each other at stage centre again. On our team I asked the coordinators monitoring the show from the ground to call out any small staging errors that they saw, caused by a changing wind for instance ('Solos half a second left' or 'Solos one second right' for example), and I would then factor this into my staging calculations. Every little bit helped.

There is so much more to the Snowbird experience than just the thrill – there is the

extreme challenge of performing to exact standards that are difficult to put into words. You eventually achieve a marvellous level of flying proficiency – confident and calm – flying in any attitude or under any G loading within the aircraft's flight envelope. With time and practice, the aircraft becomes a physical extension of the solo pilot, a mechanical entity that comes to life once the solo straps it to his back.

Personally, and in 10,000 flying hours since that time, I have never again experienced that level of flying confidence. At no time since then have I had the opportunity, the shear concentration of time and effort to honing one's flying skill, to feel the same way. For me, it was a once in a lifetime event!

I learned many things from flying with the Snowbirds. The last thing I learned was how fast two years could go by – amazingly fast. As challenging as the solo role was, the hardest and most difficult task that I faced was not the job itself. Ultimately, the hardest part was at the end, saying goodbye to all that I had come to love and enjoy about flying. It hurt me to the very core of my being. In spite of what I have written above, it does not begin to describe what a thorough honour and privilege it was for me to have been a Snowbird, and I thank God for it all. In all my flying before and since, there has been nothing like it! I have never flown with a better group of guys and the memories will forever nourish my soul."

John Politis

1989 saw the return of an old crowd favourite to the solo show, the Stage Cross to Carousel. Surprising the crowd from behind in line-abreast formation, the solos pulled up into a loop and split on the way down to complete a modified Co-360. (Bill Johnson)

The Groundcrew – The "Team Within a Team"

The Snowbird road crew fly from showsite to showsite with their assigned pilots. It is a unique arrangement among the world's major aerobatic teams, but one which has worked amazingly well. Shown here is the team that played an integral role in making the Snowbirds' 25th anniversary in 1995 a resounding success. (Rick Radell)

Talk to any pilot on the Snowbirds, past or present, and sooner or later the subject of the squadron's groundcrew will come up. Often referred to as "a team within a team," these are truly the unsung heroes behind the success of the Snowbirds. Like the administration staff who toil away while the team is on the road, the groundcrew are an integral component of the team whose work behind the scenes is by and large invisible to the viewing public. They too are hand-picked from a ready pool of volunteers who must come recommended from their respective units. Collectively, they represent every technical area of expertise required to service the aircraft on the road. Aside from their extraordinary dedication, what makes them particularly unique is the fact that the Snowbird technical road team consists of only 10 technicians who travel from showsite to showsite with the team pilots. They are the smallest groundcrew team among the world's major

aerobatic teams and they are the only major team that operates without a support aircraft.

Sgt Mark Keller was selected to rejoin the Snowbirds as the crew chief for the 1998 and 1999 seasons. An aero-engine technician by profession, he served an initial tour with the team in 1985 and 1986. In spite of the 12 year hiatus between tours with the team, he explains that little changed in the selection process over the first 30 years of the team:

———

"Every fall the scene was the same in Moose Jaw. Each candidate sat nervously in 431 Sqn, waiting his or her turn to go in for the dreaded interview with the commanding officer and crew chief of the Snowbirds. For some, it was their second attempt to win a position on the team, hoping their name would finally rise to the top. For most, it was their first. All new groundcrew members

were chosen from within the Base Aircraft Maintenance organization based on a combination of their work record, personal performance, aircraft experience and the results of the all-encompassing interview.

Even though new groundcrew now have to be posted in from outside the base, as a new member of the Snowbird team the initial impressions are the same. From the first time you walk into No. 7 Hangar at CFB Moose Jaw you get the feeling you are embarking on something special, something very different from any job or assignment you have had in the past. Things move quickly – there is no time to sit around and admire all of the photographs and memorabilia that surround you. Preparing the squadron's complement of 15 Tutor aircraft for the training season is a lot of work for the groundcrew, regardless of how long you have been on the team.

From the inception of the Snowbirds, the volunteer groundcrew have played an indispensable role in keeping the show safe. In the high stakes world of demonstration flying, vigilance is a constant companion. (Bill Johnson)

ished. Any snags that have shown up from the previous flight must be rectified or a spare aircraft readied for the next launch. In addition to routine maintenance duties, clothing and flight suit fittings must be accomplished well before the show season so that photographs and biographies can be completed for the brochure. For most of the new groundcrew members, the Snowbirds will be the first time they have been assigned a flying job. As a result, each will go up for a flight or two during the winter so that the demanding summer flying schedule is not so unsettling for the first time flyers.

As crew chief, aside from ensuring there are always enough aircraft to meet the daily flying program, winter duties include monitoring aircraft hours and fatigue life carefully. Great care is taken to ensure there is a spread between inspections so that the aircraft can be fit into a preventive maintenance program and cyclical inspections at different times. Up until the end of the 2000 season, major inspections were carried out by 15 Air Maintenance Sqn on our behalf. However, with the retirement of the Tutor from the basic jet training role, 15 AMS was disbanded and many of the technicians were posted onto 431 Sqn. Thus, all inspections and repairs are now completed by the team.

The more work that is accomplished during the winter equates to less disruption during the summer when on the road. Once all aircraft fatigue data is compiled from the previous year, the next task is finalizing who will fly which jet. This decision is made as early as possible so that each pilot can fly the same aircraft as early in the training season as possible. Each of the road technicians is paired up with a pilot for the season and all names and numbers are painted on the jets. Having your name painted on the side of the aircraft

Every off-season each Snowbird aircraft undergoes a major inspection, including non-destructive testing (similar to an x-ray) of critical airframe components. The work is painstaking but essential to a safe operation. Tutor 105 served 10 years on the team from 1978 to 1987 inclusive, serving its longest stint of five years in the same position as Snowbird 7. (Bill Johnson)

Initial aircraft demands start slowly with only a few jets at a time required as the pilots fly two to an aircraft for the first part of their workups. However, this soon increases to nine aircraft for every practice. Before you know it, you are battling Moose Jaw's cold winter lying on your back on the frozen tarmac pumping diesel into the aircraft smoke tanks. Between flights the jets are inspected and fluids (fuel, oil and oxygen) are replen-

Rain or shine, the work will get done to prepare the nine aircraft and two spares for the upcoming show. Teamwork is the name of the game. (Rick Radell, Rafe Tomsett)

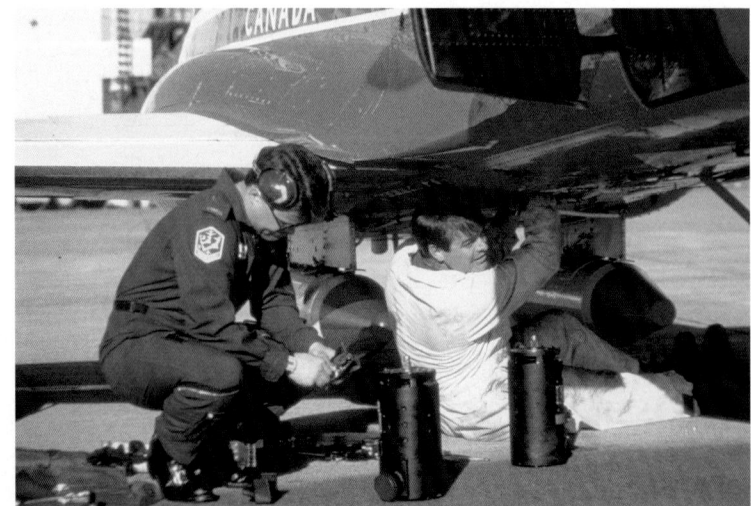

The packing and unpacking of a Snowbird Tutor has become a science in its own right. With no support aircraft, all team clothing, tools and selected spare parts are jammed within the tiny confines of each aircraft. No empty space goes unused. (Ed Drader)

is equally exciting for the groundcrew as it is for the pilot – things are really beginning to take shape when this occurs.

The winter season is the time for making sure all of the techs are fully qualified for the upcoming airshow season. This includes training new members how to safely pack up his or her jet for the road. There are many do's and don'ts of packing what seems to be an endless pile of tools, parts and clothing into the small confines of the Tutor. Obviously, we can't take every conceivable spare part with us, but from experience most of the required parts are taken. This is where the squadron supply technicians have earned their keep over the years. During the training season, they run around to the warehouse retrieving parts for the techs on a daily basis. Prior to the start of the season they ship out two large containers with extra parts – one to CFB Trenton and one to CFB Comox. When the team is in these areas, parts can be easily accessed and utilized as required. For all additional requirements, small parts are flown in on one of the team's spare Tutors or sent via courier all over North America to support the road team. For major engine snags that require an engine change, a new engine and mobile repair party will be flown

The groundcrew march-out to their respective aircraft is a signal that the Snowbird strap-in and start sequence is about to commence. The groundcrew's sharp deportment in front of the crowd is not only a sign of pride, but also an important catalyst in motivating young men and women towards technical careers in the Canadian Forces. (Top left – Roman Holowatyj, top right and bottom – Bill Johnson)

Each pilot and his assigned technician will spend an entire season travelling together, fostering a friendship that will last forever. When the pilot passes the last chance inspection and gets the final thumbs up, the adrenalin begins to flow … After landing, the technicians will be the first to greet their pilots with their assessment of the show. (Rick Radell, Bill Johnson, Garry Cotter)

in courtesy a C-130 Hercules from Air Transport Command, as will another spare Tutor aircraft. The team seldom has the luxury of waiting behind for the engine to be replaced, invariably departing for the next showsite.

The Countdown

Before you know it the days are getting longer and the 'countdown calendar' is getting shorter, next stop – Comox for spring work-ups. For first and second year techs alike, Comox is a great location for training away from home base and is a time for the aircrew and groundcrew to gel as a team. The training is intense with only one or two days off during the two-and-one-half week deployment. Heading home after Comox the team is ready for the acceptance show. Just as they have in the pre-season, each red-suited pilot will be assisted with his strap-in by his smiling blue-suited tech. During the acceptance show and each subsequent performance on the road, every member of the groundcrew takes great pride in hearing the crowd response to the show, knowing they are part of a great team.

When the big day finally arrives, you hug and kiss your family good bye and head out to the base to tow the aircraft out of the hangar. At the pre-briefed time you strap yourself in next to your pilot and wait for the boss to make his radio call, 'Snowbirds, check in.' All those little things you forgot to do at home then come racing to the forefront of your mind! As the team taxis out, family members and the odd ex-snowbird tech give the team a wave and a friendly send off, wishing they were going with you!

With each stop along the way to a new showsite the routine is the same – the jets have to be turned around as quickly as possible, often in order to make hard arrival times. In no time at all you are strapped in again for the next leg, usually wishing you had gone to the bathroom. Finally, the last hop of the day arrives and the team heralds its arrival with a pre-arranged series of flypasts over the airport or surrounding city. Upon landing and shutting down, all team members gather around the wing of an aircraft and receive a briefing for that airshow from one of the team coordinators. This will include all pertinent information for that show, from hotel directions to public relations functions such as receptions and school or hospital visits. Once the pilots have debriefed any snags on their aircraft, the

crew chief gathers the technicians to discuss maintenance operations at that showsite. Only when all of the aircraft have been readied for the next day will the groundcrew rush to the hotel, check-in, shower, change and meet in the lobby for the evening's public relations function.

Showtime!

Show day for the team technicians comes early as they normally get out to the airport three hours prior to showtime. Each aircraft is given a final inspection, emptied of all parts and tools and polished. By the time the pilots arrive to brief, the aircraft are ready to go – all in a perfect line having been inspected by the crew chief.

When the pilots arrive the team gathers at one end of the line and the friendly banter and jokes start. It is showtime and soon the groundcrew march out and stand at attention in front of their respective jet. The pilots follow shortly thereafter for the acceptance of their aircraft. The groundcrew member salutes and receives a salute and a handshake in return in a signal of mutual respect. As the start procedure takes place, the groundcrew are vigilant for any sign of a snag from their pilot. Similarly, as the aircraft taxi out, they are carefully screened as they pass the 'last chance' inspection.

Once the team is airborne, the discrete radio frequency is monitored so we can ready the spare jet should an airborne snag require a quick landing and aircraft change. If the spare is required, the pilot can be back in the air in just minutes with the assistance of the groundcrew. As the show comes to an end, the groundcrew march out in front of show centre where introductions are carried out as the nine-plane sets up for its landing.

This gives the viewing public the opportunity to meet the technicians as well which is an important part of the recruiting process carried out on behalf of the Canadian Forces. Once the aircraft are parked in front of the crowd, the entire maintenance routine begins once again. At the end of each airshow swing, which can last anywhere from 14 to 21 days, the team stops briefly in Moose Jaw for two or three days. Although it is always a relief to get home to family again, these are not days off. We use the time for preventative maintenance and change a lot of parts such as tires and brakes so that they last through the airshows of the next swing.

Bill Johnson

Rick Radell

This workload goes on for the groundcrew from April until the middle of October with very few days off; without the support of our families it would be impossible to fulfill the demands placed on the team. However, with our busy schedule the show season seems like a dream and is soon over. Once home after the season, everyone is extremely happy to be reunited with family – having a whole week off is great! But then it is tryout time for the new pilots and suddenly there are more aspiring technicians sitting in the hallway. Soon those that were first year techs suddenly find themselves the veterans responsible for training the next year's new groundcrew as the outgoing crew bid a fond farewell to the team. With that begins another new Snowbird team …

The bonds of friendship and the realization that after your second year you may never be part of such a wonderful organization again make it difficult to move on. The experience and knowledge a technician gathers in two years with 431 Sqn is an asset that is without measure. It was a pleasure to have been part of it all and I am grateful to all of the groundcrew members and their families for having played such a big part in the success of the Snowbirds."

Mark Keller

As the Snowbirds complete their 32nd season, they are more popular than ever and remain a great source of pride and inspiration for thousands of Canadians, young and old alike.

They epitomize what it is to be Canadian. Yet, in spite of their myriad accomplishments, there are more challenges on the horizon. Once again, the ultimate challenge is going to be simple survival within a military force that over the years has been devastated by cutbacks at every level. The difference now is that there is a new urgency to the Snowbird dilemma – the team cannot survive much longer on their faithful old steed, the Tutor. Nor should we expect them to. By the year 2004 the aircraft will be 40 years old and will have been the Snowbirds mount for an unparalleled 34 years. It is time the Tutor was retired along with other legendary aircraft that have served the citizens of Canada so well … and it is time the Snowbirds were equipped with new jet aircraft.

Rafe Tomsett

Rick Radell

The *Snowbirds*

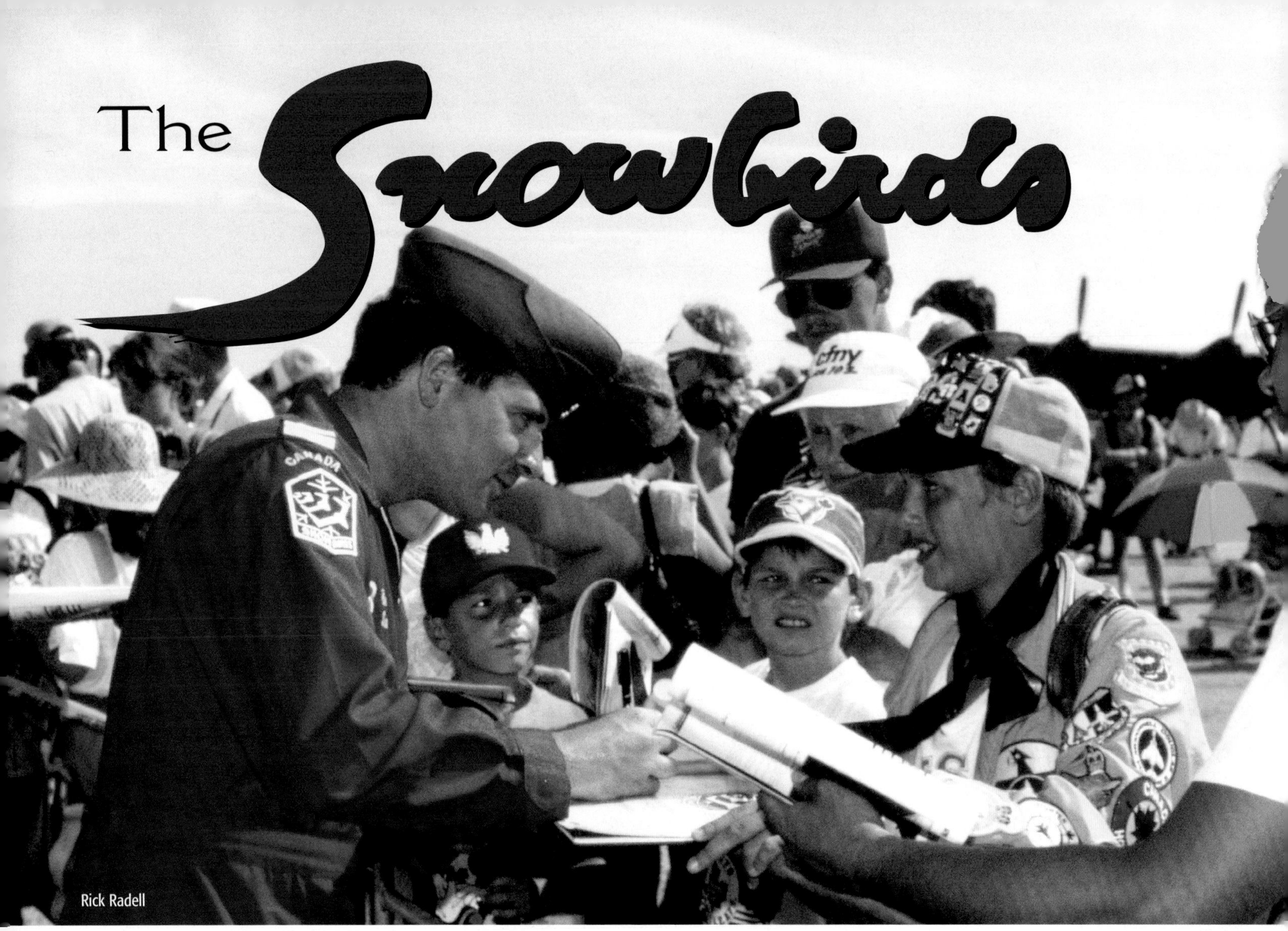

Rick Radell

The Snowbirds continue a tradition of public relations activities established decades ago by such eminent predecessors as the RCAF Golden Hawks and Golden Centennaires. From motivational presentations to autograph sessions to school and hospital visits, the team is in high demand throughout the year. As the most visible unit of the Canadian Forces, they play an indispensable role in recruiting, attracting young Canadians to rewarding professional careers in a wide variety of endeavours, whether in the army, navy or air force.

Bill Johnson

Canada's Aerial Ambassadors

Nancy Johnson

Marc Cossette

Garry Cotter

Rick Radell

Garry Cotter

Garry Cotter

Nancy Johnson

Ed Drader

Snowbird Showsites 1971 - 2002

Abbotsford, B.C.
Alexandria, Ont.
Amherstburg, Ont.
Amos, Que.
Andrews AFB, Wash.
Argentia, Nfld.
Arnprior, Ont.
Aspen, Colo.
Atlanta, Ga.
Atlantic City, N.J.
Baddeck, N.S.
Bagotville, Que.
Baie-Comeau, Que.
Barnes ANGB, MA
Barrie, Ont.
Batavia, N.Y.
Bathurst, N.B.
Battle Creek, Mich.
Beausejour, Man.
Beaverlodge, Alta.
Belle River, Ont.
Billings, Mont.
Bismarck, N.D.
Boissevain, Man.
Bonaventure, Que.
Bonnyville, Alta.
Borden, Ont.
Borden-Carleton, P.E.I.
Bouctouche, N.B.
Brandon, Man.
Brantford, Ont.
Brockville, Ont.
Bromont, Que.
Bruce Mines, Ont.
Buffalo, N.Y.
Butte, Mont.
Calgary, Alta.
Campbell River, B.C.
Campbellton, N.B.
Cardston, Alta.
Carlyle, Sask.
Carman, Man.
Caronport, Sask.
Carp, Ont.
Castlegar, B.C.
Cavendish, P.E.I.
Central Butte, Sask.
Centralia, Ont.
Chapleau, Ont.
Charlo, N.B.
Charlottesville, Va.
Charlottetown, P.E.I.
Chatham, N.B.
Chatham, Ont.
Chibougamau, Que.
Chicago, Ill.

China Lake, Calif.
Cincinnati, Ohio
Cobden, Ont.
Cobourg, Ont.
Cold Lake, Alta.
Collingwood, Ont.
Colorado Springs, Colo.
Comox, B.C.
Cookshire, Que.
Corner Brook, Nfld.
Cornwall, Ont.
Cornwallis, N.S.
Corvallis, Ore.
Courtland, Ala.
Cranbrook, B.C.
Dana, Sask.
Darlington, S.C.
Dauphin, Man.
Davenport, Ind.
Dayton, Ohio
Deer Lake, Nfld.
Denver, Colo.
Douglas, Alaska
Drummondville, Que.
Dryden, Ont.
Dubuque, Iowa
Duluth, Minn.
Ear Falls, Ont.
Edmonton, Alta.
Eganville, Ont.
El Paso, Tex.
Elliot Lake, Ont.
Elmendorf AFB, Alaska
Elmira, N.Y.
Esquimalt, B.C.
Estevan, Sask.
Eugene, Ore.
Everett, Wash.
Fairchild AFB, Wash.
Flin Flon, Man.
Fort Amherst, P.E.I.
Fort Erie, Ont.
Fort Frances, Ont.
Fort Henry, Ont.
Fort Lauderdale, Fla.
Fort McMurray, Alta.
Fort Nelson, B.C.
Fort Simpson, N.W.T.
Fort Smith, N.W.T.
Fort St. John, B.C.
Fort Worth, Tex.
Fredericton, N.B.
Fresno, Calif.
Gagetown, N.B.
Gallup, N.M.
Gander, Nfld.

Gaspé, Que.
Gatineau, Que.
Gimli, Man.
Glace Bay, N.S.
Glen Falls, N.Y.
Glendale, Ariz.
Goderich, Ont.
Goose Bay, Nfld.
Grand Beach, Man.
Grand Bend, Ont.
Grand Forks, B.C.
Grand Forks, N.D.
Grand Junction, Colo.
Grand Lake, N.B.
Grande Prairie, Alta.
Great Falls, Mont.
Greenwood, N.S.
Griffis AFB, N.Y.
Guadalajara, Mexico
Gypsumville, Man.
Halifax, N.S.
Hamilton, Ont.
Hanover, Ont.
Harbour Grace, Nfld.
Harlingen, Tex.
Harrisburg, Pa.
Havre aux Maisons, Que.
Havre St-Pierre, Que.
Hay River, N.W.T.
Hays, Kan.
High Level, Alta.
Houston, Tex.
Hudson Bay, Sask.
Inuvik, N.W.T.
Iroquois Falls, Ont.
Joliette, Que.
Juneau, Alaska
K.I. Sawyer AFB, Mich.
Kalamazoo, Mich.
Kamloops, B.C.
Kananaskis, Alta.
Kansas City, Mo.
Kelowna, B.C.
Kenora, Ont.
Kentville, N.S.
Kimberley, B.C.
Kincardine, Ont.
Kingston, Ont.
Kissimmee, Fla.
Kitchener, Ont.
La Sarre, Que.
La Tuque, Que.
Labrador City, Nfld.
Lac Beauport, Que.
Lac Etchemin, Que.
Lac St Denis, Que.

Lafayette, La.
Lake Charles, La.
Las Vegas, Nev.
Latrobe, Pa.
Leamington, Ont.
Lethbridge, Alta.
Liberal, Kan.
Little Rock, Ark.
Lloydminster, Alta.
London, Ont.
Loring, Me.
Magog, Que.
Malmstrom, Mont.
Maniwaki, Que.
Mankato, Minn.
Maple, Ont.
Markham, Ont.
Matane, Que.
McAdam, N.B.
McChord AFB, Wash.
McConnell AFB, Kan.
McGuire AFB, N.J.
Meadow Lake, Sask.
Medford, Ore.
Medicine Hat, Alta.
Melville, Sask.
Midland, Tex.
Minneapolis, Minn.
Minnedosa, Man.
Minot, N.D.
Mirabel, Que.
Moisie, Que.
Moncton, N.B.
Mont-Joli, Que.
Mont Laurier, Que.
Montmagny, Que.
Montreal, Que.
Moose Jaw, Sask.
Morrisburg, Ont.
Mosport, Ont.
Muskogee, Okla.
Muskoka, Ont.
Nackawic, N.B.
Namao (Edmonton), Alta.
Nanaimo, B.C.
NAS Fallon, Nev.
NAS Memphis, Tenn.
NAS Miramar, Calif.
NAS Oceana, Va.
NAS Patuxent River, Md.
NAS Pensacola, Fla.
NAS Point Mugu, Calif.
NAS Whidbey Island, Wash.
Nashville, Tenn.
Nellis AFB, Nev.
New Liskeard, Ont.

New York, N.Y.	Radisson, Que.	Shelburne, N.S.	Tillsonburg, Ont.
Newburg, Conn.	Rancho Murieta, Calif.	Sherbrooke, Que.	Timmins, Ont.
Niagara Falls, N.Y.	Randolph AFB, Tex.	Shilo, Man.	Tinker AFB, Okla.
Nipawin, Sask.	Reading, Pa.	Shoal Lake, Man.	Topeka, Kan.
Norman Wells, N.W.T.	Red Deer, Alta.	Simcoe, Ont.	Toronto, Ont.
North Battleford, Sask.	Red Lake, Ont.	Sioux Lookout, Ont.	Trail, B.C.
North Bay, Ont.	Redding, Calif.	Slave Lake, Alta.	Travis AFB, Calif.
North Bend, Ore.	Reese AFB, Tex.	Smithers, B.C.	Trenton, Ont.
Oklahoma City, Okla.	Regina, Sask.	Smiths Falls, Ont.	Trois-Rivières, Que.
Orillia, Ont.	Reno, Nev.	Souris, Man.	Truro, N.S.
Oshawa, Ont.	Richards Gebaur AFB, Mo.	Spokane, Wash.	Tucumcari, N.M.
Oshkosh, Wis.	Rimouski, Que.	Spartanburg, S.C.	Tyndall AFB, Fla.
Otis ANG, Mass.	Rivière-du-Loup, Que.	Springbank, Alta.	Val d'Or, Que.
Ottawa, Ont.	Roberval, Que.	Springfield, Ill.	Valcartier, Que.
Owen Sound, Ont.	Robins AFB, Ga.	St. Andrews, Man.	Valleyfield, Que.
Page/Lake Powell, Ariz.	Rockford, Ill.	St. Annes des Plaines, Que.	Vance AFB, Okla.
Paine Field, Wash.	Rockland, Ont.	St. Catharines, Ont.	Vancouver, B.C.
Parry Sound, Ont.	Rosetown, Sask.	St. Hubert, Que.	Vanderhoof, B.C.
Pasco, Wash.	Roswell, N.M.	St. Jérome, Que.	Vegreville, Alta.
Paspébiac, Que.	Rouyn, Que.	St. John's, Nfld.	Vermilion, Alta.
Peace River, Alta.	Royal Military College,	St. Louis, Mo.	Vernon, B.C.
Peachland, B.C.	Kingston, Ont.	St. Stephen, N.B.	Victoria, B.C.
Pemberton, B.C.	Royal Roads Military	St-Damien, Que.	Victoriaville, Que.
Pembroke, Ont.	College, Victoria, B.C.	St-Fréderic-de-Beauce, Que.	Ville Marie, Que.
Penticton, B.C.	Sacramento, Calif.	St-Georges-de-Beauce, Que.	Virden, Man.
Petawawa, Ont.	Saint John, N.B.	St-Isidore, Que.	Wabush, Nfld.
Peterborough, Ont.	Salinas, Calif.	St-Jean, Que.	Warwick, R.I.
Peterson AFB, Colo.	San Angelo, Tex.	Ste. Anne Des Monts, Que.	Waterloo, Ont.
Philadelphia, Pa.	San Diego, Calif.	Ste-Claire, Que.	Waterloo, Que.
Pictou, N.S.	San Francisco, Calif.	Ste-Jean-Chrysostome, Que.	Watson Lake, Yukon
Pitt Meadows, B.C.	Sandspit, B.C.	Ste-Raymond, Que.	Westover AFB, Mass.
Plattsburgh, N.Y.	Sarnia, Ont.	Stephenville, Nfld.	Wetaskiwin, Alta.
Pointe-au-Pic, Que.	Saskatoon, Sask.	Stockton, Calif.	Whitehorse, Yukon
Port Elgin, Ont.	Sauble Beach, Ont.	Stratford, Ont.	Whiteman AFB, Mo.
Port Hardy, B.C.	Sault Ste. Marie, Ont.	Sudbury, Ont.	Wiarton, Ont.
Portage la Prairie, Man.	Scott AFB, Ill.	Summerside, P.E.I.	Wilkes Barre Scranton, Pa.
Portland, Ore.	Seattle, Wash.	Swift Current, Sask.	Williamsport, Pa.
Prince Albert, Sask.	Selfridge ANG, Mich.	Sydney, N.S.	Windsor, Ont.
Prince George, B.C.	Senneterre, Que.	Syracuse, N.Y.	Winnipeg, Man.
Prince Rupert, B.C.	Sept-Iles, Que.	Tacoma, Wash.	Wolfville, N.S.
Providence, R.I.	Seymour Johnson AFB, N.C.	Terrace, B.C.	Yakima, Wash.
Quad Cities, Iowa	Shaw AFB, S.C.	Thetford Mines, Que.	Yarmouth, N.S.
Quebec City, Que.	Shearwater, N.S.	Thompson, Man.	Yellowknife, N.W.T.
Quill Lake, Sask.	Shediac, N.B.	Thunder Bay, Ont.	Yorkton, Sask.

Family...
the wind beneath our wings

Alice Drader

Ken Jubenvill

Alice Drader

Ken Jubenvill

Ed Drader

Behind every member of the Snowbirds there is a family, whether wives and children, mothers and fathers, or brothers and sisters. The Snowbird airshow season is a long one for loved ones left behind at home, but without their support the team could not function. They too become an integral component of a successful season. Family day is a joyous annual event – a last opportunity to share family togetherness, take photos and strengthen the bonds that will keep the group support network strong while the team is on the road for six months.

Alice Drader

CREWMAN- CPL MARC COSSETTE

Jacquie Perrin

PILOT - CAPT JOE PARENTE

Ed Drader

Ed Drader

Larry Milbe

Ken Jubenvill

Ed Drader

Ken Jubenvill

When Snowbirds Fly

Of all the stirring stories told,
Of ships that fly, and pilots bold,
There's one that seems to stand above
And still today, the one I love.

First "Siskins" dared, wings joined by rope
Their pilots flew on guts and hope.
Then "Sabres" formed the "Golden Hawks"
Till came the "Harvards, Goldilocks."

They tried in groups and then in pairs
When last was struck the "Centennaires"
So proud they flew that final team
Until was born the flying dream.

At first a string of twinkling lights
Rose skyward streaming plumes of white
No one before had seen this view,
Dear Lord it seemed a crowded blue.

First one, then two, and then came three
Now four, now five, now six, oh me!
And then came seven, eight and nine
I'd never seen a sight so fine.

Down and down I watched them break,
Inside I prayed there's no mistake,
Just then above me backed by blue
A diamond formed as if on cue.

And soon the air was filled with song,
As "Snowbirds" flew where they belong
And all because of someone's dream,
To give our land a flying team.

Then as the Tutors filled the skies
I watched as hundreds wiped their eyes,
It seemed as though from one display
A nation raised it's head that day.

Around me thousands glowed with pride
A people standing side by side,
Then as we watched a view sublime
Our country's finest passed in line.

That day beneath a magic sky,
The tears began to fill my eye
For as I gazed above in awe
An airborne flag was what I saw.

And sadly some did fall from space
But then another filled his place,
Because a legend does not die,
And that's the reason "Snowbirds" fly.

Pat Phillips

In Memoriam

Five Snowbirds have lost their lives while serving with the team since 1971. Their legacy lives on … they shall not be forgotten.

Capt Lloyd Waterer	Capt Gord de Jong	Capt Wes MacKay	Capt Shane Antaya	Capt Michael VandenBos
1972	1978	1988	1989	1998

John McQuarrie

The Snowbirds Gallery

As the longest serving aerobatic team in Canadian history, the Snowbirds have inspired many a portrait by artists who have attempted to capture both the beauty and grace of the Snowbird show. Following are some fine examples of dozens of works, including several by members of the Canadian Aviation Artists Association.

Graham Wragg, *Snowbirds, Smoke Now*, 1978

Rich Thistle, *Flying the Flag*, 2000

Dale Cline, *Coloured Smoke*, 1990

Don Connolly, *The Birthday Boys*, 1980

Yvette Moore, *Snowbirds – 431 Air Demonstration Squadron*, 1992
Reproduced from *A Prairie Alphabet*, art copyright, 1992 by Yvette Moore,
published by Tundra Books

Paul Tuttle, *Solid Concentration*, 1997

Geoff Bennett, *Grounded for Weather*, 1987

Jerry Davidson, *Over Home Plate*, 1994

Colin Latta, *Celebrating Twenty Years*, 1990

Robert Bailey, *Precision Pass*, 1992

William S. Phillips, *Sunward We Climb*, 1987

Carrie Friend, *Canada Burst*, 1988

R.L. Whitcomb, *Capital Performance*, 1995

John Rutherford, *Through the Valley*, 1997

William Perry, *The Art of Precision*, 2001

Tom Sinclair, *A Snowbird Salute*, 1998

Dave Leonard, *Canada's Ambassadors*, 1995

With the completion of the latest Canadian International Air Show in Toronto, well over eight decades have passed since Canadian patrons at the 1919 CNE were first captivated by a formation display of four tiny biplanes under the command of LCol William Barker. The litany of Canadian military teams that followed that first unofficial team is long and distinguished. Whereas several of these teams once existed at the same time, today the sole guardians of Canada's airshow team heritage are the Snowbirds. Yet, in spite of that extended passage of time, the human fascination that draws millions of spectators to airshows in Canada and around the world every summer has never waned. And for good reason – airshows provide outstanding entertainment as they contrast man's earliest quest to fly with the aviation technology that subsequently turned science fiction into scientific reality and sent man to the moon. It is that same spirit of human adventure and conquest that within this generation could very well put a team of astronauts on the planet Mars.

In the North American context, the International Council of Air Shows (ICAS) estimates that upwards of 18 million spectators take in airshows each year, more than any other live spectator event aside from major league baseball. Of that total, three to four million attend shows in Canada during an average season. These are impressive statistics which underscore why airshows have become a billion dollar industry. As one of the world's showcase teams, the Snowbirds constitute a vital part of that industry and belong to a very unique fraternity.

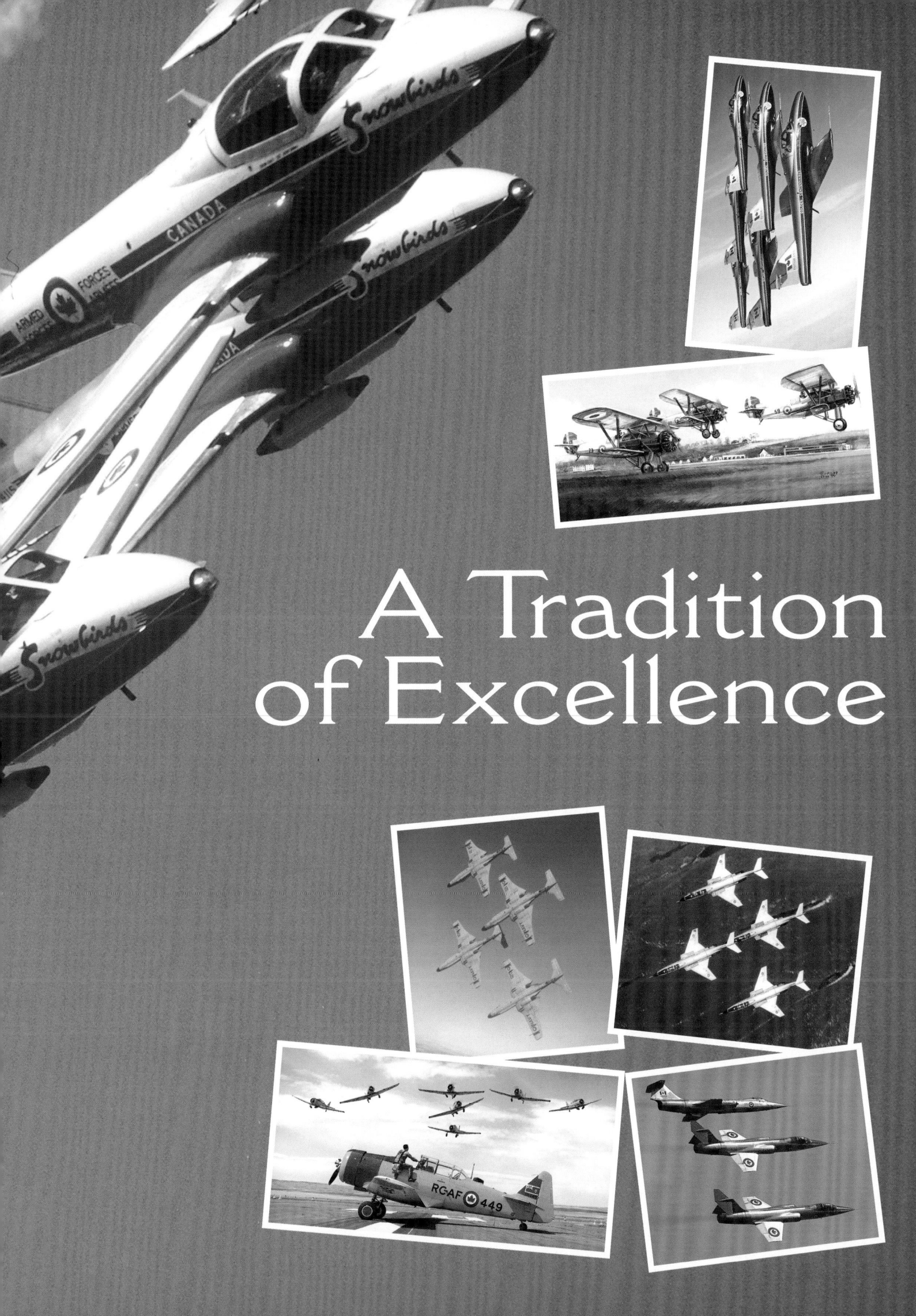

A Tradition of Excellence

The G-8 Aerobatic Teams

One manifestation of world status among the so-called Group of Eight (G-8) industrialized nations is a full-time military jet aerobatic team which is used as a means of public relations and recruiting for their military forces. Decades of exposure have also proven that these teams fulfill a much broader and popular role as aerial ambassadors for their nations, in many ways reflecting their national character as they tour allied countries. Several of the teams, notably those of the United States and Great Britain, have toured extensively worldwide over the years.

In order of their formation, the world's major teams include the United States Navy Blue Angels (1946), United States Air Force Thunderbirds (1953), *Patrouille de France* (1953), Japanese Defence Force Blue Impulse (1959), Italian Air Force *Frecce Tricolori* (1961), Royal Air Force Red Arrows (1965), Canadian Forces Snowbirds (1971) and finally the Russian Air Force *Russkiye Vityazi* (Russian Knights – 1991). Most of these teams have long and distinguished histories, many having been born of earlier predecessors such as the Canadian teams illustrated throughout this book.

What sets the G-8 jet teams apart from other aerobatic teams flying today is not only that they are each world-famous in their own right, but that they are integral components of their respective armed services whose members are posted full-time to the team for the duration of their tours, normally two to three years in most cases. With their collective numbers annually totaling fewer than 65 pilots and only several hundred technicians, it is indeed a unique fraternity. The highly competitive selection to such a team is considered a rare honour and, for many, the pinnacle of one's aviation career. With that honour however, comes the heavy mantle of responsibility to represent one's nation in a very public, and frequently heavily publicized, fashion. Along with the hundreds of hours spent perfecting aerial routines comes a myriad of public relations activities ranging from school and hospital visits to speaking engagements and lengthy autograph sessions after most shows.

Although the aerial demonstrations presented by the major jet teams are all different due to the varying types and numbers of show aircraft, they can be broadly based into two groups. The American teams have traditionally used state-of-the-art frontline fighters to present their shows which are very much focused on a "power-projection" type of display – loud and fast, normally with six fighters featuring exceptionally tight diamond formations and the ample use of booming afterburners by two opposing solos to generate crowd reaction. The Russians in their large and powerful fighters fit this mold and to a lesser extent so do the Japanese which utilize six fighter-trainers in their show.

In contrast, the major European teams eventually moved away from frontline fighters as their choice of aircraft to more economical advanced jet trainers which permitted the incorporation of larger formations of eight to 10 aircraft, while still achieving significantly lower operational costs than that of a fighter team. The benefit of the additional aircraft was that they permitted a more complicated choreography that could best be described as an aerial ballet with their larger, diverse for-

Of the eight major jet teams flying in the world today, three of them are based in North America. The Snowbirds have been flying alongside their American counterparts since 1971. (via 431 Sqn)

mations and dynamic splits and bomb bursts. Almost from their inception, each of the three main European teams have also used coloured smoke representing their national colours to further enhance their shows – with striking results. It was to this type of display that the RCAF/Canadian Armed Forces also shifted their focus with the formation of the Golden Centenaires in 1967 and subsequently the Snowbirds in 1971.

Both types of shows have their relative merits and both have generated passionate debate as to which is more appealing. There is no question that the success of these major teams and their predecessors in the years following World War II fostered the growth of what has become a phenomenal airshow industry in the west in which the major jet teams are the prime attraction. Airshows that have long been popular in North America and Western Europe, with single day audiences at the largest shows occasionally reaching hundreds of thousands of spectators, have gained popularity in Asia and were also doing so in Eastern Europe until disaster struck on July 27th, 2002. The world's worst airshow disaster at Lviv, Ukraine resulted when an air force solo demonstration pilot lost control of his Su-27 Flanker and plowed into the crowd. Clearly, the east has a long way to go in implementing the strict training regime and safety measures that have been extant in the west to protect spectators for many years. In the last dozen years, both Russia (now a junior partner in NATO) and the Ukraine have formed jet formation teams, although their status is uncertain. All military flying at the August 2002 Moscow International Air Show at Domodedovo was banned. The Chinese formed a national aerobatic team as early as 1962, and many other nations around the globe that were eager to promote their national colours and pride in their respective military forces followed suit. Although some nations such as Australia, Brazil, Chile and Poland now field turboprop teams, the aircraft of choice for the majority of national teams remains jet trainer or fighter aircraft. In recent years, there have been almost two dozen jet teams flying around the world.

The Snowbirds and the Future

In spite of the fact that the Snowbirds were the last of the original G-7 teams to join the fraternity, they were quick to achieve an enviable international reputation, building on that established by such eminent predecessors as the RCAF Golden Hawks and Golden Centenaires. In playing an indispensable role in public relations and recruiting on behalf of the Canadian Forces over the years, they have also become one of Canada's most visible and enduring national symbols. By the end of the 2002 airshow season, the team will have performed some 1,840 public demonstrations in their Canadair-built CT-114 Tutors and, based on historical averages, should complete their 2,000th performance during the 2005 season. To date, over 100 million spectators across North America have witnessed a Snowbird show while hundreds of millions more have been exposed to the team through television and video documentaries worldwide. Of significance however, is the fact that the Snowbirds are today the only G-8 team that has never conducted a trans-oceanic tour to Europe or Asia. In spite of various invitations and political initiatives,

the limited range of the Tutor aircraft and expense of transporting the team aircraft via other means has always been deemed cost prohibitive, much to the disappointment of many countries that would warmly welcome Canada's aerial ambassadors. This situation could eventually be resolved by the acquisition of a new team aircraft.

It is within the domain of demonstration aircraft that the Snowbirds also hold another unique distinction among the original teams of the world's industrial nations in that they are the only team that has never changed aircraft type. While it is a remarkable testament to the durability of the Tutor and the skill of squadron members that the team continues to enjoy such widespread popularity, the team

Snowbird pilots have been creating their aerial magic from the confines of the Tutor for over 30 years. (DND Photo, Cpl C.H. Roy)

is rapidly approaching a crossroads in its history. If the team is to continue, which most informed observers would agree it must as a national icon and the most visible unit of the Canadian Forces, then ultimately federal funds must be identified to allow the procurement of new aircraft to proceed in a timely fashion. The responsibility for identifying those funds must fall squarely on the federal government and not simply on the military leadership of the Canadian Forces who already face a daunting task in trying to meet operational commitments in the face of debilitating cuts to the Department of National Defence budget that amounted to some 23 percent between 1994 and 1999.

Each of the countries that sponsor a national aerobatic team have had to rationalize the expenses associated with maintaining their

National Jet Aerobatic Teams of the World

Country Year Formed	Team Name	Number of Show Aircraft	Present Aircraft Type
Canada 1971	Snowbirds	9	Canadair CT-114 Tutor
China 1962	81 (*Bah-yi*)	6	Chengdu F-7EB fighter
Finland 1962	Midnight Hawks	4	BAE Systems Hawk Mk 51
France 1953	*Patrouille de France*	8	Dassault/Dornier Alpha Jet E
India 1996	*Suryakiran*	9	Hindustan HJT-16 *Kiran* II trainer
Israel 1960	Israeli Aerobatic Team	4	IAI AMIT *Tzukit* (Fouga Magister)
Italy 1961	*Frecce Tricolori*	10	Aermacchi MB-399A/PAN trainer
Japan 1959	Blue Impulse	6	Kawasaki T-4 fighter trainer
Pakistan 1950s	Pakistani Aerobatic Team	6	Cessna T-37C trainer
Russia 1990	*Strizhi*	6	MiG-29A and MiG-29UB Fulcrum
1991	Russian Knights (*Russkiye Vityazi*)	6	Sukhoi Su-27 Flanker-B
Saudi Arabia 1998	Green Hawks	6	BAE Systems Hawk Mk 65
Slovakia 1991	*Biele Albatrosy*	6	L-39C Albatross trainer
South Korea 1953	Black Eagles	6	Cessna A-37B Dragonfly
Spain 1985	*Patrulla Aguila*	7	CASA C-101EB Aviojet
Sweden 1976	Team 60	6	Saab SK60 trainer
Switzerland 1964	*Patrouille Suisse*	6	Northrop Grumman F-5E Tiger II
Taiwan 1956	Thunder Tigers	7	AIDC AT-3 *Tse-Chiang* trainer
Turkey 1993	Turkish Stars	7	Canadair NF-5A Freedom Fighter
Ukraine 1997	*Ukraniskiy Sokoli*	6	MiG-29A Fulcrum
United Kingdom 1965	Red Arrows	9	BAE Systems Hawk T1
United States 1946	Blue Angels	6	Boeing F/A-18 Hornet
1953	Thunderbirds	6	Lockheed-Martin F-16C Falcon
Yugoslavia 1984	*Letece Zvezde*	7	Soko G-4 Super Galeb

The above countries have been represented by national jet aerobatic teams in recent years.

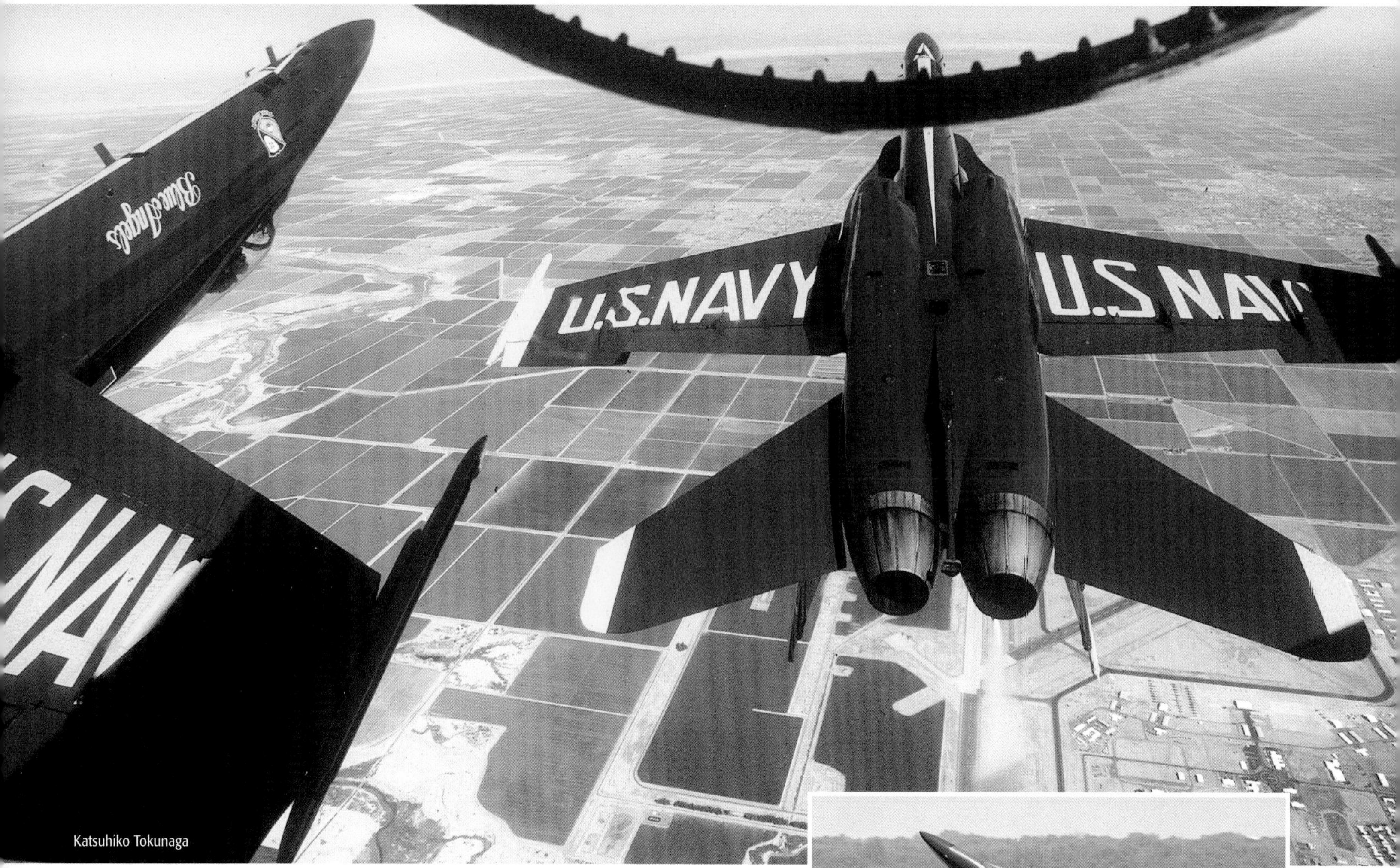

Katsuhiko Tokunaga

Blue Angels

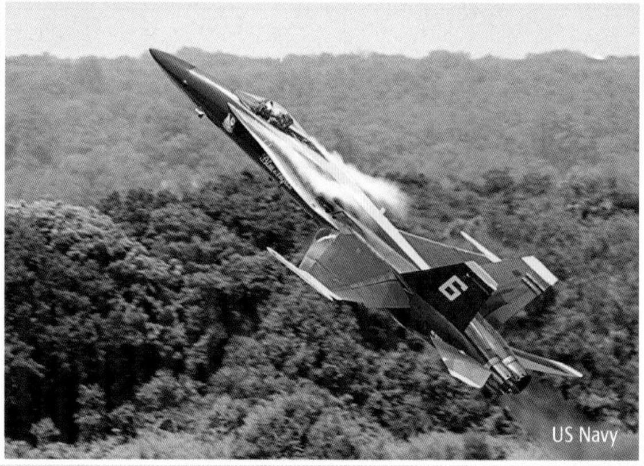

Grumman F6F Hellcat	1946
Grumman F8F Bearcat	1946
Grumman F9F-2 Panther	1949
Grumman F9F-5 Panther	1951
Grumman F9F-8 Cougar	1954
Grumman F11F-1 Tiger	1957
McDonnell Douglas F-4J Phantom II	1969
McDonnell Douglas A-4F Skyhawk	1975
McDonnell Douglas F/A-18 Hornet	1987

US Navy

Bill Johnson

Katsuhiko Tokunaga

Thunderbirds

USAF

USAF

Katsuhiko Tokunaga

Patrouille de France

Republic F-84G Thunderjet	1953
Dassault MD 450 Ouragon	1954
Dassault Mystere IV A	1957
Fouga CM-170 Magister	1964
Dassault/Dornier Alpha Jet E	1981

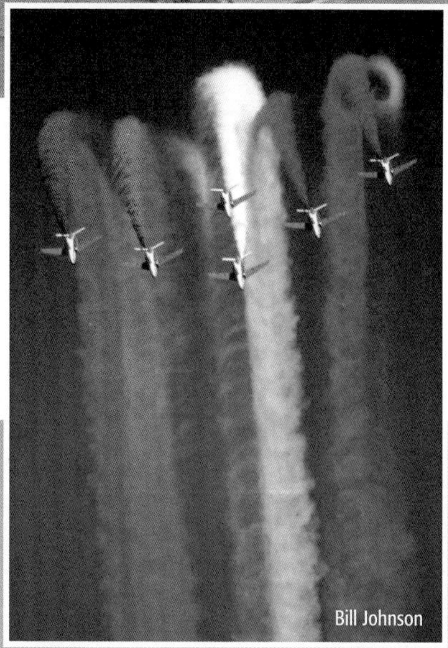

Bill Johnson

Bill Johnson

Katsuhiko Tokunaga

Katsuhiko Tokunaga

Blue Impulse

F-86F Sabre	1959
Mitsubishi T-2	1981
Kawasaki T-4	1996

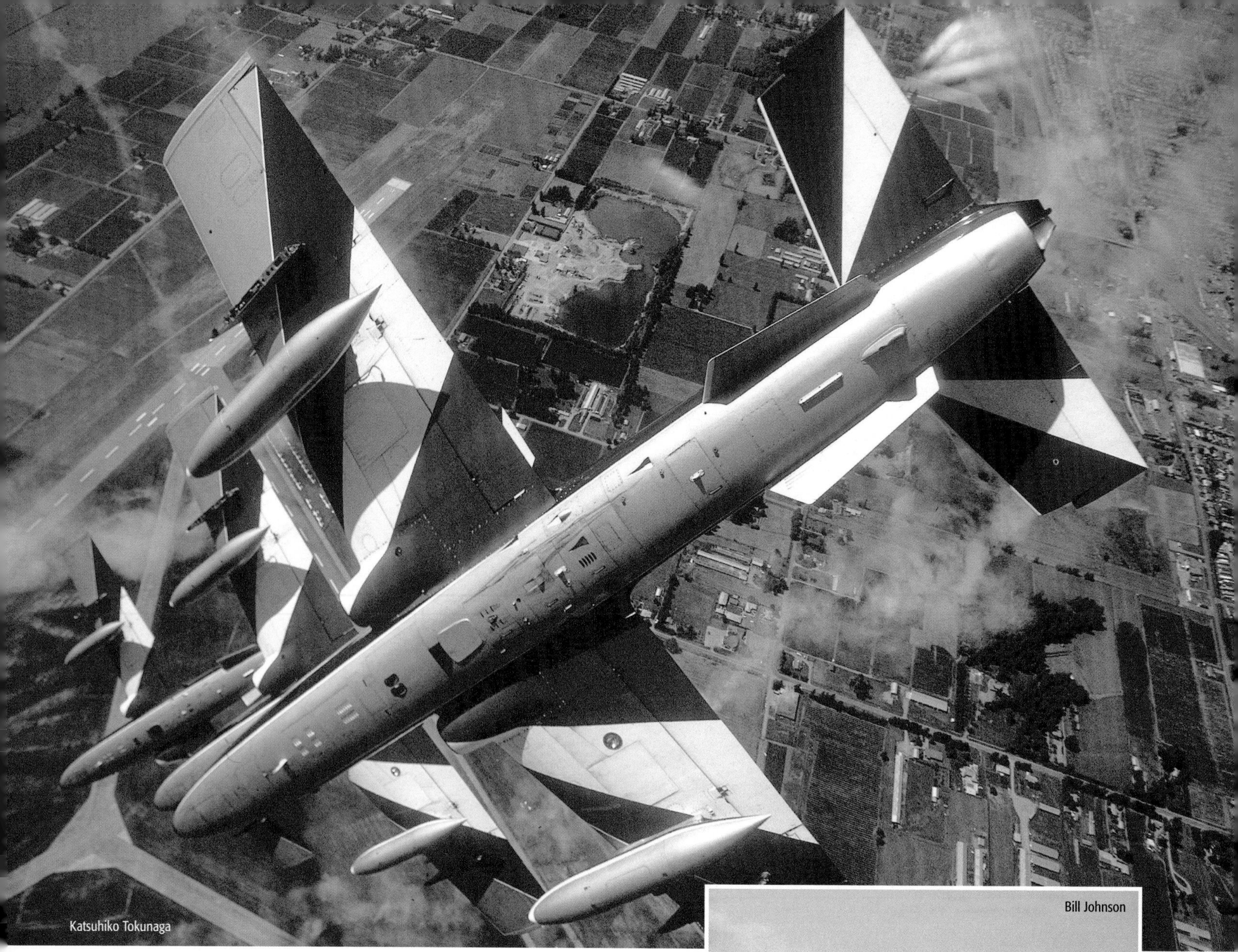

Katsuhiko Tokunaga

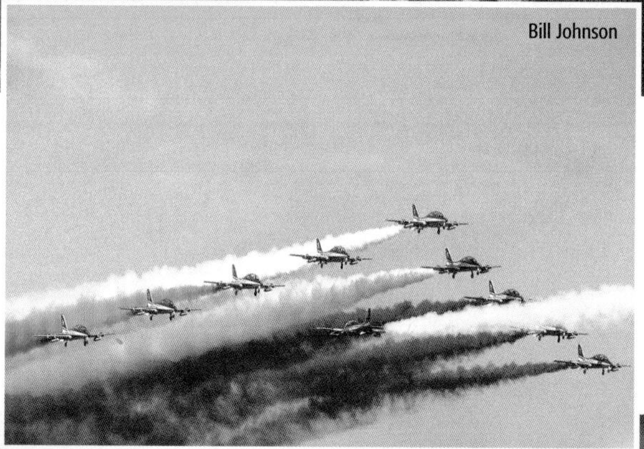

Frecce Tricolori

North American F-86E Sabre	1961
Aeritalia Fiat G-91/PAN	1964
Aermacchi MB-399A/PAN	1982

Bill Johnson

PAN via JW Jones

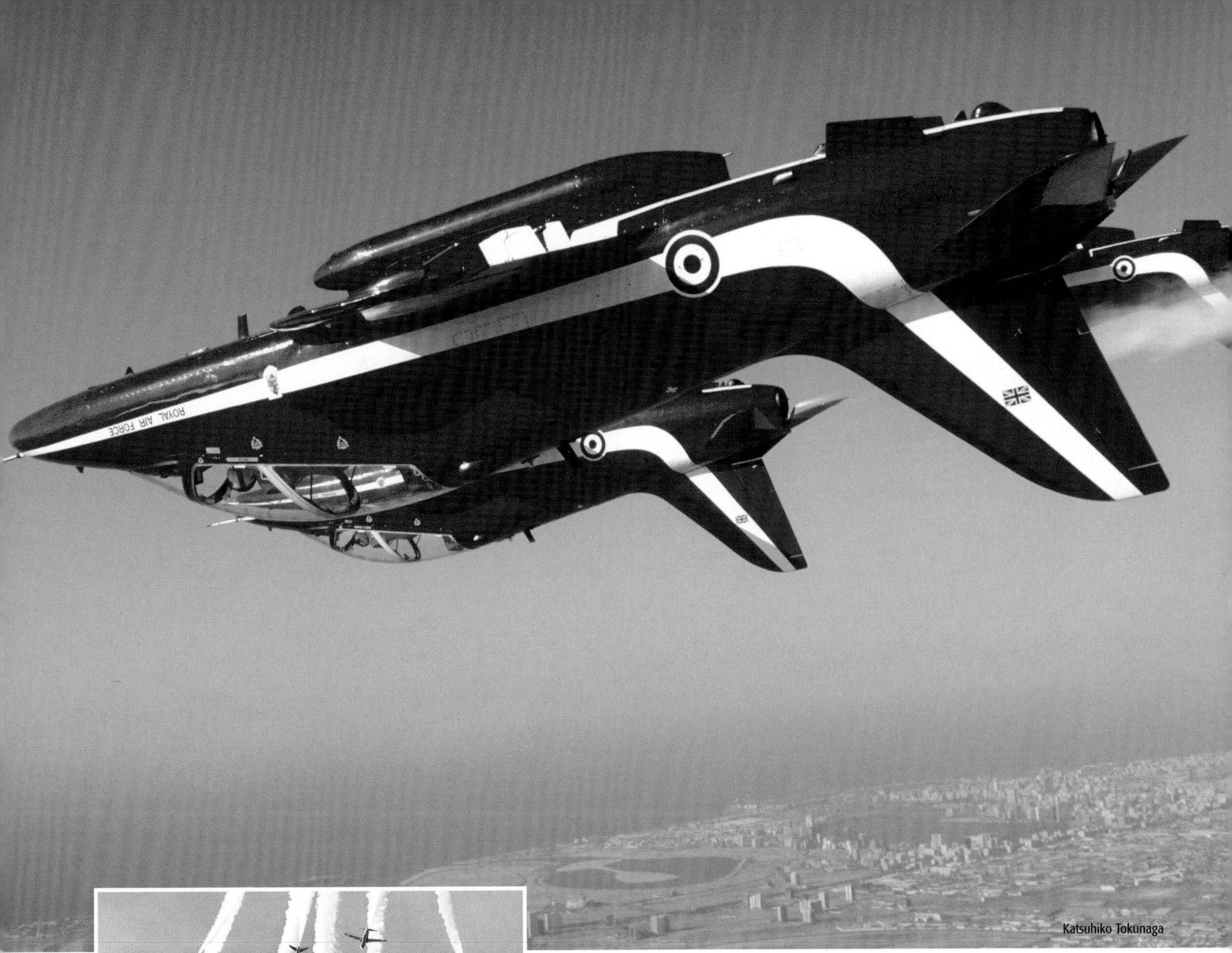

Katsuhiko Tokunaga

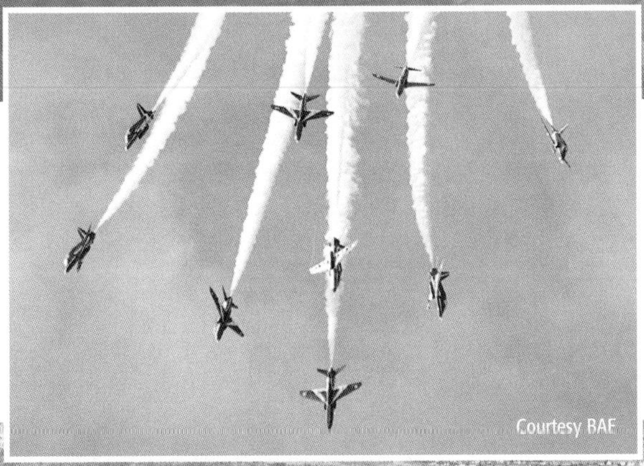

Courtesy BAE

Red Arrows

Hawker Siddeley Gnat T1	1965
BAE Systems Hawk T1	1980

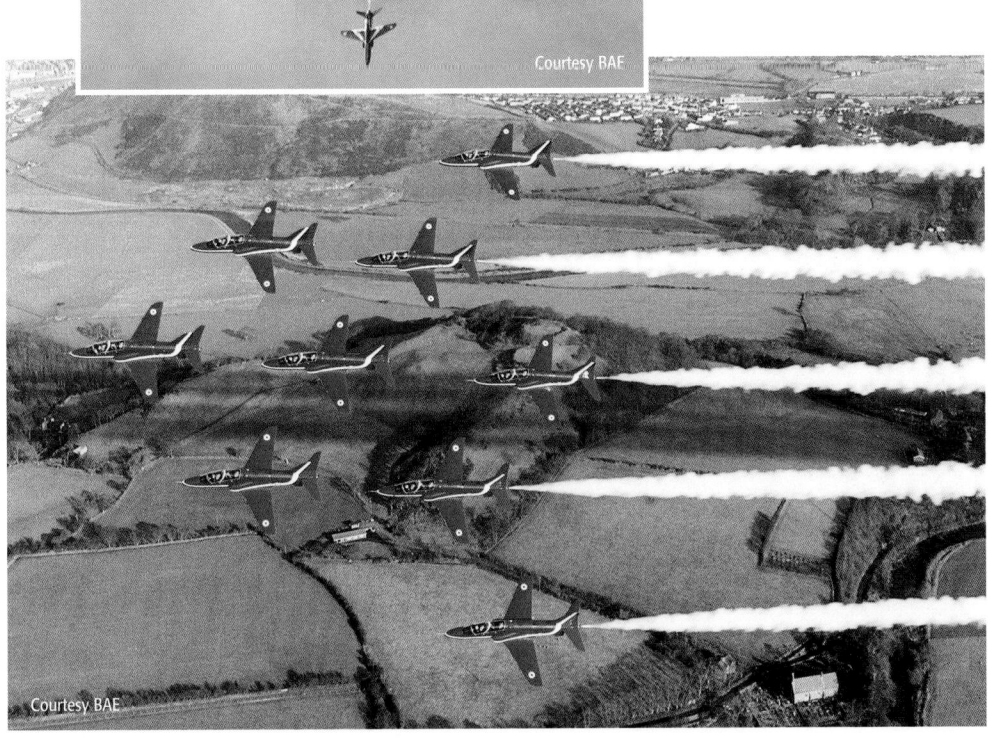

Courtesy BAE

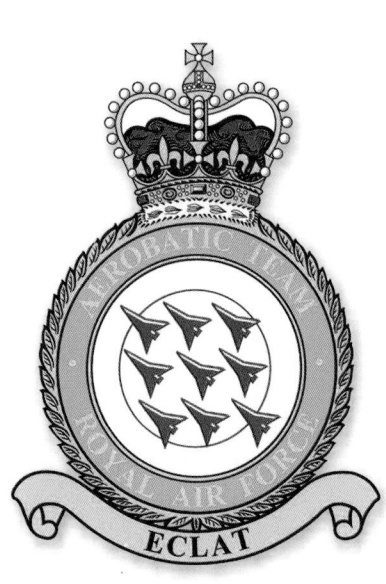

Bill Johnson

Snowbirds

Canadair CT-114 Tutor   1971

Ed Drader

Rafe Tomsett

Katsuhiko Tokunaga

Russian Knights

Sukhoi Su-27 Flanker-B   1991

Note: The future of the Russian Knights is uncertain due to financial difficulties within the Russian military.

Katsuhiko Tokunaga

Katsuhiko Tokunaga

Although the Tutor was retired as the basic jet trainer of the Canadian Forces in July 2000, the aircraft seems destined to keep looping and rolling with the Snowbirds until the end of the 2006 airshow season. (Roman Holowatyj)

team with the benefits that accrue from such investment. Invariably, those benefits have kept all of the world's major teams intact. When faced with the suggestion that the Red Arrows might not survive Ministry of Defence budget cuts in the early 1990s, the RAF's reaction was to send the team on a world tour largely funded by British industry which rallied around the team.

In September of 1999 the potential disbandment of the Snowbirds in the face of the impending retirement of the Tutor as the basic jet trainer of the Canadian Forces created widespread media attention across the country. Not surprisingly, the news generated a public outcry in Canada which resulted in a government commitment to keep the team alive indefinitely as a separate, stand-alone demonstration squadron that will continue to use the Tutor pending an in-depth analysis to consider future options. Extending the Snowbird fleet of Tutors beyond the currently planned 2006 airshow season would necessitate a complete overhaul of the aircraft to include an entire new avionics suite to replace the antiquated

instrumentation the team has now been using for three decades. Conventional wisdom would dictate that the funds necessary to complete such a refurbishment would be better spent towards a new aircraft that would give the team a new 20 to 25 year lease on life and, equally important, a fresh new image. In spite of its effectiveness over the years, the Tutor aircraft no longer depicts the modern, state-of-the-art air force that it did when it was introduced to the RCAF inventory in 1964.

Aircraft Options

The culmination of the 35th consecutive year of Snowbird performances at the end of 2005 will coincide with the 39th anniversary since the 190th and last Tutor was delivered to the RCAF on September 28th, 1966. This celebration would be a most appropriate time to mark the final retirement of the aircraft and introduction of a replacement to allow the team to move into a new era. There are presently only three possible replacement aircraft for the Snowbirds in the Canadian Forces inventory – the Boeing

CF-18 Hornet fighter, BAE Systems Hawk 115 advanced jet trainer and the Raytheon T-6A Harvard II turboprop basic trainer.

The Hornet has now been the front-line fighter of the Canadian Forces for 20 years. Current plans call for 80 of the aircraft to undergo a multi-million dollar upgrade program commencing in 2002 to keep them combat-capable until the year 2017. This is deemed the absolute minimum number of aircraft required to maintain the four operational and one training squadron currently in service. Even if surplus, unmodified Hornets were made available to the Snowbirds, the team's show complement would almost certainly be reduced to six aircraft and the day-to-day operational and maintenance costs associated with the aircraft could be cost prohibitive. Moreover, a switch to the Hornet would dictate a move of the team to Cold Lake, Alberta where maintenance facilities are already located for three Hornet squadrons. The complexity of the aircraft would also necessitate a dedicated support aircraft to transport spare parts and a large team of technicians during the six-month airshow season, something the team has always been able to avoid. Thus, while the Snowbirds could put on a very fine show with the Hornet, there seems little likelihood of ever seeing the team equipped with the CF-18.

Of the two remaining possibilities, both the Harvard II and Hawk were introduced as new trainers in 2000 as part of a unique partnership between the Canadian government and aviation industry. Significantly, both are currently based at the Snowbirds home base in Moose Jaw, Saskatchewan. While the Harvard II is a modern aircraft well suited to its basic training role, its relatively slow speed and limited range would make it very difficult for the Snowbirds to transit back and forth across the expanse of Canada in a timely fashion to meet the demands of the airshow season. And even though it would represent the cheapest option, the use of a turboprop versus a jet aircraft would represent such a fundamental step backwards in terms of prestige and overall show impact that it is highly questionable whether the team would even survive. There is no doubt the reputation and favoured status that the Snowbirds presently enjoy on the North American airshow circuit would be severely diminished by switching to a turboprop aircraft, which in turn could make it difficult for the team to fulfill its mandate and attract new volunteers to its ranks.

Although the Hornet has been the mainstay of Canada's fighter force for 20 years and remains a highly popular airshow act, it is considered unlikely that the aircraft will ever be adorned in Snowbird colours, that privilege remaining with the US Navy Blue Angels. (Garry Cotter)

The BAE Systems Hawk 115 (foreground) and Raytheon Harvard II are the newest training aircraft to join the Canadian Forces under the NFTC program. (Mike Reyno/Skytech Images)

The Hawk 115

The Hawk 115 is the latest derivative of the highly successful British Aerospace Hawk first introduced to the Royal Air Force in 1976 as an advanced jet trainer. With the introduction of the Hawk 115 (now manufactured by BAE Systems) to the Canadian Forces inventory, 18 countries around the world now utilize the aircraft as an advanced jet trainer. This popularity has led to a 30 to 36 month lead time in acquiring new Hawks, a fact government and military planners must take into account should the aircraft be selected as the Snowbirds new aircraft.

The suitability of the Hawk in the aerobatic team role is beyond question and was established long ago by the Red Arrows of the RAF who introduced the aircraft for the 1980 airshow season. In the last 22 years they have flown the Union Jack around the globe in a highly acclaimed nine-plane show that has now been witnessed in 50 different countries. Their 2002 itinerary once again included a popular visit to Canada where they performed at the Canadian International Air Show in Toronto and Nova Scotia International Air Show in Halifax. Adoption of the Hawk aircraft by the Snowbirds would allow Canada's aerial ambassadors to venture outside North America for the first time to visit allies and trading partners, repeating the flag-flying exercise every six or seven years as a showcase for Canadian talent.

Of the three aircraft under consideration to replace the Tutor, the Hawk is the only alternative that would allow the Snowbirds to maintain the integrity of the aerial demonstration they currently perform with the Tutor. Assuming a one-for-one replacement program that would permit the team to continue with nine show aircraft and two spares on the road during the airshow season, the relative cost efficiency of running the team without a dedicated support aircraft could be maintained. The Hawk is the aircraft of choice for the vast majority of ex-Snowbird team members, many senior military officers and airshow organizers alike. The millions of Canadians for whom the Snowbirds represent an irreplaceable symbol of national pride would be highly impressed with the Hawk given the opportunity to see the aircraft in Snowbird colours.

NATO Flying Training in Canada

The fact that the Hawk aircraft is even an alternative for the Snowbirds is the result of an initiative in the early 1990s that was proposed by Bombardier Inc. of Montreal. With the Department of National Defence beset by budget cuts across the board, the reduction of spending was so severe at the time that even military pilot training, one of the pillars upon which Canada's air force was built, was at risk of being contracted out abroad. The notion of losing the nation's enviable pilot training system did not sit well with senior air force officers, in or out of uniform, and a vision for a unique partnership resulted in the formation of the Canadian Aviation Training Centre (CATC) program at Portage la Prairie, Manitoba in 1992 for *ab initio*, multi-engine and rotary wing flying training for Canadian Forces pilots. Several allied nations also later joined the program. The success of the CATC initiative was a catalyst for the formation of the NATO Flying Training in Canada (NFTC) program which commenced in July of 2000, again supported by a Canadian industry team led by Bombardier.

Under the auspices of NFTC, Bombardier took over the existing infrastructure at Moose Jaw and built a world-class training facility of classrooms and simulators while simultaneously purchasing a fleet of Harvard IIs and Hawks upon which to conduct three essential phases of flying training – basic flying training and jet conversion training in Moose Jaw at 2 Canadian Forces Flying Training School and tactical fighter training in Cold Lake at 419 Tactical Fighter Training Sqn for those pilots selected to fly the CF-18. By employing civilian academic and simulator instructors (largely ex-air force) alongside currently serving air force flying instructors, the reputation for excellence developed over several decades has

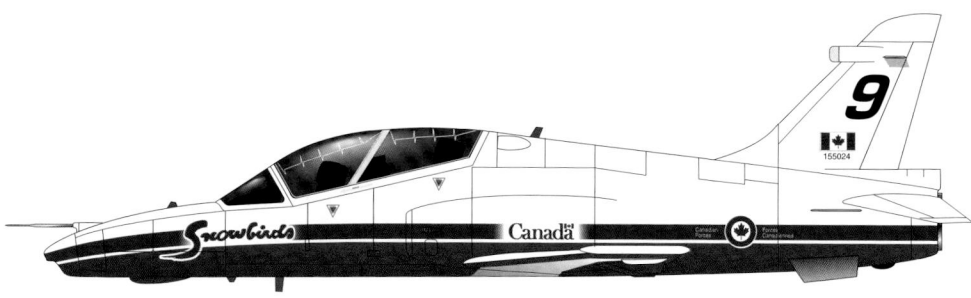

The Hawk 115 is a strong contender to replace the Canadair Tutor in the Snowbird role. Should it ultimately be selected, the Snowbirds would be the second G-8 team to adopt the aircraft, following in the footsteps of the RAF's famous nine-plane team, the Red Arrows. (Schematics courtesy BAE Systems, Snowbird adaptation by J.W. Jones)

been preserved. That reputation has also attracted multi-year contracts with a number of countries that are sending a select number of military pilots to Canada for flying training. In addition to young Canadians, national flags adorning flying suits in Moose Jaw and Cold Lake now include representation from Great Britain, Italy, Denmark, Hungary and Singapore, a reflection back to the glory days of the RCAF when Canada was also considered an international leader in flying instruction. With the enormous potential of the 20 year program to attract additional international customers, equipping the Snowbirds with the Hawk would be both logical and beneficial.

Within a few years, the first Canadian graduates of the NFTC program will have gained the requisite qualifications to compete for a position on the Snowbirds. With the future of military flying training in Canada firmly entrenched in NFTC, a team equipped with the Hawk would not only be valuable as a public relations and recruiting vehicle for the Canadian Forces, it would de facto become a roving advertisement for the merits of the NFTC concept. The synergy gained by such an arrangement could only benefit Canadian industry and local economies as more countries were attracted to the program.

Funding Alternatives

As with so many military programs over the last several decades, funding for the Snowbirds has been a constant nemesis. Yet, in comparison to the expenses incurred by the other G-8 nations that have already equipped their teams with more modern aircraft that command higher operating budgets, the Snowbirds have been a bargain for Canadians. In fact, the international reputation achieved by the team has been totally out of proportion to the funds expended in supporting it with its 1960's era jet trainer. The funds required to maintain that reputation will increase with the acquisition of a new aircraft.

Options available to the Canadian government in providing the Snowbirds with new aircraft range from the direct purchase of the 13 aircraft that would be required to continue to field a nine-plane team to a leasing arrangement similar to that now exercised through NFTC. Given the importance of the team as a national symbol, there is a compelling argument to be made for funding any future purchase of aircraft from general government revenues. At the very least, all future expenditures related to the team should be shared among those departments and ministries that benefit directly from the international recognition the team brings to Canada. These would include, among others, heritage, tourism, industry, foreign affairs and international trade as well as national defence. Representatives of many of these departments have lauded the Snowbirds over the years, both nationally and internationally, for the professional image they portray as ambassadors for Canada.

The 2002 Snowbirds met up with the 3 Wing and 4 Wing Demo Hornets in August at North Bay's Heritage Festival and Airshow. (Mike Reyno/Skytech Images)

An Integral Component

Aside from their physical presence as a national symbol, the Snowbirds also play a more subtle, but vital role within the Canadian Forces. They provide instant credibility wherever they perform and in so doing illustrate pride in profession – the same pride exemplified and so carefully protected by air force and naval traditions and the army's regimental system. It is the prospect of being part of these proud traditions that leads young men and women to don a uniform in service of their country. Indeed, the history of a unit and the essence of teamwork are two of the principals quickly ingrained in young recruits when they join the military. *Esprit de corps* and camaraderie are force multipliers. This in part explains why Canadian sailors, soldiers and airmen have traditionally done so well when given difficult operational missions, even in spite of possessing ageing equipment at times.

With the future of the Canadian Forces inexorably linked to the demographics of the country, official teams like the Snowbirds and Skyhawks will continue to play an integral and indispensable role in attracting young men and women to military careers. They face a challenging task. Statistics Canada population projections reveal that the prime target group for recruiting is in continual decline as the nation's population ages. By 2006, the percentage of the Canadian population in the 20-24 age group will have dropped to 6.68 percent, continuing to slide to 5.36 percent over the next 20 years. Combine these projections with strong competition from the civilian sector for the youth of the nation and it is clear that recruiting is going to continue to be a major challenge for the Canadian Forces. Given a new, modern aircraft and revitalized image, the Snowbirds will play a substantial role in helping meet that challenge.

Epilogue

The true significance of the Snowbirds and the legacy they represent can be measured in the hearts and minds of Canadians who turn their heads skyward year after year to marvel at the team's grace and precision as they weave their intricate patterns of smoke across the nation. Support for the team remains strong and continues to be manifested in many different ways, from the

The Snowbirds have long been recognized for their ability to relate important messages to the youth of the nation – one being to stay in school – the other being to refrain from using drugs. (via 431 Sqn)

enthusiastic applause the team receives at the dozens of airshows they perform each summer to the hundreds of letters of appreciation that have been forwarded to the team over the years – from prime ministers to school children.

It is the response of the children to the Snowbird experience that brings the greatest rewards to team members, past and present, and I am reminded of a telling experience in the stands of McMahon Stadium in Calgary in November 2000 where I was among some 45,000 Canadian Football League fans that had gathered to watch the annual fall classic, the Grey Cup. As is tradition, the national anthem before the game brought a great ovation from the masses as it concluded. What most fans had not noticed as the

last strains of *O Canada* faded out however, was that there were nine twinkling lights bearing down on the stadium from the west, the setting sun providing a spectacular backdrop. It was at this moment that master of ceremonies and CBC sports announcer Steve Armitage enthusiastically directed the fans' attention, as only he can, to "Canada's world-famous Snowbirds" as the jets rapidly approached the stadium. As heads swivelled to take in the spectacle, a surging escalation of cheers turned into a magnificent crescendo as the team swept low over the stadium trailing their characteristic smoke. The euphoria in the air was simply electric. As the deafening roar of the jets and crowd subsided, a wide-eyed youngster of about twelve sitting in front of me turned to his friend and spoke for everyone in attendance when he exclaimed, "That was totally cool!" That simple but emotionally charged statement spoke volumes about the relevance of the Snowbirds, a relevance that transcends economics.

In carrying on the legacy of their predecessors, the Snowbirds have become part of Canada's national fabric and identity, their universal appeal a force for national unity, its members role models for the youth of the nation as they demonstrate the skill, professionalism and teamwork that have earned them, and Canada, worldwide recognition. It is a legacy that simply must be preserved for future generations of Canadians to experience, not through movie documentaries or history books, but first-hand, in person, in the skies of the nation from coast-to-coast. Canada, and Canadians, deserve no less.

Per Ardua Ad Astra

Snowbird team members are looked upon as role models by thousands of young people across Canada. Team members spend hundreds of hours each year conducting public relations activities – from signing autographs at airshows to visiting schools and hospitals. (Ed Drader, Alice Drader)

The Flight of the Snowbirds

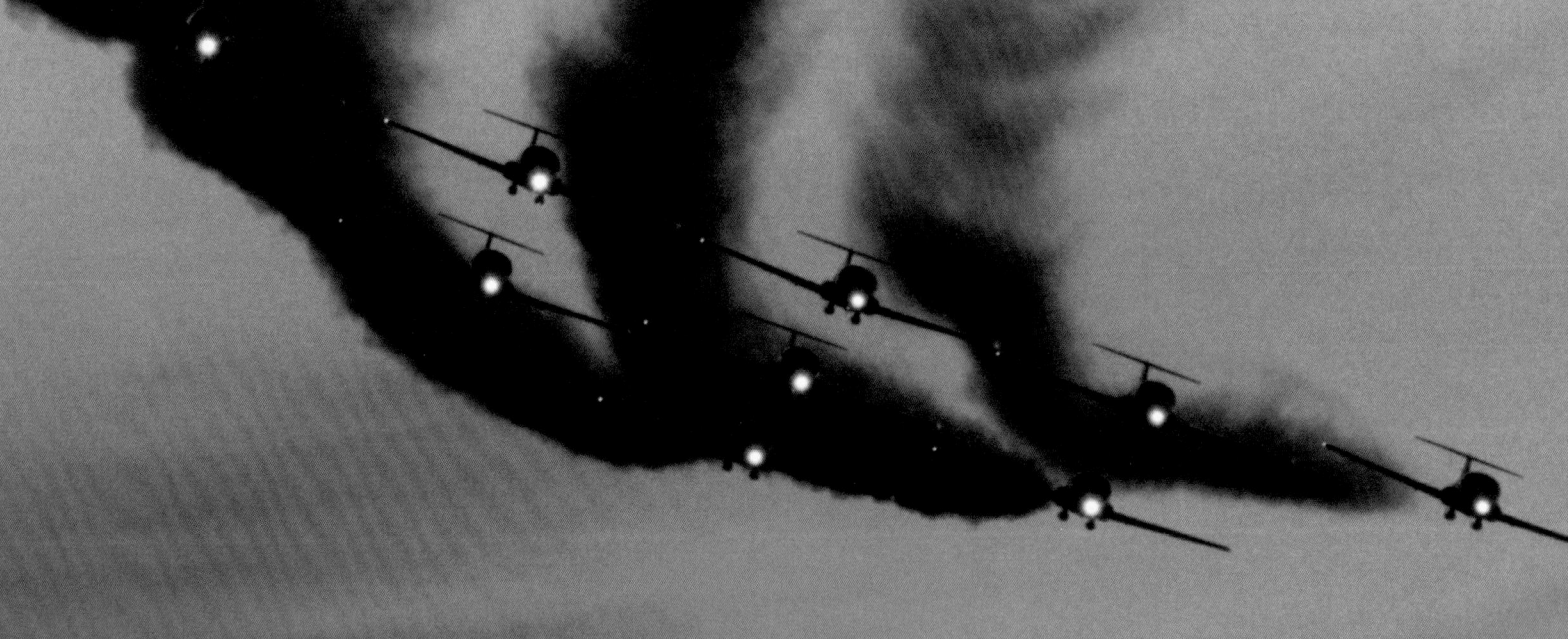

Spectators gather from far and wide,
Awaiting the Snowbirds whom they passionately pride.
The audience anticipates a magnificent sight,
They've travelled to view this sequenced flight.
The weather is perfect the sky is clear,
There is a hush over the crowd as the time draws near.
A voice over the loudspeaker welcomes the fans,
We then hear the officer give his final commands.
The pilots check in, it's time to go,
The Snowbirds are ready to fly their show.

In the distance you see nine twinkling lights,
Then the Snowbirds take off, what a spectacular sight.
These Canadian aircraft soar through the sky,
Proving the professionalism of the military as they fly.
This aerobatic team glides in perfect formation,
As they partake in manoeuvres that are of Canadian creation.
They perform the inverted wedge to big diamond loop,
And glide into the heart in a single swoop.
As the airshow progresses two jets break away,
Then the formation of seven go the opposite way.

The two aircraft partake in their solo flights,
Amazing the crowd with their passes of might.
They fly towards each other at 900 kilometres an hour,
Enduring this speed must take great will power.
Then 431 Squadron meets up one last time,
To engage in the downward burst, which is truly sublime.
This ending manoeuvre leaves white ribbons of smoke,
Drawing a trail through the sky like a perfect white cloak.
The red and white Snowbirds float down to the ground,
As the roar of their engines create a tremendous sound.
These Tutor jets coast to a calming standstill,
As the groundcrew give the thumbs up, and await the next drill.

It is now time for the pilots to unbuckle and descend.
Another splendid airshow has come to an end,
The pilots leap to the tarmac in their blazing red suits,
Giving all of their groundcrew appreciative salutes.
The Snowbird pilots then make their way to the crowd,
Offering autographs to the fans who are exceptionally proud.
These ambassadors of the sky, modest yet clever,
Have found a place in our hearts that will live on forever!

Alicia Crawford of Castleton, Ontario was a Grade 10 student when she penned this poem in January 2001.
She presented it in person to the Snowbirds later that summer.

Mike Reyno/Skytech Images

Jason Ransom, *The Ottawa Sun*

Glossary of Abbreviations

1 CAD — 1 Canadian Air Division
1 CAG — 1 Canadian Air Group
ACM — air combat manoeuvring
ADC — Air Defence Command
AEO — Aircraft Engineering Officer
AETE — Aerospace Engineering Test Establishment
AFB — Air Force Base
AFD — Air Force Day/Armed Forces Day
AFHQ — Air Force Headquarters
AFS — Advanced Flying School
AGL — above ground level
AI — airborne intercept
Air Div — No. 1 Air Division Europe
AIRCOM — Air Command
AOC — Air Officer Commanding
ATAF — Allied Tactical Air Force
ATC — Air Traffic Control
AW — All-weather
AWC — air weapons control (or, controller)
BCATP — British Commonwealth Air Training Plan
BComd — Base Commander
BFSO — Base Flight Safety Officer
BHTU — Basic Helicopter Training Unit
BOpsO — Base Operations Officer
BW1 — Bluie West 1, an airstrip in southern Greenland
CAdO — Chief Administration Officer
CAF — Canadian Armed Forces
CAS — Chief of the Air Staff
CAVOK — weather good for visual flight
CD — Canadian Forces Decoration
Cdn — Canadian
CDS — Chief of the Defence Staff
CEPE — Central Experimental and Proving Establishment
CF — Canadian Forces
CFB — Canadian Forces Base
CFFTS — Canadian Forces Flying Training School
CFHQ — Canadian Forces Headquarters
CFI — Chief Flying Instructor
CFS — Central Flying School
CFNS — Central Flying and Navigation School
CIAS — Canadian International Air Show (also referred to as the CNE Air Show)
CJATC — Canadian Joint Air Training Centre
Clunk — slang term for the CF-100 Canuck
CNE — Canadian National Exhibition
CO — Commanding Officer
COpsO — Chief Operations Officer
COS — Chief of Staff
CWH — Canadian Warplane Heritage
Det — Detachment

DComd — Deputy Commander
DFC — Distinguished Flying Cross
DFM — Distinguished Flying Medal
DGAF — Director General Air Forces
DH — de Havilland
DHC — de Havilland Canada
DND — Department of National Defence
DROs — daily routine orders
DSO — Distinguished Service Order
EA — Executive Assistant
ECM — Electronic counter measures
EFTS — Elementary Flying Training School
EO — Executive Officer
ETA — estimated time of arrival
EW — Electronic warfare
EWO — Electronic warfare officer
F — Fighter
FFAR — Folding Fin aircraft rocket
FIS — Flying Instructors School
FTS — Flying Training School
G — the force of gravity
GCA — ground controlled approach
GCI — ground control intercept
HMCS — His/Her Majesty's Canadian Ship
HMS — His/Her Majesty's Ship
HQ — Headquarters
HVARs — high velocity aircraft rockets
ICAS — International Council of Air Shows
IFR — Instrument Flight Rules
ILS — Instrument Landing System
JATO — jet assisted takeoff
KIAS — knots indicated air speed
LCC — lead collision course
M — Mach – the speed of sound
MiD — Mentioned in Despatches
Mk. — Mark of aircraft
MND — Minister of National Defence
MOT — Ministry of Transport
MP — maritime patrol or military police
MRP — mobile repair party
NAC — National Archives of Canada
NAFD — National Air Force Day
NAS — Naval Air Station
NATO — North Atlantic Treaty Organization
Nav — navigator, navigation
NCM — non-commissioned member
NCO — non-commissioned officer
NDHQ — National Defence Headquarters
NM — nautical miles
NORAD — North American Air Defence Command, latterly North American Aerospace Defence Command
OIC — Officer-in-charge
OPI — Officer of personal interest
OTU — Operational Training Unit
PFS — Primary Flying School
PMQ — permanent married quarters

PNE — Pacific National Exhibition
PR — public relations
QRA — Quick Reaction Alert
RAAF — Royal Australian Air Force
Radar — radio detection and ranging
RAF — Royal Air Force (Great Britain)
RCAF — Royal Canadian Air Force
RCASC — Royal Canadian Army Service Corps
RCN — Royal Canadian Navy
RCNAS — Royal Canadian Naval Air Station
RCNVR — Royal Canadian Navy Volunteer Reserve
RD — Repair Depot
RFC — Royal Flying Corps
RMC — Royal Military College of Canada
RN — Royal Navy
RNLAF — Royal Netherlands Air Force
RRMC — Royal Roads Military College
RT — radio transmission
SAR — search and rescue
SFOA — Staff Flag Officer Atlantic
SFTS — Service Flying Training School
Snag — a technical malfunction
SOP — standard operating procedures
SOS — struck off strength
SPAADS — Sabre Pilots Association of the Air Division Squadrons
Sqn — squadron
SSO — Senior Staff Officer
Stn — station
STOL — short takeoff and landing
ST/R — strike/reconnaissance
STU — Sabre Transition Unit
T — trainer, transport
T-Bird — T-33 Silver Star
TACAN — Tactical Air Navigation
TCHQ — Training Command Headquarters
TOT — time on target
U/S — unserviceable
UE — unit establishment i.e. the number of aircraft or personnel allotted to a unit
USAF — United States Air Force
USN — United States Navy
VC — Victoria Cross
VCDS — Vice Chief of the Defence Staff
VF — naval designation for squadron
VFR — Visual Flight Rules
VT — naval designation for training squadron
VU — naval designation for utility squadron
WComd — Wing Commander
WEE — Winter Experimental Establishment
"winco" — wing commander
W0X0F — weather - zero cloud ceiling and visibility in fog
WOpsO — Wing Operations Officer

Ranks of the Canadian Forces, Royal Canadian Air Force and Royal Canadian Navy

Canadian Forces

Officers
Gen	General
LGen	Lieutenant General
MGen	Major General
BGen	Brigadier General
Col	Colonel
LCol	Lieutenant Colonel
Maj	Major
Capt	Captain
Lt	Lieutenant
2 Lt	Second Lieutenant
OCdt	Officer Cadet

Other Ranks

CWO	Chief Warrant Officer
MWO	Master Warrant Officer
WO	Warrant Officer
Sgt	Sergeant
MCpl	Master Corporal
Cpl	Corporal
Pte	Private

RCAF Equivalent

Officers
A/C/M	Air Chief Marshal
A/M	Air Marshal
A/V/M	Air Vice-Marshal
A/C	Air Commodore
G/C	Group Captain
W/C	Wing Commander
S/L	Squadron Leader
F/L	Flight Lieutenant
F/O	Flying Officer
P/O	Pilot Officer
OCdt	Officer Cadet

Other Ranks

WO1	Warrant Officer Class 1
WO2	Warrant Officer Class 2
FS	Flight Sergeant
Sgt	Sergeant
No equivalent	
Cpl	Corporal
LAC	Leading Aircraftman
LAW	Leading Airwoman
AC 1(2)	Aircraftman
AW1(2)	Airwoman

RCN/Cdn Navy Equivalent

Officers
Adm	Admiral
VAdm	Vice Admiral
RAdm	Rear Admiral
Cmdre	Commodore
Capt (N)	Captain (N)
Cdr	Commander
LCdr	Lieutenant Commander
Lt (N)	Lieutenant (N)
S/Lt	Sub Lieutenant
Acting S/Lt	Acting Sub Lieutenant
OCdt	Officer Cadet

Other Ranks

CPO1	Chief Petty Officer 1st Class
CPO2	Chief Petty Officer 2nd Class
PO1	Petty Officer First Class
PO2	Petty Officer Second Class
MS	Master Seaman
LS	Leading Seaman
AS	Able Seaman
OS	Ordinary Seaman

Selected Bibliography

441 Tactical Fighter Squadron, *441 (F) Squadron RCAF Diary-1 Mar 51 to 30 Nov 62*, 1 Wing Marville, France, 1962.

Angelucci, Enzo and Matricardi, Paolo, *Aircraft-Combat Aircraft 1945-1960*, Sampson Low, Berkshire, England, 1980.

Banks, Capt R.D., *From White-Caps to Contrails–A History of a Modern Air Formation*, Canadian Forces Base Shearwater, Nova Scotia, 1981.

Baraton, Jean Pierre, *Snowbirds 1971-1990, a 20 year history*, J.P.B. Publications, Calgary, 1990.

Bashow, David L., *Starfighter–A loving retrospective of the CF-104 era in Canadian fighter aviation 1961-1986*, Fortress Publications Inc., Toronto, 1990.

Billing, Chevalier Jerry M.I.D., C.D., M.G.C., *A Knave Among Knights in their Spitfires*, Bunker to Bunker Books, Winnipeg, 1995.

Bucklow, Eric, *Coronation Wings–The Men & Machines of the Royal Air Force Coronation Review at Odiham 15 July 1953*, Hikoki Publications, Great Britain, 1998.

Canadian Forces Directorate of History and Heritage, *The Insignia and Lineages of the Canadian Forces Operational Flying Squadrons, Volume 4*, National Defence, Ottawa, 2000.

da Forno, Gianfranco, *Top Teams*, Howell Press Inc., USA, 1989.

Dempsey, Daniel V., *CF-104 Starfighter 1961-1986*, Canadian Forces Base Baden-Soellingen, West Germany, 1986.

Dodd, Len and Leversedge, T.F.J., *19 Wing Comox*, 19 Wing Comox, Comox, 1999.

Douglas, W.A.B., *The Creation of a National Air Force–The Official History of the Royal Canadian Air Force Volume II*, University of Toronto Press and Department of National Defence, Toronto, 1986.

Ellis, Chris, *A History of Combat Aircraft*, Optimum Books, The Hamlyn Publishing Group Limited, 1979.

Ferguson, William Paul, *The Snowbird Decades*, Butterworth & Co. (Canada) Ltd., Vancouver, 1979.

Foulds, Glen and Hisdal, David J., *"Moosemen" 419 Squadron History*, 419 Tactical Fighter Training Squadron, CFB Cold Lake, 1989.

Fuller, G.A., Griffin, J.A., Molson, K.M., *125 Years of Canadian Aeronautics–A Chronology 1840-1965*, The Canadian Aviation Historical Society, Willowdale, 1983.

Greenhous, Brereton and Halliday, Hugh A., *Canada's Air Forces 1914–1999*, Art Global and Department of National Defence, Montreal, 1999.

Hillmer, Norman, *The Creation of a National Air Force, The Official History of the Royal Canadian Air Force*, University of Toronto Press, Toronto, 1986.

Holman, R.F., *Best in the West–A History of Number 2 Canadian Forces Flying Training School and Flying Training in Canada*, 2 CFFTS, 15 Wing Moose Jaw, Moose Jaw, 1995.

Hotson, Fred W., *de HAVILLAND in Canada*, CANAV Books, Toronto, 1999.

Johnson, Bill, *Airshow!*, Superior Publishing Company, USA, 1971.

Kostenuk, S. and Griffin, J., *RCAF Squadrons and Aircraft 1924-1968*, A.M. Hakkert Ltd., Toronto and Samuel Stevens & Co., Sarasota, Florida, 1977.

Leigh, Z. Lewis, *And I Shall Fly–The Flying Memoirs of Z. Lewis Leigh*, CANAV Books, Toronto, 1985.

Marion, Normand, *Camp Borden, Birthplace of the RCAF 1917-1999*, 16 Wing Borden, Borden, 1999.

Martin, Patrick, *Canadian Armed Forces Aircraft Finish & Markings 1968-1997*, Patrick Martin, Langley, British Columbia, 1997.

McClelland & Stewart Inc., *Canadian Encyclopedia–Year 2000 Edition*, McClelland & Stewart Inc., Toronto, 1999.

McIntyre, Robert, *Canadair CF-5–Canadian Profile*, Sabre Model Supplies Ltd. Publishing, Ottawa, 1985.

McIntyre, Robert, *CF-104 Starfighter–Canadian Profile*, Sabre Model Supplies Ltd. Publishing, Ottawa, 1984.

McIntyre, Robert, *CF-101 Voodoo–Canadian Profile*, Sabre Model Supplies Ltd. Publishing, Ottawa, 1984.

McQuarrie, John, *Canadian Wings, The Passion and the Force*, McGraw-Hill Ryerson Limited, Toronto, 1990.

Milberry, Larry, *AIRCOM: Canada's Air Force*, CANAV Books, Toronto, 1991.

Milberry, Larry, *Canada's Air Force Today*, CANAV Books, Toronto, 1987.

Milberry, Larry, *Canada's Air Force, At War and Peace, Volume 1, II, and III*, CANAV Books, Toronto, 2000.

Milberry, Larry, *Sixty Years, The RCAF and CF Air Command 1924-1984*, CANAV Books, Toronto, 1984.

Milberry, Larry, *The Avro CF-100*, CANAV Books, Toronto, 1981.

Milberry, Larry, *The Canadair Sabre*, CANAV Books, Toronto, 1986.

Mills, Carl, *Banshees in the Royal Canadian Navy*, Banshee Publication, Toronto, 1991.

Nicks, Capt Don, Bradley, Cpl John and Charland, Chris (The NBC Group), *A History of The Air Defence of Canada 1948–1997*, Commander Fighter Group, Ottawa, 1997.

Organ, Richard, Page, Ron, Watson, Don and Wilkinson, Les (The Arrowheads), *Avro Arrow-The Story Of The Avro Arrow From Its Evolution To Its Extinction*, The Boston Mills Press, Erin, Ontario, Ninth printing 1986.

Oswald, Mary E., *They Led the Way–Members of Canada's Aviation Hall of Fame 25th Anniversary–1973 to 1998 and Annual Update Binder to 2001*, Canada's Aviation Hall of Fame, Wetaskiwin, Alberta, 1999.

Philp, Owen B. and Johnson, William B., *Snowbirds from the Beginning*, Porthole Press Ltd., Victoria, 1990.

Pickler, Ron and Milberry, Larry, *Canadair–The First 50 Years*, CANAV Books, Toronto, 1995.

Price, Dr. Alfred, *Late Marque Spitfire Aces 1942-45*, Osprey Publishing, England, 1996.

Ralph, Wayne, *Barker VC*, Doubleday Canada Limited, Toronto, 1997.

Robbins, Keith, *417 Squadron History*, Canada's Wings, Inc., Stittsville, Ontario, 1983.

Roberts, Leslie, *There Shall Be Wings*, Clarke Irwin & Company Limited, Toronto, 1959.

Robertson, Capt Robby, Matthews, Capt Don and Bertram, Capt Murray, *434 Squadron ... A History*, 434 Squadron "Bluenosers", Cold Lake, 1977.

Schmid, S.H. and Weaver, Truman C., *The Golden Age of Air Racing*, EAA Foundation/Times Publishing Co., Random Lake, U.S.A., 1983.

Shores, Christopher and Williams, Clive, *Aces High–A Tribute to the Most Notable Fighter Pilots of the British and Commonwealth Forces in WWII*, Grub Street, London, 1994.

Soward, Stuart E., *Hands to Flying Stations–A Recollective History of Canadian Naval Aviation, Volume 1 and Volume 2*, Neptune Developments (1984), Victoria, 1993.

Stokes, Doug, *Wings Aflame-The Biography of Group Captain Victor Beamish DSO and bar, DFC, AFC*, Crecy Publishing Limited, Manchester, 1998.

Will, Stephen, *Wings of Change–Canadian Airmen in Europe*, Hornet House Publishing, Cold Lake, 1993.

Yenne, Bill, *The Aerobats, The World's Great Aerial Demonstration Teams*, Brompton Books Corporation, USA, 1991.

Canada's Military Airshow Teams

The following represent Canadian military airshow teams and personnel identified at the time of publication.

The Pioneers

Barker Exhibition Team
Leaside, Ontario   1919
German Fokker D.VII Scouts

1919 Canadian National Exhibition
Lead	LCol W.G. Barker	
#2	Capt L.B. Hyde-Pearson	
#3	Capt W.R. James	
#4	Capt V. Dallin	

Royal Canadian Air Force

The Siskins (Siskin Exhibition Flight)
Camp Borden, Ontario	1929-1930
St. Hubert, Quebec	1931
RCAF Stn Trenton, Ontario	1932-1934

Armstrong Whitworth Siskin Mk IIIA

1929
Lead	F/L F. Victor Beamish	(RAF)
	F/L David A. Harding	(RAF)
Wing	P/O Edwin A. McGowan	(RCAF)
	P/O Ernest A. McNab	(RCAF)

For 1929 National Air Races Cleveland
Lead	F/L F. Victor Beamish	(RAF)
Wing	F/L G.R. Howsam	(RCAF)
	F/L David A. Harding	(RAF)

1930
Lead	F/L F. Victor Beamish	(RAF)
Wing	P/O Ralph C. Hawtrey	(RCAF)
	P/O Fowler M. Gobeil	(RCAF)
	P/O Ernest A. McNab	(RCAF)
Support Aircraft Pilot		
	F/O R.C. Minnes	(RCAF)

1931 Trans Canada Air Pageant
Lead	S/L Henry W. Hewson	(RCAF)
Wing	F/O Fowler M. Gobeil	(RCAF)
	F/O Ralph C. Hawtrey	(RCAF)
	F/O Ernest A. McNab	(RCAF)
Solo	F/L William I. Riddell	(RCAF)
Support Aircraft Pilots		
Ford Trimotor	F/L J.A. Boret	(RAF)
Ford Trimotor	Flt Sgt G.T. Elliot	(RCAF)
Fairchild 71	Sgt V.S. Roberts	(RCAF)

1931 RCAF Groundcrew Team
WO2 Frank Hems	LAC Bensou
Sgt Robert Laidlaw	LAC J.W. Gould
Sgt John F. Riggs	LAC S.O. Partridge
Cpl Alexander Cantlay	LAC A.J. Wilcox
Cpl George C. Ramshaw	Aircraftman Turner
Cpl Watts	Aircraftman Winden

Civilian Team - Trans Canada Air Pageant
T.M. (Pat) Reid	de Havilland Puss Moth
Godfrey W. Dean	Pitcairn Autogiro
Geoffrey O'Brien	de Havilland Puss Moth
Bernard Martin	Fairchild KR 21
W. (Bill) Resseguier	Aeronaca C3 Monoplane
George M. Ross	de Havilland Gipsy Moth
W. Jack Sanderson	Fleet Biplane
C.R. Peter Troup	Bellanca Pacemaker
Romeo Vachon	Saro Cloud Amphibian
Marshall Foss	Announcer

1932
Lead	S/L Henry W. Hewson*	(RCAF)
Wing	F/O Douglas M. Edwards	(RCAF)
	F/O Fowler M. Gobeil	(RCAF)
	F/O Larry E. Wray	(RCAF)
	F/O Ernest A. McNab	(RCAF)
	F/L William I. Riddell	(RCAF)
Solo	F/O Ralph C. Hawtrey	(RCAF)

* killed 27 Jul 32 at RCAF Stn Trenton, Ont. practicing five-ship loop for 1932 season. Replaced as leader by F/O F.M.Gobeil.

1934
Lead	F/O D. M. Edwards	(RCAF)
Wing	F/O W.A. Jones	(RCAF)
	F/O D.S. Blaine	(RCAF)
	F/O R.G. Briese	(RCAF)

RCAF Army Cooperation Flight Demonstration Team
Army Cooperation Flight
RCAF Stn Trenton, Ontario   1934
Armstrong Whitworth Atlas I

1934
Lead	F/L A. Lewis	(RCAF)
Wing	F/O H.C. Campbell	(RCAF)
	F/O R.A. Cameron	(RCAF)
	F/O W.A. Orr	(RCAF)
Narrator	F/L H.L. Pattison	(RAF)

First Jet Demonstrations

Test and Development Establishment
RCAF Stn Rockliffe, Ontario   1945
Gloster Meteor F.3

1945
Solos	F/L Jack Ritch
	F/L Bill McKenzie
	S/L Shan Baudoux

Winter Experimental Establishment
North-West Air Command
Edmonton, Alberta 1946-1947
Gloster Meteor F.3, de Havilland Vampire

1946-1947
Solo	F/L Jack Ritch

Early Harvard Teams

No. 1 FTS Harvard Team
No. 1 Flying Training School
RCAF Stn Centralia, Ontario   1948-1950
North American Harvard Mk IIB

1948-1950
Lead	F/L Lou Hill
#2	F/L Ray Greene

CFS Harvard Team
Central Flying School
RCAF Stn Trenton, Ontario   1949
North American Harvard Mk IIB

1949
Lead	F/O G.R. (Bob) Ayres
#2	F/O Ken Marlatt

No. 1 FTS Harvard Team
No. 1 Flying Training School
RCAF Stn Centralia, Ontario   1951
North American Harvard Mk IIB

1951
Lead	F/O G.R. (Bob) Ayres	
#2	F/O "Tex" Weatherly	
	Capt Marcus Tinsley	(USAF)
	F/O Chris Frost	

The Easy Aces (Centralia Aerobatic Team)
No. 1 Flying Training School
RCAF Stn Centralia, Ontario   1951-1952
North American Harvard NA-66, AT-16, Mk II, IIB or IV

1952
Lead	F/O G.R. (Bob) Ayres
#2	F/O Ernie Saunders
#3	F/O Ray Embury
#4	F/O Frank Pickles

CFS Harvard Team
Central Flying School
RCAF Station Centralia, Ontario   1953
North American Harvard

1953
Lead	F/L John Towler	(RAF)
#2	F/L Doug S.A. Bing	
#3	F/O Stu J. Allen	
#4	F/L Al Mehlhaff	

F-51 Mustang Teams

417 (FR) Sqn Mustang Team
417 Fighter/Reconnaissance Sqn
RCAF Stn Rivers, Manitoba   1947-1948
North American F-51 Mustang IV

1947-1948
Wing Cmdr	W/C S. (Stan) Turner
CO 417 Sqn	S/L J.D. (Jack) Mitchener
	S/L B. (Bev) Christmas
	F/L E.J. (Ed) Geddes
	F/L J.A. (Tony) Stephens
	F/L S. (Stan) Knight
	F/L R. (Bob) Kent
	F/L J. Rainville
	F/O B. "Duke" Warren
	F/O C. (Chuck) Keating
	F/O R. (Ray) Oldfin
Engr Officer	F/O D. Moore

416 (F) Sqn Mustang Team
416(F) Sqn
RCAF Stn Uplands, Ontario   1951
North American F-51 Mustang Mk IV

1951
Lead	F/O Roy Bamford
	F/O Ken Lewis
	F/O Bill Peterson
	F/O Ray Howey
	F/O Gerry Patterson
Solo	F/O Chuck Steacy
Rocket Firing Display	
	F/O Chuck Steacy
	F/O Harold Wilson

420 (F) Sqn Mustang Team
420 (F) Sqn, RCAF Auxiliary
Crumlin Airport, London, Ontario   1951-1952
North American F-51 Mustang Mk IV

1951
Lead	S/L G.L. (George) Lee	
#2	F/O C.J. Malone	
#3	F/L W.W. Fox	

1952
Lead	F/L D.G. Gray	
#2	F/L Jack Baxter	
#3	F/L Ivor Williams	
#4	F/O Murray Quinney	
Solo	W/C A.D. Haylett	(CO 420 Sqn)

424 (F) Sqn Mustang Team
424 (F) Sqn, RCAF Auxiliary
Mount Hope Airport, Hamilton, Ontario   1951
North American F-51 Mustang Mk IV

1951
Lead	S/L F.N. (Norm) Shrive	
#2	F/O F.T. (Fred) Allport	
#3	F/O R. (Ray) Sherk	

Vampire Teams

CFS Vampire Airshow Team
Central Flying School,
RCAF Stn Trenton, Ontario   1948-1949
de Havilland Vampire Mk III

1948

Lead	F/L J.F. "Stocky" Edwards	
#2	F/L E.G. "Irish" Ireland	

Lead	S/L F.O. (Barry) Barrett	(RAF)
#2	F/L J.H. (Jack) Phillips	
#3	F/L E.G. "Irish" Ireland	
#4	F/L L.T. (Les) Banner*	
Support Crew	F/L Norm Hoye, OC Support Crew	

killed 19 Sep 48 returning from show at Niagara Falls, New York.

1949

Lead	F/L R.L. (Hal) Knight
#2	F/O Jerry Billing

The Blue Devils
410 (F) Sqn
RCAF Stn St. Hubert, Quebec   1949-1951
de Havilland Vampire Mk III

1949

OC 410 Sqn	S/L R.A. (Bob) Kipp*
Lead	F/L Don C. Laubman
#2	F/L J.A. Omer Levesque
#3	F/O Michael F. Doyle
#4	F/O W.H.F. (Bill) Bliss
	(joined team 25 Aug 49)
Solo	F/L R.D. (Joe) Schultz
Solo	F/L W.R. (Bill) Tew
	(joined team 3 Jul 49)
Crew Chief	WO2 A.V. Charlebois

killed 25 Jul 49 at RCAF Stn St. Hubert, Que. while practicing solo inverted flight.

1950 Air Defence Group Aerobatic Team

Lead	F/L Don C. Laubman	(410 Sqn)
#2	F/O Larry E. Spurr	(421 Sqn)
#3	F/O Michael F. Doyle	(410 Sqn)
#4	F/O W.H.F. (Bill) Bliss	(410 Sqn)
Solo	F/O Fred W. Evans	(421 Sqn)
Spare	F/O W.G. (Bill) Paisley	(421 Sqn)

Note: Team disbanded 11 Sep 50 due to the impending introduction of the F-86 Sabre.

1951

Lead	S/L Don C. Laubman
#2	F/O Jerry Billing
#3	F/L Michael F. Doyle
#4	F/O W.H.F. (Bill) Bliss
Solo	F/L Dean Kelly

Note: The Blue Devils were re-formed on 8 Aug 51 for the Michigan Air Fair from 17-19 Aug. The team disbanded, for the last time, on 22 Aug 51.

Royal Canadian Navy Piston Teams

RCN Seafires
803 (F) Sqn, RCN Air Section,
RCAF Stn Dartmouth, Nova Scotia   1946
Supermarine Seafire XV

1946

Lead	LCdr C.G. "Clunk" Watson
#2	Lt Robert (Bob) Falls
#3	Lt Hal Fearon
#4	Lt Neville J. "Monk" Geary
Solo	Lt W.D. (Bill) Munro

Seafire Exhibition Flight (Watson's Flying Circus)
803 (F) Sqn /19th Carrier Air Group
HMCS Shearwater, Nova Scotia   1949
Supermarine Seafire Mk XV

1949
Red Flight

Lead	LCdr C.G. "Clunk" Watson*
#2	Lt J.J. (Joe) MacBrien
#3	Lt A.C. (Chuck) Elton*
Solo	Lt A.T. (Al) Bice
Alternate	Lt A.A. "Doc" Shellinck

killed during CNE rehearsal mid-air collision over Malton, Ont 23 Aug 49.

Black Flight

Lead	LCdr W.D. (Bill) Munro	
#2	Lt J.P. (Pat) Whitby	
#3	Lt W. (Mike) Wasteneys	
#4	Lt E.A. (Ed) Myers	
Alternate	Lt J.B. (Jack) Hartle	
Commentator	Lt H.L. (Harry) Swiggum	
Engineer	Lt B. (Brian) Dawbarn	(RN)

RCN Airshow Team
31st Support Air Group
HMCS Shearwater, Nova Scotia   1952-1953

1952
LCdr J.B. "Pop" Fotheringham
(CO 31st Support Air Group)
870 Sqn – Hawker Sea Fury FB.11

(CO 870 Sqn)	Lt D.D. (Doug) Peacocke
	Lt Mike Wastenays
	Lt Al Shimmin
	Lt Robert Falls
	Lt "Whitey" McNichol
	Lt David Tate
	Lt Ken Nicholson
	Lt "Doc" Shellinck

880 Sqn – Grumman Avenger AS-3
Crews unknown

1953
LCdr Donald W. Knox
(CO 31st Support Air Group)
VF 870 – Hawker Sea Fury FB.11

(CO VF 870)	LCdr D.M. "Pappy" Macleod
	Lt Stu E. Soward
	Lt Jeff J. Harvie
	Lt Vern J. Cunningham
	Sub Lt Jake H. Birks
	Sub Lt Marty H. Brayman

VS 880 – Grumman Avenger AS-3

(CO VS 880)	LCdr E.M. Ted Davis
(CO 31st SAG)	LCdr Don W. Knox
	Lt Stu E. Soward
	Lt Doug J. Fisher
	Lt George W. Noble

RCAF F-86 Sabre Teams

413 (F) Sqn Sabre Team
413 (F) Sqn
RCAF Stn Bagotville, Quebec   1952
North American / Canadair F-86 Sabre Mk 2

1952
12-Plane Demo Team – 28 Apr-19 May 52

Lead Section	S/L Doug Lindsay
Flt Commanders	F/L Phil Brodeur
	F/L K.C. (Ken) Lett

12-Plane Airshow Team – CNE Aug-Sep 52

Lead Section	S/L K.C. (Ken) Lett
Flt Commanders	F/L Mark Sauder
	F/L W.G. (Bill) Paisley

Additional squadron Sabre pilots that participated in one or both of the above exhibitions included:

Ken Branch	Tom Mulrooney
Art Maskell	Al Wilson
Bob Moncrief	Ernie Glover
Len Fine	Don Schneider
Dan Kaye	Brian Burns

Barney Barnett	Arnie Cavett
Jack Nichol	Jud Killoran
Gene Nixon	

Solo Aerobatics (T-33)	Harry Hrischenko

416 (F) Sqn Sabre Team
416 (F) Sqn
RCAF Stn Uplands, Ontario   1952
North American / Canadair F-86 Sabre Mk 2

1952

Lead	S/L John McKay
Solo	F/O Ray Howey

431 (F) Sqn Aerobatic Team
431 (F) Sqn
RCAF Stn Bagotville, Quebec   1954
North American / Canadair F-86 Sabre Mk 2

1954

Lead	F/O Fern Villeneuve
#2	F/O George Fulford
	F/O Rod Macdonald
#3	F/O Fred Rudy
#4	F/O Art Maskell

Operation Prairie Pacific 1954

Lead	F/O Fern Villeneuve
#2	F/O Rod Macdonald
#3	F/O Fred Rudy
#4	F/O George Fulford
Solo	F/O Al McIlraith

The Lancers
No. 1 (F) Operational Training Unit
RCAF Stn Chatham, New Brunswick   1955
North American / Canadair F-86 Sabre Mk 5

1955

Lead	F/L Garth Cinnamon
#2	F/O Dan Campbell
	F/O Doug Evjen*
#3	F/O Jack Frazer
#4	F/O Norm Garriock
Groundcrew	Cpl Jim Bleakley Elect Tech
Others unknown	

killed 13 May 55 following a mid-air collision with the leader in the landing circuit at Chatham.

Note: Only F-86 Mk 5 23286 painted in team's new colours.

"North Luff" Sabre Teams
1 (F) Wing
RCAF Stn North Luffenham, England   1952-1953
North American / Canadair F-86 Sabre Mk 2

410 (F) Sqn Aerobatic Team
1952-1953

Lead	F/L Grant Nichols	
#2	F/O Garth Cinnamon	
#3	F/O Al Robb	
#4	F/O Len Bentham	
Solos	F/O Dean Kelly	(441 Sqn)
	F/O Fern Villeneuve	(441 Sqn)
	F/O Gibson	(410 Sqn)
	F/O Potter	(410 Sqn)
	F/O Knox-Leet	(410 Sqn)

Notes: 1. Prior to the formation of the 410 team, S/L Duke Warren (CO 410 Sqn) led a 410 team at the National Air Races at Newcastle, England. His wingmen were F/L Cinnamon, F/Os Gibson, Bentham and Sylvester. 2. F/L Nichols led a 12-ship as part of 1 Wing's contribution to the Queen's Coronation flypast, RAF Odiham, England 15 Jul 53.

441 (F) Sqn Aerobatic Team
1953

Lead	F/O Gar Brine
#2	F/O Fern Villeneuve
#3	F/O Ralph Annis
#4	F/O Jean Gaudry

Column 1

Mid-summer 1953

Lead	F/O Fern Villeneuve
#2	F/O Norm Ronaasen
#3	F/O Bob Haverstock
#4	F/O Jean Gaudry
Solo	F/L Dean Kelly

439 (F) Sqn Aerobatic Team
August 1953-October 1953

Lead	F/L Harry Wenz
#2	F/O Laurie Hamilton
#3	F/O Dick Wingate
#4	F/O Len Pappas

December 1953-April 1954

Lead	F/L Harry Wenz
#2	F/O Laurie Hamilton
#3	F/O A.M. (Mac) Gillies
#4	F/O Jeb Kerr

1 (F) Wing Aerobatic Team
1954

Lead	F/O H.R. (Dick) Wingate	(439 Sqn)
#2	F/O A.M. (Mac) Gillies*	(439 Sqn)
	F/O G. (Garth) Cinnamon	(410 Sqn)
#3	F/O E.N. (Norm) Ronaasen	(441 Sqn)
#4	F/O G.J. (Jeb) Kerr	(439 Sqn)
Solo	F/L Dean Kelly	(441 Sqn)

* killed in car accident Sep 54; replaced by
F/O Garth Cinnamon (410 Sqn).

3 (F) Wing Fireballs
3 (F) Wing Aerobatic Team
RCAF Stn Zweibrucken, West Germany 1954
North American / Canadair F-86 Sabre Mk 2

1954

Lead	F/L C.E. (Chuck) Keating	(434 Sqn)
#2	F/O S.E. (Syd) Burrows*	(434 Sqn)
	F/O L.W. (Bill) Grip	(427 Sqn)
#3	F/O J.L. (Jack) Frazer	(427 Sqn)
#4	F/O E.R. (Rick) Mace	(413 Sqn)
	F/O Nick Nixon	(413 Sqn)
	(transferred before workup completed)	

* mid-air with a hawk 13 Sep 54 caused loss of vision in
one eye; replaced by F/O Grip.

2 (F) Wing Sky Lancers
2 (F) Wing
RCAF Stn Grostenquin, France 1955
North American / Canadair F-86 Sabre Mk 5

1955

Lead	F/L Tony Hannas	(421 Sqn)
#2	F/O B.R. Campbell	(430 Sqn)
#3	F/O L.M. (Len) Eisler	(421 Sqn)
#4	F/O G.C.E. (Gerry) Thériault	(430 Sqn)
Solo	F/O H.L. (Herb) Graves	(416 Sqn)
Crew Chief	F/Sgt Art Elliott	
Groundcrew	Cpl Innis	
	Cpl McCabe	
	LAC Anderson	
	LAC Bowers	
	LAC Bruce	
	LAC Hollywood	
	LAC Lunn	
	LAC Paterson	
	LAC Thibault	

4 (F) Wing Sky Lancers
4 (F) Wing
RCAF Stn Baden-Soellingen, West Germany 1956
North American / Canadair F-86 Sabre Mk 5

1956

Lead	F/O J.D. (Dale) McLarty*	(414 Sqn)
#2	F/O J.H. (Jake) Adams*	(444 Sqn)
#3	F/O E.H. (Ed) Welters*	(414 Sqn)
#4	F/O F.K. (Fred) Axtell*	(422 Sqn)
Solo	F/O L.C. (Les) Price	(444 Sqn)

* Formation team killed 2 Mar 56 during practice over France
in marginal weather. Sabre Mk 5's - 23483, 23445, 23524,
23439. Sabre 23470 later served with the Golden Hawks.

Column 2

Royal Canadian Air Force Golden Hawks
RCAF Air Display Unit

RCAF Stn Chatham, New Brunswick	1959-1962
RCAF Stn Trenton, Ontario	1963-1964

North American / Canadair F-86 Sabre Mk 5/Mk 6

1959 Golden Hawks F-86 Sabre Mk 5

CO	W/C Jake F. Easton
Lead	S/L Fern G. Villeneuve
Right Wing	F/L Jim D. McCombe
Left Wing	F/L Ed J. Rozdeba
Slot	F/L G. Jeb Kerr*
Lead Solo/Slot	F/L Ralph H. Annis
Second Solo	F/L L. "Sammy" Eisler**
2nd Solo/Lead Solo	F/O John T. Price
Spare/2nd Solo	F/O W.C. (Bill) Stewart
Spare/2nd Solo	F/O Jim A. Holt
PR Officer	S/L Russ M.L. Bowdery
Commentator	F/O George L. MacDonald
Adjutant	F/O Lorne Johnson

* killed in Calgary, Alta 10 Aug 59 in mid-air with
civilian light aircraft during landing.
** killed near Chatham, N.B. 12 Mar 59 during an
early solo practice.

1959 Groundcrew
Engineering Officer F/O C. Ray Grandy
Senior NCO   Flt Sgt O.J. Tousignant
Line Crew Supervisors

	Sgt J.A. Guy Latraverse	AFTech 4
	Cpl Norm J. Gray	AFTech 3
Crew Chiefs	LAC J.E. Arsenault	AETech 3
	LAC Wm. (Bill) Briggs	AETech 2
	LAC Rod L. Embree	AFTech 3
	LAC E. Hall	AFTech 3
	LAC Ed R. Harnum	AETech 3
	LAC J.E. McManaman	AFTech 3
	LAC J.C.R. Thompson	AFTech 3
Assistant	LAC George Bulmer	ITech 3
Crew Chiefs	LAC R.J. Campbell	SETech 3
	LAC John M. Elmose	ETech 3
	LAC D.Art Hughes	ITech 3
	LAC A.V. Johnson	ETech 3
	LAC Ed Proskin	M&WTech 3
	LAC K.J. Webber	ETech 3

Snag/Maintenance Crew

	Sgt. V.O. Campbell	ComTech 3
	Sgt F. Devins	ETech 4
	Sgt R. Johnston	SETech 3
	Sgt V.R. Metcalf	AETech 4
	Sgt D.G. Mooney	ITech 4
	Cpl Ken G. Bradley	ITech 3
	Cpl R.A. Chaignon	ComTech 3
	Cpl Fred J. Conrad	SETech 3
	Cpl L. Guy Coté	ITech 3
	Cpl G. Tom Gemmel	AETech 3
	Cpl A.G. Lapointe	SupTech 3
	Cpl H.E. Maahs	ETech 3
	Cpl F. Monteleone	AETech 3
	Cpl J.A. Oakes	ETech 3
	Cpl J. Ken Terrio	AFTech 3
	Cpl A.A. White	M&WTech 3
	Cpl R. Zinn	AFTech 3
	LAC S. Anderson	AFTech 3
	LAC D.G. Bercovitz	ClkStats 2
	LAC C.D. Curtis	ComTech 3
	LAC G.W. Donaldson	AFTech 3
	LAC R. Edgington	ARTech 3
	LAC Graham Faulkner	MtlTech 3
	LAC D.E. Fletcher	AETech 3
	LAC E.A. Hodgins	AFTech 3
	LAC J.L. Levesque	ITech 3
	LAC E.T. Lunn	AETech 3
	LAC W.H. Morrison	AFTech 3
	LAC E.B. Nickerson	ETech 3
	LAC Albert M. Pardy	AFTech 3
	LAC J.H. Savoie	ETech 3
	LAC E.A. Thompson	AFTech 3

Column 3

1960 Golden Hawks F-86 Sabre Mk 5

CO	W/C Jack F. Allan
Lead	S/L Fern G. Villeneuve
Right Wing	F/L Jim D. McCombe
Left Wing	F/L Ed J. Rozdeba
Slot	F/O Bill C. Stewart
Lead Solo	F/L Ralph H. Annis
Solo	F/L John T. Price
Second Solo	F/L Dave V. Tinson
PR Officer	F/L Rocky Van Vliet
Commentator	F/O George L. MacDonald

1960 Groundcrew
Engineering Officer F/L Dan J. McKinnon
Senior NCO   Flt Sgt O.J. Tousignant
Line Crew Supervisors

	Sgt J.A.Guy Latraverse	AFTech 4
	Cpl Norm J. Gray	AFTech 3
Crew Chiefs	LAC Wm.(Bill) Briggs	AETech 2
	LAC Rod L. Embree	AFTech 3
	LAC Ed R. Harnum	AETech 3
	LAC Dave Merriam	AFTech 3
	LAC Nick Nichols	ETech 3
	LAC Mick Nordeen	AETech 3
	LAC T.T. Thompson	AFTech 3
Assistant	LAC George Bulmer	ITech 3
Crew Chiefs	LAC John M. Elmose	ETech 3
	LAC D. Art Hughes	ITech 3
	LAC Bill Krier	AFTech 3
	LAC Art Pelltier	RTech 3
	LAC Ed Proskin	M&WTech 3
	LAC Marc Savoie	ComTech 3

Snag/Maintenance Crew

	Sgt Cooper	
	Sgt Dalton	
	Sgt D.G. Mooney	ITech 4
	Sgt Len Tesky	
	Cpl Ken G. Bradley	ITech 3
	Cpl Brad Brooks	
	Cpl Art R. Chartrand	AETech 3
	Cpl Fred J. Conrad	SETech 3
	Cpl L. Guy Coté	ITech 3
	Cpl G. Tom Gemmel	AETech 3
	Cpl Don H. Haupt	
	Cpl Lionel Higham	Clk Stats 3
	Cpl Jeeves	
	Cpl Ron Lundhal	M&WTech 3
	Cpl J.M. Murphy	ComTech 3
	Cpl Prouse	
	Cpl Sanche	
	Cpl J. Ken Terrio	AFTech 3
	LAC J.E. Arsenault	AETech 3
	LAC Chris Christensen	
	LAC Graham Faulkner	MtlTech3
	LAC Jack LaBelle	
	LAC L.O. Leblanc	
	LAC Leggett	
	LAC W.H. Morrison	AFTech 3
	LAC E.B. Nickerson	ETech 3
	LAC Albert M. Pardy	AFTech3
	LAC Ray Reid	
	LAC J.H. Savoie	SETech 3
	LAC G.A. Jack Tardiff	ComTech 3
	LAC Taylor	
	LAC Thoms	

1961 Golden Hawks F-86 Sabre Mk 6

CO	W/C Jack F. Allan
Lead	S/L Jim D. McCombe
Right Wing	F/L Borden R. Campbell
Left Wing	F/L Lloyd J. Hubbard
Slot	F/L Ed J. Rozdeba
Lead Solo	F/L Bill C. Stewart
Solo	F/L Alf F. McDonald
Second Solo	F/L Jack L. Frazer
Spare	F/O Jim E. McCann*
PR Officer	F/L Rocky Van Vliet
Commentator	F/O Bob Dobson

* killed near Chatham, N.B. 22 Feb 61 during formation
practice.

1961 Groundcrew

Engineering Officer	F/O Phil S. Perry	
Senior NCO	Flt Sgt O.J. Tousignant	
Line Crew Supervisors		
	Sgt J.A.Guy Latraverse	AFTech 4
	Cpl Willie Dunn	AFTech 3
Crew Chiefs	LAC Wm.(Bill) Briggs	AETech 3
	LAC J. Dick Clements	AFTech 3
	LAC G. W. Donaldson	AFTech 3
	LAC Ed R. Harnum	AETech 3
	LAC Gerry R. Homer	AETech 3
	LAC Dave Merriam	AFTech 3
	LAC W.H. Morrison	AFTech 3
Assistant	LAC George Bulmer	ITech 3
Crew Chiefs	LAC John M. Elmose	ETech 3
	LAC D. Art Hughes	ITech 3
	LAC Dave Morecombe	ComTech 3
	LAC E.B. Nickerson	ETech 3
	LAC Ed Proskin	M&WTech 3
	LAC Frank Clooney	ITech 3
Snag/Maintenance Crew		
	Sgt Cooper	
	Sgt Jim Hicks	
	Sgt "Red" McGillivary	
	Cpl Cann	
	Cpl Art R. Chartrand	AETech 3
	Cpl Fred J. Conrad	SETech 3
	Cpl Guy Coté	ITech 3
	Cpl "Rolly" Forget	
	Cpl G. Tom Gemmel	AETech 3
	Cpl Genovy	
	Cpl Norm J. Gray	AFTech 2
	Cpl Kahout	
	Cpl Ron Lundahl	M&WTech 3
	Cpl Jack Oakes	
	Cpl J. Ken Terrio	AFTech 3
	LAC Chris Christensen	
	LAC Bill Donohue	
	LAC Al Duggan	
	LAC Graham Faulkner	MtlTech 3
	LAC Ron Hughes	
	LAC Doug Laidlaw	
	LAC Macahoniuk	
	LAC Bill Mailaney	
	LAC Mark Marceau	AFTech 3
	LAC Mike Murphy	
	LAC Albert M. Pardy	AFTech 3
	LAC J.B.D. Racine	AFTech 3
	LAC Ray Reid	AETech 3
	LAC Spratt	
	LAC Ward	
	LAC Ken Webber	ETech 3
	LAC Ray W. West	AFTech 3

1962 Golden Hawks F-86 Sabre Mk 6

CO	W/C Jack F. Allan
Lead	S/L Lloyd J. Hubbard
Right Wing	F/L Borden R. Campbell
Left Wing	F/L Norm Garriock
Slot	F/L Jack L. Frazer
Lead Solo	F/L Alf F. McDonald
Solo	F/L George E. Miller
Second Solo	F/L Ed J. McKeogh
PR Officer	F/L Jim C. Giles
Commentator	F/L Bruce J. Lebans

1962 Groundcrew

Engineering Officer	F/O Phil S. Perry	
Senior NCO	Flt Sgt O.J. Tousignant	
Line Crew Supervisors		
	Sgt J.L. Finnigan	AFTech 4
	Cpl Willie Dunn	AFTech 3
Crew Chiefs	LAC Ed R. Harnum	AETech 3
	LAC Gerry R. Homer	AETech 3
	LAC M. Marceau	AFTech 3
	LAC Dave Merriam	AFTech 3
	LAC D.A. Osmun	AETech 3
	LAC Albert M. Pardy	AFTech 3
	LAC J.B.D. Racine	AFTech 3
Assistant	LAC J.W. Doug Brenton	Etech 3

Crew Chiefs (continued)

Crew Chiefs	LAC Frank E. Clooney	ITech 3
	LAC John M. Elmose	ETech 3
	LAC R. Emery	RTech 3
	LAC D. Morecombe	ComTech 3
	LAC J.J. St. Pierre	SETech 3
Snag/Maintenance Crew		
	Sgt J.A.Guy Latraverse	AFTech 4
	Sgt H.C. Hewitt	
	Cpl Ron T. Lundahl	M&WTech 3
	Cpl J.A. Melancon	ETech 3
	Cpl G. Paiment	AETech 3
	Cpl J. Ken Terrio	AFTech 3
	LAC Wm. (Bill) Briggs	AETech 3
	LAC G. W. Donaldson	AFTech 3
	LAC Graham Faulkner	MTech 3
	LAC D. King	ITech 3
	LAC J.G.V. Richard	ComTech
	LAC J. Risling	SETech 3
	LAC Savage	ETech 3
	LAC Ray W. West	AFTech 3

1963 Golden Hawks F-86 Sabre Mk 6

CO	W/C R. Frank Hatton
Lead	S/L Lloyd J. Hubbard
Right Wing	F/L Al Young
Left Wing	F/L Norm Garriock
Slot	F/L Clarence B. Lang
Lead Solo	F/L Ed J. McKeogh
Solo	F/L Dave J. Barker
Second Solo	F/L L. Bill Grip
PR Officer	F/L Jim C. Giles
Commentator	F/L Bruce J. Lebans

1963 Groundcrew

Engineering Officer	F/L Carl G. Peterson	
Senior NCOs	Flt Sgt J.A. Guy Latraverse	
	Flt Sgt D. Robinson	
Line Crew Supervisors		
	Sgt J.L. Finnigan	AFTech 4
	Cpl E. McEathron	AFTech 3
Crew Chiefs	LAC Wm. B. Briggs	AETech 3
	LAC J. Dick Clements	AFTech 3
	LAC Ed R. Harnum	AETech 3
	LAC Gerry R. Homer	AETech 3
	LAC M. Marceau	AFTech 3
	LAC D.A. Osmun	AETech 3
	LAC Albert M. Pardy	AFTech 3
Assistant	LAC J.W Doug Brenton	ETech 3
Crew Chiefs	LAC F.E. Clooney	ITech 3
	LAC R.J. Crown	SETech 3
	LAC John M. Elmose	ETech 3
	LAC J.G.V. Richard	ComTech
	LAC E. West	RDRTech 3
Snag/Maintenance Crew		
	Sgt G.E. Williams	AFTech 4
	Cpl Art R. Chartrand	AETech 3
	Cpl K.B. Enman	ETech 3
	Cpl Ron T. Lundahl	M&WTech 3
	Cpl R.S. McCarthy	AFTech 3
	Cpl E.R. McKinley	SupTech 3
	Cpl J.A. Melancon	ETech 3
	Cpl J.M. Murphy	ComTech 3
	Cpl J.J.M.G. Nolin	ITech 3
	Cpl J.P.G. Paiment	AETech 3
	Cpl J.H. Risling	SETech 3
	Cpl J. Ken Terrio	AFTech 3
	LAC A.W. Cameron	AFTech 3
	LAC G. W. Donaldson	AFTech 3
	LAC D.A. Kennedy	AFTech 3
	LAC Graham Faulkner	MTech 3
	LAC G.D. Fraser	RTech 3
	LAC W.N. Karachum	MTech 3
	LAC D.A. Kennedy	AFTech 3
	LAC D.J. King	ITech 3
	LAC R.C. Kurp	ETech 3
	LAC J.B.D. Racine	AFTech 3
	LAC J.J.E. St Pierre	SETech 3
	LAC A.R. Savage	ETech 3
	LAC Ray W. West	AFTech 3
	LAC W.M. Whaley	AETech 3
Admin Staff	Sgt J. Clark	ClkAdm 3
	LAC R.L. MacLellan	ClkAdm 3
	LAW D.D. McNichol	ClkAdm 1

1964 Golden Hawks F-86 Sabre Mk 6

CO	W/C R. Frank Hatton
Lead	S/L Lloyd J. Hubbard
Right Wing	F/L Al Young
Left Wing	F/L L. Bill Grip
Slot	F/L Clarence B. Lang
Lead Solo	F/L Dave J. Barker
Solo	F/O Brian H. Grover
Second Solo	F/L C.W. Beau Warrian
PR Officer	Pending at time of disbandment
Commentator	Pending at time of disbandment

1964 Groundcrew *

Engineering Officer	F/L Carl G. Peterson	
Senior NCO	Flt Sgt D. Robinson	
Line Crew Supervisors		
	Sgt J.L. Finnigan	AFTech 4
	Cpl E. McEathron	AFTech 3
Crew Chiefs	LAC Wm. (Bill) Briggs	AETech 3
	LAC J.R. Clements	AFTech 3
	LAC Ed R. Harnum	AETech 3
	LAC Gerry R. Homer	AETech 3
	LAC M. Marceau	AFTech 3
	LAC Albert M. Pardy	AFTech 3
	LAC J.B.D. Racine	AFTech 3
Snag/Maintenance Crew		
	Sgt G.E. Williams	AFTech 4
	Sgt H.G. Earle	AFTech 4
	Cpl Art R. Chartrand	AETech 3
	Cpl K.B. Enman	ETech 3
	Cpl Ron T. Lundahl	M&WTech 3
	Cpl R.S. McCarthy	AFTech 3
	Cpl E.R. McKinley	SupTech 3
	Cpl J.A. Melancon	ETech 3
	Cpl J.M. Murphy	ComTech 3
	Cpl J.J.M.G. Nolin	ITech 3
	Cpl J.P.G. Paiment	AETech 3
	Cpl J.H. Risling	SETech 3
	Cpl J. Ken Terrio	AFTech 3
	LAC J.W.D. Brenton	ETech 3
	LAC A.W. Cameron	AFTech 3
	LAC F.E. Clooney	ITech 3
	LAC R.J. Crown	SETech 3
	LAC G.W. Donaldson	AFTech 3
	LAC John M. Elmose	ETech 3
	LAC Graham Faulkner	MTech 3
	LAC G.D. Fraser	RTech 3
	LAC W.N. Karachum	MTech 3
	LAC D.A. Kennedy	AFTech 3
	LAC D.J. King	ITech 3
	LAC R.C. Kurp	ETech 3
	LAC D.A. Osmun	AETech 3
	LAC J.G.V. Richard	ComTech(A)
	LAC J.J.E. St Pierre	SETech 3
	LAC A.R. Savage	ETech 3
	LAC E. West	RDRTech 3
	LAC Ray W. West	AFTech 3
	LAC W.M. Whaley	AETech 3
Admin Staff	Sgt J. Clark	ClkAdm 3
	LAC R.L. MacLellan	ClkAdm 3
	LAW D.D. McNichol	ClkAdm 1

All personnel struck off strength Golden Hawks Unit Trenton and posted to RCAF Stn Trenton on 7 Feb 64

Known Golden Hawk F-86 Sabres / T-33 Silver Stars

Mk 5 Serials: 23001, 23037, 23042, 23043, 23066, 23073, 23080, 23083, 23096, 23133, 23135, 23164, 23205, 23301, 23313, 23320, 23353, 23358, 23359

Mk 6 Serials: 23410, 23424, 23435, 23454, 23457, 23465, 23470, 23487, 23510, 23551, 23600, 23636, 23641, 23649, 23651

T-33 Silver Star Serials: 21500, 21616

Operation Prairie Pacific Teams

1954
Commanding Officer W/C Cal Lee
Information Officer S/L Roy Wood

Silver Stars
Central Flying School
RCAF Stn Trenton, Ontario   1954
Lockheed / Canadair T-33 Silver Star

Lead	S/L Lou J. Hill
#2	F/L Russ K. Scott
#3	F/L Jack Seaman
#4	F/L Alex Bowman
Spare	F/L D.M. "Doc" Payne

Sabre Team
431 (F) Sqn
RCAF Stn Bagotville, Quebec   1954
North American / Canadair F-86 Sabre Mk 2

Lead	F/O Fern Villeneuve
#2	F/O Rod Macdonald
#3	F/O Fred Rudy
#4	F/O George Fulford
Solo	F/O Al McIlraith

CF-100 Team
423 AW(F) Sqn
RCAF Stn St. Hubert, Quebec   1954
Avro CF-100 Mk 3B

Lead	S/L L.P.S. Bing	F/O P.A. Hawkes
#2	F/L D.W. McNichol	F/O L. Parakin
#3	F/L S. K. Woolley	F/O A.R. Pratt
#4	F/O R.W. Komar	F/O A. Martin
	F/O J. Des Brisay	F/O W. Cole
Solo	F/O E.E. Hesjedahl	F/O E. McFarland
Spare	F/O Simpson	F/O K. Dorion

423 Sqn Groundcrew

F/O C.F. Barlow	Engineering Officer
Flt Sgt C. McNally	NCO i/c 423 Sqn Det
Sgt R. Cleland	2 i/c 423 Sqn Det
Cpl Goulet	Telecommunications
LAC Baldwin	Munitions Weapons
LAC Barret	Airframe
LAC Chadwick	Munitions Weapons
LAC Demers	Electrical
LAW L. de Sansoucy	Armament Systems
LAC Fontaine	Aeroengine
LAW R. Koehn	Telecommunications
LAC Langerak	Airframe
LAC Lindbloom	Aeroengine
LAC Roberts	Safety Equipment
LAC M. Roussey	Instrument
LAC Sauve	Airframe
LAC H. Wood	Aeroengine
LAC Warwick	Airframe

C-119 Flying Boxcar Support Team
F/L C.N. Agar
F/O R.H. Thiessen
F/O A. Pickering
F/O A. Edwards
F/O J.L. Nelson
LAC J. Watson
LAC J.M. Brown
LAC N.S. Justice
LAC M. LaPlante
remainder unknown

Support Aircraft:
C-119 Flying Boxcar
Canso Flying Boat

CF-100 Canuck Teams

No. 3 AW(F) OTU Solo Demos
No. 3 AW(F) Operational Training Unit
RCAF Stn North Bay, Ontario   1953-1955

1952	S/L Joe Schultz
1953-55	F/L Tony Gunter-Smith

445 AW(F) Sqn Formation Team
445 AW(F) Sqn
RCAF Stn North Bay, Ontario   1953
RCAF Stn Uplands, Ontario   1953
Avro CF-100 Mk3

1953

Lead	S/L T.R. Futer	F/O R.H. Kirkpatrick
#2	F/O W.B. Begy	P/O V.L. Bartlett
#3	F/L P.E. Etienne	F/O R.W. Baxter
#4	F/O J.C. Kitchen	F/O J. Brown
#5	F/L J.P. McGale	F/L M.L. Bolton
Solo	F/L M.J. Kobierski	F/L D.L. Turner

423 AW(F) Sqn Formation Team
423 AW(F) Sqn
RCAF Stn St. Hubert, Quebec   1954
Avro CF-100 Mk 3B

1954 – *See Operation Prairie Pacific*

Bald Eagles
No. 3 AW(F) Operational Training Unit,
RCAF Stn Cold Lake, Alta   1959-1960
Avro CF-100 Mk 4A

1959

Lead	F/L J.W. Stewart	F/O John Kuzyk
#2	F/O Don Lamont	F/O Glenn Emerson
#3	F/L Fred Hastings	F/O Al Runge
#4	F/O Stu Pollock	F/O Keith Bottoms

1960

Lead	F/L J.W. Stewart	F/O John Kuzyk
#2	F/O John Parker	F/O Lorne Jokinen
#3	F/L Paul Diamond	F/O Pete DeSmedt
#4	F/O Sam Cramb	F/O Ken Miller
Spare	F/O George Wilson	F/O Nick Chester

Golden Gigolos
433 AW(F) Sqn
RCAF Stn North Bay, Ontario   1959
Avro CF-100 Mk 4B

1959

Lead	F/L Pat Patterson	F/L Howie Sweet
#2	F/O John Rose	F/O Gerry Takach
#3	F/O Terry Harris	F/O Gerry Trudeau
#4	F/O Dave Rutka	F/O Doug Chase

Red Ravens
Electronic Warfare Unit
RCAF Stn St. Hubert, Quebec   1961-1962
Avro CF-100 Mk 5D

1961-1962

Lead	F/O K.O. Simonson	F/L Earl McFarland
#2	F/O Len Couture	F/L John Kilby
#3	F/O "Chalky" Leblanc	F/L Len Jenks
#4	F/O Bob McCraney	F/L Russ Jenkins

Royal Canadian Navy Jet Teams

VF 870 Aerobatic Team
VF 870
RCNAS Shearwater, Nova Scotia   1956-1957
McDonnell F2H-3 Banshee

1956-1957

Lead	Lt Gord Edwards
#2	Lt Frank Willis
#3	Lt Jake Birks
Lead	LCdr Bob Falls
	Lt Gord Edwards
#2	Lt Jake Birks
#3	Lt John Searle
#4	Lt Wally Sloan
Solos	Lt Frank Herrington
	Lt Frank Willis
	Lt Derek Prout[*]

[*] *killed at Shearwater, N.S. on 31 May 57
during solo airshow practice.*

Grey Ghosts
VF 870
RCNAS Shearwater, Nova Scotia   1958-1960
McDonnell F2H-3 Banshee

1958-1960

Lead	LCdr Wally Walton (leader)	
#2	Lt Walter Sloan (left wing)	
#3	LCdr A.E. (Alec) Fox (right wing)	
#4	Lt Ed Hallett (box)	(USN)
Solo	Lt Geoff Craven	

*Note: In 1959, Lt Frank Willis joined the team as an
opposing solo to Lt Geoff Craven for Shearwater shows.*

1958 Groundcrew

CPO Second Class	George Blackwell
CPO Second Class	Buck McCallum
PO First Class	Ross Steene
PO First Class	Milt Droeske
PO First Class	Robert Porter
PO Second Class	William Bruce
PO Second Class	Marvin May
Ablebodied Seaman	Ivan Pilkington
Ablebodied Seaman	Leonard Thompson
Ablebodied Seaman	Barry Whyte

T-33 Silver Star Teams

Central Flying School T-33 Demonstration Team
The Silver Stars
Central Flying School
RCAF Stn Trenton, Ontario   1953-1955
Lockheed / Canadair T-33 Silver Star

1953 CFS T-33 Demonstration Team
Lead Section (Aerobatic)

Lead	S/L Lou J. Hill	
#2	F/L Russ K. Scott	
#3	F/L Jack Seaman	
#4	Maj Mick Felts	(USAF)

Second Section (Formation)

Lead	F/L D.M. "Doc" Payne
#2	F/L R. Leather
#3	F/L A. Lehman
#4	F/L G. Frostad

1954-1955 Silver Stars[*]

Lead	S/L Lou J. Hill
#2	F/L Russ K. Scott
#3	F/L Jack Seaman
#4	F/L Alex Bowman
Spare	F/L D.M. "Doc" Payne
Crew Chief	Sgt G. Munroe

[*] *name first adopted in 1954.*

1 FIS Formation Team
Flying Instructor School
RCAF Stn Trenton, Ontario 1955-1958
Lockheed / Canadair T-33 Silver Star

1955-1956

Lead	F/L Gordon "Moe" Morrison
#2	F/O Ross McGillivray
#3	F/O Ken Blackmore
#4	F/O Dunc McLeish

1957

Lead	F/L Gordon "Moe" Morrison
#2	F/O Bill Kelly
#3	F/O Don Williams
#4	F/O Charles K. Rose III (USAF)

1958

Lead	F/L Max Preston
#2	Capt Ted Guy (USAF)
#3	F/O Doug Fraser
#4	F/O Bill Kelly

2 AFS Formation Team
No. 2 Advanced Flying School
RCAF Stn Portage la Prairie, Manitoba 1957
Lockheed / Canadair T-33 Silver Star

1957

Lead	F/L Bob Hallowell
#2	F/O Ken Castle
#3	F/O Doug Hogan
#4	F/O Marcel Vaesen
Spare	F/L Frank Wagner

Gimli Smokers
No. 3 Advanced Flying School,
RCAF Stn Gimli, Manitoba 1959-1964
Lockheed / Canadair T-33 Silver Star

1959

Lead	S/L Ken Lett
	S/L Bill Bliss
Wingmen	F/O Al Young
	F/O Tony Bosman
	F/O Ollie Fritsch
	F/O Bob Webber
	F/O Bill Arthurs
	F/O John England

1960

Lead	F/L G.N. (Gin) Smith
Wingmen	F/L Bill Mitchell
	F/L John England
	F/O Ken Kensick
	F/O Martin Sommerard
	F/O George McAffer
	F/O Fred Hope
	F/O Brian Dixon
	F/O Tony Bosman

1961

Lead	F/L G.N. (Gin) Smith
Wingmen	F/L Bill Mitchell
	F/L John England
	F/L George Shorey
	F/L Hugh Rose
	F/L "Chops" Viger
	F/O Larry Mosser
	F/O C.B. Lang
	F/O "Robbie" Robinson
	F/O Pete Trott
	F/O Elmer Dow
	F/O Len Mann
	F/O George McAffer

1962

Lead	F/L Larry Mosser
Wingmen	F/L George Shorey
	F/O Elmer Dow
	F/O Barry Dixon
	F/O C.B. Lang
	F/O Rick Flavelle
	F/O Harry Kelly
	F/O "Robbie" Robinson
	F/O Brodie Partington

1963

Lead	F/L Brodie Partington
Wingmen	F/L Walt Scott (D/Lead)
	F/L Larry Dyer
	F/O Brian Burke
	F/O Barry Dixon
	F/L Brian Evans
	F/O "Robbie" Robinson
	F/O John Kennedy
	F/O Rick Flavelle

1964

Lead	F/L Russ Bennett
Wingmen	F/L Larry Dyer (D/Lead)
	F/L Brian Burke
	F/O John Kennedy
	F/O Don Ripley
	F/O "Tommy" Thompson
	F/O Ross Mayberry
	F/O Jim Shirley
	F/O Dale Horley
	F/O Al Stuart
	F/O Doug Dargent (solo)

The Red Herring (Solo Demonstration)
VU-32
CFB Shearwater, Nova Scotia 1966-1971
Lockheed / Canadair T-33 Silver Star

1966-68, 1971	Lt (N)/Capt Ian Ferguson	(RCN/CF)
1970	Capt Wayne "Butch" Foster	(RCAF/CF)

VU-32 Jet Flight Formation Team
VU-32
CFB Shearwater, Nova Scotia 1966-1971
Lockheed / Canadair T-33 Silver Star

Lead	Lt Ian Ferguson	(RCN/CF)
Wing	Lt Hugh Fisher	(RCN/CF)
	Lt Gus Youngson	(RCN/CF)
	Lt Gerry Willis	(RCN/CF)
	F/L Tony Nichols	(RCAF/CF)

The Pink Dinks
414 Sqn Detatchment
CFB North Bay, Ontario 1967
Lockheed / Canadair T-33 Silver Star

1967

Lead	S/L Fred Tupling
	F/L Syd Burrows
#2	F/L George Morell
#3	F/L Pat Moran

Cougar T-33 Team
410 AW(F) Operational Training Sqn
CFB Bagotville, Quebec 1971
Lockheed / Canadair T-33 Silver Star

1971

Lead	Capt Earl McCurdy
#2	Capt Jim Speiser
#3	Capt Dave Speiser

Note: Due to the grounding of the Voodoo fleet for several months in 1971 due to engine problems, 410 Sqn fielded a T-33 team.

1 FTS T-Birds
1 Flying Training School
CFB Gimli, Manitoba 1970-1971
CFB Cold Lake, Alberta 1971
Lockheed / Canadair T-33 Silver Star

1970-1971

Lead	Capt Dave Thom
#2	Lt Wayne Adair
	Capt Jim Gale
#3	Capt Bobbi-Joe Hart
	Capt Bill Lynch
#4	Lt Brian Allen
Spares	Capt Gerry Hermanson
	Lt Guy Dutil

Red Herrings
VU-32 Jet Flight
CFB Shearwater, Nova Scotia 1977-1982
Lockheed / Canadair T-33 Silver Star

1977-1980

Lead	Capt John Roulston
Wingmen	Capt Bob Banks
	Capt Bob Deane
	Lt Yvon Bourdeau
	Capt Hugh Fisher
	Capt Wayne Wilhelm
	Capt Ed Beth
	Capt Ben Marcotte
	Lt Al Hutton

Tracer Reds
VU-32 Jet Flight
CFB Shearwater, Nova Scotia 1983-1992
Lockheed / Canadair T-33 Silver Star

1983 (Approx)

Lead	Maj Wayne Halliday
Wingmen	Pilots unknown

1989

Lead	Capt John Black
#2	Capt Rod Ermen
#3	Capt Tony Roeding
#4	Capt Doug Livingstone

1990-1992

Lead	Capt John Black
#2	Capt Rick Wilson
#3	Capt Dave Amberly
#4	Maj Tony Roeding

Silver Stars
Base Flight
CFB Cold Lake, Alberta 1983-1985
Lockheed / Canadair T-33 Silver Star

1983-1984

Lead	Capt Speedy Fast
#2	Capt Al Benell
#3	Capt Mike Skubicky

1985*

Lead	Capt Speedy Fast
#2	Capt Al Benell
#3	Capt Kevin German

* *Only one show was flown prior to the disbandment of all part-time airshow teams in Canada.*

Black Knights
414 (EW) Squadron
CFB North Bay, Ontario 1983-1984
CFB Comox, British Columbia 2001
Lockheed / Canadair T-33 Silver Star

1983

Lead	Capt Bob Sharpe
#2	Capt John Lahey
#3	Capt René Robert
#4	Capt Stu McAskill
Spare	Capt Lou Glussich

1984

Lead	Capt Stu McAskill
#2	Capt John Lahey
#3	Maj Bob Jones
	Capt René Robert
#4	Capt Lou Glussich

2001

Lead	LCol Yves Bossé (CO 414 Sqn)
#2	Capt Steve Wormsbecher
#3	Capt Larry Summers
#4	Maj Terry Hoffart

VU-33 T-33 Team

VU-33
CFB Comox, British Columbia,   1977-78, 1990-92
Lockheed / Canadair T-33 Silver Star

1977
Lead	Capt Pete Wittich
#2	Capt Frank Martin
#3	Capt Harry Chapin
#4	Capt Dave Lier

1978
Lead	Capt Harry Chapin
#2	Capt Terry Hallett

1990
Lead	Capt Harry Chapin
#2	Capt Franklin

1991-1992
Lead	Capt Harry Chapin
#2	Capt Blair Roe

RCAF Red Knight

Training Command Solo Demo Pilot	1958-1969
RCAF Stn Trenton, Ontario	1958-1959
RCAF Stn Saskatoon, Saskatchewan	1959-1960
RCAF Stn Portage la Prairie, Manitoba	1961-1964
CFB Moose Jaw, Saskatchewan	1965-1966
CFB Portage la Prairie, Manitoba	1967-1969
Lockheed / Canadair T-33 Silver Star	1958-1968
Canadair CT-114 Tutor	1968-1969

1958   F/L R. (Roy) Windover

Notes: First official show 14 Jun 58;
T-33 057 was painted red on 26 Aug 58

1959   F/L R. (Roy) Windover
1959   F/L C.R. (Bob) Hallowell (*Eff 10 Jul 59*)
            Crewman LAC R. (Bob) Ferguson

1960   F/L C.R. (Bob) Hallowell
            Crewman LAC J.A. (Jack) Woodhouse

1961   F/L R.J. (Ray) Goeres
            Crewman LAC J.A. (Jack) Woodhouse

            F/L D.J. (Dave) Barker (Alternate)
            Crewman LAC L.E. (Les) Matthews

1962   F/L D.J. (Dave) Barker
            Crewman LAC M. (Moe) Foote

            F/L W.C. (Bill) Fraser (Alternate)
            Crewman LAC G.G. (Grant) Harrison

1963   F/L W.C. (Bill) Fraser (Jan to Jun 63)
            Crewman Cpl P.R. (Pat) Dunn

            F/L J.W. (Bud) Morin* (Jun to Aug 63)
            Crewman Cpl P.R. (Pat) Dunn

            F/L B.W. (Wayne) MacLellan (Alternate)
            Crewman LAC R.G. (Bob) Casey

* killed 21 Aug 63 during airshow at RCAF Stn Gimli,
Manitoba in T-33 21057. Replaced by F/L MacLellan
who finished the season.

1964   F/L B.W. (Wayne) MacLellan (to Mar 64)

1964   F/O R.L. (Bill) Slaughter (from Mar 64)
            Crewman LAC Ellis Gauthro

            F/O Tex Deagnon (Alternate)
            Crewman LAC Paul Boucher

            F/L Jack Des Brisay (Officer Commanding)

1965   F/O Tex Deagnon
            Crewman LAC Jack Rathwell

            F/O Terry Hallett (Alternate)
            Crewman LAC Tom Lupton

            F/L Jim Stothard (Officer Commanding)

1966   F/L Terry Hallett
            Crewman LAC Jack Rathwell

            F/L Roger Cossette (Alternate)
            Crewman LAC Chip Lake

            F/L J.P. "Jake" Reilly
            Crewmen LACs Rathwell and Lake

1967   F/L J.E. (Jack) Waters
            Crewman Cpl Robert J. Hawes

            F/O E.R.M. (Rod) Ellis (Alternate)
            Crewmen Cpl Greg Moore
                    Cpl Vince Kavic

Canadian Armed Forces Red Knight

1968   Capt Dave Curran
            Crewman Cpl Larry H. Hunt

            Capt John Reid* (Alternate)

            Capt Joe Houlden (Commentator)
            Crewman Cpl John Hilts

* killed 22 May 68 during practice in T-33 21620
at CFB Portage la Prairie.

Note: The last T-33 Red Knight show was flown
on 9 Jun 68 at CFB Portage la Prairie in T-33 21630
at which time Capt Curran became the first Red Knight
to fly the CT-114 Tutor.

1969   Lt Brian G. Alston*
            Crewman Cpl Robert J. Hawes

            Capt Robert Cran** (Alternate)
            Crewman Cpl Larry H. Hunt

* killed 13 Jul 69 during practice in Tutor 26154
at CFB Moose Jaw.

** killed 30 Jul 69 during ejection following a student
training mishap at 2 FTS CFB Moose Jaw.

Red Knight Aircraft
T-33s 1958 – 21057; 1959 – 21057, 21201;
1960-1962 – 21057, 21574; 1963 – 21057, 21574,
21620; 1964 – 21574, 21620; 1965-1968 – 21620,
21630.

CT-114 Tutors 1968-1969 – 26153, 26154

Chipmunk and Harvard Teams

Chipmunk Synchronized Aerobatic Team (Smoke Eaters)
Primary Flying School
RCAF Stn Centralia, Ontario   1959-1962
de Havilland DHC 1 Chipmunk

1958
Lead	F/O Merv Billings
#2	F/O Jim Jotham

Note: The first shows of the season were flown
in the Harvard.

1959 - Aerobatic Team
Lead	F/O Jim Jotham
#2	F/O Don Sinel
	F/O Rene Croteau

Formation Team
Lead	F/O John Thomas
	F/O Rene Croteau
	F/O Hal Schweyer
	F/O Pete Giles

1960
Lead	F/O Jim Jotham
#2	F/O Bob Caskie
	F/O B.K. Doyle
Lead	F/L Bob Caskie
#2	F/L B.K. Doyle
	F/O Keith Chapman

1961
Lead	F/L Bob Caskie
#2	F/L B.K. Doyle
	F/O Keith Chapman
Lead	F/L Peter Caws
#2	F/O Keith Chapman
	F/O Ed McKeogh
	F/O Ron Donovan

1962
Lead	F/L Peter Caws
#2	F/O Ron Donovan

1963
Lead	F/L Peter Caws
#2	F/O Ron Donovan
	F/O Keith Chapman

2 FTS Harvard Team
2 Flying Training School
RCAF Stn Moose Jaw, Saskatchewan   1959
North American Harvard
(called themselves the "Yellow Chickens")

1959
Lead	F/L Jim Stacy
	F/O Dave Bagshaw
	F/O David Baker
Solo	F/O Robert E. (Bob) Smith

Goldilocks / Moose Jaw Harvard Aerobatic Team
Flying Instructor School
RCAF Stn Moose Jaw, Saskatchewan   1962-1964
North American Harvard Mk 4

1962
Lead	F/L Jerry Davidson
#2	F/L Bernie McComiskey
#3	F/L Murray Neilson
#4	F/L Glen "Red" Willett
	F/L Denny Lambert
#5	F/L Mike Matthews
#6	F/L Bernie Lapointe
#7	F/L Denny Lambert

Note: F/L Willett flew slot up to and including
Winnipeg AFD show on 15 Sep 62.

1962 Groundcrew
Engr Officer	F/O Roger Patey
	Sgt Moe Lyons

1963
Lead	F/L Jerry Davidson
	F/L Murray Neilson
#2	F/L Bernie McComiskey
#3	F/L Murray Neilson
	F/L Al Kucinskas
#4	F/L Denny Lambert
#5	F/L Mike Matthews
#6	F/L Bernie Lapointe
	F/L Bob Dobson
#7	F/L Moe Campbell
Team Manager	F/L Barney Hopkins
Commentator	F/L Bob Dobson

1963 Groundcrew
Engr Officer	F/L Roger Patey
Crew Chief	Sgt Rollie Muloin
AE Tech	Cpl Joe Tyers
AF Tech	LAC Denny Lank
IE Tech	LAC James Fitzhenry
Comm Tech	LAC Al Jordan
AE Tech	LAC Bill Heal

Support Aircraft: Two spare Harvards flown by
F/L Barney Hopkins and F/O Dale Bacon or
Expeditor flown by F/L Gord Wellesby.

Notes: 1. F/L Davidson led the team for the first two
shows of the season at which time F/L Neilson assumed
command. 2. F/L Dobson flew as opposing solo at
Moose Jaw AFD.

1964

Lead	F/L Murray Neilson
#2	F/L Barney Hopkins
#3	F/L Al Kucinskas
#4	F/L Denny Lambert
#5	F/L Mike Matthews
#6	F/L Bernie Lapointe
#7	F/L Moe Campbell
Team Manager	F/O Gerry Gelly

1964 Groundcrew

Engr Officer	F/L Roger Patey
Crew Chief	Sgt Rollie Muloin
AE Tech	Cpl Joe Tyers
Comm Tech	LAC Al Jordan
AF Tech	LAC Denny Lank
AE Tech	LAC Bill Heal
IE Tech	LAC James Fitzhenry
AF Tech	LAC Chuck Bishop
Telecom	LAC Mike Schmidt

CAF Golden Centenaires

Canadian Armed Forces Centennial Aerobatic Team
CFB Portage la Prairie, Manitoba   1967
Commanding Officer   W/C O.B. Philp
Public Relations   S/L Lloyd J. Hubbard
Personnel Officer   F/L J.L. Denis Gauthier

Canadair CT-114 Tutor

Team Leader	S/L Clarence B. Lang
Right Wing	F/L Tom P. Hinton
Left Wing	F/L John M. Swallow
Slot	S/L Russell C. Bennett
Outer R Wing	S/L Byron K. Doyle
Outer L Wing	S/L Robert C. Dagenais
Lead Solo	F/L R.W. (Bill) Slaughter
Opposing Solo	F/O Jim M. McKay

Note: Solo pilots F/Ls Tom Bebb and Dave Barker lost their lives in Oct 66 and Feb 67 respectively during separate training accidents prior to the start of the season.

Avro 504K	F/L George Greff
	F/L Gord A. Brown
CF-104 Solo	F/L D. René Serrao
CF-101 Solo	F/L J.E. "Jake" Miller (Pilot)
	F/O Robert M. McGimpsey (Nav)
Red Knight (T-33)	F/L J.E. (Jack) Waters
	F/O R.E.M. (Rod) Ellis (Alternate)

Golden Centenaires Groundcrew
CT-114 Tutor

F/L C.D. Grant	Engineering Officer
Flt Sgt J.M. Gibson	Avn Tech
Flt Sgt N.L. Hayward	Avn Tech
Sgt G.J. Livingston	Adm Clk
Sgt R.E. Wharton	Avn Tech
Cpl I.J. Anderson	IE Tech
Cpl L.O. Bakke	AF Tech
Cpl V.R. Bruff	M Tech
Cpl J.G. Charlebois	AF Tech
Cpl E.M. Cougle	AE Tech
Cpl H. Comtois	IS Tech
Cpl M.D. Critch	AF Tech
Cpl W.R. Doherty	Rdr Sys Tech
Cpl J.S. Green	Rdr Sys Tech
Cpl R. Haas	Sup Tech
Cpl G.B. Harding	AF Tech
Cpl W.R. Heal	AE Tech
Cpl H.L. Hunt	AE Tech
Cpl R.J. Imre	Photographer
Cpl K.F. Johnson	IE Tech
Cpl E.H. Jones	R Tech
Cpl J.W. Lapalme	S Sys Tech
Cpl C.W. Leathem	IE Tech
Cpl M.C. McAllister	AF Tech
Cpl W.G. McAskill	AF Tech
Cpl F.F. Millard	S Sys Tech
Cpl R.C. Murray	AF Tech
Cpl W.B. Nadeau	IE Tech
Cpl J.M. Ouellet	Adm Clk

Cpl C. Poirier	AF Tech
Cpl N.R. Pollon	AF Tech
Cpl C.A. Restorick	AE Tech
Cpl J. Steckler	IE Tech
Cpl W.H. Trimble	AE Tech
Cpl J.W. Veevers	AE Tech
Cpl J.D. Walker	Com Sys Tech
Cpl R.F. Weaver	IE Tech
Cpl J.W. Wighton	AF Tech
Cpl G. Yeske	Com Sys Tech
LAC R.B. Lepine	IE Tech

Avro 504K

Sgt G. Carpenter	Supervisor
Cpl D.A. Brooks	AE Tech
Cpl F.G. Doherty	AF Tech
Cpl J.A. Chermisnok	AE Tech
Cpl W.L. Ewing	AF Tech
Cpl M.R. Trimm	AF Tech

CF-104 Starfighter

W/O L. McLean	Supervisor
Flt Sgt Hempseed	Supervisor
Flt Sgt H. Richardson	Supervisor
Cpl A. Gretter	Comm Tech
Cpl A. Hughes	IS Tech
Cpl J. Hughes	Radar Tech
Cpl E. Poitras	AF Tech
Cpl Rochon	S Sys Tech
Cpl P. Valade	AE Tech
Cpl R. Wishart	IE Tech
Cpl Cardinal	
Cpl Smith	

CF-101B Voodoo

Cpl R. Stuart	IE Tech
Six others unknown	

Red Knight T-33

Cpl R.J. Hawes	
Cpl G.A. Moores	
Cpl V. Kavic	

Team Aircraft

CT-114 Tutors: 26083, 26122, 26147, 26151, 26152, 26153, 26154, 26155, 26161, 26163, 26175, 26176, 26178, 26179, 26180, 26181, 26183, 26189

CF-104 Starfighters: 12744, 12763, 12769, 12783

CF-101B Voodoos: 17459, 17395, 17483

T-33 Silver Stars (RK): 21630, 21620
                      (GC): 21592, 21490

Avro 504Ks: G-CYCK, G-CYEI

Airlift Support: C-130 Hercules (426/435 Sqns)

Snoopy Squadron

National Aviation Museum Rockcliffe and CEPE/AETE
CFB Uplands   1967

1967

W/C Paul Hartman (Chief Pilot National Aviation Museum)	Sopwith Camel
W/C David Wightman (CEPE/AETE Senior Test Pilot)	Sopwith Snipe
F/L W.R. (Bill) Long	Nieuport 17
F/L N.A. (Neil) Burns	Aeronca C-2
F/L J.F. (James) Fitzgerald	Sopwith Triplane
F/L J. (Jock) MacKay	Fleet Finch

1967 Groundcrew

S/L (Ret'd) J. Murphy	Mr. A.D. Fell
Sgt W.D. Scholey	Mr. C.E. Adams
Cpl C.S. Gallison	Mr. W. Merrikin
Cpl L.S. Moody	Mr. C.G. Aylen

Note: CEPE Uplands was redesignated AETE on 4 May 67 and the CEPE Detachment at CFB Cold Lake was redesignated 448 Test Sqn. In the fall of 1971 all test units were consolidated under AETE at CFB Cold Lake.

CF-101 Voodoo Airshow Teams

Cougars

410 AW(F) Sqn

RCAF Stn Uplands, Ontario	1962-1964
CFB Bagotville, Quebec	1968-1974
McDonnell CF-101B Voodoo	

1962 Cougar Formation

Lead	F/L Tom Murray	F/L Jeff Bingham (RAF)
#2	F/L Ted Climenhaga	Unknown
Solo	F/L Tom Murray	F/L Dave Mitton

Note: 410 Sqn was disbanded on 31 Mar 64.
The squadron re-formed in 1968 as the Voodoo OTU.

1970 Cougar Formation

Lead	Maj Carl Bertrand	Capt Chuck Wierelejchyk
#2	Capt Dave Speiser	Capt Russ Hellberg
#3	Capt Earl McCurdy	Capt John Viar (USAF)
#4	Capt Jim Speiser	Capt Charlie Gladders
#5	Capt Jerry Ryan	Capt Ron Egli
Lead	Capt Earl McCurdy	Capt Chuck Wierelejchyk
#2	Capt Dave Hickman	Capt D. Hillstrom (USAF)
#3	Capt Jim Speiser	Capt Charlie Gladders
#4	Capt John Rose	Capt Jim Lauder
Solo	LCol Hal Pike	Maj John Houghton
Nrtr	Capt Len Dodd	

Alouettes

425 AW(F) Sqn

CFB Bagotville, Quebec	1964-1972
CF-101B Voodoo	

1964

Lead	W/C Grant Nichols	F/L Brodie Templeton
#2	F/L Mike Hobbs (RAF)	F/L Stan Perry (RAF)
#3	F/O Pete Dzulinsky	F/L Doug Stuart

1966

Lead	F/L John Gray	F/L Nick Chester
	S/L Don Hutchinson	F/L Nick Chester
#2	F/O Pete Dzulinsky	Unknown
#3	F/O Bruce McIntosh	Unknown
#4	F/O Dick Lidstone	F/O Reg Howard

1967

Lead	F/L Earl McCurdy	F/L Dave Towns
#2	F/L Bill Purdy	Unknown
#3	F/L Keith Inkster	Unknown
#4	F/L Jim Speiser	Unknown

1969

Lead	Maj Bob Flynn	Capt John Lahey
#2	Capt Brian Allchin	Capt "Andy" Anderson
#3	Capt Ron D'Ambrosio	Capt Stu Morgan
#4	Capt Robert Hallin	Capt R. Jurgeson
#5	Capt R. Pashkaiewich	Capt Wilf Macleod
#6	Capt Mel Branter	Capt Lynn Housworth

1970

Lead	Maj Al Sundvall	Capt Don Parker
#2	Lt Bernie Newberry	Maj Earle Spencer
#3	Lt Ray Paul	Lt Bob LeBlanc
#4	Lt Lowell Butters	Lt Brian Drury

1971

Lead	Maj Bryce McDonald	Lt Rick Phoenix
#2	Capt Roger Ayotte	Capt Mel Felts
#3	Lt Bernie Newberry	Maj Earle Spencer
#4	Lt Lowell Butters	Lt Doug Danko
Solo	Capt Ross Betts	

1972 Alouette Reds

Lead	LCol Ron Hayman	Maj Earle Spencer
#2	Capt Ted Jackson	Capt Lance Carroll
#3	Capt John Duncan	Maj Fred Brittain
#4	Capt John Stiver	Capt Fraser Barnes
		Capt Les Taylor
Solo	Capt Jim Sorfleet	Capt Rick Alp

Larks
425 AW(F) Sqn
CFB Bagotville, Quebec   1973
CF-101B Voodoo

1973

Lead	Maj Gene Lukan	Capt Lance Carroll
#2	Capt Ken Binda	Capt Dave Crumpton
#3	Capt Marc Simard	Capt Dick Pearce
#4	Capt Dick Walker	Capt John Evans
Solo	Capt Rick Gordon	Capt Al Hamelin
Nrtr	Capt Andy Campbell	

1974
Note: No team due to runway repairs in Bagotville – 425 Sqn deployed to Val d'Or, 410 to Chatham.

Skylarks
425 AW(F) Sqn
CFB Bagotville, Quebec   1975
CF-101B Voodoo

1975

Lead	Maj Dave O'Blenis	Capt John McDonald
#2	Capt Fred Harrington	Capt Pat Nicholson
#3	Lt Bill Ruppel	Lt Al Hunter
#4	Capt Rick Engler	Lt Andre Tremblay
Spare	Capt Tim Harper	Capt Mike Lemay
Nrtr	Capt J.M. Comtois	Capt Gilbert Dubé

Warlocks
425 AW(F) Sqn
CFB Bagotville, Quebec   1976-1982
CF-101B Voodoo

1976

Lead	Maj Larry Lott	Capt Bob Borland
#2	Capt Bob Robichaud	Capt Blair Morrell
#3	Capt Mike Hardie	Capt J.J. St Pierre
#4	Capt John McNamara	Capt Doug Brown
Nrtr	Capt Jacques Nadeau	Capt Rick Sponder

1977

Lead	Maj Larry Lott	Capt Bob Borland
#2	Capt Bob Robichaud	Capt Blair Morrell
#3	Capt Mike Hardy	Capt J.J. St Pierre
#4	Capt John McNamara	Capt Doug Brown
Nrtr	Capt Roy Mould	Capt Chuck Langtry

1978

Lead	Maj Romeo Lalonde	Capt Kevin Psutka
#2	Capt Rick Galashan	Capt J.P. Paquette
#3	Capt Jacques Nadeau	Capt Bona Senechal
#4	Capt Don Bosworth	Capt Terry Cuthbert
#5	Capt Don Brodeur	Capt Serge Roy
#6	Capt Greg Mortimer	Capt Chuck Langtry
Lead	Maj Romeo Lalonde	Capt Kevin Psutka
#2	Capt Al Walker	Capt Chuck Langtry
#3	Capt Roy Mould	Capt Terry Cuthbert
#4	Capt Don Bosworth	Capt Blair Morrell

1979

Lead	Maj Romeo Lalonde	Maj Art Armstrong
#2	Capt Steve Wallace	Capt Marcel Parisien
#3	Capt Don Brodeur	Capt J.P. Paquette
		Capt Bob Cleroux
#4	Capt Dave Tower	Capt Terry Cuthbert

Note: Maj Larry Lott led the team for the Hamilton Air Show 16, 17 Jun 79 with navigator Capt Terry Cuthbert.

Lead	Maj Romeo Lalonde	Maj Jacques Boucer
#2	Capt Al Walker	Maj Bob Nagy
#3	Capt Herb Paul	Lt Reg Bossé
#4	Capt Jeff Graham	Capt Michel Gagnier

1980

Lead	Maj Keith Coulter	Maj Art Armstrong
#2	Capt Geoff Graham	Capt Rémi Picard
#3	Capt Herb Paul	Maj Val Parker
		Capt Dan Audet
#4	Capt Bob Lamb	Capt P. TenBruggencate

1981

Lead	Maj Keith Coulter	Maj Joe Sharpe
	Maj Jim Gregory*	Maj Joe Sharpe
#2	Capt Jean-Luc Sinave	Lt Mike Kyne
#3	Capt Paul Washington	Capt Ben Toenders
#4	Lt Greg Peters	Capt J.P. Dionne

* assumed command in Aug 81.

1982

Lead	Maj Jim Gregory	Capt Denis Guerin
#2	Capt Doug McLennan	Lt Gerry Lalonde
#3	Capt Daniel Pelletier	Lt René Cousineau
#4	Capt Chuck McCrea	Lt Michel Latouche

Lynx Formation
416 AW(F) Sqn
RCAF Stn Uplands, Ontario
RCAF Stn Bagotville, Quebec
RCAF Stn/CFB Chatham, New Brunswick
CF-101B Voodoo   1962-1977

1962

Lead	F/L Al Robb	F/O Chuck Verge
#2	F/O Stu Whalley	F/L Ray Jefferies
#3	F/O Roger Cossette	F/O Don Parker
#4	F/O Pete DeLong	F/O Gord Larsen
Solo	W/C Dean Kelly	F/O Mark Wiersma

1965 CNE Airshow Team

Lead	S/L Sam Millar	S/L Ron Bell
#2	F/L Bill Willson	F/L Jerry Frewen
#3	F/L Bill Webster	F/L B. Smallman-Tew
#4	F/O Jean-Guy Fortin	F/L Rod MacPherson
#5	F/O Jacques St-Cyr	F/L D.W. Smith

1966 Shearwater Airshow Team

Lead	F/L Brian Phipps	F/O Rob McGimpscy
#2	F/O Les Hare	F/O Ron Elliot

1967 Centennial Airshow Team – Ottawa

Lead	S/L Sam Millar	F/L Dick Falck
#4	F/L Pat Pattison	F/O Wayne Stuart

1967 Golden Centennaires

Solo	F/L Jake Miller	F/L Rob McGimpsey

1970 CNE Airshow Team

Lead	Maj B.K. Doyle	Capt Pete Ott
#2	Lt Don Nattress	Capt "Jake" Jacobsen
#3	Capt Dave Wilson	Capt Jim Seel
#4	Lt Ivan Morrell	Capt Don Wenzel
Solo	LCol Don MacCaul	Capt Dave Lennox

1972 CNE Airshow Team

Lead	Maj Bill Grip(409 Sqn)	Capt Al Ruttan
#2	Lt Stu Holdsworth	Lt Ron Hysert
#3	Capt Bob Cote	Capt J.P. Paquette
#4	Capt Murray Bertram	Lt Dave Buggie

1972 William Tell Airshow Team

Lead	Maj Harry Stroud	Maj B. Smallman-Tew
#2	Capt Bob Jones	Capt Joe Sharpe
#3	Capt Mike Blair	Capt Ray Harpell
#4	Capt Don Schmidt	Capt Des Larock
Solo	Capt Ivan Morrell	Capt John Allison
Nrtr	Capt Jim Thompson	F/L Dave Trotter (RAF)

1974

Lead	Maj Mike Nash	Maj Karl Robinson
#2	Lt Bob Craig	Capt Paddy O'Sullivan
	Capt Bert Doyle	Capt Harry Redden
#3	Capt Jim Thompson	Capt J.L. Clark
#4	Capt Dwayne Lung	Capt Craig Given
Spare	Capt Bert Doyle	Capt Harry Redden

1975

Lead	Maj Jim Shirley	Capt Bill Books
#2	Capt Bill Charleton	Capt Craig Given
#3	Capt Roger Arsenault	Capt J.L. Clarke
#4	Capt Bob Craig	

1976

Lead	Maj Dave Curran	Unknown
#2	Capt Terry Hunt	Capt Randy Thistle
#3	Capt Doug Moore	Capt Fred Robinson
#4	Capt Ed Kuhar	Capt Brian Salmon

Bobcats
416 AW(F) Sqn
CFB Chatham, New Brunswick   1978-1984
CF-101B Voodoo

1977

Lead	Maj Ben Macht	Capt Fred Robinson
#2	Capt Bob Gainforth	Capt Jeff Hunter
#3	Capt Earl Robertson	Capt John Haazen
#4	Capt Terry Angus	Capt Chris Ouimet
Spares	Maj Syd Rennick	Capt Randy Thistle
		Capt George Meldrum

1978

Lead	Maj Renaud Bellemare	Capt Randy Thistle
#2	Lt Terry Hoffart	Lt Norm Bonikowski
#3	Lt Dean Rainkie	Lt Don Nicks
#4	Lt Ron Dudley	Capt John Haazen

1979

Lead	Maj Renaud Bellemare	Capt Al Oostenbrug
#2	Capt Doug Cushman	Lt Steve Peach
	* Capt Tom Sabean	Lt Bob Biggart
#3	Capt Mike Stacey	Lt Bob Biggart
	* Capt Doug Cushman	Lt Steve Peach
#4	Capt Tom Dunn	Lt Mike Caron

* change effective Aug 79 due to posting.

1980

Lead	Maj Roy Mould	Capt Steve Peach
#2	Capt Terry McKenzie	Lt Ron Cooney
#3	Lt Dan Morley	Capt Jim Christie
#4	Capt Tom Sabean	Lt Dan Michailiuk
Spare	Capt Lance Carroll	Lt Bob Biggart
		Capt Hank Dielwart

1981

Lead	Capt Tom Sabean	Lt Dan Michailiuk
#2	Capt Dieter Popp	Capt Paul Zorz
#3	Capt Rick Boyd	Lt Ken Walker
#4	Capt Ron Berlie	Capt Bert Archibald

1982

Lead	Capt Dan Morley	Capt Hank Dielwart
#2	Capt Dieter Popp	Lt Jim Forbes
#3	Capt K.P. McNeil	Lt Ken Walker
#4	Capt Seldon Doyle	Capt Darrell Synnott
Spare	Capt Ron Berlie	Capt Darrell Marleau
		Capt Dan Michailiuk

Note: Capt Ron Berlie flew a solo demonstration for the CF-18 acceptance ceremony in Ottawa on 25 Oct 82. His navigator was Maj Ian Cowan.

1983
Lead	Maj Bob Olson	Capt Paul Zorz
#2	Capt Brad Dolan	Capt Darrell Marleau

1984
Lead	Maj Hayden Henwood	Capt Bob Bouchard
#2	Capt Dennis Watson	Capt Andy Graham
Spare	Lt Larry Martin	Capt Carl French

Nighthawks
409 AW(F) Sqn
CFB Comox, British Columbia   1965-1984
CF-101B Voodoo

1965
Lead	S/L Sid Popham	F/L Pete Pellow
#2	F/L Garth Foley	F/L Mike Marsh
#3	F/L Jerry Davidson	F/L Ron McDonald
		F/O Al Cooper

1966
Lead	S/L Sid Popham	F/L Pete Pellow
#2	Unknown	Unknown
#3	Unknown	F/L Bob Gillet
#4	F/L Dave Walker	F/L Jim Dale

1967
Lead	S/L Sid Popham	F/L Pete Pellow
	S/L Arnie Leiter	F/L Len Dodd
#2	Unknown	Unknown
#3	Unknown	Unknown
#4	F/L Dave Walker	F/L Jim Dale

1968
Lead	Capt George McAffer	Capt Al Cooper
#2	Capt Les Putland	Capt Fred Williams
#3	Capt Barry McLeod	Capt Brodie Templeton

1969
Lead	Capt Barry MacLeod	Capt John Emon*
#2	Capt Don Elphick	Capt Bob Merrick
#3	Capt Hugh Fischer	Lt Hank Dielwart
#4	Lt Ron Little	Capt Laurie Bastie*

* 2 navigators killed 29 May 69 following mid-air collision during practice near Comox, B.C.

Lead	Maj Sam Skinner	Capt Bill Bland
#2	Lt Harry Chapin	Lt Hank Dielwart
#3	Capt Don Elphick	Capt Don Marion
#4	Capt Stu Bains	Capt Fred Williams
	Capt George McAffer	Capt Brodie Templeton
		Capt Lynn Wagar
#5	Capt Bob Olson	Capt Fred Williams

1970
Lead	Capt George McAffer	Capt Fred Williams
#2	Capt Doug Stuart	Capt P. Dunda (USAF)
#3	Capt Ernie Poole	Capt Brodie Templeton
#4	Capt Rhinehart Koehn	Capt Hank Dielwart

1971
Lead	Capt Doug Stuart	Capt Don Middleton
#2	Capt Harry Chapin	Lt Roger Lamothe

1972
Lead	Maj Bill Grip	Capt Hank Dielwart
#2	Capt Dan Baker (USAF)	Maj Bob Conn
#3	Lt Gus Hay	Capt Marv Guile
#4	Capt Ken Carr	Capt Tim O'Rourke
Spare	Capt John Pew	Capt F. Campbell (USAF)

1973
Lead	Capt Tony Brett	Capt Tom Murray
#2	Capt John Pew	Capt Gary Raindahl
#3	Capt Gus Hay	Capt Roger Lamothe
#4	Capt Ken Carr	Capt Paul Gill

1974
Lead	LCol Ev McKay	Maj Mike Mahon
	Capt Jon Pew	Lt Mike McKay
#2	Capt Gerry MacIntosh	Lt Bart Wickham
#3	Capt Tom Potter	Capt John Molloy
#4	Capt Mike Spooner	Lt Ed Campbell

1976
Lead	Capt Tom Potter	Capt Charlie Gladders
#2	Maj Tom Goodall	Capt Pete Ott
#3	Capt J. Alexander (USAF)	Capt Trevor Wallace
		Capt Paul Gill
	Capt Lou Glussich	Capt Rich Littler
#4	Capt Les Cox*	Capt Roy Smith*
	Capt Jon Alexander	Capt Trevor Wallace

* The original crew of Hawk 4, Capts Les Cox and Roy Smith, were killed on 5 Jul 76 (Voodoo 101061) during the team's first practice when they inexplicably flew into the water. As a result, the crew of Glussich/Littler joined the team as Hawk 3 while Alexander (USAF) / Wallace moved to the solo position, Hawk 4.

1977
Lead	Maj Dave Koski	Maj Russ Hellberg
#2	Capt Jim Reith	Capt Ron Hallstrom
#3	Capt Kent Smerdon	Capt Tom Watt
#4	Capt Ron Coleman	Capt Charlie Gladders

Note: "Hawk One" (101012) was flown by Hawk 4.

1978
Lead	Capt Ron Coleman	Capt Charlie Gladders
#2	Capt George Wissler	Unknown
#3	Capt Rick Zyvitski	Capt "Jake" Jacobsen
#4	Capt Doug Evans	Capt Ray Harpell

1979
Lead	Maj Doug Evans	Capt Mel Ferraby
#2	Lt Andy Dobson	Capt Dave Taylor
#3	Capt Bill Cleland	Capt Larry Russell
#4	Capt John Wiggin	Capt G. McCluer (USAF)
Nrtr	Capt Glen Buchanan	Capt Ron Neeve

The Hawks
1980
Lead	Capt Lynn Housworth	Capt Bill Books
#2	Capt Chuck Fast	Capt Mel Ferraby
#3	Capt Dale Erhart	Capt Don Thornton
#4	Capt Brian Taylor	Capt Bernie Hughes
Spare	Capt Barry Kennedy	
Nrtr	Capt Glen Buchanan	

1981
Lead	Capt Terry Hunt	Capt Gord MacPherson
#2	Capt Joel Clarkston	Capt Bill Kolupanowicz
#3	Capt Doug Swanson	Capt Don Thornton
	Capt Barry Kennedy	Capt Bill Ricketts
#4	Capt Ed Campbell	Capt Bill Books
Nrtr	Capt Bill Motriukk	Capt Jay Jongeruis

1982
Lead	Maj Ray Dunsdon	Capt Gord MacPherson
#2	Capt Tim Strocel	Lt Andy Anderson
#3	Capt Dan Trynchuk	Capt Jay Jongerius
#4	Capt Bob Slack (USAF)	Lt Mark Forseille
Nrtr	Capt Joel Clarkston	Capt Dave Mosher

1983
Lead	Capt Eric Matheson	Maj Jon Main
#2	Capt Howard Tarbet	Lt Kurt Saladana

1984
Lead	Maj Terry Hunt	Capt Dave Reyenga
#2/4	Capt Tom Chester	Capt Doug Neill
#2	Capt Gary Soule	Capt Bernie Hughes
#3	Capt Dave Pullan	Maj Jon Main
Nrtr	Capt Kurt Saladana	

CF-104 Starfighter Teams

CEPE Starfighter Demonstrations
Central Experimental and Proving Establishment
RCAF Stn Uplands, Ontario   1962-1963
Lockheed / Canadair CF-104 Starfighter

1962-1963
F/L Lorne Tapp
F/L Frank Gilland
F/L Clive Loubser

Starfighter Demonstration Teams
No. 6 Strike/Recce Operational Training Unit
RCAF Stn Cold Lake, Alberta   1964-1967
Lockheed / Canadair CF-104 Starfighter

1964 - NAFD Rockcliffe
Lead	S/L W.G. (Bill) Paisley	
#2	F/L Don McGowan	
#3	Unknown	
#4	Unknown	
Static	F/L Lyle Kettles	

1964 - CNE Toronto
Lead	S/L Len Fitzsimmons	
#2	F/L Hugh Grasswick	
#3	F/L John Lauritsen	
#4	Capt Bob Noak	(USAF)

1965 - CNE Toronto
Lead	S/L Len Fitzsimmons	
#2	F/L Lyle Kettles	
#3	Maj Bud Jamesen	(USAF)
#4	F/L Ken Maley	
#5	F/L Moe Morrison	

1966 - CNE Toronto
Lead	S/L Grant Baker	
#2	Maj Don Gerlinger	(USAF)
#3	F/L "Gin" Smith	
#4	F/L "Buster" Kincaid	
#5	F/L "Pogo" Hamilton	

1967 - CNE Toronto
Lead	F/L Al Seitz	
#2	Capt Jamie Denard	(USAF)
#3	Capt Cebe Habersky	(USAF)
#4	F/L Tony Bosman	
#5	F/L Bob Morgan	
Solo	F/L René Serrao flew the CF-104 solo with the Golden Centennaires.	

Note: On 11 Mar 68 No. 6 Strike/Recce OTU was redesignated 417 Tactical Fighter Training Squadron.

Starfighters
417 Tac (F) Training Squadron
CFB Cold Lake, Alberta   1968-1982
Lockheed / Canadair CF-104 Starfighter

1968 Starfighters
Lead	Capt Al Seitz
#2	Capt Art Maskell
#3	Capt Bob Wood
#4	Capt Bob Morgan

1969 Starfighters
Lead	Maj Norm Garriock
#2	Capt J.W. (Bill) Stewart
#3	Maj Bill Worthy
#4	Capt Bob Morgan

1970 Starfighters
Lead	Capt J.W. (Bill) Stewart	
#2	Capt Al Heston	(USAF)
#3	Capt John Callahan	
#4	Capt Phil Engstad	
Solos	Capt Jordy Krastel	
	Capt Garry Sanderson	

Note: Flew a combined show with the 434 Sqn CF-5 Team.

1971 Starfighters

Lead	Capt Jordy Krastel
#2	Capt Eric Saunders
#3	Capt Bill Nesbitt
#4	Capt Ed Rozdeba
Solo	Capt W.C. (Bill) Stewart

Note: Flew a combined show with the 434 Sqn CF-5 Team.

1972 Deadeye Whiskeys

Lead	Capt Gord Todd
#2	Capt Ed Folks
#3	Capt Dave Bartram
#4	Capt Terry Humphries
Solo	Capt Yogi Huyghebaert

1973 Starfighters

Lead	Capt Eric Thurston	
#2	F/L Merv Paine	(RAF)
#3	Capt Terry Humphries	
#4	Capt Ray Dunsdon	
Solo	Capt John David	

1974 Deadeye Blacks

Lead	Capt Ray Dunsdon	
#2	F/L Dave Leach	(RAAF)
#3	Capt Ron Clarkson	
#4	Capt Frank Thorne	
Solo	Capt Gord Todd	
Narrator	Capt Bob Morris	

1975 Starfighters

Lead	Capt John David	
#2	F/L Rojer Wholey	(RAF)
#3	Capt Dave Bligh	
#4	Capt Frank Thorne	
Solo	F/L Dave Leach	(RAAF)

1976 Deadeye Zips

Lead	Capt Ron Doyle
#2	Capt Dave Burroughs
#3	Capt John Bagshaw

1977 Deadeye Zips / Alberta Arrows

Lead	Capt John Bagshaw
#2	Capt Laurie Hawn
#3	Capt Dave Bligh
#4	Capt Dave Burroughs

1978 Deadeye Blues

Lead	Capt Lloyd Campbell
#2	Capt Ted Lee
#3	Capt Harv Wregget
#4	Capt Dave Burroughs
Solo	Maj Walt Pirie

1979 Deadeye Zips

Lead	Capt Wally Peirson
#2	Capt Dan Bouchard
#3	Capt Don Leonard
#4	Capt Don Robinson

1980 Deadeye Zips

Lead	Capt Gus Youngson	
#2	Capt Dan Bouchard	
#3	Capt Cash Poulson	
#4	*Hauptmann* Harald Riedel	(GAF)
Narrator	Capt Dudley Larsen	(USAF)
Crew Chief	Sgt Mike Middleton	

1981

No team due to lack of resources; solo displays only.

Solo	Maj John Laidler

1982 Deadeye Zips

Lead	Capt Dave Owen
# 2	Capt Keith Robbins
Solo	Maj John Laidler

Note: Capt Dave Owen also flew a solo demo at Ottawa on 25 Oct 82 during the official acceptance ceremony for the CF-18 Hornet.

1983 Canadian CF-104 Closeout Team

Lead	Capt Phil Murphy	(417 Sqn)
#2	Capt Rob Martin	(441 Sqn)
#3	Capt John Roulston	(439 Sqn)
#4	Capt Jim Grecco	(421 Sqn)

European CF-104 Starfighter Teams

The Starfighters

1 Air Division/1 Canadian Air Group
CFB Baden-Soellingen, West Germany   1966-1983
CF-104 Starfighter

1966 430 Sqn Eagles

Lead	S/L Mo White
#2	F/L Leo O'Donovan
#3	F/L Dave Mills
#4	F/L Don Bergie
Spare	F/L Ken Castle

1967 439 Sqn Tigers

Lead	F/L Bill Graves
#2	F/O Bob Garry
#3	F/L Ray Learmond
#4	F/O Guy Fabi

1970 Red Indians (421 Sqn)

Lead	Maj Brian Titterton
#2	Capt Tony Blake
#3	Capt Don Slimman
#4	Capt John David
Solo	Maj Ed McKeogh

1971 Red Indians (421 Sqn)

Lead	Maj Ed McKeogh	
#2	Capt Jacques Desbiens	
#3	Capt Bruce Lunquist	
#4	Maj Billy Sparks	(USAF)
#5	Capt John David	
#6	Capt Jack McLean	
#7	Capt Len Sherwood	
#8	Capt Grant Dunn	
#9	Capt Tony Blake	

Note: Number of aircraft varied.

1973 Red Indians (421 Sqn)

Lead	Maj John England
#2	Capt Ed McGillivray
#3	Capt Cec Hume
#4	Capt Brian Allen
Solo	Capt Willy Floyd

1976 Tiger Romeos (439 Sqn)

Lead	Maj Bill Fuoco
#2	Lt Marty Abbott
#3	Capt Keith McDonald
#4	Capt Guy Dutil

1977 Tiger Romeos (439 Sqn)

Lead	Maj Keith McDonald
#2	Capt Lawrence Sianchuk
#3	Capt Brian Bainbridge
#4	Capt Keith Robbins

Note: Capt Guy Dutil led the team for one show on 30 May 77 at Achern in the absence of Maj McDonald.

1977 Check Whiskeys (441 Sqn)

Lead	Maj George Landry
#2	Capt Gus Youngson
#3	Capt Bob Wade
#4	Capt Bruce Reid
Coordinator	Capt Dave Trask

1977 Red Indians (421 Sqn)

Lead	Capt Jim Graham
#2	Capt Norm Shaw
#3	Capt John Duncan
#4	Capt Stan Jones
Solo	Capt Don Leonard

1978 Check Whiskeys (441 Sqn)

Lead	Capt Rick Martin
#2	Capt Ted Delange
#3	Capt Bob Wade
#4	Capt Ted Bain
Solo	Capt Dave Owen
Narrator	Capt Dave Trask

1978 Red Indians (421 Sqn)

Lead	Capt Jim Graham
#2	Capt Norm Shaw
#3	Capt Paul Deacon
#4	Capt John Duncan
	Capt Stan Jones
Solo	Capt Don Leonard
Narrator	Capt Ed Karpetz

1978 Canadian Reds

Lead	Capt Jim Graham	(421 Sqn)
#2	Capt Brian Bainbridge	(439 Sqn)
#3	Capt Bob Wade	(441 Sqn)
#4	Capt Gus Youngson	(GTTF)
Solo	Capt Nev Symonds	(421 Sqn)
Narrator	Capt Ed Karpetz	(421 Sqn)

Note: The 1978 team was the first 1 CAG team formed with pilots from all three Sqns.

1979 Tiger Romeos (439 Sqn)

Lead	Capt Brian Bainbridge
#2	Lt Al Camplin
#3	Maj Larry Hill
#4	Capt Tony Jozefowicz
Solo	Capt Dan Bouchard

Note: The "Tiger Bird" (104862) was flown by the solo.

1979 1 CAG Starfighters

Lead	Maj John David	(441 Sqn)
#2	Capt Stan Jones	(421 Sqn)
#3	Capt Norm Shaw	(421 Sqn)
#4	Capt Henry Van Keulen	(439 Sqn)
Solo	Capt Dave Owen	(441 Sqn)
Narrator	Capt Clive Ken	(439 Sqn)
Groundcrew	MCpl Jim Craik	
	Cpl Ron Pinke	
	Cpl B. Hayman	

1980 1 CAG Starfighters

Lead	Maj Eric Thurston	(421 Sqn)
#2	Capt Al Camplin	(439 Sqn)
#3	Capt Rick Bollinger	(421 Sqn)
#4	Capt Scott Bowes	(439 Sqn)
Solo	Capt Gary Lacroix	(441 Sqn)
Narrator	Capt Rick Gelinas	(441 Sqn)

1981 1 CAG Starfighters

Lead	Maj Chris Tuck	(441 Sqn)
#2	Lt Kerry Cranfield	(421 Sqn)
#3	Capt Curt Johnston	(439 Sqn)
#4	Lt Ron Platt	(439 Sqn)
	Capt Harry Chapin	(441 Sqn)
Solo	Capt Mex Tremblay	(441 Sqn)
Narrator	Capt Bob Saunders	(421 Sqn)
Crew Chief	Sgt Frank Kennedy	
Groundcrew	MCpl Ed Holloway	
	MCpl Pete Turgeon	
	Cpl Jacques Caron	
	Cpl Jim Dunham	
	Cpl John Gough	

1982 1 CAG Starfighters

Lead	Maj Fred Mueller	(439 Sqn)
#2	Capt Bob Saunders	(421 Sqn)
#3	Capt Scott Ritchie	(439 Sqn)
#4	Capt Tom Lawson	(421 Sqn)
Solo	Capt Doug Erlandson	(441 Sqn)
Narrator	Capt Mike Hoch	(441 Sqn)

1983 1 CAG Starfighters

Lead	Capt Rick Martin	(441 Sqn)
#2	Capt Dave Anderson	(441 Sqn)
#3	Capt Steve Green	(421 Sqn)
#4	Capt Neale Nowosad	(441 Sqn)
Solo	Capt Al Stephenson	(439 Sqn)
Narrator	Capt Glen Huxter	(421 Sqn)

CF-5 Freedom Fighter Teams

Schooner Bluenose
434 Tactical Fighter Sqn
CFB Cold Lake, Alberta
CFB Bagotville, Quebec
CFB Chatham, New Brunswick
Northrop / Canadair CF-5A Freedom Fighter

1970
Lead	Capt Don Bergie	
#2	Capt Ken Mowbray	
#3	Capt Tom Tilghman	(USAF)
#4	Capt Jake Miller	

1971
Lead	Capt Ron Clayton
#2	Capt Wally Peel
#3	Capt Barry Krall
#4	Capt George Adamson
Solo	Capt Jake Miller

1972
Solo	Capt Jake Miller

1973
Solo	Capt Jake Miller

1983
Lead	Capt Dave Wilson
#2	Lt Ward MacKenzie
#3	Capt Dave McCabe
#4	Capt Ron Huzarik

1984
Lead	Maj George Landry
#2	Capt Steve Whitely
Spare	Capt Dennis Beselt

1985
Solo	Capt Dennis Beselt

Saguenay Manics
433 Tactical Fighter Sqn
CFB Bagotville, Quebec   1971-1974
Northrop / Canadair CF-5A Freedom Fighter

1970
Solo	Capt Romeo Lalonde

1971
Lead	Capt Joe Gagnon
#2	Capt Cole Harvey
#3	Capt Romeo Lalonde
#4	Capt Jean-Guy Beaumont
Solo	Capt Denis Gauthier

1972
Lead	Maj Denis Gauthier
#2	Capt Jean-Guy Blouin
Solo	Capt Jean-Pierre Ferron

1973
Lead	Maj Denis Gauthier
#2	Capt Mike King

CDN Forces CF-5 Demo Team
1972
Lead	Maj Denis Gauthier	(433 Sqn)
#2	Capt Jean-Guy Blouin	(433 Sqn)
#3	Capt Len Harding	(434 Sqn)
#4	Capt Wally Peel	(434 Sqn)
Solo	Capt Jake Miller	(434 Sqn)
Spare	Capt Jean-Pierre Ferron	(433 Sqn)

Saguenay Expos
433 Tactical Fighter Sqn
CFB Bagotville, Quebec   1975-1977
Northrop / Canadair CF-5A Freedom Fighter

1975
Lead	Maj Roger Maltais
#2	Capt Claude Thibault
#3	Capt Ray Ferguson
#4	Capt Bill Boucher
	Capt Richard Brosseau
Solo	Capt George Hawey

1976
Lead	Maj Len Couture
#2	Capt Joe Kupecz
#3	Capt Ray Levasseur
#4	Capt Richard Brosseau
Solo	Capt George Hawey

1977
Lead	Maj Len Couture
#2	Capt Ray Levasseur
#3	Capt Larry Kinch
#4	Capt Richard Brosseau

For CNE Airshow
Lead	Capt Richard Brosseau
#2	Capt Larry Kinch*

killed near Forestville, Que 10 Aug 77.
Capt Brosseau flew a solo show thereafter.

1978
Lead	Maj Len Couture
	Capt Denis Rivard
#2	Lt Mag Dumais
#3	Capt Jean Egan
#4	Lt Jacques Thibaudeau

Saguenay Pogos
433 Tactical Fighter Sqn
CFB Bagotville, Quebec   1979
Northrop / Canadair CF-5A Freedom Fighter

1979
Lead	Maj Richard Bastien
#2	Capt Michel Boivin
#3	Lt Jacques Thibaudeau
Solo	Capt Chuck Caron

Saguenay Quebec
433 Tactical Fighter Sqn
CFB Bagotville, Quebec   1980-1983
Northrop / Canadair CF-5A Freedom Fighter

1980
Lead	Maj Marc Dumontet
#2	Capt Réginald Décoste
#3	Capt Dan Leboeuf
#4	Capt Michel Boivin
Lead	Maj Marc Dumontet
#2	Capt Dan Leboeuf
#3	Capt Jacques Thibaudeau
#4	Capt Bob Archambault

1981
Lead	Maj Jean Boyle
#2	Lt Alain Lacharité
#3	Lt Carl Turner

1982
Lead	Maj Bob Archambault
#2	Capt Serge Boudreault
#3	Capt Michel Carter
#4	Capt Alain Lacharité
Narrator	Capt André Viens

1983
Lead	Maj Yves Bossé
#2	Capt Jeff Beckett

Cobras
1 Canadian Forces Flying Training School
CFB Cold Lake, Alberta   1974-1975
Northrop / Canadair CF-5A/D Freedom Fighter

1974
Lead	Maj Bill Worthy
#2	Capt Dave Wilson
#3	Capt Al Currie
#4	Capt Glenn Heaton
	Maj Gord Hatch

1974 Groundcrew
MCpl Charko	Cpl Anderson
Cpl Finley	Cpl George
Cpl Woolgar	

1975
Lead	Maj Bill Worthy
#2	Capt Ted Delanghe
#3	Capt Paul Deacon
#4	Maj Doug Stuart
Spare	Capt Al Currie

1975 Groundcrew
MCpl Bethune	Cpl C.W. Hills
MCpl G.W. Dansereau	Cpl P.D. Macdonald
MCpl J.R. Hunter	Cpl N.J. Powers
Cpl J.J. Boudreau	Pvt Kostyan
Cpl A. Greter	Pvt J.D. Martin

Rut Zulus
419 Tactical Fighter Training Sqn
CFB Cold Lake, Alberta   1976-1985, 1993
Northrop / Canadair CF-5A/D Freedom Fighter

1976
Lead	Maj Doug Stuart
#2	Capt Stu Holdsworth
#3	Capt Bob Archambault
	Capt Paul Deacon
#4	Maj George Adamson

1977
Lead	Maj Doug Stuart
#2	Capt Bob Lake
#3	Capt Bob Archambault
#4	Capt Stu Holdsworth

1978
Lead	Capt Bob Lake
#2	Capt Roy DeWolfe
#3	Capt Les Koski
#4	Capt Bob Archambault
Narrator	Capt Bill Matthews

1979
Lead	Capt Roy DeWolfe
#2	Capt Doug Moore
#3	Capt Duffy McCallum
#4	Capt Richard Brosseau

1980
Lead	Maj Roger Ayotte
#2	Capt Denny Funnemark
#3	Unknown
#4	Capt Richard Brosseau

1981
Lead	Maj Claude Thibault
#2	Capt Dave Dares
#3	Capt Bruce Wickware
#4	Capt Duffy McCallum

1982
Lead	Maj Roger Ayotte
#2	Capt Jack Orr
#3	Capt Ray Ferguson
#4	Capt Réginald Décoste

1982 Groundcrew
MCpl Fisher	Cpl Smith
Cpl Brunt	Pte Provender
Cpl Paton	Pte Quinn

1983
Lead	Maj Ray Ferguson
#2	Capt Chuck Fast
#3	Capt Don Brodeur
#4	Capt Réginald Décoste

1984
Lead	Capt Réginald Décoste	
#2	*le capitaine* Christian Aubré	(FAF)
	Capt Don Brodeur	
#3	Capt Frans Blosser	(RNLAF)
#4	Capt Rick Zyvitski	

1993
Lead	Maj Les Koski
#2	Capt Bill Brown
#3	Capt Ben Lavergne
#4	Capt Ron Vandervoort
Solo	Capt Sylvain Larue

419 Tactical Fighter Training Sqn
CF-5 Solo Demo Pilots

1988	Capt Steve Charbonneau
1989	Capt Raimo Kujala
1990	Capt Steve Green
	Capt Tim Jordan
1991	Capt Bob Painchaud
1992	Capt Dave Deere
1993	Capt Greg Carlow
	Capt Sylvain Larue
1994	Capt Ron VanderVoort
	Capt Marcus Walton

Note: The popular 419 Sqn "Moose" CF-5 was introduced in 1989 and performed through the end of the 1994 airshow season. Three CF-5As were finished in the red and white scheme: Serials 116703, 116740, 116721.

CT-134 Musketeer Teams

Musket Gold
3 Canadian Forces Flying Training School
CFB Portage la Prairie, Manitoba   1971-1984, 1992
Beechcraft CT-134 Musketeer

1971
Lead	Capt Gary Swiggum
#2	Lt Mike Gammon
#3	Capt Steve Hemenway
#4	Lt Gary Tulipen
Spare	Capt Ian Stenberg

1973 The Muskrats
Lead	Capt Bill Vermue
#2	Capt Cajo Brando
Groundcrew	Cpl Wayne Vrooman

1974
Lead	Capt D.A. (Don) McLeod
#2	Capt R.R. (Roy) Mould
#3	Capt J.L. (Marcel) Belzil
#4	Capt D.A. (Don) Bosworth
Narrator	Lt A.J. (Adrian) Walker
Groundcrew	Cpl Wayne Vrooman

1975
Lead	Capt G.E. (Glen) Buchanan
#2	Capt Atilla (At) Kostya
#3	Capt R. (Bob) Jones
#4	Capt R. (Bob) Gottfried
Narrator	Lt A.J. (Adrian) Walker
Groundcrew	Cpl Wayne Vrooman

1976
Lead	Capt G.E. (Glen) Buchanan
#2	Capt P.S. (Pete) Francis
#3	Capt R. (Bob) Jones
#4	Capt R. (Bob) Gottfried
Narrator	Capt R. (Dick) Reid
Groundcrew	MCpl Wayne Vrooman

1977
Lead	Capt P.S. (Pete) Francis
#2	Lt M. (Mark) Hollman
#3	Lt J.A. (John) Valade
#4	Capt R.T. (Bob) Crosty
Narrator	Capt G.E. (Glen) Buchanan
Groundcrew	MCpl Wayne Vrooman

1978
Lead	Capt P.S. (Pete) Francis	
#2	Lt M. (Mark) Hollman	
#3	Lt J.A. (John) Valade	
#4	Capt Leo Jespers	(RNLAF)
	Capt Jim Oke	
Narrator	Capt John Calder	
Groundcrew	MCpl Wayne Vrooman	
	MCpl Jim Smith	
	Cpl "Mitch" Mitchell.	

1979
Lead	Capt Gilles Trepanier	
#2	Lt André Deschamps	
#3	Tom Whistance	
#4	Capt Leo Jespers	(RNLAF)
	Lt Steve James	
Narrator	Capt Ron Sarich	
Groundcrew	Sgt Wayne Vrooman	
	MCpl Rick Adams	
	MCpl Gord Bugden	

1980
Lead	Capt Leo Jespers	(RNLAF)
#2	Capt Bill Collier	
#3	Lt André Deschamps	
#4	Capt Steve James	
Spare	Lt Chuck Pym	
Narrator	Capt Ron Sarich	
Groundcrew	Sgt Wayne Vrooman	
	MCpl Rick Adams	
	MCpl Gord Bugden	

1981
Lead	Capt Paul Baldasaro
#2	Capt Bob Struthers
#3	Capt Greg McQuaid
#4	Capt Charles Pym
Spare	Lt Marc de van der Schueren
Narrator	Lt Rob Slinger
Groundcrew	MCpl Don Edwards
	MCpl Henry Devison
	Cpl John Richkun
	Pte Steve Morden

1982
Lead	Capt Greg McQuaid
#2	Lt Jim Manton
#3	Capt Bob Struthers
#4	Lt Marc de van der Schueren
Spare	Capt Greg Newmarch
	Lt Ryan Lepalm
Groundcrew	MCpl Henry Devison
	MCpl Rod MacKinnon
	Cpl John Richkun
	Pte Barry Bracegirdle

1983
Lead	Capt Marc de van der Schueren
#2	Capt Jim Manton
#3	Lt Ryan Lapalm
#4	Capt Ab Jaget
Spare	Lt Grant Griffiths
	Lt Hughie Niewiadomski
Groundcrew	MCpl Henry Devison
	MCpl Rod MacKinnon
	Cpl John Richkun
	Pte Barry Bracegirdle
	MCpl Gord Bugden

1984
Lead	Capt Ab Jagat
#2	Capt Grant Griffiths
#3	Capt Ryan Lapalm
#4	Capt Jim Manton
	Capt Steve Hale
Spares	Capt J.D. Fontaine
	Lt Kevin Stewart
Narrator	Capt John Haazen
	Lt Rob Slinger
Groundcrew	MCpl Rod MacKinnon
	MCpl Gord Bugden
	Cpl John Richkun
	Pte Barry Bracegirdle

1992
Lead	Maj Greg McQuaid
#2	Capt Linton Sellen
#3	Capt Russ Williams
#4	Capt Rob Carter

Rotary Wing Teams

Hillers
No. 3 Flying Training School
CFB Portage la Prairie, Manitoba   1971
Hiller CH-112 Nomad

1971
Lead	Capt Walt Morris
#2	Capt Ross Craddock
#3	Capt George Fawcett
#4	Capt Ron Aumonier

HS 50 Sea King Team
HS 50
CFB Shearwater, Nova Scotia
Sikorsky CH-124 Sea King   1973

1973
Lead	Maj Rodger Sorsdahl
	Capt Tony Jenkins
#2	Capt George Lucas
	Capt Don Pearsons

Green Gophers
403 Tactical Helicopter (Operational Training) Sqn
CFB Gagetown, New Brunswick   1975-1976
Bell CH-136 Kiowa

1975
Lead	Capt Jim White
#2	Capt Jim Ongman
#3	Capt Dave Winmill
#4	Capt Jim Thompson

1976
Lead	Capt Dave Winmill
#2	Capt Grant Whitson
#3	Capt John McWhirter
#4	Capt Jim Thompson

Dragonflies
3 Canadian Forces Flying Training School
CFB Portage la Prairie, Manitoba   1972-1983
Bell CH-136 Kiowa
Bell CH-139 Jet Ranger

1972
Lead	Capt Walt Morris
#2	Capt E.R. Schmidt
#3	Capt Fred D'Amico
#4	Capt Ron Aumonier

1973
Lead	Capt George Fawcett	
#2	Capt Bob Johnston	(USAF)
#3	Capt Stu Russell	
Spares	Capt Jim Kendall	
	Capt Gary Flath	
Crewman	Cpl Wray Palmer	

Eff July 1973
Lead	Capt George Fawcett	
#2	Capt Jim Kendall	
#3	Capt Bob Johnston	(USAF)
#4	Capt Gary Flath	

1974
Lead	Capt Jim Kendall	
#2	Capt Gary Flath	
#3	Capt Jim Carnegie	
#4	Capt Bob Johnston	(USAF)
Narrator	Capt Jim Barfield	(USAF)
Crewmen	Cpl Wray Palmer	
	Cpl Ron Black	

1975
Lead	Capt Jim Kendall	
#2	Capt Bill Matthews	
#3	Capt Jim Carnegie	
#4	Capt Gary Flath	
Narrator	Capt Jim Barfield	(USAF)
Crewmen	Cpl Wray Palmer	
	Cpl Ron Black	

1976

Lead	Capt Gary Flath	
#2	Capt Fred Holtslag	
#3	Capt Bill Matthews	
#4	Capt John Zuurbier	(RNLAF)
Narrator	Capt Dennis Carey	
Crewmen	Cpl Wray Palmer	
	Cpl Ron Black	
	Cpl Bill Ewing	

1977

Lead	Capt Fred Holtslag	
#2	Capt Bill Matthews	
#3	Capt Mike Wansink	
#4	Capt John Zuurbier	(RNLAF)
Narrator	Capt Dennis Carey	
Crewmen	Cpl Ron Black	
	Cpl John Zado	
	Cpl Mike Garepy	

1978

Lead	Capt Mike Wansink	
#2	Capt Jim Hunter	
#3	Capt Dennis Carey	
#4	Capt John Zuurbier	(RNLAF)
Narrator	Capt Bill Michael	
Crewmen	Cpl Wray Palmer	
	Cpl Ron Black	

1979

Lead	Capt Jim Hunter
#2	Capt Ed Ukrainetz
	Capt Pete Campbell
#3	Capt Bill Michael
#4	Capt Gary Miller
Narrator	Capt Pete Campbell
Crewmen	MCpl Cal Jefford
	Cpl Steve Gregory
	Cpl Paul Clark

1980

Lead	Capt Gary Miller
#2	Capt Rene Morrissette
#3	Capt Pete Campbell
#4	Capt Ed Ukrainetz (Solo)
Narrator	Capt Dennis Carey
	Capt Marcel Belzil
Crewmen	MCpl Cal Jefford
	MCpl Rick Therrien
	Cpl Jack Remenda
	Pte Steve Morden
	Pte Rick Pay

1981

Lead	Capt Gary Miller
#2	Capt Ron Carter
#3	Capt Wayne Norris
#4	Capt Ed Ukrainetz
Narrator	Capt Richard Archambault
Crewmen	MCpl Cal Jefford
	MCpl Rick Therrien
	Pte Paul Blinn
	Pte Steve Morden

1982

Lead	Capt Wayne Norris
#2	Capt Denis Panneton
#3	Capt Greg Reiser
#4	Capt Dan Shank
Narrator	Capt Phil Campbell
Crewmen	MCpl Rick Therrien
	Cpl Paul Blinn
	Pte Steve Morden

1983

Lead	Capt Greg Reiser
#2	Capt Kelly Jamieson
#3	Capt Stu Metcalfe
#4	Capt Peter McKeage
#5	Capt Bernie Faguy
Narrator	Capt R.J. Payette
Crewman	Cpl Steve Morden

1984

Lead	Capt Greg Reiser
#2	Capt Kelly Jamieson
#3	Capt Stu Metcalfe
#4	Capt Peter McKeage
Narrator	Capt Peter Graham
Crewmen	Cpl Rick Pay
	Cpl Rick Chevere

1992

Lead	Capt Jacques Girard
#2	Capt Gab Pomerlau
#3	Capt Brian Wicks
#4	Capt Miles Mozel
Narrator	Capt Craig Bessler

Air Reserve Teams

2 Air Reserve Wing
CFB Toronto, Ontario   1982
Bell CH-136 Kiowa

1982 Hummingbirds

Lead	Capt Dave Miller	(2 RSU)
	Capt John McClenaghan	(411 ARS)
#2	Capt Henry Van Keulen	(411 ARS)
#3	Capt Bob Fenn	(411 ARS)

1983 Lazer Blues Formation

Lead	Capt Dave Miller	(2 RSU)
	Capt Mark Shaddock	(411 ARS)
#2	Maj John McClenaghan	(411 ARS)
#3	Capt Bob Fenn	(411 ARS)
Crewmen	MCpl Marc Marcotte	
	MCpl Lawrence Livesey	
	Cpl Joe Grech	
	Cpl Dave Fisher	
	Cpl Diana Hooper	
	Cpl Zaid Mohammed	

1984 TAC ADS Formation

Lead	Maj Fred Holtslag	(2 RSU)
#2	Maj Bob Fenn	(411 ARS)
#3	Capt Mark Shaddock	(411 ARS)
	Maj Brian Chamberlain	(400 ARS)

C-130 Hercules Teams

Tactical Tigers Demonstration Team

Tactical Airlift School
CFB Edmonton, Alberta   1982-1984
C-130 Hercules

1984

Lead	Maj Frank Fay	
#2	Capt Bill Nesbitt	
#3	Capt Lonnie Register	(USAF)
#4	Capt Jay Olson	

CT-114 Tutor Teams

Golden Centennaires

See separate listing above

B Flight Jesters

2 Flying Training School
CFB Moose Jaw, Saskatchewan   1969-1970
Canadair CT-114 Tutor

1969-1970

Lead	Capt Neal Pringle
#2	Capt Claude Thibault
#3	Capt Keith Mirau
#4	Capt Robie Robichaud
	Capt Michael Marynowski
	Capt Tony Roeding
	Capt Speedy Fast
	Capt Wayne Ralph
Narrator	Capt Joe Houlden

2 CFFTS Formation Demonstration Team
The Tutor Whites

2 Canadian Forces Flying Training School
CFB Moose Jaw, Saskatchewan   1970-1971
Canadair CT-114 Tutor

1970

Lead	Maj Bing Peart
#2	Capt Bill Cowan
#3	Capt Fred McCague
#4	Lt Doug Zebedee
Narrator	Capt Joe Houlden

1971

Lead	Maj Glen Younghusband
Wingmen	Capt Tom Gernack
	Capt Gord Wallis
	Capt Fred McCague
	Capt Chester Glendenning
	Capt Laurie Illingworth
	Capt George Hawey
	Capt Michael Marynowski
	Capt Lloyd Waterer
	Capt Bob Sharpe
	Lt Doug Zebedee

Note: The 2 CFFTS Formation Team was renamed the Snowbirds on 25 Jun 71. The first major exposure for the new team took place at the Saskatchewan Homecoming Air Show held at CFB Moose Jaw, Saskatchewan on 11 Jul 71.

Vikings

Flying Instructor School	
CFB Portage la Prairie, Manitoba	1969
CFB Moose Jaw, Saskatchewan	1976-1981
CFB Portage la Prairie, Manitoba	1981-1984
Canadair CT-114 Tutor	

1969 Viking Reds

Lead	Maj Ron Beehler	
Wingmen	Capt Tom Bugg	
	Capt Gerry Thorneycraft	
	Capt Clancy Sheldrup	
	Capt Guy Childress	(USAF)
	Capt Tom Byrne	
	Capt Tom Hinton	
	Capt Pat Barrett	

1976 Vikings

Lead	Maj Ed Rozdeba
Wingmen	various FIS staff instructors

1977

Lead	Maj Ed Rozdeba	
#2	Capt Ray Hansford	
#3	Capt Roy DeWolfe	
#4	Capt Jean-Guy Beaumont	
	Capt Mike Thompson	(RAF)
	Capt Roy Wansink	
Narrators	Capt Don McLeod	
	Capt Gerry Bayles	
	Capt Jim Fowler	

1978

Lead	Maj Ed Rozdeba	
#2	Capt Don McLeod	
#3	Capt Speedy Fast	
	Maj Dave Currie	
#4	Capt Roy Wansink	
	Lt Dick Bos	(RNLAF)
Narrators	Capt Jim Fowler	
	Capt Don Hollington	

Mid-summer

Lead	Capt Speedy Fast	
#2	Capt Bob Drake	
#3	Capt Don Hollington	
#4	Capt Dick Bos	(RNLAF)
Narrator	Capt Jim Fowler	

1979

Lead	Capt Speedy Fast	
#2	Capt Bob Drake	
#3	Capt Don Hollington	
#4	Capt Dick Bos	(RNLAF)
	Capt Bin Bonnema	(RNLAF)
Narrator	Capt Dan Dempsey	

Eff 7 Aug 79

Lead	Maj Roger Maltais	
#2	Capt Dan Dempsey	
#3	Capt Don Hollington	
	Capt Michel Gareau	
#4	Capt Bin Bonnema	(RNLAF)

1980

Lead	Capt Dave Burroughs
#2	Capt Andy Fok
#3	Capt Mel Warren
#4	Capt J.C. Gagne

1981

Lead	Maj Murray Bertram
#2	Capt Mel Warren
	Capt Andy Fok
#3	Capt Bill Carswell
#4	Capt Roy Wansink
	Capt J.C. Gagne

1982

Lead	Maj Murray Bertram
	Capt Guy Trudeau
#2	Capt Mel Warren
	Capt Guy Trudeau
#3	Capt Bill Carswell
#4	Capt Roy Wansink
	Capt J.C. Gagne

1983

Lead	Maj Murray Bertram
	Maj Ken Carr
#2	Capt Mel Warren
	Capt Andy Fok
#3	Capt Guy Trudeau
	Capt Gilles Raiche
#4	Capt Roy Wansink
	Capt Geoff Graham

1984

Lead	Maj Ken Carr
#2	Capt Bernie DeGagné
	Capt Andy Fok
#3	Capt Gilles Raiche
#4	Capt Geoff Graham
	Capt Steve Gignac
#5	Capt Andy Maziarski
Crew	MCpl Bill Spencer
	MCpl Henry Devison

Canadian Air Force Heritage Flight

Sponsored by 1 Canadian Air Division HQ
17 Wing Winnipeg, Manitoba   1998-1999
North American Harvard Mk IV
Lockheed/ Canadair T-33 Canadair CT-114 Tutor

1998

Harvard	F/L William E. Lamon	
	Capt Ian Searle	2 CFFTS
	Capt Tim Rawlings	2 CFFTS
T-33	Capt Brehn Eichel	417 (CS) Sqn
Tutor	Capt Tim Rawlings	2 CFFTS
	Capt Ian Searle	2 CFFTS

Note: Capts Searle and Rawlings took turns flying in the Harvard and Tutor.

1999

Harvard	F/L William E. Lamon	
	Capt Mike Ayling	2 CFFTS
T-33	Capt Pat Boyle	414 (CS) Sqn
	Capt Sheldon Tuttosi	417 (CS) Sqn
Tutor	Lt Darcy Molstad	2 CFFTS

CF-18 Hornet Demo Teams

Canada

1983	Capt Gary Liddiard	410 Sqn
1984	Capt Dale Erhart	410 Sqn
	Capt B.J. Ryan	410 Sqn
1985	Capt Guy Dutil	410 Sqn
	Capt Chuck Caron	425 Sqn
1986	Capt Bob Wade	410 Sqn
	Capt Tristan deKoninck*	425 Sqn

* killed May 1986 departing CFB Summerside in poor weather.

Year	Name	Sqn
1987	Capt Neale Nowosad	410 Sqn
	Capt Jacques Thibaudeau	425 Sqn
1988	Capt Terry Shortt	410 Sqn
	Capt Pierre Blais	425 Sqn
1989	Capt Rich Lancaster	410 Sqn
	Capt Richard Duguay	433 Sqn
	Maj Jacques Thibaudeau	425 Sqn
1990	Maj Mark Holmes	410 Sqn
	Capt Yves Tessier	433 Sqn

Crew: Sgt Cormier, Cpl Lemieux, MCpl Boulianne, Cpl Dufour, Cpl Banset, Cpl Marcoui, Cpl Henry

Year	Name	Sqn
1991	Capt Louis DeGagne	410 Sqn
1992	Capt Jon Graham	425 Sqn

Crew: WO Dufort, MCpl Pilon, MCpl Maltais, MCpl Rompré, Cpl Paré, Cpl Bergeron

Year	Name	Sqn
1993	Capt Keith Moore	410 Sqn
	Capt Marc Charpentier	433 Sqn

Crew: Sgt Cormier, MCpl Duchenes, MCpl Coté, MCpl Fugère, Cpl Fournier, Cpl Borduas

Year	Name	Sqn
1994	Capt Kevin Stewart	410 Sqn
	Capt Grant Cossey	425 Sqn
	Capt Marc Charpentier	433 Sqn

Crew: MCpl Palardi, MCpl Plourde, Cpl Raymond, Cpl Lopez

Year	Name	Sqn
1995	Capt Mike Woodfield	410 Sqn
	Capt J. Bzrezinski	433 Sqn

Crew: MCpl Paré, Cpl Morin Cpl Charbonneau

Year	Name	Sqn
1996	Capt Duane Lecaine	410 Sqn
	Capt Greg Morris	425 Sqn

Crew: Sgt Bélanger, MCpl Garceau, Cpl Séguin, Cpl Charron, Cpl Lessard

Year	Name	Sqn
1997	Capt Doug Carter	410 Sqn
	Maj Norm Gagne	410 Sqn
	Capt Steve Langille	433 Sqn

Crew: MCpl Ghislain Maldemay, Cpl Alain Fortin, Cpl Robert Chrétien

Year	Name	Sqn
1998	Capt Steve Nierlich	410 Sqn
	Capt Miguel Bernard	410 Sqn
	Capt Bill Moffat	425 Sqn

Crew: MCpl Ayotte, MCpl Boulianne, Cpl Deroy, Cpl Lavoie, Cpl Richard

Year	Name	Sqn
1999	Capt Rob Mitchell	410 Sqn
	Capt Mike Mirza	410 Sqn

Crew #1 Sgt Steve Horton, MCpl Bob Dealy, Cpl Ellen Berger, Cpl Todd Giles;
#2 Sgt Kevin Smith, MCpl Tom Shier, Cpl Tim Blackwell, Cpl Tom Wilton;
#3 Sgt Chris Sawatzky, MCpl Janique Lafond, Cpl Nelson Legace, Cpl Mark Riach

Year	Name	Sqn
2000	Capt Scott Greenough	410 Sqn

Crew: #1 Sgt Wolf Hubmann, MCpl Kurt Lawrence, Cpl Carmen Bear, Cpl Todd Raycraft, Cpl Scott Marsh;
#2 Sgt Dave Wilkinson, MCpl Dean Marta, Cpl Eric Braun, Cpl Chris Hall, Cpl Mike Lafitte

Year	Name	Sqn
2000	Capt Patrice Hervieux	433 Sqn

Crew:MCpl J.C. Parent, Cpl Yanick Daigle, Cpl Mario Grandmont

Year	Name	Sqn
2001	Capt Rick Williams	410 Sqn
	Capt Lee Vogan	410 Sqn

Crew: Sgt Wolf Hubmann, MCpl Scott Kane, Cpl Yannick Debreuil, Cpl Dawn-Marie Pinkney, Cpl Richard Coltart, Cpl Ellen Berger, Cpl Mark Riach, Cpl Darren Reuer, Cpl Todd Giles, Cpl Ron Wicht

Year	Name	Sqn
2001	Capt Gary Schwindt	433 Sqn

Crew: MCpl Guy Boileau, Cpl Marc Lemelin, Cpl Sylvain Bolduc

Year	Name	Sqn
2002	Capt Doug Clements	410 Sqn

Crew: Sgt Wolf Hubmann, Cpl Tim Blackwell, Cpl Kerry Egbert, Cpl Richard Mason, Cpl Terry Looker

Year	Name	Sqn
2002	Capt Scott Shrubsole	425 Sqn

Crew: MCpl Jean Lavoie, Cpl Pierre Beaulieu, Cpl Steve Antonacci

Note: Groundcrew support teams for 410 Sqn Hornet demos varied up until 1999 at which time dedicated teams were assigned to travel with the squadron's CF-18 demo pilots.

1 Canadian Air Group/ 1 Air Division,
CFB Baden-Soellingen/ 4 Wing, West Germany

Year	Name	Sqn
1985	Maj Gary Liddiard	409 Sqn
1986	Capt Paul Noack	409 Sqn
	Capt Ron Platt	439 Sqn
1987	Capt Billie Flynn	409 Sqn
	Capt Grant Youngson	439 Sqn
1988	Capt Don Thornton	409 Sqn
	Capt Bob Painchaud	421 Sqn
1989	Capt Chris Glover	421 Sqn
	Capt Kirk Leuty	439 Sqn
1990	Capt Mal Macnair	409 Sqn

Snowbirds

CFB Moose Jaw, Saskatchewan   1971 - Present
Designated 431 (Air Demonstration) Sqn 1 Apr 78
Canadair CT-114 Tutor

Travelling Show Team

1971	Maj Glen Younghusband
	Capt Tom Gernack
	Capt Gord Wallis
	Capt Fred McCague
	Capt Chester Glendenning
	Capt Laurie Illingworth
	Capt George Hawey
	Capt Michael Marynowski
	Capt Lloyd Waterer
	Capt Bob Sharpe
	Lt Doug Zebedee

Notes: 1. Groundcrew for the Snowbirds first year of operation did not travel with the team on a regular basis. However, they included: Sgt Dick Gaff, Sgt Lorne Foster, Cpl Don Anderson, Cpl Wayne Adams, Cpl Al McFadden, Cpl Ed Torfason, Cpl Bob Nixon and Cpl Mike Thompson. 2. The aircraft flown by the Snowbirds for the first three seasons were exclusively ex-Golden Centennaires aircraft that had been repainted white with red trim. Tutor 114153 had also served as the Red Knight spare aircraft in 1968 and 1969. The aircraft carried "The Big 2" crest on the tail in 1971 and 1972. Known Serials: 114122, 114147, 114151, 114152, 114153, 114155, 114175, 114179, 114180, 114181, 114183.

1972

No	Name	Serial
1	Maj Glen Younghusband	
	Sgt Bob Holloway	114175
2	Capt Tom Gernack	
	MCpl Ron LaGrange	114147/152
3	Capt Laurie Illingworth	
	MCpl Larry Legault	114122
4	Lt Larry Currie	
	Cpl Mike Thompson	114153
5	Capt Chester Glendenning	
	Cpl Chuck Mikkelson	114155
6	Capt Fred McCague	
	Cpl Pete Hennicke	114181
7	Capt Gord Wallis	
	Cpl John McCluskey	114179/147
8	Capt Lloyd Waterer*	
	Cpl Dwight Vaughan	114183
9	Capt Michael Marynowski	
	Cpl Reg Bach	114180
10	Capt John Hackett	
	Cpl Bob Nixon	T-33 133275

* killed during airshow at CFB Trenton on 10 Jun 72.

1973

1	Maj George Miller	
	Sgt Bill Holloway	114175/083
2	Capt Larry Currie	
	Cpl John Doerksen	114153
3	Lt Mike Murphy	
	Cpl Ely Bowen	114152
4	Capt Carl Stef	
	Cpl Ed Torfason	114179/181
5	Lt Bob Wade	
	Cpl Chuck Wicks	114155
6	Capt George Hawey	
	Cpl Bob Leblanc	114180
7	Capt Gord Wallis	
	Cpl Pete Hennicke	114151
8	Capt Tom Griffis	
	Cpl Chuck Mikkelson	114147
9	Capt Laurie Illingworth	
	MCpl Larry Legault	114122
10	Capt John Hackett	
	Cpl Rusty Rutherford	T-33 133275

Note: The Snowbird crest was introduced in 1973 and replaced the Big 2 crest on the tail.

1974

1	Maj George Miller	
	Sgt Doug Marshall	114151
2	Capt John Shaw	
	Cpl Ray Lund	114147
3	Capt Mike Murphy	
	Cpl Ely Bowen	114152
4	Capt Carl Stef	
	Cpl Rusty Rutherford	114181
5	Capt Bob Wade	
	Cpl Al Boyce	114155
6	Capt Murray Bertram	
	Cpl Mike Thompson	114180
7	Capt Harry Chapin	
	MCpl Cal Wanvig	114175
8	Capt Tom Griffis	
	Cpl Pete Hennicke	114153
9	Capt Yogi Huyghebaert	
	Cpl Ed Torfason	114122
10	Capt Greg Bruneau	
	Cpl Bud Peters	T-33 133275
11	Capt Andy Bessette	
Spare Tutors		114083, 003

Note: The distinctive Snowbird paint scheme was introduced for the 1974 airshow season, including numbers 1 to 9 on the tails of the show aircraft.

1975

1	Maj Denis Gauthier	
	Sgt Bill Holloway	114151/153
2	Capt John Shaw	
	Cpl Ray Lund	114147
3	Capt Chris Tuck	
	Cpl Fred Broderick	114152
4	Capt Dave Wilson	
	Cpl Garth Suitor	114181
5	Capt Carl Stef	
	Cpl Al Boyce	114155
6	Capt Murray Bertram	
	Cpl Wayne Swayze	114180
7	Capt Harry Chapin	
	MCpl Cal Wanvig	114175
8	Capt Ken Carr	
	Cpl Pete Hennicke	114153/003
9	Capt Yogi Huyghebaert	
	Cpl Ed Torfason	114122
10	Capt Greg Bruneau	T-33 133275
11	Capt Jack Girard	114083

1976

1	Maj Denis Gauthier	
	Sgt Doug Marshall	114153
2	Capt Gerry Nicks	
	Cpl Wayne Swayze	114147
	Cpl Lou Doan	
	Cpl John Zorn	
3	Capt Chris Tuck	
	Cpl Moe Taylor	114152
4	Capt Dave Wilson	
	Cpl Ross Chapman	114181
5	Capt Paul Beaulieu	
	Cpl Gary Freisen	114155
6	Capt Jim Sorfleet	
	MCpl Nick Nichols	114180
7	Capt Harry Chapin	
	Cpl Chuck Wicks	114175
8	Capt Ken Carr	
	Cpl Vern Opperman	114151
9	Capt Eric Fast	
	MCpl Cal Wanvig	114122
10	Capt Jack Girard	
	Cpl Ian Neilson	T-33 133625
11	Capt Mike Jephcott	T-33 275 / Tutor 129
Spare Tutors		114083, 003

1977

1	Maj Gord Wallis	
	Sgt Harold Breadner	114178
2	Capt Gerry Nicks	
	Cpl Barry Dickson	114036
3	Capt Wayne Thompson	
	Cpl Ron Venables	
	MCpl Bob O'Reilly	114177
4	Capt Jim Sorfleet	
	MCpl Wally Corbin	114082/055
5	Capt Joe Molnar	
	MCpl Nick Nichols	114163
6	Capt Keith Coulter	
	Cpl Moe Taylor	114030
7	Capt Paul Beaulieu	
	Cpl John Zorn	114088/043
8	Capt Gord de Jong	
	Cpl Ross Chapman	114132/118
9	Capt Eric Fast	
	MCpl Garth Suitor	114114
10	Capt Mike Jephcott	
	Cpl Ian Neilson	114003
11	Capt Stu Morgan	114129(T)

Note: In 1977 four of the team positions were renumbered. SB 4 became first line-astern, SB 5 second line-astern, SB 6 outer right wing and SB 7 outer left wing. 1977 was also the first year that one of the team aircraft was equipped with under-belly fuel tanks (T) for extended range use by one of the team coordinators.

431 (Air Demonstration) Squadron Snowbirds

1978

1	Maj Gord Wallis	
	Sgt Cec Keddy	114178
2	Capt Marc Ouellet	
	Cpl Michel Poisson	114036
3	Capt Wayne Thompson	
	Cpl Garry Ward	114177
4	Capt Terry Hunt	
	Cpl Al Dillman	114043
5	Capt Joe Molnar	
	MCpl Wally Corbin	114163
6	Capt Keith Coulter	
	Cpl Kevin Buell	114030
7	Capt John McNamara	
	MCpl Bob O'Reilly	114110
8	Capt Gord de Jong*	
	Cpl Fred Broderick	114118
9	Capt Ray Hansford	
	Cpl John Zorn	114105
10	Capt Stu Morgan	
	Cpl Ian Neilson	114114
11	Capt Yves Bossé	114164(T)
Spare Tutors		114055, 129(T)

Note: The Snowbirds were granted squadron status on 1 Apr 78, the first official aerial demonstration team in Canadian history to receive such distinction.
* killed during airshow at Grande Prairie, Alta on 3 May 78.

1979

1	Maj Tom Griffis	
	Sgt Cec Keddy	114178
2	Capt Marc Ouellet	
	Cpl Michel Bernier	114036
3	Capt Graham Miller	
	Cpl Mike Roy	114114
4	Capt Terry Hunt	
	Cpl Fred Rockall	114043
5	Capt Jim Reith	
	MCpl Garry Ward	114163
6	Capt Frank Thorne	
	Cpl Ed Gammon	114049
7	Capt John McNamara	
	MCpl Kevin Buell	114110
8	Capt Larry Rockliff	
	Cpl Michel Poisson	114030
9	Capt Ray Hansford	
	Cpl Al Dillman	114177
10	Capt Yves Bossé	
	MCpl Ian Neilson	114105
11	Capt Jim Fowler	114164(T)
Spare Tutors		114055, 129(T)

1980

1	Maj Tom Griffis	
	Sgt Dutch Simms	114178
2	Capt Chuck Gillespie	
	Cpl Al McGrath	114036
3	Capt Graham Miller	
	Cpl Rocky White	114114
4	Capt Bob Drake	
	Cpl Mike Langevin	114043
5	Capt Yves Bossé	
	Cpl Jack Gariepy	114163
	MCpl Kevin Buell	
	Cpl Michel Poisson	
6	Capt Frank Thorne	
	Cpl Ed Gammon	114030
7	Capt Wally Stone	
	Cpl Michel Bernier	114105
8	Capt Larry Rockliff	
	Cpl Mike Roy	114049
9	Capt Dan Dempsey	
	Cpl Fred Rockall	114110/055
10	Capt Denis Mercier	
	MCpl Gary Ward	114177
11	Capt Jim Fowler	114164(T)
Spare Tutors		114055, 129(T)

1981

1	Maj Mike Murphy	
	Sgt Dutch Simms	114049
2	Capt Chuck Gillespie	
	Cpl Paul McKeen	114036
3	Capt Dennis Beselt	
	MCpl George Beck	114114
4	Capt Bob Drake	
	Pte John McCanna	114177
5	Capt Sonny Lefort	
	Cpl Perry Luchia	114163
6	Capt Dean Rainkie	
	Cpl Tony Vanderberg	114030
7	Capt Wally Stone	
	Cpl Dick Bennett	114105
8	Capt John Politis	
	Cpl Bob Bauer	114178
9	Capt Dan Dempsey	
	Cpl Al McGrath	114055
10	Capt Denis Mercier	
	Cpl Barry Fremont	114043
11	Capt Wally Peters	114164(T)
Spare Tutors		114110, 129(T)

1982

1	Maj Mike Murphy	
	Sgt Alex Cameron	114178
2	Capt Geoff Gamble	
	Cpl John McCanna	114030
3	Capt Dennis Beselt	
	Cpl Barry Fremont	114114
4	Capt Tristan deKoninck	
	Cpl Dick Bennett	114177
5	Capt Sonny Lefort	
	Cpl Harry Partridge	114163
6	Capt Dean Rainkie	
	Cpl Bob Bauer	114049
7	Capt Rob Chapman	
	Cpl Perry Lucia	114105
8	Capt John Politis	
	Cpl Marty Cornfield	114036

9   Capt Jon Graham
        Cpl Tony Vanderberg   114043
10 Capt Ron Carter   114129(T)
11 Maj Wally Peters
        Sgt George Beck   114055
Spare Tutors   114110, 164(T)

1983

1	Maj George Hawey	
	Sgt Alex Cameron	114036
2	Capt Geoff Gamble	
	Cpl Mike Landers	114030
3	Capt Bill Ryan	
	MCpl Bill MacPhee	114114
4	Capt Tristan deKoninck	
	Cpl Pat Messaoud	114177
5	Capt Holmes Patton	
	Cpl Georges Ménard	114055
6	Capt Richie Clements	
	Cpl Harry Partridge	114049
7	Capt Rob Chapman	
	Pte Tim Payne	114105/043
8	Capt Bob Stephan	
	Cpl Marty Cornfield	114163
9	Capt Jon Graham	
	Cpl Ron Bernard	114190
10	Capt Ron Carter	
	MCpl Bob Bauer	114110
11	Maj Norm Fraser	114164(T)
Spare Tutors		114105, 129(T)

1984

1	Maj George Hawey	
	Sgt Rick Harvey	114036
2	Capt Al Merrick	
	Cpl Mike Landers	114098
3	Capt Bill Ryan	
	MCpl Bill MacPhee	114114
4	Capt Dave Forman	
	Cpl Pat Messaoud	114177
5	Capt Holmes Patton	
	Cpl Georges Ménard	114055
6	Capt Richie Clements	
	Cpl Doug Dennison	114049
7	Capt Carl Shaver	
	Cpl René Petit	114043
8	Capt Bob Stephan	
	Cpl Dan Jean-Marie	114030
9	Capt Steve Wallace	
	Cpl Ron Bernard	114190
10	Capt Mike Bell	114164(T)
11	Maj Norm Fraser	
	Cpl Tim Payne	114110
Spare Tutors		114105, 129(T)

1985

1	Maj Yogi Huyghebaert	
	Sgt Rick Harvey	114036
2	Capt Al Merrick	
	Cpl Mark Keller	114030
3	Capt Steve Purton	
	MCpl Brian Herde	114114
4	Capt Dave Forman	
	Cpl Bert Hargreaves	114190
5	Capt Gino Tessier	
	Cpl Al Herron	114055
6	Capt Steve Hill	
	Cpl Doug Dennison	114177
7	Capt Carl Shaver	
	Cpl René St. Laurent	114105
8	Capt Mike Skubicky	
	Cpl Dan Jean-Marie	114049
9	Capt Steve Wallace	
	Cpl John Mahoney	114098
10	Capt Mike Bell	
	Cpl René Petit	114110
11	Capt Eric Dumont	114129(T)
Spare Tutors		114043, 164(T)

1986

1	Maj Yogi Huyghebaert	
	Sgt Alex Bouzane	114036
2	Capt Joe Parente	
	Cpl Mark Keller	114043
3	Capt Steve Purton	
	MCpl Brian Herde	114114
4	Capt Jim Fowlow	
	Cpl Don Brak	114177
5	Capt Gino Tessier	
	Cpl Al Herron	114190
6	Capt Steve Hill	
	Cpl Mark Doane	114055
7	Capt Howard Tarbet	
	Cpl Gilles Dubé	114110
8	Capt Mike Skubicky	
	Cpl Gord Neave	114049
9	Capt Don Brodeur	
	Cpl John Mahoney	114098
10	Capt Bob Curran	114129(T)
11	Capt Eric Dumont	
	Cpl Bert Hargreaves	114041
Spare Tutors		114105, 164(T)

1987

1	Maj Dave Wilson	
	W/O Alex Bouzane	114108
1	Maj Dennis Beselt	
	W/O Alex Bouzane	
2	Capt Joe Parente	
	MCpl Dan Bergeron	114055
3	Capt Paul Giles	
	Cpl Mike Cook	114098
4	Capt Jim Fowlow	
	Cpl Chris Detta	114115
5	Capt Don Barnby	
	Cpl Wally Marshall	114110
6	Capt Boyd Smith	
	MCpl Mark Doane	114043
7	Capt Howard Tarbet	
	Cpl Gilles Dubé	114098
8	Capt Wes MacKay	
	Cpl Gord Neave	114036
9	Capt Don Brodeur	
	Cpl Serge Pilote	114141
10	Capt Richard Lapointe	114049(T)
11	Capt Eric Dumont	
	Cpl B. Duivenvoorde	114164
Spare Tutors		114190, 105

Notes: 1. Maj Wilson was replaced by Maj Beselt on 12 Apr 87. 2. The new stylized Snowbirds logo was introduced on the nose.

1988

1	Maj Dennis Beselt	
	Sgt Jerry Unrau	114108
2	Capt Shane Antaya	
	Cpl Mike Cook	114055
3	Capt Paul Giles	
	Cpl Guy Fortin	114098
4	Capt Bjorn Kjaer	
	Cpl Serge Pilote	114115
5	Capt Don Barnby	
	Cpl Marc Cossette	114052
6	Capt Boyd Smith	
	Cpl Oswald Lindsay	114036
7	Capt Darryl Shyiak	
	Cpl Wally Marshall	114041
8	Capt Wes MacKay*	
	Cpl Denis Fontaine	114037
9	Capt Ken Rae	
	MCpl Dan Bergeron	114023
10	Capt Richard Lapointe	
	Cpl Chris Detta	114100
11	Capt Kevin Kokotailo	114049(T)
Spare Tutors		114190, 164(T)

Note: The Snowbirds flew the colours of the olympic rings to open the 1988 Winter Olympics in Calgary.
* killed in automobile accident in Latrobe, PA on 25 Sep 88.

1989

1	Maj Dan Dempsey	
	Sgt Jerry Unrau	114055
2	Capt Shane Antaya*	
	Cpl Mario Deshaies	114098
3	Capt Steve Will	
	MCpl Guy Fortin	114037
4	Capt Bjorn Kjaer	
	Cpl Jim Burton	114046
5	Capt John Low	
	Cpl Marc Cossette	114023
6	Capt Dale Hackett	
	MCpl Oswald Lindsay	114052
7	Capt Darryl Shyiak	
	Cpl Dave Scharf	114115
8	Capt Les Racicot	
	MCpl Doug Dennison	114108
9	Capt Bob Stephan	
	Cpl Leo Jenkins	114080
10	Capt Dominic Taillon	114049(T)
11	Capt Kevin Kokotailo	
	MCpl Denis Fontaine	114041
Spare Tutors		114110, 036(T), 164(T)

* killed in Toronto, Ont on 3 Sep 89 on the second day of the annual Canadian International Air Show.

1990

1	Maj Dan Dempsey	
	Sgt Dan Bergeron	114100
2	Capt Ross Granley	
	MCpl Mario Deshaies	114041
3	Capt Steve Will	
	Cpl Tony Edmundson	114037
4	Capt Vince Jandrisch	
	Cpl Jim Burton	114108
5	Capt John Low	
	Cpl Dan Seguin	114080
6	Capt Dale Hackett	
	Cpl Rick Macnab	114115
7	Capt Brooke Lawrence	
	Cpl Dave Scharf	114052
8	Capt Les Racicot	
	Sgt Doug Dennison	114164
9	Capt Rich Lancaster	
	Cpl Leo Jenkins	114046
10	Capt Dominic Taillon	
	MCpl Dave Fischer	114023
11	Capt Jeff Hill	114049(T)
Spare Tutors		114075, 011, 055, 084(T)

Note: The team used coloured smoke (red and white) at all major shows in 1990 to celebrate the team's 20th anniversary.

1991

1	Maj Bob Stephan	
	Sgt Dan Bergeron	114011
2	Capt Ross Granley	
	Cpl Mario Asselin	114080
3	Capt Marc Robert	
	Cpl Tony Edmundson	114052
4	Capt Vince Jandrisch	
	Cpl Rick Murray	114108
5	Capt Nick Cassidy	
	Cpl Dan Seguin	114100
6	Capt Bill Watts	
	Cpl Rick Macnab	114046
7	Capt Brooke Lawrence	
	Cpl Doug Wray	114115
8	Capt Glen Oerzen	
	MCpl Dave Fischer	114075
9	Capt Rich Lancaster	
	MCpl Ed Dillon	114094
10	Capt Réal Turgeon	114084(T)
11	Capt Jeff Hill	
	Cpl Stu Gilchrist	114164
Spare Tutors		114023, 037, 041, 049(T)

1992

1	Maj Bob Stephan	
	Sgt Joe Maillet	114011
2	Capt Rob Martin	
	Cpl Stu Gilchrist	114094

3 Capt Marc Robert
Cpl Tony Edmundson — 114108
4 Capt Glenn Kerr
Cpl Rick Murray — 114046
5 Capt Nick Cassidy
Cpl Vince Leather — 114100
6 Capt Bill Watts
Cpl Terry Spence — 114080
7 Capt Frank Bergnach
Cpl Doug Wray — 114075
8 Capt Glenn Oerzen
Cpl Marco Asselin — 114052
9 Capt Bob Painchaud
MCpl Ed Dillon — 114115
10 Maj Réal Turgeon
Cpl Kori Ibey — 114023/078
11 Capt Mike Lenehan — 114084(T)
Spare Tutors — 114164, 041, 049(T)

1993

1 Maj Dean Rainkie
Sgt Joe Maillet — 114011
2 Capt Rob Martin
Cpl Pierre Turgeon — 114094
3 Capt André Lortie
Cpl Mike Ubell — 114108
4 Capt Glenn Kerr
Cpl Denis Houde — 114046
5 Capt Derek Mosher
Cpl Vince Leather — 114100
6 Capt Chris Granley
Cpl Terry Spence — 114080
7 Capt Frank Bergnach
Cpl Marlene Shillingford — 114075
8 Capt Michel Cliche
Cpl Kori Ibey — 114052
9 Capt Bob Painchaud
MCpl Jim Flach — 114115
10 Capt François Cousineau
Capt Ménès Pierre-Pierre — 114049(T)
11 Capt Mike Lenehan
Cpl Mike Crickmore — 114076
Spare Tutors — 114041, 164

1994

1 Maj Dean Rainkie
Sgt Mark Doane — 114188
2 Capt Mario Hamel
Cpl Pierre Turgeon — 114075
3 Capt André Lortie
Cpl Rick Ouellette — 114100
4 Capt Will McEwan
Cpl Denis Houde — 114076
5 Capt Derek Mosher
Cpl Richard Jack — 114079
6 Capt Chris Granley
Cpl Mike Crickmore — 114080
7 Capt Dave Deere
Cpl Marlene Shillingford — 114164
8 Capt Michel Cliche
Cpl Gord Tulloch — 114094
9 Capt Norm Dequier
MCpl Jim Flach — 114078
10 Capt Ménès Pierre-Pierre — 114049(T)
11 Capt Mike Lenehan
Cpl Ron Kleim — 114011
Spare Tutors — 114052, 108, 115, 041(T)

1995

1 Maj Steve Hill
Sgt Mark Doane — 114188
2 Capt Mario Hamel
Cpl Tony Solimine — 114012
3 Capt Greg Carlow
Cpl Tim Woodward — 114115
4 Capt Will McEwan
Cpl Daniele De Luca — 114076
5 Capt Jeff Young
Cpl Richard Jack — 114100
6 Capt Ian Searle
Cpl Rick Ouellette — 114108
7 Capt Dave Deere
Cpl Ron Kleim — 114164
8 Capt Steve Dion
Cpl Gord Tulloch — 114080
9 Capt Norm Dequier
MCpl Martin Singher — 114078
10 Capt Ménès Pierre-Pierre
Cpl Éric Bissonnette — 114011
11 Capt Claude Lebel — 114156
Spare Tutors — 114174, 035, 041, 049(T)

1996

1 Maj Steve Hill
Sgt Pete Henry — 114188
2 Capt Rod Erman
Cpl Tony Solimine — 114080
3 Capt Greg Carlow
Cpl Peter Dueck — 114174
4 Capt Dan Robinson
Cpl Daniele De Luca — 114078
5 Capt Jeff Young
Cpl Ian McLean — 114076
6 Capt Ian Searle
Cpl Tim Woodward — 114108
7 Capt Brock Andrew
Cpl Éric Bissonnette — 114099
8 Capt Steve Dion
Cpl Ken Marcicki — 114156
9 Capt Jean Guilbault
MCpl Martin Singher — 114035
10 Capt Chris England — 114164
11 Capt Claude Lebel
Cpl Greg Turcotte — 114011
Spare Tutors — 114012, 100, 049, 041(T)

1997

1 Maj Darryl Shyiak
Sgt Pete Henry — 114188
2 Capt Rod Ermen
Cpl Gary LeCourtois — 114080
3 Capt Derek Miller
Cpl Ken Marcicki — 114156
4 Capt Dan Robinson
Cpl d'Arcy Monaghan — 114078
5 Capt Mike Ayling
Cpl Ian McLean — 114011
6 Capt Scott Shrubsole
Cpl GregTurcotte — 114174
7 Capn Brock Andrew
Cpl Troy Bartlett — 114172
8 Capt Marcus Walton
Cpl Peter Dueck — 114035
9 Capt Jean Guilbault
MCpl Marco Asselin — 114099
10 Capt Chris England
Cpl Brian Doll — 114164
11 Capt Richard Walsh — 114076 / 041(T)
Spare Tutors — 114076, 012, 108, 041(T), 049(T)

1998

1 Maj Darryl Shyiak
Sgt Mark Keller — 114188
2 Capt Michael VandenBos
Cpl Gary LeCourtois — 114099
3 Capt Derek Miller
Cpl Travis Laslo — 114035
4 Capt Mike Ayling
Cpl Brian Doll — 114078
5 Capt Jayson Miles-Ingram
Cpl d'Arcy Monaghan — 114142
6 Capt Scott Shrubsole
Cpl Mike Sanikopoulos — 114156
7 Capt Ian McLean
Cpl Troy Bartlett — 114174
8 Capt Marcus Walton
Cpl Gérard Menard — 114019
9 Capt Ian James
MCpl Marco Asselin — 114145
10 Capt Emmanuel Bélanger — 114076
11 Capt Richard Walsh
Cpl Corey Stangeland — 114012
Spare Tutors — 114108, 172, 041(T), 049(T)

1999

1 Maj Bob Painchaud
Sgt Mark Keller — 114078
2 Capt Ian Searle
Cpl Rich Slonski — 114172
3 Capt Norm Dequier
Cpl Paul Bourgoin — 114035
4 Capt Jayson Miles-Ingram
Cpl Corey Stangeland — 114142
5 Capt Tim Rawlings
MCpl Travis Laslo — 114188
6 Capt Craig Brown
Cpl Mike Sanikopoulos — 114076
7 Maj Ian McLean
Cpl Brad Fulton — 114174
8 Capt Patrick Ouellet
Cpl Gérard Menard — 114099
9 Capt Ian James
MCpl Marc Elder — 114145
10 Capt Emmanuel Bélanger — 114108
11 Capt Eric Pootmans
Cpl Chris Hardy
Spare Tutors — 114012, 019, 159, 041(T), 049(T)
Note: Capt Michael VandenBos, the incumbent SB 2 for 1999, was killed in a pre-season training accident south of Moose Jaw, Sask on 10 Dec 98.

2000

1 Maj Bob Painchaud
Sgt Jim Flach — 114006
2 Capt Warren Wright
Cpl Harold Duff — 114099
3 Capt Ian Searle
Cpl Paul Bourgoin — 114019
4 Capt Chris Van Vliet
Cpl Chris Hardy — 114076
5 Maj Tim Rawlings
Cpl Dean Gullacher — 114142
6 Capt Craig Brown
Cpl NancyAnderson — 114145
7 Capt Rob Mitchell
Cpl Brad Fulton — 114013
8 Capt Patrick Ouellet
Cpl Rich Slonski — 114173
9 Capt Bob Reichert
MCpl Marc Elder — 114174
10 Capt Emmanuel Bélanger — 114041
11 Capt Andrew Cook
Cpl Kevin Madower — 114012
Spare Tutors — 114078, 159, 172, 035, 049(T)

2001

1 Maj Bob Painchaud
Sgt Jim Flach — 114006 / 078
2 Capt Wayne Mott
Cpl Richard Pilon — 114099
3 Capt Maryse Carmichael
Cpl Kevin Madower — 114019
4 Capt Chris Van Vliet
Cpl Martin Martel — 114076
5 Capt Warren Wright
MCpl Dean Gullacher — 114142
6 Maj Ian Searle
Cpl Mike Grimard — 114145
7 Capt Rob Mitchell
Cpl Harold Duff — 114159
8 Capt Craig Brown
MCpl NancyAnderson — 114173
9 Capt Bob Reichert
MCpl Mark Gegner — 114174
10 Capt Jean-Pierre Turcotte
Cpl Jean-Pierre Bérubé — 114172
Capt Eric Pootmans
11 Capt Andrew Cook — 114012
Spare Tutors — 114104, 035, 013, 081, 049(T), 041(T)

2002

1 Maj Steve Will
Sgt Dan Ross — 114013
2 Maj Maryse Carmichael
Cpl Mike Pelletier — 114019
3 Capt Chris Bard
Cpl Richard Pilon — 114099

4	Maj Steve Melanson	
	MCpl Mike Grimard	114076
5	Capt Warren Wright	
	Cpl Harold Duff	114085
6	Capt Andy Mackay	
	Cpl Chris Martin	114058
7	Capt Rob Mitchell	
	Cpl Rick Probetts	114172
8	Capt Wayne Mott	
	Cpl Martin Martel	114146
9	Capt Bob Reichert	
	MCpl Dean Gullacher	114159
10	Capt Lyle Holbrook	
	Cpl Jean-Marc Brien	114009
11	Capt Andrew Cook	114173
14	Lt Jay Walker	
Spare Tutors	114104, 174, 035, 145, 081, 041(T),	
	064(T), 120(T), 089(T)	

Snowbirds Alumni

Officers

Major Glen Younghusband — Summerland, B.C. — Team Lead — 71,72

Captain Tom Gernack — Maple Creek, Sask. — Inner Right — 71,72

Captain Laurie Illingworth — Truro, N.S. — Inner Left/Solo — 71,72,73

Major George Hawey — Québec City, Qué. — First Line Astern 71, 73 — Team Lead 83,84

Major Gord Wallis — Wetaskiwin, Alta. — Second Line Astern 71-73 — Team Lead 77,78

Captain Chester Glendenning — Bathurst, N.B. — Outer Left — 71,72

Captain Fred McCague — New Westminster, B.C. — First Line Astern — 71,72

Captain Mike Marynowski — Paynton, Sask. — Left Wing/Solo — 71,72

Captain Lloyd Waterer — Invermere, B.C. — Right Wing/Solo — 71,72

Captain Bob Sharpe — Fort Erie, Ont. — Wing — 71

Captain Doug Zebedee — East Coulee, Alta. — Wing — 71

Captain Larry Currie — Loring, Ont. — Outer Right/Inner Right — 72,73

Captain John Hackett — Ottawa, Ont. — Coordinator — 72,73

Major George Miller — Ottawa, Ont. — Team Lead — 73,74

Major Mike Murphy — Dartmouth, N.S. — Inner Left 73,74 — Team Lead 81,82

Captain Carl Stef — Weyburn, Sask. — Outer Right/Outer Left — 73,74,75

Captain Bob Wade — Evansburg, Sask. — Outer Left — 73,74

Major Tom Griffis — Toronto, Ont. — Solo 73,74 — Team Lead 79,80

Captain John Shaw — Ottawa, Ont. — Inner Right — 74,75

Captain Murray Bertram — Eston, Sask. — First Line Astern — 74,75

Captain Harry Chapin — Vancouver, B.C. — Second Line Astern — 74,75,76

Major Yogi Huyghebaert — Fir Mountain, Sask. — Solo 74,75 — Team Lead 85,86

Captain Greg Bruneau — Montréal, Qué. — Coordinator — 74,75

Captain Andy Bessette — Montréal, Qué. — Coordinator — 74

Captain Mike Savard — Québec City, Qué. — Coordinator — 74

Major Denis Gauthier — Sherbrooke, Qué. — Team Lead — 75,76

Captain Chris Tuck — Victoria, B.C. — Inner Left — 75,76

Major Dave Wilson — Dartmouth, N.S. — Outer Right 75,76 — Team Lead 87

Captain Ken Carr — Port Elgin, Ont. — Solo — 75,76

Captain Jack Girard — Ste Foy, Qué. — Coordinator 75,76 — Executive Officer 77,78

Captain Roy Gately — Saskatoon, Sask. — Administration Officer — 75,76

Captain Gerry Nicks — Vancouver, B.C. — Inner Right — 76,77

Captain Paul Beaulieu — Montréal, Qué. — Outer Left — 76,77

Captain Jim Sorfleet — Winnipeg, Man. — First Line Astern — 76,77

Captain Speedy Fast — Spiritwood, Sask. — Solo — 76,77

Captain Mike Jephcott — Vancouver, B.C. — Coordinator — 76,77

Captain Wayne Thompson — London, Ont. — Inner Left — 77,78

Captain Joe Molnar — London, Ont. — Second Line Astern — 77,78

Captain Keith Coulter — Golden, B.C. — Outer Right — 77,78

Captain Gord de Jong — Edmonton, Alta. — Solo — 77,78

Captain Stu Morgan — Brantford, Ont — Coordinator — 77,78

Captain Marc Ouellet — Ottawa, Ont. — Inner Right — 78,79

Captain Terry Hunt — Lethbridge, Alta. — First Line Astern — 78,79

Captain John McNamara — Hamilton, Ont. — Outer Left — 78,79

Captain Ray Hansford — Galt, Ont. — Solo — 78,79

Captain Yves Bossé — Brownsburg, Qué. — Coordinator 78,79 — Second Line Astern 80

Captain Ron Duckworth — Dundas, Ont. — Executive Officer — 78,79,80,81

Captain Graham Miller — Hamilton, Ont. — Inner Left — 79,80

Captain Jim Reith — Edmonton, Alta. — Second Line Astern — 79

Captain Frank Thorne — Thompson, Man. — Outer Right — 79,80

Captain Larry Rockliff — Edmonton, Alta. — Solo — 79,80

Captain Jim Fowler — Calgary, Alta. — Coordinator — 79,80

Captain Jim "Chuck" Gillespie — Toronto, Ont. — Inner Right — 80,81

Captain Bob Drake — Edmonton, Alta. — First Line Astern — 80,81

Captain Wally Stone — Kemptville, Ont. — Outer Left — 80,81

Major Dan Dempsey — Edmonton, Alta. — Solo 80,81 — Team Lead 89,90

Captain Denis Mercier — Valleyfield, Qué. — Coordinator — 80,81

Major Dennis Beselt — Calgary, Alta. — Inner Left 81,82 — Team Lead 87,88

Captain Sonny Lefort — Fort Frances, Ont. — Second Line Astern — 81,82

Major Dean Rainkie — Melville, Sask. — Outer Right 81,82 — Team Lead 93,94

Captain John Politis — London, Ont. — Solo — 81,82

Major Wally Peters — Litchfield, N.S. — Coordinator — 81,82

Lieutenant Heather Campbell — Bridgetown, P.E.I. — Executive Officer — 81,82

Captain Geoff Gamble — St Laurent, Qué. — Inner Right — 82,83

Captain Tristan deKoninck — Ladysmith, B.C. — First Line Astern — 82,83

Captain Rob Chapman — St Catharines, Ont. — Outer Left — 82,83

Captain Jon Graham — Sault Ste Marie, Ont. — Solo — 82,83

Captain Ron Carter — Saint John, N.B. — Coordinator — 82,83

Captain Leslie Whan — Winnipeg, Man. — Admin Officer — 82,83,84,85,86

Captain Bill Ryan — Greenwood, N.S. — Inner Left — 83,84

Captain Holmes Patton — Moose Jaw, Sask. — Second Line Astern — 83,84

Captain Richie Clements — Calgary, Alta. — Outer Right — 83,84

Major Bob Stephan — London, Ont. — Solo 83,84,89 — Team Lead 91,92

Major Norm Fraser — Chambly, Qué. — Coordinator — 83,84

Captain Al Merrick — Beaconsfield, Qué. — Inner Right — 84,85

Captain Dave Forman — Dartmouth, N.S. — First Line Astern — 84,85

Captain Carl Shaver Outer Left	Ottawa, Ont. 84,85	
Captain Steve Wallace Solo	Toronto, Ont. 84,85	
Captain Mike Bell Coordinator	Toronto, Ont. 84,85	
Captain Steve Purton Inner Left	Merthyr Tydfil, S.Wales 85,86	

Captain Carl Shaver — Ottawa, Ont. — Outer Left — 84,85

Captain Steve Wallace — Toronto, Ont. — Solo — 84,85

Captain Mike Bell — Toronto, Ont. — Coordinator — 84,85

Captain Steve Purton — Merthyr Tydfil, S.Wales — Inner Left — 85,86

Captain Gino Tessier — Joliette, Qué. — Second Line Astern — 85,86

Major Steve Hill — Toronto, Ont. — Outer Right — 85,86 — Team Lead — 95,96

Captain Mike Skubicky — Toronto, Ont. — Solo — 85,86

Captain Eric Dumont — Laval, Qué. — Coordinator — 85,86,87

Captain Joe Parente — Vancouver, B.C. — Inner Right — 86,87

Captain Jim Fowlow — St. John's, Nfld. — First Line Astern — 86,87

Captain Howard Tarbet — Trail, B.C. — Outer Left — 86,87

Captain Don Brodeur — Vancouver, B.C. — Solo — 86,87

Captain Bob Curran — Courtenay, B.C. — Coordinator — 86

Captain Paul Giles — Ottawa, Ont. — Inner Left — 87,88

Captain Don Barnby — Timmins, Ont. — Second Line Astern — 87,88

Captain Boyd Smith — Abbotsford, B.C. — Outer Right — 87,88

Captain Wes MacKay — Camrose, Alta. — Solo — 87,88

Captain Richard Lapointe — Black Lake, Qué. — Coordinator — 87,88

Captain Ross Fetterly — Pointe Claire, Qué. — Admin Officer — 87,88,89,90

Captain Shane Antaya — Stratford, Ont. — Inner Right — 88,89

Captain Bjorn Kjaer — Nanaimo, B.C. — First Line Astern — 88,89

Major Darryl Shyiak — Portage la Prairie, Man. — Outer Left — 88,89 — Team Lead — 97,98

Captain Ken Rae — Toronto, Ont. — Solo — 88

Captain Kevin Kokotailo — Regina, Sask. — Coordinator — 88,89

Major Stephen Will — North Bay, Ont. — Inner Left — 89,90 — Team Lead — 02

Captain John Low — Chatham, Ont. — Second Line Astern — 89,90

Captain Dale Hackett — Burlington, Ont. — Outer Right — 89,90

Captain Les Racicot — North Battleford, Sask. — Solo — 89,90

Captain Dominic Taillon — St-Prime, Qué. — Coordinator — 89,90

Captain Ross Granley — Red Deer, Alta. — Inner Right — 90,91

Captain Vince Jandrisch — Winnipeg, Man. — First Line Astern — 90,91

Captain Brooke Lawrence — Barrie, Ont. — Outer Left — 90,91

Captain Rich Lancaster — St. Catharines, Ont. — Solo — 90,91

Captain Jeff Hill — Toronto, Ont. — Coordinator — 90,91

Captain Paul Richards — Oromocto, N.B. — Logistics Officer — 90,91,92,93

Captain Marc Robert — Montréal, Qué. — Inner Left — 91,92

Captain Nick Cassidy — Kemptville, Ont. — First Line Astern — 91,92

Captain Bill Watts — Alexandria, Ont. — Outer Right — 91,92

Captain Glenn Oerzen — Victoria, B.C. — Solo — 91,92

Major Réal Turgeon — St-Isidore, Qué. — Coordinator — 91,92

Captain Rob Martin — Ottawa, Ont. — Inner Right — 92,93

Captain Glenn Kerr — Wetaskiwin, Alta. — First Line Astern — 92,93

Captain Frank Bergnach — Ottawa, Ont. — Outer Left — 92,93

Major Bob Painchaud — Lac Saguay, Qué. — Solo — 92,93 — Team Lead — 99,00,01

Captain Mike Lenehan — Windsor, Ont. — Coordinator — 92,93,94

Captain André Lortie — Rouyn-Noranda, Qué. — Inner Left — 93,94

Captain Derek Mosher — Halifax, N.S. — Second Line Astern — 93,94

Captain Chris Granley — Bellevue, Wash. — Outer Right — 93,94

Captain Michel Cliche — Beauceville, Qué. — Solo — 93,94

Captain François Cousineau — Repentigny, Qué. — Coordinator — 93,94

Captain Mario Hamel — Montréal, Qué. — Inner Right — 94,95

Captain Will McEwan — Toronto, Ont. — First Line Astern — 94,95

Captain Dave Deere — Georgetown, Ont. — Outer Left — 94,95

Captain Norm Dequier — Haywood, Man. — Solo — 94,95 — Inner Left — 99

Captain Ménès Pierre-Pierre — Ottawa, Ont. — Coordinator — 94,95

Captain Tana Beer — Saskatoon, Sask. — Logistics Officer — 94,95

Captain Greg Carlow — Brantford, Ont. — Inner Left — 95,96

Captain Jeff Young — Bracebridge, Ont. — Second Line Astern — 95,96

Major Ian Searle — Belfountain, Ont. — Outer & Inner Right — 95,96 — Inner Left/Outer Right — 99,00,01

Captain Steve Dion — Pincourt, Qué. — Solo — 95,96

Captain Claude Lebel — Grand Mère, Qué. — Coordinator — 95,96

Captain Rod Ermen — Moncton, N.B. — Inner Right — 96,97

Captain Dan Robinson — Vancouver, B.C. — First Line Astern — 96,97

Captain Brock Andrew — Virden, Man. — Outer Left — 96,97

Captain Jean Guilbault — Drummondville, Qué. — Solo — 96,97

Captain Christopher England — N. Vancouver, B.C. — Coordinator — 96,97

Captain Shirley Grenier-Greenwood — Iroquois Falls, Ont. — Logistics Officer — 96,97

Captain Derek Miller — Langley, B.C. — Inner Left — 97,98

Captain Mike Ayling — N. Vancouver, B.C. — Second Line Astern — 97,98

Captain Scott Shrubsole — Nepean, Ont. — Outer Right — 97,98

Captain Marcus Walton — North Bay, Ont. — Solo — 97,98

Captain Richard Walsh — Niagara-on-the-Lake, Ont. — Coordinator — 97,98

Captain Michael VandenBos — Whitby, Ont. — Inner Right — 98,99

Captain Jayson Miles-Ingram — Quill Lake, Sask. — Second Line Astern — 98,99 — Standards Pilot — 01,02

Major Ian McLean — London, Ont. — Outer Left — 98,99

Captain Ian James — Calgary, Alta. — Solo — 98,99

Captain Emmanuel Bélanger — Rivière-du-Loup, Qué. — Coordinator — 98,99,00

Captain Michael Perry — Sidney, B.C. — Logistics Officer — 98,99

Major Tim Rawlings — Barrie, Ont. — Second Line Astern — 99,00

Captain Craig Brown — Hamilton, Ont. — Outer Right, Solo — 99,00,01

Captain Patrick Ouellet — Charlesbourg, Qué. — Solo — 99,00

Captain Eric Pootmans — Beaconsfield, Qué. — Coordinator — 99 — Standards Pilot — 00,01

Captain Warren Wright — Delta, B.C. — Inner Right/Second Line Astern — 00,01,02

Captain Chris Van Vliet — Spruce Grove, Alta. — First Line Astern — 00,01 — Standards Pilot — 02

Captain Robert Mitchell	Victoria, B.C.	
Outer Left	00,01,02	

Captain Robert Mitchell — Victoria, B.C. — Outer Left — 00,01,02

Captain Bob Reichert — Saskatoon, Sask. — Solo — 00,01,02

Captain Andrew Cook — Cobourg, Ont. — Coordinator — 00,01,02

Captain Dan Morrison — Barrie, Ont. — Logistics Officer — 00 — Deputy Commanding Officer — 01,02

Captain Wayne Mott — Miramachi, N.B. — Inner Right/Solo — 01,02

Major Maryse Carmichael — Beauport, Qué. — Inner Left/Inner Right — 01,02

Captain Jean-Pierre Turcotte — Chicoutimi, Qué. — Coordinator — 01

Captain Arlene McGuire — Sudbury, Ont. — Logistics Officer — 01,02

Captain Rick Thompson — Timmins, Ont. — Sqn Maintenance Engineering Officer — 01,02

Captain Chris Bard — Guelph, Ont. — Inner Left — 02

Major Steve Melanson — Moncton, N.B. — First Line Astern — 02

Captain Andy Mackay — Orleans, Ont. — Outer Right — 02

Captain Lyle Holbrook — Grand Bend, Ont. — Coordinator — 02

Lieutenant Jay Walker — Scarborough, Ont. — Public Affairs Officer — 02

Captain Charles Mallett — Edmonton, Alta. — Standards Pilot — 02

Major Stu McIntosh — Abbotsford, B.C. — Deputy Commanding Officer — 02

Captain Stephanie Godin — Pointe-Claire, Qué. — Public Affairs Officer — 02

Note: Ranks reflect the highest rank achieved while serving with the team.

Groundcrew Support Team

Sergeant Dick Gaff — Burnaby, B.C. — Crew Chief — 71

Sergeant Lorne Foster — Crew Chief — 71

Corporal Wayne Adams — Safety Systems — 71

Corporal Don Anderson — Airframe — 71

Corporal Al McFadden — Instrument Electrical — 71

Corporal Bob Nixon — Brooks, Alta. — Airframe — 71,72

Corporal Mike Thompson — Toronto, Ont. — Aero Engine — 71,72 / 74

Corporal Ed Torfason — Hecla, Man. — Communication Systems — 71 / 73,74,75

Sergeant Bill Holloway — Vancouver, B.C. — Crew Chief — 72,73 / 75

M/Corporal Ron LaGrange — New Westminster, B.C. — Instrument Electrical — 72

M/Corporal Larry Legault — Radville, Sask. — Deputy Crew Chief — 72,73

Corporal Reg Bach — Penticton, B.C. — Instrument Electrical — 72

Corporal Pete Hennicke — Berlin, Germany — Aero Engine — 72,73,74,75

Corporal Claude Mikkelson — Strome, Alta. — Airframe — 72,73

Corporal Joe McCluskey — Boisetown, N.B. — Safety Systems — 72

Corporal Dwight Vaughan — Dartmouth, N.S. — Communication Systems — 72

Corporal Ely Bowen — Winterbrook, Nfld. — Instrument Electrical — 73,74

Corporal John Doerksen — Niverville, Man — Aero Engine — 73

Corporal Bob LeBlanc — Ottawa, Ont. — Instrument Electrical — 73

Corporal Rusty Rutherford — Lloydminster, Sask. — Safety Systems — 73,74

Corporal Chuck Wicks — Innisfail, Alta. — Airframe — 73 / 76

Sergeant Doug Marshall — Eston, Sask. — Crew Chief — 74 / 76

M/Corporal Cal Wanvig — Calgary, Alta. — Deputy Crew Chief — 74,75,76

Corporal Al Boyce — Selkirk, Man. — Instrument Electrical — 74,75

Corporal Ray Lund — Vancouver, B.C. — Airframe — 74,75

M/Corporal Garth Suitor — Blackie, Alta. — Airframe/Deputy Crew Chief — 75 / 77

Corporal Fred Broderick — Penticton, B.C. — Instrument Electrical — 75 / 78

Corporal Bud Peters — Victoria, B.C. — Safety Systems — 75

Corporal Wayne Swayze — Reston, Man. — Aero Engine — 75,76

M/Corporal Ian Neilson — Lethbridge, Alta. — Safety Systems — 76,77,78,79

M/Corporal Nick Nichols — Kentville, N.S. — Instrument Electrical — 76,77

Corporal Ross Chapman — Regina, Sask. — Instrument Electrical — 76,77

Corporal Lou Doan — Comox, B.C. — Aero Engine — 76

Corporal Gary Friesen — Calgary, Alta. — Airframe — 76

Corporal Vern Opperman — Comox, B.C. — Aero Engine — 76

Corporal Moe Taylor — Ladner, B.C. — Airframe — 76,77

Corporal John Zorn — Yorkton, Sask. — Aero Engine — 76,77,78

Sergeant Harold Breadner — Tisdale, Sask. — Crew Chief — 77

M/Corporal Wally Corbin — London, Ont. — Airframe/Deputy Crew Chief — 77,78

M/Corporal Bob O'Reilly — Eganville, Ont. — Comm Systems/Avionics Technician — 77,78 / 01,02

Corporal Barry Dickson — Weyburn, Sask. — Aero Engine — 77

Corporal Rod Venables — Lethbridge, Alta. — Airframe — 77

Sergeant Cec Keddy — Kentville, N.S. — Crew Chief — 78,79

M/Corporal Kevin Buell — White Rock, B.C. — Airframe — 78,79

M/Corporal Garry Ward — Duff, Sask. — Airframe/Deputy Crew Chief — 78,79,80

Corporal Al Dillman — Glidden, Sask. — Aero Engine — 78,79

Corporal Michel Poisson — Plessisville, Qué. — Instrument Electrical — 78,79

Corporal Michel Bernier — Sorel, Qué. — Airframe — 79,80

Corporal Ed Gammon — St. Catharines, Ont. — Communication Systems — 79,80

Corporal Fred Rockall — Toronto, Ont. — Aero Engine — 79,80

Corporal Michael Roy — Moose Jaw, Sask. — Instrument Electrical — 79,80

Sergeant Dutch Simms — Liverpool, N.S. — Crew Chief — 80,81

Corporal Jack Gariepy — Ottawa, Ont. — Instrument Electrical — 80

Corporal Michel Langevin — Azilda, Ont. — Aero Engine — 80

Corporal Al McGrath — Vancouver, B.C. — Aero Engine — 80,81

Corporal Rocky White — Stephenville, Nfld. — Safety Systems — 80

M/Corporal George Beck — Parkbeg, Sask. — Deputy Crew Chief — 81,82

Sergeant Bob Bauer — Toronto, Ont. — Safety Systems — 81,82,83 — Aviation Technician — 01,02

Corporal Dick Bennett — Stephenville Crossing, Nfld. — Airframe — 81,82

Corporal Barry Fremont — Comox, B.C. — Instrument Electrical — 81,82

Corporal Perry Luchia — Nobleford, Alta. — Communication Systems — 81,82

Corporal John McCanna — Renfrew, Ont. — Aero Engine — 81,82

Corporal Paul McKeen — Victoria, B.C. — Airframe — 81

Corporal Tony Vanderberg — Portage la Prairie, Man. — Instrument Electrical — 81,82

Sergeant Alex Cameron — Saskatoon, Sask. — Crew Chief — 82,83

Corporal Marty Cornfield — Victoria, B.C. — Aero Engine — 82,83

Corporal Harry Partridge — Fort Qu'Appelle, Sask. — Airframe — 82,83

Corporal Frank Pineau — Carberry, Man. — Supply Technician — 82,83

M/Corporal Bill MacPhee — Shubenacadie, N.S.
Deputy Crew Chief — 83,84

Corporal Ron Bernard — Trenton, Ont.
Instrument Electrical — 83,84

Corporal Mike Landers — Kirkland Lake, Ont.
Aero Engine — 83,84

Corporal Georges Ménard — Montréal, Qué.
Airframe — 83,84

Corporal Pat Messaoud — Montréal, Qué.
Communication Systems — 83,84

Corporal Tim Payne — Brandon, Man.
Instrument Electrical — 83,84

Sergeant Rick Harvey — Lebret, Sask.
Crew Chief — 84,85

Sergeant Doug Dennison — Montréal, Qué.
Airframe — 84,85
Deputy Crew Chief — 89,90

Corporal Dan Jean-Marie — Yorkton, Sask.
Aero Engine — 84,85

Corporal René Petit — Montréal, Qué.
Safety Systems — 84,85

Sergeant Mark Keller — Balmertown, Ont.
Aero Engine — 85,86
Crew Chief — 98,99

M/Corporal Brian Herde — Melville, Sask.
Deputy Crew Chief — 85,86
Aviation Technician — 01,02

Corporal Troy Canam — Upper Kent, N.B.
Supply Technician — 85,86

Corporal Bert Hargreaves — Winnipeg, Man.
Communication Systems — 85,86

Corporal Al Herron — Milton, Ont.
Airframe — 85,86

Corporal John Mahoney — Ottawa, Ont.
Instrument Electrical — 85,86

Corporal René St. Laurent — Québec, Qué.
Instrument Electrical — 85

Warrant Officer Alex Bouzane — Bishops Falls, Nfld.
Crew Chief — 86,87

Corporal Donald Brak — Paisley, Ont.
Safety Systems — 86

Sergeant Mark Doane — Oakville, Ont
Airframe — 86,87
Crew Chief — 94,95

Corporal Gilles Dubé — Quebéc, Qué.
Instrument Electrical — 86,87

Corporal Gord Neave — Victoria, B.C.
Aero Engine — 86,87

Sergeant Dan Bergeron — Montréal, Qué.
Deputy Crew Chief — 87,88
Crew Chief — 90,91

Corporal Mike Cook — East Dieppe, N.B.
Airframe — 87,88

Corporal Chris Detta — Devon, Alta.
Safety Systems — 87,88

Corporal Brian Duivenvoorde — Barrie, Ont.
Communication Systems — 87

Corporal Wally Marshall — St. John's, Nfld.
Airframe — 87,88

Corporal Serge Pilote — Chicoutimi, Qué.
Instrument Electrical — 87,88

Corporal Darren Schuszter — Victoria, B.C.
Supply Technician — 87,88

Sergeant Jerry Unrau — Winnipeg, Man.
Crew Chief — 88,89

M/Corporal Denis Fontaine — Montréal, Qué.
Airframe — 88,89

M/Corporal Guy Fortin — Bishopton, Qué.
Aero Engine — 88,89

M/Corporal Oswald Lindsay — Regina, Sask.
Communication Systems — 88,89

Corporal Marc Cossette — Coderre, Sask.
Instrument Electrical — 88,89

M/Corporal Mario Deshaies — Ste-Gertrude, Qué.
Safety Systems — 89,90

Corporal Jim Burton — Cold Lake, Alta.
Instrument Electrical — 89,90

Leading Seaman Darcy Gallipeau — Regina, Sask.
Supply Technician — 89,90,91

Corporal Leo Jenkins — St. John's, Nfld.
Aero Engine — 89,90

Corporal Dave Scharf — St. Albert, Alta.
Airframe — 89,90

M/Corporal Dave Fischer — Formosa, Ont.
Aero Engine — 90,91

Corporal Tony Edmundson — Medicine Hat, Alta.
Airframe — 90,91

Corporal Rick Macnab — Thompson, Man.
Communication Systems — 90,91

Corporal Dan Séguin — Montréal, Qué.
Instrument Electrical — 90,91

M/Corporal Marco Asselin — St-Siméon, Charlevoix, Qué
Aero Engine — 91,92
Deputy Crew Chief — 97,98

M/Corporal Ed Dillon — Summerside, P.E.I.
Deputy Crew Chief — 91,92

Corporal Stewart Gilchrist — Moose Jaw, Sask.
Safety Systems — 91,92

Corporal Rick Murray — Cornwall, P.E.I.
Instrument Electrical — 91,92

Corporal Doug Wray — Scarborough, Ont.
Airframe — 91,92

Sergeant Joe Maillet — Moncton, N.B.
Crew Chief — 92,93

Corporal Earle Bourgeois — New Westminster, B.C.
Supply Technician — 92,93,94

Corporal Kori Ibey — New Liskeard, Ont.
Aero Engine — 92,93

Corporal Vince Leather — Scarborough, Ont.
Instrument Electrical — 92,93

Corporal Terry Spence — Chemainus, B.C.
Communication Systems — 92,93

Corporal Mike Ubell — Luseland, Sask.
Airframe — 92,93

Warrant Officer Jim Flach — Rosetown, Sask.
Deputy Crew Chief — 93,94
Crew Chief — 00,01

Corporal Mike Crickmore — Rockton, Ont.
Safety Systems — 93,94

Corporal Denis Houde — Charlesbourg, Qué.
Instrument Electrical — 93,94

Corporal Marlene Shillingford — Newmarket, Ont.
Airframe — 93,94

Corporal Pierre Turgeon — Sherbrooke, Qué.
Aero Engine — 93,94

Corporal Richard Jack — Penticton, B.C.
Instrument Electrical — 94,95

Corporal Ron Kleim — Medicine Hat, Alta.
Airframe — 94,95

Corporal Rick Ouellette — Elm Creek, Man.
Communication Systems — 94,95

Corporal Gord Tulloch — St. John's, Nfld.
Aero Engine — 94,95

M/Corporal Martin Singher — Val Belair, Qué.
Deputy Crew Chief/Airframe — 95,96

Corporal Éric Bissonnette — Sept Iles, Qué.
Airframe — 95,96

Corporal Daniele De Luca — Montréal, Qué.
Instrument Electrical — 95,96

Corporal Tony Solimine — Toronto, Ont.
Aero Engine — 95,96

Corporal Liz Vella — Kingston, Ont.
Supply Technician — 95,96

Corporal Tim Woodward — Madge Lake, Sask.
Safety Systems — 95,96

Sergeant Pete Henry — Bathurst, N.B.
Crew Chief — 96,97

Corporal Peter Dueck — Elm Creek, Man.
Airframe/Aviation Technician — 96,97

Corporal Ken Marcicki — McCreary, Man.
Aero Engine/Aviation Technician — 96,97

Corporal Ian McLean — Swift Current, Sask.
Instrument Electrical/Aviation Technician — 96,97

Corporal Greg Turcotte — Trenton, Ont.
Communication Systems/Avionics Technician — 96,97

Corporal Troy Bartlett — Grand Bank, Nfld.
Aviation Technician — 97,98

Corporal Brian Doll — Warman, Sask.
Aviation Technician — 97,98

Corporal Gary LeCourtois — Saint-Godefroi, Qué.
Aviation Technician — 97,98

Corporal Margaret McPherson — Oromocto, N.B.
Supply Technician — 97

Corporal d'Arcy Monaghan — Summerside, P.E.I.
Aviation Technician — 97,98

M/Corporal Travis Laslo — Moose Jaw, Sask.
Avionics Technician — 98,99

M/Corporal Ken Mick — Edmonton, Alta.
Supply Tech — 98,99,00,01

Corporal Gérard Ménard — Drummondville, Qué.
Aviation Technician — 98,99

Corporal Mike Sanikopoulos — Sept-Iles, Que.
Avionics Technician — 98,99

Corporal Corey Stangeland — Birch Hills, Sask.
Aviation Technician — 98,99

Sergeant Marc Elder	Edmonton, Alta.	
Deputy Crew Chief/Aviation Technician	99,00,01,02	

Sergeant Marc Elder — Edmonton, Alta.
Deputy Crew Chief/Aviation Technician — 99,00,01,02

M/Corporal Rich Slonski — Vernon, B.C.
Aviation Technician — 99,00,01,02

Corporal Paul Bourgoin — Rivière-verte, N.B.
Aviation Technician — 99,00,01

Corporal Brad Fulton — Trenton, Ont.
Aviation Technician — 99,00,01

Corporal Chris Hardy — Sarnia, Ont.
Aviation Technician — 99,00,01

M/Corporal Nancy Anderson — Carmangay, Alta.
Avionics Technician — 00,01,02

M/Corporal Dean Gullacher — Cranbrook, B.C.
Avionics Technician/Deputy Crew Chief — 00,01,02

Corporal Harold Duff — Gagetown, N.B.
Aviation Technician — 00,01,02

Corporal Kevin Madower — West St. Andrews, N.S.
Aviation Technician — 00,01,02

Chief Warrant Officer Randy Doan — Regina, Sask.
Sqn Warrant Officer — 01,02

Warrant Officer Roger Arseneau — Chatham, N.B.
Avionics Technician — 01,02

Warrant Officer Barry Silk — Moose Jaw, Sask.
ARO/Aircraft Structures — 01,02

Sergeant Al Beasley — Comox, B.C.
Aviation Technician — 01,02

Sergeant Grant Beeber — Lethbridge, Alta.
Supply — 01,02

Sergeant Allan Ecker — Saskatoon, Sask.
Chief Clerk — 01

Sergeant Jerry Erickson — Moose Jaw, Sask.
Supply Technician — 01

Sergeant Mark Gegner — Watrous, Sask.
Deputy Crew Chief/Aviation Technician — 01 / 02

Sergeant Dan High — London, Ont.
Aviation Technician — 01

Sergeant Meme LaChapelle — Saint-Césaire, Qué.
Aviation Technician — 01

Sergeant Jean LaFramboise — Hawkesbury, Ont.
Avionics Technician — 01

Sergeant Mary Meier — London, Ont.
Aviation Technician — 01,02

Sergeant Dan Ross — Brooksby, Sask.
Aviation Tech/Crew Chief — 01 / 02

Sergeant Phil White — Dartmouth, N.S.
Aviation Technician — 01

M/Corporal Dwain Barcier — Bonville, Ont.
Vehicle Technician — 01,02

M/Corporal Dave Bell — Nepean, Ont.
Aircraft Structures — 01

M/Corporal Tom Critchley — Stephenville Crossing, Nfld.
Aircraft Structures — 01,02

M/Corporal Russ Davies — Ashton, Ont.
Aircraft Structures — 01,02

M/Corporal Glen Duvall — Cutknife, Sask.
Avionics Technician — 01,02

M/Corporal Mike Grimard — Brock, Sask.
Aviation Technician — 01,02

M/Corporal Pat Gugel — Moose Jaw, Sask.
Avionics Technician — 01,02

M/Corporal Warren Hruska — Morris, Sask.
Clerk — 01

M/Corporal Mike Kelly — Hamilton, Ont.
Avionics Technician — 01

M/Corporal Dave Lott — Stratford, Ont.
Aviation Technician — 01

M/Corporal Fred Martin — Sheet Harbour, N.S.
Aviation Technician — 01,02

M/Corporal Rick Perron — St-Alban, Que.
Aircraft Structures — 01

M/Corporal Paul Silvey — Calgary, Alta.
Aviation Technician — 01,02

M/Corporal Cindy Singleton — Chester, England
Supply Technician — 01,02

M/Corporal Shawn Stone — Corner Brook, Nfld.
Aviation Technician — 01,02

M/Corporal Mike Underwood — Toronto, Ont.
Aviation Technician — 01,02

M/Corporal Dawn Williams — Kingston, Ont.
Resource Management Support Clerk — 01,02

Corporal Terry Allain — St-Louie, P.E.I.
Aviation Technician — 01,02

Corporal Cheryl Beaulieu — Halifax, N.S.
Resource Management Support — 01

Corporal Duane Benz — Craik, Sask.
Aviation Technician — 01,02

Corporal Jean-Pierre Bérubé — Bic, Qué.
Aviation Technician — 01,02

Corporal Steve Bird — Goose Bay, Nfld.
Aviation Technician — 01

Corporal Donald Cathcart — Halifax, N.S.
Avionics Technician — 01,02

Corporal Dallas Cave — Calgary, Alta.
Aviation Technician — 01

Corporal Joel Charron — Saint-André-Est., Qué.
Aviation Technician — 01,02

Corporal Al Cole — Cole's Island, N.B.
Aviation Technician — 01,02

Corporal Dave Corry — New Delhi, India
Avionics Technician — 01

Corporal Lee Devine — Seaforth, Ont.
Aviation Technician — 01

Corporal Lisa England — Harry's Harbour, Nfld.
Aircraft Structures — 01

Corporal Brad Fayant — Melville, Sask.
Avionics Technician/Aircraft Structures — 01,02

Corporal Greg Folliott — Moose Jaw, Sask.
Aviation Technician — 01,02

Corporal Darrell Fournier — Meadow Lake, Sask.
Aviation Technician — 01,02

Corporal Steve Hawkins — Scarborough, Ont.
Aircraft Structures — 01,02

Corporal Micky Kelly — Balmertown, Ont.
Avionics Technician — 01,02

Corporal Dieter Kempter — Oshawa, Ont.
Aviation Technician — 01

Corporal Dave Kopp — Simpson, Sask.
Supply Technician — 01,02

Corporal Mike LaChapelle — Montréal, Qué.
Aviation Technician — 01

Corporal Maryse LaFramboise — Mont-Laurier, Qué.
Avionics Technician — 01

Corporal Wanda Madower — Warren, Man.
Aviation Technician — 01,02

Corporal Pat Marceau — St-Joseph Island, Ont.
Aircraft Structures — 01,02

Corporal Martin Martel — Joliette, Qué.
Aviation Technician — 01,02

Corporal Chris Martin — Toronto, Ont.
Aviation Technician — 01,02

Corporal Terry McLaren — Hamilton, Ont.
Supply Technician — 01,02

Corporal Eric Moisan — St. Rédempteur, Qué.
Avionics Technician — 01,02

Corporal Rob Oddy — Penticton, B.C.
Avionics Technician — 01,02

Corporal Mike Pelletier — Ottawa, Ont.
Aviation Technician — 01,02

Corporal Brian Phillips — Saint John, N.B.
Aviation Technician — 01,02

Corporal Richard Pilon — St-Jérome, Qué.
Aviation Technician — 01,02

Corporal Rick Probetts — Winnipeg, Man.
Avionics Technician — 01,02

Corporal Ian Rensby — Moose Jaw, Sask.
Avionics Technician — 01,02

Corporal Ronald Robson — Brandon, Man.
Aviation Technician — 01,02

Corporal Kam Singh — Winnipeg, Man.
Aviation Technician — 01,02

Corporal Sheldon Stotz — Golden, B.C.
Non-destructive Testing Technician — 01,02

Corporal Ryan Willett — New Liskeard, Ont.
Aviation Technician — 01,02

Corporal Rick Yuke — Hanover, Ont.
Aviation Technician — 01,02

Private Zack Crawshaw — Calgary, Alta.
Aviation Technician — 01,02

Private Christian Lentz — Nancy, France
Aviation Technician — 01,02

Sergeant Luc Labrecque — Asbestos, Qué.
Chief Clerk — 02

Corporal Jean-Marc Brien — Montréal, Qué.
Aviation Technician — 02

Corporal Daniel McIntyre — Saint John, N.B.
Aviation Technician — 02

Corporal Ian McIvor — Winnipeg, Man.
Aircraft Structures — 02

Private Matthew Faulkner — Stirling, Ont.
Aviation Technician — 02

Note: Ranks reflect the highest rank achieved by personnel while serving on the team.

Squadron Secretary

Mrs. Sue Richard — 78-80
Mrs. Maryanne Langevin — 79
Mrs. Sally Hazleton — 79
Mrs. Marg Fowler — 80 - present

Honorary Snowbirds

LGen (Ret'd) F.R. Sutherland
(Honorary Colonel 431 (AD) Squadron)
Col (Ret'd) O.B. Philp
Col (Ret'd) Ralph Annis
Col (Ret'd) Dave Tate
LCol (Ret'd) Terry Lyons
Bill & Nancy Johnson
The Pietsch Family
(Al, Barb, Warren, Jolene, Kent)
Art & Judy Scholl
Ed & Alice Drader
Lois Boyle
Jack & Myrna Kingscote
Joann Osterud
Bob Hoover
Gary McMahon
Rick Grissom
Bud Granley
Marg Fowler
Alice Biegler

Ray Ban Gold
    Rod Ellis
    George Kirbyson
    Bill Cowan
    Al Hauff
Rafe Tomsett
Les Gould
Tom Nevison
Dan McLaren
Jacquie Perrin
Larry Milberry
Don Chapman
Johnny Friend
French Connection
    Daniel Heligoin
    Montaine Mallet
Bernie Geier
Katsuhiko Tokunaga
Ed Ruthe
Milton Berger

Col (Ret'd) Frank Hanton
BGen (Ret'd) Claude Thibault
Col (Ret'd) Terry Humphries
David Foster
Steven Vitali
Jack Reilly
Lyn Johnston
Gary Sloane
Danny Clisham
Jerry Davidson
Terry Venables
Ian Smith
Marianne Hoffart
Rod Hillman
Larry & Kathy Doak
David Tavenor
Dale Cline
John McQuarrie
Sean Tucker
Bob Singleton

Canadian Forces SkyHawks
Julie Clark
BGen Jim Hunter
Bill & Judy Carter
Capt Rick Thompson
Bob Granley
Bob Thomson
Dr. Robert Conn
Don Pearsons
Col Terry Leversedge
Wayne Harper
Maj Norm Bell
Garry Cotter
Tom Lawson
Rick Radell
Don Fynn
Larry Rymal
Risto Laamanen
Martina Chapman
Mark Sargent

Index

Garry Cotter